WITHDRAWN
HARVARD LIBRARY
WITHDRAWN

THE COLLECTED
WORKS OF
JEREMY BENTHAM

General Editor
Philip Schofield

RELIGION AND THE CHURCH

Church-of-Englandism and its Catechism Examined, printed in 1817 and published in 1818, was part of the sustained attack on English political, legal, and ecclesiastical establishments undertaken by Bentham following his transition to political radicalism in the first decade of the nineteenth century. The focus of the work is the educational practice of the Church of England, particularly in the schools sponsored by the National Society for the Education of the Poor in the Principles of the National Church, where the Catechism was substituted to the Bible as the standard of rectitude, and hence the religion of the Church of England substituted to the religion of Jesus. The purpose of the Church's system of education, according to Bentham, was to instil habits of insincerity into the population at large. The Church had an interest in promoting moral depravity, in order to protect the abuses which were profitable both to the clergy and the ruling classes in general. Bentham goes on to recommend the 'euthanasia' of the Church, and argues that government sponsored proposals were in fact intended to propagate the system of abuse rather than reform it. An appendix based on original manuscripts, which deals with the relationship between Church and state as revealed in official papers documenting the discontinuance of a series of excise prosecutions, is published for the first time. The volume also contains the text of *The Book of Church Reform* (1831), extracted from *Church-of-Englandism*, but for which Bentham composed a new preface and conclusion. This authoritative version of the text is accompanied by an editorial introduction, comprehensive annotation, collations for several extracts published during Bentham's lifetime, and subject and name indexes.

The Collected Works of Jeremy Bentham

The new critical edition of the works and correspondence of Jeremy Bentham (1748–1832) is being prepared and published under the supervision of the Bentham Committee of University College London. In spite of his importance as jurist, philosopher, and social scientist, and leader of the utilitarian reformers, the only previous edition of his works was a poorly edited and incomplete one brought out within a decade or so of his death. The overall plan and principles of this edition are set out in the General Preface to *The Correspondence of Jeremy Bentham*, vol. 1 (Athlone Press), which was the first volume of the *Collected Works* to be published.

Volumes published by Oxford University Press

Constitutional Code Volume 1
Edited by F. Rosen and J. H. Burns

Deontology, together with A Table of the Springs of Action and Article on Utilitarianism
Edited by Amnon Goldworth

Chrestomathia
Edited by M. J. Smith and W. H. Burston

First Principles preparatory to Constitutional Code
Edited by Philip Schofield

Securities against Misrule and other Constitutional Writings for Tripoli and Greece
Edited by Philip Schofield

Official Aptitude Maximized; Expense Minimized
Edited by Philip Schofield

Colonies, Commerce, and Constitutional Law: Rid Yourselves of Ultramaria and other writings on Spain and Spanish America
Edited by Philip Schofield

'Legislator of the World': Writings on Codification, Law, and Education
Edited by Philip Schofield and Jonathan Harris

Political Tactics
Edited by Michael James, Cyprian Blamires, and Catherine Pease-Watkin

Rights, Representation, and Reform: Nonsense upon Stilts and other writings on the French Revolution
Edited by Philip Schofield, Catherine Pease-Watkin, and Cyprian Blamires

Writings on the Poor Laws Volumes I & II
Edited by Michael Quinn

Of the Limits of the Penal Branch of Jurisprudence
Edited by Philip Schofield

Correspondence, volume 6: January 1798 to December 1801
Edited by J. R. Dinwiddy

Correspondence, volume 7: January 1802 to December 1808
Edited by J. R. Dinwiddy

Correspondence, volume 8: January 1809 to December 1816
Edited by Stephen Conway

Correspondence, volume 9: January 1817 to June 1820
Edited by Stephen Conway

Correspondence, volume 10: July 1820 to December 1821
Edited by Stephen Conway

Correspondence, volume 11: January 1822 to June 1824
Edited by Catherine Fuller

Correspondence, volume 12: July 1824 to June 1828
Edited by Luke O'Sullivan and Catherine Fuller

CHURCH-OF-ENGLANDISM
AND ITS
CATECHISM EXAMINED

edited by
JAMES E. CRIMMINS
and
CATHERINE FULLER

CLARENDON PRESS · OXFORD

OXFORD
UNIVERSITY PRESS

Great Clarendon Street, Oxford OX2 6DP

Oxford University Press is a department of the University of Oxford.
It furthers the University's objective of excellence in research, scholarship,
and education by publishing worldwide in

Oxford New York

Auckland Cape Town Dar es Salaam Hong Kong Karachi
Kuala Lumpur Madrid Melbourne Mexico City Nairobi
New Delhi Shanghai Taipei Toronto

With offices in

Argentina Austria Brazil Chile Czech Republic France Greece
Guatemala Hungary Italy Japan Poland Portugal Singapore
South Korea Switzerland Thailand Turkey Ukraine Vietnam

Oxford is a registered trade mark of Oxford University Press
in the UK and certain other countries

Published in the United States
by Oxford University Press Inc., New York

© Oxford University Press 2011

The moral rights of the authors have been asserted
Database right Oxford University Press (maker)

First published 2011

All rights reserved. No part of this publication may be reproduced,
stored in a retrieval system, or transmitted, in any form or by any means,
without the prior permission in writing of Oxford University Press,
or as expressly permitted by law, or under terms agreed with the appropriate
reprographics rights organizations. Enquiries concerning reproduction
outside the scope of the above should be sent to the Rights Department,
Oxford University Press, at the address above

You must not circulate this book in any other binding or cover
and you must impose the same conditions on any acquirer

British Library Cataloguing in Publication Data

Data available

Library of Congress Cataloging in Publication Data

Data applied for

ISBN 978-0-19-959025-4

1 3 5 7 9 10 8 6 4 2

Typeset by Anne Joshua, Oxford
Printed in Great Britain
on acid-free paper by
MPG Books Group, Bodmin and King's Lynn

PREFACE

The Bentham Committee wishes to thank the Arts and Humanities Research Council whose generous grant allowing for the appointment of Catherine Fuller as co-editor has made possible the preparation of the present volume. The Bentham Committee is grateful to the British Academy, the Economic and Social Research Council, and University College London for their continuing support of *The Collected Works of Jeremy Bentham*.

Thanks are due to University College London Library for permission to publish material from its collection of Bentham Papers.

The initial editorial work on this volume was undertaken by James Crimmins, who provided a typescript of the printed text, a draft transcription of the manuscripts for the Andrewes Appendix, and draft Editorial Introduction, annotation, collations, and subject index. Catherine Fuller then undertook the enormous task of reviewing, revising, and supplementing the annotation. The text of the Andrewes Appendix was established by me, and the annotation drafted by Catherine Fuller. A revised version of the collations was prepared by Catherine Fuller, Catherine Pease-Watkin, Dr Oliver Harris, and me. The burdensome task of checking the annotation was undertaken by Irena Nicoll, Dr Oliver Harris, and Catherine Pease-Watkin. I reviewed and revised the annotation and the Editorial Introduction, and undertook the final preparations for the press. The proofs were read by me, with help from Dr Harris, Ms Pease-Watkin, Dr Michael Quinn, and Dr Valerie Wallace. Thanks are due to Mrs Kate Barber and Ms Anna Schüle for administrative assistance.

The Index of Subjects pertaining to *Church-of-Englandism* was prepared by Professor Crimmins and revised by me. The Index of Subjects pertaining to the Andrewes Appendix and 'Book of Church Reform' was prepared by me. I am grateful to Mrs Pease-Watkin for assisting me in the preparation of the Index of Names.

Professor Crimmins would like to acknowledge the assistance received from the late Professor Robert Fenn, Harold Tesch, Jane Caskey, Anne Skoczylas, Toby Schwartz, and Patrick Carter, and to thank the Social Sciences and Research Council of Canada for financial support.

Catherine Fuller and I would like to acknowledge the help received in the elucidation of certain references in the text from

PREFACE

the following: Mr Kristopher Grint; Dr Clare Haynes; Professor Simon Hornblower; Professor Andrew Lewis; Professor Michael Lobban; Inez T.P.A. Lynn; Mr D.R.S. Richards; Dr Renate Sohnen-Thieme; and Professor Richard Whatmore.

We are grateful to Ms Gillian Furlong, Ms Susan Stead, and their colleagues in the Special Collections department of UCL Library for their never-failing assistance and advice.

P.S.

CONTENTS

SYMBOLS AND ABBREVIATIONS ... ix

EDITORIAL INTRODUCTION ... xi

CHURCH-OF-ENGLANDISM AND ITS CATECHISM EXAMINED

Contents	3
Preface on Publication	7
Preface	28
Plan of the Work	43
Introduction	56
Part I	56
Part II	88
Part III	99
Part IV	102
Part V	195
The Church of England Catechism Examined	203
Recapitulation	253
Appendix. No. I	257
Appendix. No. II	312
Appendix. No. III	333
Appendix. No. IV	343
Appendix. No. V	494

EDITORIAL APPENDIX: THE ANDREWES APPENDIX

Appendix N° III. Dean Andrews and Mr Vansittart. Affections manifested by them towards the people—from the papers of the House of Commons ... 539

CONTENTS
THE BOOK OF CHURCH REFORM

Table of Contents	579
Preface	580
[Conclusion]	587
COLLATIONS	595
A. Church-of-Englandism and its Catechism Examined (1817)	596
B. On Blasphemy	598
C. Mother Church Relieved by Bleeding	603
D. The Church of England Catechism Examined	605
E. The Book of Church Reform	613
INDEX OF SUBJECTS	619
INDEX OF NAMES	641

SYMBOLS AND ABBREVIATIONS

Symbols
| |	Space left in manuscript.
[to]	Word(s) editorially supplied.
⟨...⟩	Word(s) torn away.
⟨so⟩	Conjectural restoration of mutilated word.
[?]	Reading doubtful
[...?]	Word(s) proved illegible.

Abbreviations

CW	This edition of *The Collected Works of Jeremy Bentham*.
UC	Bentham Papers in the Library of University College London. Roman numerals refer to boxes in which the papers are placed, Arabic to the folios within each box.
Bowring	*The Works of Jeremy Bentham*, published under the superintendence of . . . John Bowring, 11 vols., Edinburgh, 1843.
1817	'Church-of-Englandism and its Catechism examined. . . . By An Oxford Graduate. London: Printed in the Year 1817.
1818	*Church-of-Englandism and its Catechism examined*. . . . By Jeremy Bentham, Esq. London: Printed, 1817: Published, 1818.
Errata	'Table of Errata' issued with 1818.
First Annual Report	*First Annual Report of the National Society, for Promoting the Education of the Poor in the Principles of the Established Church*, London, 1812.
Second Annual Report	*Second Annual Report of the National Society, for Promoting the Education of the Poor in the Principles of the Established Church*, London, 1814.
Third Annual Report	*Third Annual Report of the National Society, for Promoting the Education of the Poor in the Principles of the Established Church*, London, 1815.

SYMBOLS AND ABBREVIATIONS

MS add.	Text added to the original manuscript reading.
MS alt.	Alternative manuscript reading, usually interlinear or marginal.
MS del.	Word(s) deleted in manuscript.
MS orig.	Original manuscript reading.

EDITORIAL INTRODUCTION

Church-of-Englandism and its Catechism Examined was printed in 1817, under the pseudonym 'An Oxford Graduate', and was published in 1818, under Bentham's own name. The work was part of a wider project to undermine the whole political, legal, and ecclesiastical establishment of England, and complemented *Plan of Parliamentary Reform*,[1] in which Bentham advocated 'democratic ascendancy', to be accomplished through reform of the electoral system. While *Plan of Parliamentary Reform* criticized the existing political system and made proposals for its radical reform, *Church-of-Englandism* advocated the 'euthanasia' of the religious establishment, and while *Plan of Parliamentary Reform* contained Bentham's own 'Catechism of Parliamentary Reform' in which he outlined and justified his proposals, *Church-of-Englandism* contained a scathing, clause-by-clause attack on the Church's Catechism. Bentham emphasized the link between the two works in a letter to his amanuensis John Herbert Koe:[2] 'Church cat. follows up the blow given in Plan Cat.: it goes to the destroying of the whole mass of that matter of corruption which while the Tories feed upon in possession, the Whigs feed upon, and will continue feeding upon while they are any thing, in expectancy.'[3] He reiterated the point in the 'Preface on Publication' to *Church-of-Englandism*: 'In the Introduction to the work intituled *Plan of Parliamentary Reform*, &c., a sort of sketch was given of one of the two *natures*, of which our constitution, such as it is, is composed, viz. the *temporal* one. In the present work may be seen a portrait of the other nature, viz. the *spiritual* one.'[4]

The main target of *Church-of-Englandism* was the system of education sponsored by the Church, and more particularly the schools of the National Society for the Education of the Poor in the Principles of the National Church. The National Society had been founded in 1811 to promote the teaching of the doctrine of the Church of England by means of the 'monitorial' system of education,

---

[1] *Plan of Parliamentary Reform, In the Form of a Catechism, with Reasons for each Article, with an Introduction, shewing The Necessity of Radical, and the Inadequacy of Moderate, Reform*, London, 1817 (Bowring, iii. 433–557).

[2] John Herbert Koe (1783–1860), Bentham's protégé and former secretary, who was admitted to Lincoln's Inn 1804, called to the Bar 1810, QC 1842, and served as a County Court Judge 1847–60.

[3] Bentham to Koe, 14 January 1818, *The Correspondence of Jeremy Bentham*, vol. ix, ed. S. Conway, Oxford, 1989 (*CW*), p. 145.

[4] 'Preface on Publication', p. 8 below.

whereby the master taught the senior pupils and they taught the rest. Bentham argued that the schools of the National Society represented an 'exclusionary system of education'. Only the children of those parents who consented to their being taught the Catechism of the Church of England were admitted, while Jews, Catholics, and dissenting Christians were excluded. Bentham claimed, moreover, that by making children learn the Catechism by heart and thus encouraging false declarations of belief, the Church was purposely instilling habits of insincerity and mendacity. The Church had an interest in engendering moral depravity in the people, and in maintaining the 'prostration of the understanding and will' advocated by the Bishop of London.[1] By encouraging pupils to learn the Catechism by heart, the aim of the National Society was not to advance education, nor even to promote the religion of Jesus, but to preserve the abuses which characterized the Church of England.[2] In the Appendices to *Church-of-Englandism* Bentham examined some of those abuses in detail, showed the inadequacy of some of the proposed measures of reform, and put forward a systematic programme of his own.

HISTORY OF THE WORK

As Bentham explained in the 'Preface', *Church-of-Englandism* had its genesis in his experience of the discipline and doctrines of the Church while a student at the University of Oxford in the 1760s.[3] He recalled with particular asperity the obligation he had been under to subscribe to the Thirty-nine Articles of the Church of England in order to take his degree, an intellectual ordeal that never ceased to trouble him, and constituted a pivotal moment in the development of his views on organized religion. He later recounted that when told he would have to subscribe to the Articles, he had set out to examine them: 'The examination was unfortunate. In some of them no meaning at all could I find; in others no meaning but one which, in my eyes, was but too plainly irreconcileable either to reason or to scripture.' He had gone to the Fellow of his College responsible for clearing up doubts in the minds of students, only to be told that it was presumptuous for one so young to question that which had been

---

[1] See William [Howley], Lord Bishop of London, *A Charge delivered to the Clergy of the Diocese of London at the Primary Visitation of that Diocese in the Year 1814*, London, 1814, p. 16.
[2] For Bentham's own educational proposals see *Chrestomathia*, ed. M.J. Smith and W.H. Burston, Oxford, 1983 (*CW*).
[3] See pp. 32–9 below.

EDITORIAL INTRODUCTION

framed 'by some of the holiest as well as best and wisest men that ever lived'. Bentham had remained dissatisfied, but had subscribed.[1] He described the writing of *Church-of-Englandism* as an '*expiation*'.[2]

In 1812 Bentham began to draft a work entitled 'Church-of-Englandism examined' which he never printed or published,[3] and which survives as a set of text sheets, rudiments, plans, and marginal summary sheets,[4] written under the main heading 'Church'.[5] According to the earliest plan, the proposed title of the work was:

Church-of-Englandism examined: in respect of influence on happiness, morality and useful learning. Influence on 1. General Morality. 2. Habitual sincerity. 3. Education of the many. 4. Education of the governing and influencing few. 5. Fulfilment of official duty. 6. Professional Zeal. 7. Political probity. 8. Financial Economy. 9. Requisition and diffusion of useful learning. With a continual Parallel between Church of Englandism and Scottish Presbyterianism under those several heads. And An enquiry into the most eligible remedy for whatever imperfections may be discernible. By an Oxford Graduate.[6]

Many of the themes mentioned in the title and accompanying plan would be touched upon in *Church-of-Englandism*.[7] It appears that Bentham, having begun work on the text in the autumn of 1812, continued to work on it into the spring of 1813, and then returned to it in late 1813.[8] The surviving text sheets correspond to only a small proportion of the planned work. On the other hand, the marginal summary sheets point to a significant number of text sheets which are no longer extant. This suggests either that a number of text sheets have been lost, or that Bentham drew on them for *Church-of-Englandism*, and having used them in that way, destroyed them. The

---

[1] See pp. 35–6 below and Bowring, x. 37.

[2] See 'Preface', p. 40 n. below.

[3] See the note of July 1818 added to a plan headed 'Church. Titles of Chapters and Sections' at UC vi. 27a & b (6 September 1813): '☞ This written before Church of Englandism. Not published nor finished.'

[4] For Bentham's normal working practice, and the relationship between text, marginal summary, and rudiment sheets, see pp. xxix–xxx below.

[5] See UC v. 94–316, vi. 1–209.

[6] UC vi. 1 (14 March 1812).

[7] Bentham drew up several more plans during the course of the composition of the work, and suggested several alternative titles: see, for instance, UC vi. 2 (12–13 September 1812); vi. 4 (6 October 1812); vi. 6 (7 December 1812); vi. 7 (2 February 1813, with additions dated 14 September and 28 November 1813); and vi. 27a & b (6 September 1813).

[8] Text sheets are at UC v. 94–316, vi. 24–6, 43, 144–7, most of which are dated between 29 December 1812 and 17 March 1813, and between 18 September and 11 December 1813. Marginal summary sheets are at UC vi. 28–42, 44–9, 51, 53–143, 148–209, most of which are dated between 23 September 1812 and 5 May 1813, and between 31 October and 7 December 1813. A further group of seven text sheets is located in James Mill's Commonplace Books, 4 vols., London Library, ii. 61–7. A sequence of 'Rudiments', which present an outline of the work, are at UC vi. 10–23 (27 October–1 November 1812).

EDITORIAL INTRODUCTION

fact remains, however, that Bentham regarded 'Church-of-Englandism examined' and *Church-of-Englandism and its Catechism Examined* as separate works, even though the two works had many themes in common.

While no text sheets survive corresponding to the published text of *Church-of-Englandism*, in accord with Bentham's practice of destroying the manuscripts for works he printed, there does survive a very large proportion of the marginal summary sheets. The dates on the marginal summary sheets usually reflect the dates on which they were compiled, rather than the dates on which the corresponding text sheets were written, but there is not usually more than a few days' discrepancy between the two. Hence, the marginal summary sheets reveal that the first part of 'Catechism Examined' was written in September 1813,[1] and, therefore, may have been intended for 'Church', on which Bentham was working at this time.[2] The remaining part of 'Catechism Examined' was written in early December 1814.[3] The marginal summaries for the 'Preface' were compiled at the end of August 1815.[4] The 'Introduction', or at least a very large proportion of it, was written in March 1816.[5] The bulk of the work on what was eventually printed as Appendix IV was undertaken in the summer and autumn of 1816.[6] Given that the omitted Andrewes

---

[1] See UC clviii. 123–5 (25 September 1813).

[2] Fragments at UC vi. 101–2 (18 September 1813) and 103–6 (20 September 1813) show that Bentham had, a few days earlier, been working on a commentary on the Thirty-nine Articles, under the more general heading 'Doctrine'.

[3] See UC clviii. 128–33 (4–7 December 1814). The marginal summary sheet at UC clviii. 127, which corresponds to the pages Bentham omitted from the text (see p. 212 n. below) when it was printed, is dated 29 December 1814.

[4] UC clviii. 138–40 (30 August 1815). These marginal summaries correspond to 'Preface', pp. 28–40 below, that is up to the 'Recapitulation'. The 'Plan of the Work', which follows the 'Recapitulation', pp. 43–55 below, must have been written and printed at a late stage in the preparation of the text.

[5] UC clviii. 141–4, 146–51 (15–18 March 1816) constitute the marginal summaries for Parts I and II, pp. 56–98 below, together with clviii. 145 (11 May 1816), which constitutes the marginal summaries for pp. 71–3, and was, therefore, a later insertion. UC clviii. 154 (18 March 1816) constitute the marginal summaries for Part III, pp. 99–101 below.

[6] The corresponding marginal summary sheets are at UC clviii. 158–62, 164–77, 182–3, 197–9, 202–12, 215–18, 221, with various dates in August, September, October, and November 1816.

There are a number of marginal summary sheets for which the relevant text has not been identified, and for which no corresponding text sheets appear to survive. A series of marginal summary sheets at UC clviii. 184–96 (20, 22, 24–9 August 1816) corresponds to the 'brief sketch' discussing the 'effects' of the system of government adopted by the Church of England which Bentham wrote for Appendix IV, but decided to exclude from the work (see p. 345 below). A series at UC clviii. 135–7 (1, 7 February 1815), and intended for the 'Introduction', Part I, pp. 56–87 below, contains an examination of *A Catechetical Instruction: Being an Account of the Chief Truths of the Christian Religion, Explained to the Meanest Capacity; By Way of Question and Answer*, first published at London in 1728, and *The Church Catechism Broke into Short Questions, with An Explanation of some Words, for the Easier Understanding of it: To which are added, Prayers for the Charity-Schools*, first published at London in 1709, new editions of both of which

EDITORIAL INTRODUCTION

Appendix was written in April 1816,[1] it is possible that Bentham worked on Appendices II–III at the same time, though Appendix I appears to have been written a year or so earlier.[2] The first three of the six sections of Appendix V were written in January 1817, and the final three sections in August 1817.[3] The final part of the text to be written was the 'Preface on Publication', comprising two letters from Bentham to William Smith[4] dated 24 January 1818 and February 1818 respectively, with a response from Smith to the first of Bentham's letters, dated 16 February 1818. This material was added when it became apparent to Bentham that he would have to publish the work under his own name, in the hope that it would lessen the likelihood of his being prosecuted for libel.[5]

As well as the majority of the marginal summary sheets, various fragments of unpublished text and other material survive. In the 'Introduction', Part IV, Bentham claimed that the conduct of the National Society, as it appeared in its first three *Annual Reports*,[6] was 'a tissue of *imposture*',[7] as evidenced by the lack of the usual 'Marks of Authenticity', such as time and place of meeting and list of persons present, attached to reports of proceedings.[8] His analysis of the 'Marks of Authenticity' given in the accounts of the various meetings in Part IV, §11[9] is based on a Table which he compiled, listing the proceedings in question, and recording the title as given in the

were later reissued by the Society for Promoting Christian Knowledge and subsequently recommended by the National Society. At UC clviii. 155 (5 April 1816) Bentham explained that he would not comment on Thomas Belsham, *Letters addressed to the Right Reverend the Lord Bishop of London, in Vindication of the Unitarians from the Allegations of his Lordship in the Charge delivered to the Clergy of the Diocese of London at his Lordship's Primary Visitation*, London, 1815, and an article in the *Quarterly Review*, vol. xiv, no. xxviii (October 1815), 39–53, reviewing [Howley], *Charge delivered to the Clergy of the Diocese of London* and Belsham's response, as *Church-of-Englandism* was already too bulky. Marginal summary sheets at UC clviii. 163 (9 September 1816), 178 (27 March and 17 September 1816), 179–80 (26 August 1816), 181 (15 September 1816), 213 (1 November 1816), 214 (22 October 1816), 219 (19 September 1816), 220 (17 November 1816), 222 (3 October 1816), and 224–8 (4, 14, 18, 23, 26 October 1816) contain material intended for Appendix IV, pp. 343–493 below, and clviii. 229 (6 October 1816) and 230 (11 October 1816) material intended for Appendix V, pp. 494–536 below.

[1] See p. xxv below.
[2] See UC clviii. 152–3 (25–6 March 1815), which constitute the marginal summaries for a part of Appendix I, pp. 261–71 below.
[3] See Bentham to Koe, 2 January and 25–7 August 1817, *Correspondence*, ix. 4–5, 51, discussed at pp. xviii–xix below.
[4] William Smith (1756–1835), MP for Norwich, Unitarian, and campaigner for the removal of religious disabilities.
[5] See pp. xxii–xxiii below.
[6] *First Annual Report of the National Society, for Promoting the Education of the Poor in the Principles of the Established Church*, London, 1812; *Second Annual Report of the National Society, for Promoting the Education of the Poor in the Principles of the Established Church*, London, 1814; and *Third Annual Report of the National Society, for Promoting the Education of the Poor in the Principles of the Established Church*, London, 1815.
[7] See p. 102 below.   [8] See pp. 104–6 below.   [9] See pp. 168–86 below.

EDITORIAL INTRODUCTION

contents page of the relevant *Annual Report* and on the paper itself as reproduced therein, the time and place of meeting, the signature of the secretary, the person or persons by whose order the paper was issued, and the persons listed as present.[1] Related to this material is a sequence, with the marginal subheading 'Archbishop & Co.', in which Bentham expanded on his claim that the Archbishop of Canterbury[2] was the 'contriver-in-chief and conductor-in-chief' of the fraud, and which may be an early draft of 'Introduction', Part IV, §10.[3] A further group of manuscripts deals with a speech of the Archbishop of Canterbury given at a meeting of the National Society held on 31 May 1816, and reported in the *Morning Chronicle*, 5 June 1816. Bentham concentrated on two statements in particular, first that 'no fixt principles of religion were inculcated' in schools other than those of the National Society, and that 'there was not common sense in any system of education, which brought up the people in indifference or hostility' to the established Church.[4] Bentham, in response, argued that the principles of the Church of England were not those of Jesus, but those fixed by the Act of Uniformity of 1662, and that if the Church of England wished to have fixed principles, it should adopt those of the Church of Rome. He pointed out that insofar as dissenters were schismatics and heretics from the Church of England, as claimed by the Bishop of London,[5] then the Church of Englandists were schismatics and heretics from the Church of Rome.[6] A short sequence headed 'Communion of Saints', which

---

[1] See 'Table shewing the instances, and the manner, in which, in the three extant Reports of the acts of the Society, self-styled The National Society, the proper and usual tokens of authenticity have respectively been omitted or truncated', at UC vii. 129–31.

[2] Charles Manners-Sutton (1755–1828), Archbishop of Canterbury from 1805.

[3] See UC vii. 108–18 (27 April, 2, 20, 28–9 May 1816) and pp. 160–8 below. A fragment, in which Bentham argued that the purpose of the imposture was to evade responsibility, extend patronage, and multiply salaries and emoluments, is at UC vii. 132–3 (2 May 1816). A related fragment is at UC vii. 154 (9 June 1816). Further fragments on the theme of 'Archbishop & Co.' are at UC vii. 119 (13 May 1816) and vii. 120 (17 May 1816). An extract, in the hand of a copyist, of *First Annual Report*, pp. 13–17, detailing the commencement of the National Society, is at UC vii. 123–7 (12 May 1816). A marginal summary sheet at UC vii. 159 (16 June 1816), for which the four corresponding text sheets have not been located, argues that the inconsistent use of tokens of authenticity was probably due to a combination of improbity and incapacity on the part of the Archbishop.

[4] A copy of the speech is at UC vii. 155 (7 June 1816). A copy of a further extract concerning the re-election of members of the National Society's General Committee is at UC vii. 156 (the date of 7 May 1816 is presumably a slip for 7 June 1816).

[5] See [Howley], *Charge delivered to the Clergy of the Diocese of London*, pp. 15–16.

[6] See UC vii. 136–49 (6–7 June 1816). Further fragments dealing with the Archbishop of Canterbury's speech of 31 May 1816 are at UC vii. 150, 157–8 (8–9 June 1816) and vii. 151–2 (19 June 1816). An extract from *The Examiner*, 19 May 1816, p. 312, itself taken from the *Chester Courant*, which reports the sacking of workmen because they were dissenters, and which, Bentham remarked, showed the Church 'in her true colours', is copied at UC vii. 121 (20 May 1816).

EDITORIAL INTRODUCTION

Bentham originally wrote for his examination of the Catechism, but which he decided to omit, deals with the etymology of the terms angels, saints, and prophets.[1]

Prior to the printing of *Church-of-Englandism* in mid-1817, Bentham decided to omit two of the projected appendices. He noted in the 'Plan of the Work' that because of the 'inordinate length' to which the work had grown, those parts 'designed for a prospectus' had been omitted, but that the material relating to the chief issues it contained could be found 'in some part or parts of this work as it stands at present'.[2] Bentham then explained that the omitted manuscripts concerned the activities of Thomas Kipling, Dean of Peterborough,[3] Gerrard Andrewes, Dean of Canterbury,[4] and Nicholas Vansittart, Chancellor of the Exchequer,[5] and indicated the pages in *Church-of-Englandism* where these were discussed.[6]

The original Appendix II is a commentary on a letter written by Kipling and published in the *Monthly Magazine*, July 1815, p. 580. One short sequence of text survives, which carries the heading 'Specimen of the Church of England intended mode of dealing with persons tainted with the guilt of Schism, as announced by the Dean of Peterborough, Dr Kipling'.[7] In the printed version of 'Church-of-Englandism', Bentham incorporated in Appendix I a brief discussion of Kipling's letter, the text of which he reproduced in a footnote.[8]

The manuscripts containing the original Appendix III, dealing with

---

[1] See UC vii. 103–6 (9 June 1814) and pp. 219–21 below.

Several other fragments have survived: UC vii. 153 ([?] March 1816) comparing the policies of William Laud (1573–1645), Archbishop of Canterbury 1633–45, with those of Manners-Sutton; vii. 101 (2 April 1816) on the giving of reward, not for telling the truth, but for supporting established doctrines; vii. 128 (13 May 1816) explaining that the purpose of the 'sketch here given . . . of the Excellent Church' was to prepare minds for the reforms proposed in Appendix IV; vii. 102 ([?] June and 9 July 1816) on Thomas Burgess, *A Brief Memorial on the Repeal of So much of the Statute 9. and 10. William III. as relates to Persons denying the Doctrine of the Holy Trinity: addressed to all who believe the Christian Religion to be a True Religion, and who are desirous of maintaining the religious institutions of their ancestors. To which is prefixed, A Demonstration of the Three Great Truths of Christianity, together with Specimens of Unitarian Rejection of Scripture and of all Antiquity*, London, 1814, in which the author, argued Bentham, condemned as blasphemous the opinions of anyone who happened to disagree with him; vii. 122 (21 May 1816) on the withdrawal of children from the National Society's school in Colchester; and vii. 134–5 (4 May 1816) on the persecution of Protestant school masters in France. UC vii. 107 (2 July 1816) contains a copy of I Corinthians 11: 17–34.

[2] See p. 48 n. below.

[3] Thomas Kipling (*c.* 1745–1822), Dean of Peterborough 1798–1822.

[4] Gerrard Andrewes (1750–1825), Rector of St James's, Piccadilly 1802–25, Dean of Canterbury 1809–25.

[5] Nicholas Vansittart (1766–1851), created Baron Bexley in 1823, Chancellor of the Exchequer 1812–23.

[6] See pp. 48–9 n. below.

[7] See UC vii. 3–7 (28 April 1816), with a corresponding marginal summary sheet at vii. 2 (29 April 1816).

[8] See p. 295 & n. below.

EDITORIAL INTRODUCTION

Andrewes and Vansittart, are more extensive. Bentham drew on a series of parliamentary papers, which gave an account of the discontinuance of a number of excise prosecutions on the orders of the Treasury, in order to illustrate the corrupt nature of the relationship between Church and state. The particular focus of Bentham's commentary was a letter sent by Andrewes to Vansittart on behalf of a Canterbury brewer.[1] Andrewes claimed to be protecting the brewer from a miscarriage of justice, but, according to Bentham, he was exercising an undue influence on government in order to prevent justice from taking its proper course. In the present edition, the original manuscript version of the Andrewes Appendix has been reproduced in an Editorial Appendix.[2]

Bentham composed a considerable portion of *Church-of-Englandism* while at his country retreat, Ford Abbey in Devon.[3] His amanuensis John Herbert Koe remained at Bentham's house at Queen's Square Place, Westminster in order to deal with Bentham's affairs, and to send him manuscripts, books, newspapers, and other items as and when he requested them. On 1 January 1817 Bentham informed Koe that *Church-of-Englandism* was almost ready for the press,[4] though the following day he asked him to provide information in relation to recent legislation augmenting the salaries of the clergy,[5] which he went on to discuss in Appendix V. Bentham returned to London later in January 1817, but does not seem to have delivered the manuscript to the printer, John McCreery,[6] until just before he returned to Ford Abbey at the end of July 1817. Once back in Devon, he reported to Koe: 'The lost sheep of Church Cat are found here.'[7] This is most probably an allusion to the manuscripts for the passage dealing with the Apostles' Creed which was printed out of sequence, and the note dealing with the value of Church livings, which was mislaid.[8] The passage dealing with the Apostles' Creed was printed with the initial issue, which went up to p. 441, where the printer added an explanatory comment concerning the incomplete state of the work.[9] The appearance of the note on Church

[1] See 'Further Papers Relating to Excise Prosecutions &c.,' *Commons Sessional Papers* (1816), xviii. 69.
[2] For further details see p. xxv below. A brief account of the affair appears in Appendix II, pp. 323–7 n. below. The remaining Appendices were renumbered accordingly when the Kipling and Andrewes Appendices were discarded.
[3] Bentham was at Ford Abbey 17 July 1814–mid-March 1815; 6 July 1815–January 1816; 26 July 1816–31 January 1817; and 31 July 1817–February 1818.
[4] Bentham to Koe, 1 January 1817, *Correspondence* (CW), ix. 3.
[5] Bentham to Koe, 2 January 1817, ibid. 4–5.
[6] John McCreery (1768–1832) of Black Horse Court, London.
[7] See Bentham to Koe, 9 August 1817, *Correspondence* (CW), ix. 34.
[8] See pp. 212 n., 523–4 n. below.
[9] See Collation A, pp. 596–7 below.

EDITORIAL INTRODUCTION

livings was delayed until the final three sections of Appendix V were printed, probably at the end of August 1817, when Bentham informed Koe that he had sent McCreery the final sixteen pages, 'forming the conclusion of Church Cat.'[1] At the same time, he gave instructions that the pages 'must come to *me* for revision'.[2] The title page of the printed version was dated 1817, and attributed authorship to 'An Oxford Graduate'.[3]

In late September 1817 Bentham was visited at Ford Abbey by Samuel Romilly,[4] who began to read what appears to have been a proof copy, or perhaps a revised proof, of 'Church-of-Englandism'. Bentham wrote to Koe on 29 September 1817:

He read it while here as far as the comment on the Creed in the body of the work:[5] the introduction however (he said) but cursorily. I told him how I had received a copy from Macreery. It was plainly impossible he said that any man could have written it but myself. I offered to lend him my copy for a limited time saying (what was very true) that I was reading it myself and had not finished it. But he was not to be so put off and insisted upon having a copy to keep by some means or other. He spoke of it to me at several different times spontaneously: first—it was a sad thing such a work could never be published: then it was most admirable: and at last he never had been so much captivated with any thing he had ever read in his life. Why could it not be published? Because in speaking of Jesus's descent into hell I had said as well might the Devil have ascended into heaven.[6] A mighty idle proof of libel! but I took advantage of it to desire him as he read to mark the dangerous passages which he readily promised: and upon my desiring some time afterwards that if any where he found the poison confined to a word or two he would set down in the margin what he regarded as safe substitutes, he consented without difficulty. It ended with a promise which he several times made me repeat, that you should forthwith cause Macreery to send a copy to his house....

It is not clear whether it was Romilly's comment that first raised the possibility of prosecution in Bentham's mind, but, as he went on to

---

[1] i.e. Appendix V, §§ 4–6, pp. 525–36 below. The relevant pages in the original edition are 442–56, but p. 441, the recto of p. 442, had also to be reissued. See Collation A, pp. 596–7 below.

[2] Bentham to Koe, 25–7 August 1817, *Correspondence* (*CW*), ix. 51.

[3] The printed version of 1817 carries the printer's imprint: 'J. M'Creery, Printer, Black-Horse-Court, London'. A copy sent to John Quincy Adams (1767–1848), United States Secretary of State 1817–25, President 1825–9, who had been Envoy Extraordinary and Minister Plenipotentiary to Britain from 1815 to 1817, is collected with thirty-five other Bentham tracts in the Stone Library, Adams National Historical Park, Quincy, Massachusetts. The copy owned by Francis Place (1771–1854), master tailor and radical politician, now in the British Library, shelfmark 4106.bb.6, is an amalgam of the 1817 and 1818 issues.

[4] Sir Samuel Romilly (1757–1818), Solicitor-General 1806–7, lawyer, law reformer, and MP, and his wife, Lady Anne Romilly (*c.* 1773–1818), stayed at Ford Abbey from 25 to 29 September 1817.   [5] See pp. 212–22 below.

[6] See p. 215 below.

EDITORIAL INTRODUCTION

explain, he decided to try to turn Romilly's reputation to advantage: 'the use of his revision is—that as to so much as remains uncondemned, it will serve for the encouragement of booksellers'.[1] Romilly, it seems, agreed to point out the 'dangerous passages', and amend any problematic words. Later, however, he stated that he had been unable to carry out this task, as there were too many of them.[2] On 11 November 1817 Bentham was still expecting to hear from Romilly, and complained to Koe that Romilly had not contacted him.[3] Koe replied that Romilly 'speaks in terms really of enthusiastic admiration' of the book, but had not had time to read it.[4] On 29 November 1817 Bentham again complained that he had not heard from Romilly.[5]

Having begun to circulate the text,[6] and having still not heard from Romilly by 7 January 1818, Bentham decided to wait no longer, and asked Koe to retrieve Romilly's copy of the work so that he could make use of whatever comments Romilly had made.[7] Soon afterwards Bentham explained to Koe that he no longer expected to hear from Romilly, and lamented that 'he has broke his word to me'. He speculated that Romilly had disapproved of his criticism of the Whigs in *Plan of Parliamentary Reform*, had realized that the attack was continued in *Church-of-Englandism*, and so had laid the book aside.

As to Romilly when he came to the part in which Sinecures and the overpay of overpaid Offices, with all the other parts of the Mammon of unrighteousness, which he toils to have his share in the disposal of are rolled in the kennel, not improbably, being galled and alarmed, and hence foreseeing more vexation than amusement he stopped there.[8]

Romilly did, however, eventually speak to Bentham about the work. Bentham later recounted to Francis Place that he had been sent for by Romilly, who had 'travelled through' *Church-of-Englandism*,

---

[1] Bentham to Koe, 29 September 1817, *Correspondence* (*CW*), ix. 66, 67.
[2] See p. xxi below.
[3] Bentham to Koe, 11 November 1817, *Correspondence* (*CW*), ix. 117.
[4] Koe to Bentham, 13 November 1817, ibid. 118.
[5] See Bentham to Koe, 29 November 1817, ibid. 126.
[6] On several occasions Bentham referred to *Church-of-Englandism* as 'Ensor's Book': see, for instance, Bentham to Koe, 11 November 1817, Bentham to Place, 11 November 1817, and Bentham to Koe, 29 November 1817, *Correspondence* (*CW*), ix. 117, 126. The allusion is to George Ensor (1769–1843), the Irish radical writer, author of *On National Government*, 2 vols., London, 1810, and *An Inquiry concerning The Population of Nations*, London, 1818, whom Bentham had known since at least 1815 (see *The Correspondence of Jeremy Bentham*, vol. viii, ed. S. Conway, Oxford, 1988 (*CW*), p. 503). It appears that someone, who had presumably seen a privately circulated copy, had suggested that Ensor was the author, and hence Bentham's ironic allusions to it as such.
[7] Bentham to Koe, 7 January 1818, *Correspondence* (*CW*), ix. 143.
[8] Bentham to Koe, 14 January 1818, ibid. 144–6. The sections on sinecures to which Bentham refers are at Appendix IV, pp. 343–493 below.

and pronounced these very words: 'Bentham, I am sure as I am of my existence that, if you publish this, you will be prosecuted; and I am as sure as I am of my existence that, if you are prosecuted, you will be convicted. There is scarce a sacrifice that I would not make rather than that you should publish.' Not but that he agreed with it in every tittle, and declared it to several persons the most captivating book he ever read. He suggested precautions which for some time were observed, but have for some time been discontinued.[1]

According to the account in Romilly's diary, the meeting took place on 5 April 1818:

Bentham wrote, some little time ago, and printed a work, which he has entitled 'Church-of-Englandism and its Catechism examined.' He allowed me to see it after it was printed. The work is written against the National School Society, whose aim is to proscribe all education of the poor, except that in which the religion of the Church of England forms an essential part; and the work, therefore, undertakes to prove, that Church-of-Englandism is wholly different from true Christianity, as it is to be learned from the gospel. The subject, however, is treated with so much levity and irreverence that it cannot fail to shock all persons who have any sense of religion. I had prevailed on Bentham till now not to publish it. He desired me to strike out the passages I thought most likely to give offence; but they were so numerous that I was obliged to decline the task; and I understood that he had given up all thoughts of publishing the work. To my astonishment, however, I learned yesterday that it had been advertised the day before with his name, and had been publicly sold. I have made a point of seeing him today, and, by the strong representation I have made to him of the extreme danger of his being prosecuted and convicted of a libel, I have prevailed on him to promise immediately to suspend, if not to stop altogether, any further sale of the book.[2]

It appears from this that one of the 'precautions' alluded to by Bentham in his letter to Place consisted in suspending the sale of the book, but it is also apparent that, if Bentham did implement a suspension, it was only temporary.

While waiting for Romilly's comments on the book, Bentham had decided to proceed with publication, and as early as January 1818 had begun to look for a publisher, using Koe, Place, and Mark Wilks[3] as

---

[1] Bentham to Place, 6 December 1818, *Correspondence* (*CW*), ix. 294. This letter was written immediately after Romilly's suicide on 6 December 1818. Bentham later repeated this account, adding that the interview took place 'a short time' before Romilly's death, and that his warnings about prosecution and conviction were among 'his very last words' to him: see Bentham to Diego Colón, 6 December 1820, *The Correspondence of Jeremy Bentham*, vol. x, ed. S. Conway, Oxford, 1994 (*CW*), pp. 229–30.
[2] *Memoirs of the Life of Sir Samuel Romilly, written by himself; with a selection from his Correspondence. Edited by his Sons*, 3 vols., London, 1840, iii. 336–7.
[3] Mark Wilks (1783–1855), writer and congregational minister.

EDITORIAL INTRODUCTION

intermediaries.[1] Indeed, a sample of the work, consisting in extracts on the subject of blasphemy, had been published in *The Examiner* on 18 and 25 January 1818.[2] Bentham had hoped to issue this material before William Hone was tried for blasphemy, but he had been overtaken by events, and the trials had taken place on 18, 19, and 20 December 1817.[3] Bentham, therefore, had composed an introductory paragraph for the extracts, explaining that he had sent them for publication because of the interest that the subject had generated 'in consequence of the late prosecutions'.[4] Having decided to publish *Church-of-Englandism*, Bentham developed a strategy which he hoped would provide some protection from the threat of prosecution. On 14 January 1818 he wrote to Koe:

I have employed the greatest part of this morning in writing a letter to W. Smith M.P. to ask for his story, which I have heard of the good behavior of the Archbp of Canterbury[5] on the occasion of the repeal of the Trinitarian Act of William: the lawyers having put in their claws and bedeviled it into its present shape after the Archbishop had drawn it or consented to it in a much less bad one. If W. Smith will furnish me with the information requested or any part of it, I mean to publish it in the form of an Advertisement or additional Preface to Church Cat.[6]

The Doctrine of the Trinity Act of 1813,[7] which Smith had introduced into the House of Commons, permitted Unitarians to hold public office and repealed provisions subjecting the expression of anti-Trinitarian views to punishment on the grounds of blasphemy and profanity. Bentham sent his letter to Smith on 24 January 1818,[8] receiving a response dated 29 January 1818, in which Smith agreed to provide the information requested,[9] which was eventually sent on 16

---

[1] Bentham to Koe, 14 January 1818, *Correspondence (CW)*, ix. 145. See also Bentham to Place, 14 January 1818, ibid. 147.

[2] The extracts, taken from Appendix IV, §3, pp. 367, 367–70 n. below, 'Recapitulation', p. 255 below, and Appendix IV, §3, pp. 365–7 below, appeared under the title 'On Blasphemy' in *The Examiner*, 18 January 1818, pp. 34–5, and 25 January 1818, p. 52. For further details see Collation B, pp. 598–602 below.

[3] Having published in 1817 a collection of parodies on religious texts, including the Catechism, William Hone (1780–1842), writer and bookseller, had been charged with blasphemous libel. At each of the three trials, Hone had been acquitted. It is possible that the trials of Hone similarly encouraged Bentham to publish *'Swear not at all:'* containing an exposure of the Needlessness and Mischievousness, as well as Antichristianity, of the Ceremony of an Oath, London, 1817 (Bowring, v. 187–229), which had been printed in 1813: see Advertisement (Bowring, v. 189).

[4] See *The Examiner*, 18 January 1818, p. 34. For Bentham's instructions to insert the introductory paragraph see Bentham to Koe, 22 December 1817, *Correspondence (CW)*, ix. 138–9.   [5] i.e. Manners-Sutton.

[6] Bentham to Koe, 14 January 1818, *Correspondence (CW)*, ix. 145–6.

[7] 53 Geo. III, c. 160.

[8] See pp. 10–12 below, and Bentham to Smith, 24 January 1818, *Correspondence (CW)*, ix. 151–3.   [9] Smith to Bentham, 29 January 1818, ibid. 153–4.

EDITORIAL INTRODUCTION

February 1818.[1] In the meantime Bentham reiterated his strategy to Place:

> By this means while I display candour and a whole heap of other virtues of which my heart is composed, I render it more difficult for an Atty General to obtain a conviction, even at the hands of a trained Middlesex Jury, and thereby diminish in proportion the risk if there be any on the part of the Bookseller. . . . Moreover this little bit of correspondence will by God's blessing by means of the additional bits of personality given to it, afford a promise of increasing the circulation.

While awaiting Smith's response, Bentham continued his search for a publisher, hoping that Wilks would be able to recommend one, but also considering a contact of McCreery's, who would publish the work 'if it had a name to it'. Bentham explained to Place that he had 'for some time' intended to publish the work under his own name, since the publication of his correspondence with Smith would have rendered any 'concealment' of his name 'out of the question'.[2]

In the event, the book was published by Effingham Wilson.[3] A collation of the printed text of 1817 with the published text of 1818 shows that they are for the most part the same issue,[4] though some changes were made. The respective title-pages and contents pages were reissued, the former with Bentham's own name rather than 'An Oxford Graduate' (the text itself retains allusions to the author as 'An Oxford Graduate'), and an indication that the work now included a discussion of 'the proposed new churches', namely the final three sections of Appendix V, amounting to the sixteen pages that Bentham mentioned in his letter to Koe of 25–7 August 1817.[5] For the published edition, Bentham added the 'Preface on Publication' (though it is not mentioned in the reissued contents pages) and a 'Table of Errata', consisting of two unnumbered pages and inserted at the end of the 'Preface on Publication'. The work was eventually printed and published with four discrete sets of pagination, the first two in Roman and the last two in Arabic numerals. The first was for the 'Preface on Publication'; the second for the 'Preface'; the third for the 'Introduction'; and the fourth for 'The Church of England Catechism Examined' and the five Appendices.[6]

---

[1] See pp. 12–16 below, and Smith to Bentham, 16 February 1818, *Correspondence* (*CW*), ix. 162–5. Bentham's response to Smith was published as an open letter in *Church-of-Englandism*: see pp. 16–27 below, and Bentham to Smith, February 1818, *Correspondence* (*CW*), ix. 168–77. The marginal summaries for Bentham's letters to Smith are at UC vi. 210 (20 January 1818) and vi. 211 (5 March 1818) respectively.
[2] Bentham to Place, 6 February 1818, *Correspondence* (*CW*), ix. 157–8.
[3] Effingham Wilson (1785–1868) of 88 Cornhill (in the Royal Exchange).
[4] See Collation A, pp. 596–7 below. [5] See p. xix above.
[6] i.e. pp. 7–27, 28–55, 56–202, and 203–536 below respectively.

EDITORIAL INTRODUCTION

The precise date of publication of *Church-of-Englandism* is not known, but it appeared either in March or early April 1818. In a letter to Sir Francis Burdett of 25 February 1818, Bentham stated that he hoped to publish a work which he did not identify, but which must have been *Church-of-Englandism*, 'in less than a fortnight'.[1] It had not, however, appeared by 4 March 1818, since the 'Preface on Publication' contains a reference to a report in the *Morning Chronicle* of that date.[2] Samuel Romilly, as noted above, had been informed that the work had been advertised on 3 April 1818 and 'had been publicly sold'.[3] Moreover, on 11 April 1818, Bentham sent Jean Baptiste Say 'what is wanting to compleat the two copies of my *"Church of Englandism etc examined"* which I understand were conveyed, as I desired, to your care some 6 or 8 months ago'.[4] This additional material did include the 'Preface on Publication',[5] but may have also included the reissued title and contents pages, and possibly the final three sections of Appendix V.

In view of the fact that the work was published in the spring of 1818, it is unclear why an advertisement for *Church-of-Englandism* appeared in the *Morning Chronicle*, 19 January 1819, under the heading 'Books Published This Day'.[6] It is possible that this was an attempt to garner some additional publicity for the book, since two reviews had already been or were about to be published. One of these, making 'a most furious attack upon it', but consisting—so Bentham had been informed, as he had not himself read it—in 'vague generalities',[7] appeared in the *Quarterly Review*,[8] and the other in the *Monthly Review*.[9] John Bowring, Bentham's literary executor,[10] omitted the work, along with Bentham's other published writings on religion,[11] from his edition of *The Works of Jeremy Bentham*, and

---

[1] Bentham to Burdett, 25 February 1818, *Correspondence* (*CW*), ix. 167.
[2] See p. 19 below.
[3] See p. xxi above. It was common practice to advertise books on the day of publication, so it is possible that the work was in fact published on 3 April 1818, though no newspaper advertisement has been traced.
[4] Bentham to Say, 11 April 1818, *Correspondence* (*CW*), ix. 189. Jean Baptiste Say (1767–1832), French economist and political philosopher.
[5] Bentham confirmed that he had sent a copy of 'Preface on Publication' to Say in Bentham to Samuel Bentham, 14 January 1820, *Correspondence* (*CW*), ix. 376.
[6] The listed price was 20s.
[7] Bentham to José Joaquín de Mora, 15–17 November 1820, *Correspondence* (*CW*), x. 154.
[8] *Quarterly Review*, vol. xxi, no. xli (January 1819), 167–77.
[9] *Monthly Review*, vol. lxxxviii (January 1819), 52–62.
[10] Sir John Bowring (1792–1872), merchant, first editor of the *Westminster Review*, later MP and diplomat, had been introduced to Bentham in August 1820.
[11] Philip Beauchamp, *Analysis of the Influence of Natural Religion on the Temporal Happiness of Mankind*, London, 1822, and Galamiel Smith, *Not Paul, but Jesus*, London, 1823. Both works appeared pseudonymously: the former was edited by George Grote (1794–1871), historian of Greece, while Francis Place claimed to have helped Bentham with the latter.

EDITORIAL INTRODUCTION

made no mention of them in the 'Memoirs and Correspondence' he compiled for it.[1] They were, presumably, among those writings that Bowring deemed too 'bold and adventurous' for publication.[2]

Andrewes Appendix

Bentham's original intention, as noted above, was that the essay on Andrewes should form Appendix III, but he decided to omit it when he concluded that the work was overlong. The text, written at the end of April 1816, has been reproduced from the original manuscripts, which carry the main heading 'Cat.'[3] The title appears at the head of the first text sheet, while the titles for the two sections of the essay are taken from the marginal subheadings on the corresponding text sheets.[4]

Reissued Extracts

Extracts from *Church-of-Englandism* were reissued on four occasions during Bentham's lifetime. Three reissues of Appendix IV, §§ 9–10 appeared in 1823, 1825, and 1831 respectively, the first two under the title *Mother Church Relieved by Bleeding*,[5] and the third under the title *The Book of Church Reform*.[6] A reissue of Bentham's critique of the Catechism was published in 1824, under the title *The Church of England Catechism Examined*.[7] His purpose in reissuing the two sections from Appendix IV in 1823, as he explained to Place, was to

---

[1] See Bowring, x. *passim*, xi. 1–170.

[2] See *Autobiographical Recollections of Sir John Bowring. With a brief Memoir by Lewin B. Bowring*, London, 1877, p. 339.

[3] The text sheets are at UC vii. 16–37, 91, 38–80 (21–7, 30 April 1816), and are paginated 1–13, 13*, 14–21, 21*, 22–64 respectively. Marginal summary sheets at UC vii. 8–9, 11–13, 1, 10, 14 (28, 30 April 1816) correspond to the text at vii. 16–60, and a marginal summary sheet at vii. 15 (30 April 1816) to the text at vii. 70–4. The remaining text sheets do not contain marginal summaries.

[4] A number of subheadings appear on the text sheets, but these have not been reproduced in the present edition.
Related fragments are at UC vii. 92 (25 April 1816); vii. 87–90, 94–5, 81–6 (29 April 1816); vii. 96–8 (7 May 1816); vii. 99 (8 May 1816); vii. 100 (9 May 1816); and vii. 93 (n.d.).

[5] *Mother Church Relieved by Bleeding; or, Vices and Remedies: Extracted from Bentham's Church of Englandism, &c. Examined: being matter Applying to Existing Circumstances, and Consisting of a Summary Recapitulation of the Vices, Therein Proved to have Place in the Existing System, and of the Particulars of the Remedial System Therein Proposed*, London, 1823; and *Mother Church Relieved by Bleeding; or, Vices and Remedies: Extracted from Bentham's 'Church of Englandism.' &c.*, London, 1825. See Collation C, pp. 603–4 below.

[6] *The Book of Church Reform: containing the most essential part of Mr. Bentham's 'Church of Englandism Examined', &c. Edited by one of his Disciples*, London, 1831. See Collation E, pp. 613–18 below.

[7] *The Church of England Catechism Examined. A New Edition*, London, 1824. See Collation D, pp. 605–12 below. The work was later republished as *The Church of England Catechism Examined*, Ramsgate, 1868; and *The Church of England Catechism Examined. Reprinted with a Biographical Introduction by J. M. Wheeler*, London, 1890.

EDITORIAL INTRODUCTION

support a motion in the House of Commons proposed by Joseph Hume[1] respecting tithes in Ireland, and scheduled for 4 March 1823.[2] Bentham sought Place's advice on the content and presentation of the proposed tract: 'tell me, *what* to reprint, *how much*, in what *order*, at what *price*, how to be *circulated*?' He considered handing a copy to MPs as they entered the House for the debate, and in that case wondered whether the extract should be published anonymously, on the grounds that some would refuse to receive it if it were known to be by Bentham.[3] According to Bentham's amanuensis John Colls,[4] the extract was taken to the printers on 6 February 1823 with an order to print 1,000 copies, and the printed copies were received by 19 February 1823.[5]

Nothing is known about the second reissue of Appendix IV, §§ 9–10 in 1825, but the third reissue as *The Book of Church Reform* in 1831 contained new material in a preface and a conclusion.[6] The title-page announced that the tract was 'Edited by one of his Disciples', though the 'Disciple' has not been identified. Bentham was in part inspired to publish *The Book of Church Reform* by his belated discovery of Robert Southey's defence of the established religion in *Book of the Church*, which had appeared in 1824.[7] He was annoyed that Southey had entirely ignored *Church-of-Englandism*, especially those sections devoted to Church reform. Convinced that Southey had read the book, Bentham concluded that he had not mentioned it because the remedies proposed there were 'incontrovertible'.[8] Bentham then added a comment on Robert Mackenzie Beverley's *Letter to his Grace the Archbishop of York, on the Present Corrupt State of the Church of England*, which was published at Beverley in 1831, and which was critical of the Church.[9] Beverley was essentially correct, stated Bentham, in identifying the Church's faults, but his 'plan of *reform*' was 'immethodical; and however justifiable, unjustified and

---

[1] Joseph Hume (1777–1855), radical politician, MP for the Aberdeen Burghs 1818–30.

[2] For Hume's motion see *Parliamentary Debates* (1823) viii. 367–416. A previous motion on the same subject had been introduced by Hume in the House of Commons on 19 June 1822 (see ibid., (1822) vii. 1147–98).

[3] Bentham to Place, 29 January 1823, *The Correspondence of Jeremy Bentham*, vol. xi, ed. C. Fuller, Oxford, 2000 (*CW*), pp. 197–8.

[4] John Flowerdew Colls (1801–78) entered Bentham's service in the summer of 1816, and remained until 1829. He later became a Church of England clergyman and was author of *Utilitarianism Unmasked*, London, 1844.

[5] Colls's Journal, BL Add. MS 33,563, fos. 118–19.

[6] For the text see pp. 577–93 below and Collation E, pp. 613–18 below.

[7] Robert Southey, *The Book of the Church*, 2 vols., London 1824. Southey (1774–1843), poet, historian, contributor to the *Quarterly Review* from 1809 until 1839.

[8] See p. 581 below.

[9] Bentham explained that the tract had been brought to his attention by a reference to it in the *Morning Chronicle*, 11 June 1831: see p. 585 below.

EDITORIAL INTRODUCTION

incomplete'. In contrast, *Book of Church Reform* provided systematic proposals for reform.[1]

The concluding material added to *Book of Church Reform* was prompted by a petition to Parliament, agreed at a public meeting at York (now Toronto), Upper Canada of 10 December 1830, signed by over 10,000 citizens,[2] which came to Bentham's notice while the *Book of Church Reform* was being prepared for the press. The petitioners objected to the fact that the Church of England would be the sole beneficiary of the proceeds raised by the sale of the clergy reserved lands, amounting in effect to the creation of an established church, and requested instead an equality of treatment between the various churches, the removal of religious tests for admission into King's College, York, and the diversion of the funds raised from the sale of the lands 'to the purposes of general education and various internal improvements'.[3] Bentham saw close parallels between the demands of the petitioners in Canada and his own proposals for the 'euthanasia' of the Church of England at home, and hence the addition of his concluding comments.

TEXT

Printed Text

The present edition of *Church-of-Englandism and its Catechism Examined* and of *The Book of Church Reform* corresponds as closely as possible with the style and conventions, including spelling, capitalization, punctuation, and the use of italics and other devices, of the texts published in 1818 and 1831 respectively. There are some minor variations: double inverted commas indicating quotations are replaced here with single inverted commas (consequently, single inverted commas usually indicating quotations within quotations are replaced with double inverted commas); the symbols used in the 1818 edition to

---

[1] Two sheets of an early draft of the final few paragraphs of the 'Preface' dealing with Beverley's *Letter* are at UC viii. 162^v, 164^v (16 June 1831). One sheet of a second draft of the 'Preface' is at UC viii. 153^v (20 June 1831), and an abandoned draft of the title page and opening paragraphs is at viii. 149^v. The bulk of the final draft of the 'Preface' is at UC viii. 160^v, 157^v, 163^v, 173^v, 161^v, 158^v (21–3 June 1831). Two sheets which were omitted from the printed text of the 'Preface' are at UC viii. 169^v, 168^v (22 June 1831).

[2] The petition was presented to the House of Commons by Joseph Hume on 14 October 1831, and ordered to be printed: see *Parliamentary Debates* (1831) viii. 774–81, and *Commons Journals* (1830–1) lxxxvi, Part II, 917–18.

[3] See 'Upper Canada. Copy of a Petition to the Imperial Parliament, respecting the Clergy Reserved Lands, and the King's College, In that Province, agreed to at a Public Meeting at York, On the 10th of December, 1830; with Copies of other Documents relating thereto', London, 1831.

EDITORIAL INTRODUCTION

indicate Bentham's own footnotes and subfootnotes are replaced here with suprascript letters (editorial footnotes are indicated by suprascript numerals), with a separate sequence for each page; and some minor errors of typography and punctuation have been silently corrected. The only parts of the 1818 edition to carry running headings are the 'Preface on Publication', the passages dealing with 'Oxford Graduate's Maxims' and 'Excellent Church's Maxims' and the accompanying notes, and the notes accompanying the 'Non-Residence Table'. Elsewhere, the running headings in the present edition of *Church-of-Englandism* have been editorially supplied. The original issue of *Book of Church Reform* does carry running headings, and these have been reproduced on the rectos of the text in the present edition. Editorial apparatus is confined to the use of square brackets to indicate editorially inserted words, accompanied where necessary by an explanatory editorial footnote. Variations between the 1817 and 1818 issues, and between the 1818 issue and the later published extracts, are indicated in the Collations.[1] Where Bentham has inserted a cross reference in the form of a page number, the correct page number in the present edition has been supplied, and the original silently suppressed.

Bentham frequently quotes passages from other published works, in particular the first three *Annual Reports* of the National Society. Minor discrepancies between the original and the reproduction in the present text, including the use of italics, which are most commonly Bentham's, have not been noted. Bentham's page references to passages in other works are usually made only to the first page from which the quotation is taken. Where the reference is accurate, it has usually not been considered necessary to indicate the full extent of the quotation.

The 1818 issue of *Church-of-Englandism* was accompanied with a two-page Table of Errata (bound after the 'Preface on Publication') headed by the statement: 'The following Table of Errata, the number of which can not but be matter of regret, has been occasioned by a weakness in the author's eyes, coupled with his distance from the press:[2] occasion has been taken to intersperse a few amendments.' These errata have been incorporated into the text, with the original text indicated in editorial footnotes. In place of the four series of paginations of the 1818 edition, the present edition has one continuous series.

---

[1] See pp. 595–618 below.
[2] Bentham was residing at Ford Abbey, Devon.

EDITORIAL INTRODUCTION

Manuscripts

The Andrewes Appendix has been reconstructed from Bentham's manuscripts. The text is written on single sheets of foolscap, which are ruled with a wide margin and with a double line at the top, where Bentham inserted the date and the main heading. At the top of the margin he added a subheading or series of subheadings. He wrote only on the rectos of the text sheets, which he paginated consecutively with Arabic numerals. For the bulk of the material he added marginal summary paragraphs, that is short summaries of the subject-matter of the text. These marginal summaries are not reproduced in the present text, since they were not intended for publication, but were used by Bentham as a means of organizing his material. Once he had drafted a body of material corresponding to an intended section or other division of the text, it was Bentham's practice to transfer the marginal summaries to other sheets of foolscap known as marginal summary sheets. These sheets are ruled into four columns with a double line at the top for headings. There survive a handful of sheets containing 'rudiments', often referred to by Bentham as 'brouillons'. These sheets, which contain general statements or positions, notes of ideas and themes for possible development, examples for illustration, and plans, are normally written on double sheets of foolscap, each sheet being ruled into four columns with a double line at the top for headings.

It has been editorial policy to reflect as far as possible the manuscript sources on which the Andrewes Appendix is based, but without sacrifice thereby of clarity and sense. Bentham's spelling and capitalization have been retained in most instances, although editorial discretion has been exercised with regard to his punctuation, which is often inconsistent and sparse. Punctuation marks have been adjusted and supplied where clearly indicated by the sense, or required for the sake of clarity, but not in cases where this might involve a dubious interpretation of the meaning. The words and phrases underlined by Bentham for emphasis have been rendered in italics, as have all foreign words and phrases, some of which Bentham underlined and some of which he did not.

The manuscripts contain many additions (either interlinear or marginal), deletions, and emendations which represent Bentham's later corrections to the text. The latest variant has usually been preferred, while original readings have not usually been indicated. Where there is no text corresponding to some part of a marginal summary paragraph, the appropriate marginal summary is reproduced in an editorial footnote. Square brackets in the text are

EDITORIAL INTRODUCTION

reserved for editorially inserted words, while Bentham's original is, where appropriate, given in an editorial footnote. Bentham's square brackets are replaced by braces. Round brackets are those supplied by Bentham. Vertical strokes indicate a gap or blank space in the manuscript. Bentham's own footnotes are indicated by superscript letters, and editorial footnotes by superscript numerals, with a separate sequence for each page of text. The organization of the text has been ascertained by paying regard, where applicable, to the pagination of the text sheets, the numbering of the various sections, the numbering of the marginal summary paragraphs, and of course the sense. The location of any related fragments has been indicated above.[1]

[1] For the manuscripts used in the present edition see p. xxv n. above.

CHURCH-OF-ENGLANDISM
AND ITS
Catechism examined:
PRECEDED BY
STRICTURES ON THE EXCLUSIONARY SYSTEM,
AS PURSUED IN THE
NATIONAL SOCIETY'S SCHOOLS:
INTERSPERSED
WITH PARALLEL VIEWS OF THE
ENGLISH AND SCOTTISH ESTABLISHED AND NON-ESTABLISHED CHURCHES:
AND CONCLUDING WITH
REMEDIES PROPOSED FOR ABUSES INDICATED:
AND
AN EXAMINATION OF THE PARLIAMENTARY SYSTEM OF CHURCH REFORM LATELY PURSUED, AND STILL PURSUING:
INCLUDING THE PROPOSED NEW CHURCHES.

BY
JEREMY BENTHAM, ESQ.
BENCHER OF LINCOLN'S INN,
AND LATE OF QUEEN'S COLLEGE, OXFORD, M.A.

CONTENTS.

	Page
[PREFACE ON PUBLICATION]	7
PREFACE	28
[PLAN OF THE WORK]	43

INTRODUCTION.

PART I.—THE CATECHISM—A BAD SUBSTITUTE TO THE BIBLE—IS SUBSTITUTED TO IT	56
§1.—Church of England Catechism—this perhaps the First Censorial Commentary ever applied to it	56
§2.—On Religion, in a Christian Free-School, the Bible the only fit Lesson-Book	58
§3.—No Substitute to the Bible should be there taught—the Catechism is made a Substitute to it	62
§4.—Badness of this Substitute in every respect: I. As to Faithfulness.—No Tests of it	67
§5.—II. Badness in respect of Matter	74
§6.—III. Badness in respect of Form	75
§7.—Of the Badness of this Formulary, in respect of Matter, the Framers of it were conscious	77
§8.—Of the Badness of this Formulary, in respect of Faithfulness, Matter, and Form, the Imposers of it on the Schools are conscious	77
[§9.—The Religion thus taught by the Rulers of the Church of England, is not the Religion of Jesus]	82
PART II.—EXCLUSIONARY SYSTEM OF INSTRUCTION—ITS ESTABLISHMENT—ITS BAD TENDENCIES	88
PART III.—EXCLUSIONARY SYSTEM—GROUNDS FOR THE HOPE THAT THE APPROBATION OF IT IS NOT GENERAL	99
PART IV.—NATIONAL SOCIETY—GROUNDS FOR REGARDING THE EXCLUSIONARY ACTS AS SPURIOUS, AND ITS REPORTS AS PURPOSELY DECEPTIOUS	102

§1.—Cause and Ground of Suspicion as to Authenticity   102

§2.—Marks of Authenticity, proper and usual, in Reports of Proceedings of Public Bodies   104

§3.—Positions and Plan of Proof—Ends pursued by the Institution—Means employed   106

§4.—I. Proofs of the System of Exclusion   109

[§5. II.][1]—Proofs of the System of Imposition—[I.][2] General Committee—Meetings none   123

§6.—Proofs of the System of Imposition continued— II. Sub-Committees and their Meetings, none   130

§7.—Proofs of the System of Imposition continued— III. Acts spurious   133

§8.—Securities against Spuriousness—Cause of the Omission of them, Necessity and Design—not Inadvertence   146

§9. [III.]—Authors, acting and consenting, of the combined Systems of Exclusion and Imposition   153

§10.—Authors, &c. continued—Dr. Manners Sutton, Archbishop of Canterbury   160

§11.—How to organize a Chaos—Forms of Disorder exemplified in these Reports   168

§12.—General Committee—Fraud involved in the Title thus given to the Managing Body   186

PART V.—BAPTISM AND SPONSORSHIP PROPER, WHEN INSTITUTED—BAPTISM USELESS, SPONSORSHIP IMPROPER NOW   195

THE CHURCH OF ENGLAND CATECHISM EXAMINED   203

APPENDIX, No. I.

REMARKS ON THE OBJECT OF THE CHURCH OF ENGLAND RELIGION, AS AVOWED BY THE BISHOP OF LONDON   257

---

[1] 1818 '§II. (should be) §5.'
[2] 1818 '2.'

CONTENTS

No. II.

LORD'S SUPPER—NOT DESIGNED BY JESUS FOR GENERAL IMITATION—ITS UTTER UNFITNESS FOR THAT PURPOSE   312

No. III.

REMEDIES TO THE [MISCHIEFS OF THE] EXCLUSIONARY SYSTEM AS APPLIED TO INSTRUCTION   333

No. IV.

REMEDY TO ALL RELIGIOUS AND MUCH POLITICAL MISCHIEF—EUTHANASIA OF THE CHURCH   343
§1.—Plan of this Paper   344
§2.—Euthanasia, in Contradistinction to Cacothanasia, what?— UTI POSSIDETIS Principle—its Application to this Case   346
§3.—I. Service   351
§4.—II. Pay   371
§5.—Pay continued—Merit, whether producible by Sinecures   399
§6.—III. Discipline   415
§7.—State of Discipline, as exhibited by Authority, and elucidated by a Diocesan Secretary   428
§8.—Ulterior Information from Mr. Wright   460
§9.—Vices of Excellent Church recapitulated   471
§10.—Facienda in the way of Reform   482

No. V.

RECENT MEASURES OF PRETENDED REFORM OR IMPROVEMENT—THEIR INUTILITY AND MISCHIEVOUSNESS   494

INTRODUCTION   494
§1.—I. Giving Increase to the Number of Non-Resident Incumbents   496
§2.—II. Increasing the Number of Resident Curates   499
III. To that End, out of the Pockets of Incumbents and Patrons, taking Money, and forcing it into the Pockets of Curates   499

§3.—IV. For Increasing the Value of English Livings, exacting from the Population of the Three Kingdoms the Annual Sum of 100,000*l*.   518

§4.—V. Regulating the [occupations][1] of Agriculture, in the case of a Parish or other Priest   525

§5.—VI. Over Incumbents and Curates, lodging despotic power in the hands of Bishops   530

§6.—VII. Announced, and remaining to be executed. From Christians, and others of all persuasions, money to be exacted, sufficient to render the number of Church-of-England Churches commensurate to the whole population   535

[1] 1818 'operations'.

PREFACE
ON PUBLICATION.

NOT without regret, in a manner so contrary to what will be seen to have been his original intention, is the personality of the author at length exposed to the view of the company,[1]—a company, not small either in eminence or numbers,—of those who in so many parts of the work, will find more or less cause to be dissatisfied with it.

From the view of a determinate individual, in the character of the instrument by which the reproach is cast, the dissatisfaction can not but receive more or less increase: and, assuredly, of the object which he has all along been aiming at, never has the production of pain in any shape, to so much as a single individual, formed any part: never any more than of that of the surgeon in the probing of a wound.

To the regret thus expressed one alleviation however remains: viz. that among existing individuals scarcely could any one be found, from whose personality any uneasiness, in the production of which he may thus have been instrumental, could receive less increase. Coming from a recluse, who forms no part of society—whose destiny keeps his person as completely, as if he were immured in a solitary cell, out of all chance of offending the eyes of any of the distinguished functionaries and other personages, to whose minds the offence, such as it is, will have been *given*—a work presenting no name but that of a person so circumstanced, will in the scale of inoffensiveness be found to stand next in order to an anonymous one.

With the exception of the title and of this last-written though first stationed preface, the whole contents of this volume will here be seen in the exact state in which, more than a twelvemonth ago, having passed through the press, they were made ready for the bookseller.

From booksellers, to whom the work had been either shewn or mentioned by description, the answer was—'Yes, with a name readily: but not otherwise:' with a name, meaning the name of the author

---

[1] The work had been printed in 1817 by John McCreery (1768–1832), of Black Horse Court, London, but was not published until the following year by Effingham Wilson (1785–1868), bookseller, of 88 Royal Exchange, London, as Bentham goes on to explain. The printed text of 1817 appeared under the pseudonym of 'An Oxford Graduate', whereas Bentham identified himself as the author in the published text of 1818. Bentham composed this 'Preface on Publication' in February and March 1818. For further details see the Editorial Introduction, pp. xxii–xxiii above.

whoever he might be: for, as to the name of the real author it was not, it is believed, mentioned.

In the Introduction to the work intituled *Plan of Parliamentary Reform*, &c.,[1] a sort of sketch was given of one of the two *natures*, of which our constitution, such as it is, is composed, viz. the *temporal* one. In the present work may be seen a portrait of the other nature, viz. the *spiritual* one. The sketch was but a miniature, and that a mere outline: the portrait will be found to be of a larger size, and more particularly delineated as well as coloured.

In this instance, as in that other, whether it be with an immediate view to reformation,—or, as an indispensable means to that end, in the character of an object of censure,—the *system*—against *that* it is, and that alone, had there been any choice, the censure could have been pointed. The system, yes; individuals, no: because, the individuals, being but the children of the system—bred under the system,—had the existing individuals never had existence, under that system others exactly like them, differing in nothing but in name, would have occupied their places.

But of the system—a system in the abstract—without bringing to view any of the individuals acting under it, to give any intelligible representation—any representation on which any hope of good, how faint so ever, could have grounded itself, was not found practicable. Of all that, which will here be seen to have been *done*, (saying included) by an Archbishop of Canterbury,[2] a Bishop of London,[3] a Rector of St. James's,[4] a Lord President of the Council,[5] a Chancellor of the Exchequer,[6] a Chief Judge of the Roman law, Civil and Canon[7]—a Rector of St. James's[8]—with their *et cæteras* upon *et cæteras*,—scarce is there any thing, that, by any person, if any such there be, in whose judgment it had been better left undone than done,

[1] *Plan of Parliamentary Reform, in the form of a Catechism, with reasons for each article, with an Introduction, shewing the necessity of radical, and the inadequacy of moderate, reform*, London, 1817 (Bowring, iii. 433–557), consisted in a shorter 'Catechism of Parliamentary Reform', composed in 1809–10, preceded by a longer 'Introduction', composed in 1816–17.

[2] Charles Manners-Sutton (1755–1828), Archbishop of Canterbury 1805–28.

[3] William Howley (1766–1848), Bishop of London 1813–28, Archbishop of Canterbury 1828–48.

[4] Gerrard Andrewes (1750–1825), Rector of St James's, Piccadilly 1802–25, Dean of Canterbury 1809–25.

[5] Dudley Ryder (1762–1847), created Earl of Harrowby in 1809, Vice-President of the Board of Trade 1790–1801, Paymaster General 1791–1800, Foreign Secretary 1804, Lord President of the Council 1812–27.

[6] Nicholas Vansittart (1766–1851), created Baron Bexley in 1823, Chancellor of the Exchequer 1812–23.

[7] Sir William Scott (1745–1836), created Baron Stowell in 1821, Judge of the Consistory Court of London and Vicar-General of the Province of Canterbury 1788–1821, and Judge of the High Court of Admiralty 1798–1828.

[8] Bentham has (presumably unintentionally) repeated himself.

PREFACE ON PUBLICATION

would have been recognized as possible, or at any rate as likely to have been done, if it had not been seen actually done: actually done by certain individuals, such as those by which those same characters will be seen to have been actually performed.

Had it not then been for individual acts and discourses, such as those here exhibited and held up to view in detail, the author would have been called to order for seeking, on grounds so purely imaginary, to destroy all confidence in public men. This for reproof: while for refutation, the words *abstract, visionary, utopian, speculative, enthusiastic*, with their respective conjugates, on one side of the field,[1]—with the names of Marat and Robespierre[2] on the other, would have been uttered and received—as so many instruments, not less sufficient than simple and concise.

As to *accusation, imputation, crimination, condemnation, censure*—whatsoever may be regarded as seeking to attach itself, in a strain expressed by any of those words, to this or that individual,—to the acts or discourses of the individual in question, as exhibited by the documents all along quoted or referred to—documents all along of the most authentic and unquestionable nature—every thing of that sort not only is now, but from first to last has all along been meant to be confined. Of this meaning and intention, notice, it is believed, will, in places more than one, be found given in the body of the work. But, for further assurance, a declaration thus all-comprehensive, and placed at the very threshold, may perhaps be found not altogether misemployed.

In so melancholy a state of things as will be seen here depictured, the following correspondence will in some sort serve to shew, viz. that the scene, how dark so ever, is not completely destitute of all lighter shades, and at the same time with what alacrity has been laid hold of, and with what perseverance improved, whatsoever opportunity offered a prospect of placing the conduct of the distinguished persons in question, or any of them, in any light more agreeable to a philanthropic eye. Every other opportunity of the like nature that came within his reach, would be noticed by the author with the like alacrity, and whatever occasion it afforded of doing the like justice, improved with the like solicitude.

---

[1] For a further discussion of these and similar terms see *The Book of Fallacies*, London, 1824, pp. 295–313 (Bowring, ii. 457–62).

[2] Jean Paul Marat (1744–93) and Maximilien François Marie Isidore Joseph de Robespierre (1758–94) were figures associated with the worst excesses of the French Revolution.

CHURCH-OF-ENGLANDISM

'JEREMY BENTHAM, ESQUIRE, *to* W. SMITH, ESQUIRE, M.P.[1]

'Ford Abbey, near Chard,[2] *Jan.* 24, 1818.

'SIR,

'THE occasion, of the application I am hereby taking the liberty of troubling you with, is—my having in immediate readiness for publication a work of considerable bulk, in the course of which, though on grounds of the utmost publicity, the conduct of the *Archbishop of Canterbury*,[3]—on a certain occasion also of an eminently public nature,—is held up in a point of view, such as, in some eyes, howsoever it may be in others, seems not likely to be an altogether favourable one. Since the completing of the impression, it has happened to me to hear—and on what seemed to me good authority—through the medium of some friends of yours and mine, that his Grace's conduct, on the occasion of that *Toleration Act*, for which the *religion* and *liberty* of the country are so eminently indebted to yourself,[4] was such, as in proportion as it is known, can not but recommend him, in a very high degree, to the admiration of the friends of *both*.

'What *has* been done by a man on *one* occasion does not cause *not* to have been done that which has been done by him on *another*. But it would be a conduct not consistent with my notions of generosity, or even of justice, if, while thus, by the considerations that will be seen, compelled to hold up to view what seemed to be the ill deserts of a person in so high and influential a situation, I suffered the occasion to go by, without endeavouring to make known, to the same extent, what it has fallen in my way to be apprized of, and to regard as possessing an incontestable claim, to be placed to the per contrà side of the account.

'Assured of finding the like sentiments on your part, I take the liberty of addressing to you this letter, for the purpose of requesting the favour of your enabling me to give effect to the above wish. As to the being accessory in any way to any accusation, which it may happen to you to see contained in the work in question,—to no such imputation can a compliance with any such request as this expose

---

[1] William Smith (1756–1835), Unitarian, first elected to Parliament in 1784, was MP for Norwich 1807–30. The letter is reproduced in *The Correspondence of Jeremy Bentham*, vol. ix, ed. S. Conway, Oxford, 1989 (*CW*), pp. 151–3.

[2] Bentham rented Ford Abbey in Devon from 1814 until 1818, and resided there for about six months each year.

[3] i.e. Charles Manners-Sutton.

[4] The Doctrine of the Trinity Act of 1813 (53 Geo. III, c. 160) extended the exemptions given to dissenters from the Church of England in the Toleration Act of 1689 (1 Wm. & Mary, Sess. I, c. 18) to Unitarians, and removed the penalties attached to the denial of the Trinity by the Blasphemy Act of 1698 (9 & 10 Wm. III, c. 32).

PREFACE ON PUBLICATION

you: for, supposing such compliance declined by you, the work in question will not be the less published. With *your* motives on the occasion, his Grace could not therefore but feel satisfied, whatsoever might be the case in regard to *mine*.

'What I heard was to this effect: viz. that, on the occasion of the Unitarian Toleration Bill, which has so happily passed into an act (53 Geo. III. c. [160].)[1] it was in concert with his Grace that the Act passed both Houses: passed, and in that tranquillity which was at once so decorous and so admirable: that, in the state in which it was originally *drawn* or *approved* by his Grace (I am not enabled to say exactly which of the two was the case) it was so congenial to your wishes, as to have in no inconsiderable degree surpassed your expectations: and that it was so, in a degree much beyond what the Act is, in the form into which it has been moulded: that it went so far as to give a compleat indemnity not only to Unitarianism, but to all opinions without distinction respecting the constitution of the Godhead: (alack, what a subject for pretended knowledge! what a ground for punishment on the score of imputed ignorance!) and this, not only as against punishment under *statute law*, but also as against punishment at *common law*. No effect approaching to this (I have the mortification to see) has been produced by the Act as it stands at present. This difference—this sad difference between that which it is, and that which, I think, you can not but join with me in wishing that it had been, had (I understand) for its cause the interposition—not of any Bishop, nor of any other spiritual person—but of some wearer of a long robe of a different cut.[2]

'Under these circumstances, the following are the particulars of the information which I am taking the liberty of requesting at your hands.

'1. Whether it be not true, that a Bill, either drawn or approved by the *Archbishop of Canterbury*, gave to the liberty of *printing* and publishing—(or, as Bishop Taylor, using the Scriptural term, more emphatically, as well as concisely phrases it, the *liberty of prophesying*)[3]—a basis, broader, in some and what direction, than that which by the Act in question has been given to it.

'2. Amongst the effects of that Bill, was not that of rendering the

---

[1] 1818 '136' is a slip.

[2] In his reply (see pp. 14–15 below), Smith explains that the Bill was amended at the behest of Edward Law (1750–1818), first Baron Ellenborough, Chief Justice of King's Bench 1802–18, and John Scott (1751–1838), first Baron and first Earl Eldon, Lord Chancellor 1801–6, 1807–27.

[3] Jeremy Taylor (bap. 1613, d. 1667), Bishop of Down and Connor and Administrator of Dromore 1661–7, was author of ΘΕΟΛΟΓΊΑ ἘΚΛΕΚΤΙΚΉ. *A Discourse on the Liberty of Prophesying*, London, 1647.

liberty in question secure, as well against prosecution at *common law*, as against prosecution on *statute law*?

'3. Between that Bill and the aforesaid Act were there any and what other differences?

'To these questions, the shortest as well as most compleat and correct answer the nature of the case admits of, (if no decisive objection to your favouring me with it occurs to you,) would be—a copy of the Bill itself, in the state in which it received the approbation of his Grace.

'4. By what cause or causes did that difference appear to you to have been produced?

'Of the above four questions, the three first, you will be aware, are the only ones which have any immediate bearing, on the purpose of this application, as above declared. But, surely, whatsoever regard for religious liberty was, in the first instance, manifested by his Grace, can not but receive additional lustre, from whatsoever contrast may have had place between it and any oppositeness in sentiment and conduct which may have been manifested elsewhere:—manifested from a quarter less exposed, on this ground, to the seductive influence of sinister interest, and interest-begotten prejudice.

                    'I am, Sir,
              'With very sincere respect,
                'Your obedient servant,
                    'JEREMY BENTHAM.'

'W. SMITH, ESQ. M.P.
  '*Park Street, Westminster.*'

'W. SMITH, ESQ. M.P. *to* JEREMY BENTHAM, ESQUIRE.[1]

'*Park Street, Westminster, 16th February,* 1818.

'MY DEAR SIR,

'I HAVE received your favour enquiring into the particulars of what passed between the Archbishop of Canterbury and myself, on occasion of the introduction of the Bill for repealing the Penal Statutes against the impugners of the Trinity, which was passed into a law in the year 1813: and having still in my mind a pretty clear

[1] The original letter, which is at BL Add. MS 33,545, fos. 262–6, is reproduced in *Correspondence* (*CW*), ix. 162–4. Smith had initially acknowledged Bentham's letter in a brief response on 29 January 1818: see ibid. 153–4.

recollection of the affair, I apprehend that I shall afford the most satisfactory reply to your questions, by a connected relation of the circumstances as they occurred. And this I shall do with the greater pleasure, as it gives me the opportunity of acknowledging the obligation which his Grace then conferred upon me by the uniform frankness and liberality of his conduct throughout the whole of the proceeding. As soon as I had determined on attempting the measure, my first step was to wait on the Archbishop at Lambeth, to acquaint him of my intention, and to receive from him such communication as he should think fit to make. The result of a very open and friendly conversation on the subject, with his Grace, was a clear conviction in my own mind that I needed not to be uneasy about any opposition to be expected from him;—but he explicitly declared his disinclination to pledge himself to any particular point, till he had taken the sentiments of his brethren, whom, on such matters, it was his wish to consult; and said, that as the spring was then pretty far advanced, and several of the Bishops had left London (probably without any intention to return during the Session of Parliament,)[1] he would be glad to have the business postponed till the next year, if it were not inconsistent with my views or convenience:—with which suggestion, as the matter could not be considered as immediately urgent, I, of course, complied. Early in the ensuing session,[2] I again waited on his Grace, whom I had the pleasure to find in the same disposition. He then told me, that supposing my object was only to remove every obstruction to fair argument and discussion, he was willing to consent to the repeal of all the statutes, inflicting penalties, or disabilities for impugning or denying the doctrine of the Trinity, either by writing or advised speaking:—but that he supposed I did not, any more than himself, intend to open a door for the admission of all manner of profaneness and impiety in *the mode of treating* subjects of so solemn a description; and therefore that the crime of blasphemy should still be left open to the animadversion of the common law:—I, and I have no doubt his Grace also, understanding by the term "Blasphemy," of course, not that constructive and inferential imputation of the crime which might be fastened on every doctrine relative to the Divine Nature differing in any respect or degree from that of the Established Church, (an interpretation wholly subversive of the very liberty and relief intended to be granted,) but that which is its common, and, I imagine, also its legal import;—the use of language and epithets in themselves reproachful, reviling and abusive, levelled

[1] i.e. the parliamentary session that ran from 7 January 1812 to 4 May 1812.
[2] Parliament reassembled on 24 November 1812.

immediately at the majesty and character of the Supreme Being.[1] On this footing, I most readily agreed to place the question;—persuaded that, however plausible an argument may be raised for the abstract right of using, in any controversy, such terms as disputants may think most applicable to the subject, yet that such latitude is not here necessary, or even advantageous to the legitimate object of all controversy, the successful investigation of truth: and therefore that respect to the national worship, tenderness to the opinions, or even prejudices of serious and sincere religionists, and, above all, the venerable nature of the subjects in question, completely justify, if they do not absolutely demand, the prohibition of such language, as useless, indecent, and mischievous.

'I next informed his Majesty's Ministers of my design, and the progress I had made; and learned from them, with great satisfaction, that they were equally inclined to acquiesce in the measure: and only desired that, in the progress of the Bill, I would not, by unnecessary discussion, incur the risk of exciting a spirit of alarm and opposition which then appeared to lie dormant, but pursue my object as quietly as circumstances should permit. In this reasonable proposition I also cheerfully acquiesced; and soon after, had an interview with the Archbishop and the Chancellor of the Exchequer,[2] when the Bill was moulded into that shape in which it passed, unopposed, through the House of Commons.[3]

'In the Lords however an objection was taken by the Ch. and the Lord C.I.[4] not to the principle, but merely to the mode—the two Noble Lords disapproving the sweeping repeal of all the statutes by which the penalties, &c. were imposed, and preferring that they should be described and repealed, *nominatim*;[5] dwelling so much on this, as to insist on the rejection of the Bill as it then stood;[6] by which,

---

[1] According to William Blackstone, *Commentaries on the Laws of England*, 4 vols., Oxford, 1765–9, iv. 59, blasphemy was an offence 'against the Almighty, by denying his being or providence; or by contumelious reproaches of our Saviour Christ. Whither also may be referred all profane scoffing at the holy scripture, or exposing it to contempt and ridicule.'

[2] Vansittart.

[3] Smith gave notice to move a Bill for the Relief of Persons Denying the Doctrine of the Trinity on 5 May 1813: see *Parliamentary Debates* (1813) xxv. 1147–8. The Bill was presented to the Commons by Smith and ordered to be printed on 15 June 1813. It received its Second Reading, was amended, and ordered to be reprinted on 23 June 1813. The amendments were considered and read a second time on 28 June 1813. The amended Bill received its Third Reading and was sent to the House of Lords on 29 June 1813. See *Commons Journals* (1812–13) lxviii. 567, 595, 611, 618.

[4] i.e. Lord Chancellor Eldon and Lord Chief Justice Ellenborough.

[5] i.e. 'by name' or 'one by one'.

[6] The amended Bill had received its First Reading in the House of Lords on 30 June 1813, and its Second Reading on 2 July 1813, whereupon it was discussed in committee, but was abandoned on 7 July 1813: see *Lords Journals* (1812–14) xlix. 551, 561, 587.

PREFACE ON PUBLICATION

as the session was drawing to a close, I was somewhat embarrassed:—but they both had the goodness to assure me that they would consent to pass, with all expedition, a new Bill drawn on the plan they suggested. The first was accordingly negatived, and the new one, so drawn and settled, immediately introduced into the Commons, carried through every stage, and passed without delay:—from whence it went up to the Lords, where, to my infinite content, it was equally successful.[1]

'One only material difference in the operation of the two Bills has since appeared:—that, whereas the former, from the generality of its terms, extended to Ireland,—the latter does not; from the inadvertent omission to repeal specifically the Irish penal statute.[2]

'At the moment of the rejection of the first Bill in the House of Lords, the Archbishop took the occasion to say to me, that, having originally given his assent to the measure, he certainly should not think of retracting it, merely because it was thought expedient to effect the purpose by means somewhat different from those which he himself had agreed to; and that I might rely on his support of the new Bill—a pledge which, it is needless to say, was strictly observed.

'You have now, Sir, as accurate an account as my memory will furnish, of a transaction on which I have ever reflected with unmixed satisfaction; regarding it as affording an irrefragable proof of the increasing justness and liberality of the sentiments of the age, on principles of the highest importance, and strong ground of hope, that the last lingering remains of intolerance will, ere long, be swept clean away. Happy, too, in having been the active and fortunate, though humble instrument, through whose agency the occasion was presented of effectuating so considerable an advantage.

'As for the Reverend Metropolitan, whose part in this business must have been so influential, I shall not easily be convinced that, in other affairs, he can have been induced to adopt courses inconsistent with the principles which appeared to me to guide his conduct in this. But even could I suppose such a conviction effected, I should think it certainly not the less incumbent on me fully to represent, in its just colours, that portion of his Ecclesiastical Administration which,

---

[1] The new Bill was presented to the House of Commons and received its First Reading on 10 July 1813. It received its Second Reading and was amended on 12 July 1813. The amendments were agreed on 13 July 1813. The Bill received its Third Reading and was sent to the House of Lords on 14 July 1813. In the Lords, it received its First Reading on 14 July 1813 and its Second Reading on 16 July 1813. It was discussed in committee on 19 July 1813, and was passed on 20 July 1813. See *Commons Journals* (1812–13) lxviii. 657, 659, 661, 666, 673, and *Lords Journals* (1812–14) xlix. 615, 619, 649–50, 653.

[2] The Irish Unitarians were relieved from the penalties for impugning the Trinity by an Act passed in July 1817 (57 Geo. III, c. 70).

having had the opportunity of closely observing it, I thought strongly marked with every quality by which the true interests, not merely of the National Establishment, but of Christianity itself, can best be promoted.

'I am, my dear Sir,
'Very faithfully your's,
'WILLIAM SMITH.'

'P.S. I must also record on this subject that for which I have sufficient authority to induce my own entire belief; that, at a Meeting of the Right Reverend Bench, convened to determine on the conduct proper to be pursued with respect to the Bill, the Bishop of Norwich[1] alone professed his approbation of it, and his determination to support it: but this I should never have learned or suspected from any the slightest change in the conduct or language of the Archbishop of Canterbury.'

LETTER II.

MR. BENTHAM *to* MR. SMITH.[2]

Queen Square Place, Westminster,[3] *Feb.* 1818.

'DEAR SIR,
'I HAVE to acknowledge the favour of your very obliging Letter. So far as concerns the Archbishop, it is truly gratifying to me to see the account I had received from *unimmediate,* so fully confirmed by such respectable, as well as *immediate,* evidence. At the same time, in regard to the general result, I wish it were in my power to indulge in any such comfortable view, as that which, it seems to me, you have taken of it. Concurring with every thing you say with regard to the Archbishop,—still, in the state of things, as reported by you, I am unable to see any such security, as you (it seems to me) not only have seen, but continue to see in it.

'What you count upon (so it seems to me) is in the first place, absolute security as against statute law; in the next place, like security as against common law.

---

[1] Henry Bathurst (bap. 1744, d. 1837), Bishop of Norwich 1805–37.
[2] The letter is reproduced in *Correspondence* (*CW*), ix. 168–77.
[3] Bentham inherited Queen Square Place on his father's death in 1792, and continued to live there until his own death on 6 June 1832.

PREFACE ON PUBLICATION

'Neither against the one nor against the other scourge, is it my good fortune to be able to see any such security for you: and the liberty I take of mentioning the matter here, is accompanied with the less hesitation, because, though, perhaps, not exactly relevant to the purpose of my first Letter to you, it is completely so to the purpose of the present work.

'1. First as to statute law. As to bills, upon a careful search among the House of Commons' papers, I find two, and no more than two, both of the year 1813: one, the original bill, date, June 15; the other, the amended bill, date, June 23.[1] One you speak of, of course the latter, as rejected;—of course in the Lords: rejected, in the manner you describe. This rejection—what then is the peccant matter by which it was produced? A comparison of the amended bill with the act will shew it. In the bill it is the clause, by which, to the repeal of the particular act, which *pro tanto*, is by that clause accordingly repealed, is added a sweeping clause, repealing "so much of the said act of the ninth and tenth of King William, and of all or any other act or acts of the English, Scotch, British, Irish, or United Parliaments, as imposes penalties on those who, &c.—(except, &c.)"[2] Having this sweeping clause in it, the bill was rejected. The act which afterwards passed, and which we have, has no such sweeping clause.

'Nor yet was the clause got rid of in the ordinary way, by amendment; instead of this, the whole bill, as it stood, was thrown out: an intimation having, however, been previously given—and *that*, as it should seem a secret one—that, provided this obnoxious clause were omitted, another bill might be less unfortunate.

'Now, Sir, on the subject of this manœuvre, I will venture to submit to you an observation or two.

'In the first place, that sweeping and completely tranquillizing clause, for what cause was it not permitted to stand? For this cause, or for none: because in the pre-eminently learned eyes in question,[3] even as against statute law, it would have rendered if not security too secure, at any rate tranquillity too tranquil.

'To leave you still in a state of insecurity, anxiety, and depen-

---

[1] For the texts of the original Bill of 15 June 1813, and the Bill as amended on 23 June 1813, see *Commons Sessional Papers* (1812–13) ii. 1095–8, 1099–1102 respectively.

[2] The original Bill as amended, dated 23 June 1813, provided that 'so much of the said Act of the ninth and tenth of King *William*, and of all or any other Act or Acts of the English, Scotch, British, Irish, or United Parliaments, as imposes penalties on those who interpret the Holy Scriptures inconsistently with the doctrines of The *Holy Trinity* as laid down in the thirty-nine articles of the United Church of England and Ireland, be and the same are hereby Repealed; except so far as may relate to Ministers of the said United Church.' See *Commons Sessional Papers* (1812–13) ii. 1100.

[3] i.e. Eldon and Ellenborough.

CHURCH-OF-ENGLANDISM

dance—either this was the object of the *veto*, or it had none. In the statute book is there any other statute, by which punishment, in any shape, is attached to the sort of act in question? If, yes, here then the persecuting intention stands confessed. Is there no such statute? Then is the omission useless and indefensible.

'So much for the design. Now as to the mode.

'This clause being then, by the persons in question, let us suppose, regarded,—at any rate professed to be regarded, as improper, or at least as needless,—then why not get rid of it in the ordinary way? For what cause decline getting rid of it by an amendment? Sir, I will assign a cause: let any other supposable cause be found, I will acknowledge my mistake. Sir, it was the fear—the well-grounded fear—of that sentiment, which would be the necessary result of their being seen to do that, which in fact, they were doing.

'To neither of the pre-eminently learned persons in question, would it have been agreeable to see his name upon the journals, in quality of mover of such an amendment: an amendment by which the mind of the mover would thus far have stood depicted upon record, in its real colours. No: they insisted on your doing against yourselves, what they were ashamed to do: they insisted on your employing your own hands in cutting the ground from under your own feet.

'Speaking of the persons in question, on occasion of the penalties in question,—after saying, "disapproving the sweeping repeal of all the statutes, by which the penalties, &c." were imposed, *preferring* (you add) that they should be described and repealed *nominatim*.[1]

'Pardon me, if in this word *preferring*, I see the source of a misconception, which it seems to me necessary to obviate. An intimation, which by implication, this word presents to me, as likely to convey, is—that, between the courses thus put in opposition to one another, there existed—at any rate in the learned eyes in question—some natural incompatibility: that of these same two courses one, and that alone, was regarded as legally proper, the other legally improper: and that the two being, as above, naturally incompatible, that which was regarded as the proper one—that, and that alone—was accordingly consented to, the other rejected.

'Such being the conception presented, how stands the fact? Incompatibility, manifestly there was none. In the *preference*, carried as it was into effect, two things were contained: rejection put upon one mode, admission given to the other. What was the mode rejected? the only one that could be completely effectual to the professed purpose. What was the mode—the only mode—which

---

[1] See p. 14 above.

PREFACE ON PUBLICATION

the *goodness* you speak of,[1] would admit? It was a mode, in the first place, insufficient to its declared purpose; in the next place, pregnant with collateral inconveniences.

'First then the mode thus rejected would, I say, have been completely effectual to the professed purpose. What was that mode? It was what you so properly denominate the *sweeping* mode: the repeal of all the obnoxious statutes by one sweeping clause.

'This mode (so you say, and truly) was rejected. The proof is, that a clause to this effect may be seen in the amended bill, (the bill of [23d][2] June, 1813) as it came from the Commons, and that no such clause is to be seen in the act, (53d George III. c. 160.)—So much (says this same clause) "So much of the said act of the 9th and 10th of King William, and of all or any other act or acts of the English, Scotch, British, Irish, or United Parliaments, as imposes penalties, &c. are hereby repealed."

'This mode was, I say, the only mode which to that same purpose could be completely effectual. For, the repeal of any thing less than the whole number of the penal provisions, bearing upon the point in question, how could it be effectual? Repealing them all, one by one, (this I call the *particularizing mode*) would, indeed, supposing it known by every body that they were all repealed, have been equally effectual. But to whom could this be known? To nobody. Not even to the pre-eminently learned persons, who refused to admit of any other mode.

'How should it be known? On the contrary, is it not known, that in the existing legislative chaos, we possess a sort of *terra incognita*,[3] in which, as within the Arctic and Antarctic circles, discoveries may from time to time be made? Have we not a very notorious evidence of this, in the statute, 13th Charles II. cap. 5, by the discovery of which the number of signatures to a petition for reform has so recently— (and—I beg Sir Samuel Romilly's pardon, see Commons' debate, Morning Chronicle, 4th March, 1818, for saying so prudentially)— been reduced to twenty?[4]

'In the particular case in question, one reason why, even to these pre-eminently learned persons themselves, the sufficiency of the only mode they would admit of, could not be known, is—that it had no

---

[1] See p. 15 above.   [2] 1818 '25th' is a slip.   [3] i.e. 'unknown land'.
[4] In the House of Commons on 3 March 1818, Sir Samuel Romilly (1757–1818), law reformer, Solicitor General 1806–7, presented forty-six petitions for parliamentary reform from Bristol, each petition containing twenty names. Romilly explained that the petitioners had mistakenly believed that, under the Act against Tumultuous Petitioning of 1661 (13 Car. II, c. 5), petitions of more than twenty names were prohibited. The statute, however, merely prohibited active solicitation on behalf of petitions with more than twenty signatures. See *Morning Chronicle*, 4 March 1818, and *Parliamentary Debates* (1818) xxxvii. 752–3.

existence. For proof, I give you back the case of Ireland, the case to which your own letter alludes.

'While the ink is yet wet, comes from the bookseller my copy of the statutes of last session, and in it the statute of the 7th July, 1817, 57th George III. cap. 70, which then, for the first time, extends to that island the relief which, such as it is, had four years before been vouchsafed to ours.[1]

'Now, as to the *collateral inconveniences*. One of these likewise, this letter of yours, Sir, supplies me with: *delay* and *vexation*, are their names. When the only completely effectual mode was rejected, you were (you say) "somewhat embarrassed." Well might you so be: and this, notwithstanding "the goodness," with which they "assured you (these pre-eminently learned persons) that they could consent to pass with all expedition a new bill drawn on the plan they suggested:"[2] viz. that plan, the insufficiency of which has just been demonstrated. Insufficient as it was,—by the passing of this bill, this embarrassment of yours, if not removed, was, at any rate, to a certain degree relieved. So far as it regarded yourself, and your brethren in *this* island, it continued not more than about a couple of months: for, the 21st of July is the date of the act, by which so much as could be removed by it was removed. But your brethren in Ireland, what to them has been the effect of all this learned goodness? In hot water were they kept by it full four years. In hot water? Yes, Sir, and, moreover, in jeopardy. For, in the mean time, who could say what might not happen? As Providence would have it, your sheet-anchor, the archbishop, continued serviceable. But all men are mortal, and the holiest men (ask Saint Peter else) not unchangeable.[3] What, if in the course of these four years, his Grace had died? Sir, your postscript gives the answer.[4] For successor he would have had one of those bishops, who are against the measure. Behold then the effect, and not improbably the object—or what else was the object? of the learned *goodness*, before which you had to bow.

'First collateral inconvenience. Delay and vexation combined.

"2. Another *collateral inconvenience*. It is composed of the *expence*, public and private together, which cannot but have been attendant, on the interval of delay, and the two additional processes, which all this goodness and learning filled it with: viz. the preparing and bringing in to the Commons that fresh Bill, which became the *Act;* and moreover the whole manufacture of the fresh Bill which was made necessary for Ireland.

[1] See p. 15 n. above. [2] See p. 15 above.
[3] An allusion to Peter's denial of Jesus: see Matthew 26: 34–5, 69–75; Mark 14: 66–72; Luke 22: 54–62; and John 18: 15–18, 25–7. [4] See p. 16 above.

PREFACE ON PUBLICATION

'In *my* account, this expence, Sir, *is* an inconvenience: how many hundred pounds it may have amounted to, I cannot pretend to say: a mere drop in the ocean: in the ocean of industriously begotten and (except in so far as, for example, the voice of a petitioning people may be smothered by economy,) anxiously nursed, unnecessary expence. In *my* account I say it *is* an inconvenience. In the account of the pre-eminently learned persons in question, can it have been placed on that same side?—Alas, no: on no other than the opposite side. To all those who fatten upon fees—official men, judges, professional lawyers of all sorts—to all these belongs a common cause—an habitual, and, from habit, almost an instinctive sympathy. When I see either of the two pre-eminently learned persons ready and willing, to see exchanged for salary, all fees, from which, either in pocket or in patronage, he derives a profit,—*then* will I acknowledge, that the burthen, with which in that shape, they, on this occasion, concurred, according to you, in forcing upon the public, as well as individuals, formed no part of the inducement to the conduct by which that burthen was imposed.

'Second collateral inconvenience—result of the delay, *expence*.

'Sir!! Sir! (I think I hear you cry) Sir, what is this you are about?—Bad motives?—are you not imputing *bad motives?*

'Good Sir, no: not I, indeed: I impute no *bad motives. Love of money, and money's worth*—a branch of self-regarding interest—this, and this alone, is the motive I impute. Sir, I love money myself: and not the less for my having so little of it.—Sir, do you think I would impute to myself *bad motives?*

'No, Sir; if you want to see a man who has no love for money, go to my Lord Chancellor, go to my Lord Chief Justice,[1] they perhaps, may be able to direct you to one.

'A motive, the general predominance of which over every other, is necessary to the very existence of the species, can this, with any thing like propriety, be termed a *bad motive?* Were it not for this predominance, think, Sir, what would become of the whole species in a month's time. *Bad motive?* No, Sir; there is no such thing as a *bad motive*. This—so delusive in the current language—this may, perhaps, appear to you a mystery. But the present is not a time, or place, for clearing it up: in a small tract of mine, intituled, *Table of the Springs of Action*, you may see it cleared up, whenever you please:[2] —Dear Sir—why, if I were to impute bad motives to any body—to any body

---
[1] Eldon and Ellenborough, again.
[2] See 'A Table of the Springs of Action' (printed 1815, published 1817) in *Deontology together with A Table of the Springs of Action and Article on Utilitarianism*, ed. A. Goldworth, Oxford, 1983 (*CW*), pp. 79–115, esp. 105–11.

that ever lived—to Scroggs for example, or Jefferies[1]—Sir, I might be put in jail for it, and perhaps in irons. No, Sir, nobody shall ever catch me imputing to any body a bad motive.

'Sir, I will do no injustice. Insufficient as it is, I will not say that the only mode which all this learning would endure—the mode which they "dwelt on so much as to insist on the rejection" of the only sufficient one[2]—I mean the *particularizing* mode—was, in its nature, to every purpose useless. One purpose there is, with reference to which it is in some degree useful,—useful as being to this same purpose more conducive than the sweeping mode:—I mean the clearing the text of the statute-book of the dead bodies of the statutes undertaken to be killed. But this which, besides being a minor one, is compleatly foreign to the only purpose ever mentioned, was it ever in the view of those pre-eminently learned persons, or either of them? Sure I cannot be, but my belief is in the negative. One reason is—that, whereas, for want of all divisions into numbered parts, it depends, in the instance of each statute professed to be repealed, upon chance Editors,—in the first place, whether any such disburthenment shall be attempted,—in the next place, whether that which, if any thing, is done to that end shall be correctly done,—it follows not that, in regard to the statutes in question, now that they are as you observe "*described and repealed nominatim,*" the text of the statute-book will ever be disburthened of them after all. Now, Sir, under these circumstances, on the occasion in question, on the part of the pre-eminently learned persons in question, did any such desire or view exist, as that of procuring to the public, in relation to so much as this one short statute, this collateral and minor benefit? Of any such wish I must confess myself unable to descry any the least symptom. Why? Because if there had been any such wish, nothing could have been easier than for one of them, without giving any trouble to the other, at the expence of a few words interchanged with the speaker of the House of Commons, to procure a regulation, by which, giving authority to the numbered divisions inserted by all editors, this principle of simplification might, in the only authentic and sufficient manner possible, be applied to all statutes whatsoever, existing as well as future.

'Another reason is—that, during the conjunct, and alas! how

---

[1] Sir William Scroggs (*c.* 1623–83), Chief Justice of King's Bench 1678–81, presided over the infamous 'popish plot' trials in 1678, when he was considered to have displayed partiality towards the prosecution and disregarded perjury on the part of Crown witnesses, while George Jeffreys (1645–89), first Baron Jeffreys, Chief Justice of King's Bench 1683–5, Lord Chancellor 1685–8, was noted for his cruelty, particularly during the 'Bloody Assizes' following the defeat of the Monmouth rebellion in 1685 when he condemned several hundreds to death.

[2] See p. 14 above.

tediously protracted reign of these two prodigiously learned persons,—in compensation for the multitude of good measures which they have either killed outright, or in the manner of this of yours, wounded,—my memory will not serve me for recollecting (much as the law needs amendment) so much as any one measure for the amendment of the law introduced or served by either of them—no, not one; unless *that* be reckoned an amendment, by which, in the true *Draco* style,[1] a bounty is given upon murder, by setting *attempt* and *perpetration* at the same price.[2]

'Described you say, and repealed *nominatim*. Forgive me another remark—it is not for want of respect where so much is due—it is not for the sake of cavil, it is for the sake of public instruction, that I make it. Described, yes; repealed *nominatim*, no. Repealing a statute, or portion of statute, *nominatim*, is repealing it by name. Sir, no portion of a statute ever has a name. If it had but a *number*, a name it would thereby have, and that a sufficient one. In the legislation of every civilized country but this—Sir, I say it with full assurance—portions of statutes *are* authoritatively distinguished—*names* of this sort *are* employed. In this proud country alone not. And why not? Sir, I have given the reason so often, and with so little fruit, I am quite tired of giving it. Nothing in this way is ever done, but under the direction of those whose interest it is that it should be as badly done as possible. Uncognoscibility being the end, indistinctness, voluminousness, confusion, uncertainty, are so many means. Designate a clause by a *number*, you designate it at the expence of a few figures; and, errors of the press excepted, without possibility of mistake. Designate it by "*description*," it is sure to be verbose: it is not sure to be either clear or adequate; nor, be it ever so clear and adequate, to escape being misconceived.

'And now, Sir, in so far as concerns *statute*-law, you see, perhaps, a little more distinctly than before, the *effect*—and,—if it had any *object* other than that of displaying power, creating dependance, and exciting unmerited gratitude,—the *object* or *objects* of all this "goodness."

'So much for statute-law. [2.][3] Now, Sir, as to *common law*. If that *tranquillity*, in which you seem to have so comfortably wrapt yourself, had *security* for its accompaniment, no one could be further than I should be from seeking to disturb it. Alas, would that were really the

---

[1] Draco drew up a code of laws for Athens in 621/620 BC which prescribed the death penalty for most offences.

[2] The so-called Ellenborough Act of 1803 (43 Geo. III, c. 58) had created the capital felony of attempted murder.

[3] Bentham has failed to continue the enumeration begun at p. 17 above.

case! This comfort of yours, what is the basis on which it rests? On a definition of the word *blasphemy*.[1] On a definition?—very good, if from competent authority,—so good, that no other can compare with it. But—this same definition by which you seem thus tranquillized,—who have you to own it? One person you are sure of, yourself: another person you moreover regard yourself sure of, viz. the Archbishop. I could give you another, if so insignificant an one could be of any use to you. But—make the most of it, *of what* is this the definition? Of what the law *is?*—Alas! no: only of what the law, as *we* say, *ought to* be. But, Sir, what is it that this supposed security of yours depends upon? On what the law *ought to be?* No, Sir: but on what it *is:* the *law*, meaning *now* the *common law*. And what, Sir, is *common law?* Sir, I will tell you what it is. It is on this, as on all other occasions, the expression of the will and pleasure of one or more of a set of men, whose interest is, on this ground, in a state of diametrical opposition to the universal interest;[2] who, on every occasion, to that same will and pleasure,—without any other controul than that nominal one which, not being real, is so much worse than none,—give the effect of law: that effect which,—without the aid of those pre-eminently learned persons,[3]—that body in which the plenitude of power is supposed to reside,[4] never finds itself able to give.

'On this very occasion, whose would the will and pleasure be? Whose but that of these same pre-eminently learned persons, whose wisdom, or whose sincerity, refused to suffer you to grasp so much as the shadow of a security, unless to the adequate relief you had prepared for yourselves, you would yourselves be the instruments of substituting an inadequate one? Now, Sir, forgive the liberty I take in asking you,—have you any assurance—any tolerably-grounded assurance—that this definition of yours—even suppose it not only approved, but signed by the Archbishop, would be adopted by common law?—would, in addition to *law as it ought to be*, be made *law as it is?* Alas, Sir, proof of the contrary is staring you in the face. Sir, have you not heard of Mr. *Hone* and *his* blasphemy?[5] Sir, have

[1] For Smith's definition of blasphemy see pp. 13–14 above.
[2] i.e. the Common Law judges.
[3] i.e. Eldon and Ellenborough.
[4] i.e. Parliament.
[5] William Hone (1780–1842), London bookseller, having in 1817 published a collection of parodies on religious texts, including the Catechism, was charged with blasphemous libel, and prosecuted at three trials held before the Court of King's Bench at the Guildhall, London on 18–20 December 1817. Hone defended himself at each trial, and, despite the judges' charges to the jury to convict him, was acquitted on each occasion. For an account of the trials see [William Hone], *The Three Trials of William Hone, for publishing three parodies; viz. the Late John Wilkes's Catechism, The Political Litany, and the Sinecurist's Creed; on three Ex-Officio Informations, at Guildhall, London, during three successive days, December 18, 19, & 20, 1817; before three Special Juries, and Mr. Justice Abbot, on the first day, and Lord Chief Justice Ellenborough, on the last two days*, London, 1818.

PREFACE ON PUBLICATION

you not heard of Mr. *Wright* of Liverpool, and *his* blasphemy?[1] Mr. Wright—a divine, whose blasphemy is, if I mistake not, pretty exactly of the same stamp with your own piety and that of Dr. Belsham?[2]

'Know you not that by the piety of common law, every scribbler,—with or without a name, with a true name, or with a false one,—whose scribble it has pleased, or shall please, King, Lords, and Commons, to put into a book, called the *Liturgy*, is to the purpose in question, put upon a level with God? his scribble with the word of God,—and, as in the course of this present work of mine you may see demonstrated, employed as an improved substitute to that same holy word?[3]—Know you not how, within these few months, being duly put in motion, by fees supplied by a pious Cabinet, the piety of common law, did actually speak to this effect by the mouth of a pre-eminently learned person, whose learning was so lately and effectually covered with shame by the ignorance of Mr. Hone?[4]

'Know you not that the piety of *common law* has a maxim of its own, by force and virtue of which, under the name of *blasphemers*, or any other name, it can at any time grind to powder all such christians as yourself, as well as all other persons, who have or profess to have a religion of their own in any shape? Know you not that, according to the tenor of this maxim, "*Christianity is part and parcel of the law of England?*"[5] that any thing and every thing, which it shall please the piety of this or that bench to call *christianity* will thereby be so? that

---

[1] John Wright, a Unitarian, had been charged with blasphemy for denying the doctrine of the Trinity, the idea that the soul survived the body, and that Christ's death could atone for sins: see John Wright, *A Sermon, delivered at the Long Room, Marble Street, Liverpool, on Tuesday Evening, April 8th, 1817. For which a prosecution is commenced on a charge of blasphemy*, Liverpool, 1817. The case against Wright was subsequently abandoned.

[2] Thomas Belsham (1750–1829), Unitarian clergyman and author of numerous defences of Unitarianism, including *Letters addressed to the Right Rev. the Lord Bishop of London, in Vindication of the Unitarians, from the Allegations of his Lordship in the Charge delivered to the Clergy of the Diocese of London, at his Lordship's primary Visitation*, London, 1815.

[3] See pp. 56–87 below.

[4] Sir Samuel Shepherd (1760–1840), Attorney-General 1817–19, who unsuccessfully prosecuted Hone at all three trials, in his closing speech at the first trial, effectively equated the ridiculing of the Church of England's Liturgy with the ridiculing of the Holy Scriptures, in the sense that both activities were illegal and libellous: see the report of the trial in the *Morning Chronicle*, 19 December 1817, and *Three Trials of William Hone*, pp. 4–5.

[5] The maxim was referred to on several occasions by Shepherd at Hone's trial on 19 December 1817. It is a conflation of two reports of a judgment given by Sir Matthew Hale (1609–76), Chief Baron of the Exchequer 1660–71, Chief Justice of King's Bench 1671–6, in which he is said to have remarked that 'Christian Religion is a part of the Law itself', and that 'Christianity is parcel of the Laws of England': see *R. v. Taylor* (1676), Jos. Keble, *Reports in the Court of Kings Bench at Westminster, From The XII to the XXX Year of the Reign of our Late Sovereign Lord King Charles II*, 3 pts., London, 1685, iii. 607, and *The Reports of Sir Peyton Ventris K*[t.] *Late One of the Justices of the Common-Pleas*, 2 pts., London, 1696, i. 293, respectively. According to Blackstone, *Commentaries on the Laws of England*, iv. 59, the offences gathered under the heading of blasphemy were 'punishable at common law by fine and imprisonment, or other infamous corporal punishment: for christianity is part of the laws of England'.

every thing that it shall please that same piety to call an *offence* against the said *christianity* will thereby be so, and the offender liable to be *visited*, as the phrase is,[1] with any or all such instruments of destruction as the hand of *precedent* has now presented to the piety of that same pre-eminently learned bench?

'Know you not, Sir, that,—besides all purposes such as the one in question,—the piety and wisdom of common law,—not to speak of other branches,—has, in its penal branch, an assortment of phrases applicable to all imaginable purposes? phrases covering, when taken together, the field of law in its whole extent? *(Contra bonos mores*[2]— *Conspiracy, Libel,* &c. I have somewhere got a list or the commencement of a list of them).—Know you not, Sir, in a word, that wheresoever *common law* reigns, *security*—whether it be for life, liberty, property, or any thing else—is an empty name? Shew me, Sir, if you can find one, that proposition in Euclid which is more uncontrovertibly demonstrated[3] than is this one, melancholy as it is, in my letter to the people of the American United States, published in my late work, intituled *Papers on Codification, &c.*[4]—I wish it were in my power to give you any better authority: I mean in black and white. But, now and then it may happen to you, in the house, to find yourself within a whisper of Sir Samuel Romilly. On any such opportunity, ask him whether, in the picture above drawn of the goddess of so many idolatries,[5] there be any considerable overcharge: and, if for answer you should receive nothing but a sigh or something equivalent, you will not be at much loss to know what to conclude.

'I am, my dear Sir,
'Yours very thankfully,
'J.B.'

'P.S. On the subject of *blasphemy*,—in the overgrown volume, to which in thus writing to you I am writing a last preface,—in this volume, pages from 367 to 370, you may see how perfect the agreement is between your notions and mine. Judge from hence

---

[1] See, for example, Exodus 20: 5; Jeremiah 8: 12; and Hosea 9: 7.

[2] i.e. 'against good morals'.

[3] Bentham is referring to ὅπερ ἔδει δεῖξαι, more familiar in the Latin *quod erat demonstrandum*, used by Euclid (dates uncertain, between 325 and 250 BC), the celebrated mathematician: see, for example, *Elements*, I. iv.

[4] See 'Jeremy Bentham, an Englishman, to the Citizens of the several American United States', dated July 1817, apart from the Postscript which is dated 26 August 1817, which appeared as Supplement No. V in *Papers relative to Codification and Public Instruction: including Correspondence with the Russian Emperor, and divers Constituted Authorities in the American United States*, London, 1817, and is reproduced in *'Legislator of the World': Writings on Codification, Law, and Education*, ed. P. Schofield and J. Harris, Oxford, 1998 (*CW*), pp. 113–72, esp. 128–36, 162–7.

[5] See *Romeo and Juliet*, II. ii. 114.

PREFACE ON PUBLICATION

of the pride and pleasure which that part of your letter afforded to me.

'You will not see this my second letter till after it is made public. You shall not have been party or privy to any of my enormities.'

PREFACE.

On the formulary, which forms the subject of the ensuing tract,[1] the judgment here pronounced, it will immediately be seen, is far indeed from favourable.

Of the whole system, doctrine and discipline together, of which that formulary forms a part, the opinion entertained, it may still earlier be seen, is correspondently unfavourable.

Question.[2] An Oxford Graduate![3]—This from an Oxford Graduate? If such indeed he be, and not an impostor, falsely assuming so respectable a character,—by what disastrous impulse can the pupil of so excellent and so holy a school of instruction, have been precipitated into apostasy? . . . .

Answer. Be the author of the book in himself honest or dishonest,—be the inducements by which he was engaged in it praise-worthy or blame-worthy,—the formulary, which is the subject of it, is in either case exactly what it is, neither better nor worse: the observations, to which in the present instance it has given rise, neither worse nor better grounded.

So manifestly as well as correctly true is the matter of these answers, that the person, who will be either able or disposed to controvert them in any point, seems not very likely to be found.

Yet, by any answers of this sort,—pertinent as they are, though not less trivial than pertinent,—scarce in any instance, perhaps, will the sort of curiosity, of which the above questions are the expression, be likely to be extinguished, or so much as damped.

That the causes in question are of a complexion discreditable to the author, and to the sort of persuasion in favour of which the work tends to operate, is in a manner included in any such questions as the above: in the character or situation of the author, what (say they) is

---

[1] i.e. the Catechism of the Church of England, which appeared under the title of 'A Catechism. That is to say, An Instruction to be learned of every person before he be brought to be confirmed by the Bishop', in *The Book of Common Prayer, and Administration of the Sacraments, and other Rites and Ceremonies of the Church, According to the Use of The Church of England*, authorized by the Act of Uniformity of 1662 (13 & 14 Car. II, c. 4).

[2] The first question of the Catechism is: 'What is your name?'

[3] The version of the work printed in 1817 attributed its authorship to 'An Oxford Graduate'. Bentham had been entered into Queen's College, Oxford, aged 12, in 1760. When he graduated as Bachelor of Arts in 1764 he was reputedly the youngest person ever to have done so. He took the degree of Master of Arts in 1767.

PREFACE

there, that affords a hope of its being found capable of serving, in the place of argument, to throw discredit on the work? for it is only by a view of that sort,—and therefore only from that quarter of the religion-professing world,—that any considerable curiosity seems, in the present instance, very likely to be excited. In the eyes of any person, should the observations of which the work is composed wear the air of truth, by the truth will his attention not only be preferably engaged, but probably nearly if not altogether engrossed.

When, on an occasion of this sort, a question of this sort is thrown out, the author is commonly among the very last persons to whom it is addressed. Ground for condemnation is what is wanted: and, from the party on whom it is to be passed, no such ground, in the way of voluntary contribution, can naturally be expected.

Under these circumstances, curiosity—the sort of curiosity here in question—must content itself, as well as it can, with the not only scanty but partial supply, which, under such circumstances, human nature can find motives for affording.

By any notoriety given to the individual, no effect, in any point of view beneficial, could be produced.

This being the case, to what use (it may be asked) profess to offer to the appetite of curiosity any the smallest part of the aliment of which it is in quest?

An Apostate is every thing that is bad. By your own confession, you are no better than *an apostate.* You are an enemy—an enemy to the *Church,* under which you were bred and fostered—of that *established Church,* of which the '*excellence*' has so truly been declared, and so nobly proclaimed, by the Right Reverend persons, by whom in one sense it is governed, and of whom in another sense it is composed.[1] Being an enemy to this holy Church, nothing that you say of any thing—nothing that you say of any body—but most of all, and in particular, nothing that you say of yourself, can be entitled to any sort of credence, unless it be to that sort, which, in so far as it makes against himself, may be given to the assertion of any other malefactor, whom, through the veil of mendacious discourse, which he

---

[1] Bentham refers throughout this work to the attribute 'excellence' or 'excellent' which was used in connection with the Church of England by laymen and churchmen alike at this time. As well as this general use of the term, Bentham appears to have had particularly in mind the opening statement in *First Annual Report of the National Society, for Promoting the Education of the Poor in the Principles of the Established Church,* London, 1812, p. 5: 'That the NATIONAL RELIGION should be made the Foundation of NATIONAL EDUCATION, and should be the first and chief thing taught to the Poor, according to the excellent *Liturgy and Catechism* provided by our Church for that purpose, must be admitted by all friends to the Establishment. . . .' Bentham quotes the passage at length in Introduction, Part IV, §4, pp. 110–14 n. below. This statement appeared in advertisements for the National Society, including that in *The Times,* 11 January 1812.

spreads over his deportment, the condemnatory truth may here and there be descried.

The answer is—though, if his wishes and endeavours prevail, his name will not transpire during his life-time, yet at his death his motives for concealment will be at an end. He will then be known: and in proportion as he *is* known, he will be known for one, to whom that part of probity which concerns veracity, never could have been an object of indifference.

Unfortunately, in a case of this sort, even during the author's lifetime, wishes of this sort, how anxious soever, are not unfrequently frustrated.

This, then, is a mischance, which, from the nature of what is disclosed, it will plainly be seen he could not but have in view: and against which he accordingly could not fail of being provided.

But why then say any thing at all of yourself? Why—to what good end—give any the most imperfect outline, of that personal individuality, which, by your own acknowledgement, is nothing to the purpose?

The answer is—no such apparently irrelevant matter would have found admittance,—no such personal hazard been encountered,—but for the instruction—the useful instruction—which, in this shape, it seemed, might perhaps be afforded: and for the sake of that object, he must, under these circumstances, as to what concerns credence, content himself with trusting to that superiority, which, in its contest for credence, truth possesses over falsehood,—and to that complexion of sincerity, which, upon a view taken of the whole work, the wishes and desires that gave birth to it, will, it is hoped, be found to have given, to the language in which it is expressed.

Be the opinions and assertions what they may, the cause of their being published is one thing:—the cause of their having been framed and entertained, another,—and in respect of *time*, frequently a very different one.

As to the opinions and assertions here brought to view, the cause of their being thus made public,—the principal at least, if not the only cause, or at any rate, the occasion, is—the observation made of that system of exclusion, of which the formulary in question has been and continues to be the instrument: the exclusion, by which the benefit of the capital and new-invented instrument of virtue and happiness[1] is denied to all those children whose parents choose not to see it perverted, as it seems to them, to the production of the opposite ill effects. But of this, more in its more appropriate place.

In the formation of these opinions and these affections, no prepossessions adverse to the system thus censured can have had

---
[1] i.e. the monitorial system of education.

PREFACE

any the smallest share. In the instance here in question, all prepossessions were, in an eminent degree, favourable to it.—But it is time to substitute the first person to the third.

Of my four great-grandfathers, two were Clergymen of the Established Church: both beneficed:[1] both of them men of more than ordinary estimation in their calling: men whose love and reverence for that establishment, to the reputation of which their own deportment gave increase, stood abundantly expressed in the deportment and language of their respective daughters.[2] In the lap of one of these daughters, I learnt for my first lesson, the matter, in so far as it was learnable—of this formulary.[3] Of their devotions,—and those, not weekly only but daily—and in every part accordant to the rites of the established Church,—was I, at all times when the suspension of school-instruction renewed the domestic intercourse, in the instance of both of them, an affectionate, reverential, and continual witness: and by these passionately beloved, eminently virtuous, as well as pious authors of my being, were the same affections and opinions transmitted to both my immediate parents,—to the son of the one, and the daughter of the other.[4]

At my birth, and till he quitted the neighbourhood,[5] which was not till I had been some years at the university, my father belonged to a club, in which he was the only member that was not a clergyman—a clergyman of the Church of England.

Walking one day with him in London, upon our passing near a building, which had something public in its appearance, he motioned to go in. To a question of mine, what it was, the answer was—*a Dissenting Meeting House.*—'Sir,' said I, '*would it be altogether right for us to enter into such a place?*'—His answer was a smile:—but the departure was immediate.[6]

A recollection,—but though considerably less remote, much less distinct,—is that of the period at which, on the occasion of a ceremony called *a Confirmation*, my head received the sanctifying

---

[1] William Woodward (*c.* 1640–1703), Bentham's mother's maternal grandfather, was Rector of St Stephen's Church, Baughurst, Hampshire from 1668 until his death, and John Tabor (1649–1709), his father's maternal grandfather, was Rector of St Stephen's, South Hanningfield, Essex from 1672 until his death.

[2] i.e. Bentham's paternal grandmother Rebecca Tabor, who married Jeremiah Bentham Senior (1684–1741), and his maternal grandmother Alicia Woodward, who married Thomas Grove (d. 1751).

[3] For Bentham's later reminiscences, recorded by John Bowring (1792–1872), merchant, later radical MP, diplomat, and Bentham's literary executor, on 'the catechetical course of examination' which he received from his grandmother Rebecca see Bowring, x. 17–18.

[4] Jeremiah Bentham (1712–92), Bentham's father, who married Alicia Whitehorn, née Grove (d. 1759), in 1745.

[5] Jeremiah Bentham moved from Aldgate to Queen Square Place, Westminster in 1762.

[6] This anecdote also appears in Bowring, x. 36–7.

touch of a Right Reverend hand. On the occasion, and for the purpose of its receiving this mysterious touch, the supposition is, that the contents of the Catechism have all of them received a permanent, and, by divine grace, an everlasting habitation in every head thus sanctified. For my own part, I remembered as well as I could—I understood as much as I could—I believed as hard as I could—and if any thing was wanting to belief, it was made up by trembling.

In the Church itself—in its discipline and its doctrine—and, in particular, in a particular exercise, which, in the last stage and highest seat of my education, I saw given to that discipline,[1]—in those things which, in relation to those objects, my own individual observation, not only uninfluenced, but unaccompanied by the application of any exterior influence, presented to my reflection,— did the unfavourable impressions,—the unfavourable opinions, and thence, and thence only, the unfavourable affections, in which this work originated, take their rise.

No: incredible as it may appear—incredible as it may so naturally be pronounced, by those whose orthodoxy is made sure, by the hope of preferment, combined with the fear of ruin,—to no motive, to which any such epithet as *sinister* is wont to be affixed,—no, not to prospect of profit in any shape—not to resentment, envy, or any affection of the dissocial stamp, can either the affections or the opinions, have, in the smallest degree, been indebted for their existence.

In the seat of instruction, in which these opinions and these affections (adverse as they unwillingly were and are) were formed, no cause of personal enmity, or so much as ill humour,—no disappointment—unless it were the finding bad instruction where I had expected good, and next to no instruction where I had expected much,—did I ever experience. Of no one member of the governing body did I ever so much as imagine myself to have, on any personal account, any reason to complain. On the contrary, from that quarter more offers did it happen to me to receive, and those of a very friendly and substantial nature, than I thought it advisable to accept. Even to this hour I continue, and without any intervening interval of an opposite description, on terms of friendship with some—on terms other than those of friendship, with none.

The first cause was this. Of the University of Oxford I had not been long a member, when, by a decree of the Vice-Chancellor in his court, five students were, under the name of Methodists, expelled from it. Heresy and frequentation of *conventicles* were the only offences

---

[1] Presumably the expulsion of the Methodist students, to which Bentham refers below.

PREFACE

charged upon them.[1] Taking the word *conventicle* for the place of meeting—these conventicles were so many private rooms, the small apartments of the several poor students, for poor they were. The congregation consisted of these same poor and too pious students, with the occasional addition of one and the same ancient female. The offence consisted in neither more nor less than the reading and talking over the Bible. The heresy consisted in this—viz. that, upon being, by persons sent to examine them, questioned on the subject of the thirty-nine Church of England Articles, the sense which they put upon these articles were found to be in some instances different from the sense put upon those same articles by those their interrogators.

The mode of inquiry employed was thus the very mode which, in foreign parts, under the Catholic so called *Inquisition*, was employed for clearing the country of persons guilty of thinking differently from what was professed to be thought by the Church of Rome:[2] the very mode which, here in England, by Elizabeth and James, was under the Church of England *not* so called *Inquisition*, employed for clearing the country of persons guilty of thinking differently from what was professed to be thought by the Church of England.[a] The judges made

[a] See Neale's History of the Puritans.[3]

[1] Bentham has misrecollected the date of this incident, since it took place after he had left Oxford and taken up residence in Lincoln's Inn. In 1768 seven students were ordered to appear before the Vice-Chancellor's Court, of whom six were charged with attending illicit conventicles, associating with Methodists, and holding doctrines contrary to the Thirty-nine articles. Three of the seven were additionally accused of having been bred to trades, five of being insufficient in learned languages, and three of behaving badly towards their tutor. The hearing on 11 March 1768 was presided over by the Vice-Chancellor, David Durell (1728–75), and four assessors, who had intended to hear the case in private, but were forced by the presence of a large crowd to examine the accused and witnesses in public, in the dining hall at St Edmund Hall. The charges against one student were dropped because he was 'a man of fortune and not designed for Holy Orders', but the remaining six were expelled from the University. See S.L. Ollard, *The Six Students of St Edmund Hall Expelled from the University of Oxford in 1768*, London, 1911, and V.H.H. Green, 'Religion in the Colleges 1715–1800', in *The History of the University of Oxford: Vol. V. The Eighteenth Century*, ed. L.S. Sutherland and L.G. Mitchell, Oxford, 1986, pp. 459–61.

[2] The Inquisition, originally established by the Roman Catholic Church in the thirteenth century to detect and prosecute heresy, had been reinstituted in 1542 by Paul III (1468–1549), Pope from 1534, as the Roman Inquisition, or Holy Office, in order to eradicate Protestantism. The Roman Inquisition and the Court of High Commission (see below) were ecclesiastical courts which employed the Canon Law's inquisitorial mode of procedure.

[3] The Court of High Commission, established in 1559, had wide-ranging powers to deal with ecclesiastical offences and to suppress movements considered to be dangerous to the established Church. The Court was summoned by Letters Patent during the reigns of Elizabeth I (1533–1603), Queen of England and Ireland from 1558, James VI (1566–1625), King of Scotland from 1567, as James I King of England and Ireland from 1603, and Charles I (1600–49), King of England, Scotland, and Ireland from 1625, but was abolished in 1641.

Daniel Neal (1678–1743) was the author of *The History of the Puritans or Protestant Non-Conformists*, 4 vols., London, 1732–8. Bentham used Joshua Toulmin's edition, published in 5 volumes at Bath from 1793 to 1797. For Neal's discussion of the work of the Court of High Commission see vols. i and ii, as index.

the crime; those same judges punished it. *Bishop Taylor*, had it happened to him, being then in being, to have exercised, in company with these poor students, that liberty, in defence of which he wrote—[a]*Bishop Taylor*, would, if like them he had been undignified and unprotected, have shared their fate.

This cause, what was it?—Exactly that and no other, the multiplication of which is the sole and professed object of all our Bible Societies. No, not any the slightest difference: unless while the study of that source of salvation is, when pursued by one's self a merit, the study of it, with the assistance, or in the company of a friend or two, is a crime: in which case it might not be amiss, that by due warning given, all persons should, as effectually as possible, be preserved from the commission of this crime; and, in particular that to that end, the stereotype edition should be corrected, by the erasure of that text, in which Jesus is stated as promising to be in the midst of any two or three persons gathered together in his name.[b]

At this time, most strictly and literally true as it is, this statement will, upon the face of it, be apt to appear incredible.—But *these young men*, (it was asked), *were they not really Methodists?*—To this question no answer could, with truth, be given otherwise than in the affirmative. For what was *then*, what is even *now*, a Methodist? What but a zealous and consistent Church of Englandist? Even now, let any one be generally recognized as being zealous as well as assiduous in the practice of the rites of the Church of England, holding up to view, at the same time, on all occasions, in the language of the Bible, the ideas of *salvation* and *damnation*, will he not be as generally styled *a Methodist?* Any known peculiarity of doctrine—any thing else whatever—is it necessary to his being considered as justly designated by that name?

And the place of meeting, was it not a Conventicle? Yes: for a Conventicle is *any* place, in which persons in any number are *gathered together*. Nay, and among the *University statutes*—those statutes, of which these youths had been made to swear to the observance, and which by no man who ever was or is made to swear to them, were or are ever observed,[c] is there not one by which all *illicit Conventicles* are

---

[a] 'On the Liberty of Prophesying.'[1]
[b] Matt. xviii. 20. For where two or three are gathered together in my name, there am I in the midst of them.
[c] See Knox's Essays; viz. in the 17th of those editions, in all which, for these thirty or forty years, a practice, which in these their own statutes is styled *perjury*, has been

---

[1] Taylor, ΘΕΟΛΟΓΊΑ ἘΚΛΕΚΤΙΚΉ. *A Discourse on the Liberty of Prophesying.*

PREFACE

prohibited in express terms?[1] and were not these their Conventicles *illicit?* Yes: for in them used to be done, that which, had he known of it, the Vice-Chancellor would rather should not have been done, viz. the reading of, and conversing on the subject of the Bible.

Be this as it may, by the sentence, by which those readers of the Bible were thus expelled from the University, that affection which at its entrance had glowed with so sincere a fervor,—my reverence for the Church of England—her doctrine, her discipline, her Universities, her ordinances,—was expelled from my youthful breast. I read the controversy: I studied it: and, with whatsoever reluctance, I could not but acknowledge the case to stand exactly as above.

Not long after—(for at my entrance, that immaturity of age, which had excused me from the obligation of signature, had excused me from the necessity of perjury)—not long after came the time for the attaching my signature to the *thirty-nine Articles*.[2] Understanding that of such signature the effect and sole object was—the declaring, after reflection, with solemnity and upon record, that the propositions therein contained were, in my opinion, every one of them true, what seemed to me a matter of duty was—to examine them in that view, in order to see whether that were really the case. The examination was unfortunate. In some of them no meaning at all could I find: in others, no meaning but one which, in my eyes, was but too plainly irreconcilable either to reason or to Scripture. Communicating my distress to some of my fellow collegiates, I found them sharers in it. Upon

charged upon these rulers, and the truth of the charge acknowledged by their silence.[3]

---

[1] See Tit. xv, §13. De Conventiculis illicitis reprimendis, *Corpus Statutorum Universitatis Oxoniensis*, ratified in 1636.

[2] Bentham has misrecollected the order of events. He subscribed to the Thirty-nine Articles of the Church of England on his graduation in 1764.
The remainder of this paragraph, and the final sentence of the following, are reproduced at Bowring, x. 37.

[3] Vicesimus Knox, *Essays, Moral and Literary*, first published in two volumes in 1778–9, which had reached its seventeenth edition in three volumes in 1815, does not in fact contain this section. Bentham makes the same point in '*Swear not at all:' containing an exposure of the needlessness and mischievousness, as well as Antichristianity, of the ceremony of an oath*, London, 1817, Appendix, pp. 13–14 (Bowring, v. 195–6), where he identifies the text as Vicesimus Knox, *Liberal Education: or, a practical treatise on the methods of acquiring useful and polite learning* (first published 1781), 10th edn., 2 vols., London, 1789. He reproduces material from §XXXIX. On the universities, ii. 120–1, of which the relevant passage is as follows: 'To give a just account of the state of the university of Oxford, I must begin where every fresh-man begins, with admission and matriculation; for it so happens, that the first thing a young man has to do there, is to prostitute his conscience, and enter himself into perjury, at the same time that he enters himself into the university.' Vicesimus Knox (1752–1821) graduated as Bachelor of Arts from Oxford in 1775, and was Headmaster of Tonbridge School 1778–1812. For Bentham's further discussion of perjury among the 'rulers' of the University of Oxford see '*Swear not at all*', Appendix, pp. 85–97 (Bowring, v. 224–9).

inquiry it was found, that among the Fellows of the College there was one, to whose office it belonged, among other things, to remove all such scruples. We repaired to him with fear and trembling.[1] His answer was cold: and the substance of it was—that it was not for uninformed youths such as we, to presume to set up our private judgments against a public one, formed by some of the holiest, as well as best and wisest men that ever lived.

When, out of the multitude of his attendants, Jesus chose twelve for his Apostles, by the men in office he was declared to be possessed by a Devil: by his own friends, at the same time, he was set down for mad.[a] The like fate, were my conscience to have shewed itself more scrupulous than that of the official casuist, was before my eyes. Before the eyes of Jesus stood a comforter—his Father—an Almighty one. Before my weak eyes stood no comforter. In *my* father, in whom in other cases I might have looked for a comforter, I saw nothing but a tormenter: by my ill-timed scruples, and the consequent public disgrace that would have been the consequence, his fondest hopes would have been blasted, the expenses he had bestowed on my education bestowed in vain. To him, I durst not so much as confess those scruples. I signed:—but, by the view I found myself forced to take of the whole business, such an impression was made, as will never depart from me but with life.

Mendacity and *insincerity*—in these I found, and it will be seen how far I experienced,—the effects—the sure and only sure effects—of an English University education: of a Church of England education of the first quality: these, sooner or later, I could not but see in the number, not only of its *effects*, but of its *objects:* of mendacity, a forced *act* or two: and the object of it the securing of an *habit* of insincerity throughout life.

Another thing, which I moreover beheld most certainly among the effects, and but too probably among the objects, of Church of England doctrine, enforced by Church of England discipline, was,—that 'humble docility' as towards its rulers and their subordinates—that 'prostration of the understanding and will,' which, in so many words, with an intrepidity that cannot sufficiently be admired, the *Bishop of London*, on a late *Charge*, some passages of which will

---

[a] Mark iii. 14 to 22. And he ordained twelve . . . . (14.) and they went into a house (19.) And the multitude cometh together again, so that they could not eat bread. And when his friends heard of it, they went out to lay hold on him: for they said, he is beside himself. And the Scribes which came down from Jerusalem said, he hath Beelzebub . . . . (20, 21, 22.)

[1] See, for instance, Mark 5: 33; II Corinthians 7: 15.

PREFACE

here be more particularly brought to view, has published as the avowed object of their endeavours:[1] their *National Society*'s Schools,[2] and this their Catechism, being employed as instruments to this purpose.

The more closely I looked into the controversial doctrine thus forced into my hands, the more fully I saw reason to be substantially confirmed, in that general conception of them, which had from the first presented itself to me:—some of them not true—others, whether true or false, not susceptible of application to any particularly useful purpose: many of them to much bad purpose: those, which were at the same time true and useful, so plainly true and so plainly useful, that no fear could be entertained of their commanding instantaneous assent, but for that suspicion, which is the natural concomitant of bribery and intimidation—of reward—of punishment—or of a compound of both—when seen to be employed to operate upon conscience.

In mendacity and habitual insincerity is there any thing of vice? He who has entered into *that* fold[3] cannot have entered into it without having sold himself to the practice and service of vice. This done, to drag down into the same abyss as many others as possible, is a policy, the urgency of which cannot reasonably be expected ever to be resisted. In any one who follows the same course, instead of that accuser or condemning judge which he would have beheld otherwise, each man beholds an accomplice: an accomplice, the surest and most zealous of all advocates and defenders.

Trained up in *insincerity*—attached to it by principle—by practice—and above all, were it only because before all, by interest—that

---

[1] See William [Howley], Bishop of London, *A Charge delivered to the Clergy of the Diocese of London at the Primary Visitation of that Diocese in the Year 1814*, London, 1814, p. 16, referring to the 'Unitarian system': 'Its influence has generally been confined to men of some education, whose thoughts have been little employed on the subject of religion; or who, loving rather to question than learn, have approached the oracles of divine truth without that humble docility, that prostration of the understanding and will, which are indispensable to proficiency in Christian instruction.'

[2] The National Society for Promoting the Education of the Poor in the Principles of the Established Church throughout England and Wales opened its first school, Central School in Baldwin's Gardens, Gray's Inn Lane, London, on 19 June 1812: see *Second Annual Report of the National Society, for Promoting the Education of the Poor in the Principles of the Established Church*, London, 1814, pp. 5, 14–15. At the school, students were taught using the Madras system, and teachers were trained in the use of the system. For reports from the schools which opened in England and Wales in association with the National Society in the two years following the Society's foundation see ibid., Appendix I, pp. 23–77, and *Third Annual Report of the National Society, for Promoting the Education of the Poor in the Principles of the Established Church*, London, 1815, Appendix I, pp. 25*–164. This *Report* mistakenly repeats page numbers 25 to 30 at the commencement of the Appendices.

For the establishment of the National Society see p. 43 n. below.

[3] Possibly an allusion to John 10: 16.

sinister interest, to which the vicious principle owed its birth,—the more acute his sense is of the absurdity, and groundlessness, and mischievousness, of the doctrines to which his outward assent has been compelled, the more determinately—taking the weakness of St. Peter for the model of his strength,[1]—yes—the more determinately, will he insist on the reasonableness of them—on their necessariness to salvation—and on the impossibility, that either of those qualities can really experience a denial, from any cause, but either a degree of profligacy deserving of punishment under the name of punishment,—or insanity, calling for the like punishment under the name of necessary care.[a]

Be this as it may, as in the exclusion put upon all children whose parents will not force lies into their mouths, (for though the things themselves were ever so true, the assertion made by the child, that he understands them, and believes them so, would not the less be a lie),—as, in the observation made of this exclusionary system, the publicity given to the opinions and assertions manifested in the ensuing tract, has found its proximate cause,—so, in the witnessed expulsion of the Methodists, and the experience had of the forced

---

[a] In regard to these *Articles* and these *Subscriptions*, a few words, having for their object the mitigation of the evil, may perhaps be not altogether without their use. In and by the act of *subscription*, what is the fact asserted? It is—for what else can it be?—It is—that at the moment at which the last stroke of the pen is given to the signature, the persuasion, of the person whose signature is attached to it, is—that the propositions, to which it is thus attached are, all of them, true:—At that same moment?—Yes?—At any subsequent one? No:—for to no subsequent one is it possible that the assertion thus expressed can have any application. The very next moment,—or if this be as yet too near for sincerity, the next moment after that which closed the consultation with the pillow—that very moment, without mendacity, or any the least approach to it, supposing any one or every one of these articles to have become in his eyes a subject of disbelief, he is no less free to declare it—such his disbelief—than if he had never set his hand to any thing. That because at one moment he was a liar, a man should continue to be a liar—that he should so much as continue to be a dissembler—all his life—a doctrine to any such effect is surely as far from belonging to the case, as it is from being true: howsoever it may be of the number of those notions which, to preserve the Church from its dangers,[2] have been invented and propagated by its defenders, and slipt into the ceremony, in such a manner as to make people look upon them as necessarily contained in it. That because, by whatsoever means thou hast been led to defile thyself with this lie,

---

[1] For Peter's denials of Jesus see p. 20 n. above.

[2] Cf. [Howley], *Charge delivered to the Clergy of the Diocese of London*, p. 13: 'We are indeed exposed to dangers, and those of no ordinary magnitude. The opposite extremes of defect or excess of religious belief and feeling prevail among us, in a variety of modifications and degrees, to an alarming extent. The partizans of these several errors, disjoined in all other respects by discordancy of principle, sentiment, and ultimate views, are not the less disposed to unite in offensive alliance against the object of their common aversion, the Established Church.'

PREFACE

injection[1] of the matter of the thirty-nine Articles, did this same publicity, as well as those opinions and affections themselves, find its remoter and original cause.

For the momentary mendacity, into which puerile weakness had been betrayed and forced, abjuration was, as it seemed, the only reparation—nor that an useless one—that could be made. By a consequent, and persevering, and unbroken habit of insincerity, continued during life,—the vice of the moment might have remained hidden from the eyes of men: but there would have been eyes—there are eyes—from which it could not have been concealed. When perseverance is wickedness, apostacy is a duty: and, unless followed by reparation, as far as reparation can be made, repentance cannot be stated as sincere.

Never was defection more completely unbought:—assuredly no worldly fruits have either been received or sought from it. Not so much as thanks can be received for it by the author, so long as his personality continues under the shade, in which it is his anxious care to bury it: far different from thanks would be the retribution, were the secret ever to transpire.

Even of the minute profit,—which, if any, is all which, in the present state of the press, can be expected to flow from such a publication,—no part will ever find its way into the hand by which this pen is guided. It will be divided by the bookseller between Schools and Missions.

The ensuing *Introduction* was not, any more than this Preface, written till after the completion of the short work,[2] which it is

thinkest thou, Young Man, that thou art bound in conscience to persevere in it?—An assertion is one thing: a promise is another. An *assertion* is confined to what is *past* or *present:* a *promise*, to what is *future*.—But, in addition to the lie in this manner *once* told, suppose even a *promise* given—an express promise—to persevere in it;—a promise to any such effect, would it be binding?—Yes; if because, with a pistol to your throat, you had sworn to murder your father, you would be bound in conscience to improve upon Jephtha, and perform your vow.[3]—Yes: if, because if in one unguarded moment she had yielded to the solicitation of unhallowed appetite, a woman would be bound in conscience to engage in a habit of prostitution, and persevere in it during life.

Accordingly, in my own instance, the sin of my boyhood—which every hour that it forces itself upon recollection, brings shame with it, it is true, but a shame which is almost lost in the accompanying indignation kindled by the thought of the so much more heinous sin—the sin of my corrupters—the hoary authors of that venial one,—this transgression, does it consist in the declaration I am thus making, that in more parts of it than one the matter of this formulary is the subject of my disbelief, and

---

[1] 1818 'injustice'. The text follows the 'Errata'.
[2] i.e. 'Church of England Catechism Examined', pp. 203–56 below.
[3] For the story of Jephthah and his daughter see Judges 11: 30–40.

employed to introduce. Under these circumstances, it was scarce possible, in writing the Introduction, altogether to avoid proceeding upon what is done in the work, as upon a ground already laid, and thereby exposing it, more or less, to the imputation of affirming that, which remained as yet unproved. Hence the danger, lest all these conceptions, which have in fact been the result of the coolest reflection, as well as the closest attention, should present themselves to the reader in the character of a tissue of loose declamation, the offspring of unreflecting passion:—present themselves thus at the first, and thence—such is the effects of first impressions—to the last.

To obviate this inconvenience, what follows is the reprint of a paragraph, which, being written after the comment on the Catechism, is there given in the character of a *'Recapitulation:'* viz. a Recapitulation of the charges brought against that formulary; accompanied with references to the several *observations* or *sets of observations*, which at that stage of the inquiry had presented themselves as *proofs*, demonstrative of the justice of those several charges. In that place the character in which it presents itself is that of a list of charges *already proved:* in this place this same document may be considered as a list of charges *undertaken to be* proved; and of which, as the inquiry advances, it is expected by the writer, that in the eyes of a candid and discerning reader, they will severally, when the time comes, appear to *have been* proved.

RECAPITULATION.[1]

On recurring to the Observations contained in the preceding pages, the following are the *vices* which will, it is believed, be found to have been proved upon this formulary, the peccant matter of which is, with a diligence unhappily so successful, injected, by the hand of power, into the breasts of the great majority of the instructed part of the population, at the very first dawn of the reasoning faculty—

I. BAD GRAMMAR. For a passage teaching bad grammar by example, see p. 238.

tainted as it is with that sin, the whole together the object of my abhorrence?—A confession of this sort a sin?—so far from being a sin, it is an *expiation;* an atonement for that early sin,—and the only atonement, which, in a case like this, it can be in a man's power to make.

---

[1] The Recapitulation reproduces 'Church of England Catechism Examined', pp. 253–4 below.

PREFACE

II. BAD LOGIC; viz.
  1. By inculcation of matter plainly useless. See p. 215 to 219.
  2. By inculcation of manifest surplusage. See p. 245. 246.
  3. By inculcation of matter plainly unintelligible. See p. 206 to 210. 214 to 222. 224. 225.
  4. By inculcation of propositions inconsistent with one another. See p. 209. 210.
  5. By inculcation of instruction, which is either erroneous, or at best useless. See p. 230. 231.
  6. By exemplification and consequent inculcation of the art and habit of gratuitous or unfounded assertion, and groundless inference. See p. 222. 223. 228. 229. 230.
  7. By inculcation of matter, repugnant to those thirty-nine Articles, to which the whole body of the Clergy—Bishops and Archbishops included—together with all other ruling and otherwise influential persons,—who become partakers of that course of education which is in highest repute, will, upon entrance into that course, after being thus impregnated with the repugnant matter of this formulary, be forced to declare their assent and approbation on record. See p. 222. 223.
  8. By inculcation of matter savouring of Popery. See p. 245 to 248.

III. Matter, the tendency of which is—to operate, in various *other* ways, to the depravation of the INTELLECTUAL part of man's frame, viz.
  1. Matter, by which the principle of *vicarious obligation* is inculcated: i.e. by which children are commanded to believe, that it is in the power of two or three self-appointed persons, by agreeing together, to oblige a young child, in conscience, to pursue to the end of his life, any course of conduct, which, at that time, it may please them to prescribe. See p. 205. 206.
  2. Matter, by which the young child is himself forced to utter *a rash promise*, binding him, during life, to pursue the course of conduct therein and thereby prescribed. See p. 210. 211.
  3. Matter, by which the child is initiated in the art and habit of *lax interpretation:* i.e. of declaring, in relation to the discourse in question, whatever it may be, his persuasion, that such or such was the meaning, intended by the *author* to be conveyed by it: viz. whatever meaning it may at any time happen to suit the personal purpose of the *interpreter* so to convey, how wide soever of the import really so intended to be conveyed. See p. 232. 233 to 252.

4. Matter, by which the *intellectual* part of the child's frame is destined to be *debilitated* and *depraved* by groundless and useless *terrors*. See p. 207 to 209. 237.

IV. Matter, the tendency of which is to operate, in various other ways, to the DEPRAVATION of the MORAL part of man's frame: viz.
1. Matter, in the texture of which *Hypocrisy* is plainly discernible. See p. 209. 210.
2. Matter, by which *lying* is inculcated as a duty:—a duty, which the child is forced to declare himself bound to persevere in the performance of. See p. 203. 204. 211. 215. 224. 232. 233. 237.
3. Matter, by which *Imposture* may be seen to be promoted. See p. 233 to 252.
4. Matter, by which *Forgery* may be seen to be knowingly uttered. See p. 212. 213.
5. Matter, by which encouragement is given to sin and *wickedness in every shape*. See p. 250 to 252.

V. Matter, the tendency of which is to operate, in an immediate way, to the injury of the SENSITIVE part of man's frame.
Matter, by which groundless and useless terrors are infused, as above.

PLAN OF THE WORK.

Plan[1] of the Work.
To the end that, from the first, not only the design of this work, but the connexion between the several parts of it, may be plainly understood, a brief sketch, explanatory of the plan pursued in the course of it, may be not without its use.

I. As to the Introduction:—It is divided into five parts.

I. Part I. In this part will be maintained that, as applied to the purpose of instruction, the Church of England Catechism, in so far as it is substituted to the Bible, is a bad substitute: and that, in the National Society's Schools,[2] in effect it actually is substituted to it:— substituted, not simply added. What will thereupon be shewn is—that Church of Englandism is a religion different from the religion of Jesus, and that in these Schools, principally by means of that Catechism, this spurious religion actually is substituted to the religion of Jesus. Short title—*The Catechism—a bad substitute to the Bible—is substituted to it.*[3]

II. Part II. In this part will be shewn that, by express provision anxiously made, by the persons, whoever they are, by whom, in the name of the Society, self-styled *The National Society*,—as if in the whole nation there were no other Society,—the system of instruction carried on in these Schools is directed,—the children of all members of the nation who are not Church-of-Englandists stand excluded from the benefits of it. For the designation of the system by which the accomplishment of this object is aimed at, the appellation of *The Exclusionary System*, will, in the course of this work, be all along applied. Antecedently to the proofs afforded of the establishment of this exclusionary system, the true nature and tendency of this system will be developed and held up to view.

Short title—*The Exclusionary System—its bad effects—its establishment.*[4]

---

[1] 1818 'II. Plan'. The enumeration is redundant.
[2] The meeting to propose the foundation of the National Society for Promoting the Education of the Poor in the Principles of the Established Church, throughout England and Wales was held on 16 October 1811, and the first General Meeting, which approved the rules and regulations for the constitution and government of the Society, was held on 21 October 1811. For the opening of the first school see p. 37 n. above.
[3] See pp. 56–87 below. [4] See pp. 88–98 below.

III. Part III. If, in the majority of the English nation, the spirit of antichristian hostility thus manifested towards 1,500,000 of their fellow subjects, were universal, the spectacle so exhibited would be still more melancholy than it is believed to be. Evidence has been noted, by which the contrary hope has been produced. To bring to view the grounds on which this hope rests, is exclusively the business of this third, as well as in some sort that of the next succeeding part.—Short title—*Exclusionary system—Grounds for the hope, that the approbation of it is not general.*[1]

IV. Part IV. On the subject of the proceedings of the National Society in relation to the Schools in question, three *Reports* have been published, purporting to contain accounts of those proceedings, as carried on respectively, in the first, second, third, and fourth years of its age, being the years 1811-2, 1812-3, 1813-4, and 1814-5.[2] In these Reports, a notion all along held up to view, is—that, in the character of Committee-men—Members, some of them of this or that one, others of this or that other, of a variety of Committees,—so many different branches of the business have all along been performed: so many different minds having in each instance applied themselves to the subject, and given their concurrence to what has been done. A suspicion, which by the complexion of the published documents has been produced, is—that in the intimation thus conveyed, there is no truth: for that it is always by some one Member alone, or, at the utmost, with the general, and not any special concurrence of some one other Member, or very small number of Members, and without means of resort allowed to Members at large, that every thing has been done: and that of this imposture a principal, if not the only object, has been the screening of the exclusionary system, with its principal author or authors, from the reproach so justly due. In this fourth part of the Introduction, the circumstances by which this suspicion has been produced will be laid open to view. Short title—*National Society—Grounds for regarding its Reports as spurious, and purposely deceptious.*[3]

The persons to whom the suspicion more particularly points, in the character of authors and conductors of the supposed system of

---

[1] See pp. 99–101 below.
[2] See 'Report of the General Committee', in *First Annual Report of the National Society*, pp. 13–19; 'Report of the General Committee 1813', in *Second Annual Report of the National Society*, pp. 5–20; 'Report of the General Committee 1814', in *Third Annual Report of the National Society*, pp. 9–30; 'Report of the General Committee 1815', in *Fourth Annual Report of the National Society for Promoting the Education of the Poor in the Principles of the Established Church*, London, 1816, pp. 9–33.
[3] See pp. 102–94 below.

PLAN OF THE WORK

misrepresentation, are the Archbishop of Canterbury, President of the Society, and the Reverend T.T. Walmsley, Secretary.[a]

V. *Part V.* In the tenor of the Catechism in question, reference is made, and great stress laid, on a portion of Church service, in which are contained a ceremony called *Baptism*, and a species of engagement, distinguished or distinguishable by the appellation of *Sponsorship*. In the tenor of the Catechism, such are the virtues and the consequent indispensability ascribed to this ceremony, and this engagement,—such, on the other hand, the mischiefs with which in the present state of things they seemed pregnant, that, antecedently to a general examination of the contents of the Catechism at large, a few observations, explanatory of the true nature of these two objects, presented themselves as forming an indispensable preparative. In this fifth part of the Introduction, this explanation has been submitted to the sincere reader's view. Short title—*Baptism and Sponsorship—proper when instituted,—Baptism now needless, Sponsorship improper.*[1]

Thus much for shortness. But when the observation thus made comes to be developed, the particular imports requisite to be attached to the word *improper*, as applied to the two objects, will be seen to be very materially different: the *baptism needless*, but with the exception of accidental, though but too natural, abuses, *innoxious:* the *sponsorship*, rendered by change of circumstances not merely *needless* and *useless*, but essentially *immoral* and *noxious*.

VI. *Body of the work.*

Immediately after Part the Fifth of this Introduction, comes the body of the work, intituled, *The Church of England Catechism examined*. At the end of the Preface, it was thought necessary that the *Charges*, which have been the result of this examination, should in the first place be brought to view.[2] In the course of it, the question which the sincere reader will all along have to propose to himself, is—how far, by the considerations so brought to view, these charges are respectively made good. Attached to each Charge, be it remembered, is a reference to the passage or passages, text and comment

---

[a] The gaps thus visible in the Christian names of the Reverend Divine would not have been left, had any means been any where furnished, whereby they could have been filled up.[3]

---

[1] See pp. 195–202 below.   [2] See 'Recapitulation', pp. 40–2 above.
[3] Tindal Thompson Walmsley (1758?–1847), Rector of St Martin, Ludgate 1805–19 and of St Vedast, Foster Lane and St Michael-le-Querne 1815–47 in the City of London, was elected Secretary of the National Society at the undated first meeting of the General Committee: see *First Annual Report of the National Society*, p. 14.

together, in which it originated, and by which it is regarded as justified.

In this Introduction and the body of the work together, for the purpose of affording a warrant for the several above-mentioned Charges, viz. by proof made of the allegations contained in them, little more than tendencies—general *tendencies*—could, without digression and confusion, have been brought to view. How melancholy soever be the complexion of it, to the sincere reader, it cannot but, in another sense, be matter of satisfaction,—viz. in respect of the proof afforded of the justice of the respective charges,—to behold these same *tendencies* ripened into *act*: the moral diseases, which such instruction is shewn to have a tendency to produce, breaking out and manifesting themselves in the conduct of determinate individuals, occupants of public and influential situations. For denial or doubt on the question of *fact*, no room will here be left: of whatsoever observations may here be found, the ground will be seen to be throughout composed of printed and published documents, of which the authenticity—and so far as concerns the imputation upon those persons whose discourses they respectively present to view, the verity,—will be seen to stand undisputed and indisputable. Of these documents, with the observations that seemed requisite to bring to view the connexion between the alleged cause and the inferred effect, will be seen to be composed the matter of the *Appendix*.

In this Appendix, five public characters, or groups of public characters, will in the first place be more or less brought to view: 1. Dr. Howley, Bishop of London; 2. Dr. Kipling, Dean of Peterborough;[1] 3. Dr. Andrews, Dean of Canterbury, and Rector of St. James's, Westminster;[2] 4. Mr. Vansittart, Chancellor of the Exchequer; 5. The Archbishop of Canterbury, President of the New-Instruction Society, self-styled *The National Society*, and in each year his one and fifty Colleagues in the office of Members of the governing body of that Society—styled, *The General Committee*.[3]

---

[1] Thomas Kipling (*c.* 1745–1822), Dean of Peterborough 1798–1822.

[2] St James's, Westminster was more commonly called St James's, Piccadilly.

[3] The General Committee was composed of fifty-two members: the Archbishop of Canterbury, who was President *ex officio*; the Archbishop of York; the twenty-four bishops eligible to sit in the House of Lords; ten temporal Lords or members of the Privy Council, from among whom Vice-Presidents were appointed for indefinite terms; and sixteen other members who were appointed by the President and the Vice-Presidents, a fourth part of whom were scheduled to resign annually but who were eligible for immediate re-election. For the resolutions constituting the National Society see *First Annual Report of the National Society*, pp. 6–8, especially Resolutions 3–7 at p. 7, which deal with the composition of the General Committee. For a list of the members of the first General Committee see ibid., pp. 13–14.

PLAN OF THE WORK

VII. Appendix, No. I. Among the above-mentioned accusations against the Catechism, is that of containing matter, tending in various ways to the depravation of the intellectual part of man's frame. Of such a depravation a more comprehensive or conclusive symptom cannot surely be imagined than '*a prostration of understanding and will*,'[1] the morbific cause of prostration being in this case applied in the first instance to the *understanding*, and thence to the *will*, by the movements of which last-mentioned faculty are directed those of the other. Applied to the corporeal part of man's frame, *prostration of strength* is an appropriate term, employed by medical men to express the lowest stage of weakness. The benefit of experiencing, at the hands of the prostrate mind, undue obsequiousness, ready to minister in every shape to his own private and sinister interest—is not this the only motive, by which, in the breast of any human being, a wish, to create or find any such disease in the mind of any other human being, can reasonably be supposed to be produced? *undue obsequiousness*, in which is included practice of every folly, every vice, and every crime which in furtherance of such sinister interest it can happen to a man to wish to see practised.

'*Prostration of understanding and will*,' is in one word *slavery:* but that sort of slavery, in comparison of which the most absolute that is to be found in Barbary or the West Indies is freedom. Except for the purpose of beholding in himself the correspondent *tyranny*, is it in human nature that any man should wish to behold in any other, any such *slavery?* and, in the import of one word, *tyranny*, is condensed the presence of every thing that goes by the name of *vice*, and the absence of every thing that goes by the name of *virtue*.

In the discourse in question, the rendering this prostration of understanding and will general among all Church-of-Englandists, is an object which will be seen avowed by the Bishop:[2] an object not merely of his own wishes, but an object, for the attainment of which the system of instruction, of which this Catechism forms the principal part, is the intended instrument.

By the author's own hand, in the course of this his *Charge*, the frame of mind, intellectual and moral, that gave birth to it,—but more particularly the moral,—may be seen to a considerable degree developed and laid open to view. With the exception of Church-of-Englandists,—whose understandings and wills it is his warmest hope and endeavour to lay prostrate at the feet even of his subordinates, all Christians as well as Non-Christians will be seen spoken of by him as

---

[1] See p. 37 n. above.
[2] i.e. William Howley, Bishop of London.

CHURCH-OF-ENGLANDISM

'*enemies*;'[1] Christians moreover as schismatics, and, as such, men of '*guilt*:'[2]—practical inference, oppression under the name of *punishment*.

Thus then may be seen some of the tendencies of the Catechism ripened into act.

In support of the self-styled *Excellent Church*, war, offensive as well as defensive, upon all other Churches, being thus the business of that truly Episcopal Charge,—observations, tending to shew more or less of the title of that Idol to that its assumed attribute,—particularly when viewed in comparison with the equally established Church of Scotland,—will naturally be found interspersed.

Short title of this first article in the Appendix[3]—*Remarks on the Object of Church-of-England Religion, as avowed by the Bishop of London.*[a]

[a] In consideration of the inordinate length, to which the work would be swelled by the addition,—the papers, of which what follows between the mark inserted in this part of the text, and the correspondent mark in a succeeding page was designed for a prospectus, have for the present been omitted.[4] But, in relation to every one of the topics therein touched upon,—and in confirmation of every one of the opinions or suspicions therein advanced,—matter will be found, in some part or parts of this work as it stands at present.

For *Dean Kipling*, see as in the text App. No. I. pp. 295, 296: for *Dean Andrews*, see App. No. II, the pages not difficult to find.[5] For *Archbishop Manners Sutton*, see Introduction, from beginning to end:[6] for *Mr. Vansittart*, see the same pages in which mention is made of his friend Dean Andrews: for *Bishop Burgess*—not less worthy than any of these illustrious persons to be had in remembrance—see App. No. I. p. 294, and perhaps elsewhere. But above all see his 'BRIEF MEMORIAL,' &c., including his 'DEMONSTRATION' &c., by which any one thing as well as any other may be demonstrated: year of date 1814:[7] and therein, as in a mirror, behold him rending his

---

[1] See [Howley], *Charge delivered to the clergy of the diocese of London*, p. 22: 'In the mean while every populous village, unprovided with a national school, must be regarded as a strong hold abandoned to the occupation of the enemy.'

[2] See ibid., p. 1, referring to the work of Howley's predecessor John Randolph (1749–1813), Bishop of Oxford 1799–1807, Bangor 1807–9, and London 1809–13: 'From the period of his first entrance on the higher departments of the church he opposed a determined resistance to the spurious liberality, which in the vain desire of conciliation increases division and multiplies heresy, by palliating the guilt of schism, or by diminishing the number and undervaluing the importance of doctrines essential to Christianity.'

[3] See pp. 257–311 below.   [4] i.e. ☞ p. 49 and ☜ p. 53 below respectively.

[5] See p. 323 below, as identified by the 'Errata'. Bentham's comment refers only to the discussion of Andrewes at pp. 323–7 n. below. The full version of the Andrewes Appendix is reproduced at pp. 537–75 below.

[6] See pp. 56–202 below.

[7] Thomas Burgess (1756–1837), Bishop of St David's 1803–25 and Salisbury 1825–37, was author of *A Brief Memorial on The Repeal of so much of the Statute 9. and 10. William III. as relates to Persons Denying the Doctrine of the Holy Trinity: addressed to all who believe the Christian Religion to be a True Religion, and who are desirous of maintaining the religious institutions of their Ancestors. To which is prefixed, A Demonstration of the Three Great Truths of Christianity, together with Specimens of Unitarian Rejection of Scripture and of all Antiquity*, London, 1814.

PLAN OF THE WORK

☛ In Appendix, No. I. pages 295, 296, mention will be found incidentally made, of Dr. Kipling, Dean of Peterborough, and a threatening letter of his, privately addressed to a Catholic Clergyman.[1] In the Bishop's Charge, as above, we have the theory: in this letter of the Dean's, we may see that theory reduced to practice. In the Charge we shall see Non-Church-of-Englandists marked out as 'enemies' and men of 'guilt:' in the private letter, now very properly made public, we shall see them treated as such. Whether the threat of prosecution contained in it was executed, does not appear: but to the present purpose the threat is quite sufficient. It may serve as an example of that intellectual imbecility, as well as of that moral pravity, with which it is the tendency of this Catechism to infect the mind. The offence consisted in the having applied the epithet *new* to the Church of England.

In the sight of Jesus, if any credit be due to the Gospel History, all men were equal.[2] On this principle, on the part of any assemblage of men, the claim to regard at the hands of the ruling powers increases and diminishes in exact proportion to the number of the persons of which the assemblage is composed. As between one such assemblage and another, numbers in each being equal, the comparative claim to the benefit of that social affection at those same hands will, by a title equally indisputable, increase and diminish in proportion to the *need* they have of the beneficial effects of that affection, in all the several ways in which they can be made to flow. On both these titles, taken together, the claim of the poor was, in the eyes of Jesus, superior to that of the rich.[3] Not so in the eyes of Dean Andrews. In those seats of instruction, in which, for the creation and preservation of pride on the part of the richer, and servility and undue obsequiousness on the part of the poorer classes, rank and riches are distinguished by those external marks of superiority, which, even by the proudest of the proud, have every where else been discarded,—Dean Andrews, as well as the two other dignitaries above-mentioned,[4] had

breast, if not his garments,[5] at the thoughts of the end, now at length put, to the oppression for so many generations exercised upon *Arians* and *Unitarians*.

---

[1] Kipling's letter to John Lingard (1771–1851), Roman Catholic priest and historian, was published in *Monthly Magazine; or, British Register*, vol. xxxix, no. 270 (1 July 1815), 580, and is reproduced in Appendix I, pp. 295–6 n. below.

[2] See, for instance, Galatians 3: 28: 'There is neither Jew nor Greek, there is neither bond nor free, there is neither male nor female: for ye are all one in Christ Jesus.'

[3] Bentham perhaps had in mind Jesus' injunction to the rich ruler to 'sell all that thou hast, and distribute unto the poor': see Luke 18: 18–30, esp. 22.

[4] Kipling and Howley.

[5] See Joel 2: 13.

been taught to regard, as so many objects of just contempt, all persons less loaded than they themselves were, or hoped to be, with the pomps and vanities of this world.[1] In his stall at Canterbury, chief of a set of idlers, paid for doing nothing, under the name of Prebendaries—in this his slumbering place,—but still more impressively in his Rectorial mansion, in the purlieus of the Palace,[2] in and by his familiar and confidential intercourse with the Chancellor of the Exchequer, and his Colleagues, and Subordinates, at the Treasury Board,—he had learnt to behold, in the individuals belonging to the middling ranks, so many objects of profound contempt,—of contempt proportionably more profound,—the subject and abject multitude.

To the sportive genius of this Receiver of the Holy Ghost, as displayed in a confidential address of his to those Receivers of taxes,[3] the middling classes are indebted for the nick-name, under which they will be seen held out by him as fit objects of those antisocial affections. At the dawn of the reformation, by the Dignitaries of the Church of Rome, Protestants were stigmatized with the name of *Guex* or *Geuses*, i.e. beggars.[4] In the same spirit, by this Dignitary of the *Daughter* Church—or not to offend Dean Kipling, say the *Sister* of the *Mother* Church[5]—men who are neither so rich, nor so wedded to wine as to loath all cheaper liquors, will be seen marked out as objects of scorn, and their health as an object of just disregard, under the name of *Ale-drinkers*.[6]

---

[1] In the Catechism, the child states that his parents 'did promise and vow three things in my name. First, that I should renounce the devil and all his works, the pomps and vanity of this wicked world . . . .' This refers in turn to the service of baptism authorized by the *Book of Common Prayer*, where parents are asked: 'Dost thou, in the name of this Child, renounce the devil and all his works, the vain pomp and glory of the world . . . .'

[2] The Rectory at St James's, Piccadilly, a three-storey brick house built in 1685–6 situated in the north-east corner of the churchyard, was about a third of a mile from St James's Palace, at this time the principal Royal residence in London, situated at the corner of Green Park and St James's Park.

[3] For Andrewes's letter of 6 February 1815 to Stephen Rumbold Lushington (1776–1868), Joint Secretary to the Treasury 1814–27, later Governor of Madras 1827–32, in support of John Abbott, a magistrate and brewer in Canterbury, accused of adulterating his beer, see 'Further Papers Relating to Excise Prosecutions; &c.', *Commons Sessional Papers* (1816) xviii. 65–74, at 69. The case of Abbott is referred to again in Appendix II, pp. 323–7 n. below, and is the subject of the Andrewes Appendix, pp. 537–75 below.

[4] 'Ce ne sont que des gueux' are reputedly the words used by Charles de Berlaymont (1510–78) to describe the Dutch nobles who on 5 April 1566 presented a petition opposing the civil and religious rule of Spain in the Netherlands to Margaret, Duchess of Parma (1522–86), Governor-General of the Netherlands 1559–67, who had been appointed by her half-brother Philip II (1527–98), King of Spain from 1556. Berlaymont was not an official of the Church of Rome as Bentham suggests, but one of three special advisers to Margaret who were responsible directly to Philip II. The term he used as an insult was within three days adopted by those who resisted the rule of Spain in the Netherlands.

[5] See Appendix I, p. 295 & n. below.

[6] For Andrewes's use of the term 'ale drinkers' see *Commons Sessional Papers* (1816) xviii. 69:

PLAN OF THE WORK

In the person of *Mr. Nicholas Vansittart*, the public have long viewed (alas, very long!) a Right Honourable Gentleman, scarcely more distinguished by his situation of *Chancellor of the Exchequer*, than by the splendor of his piety, according to the forms and rites of the Church of England. In the list of members of the governing Committee of that *Episcopal Society*, which will be seen taking for its principal, if not sole object, the converting, by means of the abovementioned exclusionary system, the new invented engine of instruction into a buttress for the support of the tottering Church, this lay name may accordingly be seen, while others vanish, occupying a constant place.[1]

It was for the eyes of this Right Honourable and conspicuously pious Gentleman, that the letter in which, by the style and title of *Ale-drinkers*, all ranks of men beneath the level of the most opulent are, in manner abovementioned, pointed to, as being of the number of those whose health possesses not, at the hands of their superiors, any title to regard. On this letter of spiritual advice, in conjunction with others, written by other persons in pursuit of the same object,[2] certain *Treasury Minutes* will be seen grounding themselves: Minutes, penned under the direction of the piety of Mr. Vansittart.[3] In these Minutes, certain maxims of government and judicature will be seen avowed and acted upon: and in regard to these maxims, it will be seen that for the utter dissolution of this or any other government, nothing more can, at any time, in addition to these maxims, be requisite and necessary,—provided always, that the observance given to them be impartial, constant, and inflexible.

Supposing these maxims uniformly acted up to, such, it is shewn, would be the inevitable effect. But at the same time, the intention of producing any such effect is obviously that sort of intention, which consistently with reason can not be imputed to any man who is not out of his senses, much less to a man so situated.—On the other hand, let but the application of these same maxims be *partial*, and at the same time *arbitrary*, government is *not* dissolved: it is only

'[Abbott] has appeared to me so good a man, and so useful a magistrate that I should be very sorry to have that usefulness diminished by his being brought forward to the public in a matter which concerns only ale drinkers, and I fear has its source in malice.' See also p. 540 n. below.

[1] Vansittart was listed as a donor of funds to the National Society for Promoting the Education of the Poor from 1811 to the time when Bentham was writing. He does not, however, appear to have been a member of the General Committee, as Bentham here suggests.

[2] Five other letters in addition to that from Andrewes were submitted: see *Commons Sessional Papers* (1816) xviii. 69–71, and p. 540 below.

[3] For a copy of the Minute, dated 10 February 1815, and the warrant of the Lords Commissioners of His Majesty's Treasury, dated 25 February 1815, and signed by three Commissioners of the Treasury—Vansittart, Berkeley Paget, and Charles Grant—see *Commons Sessional Papers* (1816) xviii. 72, and pp. 325 n., 547, 558–71 below.

rendered corrupt and despotic, and the corruption and despotism supported and secured: and, such it is shewn, is the value of these maxims, so long as they are observed,—that to such partiality, corruption, and despotism, no check can be applied. If, of the setting up the maxims in question, the object was not the rendering the exercise of the power in question thus partial and corrupt, it will be for the reader to judge whether the establishment and exercise of it was not an act without an object: an effect without a cause.

At the same time, what is obvious enough is—that any such intention as that of exercising government with partiality, corruption, and despotism, can never be professed, or so much as admitted, consistently with any pretensions to the reputation either of probity or of piety. To a public man, who lays claim to either, what is therefore altogether necessary is—that an habitual cloak of insincerity shall be carefully worn by him, and all his acts and words enveloped in it. But, to the formation of such a habit, nothing (it will have been shewn), can more effectually contribute, than a thorough and continued impregnation with the matter of this Catechism. Accordingly, whether the complexion of the Right Honourable mind, here in question, be not to be numbered among the exemplifications of the baleful effects of this formulary, is among those points, on which the sincere reader will have to pronounce.

In the Introduction, Part IV. will, as above,[1] have been brought to view the grounds of the suspicion entertained, that the Reports published under the name of *the National Society*, have been spurious, and at the same time purposely deceptious: *spurious*, in as much as the acts, therein represented as having had the actual concurrence of the whole body,—or such and such large portions of it,—have, in the most important instances, and in particular in the instance of the *exclusionary acts*, been the work of no more than one member of those bodies respectively: viz. the Archbishop of Canterbury, the President: *purposely deceptious*, in as much as a system, composed of general concealment and occasional disclosure, has all along been carried on, having for its object the producing a persuasion, that the acts in question have all along had the actual concurrence—in the first place, of this or that particular Committee,—in the next place, of the General Committee, of the Members of which the list is published in every such Report.[2]

Supposing the case to be such as it is thus suspected to be, here would be guilt in two different shapes to be divided among those whom it concerned: of active misrepresentation, and purposed

---

[1] See pp. 44–5 above.   [2] See p. 46 n. above.

PLAN OF THE WORK

imposture and deception, the charge would fall upon the Archbishop of Canterbury, the President: of connivance with this active guilt, upon the rest of the Bishops and their lay-coadjutors.

Upon this supposition, the connection,—between the disposition, above stated as formed by the instrument in question on the one hand, and the language and conduct of men in high places on the other,—will be found still more particularly close in this, than in any other of the abovementioned five instances.[1]

In the other cases, the disease produced is rather a general laxity of the moral frame,—with or without its naturally, though not constantly concomitant symptom—general debility of the intellectual frame: in this last case it is immorality in a determinate shape: viz. insincerity and fraud, or in one word *falsehood*—and this practised on a specific occasion, for a specific purpose.

VIII. Appendix, No. II. In the course of the examination made of this Catechism in the body of the work, occasion was found for bringing in some degree to view the abuses, of which the Church ceremony, called *the Lord's Supper*, has been the source: on which same occasion, another ceremony,—issuing beyond doubt from the same sacred source, and of the two the only one properly applicable to the situation of the followers of Jesus taken at large,—is there held up to view, in comparison and competition with it.[2] The more thoroughly the two ceremonies were thus conjunctly considered, the more impressive was the conception formed, of the advantages which would result, from the substitution of the perfectly innoxious, and at the same time eminently and usefully instructive ceremony, to the unfaithful imitation of a scene in private life, in which no generally applicable instruction was contained, and the imitations of which have, in experience, been found to be in so deplorable a degree noxious.

On maturer consideration however, for the reason that will be seen, the *feet-washing*,—though preferable in every respect—and in a high degree—to the *wine-drinking* ceremony—and though in use, and even in practice, not altogether unknown in Catholic countries,—seemed not to afford a sufficient promise either of its being instituted by any class of Christians in this country,—or, if instituted, of its being decidedly useful. Hence, this being dropt, remains for the Short Title.—*Lord's Supper—not designed by Jesus for general imitation—its utter unfitness for that purpose.*[3]

---

[1] See p. 46 above.   [2] See pp. 322–31 below.   [3] See pp. 312–32 below.

IX. Appendix, No. III. Against mischiefs, so enormous as these which will have been seen to flow from the *exclusionary system*,—hard indeed would be the condition of the people of this country, if such were the nature of the case, as to deny all remedy. From two sources alone can any such remedy be looked for: one is, *repentance* at the hands of the authors of the system; the other is, a course, the taking of which is already in the hands of the persons most immediately affected by it, viz. the parents and guardians of the children to whom the poisonous cup is held out.

Of these two remedies, for form sake, the first mentioned is indeed held up to view: but, of course, with scarce a ray of hope to gild it with.

The other will be seen presented for adoption: presented in the character of a lawful, safe, effectual,—and, when well considered, an unobjectionable one.

Short title. *Remedies to the mischiefs of the Exclusionary System as applied to Instruction.*[1]

X. Appendix, No. IV. Throughout the whole field of morals, dissocial and social affection afford a test,—by which, in so far as circumstances admit of the application of it, they may be distinguished from each other. Dissocial, finds in the exposure of abuses and other imperfections, its ultimate gratification: social affection, whether operating upon a private or a public scale, puts, and keeps itself upon the look out for a remedy: and, howsoever remote and uncertain, it is only by the cheering prospect of a remedy in the back ground, that it can bring itself to face and dwell upon the afflicting spectacle, of the stream of sufferings so generally flowing from the abuse.

It is thus that,—where the mischief produced by the injection of the matter of this Catechism has been brought to view,—a remedy— and that such as it is, one which it is in the power of all fathers and guardians to administer—has been sought for, found, and just now referred to.—It is thus that,—where the mischief, produced by *subscription* to articles of faith, was, though but incidentally, brought to view,—a remedy to that mischief was, with like care, pointed out.[a] But, of every abuse and every imperfection, which has place in the field of religion,—not to speak of the field of government,—the main root—not to say the only root—has all along been seen to lie in that remnant of Popery, *the Excellent Church,* as viewed in its present

---

[a] See Preface, p. 38.

---

[1] See pp. 333–42 below.

state. For the application of a radical remedy to this radical evil, the times, even by the confession, or rather proclamation, of those by whom it is most cherished, seem ripening apace.

On this subject, and on this state of things, *remediation,*—the object thus all along looked to as a first principle of direction—requires that something should be said: were it only in the view of giving some intimation, how slight so ever, of the course necessary to be pursued, for reducing to its *minimum* the mass of evil inseparable from so great a change.

At the same time, consideration being had of the scattered state, in which the grounds of the demand for this change, such as in the course of this work will have presented themselves, will have been brought to view,—a task, which could not wholly be put by, has been—the giving a sort of compressed recapitulation of those grounds; together with a few additions, to give roundness to the whole.

Short title—*Remedy to all religious, and much political mischief—Euthanasia of the Church.*[1]

XI. Appendix, No. V. Conscious—if not of the primeval, at any rate of the present, rottenness of the whole fabric—alarmed by the symptoms of dissolution which have been continually pressing themselves upon observation,—men in power have, of late years, betaken themselves to several expedients for warding off the impending catastrophe. Of these expedients, the adoption thus given to the new system of instruction, with the exclusionary system grafted upon it, may be stated as being by far the one best adapted to the purpose. Of the others, a short view will form the *fifth* and last article of this Appendix.

Short title—*Measures recently instituted or proposed for meliorating the state of the Church—efficient to bad, inefficient to good purposes.*[2]

END OF THE PLAN OF THE WORK.

[1] See pp. 343–493 below.   [2] See pp. 494–536 below.

INTRODUCTION.

PART I.

THE CATECHISM—A BAD SUBSTITUTE TO THE BIBLE—IS SUBSTITUTED FOR IT.

§I. *Church of England Catechism—this perhaps the first Censorial Commentary ever applied to it.*

THE *Catechism* forms part of that authoritative system of religious discourse, which, by the style and title of '*The Book of Common Prayer, and Administration of the Sacraments, and other Rites and Ceremonies of the Church, according to the use of the Church of England*,' has now, for about two centuries and a half, possessed the exclusive privilege of supplying the matter of devotion to the members of that established church:[1] and this in particular is the part, and the only part, the imprinting of which, or rather the words of it, on their memories, has generally been the object of the first literary task, which, at the commencement of the career of intellectual, or at any rate of literary, instruction,—has given exercise to the faculties and patience of children of both sexes.

Under the pretence of *exposition*, i.e. *explanation*, yet not the less in the style and tone of eulogy, it has received comments in abundance, in all which those merits have been ascribed to it, with the existence of which, supposing them to exist, the existence of any utility, whether on the part of the exposition in question, or on the part of any thing else that could have been exhibited in the name or character of *an exposition*, would have been incompatible.

The thing thus undertaken to be expounded is, in so far as it has any claim to regard, an extract—and that, so far as it goes, a correct one—from the sacred original. *Correctness—clearness*—does it fail in either of these points? It fails of answering any good purpose to which

[1] The *Book of Common Prayer* had been authorized by the Act of Uniformity of 1662 (13 & 14 Car. II, c. 4).

INTRODUCTION. PART I. §I.

it can have been directed. Instead of being expounded, it should be discarded. Were it the original, yes: in so far as, by change in language or manners, obscure allusions to past events or states of things, exposition is found to be requisite. But, an *exposition?*—*expound* an *exposition?*—No: absurdity is involved in the very idea of it.—Expound the inadequate exposition?—No: but, instead of it, give an adequate one, and send the inadequate one to the trunk-makers.

The Scottish Church has its Catechism. It has even two of them, the longer and the shorter[1]—the shorter, had it been still shorter, longer than could[2] have been wished. The longer a text, the greater the quantity of matter, for commentators and expositors to crawl over and cover with their slime. Yet, who ever heard of comments or expositions to either of these formularies?

To the Scottish Church this, however, is but the beginning of triumphs. As we advance, many are the points of difference that will present themselves: and, on each point, will an addition be seen made to the number of her merits.

As to this formulary, whether, amidst the multitude of comments and expositions, with which, under different names, it has been covered, it has ever seen so much as one,—other than of that sort which commences with a secret vow, to keep the door of the mind inexorably shut against every idea, the effect of which might be to beget any the least suspicion, of imperfection in any shape, in the consecrated text,—is more than has happened to find its way to the cognizance of the author of these pages.

Upon the whole, the abundance of comments of the laudatory cast, coupled with the paucity, or utter non-existence, of any of an

---

[1] In July 1648 the General Assembly of the Church of Scotland approved both the Longer and the Shorter Catechisms (having previously approved the Confession of Faith in August 1647). All three texts had been prepared by the Westminster Assembly of Divines, appointed by the Long Parliament in 1643 to reform the Church of England, and to bring a closer union with the Church of Scotland and other Reformed Churches in Europe. The Catechisms and Confession of Faith were ratified by the Scottish Parliament in 1649, but were rescinded and annulled, like all other acts passed between 1640 and 1660, following the Restoration. In 1690, however, the Catechisms and the Confession of Faith were restored and the Church of Scotland confirmed as Presbyterian. See *The Acts of the Parliaments of Scotland 1124–1707*, ed. T. Thompson and C. Innes, 12 vols. in 15, Edinburgh, 1814–75: Act 58, 7 February 1649, vi. Part ii. 161; Act 126, 28 March 1661, vii. 86–7; and Act 7, 7 June 1690, ix. 133–4. The Shorter Catechism remained the most common text for catechetical instruction until well into the nineteenth century. For the text of the Catechisms and the Confession of Faith see *The Confession of Faith And the Larger and Shorter Catechisme, First agreed upon by the Assembly of Divines at Westminster, And now appointed by the Generall Assembly of the Kirk of Scotland to be a part of Uniformity in Religion between the Kirks of Christ in the three Kingdomes*, Edinburgh, 1649. For Bentham's further discussion of the Scottish Catechisms and the work of the Westminster Assembly of Divines see pp. 69–73 below.

[2] 1818 'would'. The text follows the 'Errata'.

accusative, or so much as a critical complexion,—these two naturally connected phenomena present themselves as the altogether natural result of two very obvious causes. Vast must have been the number of professional men, each of whom beheld advantage to himself in many a shape, from the merit of covering it with his praise:[a] small indeed, if any, of those, to whose eyes advantage can have presented itself in any shape, as capable of being derived by them from the exposure of any imperfection that might be to be found in it.

Of what benefit, either to the critic himself in any ordinary shape, or so much as to the public at large, in any measurable compass of time, could any such criticism afford a prospect of being productive? That, supposing the formulary ever so full of imperfections, and those imperfections ever so completely demonstrated, the removal of any so much as the minutest, particle of them by authority would ever be the consequence;—at what time could any such result present, to any intelligent mind, any, the faintest colour of probability? And, as to the audacious individual, by whom any such imperfections should have been held up to view, from what quarter could he expect any return more acceptable, than neglect? To Church of Englandists he and his criticism would be objects of blind aversion,—to all but Church of Englandists, (but for some such awakening conjuncture as the present,) objects of indifference.

§II. *On Religion—in a Christian Free-School—the Bible the only fit Lesson-Book.*

In the sort of school in question, the arts to be taught are—besides Arithmetic, those of Reading and Writing. For furnishing lessons for this purpose, a book—one book at least—is necessary. If one book alone, what shall this book be?—If more books than one, to which of them shall the preference—in the first place—be given?

To both these questions one and the same answer may serve—*the Bible*.

On this occasion, as on every other, for proof of the position, which is advanced, the broader the ground is that is laid, the better: the

[a] At school—well do I remember—the only danger I ever felt myself in of punishment, was from my inability to beat into my memory the words—for as to sense, it was out of the question—of a Comment, or Exposition of this formulary, by some *Archbishop:* his name began with a W, which is all [I] now recollect about this night-mare, by which my sleep was so long disturbed. I should expect to find it either *Wake* or *Williams*.[1]

[1] William Wake (1657–1737), Archbishop of Canterbury 1716–37, was author of *The Principles of the Christian Religion Explained: In a Brief Commentary upon the Church Catechism*, London, 1699.

broader the ground—in other words, the greater the number of the persons, at whose hands, by means of the proof, the position may reasonably be expected to obtain acceptance.

The Bible then—the Bible, were it only in consideration of its being that book which, in this country, has, beyond comparison, more readers, as well as more hearers, than any other, might, even from this circumstance alone, be naturally regarded as presenting an indisputable claim to preference and precedence.

To the preference thus proposed, from any person by whom the religion of Jesus is believed in, could any such objection come? No, surely:—unless perhaps it were on account of the immature state of the intellectual faculties, at the time of life, at which, on a subject so fraught with mystery, instruction will, on the supposition in question, be endeavoured to be administered.

But assuredly, so long as, in the matter, of which the book in question is composed, a sufficient quantity can be found, of that which, with reference to the mind in question, is sufficiently clear; so long, from the obscurity of any part not employed, no valid objection can be derived against the employment of any part of it, which, being clear, is employed accordingly.

Nor,—supposing the clouds, which hang over the import, whatever they may be, sooner or later dispelled,—will the existence of it,—howsoever, at the commencement of the course of instruction, and even for a considerable time thereafter unquestionable,—be, upon due reflection, found to constitute any sufficient objection to the employing of it to this purpose. For some time indeed, by the supposition, it is without being accompanied by the ideas which they are meant to designate, that the signs present themselves to the *conception*, and lodge themselves in the *memory*. Be it so. But, at any rate, the *signs* are *there:* and, for the purpose of grammatical instruction,—which, in the order of time, is the first purpose,—they serve as well as any others: thereupon, as the faculties of the mind acquire maturity, and the storehouse of the mind receives its stock, little by little, the desirable and desired *ideas* drop in and attach themselves to the *signs*.

In a place of instruction, designed, as are the schools in question, for children, to whom, in so large a proportion, but for the means thus afforded, instruction on religion would not in any shape whatever be afforded,—the reason for taking, for the source of instruction in *reading* and *writing*, that same book, which is the source of instruction in *religion*, operates with a degree of force far beyond any with which it can apply in another situation:—in any situation, in which, whether the means here in question were or were not employed, instruction in religion might reasonably be expected to flow in from other sources.

Thus much as to *believers*. And even the few in whose eyes either religion in general, or the religion of Jesus in particular, is not conducive, but prejudicial, to real happiness and useful morality, and by whom religious instruction is accordingly regarded as worse than useless,—even these, so long as no school, from whence all religious instruction is excluded, were to be found, might still find it not inconsistent with their views to send their children to a school in which the book containing the religion of Jesus is taught: inasmuch as the same instrument, viz. the art of reading, which, in the first instance, will thus have been employed in the implanting of the supposed mischievous instruction, might, at a succeeding period, be equally made to serve in the eradicating of it:—might,—and, in their view of the matter, naturally would,—and with more than equal promise of success.

Thus much then being considered as settled, viz. that the book containing the religion of Jesus is the most proper book, from which the first lessons in the arts of reading and writing can be extracted, the next question is—in that same whole, of what description are the parts, from which they may with most propriety be extracted.

Neither in this does there seem much difficulty. The religion of Jesus—and not the religion of any other person—is the religion to be taught. But the religion of Jesus—in whose words shall it be sought for, but in the words of Jesus?

Here then we have two bodies of doctrine, to which, by an altogether indisputable title, the precedence and preference seems to be due: viz. the '*Discourses*'[a] at large, (headed by the 'SERMON *on the Mount*'),[a] these 'Discourses' and the '*Parables*.'[a]

Next to these, in the conjunct order of authenticity and importance, and thence in the order of preference, come those, in which is contained the description of the *acts* of Jesus, as delivered by the same biographical historians to whom we are indebted for his *Discourses:* and among these acts, a prominent place is naturally occupied by the *miraculous* ones—in one word, the '*Miracles*.'[a]

Thus, in a *direct* way, the determination, on the question, which of those parts are most proper, being made, if so it be, that, for the

---

[a] Under these same names, these are the lists of books, recommended and said to be employed in their central School, by the *National Society*.[1] See Part II. in which that part of the Report, made by that Society, is animadverted upon.[2]

---

[1] See *Second Annual Report of the National Society*, Appendix VIII, p. 196. Bentham reproduces the relevant passage from the *Report* at p. 64 n. below.

[2] See p. 91 below.

INTRODUCTION. PART I. §II.

purpose in question, in the place of instruction in question, at the time of life in question, this portion of the religion of Jesus, to which no believer in the religion of Jesus does or can object, is sufficient—and it seems difficult to say, why, in that same place, and at that same time of life, it should not be sufficient—every such invidious task as that of inquiring, whether,—in the consecrated miscellany, in the composition of which, in an age of darkness, the hand of the bookbinder, under the rod of the to us unknown ruling power, took so large a part, this or that article be not more or less unfit to be placed upon a level with the undisputed words of the discourses, and the undisputed narratives of the acts of Jesus,—will thus be rendered needless.

On the other hand, a consequence, which cannot be thought of without regret, is—that, by this means, an exclusion, and that an insuperable one—seems to be put upon the whole race of the Jews: more particularly when it is considered, in how large a proportion in this fraternity are to be found those members, who, but for this means, are likely to remain altogether destitute of so many invaluable benefits: destitute not only of instruction in reading and writing, but even, with the exception of a few burthensome and worse than useless rites and ceremonies, (in a considerable proportion of modern date) from instruction in *all* religion—from instruction in the very religion, of which their parents are nominally professors.

On the part of the bulk of the population—on the part of the Christian subscribers to these schools,—at least without some assistance and co-operation on the part of those dissidents themselves—it appears not how this cause of exclusion can admit of any remedy.

On the part of the Jewish parents themselves—that is to say, on the part of such of them, if any, as have strength of mind sufficient for the application of it—a remedy, by which the force of the exclusionary principle might, without a departure from the line of probity, be eluded, might be applied.—*Fables—under the name of fables—other fables under the name of histories—such are the discourses, which, in every school, in which instruction is given in the learned languages, are employed as sources and vehicles of instruction: among these, if you are true children of our Father Abraham, will you rank whatsoever they put into your hands to read or hear, concerning that Jesus, whom with such good reason our forefathers hanged upon a tree.*[1]—To some such effect as this is, would be the[2] caution, which, on sending his child to any

---

[1] 1818 '*tree?*' The text follows the 'Errata'.
[2] 1818 'would the'. The text follows the 'Errata'.

such place of Christian instruction, might, for keeping the imagined tares from mixing themselves with the undisputed wheat,[1] be given to him by a conscientious and consistent father.

True it is, that, on the part of the rulers of the Christian Church of England, for leaving the door completely open to the use of any such expedient, a departure in some sort from the present practice would be necessary. At present—such is the form of words in which the instruction is administered—on this subject, whatsoever is delivered to a child as true, he is all the while, not only taught, but compelled to declare, that he believes it to be true. Though (what in this or that part may be the case) in his eyes it may be false—though (what in a great part cannot but be the case) in his eyes it may be inconceivable—still what he is always forced to do is—over and over again, and in relation to every part without exception, to declare, that, in his eyes, it is true. But this is neither more nor less than to take the child in hand, and force him to *tell lies:* and not only, as in the case of *subscription* to Articles,[2]—at some one moment, to utter in the lump one enormously extensive lie, but to contract the *habit* of lying: yea, and in that most mischievous of habits, to persevere, till all regard for truth has been expelled, and the poison of mendacity has worked itself into the very marrow of the bones.

If these observations be correct, then, to make the only advance, requisite to the opening the door of any such school, to the child of a conscientious and consistent Jew, all that is necessary on the part of the rulers of the Church of England is—to cease acting in the character of suborners of juvenile mendacity. But, on this subject, occasion will present itself for speaking more largely in the sequel of this work.[3] This is no greater nor other concession, than that which would be necessary to the removing of the bar, by which an exclusion is endeavoured to be put, even upon all *Christian* children, whose lot it has not been, to have had for their parents members of the Church of England.

§III. *No substitute to the Bible should be there taught—the Catechism is made a substitute to it.*

The sacred text ought not to have a substitute. The reason is simple enough: and as conclusive as it is simple. In so far as it is different from the genuine and sacred original, by this difference, and

---

[1] For the parable of the tares and wheat see Matthew 13: 24–30, 36–43.
[2] i.e. the Thirty-nine Articles of the Church of England.
[3] See Appendix III, pp. 333–42 below.

by the whole amount of this difference, the substitute stands condemned: in so far as it is *not* different, there is no use in it.

Whether as a *postulate*, or as a *thing proved*, in a Protestant Country, may not then this position be stated as uncontrovertible?—In a Christian and Protestant Free School, the book in which is contained the whole religion of Jesus, ought not to have a substitute.

In the Central Free School, conducted in the name of the National Society,[1] the Bible *has* a substitute. The *Catechism*—that formulary, the poisonous nature of which it is the business of this tract to lay open to view, is made to operate as this substitute.

By the proof that follows, the truth of this position will be seen manifested: manifested—to a degree beyond any, which, by a person who had not scrutinized into the documents, and with this particular view, could easily have been imagined. With the single exception of the very short prayer, called *the Lord's Prayer*, which it was impossible to put aside,—of the sacred text, not a syllable is administered,—if indeed it be administered,—but for show and to save appearances. The only matter of a religious cast which is really intended to be administered with effect—the only matter of that description, which is so much as professed to be administered, in a manner calculated to produce the effect—is the matter composed of the words of *Holy Mother Church:* and this, in the instance of this Catechism, in such a manner as to throw all the rest, even of that pretious matter, into the back ground.

'*Our Saviour's Sermon on the Mount—Discourses of ditto—Miracles of ditto—Parables of our Blessed Saviour*'—these collections have already been stated as really proper for the purpose.[a] It was even from the list of Books recommended in the Report, styled *the National Society's 2d Report*, that these titles have been transcribed. Had this been all, in no other character than that of an object of approbation and applause, would this part of the management have here been mentioned.

But these discourses and acts of this '*Blessed Saviour*,' are they so

---

[a] See p. 190, 193.[2]

---

[1] Central School in Baldwin's Gardens, Gray's Inn Lane, London was opened by the National Society for Promoting the Education of the Poor on 19 June 1812: see p. 37 n. above.

[2] The references are to two lists of books, the first dated August 1812 and the second February 1813, which appear at *Second Annual Report of the National Society*, Appendix VI, p. 190, and Appendix VII, p. 193, respectively. The list dated August 1812 is reproduced at *First Annual Report of the National Society*, p. 198, and *Third Annual Report of the National Society*, Appendix IV, p. 169, and the list dated February 1813 at ibid., Appendix V, p. 172. Bentham reproduces the latter at p. 67 n. below.

CHURCH-OF-ENGLANDISM

much as *read?* Perhaps so: though scarcely even of this is any altogether unequivocal assurance to be found.[a]

But, the genuine matter of the original—suppose it *read*, what would it avail? what could the children be the better for it, when it is *the substituted matter*—the spurious matter—when it is this alone that

---

[a] In the National Society's Second Report—in that article of the Appendix which is intituled, 'No. VIII. The present state*a* of the CENTRAL SCHOOL, BALDWIN'S GARDENS,' the passage stands as follows:—Page 196. 'The *Religious exercises* learnt by heart are—the Lord's Prayer—Grace before and after meat—2d and 3d Collects of the Morning and Evening Service—Prayer on entering and leaving Church—the Catechism entire—and the same broken into short questions.

'The Books in *reading*, for which the Children are prepared by previous instruction on the *sand-trays*, are—National Society, Central School, No. 1. on cards (taught card by card, first by previous spelling, then by words)—National Society, Central School, No. 2.—National Society, Central School, No. 3.[1]—the Sermon on the Mount—the Parables—the Discourses—and the Miracles of our Blessed Saviour—Ostervald's Abridgment of the Old Testament[2]—and Mrs. Trimmer's Abridgment of the New[3]—all taught in the usual way, except that the spelling columns, No. 3. are first read syllabically and then by words: then follow the Bible and Prayer Book, to be put into the hands of such as by means of this initiatory course have attained to good reading.'

These then—all these without discrimination—are the Books, for the *reading* of which the Children are '*prepared.*' But in so long a list of Books—and some of them so voluminous—for example the Bible and the Prayer Book—that all should be read throughout is not possible. The consequence is—that by those which *are*, those which are *not* the favourites, will, in a greater or less degree be pushed out: and these favourites which are they?—that the portion of the Bible, in which are contained the accounts of the discourses and acts of Jesus are not of the number,—is already but too manifest. One of them, however, we shall soon see, and in CAPITALS.[4]

---

[a] '*The present State* of the *Central School*'—Present?—at what time? Ask those who are in the secret. Look for it in this same No. VIII[5]—Look for it in any other part of this same Report—you may look long enough. But, this and so many other such reserves, have their sufficient reason; concerning which, see Part IV.[6]

---

[1] For an example of one of these books see *National Society Central-School Book. No. 2*, Pts. I & II, n.d., printed and sold by Thomas Varty, 31 Strand, London, at British Library shelf-mark 863.i.22.(28). The books are approximately 3″ × 5″ in size (duodecimo), comprising 12 pages. Part I contains one simple reading exercise, and nine short texts on how to lead a moral and religious life. Part II contains four short stories from which morals are drawn.

[2] Jean Frédéric Ostervald (1663–1747), Swiss Reformed pastor, was author of *An Abridgment of the History of the Bible*, which is referred to as 'Ostervald's Abridgement of the Bible' at *Second Annual Report of the National Society*, Appendix VI, p. 190. The work, translated from *Abrégé de l'histoire sainte et du catéchisme* (first published in 1734), appeared in many editions.

[3] Sarah Trimmer, née Kirby (1741–1810), educationalist, was author of *An Abridgment of the New Testament; consisting of Lessons composed from The Writings of the Four Evangelists, for the use of schools and families*, London, [1805].

[4] See pp. 65–6 below.

[5] 'The present State of the Central School, Baldwin's Gardens', *Second Annual Report of the National Society*, Appendix VIII, pp. 194–6.

[6] See pp. 102–94 below.

INTRODUCTION. PART I. §III.

is *got by heart:* and not merely in the *common* way got by heart, but, by all the power of the new engine of instruction—by question and answer and by *challenging*—alias, competition and *place-taking—injected:* injected, as hath been observed into the very marrow of their bones. '1. *Grace before and after meat.*¹ 2. *Second and Third Collects of the Morning and Evening Service.* 3. *Prayers on entering and leaving Church*'ᵃ—all these put together, whether considered in respect of quantity or quality, are of little moment.

For now comes the one thing needful²—*the Catechism.*ᵇ This is injected no less than *three times over.* For these are the words, in and by which it is spoken of as *learnt by heart.—'The Catechism entire— and the same broken into short questions.'*³—Upon the face of this statement, what might naturally be supposed, is—that it was but *twice.* But, turn to the Book, intituled *'The Catechism broken into short questions,'* and you will find that in *that* book the whole matter of this same Catechism is administered twice over, viz. in the first plan in *larger* portions, and then the same matter in smaller portions, into which, by the interposition of questions, each larger portion is broken down. Thus then we have the same matter administered three times over, viz. 1. unbroken; 2. broken into larger fragments; 3. broken into smaller ones.

In this most impressive manner, though it had been administered no more than once, it would have been quite sufficient to throw out into the back ground—every thing that came from Jesus: but in this same most impressive manner it is administered (we see) no less than thrice.

Even this was not thought sufficient. To provide the more effectually for the exclusion of every thing that belonged to Jesus,—under the name of 'A CATECHETICAL INSTRUCTION, being an ACCOUNT of the CHIEF TRUTHS of the CHRISTIAN RELIGION, explained to the *MEANEST CAPACITY*, by way of Question and Answer'⁴—or (to call it by the

ᵃ P. 196.
ᵇ Ibid.

---

[1] 1818 *'ment'*. The text follows the 'Errata'.
[2] An echo of Luke 10: 42.
[3] Probably first published at London in 1726, a new and corrected edition, with the title *The Church Catechism Broke into Short Questions: To which is added, An Explanation of some Words, for the easier Understanding of it. Together with Prayers for the Use of the Charity Schools*, was published in 1756 under the auspices of the Society for Promoting Christian Knowledge. Subsequent editions of the work were recommended by the National Society.
[4] *A Catechetical Instruction: Being an Account of the Chief Truths of the Christian Religion, Explained to the Meanest Capacity; By Way of Question and Answer* was first published at London in 1728. In 1770 a new, fourth edition was published under the auspices of the Society for Promoting Christian Knowledge. Subsequent editions of the work were recommended by the National Society.

shorter title given to it) CHIEF TRUTHS,—to make certainty more sure, provision is made of *another body of divinity*, and that a *new* one,—to co-operate with the Catechism, and act under it, in the character of a *sub-substitute* to every thing that came from Jesus. Suppose the manner in which this *sub-substitute* is taught—suppose it even not more impressive than the manner in which, as above, the Discourses and Acts of Jesus are taught, how effectually the genuine matter might be elbowed out by this spurious matter, may easily be imagined. But it is in that same peculiarly impressive form, that this new portion of spurious matter—this sub-substitute to every thing that ever came from Jesus (the one short and unexcludible prayer excepted)[1] is also fitted to be administered.[a]

As to these self-styled CHIEF TRUTHS—as to this new Supplement to the Old Catechism—who the author of it is, my Lords the Bishops have not vouchsafed to inform us. Who the author is, and what the contents are—these are among the *truths*, as well as who the author is, among the *secrets*—which for the present purpose are not worth knowing. What, to the present purpose, it is quite sufficient to know, is—that in conjunction with, and subordination to, the Old Catechism, this new body of divinity, begotten by we know not who, but at any rate *adopted* by *My Lords the Bishops*,—is employed in the character of a sub-substitute to the only authentic and genuine accounts of the *discourses* and *acts* of Jesus—or, to speak more shortly and not less truly, to *the religion of Jesus*.

What, on this occasion, is moreover curious enough is—to see

---

[a] In the abovementioned Report,[2] of which so much more will come to be said, it is in two places recommended to all the Schools carried on in subordination to that National Society, and, to inforce the recommendation, therein mentioned as being sold to them by the Society at reduced prices: viz. in Appendix, No. VI. p. 190. under the name of *Chief Truths of the Christian Religion;* and again in No. VII. p. 193, under the shorter name of *Chief Truths.* In No. VI. it stands next but one to '*Catechism broken into short questions.*' This was in August, 1812. At this time nothing of *Our Saviour* was included in the list but the '*Sermon on the Mount.*' In No. VII. p. 193. come 'Parables of our Blessed Saviour; Miracles of ditto; and Discourses of ditto:' over all these discourses and acts of the *'Blessed Saviour'* precedence is given to this National Society's *Chief Truths.* In the list of the abovementioned Books, mentioned in this same Report, No. VIII. p. 196, as being employed in the instruction administered in the *Central School,* situated in the Metropolis, it is not visible.—*Is it then employed there, or is it not?* If yes, why suppress the mention of it? If not, why refuse to the children of this one School the benefit of a source of instruction recommended to every other? In p. 192. '*to preserve uniformity of proceeding,*' stands at the head of the list of those which the Society is there made to declare to be '*its only objects.*'

---

[1] i.e. the Lord's Prayer.
[2] i.e. *Second Annual Report of the National Society.*

INTRODUCTION. PART I. §IV.

how, as if by the shuffling of a pack of cards, the works of the *'Blessed Saviour'* are, without any the smallest distinction, huddled together in a promiscuous bundle along with those of *the Rev. Mr. Ostervald*, and the anonymous author of the CHIEF TRUTHS.

Not so those of MRS. TRIMMER. Her more holy name is distinguished and illustrated by capitals. What the *Blessed Virgin* is to *the Church of Rome*, this *Blessed Matron* is to the *Church of England*. In the Mother the Son finds a rival, and that rival a preferred one.[a]

§ IV. *Badness of this substitute in every respect:* I. *as to faithfulness. No tests of it.*

That which a formulary, employed in the way in which this Catechism is employed, ought to be,—that which it of course professes to be, is—a true picture of the religion of Jesus: a miniature picture indeed; but, as far as it goes, a true one.

Of the religion, of which they thus undertook to give a picture, to give a true picture did *not* suit the personal interests, nor therefore the purposes and designs, of the authors of this formulary. From external circumstances this will, it is believed, be seen ere this Introduction is at an end; and from the formulary itself in the *body* of this work.

That which *did* suit their purposes was—to employ it as an instrument of corruption, for corrupting altogether the intellectual

---

[a] 'With a view to furnishing initiatory Books with greater convenience, and at reduced prices, the Committee' (says the Report, p. 192)[1] 'have ordered to be deposited at Messrs. Rivington's, St. Paul's Church-Yard, Books of that description, in sets of 50 each, for 100 Children, of which a list is subjoined.'

In p. 193, after other matter, without any further title, comes what follows—

	£.	s.	d.
'50 dozen Cards or Leaves, or National Society Central School Book, No. 1	0	4	3
'50 National Society Central School Book, No. 2	0	2	0
'50 Ditto, No. 3	0	2	0
'50 Sermon on the Mount	0	2	0
'50 Broken Catechism	0	3	9
'50 Ostervald's Abridgment	0	2	0
'Arithmetical Tables, per dozen	0	0	$4\frac{1}{2}$
'50 Chief Truths	0	2	0
'50 Parables of Our Blessed Saviour	0	2	0
'50 Miracles of ditto	0	2	0
'50 Discourses of ditto	0	2	0
And MRS. TRIMMER'S 'Teacher's Assistant, 2 vol.[2] in double sets at.	0	7	0 each set.'

---

[1] *Second Annual Report of the National Society*, Appendix VII, p. 192.
[2] Mrs Trimmer, *The Teacher's Assistant: consisting of Lectures in the catechetical form, being part of a plan of appropriate instruction for the children of the poor*, 2 vols., London, 1803.

part, and to a great extent the moral part, of the minds thus impregnated: the *intellectual*, through the medium of the *sensitive* part, that by weakness they might be rendered *unable*, because by terror they had been rendered *unwilling*, to discern the mischievousness of the dominion exercised at their expense: the *moral* part, that by their being themselves habituated to the practice of mendacity and insincerity in their own sphere, the spectacle of those vices, when practised at their expense in higher spheres, might in their eyes be rendered an object of indifference.

Not only that this object *was* pursued, but in particular by what precise means it was pursued, may be seen in the *body* of this work.

For those purposes, what was necessary was—that, in the composition of this formulary, their hands should be as free as possible from all checks, the effect of which might be to obstruct them in the pursuit of those same purposes.

For the fidelity of any picture, undertaken to be given of any mass of the matter of discourse, the nature of the case offers a sort of *security*, of which neither the nature nor the importance, nor, in so far as the reputation of sincerity is regarded as necessary, the necessity, either is now, or was then unknown to any one. This is—need it be mentioned?—an accompaniment, composed of *references* and *quotations*. Intimately connected as are those two securities in their nature,—frequently as they are connected in practice,—either of them is, however, not the less capable of being afforded without the other.

References without quotations present the most common case.

Quotations without references are much less common, because much less natural: much less natural, because the object is—not merely that misrepresentation may not have place, but that all suspicion of its having had place may be excluded.

On ordinary ground—in the case of an ordinary *history* for example—references *without* quotations are commonly and may reasonably be accepted, as affording a security, sufficient for the nature and importance of the case.

But, in the instance here in question, no security, short of the very best and most efficient that the nature of the case affords, could either be sufficient, or by any intelligent person be regarded as sufficient, or by any honest person—by any person who were not, for the sake of the profit of misrepresentation, content to expose himself to the just suspicion of it—be offered as sufficient.

References *with* quotations,—*quotations*, that it might be seen by every one, whether the picture were a faithful, or if unfaithful, how far an unfaithful one—*references*, that it might be seen that the quota-

INTRODUCTION. PART I. §IV.

tions were, as far as they went, genuine, and, at the same time, untainted with partiality—with that sort of *deficiency*, which, whether it has design or accident for the cause, has misrepresentation for its effect,—such and such alone could be the securities, to which, in a case such [as] the present, any such quality as that signified by the word *adequate*, could be ascribed.

The importance of the subject, is it not such—that, in comparison of it, all others put together shrink into insignificance?

Proportioned to this real importance, was not the sense entertained of it in the minds of all classes of the community?—proportioned to that sense, the warmth of the dissensions that prevailed?—proportioned to that warmth, were not the suspicions of misrepresentation?—of misrepresentation, intended as well as unintended?

Here for the second time, may be seen the difference between *Church-of-Scotlandism* and *Church-of-Englandism:*—between *Puritanism*, since that must be the name, and *Impuritanism:* between *Presbyterianism* and *Episcopacy*: between the management of the *equal many*, and the domination of the *ruling few*.

By no British—by no Scottish—by no Irish—but above all by no English readers, ought this contrast to be lost sight of. In no part of this work has it ever been lost sight of. It runs through the whole extent of the field of Church discipline. It will present itself again and again in the course of these pages: and all along what *purity* and *impurity* are, will be shewn—not by declamation, but by example.

The Scottish Church has, as above (§ [I.]),[1] its two Catechisms. In the one, as in the other, not a proposition without its *quotation:* not a quotation without its *reference*.[2]

How far the pictures drawn under these checks are correct, is matter of debate. But *that* about which there can be no debate is—the conclusiveness of the proof thus afforded of the sincerity of those who draw them.

By the penners of the *Church of England* Catechism,—unless the *Creed*,[3] the Ten Commandments,[4] and the Lord's Prayer[5] be taken for quotations,—neither quotation is given, nor so much as a reference.

---

[1] 1818 '4' is a slip. See p. 57 above.

[2] On 25 November 1647 the House of Commons instructed the Westminster Assembly of Divines to add scriptural proofs to the Larger and Shorter Catechisms. On 14 April 1648 the Assembly presented the Catechisms to the House of Commons with scriptural proofs affixed. See *Commons Journals* (1646–8) v. 368, 530.

[3] The affirmations in the so-called Apostles' Creed, reproduced in the Catechism, had a scriptural basis in the New Testament.

[4] Exodus 20: 1–17.

[5] Matthew 6: 9–13; Luke 11: 1–4.

CHURCH-OF-ENGLANDISM

They made their choice. They chose rather to incur the just suspicion of misrepresentation, than to forego the benefit of it.

In the order of time, the date of the contents of the Scottish Catechisms was posterior to that of the English:[1] the state of the public mind, maturer.—True: but, at least since printing came into use, at what period was the state of the public mind—of the lettered part of it at least—so immature as not to see, that by references and quotations, a surety against misrepresentation, and that the only one, is afforded?

To keep the Bible as much as may be out of sight, is a policy, which, as far as circumstances have admitted, has ever been pursued in common, by Church-of-Romanism and Church-of-Englandism.

By Church-of-Romanism it was originally pursued in that coarse and clumsy way, which, for so many centuries, continued to be not ill-suited to the coarseness, and ignorance, and stupidity of the times.[2] By Church-of-Englandism,[3] in the instance here in question, it was pursued in that sort of way which was suited to the state of the public mind, at that less immature period of its existence.

The Established Church of *Scotland* is a *Presbyterian* Church: the Established Church of *England* is an *Episcopalian* Church.—True: but this difference between the two forms of government, what is it to the purpose?—What?—unless it be, that while to the nature of a Presbyterian Church, it is *not* congenial to palm upon the people a spurious substitute for a genuine abridgment, to the nature of an Episcopalian Church in general, or at least to that of the Church of England in particular, an imposition of this sort *is* congenial.

Oh! but,—if in this summary, not only the references to the texts, on which it is grounded, and by which it is justified, but the texts themselves, were inserted,—there would be no end to it: it would not be the thing, which is so indisputably needful, and what it professes

---

[1] The Church of England Catechism incorporated in the *Book of Common Prayer* of 1552 was confirmed by the Act of Uniformity of 1559 (1 Eliz. I, c. 2), while the Church of Scotland Catechism was approved by the General Assembly of the Church of Scotland in 1648.

[2] Before the Protestant and Catholic Reformations the Latin Bible (the Vulgate) was in use in all churches. In an attempt to curb both public and private interpretations of the Bible that were contrary to the teaching of the Roman Catholic Church, the Council of Trent in 1546 confirmed the Vulgate as the authentic text, and forbade the use of the Bible without ecclesiastical authority. For decrees concerning the canonical scriptures, and the edition and use of the sacred books (Fourth Session, 8 April 1546), and decrees concerning lectureships in Holy Scripture and preaching (Fifth Session, 17 June 1546), see *Canons and Decrees of the Council of Trent*, trans. H.J. Schroeder, Rockford, Ill., 1978, pp. 17–20, 24–8.

The first English version of the Bible to receive authorization was the so-called Matthew's Bible in 1537, and in the following year the Great Bible was ordered by Royal Injunction to be set up in every church. The Authorized Version of the Bible of 1611 superseded all previous versions.

[3] 1818 'By the Church-of-Englandism'.

and is designed to be: it would not be fit for—it would be by much too large for—the young and tender mouths for which it is intended.

True enough: but what is the consequence.—That no summary with the text attached to it, should on any occasion, or for any purpose, be employed? That the pretended quintessence should remain at all times, and be circulated in all places, without a syllable from the sacred original to justify it?—No surely. But that there should be *two* publications: one with the *texts*, as well as the *references*; the other with the references alone. The one would serve for justification, the other for instruction: the one for those whose acquirements enabled them to judge for themselves; the other for those, whose time of life and want of acquirements, rendered them unable, for the present at least, to apply the rational faculty to this most important indeed, but unhappily proportionably arduous use.

To his Lordship of London, (see Appendix, p. 304.) the *Puritans* may be seen presenting themselves in no other character than that of '*exciters of troubles.*'[1] To some eyes it may, perhaps, be more agreeable to behold in those same Sectaries, men of principle, manifesting for years together, the qualities of sincerity, piety, zeal, patience, and perseverance. To these same persons, on this same field, it may moreover, perhaps, be not unacceptable, to behold the difference between *Puritans* and *Impuritans*. If so, let them, in the following extracts, or—what will be still better—in the original, see the account given of the matter, in *Neale's* History of the *Puritans, Toulmin's* Edition, iii. 354.[2]

Anno 1648, September 15, of the two Scottish Catechisms, the larger was, by order of the two Houses of Parliament, printed for public use. It was at the express '*desire*' of the two Houses, that the '*marginal references* to Scripture were *inserted*.'[a] It was for this cause alone that from November the 5th, 1647, being the day on which 'the shorter Catechism was presented to the House of Commons,' the presentation of this larger Catechism had been deferred for upwards of four months, viz, 'till the 14th of April,' 1648.[3]

[a] The *quotations* being at present printed, as well as those words and figures to which alone, perhaps, in strictness of speech, the term *reference* can with propriety be applied,—by the words '*marginal references*,' were meant to be designated (it should seem) by Neal, the *quotations*, as they now stand, as well as the *references*.

---

[1] See [Howley], *Charge delivered to the Clergy of the Diocese of London*, p. 17: 'I do not affect to dread a renewal of the excesses committed by the Donatists of old, or even of the troubles excited by the Puritans in later times.'

[2] i.e. Neal, *History of the Puritans*, ed. Toulmin, 1795, iii. 354.

[3] Neal's account is slightly inaccurate. As stated above (p. 69 n.), the House of Commons ordered scriptural proofs to be attached to both the Longer and Shorter Catechisms on 25

CHURCH-OF-ENGLANDISM

'The shorter Catechism,' (furnished, it may in like manner be presumed, with its quotations,) 'the King, after many solicitations, at the treaty of the Isle of Wight, offered' (says Neale) 'to license with a suitable preface:[1] but, that treaty proving unsuccessful, it was not accomplished.'

About fourteen years afterwards, viz. in the year 1662,—two years, or thereabouts, after the Restoration of Charles the Second,[2]—comes the *Act of Uniformity.* (13 and 14th Ch. 2. c. 4.) and now it is, that *that* picture of the religion of Jesus, which bears upon the face of it the most perfect test of its faithfulness that the nature of the case admits of, is cast out: cast out, and in the place of it, the old daubing, on the face of which not so much as any the least pretence to the character of faithfulness is visible, is forced into use.[3]

Thus it was that, for fourteen years, or thereabouts, viz. from 1648 to 1662,[4] the Bible was in honour in England, as, before it came to be so in England, it had already been in Scotland. In comes the profligate King, with his Church-of-Englandism on his front, and his Church-of-Romanism in his heart,[5]—and now the Bible is cast out, and this breviary of the Church-of-England religion once more seated in the place of it.

One thousand six hundred and sixty-two is the year, in which, under the notion of its being the more trust-worthy, this account without vouchers was substituted to that to which so ample a stock of vouchers may be seen thus carefully and anxiously annext.

Four and thirty years had the first volume of the Institute of Human Law,—for which, such as it is, the world of law is indebted

---

November 1647 (not 5 November as Neal states), whereupon both Catechisms, with proofs, were presented to the House of Commons on 14 April 1648 (see *Commons Journals* (1646–8) v. 368, 530). On 25 September 1648 the Shorter Catechism only was ordered to be printed and published by the House of Commons and the House of Lords (see *Lords Journals* (1647–8) x. 511), while the Longer Catechism was approved by the House of Commons on 24 July 1648, but never received approval from the House of Lords (see *Commons Journals* (1646–8) v. 645).

[1] Charles I (1600–49) was held on the Isle of Wight, from November 1647 until December 1648. In a final attempt by Parliament to reach a settlement with him, Charles I was released from Carisbrooke Castle and taken to a house in Newport, where during negotiations of the so-called Treaty of Newport held between September and November 1648, the King, in a paper dated 10 November 1648, gave his approval to the Shorter Catechism. The paper appears in *Lords Journals* (1647–8) x. 589.

[2] Charles II (1630–85), King of England, Scotland, and Ireland from 1660.

[3] The Act of Uniformity of 1662 (13 & 14 Car. II, c. 4, §II) discarded the work of the Westminster Assembly of Divines, and authorized the *Book of Common Prayer* of 1662, closely based on the *Book of Common Prayer* of 1552, with its catechism devoid of scriptural proofs.

[4] i.e. from the date that the Shorter Catechism was approved by Parliament to the passing of the Act of Uniformity.

[5] As reigning monarch, Charles II was Supreme Governor of the Church of England, but on his death-bed in February 1685 he was received into the Roman Catholic Church.

INTRODUCTION. PART I. §IV.

to Sir Edward Coke,[1]—been in the knowledge, if not in the hands, of every man by whom any part was taken in this disastrous change. *Quotations* at length? no: room could not admit of it: importance did not require it. But, without indication given of his authorities, indication given in the usual way of *reference*, that lawyer, with all his confidence, would never have dared to encounter the public eye.

Not to speak of the *Hales*, the *Hawkinses*, the *Burns*, the *Blackstones*[2]—by what one English lawyer, that, from that time ever wrote, was ever betrayed any such presumptuous and absurd conceit, as that, without reference to the original sources, from which the matter of his abridgments was respectively drawn, any work of his would either experience, or deserve to experience, any the smallest particle of regard?

No:—*man's law* is not to be thus dealt with:—it is only of *God's law*, that profligate men, when the power is in their hands, dare make what they please.[a]

---

[a] On a subject, on which according to all parties the difference between heaven and hell is at stake, the conscientious sincerity and carefulness, of the republicanism of those times, forms so striking a contrast with the profligate and careless despotism, of the monarchy of those same times—not to speak of other times,—and moreover so instructive a lesson to all times,—that insertion could not here be refused to the two here following anterior pages in *Neal*, by which the account is taken up at a somewhat anterior period. Vol. iii. c. viii. pp. 350, 351, 352.[3] To Rushworth, Whitlocke,[4] and other unexceptionable authorities, are the references all along made.

'The Reverend Mr. Charles Herle succeeded to the Prolocutor's chair by order of

---

[1] Sir Edward Coke (1552–1634), Chief Justice of Common Pleas 1606–13, Chief Justice of King's Bench 1613–16, was author of *The First Part of the Institutes of the Lawes of England, Or, A Commentarie upon Littleton, not the name of a Lawyer onely, but of the Law it selfe*, London, 1628.

[2] These figures were authors of important expositions of the English law. Hale was author of *Historia Placitorum Coronæ. The History of the Pleas of the Crown*, 2 vols., London, 1736; William Hawkins (1681/2–1750), sergeant-at-law, was author of *A Treatise of the Pleas of the Crown: Or A System of the Principal Matters relating to that Subject, digested under their proper Heads*, 2 vols., London, 1716–21; Richard Burn (1709–85), legal writer and clergyman, was author of *The Justice of the Peace, and Parish Officer*, 2 vols., London, 1755, and *Ecclesiastical Law*, 2 vols., London, 1763; Sir William Blackstone (1723–80), first Vinerian Professor of English Law at the University of Oxford 1758–66, Justice of Common Pleas 1770, 1770–80, Justice of King's Bench 1770, was author of *Commentaries on the Laws of England*, 4 vols., Oxford, 1765–9.

[3] i.e. Neal, *History of the Puritans*, ed. Toulmin, 1795, iii. 350–2.

[4] John Rushworth, *Historical Collections Of Private Passages of State. Of Weighty Matters in Law. Of Remarkable Proceedings in Five Parliaments. Beginning The Sixteenth Year of King James, Anno 1618. And ending the Fifth Year of King Charls, Anno 1629. Digested in Order of Time*, 4 pts. in 7 vols., London, 1659–1701; and Bulstrode Whitelock, *Memorials of the English Affairs: or, An Historical Account of What passed from the beginning of the Reign of King Charles the First, to King Charles the Second His Happy Restauration. Containing the Publick Transactions, Civil and Military. Together with The Private Consultations and Secrets of the Cabinet*, London, 1682.

CHURCH-OF-ENGLANDISM

§ V.—II. *Badness in respect of Matter.*

For the proof of this, see the body of the work,[1] which, from first to last, is directed to this office.

Parliament, July 26, 1646,[2] in the room of the late Dr. Twisse, when, the discipline of the Church being pretty well settled, it was moved to finish their *confession of faith*.[3] The English Divines would have been content with revising and explaining the thirty-nine articles of the Church of England, but the Scots insisting on a system of their own, a committee was appointed to prepare materials for this purpose, May 9th, 1645; their names were, Dr. Gouge, Dr. Hoyle, Mr. Herle, Gataker, Tuckney, Reynolds, and Vines,[4] with the Scots Divines,[5] who having first settled the *titles* of

---

[1] See pp. 203–56 below.
[2] Neal, *History of the Puritans*, iii. 350, gives the correct date of 22 July 1646.
[3] William Twisse (1578–1646), Rector of Newbury, Berkshire from 1620, who had been Prolocutor of the Westminster Assembly of Divines since July 1643, died on 20 July 1646. He was succeeded on 22 July 1646 by Charles Herle (1598–1659), Rector of Winwick, Lancashire from 1626. The House of Commons took the opportunity to encourage the Assembly to complete the Confession of Faith. See *Commons Journals* (1644–6) iv. 622; *Lords Journals* (1645–6) viii. 437.
[4] On 17 April 1645 the House of Commons had instructed the Westminster Assembly of Divines to prepare a Confession of Faith for the Church of England: see *Commons Journals* (1644–6) iv. 114. On 9 May 1645 the Assembly considered the best way to proceed, in consequence of which on 12 May 1645 seven members were appointed to a Committee to draw up a Confession of Faith: Charles Herle; William Gouge (1575–1653), preacher and subsequently minister of St Anne, Blackfriars, London, who also served as one of the assessors of the Assembly from November 1647; Joshua Hoyle (bap. 1588, d. 1654), Professor of Divinity at the University of Dublin from 1623, Vicar of Stepney, Middlesex 1642–54, Vicar of Sturminster Marshall, Dorset from 1643, Master of University College and Regius Professor of Divinity at the University of Oxford from 1648; Thomas Gataker (1574–1654), scholar and Rector of Rotherhithe, Surrey from 1611; Anthony Tuckney (1599–1670), Vicar of Boston 1633–60, Rector of St Michael-le-Querne, London from 1643, Master of Emmanuel College, Cambridge 1645–53, Master of St John's College, Cambridge 1653–61, Vice-Chancellor of the University of Cambridge 1648–9, Regius Professor of Divinity at the University of Cambridge 1656–61; Edward Reynolds (1599–1676), Rector of Braunston, Northamptonshire 1631–61, Minister at St Lawrence Jewry, London 1657–61, Dean of Christ Church, Oxford 1648–51, 1659–60, Warden of Merton College, Oxford 1660–1, Vice-Chancellor of the University of Oxford 1648–50, Bishop of Norwich from 1661; and Richard Vines (1599/1600–1656), Rector of Weddington, Warwickshire 1628–43, Rector of Caldecote, Warwickshire 1630–43, Rector of St Clement Danes, London 1643–5, Rector of Walton, Hertfordshire 1645–50, Vicar of St Lawrence Jewry, London 1650–6, Master of Pembroke College, Cambridge 1644–50. See *Minutes of the Sessions of the Westminster Assembly of Divines while engaged in preparing their Directory for Church Government, Confession of Faith, and Catechisms (November 1644 to March 1649) From Transcripts of the Originals procured by a Committee of the General Assembly of the Church of Scotland*, ed. A.F. Mitchell and J. Struthers, Edinburgh and London, 1874, Session 433, 9 May 1645, p. 90; Session 434, 12 May 1645, p. 91.
[5] The Commissioners from the Church of Scotland were ordered to assist the Committee in drawing up the Confession of Faith: see *Minutes of the Sessions of the Westminster Assembly of Divines*, Session 434, 12 May 1645, p. 91. Originally five ministers and three elders had been nominated by the General Assembly of the Church of Scotland as Commissioners to the Westminster Assembly. The Commissioners declined to become full members of the Assembly, but entered into debates. Four out of the five ministers and two out of the three elders attended and participated in the debates: Robert Baillie (1602–62), minister of Kilwinning in the Presbytery of Irvine 1631–42, Professor of Divinity at the University of Glasgow 1642–60,

INTRODUCTION. PART I. §VI.—III.

§VI.—III. *Badness in respect of Form.*

For the proof of this, see §8.[1] in which the consciousness, of its unfitness in this respect, is proved—proved upon those, who the several chapters, as they now stand in their confession of faith, in number thirty-two,[2] distributed them for greater expedition, among several *sub-committees*, which sat two days every week, and then reported what they had finished to the committee, and so to the Assembly, where it was debated paragraph by paragraph. The disputes about *discipline* had occasioned so many interruptions, that it was a year and a half before this work was finished; but on Nov. 26, 1646, the *prolocutor* returned thanks to the several committees, in the name of the Assembly, for their great pains in perfecting the work committed to them.[3] At the same time Dr. Burges[4] was appointed to get it transcribed, in order to its being presented to Parliament, which was done, Dec. 11, by the whole Assembly in a body, under the title of, *The Humble Advice of the Assembly of Divines and others, now, by authority of Parliament, sitting at Westminster, concerning a Confession of Faith.*[5] The House of Commons having voted the Assembly thanks, desired them to insert the *proofs* of the several articles in their proper places, and then to print six hundred copies, and no more, for the perusal of the houses.[6] The Reverend Mr. Wilson, Mr. Byfield, and Mr. Gower,[7] were appointed, Jan. 6, to be a committee, to collect the scriptures for confirmation of the several articles;[8] all which, after examination by the Assembly, were inserted in the margin. And then the whole *confession* was committed once more to a review of

---

Principal of the University 1661–2; George Gillespie (1613–48), minister at Wemyss in the Presbytery of Kirkcaldy 1638–42, Greyfriars Church, Edinburgh 1642–7, and St Giles', Edinburgh from 1647; Alexander Henderson (1583–1646), minister at Leuchars in the Presbytery of St Andrews, *c.* 1612–32, Greyfriars Church, Edinburgh 1638, and St Giles', Edinburgh from 1639; John Maitland (1616–82), second Earl and first Duke of Lauderdale; Sir Archibald Johnston (bap. 1611, d. 1663), Lord Wariston; Samuel Rutherford (*c.* 1600–61), theologian, Professor of Divinity at St Mary's College, St Andrews 1638–61, and Rector of the University of St Andrews from 1651.

[1] See pp. 146–53 below.
[2] In fact, thirty-three articles of faith were debated and approved by the Westminster Assembly of Divines.
[3] See *Minutes of the Sessions of the Westminster Assembly of Divines*, Session 746, 26 November 1646, p. 303.
[4] Cornelius Burges (d. 1665), Vicar of Watford, Hertfordshire 1618–45, lecturer at St Paul's, London 1643–56, preacher at St Andrews, Wells 1656–60, had been appointed one of the Assessors of the Westminster Assembly of Divines in 1643.
[5] The Confession of Faith was presented to the House of Commons in instalments on 25 September 1646 and 4 December 1646: see *Commons Journals* (1644–6) iv. 677, 739.
[6] On 7 December 1646 the House of Commons ordered that 600 copies of the Confession of Faith be printed for the service of the House, and that the Westminster Assembly send the scriptural proofs as soon as possible: see *Commons Journals* (1646–8) v. 2.
[7] Thomas Wilson (*c.* 1601–53), Rector of Otham, Kent 1631–5 and from 1639, Perpetual Curate at Maidstone, Kent from 1644; Adoniram Byfield (d. 1658x60), Vicar and Rector of Fulham, London *c.* 1646–52, Rector of Collingbourne Ducis, Wiltshire from 1652, had been appointed in July 1643 as one of the two Scribes of the Assembly; and Stanley Gower (bap. 1600, d. 1660), Rector of Brampton Bryan, Herefordshire from 1634, Rector of Holy Trinity, Dorchester, Dorset from 1649.
[8] See *Minutes of the Sessions of the Westminster Assembly*, Session 768, 6 January 1647, pp. 318–19.

persevere but the more strenuously in thus forcing into the mouths of babes, almost as soon as they cease to be sucklings,[1] the pill, the bitterness of which is all the while endeavoured to be gilded over by a covering of praise.

the three committees,[2] who made report to the Assembly of such further amendments as they thought necessary; which being agreed to by the house,[3] it was sent to the press, May 11, 1647. Mr. Byfield, by order of the House of Commons, delivered to the members the printed copies of this *confession of faith*, with *scripture notes*, signed—

CHARLES HERLE, *Prolocutor.*

COR. BURGES,
HERBERT PALMER,[4] } *Assessors.*

HENRY ROBOROUGH,[5]
ADONERAM BYFIELD, } *Scribes.*

And because no more were to be given out at present, every member subscribed his name to the receipt thereof.

The House of Commons began their examination of this confession, May 19,[6] when they considered the whole first chapter, article by article; but the disturbances which arose between the parliament and the army interrupted their proceeding the whole summer; but when these were quieted, they resumed their work, and October 2,[7] ordered a chapter of the confession of faith at least to be debated every Wednesday, by which means they got through the whole before the end of March following; for at a conference with the House of Lords, March 22d, 1647–8, the Commons presented them with the *confession of faith*, as passed by their House, with some alterations: they agreed with the Assembly in the doctrinal part of the confession, and ordered it to be published, June 20th, 1648, for the satisfaction of the foreign churches, under the title of *Articles of Religion, approved and passed by both Houses of Parliament, after advice had with an Assembly of Divines, called together by them for that purpose.*[8]

---

[1] Psalm 8: 2.

[2] See *Minutes of the Sessions of the Westminster Assembly*, Session 820, 5 April 1647, p. 345. At the inception of the Westminster Assembly, its members were distributed among three committees, which undertook preliminary discussions on matters before the Assembly, and prepared propositions to be debated in plenary sessions. For a list of members of the three committees see ibid., p. lxxxv.

[3] The Confession of Faith with scriptural proofs was ordered to be printed for the service of the House of Commons on 29 April 1647: see *Commons Journals* (1646–8) v. 156.

[4] Herbert Palmer (1601–47), Rector of Ashwell, Hertfordshire from 1632, and Master of Queens' College, Cambridge from 1644.

[5] Henry Roborough (d. 1649), Curate and subsequently Vicar of St Leonard, Eastcheap, London from 1617.

[6] See *Commons Journals* (1646–8) v. 177–8.   [7] See ibid. 323.

[8] 1818 omits closing quotation mark. The text follows the 'Errata'.

The House of Commons completed consideration of the Confession of Faith on 17 March 1648 and, following a conference with the House of Lords on 22 March 1648, the text was ordered to be printed and published on 20 June 1648: see *Commons Journals* (1646–8) v. 502, 608; *Lords Journals* (1647–8) x. 130. The text was published on 27 June 1648 as *Articles of Christian Religion, Approved and Passed by both Houses of Parliament, After Advice had with the Assembly of Divines by Authority of Parliament sitting at Westminster,* London, 1648.

INTRODUCTION. PART I. §VIII.

§VII. *Of the Badness of this Formulary in respect of Matter, the Framers of it were conscious.*

Of this consciousness the proof consists—partly in the real badness of it, as displayed in the body of the present work;[1] partly in the fact of their avoiding, as above, to afford, for the faithfulness of their picture, those[2] securities, which the nature of the case presented to every man's view as well as their own,—and which, by the framers of the Scottish Catechisms, and their collaborators the *English Puritans*, were accordingly, as hath been seen, (§4.)[3] attached to their works.

§VIII. *Of the Badness of this Formulary, in respect of Faithfulness, Matter, and Form, the Imposers of it on the Schools are conscious.*

I. First, of the badness of that one of its features, which consists in its being destitute of the above-mentioned necessary *securities for faithfulness*.

To the weight of those considerations, which, to all thinking minds, could not but have been present from the first,—and by which, as above shewn, the conduct of the Scottish Church, as applied to this very species of instrument, had, in so conspicuous a manner and degree, been governed,—let any one judge whether, at this time of day, it was possible for the rulers of any Christian church to escape being sensible.

But the proof rests not in any such universally applicable presumption. Behold it in their own practice.

Of the new system of religion, which, as above seen,[4] under the name of *Chief Truths of the Christian Religion*, out of the funds raised by subscription, the Church of England Bishops pay subscribers for adopting, mention has there been made. In this '*Catechetical Instruction*' (for such it is, and on the title-page is said to be)—meaning a discourse in the form of *question and answer*,—may be seen a cluster of *references*—nor that a scanty one—with which each answer is garnished.

Of the intimation thus, howsoever unintendedly afforded, what is the import?—What but an acknowledgement—an acknowledgement, tacit indeed, but not the less expressive—that, in administering, in the instance of the old catechism, in lieu of the matter of the Bible, the produce of their own brains,—without a shadow of proof, either of its being in reality, or so much as of its being by them really regarded as being, a fair deduction from the text of the sacred

---

[1] See pp. 203–56 below. [2] 1818 'these'. The text follows the 'Errata'.
[3] See pp. 67–73 above. [4] See pp. 65–7 above.

original,—the course taken by their predecessors, and persevered in by these their successors, was altogether an unwarrantable one.

Of this so newly adopted practice what has been the object? Manifestly to do what was found convenient,—and deemed as little inconsistent as might be, with the spirit of their policy and the constant tenor of their practice,—towards providing themselves, if not with a defence, with something like a screen, behind which to hide themselves, in this one instance, from a reproach so just and obvious.

But, of this expedient what is the fruit?—Justification? No: nor any thing but greater condemnation. Except another tacit and unintended, but not the less indisputable, acknowledgement—an acknowledgement of the insufficiency and inaptitude of the old *mumpsimus*, on the back of which they thus clap this their new *sumpsimus*,—what good purpose does it answer?—None whatever. The passages to which these references are made—had these passages themselves, as in the Scottish Catechism, been subjoined *in terminis*,—such appendages as these would indeed have served as *tests*—as tests of the justness of the interpretation put all along upon the sacred original, and of the legitimacy of the inferences deduced from it: as tests of the justness of the representation all along actually so given, and thereby as securities against misrepresentation and spurious addition. In that case, to no eye would the alleged copy ever have presented itself, but to that same eye would the test of the faithfulness of that same copy have presented itself at that same time.

Such would have been the case, if, for their accompaniment and support, the passages respectively referred to had been added to these references. But these references, as they stand naked—these strings of figures, by all which put together, no idea but those of *number* and *place* is conveyed—to any such good purpose, or to any other good purpose, in what way is it that they can serve? To no eye, at the same time with the pretended picture, will the *test* thus pretended to be applied be present:—to no eye, at the same time with the pretended picture, will the sacred original be ever thus made visible. Of the thousands and myriads of eyes, under which these dead-letter figures are placed, by how many is there any the least probability, that, between the original and this pretended miniature, any confrontation will ever be made?

By curiosity or sectarian jealousy, suppose here and there an individual—suppose this or that professional, or any other scrutinizer, led to undertake the confrontation. By this eye suppose—what at least, for argument's sake, may be supposed—an instance of unfaithfulness discovered. What matters it?—What care the authors of it? Nothing. The answer is ready. So many men, so many minds. Of the subject in question, many parts are confessedly as obscure and 'hard to be understood'—so St. Peter says of St. Paul[1]—as they are sacred and important. Such and such are the interpretations, which to those eyes presented themselves as the true and proper ones. As for *themselves*, as *men*, they are but fallible. Be it so: but, as *rulers* of the Church of England, theirs is the interpretation, which, at every hazard, the other members—the *subject*-members of the same Church—are, as well by law as by conscience, bound to follow.

Here then are references: but here are no quotations. What was wanted was—the semblance of a test: what could not be endured was—the reality of a test. Meantime the acknowledgement remains: the acknowledgement given of the need of a test:—of the need of such a test in such a case:—the untrustworthiness of every picture, the faithfulness of which, as towards the original, bears not this sort of testimony upon the face of it. This acknowledgement stares their *old* catechism in the face, and testifies against it.

Another truth, these *Chief truths* serve to prove, and this too without the need of any very close inspection. This is—that *innovation* is not regarded by them as a plea in bar, where the matter of it accords with their convenience: for example, that, if it did accord with their convenience, *means* would not be wanting for the abolishing of this old Catechism, or for the reform of some of the acknowledged imperfections, of that Liturgy, of which it makes a part:—not to speak of any such radical reform, as that of laying that whole[2] body of solid laudanum upon the shelf.

The sort of regard, shewn by these upholders of the Church of England religion to this handiwork of their predecessors—to this substitute to the book containing the religion of Jesus—compare with it (for the contrast is not an uninstructive one) the sort of regard, paid by these same persons to that sacred book itself.

In the Catechism they continue to exhibit—and by their own sole authority (this of course regards the whole corporation from the beginning, and not merely the present members) a substitute to the Bible:—to both Testaments, Old and New. The words, from beginning to end, their own: not one quoted from the original: not one so much as referred to, from beginning to end, except it be the obscure *allusion* to that part of the Jewish Code, in which is contained what are called the *Ten Commandments:* not a syllable, by which, in any mind, to which the matter was not made known from other sources, so much as a suspicion could be produced, that any such book had ever been in existence.

---

[1] See II Peter 3: 16.
[2] 1818 'same'. The text follows the 'Errata'.

So much for the Bible. Its substitute was not to be so dealt with. In their lesser book, called *The Broken Catechism*—otherwise called *The Catechism broken down into Short Sentences*,[1]—of these sentences, not so much as a single group is ever brought to view, till after the correspondent part of the original has been brought to view, in its original and unbroken state.

It is not, therefore, through ignorance or heedlessness, that, in so far as it is pursued, the plan of substitution is kept up. Where regard is to be manifested, full well do they know how to manifest it: to the object to which it suits their purpose to pay regard, the strictest regard is paid accordingly: to the object, which it suits their purpose to treat with *neglect*, neglect, not to say contempt, continues to be manifested: it continues to be, as all along it has been, kept in the back ground.

Even in the case of merely human laws, regulating the comparatively insignificant concerns of the present life, what abridgment-maker is ever either presumptuous enough, or careless enough, to neglect giving to his work this test, and in his opinion this proof and certificate of fidelity? If such were the marks of presumption or negligence, apparent on the face of his work, what regard would any one pay to it?

II. Of what remains to be proved of this evil consciousness, the proof will not consume much time.

The thing, viz. the Old Catechism, is bad in *matter*. Those by whom it is thus forced into the mouths of these innocents are conscious of its being so. The proof of evil consciousness is their forcing into the same tender and much injured mouths their newly made up bolus—the '*Catechetical Instruction*' above spoken of.

The Old Catechism is what it is: this cannot be denied.'*Excellent*' in all unassignable particulars—'*excellent*' as the church from which it sprung is '*excellent*'[2]—still, on one point, viz. that of plainness, it was not altogether so perfect as could be wished. By this new *Catechetical Instruction*, all that remained to fill up the measure of excellence is supplied. In this fruit of still maturer wisdom, '*the Chief truths of the Christian Religion,*' (says the title-page,) '*are explained to the MEANEST CAPACITY.*'[3]

The composition of the indivisible Godhead—the identity of the numbers *three* and *one*, when applied to the same object—the impregnable truth of a cluster of self-contradictory propositions—all this, and abundance more of the same stamp, made *plain* to the *meanest capacity!*—Of the assurance thus given what is the result?—

---

[1] See p. 65 n. above.   [2] See p. 29 n. above.   [3] See p. 65 n. above.

INTRODUCTION. PART I. §VIII.

That if at the time when this new Catechism is first put into his hand,—much more if, at any more advanced period of his life,—any thing like a doubt should, in the breast of any one of these hapless children, happen to arise, respecting the meaning of any one of the things thus completely and finally explained, a further assurance he thus receives is—that his *'capacity'* is *meaner* than *'the meanest.'* But, in relation to his own *capacity*, to no man is it in any degree agreeable, that any such opinion should be entertained:—entertained either by himself or others. To avoid every such unpleasant sensation, what then is the course he takes?—To save himself from being seen *by himself* not to understand it, he strives to smother doubts as fast as they spring up: to save himself from being seen *by others* to be in any such humiliating condition, whatsoever of these doubts, spite of all his efforts, happen now and then to spring up, he takes effectual care to keep them to himself. And thus the grand and avowed object of the Bishop of London's labours—the prostration of understandings and wills[1]—is accomplished.

In some such way it is that the *Chief truths* of the Church of Rome's religion gain credence. In this same way it is, that the *Chief truths* of the Church of England religion—including the truths of chief importance to its rulers—gain credence.

This Catechism—this antique breviary—Of all the persons, Reverend, and Very Reverend, and Right Reverend, and Most Reverend—Honourable and Right Honourable—who, with admiration so passionate, and zeal so ardent, concur in the worship of this substitute to the Bible,—is there a single one, who, at this time of day, would be capable of giving birth to a composition in every respect so ill-penned—in every respect so ill-adapted to every useful purpose—so well adapted to so many mischievous ones? Is there so much as a single one, who, were it now brought forward for the first time, would bring himself, or could be brought, so much as to set his name to it?—The ensuing *Examination*[2] read, let any one of them ask himself this question, and then answer it. In print he will not venture to answer it. No: explicitly he will not venture to answer it. But implicitly his answer to it is already given: given, by his concurrence in the slipping in of this *Supplement* to it.

III. Thirdly and lastly, the thing is bad in *form*. In its sentences it is *long-winded*. In virtue of this imperfection—not to speak of others—it has at all times been bad for all men, for all women, as well as for all children. But at the present time, and for the present purpose—for

---
[1] See p. 37 n. above.
[2] i.e. 'Church of England Catechism Examined', pp. 203–56 below.

the children who are to be instructed according to the new system—it is more particularly bad.

Of this badness likewise, those who not the less anxiously persevere in forcing it into those tender mouths, are fully, howsoever reluctantly, conscious.

Of this branch of their evil-consciousness, as in the case of the foregoing ones, the proof is furnished by their own practice.

To this altogether indigestible and scarcely swallowable morsel, in its entire state, they have, as abovementioned (§ [3.])[1]—they have—what?—*substituted?*—No: but *added*—the same in a mixed state. To the entire Catechism, they have added, that of which the title at length is—*The Church Catechism broken into Short Questions:* or—to call it by its more commodious and only usual name—the name by which also they themselves style it—*The Broken Catechism.*

This short name is an apt and useful one: the work itself is, in this its characteristic respect, well-adapted to its purpose.—But, whether it be in its minced or its unminced state that the mass presents itself, the parable of the *broken reed*[2] will stick by it.

Note, that, before they are allured thus to feed upon the mass, in the shape of minced meat, they are forced (as hath been seen)[3]—these tender mouths—to swallow it whole. Yes: *twice* to swallow it whole. Such is the relief afforded by the breakage.

That, in so far as concerns *form*, the alteration thus made is an improvement—and that a most capital one—is out of all dispute. Compared with the *old* Catechism, in so far as concerns *form*, this *new* one is therefore an eminently good thing: but this it could not be, if that original were not as eminently a bad one.

§IX. *The Religion thus taught by the Rulers of the Church of England, is not the Religion of Jesus.*

In this state of things,—the religion, which in these same schools is thus taught, is it the religion of Jesus?—Not it indeed—it is a quite different thing. Of this proposition, the proof rests—not on any points of detail—not on inferences drawn, on such or such particular subjects, from such or such particular texts. It applies not to this or that opinion—to this or that word. It goes to the whole together. The ground it rests upon is the broadest of all grounds: viz. that, administered as they are, and as above they have been seen to be administered, the portions of discourse thus forced into the minds, or at least into the mouths, of these poor children, form altogether a *substitute*—not a mere *additament*, but a complete

---

[1] 1818 '4' is a slip. See p. 65 above.
[2] See Isaiah 36: 6.
[3] See p. 65 above.

substitute—to the religion, which would be composed of the discourses of Jesus.

Not being the religion of Jesus, whose religion then is that substitute?—By *invention*, so far as depends upon this Catechism, it is the religion of the authors of this Catechism; so far as depends upon the Thirty-nine Articles, of those who respectively gave the force of law to that Catechism and to the Thirty-nine Articles: by *adoption*, it has, in each succeeding portion of time, been the religion of their successors—the rulers of that portion of time,—and is now the religion of their successors—the rulers of this present time.

That part of the religion, which is contained in the Thirty-nine Articles not being at present in question,—(for how consistently soever it might be, it appears not that any such security for orthodoxy, as that of a subscription to the Thirty-nine Articles, has yet been put about the necks of the National Society's Scholars),— what, on the present occasion, remains to be said on this subject, will have to confine itself to this Catechism.

In such a place—administered to minds so circumstanced—how repugnant soever to the original—any *Exposition*,—any discourse, professing to give an account of that original,—supersedes it. The child is to understand it—Yes: but *this* is the sense in which he is to understand it. The child is to believe it—Yes: but *this* is the sense in which he is to believe it.

Of any persuasion that can be entertained by the child, where is the immediate source? In any assurance given by the person whose discourse the original was? No: but in the assurances given by the person, by whom the original, if it be the original,—the exposition, if it be the exposition,—is put into the child's hands. The person who is present to his senses, in whose presence he stands, and by whose authority he is governed, he *is* the person—in the nature of the case he alone *can be* the person—in whom the trust of the child is placed. The person, whose discourse, the discourse expressed by the sacred original was, is *not* present to his senses. Unless by mere accident, even the person, whose discourse the *exposition* is, is *not* present to his senses. The person—the only person—constantly and necessarily present to his senses, is the *Schoolmaster*, by whom the *exposition* is put into his hands. A person incidentally present to his senses, may indeed be this or that person in still higher authority, by whom the school is now and then visited, and to whose authority the child sees the master bow. But these two—the master and the master's superior—are, to this purpose, one.

Now then, by all these powers, it is either *in lieu of*, or at any rate *in conjunction with*, the sacred original,—that into the child's hands the non-sacred *exposition* is thus put. If, in lieu of it, then clearly the exposition alone, and not the sacred original, is the object of his faith. In the words of the exposition, and in the discourse of those, by whom and by whose authority, it is put into his hands—in these alone, and not in any words of him whose words the words of the sacred original purport to exhibit—are to be seen or heard the sources of their faith.

But even if, at the same time with the *exposition*, the sacred original be put into the child's hands,—still, as above—still, in effect it is as if the exposition had, *without* the original, been put into his hands. Say to a child—'*this paper* (No. I.) *is not to be believed, but in the sense, which, in this paper* (No. II.) *is put upon it*'—in *words*, this is telling the child to believe in No. I.: but, in *effect*, it is just the same thing as telling him to pay no regard to it.

If the sacred original thus dealt with be the religion of Jesus, what is it then but mere mockery, to call the religion thus taught the religion of Jesus? It is the religion of the persons, under whose authority the *Exposition* is put into the child's hands.

The *person* of Jesus is not present to them: hence it is, therefore, that his person is not the object of their mockery. But the *words* of Jesus *are* present to them: and these words are not in effect less truly the objects of this their mockery, than his person was the object of the mockery of those men, by whom, while on the cross, he was hailed '*King of the Jews.*'[1]

A thing conceivable indeed is—that the sense, put upon the original by the Exposition, is the sense that *truly* belongs to it:—in a word, that it is a *faithful* one: and, in so far as this is the case, so far (except it be the *absurdity* and *presumption* of putting men's word above God's word,—the *oppression* thus exercised upon those who are compelled to do the same,—and the evil example set in both these ways) no mischief is done.

Note, that the less advanced the age in which the *Exposition* was penned, the less the probability of its being a faithful one. But, be it ever so faithful, where is the advantage that a copy has over the original?

Meantime, the *security* for this faithfulness, where is it?—The *ground* made for its being a faithful one—the *evidence* of its faithfulness, where is it?

One such security—one such ground—one such evidence, and no other—does the nature of the case admit of, and what is it?—Nothing can be more obvious.

---

[1] See Matthew 27: 29; Mark 15: 18; Luke 23: 38; John 19:19.

INTRODUCTION. PART I. §IX.

This security—need it any more be mentioned? is no other than the *test* above brought to view (§3 and 8)[1] consisting of the undiscontinued assortment of *quotations:* of quotations, supported by a correspondent accompaniment of *references*. But—once more—under the full view and consciousness of its importance, this test, which the framers of the Catechism knew better than to give, hath, as hath been seen all along, been studiously avoided to be given by their successors, and more especially by the present generation of their successors.[a]

Thus would the matter stand, even though, in respect of the efficiency of the means respectively employed for the inculcating them, the Bible and the Catechism were suffered to stand upon the

---

[a] So in the case of *Subscriptions*. To the extent of the whole of the matter contained in the Exposition, the moment any discourse, purporting to be the Exposition of an original, by which a system of religion is delivered—the moment any such paper is subscribed to, as prescribing the true and only true sense of the original, the religion delivered in the original is renounced. The object of the belief thus declared is—not the original, in any part of it, but the *Exposition*. Suppose—(for argument sake, at any rate, a supposition to this effect may be put)—between the original and the *Exposition*, suppose, in any part, a difference—insomuch that, to the extent of the difference, if the one is adhered to, the other is renounced. In such case, which is adhered to? Evidently the *Exposition:*—for *that* is the instrument subscribed to:—which is renounced? Evidently the *original*, for the original is *not* subscribed to. Be your original what it may—be your Exposition what it may—thus will the matter be. In the present case, the original is *the Bible*—the Exposition is the set of *Church of England Articles*. What follows?—Need it be repeated? To the whole extent of that formula, the religion of its unknown penners is by every such subscriber adhered to—the religion of Jesus renounced.

It is therefore mere mockery, to call this part of the religion of Church of Englandists the religion of Jesus. It is the religion of the penners of the Thirty-nine Articles,—adopted, and down to this time received and sanctioned, by the several successive rulers, for the time being, of the Established Church of England.

So in *Scotland*. What is it that Church-of-Scotlandists believe in? Is it the religion of Jesus?—No: *that* they are precluded from believing in by *their* Catechisms. It is the religion of those who penned, and of those who, since them, have been subscribers to those Catechisms:—in one word it is the religion of the Kirk.

This is not the less true, be the *discipline* of the Church of Scotland ever so much better (and, even before these pages are at an end, it will be seen to be beyond all comparison better) than that of the Church of England.

Between the two churches, taken at their origin, in this lies the great difference—the great moral difference. Whatever else they were—the authors of the religion of the Church of Scotland were honest men:—men firmly believing,—as the proof given by them, as above, shews,—that every thing contained in the religion of their making was contained in the religion of Jesus: while the others were—what their works, as above, shew them to be.

---

[1] See pp. 62–7, 77–82 above respectively.

same level. But how wide this supposition is of the truth has been seen already.

Question to my Lords the Bishops—and to the Lay-Saints, Co—or Sub—Rulers of the self-styled 'Excellent Church.'—Suppose two Books, the *Koran* and the *Bible:* each of them furnished with an *accompaniment,* consisting of an *Exposition,* composed of a *Catechism,* injected by the new engine into the mind in its infant state, and a set of *Articles,* his belief of which, with the starvation pistol at his throat, each youth, at his entrance upon the road to preferment, is, by a writing under his hand, forced to declare. The Catechism and Articles attached to the *Koran* are—every proposition of them—so many extracts composed of the most essential parts of the four Gospels. The Catechism and Articles attached to the *Bible* are—so many extracts composed of the most essential parts of the *Koran.* In both cases, as above, the Exposition got by heart, and subscribed to,—the original not. For the purification of morals—for the salvation of souls—which of the two apparatus would your Graces, your Lordships, and your Honours, be pleased to recommend in preference?

Suppose your Lordships' temporalities at stake: suppose, moreover, that, for the preservation of *'decency'* in the Church,[1] these instruments of the renounced 'pomps and vanities'[2] were become objects of your Lordships' care.—A *law* which *gave* them; accompanied by an *interpretation,* composed of a judgment, viz., in dernier resort, by a competent court of law, which *took them away:* or a *law* which *took them away,* accompanied with an *interpretation,* which, in the way just mentioned, *restored them:* Of the two laws,—all prospect of any others out of the question,—which would be your Lordships' choice?

A reproach, often mentioned, as having been cast, by their adversaries, upon such of the Hollanders, who, in former days, had been admitted as traders into the *Japanese* Empire, is—that, in the character of a token necessary to their being so admitted, they had trampled on the cross.[3] The case is—that the Romanists, by the

---

[1] Bentham is alluding to *Substance of the Speech of the Earl of Harrowby, on moving for the recommitment of a Bill for the better support and maintenance of Stipendiary Curates, on Thursday, the 18th of June, 1812,* London, 1812, p. 16: 'How can we expect that persons, whose incomes hardly afford the means of subsistence, will be able to keep up that decent appearance which is almost indispensably necessary to secure the respect of their parishioners?' For Bentham's discussion of Harrowby's Curates Bill see pp. 388–97 n., 499–518 below.

[2] See p. 50 & n. above.

[3] As proof of their renunciation of Christianity, all Japanese working for the Dutch East India Company at the trading post of Deshima, an artificial island in the harbour of Nagasaki, had to perform the act of trampling on an image of the crucifixion, in conjunction with swearing an oath to deny the Dutch all friendship, credit, and communication: see Engelbertus Kaempfer, *The History of Japan,* trans. J.G. Scheuchzer, 2 vols., London, 1727, i. 334–5.

INTRODUCTION. PART I. §IX.

course which, in those days, they took for the propagation of their religion in those countries, having rendered their religion an object of alarm to the rulers of that empire,—this ceremony, supposing the story founded in fact, must have had for its object the furnishing what was regarded as conclusive evidence, of their not being votaries of a religion which had rendered itself thus formidable.[1]

For my own part, supposing, under these circumstances, supposing it to contribute any thing towards a prospect of spreading the religion of Jesus in those as yet untried countries, I see not what prevalent objection, unless he were a Catholic, the most zealous missionary need have to the joining in such a ceremony.

In this, if taken by itself, there is nothing more than an imputed—there is not any real and effectual—renunciation of the religion of Jesus. But, by a subscription to any such pretended *Exposition* and real substitute, as has just been brought to view, not only a renouncement is made, but that renouncement a substantial and effectual one.

---

[1] The Jesuit St Francis Xavier (1506–53) first took the Roman Catholic religion to Japan in 1549, but in 1587 Toyotomi Hideyoshi (1536–98), ruler of Japan from 1583, suspecting their growing mercantile and political influence, denounced the Jesuits as traitors and ordered their expulsion from the country, although in the event most remained. The persecution of Christians persisted, and converts were forced to swear an oath of apostasy, accompanied by the act of trampling on a holy image, upon pain of death. Tokugawa Iemitsu (1604–51), Shogun from 1623, pursued the policy of Sakoku or 'closed country', whereby Japanese were forbidden to leave and all foreigners were excluded from the country, and only the trading post at Deshima, limited to Dutch and Chinese, was permitted.

PART II.

EXCLUSIONARY SYSTEM OF INSTRUCTION—ITS ESTABLISHMENT—ITS BAD TENDENCIES.

EXCLUSION, and compulsory or seductive proselytism,—exclusion of one part of the community of the poor from the benefits of education—compelling the other part to come within the pale of the church dominion,—such are the two intimately connected, though perfectly distinct, and even contrasted, objects, in the pursuit of which this formulary is made a principal instrument.

Presently will be seen the particular measures,—which, in the pursuit of these objects, have been, and continue to be, employed. But, in the mean time, a short view of the circumstances, which led to the application thus made of that instrument, may be not altogether without its use.

In that part of education, which consists in intellectual instruction, the moralist beholds the means of virtue and happiness,—the politician, the means of internal peace, tranquillity, and rational obedience,—the Christian, the means of salvation.

In the new-invented system of instruction, all join in beholding an instrument of matchless and never-before-imagined efficiency, for the communication of that blessing, the value of which is so universally acknowledged.

From the first, the inventor of it—*Dr. Bell*—from his station in Hindostan, saw in it all these capacities: but many and many were the years that had elapsed, before any the faintest prospect of seeing these capacities ripened into act in these northern regions could have opened to his view.[1]

---

[1] Andrew Bell (1753–1832), educationalist, Chaplain at Fort St George, Madras 1787–96, Rector of Swanage, Dorset 1801–9, Master of Sherburn Hospital, Durham from 1809, Canon of Hereford Cathedral 1818, Canon of Westminster Abbey 1819–28, developed the monitorial system of education at the Male Orphan Asylum in Madras at which he taught from 1789 to 1796. On his return to London, he described the system in *An Experiment in Education, made at the Male Asylum of Madras*, London, 1797. The Madras system was first used at St Botolph's Charity School, Aldgate, London in 1798, and the National Society adopted the system in its schools, the first of which opened in 1812 (see p. 37 n. above).

INTRODUCTION. PART II.

Lancaster,—the first adopter, and, in some particulars, the improver, of the intellectual mechanism,—saw in it an instrument of that reputation, that opulence, and that power, which he actually attained, and so notoriously and scandalously abused.[1]

His supporters—his generous and public spirited supporters[2]—saw in it those admirable capacities which it possesses, and pushed on the application of it to the utmost of their power.

The personal and perhaps the public views of Lancaster, concurred with the public views of those his supporters, in giving to it the utmost extension possible: in giving to it an extension, which, by no factitious limitation whatsoever, was, or was intended to be, narrowed.

The dew of *royal favour*[3]—who could have thought it?—the dew of royal favour was seen at length to fall upon the head of this schismatic.

The Bishops—the rulers of that church, of the *excellence* of which the sole proof lies in the epithet so hardily and unweariedly bestowed upon it—awakened and alarmed by this self-styled Quaker, these rulers, after a sleep of so many years,—during which the invention was experiencing that treatment, of which, at such hands, merit, in proportion to its usefulness, might, from the signs of the times, have assured to itself,—saw in it, as soon as they saw any thing in it, an instrument of defensive—of defensive?—yea, and moreover, by the grace of God, offensive—prosperously offensive—warfare.

The Church was then—as it still is—and, so long as it stands, will

---

[1] Joseph Lancaster (1778–1838), a Quaker, developed the monitorial system at the Royal Free School, Borough Road, London, which opened in 1801, accepting pupils from all religious denominations. In 1810 the Royal Lancasterian Institution for the Education of the Poor of Every Religious Persuasion was formed with the purpose of establishing a national system of Lancasterian Schools. Following disputes between Lancaster and the managing committee, a constitution and rules were approved for the renamed Institution for Promoting the British System for the Education of the Labouring and Manufacturing Classes of Society of Every Religious Persuasion, with Lancaster as a salaried superintendent. Lancaster was frequently in debt, and, following a scandal involving accusations of physical abuse of trainee teachers, he resigned in 1814 from the Institution, which was subsequently renamed the British and Foreign School Society. See also p. 101 n. below.

[2] Those who supported Lancaster included Bentham's friends William Allen (1770–1843), Quaker philanthropist; Henry Peter Brougham (1778–1868), first Baron Brougham and Vaux, Lord Chancellor 1830–4; James Mill (1773–1836), philosopher, economist, and historian; and Francis Place (1771–1854), master tailor and radical politician.

[3] According to Lancaster, following an interview in 1805, George III (1738–1820), King of Great Britain and Ireland from 1760, promised Lancaster annual subscriptions of £100 from himself, £50 from Charlotte (1744–1818), Queen of Great Britain and Ireland, and £25 from each of the princesses: see William Corston, *A Brief Sketch of the Life of Joseph Lancaster; including the Introduction of his System of Education*, London, [1840], pp. 15–17. George III's sons, Edward (1767–1820), Duke of Kent and Strathearn, and Augustus Frederick (1773–1843), Duke of Sussex, also supported Lancaster's work. For the support of the Duke of Kent, for example, see p. 101 n. below.

ever be—*in danger.*[1] They saw it was so: they said it was so: they keep saying it is so: nor can falsehood be imputed to them, so long as they confine themselves to the repetition of this dirge.

The Church of England is in danger now, as the Church of Rome was three centuries ago, and exactly from the same cause.[2] The spiritual edifice is in danger, as a wooden one is in danger when the dry-rot is in all its timbers.

The Established Church is in danger, and from all the non-established ones. Why?—Because, in England, from the very nature of the two opposite sorts of Churches, it follows, that, by their respective ministers, in the one case, all their useful duties should to the utmost be fulfilled, in the other that to the utmost those same duties should be neglected. But of this elsewhere.[a]

In the hands of *Lancaster*, with or without intention, the Bible, put into action by the instrument invented by Dr. Bell, worked as a battering-ram against the Established Church.—What was to be done? The Bible suited not the purposes of the Church of Rome: they forbad the use of it.[3] As little did it or does it suit the purposes of the present rulers of the Church of England. What then was to be done?—Forbid the use of it they could not. What, in that same view, they could and did was—to teach, in the new way, the old thing which they found already in use—the Catechism:—the Catechism, which, having so long ago been taken in substance from the Church of Rome, was now seen to be so commodiously suited to those same purposes. The Bible was taught by Lancaster: the Church of England Catechism was not taught by him.[4] Should the system of Lancaster spread, and become universal,—the Bible might prevail over the Catechism, and the Church of England might thus be brought to an end.—*Dr. Bell* was taken up,—and, with the Catechism in his hand, employed to defend the *Church* against the *Bible*.

The war thus secretly carried on against the Bible, common prudence forbade to become an open one. Appearances required

---

[a] See Appendix, No. I.[5]

[1] See p. 38 n. above.
[2] i.e. from reformation.
[3] See p. 70 n. above.
[4] The Lancasterian schools used the Bible, hymnals, and Mrs Trimmer, *An Easy Introduction to the Knowledge of Nature, and reading the Holy Scriptures, adapted to the capacities of children*, London, 1780, and John Freame, *Scripture-Instruction; Digested into Several Sections, By Way of Question and Answer*, London, 1713: see Joseph Lancaster, *Improvements in Education, as it respects the industrious classes of the Community, containing, among other important particulars, An Account of the Institution for the Education of One Thousand Poor Children, Borough Road, Southwark; and of the new system of education on which it is conducted* (first published 1803), 3rd edn., London, 1805, pp. 155–61, 187.
[5] See pp. 257–311 below.

INTRODUCTION. PART II.

that some use should appear to be made of it. Selected and cooked up in the manner which was judged a proper one, the *Parables*, the *Miracles*, the *Discourses of Jesus*,—sooner or later, (for, in the accounts published, *times* are throughout kept, as will be seen, in a state of the most convenient darkness)—sooner or later, some of each, at any rate, were professed at least to be taught.—Taught—but how? Taught by being caused to be repeated? Oh, no: that was a privilege, reserved (as in Part I. §[3,][1] as hath been seen)[2] for compositions of superior worth and use: for the *Graces*, the *Collects*, the *Prayers*, the *Catechism*,—the Catechism *'entire and broken'*—of the Church of England. Under the impossibility of suppressing it altogether, the shortness of one short discourse—the Lord's Prayer—saved it from the exclusion, so resolutely put upon every thing else that was ever said by him.[a]

By weight of metal, if employed in the working of this new engine—by weight of metal, could a sufficiency of it be provided—not only might the danger, the pressure, be stopped,—but, with hopes—not only of increase of dominion, but of the complete subjugation of the enemy, and the complete extirpation of schism—the war carried into his quarters.

Open force could not be applied. The Lancaster Schools were indeed *Meetings*, and any meetings might be converted into *Conventicles*. But, every where but at *Oxford*,[3] *Conventicles* were protected by the *Toleration Act*:[4] protected in some sort, by that law, but still more effectually by the spirit of the times,—or, to speak more plainly, by the ever encreasing multitude and intelligence of the Dissenters.

Other methods were therefore to be resorted to. The rival manufacture—the manufacture of *minds*—was to be crushed by weight of capital. Capital was accordingly to be the instrument: competition, the mode of working it: competition, the mode;—and that competition such as should be an irresistible one.

The exertions were unexampled: had the object been less scandalous, the term *miraculous* might almost have been ventured to be given to them.

The *Convocation* system was revived.[5] The Lower House was

[a] Second Report of the National Society, anno 1814, p. 196.[6]

---

[1] 1818 '4' is a slip.   [2] See pp. 62–7 above.
[3] An allusion to the expulsion of the Methodists from the University of Oxford: see pp. 32–5 above.
[4] i.e. 1 Wm. & Mary, c. 18, §4 (1689).
[5] The Convocations of Canterbury and York, composed of an Upper House for Bishops and a Lower House for the rest of the clergy, had last been summoned in 1717. They had enjoyed the right to assent to taxation of the clergy until 1664, when they submitted to taxation by Parliament (16 & 17 Car. II, c. 1).   [6] See p. 64 n. above.

CHURCH-OF-ENGLANDISM

indeed untaxable. But the Upper House—the Bishops, headed by the Archbishops—taxed themselves.[1] Taxing themselves individually, they did in this way what they could not have done by taxing themselves collectively—they taxed laymen along with them. The *Alarm Bell* rung: and all who either felt, or felt themselves under the obligation of appearing to feel, for an Ecclesiastical Establishment, the gigantic abuses of which form so powerful a rampart for the comparatively pigmy abuses of the Civil, flocked round the *Church* and laid their offerings upon its altars.

The difficulty was to get the money. The money once got, the means were obvious. All that was wanting was a set of brazen fronts, and well seared consciences.[2] Of these there was no want; nor under such a system ever can be.

Search the Liturgy all over, and from among those of its formularies that are peculiar to the Church of England, pick out that which is the most palpably absurd and mischievous. Set up a number of Free Schools upon the new system,—and among the conditions of admittance, require, at the hands of parents, a consent that their children shall receive a thorough impregnation with the matter of this formulary.—What follows?—Evidently this: viz. that, by all who are not reconciled to the abomination by blind habit, or won over by prospects of temporal advantage, the proffered boon will be rejected.

Here then comes already into view exclusion and proselytism, the double fruit of so obvious and efficient a measure: two intimately connected advantages,—so flattering, so soothing—the one to the *irascible*, the other to the *concupiscible* appetite:—the enemies of the Church cast out into outer darkness;—the golden sceptre held out to those and those alone, whom repentance should lay prostrate, to help form her footstool. Who could say, to what a length a consummation so devoutly to be wished,[3] might—always by the grace of God—in time extend itself?

Such were the promised effects of the plan, upon the interest of the Church:—meaning always the governing part of the Church. The effects of it upon the interest of the community at large were of a very different complexion. But these have never been worth a thought.

I. First as to the *exclusion*.

The persons most immediately, and therefore most obviously, suffering are the persons thus excluded. But these form but a part

---

[1] The Archbishops and Bishops were *ex officio* members of the General Committee of the National Society (see p. 46 & n. above), and contributed generously to the Society, which was funded from annual subscriptions and donations. A list of the subscribers and sums raised was published in the *Annual Reports*.

[2] An echo of I Timothy 4: 2. [3] *Hamlet*, III. i. 63–4.

INTRODUCTION. PART II.

of the community, and that the smallest part: the persons next in sufferance form the whole of it: nor, at the same time, are the excluded part excluded from their share in this sufferance; so that *their* sufferance comes upon them in a double shape.

Destitute of intellectual instruction, man, even in the bosom of the most civilized country, is often found appearing in no better a character than that of a savage. Of the Hulks, and the Penal Colonies—not to speak of the home Prisons—the population is, for the most part, composed of human beings thus abandoned to ignorance, vice, and wretchedness. Such, as to the far greater part, appears to be the state of the population under the Church of England.

Under the Church of Scotland, a person altogether destitute of intellectual instruction is hardly to be found. Upon a careful examination of the Returns that have been made to Parliament,—allowance made for difference of population,—compared with that of Scotland, the number of persons in England within the same period, committed on criminal charges, was found to be as rather more than *eleven* to *one*.[1]

II. Next as to the *compulsory proselytism*.

Applied to the dissenting part of the population, corresponding to the differences in respect of education, situation, and temper, which the regulation chanced to meet with on the part of different individuals, would be the effect produced by it. Some would not be able to prevail upon themselves to become purchasers of the proffered benefit, at the price thus demanded for it: in all these instances *exclusion* would be the result. Others, unable to withstand the temptation, would sacrifice their offspring to the inviting Moloch.[2]

But by any profit thus reaped from the sacrifice, the magnitude of that sacrifice would not, in all eyes, be lessened. In some it would rather be increased: and of the sort of sensation thus producible in a

---

[1] In the seven years from 1805 to 1811 a total of 33,945 persons were committed for trial in England and Wales, while in the six years from 1805 to 1810 a total of 543 persons were committed for trial in Scotland. See 'A return of the number of Persons, charged with Criminal Offences, Who were committed to the different Gaols in England and Wales, for trial ... in the Years 1805,—1806,—1807,—1808,—1809,—1810, —&1811', and 'Scotland. A Return of Persons, Male and Female, Committed, in the years 1805, 1806, 1807, 1808, 1809, & 1810, To the several Gaols in Scotland', in *Commons Sessional Papers* (1812) x. 233–6, 217–32 respectively. According to the census of 1811, the population (excluding those serving in the Army and Navy) of England and Wales was 10,106,780, and of Scotland 1,804,864: see *Commons Sessional Papers* (1812) x. 171–4.

Adjusting the calculation to take into account the unequal periods of time and the difference of population, the number of persons committed on criminal charges according to the above figures is, as Bentham claims, in a ratio of 11.16 to 1. Bentham gives the sources for his calculation at p. 291 n. below.

[2] The worship of Moloch was widely associated with the sacrifice of children: see Leviticus 18: 21, and John Milton, *Paradise Lost*, I. 392–3.

religious and reflecting breast, memory, with little aid from imagination, has sufficed—in one instance at least—to present a picture.[1]

The larger that part of the population, by which the benefit came in this and other ways to be purchased, the deeper the humiliation of such as should be left destitute of it: and thus, in the character of an instrument of compulsory proselytism, the benefit would continue to operate with continually increasing force. Such was and is the Machiavelism of this tyranny.

If there be a maxim of government, thoroughly rooted in the honest and thinking part of the English public mind,—one might even venture to say in by far the greater portion of that mind,—it is this:—that, at any rate in a country, the population of which is civilized, in[2] the degree in which that of the British Isles is civilized, the securing the temporal well being of mankind—this, and not the salvation of souls, is the proper ground—the only proper ground—for the application of the powers of government to matters of religion.

Is it then that an eternity of infinite felicity or infinite misery, is of less importance than three or fourscore years of chequered existence?—No: but that, of the opposite doctrine,—supposing it but pursued with consistency,—instead of the object aimed at, tyranny—everlasting and universal tyranny—tyranny worse than Romish, followed by war for the purpose of universal subjection—would be the result. Instead of the object aimed at? Yes: for, even at this price, the attainment of it—so far from being promoted—would be counteracted. If for example, either in England, Scotland, or Ireland,—Dissenters from the established Church being termed *Schismatics,—Schismatics* were to be treated, as the present, pursuing the maxims of the late, Bishop of London,[3] calls upon Government to treat them—treated as men of '*guilt*'[4]—treated as criminals. With sword in one hand, and purse in the other, Englishmen would be to be sent to Scotland to convert Scotchmen to Episcopacy,—Scotchmen at the same time into England to convert Englishmen to

---

[1] Bentham is probably referring to one of the Mortlake tapestries, made after the cartoons by the Italian Renaissance painter Raffaello Sanzio (1483–1520) which hung at Ford Abbey (for which see p. 10 n. above), entitled 'The Sacrifice At Lystra before St Paul and St Barnabas'. In a letter written at Ford Abbey, Bentham refers to the tapestry as the 'Sacrifice Cartoon': see Bentham to Koe, 29 October 1817, *Correspondence* (*CW*), ix. 95.

[2] 1818 'civilized in'. The text follows the 'Errata'.

[3] John Randolph, Bishop of London from 1809 until his death in July 1813, the immediate predecessor of William Howley, had warned of 'a new schism' which had been engendered between the church and those who dissented from it: see *A Charge delivered to the Clergy of the Diocese of London, by John, Lord Bishop of that Diocese, at his Primary Visitation in* MDCCCX, Oxford, 1810, pp. 11–19, esp. 12.

[4] See p. 48 above.

INTRODUCTION. PART II.

Presbyterianism,—while on the like mission both together were sent to Ireland,—there to be kept, till, reclaimed from the errors of the Church of Rome, the Irish were, to a man, made to acknowledge, in the same breath, the unrivalled excellence of the English Episcopalian and Scottish Presbyterian Churches.

The thing, in the production of which the powers of Government are on this occasion professed to be employed, is—*religion:* but, if insincerity, mendacity, and mischievous obsequiousness be vices, the thing, and the only thing, in the production of which they are really and effectually employed is—*vice*. On the field of *religion*, the thing, to which, on this occasion, these powers are specifically employed, is—the production of a *declaration of persuasion*. But, in so far as the declaration so made is *true*, whatever is thus bestowed—whether it be in the shape of reward or punishment—is spent without need, effect, or use:—spent in causing that to have place, which has place already. In what way then, when thus employed, are they employed with effect?—In one way, and in one way only:—in the production of such declarations in the case in which they are *not* true: in the production of *mendacity:* in the production of *vice:* in the production of that vice, which is the instrument of every other vice, as well as of every sort of crime.

That, which causes a persuasion to be really entertained, is that which applies to the *understanding*. That which applies to the understanding is *argument*. Employing *argument* for securing welfare, whether temporal or eternal,—whether through persuasions entertained, or by other means,—is a course which,—after substraction made of all punishment and all reward, applied to the *will* as above,—would remain no less open to rulers than to subjects: and, on this ground these same rulers can not but act to prodigious advantage. Not to speak of *punishment*—in their hands, though in an indirect, though not the less efficient way, applicable to this, as to any other purpose—in the production of argument they are free, and will in any case remain free, to employ the powers of *reward*—and that without need of any expense on purpose—in a quantity greater than any that to the same purpose can be applied by any individual, or association of individuals;—reward, to an amount altogether unlimited:—and in this same way are they continually producing argument, true and false, believed or not believed to be true by him who utters it,—and at all times in *any quantity they* choose to have. For money, for power, for dignity,—for the mere hope, however distant, of any of these good things,—argument is to be sold and may be bought by them, at all times, on any subject, and for the use of any side. And thus, in *their* hands,—without need of their employing their powers in the production of vice,—argument, in support of virtue, religion, and happiness, may if that be their real object, be purchased and set to work, with a degree of advantage altogether matchless.

But, though the best arguments that the nature of the case will admit of, and the state of the public mind, at the time supplies, is always at their command,—yet, when the best arguments that the nature of the case admits of on their side, are good for nothing, argument will not suit their purpose: and thus it is, that in spite of the immorality, and in spite of the just reproach,—in support of their cause, whatever it is,—and with a degree of energy and constancy, rising with the degree of badness, which, even in their own view of it, belongs to it,—thus it is that, according as opportunities and means present themselves, they persist in employing the powers of reward, and even of punishment, in support of it.

Thus then is an exclusion put at once upon the children of all those parents, in whose view of the matter the absence of all such instruction, as is not to be had but through the channel in question, is better than the presence. As to what ground there may be for any such view, it is what the body of this work is designed to shew.

All this while, let it not, however, be imagined, that to the use of this or any other such comparatively indirect means, the exertions made for this double and doubly pernicious purpose have been confined.

From their own accounts of their own proceedings, take the following extracts:—

I. In p. 187, of the National Society's Second Report, dated in 1813, and 1814, of a string of Resolutions, eight in number, which, on some day of the month of February, 1812, (day not named) are, in No. IV. of the Appendix, printed under the title of PLAN *of* UNION,[a] that which stands eighth and last is in the words following:—

'That the Society itself being instituted principally for educating the Poor in the doctrine and discipline of the Established Church, according to the excellent Liturgy and Catechism provided for that purpose, it is required that all the Children received into these Schools be instructed in this Liturgy and Catechism, and that, in conformity with the directions in that Liturgy, the Children of each School do constantly attend Divine Service in their parish Church, or other place of public worship under the Establishment, wherever the

---

[a] In Report I. p. 27, without Month or Year.[1]

[1] i.e. the resolution in question appears both under 'No. IV. National Society. Plan of Union. February 1812', in *Second Annual Report of the National Society*, Appendix IV, pp. 186–7, and under 'Plan of Union', in *First Annual Report of the National Society*, Appendix III, pp. 27–8.

INTRODUCTION. PART II.

same is practicable, on the Lord's Day; unless such reason for their non-attendance be assigned, as shall be satisfactory to the persons having the direction of that School; and that no religious tracts be admitted into any School, but such as are, or shall be contained in the Catalogue of the SOCIETY FOR PROMOTING CHRISTIAN KNOWLEDGE.'[1]

'T.T. WALMSLEY, Sec.'

II. In p. 197, of this second Report, (it is not in the first) without introduction or other explanation, comes an article, of which the following is a reprint.[2]

No. IX.

Form of Certificate for Masters.

NATIONAL SOCIETY CENTRAL SCHOOL.

'This is to certify that   who is desirous of being admitted into the NATIONAL CENTRAL SCHOOL, for the purpose of learning the System of Education there practised, is a Member of the UNITED CHURCH of ENGLAND and IRELAND as by law established, and of a sober and religious life and conversation.

Signed   Rector,
                  Vicar, or } of
                  Curate

"*⁎* It is requested that no Clergyman will sign the above Certificate as *a matter of form*, but that he will make the strictest enquiries into the character of the person applying for his signature, and *into the regularity of*   attendance upon the Service of the Church.'

A curious circumstance is—if interest-begotten bigotry were any thing less than stone-blind—if it were capable of reading any thing that accorded not with its own purposes—a curious enough circumstance is—that, in that very fabrication of their own, which with such anxious care they substitute to the Bible, they may read their own condemnation:—they may read the condemnation of that very system of exclusion, which, by means of it, they are there so diligently putting in practice.

Question in the *Catechism*. 'What dost thou chiefly learn in these Articles of thy Belief? Answer. First, I learn to believe in God the

[1] The chief aims of the Society for Promoting Christian Knowledge, founded in London in 1698, were to encourage education and to publish and distribute Christian literature in Britain and the wider world. At this time the Society was the principal publisher of Christian literature in Britain.

[2] The certificate is also reproduced in *Third Annual Report of the National Society*, Appendix VII, p. 176.

CHURCH-OF-ENGLANDISM

Father, &c. Secondly, in God the Son, who hath redeemed me and all mankind.'

Questions thereupon in the *'Broken Catechism.'* '*Question.* What did God the Son for you? *Answer.* He redeemed me. *Question.* Did he redeem any besides you? *Answer.* Yes; all mankind.'

By Jesus himself, the benefit bestowed by his coming was intended—was, according to these very formularies of theirs, intended—for all mankind. By these rulers of the Church of England is that same benefit intended for all mankind?—So far from its being so, it is not (witness these exclusionary laws) intended for any but a comparatively minute portion of those who profess the religion of Jesus. Is it intended for all mankind? No: not so much as for all Christians. For all Christians? No: not so much as for all Protestants. For whom then is it intended by them? Not for so much as a single soul, other than those who, in the character of subjects to their governance, are content to be perpetual contributors to those *riches*, in which they put their trust;[1] to that *power* which they abuse; to those *factitious dignities*, with which they deck their names; to that *purple*, and that *fine linen*,[2] in which they strut; to those *pomps and vanities*, which in their babe-and-suckling[3] state they renounced,[4] and which they are seen with so much anxiety mounting guard upon, in their Church regnant and Church militant state.

The instruction which the Gospel contains, is it, or is it not conducive, to private virtue, to private happiness, to rational obedience, to internal tranquillity, to external peace, to salvation of souls? If not, then why, at all this pains and expense, profess to teach it?—If yes, then why refuse to so much as a single soul the benefit of it?

'Perish bodies! perish souls! Yea, in any numbers let them perish,—rather than a feather should risk the being shaken from the down on which we repose!'—Such, ye hypocrites, are your vows. Can you deny them? Behold them in your own acts: behold them in those acts of yours, which are now staring you in the face.

---

[1] Mark 10: 24.   [2] Luke 16: 19.
[3] Psalm 8: 2.   [4] See p. 50 & n. above.

PART III.

EXCLUSIONARY SYSTEM—GROUNDS FOR THE HOPE THAT THE APPROBATION OF IT IS NOT GENERAL.

THESE grounds are composed of two articles of documentary evidence: one of them *direct;* the other *circumstantial* evidence.

The *direct* is furnished by an express declaration of *Sir Thomas Bernard*.[1]

Of the ardency and activity of the zeal of the worthy Baronet, in favour of the new instruction system; and at the same time of his orthodoxy, in the character of a son of the Church of England,—without which latter character, his testimony, however respectable in itself, would scarcely be applicable to the present purpose,—that work of his, in which so interesting an account is given of the Schools, instituted for this purpose at Durham, by his friend the Bishop, affords ample proof:[2] and, considering that intimacy, the marks of which are upon the face of that publication so apparent, it seems as difficult as it would be unpleasant to suppose, that in the opinions and assertions, so strenuously, as well as plainly manifested by one of the two friends, the other should be altogether without a share.

In proof of the disapprobation—not to say the abhorrence—with which the system of exclusion and compulsory proselytism is, or at least not long ago was, regarded by Sir Thomas Bernard, I have the satisfaction of finding the two altogether explicit passages, which here follow.

They are, both of them, copied from a printed paper, signed *Thomas Bernard*, and, in the character of a preface, to a work *'On*

---

[1] Sir Thomas Bernard (1750–1818) had been called to the Bar in 1780, but following marriage to an heiress in 1782, and a successful career in conveyancing, he retired and devoted himself to philanthropic work. In 1796, together with Shute Barrington (1734–1826), Bishop of Llandaff 1769–82, Salisbury 1782–91, and Durham 1791–1826, and Edward James Eliot (1758–97), he founded the Society for Bettering the Condition and Increasing the Comforts of the Poor.

[2] Sir Thomas Bernard, *The Barrington School; being an illustration of the principles, practices, and effects, of the new system of instruction, in facilitating the religious and moral instruction of the poor*, London, 1812. Barrington School, established at Bishop Auckland in 1810, and named after its founder Shute Barrington, Bishop of Durham, educated children by means of the monitorial system, and trained teachers in its use.

the Education of the Poor,' published by '*The Society for bettering the Condition of the Poor.*'[a]

In the first of them stands in the text the following passage.

'With such abundant sources of corruption,' (says the worthy Baronet, p. 52) 'where can the patriot, who desires the happiness, or even the existence of his country,—where can he look for security,—to what can he direct his hopes, but to education, formed on the general principles of Christianity,—bestowed impartially upon all our fellow-subjects, and connected in amity with our civil and religious establishment?' and to this passage is subjoined, in form of a note, the following one. 'When I speak of a national system of education, connected in *amity* with our religious establishment,—and while I wish it to receive the aid, and be under the direction of that establishment, I do not mean that the system shall be subservient to its power, or instrumental of conversion to its tenets. To deal out education to the poor, only on the terms of *religious conformity*, is, in my opinion, a species of persecution, differing not greatly from the supplying of bread to the hungry and necessitous on similar conditions,—and being as defective in true policy as it is unjust in principle.'

In the other passage—(it is in a preceding page, p. 48 of that same Preface)—speaking of 'the *Charter Schools* in *Ireland*, I have been very much misinformed,' (says he) 'if the impolitic and intolerant condition, on which education in them is given to the Catholic poor, contributes so much to conversion as to violent and bitter prejudice against the Established Church.'[1]

Such are the opinions and affections expressed—and by whom?— Not merely by an individual, but by an individual writing and

[a] It constitutes the first part of 'a Digest of the Report of that Society,' and contains a selection of those articles which have a reference to education. The date of it is *London*, 1809.[2]

---

[1] The Protestant Charter Schools, run by the Incorporated Society in Dublin, for Erecting and Promoting English Protestant Schools in Ireland, had been granted a Royal Charter in 1733. Protestant and Catholic pupils were taught literacy and numeracy, received Protestant religious instruction, and undertook manual labour. Catholic children were frequently removed entirely from their parents' care in order to eliminate any 'popish' influences, and were later apprenticed to Protestant masters. Abusive practices in these schools were criticized by John Howard (1726?-90), philanthropist and prison reformer, who visited Ireland in 1783, 1787, and 1788: see John Howard, *The State of the Prisons in England and Wales, with Preliminary Observations, and an account of some foreign prisons and hospitals*, 3rd edn., Warrington, 1784, pp. 208-9; and *An Account of the Principal Lazarettos in Europe; with various papers relative to the plague*, Warrington, 1789, pp. 101-17.

[2] [Thomas Bernard], *Of the Education of the Poor; being the first part of a Digest of the Reports of the Society for Bettering the Condition of the Poor: and containing a Selection of those Articles which have a reference to Education*, London, 1809. There are a number of minor inaccuracies in the rendering of the passages.

INTRODUCTION. PART III.

publishing them in the character of the organ of a numerous society—*The Society for the Bettering the Condition of the Poor:*—the members of it distinguished—most, if not all of them—scarcely more by this testimony of their benevolent zeal, in behalf of this most important object, than by their attachment to the doctrine and discipline of the Church of England.[a]

---

[a] The text was on the point of being sent to the press when, in the person of the *Bishop of Norwich*,[1] the paper of the day brought to view the cheering spectacle of so illustrious an addition to the declared adversaries of the exclusionary system.

Morning Chronicle, 10th May, 1816.
{Advertisement.}

PUBLIC EDUCATION.—The Right Reverend the Lord Bishop of Norwich will preach a sermon on Sunday next,[2] at the parish church of St. Botolph, Aldersgate, London, before his Royal Highness the Duke of Kent, the Right Honourable the Lord Mayor,[3] and other illustrious personages who have promised to attend on behalf of the Royal Institution, for the gratuitous education, on the British system, of one thousand children *of all religious denominations*, within the Wards of Aldersgate, Bassishaw, Coleman-Street, Cripplegate, and the parishes of St. Luke and St. Leonard-Shoreditch, Middlesex, established in North-Street, City-Road.[4]

JOHN WILKS, *Secretary.*[5]

Finsbury-Place, May 7th, 1816.

---

[1] i.e. Henry Bathurst.

[2] i.e. 12 May 1816.

[3] Sir Matthew Wood (1768–1843), druggist and politician, Lord Mayor of London 1815–16, 1816–17, and MP for the City of London 1817–43.

[4] Under the auspices of Lancaster's subsequently renamed British and Foreign School Society (for which see p. 89 n. above), a school for the education of 1,000 poor children from any religious denomination had opened in North Street, City Road, Finsbury, London in 1813. For other notices concerning the School see, for example, *Morning Chronicle*, 27 February 1813, 12 March 1814, 10 May 1816.

[5] John Wilks (1766?–1854), son of a dissenting minister, attorney, later MP for Boston 1830–7, had been Secretary of the Protestant Society for the Protection of Religious Liberty since its foundation in 1811.

PART IV.

NATIONAL SOCIETY—GROUNDS FOR REGARDING THE EXCLUSIONARY ACTS AS SPURIOUS, AND ITS REPORTS AS PURPOSELY DECEPTIOUS.

§I. *Cause and Ground of Suspicion as to Authenticity.*

FOR the hope that the approbation bestowed upon the *exclusionary* system has not been general, the direct ground has just been seen. The circumstantial ground is of a very different cast. It involves in it the character of a whole society.—And what society?—A domineering, an overbearing society—self-designated, as if by a charter, by the imposing and exclusive name of *The National Society:*—a society, of which the whole bench of English *Bishops* form—what?—a part?— Yes, in appearance indeed but a part: but in effect, as will be seen, the whole.[1]

The ordinances by which all children, whose parents will not suffer them to be impregnated with the matter of the Church of England Liturgy, stand excluded from schools either founded or directed by this society, have been seen.[2]

Of the evidence now to be produced, the tendency is to shew—that of the whole business of this society the conduct has been throughout, and in particular in what concerns the above-explained *exclusionary* system, a tissue of *imposture:* of imposture, and if not of direct *forgery*, something extremely like it, and productive of the same effect: that, of the vast multitude of the members, of whom the society appears to be composed,—and whose minds are supposed to apply themselves, more or less to, and in general, as testified by their contributions, approve of, what is done,—commonly by no more than a minute number, perhaps, in all material instances, and in particular in all instances in which the *exclusionary system* is concerned, by not more than one for a constancy,—scarce ever by more than two, unless a dependent Secretary, if not a substitute to both, may be taken for a third,—what has been done has been either done or specifically approved.

Should this turn out to be the case, what follows?—That, by

---

[1] For the composition of the General Committee see p. 46 above.
[2] See pp. 88–98 above.

conniving at what is done for the purpose of the exclusion, without taking any publicly apparent part in it, the intolerant part of the Bishops and their adherents, being but too probably the major part, contrive in this way to enjoy the benefit of the wickedness, without standing exposed to the disgrace so justly due to it: while the minority,—feeling their inability to oppose the torrent with effect, and,—sensible that, of any appearance of dissension, in a body which has so little reputation to lose, a loss of more or less of that little might be but too natural a consequence,—keep their eyes and ears as fast shut as possible, and leave the whole matter to run on in its own course.

Far be it from this pen to convey any such imputation as shall stretch beyond the proof: and, therefore, it is that this first opportunity is embraced for declaring, that in what the reader will here see, is contained the whole of the ground in which the suspicions of spuriousness, as here stated, have their source. By particular inquiries to have sought for confirmation or disproof, besides danger of betraying the person of the author, would, so far as concerns confirmation, have been mere lost labour. For, what credence could have been expected for anecdotes without a name?

Under these circumstances, what in relation to this subject is here said, is said with the less reserve, because secure, if not against the reproach, at any rate against the guilt, of injustice. In the account given, in the name of the Society itself, of its own proceedings—in that document may be seen the ground, and the only ground, of those inferences, of the legitimacy of which the reader will be the judge. Out of their own mouths, and no others, will, if condemned, their condemnation come.[1]

Not even upon the supposition, that the suspicions here stated as conceived have been altogether erroneous,—for that to every thing that has been done the minds of the majority of the Society have, as far as in so numerous a Society could reasonably have been expected, been actually applied and consenting,—not even upon this supposition, will the evidence (the display here made) be without its fruit, any more than without its ground. The fruit will be—that of the business of the Society the conduct has been,—and, if it be still in the same hands,—still is—in altogether unfit hands: in hands by which, though, by the supposition, without the *guilt*, they themselves have been exposed—and with them the whole Society of which they are the instruments—to the reproach—nor that, howsoever erroneous, the unjust reproach—of impostors.

[1] An echo of Job 9: 20 and 15: 6.

CHURCH-OF-ENGLANDISM

§ II. *Marks of Authenticity, proper and usual, in Reports of Proceedings of Public Bodies.*

1. *Members concurring,* as evidenced by their signatures—2. Members *present*—3. Person or persons officiating as *Secretary* or Secretaries—4. *Place* of operation—5. *Time* of operation—Of the proceedings of public bodies in general, and of delegated bodies in particular—under every one of these heads it will be seen to be matter of undeniable use and advantage that entries should be made: and accordingly, under all or most of them, are entries commonly made. *Spuriousness* and *mismanagement*—in every instance, in the prevention of one or both these mischiefs will the use of the labour thus bestowed be found.

1. Members concurring, as evidenced by their signatures.—Why this head?—*Answer*. 1. That it may be seen, that the *operations* exhibited as performed, and the *instruments* exhibited as concurred in by the body, if a *delegated* body—or say a *Committee*—i.e. by the majority of the members present—had really for their sanction that concurrence. 2. That, by every member of the body at large—the principal body—it may be known, not only of what *number* of the members of the delegated body, but by what *individuals* of that body, whatsoever has been done was approved: that thus that *responsibility*, on the reality and efficiency of which depends the only security for good management, may, in both its stages, be exhibited: viz. the responsibility of the delegated body as towards the principal body; and the responsibility of the principal body itself—as towards the body of which it forms a part, and but a part—viz. the universal body of the community at large.

2. *Members present*—Why this head? *Answer*. 1. That it may be seen, that of the whole number of the members, by whom cognizance was taken of the business, the members concurring really formed the majority. 2. That, in case of dissent, it may be seen, not only *how many*, but *who*, were on the dissenting side: and thus authorities be not only *counted* but *weighed*.

3. *Member, or other person officiating as Secretary*. Why this head? *Answer*. In every political body some one person at least is required, in whose instance constant, or otherwise adequate, attendance may be looked for: looked for, viz. in respect of that continuity and uninterruptedness of attention, which is so necessary for the securing—not only the *regularity* and *consistency* of their proceedings, but the *authenticity* of the *operations* and *instruments*, represented as duly sanctioned, viz. by having received the necessary concurrence.

Another sort of person, whose signature may, on an occasion of this sort, naturally be looked for—and whose signature is accordingly, on such occasions very commonly attached—is *the Chairman.* But in this instance the necessity of such signature is not quite so constant and so urgent as in the other.—*Why?*—1. Because, if, at the meeting in question, of the delegated body in question, there be a person by whom the *Chair* is said to be taken—a person who is spoken of in the character of *Chairman* of the meeting,—as, for the sake of *good order* and *authenticity* there ought in every instance to be,—of this person if by the Secretary any minutes are taken, mention is naturally made in the *minutes:* and if, as above, so it be that to the several *operations* and *instruments* the signatures of the members concurring are attached, his signature will, of course, appear among the rest. 2. Because, unless in the case of a special regulation to the contrary, that which,—be the number of successive meetings ever so great,—may very well happen, is—that, in any proportion of that number, the person officiating in the character of *Chairman* may be each time a *different* one:—and the performance of a duty may much more certainly be depended upon, at the hands of a person certain constantly stationed for that purpose, than at the hands of every individual of an everchanging multitude.

4. *Place of Meeting.*—Why this head? *Answer.* That it may be seen that, in each instance, whether fixed or varying, the *place*, at which the meeting was held, was the place at which all such members, as were inclined to attend, could be apprised that it was to be held: otherwise, such as should be disposed to attend, might in any numbers be deprived of the opportunity, and, in a manner opposite to the wish and opinion of the *many*, the business be performed by the *few*, who were in the secret of the intended place.

5. *Time of meeting.*—Why this head? *Answer.* 1. For a reason, corresponding to that just mentioned under the head of *place:* viz. that it may be seen that every member, inclined to attend, had knowledge at what *time*, as well as what *place* to attend. 2. That no operation or instrument, to which no due sanction was really attached, may ever, by the secretary, or any other person, be stated as having actually been sanctioned.

If either of the place or of the day the mention be omitted,—much more if of both those necessarily concomitant circumstances all mention be omitted,—at the same time that all mention of any member or members, as having, on the occasion in question, been attendant, is omitted,—what is the consequence? That, by his own single act, with or without the instruction or suggestion of some irresistibly influential person behind the curtain, the secretary feels himself at liberty to manufacture what operation and instrument he pleases. That on no day, at any place where any such business, as is stated to have been done, could lawfully be done, it had ever happened to himself to be present,—thus much is what to every member cannot but be perfectly well known. But, that on some day or other, at some proper place or other, a competent number of other members may not have been present, and giving their concurrence to this same business,—this is what, unless by inquiry, and that inquiry produced by suspicion, seldom can it happen to any member to be apprized of.[a]

§ III. *Positions and Plan of Proof—Ends pursued by the Institution—Means employed.*

By a number of blanks observed in the dates, a suspicion was very soon produced, that all was not right: and, from a review thereupon made of the whole, the following conclusions seemed to follow: viz. 1. that, of the business represented by the Report as having been done by the persons to whom it is there ascribed, namely, the persons in whom the right of management is represented as being lodged, which persons are the two-and-fifty persons, half Bishops, half Laymen, and other Clergymen, of whom the managing body, styled *The General Committee*, is stated as composed,[1]—or, for this or that particular purpose, by Sub-Committees nominated by that General Committee,—no part of the business has ever been done, but what has been mere *matter of form:*—for that every thing which has been in any degree material, and in particular every thing by which the *exclusionary system* has been established, have been the work of a single person, with or without occasional consultation with another;—of one principal person, or of a secretary, acting under his orders: that, in a word, this most public business has been managed just in the way in which any business belonging exclusively to the person in question in his private capacity would have been conducted: viz. at one or other of his own residences, or at the residence of such his secretary as it might happen: the principal person, incidentally and accidentally talking the matter over with this or that confidential person, who is in the secret; but nothing in any way material being ever done in any such regular form, as that in

[a] As to *place* and *time* of meeting—if those circumstances respectively are *variable*, it is matter of necessity for information,—and even if they are *fixed* it may be matter of convenience for remembrance,—that previous *notices* should be given: and, by the avoiding to give such notice, the same frauds may be practised, as those which, when practised, may, by avoiding to make the requisite entries, be concealed. But the subject of *notices* belongs not to the present purpose.

---

[1] See p. 46 n. above.

which by every body it would of course be supposed to have been done.

By a plan of this sort, supposing it conceived and acted upon, a correspondent hue would necessarily be spread over the accounts given of the proceedings. In the few instances, and those insignificant, and purely formal, in which what was done was actually the work of the sort of body to which it is ascribed,—viz. either of the above-mentioned *General Committee*, or of any *particular* Committee, or of any person or persons regularly authorized by any such body,—the *day* and *place* of meeting, if it were a Committee, or the *persons*, if they were persons authorized by a Committee—the persons with the times of their respective acts—would be brought to view. On the other hand, in an instance in which what was done was not the work of any such body, or of any person regularly authorized as above, but the private work of a manager behind the curtain,—in any such instance no token of authentication would naturally be, because without a positive and glaring falsehood it could not be, held up to view.

On this supposition, the several instruments, which came to be brought to view, as having received the sanction of the Society, would naturally present themselves under one or other of two appearances:—1. when, for any purpose, it was deemed necessary, that the circumstance of *time should* be brought to view,—in this case a *time* would indeed be mentioned: but in expressions still indeterminate, such as those designative of the *year* and *month*, without the *day* of the month. But, in this case, by the supposition, no such business having, on any day of the month in question, really been done, either by the Society itself, or by any person regularly and openly appointed for that purpose—no day could safely be mentioned as the day on which that same business was done: 2. where it was *not* deemed necessary that the circumstance of *time* should in any way be brought to view,—in this case no expression designative of *time*, how loosely soever designative, would be hazarded.

Of these two courses, when on other accounts it seemed admissible, the latter was on one account manifestly the more commodious. On the subject of *time* suppose nothing said—nothing by which the attention would necessarily be drawn to the subject of time is uttered: whereas, in the only way in which on this supposition it is practicable, let the circumstance of time be mentioned, the danger is—that, by the singularity of the appearance exhibited,—which, on this supposition, consists of *blanks*, substituted in a case in which generally, not to say universally, *figures* are employed,—the attention of this or that reader may be drawn to the subject, and suspicion raised:—suspicions such as in fact have been raised, and are here, with the grounds of them, brought to view.

Of the transactions of this Society, at this time, viz. May, 1816, three Reports, and no more than three, have been published. Report I., date on the title-page, 1812: date of the earliest transactions recorded in it, 16th Oct. 1811; latest date discoverable in it, (p. 198) Aug. 5, 1812.[1] Report II., date on the title-page, 1814. Report III., date on the title-page, 1815. From the matter of these three Reports, and from no other source, have been drawn the inferences of which the following terms contain the expression, and of the justness of which the sincere reader will have to judge.

I. By the person or persons acting in the name of *The National Society*, the establishment of the *Exclusionary System*, as above explained, has from the first been designed to be carried into effect, and been carried into effect accordingly. For the quotations and observations, from which this inference has been deduced, short title—*Proofs of the System of Exclusion*.[2]

II. In the accounts all along published of their proceedings, a system of *imposition* has all along been carried on: of imposition, by which, when exposed, it will appear—that,—whereas, all that is material in the business has been carried on by a *single* person,—with or without occasional concert, but, at any rate, without any regular and regularly recorded co-operation with any other person or persons,—with the assistance of a secretary acting under his orders, or in his stead,—the representation, all along made, of the manner in which it has been carried on, has had for its object the inducing a general persuasion—that, in every act that has been done, a *number of persons*, in the character of members of one or more bodies, more or less numerous, under the names of *The General Committee* and its *Sub-Committees*, have participated. Short title—*Proofs of the System of Imposition*.[3]

III. *Proofs, shewing the actors—the principal actors—in the system of imposition.*

Of the proofs, brought to view under the above two heads, the effect will not, (it is believed) on an unprejudiced mind, be purely and simply the persuasion respectively expressed in the above terms. Indeed, had this been all, so much at least as concerns the exclusionary system would have been superfluous and useless: a design to that effect being no more than what, on a variety of occasions, will be

---

[1] The latest date in *First Annual Report of the National Society* is in fact 19 November 1812 at p. 39.
[2] See pp. 109–22 below.
[3] See pp. 123–53 below.

seen to have been not merely acknowledged, but studiously proclaimed. An ulterior effect will be—a conception of the extraordinary ardency of that zeal, with which, by the immoral means spoken of, under the second of the above two heads, this design appears to have been pursued.

From the ardency of this zeal,—coupled with the extraordinary nature of those same means,—and the notorious history of the whole business, in respect of the long continued neglect, with which the new system of instruction and the inventor were viewed, until the time when, without being confined to Church-of-Englandism, it had been employed in other hands with success in the joint advancement of intellectual instruction and the religion of Jesus,[1]—from all these considerations put together have been deduced two other inferences, the truth and justice of which are here submitted to the sincere reader in the terms following.

1. *Of the institution of this Society, the ultimate object has not been the advancement—either of intellectual instruction in general, or of the religion of Jesus.*

2. *Of this same institution the sole ultimate object has been—the preserving from reformation the abuses, with which the Church of England establishment is replete.*

In relation to neither of these two inferences will any separate documents or observations be, in this part of this Introduction, brought to view in the character of proofs.

Under the system, here styled *the system of imposition*,—the acts being all along ascribed (it will be seen) to sets of persons by whom they were not performed,—came of course the question—by whom then have they been performed? In answer to this question, lights will be afforded from the matter of the above mentioned Reports, elucidated by such observations as have seemed requisite.

III. Short title repeated—*Proofs, shewing the real actors in the system of imposition.*[2]

§IV.—I. *Proofs of the System of Exclusion.*

So openly and repeatedly avowed, and even so ostentatiously displayed, is the design there indicated,—that, but for the ardency of the exclusionary zeal so expressed, and the inferences, for which, as above, that ardency forms so strong and conspicuous a ground, it might have been waste of time and space, thus to bring the evidence of it to view.

It blazes forth in the very title-page, and at the very first sentence of

---

[1] For Bentham's account of the history of the monitorial system see pp. 88–92 above.
[2] See pp. 153–68 below.

that page.—*'First Annual Report of the National Society for promoting the Education of the Poor* IN THE PRINCIPLES OF THE ESTABLISHED CHURCH.'

Thereupon, after one unnumbered page, in which nothing is contained, but the words *'Account of the Proceeding for the formation of the National Society,'* comes another unnumbered page, (it stands the *fifth*) at the head of which stand these words, viz. *Education in the* PRINCIPLES *of the* ESTABLISHED CHURCH. Thrusting itself in immediately after the simple and characteristic title just now mentioned, this uncharacteristic phrase it is, that, like a Lottery-Office puff,[1] serves instead of a title to what follows.

Thereupon follow three paragraphs, which, all of them boiling and flaming with that same zeal, present an indubitable claim to a place under this head, and will accordingly be found, in the margin:[a] and,

[a] *National Society's Report I. Last date,* 5th August, 1812.[2]

That the NATIONAL RELIGION should be the foundation of NATIONAL EDUCATION, and should be the first and chief thing taught to the Poor, according to the *excellent Liturgy and Catechism* provided by our Church for that purpose, must be admitted *by all friends to the Establishment;* for *if the great body of the people*[3] *be educated in other principles than those of the Established Church,* the natural consequence must be to alienate the minds of the people from it, or render them indifferent to it, which may, in succeeding generations, prove *fatal to the Church,* and to the State itself.*[a]*

[a] {*State itself.*} For their object, howsoever covertly aimed at, this and the two next paragraphs have (it may be seen) the justification of the Exclusionary system.

In Part [III.][4] the objection[s], urged against that system by *Sir Thomas Bernard,* in the name of the *Poor-bettering* Society, have been seen already.[5] Three years, or thereabouts, had they stood full in the view of the penners and sanctioners of this Report. To these objections,—they being in their very nature unanswerable,—no answer is here, any more than elsewhere, so much as attempted. No notice is here taken of it.

Note well the principle, upon which this justification grounds itself.—It is—that if, at a time of life, at which it is not possible for the human mind to form any judgment at all on the subject of a system of religion, with the system of *history* it depends upon, and the system of *morality* which it includes,—nor consequently to entertain any real belief on such a subject,—the great body of the people have not been made to get by heart the formulary, containing the system in question of religion,—declaring at the same time, all along, that they do firmly believe it,—the Established Church, as established, will not be able to stand its ground:—in short, that it will fall:—and from thence the inference is—that the *State,* i.e. the *Constitution* of the State, will fall along with it.

Note, moreover, that, by this same course support equally effectual might be given

---

[1] Advertisements were routinely placed in the press by the appointed contractors in order to attract customers for the government lotteries.

[2] See *First Annual Report of the National Society,* pp. 5–7. For the latest date mentioned in this document see p. 108 n. above.

[3] *First Annual Report* 'Nation'.   [4] 1818 'II.' is a slip.

[5] See pp. 99–101 above.

INTRODUCTION. PART IV. §IV.

immediately after the sort of introduction so composed, comes thereupon the above promised '*Account*,'—the *Account*, such as it is, *of the proceedings*, by which the Society of invisibles will presently

It must indeed be admitted in this country of civil and religious liberty, that every man has a right to pursue the plan of education, that is best adapted to the religion which he himself professes. Whatever religious tenets therefore men of other persuasions may think proper to combine with the mechanism of the new system, whether tenets peculiar to themselves, or tenets of a more general nature, they are free to use the new system so combined, *without reproach or interruption*,[a] from the

---

to the religion of the *Church of Rome,*—to the religion of *Bramah*—or to the religion of *Mahomet*. That by this same course—supposing it to be, with relation to the end it aims at, an effectual one,—any system of religion, or no religion whatever—one as well as any other—might with equal success be forced into the minds of the rising generation—this the authors and sanctioners of this paragraph, whoever they are, cannot deny. That, *unless* this same course be taken, the Church they are thus labouring to support, will not be able to stand its ground—this they here declare themselves apprehensive of.

[a] {*Without reproach or interruption.*} *Without reproach,* viz. from such of the Members of the Establishment as do *not* reproach them, true:—but *not* without reproach from such as *do* reproach them: for example the present *Bishop of London:* by whom, from the pulpit his Clerical subordinates, and from the press all who read English, are informed—that all tenets different from those of the Church of England are *schism*, and that all schism is *guilt:* (Charge, p.1.)[1] and by whom the system of instruction in question is expressly referred to, in the character of an instrument, and that a most desirable one, for the applying of these principles to practice.—See below §9, and Appendix, No. I.[2]

Without interruption, yes. But why? Because they chose not to offer it? No: but because they durst not. Witness the Secretary of State, *Lord Viscount Sidmouth:*[3] who, with *Bill* in hand, offering to commence *his* course of interruption was, by the Bench of English Bishops, treated,—such, notwithstanding the willingness of the spirit, was the weakness of the flesh,[4]—treated as Jesus was by the Saint, of whom the Bishops of Rome are successors.[5]

As to *power*, the only interruption which it was in the power of these Church-of-

---

[1] See p. 48 n. above.   [2] See pp. 153–60 and 257–311 below respectively.

[3] Henry Addington (1757–1844), created Viscount Sidmouth in 1805, Speaker of the House of Commons 1789–1801, leader of the administration as First Lord of the Treasury and Chancellor of the Exchequer 1801–4, Lord President of the Council 1805, 1806–7, 1812, Lord Privy Seal 1806, Home Secretary 1812–22.   [4] Matthew 26: 41.

[5] Bentham is alluding to the rejection by the House of Lords, on the advice of Manners-Sutton, Archbishop of Canterbury, of the Protestant Dissenting Ministers Bill, which required all dissenting ministers to be licensed, and which had been introduced in the House of Lords by Sidmouth on 9 May 1811. When Sidmouth presented the Bill for its Second Reading on 17 May 1811, the debate was postponed to allow for consideration of the Bill throughout the country. When Sidmouth again presented the Bill for its Second Reading on 21 May 1811, some 500 petitions had been received objecting to the Bill, whereupon the Archbishop of Canterbury advised that it would be unwise to proceed, and the Bill was lost. See *Parliamentary Debates* (1811) xix. 1128–33, xx. 196–8, 233–55.

Bentham is comparing the House of Lords' rejection of Sidmouth's Bill to the denial of Christ by Peter, traditionally considered to be the founder and first Bishop of the Church of Rome. For Peter's denial see p. 20 n. above.

be seen to have been formed.—Date thereupon assigned to the first meeting, 16th Oct. 1811.

Next to the above-mentioned matter, and in the same page, (p. 6,)

members of the Establishment. On the other hand the *members of the Establishment* are not only warranted, but in duty bound to *preserve that system, as originally practised at Madras,*[a] in the form of a *Church of England Education.*

The *friends,* therefore, *of the Establishment* throughout the kingdom are earnestly requested to associate and co-operate, for the purpose of promoting the Education of the Poor in the *doctrine and discipline of the Established Church.*—It is hoped that such co-operation will not be wanting, when the object in view is *nothing less than the* preservation[b] of the National Religion, by ensuring to the great body of the people an education adapted to its principles.

Englandists to give to the new system of instruction, in so far as carried on upon a principle other than [the] exclusionary principle, they did give to it: viz. a competition set up against it, on the ground of that hostile principle. Not a finger did they stir in aid of it, till, upon the all-comprehensive principle it had been set on foot,—and with such formidable success established,—by Lancaster, and his supporters. Unless the taking of passages out of the Bible for lessons was an exclusion, the Lancasterian scheme put no exclusion upon Church-of-Englandists. These Church-of-Englandists, in this their course, have been all along not only anxious, but declaredly anxious, to put an exclusion upon all Non-Church-of-Englandists.— The contributions which otherwise would have been given for the support of a non-exclusionary system, they draw off to the support of this their exclusionary system. Thus, all the interruption, which it is possible for them to give, they do give.—And the enormous force of their influence considered, is it an inconsiderable one?

[a] {*Bound to preserve . . . as . . . at Madras.*} Destitute of all argument, in their endeavours to produce the effect of argument they are thus forced, or if they please '*bound,*' thus to steal in, as it were, in lieu of argument, insinuations thus obscure and irrelevant. They are *bound* (say they) amongst other things,—for this is what is meant, if any thing,—to teach this their Catechism. Why?—because it was taught at Madras.—What a reason!—But why was it taught at Madras? Why?—only because at Madras, i.e. in the eyes of the inventor of the new system,[1] there could not have been any so much as the faintest hope of temporal reward or encouragement in any shape, on any other condition than that of teaching this same Catechism. By the very nature of their Establishment,—without saying this, because altogether without need of saying any such thing,—they had thus set the law to Dr. Bell:—and now— such, for want of argument, is their distress—such thereupon their humility—it is *Dr. Bell,* that by his practice has set the law to them: viz. to the *Bench of Bishops.* Of the stone, which, for so long a course of years,—some thirteen or fourteen years to wit,[2]—these tardy and unworthy builders refused, thus glad are they at length to make the headstone of their corner.

[b] {*preservation.*} Thus explicity do they declare, that, in the exclusionary, and 'understanding-and-will-prostrating' system,[3] as above and hereinafter described, they behold an indispensable instrument, for the preservation of what they call *the National Religion:* viz. their own worldly and anti-Christian power, their own

---

[1] i.e. Andrew Bell.

[2] While the first school in England to adopt the Bell or Madras system of education was established in 1798, the National Society was not established until 1811, and its first school not opened until 1812.

[3] See p. 37 n. above.

INTRODUCTION. PART IV. §IV.

comes a string of numbered Resolutions, fourteen in number, stated as having been come to at two subsequent meetings, held at two specified days, by the same imaginary persons, in the same or some

> With a view of promoting such co-operation, and with the intent of laying the foundation of a Society, which shall extend its influence over the whole kingdom, a number of persons, *friends to the Establishment,*[a] at a meeting holden 16th October, 1811,
> His Grace the Archbishop of Canterbury in the Chair,——Resolved,

factitious dignities, their own overpaid places, their own useless places, and their own sinecures.

With such an immense mass of the matter of wealth, constantly, in the shape of the matter of corruption, applying itself to the minds of all persons, who, by their condition in life, are rendered susceptible of literary education,—applying itself to them in such manner, as to invite and urge them to throw off the yoke of the law of sincerity, and, by *subscription* and conformity, to place themselves in the track[1] of preferment;—with so enormous a mass of the matter of corruption, thus continually employing itself, not only in the fixing of adherents, but in the purchase of converts;—to what imaginable circumstance can we look for the source of the so much apprehended danger—the danger, from which the proposed remedy is designed to operate as a preservative?[2] To what imaginable circumstance, unless it be the real worthlessness of this perpetually self-styled *Excellence?*

If to any other circumstances, what can be the hypothesis, on which this notion of *danger* grounds itself? It must be—that a state of universal mental depravation, is the state—not only of all Non-Church-of-Englandists;—but in short of the great majority of the whole population of the country: that the propensity towards error is so strong and general, that the millions a year, which, after being levied by forced contributions, are employed in the preservation of the doctrine and discipline of the Church from destruction, will still be unavailing, but for the additional 20,000*l.* or 30,000*l.* a year, thus raised—with the additions thus endeavoured to be raised—by voluntary contributions:[3]—in a word, that—such is the system they are thus striving to uphold—no man would embrace it *gratis,* and upon conviction,—no man would ever embrace it [at] all, if he were not either paid for so doing, or living under the expectation of being paid for it. Thus, in the blindness of their zeal, do these men pass condemnation on themselves.

[a] *Add*—but who are afraid or ashamed to shew themselves to any body but themselves.

---

[1] 1818 'tract'. The text follows the 'Errata'.
[2] 1818 'preservation'. The text follows the 'Errata'.
[3] In 1810 the Governors of Queen Anne's Bounty set aside £20,000, taken from the grants of £100,000 made to them annually by Parliament for the eleven years 1809–16 and 1818–20, for the purpose of increasing the sum given to augment the livings of poor clergy from £200 to £300, where any person would contribute £200 or more in cash, lands, or tithes. For a report of the first payment see *Commons Sessional Papers* (1810) xiv. 99–100, and for an account of the annual Parliamentary grants see Christopher Hodgson, *An Account of the Augmentation of Small Livings, by 'The Governors of the Bounty of Queen Anne, for the augmentation of the maintenance of the Poor Clergy,' and of benefactions by corporate bodies and individuals, to the end of the year 1825; also the Charters, Rules, and Acts of Parliament, by which the proceedings of the Governors are regulated,* London, 1826, pp. 32–8. For Queen Anne's Bounty see also pp. 293 n., 518–25 below.

other concealed place, *the Bishop of London*[1] in the Chair.[2] Of these Resolutions the two first are—'1. *That the title of the Society now constituted, be* "THE NATIONAL SOCIETY FOR PROMOTING THE EDUCATION OF THE POOR, IN THE PRINCIPLES OF THE ESTABLISHED CHURCH, THROUGHOUT ENGLAND AND WALES." 2. That the sole object of this Society, (p. 7,) shall be to instruct and educate the Poor in suitable learning, works of industry, and the Principles of the Christian Religion, according to the Established Church.' Thus far the Resolution.

Now, in the matter therein manifested, what eye is there but theirs that does not behold and observe three perfectly distinct objects, whereof to some millions of eyes, two are not only opposite but irreconcilable, viz. *'education of the Poor in suitable learning,'* and ditto *'in the principles of the Established Church?'*—Thus there are three objects. But in these *three* objects the zeal of these anonymous and self-concealed persons—such is its blindness—could see but *one*. The sole object—*any* sole object—can it be any more than *one*? With respect to this *one* then can there be any doubt what it is? Can it be any thing but the educating the Poor *in the principles of the Established Church,*—that ultimately declared one sole real ultimate object, in the contemplation of which the two others, even at the very time of speaking of them, are so perfectly lost sight of? In their lips and on their papers, *'suitable learning,'* and *'works of industry:'*—in their hearts, *'Established Church,'* and nothing else.

After this account of the Genesis of the Society, follows, (p. 13) under the title 'REPORT of the GENERAL COMMITTEE,' an account of the earliest proceedings of the managing body by which that title was assumed. From this paper five several masses of exclusionary discourse will be brought to view: and in no one of all these instances is any evidence to be found of its having received the sanction of the governing body, antecedently described under the name of *The General Committee*. On the contrary, in every one of these instances, in support of the opposite position, there exists the sort of evidence,

---

That such a Society be now constituted, and that measures be taken for carrying the same into effect.

That for this purpose the ARCHBISHOP of CANTERBURY, for the time being, be President; and,

That a special Committee be appointed, and requested to meet to-morrow, and on Friday, to consider of Rules and Regulations for the construction and government of the Society, and to make their Report to a general meeting, which is to be holden on Monday next.[3]

---

[1] John Randolph.
[2] For the resolutions see *First Annual Report of the National Society*, pp. 6–8.
[3] i.e. 17, 18, and 21 October 1811 respectively.

INTRODUCTION. PART IV. §IV.

above-mentioned by the name of the *negative circumstantial evidence:* viz. absence of the ordinary and requisite marks of authenticity, as above described.[a]

---

[a] Report I. p. 16.—'In one particular quarter, viz. the Deanery of Tendering, in the County of Essex, a plan has been laid down for carrying the benefit[1] of the system into the several country Parishes, which is inserted in App. No. 5.[2] with the approbation of the Committee annexed; so published as an useful example to others. In the above Deanery, this plan is now carrying into effect with great spirit, and the execution of it is in great forwardness.'[a]

P. 18—'2. They look forwards for farther support from those who are *attached to the Constitution of Church and State; the sole object in view* being to communicate to the Poor, generally, by means[3] of a summary mode of education, lately brought into practice, such knowledge and habits as are sufficient to guide them through life, in their proper stations, especially to teach the doctrines of religion, *according to the principles of the Established Church,* and to train them to the performance of their Religious duties by early discipline.

3. It is unnecessary[b] for this Committee to enlarge upon the necessity of good instruction, and of the benefit which would accrue to Society, in proportion as its

---

[a] Of these proceedings further mention will occur presently. Particular indeed is the importance attached to them. No wonder.—No where else does the exclusionary zeal blaze out more fiercely. They had for their conductor—not indeed the present Bishop of London, but his immediate predecessor—the Church of England hero with whose eloquence his charge (anno 1814) (p. 1) opens:—the Bishop, in whose eyes *'schism'* was *'guilt,'* whose *'endeavour* was to replace ecclesiastical discipline on its antient footing'—that discipline of which the *'benefit'* is *'lost'* if *'the discretion of the ruling power'* be *'fettered.'*[4] This, however, is but a small part of what in that one paragraph may be seen breathing the same spirit. A more finished picture of a persecuting despot, held out in that very character, as an object of admiration and instruction, could scarce have been drawn by a French Court Catholic of the day, under the orders of the Duke and Duchess of Angoulême.[5]

[b] {*Unnecessary.*} Yes: and fruitless likewise. So long as they had their choice (what can be more notorious?) what they chose was—that the body of the people should have no instruction. So long as they had their choice, Dr. Bell and his system were, in their eyes, objects of scorn or indifference. When the system of *no-instruction* was seen to be no longer tenable, then came this system of *bad instruction,* the badness of

---

[1] *First Annual Report* 'benefits'.
[2] See *First Annual Report of the National Society,* Appendix V, pp. 49–54.
[3] *First Annual Report* 'by the means'.
[4] See [Howley], *Charge delivered to the Clergy of the Diocese of London,* p. 2, paying tribute to the work of John Randolph: 'His endeavour to replace ecclesiastical discipline on its ancient footing, to recover the rights and assert the legitimate authority of the Spiritual Governor, originated in the same views. For he had been taught by the records of antiquity no less than by the deductions of reason, that the prosperity of our institutions depends on attention to the spirit of their laws, and that the vigour of discipline is relaxed, and its benefit lost, by weakening the hands and fettering the discretion of the ruling power.'
[5] Louis Antoine de Bourbon, Duc d'Angoulême (1775–1844), and Marie Thérèse Charlotte, Duchesse d'Angoulême (1778–1851), known for their fierce loyalty to Louis XVIII (1755–1824), King of France from 1814. Bentham refers again to Louis XVIII, the Angoulêmes, and the piety of the French court at pp. 331–2 n. below.

6. As yet, for support of the exclusionary system nothing more has been seen than a series of general and theoretical *declarations*. The first exclusionary *act*, of which, in the proceeding inserted in this first Report, any trace is to be found, is an act, the mention of which comes

members are governed by a sense of Religious duty, and to the members themselves in respect both of their present happiness and eternal welfare. If this obtains at all times, more especially in the present, when, on the one hand, indifference to Religion, in the neglect of the regular performance of sacred duties, is but too

which is thus varnished by the word *good,* as that of its Church is by the word *excellent,* and that of Church 'pomps and vanities'[1] by the word *decency.*[2]

'*Necessity of good instruction!*'—*They* enlarge upon the *necessity* of it?—they, whose most strenuous endeavours have so openly been employed, in excluding from the benefit of it all children, whose parents will not purchase it on the terms of forcing them to put from them what they think good, and embrace what they think evil? In one and the same breath, the necessity of granting it and the necessity of refusing it:—this is what they *preach:*—to hundreds of thousands they accordingly do refuse it:—this is what they *practise.*

Note, that in any such character as that of the ultimate object of the system of instruction, throughout the whole course of these effusions, scarcely is morality, scarcely is even Christianity, so much as professed to be held up to view: scarcely any thing whatever but the support so much needed by the Church of England. With the exception of that *decency,* which is composed of the so solemnly renounced[3] '*pomps and vanities,*' to such a degree has worldly anxiety got the ascendant even over DECENCY—scarcely in any other character is Christianity so much as professed to be regarded, than that of a state engine:—an engine, employed in the manufactory of the matter of corruption, for a cement to the *Warburton Alliance* between *Church* and *State:*[4] a cement for the wall of defence, built up for the protection of the whole stock of over-paid places, needless places, mischievous places, and sinecure places, sacred and profane.

Indeed, with what face, or prospect of success, could either morality or Christianity have been mentioned,—mentioned as main and ultimate objects of the instruction,—when, in both instances, in the same breath, that same instruction is so anxiously withholden from all those who will not accept of Church-of-Englandism, in lieu of both those benefits?

Be moral men—i.e. on condition of your being, '*in understanding and will, prostrate*'[5] under us:—not otherwise.

Be Christians—i.e. on condition of your being, '*in understanding and will, prostrate before our interpretations of Christianity:*' otherwise, be as un-Christian as you will—what care we?—Such are the conditions, which will be seen constantly intended, and almost as constantly expressed, when, by these holy men, either morality or Christianity are spoken of as qualities desirable on the part of the people.

---

[1] See p. 50 n. above. [2] See p. 86 n. above.
[3] 1818 'announced'. The text follows the 'Errata'.
[4] William Warburton (1698–1779), Bishop of Gloucester from 1760, was author of *The Alliance between Church and State, Or, the Necessity and Equity of an Established Religion and a Test-Law Demonstrated, From the Essence and End of Civil Society, upon the fundamental Principles of the Law of Nature and Nations,* London, 1736, regarded as the classic statement of the relationship between the Church of England and the British state.
[5] See p. 37 n. above.

INTRODUCTION. PART IV. §IV.

in towards the close, viz. in p. 17: and of this the exclusionary nature is as yet disguised, not being visible to any eyes, but such, if any, by which a search shall have been made for it in the Appendix. In the body of the Report, all you see is *a donation:*—a donation—made to a apparent, and, on the other, men's *minds are distracted by an infinite variety of opinions,*[a] studiously propagated by their respective advocates.

P. 19.—'If the plan, of which they have now detailed the progress for a few months, be cordially supported and encouraged *by those who are friends to the Communion of the Church*, they have good reason to hope, that it will accomplish a considerable improvement in the condition, and in the moral and religious habits of the poorer branches of the Community, and give a new character to Society at large.

---

[a] {*Minds—distracted by an infinite variety of opinions.*} As if, in all ages of Christianity, from the earliest down to the present, this '*distraction,*' as it is called, had not had place:—as if, so far from being prejudicial, this *variety*, except in so far as it is productive of hostility or oppression, were not even conducive—in an eminent degree conducive—to true morality and happiness. Differing one from another in respect of such their opinions, each strives to prove against his competitors the truth of his opinions by the goodness of his practice.

In England, the morality of the Established Clergy—will any one of them dare to bring it into comparison with that of the Sectarian Clergy, of any of the sects? Among the Established Clergy, is not attention to professional duties—any thing like constant and zealous attention—a rare case?—Among the Sectarian Clergy, inattention, an unexampled one?—Why? because, for respect, for affection, even for subsistence, the Sectarian Clergy—what have they to trust to but their good behaviour?—while to the Established Clergy, good behaviour is comparatively of no use. Yes:—what they have to trust to is what they do trust in:—their riches,[1] their factitious dignities, their temporal power: to secure to them respect—respect without desert, and independently of good behaviour—such was and *is* the *object*—such, unhappily, in too great a degree, is still the *effect*,—of those ill-placed powers—of those factitious dignities, and of the enormous masses of the matter of wealth, added for the support of those same ill-placed dignities.

Under these circumstances, what matters it how great the variety of opinions is? Of these opinions, what are the subjects?—Matters which, for the most part, not only none of them understand, but for the understanding of which, were they capable of it, none of them would, any more than any body else, be any thing the better. The times when this variety was at its *minimum*, what were they? Precisely the times—say from the 8th or 9th to the 12th or 13th centuries—when Church power, and with it ignorance and immorality, were at their *maximum*. Such is the state of minds—such the universal '*prostration of understanding and will*'—such the *uniformity*, to the production of which this their system of instruction is thus avowedly directed.

On the field of theology is variety—variety of opinions—a spectacle so unendurable to them?—Let them go to *Spain:* there they will find none of it: there they may behold uniformity—perfect uniformity—with all its blessings: there they may reconcile themselves to that original and venerable Church, from which their own is but a schism: a schism not to be justified but on those principles—yes, on those very principles—which, when appealed to in favour of any but themselves, are the objects of their abhorrence.

---

[1] Mark 10: 24.

Benefit Society of Schoolmasters, and without any *condition* that in this place is so much as hinted at.[1] Turn to the article in the Appendix, (it stands in p. 66, is numbered No. XI. and forms the last number,) what

P. 26. No. II. of Appendix. *(Address to the Public.)*[a]—Under these circumstances the Committee is persuaded, that, in calling for a more general and extended support of an institution, in which *the best interests of the Established Religion and Constitution of the Country* are so deeply involved, they shall not appeal in vain to the friends of both.

P. 49. *(No. V. of Appendix.)*—THE GENERAL COMMITTEE of the NATIONAL SOCIETY[b] consider that the most ready and satisfactory answer they can give to the numerous inquiries transmitted to them, from various parts of the Kingdom, as to the best and most effectual method of carrying into execution the great and important designs of the Society, will be by offering to such as seek for this information a practical illustration of the system. With this view, they have selected, from among the many Reports, communicated to them from local Societies already formed, or now forming, the proceedings of the DEANERY of TENDERING, in the County of Essex, and Diocese of London, which appear, on the whole, *the best adapted for general imitation,* and which, if extensively adopted, with the laudable exertion and judicious regard to co-operation, as hath been manifested both by the clergy and laity in that district, cannot fail, under the blessing of Divine Providence, to diffuse the inestimable benefits of moral and religious Education among the lower orders of Society throughout the kingdom, by a method at once easy in its operation and certain in its effects.

With this view the Committee are desirous to call the attention of the parochial clergy at large to these Resolutions, not only as affording an example of the valuable benefits that must result from such combined efforts in a work alike important to all, but with a further design to promote that uniformity of System, which is one of the fundamental objects of the National Society.

P. 50 continued.

NATIONAL SOCIETY.
'His Royal Highness the Prince-Regent, Patron.[2]

DISTRICT SOCIETY at COLCHESTER.
The Right Honourable and Right Reverend the Lord Bishop of London, Patron.

{Note well the two patrons. Thus to the Empire of Japan (it is said) there are two Emperors—a Temporal and a Spiritual one.}[3]

Deanery of Tendering.
'At a meeting of the CLERGY only of the said Deanery, held at Thorpe, on Monday,

---

[a] 29th January, 1812.
[b] No place, no time, no signature.

[1] According to the *First Annual Report of the National Society,* p. 17, the National Society had made a donation of £50, and granted an annual subscription of £10 10s., to the Society of Schoolmasters, who had undertaken to form themselves into a Benefit Society, and adopt the Madras system of education.
[2] i.e. George (1762–1830), Prince of Wales, Prince Regent from 1811, and as George IV, King of Great Britain and Ireland from 1820.
[3] See Kaempfer, *The History of Japan,* i. 149, for the several titles given to Japanese hereditary emperors, and i. 182, where the first secular Emperor is referred to as *Seogun.*

INTRODUCTION. PART IV. §IV.

you see to a certainty (for so in express terms it is declared) is— *'These Schoolmasters must belong to the Established Church.'*[1] what you see to little less than a certainty is—that it was at the suggestion and instance of the concealed doers of the great Society, that this little

the 2d day of March, 1812, to consider of the best means of carrying into effect the objects of the above Society in the said Deanery,

'Present *(nearly every officiating Clergyman in the Deanery,* three of whom were members of the Special Committee for the said Deanery.)

'.... The following Resolutions were proposed to the meeting, and unanimously agreed to:

'1st. That this meeting, convinced of the urgent necessity, in these times, of some system of general education *in the principles of the Established Church,* have observed with a lively interest the formation of a National Society with that view, and approve highly of the *enlarged and comprehensive scale* on which it is formed.'

P. 52—'In consequence of the above Resolutions, a general and numerous Meeting of the Clergy and also of the Laity of the Deanery, was subsequently held at the same place, March 16th, when, after *the principles on which the National Society* is founded had been stated fully to this meeting, its objects particularly pointed out, and the resolutions, by which it is constituted, as well as the regulations by which it is to be conducted, read,—

'IT WAS UNANIMOUSLY RESOLVED, 1st. That such a Society, is, from the complexion of the times and the[2] circumstances of the poor, become particularly necessary in these kingdoms, as calculated to propagate and maintain the *scriptural doctrines and sound religion of our Reformed Church* amongst the now uninstructed part of the community, to inculcate early habits of piety, decency, sobriety, and virtue, upon the rising generation, and thus to promote, in profession and practice, pure and unadulterated Christianity.'—{Pure and unadulterated Christianity!}

'3d. That in conformity to a Resolution of the said District Society, of the 8th January last, this meeting do now proceed to the nomination of a Sub-Committee for this Deanery, to co-operate and communicate with the General Committee at Colchester, on the points stated in the said Resolution.

'4th. That such Sub-Committee shall consist of *all the Clergy* within the Deanery, and of *two of the Laity,* or, where *necessary,* a greater number, of each parish.

P. 53—9th. 'That in whatever way the said subscriptions may be applied, particular care shall be taken that *all the children* reaping the benefit of this most charitable Institution, *shall without exception,* be *instructed in the excellent Liturgy and Catechism of the Church of England,* shall constantly attend Divine Service in their Parish Church, or in some Chapel *under the Establishment,* on the Lord's Day, unless such reason for their non-attendance be given as shall be *satisfactory to the parochial Members of the Sub-Committee.*

'(Signed by the Chairman.)'

---

[1] See *First Annual Report of the National Society,* Appendix XI, p. 66: 'The object of the Society of Schoolmasters is to afford relief to their superannuated Members, and to assist the Widows of Members deceased. These Schoolmasters must belong to the established Church, and practice the Madras System of Education. A Donation of £10., or an annual Subscription of £1. 1s., constitutes an honorary Member of the Society. The other Members subscribe 10s. 6d. quarterly, for the accumulation of a fund, out of which the object of the Society is to be accomplished. No Schoolmaster can be admitted a member after the age of 50, or receive any benefit from the fund till he has been two years in the Society.'

[2] *First Annual Report* 'and from the'.

Society was formed,—that the prospect, of the advantage afforded to the exclusionary system, by loading the donation with this exclusionary condition, was the motive for this suggestion,—and that the donation was the purchase-money paid for that advantage.

Mark here the progress of the exclusionary system: with the intolerance, and the corruption, by which it is characterized. In the infancy of the Society, before it had learnt to feel its strength, conformity on the part of Schoolmasters being to be secured by any means, bribery was the instrument employed: and on that occasion, in the body of the Report,—being that part, which, unless with some particular view, is all of it that any body reads,—this instrument, it may have been seen as above, was kept compleatly out of sight. Free and unconditional was the liberality then and there displayed. This then was what was designed for the eyes of readers at large. But, to the Schoolmasters, at whose hands, compliance with the terms of the donation was to be obtained—it was necessary that those terms should be made visible: accordingly, after notice given to persons of this description in[1] the *Table of Contents*, that in the Appendix they will find something that will interest them, in the Appendix accordingly, the benefit held out to them is displayed, but with terms fastened on it.[2]

Further than this, in the first year of the Society's age, it was not thought advisable to go: and, at that early stage, even this was kept hidden from as many eyes as, consistently with its purpose, it could be hidden from.

But, in the interval between the penning of the first and that of the second Report, success, as will be seen in so many other instances besides this, had given birth to boldness. Accordingly, in Report II. and not before, comes out the exclusionary regulation, (above brought to view in Part II. of this Introduction)[3] by which, payment to *Conformists* for coming in not being sufficient, *Nonconformists* are inexorably shut out.

When the *principles* are disseminated, the trumpet is blown in Sion,[4]—because it is by this trumpeting that men's passions are to be

---

[1] 1818 'on'. The text follows the 'Errata'.

[2] The Table of Contents at *First Annual Report of the National Society*, p. 22, lists the following item: 'Extract from the Statement of the Society of Schoolmasters'.

[3] See p. 97 above.

[4] See Joel 2: 15: 'Blow the trumpet in Zion, sanctify a fast, call a solemn assembly'. According to *First Annual Report of the National Society*, p. 17, and *Second Annual Report of the National Society*, p. 17, the Society held its first and second annual meetings at Sion College, London. The College was established by Royal Charter in 1630 following a bequest of £3,000 made by Thomas White (*c.* 1550–1624), Vicar of St Dunstan-in-the-West, Fleet Street, in order to endow a college where the London clergy could meet and 'maintain love in conversing together'.

INTRODUCTION. PART IV. §IV.

exerted, and prepared, as effectually as may be, for the endurance of the acts—these immoral and anti-christian acts—without which such principles could not have been carried into effect. When of the *acts* themselves the necessity comes of making the disclosure, the greater the number of eyes from which they could still be kept hidden, the less copious (it was seen) would be the torrent of that reproach, which is so justly due to the system to which those acts was to give effect.

Of the measure,—the mention of which, but in its purified state, as just explained, is slid in at so early a part of the Report,—slight is the importance, in comparison of the importance of those other measures, the reference to which, obscured to such a degree, as to disclose nothing of their nature, may be seen reserved for the very last paragraph (p. 19.) of this same Report. The Rules of the Society, and *terms of Union* (it is there said) 'are before the public in the papers now published, as examples of the mode in which they wish the plan to be carried into effect.'—*Rules of the Society?*—Good:—but what rules?—where are they to be found?—No reference. No where in the Appendix is any No. to be found, having for its title any such phrase, or for its contents any such Contents.—*Terms of Union?*—good: but these too where are they to be found? Again no reference. Search, however, (which without special motives adequate to the trouble you will not do)—search, however, into the Appendix, and there indeed, p. 27, No. III. you will find a paper having the words *Plan of Union* for its title. And here, but too truly, in the last of its eight unnumbered articles will you find, introduced as it is by an exclusionary preamble, the first of these two exclusionary acts, which in Part II. of this Introduction, it was found necessary to present to view.[1]

By whom sanctioned? at what meeting? who concurring? who present? held at what time, or what place?—all these particulars remain buried in darkness. But the system of imposition, of which this darkness is one of the proofs, belongs not to the present, but to the next succeeding head.

With this first Report stops for some time, the torrent of exclusionary eloquence. The system, in the support of which it was employed, had passed unquestioned:—it had produced its fruits: those fruits had, as we see, been ripened into *acts*.

In Report II. nothing at all in this strain, or nothing worth noticing, has been found. But in Report II. that same exclusionary rule may be seen reprinted:—reprinted, with no other amendment than the addition of a fragment of a date, which, ere long, there will be

---
[1] See pp. 96–7 above.

occasion to bring to view:[1] reprinted in that same Report II. in which the design of it may be seen consummated by that other act (the one regarding *Masters*,) which in Part II. of this Introduction follows it.[2]

In Report III. however, three additional masses of exclusionary doctrine may be seen presenting themselves.—Results prosperous, hopes realized;—in the fulness of the heart, the mouth and the pen now speak.

The acts by which the doctrine is applied to practice are also of course persevered in. Witness those same two exclusionary acts, reprinted from Report II. word for word.[3]

National Society's Third Annual Report for 1815, p. 19.

'The schools now conducted under the Society's auspices, and according to the doctrine and discipline of the Established Church, which were stated in the last Report to be 230, now amount to 360; and the number of Children comprised in them, which was last year computed at upwards of 40,000, is now 60,000.'

P. 21. 'Sheffield, Leicester, Halifax . . . . Scarcely any of our large manufacturing towns can be named, in which the objects of gratuitous education are more[4] numerous than the three above specified, or more beyond the means of that part of the Inhabitants who take a lively interest in the education of the poor, and who feel it their duty to combine Religious Instruction with useful learning, and to dispense the former according to the Liturgy and Catechism of the Church of England.'

P. 29. 'Of the debt of gratitude due to Dr. Bell, for devising and bringing to maturity a method of general education, which has enabled the Governors of the Church to execute what our Reformers projected—the giving to the whole population of the Realm, a competent measure of useful learning, seasoned with religious instruction in the principles of our National Faith—the Committee feel that it is quite out of date for them to offer any *computation.*'

A good fat Bishoprick;—or,—if the elements of Church-of-England Episcopal decency, such as nobility of descent, relationship to nobility, &c. are judged deficient in Dr. Bell,—a snug Deanery;—would be better worth than any such '*computation*' or any other such barren panegyric. But, to attach to merit in any shape any such privileged rewards, would be setting a dangerous precedent, and encouraging that spirit of *innovation*, of which Atheism and Jacobinism are the sure ultimate results.

---

[1] See p. 134 below. [2] See p. 97 above.
[3] 'Plan of Union', *Second Annual Report of the National Society*, Appendix IV, pp. 186–7, was reprinted in *Third Annual Report of the National Society*, Appendix III, pp. 166–7, while 'Form of Certificate for Masters', *Second Annual Report of the National Society*, Appendix IX, p. 197, was reprinted in *Third Annual Report of the National Society*, Appendix VII, p. 176.
[4] *Third Annual Report* 'are probably more'.

INTRODUCTION. PART IV. §V.

§ [V.] II. *Proofs of the System of imposition*—[I.][1]*General Committee, Meetings none.*

Misrepresentation—deception—purposed misrepresentation—studied misrepresentation—imposition—imposture—by whichsoever of all these names on this or that occasion it may happen to be called, the nature of it will not be varied—the system will be still the same.

1. Meetings of the General Committee—their existence. 2. Sub-Committees—their existence and meetings. [3.][2] Acts represented as acts of the General Committee, or of a Sub-Committee—their genuineness. Such are the distinguishable subjects, of the examination, from which the suspicion of imposition has received its confirmation.

I. As to the Meetings of the General Committee—their existence.—Matter of fact as *represented* in the Reports,—Meetings of their body held on such and such particular days, and such and such business done by it. *Real* matter of fact as suspected and inferred,—no such Meetings held.

II. Existence and Meetings of Sub-Committees.—Matter of fact as *represented* in these same Reports, these Sub-Committees severally formed, and, on such and such days,—Meetings of the Members in competent number duly held, and such and such business done by them. *Real* matter of fact as suspected and inferred,—no such Sub-Committees formed; or, if formed, no such Meetings held by them.

III. Sanctionment given to acts represented as being acts of the *General Committee*, or acts of this or that *Sub-Committee*, or of both.—Matter of fact, as *represented* in these Reports, appropriate sanctionment given to each of these sorts of acts respectively: *real* matter of fact as suspected and inferred,—in the instance of these several acts, with few or no exceptions, no such sanctionment ever given.

I. First then as to the *existence* of Meetings on the part of the General Committee.

Of the birth of this public body, in and by Report I. p. 13, and the account antecedently given (as hath been seen)[3] of the preparatory proceedings,—October 21, 1811, is stated as the day. To the first meeting, held by the body so constituted, certain acts are (Report I. p. 14,) ascribed: but, to the meeting itself, neither will *place*, nor *day*, nor *month*, on that or any other occasion, be found assigned. On that same occasion, viz. in p. 13 of that same first Report, and in the very

---

[1] 1818 '2'.
[2] According to the 'Errata', '2' should be inserted here, but this is plainly a slip for '3'.
[3] See p. 113–14 n. above.

first paragraph, in speaking of the General Committee, after saying to whom the management of its (the Society's) affairs was 'by the Constitution intrusted,' (it has already been seen what constitution) what is said of it is in these words—'*who have held weekly meetings for that purpose: the Committee consisting of*'—and thereupon come the names or descriptions of the Members.

Now, of this statement what can have been the object, unless it be the producing of this conception—viz. that, in general at least, and bating special exceptions, meetings of the Members of this Committee had place from first to last once a week, and that at those weekly meetings it was that every thing, which thereafter comes to be stated as having been done, was ultimately done. Such is the conception, which, to all appearance, it was the intention to produce. Now, to judge from the Report itself, how stands the fact? *Answer*—No such weekly meetings were ever held. From whence this inference? *Answer*—From these circumstances.—To the supposed meeting thus spoken of, neither of *place*, nor of *time*, nor of *members concurring*, nor of members *present*, is any assignment to be found: whereas of such meetings mentioned in this Report as appear to have been really held, both *time* and *place* have been mentioned:— mentioned, and with that degree of particularity, which is sufficient for the purposes of indication, and which accordingly, in Reports of the proceedings of public bodies, is customarily exemplified.

On the other hand, true it is that,—immediately after the enumeration made as above, of the members of the General Committee,—in this same Report (Rep. I. p. 14,) mention may be seen made of certain acts—certain specific acts—in the character of acts performed by that same Committee. 'The Committee (it is said) at its first meeting elected the Rev. T.T. Walmsley, Secretary, and J. Watson, Esq. Treasurer,[1] (for the regular management of [which offices][2] Rules and Regulations were afterwards made,) and appointed a Sub-Committee, to take measures for establishing a Central School in the Metropolis:'—and at bottom the Note referred to by the * is—See App. No. 8.[3]

Under these circumstances, what, as far as appears, was the truth of the case?—*Answer*—That, of no such body as the fifty-two persons of whom the General Committee is there stated as having been composed,[4]—and who, in their quality of Members of it, had, each of

---

[1] Joshua Watson (1771–1855), wine merchant and philanthropist, Treasurer of the National Society 1811–42.

[2] 1818 'which, other'. The text follows *First Annual Report*.

[3] i.e. 'Duties of the Treasurer and Secretary', *First Annual Report of the National Society*, Appendix VIII, pp. 60–1.

[4] For the composition of the General Committee see p. 46 n. above.

them, at any meeting held of their body, the right of being present,—nor of any considerable number of that body, (summonses given or not given,) was any such General Meeting held: but that, at the residence of some particular individual,—he being, indeed, one member of that body,—with or without the concurrence of some one other member, or some other such small numbers of Members, not sufficient to constitute a regular meeting of that body,—were those acts really passed, which, as above, are there *stated* as having passed.

So much as to this *first* meeting. And, from the fictitiousness of this *first* meeting, results the equally probable fictitiousness of several *other* meetings, the times of which are no otherwise designated, than by reference to the time of this *first*.

These supposed fictitious meetings are those which are represented as having been held between the time of the above *dateless* meeting, and June 3, 1812.[1] Of these the one first mentioned, is one which, in Report I. p. 14, 15, may be seen mentioned by the name of *'the next meeting.' Place, time, members present*, none.—Divers *acts* or things are not the less represented as having been done at this same meeting.—These are—1. Resolution concerning the use of the intended Central School; 2. Ditto, concerning the use to be made of existing Schools for the training of Masters. 3. Renewal and instruction of a therein above mentioned Committee, afterwards designated by the name of the *Committee for Building*, or *Building Committee*. 4. Measures taken for spreading the system, by a recommendation to form trustees, &c.

From this second or *'next* Meeting,'—which, it should seem, was never held,—from this it is that another anonymous meeting takes its date: for it is *'soon after'* the abovementioned *next* (p. 15.) that this other performs its acts. These are, 1. Appointment of a *'Committee of Correspondence.'* 2. Publication of 'an *Address to the Public*,' for which reference is made to App. No. 2.[2]

To this probably imaginary meeting, which immediately succeeded that which was next to the first, succeeded *another*, in which, under the name of *a Plan of Union*, certain Resolutions were passed, for which, reference is there made to App. No. 3.[3] It is the same string of Resolutions, as that, the eighth and last of which has, in Part II. of this Introduction, been brought to view by the name

---

[1] i.e. the date of the National Society's first annual meeting: see *First Annual Report of the National Society*, p. 17.
[2] 'Address to the Publick, 29*th January*, 1812', *First Annual Report of the National Society*, Appendix II, pp. 25–6.
[3] 'Plan of Union', *First Annual Report of the National Society*, Appendix III, pp. 27–8.

of *Exclusionary act the first*.[1] Of this supposed imaginary meeting, the time, supposing it real, must have been subsequent to, and therefore distinct from, that at which, as above, the Sub-Committee, styled a *Committee of Correspondence*, was appointed: since it is upon the Report made by that same Sub-Committee, that the meeting in question is stated as doing what is ascribed to it.

The first meeting, to which any place is assigned, is one which is stated (Report, p. 17,) as having had place at *Sion College*. To this meeting is assigned not only a *month*, viz. June, and a *day* of that month, viz. the 3d. but a day of the week, viz. *Wednesday*. To an addition thus superfluous, mention of the *year* might have been a not unuseful substitute. No such mention is made. But by ratiocination it may be sufficiently ascertained, that the year meant must have been 1812. Not till October, 1811, did the Institution receive its existence. And, at this same Sion College, in the year 1813, will be seen, held in the same month, a meeting which is plainly not *this* but a different one.[2] Remains therefore for the year of *this* meeting, the year 1812.

Such, as if the year sought had been the year of the first Olympiad, is the demand for criticism. Such is the ingenuity, with which the history of this self-closed conclave of Church-of-England Cardinals has been wrapt in clouds.

At this 'annual meeting of the Society,' (for such it is styled) five distinguishable acts are represented as having had place:—1. Receipt of a 'Report made of the proceedings,' (viz. the intermediate proceedings) 'of the Committee,' (the General Committee)—viz. the above, and God knows what other proceedings, in which it seems probable that no such Committee was ever suffered to take part. 2. Receipt of 'a statement of the account for the year,' (meaning the fraction of the year from 11th October, 1811, to this 3d June, 1812). 3. Election of four Members, in the room of four retiring Members. 4. Election of an Auditor in the room of one who had become a Member of the Committee. 5. 'Determination' taken 'that the vacancies happening in the course of the year should be reckoned among the resignations.'[3]

So much, for the present, as to Report I. Proceed we now to Report II.

The first day in this Report, mentioned as a day on which a meeting styled *a General Meeting* was held, is 2d June, 1813: on which day, as above, the *place* mentioned as the *place of meeting* is *Sion College*. This is in Report II. p. 17: and it is here for the first time that any

---

[1] See pp. 96–7 above.

[2] The second annual meeting of the National Society was held at Sion College on 2 June 1813: see *Second Annual Report of the National Society*, p. 17.

[3] See *First Annual Report of the National Society*, p. 17.

INTRODUCTION. PART IV. §V.

specific tokens of a real meeting make their appearance. Not that any such thing as a list, purporting to be a list of *Members present*, is to be found in it. But *three* persons by name, are mentioned as making *motions* there: a circumstance by which it is rendered *probable*,—though it might be too much to say *certain*,—that, at that same *time, there* they, all of them, actually were. Of these, those whose names may, in a paper prefixed to this second Report, be seen standing upon the list, intituled 'List of the Committee and Officers of the National Society,' are—1. *President, the Archbishop of Canterbury,* and 2. *the Earl of Shaftesbury, V. P.*[1] Of these same motion-makers, the third, and only other, is *Earl Nelson,*[2] whose name is *not* upon that same list.

To judge from this same Report, it may even be matter of some doubt, whether on this grand and prepared occasion,—at this *'general'* annual meeting of the Society' at large,—these three illustrious persons gave themselves the satisfaction of beholding, any one of them, any comrades besides the two others. Of not so much[3] as a single person,—over and above the number, without which that could have been done which is stated as being done,—are any tokens to be found. To seven persons, or sets of persons, by that same number of different *Resolutions, thanks* are ordered, on the motion of *the 'President.'* Thus all that, in the way of thanksgiving, could be done by the President, it is by the President that it is done.— By him, by whom so many thanks were given, it had been hard if no thanks had been received. But the President could not move thanks to the President. For the execution of this important office, provision is accordingly made of *The Earl of Shaftesbury.*—Similar to the demand for thanks,—which had thus produced itself, and thus received its supply, in the instance of the President,—was a correspondent demand in the instance of the *General Committee*. In the persons of the pair of illustrious Members just named,—in these, and, for aught appears, in no others,—was embodied at this time the said General Committee. But the modesty of these two illustrious persons would not suffer either of them to move thanks for the joint use of himself and the other: for the supply of this demand for thanks, their prudence had accordingly made provision of *Earl Nelson;* whose name, illustrious as it is,[4] does not display itself upon the list of the 52

---

[1] Cropley Ashley-Cooper (1768–1851), sixth Earl of Shaftesbury, was a Vice-President and founding member of the National Society.

[2] William Nelson (1757–1835), created Earl Nelson in 1805, Rector of Hilborough, Norfolk 1797–1806?, and Canon of Canterbury 1803–35.

[3] 1818 'Of so much'. The text follows the 'Errata'.

[4] Nelson was the older brother of Horatio Nelson (1758–1805), Viscount Nelson, famous Admiral and victor of the Battle of Trafalgar (1805).

Members, of whom the General Committee is stated as being at that time composed.[a]

Of the suspicion,—that the Meeting, stated in Report I. as being held in June 1812 at Sion College, being the first of the Meetings stated as being held at that place, was—if any such Meeting really had place—a private one,—present only the few that were in the secret,—a confirmation may, as it should seem, be afforded, by a comparison of the terms by which the Meeting of 1812 is designated, viz. in Report I.;—compared with the terms in which the Meeting of 1813 is designated, viz. in Report II. In Report II. the Meeting there mentioned as held at Sion College in June 1813, is styled the *'General Annual Meeting'* of the Society. Yet,—though at that same place a meeting, styled the Annual Meeting of the Society, had in Report I. been stated as held in 1812,—this of 1813 is not styled *the second.* On the other hand, the Meeting stated in Report I. as held in 1812—this Meeting, though there styled the *'Annual Meeting'* of the Society, is *not* there styled the *general* annual meeting, nor is the word *general* at all applied to it. By the name of *The first of the intended General Annual Meetings of the Society at large*—by this, or by some equivalent name, would not this meeting have been designated,—if it had been what the second annual meeting, held at that same place, seems to have been intended to be passed upon the public for?—That is to say, not a *close* meeting,—such as those of the governing body, the General Committee, avowedly are,—but an *open* meeting, into which all persons, being members of the Society at large, should find entrance: in other words, 'all Subscribers of not less than one guinea annually, or Benefactors to the amount of ten guineas:' all these being persons, who, by the 10th of the fourteen Resolutions reported in Report I. p. 8, as come to at a meeting preliminary to the formation of the Society, are declared to be 'qualified to attend such meeting:' viz. per 'Resolution 8, a *general* meeting to be holden annually.'[1]

In the account given of the meeting of 1812, not so much as the appearance, any more than the name, of a *general* meeting, i.e. of an *open* meeting, is attempted to be given to it. But, in the account

---

[a] In addition to the above acts of thanksgiving, the only two acts which, on that occasion, are stated as having had place, are—One, for the 'forthwith' publishing 'a correct statement of the proceedings of the Society for the last year;'—the other, an appointment made of Auditors. It is at the motion of that same most Reverend President that, on both those occasions, the requisite *Resolutions* are stated as having been come to.

---

[1] For Resolution 8 see *First Annual Report of the National Society*, p. 7.

INTRODUCTION. PART IV. §V.

given, as above, of the meeting of 1813, not only the name of a *general* meeting, but the appearance of an *open* meeting is actually given to it.

Members of the General Committee, two at the least,—viz. the Archbishop President and the Earl of Shaftesbury,—whose business it is to thank the one of them the other,—there they are:—Non-Member of that same illustrious Committee, Earl Nelson,—brought thither to thank them both,—there he is:—the noble and not the less Reverend Non-Member of the Committee—Orator and self-deputed Representative of all the other Members of this National Society of England—as, upon another occasion, *Orator Cloots* was of the whole human race.[1]

From the comparison thus made, the inference is it an ill-grounded one, viz. that of the wording thus employed, at least in the instance of the meeting of 1812, the object was to cause a close meeting to be taken for an open one? For the variation,—observable as above, in the expression,—on this hypothesis an adequate cause will be found: on any other hypothesis, no such cause will (it is believed) be to be found for it.

Be this as it may, this,—as it appears to have been the first, so does it appear to have been, and moreover to be likely to remain, the last—representation of the Melo-drama, intituled, *A General Annual Meeting of the National Society.*—Out comes Report III., date in the title-page 1815: and in it neither as holden at *Sion College*, nor as holden at the National Society's *Central School*, nor in short as holden at any other place, has any trace of any such meeting been found.

The year 1814 is passed away,—the month of June in that year—the appointed month of annual thanksgiving—is passed away,—and no more such thanks have been given at any such place. No more Earls of Shaftesbury:—no more Earls Nelson.—Exhausted by that one[2] grand effort, the stock of thanksgivers is gone. Happily, not yet exhausted is the stock of thanks. But, no more Earls being found to administer them to either, the most Reverend President and his Reverend Secretary,—confined to the theatre furnished by their own Report,—add now, to their severer labours, the more agreeable task of thanking one another and themselves. The thanks, so justly due to the most Reverend the President, may be seen in p. 30: the thanks not

---

[1] Jean Baptiste du Val-de-Grace, Baron von Cloots (1755–94), Prussian nobleman, later known as Anacharsis Cloots, promoted the idea of a universal federation of all peoples and, following his address to the National Assembly of France on the subject in June 1790, became known as the 'Orator of the Human Race'. A fervent supporter of the French Revolution, on 26 August 1792, along with Bentham, he was made a citizen of France, but was then guillotined during the Reign of Terror.

[2] 1818 'same'. The text follows the 'Errata'.

less justly due, though in his subordinate sphere, to the Reverend the Secretary, may be seen in page the twenty-eighth.[1]

§ VI. *Proofs of the system of imposition continued,* II. *Sub-Committees and their meetings, none.*

Thus much as to the *General Committee*—its meetings and proceedings.—Now as to *Sub-Committees*.

Not inconsiderable is the importance of the functions, and thence of the existence, of these Sub-Committees. Not indeed in the *first* Report, but, however, in Report II. (p. 5) the information is given—that 'of the business of the General Committee (from a time not discoverable), every branch had *been prepared for them by their Sub-Committees.*'[2]

And thus it is—that, for a General Committee—which, though meeting 'in weekly meetings' throughout the whole year, meets not at any time or place,—the business is with equal regularity prepared by a set of Committees,—number unascertainable,—of which the meetings could also have been held, had it happened to them to have been held at any time or place.

Following this course is what, in the same passage (Rep. II. p. 5) is termed 'following the same course which they' (the Committee) 'had prescribed to themselves last year.'

In regard to Sub-Committees, to the truth of this state of presumable non-existence, one exception indeed, but one exception alone, is to be found. This is *The Sub-Committee for Building*, more briefly and familiarly *The Building Committee*. Under both these names, in Report I. Appendix, No. I. p. 23, mention may be seen made of it, with not only year (1812) and month (May) of its operation, but also day of the month (9th), place (London House),[3] and Members, five in number, all of them with names—of whom, as might well be imagined, the Right Reverend occupant—not the present Lord of London, it is believed, but his immediate predecessor—was one.[4]

---

[1] i.e. *Third Annual Report of the National Society*, pp. 30, 28. The *Third Annual Report of the National Society* mistakenly repeats page numbers 25 to 30 at the commencement of the Appendices.

[2] See *Second Annual Report of the National Society*, p. 5: 'The Committee have in their general designs followed the same course which they had prescribed to themselves last year; every branch of their business having been prepared for them by their Sub-Committees'.

[3] The Bishop of London had his chambers at London House, Aldersgate Street, London.

[4] i.e. John Randolph, Howley's predecessor as Bishop of London. The other members of the Building Committee who were present were Francis Burton (1744–1832), MP for Heytesbury 1780–4, New Woodstock 1784–90, Oxford 1790–1812, appointed a Commissioner for Church Building in 1818; George Owen Cambridge (1756–1841), Archdeacon of Middlesex 1806–41; William Waldegrave (1753–1825), Baron Radstock (I), naval officer; and William Davis, not further identified.

INTRODUCTION. PART IV. §VI.

In this Report, and in that same page of it, (p. 23.) mention may, moreover, be seen, not only of the existence of the Sub-Committee, of which it is the Report, on that day, but, moreover, of its existence at a former day, viz. '26th December, 1811:' its operations on that former day having been performed 'in consequence of instructions received from the General Committee.'

Of these tokens of existence,—which, in this one instance out of so indeterminable a multitude, were producible,—we see the display that has been made. And why made? Even that,—from the existence of the sort of bodies in question, in this one instance in which they had existence, their existence being demonstrated by these tokens,—their existence might be *inferred* in all that variety and multitude of instances in which, they not having existence, no such *tokens* of existence in relation to them could be displayed.

Such being the *motive*, by what ulterior interpretation shall the *mode* be adumbrated? Let experiment be made. On this important day[1] a dinner was given at London-House: and there it was that, at an altar covered with at the least a decent assemblage of those elements, of which Church-of-England *decency* is composed,—with or without other communicants,—members of the General Committee of the National Society, in a number which was found or deemed competent to the formation of a Sub-Committee for the purpose in question, found themselves assembled and met together. Whether it was the idea of the Sub-Committee that gave birth to the dinner, or the dinner that gave birth to the idea of the Sub-Committee, this is among the secrets to the revealing of which the hypothesis dares not aspire. Be this as it may, here was a number, which,—to judge from appearances, as above,—was greater than the greatest which were chosen, and at the same time chose, to be assembled for the meeting, afterwards mentioned as the *General Annual Meeting of the Society:* meaning the whole Society, composed of so many thousands, of whom the members of the General Committee, fifty-two in number, formed a part.

Of so many of which mention is made, this being the only Sub-Committee that, it should seem, was ever fortunate enough to possess the attribute of existence, no wonder it should thus have been made the most of.

But even of this one Sub-Committee, the existence could not hold out long. Metamorphosis is the work of fable. This Sub-Committee had not long been in possession of that distinguishing attribute, when, for lack of other appropriate matter, it was (Rep. II. p. 6) *turned into a Finance Committee:* thus was it turned, and, as it was turning,

[1] i.e. 9 May 1812.

its existence vanished: for neither at any *place*, nor at any *time*, nor by any person or persons, was the metamorphosis performed.

The following are the only Sub-Committees, of which,—either in Report I. or in Report II.,—after a careful search, mention is found made, as if they had had existence:

I. In Report I.

1. P. 14.—A Sub-Committee, in that place without a name, mentioned in Appendix, No. I. p. 23, under the title of *The Sub-Committee for Building;* and in the body of the article, *'The Building Committee.'*

2. P. 15.—A Sub-Committee, styled a *'Sub-Committee of Correspondence.'*

3. P. 14.—A Sub-Committee in that place also without a name, but of which the Report, printed in the Appendix, No. VI. p. 54, is styled, 'Report of the School-Committee.'[1]

These are all the Sub-Committees, of which any mention has been found in Report I.

Now, as to Report II.—In this Report, mention has been found made of the two following additional Sub-Committees—or at least names of Sub-Committees.

4.—1.—P. 6.—*A Finance Committee.*—In the page next preceding, (p. 5) *The Committee for Building* had re-entered upon the stage. Now then comes in a metamorphosis, and thereupon a question of identity. In page 6, 'This Committee,' (it is said) 'was *then* turned into a Finance Committee,' for a purpose thereupon mentioned.[2] This is as who should say—*at that time.* What was *that* time? *Answer*, no time: for none is to be found.

5.—2. ib. PP. 15, 16. A Committee of *Ladies:*—of which the institutions and functions are thereupon stated:[3] the same having been established by acts,—that is to say, by *'Resolutions* of the General Committee,'—Resolutions[4] come to at one of its inscrutable meetings,—held in their usual manner,—present nobody, at no time, and in no place.[a]

---

[a] Under these circumstances, we have the satisfaction of being informed (p. 16)

[1] 'Report of the School Committee', *First Annual Report of the National Society*, Appendix VI, pp. 54–8.

[2] According to *Second Annual Report of the National Society*, p. 6, the Finance Committee was formed 'in order to ascertain as nearly as might be the annual charge of their establishment in London, and to compare it with the amount of the Donations and Subscriptions for defraying that and other expences, that the Society might the better judge what would remain for them to distribute through the rest of the Country, for founding schools in other places, or for other purposes of the Charity'.

[3] See ibid., pp. 15–16, which contains six resolutions approved by the General Committee for the formation of a Ladies' Committee to regulate and inspect 'the employment and work of the Girls'.   [4] 1818 omits 'Resolutions'. The text follows the 'Errata'.

INTRODUCTION. PART IV. §VII.

§VII. *Proofs of the System of Imposition continued.*—III. *Acts spurious.*

III. Thus much as to the meetings or non-meetings of the General Committee,—and the existence or non-existence—meetings or non-meetings—of Sub-Committees: now as to the existence or non-existence of certain *instruments*, represented as having received the sanction of these several non-existent or non-acting authorities. Of *operations* and *instruments* taken together, mention has already, and *that* of necessity, been made,—viz. on the occasion, and for the purpose, of shewing the non-existence of the several authorities, from which, in these Reports, *acts*, coming respectively under both these names, are spoken of as having emaned.

Of *operations*, the nature being rather fugitive, there would be more or less of difficulty in dealing *with them. Instruments*, however, *remain:* and, so long as they do remain, an account of some sort may at any time be respectively taken of them.

Of acts of this indisputable tenor, Report I. furnishes *eleven:* of which *four* are, upon the face of them, acts of the *General Committee:* papers, exhibiting marks of discourse, purporting to be the discourse of the *General Committee:*—*two*, papers purporting to be, respectively, the discourses of two *Sub-Committees:* four others, so many papers purporting to be the discourses of so many other persons or sets of persons; and the remaining one, a list, formed (of course by the Secretary)[1] from the communications received by him in the name of the Society, under the orders of the General Committee: viz. the paper intituled, in the 'Contents of the Appendix,' '*List of Diocesan, District, and other Societies, united to the National Society.*'[2]

1. The instruments, purporting respectively to be so many discourses sanctioned by and delivered as theirs by the managing body—the General Committee,—are all that belong to the present purpose. They are the following, viz.

that 'The Dowager Countess of Spencer,[3] and *other* her Colleagues' (she herself being one of them her said Colleagues) 'have been so kind as to undertake this charitable work, and have executed their task much to the benefit of the school, and to the satisfaction of the Committee.' Since that time, the Dowager Countess is gone to receive her reward in heaven: as to 'other her Colleagues,' they not improbably still continue—where, not improbably, they have been from the first—*in nubibus.*[4]

---

[1] i.e. Walmsley.
[2] See Table of Contents and Appendix IV in *First Annual Report of the National Society*, pp. 22, 29–49 respectively.
[3] (Margaret) Georgiana Spencer, née Poyntz (1737–1814), Countess Spencer, philanthropist, had married John Spencer (1734–83), first Earl Spencer, in 1755.
[4] i.e. 'in the clouds'.

CHURCH-OF-ENGLANDISM

I. *'Address to the Public.'*—In Report I. this stands No. II. pages 25 and 26. This has for its object the compelling contributors to come in. To this instrument a time certain is indeed assigned: viz. 29th January, 1812. But, as far as appears, by no body of persons, sitting together in the character of *Committee-men*, was it sanctioned, nor, therefore, at any *place*. The signature it bears is that of the Secretary:[1] and of his office the place is mentioned, viz. No. 13, Clifford's Inn. The *time* then, viz. the time mentioned as above, is the time which it seemed good to him,—taking, doubtless, the pleasure of the Most Reverend President[2] on the subject,—to assign to it. For the purpose of getting in the money, this was the act of The General Committee. Ask the Secretary at what meeting of the General Committee this address was sanctioned,—his answer is, doubtless, ready.—*No such meeting:* no occasion for any. By himself,—the pleasure of the President being taken on the subject,—the instrument was penned.

In Report II. this paper is not to be found.

Nor yet in Report III.

II. *'Plan of Union.'* In Report I. this stands, No. III. pages 27, 28. Signature to it, *T.T. Walmsley, Sec. Place,* none; *day,* none.

Of this instrument, occasion for making mention has presented itself already more than once.[3] But the subject is not yet exhausted.

In Report II. this paper is reprinted. It there stands, No. IV. pages 186, 187.; and now presents itself—a curious enough circumstance.

At the time when this instrument was first made public, neither could the Most Reverend President, whose signature is *not* attached to it in this Report,—nor the Reverend Secretary, whose signature *is* attached to it in this Report,—tell at what time it became the act of the Society. Between one and two years elapse, and now, viz. at the time of getting up this second Report, the discovery had been made by them, that the year was 1812 and the month February: information which is accordingly immediately after the title made public: of the veil, by which the *time* had been concealed from them, a corner having been removed. Revealed to them are now the year—1812, and moreover the month—*February.* Still, however, another corner of the veil,—viz. that which covered the day of the month,—remains, and keeps it involved in mystery: nor even now does the revelation extend to the *place,* at which, by that important instrument, the sanction of the Society was received.

In this, however—such is its importance—is contained—let it not be forgotten—that which has already been brought to view, (Part II.)[4] in the character of the first of the *exclusionary acts.* This then, in

[1] i.e. Walmsley.   [2] i.e. the Archbishop of Canterbury.
[3] See pp. 96–7, 121, 125–6 above.   [4] See pp. 96–7 above.

INTRODUCTION. PART IV. §VII.

so far as concerns the *Society* and the *General Committee*, may be set down, it should seem, and without much danger of error, in the category of imposture. In the character of an act of the Most Reverend *President*, it might, at the same time, without much greater danger of error, be set down, it should seem, be set down as genuine.

In Report III. it is again reprinted:[1] and, neither in regard to *time* nor *place*, is any addition there made, to the revelations, reprinted as above in Report II.

III. '*Advertisement of the Society, April 8th,* 1812:' so intituled and dated, in the Contents, and at the head of the paper itself.—In Report I. this stands No. VII. pages [58, 59:][2] signature, *T.T. Walmsley, Sec.;* place, No. 13, Clifford's Inn.

The discourse, with which this instrument opens, and which is thus (be it observed) put in the front of it, is of a sort which, it is true, might without impropriety, come from the Secretary.—Why?— Because, for its first and principal object, what it has is—mere conveyance of information: the giving notice of a matter of fact:—of a fact which had just taken place; and of which, as soon as it had taken place, it was proper and material that the public at large should be apprized: viz. the fact of the opening of a new school.

But this discourse—a discourse, to the delivery of which, in the character of a discourse of the Secretary, no charge of incompetence could be applied—at the heels of it comes in a string of other discourses:—discourses delivered, and with the most perfect composure, in the name—not merely of the General Committee, but of the National Society itself. The National Society having appeared to the Reverend Secretary,—(but, in the first place, according to the best interpretation, to the Most Reverend President) in a dream,— and laid open to him its or their whole mind, no difficulty, on this occasion, does he find in making them say whatsoever it is found convenient for them to have said. '*They are of opinion*' ... so and so— '*they think also,*' so and so ... '*they trust*' so and so ... '*they are ready and willing*' so and so ... ; and finally '*they earnestly exhort*' so and so.[3] Of the mind of this excellent person of their own creation, the whole

[1] *Third Annual Report of the National Society,* Appendix III, pp. 166–8.
[2] 1818 '88, 59'. 'Errata' states 'for 59 put 89', but the correct reference is pp. 58–9.
[3] For the 'Advertisement of the Society. *April 8th,* 1812', from which the quoted phrases are taken, see *First Annual Report of the National Society,* Appendix VII, pp. 58–9, and *Second Annual Report of the National Society,* Appendix V, pp. 188–9. The Advertisement announced that the preparations for the building of the Central School at Baldwin's Gardens, Gray's Inn Lane, London (for which see p. 37 n. above), were well advanced, and that a school at Holborn Hill, London was being used temporarily. The Advertisement also stated that the Society had no plans to build more schools at present, but encouraged parishes to establish their own schools, offering to provide advice in the manner of construction and to provide teachers trained in the Madras system of education.

CHURCH-OF-ENGLANDISM

stock of furniture—*opinions, thought, belief, desire and readiness, exhortations*—are known to these reverend and inspired persons:—from their eyes none of these secrets are hid.[1]

On the subject of this *Advertisement*, as it is called,—or that of the above-mentioned *Address to the Public*,[2] press the Reverend Secretary, one and the same answer may serve. According to the convenience of the moment, it is, or is not, the act of the Society: of that Society whose Advertisement it calls itself. That it *is*, may be proved by all but the commencement: that it *is not*, may be proved by the commencement.

In Report II. this paper is reprinted. It there stands No. V. pages [188, 189].[3] Of the word *new*—in a Report, published a twelvemonth after its first appearance,—the import might admit of discussion:[4] under these circumstances, it seems to be of the ambulatory cast. But the National Society is still in the same most Reverend pocket; and its mind, as expressed on the former occasion, undergoes no change. In Report III. this paper is not reprinted.

IV. *Rules for the Office of Treasurer and Secretary.*—Such is the title in the 'Contents of the Appendix.' In Report I. this paper stands No. VIII. pages 60, 61. The title of it is, however, there changed into *'Duties of the Treasurer and Secretary.'* To this is affixed the signature—*T.T. Walmsley, Secretary.* But, on this occasion, he appears not in any *place*. In Report II. this paper is not reprinted.

Nor yet in Report III.

As to the *duties* themselves they belong not to the present purpose.—By whom were they prescribed?—this is what belongs to the present purpose; and, by the all pervading silence, the answer is supplied.

V. In Pages 197, 198, may be seen a paper, with which this first Report concludes. A circumstance, that calls for remark, is—that, notwithstanding its importance,—or rather perhaps, as will be seen, by reason of its importance,—no title is put at the head of it. In it is contained a *list of books*,—which, in the Schools under the immediate direction of the General Committee, were at that time employed, or intended to be employed, as *lesson-books;* and of which, in that same character, a recommendation is given,—addressed to the managers

---

[1] An echo of the Collect recited at the start of 'The Order for the Administration of the Lord's Supper or Holy Communion', *Book of Common Prayer*: 'Almighty God, unto whom all hearts be open, all desires known, and from whom no secrets are hid'.

[2] See p. 134 above.

[3] 1818 '27, 28'. See 'Advertisement of the National Society. *April 8th*, 1812', *Second Annual Report of the National Society*, Appendix V, pp. 188–9.

[4] See ibid.: 'They are ready and willing . . . to offer every assistance . . . more especially in providing proper Teachers to instruct them in the new System'.

INTRODUCTION. PART IV. §VII.

of all such Schools as, in pursuance of the *'Plan of Union,'* above-mentioned, had then placed, or shall have placed themselves, under the guidance of the Committee.

Of the nature and importance of this paper, the sincere reader will perceive how materially it concerns him to be well apprized. By this recommendation it is that the whole mass—of the literary instruction, intellectual and moral, administered to the whole multitude of Scholars of which the population of these Schools, (number amounting, half a year[1] ago, to no less than 60,000)[2] is or will be composed,—is determined.

In and by this recommendation is consummated, (as hath been seen in Part II.)[3] the *exclusionary system,*—and that substitution of Church-of-Englandism to the religion of Jesus, in the effectuation of which as above, the exclusionary system is the main instrument employed.

Such may be stated as the *end* or *object.* Observe now the *means.* Nothing could be more snug, nothing could be more dextrous, than the contrivance.

These, it is stated, are the books, which for the purpose in question are 'recommended' (Rep. I. p. 197.). Recommended—good: but by whom? By the governing body of the self-styled National Society, the General Committee?—Oh no: this not being true could not without a gross, and to many a manifest falsehood, have been affirmed. Affirmed accordingly it is not. It is but insinuated: and for this purpose, the form of words employed is such, that, unless by any one who shall have been put upon his guard against the system of imposture, an inference in the affirmative would be made of course. 'Many applications' (p. 197.) says this paper, 'having been made to the COMMITTEE of the NATIONAL SOCIETY for lists of Elementary and other Books, proper to be used in Schools upon the Madras system—the following *are recommended* as a convenient set for a School of 100 children at its commencement,' . . . &c.

For the sanctioning an act, of this radical and all-embracing importance, have we then any Meeting of the General Committee?—that General Committee, which (says the same Report, p. 13,) 'have held weekly Meetings' . . . 'for the arrangement[4] of its affairs?'—have we so much as any such thing as a Report, from the existing or non-existing *School-Committee?*—or from any one other of

---

[1] 1818 'one half year'. The text follows the 'Errata'.
[2] *Third Annual Report of the National Society,* p. 20. The passage is quoted by Bentham at p. 122 above.
[3] See pp. 88–98 above.
[4] *First Annual Report* 'management'.

those *Sub-Committees*, by which (says Report II. p. 5,) 'every branch of its business has been prepared for the *Committee?*' viz. 'according to the course which the Committee had prescribed to itself,'[1] at the time of the transaction, of which this Report I. gives the accounts?—Oh no: nothing have we of any of these.—What is it then, if any thing, that we have?—Oh, as usual, *T.T. Walmsley, Sec.* Here too, and on this same first occasion, we have—what in company with that same signature we have not always,—viz. a determinate *day* and even *place*. Day, August 5, 1812: Place, National Central School, Baldwin's Gardens, Gray's-Inn-Lane.[2]

In regard to the designation of *place* and *time* of meeting, why all this variety? In relation to a pair of adjuncts so essential, why, on the part of the Reverend Secretary, all this apparent indifference?—*Answer*—To this end: viz. that, by readers in general, these same adjuncts may be regarded as matters of indifference. Yes: and in a certain class of instances, so far as concerns *place* at least, matters of indifference—perfect indifference—they may, without difficulty, be allowed to be: viz. in all instances, in which the will of the Reverend Secretary himself, is the source, from which they may without impropriety be acknowledged to flow. But in all those instances, where the only source, from which with propriety they can have issued, is an aggregate of minds—the minds of a certain number of the members of the General Committee, acting as such,—there the importance of these adjuncts stands upon a footing somewhat different. In these instances (need it be repeated?) in the designation of *place*, *time*, and *Members concurring*—in the conjunct exhibition of these adjuncts—may be seen not only a security against forgery, but the only security which the nature of the case admits of.

Note here a further circumstance, which possibly may have been the result of accident, but rather more probably has been among the fruits of the ingenuity of T.T. Walmsley, Sec. This Report, Report I. closing with the above paper, this signature, with all its marks of authentication as above, is still capable of being regarded in either of two characters: viz. as applied to this recommendatory paper alone, or as applied to the whole contents of the Report. The desirable thing is, of course, that it shall be generally considered as applied to both. On the other hand, suppose any such consideration to occur to any person, as the following:—'*Considered in itself, this list of books may be a more or less proper or improper one. But, be the books ever so proper, the recommendation thus given of them, is it not rather too much for T.T. Walmsley, Sec.*', not only out of his own head, but on his own

[1] See p. 130 n. above.
[2] See *First Annual Report of the National Society*, p. 198.

INTRODUCTION. PART IV. §VII.

authority, to give?'—Such is the question, to which, in case of need,—whether by prudence or good fortune,—an answer may already be seen provided.—'*Oh no: of the signature with the* place *and* time *to it which you see, the only design and meaning is—to shew that the Report, such as you see it, comes out in the name of, and by authority from, the excellent Society,—of the proceedings of which it purports to be the Report, and of which the Reverend Gentleman has the honour to be Secretary: and as to this particular paper, what you see is—that a multitude of applications had been made about these books;—such a multitude, that it became absolutely necessary to give satisfaction to so laudable a desire:—and this, you see, is accordingly given, in and by the article which you see.*'—Divested thus effectually of his personality, where is the shaft, to which the Reverend Secretary can now be said to afford a mark?

Note here the progress of overweaning self-assurance.

In Report I, the Society being as yet but in its cradle—in this prudentially obscure form,—viz. that of a sort of Bookseller's advertisement, to which the signature of the Society's Secretary might or might not be considered as specially applicable,—a mere advertisement, and that without a title,—was this act of radical and all-embracing importance smuggled in.

Between the publication of Report I. and the completion of Report II. for the press,—it had, it should seem, passed either altogether unobserved; or at any rate without any objection, from any formidable quarter, made to it. Thereupon, out comes Report II,—and in it comes this same article,—now for the first time furnished, like the others, with its No.—viz. No. VI. (pp. 189, 190),—and at the head of it, now for the first time, with *a title:* a title, during the penning of which, all conception of the contents, seems to have been drowned in the exultation which gives birth to it. *NATIONAL SOCIETY,* 'For the Education of the Poor in the Principles of the ESTABLISHED CHURCH,' placarded in blazing capitals—these are the words which, on this occasion, occupy the place of a characteristic title. At the conclusion, here too we have *T.T. Walmsley, Sec.—Year* 1812; *month,* August;—*day,* none:—*place,* for this time, No. 13, Clifford's Inn; that being by this time the Reverend Secretary's Official Residence.

Thus far the form of the signature is such as it was wont to be. But,—being called for by the importance of the occasion,—now comes, on the part of the Reverend divine, an exertion of fortitude, such as had not till now been manifested by him: but which, having now been manifested, will presently be seen repeated. '*By order of the Committee*'—Yes: these are the very words, which in Report II. p. 190, may be seen standing immediately before the words *T.T. Walmsley, Sec.*

Well then good Mr. T.T. Walmsley, Sec.—forasmuch as this is a paper, for the publication of which in their name, there exists an Order of the Committee—Good Mr. T.T. Walmsley, Sec., tell us then *of whom* this Committee was composed; and by whom, by authority from this Committee, this Order was signed: tell us this,—or if this be too much trouble, not to speak of difficulty,—tell us when was *the day*, on which, as appears by the entry in your books, the Committee sat.—Alas! alas! put these questions to Mr. Sec. ever so home, no answer from him will you get. What his invention,—with or without his books,—here shews is—the year and the month: what neither his invention,—nor, without a forgery, his books,—will ever shew, is—the day of the month. Why?—Because, in a case such as that in question, the fact in question,—being a fact which in truth never happened,—cannot without manifest falsehood be asserted to have happened, on any individual day, at any individual public and particularised place.

All this, however, having, in the mean time, (it may be presumed) passed off smoothly and without adverse observation,—in Report III. we have this same paper reprinted word for word. In that Report it may be seen standing under the head of No. IV. pages 168, 169.

Such are the marks of exultation,—produced, at the time in question, by the thus already experienced success of the system of imposture, employed in the giving effect to the exclusionary system of instruction—the last defence of the rotten and tottering Church,—marks of exultation—with the assistance of the Printer and his Devils thus placarded,—the words *Principles of the* ESTABLISHED CHURCH offering themselves to the eye in flaring capitals,—and such is the delight with which this title continued to be contemplated,—that, in the very next article, (viz. No. VII. Rep. II. p. 191,) this same irrelevant title is made to serve instead of a relevant one.

But, proportioned to the undue exaltation, will be the due humiliation,—now that the imposture (if such it be) is brought to light, and the exclusionary system covered with the so well merited reproach.

Of these instruments Report II. furnishes three others, no one of which had been antecedently printed in Report I. All of these may [be] seen subsequently reprinted in Report III.

I. Page 191, 192, 193, No. VII. Paper,[1] as intituled in the Table of Contents, *Advertisement, August* 1812. On the paper itself, *title*, the same as the flaming one, just mentioned as being prefixt to the last preceding No., No. VI., viz. *'National Society, for the Education of the Poor in the Principles of the Established Church:'* Contents, miscellaneous: viz.—1. Notice—that a School is opened for general inspec-

---
[1] 1818 'VII. 1. Paper.' The enumeration is redundant.

INTRODUCTION. PART IV. §VII.

tion:—2. that persons sent from Country Parishes for that purpose will be gratuitously trained by the General Committee, to serve in the capacity of Masters or Mistresses in the Country Schools:—3. that, for the supply of deficiencies, a stock of persons ready trained is in store:—4. here too the information given of the *books recommended* is repeated:—5. Information—that Report I. is printed, and where it may be had: 6. Information—that, as there declared, the General Committee are able and ready to furnish money *to* the Country Societies,—and that they desire none *from* them:—7. Declaration of general prosperity in general terms; exhortation to give encrease to it by ever increasing Contributions:—8. and lastly, reprint of the list of *Lesson books* recommended.

By the tide of the success, it looks as if the head of the Reverend Secretary—not to speak of the most Reverend President—had by this time been somewhat turned. For this communication,—after six months or thereabouts, employed or at least employable in consideration,—no more apposite title can he find than the exulting, and in every other respect uncharacteristic, title above mentioned. Indeed, for a farrago, such as hath been seen—(but why make up any such farrago?) no characteristic title could very easily have been found.

Here too may be seen the same imposition, and the same clue—(such is the boldness produced by success)—the same so imprudently flaring mark, by which it may be detected. This too '*By order of the Committee:*'—and there we have the imposture.—Year, 1813; month, February; instead of the *day*, a *blank:*—and thus we have the clue, whereby the imposture may be or rather already is—detected.

In this paper, one declaration,—which as it stands expressed, forms a sort of a parenthesis, arising as it were incidentally out of the declaration made of disinterestedness as above,—must here be brought a little more into the light before it is dismissed. In this parenthesis is given a list of the Society's '*only objects*' (p. 192.) viz. '1. To preserve an uniformity of proceeding. 2. To adopt the most improved system of educating the Poor that can be devised. 3. To afford to the Country Societies pecuniary assistance where requisite. 4. To furnish them with *competent* Masters and *proper* Books, at a reduced expense.'

'*Competent Masters*'—O yes: but in this word *competent* is contained, as hath been seen, (Report II. No. IX. p. 197.)[1] the essence of the exclusionary system.—'*Proper Books.*'—O yes: but in this one word *proper* are included—the essence of the Exclusionary System, the scheme of substitution of Church-of-Englandism throughout

[1] See p. 97 above.

England, to the religion of Jesus, (see Part II.)[1] and the furnishing a new support to the rotten and crazy edifice.

Uniformity on the one hand, and the maximum of improvement on the other—for preventing these two objects from clashing, some little consideration and adroitness is, in the nature of the case, necessary. How far, by the Reverend Secretary, or most Reverend President, these requisites were on this occasion possessed, will now be seen. By *Uniformity,* alas!—by *Uniformity,* the serpent idol of Church-of-England worship—poor *Improvement* will be seen swallowed up.[a]

[a] National Society Report III. p. 14. Speaking of Training Masters, it goes on and says, 'for whose guidance a recommendation has been generally given, that, in the conduct of schools placed under their superintendence, they in no case take *upon themselves* to originate any variations from the practices of the Central Schools. This precautionary regulation' (it continues) 'has been adopted to provide against a prevailing propensity in the Masters to the making what may be deemed *improvements,* from the introduction of which the beautiful and efficient simplicity of the System would more[2] probably receive injury than advantage. And in pressing the general desirableness of *uniformity* in practice, as well as in principle,[3] where it can be conveniently had, the Committee have great satisfaction in the belief that an inspection of the daily process of education at the Central School, will satisfy examiners, that deviations from the mode there practised are in general more likely to injure, than to improve the most effective system of education that has ever been[4] devised for the Poor.'

Thus far the nameless Reporter and his invisible Committee. Four years have not elapsed since the birth of this Society—*Improvement,*—as the own mother of her—has not only been acknowledged but trumpeted—continually trumpeted—in that character,—and already does the unnatural offspring thus order her to be smothered. Smothered? Why? Oh! because such is the requisition made by *Uniformity:*—dear *Uniformity,* the restorer and saviour of the 'Excellent Church.'

What then? (exclaims somebody)—so admirable an instrument—would you have it spoilt by ignorant and presumptuous hands?—In uniformity—howsoever it may be, when a *declaration of persuasion* is the subject—in uniformity, when applied to a system of instruction, radiating over the whole country, from one central source, can there be any thing but what is salutary?—Say what you will, is not *uniformity* an advantage?

O yes:—but to the rule thus nakedly laid down, the nature of the case afforded an obvious appendage, having the effect of a *temperament:*—a temperament, which, while it secured to the rule all the good professed to be aimed at by it, would have cleared it of all mischief.

Practise nothing of your own invention, or any body's but Dr. Bell's, says the rule:—*propose to us any thing of your own, or any body else's invention, that you think useful,* would have said the temperament. The rule was the natural product of that mixture of pride, and jealousy, and fear, and indolence, and imperiousness, which characterizes little minds in great places:—the temperament is strange and abhorrent to such minds.

Dr. Bell—is he not only the first of all existing ingenious Schoolmasters, but the last of all possible ones?

---

[1] See pp. 88–98 above.　　　　　　　　　[2] *Third Annual Report* 'would much more'.
[3] Ibid. 'as principle'.　　　　　　　　　　[4] Ibid. 'ever yet been'.

INTRODUCTION. PART IV. §VII.

II. Report II. No. VIII. pages 194, 195.—Title, *The present State of the Central School, Baldwin's Gardens.*—*The present?* At what time? *Answer.* At no time: for, on the subject of *time*, not any the faintest elucidation is here to be found. This being established, every thing that might otherwise have been to be said, in relation to that same '*state*,' may, with the less loss and cause of regret, be omitted.

At *no time?* Yes: but, at the same time, at *all* times. For, word for word, with no other exception than that of a few words of addition on the subject of *holidays*,[1] is the same paper reprinted in Report III.— reprinted about a twelvemonth afterwards. No. VI. (pp. 173, 174, 175,) designates the place, in which, and under the same title, it will there be found. In this sample, behold one of the ways in which *uniformity*—dear *Uniformity*—may be preserved.

A determination having been already taken, that no such troublesome intruder as *Improvement* shall be suffered to come in, the picture here given of that '*present state*,' which the school was in at *no* time, may, and with signal economy in the articles of mental and manual labour, serve for any number of successive years: in a word, so long as the *Excellent Church*, with its *Excellent Schools*, and their *Excellent Managers*, shall endure.

Note, that in this *perpetual calendar* may be seen that list of '*Religious exercises*,'[2] by which, as shewn in Part II. of the present Introduction,[3] so much light has been thrown, upon the excellent plan, for substituting to the less Excellent religion of Jesus, the more Excellent religion of that Excellent Church, by which all these Excellencies are displayed.

Congenial to the tenor of the evidence itself, is, on this occasion, the mode, in which—no—not the mode in which it is *authenticated*— but the mode in which the task of giving to it the marks of authenticity is either forgotten or avoided. With perfect consistency, of the picture of the state of the school, as it *stood* at no *time*, the *verity* is *certified* in no *place*, by no *person*, at no *time:* by no *person*, not so much as by the person, by whose evidence so very little seems throughout to be added to any ground of credence:—no, not so much as by T.T. Walmsley, Sec.

III. Report II. page 197, No. IX.—*Form of Certificate for Masters.*

This is the instrument, which, in Part II. has been held up to view in its character of the second of the instruments of the exclusionary system.[4]

---

[1] The addition concerns the dates of the annual Summer and Winter holidays: see *Third Annual Report of the National Society*, p. 175.
[2] The list of 'Religious Exercises' is reproduced at p. 64 n. above
[3] See pp. 88–98 above.
[4] See p. 97 above.

Time and *Place* are as completely absent, as every object that comes under the denomination of *person*.—No:—nobody knows any thing about the matter: not even T.T. Walmsley, Sec.

Number of persons of whom God is composed—that God, whom, if St. John is to be believed, (John, i. 18—I. John, iv. 12) no one ever saw—this number is no less correctly known to the Reverend Secretary, than to the Most Reverend President. Number of the persons, over whom, on this occasion, the Most Reverend President presided—and under whom, on this same occasion, the Reverend Secretary officiated—this article remains, and for ever will remain, in the clouds.

All the while it is by this non-entity, in conjunction with so many other non-entities, that the Society with all its schools is governed.

In Report III. this paper is likewise reprinted. Reprinted, and, word for word, without omission, alteration, or addition, under the head of No. VII.[1]

IV. Report II. pages 197, 198, No. X. Title, in the Table of Contents, *Regulations for training Masters*.—Title on the paper itself, *Rules and Regulations for training Masters*.[2]

In this case, in the same form, or rather no form, as in the one last mentioned, the same draught may be seen drawn upon the public, by the Reverend Secretary, for the requisite competent stock of ungrounded faith. Established by *nobody*, on *no day*, at *no place*,—signed by nobody, not even by T.T. Walmsley, Sec.,—not so much as garnished by the words NATIONAL SOCIETY—*Central School*—stationed at the head of the preceding paper,[3] instead of a date,—they stand, in other respects—these 'Rules'—or these 'Rules and Regulations'—upon exactly the same imaginary ground as the *Form of Certificate for Masters*.

In Report III. pages 176, 177, under No. X. (by inadvertence put instead of No. VIII.) this paper stands reprinted word for word.

Of these Rules, the main body is foreign to the present purpose. Not altogether so either the Introductory passage, or the first of the Rules.

'The conduct and improvement:' it begins with saying—'The conduct and improvement of the Masters being objects to which the very particular attention of the Committee' (viz. the imaginary Committee) 'is directed, it is ordered—

'That a book shall be kept, to be called *The Report of the Masters*,

---

[1] See *Third Annual Report of the National Society*, Appendix VII, p. 176.

[2] See *Second Annual Report of the National Society*, pp. 1, 197 respectively.

[3] i.e. 'The present State of the Central School, Baldwin's Gardens', *Second Annual Report of the National Society*, Appendix VIII, pp. 194–6.

which shall be a faithful register of their conduct, and be laid weekly before the Committee, during whose sitting every master is required to be in waiting.'

The case being (as, long before this, must, it is believed, have been clear enough to every body)—the case being, that no real Committee is ever sitting,—how is it that, in this way, an intercourse is thus constantly kept up between two assemblages of persons—the one visible, composed of the *Schoolmasters*—the other invisible, composed of the illustrious, but never-assembled *masters* of those same *Schoolmasters*.

Another look, and you will see how it is:—i.e. how it cannot but be.—Somewhere or other in the building, conceive a room, called the *Committee-Room:*—in that same building conceive another room, called the *Waiting-Room:* conceive, moreover, a third room, called the *Secretary's Room*. The Committee-Room is the supposed seat of the many-headed Idol.—T.T. Walmsley, Sec. is the High Priest.

When a *Schoolmaster* comes, he is ordered to the High Priest, by whom he is sent to the *Waiting-Room*, where he sits kicking his heels with his fellows. If at that time so it happens that a special order is to be given to him,—in goes the High Priest, shuts himself up with his invisible God,—takes his Godship's pleasure, and delivers to the bowing Master,—or, if his Lordship of London is understood to form one person of the godhead, the *'prostrate'*[1] master,—the result of it.

Do what I preach, and not as I do, is an old adage, put into the mouths of such Reverend Gentlemen as do preach.—According to the above rule, the book kept by the Masters is to be '*a faithful Register of their conduct:—of the conduct of these same Masters.*'—Faithful?—In what sense and manner *faithful?*—In the same manner as these Reports, which are so regularly published by the Secretary, and for which, when published, he is at the motion of the Most Reverend President so regularly thanked?—Alas! no: but in the opposite manner. In the way of contrast, however,—should it ever happen to a copy of this work to meet the eyes of any one of these Masters,—in the way of contrast the conduct of the real conductors of the institution might be of use to him. To the National Society's Schoolmasters, the peep here given behind the curtain may afford a lesson of *'faithfulness,'*—as the deportment of the Helots when in a certain state, was made to afford a lesson of *sobriety* to the children of their masters.[2]

---

[1] See p. 37 n. above.
[2] See Plutarch, *Life of Lycurgus*, xxviii. 4.

§VIII. *Securities against Spuriousness—Cause of the Omission of them, Necessity and Design—not Inadvertence.*

So many tokens of authenticity, so many instruments of authentication, so many securities against spuriousness. Of the use or value of these securities, is it that the authors of these Reports were unapprized or insensible?—Not they indeed.

If in any case they have omitted to exhibit them, it is because,—with a few inconsiderable exceptions, which will here be brought to view,—in all cases, from first to last, in the case in question among the rest, they have found themselves unable to exhibit them: and the cause why they have found themselves unable to exhibit them is—that, without a glaring falsehood, these securities could not have been exhibited:—a falsehood, which, if uttered, would have been recognized as such:—recognized by a number of persons so considerable, that all prospect of its remaining ultimately concealed from the eye of the public at large would have been manifestly hopeless.

The falsehood in question, in what then would it have consisted?—*Answer*—In this: viz. in the assertion, that, on such or such a day, such or such an act received the sanction of a certain number of members of the governing body in question, styled *The General Committee of the National Society,*—assembled together in one room, in one or other of two characters,—viz. that of Members of the *General Committee* acting *as such* (total number of those[1] who had a right to meet, 52) or that of Members of one or other of the *Sub-Committees*, formed out of that same number, and acting under the authority of that same *General Committee*.

If, on any determinate day—say 1st January, 1813—the case was, that, on that same day, no meeting of the General Committee was held,—any portion of discourse, by which intimation were given, that, on that same day, an act of such or such a tenor received the sanction of the General Committee, would be a palpable, and, sooner or later, a universally notorious, falsehood,—and, unless by some accident too extraordinary to be repeated, a wilful falsehood.

In this then may be seen the reason—the sole reason—why, with very few exceptions indeed, in every instance, in which the act in question is, on the Report represented as being the act of the *General Committee,*—or of a *Sub-Committee*, acting under the authority of that governing body,—no *day* is mentioned as being the day on which such act received the sanction of the one or the other of these same bodies respectively: the act being, in each such instance, the act either of some one individual, or some small number of individuals,

---

[1] 1818 'these'. The text follows the 'Errata'.

not competent to the formation of those same bodies respectively.—Being exercised by, or by or under the orders of, some one individual, or incompetent number of individuals respectively,—it could not, without a palpable falsehood, have been stated as having, on this or that determinate day, received the sanction of either of these same bodies respectively; and, therefore, it was, that to the statement, by which it is represented, as if it had received that sanction, no determinate day was ventured to be assigned.

Follows now the proof—that the omission in question—the non-exhibition of these securities against spuriousness—of these evidences of authenticity—had not inadvertence for its cause, nor, therefore, any other cause than design—the offspring of necessity, as abovementioned.

1. By the omission of these securities, the exhibition of which is so general, not to say universal—by this omission,—if, in any one instance, much more if in a number of instances, total—extending to all the several distinguishable securities in question—a risk, more or less considerable, could not but,—in the eyes of any reflecting, though it were an ever so moderately intelligent, mind,—appear to be incurred.

2. From the omission of the *principal* security—of that security, without which all the others would be unavailing,—viz. the security afforded by the statement of an individual *day*, as the day on which the act in question received the sanction in question—a suspicion of the sort in question could not but receive[1] additional strength and confirmation.—Why?—*Answer.*—Because, by the omission of this major and ultimate security, while the minor and introductory securities were afforded,—this major security being one, in the giving of which, supposing the act genuine, there could not, unless by some extraordinary accident, have been any difficulty,—demonstration was afforded, that the attention of the penner of the Report had actually applied itself to the subject.

Under these circumstances, of the most perfect proficiency in the arts of imposture and deception, the resource, supposing circumstances to admit of it, would naturally be—in relation to all such incidents as it became necessary to bring to view, the putting a complete exclusion upon every expression, that could be conducive to the bringing to view, as and for the time in which any act was exercised by the body or individual in question, any portion of time so determinate as that which is comprized within the limits of a single day: and, in a word, on every occasion to keep the designation of time as indeterminate as possible.

[1] 1818 'not receive'. The text follows the 'Errata'.

Accordingly, in the paper, intituled 'Summary of Reports from Diocesan and District Societies, and Schools in union with the National Society,' the sort of chronological intimation in question is, with very *few* exceptions, excluded from Report II. and, it is believed, without *any* exception from Report III.[1]

But, in verbal as in material fortification, if by being left unguarded, any one spot is left defenceless, as well might the whole be left defenceless. Accordingly,—in a certain number, though, comparatively speaking, in but a small number, of instances,—this measure of precaution, whether through necessity or through inadvertence, has been left unemployed:—to the mention made of the incident in question, it being real, and as such susceptible of a determinate chronological date,—a determinate chronological date has accordingly been attached: and thus it is, that, by the token of authenticity thus exhibited in certain instances, the attention of *one* reader at least has been drawn to the non-appearance of it in so many other instances.

The cases in which this departure from the prudential practice of a general suppression of dates may be seen to have place, will, it is believed, be found referable to one or other of the heads following:—

1. Cases in which, the National Society not having as yet received a regular form, the demand for the sort of misrepresentation here in question has not yet commenced. In this state of things, the case being that, by certain persons, in relation to the subject in question, business of the sort in question was, on the days in question, actually done,—no such purpose could, by the sort of omission in question, be as yet answered. Accordingly, in the case of the assemblage of persons here in question, in a publication purporting to be an account of what they did,—in this case, as in the case of any other assemblage of persons meeting for a purpose of a public nature, the time of meeting was in this way, as of course, particularized. True it is, that thus, even at the very commencement of the business, they saw reason for concealing *themselves*, and accordingly did take effectual care to conceal themselves. But, this species of concealment being thus far sufficient for the purpose, imposition was not as yet resorted to.[a]

[a] To this head may be referred the following instances of an adequate designation of time:—

I. Anno 1811, Oct. 16.—Preparatory meeting of some unknown persons, antecedently to the formation of the self-styled National Society. Report I. p. 6.—N.B. The

[1] For the relevant reports see *Second Annual Report of the National Society*, Appendix I, pp. 23–177, and *Third Annual Report of the National Society*, Appendix I, pp. 25–164.

INTRODUCTION. PART IV. §VIII.

II. Cases in which, it having thus far been deemed necessary, at first to set up, and then to keep up, the appearance of a meeting, open to Subscribers at large,—and a meeting of some sort having been held accordingly,—stating the day on which such meeting was held, would naturally present itself as an act of necessity.[a]

III. Case, in which,—a meeting, regarded, and accordingly re-meeting, in this instance, a *close*,—and, except as to the day, a perfectly *secret* one. *Place* not mentioned.—No one *person* mentioned as *present*.[1]

II. Anno 1811, Oct. 21.—Meeting, on the occasion on which the Society was declared to be formed. Report I. pp. 9–13.[2]—N.B. Between these two meetings, indication is given of two or three others, but with less clearness: being given, not in an independent form, as these two are, but by relation made to the first of them.[3]

N.B. All these meetings close.—At the meeting of Oct. 21. *Place* mentioned, *Bow Church*. 'In the Chair,' the Archbishop of Canterbury. No other person mentioned as present.[4]

[a] To this class may be referred the following instances:—

III.—1. Anno 1812, June 3d.—Meeting, styled in Report I. p. 17, '*Annual Meeting of the Society*,' without the word *General*; in Report II. No. II, p. 178, '*General Annual Meeting of the Society:*' also in Report III. p. 165, '*General Annual Meeting of the Society.*'[5] According to appearance, this first of all meetings, by which any such character as that of an *open* meeting has ever been assumed, was in fact *not* an open meeting, but a close one: admittance not being given to any person, who was not either himself a member, or introduced by some person who was a member, of the '*General*,' i.e. the governing '*Committee*.' *Afterwards*, however, viz. in the two subsequent Reports,—and, as it should seem, for the purpose of qualifying it for presenting to readers, not in the secret, the idea of an *open* meeting,—the word *general* (being the same word which, in speaking of the next year's meeting, is employed for the purpose of representing it as an open one)—was slipped in, as above. *Place* mentioned, *Sion College*.

IV.—2. Anno 1813, June [2].[6]—Meeting, styled in Report II. p. 17, as above,—'*General Annual Meeting of the Society*.' Place, Sion College. In and by the account there given of it, in relation to *this* meeting, the conception manifestly intended to be conveyed, is—that it was an *open* one: and to this purpose it seemed unavoidable, that a determinate day should be stated as the day on which it was holden. But that, in effect, it was no other than a *close* one, is a suspicion, the ground of which may be seen above, viz. in §5.[7]

---

[1] In his discussion of this meeting at p. 161 below, Bentham records that the Archbishop of Canterbury was in the Chair.
[2] i.e. reports of the meeting held at Bow Church on 21 October 1811 appear at *First Annual Report of the National Society*, pp. 9 and 13.
[3] At the meeting on 16 October 1811, two further meetings were planned for 17 and 18 October 1811: see *First Annual Report of the National Society*, p. 6.
[4] See ibid., p. 9.
[5] More precisely, the meeting on 3 June 1812 is referred to as 'annual meeting' at *First Annual Report of the National Society*, p. 17, and 'annual General Meeting' at *Second Annual Report of the National Society*, Appendix II, p. 178. The meeting of 2 June 1813 is referred to as 'annual General Meeting' at *Third Annual Report of the National Society*, Appendix II, p. 165.
[6] 1818 '3' appears to be a slip.
[7] See pp. 128–9 above.

presented, as a regular one, viz. a meeting of a *Sub-Committee*, having really been held,—indication was given of the day on which it was held: viz. either because,—(the plan of carrying on the business by secret Agents, without the intervention of meetings of the General Committee or of Sub-Committees, not having yet been formed),—the designation of the day was, in conformity to general usage, given as of course,—or because a hope was at that time entertained, that the demonstration thus given of correctness, in this one case, might operate not only as presumptive, but as conclusive, evidence of actual correctness, in other cases: in cases in which such tokens of correctness, not being capable of being afforded without a palpable falsehood, are accordingly *not* visible.[a]

IV. Cases, in which the acts in question neither were,—nor, for the deceptious purpose in question, required to be believed to be,—acts of the Society at large: being manifestly so many acts of certain officers, acting under the authority of the Society,—in a matter, to which, without contravening established usage, the proper tokens of authenticity and correctness could not be refused.[b]

V. Case, in which the instrument in question,—though in reality not competent to be issued by any person, otherwise than with the express sanction of the governing Committee,—yet, being, upon the face of it, in respect of the foremost and most prominent part of it, within the competence of the Secretary,—received, in conjunction with the signature of the Secretary, a determinate day of date: viz. under the assurance, that,—howsoever it might be known to the members of the said Committee in general, that, at that day, there was no meeting of the said Committee,—yet, under the notion of its being given as and for the act of the Secretary alone, without its having received, because without its having stood in need of receiving, the sanction of the Committee,—or under the notion of its having received the sanction of the Committee on some former occasion or occasions,—no such reproach as that of wilful misrepre-

---

[a] V.—1. Anno 1812, May 9.—Report I. p. 23.—Report of the Committee, called the Building Committee: of which mention has already been made in §6. and elsewhere.[1]

[b] VI.—1. Anno 1812, May 19.—Auditors' allowance of the Accounts.—Report I. pp. 58, 59.[2]

VII.—2. Anno 1813, June 1.—Ditto.—Report II. pp. 200, 201.[3]

VIII.—3. Anno 1814, June 1.—Ditto.—Report III. pp. 182, 183.[4]

---

[1] See pp. 125, 130–2 above and 176, 180, 181, 183–6, 193 below.
[2] See *First Annual Report of the National Society*, Appendix IX, pp. 62–3.
[3] See *Second Annual Report of the National Society*, Appendix XI, pp. 200–1.
[4] See *Third Annual Report of the National Society*, Appendix X, pp. 182–3.

sentation would, in the eyes of any of those persons, appear imputable to it.[a]

VI. Cases in which the acts reported, being acts of other assemblages of persons,—viz. bodies acting, in various parts of England, in union with this Society, and under directions from the General Committee,—and these acts having, in the usual manner, received, of course, the usual marks of authentication, and, amongst others, the designation of the determinate days, on which they respectively received the sanction of the several bodies,—under these circumstances, to have truncated the form of authentication, by leaving out the designation of the day, would naturally have called forth attention and surprise, on the part of readers in general; but more particularly on the part of the persons of whom the local meetings in question had been composed. The designation of the day was accordingly, in these instances, left to stand. Standing as it does, true it is that,—by the contrast it forms with the totally unauthenticated state of some of the acts given as the acts of the General Committee, in some instances, and the mutilated state of the form of authentication in others,—it operates in some sort in confirmation of the suspicion of spuriousness, when once brought to view. But, lying as they do, dispersed in so vast a body of matter, an assurance which under these circumstances might naturally enough be entertained, is—that under such circumstances, these indications[1] of spuriousness would escape notice. On the other hand, had the designation of the days been in these instances truncated,—viz. for the purpose of cutting them down, to a conformity with the pattern, exhibited in the representation given in these Reports, of the acts therein ascribed to the

---

[a] IX.—1. Anno 1812, April 8th.—Paper, intituled *'Advertisement of the Society;'* Report I. p. 58. No. VII.—What it *opens* with is,—an article of information, such as the Secretary would of himself be competent to give: viz. information of a matter of fact,—the opening of a school,—which had just then taken place. So far so good. But thereupon, as already observed,[2] comes a quantity of matter, which,—being delivered, as speaking, upon a variety of subjects, the mind, not merely of the governing Committee, but of the whole Society,—could not with propriety have been delivered in any such character, without an act of the governing body to sanction it. The matter of fact being, however, of such a nature, as naturally to call, not only for a determinate *year* and *month*, but for a determinate *day* in which to place it,—the deficiency would have been apt to excite attention and remark, if, in this instance, as in so many others, the mention of the determinate day had been omitted. The risk of suspicion incurred by insertion, presenting itself as being inferior to the risk that would have been incurred by omission, mention of the particular day may accordingly be seen inserted.

---

[1] 1818 'tokens'. The text follows the 'Errata'.
[2] See pp. 135–6 above.

governing bodies of the Metropolitan Society; in this case the probability would have been—that, by the bare appearance of such truncation, in the face of each such instrument standing singly, the suspicion thus produced would have been much stronger, than would have been produced by an indication, for the furnishing of which the confrontation and comparison of two different classes of instruments would have been, and has accordingly been here, found necessary.[a]

VII. Cases in which the act reported is the act of a party, not in connexion with the Society.[b]

Such are the circumstances, under which the sincere reader will have to pronounce his judgment, on the subject of the omissions and truncations which have thus been brought to view:—to pronounce—in the first place, whether they had for their cause mere *accident* or

---

[a] X.—1. 1812, January 29.—Proceedings at a Country Meeting, at Exeter. Report I. p. 39.

XI.—2. 1812, March 2.—Proceedings at Thorpe, in the Deanery of Tendering, in Essex. Report I. p. 50.

XII.—3. 1812, March 6.—Proceedings at Winchester. Report I. p. 49: with several antecedently mentioned dates.

XIII.—4. Anno 1812, October 14.—'Paper, circulated by the Norfolk and Norwich Society, for the Education of the Poor in the Principles of the Established Church.' In Report II. p. 179 to 182, under the above title, this Paper forms in this Report a separate article of itself, having for this purpose been detached from the paper, to which it properly belongs, viz. No. I. 'Summary of Reports from Societies, &c. in Union with the National Society.' In this detached paper, (p. 181.) not only is the day, as above, designated, but prefixt to the names of the three persons officiating as Secretaries, are the words, 'By order of the Committee.'—Thereupon in the next page (p. 182,) follow three paragraphs, to the last of which is attached another date, viz. Norwich, 28th October, 1812, but without signature, or any mention of any Committee.

XIV.—5. Anno 1812, October 19.—Proceedings at a Meeting at North Walsham, in Waxham Deanery, Norfolk. Report II. p. 183 to 185.—Concerning persons present, information is here given in these words: viz. 'Present, the Honourable Colonel Wodehouse,[1] in the chair,—Rev. Dr. Hay,[2] and others of the Clergy and Laity.' Quere, Who is this Dr. Hay, who, after the Honourable Chairman, is every body, while all the '*others*,' Clergy and Laity together, are nobody? It looks as if these *others* were such, that on account of the smallness of their number, or on some other account, prudence forbad the bringing of their names to view.

[b] XV.—1. Anno 1813, March 9.—Application made in the name of the East-India Company, for two Schoolmasters trained by the Society, to be sent to St. Helena. Report II. p. 16.

---

[1] John Wodehouse (1771–1846), later succeeded as second Baron Wodehouse in 1834, was MP for Great Bedwyn 1796–1802 and Marlborough 1818–26, and Colonel of East Norfolk Militia from 1798.

[2] Thomas Hay (1759–1830), Rector of Belton, Suffolk from 1790, Canon of Christ Church, Oxford from 1795, and Rector of North Repps, Norfolk from 1813.

design: and, if design, *what* that design was: in a word, whether it can have been any other, than the design of causing a multitude of acts to be generally regarded as acts of the Society in question, whereas in truth they were not: and in particular the acts here held up to reprobation, under the name of *exclusionary* acts, and under the notion of their being repugnant to morality and to the religion of Jesus.

§ IX. [III.] *Authors, acting and consenting, of the combined systems of exclusion and imposition.*

Of that system of ill-will towards men, by which the benefits of religious and moral instruction have been withholden from so many, and by which that security which depends upon the religion and morality of all, has been denied to all,—we have seen the authors—active authors and connivers together: viz. those in whom, under the name of members of the *General Committee*, is vested the sole right of conducting the affairs of the self-styled *National Society:* Archbishops and Bishops, 26; nominees of the said Archbishops and Bishops, 26 others.[1] Of that system of misrepresentation and imposition, by which the main actors in that anti-christian and anti-social system have endeavoured to hide themselves in the crowd of passive connivers, and by that means to become screened from that pre-eminent share in reproach, which is so justly due,—the existence has also been proved, and the contrivance developed and brought to light.

These main actors then, who are they?—This is what remains to be shewn in the present Section.—These main actors, who are they?—*Answer*—1. In the first place, constantly and regularly, the *President* of the self-styled *National Society*, Dr. Manners Sutton, *Archbishop of Canterbury*, and under him the so often mentioned and no otherwise denominable, T.T. Walmsley, Sec. [2.] In the next place, occasionally,—and though probably with not less than equal zeal, yet not with equal assiduity—equal assiduity on the part of any other agent not being deemed necessary,—Dr. William Howley, Lord Bishop of London:—self-constituted *Prostrator-General*—as there will be such frequent occasion to shew and to remember—*Prostrator-General of understandings and wills.* (See below, p. 257, &c.)

I. First in order, though neither first in dignity nor equally constant in operation, let us behold his Lordship of London. By this transposition, we shall from the first be rendered the better acquainted, not only with the zeal by which these combined systems have been

---

[1] For the composition of the General Committee see p. 46 n. above,

CHURCH-OF-ENGLANDISM

produced, but with the nature and extent of the designs to the accomplishment of which they have been and are directed.

On all these accounts, what seems matter of indispensable necessity is—that in this place the reader should be presented with a specimen of the graphic art,—in which, by a sort of spiritual imitation of one of the temporal curiosities of *Bullock's Museum*,[1] two portraits—viz. that of the late Bishop and that of the present—himself being the limner—are so conjoined, that by a slight shifting of position, either the one or the other may be contemplated: both of them being not only enclosed in the same frame, but, like two colours of a changeable silk, both occupying one and the same portion of space. After the examination of this double portrait—and let it be with that attention to which it presents so irresistible a claim—it will rest with the sincere reader, to form his judgment on several points, the importance of which will scarcely be dubious in his eyes:—for example,—

1. Whether it be the fault of either of these Lords of London, any more than of *the Bishop of St. David*'s,[2] if either London or Country still continue to be infested, with any persons who, in *opinion* (1)[a] or in *practice*, (2) by *heresy* (3) or by *schism* (4), are separated from the *Established Church:*—

2. Whether, in this view of the matter, all such persons are not men of '*guilt:*' (6)—

3. Whether any such *guilt* ought to be '*palliated:*' (7)—

4. Whether any '*desire of conciliation*,' by which such palliation may be suggested, is not in their view, a '*vain desire:*' (8)—

5. Whether, according to the principles of the two Prelates, for the purpose of clearing the country from such *guilt*, (6) the growth of every '*opinion*' (1) or '*practice*, (2) which even by remote consequence might unsettle the faith of the inexperienced, or introduce confusion and disorder into the Church, (9) ought not to be *checked:*' (10)—

---

[a] Of this and the ensuing figures of reference, the use is—to guide the eye the more promptly to the passage in the ensuing original, from whence the words here quoted have respectively been extracted.—To some readers it may perhaps be found more convenient to peruse the original in the first instance.[3]

---

[1] William Bullock (b. early 1780s, d. 1849), naturalist, traveller, and antiquary, opened a museum containing works of art, objects of natural history, and curiosities at Liverpool in 1795. In 1809 he moved the museum to Piccadilly in London, and in 1819 sold his collection before travelling in Mexico.

[2] Thomas Burgess.

[3] The words and phrases corresponding to references 1–19 are from [Howley], *Charge delivered to the Clergy of the Diocese of London*, pp. 1–3, which, as Bentham states, is reproduced at p. 157 below.

INTRODUCTION. PART IV. §IX.

6. Whether, for this purpose it has not been the desire, design, and endeavour, of these two Right Reverend persons to *'replace ecclesiastical discipline upon its ancient footing:'* (11)—

7. Whether that *ancient footing* be not to be found in the principles[1] and practice of *Archbishop Laud*, and his predecessors in the days of *Elizabeth*,[2] or, in respect of every thing but bodily torture, in the practice of the *Spanish Inquisition:*—

8. Whether among the purposes, for which, in this same Charge, it is declared that the aforesaid *'discipline'* ought to be,—and which, if the necessary power is to be had, of course will be,—employed, be not the *'recovering the rights of the Spiritual Governor:'* (12)—

9. Whether, among these rights, which, having once been possessed and exercised, have since been lost, and now remain to be thus *'recovered,'* be not the right of governing, without the concurrence of Parliament all persons in all *ecclesiastical* matters: that is, in all matters to which it shall be the pleasure of the persons so in power to give that name: that same right being the right formerly possessed and exercised, under the name of *Heads of the Church*, (successors thereby in England to the *Popes,*) by *Henry the Eighth* and his worthy daughters and successors, *Mary* and *Elizabeth*;[3] amongst other branches of that same right, that of *burning heretics*, as exercised by the aforesaid *Henry, Mary,* and their successor *James:*—[4]

10. Whether it be not the declared opinion of both these Lords of London, that, in the prosecution of such designs, the *'discretion of the ruling power,'* ought not to be *'fettered:'* (13).—11. Whether, by the present Lord, this policy be not pronounced a *'wise policy;'* (14)—and such a policy that, in the *'pursuance'* of it, *'resolution'* ought to be *'inflexible,'* (15) and not to be *'discouraged by resistance:'* (16)—

---

[1] 1818 'principle'. The text follows the 'Errata'.
[2] As Archbishop of Canterbury and chief adviser to Charles I, William Laud (1573–1645), Archbishop of Canterbury from 1633, was responsible for pursuing a policy of religious uniformity, and was notorious for his hostility to Puritanism. Laud's predecessors during Elizabeth's reign were Matthew Parker (1504–75), Archbishop of Canterbury from 1559; Edmund Grindal (1516x20–83), Archbishop of Canterbury from 1576; and John Whitgift (1530/31?–1604), Archbishop of Canterbury from 1583.
[3] By the Act of Supremacy of 1534 (26 Hen. VIII, c. 1), Henry VIII (1491–1547), King of England from 1509 and King of Ireland from 1541, was declared Supreme Head of the Church of England, and authorized to act in ecclesiastical matters without the consent of Parliament. Following the accession in 1553 of Mary I (1516–58), Queen of England and Ireland from 1553, the Act of Supremacy was repealed (1&2 Ph. & Mar., c. 8), but in the Act of Supremacy of 1559 (1 Eliz. I, c. 1), Elizabeth was proclaimed Supreme Governor of the Church of England, and supreme governor of all spiritual or ecclesiastical things or causes.
[4] Around eighty heretics were burned during the reign of Henry VIII under the authority of 25 Hen. VIII, c. 14 (1534); around 290 heretics were burned during the reign of Mary under the authority of 1&2 Ph. & Mar., c. 6 (1554); and two heretics were burned during the reign of James I using the writ *de heretico comburendo*.

CHURCH-OF-ENGLANDISM

11.[1] Whether, by the present Lord Bishop's own avowal, it be not in the character of an instrument to be successively employed in the prosecution of these designs, that by both their Lordships, under the name of '*the National System* of Education,' (17) the system, (including the exclusionary system, as above,) pursued by the Society self-styled *the National Society*, has been supported:—

12. Whether, by the same avowal, all this be any thing more than a sample, of the '*advantage*, (18) which, had the late Bishop lived longer, might, with the predestinated approbation and applause of the present Bishop, have been expected from his said predecessor,—had not '*the dispensations of Providence*' deprived the world of it, by preventing '*the complete expansion of his plans:*' (19)—

13. Whether, of all the interpretations herein above put upon the words of the Bishop, there be any one, of which,—if received as they stand delivered, i.e. without limitation,—they might not, without any impropriety be regarded as susceptible:—

14. Whether, without giving up any the least of its claims or wishes, the most tyrannical and inhuman ecclesiastical despotism that ever raged, might not employ these same terms in the giving expression to such its claims or wishes:—

15. Whether it has been his Lordship's pleasure, to vouchsafe to subjoin to these his words so much as a single word of limitation,—having, for its effect or for its object, the clearing of this his predecessor or himself, of the wish or the design to endeavour at the establishment of such a despotism:—

16. And whether it be not among the artifices, of the *Lords of Misrule*, on whatever *Benches* seated,—for the purpose of feeling their way, and judging how far they may hope to see others follow them, to express themselves in words of studied generality, to which, as occasion serves, any meaning, between the most perfectly innoxious, and the most perfectly atrocious, may, without verbal impropriety, be attached:—their partizans, according to the disposition eventually manifested by those on whom success depends, being prepared to receive, either with willing applause, or with forced cries of unwarrantableness, the interpretation, which it is their wish to see carried into effect.

After the indications thus afforded of the strokes of character discernible in the two originals, here follow, in one frame as above, the two originals themselves.

Portrait of *Dr. Randolph*[2] and *Dr. Howley*, successively *Lords of*

[1] This is the second point 11.
[2] 1818 '*Dr. Porteus*'. The text follows the 'Errata'. Beilby Porteus (1731–1809) was Bishop of London 1787–1809.

INTRODUCTION. PART IV. §IX.

London,[1] as drawn by the said *Dr. Howley:*—copied from his *'Charge,'* &c. Anno 1814, pp. 1, 2, 3.[2]

'From the period of his' (the then late Bishop of London's) 'first entrance on the higher departments of the Church, he opposed a determined resistance to the *spurious liberality*, which in the *vain desire* (8) of *conciliation* increases division and *multiplies heresy*,(3) by *palliating* (7) *the guilt* (6) *of schism*,(4) or by diminishing the number and undervaluing the importance of doctrines essential to Christianity. The principal aim of all his labours was the maintenance of *sound doctrine* and the *security of the Established Church*,(5) which he justly considered as the bulwark of pure religion, the pillar of divine truth. To this conviction deeply rooted in his mind must we attribute his jealousy of innovation, however specious, his vigilance in exposing the tendency and *checking* (10) *the growth of opinions* (1) *or practices*,(2) *which even by remote consequence might unsettle the faith of the inexperienced, or introduce confusion and disorder into the Church*.(9) His *endeavour to replace ecclesiastical discipline on its ancient footing*,(11) *to recover the rights and assert the legitimate authority of the Spiritual Governor*,(12) originated in the same views. For he had been taught by the records of antiquity no less than by the deductions of reason, that the prosperity of our institutions depends on attention to the spirit of their laws, and that *the vigour of discipline is relaxed, and its benefit lost, by weakening the hands and fettering the discretion of the ruling power*.(13) In pursuance of this *wise policy* (14) he manifested an *inflexibility of resolution*,(15) a firmness of spirit, which could neither be daunted by clamour, nor discouraged by resistance;(16) a perseverance in labour which was never relaxed or interrupted by disgust or lassitude. In proof of the judgment which directed his views, and *the zeal* which animated his exertions in matters of general utility, we have only to cite *his effective co-operation with other distinguished prelates in establishing the National System of Education*,(17) and his paternal attention to the numerous cions of this institution, which sprang beneath his fostering care in every part of the diocese.

But I will trespass no longer on your attention, by expatiating on claims to your gratitude of which you are deeply sensible, or endeavouring to estimate the sum of *advantage* (18) which might have accrued from his active piety, *had* the dispensations of *Providence allowed a longer time* for the effect of his labours, and *the complete expansion of his plans.*'(19)

Thus far his present Lordship—Nor need we torment ourselves with any such endeavour, as that of forming an estimate, of the loss sustained by the suppression of that estimate. Never did the mantle of *an Elijah* fit more exactly the shoulders of an *Elisha*.[3] For the *Grand Lama* of to-day is not more truly one with the Grand Lama of

---

[1] i.e. John Randolph, Bishop of London 1809–13, and William Howley, Bishop of London 1813–28.
[2] See [Howley], *Charge delivered to the Clergy of the Diocese of London*, pp. 1–3.
[3] II Kings 2: 12–15.

the other day,[1] than the *Lord Bishop of London* of these same periods. Not more instructively could the 'plans' of the departed Lord-Saint have been 'expanded' by himself, than they have been, and continue to be by his Right Reverend successor. Behold what you will find written, or at least read by him, in 'a Sermon preached in the Cathedral Church of St Paul, on Thursday,' (in the same year with the year of the date, of the above Charge, but whether before or after, the Charge being without date, is among the unrevealed mysteries,) viz. on Thursday, 'June 16, 1814, being the time of the yearly meeting, of the Children educated in the Charity Schools, in and about the Cities of London and Westminster:' and printed in the 'Annual Report of the Society,' calling itself the Society 'for promoting Christian Knowledge, for the year 1814.'—Year in the title page 1815.[2]

After mention made of the self-styled *National Society* and its achievements—'On this ground' (continues his Lordship, p. 15,) 'let us manfully take our stand;'[3]—and in this stand let us not only behold but accompany him;—endeavouring, at the expense of here and there a word or two of interpretation, to render this expansion of these his plans, if not the more complete, at any rate the more clearly, and readily, and extensively intelligible.

'On this ground,' (then says he) 'let us manfully take our stand; in the fixed resolution, neither to swerve from the example of our fathers,' {add *whether Protestant or Popish,*} 'nor disregard the admonitions of scripture' {add, *where they condemn that same example*}. 'The diffusion of knowledge,' (continues he) the diffusion of knowledge 'disjoined from religious instruction,' {add, *viz. as you will see presently, in that profession, and that alone, in which under the name of the profession of our ancestors, we Bishops and those under us administer it*}—this diffusion of knowledge 'stands in the same relation to ignorance, as positive evil to the absence of good. It is an enormous encrease of power, without any adequate check or controul; injurious to the individual, injurious to the community, and thus destructive of happiness, the only reasonable end of all attempts at improvement.' {Add, *and herein we adopt, and in and by our adoption strengthen, as well as purify, the doctrine of that successor of Mahomet, by whom the library of Alexandria was purified of its contents. Either they are the same, says he, with those of the Koran, or they are*

---

[1] Each succeeding Grand Lama of Tibet was considered to be the reincarnation of a deity.

[2] William [Howley], Bishop of London, 'A Sermon preached in the Cathedral of St. Paul, on Thursday, June 16, 1814, being the time of the yearly meeting of the children educated in the charity schools in and about the cities of London and Westminster', was printed in *The Annual Report of the Society for Promoting Christian Knowledge, for the year 1814*, London, 1815, pp. 1–18.

[3] The following extract is at ibid., pp. 15–16.

INTRODUCTION. PART IV. §IX.

different:—if the same, they are useless, if different, worse than useless.}[1] 'And here' (continues his Lordship) 'we should carefully guard against the dangerous maxims, too often recommended, by the specious names of liberality, charity, and love of peace. INDIFFERENCE TO FORMS OF FAITH IS INDIFFERENCE TO TRUTH OR FALSEHOOD. The Gospel we receive with reverential acquiescence as the word of God. But the doctrine which rests on erroneous interpretation,' {add, *and every interpretation but our own is of course erroneous,*} 'or perverse exposition, of the sacred text,' {add, *and every exposition but our own is perverse,*} 'is the vain imagination of man, usurping the authority of scripture, and extruding divine truth. From our ancestors,' {add, viz. *from those among them who stood up in opposition to those principles of immutability, which I am inculcating,*} 'we have inherited the profession' {add, *in opposition to the practice*} 'of primitive and genuine Christianity; and in neglecting to secure its transmission, in unabated purity, to after-ages, we should be guilty of the most unprincipled injustice to our children, the most criminal disregard to the interests of posterity. A definite system of doctrines' {add, viz. *presented by us*} 'is of equal necessity, to maintain the integrity of revelation,' {add, *revelation being unable to maintain its own integrity,*} 'and to prevent the introduction of dangerous and corrupt novelties. Nor can we have rational assurance, that any succeeding generation will be trained in the genuine principles of Christianity, but in the indissoluble connexion of National Education with our National Faith:' {add, viz. *of an Education which forces children to say they believe, without knowing what it is, every thing which we Bishops are paid, from* 2,500*l.* to 25,000*l. a year, for professing to believe*}.[2]

Bravo, Lord of London!—'Disjoined from religious instruction'—viz. instruction in 'the religion of our ancestors'—Protestant and Popish—not to mention Heathen—and to the exclusion of all other instruction,—*knowledge* is then, according to your Lordship, so much '*positive evil.*'—Annihilate, oh Lord, all human learning!—This is *Baker* out-*Bakered*.[a] Annihilate all human learning?—and for

---

[a] Under some such title as *Reflexions upon Human Learning*, an 8vo. written by a

[1] The account of the burning of the books of the Library of Alexandria in 641 on the orders of Caliph Omar of Damascus, following the capture of the city by Muslim forces, had its source in Arabic writers. It was from the work of Bar Hebræus, Arabic Abû-l-Farağ (1226–86) that the relevant passage was translated into Latin in Edward Pocock, *Historia Compendiosa dynastiarum,* Oxford, 1663, p. 114. Doubt was, however, cast on the account by Edward Gibbon, *The History of the Decline and Fall of the Roman Empire,* 6 vols., London, 1776–88, v. 342–5.

[2] For the salaries of the Bishops, which in fact ranged from £900 to £24,000 per annum, see pp. 409–11 n. below.

what?—Only to save from the melting-pot a few hundreds of antichristian and vice-engendering Sinecures.—Ye Gods, annihilate but *space* and *time*, and make two lovers happy![1]—Compared with the inward Episcopal prayer included in the above doctrine, this amorous one was a rational one. But why speak of such a wish as if it were peculiar to lovers? The miracle which the amorous religionist only prayed for, his Lordship's friend the Archbishop, we have seen—if not atchieving, at least labouring at. In his way we have been seeing both *time* and *place*—if not annihilated, suppressed. Suppressed?— and for what? Only to save from the light of day the work of his hands—the exclusionary system—the mind-extinguishing system— that sanctified and so well-elaborated production of the modern den of CACUS.[2]

§X. *Authors, &c. continued. Dr. Manners Sutton, Archbishop of Canterbury.*

II. Next, as to the Archbishop of Canterbury.

In the tract so often referred to by the title of Report I, year of date 1812,—after a page occupied by the words '*Account of the Proceedings for the Formation of the National Society,*' the five next succeeding pages are occupied by a paper bearing at the top of the page in the form of a title, (p. 5,) the words—*Education in the Principles of the Established Church*.[3] Upon examination, what this paper is found to contain, is—an Account of so much of those same proceedings, as was antecedent to those spoken of in the *Report* by which by the several titles of '*Report of the General Committee of the National Society,*' in a preceding page,[4]—and *Report of the General Committee,* at the head of the commencing page,—it is immediately followed.[5]

For the authentication of this Account no name is visible. True it is, that at the end of it may be seen, though without *day* or *place*, the

Reverend Mr. Baker, to shew the *uselessness* of any other knowledge than that of things which are above knowledge, is still to be seen now and then in Catalogues.[6]

---

[1] For these lines, usually attributed to Jonathan Swift (1667–1745), see '$\Pi EPI\ BA\Theta OY\Sigma$: Of the Art of Sinking in Poetry', in *Miscellanies. The Last Volume,* London, 1728, Ch. XI, p. 52.

[2] In classical mythology Cacus was a savage monster who lived in a dark cave on Mount Aventine, until slain for stealing cattle by Heracles. When Heracles tore apart the rocks concealing the cave, Cacus was suddenly exposed to daylight. See Virgil, *Aeneid,* VIII. 184–305, esp. 194–5, 247–9.

[3] See *First Annual Report of the National Society,* pp. 5–9.

[4] i.e. ibid., p. 11.

[5] For 'Report of the General Committee of the National Society' see ibid., pp. 13–19.

[6] Thomas Baker (1656–1740), clergyman and antiquarian scholar, was the anonymous author of *Reflections upon Learning, Wherein is shewn the Insufficiency thereof, in its several Particulars. In order to evince the Usefulness and Necessity of Revelation,* London, 1699. The work had reached its eighth edition in 1756.

words '*H.H. Norris, Acting Secretary:*'[1] but what is thus authenticated, if by it any thing can be said to be authenticated, is—not [an][2] account of those same proceedings, but of some other proceedings subsequent to them: viz. the laying them (at no *time*) before the Prince Regent,[a] who (at no *time*) has been pleased to signify his entire approbation of the same, and (at the same or some other such *no time,*) 'has condescended to offer to become the Patron of the Society:' nor, such as it is, does the authentication,—thus given by this Mr. *Norris*, whoever he is, and supposing a person at that time in existence to have written that word, as and for his name,—appear to have been given at any *time* or *place*.

In the Account, given as above of the Society in its Pre-Adamitic state,—in this Account, such as it is (viz. in p. 6,) the first fact that presents itself is—that, for the purpose therein previously described, 'a number of persons, *friends to the Establishment* at a meeting holden on the 16th day of October, 1811,' (*persons* and *place* kept concealed) 'His Grace the Archbishop of Canterbury, in the Chair, Resolved, That such a Society be now constituted, and that measures be taken for carrying the same into effect. That for this purpose the Archbishop of Canterbury for the time being be President:'—all future Archbishops of Canterbury being it seems for this purpose, thus disposed of by his said Grace and the other Members of this Secret Association, whoever they were.

Thereafter, at two succeeding meetings, (page 6, 7,)[3] neither of which was any more than the first, held at any *place*, divers functions are assigned to the said President, in conjunction with a set of persons therein described under the name and title of *Vice-Presidents*, among whom the Bishop of London, viz. the late Bishop, whose portrait has just been seen,[4] occupies a prominent place.

In the last place comes an account of a meeting, styled *a general meeting*, which appears to be the fourth meeting held by these anonymous persons, who are so constantly and so justly ashamed

---

[a] Page 9.[5]

[1] Henry Handley Norris (1771–1850), writer and philanthropist, was Curate of St John's, South Hackney 1806–31 and Rector 1831–50. Norris was Acting Secretary at the first General Meeting, which approved the constitution and the rules of the Society, held on 21 October 1811. Subsequently, Walmsley was elected as Secretary to the General Committee, and Norris elected to the General Committee. For an earlier reference to the first General Meeting see p. 149 n. above.

[2] 1818 'on'.

[3] For a report of the two meetings held on 17 and 18 October 1811, at which appointments were made of president, vice-presidents, auditors, and a committee of sixteen members to manage the affairs of the Society, see *First Annual Report of the National Society*, pp. 6–8.

[4] See pp. 156–7 above.

[5] *First Annual Report of the National Society*, p. 9.

of themselves, viz. 'October 21, 1811.—At a general meeting of the National Society,' (then follows its long winded title),—therein said to be holden at *Bow Church*, but if really held there, held, it is sufficiently manifest, with close doors, 'His Grace the Archbishop of Canterbury, in the Chair,'—of four unnumbered Resolutions, the *second* is—that 'he be requested to lay the proceedings of this meeting' (this meeting of anonymous and self-concealed confederates) 'before . . . the *Prince Regent:*'—the *third*, that the foregoing Resolutions (numbered Resolutions, fourteen in number, declared at a former secret meeting,) 'be made public as soon as the *Archbishop and Bishop of London* shall direct:' and the fourth and last, 'That the thanks of this meeting be given to the Most Reverend the Lord Archbishop of Canterbury, for the zeal and ability manifested by him in the formation of this Society.'[1] And from and after this day, 21st October, 1811, the Society, it seems, is regarded as formed.

In Report II, in relation to his Grace of Canterbury, nothing material has been found.

But now comes Report III: and now the number of Schools having by this time been raised to 360, and that of Scholars to 60,000, (p. 19.),—and the blindness of the public at large to the Exclusionary system and its abominations sufficiently established,—now comes the time, when the veil is to be taken off, and the glory ascribed to him to whom it is most due.[2] Now accordingly it is that we are informed (p. 30,) that *'at all their deliberations'* (the deliberations of nobody knows who,) *'his Grace was constantly presiding.'*—Presiding?—Yes—*presiding:* and this being Report III, and that the latest Report extant, the deliberations thus spoken of are the deliberations, by which all the several portions of time, the accounts of which are given in these three Reports are supposed to have been occupied.

'*Presiding?*' Yes, presiding.—'*Deliberations?*'—Yes, deliberations.—To any of those cursory glances, which alone were calculated upon by these Reports, all this shews clear enough. Look a little closer, lights true and false, it will be seen, have here been blended together.

Apply the discriminating prism, the false may be separated from the true.—*Presiding?*—Yes, in this one convenient word are conjoined two different propositions: 1. that on each occasion, what was done received the sanction of the person, whose official name was *the President:* 2. that it received the sanction of certain *other* persons, in every instance, in a number sufficient to constitute, according to the nature of the case, a *Committee*, or a *Sub-Committee*. To the first of

---

[1] See *First Annual Report of the National Society*, p. 9.
[2] An echo of Psalm 29: 2.

these two propositions, credence may, with little danger of error, be attached. That with any thing like equal security it cannot be given to the others, is a proposition, the truth of which will, it is believed, by this time be found pretty well established.

'Deliberations?'—What then, and amongst whom, were these deliberations? Of non-existing public bodies, such as Committees and Sub-Committees, the deliberations will also have been non-existing. But that on a subject thus interesting, by his Grace of Canterbury no deliberations at all were ever held, this would be too much to affirm. *Deliberations?* Oh yes, in the course of the three or four years in question, deliberations doubtless not a few.—Deliberations, with his Lordship of London, at a dinner, or an evening party— at Court, or at the House: deliberations with his Grace's pillow, meaning the nightly pillow: deliberations with his said Grace's daily pillow,—the ever ready 'T.T. Walmsley, Sec.' Of any more regular deliberations—of any deliberations of any one Committee at which his Grace presided, search the Reports—all three of them—no traces will you find.

The ————, thus carried on against the religion and morality of the people, having, under the smiles of the government been entered into and organized, with little less secrecy than if it had been a ———— against the Government, hence it is, that when the documents fail—documents all along furnished, after having been fabricated, garbled, or truncated, in such manner as was deemed most conducive to their designs—fabricated, garbled, truncated, by the ———— themselves—opinion, on the part of one who is not in the secret, should not, and therefore, on this occasion, will not, venture beyond the limits of conjecture.

But—once more—*Deliberations?*—Yes: by this happily chosen ambiguous word, in addition to so many other happily chosen ambiguous words, that which, if so many suppressions as have been seen, had any object, could not without manifest falsehood have been directly *affirmed*, is most effectually insinuated: viz. the existence,—and *that* the *constant* existence,—of *Sub-Committees*, and of regular and frequent *meetings* of such Sub-Committees, as well as of the *General Committee:* Sub-Committees proposing and preparing; (Report II. p. 5.) General Committee approving and adopting: while by all that has been said, not so much as of a single Sub-Committee— (over and above the singular one so often mentioned)[1]—not to speak of the *General Committee*—for any purpose of business, will the existence of any *one* meeting be found ventured to be affirmed.

---

[1] i.e. the Building Committee: see pp. 125, 130–2, 149–50 above.

No: never, at the commencement of any enterprize which probity would have shrunk from, never were such marks of trepidation exhibited, exhibited under so perfect an assurance of impunity. Of this meeting, as well as of two preceding meetings, the *time* indeed disclosed, but by the concealment of the *place*, the disclosure rendered useless. The place, at any rate, was one that had bars and bolts to it. What was that place? Was it Lambeth Palace?[1] Was it *London Palace*, with such extraordinary and ill-assorted humility, lowered down to '*London House?*'[2]—Enquire of the Angels,—winged or not winged,—inhabitants of those holy places.

Archbishop of Canterbury, *President*—Archbishop of York and the other Bishops, sole original *Vice-Presidents*—of the all-governing Committee;—*Ten* temporal *Peers* or *Privy-Counsellors*, profane indeed, but sanctified by the nomination made of them by these consecrated persons;—*Sixteen* other members, sacred and profane together, *below* the rank of Vice-President, but still nominated by the same sacred persons;—Four vacancies to be made in each year;—but the filling up of these vacancies not to be trusted, even to a 'General Meeting' howsoever composed, but out of '*a double list*' (whatsoever be meant by a double list) formed by the President and Vice-Presidents,—of the first set of sixteen the initiative appointment not having been trusted to any less sure and zealous hands, than those of his Grace of Canterbury and his Lordship of London; .... —penetrate who can, into the interior of the fortress thus reared and entrenched.[a]

[a] After stating what was done at the meeting of 16th Oct. 1811, being the first meeting of all, and that a secret one,—viz. the Resolution for the constituting a Society for the purposes above mentioned,—the choice of the Archbishop of Canterbury for President,—the appointment of a Special Committee to consider of a Constitution, and make report to a meeting called a *General Meeting*,—and that the Committee had met accordingly, and, the Bishop of London being in the Chair, had come to certain Resolutions, of which those herein above printed, p. 114, are two, (being Resolutions declarative of the title and object of the Society),—the string of Resolutions is contained (Report I. p. 6.)[3] in the words following, viz.—

'3. That His Grace the Archbishop of York, and the Right Reverend the Bishops of both Provinces,[4] for the time being, be Vice-Presidents, together with ten temporal Peers, or Privy-Counsellors, to be nominated by the President and other Vice-Presidents for the present, and as vacancies may happen in future.

'4. That a Committee of sixteen, besides the President and Vice-Presidents, who are members *ex officio*, be appointed to manage the affairs of the Society.

'5. That the appointment of the Sixteen, for the present year, be left to the

---

[1] The London residence of the Archbishop of Canterbury.
[2] The chambers of the Bishop of London in Aldersgate Street, London.
[3] *First Annual Report of the National Society*, pp. 6–8.
[4] i.e. the provinces of Canterbury and York: in other words, the twenty-four Bishops of England and Wales and the Bishop of Sodor and Man.

INTRODUCTION. PART IV. §X.

Of all this *secrecy*,—secrecy in the conduct of a concern in itself of the most public nature,—of all this mystery, what was the final cause and motive.

Several may in conjunction be assigned to it:

1. Fear of the odium, so justly attached to the *exclusionary system:*—an odium, of which the Confederates had already had a foretaste, in the above reported passage, (see above, Part III,) in the preface to the publication of the *Poor-bettering Society:*[1]—2. Unwillingness to let it be seen, by how *small* a portion, of those to whom the right of co-operating could not but be imparted, any such exertion as that which would be necessary to the exercise of that right would ever be made:—3. Advantage seen, in the great facility afforded by the darkness with which the face of this deep[2] was covered:—the facility of practising upon the country that imposition, which from first to last has been seen practised upon it; viz. the imposition that consists in causing men to believe, that bodies of men—organized and elected bodies—have throughout been bearing a part—in a business, which throughout has been in truth the work of one and the same single

President and the Bishop of London, and such other Bishops as shall be in town; and on all future occasions to the President and Vice-Presidents, according to the manner hereinafter specified.

'6. That the Sixteen now be appointed to continue[3] in office till the first General Meeting.

'7. That a fourth part of the said Sixteen resign their office at the end of the year, but be capable of immediate re-election.

'That a double list be formed by the President and Vice-Presidents, out of which the annual general meeting shall elect the persons, who are to fill up the vacancies.

'8. That a general meeting be holden annually in the month of May or June, or oftener, if the Committee shall think it expedient.

'9. That at the same a report of the Society's proceedings be made, a Statement of the accounts for the year be laid before the Meeting, and the vacancies in the Committee be filled[4] up as above stated.

'10. That all Subscribers of not less than one guinea annually, or Benefactors to the amount of ten guineas, be qualified to attend such meeting.

'11. That a Treasurer and a Secretary be appointed by the Committee; the former to be *ex officio* a member of the Committee.

'12. That Sir Thomas Plumer, Solicitor-General,[5] and J. A. Park, Esq.[6] be Auditors for the present year, and that new auditors be elected at each general meeting for the ensuing year.

'13. That the Committee have power to make such Rules and Regulations as may be expedient for carrying into execution the designs of the Society.'

14. Naming Banking-Houses for receipt of Benefactions.

---

[1] See pp. 99–100 above.
[2] See Genesis 1: 2.
[3] *First Annual Report* 'now to be appointed continue'.
[4] Ibid. 'Committee filled'.
[5] Sir Thomas Plumer (1753–1824), Solicitor General 1807–12, Attorney General 1812–13.
[6] Sir James Alan Park (1763–1838), Justice of Common Pleas 1816–38.

individual, with or without the occasional and irregularly afforded encouragement and support, of this or that other at pleasure,—the drudgery part of the business being all along the work of a subordinate and effectually obsequious mind:—4. Convenience, afforded by the exclusion, applied not only to all witnesses to discussion, but even to all discussion itself;—to all discussion, under any circumstances, which should leave it to so much as the pretence of being *free*.—In this list behold a set of causes, abundantly adequate to the production of all these symptoms of self-conscious improbity:—and, by him who thinks he can find them, let any other less dishonourable ones be found.

On this occasion, the most Reverend the Archbishop, and his Reverend right-hand man, the Secretary, found two not very readily accordant duties, waiting to be moulded into consistency. One was— of the parcel of glory,—to which, after surrender thereof made into the hands of God in quality of Lord of the Manor, the Tenant is regularly re-admitted, with the glory of humility annext to it,—to allot the largest portion possible to the one most deserving person: i.e. (for, under the Church of England hierarchy, these are synonymous terms) to the person whose place stands highest in the joint scale of power, dignity, and opulence:—the other was—to avoid saying any thing, that should stand in direct contradiction to the all along continued notion, so plainly (Rep. II. p. 5.)[1] meant to be conveyed, viz. that, whatsoever has been done, it is by a *Committee* that it has been done: a Committee of the one sort or the other, in the composition of which, in either case, to make the least of it, members, more than one or two must on each occasion have been included.

To change the figure—it is truly edifying to observe the steersmanship displayed by the Reverend Secretary in his passage through these straits. The conclusion of the paragraph has already been seen:[2] and, down to this conclusion, here follows the commencement—(Report III. p. 30.)—'Here they' (viz. the General Committee, i.e. the Archbishop and this his well matched Secretary) 'would close their Report, if they did not deem it of importance to let it be known to the Public, that the conduct and management of the Institution has never ceased to *engage the consideration* of many of the *first characters* both in Church[3] and State, *who have been selected for that purpose by*

---

[1] See 'Report of the General Committee', *Second Annual Report of the National Society*, p. 5: 'The General Committee, to whom the management of the concerns of the National Society is entrusted, have proceeded according to the plan laid down in their former Report, and have now to submit to the Publick the progress they have made during the last year, which they trust will be found to be considerable.'

[2] See p. 162 above.

[3] *Third Annual Report* 'both of Church'.

INTRODUCTION. PART IV. §X.

the Society at large.[a] It would be *superfluous* to enumerate individually *all those whose exertions have been eminently serviceable;* but it must be satisfactory to the Public to learn, and therefore it is their duty not to withhold the fact, that, notwithstanding the .... demands on the time of' .... &c.:—and then comes the above-mentioned passage (see p. 162 of this) about the *constant presidence.*

Such is the mention made of the persons, in relation to whom, the design appears to have been—that, of these same persons, by us who are not in the secret, it should be understood,—that the several Sub-Committees and meetings of the General Committee have all along been composed. To have said as much in direct terms, would have been a direct falsehood; and *that*,—to several persons in the first instance, and by means of some of them to persons in general,—sooner or later, a notorious one. But, by the phraseology thus ingeniously and happily contrived, the scandal, that would have resulted from any such discovery, was avoided.

The National Society!—not merely *a* National Society, but *the* National Society!—as if in the whole *nation* there neither ever was, nor ever can be any *other* Society?—*The National Society?*—No: to a Society constituted for such ends—in such manner and form—and by such means—to give the style and title of *the National Society,*—is a libel upon the Nation.—A Society, of which the end in view is oppression, the form despotic, the first means secresy, the ulterior means imposture?—a Society set on foot by a knot of persons, who were and are ashamed or afraid to own themselves? a Society, of which, from first to last, the business has been done, by persons who from the first to the last, have been and still are, ashamed or afraid to make known the parts they respectively had in it?—this, in England, a *National* Society?—and not only *a* National Society but *the* only one?—Yes:—self-assumed names, long and short—members—operations—in this Society, such as it has been already seen to be, every thing is of a piece.

---

[a] *'Selected by the Society at large?'* Unhappily this is a .... what shall we say?—a mere invention; alas! and *that* a studied one: it is in pursuance of the plan which gave birth to this untruth, that, to the governing body, the appellation of *The General Committee*—by which was to be understood The General Committee *of* the Society at large—has been all along applied. General Committee *of* the National Society at large—*nominated by* the Society at large—(i.e. as per Resolution 8, 9, 10, p. 165 of this, by the whole body of the Contributors)—such is the false notion endeavoured to be conveyed.—The truth is—that never has any thing been done by the Society at large. No such *nomination* made: no such *'selection'* made, as is above stated in the text. For a compleat exposure of this fraud, see below, §12.[1]

[1] See pp. 186–94 below.

The Bishops' Society—the Members of it, all of them, either themselves Bishops, or nominees of Bishops—*The Bishops' Society*—a job for the Bishops, set on foot by the Bishops—carried on by and for Bishops—such, it has been seen, is its *nature*—such and such alone is the *name*, by which it should be called.

§XI. *How to organize a Chaos—Forms of Disorder exemplified in these Reports.*

Thus much concerning the supposed system of *imposition*, considered in that same character,—as also concerning its author or authors. But even supposing all sinister design out of the question,—every thing that is amiss having imbecility for its sole cause,—even on this supposition the few additional pages that may be necessary to the placing of this imbecility in its true light, will scarcely be thought to lie open to the charge of being wasted on an unworthy subject. Yes—if the Reverend T.T. Walmsley, Sec., so often mentioned, were the only person to whom the symptoms of incapacity about to be displayed were imputable. But, among the persons whose fitness for these respective offices is at stake, in the character either of penners or approvers,—are those who, taken together, form no small portion, of those members of the great community, on whose fitness for the functions respectively exercised by them, the lot of all the others,—not to speak of those persons themselves,—is in so great a degree dependent.

1. First, as to *the Archbishop of Canterbury*. Whether, for the general scheme of execution, as well as for the original design,—it be not to his Grace, in conjunction with the two successive Lords of London, that the acknowledgements of the public are, in the first place, if not exclusively due—is a point, which, with such grounds for decision as presented themselves, has already been submitted to the judgment of the sincere reader. But the point now in question is the *penmanship:* and it will now be to be seen—whether, of whatsoever glory may be derivable from this source, either the entire mass, or at least by far the principal portion, belongs not by an indisputable title to his said Grace.

In relation to the body, in which, in and by these Reports, his Grace is throughout represented as acting in the character of *President*,—the doubts which have presented themselves, as attaching to its title to its assumed appellative of *a Committee*, will presently be brought to view. But, be this as it may, *Committee* is the name there given, to a body to such a degree *Parliamentary*, that the whole body of *Lords Spiritual* formed but a part of it. Now then,—as in the House of Commons, so in the House of Lords,—as often as a paper, under the

INTRODUCTION. PART IV. §XI.

name of *a Report*, is penned, *a Committee* being the authority, in the name of which it appears, the hand of the *Chairman* of that same Committee is the hand, by which, at any rate it is always *supposed* to be penned,—and, unless by accident, always *is* penned.

In the penning of these papers, suppose even any subordinate hand—suppose, as next in course, the hand of T.T. Walmsley, Sec. to have been ever so busy—suppose accordingly that in the main they belong not to his Grace on the score of *generation*,—at any rate they cannot but have belonged to his said Grace on the score of *adoption:* which circumstance, even without any direct evidence,—if not for all purposes of admiration, at any rate for all purposes of commiseration,—suffices to render it as much his Grace's work as if it had been by his Grace's most Reverend hand that the characters had been penned, or by his Grace's most Reverend lips, that the sounds of which they are expressive had been dictated.

Not, however, to any such ground of inference, is his said Grace's claim to the title of adoptive parent of this intellectual progeny confined. In Report II. p. 18., at his Grace's motion, &c. &c. a Resolution passed, ordering that 'of the proceedings of this Society a correct statement for the' {then} 'last year be published forthwith:'—and, in Report III. p. 28., in the discharge of the duties of his 'peculiarly laborious office,' among which are particularized the having 'to attend upon all its (the Society's) Committees, and to record all its proceedings:' his *'merits'* are stated as being such on which 'it may be thought unnecessary to enlarge.'[1]

Of the work in question, be it what it may, the paternity, by a title thus indisputable, belongs then to his said Grace.

What the work consists of is—a *Report*,—i.e. a statement—summary statement—of the proceedings of a public body,—followed, as usual, by an *Appendix*, composed of a number of separate papers, or written discourses,—which, instead of being interwoven in the narrative, are, for shortness, discarded out of it,—and in each instance are, or at least ought to be, referred to in it. On the present occasion, the *body* of the Report is out of the question: all that belongs to the occasion is the *Appendix*.

Even in the Appendix, all that belongs to the present purpose is comprehended under two heads, viz. 1. giving,—in or in connexion with the body of the Report,—in relation to each article in the Appendix, that brief indication of the distinguishing nature of its

---

[1] See *Third Annual Report of the National Society*, p. 28: 'On the merits of their Secretary, the Rev. T.T. Walmsley, whose office is peculiarly laborious, from having to conduct the whole correspondence of the Society, to attend upon all its Committees, and to record all its proceedings, it may be thought unnecessary to enlarge'.

contents, which is commonly denominated *a title:* and 2. the attaching to it, in some way or other, according to the nature of it, those *tokens of authenticity*, which lead to the proof that it is what it assumes to be: and in particular that it is the discourse of the person or persons whose discourse it assumes to be:—and, in so far as, with relation to the contents of the individual article in question, independently of the question of authenticity, the circumstance of time is on any other account material, at what point of time the paper received its existence, or its currency, as the case may be.

On this occasion, the difficulty that belongs to the occasion consists—not so much in the keeping to the track of propriety,—but in the conceiving how, in relation to either of the two just mentioned points, it could have happened to a man to depart from it. This track is no other than what every man, one should have thought, would have fallen into, and continued in of course. Among so many *Reports*, as, in every session, are given in by so many *Committees* of the House of *Commons*—not to speak of the House of great dignity and small use[1]—among all these instruments, not so much perhaps as one would be to be found, which, how indifferently soever penned in other respects, might not in these two particulars have afforded to the penner of the Reports here in question a pattern for imitation:—a pattern, and that so plain and complete an one, that, so long as the author kept his work in a state of conformity to it, the work could not go amiss.

In this sort of parliamentary composition are included both the above points—viz. *title* and *tokens of authenticity:* but, as to what concerns the tokens of authenticity, and in them as to what concerns the *date*,—among the letters, which, under the direction of the master, a boy at a Boarding School writes to his parents, scarcely would any one be found, that did not present a pattern, the non-observance of which, together with the darkness of which it has been productive, has already been seen exemplified in this performance of the head of the Church-of-England Clergy. Obviating any such imputation as that of spuriousness, would not indeed be either within the school-boy's view, or congenial to the nature and purpose of such his performance: but, when applied to the case of a public body, these circumstances, mention of which would, by the school-boy, be made of course, are not the less applicable to the public purpose now before us.

It is now time to give a sort of general outline of the chaos, the particular features of which have already, most of them, been separately brought to view. The forms of disorder, which will be

---

[1] i.e. the House of Lords.

INTRODUCTION. PART IV. §XI.

seen exemplified, will, it is believed, be found referable to one or other of the thirteen ensuing heads:—

1. *Form of Disorder* 1.—To the article in question,—though in the Appendix shot down in the midst of a set of titled articles,—in no fewer than *nine* instances, no *title* any where. None to the article itself: none in the *Table of Contents:* accordingly, the articles in that Table being, in the customary way, distinguished by Nos., no *No.* to it there or elsewhere:—consequently, no reference to it in the body of the Report.[a]

[a] I. Instances in Report I.

I. Report I. p. 54.—Advertisement, declaring how Parishes, &c. may *unite* themselves to this Society, (i.e. place themselves under the direction of the governing body), viz. through the *Bishop* of the Diocese: and correspond with it; viz. through its *Secretary*.

II. Report I. p. 64.—Advertisement, stating who the *Trustees* are, in whose names the government annuities belonging to the Society are invested.

III. Report I. p. 64.—Advertisement, mentioning who the *Bankers* are, in whose hands such part of the Society's money, as is destined for current expenses, is lodged.

IV. Report I. p. 197.—List of *Country Schools*, to which pecuniary *aid* has been afforded by the governing body.

V. Report I. pp. 197, 198.—List of Books recommended as *Lesson-Books* for the Schools.—N.B. In Report II. pp. 189, 190, this article will be found: and in that place with a *title*, such as it will be seen to be; and moreover accordingly with a No. in that place, as well as in the Table of Contents. And so likewise again in Report III. pp. 168, 169. See above p. 136.

II. Instances in Report II.

None, except as underneath.

III. Instances in Report III.

VI.—1. Notices to Country Parishes, concerning the *terms of Union*. It consists of an Extract from Report I. (viz. from the body of the Report), p. 19, *that* being the last. At the conclusion are the following words in Italics—'*Extract from the first Report of June* 1812:'[1] as if there had been two Reports, both issued at that same no-time. Whence this date was taken,—imperfect as, for want of the day of the month, it is,—does not appear: no such date has been found any where attached to this Report. The page in which the Extract is printed, is, as above, p. 19. But, in the reference thus made, the No. of the page is not comprized. Of this Extract, such as it is, the rationally expectable use seems not very easy to discover. Without mention made of it in the *body of the Report*,—without No. to lead to it in the *Table of Contents*, or consequently to the paper itself in the Appendix in which it is placed,—without so much as a title to attract the eye, unless a pair of words, so completely uncharacteristic as the words NATIONAL SOCIETY, be regarded as a title,—it lies thus buried in the Appendix, where the chances are, in each

---

[1] See *Third Annual Report of the National Society*, p. 168. The extract from the Report of June 1812 stated that the National Society sought 'no controul over the Schools established in the several Districts, nor any thing more than an assurance that they are founded on the same general Principles, on which sole condition they are willing to receive them into Union, and to give them such advice and assistance as may occasionally be required'.

2. *Form of Disorder* 2.—In *three* instances, Title,—and accordingly a No. in the Table of Contents: No., but no title to the article itself.[a]

3. *Form of Disorder* 3.—In *ten* instances, *Title* of the article more or less *uncharacteristic* of its contents.[b]

    instance—who shall say how many?—against its being descried by the eye, for which, if for any thing, it must have been intended. Had it been inserted in the *body* of this *third* Report, as it was in that of the *first* Report, the probability of its answering its purpose would have been at its *maximum:* as it is, it is at its *minimum:*—in the *body*, the number of pages being but 30; in the *Appendix*, 158,—besides a long series of unnumbered ones.[1]

VII. 2. Report I. p. 64.—'*Form of leaving a legacy to the Society.*'—Furnished as it is with this *title* upon the face of the paper itself, this article will not in strictness come exactly under the form of disorder here in question, according to the description above given of it. It does however in essentials: for, in the *Table of Contents* it has no place: nor consequently, in the Appendix, into which it has found its way by a chance throw, has it any No. to distinguish it. In this Report it comes next after the abovementioned Notes about the Bankers.

VIII. 3. Report II. p. 199.—In this Report, viz. in this place in the Report, this same article is reprinted in the same manner. It here stands last but one; having no articles after it but that which exhibits the allowance given to the Year's Account by the Auditors.

IX. 4. Report III. p. 181. So likewise in this third Report. Position, the same as in Report II.

[a] Instances in Report I.

I. Report I. p. 49. No. 5.—Proceedings of the Deanery of *Tendering*, in the County of Essex.

II. Report I. p. 65. No. 10.—Substance of the Applications from the Forest of *Dean*.

III. Report I. p. 66. No. 11.—Extract from the Statement of the Society of *School-Masters*.

Of this form of disorder no instance has been found, either in Report II. or in Report III.

At the time of the penning of Report II., the penman had become aware, of the incongruity of omitting to give any title to the article itself, in a case in which a title stood attached to it in the Table of Contents. But, among the things that remain still to be learnt by him are—1. the incongruity of attaching to the article itself a title which is not *characteristic* of its contents: and 2. the incongruity of employing, for the designation of an article in the Table of Contents, a title which is otherwise than exactly *conformable* to the title attached to the article itself.

[b] Instances in Report I.

I. 1. Report I. p. 25. No. 2.—'Address to the Public. January 29th, 1812.'—*Object*, soliciting Contributions.

II. 2. Report I. p. 58. No. 7.—'Advertisement of the Society, April 8th, 1812.' *Object*, in the foreground—notice of the opening of a School: Object, in the back-ground—*opinions, thought, belief, desire and readiness, exhortations*—ascribed to the whole Society.[2]

---

[1] *Third Annual Report of the National Society* is mispaginated: it begins with the Report at pp. 1–30, continues with ten Appendices at pp. 25–183, and concludes with sixty-five unnumbered pages containing a list of benefactors and annual subscribers, and an index.

[2] For Bentham's discussion of this paper see pp. 135–6 above.

INTRODUCTION. PART IV. §XI.

4. *Form of Disorder* 4.—In *three* instances, *Contents* of the article *heterogeneous:* the title applicable to no more than a *part* of them.[a]

Instances in Report II.

I. 3. Report II. pp. 179 to 185. No. 3.—'Paper circulated by the Norfolk and Norwich Society, for the Education of the Poor in the Principles of the Established Church.'—*Subject*, Plan for the extension of the system. Proceedings at North Walsham, in Norfolk.

II. 4. Report II. p. 188. No. 5.—'Advertisement of the National Society, April 8th, 1812.' See above, instance 2.

III. 5. Report II. p. 189. No. 6.—'NATIONAL SOCIETY, For the Education of the Poor in the Principles of the Established Church.' *Object*, recommendation of Lesson-Books.[1]

IV. 6. Report II. p. 191. No. 7.—'NATIONAL SOCIETY, For the Education of the Poor in the Principles of the Established Church.' *Object*, miscellaneous: *School opened—Masters trained—Books recommended—Report I. printed—Money offered—Prosperity declared.* See above, p. 140.

Instances in Report III.

I. 7. Report III. p. 168. No. 4.—'NATIONAL SOCIETY, For the Education of the Poor in the Principles of the Established Church.' *Object*, recommendation of Lesson-Books. See above, instance 5.

II. 8. Report III. p. 170. No. 5.—'NATIONAL SOCIETY, For the Education of the Poor in the principles of the Established Church.' *Object*, miscellaneous. See above, instance 6.

III. 9. Report III. p. 178. No. 9.—'SOCIETY OF SECRETARIES.' *Contents*, Resolution passed in London, by a Society composed of Secretaries to Local Societies. *Objects—Concentrating in London information of the state of the Country Education—Appointment of a Visitor-General.*

IV. 10. Report III. p. 182. No. 10.—'NATIONAL SOCIETY, For the Education of the Poor in the Principles of the Established Church.' *Contents*, Auditor's allowance of the Accounts. N.B. To the corresponding article of the *first* year, a *characteristic* title may be seen attached in Report I.[2]

In no one of these instances, as far as appears, would the talent of the penman serve him, for conveying any the most general information, concerning the *contents, object*, or *subject* of the article. Instead of it, what he gives is—what appears to have been constantly in his thoughts—a puff, expressive of the personal and party feelings, in which, the whole design so manifestly originated. Church for ever! Excellent Church for ever! Huzza! Hallelujah!

[a] Instances in Report I.

I. [1.] Report I. p. 58. No. 7.—Title uncharacteristic:—viz. '*Advertisement of the National Society, April* 8, 1812.' Contents, 1. *One London School opened, viz. in Baldwin's Gardens:*—2. *another about to be:*—*no more intended.*—3. *Local Schools recommended.*—4. *Union and pecuniary assistance offered to them.*—5. *Exhortations to all, especially Clergy, to become contributors.*—To no more than the two first of these articles, does the appellation *Advertisement* seem applicable. See above, *Form of Disorder* 3: where, the purpose being different, the summary is slightly different.

---

[1] For Bentham's discussion of books recommended by the National Society see pp. 62–7 above.

[2] See 'National Society's Account of Receipt and Expenditure, From 21st of October, 1811, to 18th of May, 1812', in *First Annual Report of the National Society*, Appendix IX, pp. 62–3.

CHURCH-OF-ENGLANDISM

5. *Form of Disorder* 5.—In *twenty-one* instances, Title in the *Table of Contents* not conformable to the title at the head of the *article* itself.[a]

Instances in Report II.

I. 2. Report II. p. 188. No. 5. The same as the above.

II. 3. p. 191. No. 7.—Titles uncharacteristic: viz. the standing puff, *National Society*, &c. as above, *Form* 3.—Contents—1. *The Baldwin's Gardens School opened and inspectable*. 2. *For Masters and Mistresses, persons will be received and trained in London*. 3. *Lesson-Books on what terms furnished*. 4. *Society's object, what*. 5. *Contributions solicited*. 6. *Progress reported*. 7. *Pecuniary aid offered to local Schools*. 8. *Success declared*. 9. *Contributions when and where receivable*.

N.B. Most of these articles seem to present matter for so many separate advertisements. But any attempt to decompose the mass and give arrangement to its contents would be lost labour here.

[a] *Titles in the Tables of Contents.*   *Titles at the Head of the Papers themselves.*

Instances in Report I.[1]

I. (Report I. p. 25.) 'No. II.—Address to the Public.'   'No. II.—Address to the Public, 29th January, 1812.'

II. (Report I. p. 29.) 'No. IV.—List of Diocesan, District, and other Societies, united to the National Society.'   'No. IV. Summary of Reports from Diocesan, District, and other Societies, united to the National Society.'

III. (Report I. p. 60.) 'No. VIII.—Rules for the Office of Treasurer and Secretary.'   'No. VIII.—Duties of the Treasurer and Secretary.'

N.B. It should have been *Offices:* though by the phraseology the opposite meaning is, in both places, expressed.

IV. (Report I. p. 62.) 'No. IX.—Audit of the Accounts from Oct. 21, 1811, to May 18, 1812.'   'No. IX.—National Society's Account of Receipt and Expenditure, from 21st of October, 1811, to 18th of May, 1812.'

Instances in Report II.[2]

V. (1. Report II. p. 178.) 'No. II.—Grants of Money made by the National Society to Diocese[3] and District Societies and Schools in Union with it.'   'No. II.—Grants of Money made by the National Society to Diocesan and District Societies and Schools in Union with it, since the annual General Meeting, 3d of June, 1812.'

VI. (2. Report II. pp. 179 to 185.) 'No. III.—Paper circulated by the Norfolk and Norwich Society.'   'No. III.—Paper circulated by the Norfolk and Norwich Society, for the Education of the Poor in the Principles of the Established Church.'

VII. (3. Report II. p. 186.) 'No. IV.—Plan of Union.'   'No. IV.—National Society—PLAN of UNION. February, 1812.'

VIII. (4. Report II. p. 189.) 'No. VI.—Ditto, August, 1812.'   'No. VI.—National Society, For the Education of the Poor in the Principles of the Established Church.'

IX. (5. Report II. p. 191.) 'No. VII.—Ditto, February, 1813.'   'No. VII.—National Society, For the Education of the Poor in the Principles of the Established Church.'

---

[1] The Table of Contents appears in *First Annual Report of the National Society* at p. 22.
[2] The Table of Contents appears in *Second Annual Report of the National Society* at p. 1.
[3] *Second Annual Report* 'Diocesan'.

INTRODUCTION. PART IV. §XI.

6. *Form of Disorder* 6.—Out of *twenty-six* instances, in all of which, if in any one, a demand for the form of words *By order of the Committee* had place, (viz. at the end of the article, and immediately before the signature,) this same form of words attached to the article in *four* instances, not attached to it in the remaining *twenty-two*.[a]

Titles in the Tables of Contents.	*Titles at the Head of the Papers themselves.*
X. (6. Report II. p. 194.) 'No. VIII.—Present State of the Central School in Baldwin's Gardens.'	'No. VIII.—The present state of the Central School in Baldwin's Gardens.'
XI. (7. Report II. p. 197.) 'No. IX.—Form of Certificate for Masters.'	'No. IX.—Form of Certificate for Masters, National Society Central School.'
XII. (8. Report II. p. 197.) 'No. X.—Regulation[1] for Training Masters.'	'No. X.—Rules and Regulations for Training Masters.'
XIII. (9. Report II. p. 200.) 'No. XI.—Audit of the Accounts from May, 1812, to June, 1813.'	'No. XI.—National Society for the Education of the Poor in the Principles of the Established Church.'

Instances in Report III.[2]

XIV. (1. Report III. p. 165.) 'No. II.—Grants of Money made by the National Society to Diocesan and District Societies and Schools in Union with it.'	'No. II.—Grants of Money made by the National Society to Diocesan and District Societies and Schools in Union with it, since the annual General Meeting, 2d June, 1813.'
XV. (2. Report III. p. 166.) 'No. III.—Plan of Union.'	'No. III.—National Society.—Plan of Union, February, 1812.'
XVI. (3. Report III. p. 168.) 'No. IV.—Advertisement of the National Society, Aug. 1812.'	'No. IV.—National Society, For the Education of the Poor in the Principles of the Established Church.'
XVII. (4. Report III. p. 170.) 'No. V.—Ditto, February, 1813.'	'No. V.—National Society, For the Education of the Poor in the Principles of the Established Church.'
XVIII. (5. Report III. p. 173.) 'No. VI.—Present State of the Central School in Baldwin's Gardens.'	'No VI.—The present State of the Central School, Baldwin's Gardens.'
XIX. (6. Report III. p. 176.) 'No. VII.—Form of Certificate for Masters.'	'No. VII.—Form of Certificate for Masters, National Society Central School.'
XX. (7. Report III. p. 176.) 'No. VIII.—Regulations for Training Masters.'	'No. VIII.[3]—Rules and Regulations for Training Masters.'
XXI. (8. Report III. p. [182].)[4] 'No.X.—Audit of the Accounts from May, 1813, to June, 1814.'	No. X. National Society, For the Education of the Poor in the Principles of the Established Church.'

[a] By order of the Committee,—what?—Here is an ellipsis; how is it to be supplied?—What is it that, by the body thus denominated, is meant to be represented as having been ordered to be done?

---
[1] *Second Annual Report* 'Regulations'.
[2] The Table of Contents appears in *Third Annual Report of the National Society* at p. 5.
[3] Appendix VIII is mistakenly numbered X in ibid., p. 176.
[4] 1818 '176' is a slip. Appendix X commences at *Third Annual Report of the National Society*, p. 182.

CHURCH-OF-ENGLANDISM

1. If the article in question be meant to be represented as being an act of that same body, is it that the effect of the order is meant to be the *making entry* of the article upon the books?—upon the books in which the acts of the body are registered?

2. Is it, that, on the particular occasion in question, *publication*—separate publication—shall be made of it?—The act being of the nature of an Advertisement, and so intituled, this is what in some instances—and in particular in the present one—must, it should seem, have been meant.

3. Is it, that in the next Report published of the proceedings of the body, insertion shall be given to it?—For this purpose, one general order, comprehending all the papers proposed to be inserted in the Report, might suffice. Even without any such express order, an order calling upon the Chairman, the Secretary, or any other person belonging to the body, to draw up the Report, will naturally, supposing no limitation attached, be understood as giving him authority for the insertion of all such papers, the insertion of which shall, in his view of the matter, be requisite.

1. One case there is, in which the *first* of the above three meanings cannot be the proper one. That is—where the discourse in question is not an act of the body itself, but the discourse of some person or persons not members of the body: in which case it will from him or them have been received by the body itself, or by some person or persons commissioned for that purpose: as in the case of communications made from particular local bodies, acting in union with this general body.

2. So, if the article be the discourse of this or that person, or assemblage of persons, acting in some official character under the directions of the governing body itself: as here in the instance of the *Secretary*, and the two *Auditors* of the Accounts.

3. If in any instance the declaration made in Report II. p. 5. has been true, viz. that, for this self-styled *Committee*, 'every branch of their business has been prepared for them by their Sub-Committees;'[1] then in so far as this is true, for every act of the Committee itself, there must have been *two* orders given: viz. one, for the entering of the Report made by the Sub-Committee; and another, for the adoption of the matter of that Report by the Committee.

For example, on the occasion of the article, which stands first in the first of these three Reports,—the article being a Report made by a *Sub-Committee*, viz. the Building Committee, certifying an opinion formed by that same Sub-Committee,[2]—*that* opinion destined indeed to form a *ground* for some act of the principal Committee, but not being itself a discourse destined to become an act of that same Committee,—this case is *not* of the number of those, which admit of any such pair of corresponding orders.

But, next to that comes an '*Address to the Public*,' 29th January, 1812, calling for contributions from persons at large: next to that again (to go no further) the '*Plan of Union*' according to which the Country Societies are called upon to take upon them the yoke prepared for them by these Bishops:[3] and, in each of these instances, if the declaration made as above was true, there must have been *two* orders: one, according to which the paper became the act of the appropriate *Sub-Committee*;—the other, by which it thereupon became the act of the principal body, self-styled *the Committee:* and, as to *publication*, if, in the instance of the *Address*, entry and *publication* will be understood, as being of course comprized in one and the same order,—in the instance of the *Plan* this will hardly be the case: and if so, here then is a demand for *one more* order, viz. *a third*.

---

[1] See p. 130 above.
[2] See *First Annual Report of the National Society*, Appendix I, pp. 23–4.
[3] See ibid., Appendix II, pp. 25–6, and Appendix III, pp. 27–8.

INTRODUCTION. PART IV. §XI.

Instances in Report I. none.

In Report I. p. 54. may, however, be seen one article, though without a number, by the commencement of which, the conception of its having received the sanction of the governing body seems intended to be conveyed. '*The General Committee of the National Society*' (it is said) '*wish* the parochial clergy to understand'—viz. how union with the Society so called may be effected, and correspondence with it carried on.

This, it is manifest, though it might have been rendered, is not as it stands, the discourse of the body thus described. It is not even given as such by the penman by whom it is thus penned. For, where it is really his intention so to do, he finds no difficulty in giving expression and effect to such intention:—witness the ensuing articles. What he wishes is—that it may notwithstanding be taken for an act which has received the sanction of the Society, he himself knowing that it is not so.

Instances in Report II.

1. Report II. p. 189, No. VI.—Title in the Table of Contents, '*Ditto, August,* 1812.'—Title on the article itself, '*National Society,*' &c.—Words of the authenticating clause, just before the signature, '*By order of the Committee.*'—Signature, '*T.T. Walmsley, Sec.* No. 13, Clifford's Inn.' N.B. This is the article for the recommendation of Lesson-Books.[1] What the word *Ditto* is meant to represent is '*Advertisement of the National Society:*' these words forming part of the words of which the last preceding article is composed.

2. Report II. p. 191. No. VII.—Title in the Table of Contents, '*Ditto, February,* 1813.' Title to the article itself, '*National Society,*' &c.—Signature, '*T.T. Walmsley, February,* 1813.' This is one of the miscellaneous articles.[2]—N.B.—Here are three articles following, to each of which the appellation of an *Advertisement of the National Society* is applied; yet only to the two last of them is the formula of authentication *By order,* &c. applied.[3]—Is it then that the first of them, though not the act of the body in question, was yet meant to be given as such?

Instances in Report III.

3. Report III. p. 168. No. IV.—A reprint of the article No. VI. in Report II. Signature, T.T. Walmsley, Sec. August, 1812.

4. Report III. p.170. No. V.—A reprint of the article No. VII. in Report II. Signature (this time) '*T.T. Walmsley, Sec. February,* 1813.'

Instances in which, in all three Reports taken together, the demand for this formulary, if in any, had place,—the article being an instrument which, besides the order for the publication of it, received, or should have received, its existence from the governing body:—These are—

1. Instances in which (as per *Form I.*) the article has not any No., or, except in three of them, any title, either in the *Table of Contents* or to the *article* itself   6[4]
2. Instances in which (as per *Form I.*) the article has not any No. in either place, nor any title in the Table of Contents, but has a title to the article itself   -   3[5]
3. Instances in which the article has a No. in both places, and a title in both or one   - - - - - - - - - - - - - 17[a]

Total   26

[a] Articles of this description appear to be—in Report I. Nos. 2, 3, 7, 8:—in Report II. Nos. 4, 5, 6, 7, 8, 9, 10:—in Report III. Nos. 3, 4, 5, 6, 7, 8.[6]

[1] See p. 63 n. above.   [2] See pp. 140–1 above.
[3] See *Second Annual Report of the National Society*, Appendices V, VI, VII, at pp. 188–9, 189–90, 191–3, respectively.   [4] i.e. '*Form of Disorder* I', nos. I–VI, pp. 171–2 n. above.
[5] i.e. '*Form of Disorder* I', nos. VII–IX, p. 172 n. above.
[6] The numbers refer to the Appendices within each *Report.*

7. *Form of Disorder* 7.—Secretary's attestation—in some instances, viz. *fourteen*, or thereabouts, attached; in others, viz. *twenty-two*, or thereabouts, not.[a]

Deduct instances in which, as above, that same demand is satisfied - - 4

Remain instances in which it is not satisfied - - - - - - - 22

[a] Follows an account of the instances in which, in all the Reports taken together, the demand for this formulary, if in any, had place:[1]
1. Instances in which (as per *Form of Disorder I.*) being, as above, *unnumbered*,[2] the article appears, as above (*Form* 6.)[3] to be an instrument requiring to receive its existence from the governing body—say, among the exemplifications of *that* form, articles 1, 5, 7, 8, 9: making together - - 5
2. Instances in which, being *unnumbered*, the article appears to be such, as to be capable of receiving its existence, without impropriety, from the Secretary alone;—at any rate, on the supposition of an order to that effect, from the governing body, to pen and publish an article of the description in question:—say, among the exemplifications of *that* form,[4] articles 2, 3, 4, 6: making together - - - - - - - - 4
3. Instances, in which (as per *Form* 6) the article *having a No.* attached to it, and being such as required to receive its existence from the governing body, required accordingly the signature of the Secretary: though to no other purpose than that of certifying the article to be of the number of those instruments, for the publication of which,—they being moreover such as had received their existence from the governing body,—an order from that same body had been given - - - - - - - - - - 17[5]
4. Instances in which (the article *having* moreover its *number)* the signature of the Secretary appears requisite: viz. according to the nature of the case, either for the certifying it to have been penned by himself,—under an order, or permission, of the governing body for that purpose, together with a corresponding order for publication;—or, in the case of such of them as came to the Society from other hands, for the certifying the existence of an order for the publication of it - - - - - - - - - - 10[a]

Total number of the instances in which the demand for his attestation appears to have had place - - - - - - - - - - - - 36

[a] Articles, to the penning of which the Secretary may have been competent.—Say, in Report I. Nos. 4 and 10: in Report II. Nos. 1 and 2:—in Report III. Nos. 1 and 2: together 6.

Articles, sent in to the Society from other quarters.—Say, in Report I. Nos. 5 and 11:—in Report II. No. 3:—in Report III. No. 9: together 4.—Total 10.

N.B. In this account, are not included the three articles exhibiting the allowances given to the Accounts by the *Auditors*, in and for the three years: viz. in Report I. No. 9:—in Report II. No. 3:—in Report III. No. 10.

[1] 1818 'places'. The text follows the 'Errata'.
[2] See pp. 171–2 n. above.
[3] See p. 175 above.
[4] i.e. '*Form of Disorder* 1.'
[5] For the seventeen instances in question see p. 177 n. above.

INTRODUCTION. PART IV. §XI.

8. *Form of Disorder* 8. Secretary's attestation differently expressed in different instances.[a]

Deduct, instances in which his attestation is accordingly attached: for the particulars of which see the *Form of Disorder* next ensuing[1] - - - - } 14[a]
Remain, instances in which it is not attached - - - - - - - 22

[a] N.B. A preliminary question is—what is the name of the Reverend Gentleman thus designated?—Look for it who will, no where will he find it in any one of these three Reports. The Surname, yes: but as to the Christian name, look for it where you will, no where will you find any more of it than T.T.

In so small a total number as fourteen, as above, no fewer than *five* different forms or modes of signature may these three Reports, when taken together, be seen to exhibit.

1. First behold him T.T. Walmsley, Sec.; signing in no *place*, and at no *time*. Instances, six: viz. in Report I. No. 1, 3, 0:[2]—in Report II. No. 4:—in Report III. Nos. 3, 0:[3]—together, 6.

2. Next behold him signing at a certain *place*, but at no time. Instances, five:—viz. in Report I, Nos. 2 and 7—in Report II, Nos. 5 and 6:—together, 4.—*Place* in all these instances, No. 13, Clifford's Inn.

3. In the third place behold him signing in no *place*, but however at some time, though *that* a most unfortunately as well as remarkably uncertain one. Instances two: viz. in Report II. No. 4: *Place* none; *Time*, as to month and year, February, 1813, but not on any day of the month:—in Report III. No. 5, article the same: Topography and Chronology the same. This ignorance or oblivion respecting the time at which he wrote his own signature, had it for its purpose any such design as that of giving accompaniment and apology to the like ignorance or oblivion, in respect of so many imaginary acts, given as acts of his imaginarily acting body, self-styled *the General Committee?*

4. In the fourth place,—such is the advance at this time made by him, in the kindred sciences of Geography and Chronology—behold him informed of the *place*, as well as (though still with the former exception as to the day) of the *time* in which he wrote. Of this degree of perfection we have however but one exemplification: viz. in Report III. No. 4. *Place*, No. 13, Clifford's Inn: *Time*, August, 1812:—but as to what day it was in the month,[4] this in the scale of Chronological science, is a point to which at the penning of this last of the three Reports he had not yet attained. In the Report which is next to come, one step more may give the deficiency its supply. Thus it was,

[a] Say, in Report I. Nos. 1, 2, 3, 7, 8:—in Report II. Nos. 4, 5, 6, 7:—in Report III. Nos. 3, 0, 4, 5.—Total 13.—N.B. By the 0 is designated the article consisting of an *Extract from the conclusion of Report I.* to which Extract no No. is attached, nor is any notice taken of it in the Table of Contents.[5]

---

[1] i.e. '*Form of Disorder* 8'.
[2] For this untitled article, mentioned at pp. 171 n., 177 n. above, see *First Annual Report of the National Society*, p. 54. A place, however, is given, namely 13, Clifford's Inn.
[3] For this untitled article, mentioned at pp. 171-2 n. above, see *Third Annual Report of the National Society*, p. 168. It does, however, carry the heading 'National Society'.
[4] 1818 'in month'. The text follows the 'Errata'.
[5] For this unnumbered article see *Third Annual Report of the National Society*, p. 168. This article is an extract from the final paragraph of 'Report of the General Committee of the National Society', *First Annual Report of the National Society*, pp. 13–19, at p. 19.

CHURCH-OF-ENGLANDISM

A circumstance not a little remarkable is—that, of all the meetings, of the proceedings of which an account is given in the Appendix to any one of these three Reports,—that which comes *first*—date of it, 'May the 9th, 1812'[1]—and that which comes *last*, viz. 'May 31, 1814,'[2] are the only ones, in the instance of which the aggregate of the tokens of authenticity is exhibited in its proper, and elsewhere customary, degree of plenitude. At the first of these two meetings, the Reverend Divine,—who, under the direction of the Most Reverend one, appears in the character of penman to all these three Reports,—officiated as such with the title of *Secretary;* in this same first recorded meeting,—the number of the members, viz. *five*, not being regarded (it should seem) as being sufficiently great to stand in need of a Chairman,—no person is exhibited in express terms by the title of *Chairman:* that character being moreover understood to belong, as of congruity, and thence by implication, to a person so manifestly pre-eminent, as the Right Reverend Prelate, the Lord Bishop of London, Lord of the Palace in which at this first-recorded meeting this first of Sub-Committees sat.[3]—On the other hand,—at the last of these same two meetings the number being so considerable, (sixteen) and the company so miscellaneous,—flocking together to this metropolitan and central spot from all corners of this National Society's world,—the occasion was deemed a proper one for a *Chair*, and moreover the Secretary of the center Society, a proper person to be seated in it.

it may be remembered, with the *Plan of Union*, when the Committee were putting the last hand to this important act, nobody knew any thing about the time: it might be one year; it might be another year. But in the course of the next year a discovery was made: a discovery not only of the *year*, but of the *month*. But this was all: the day is still in darkness, and there the matter rests.[4] However on *that* occasion *two* steps were made: and the present occasion requires but *one*.

5. In the fifth place, behold him informed indeed of the year and the month: but by reason of some failure, which happily (it has been seen) was but a temporary one, unconscious of the *place* in which he was writing, as well as of the day of the month: and moreover at this time, though acting in the character of Secretary, and though, as upon this same occasion, he expressly assures us, it is 'by *Order of the Committee*' that he is writing, yet either divested of that office, or unconscious of his possessing it.—Report II. p. 193. No. VII. '*T.T. Walmsley*, February, 1813.' Thus much and nothing more:—except the words '*By order of the Committee.*'

---

[1] i.e. 'Report of the Sub-Committee for Building', *First Annual Report of the National Society*, Appendix I, pp. 23–4. For Bentham's discussion of the Building Committee see pp. 125, 130–2, 149–50, 176 n. above and 181 n., 183–6, 193 n. below.

[2] i.e. 'Society of Secretaries', *Third Annual Report of the National Society*, Appendix IX, pp. 178–80. For Bentham's discussion of the Society of Secretaries see pp. 173 n. above and 181 n., 184 n. below.

[3] i.e. London House, Aldersgate Street, the chambers of the Bishop of London.

[4] For Bentham's discussion of this document see pp. 96–7, 134–5 above.

INTRODUCTION. PART IV. §XI.

But the curious, as well as to the present purpose the material, circumstance is—that, as at the first so at the last, when a *real* meeting,—of the persons, whom it is the endeavour of these Reports throughout, to cause the public to believe to have met,—has indubitably had place,—in these instances and in no other, have the proper and customary tokens of authenticity been inserted.

9. *Form of Disorder* 9.—Of the *Persons present,* (viz. at the meeting in which the act, being an act of the Governing body,—or of a body acting in direct subordination to the Governing body,—received its existence,) out of *four-and-twenty* instances, mention made in *one* alone,—in every other, not.[a]

10. *Form of Disorder* 10.—*Place of Meeting*—out of *four-and-twenty* instances, in *one* instance mentioned;[1] in the remaining three-and-twenty, not.[b]

11. *Form of Disorder* 11.—*Time of Meeting*—out of the above

---

[a] Instances in which the act comes under the first of the two descriptions just mentioned—viz. as per Form 1.

Articles without Nos. to them[2]	5
Articles with Nos. to them[3]	17
Instances in which the act comes under the other of these two descriptions—viz. those of the two *Sub-Committees*	2
Total number of the instances, in which the demand for the information in question had place	24
Deduct the one instance on which this demand is satisfied, viz. that of the Building Committee, Report I. No. 1.	1
Remain the number of instances in which, though having place, this demand is *not* satisfied	23

N.B. In the article, Report III. No. 9,—in which are exhibited certain Resolutions as come to by a Society styled '*Society of [Secretaries],*'[4]—the persons present, sixteen in number, are all mentioned by their names, in conjunction with the names of the *Societies,* for which they were respectively thus officiating.

☞ For another instance, in which mention is made of the *persons present.* See *Form of Disorder* 13.[5]

[b] The instances in which, in the character of a token of authenticity, this circumstance is material, being the same as those which come under the last mentioned head, viz. that of *Persons present,* for the particulars of these same instances see that same head.

---

[1] i.e. the Building Committee: see p. 180 & n. above.
[2] i.e. unnumbered articles which represent acts of the governing body (as per. no. 1, p. 178 n. above).
[3] i.e. numbered articles which represent acts of the governing body (as per no. 3, p. 178 n. above).
[4] 1818 '*Sectaries*'. See *Third Annual Report of the National Society,* Appendix IX, pp. 178–80.
[5] See p. 184 n. below.

four-and-twenty instances[, in *ten* instances] mentioned:—in the remaining fourteen, not.[a]

12. *Form of Disorder* 12.—Designation of them—out of the above *ten*, in *four* instances, compleat: in the remaining *six* incompleat: the day of the month not being mentioned in any one of them.[b]

13. *Form of Disorder* 13.—The same article presenting a different appearance, in different Reports.[c]

[a] These instances are of course the same as those comprised under the two heads last-mentioned.

Instances in which the time is mentioned are—I. In Report I. Nos. 1, 2, 7: II. In Report II. Nos. 4, 5, 6, 7: III. In Report III. Nos. 3, 4, 5. N.B. In Report II. No. 4, which has a date, is a reprint of Report I. No. 3, which has no date: also in Report II. No. 5, is a reprint of Report I. No. 7: also in Report II. No. 6, is a reprint of an Article which in Report I. has no No.: also in Report II. No. 7, is a reprint of Report I. No. 5.

[b] Instances in which the mention made of the time is compleat, are—I. In Report I. No[s]. 1, 2, 7: In Report II. No. 5.—In Report II. No. 5, is a reprint of Report I. No. 7.

[c] I. *Table of Contents.*—1. The Contents in question are the Contents of the *Appendix;* in that part of the publication are comprised all the articles thus referred to.—Accordingly in Report I., the words of the title prefixed to the list of these articles are—*Contents of the Appendix.* In Report II. the words are—*Table of Contents:* and so in Report III.

2. In the Table of Contents to Report I., no *figures of reference* are to be seen, referring to the pages, at which the papers in question respectively commence. In Report II. figures for this purpose are inserted: and so in Report III. The alteration is manifestly an improvement. But that *such* an improvement should remain to be made!!

II. *List of Books recommended.*—In speaking of Report I. p. 197, it has already been shewn[1] how the recommendation there given, of a list of books for Lesson-books, is slid in without any distinctive mark. No No., and thence no place is given to it in the *Table of Contents:*—no title at the head of the article itself.—In Report II. p. 189, as already observed,[2] enters again this same article; and at[3] this time furnished with a No.—viz. No. 6: but neither in the Table of Contents, nor at the head of the article itself has it any other than an uncharacteristic title.[4] In Report III. p. 168, it presents the same appearance as in Report II.: having in both places a No. viz. in Report II. No. 6; in Report III. No. 4: the title in the Table of Contents being the same in the later Report as in the earlier: so likewise the title at the head of the article itself: but in each Report the title in the two places is different; and in both of them uncharacteristic.[5]

In Report II. p. [189],[6] No. 6. the Secretary's signature to this article—this signature, though subscribed (it is therein said) by order of the Committee, has (it has been seen)[7] no *time* of date to it: in Report III. it has however, a time of date to it.[8] But the *time* is (it has been seen)[9] an incompletely designated one; the day of the

[1] See pp. 136–9 above.   [2] See pp. 139–40 above.
[3] 1818 'all'. The text follows the 'Errata'.
[4] i.e. 'National Society For the Education of the Poor in the Principles of the Established Church'.
[5] For the differences in title see pp. 174 n., 175 n. above, and for the uncharacteristic nature of the title see p. 173 n. above.   [6] 1818 '100' is a slip.   [7] See pp. 139–40 above.
[8] As Bentham immediately goes on to state, this article does not have a time of date.
[9] See p. 140 above.

INTRODUCTION. PART IV. §XI.

Nor is this all. For, as if to cut a figure with,—and, upon his first entrance upon his task, to impress the mind of the reader with the idea of regularity, as being a quality inherent in the whole of the proceedings, and thence in the whole of the accounts given of them,—*this* meeting[1] it is, of which, though out of its turn, the account is thus taken up, and set at the head of the articles consigned to this Appendix. May the 9th, 1812, is the day assigned, to the meeting recorded in this first recorded document. The document which thus stands first recorded, is it the document of the earliest date? Oh no: for of that which stands next recorded, and of which the mention is thus postponed to the mention of it, viz. No. II. p. 25, the '*Address to the Public*,' (it is the Address calling for Contributions,) the date is more than three months earlier—viz. '29th January,' in that same year, '1812.'

More than this, in that same first recorded document, intituled *Report of the Sub-Committee for Building*, immediately after mention of the *Members present* as above, 'The Building Committee' (continues this Report, p. 23,) 'having met the 26th of December, 1811, in consequence of instructions from[2] the General Committee, proceeded to enquire for a proper place wherein to establish a Central month being wanting: and, for[3] the fixation of the Month and Year, viz. Aug. 1812, the[4] source which Mr. Sec. has recourse to, is[5] no other than the title to this article, as printed in the *Table of Contents* of the last preceding Report, viz. Report II.: for at the time of drawing up this Table, Year and Month had it appears been revealed to him, though the Day of the Month continued, as it continues still, in darkness. In p. 136, &c. a cause for this disconformity has been endeavoured to be found.[6]

III. *Plan of Union.*—1. In Report I. the article intituled *Plan of Union*, makes its appearance without any authenticating date; in Report II. it makes its appearance for the first time, with a date, though that date is even then an imperfect one, the day of the month being wanting. In Report III. it makes its appearance with the same imperfect date.[7] In p. 180, of this, a cause for that disconformity likewise has been endeavoured to be found.

IV. *Lists of Benefactors.*—In relation to this subject, the following are the diversities exhibited by the three Reports.

1. In Report I., in the *Table of Contents*, no mention of any such article, nor

---

[1] i.e. the meeting of the Building Committee.
[2] *First Annual Report* 'instructions received from'.
[3] 1818 'wanting, and for'. The text follows the 'Errata'.
[4] 1818 '1812: and the'. The text follows the 'Errata'; except that a comma is supplied after '1812'.
[5] 1818 'recourse to for this purpose, is'. The text follows the 'Errata'.
[6] See pp. 136–40 above, and especially p. 138, where Bentham states that the reason for the 'variety' in 'the designation of *place* and *time*' is that 'these same adjuncts may be regarded as matters of indifference'.
[7] For the 'Plan of Union' see *First Annual Report of the National Society*, Appendix III, pp. 27–8; *Second Annual Report of the National Society*, Appendix IV, pp. 186–7 (where the date is given as February 1812); and *Third Annual Report of the National Society*, Appendix III, pp. 166–7.

School.' Here then is evidence of an *anterior* meeting—a meeting held on this same subject—held on a day more than four months anterior to that of this *first regularly recorded* meeting; and even more than a month anterior to the date of that *Address*, the record of which is postponed to the record of it: and *that* too a meeting, as it should seem—though perhaps not—of this same Committee: but at any rate, a meeting, the proceedings of which, for some reason or other were not thought meet to be had in any more particular remembrance.

O yes:—perhaps the same; perhaps not:—for here comes another quere;—the assembly mentioned in the title to this No. I. p. 23, under consequently any No. for the designation of any such article, is to be found. But, in p. 69, commences an article (of course without a No.), having for its title 'BENEFACTORS and ANNUAL SUBSCRIBERS,' occupying the pages from 69 to 113: and in p. 117, commences another list (without a No.) having for its title the words *Benefactors and Annual Subscribers to Societies in the Country*, occupying the pages from 117 to 196.

2. In Report II. in the *Table of Contents*, at the end of the list of numbered articles, comes an article without a No. viz. '*A List of Benefactors* and Annual Subscribers,' *with a reference* to p. 203. At p. 203, accordingly commences a list having for its title the words BENEFACTORS and ANNUAL SUBSCRIBERS; occupying the pages from 205 to 253. A remarkable circumstance is—that in this Report II., no list of *Benefactors and Annual Subscribers to Societies in the Country* is to be found.

3. In Report III., as in Report II., *in the Table of Contents*, at the end of the list of numbered articles, comes an article without a number, viz. 'A List of Benefactors and Annual Subscribers.' Here *no reference* is to be found [to][1] any page. At the end of the publication however, (the series of numbered pages closing with p. 183,) commences a list, (pages not numbered) having for its title, as in Report II., the words *Benefactors and Annual Subscribers*. But neither in this Third Report, any more than in Report II., is any list, of *Benefactors*, &c. *in the Country*, to be found. In Report I. this *Country list* is a good deal more numerous, it may be seen, than the *Town list*. Of this discontinuance would you know the cause?—Enquire of those who are in the secret.

V. *Persons present.*—In the article, Report III. No. 9, exhibiting certain Resolutions come to by a Society styled '*Society of Secretaries*'—(Resolutions tending to the communicating of information and to the appointment of a Visitor to the schools)— the persons present are all mentioned by their names, in conjunction respectively with the names of the Societies for which they were thus officiating. Moreover, in this instance, exhibition is made of the several other tokens of authenticity: viz. *Place*, 'The Central School:'—*Time*,—and *that*, as in so many of the above instances, not incompleatly, but compleatly, and even more than compleatly, designated;—viz. '*Tuesday*, the 31st of May, 1814.'—To this article is attached the following signature, viz. T.T. WALMSLEY, *Chairman.*—The body here in question,—though a body in a certain sort connected with, and acting under the influence of the governing body of the Society in question,—not being, in the manner of a *Committee*, in a state of regular sub-ordination in relation to it,—thence it was that, under the several former heads, in the character of a source of exemplification, this article could not without impropriety be brought to view.

---

[1] 1818 'in'.

INTRODUCTION. PART IV. §XI.

the name of '*the Sub-Committee for Building*,' and the assembly in line eighth of that same page mentioned under the name of *the Building Committee*, are they after all the same Committee? or—to speak more particularly, and thence more plainly—the persons who were appointed members of it, and moreover the persons who in virtue of that appointment met and acted,—were they, at both times, or in no one, or in one only, and which of those two times, these same persons?

In the body of the Report, it is in a paragraph contained in pages 14 and 15, and not in any other place, that mention is made of *this Sub-Committee*, or say of *these Sub-Committees*. Look to that place for elucidations,—and, instead of the elucidations sought, what as usual you will find is—darkness visible.

'The Committee (page 14,) *at its first meeting*. . . . appointed a Sub-Committee, to take measures for establishing a Central School in the Metropolis . . . At the next meeting' . . . 'The Sub-Committee . . . was *renewed*, and instructed to find out, &c. . . . which business was entered upon and brought to a conclusion without delay, as will be seen in the report of their proceedings under the sanction of the general Committee, printed in the App. No. I.'—viz. the so often mentioned Report of May 9, 1812.[1]

This same '*first meeting*'—on what day was it held?—*Answer.*—If on any day, on some day posterior to October 21st, 1811, and anterior to 26th December, in that same year, 1811:—posterior to the day in *October;* that being the day on which, according to p. 13, the '*Society was formed:*' anterior to the day in *December;* that being the day, on which, under the name of *the Building Committee*, a Building Committee, nominated according to p. 14, either at that same first meeting, or at the next to it, is in No. I. p. 23, '*Report of the Sub-Committee for Building*,' stated to have met.

That same '*next meeting*'—on what day was it held?—*Answer.*—If on any day, on some day posterior to that, on which the '*first*' of these same two meetings was held: as also anterior to that same day of December, viz. the 26th: since[2] it was at that same meeting of the General Committee, that 'the *Sub-Committee*,' by which *instructions*

---

[1] See *First Annual Report of the National Society*, Appendix I, pp. 14–15: 'At the next meeting it was resolved that the Central School should be large enough for the education of 1,000 children, and until such school could be provided, that the schools at Lambeth, Mary-le-bone, and Gower's Walk, Whitechapel, should be made use of for training Masters. The Sub-Committee at the same time was renewed and instructed to find out a proper situation for the Central School, with power to treat for the purchase of proper premises, and give orders for the repair or erection of a convenient building; which business was entered upon and brought to a conclusion without delay, as will be seen in the report of their proceedings, under the sanction of the general Committee, printed in the App. No. 1.'

[2] 1818 'sure'. The text follows the 'Errata'.

were thereupon *'at the same time'* received, *'was,'* as above, *'renewed:'* always supposing that the Sub-Committee, which on that same 26th of December, co-operated as above, was the *same* Committee, which on that same nameless day of the General Committee's said *'next meeting'* was so *'renewed and instructed'* as aforesaid.

These are all the *data:* and from these data, let the Chronologer, whose skill in Chronology is adequate to such an enterprize, and who at the same time wants employment, fix the date.

Concluding problem.—Of the *disorder* that has been seen, required to find, what part, if any, has been the result of *artifice,*—what part, if any, the result of *incapacity*. To this problem all along has a solution been sought:—sought—sincerely and diligently sought:—yet still, in conclusion—such is the darkness with which the face of this deep[1] is covered—must it be left unsolved. By a peep into the *books* of this self-styled *Committee*—if indeed any such books have been kept—the solution, or at any rate an approximation towards it, might probably be effected. But these books are in the custody—nominally, of the Reverend *Secretary;* effectively, of the most Reverend *President*. Enquire of them—(but, to the power, who is there that adds the inclination, necessary to the making any such enquiry with effect?) enquire of them, the answer will be—either that the voracity of some profane *rat* has taken an unhappy direction to these sacred muniments,—or that,—in virtue of one of those inscrutable decrees of an all-directing providence, the aid of which is never wanting to orthodox divines at a dead lift,—fire from heaven has come down, and consumed into a burnt sacrifice these offerings of Church-of-England devotion:—consumed them, as of old, in token of acceptance, on the very altars on which they have been offered.[2]

§XII. *General Committee.—Fraud involved in the title thus given to the Managing body.*

Of whatever in the course of this discussion there has been occasion to say of the Governing body, one source of perplexity has been a perpetual accompaniment:—this is—the impossibility of giving to it, without joining in a system of misrepresentation, the style and title given to it throughout the whole course of these Reports:—viz. *the General Committee*. By the word *Committee*, in every instance, is, or ought to be, meant to be designated a subordinate assemblage of the members of the artificial body in question,—to which assemblage, on some particular occasion, a particular portion of the

---

[1] Genesis 1: 2.   [2] See I Kings 18: 30–40, esp. 38.

INTRODUCTION. PART IV. §XII.

business is, by the whole body *committed*, i.e. *entrusted:* entrusted—viz. for the purpose of exercising some preparatory function.

A Committee is a relative term: and, though as in the case of *a trustee*, and so many others, the current language, (such is its imperfection,) has not, in the compass of a single word, afforded to it its correlative,—yet to the existence of the object thus designated, the existence of a *correlative* object is not in this instance less undeniably necessary, than in the case of *father* and *son*, or that of *grantor* and grantee. *A Committee?*—and without a person or set of persons *by whom* the business in question is *committed?*—not less self-contradictory would be the supposition of a *deputy* or set of *deputies*, without a person or set of persons by whom he or they had been deputed. As well might you speak of a *son* who had never had a *father*, as of a *Committee* to which the business performed by it had never been *committed* to it.—*Committee of the whole House?*—Yes: in the practice of Parliament this locution is to be found, though in that instance alone. And why?—only because, to the exercise of those preparatory functions, for the exercise of which a select portion of the body in question is in general regarded as most competent,—in some particular instances nothing less than the whole is regarded as being sufficient. But even in this case,—in which, for reasons foreign to the present purpose, a sort of fiction has been recurred to,—even in this case the offspring is no more unprovided of its parent than when, as in general, the Committee is a *select* one. True it is, that for any sort of purpose,—with any sort of intention, good or bad,—a set of men self-chosen may, on this or that occasion, have gone about calling themselves *a Committee*. But, for any such purpose never did any set of men ever go about under that name, by whom,—were any such question put to them as—*by whom was this business committed to you?*, the impropriety of the appellation thus assumed would not immediately have been recognized.

In this respect, how stands the matter in the present instance?

The name given to the governing body is, as above, *the General Committee*. But the expression is elliptical: and, ere any determinate import can be attached to it, the ellipsis must be filled up. Committee?—of what body?—In the business of Parliament the answer is in every case given without difficulty.—Committee *of the House:*—Committee of the House of *Lords;*—Committee of the House of *Commons*.

Well then—the filling up—how shall it be performed in the present instance? The General Committee?—of what? The answer insinuated, is—the General Committee of the Society, styled by this same pretended Committee *the National Society.*—Insinuated?—Yes.—

Asserted?—No.—Why not?—Even because, if asserted, the assertion would have been too notoriously false.—For, in addition to the Members of this self-styled General Committee, of what Members can the Society, styled the National Society, have been composed?— *Answer.*—Of those and those alone, who, from the birth of the Society down to the present time, have, by their subscriptions,[1] contributed to the formation of that fund,—which, in consequence of their acquiescence, has been disposed of by unknown persons, whom the fifty-two Members, of the body, in the name of which, under this falsely assumed, or, at any rate, falsely attributed name, the business has been conducted, have suffered to act in their names.

Now then—of this supposed governing body,—by the self-concealed person or persons, who, without any produced or probably producible warrant, have been acting in its name, so groundlessly styled *the General Committee,*—what is the true genealogy?—Supposing it to have had any real existence, by whom was it formed?—The Members of it—by whom were they nominated?—By the whole number of the Contributors, reckoning down to this or that day? or by any meeting to which that whole number had been invited?—No such thing. Of the persons, in relation to whom, by means of this fraud, the authors of it endeavour to cause it to be believed that, under the name of *the General Committee,* they were named and appointed members of the governing body by the Contributors at large, the nomination was in fact begun by an unknown small number, in which were included—of a certainty, the present Archbishop of Canterbury, as certainly the late Bishop of London,[2] and perhaps another or two of the Bishops:—by these were put down, and in each instance with or without consent, the names of the remaining Bishops and Archbishops: with or without whose concurrence, they went on to name certain Peers and Privy Counsellors: which body, in some not fully declared way and proportion, composed of Archbishops, Bishops, Peers, and Privy Counsellors, made up the nominated number, to a total of fifty-two, out of laymen and clergymen of inferior dignity.[3]

To form a fund for the purpose in question, these fifty-two,—some of them at least—not improbably, upon looking over the list of contributors,[4] it would appear all of them,—contributed respectively

---

[1] For the conditions of membership of the National Society see pp. 128, 165 n. above.
[2] i.e. Charles Manners-Sutton and John Randolph.
[3] For the composition of the General Committee see p. 46 n. above.
[4] For the lists of benefactors and annual subscribers nationally and locally see *First Annual Report of the National Society,* pp. 69–196; *Second Annual Report of the National Society,* pp. 205–54; and *Third Annual Report of the National Society,* sixty-five unnumbered pages following p. 183.

so many sums of money: inviting persons at large to become contributors along with them. But, to no one individual, other than those fifty-two persons themselves, is any part in the management—any share in the power of disposing of the money, or in any other of the powers exercised—allowed by them.

Now then, as to this principal point, what is the true state of the case?—By the whole number of the Contributors, of whom the assemblage of persons, styled in these Reports by their collective name *the National Society*, is composed—is it by *this* body, that the members of the body, in these same Reports styled *the General Committee*, were appointed?—or are so much as here represented as having been appointed?—No such thing.—It is by themselves or one another, that these members of the governing body were appointed.—Appointed?—and to what?—to the function of disposing of whatsoever monies should by the several contributors be eventually put into their hands.

Here then is a scheme of misrepresentation—a radical scheme of misrepresentation—planned and executed from the first. Represented are these men,—and by themselves, or at least by some of themselves,—as having been appointed, and invested with all these powers, which they have since been exercising. Invested? and by whom?—by a body, which, even by their own shewing, had not at the time of the supposed act of investment, any existence.

Well but—after their having thus begotten the *Society*, may not the Society have returned the favour, and begotten or adopted *them*? Begotten or adopted them—in the character which they assume, viz. that of its *General Committee?*—Oh no: no such thing:—no such incident is so much as pretended. *Thanks* and *approbation*—for these things, and these alone, has it been their pleasure to be beholden to these their children:[1] existence is too precious a possession for them to claim to be regarded as indebted for it to, or to hold it of, any persons but themselves.

Thus it is that, from first to last, the power they exercise, they exercise on a false pretence: the pretence of having received it from a set of persons from whom in truth they never have received any such thing;—to whom in truth they never chose to be beholden for any such thing.—No: no such experiment durst they venture upon: disappointment and disgrace might have been the result of it.—The scheme—is it a national scheme, or is it a party scheme?—the religion to be supported—is it the religion of Jesus, or is it Church-of-Englandism?—the means of execution—are they uncorrupt or corrupt?—To questions such as these, no answer could have been

[1] See pp. 127–8 above.

returned, but a self-condemning one;—and, for the putting of all these questions, in any one meeting, supposing it a free and open one, any one tongue would have sufficed.

Here then is a fraud: a fraud planned and executed from the beginning: a fraud in which all the Archbishops and Bishops, with the addition of Right Honourables in abundance, seem at first appearance implicated.

That as to this part of the whole system of fraud, the Archbishops and Bishops were however, generally speaking, unconscious, nothing is there in this that in the nature of the case seems incredible. What sort of a thing *a Committee* is—to an Archbishop or Bishop as such, it is not necessary to know *that* or any thing else.

But the Right Honourables?—look at the Right Honourables!—among them—not to speak of the titled Saints of lower degree—you will see the *Lord Chancellor,*—Speaker as such of the House of Lords,—the *Lord Redesdale,* quondam Speaker of the House of Commons—and *Mr. Abbot,* the present Speaker of the same Honourable House.[1] These lawyers—these veteran and wily lawyers—to them is it possible that it should have been unknown what *a Committee is?* To them is it possible that it should not have been known, that without an agent there is no such object as a patient—that without a Committ*er* there is no such thing as a Committ*ee?* This they might have learnt from *Mother Goose:* this they had actually learnt from *Mother Blackstone.*[2]—Ah no:—at the price of no such confession of ignorance would these, or any other such lawyers, be content to purchase the reputation of innocence.

Fraud, under the name of *fiction,* being the grand instrument of his power—fraud upon the legislature—fraud upon the people—fraud on every occasion—is dear to the man of law: dear to him—primarily for the sake of that same power, secondarily, and by force of habit, for its own sake. Fraud, in every licensed shape in which he has a part in the management of it—(and in what licensed shape has he not a part in the management of it?) it is his interest that to the eye of the public it should be as familiar as possible. Familiar?—Why?—even that by familiarity the deformity of it may, as nearly as possible, be rendered

---

[1] As Lord Chancellor, Eldon acted as president and prolocutor of the House of Lords. John Freeman Mitford (1748–1830), created Baron Redesdale in 1802, Solicitor General 1793–9, Attorney General 1799–1801, had been Speaker of the House of Commons from 1801 to 1802. Bentham's step-brother Charles Abbot (1757–1829), created Baron Colchester in 1817, was Speaker of the House of Commons from 1802 to 1817. All three were Vice-Presidents of the General Committee.

[2] See Blackstone, *Commentaries on the Laws of England,* ii. 140 n.: 'We may here remark ... that the terminations of "—or" and "—ee" obtain, in law, the one an active, the other a passive signification; the former usually denoting the doer of any act, the latter him to whom it is done.'

INTRODUCTION. PART IV. §XII.

imperceptible. Never *without* fraud will the man of law do any thing which he can contrive to do *by* or *with* fraud. Bad things he does by fraud, because he could not do them otherwise: good things, when they *must* be done, he chooses to do by fraud,—that by the goodness of the *effect* the blindness of the public may be deluded into a belief of the goodness of the *instrument*. And whether he is or is not conscious of them (for—no fees being to be got by the perusal of it—his own mind is an object too frightful for the man of law to be fond of looking into)—whether he is or is not conscious of them—in the *fictions*, alias the *frauds*, with which the Catechism will be seen to swarm, may be seen the cause of the fondness with which it is hugged, not only by the established priest, but by his confederate, the man of law. The Liturgy, with its Catechism and its Altar, have they not become stepping-stones not only to spiritual but to temporal benches? From interpreting, in the Church-of-England mode, according to the rules that will be seen,[a] the Oracles of God, the half-bigot, half-hypocrite comes to interpret, according to the same rules, the oracles of the grim Idol, to which, day by day, under the name of *Common Law*, so many lives and fortunes are sacrificed: the Idol manufactured by his predecessors on the same Bench, with the instrument with which Samson slew the Philistines.[1]

In addition to the *universal* objects,—common, as just above explained, to all priestly and to all lawyerly fraud,—the particular fraud in question had it not any *special* object?—Oh yes, that it had. It had for its object the blinding the eyes of the Contributors at large, by causing them to ascribe regularity to the whole system of irregularity thus organized. Referring himself to Resolution 10, Report I.—under and by virtue of his right, had it happened to any 'Subscriber of one guinea annually' to make a motion respecting the disposal of the fund—a motion tending for example to the exclusion of the exclusionary conditions—that instant would his mouth have been stopt by the observation, that by Resolution the 4th of that same string of Resolutions, 'to manage the affairs of the Society' was a function that belonged to none but the 'Committee of sixteen, besides the President and Vice-Presidents;' which President and Vice-Presidents were, by Resolution 3, the twenty-six Archbishops and Bishops, together with ten temporal Peers or Privy-Counsellors, to be perpetually nominated by the said Presidents and *other* Vice-Presidents, (these others being the said Archbishop and Bishops only,) and which said Committee of sixteen were moreover, by Resolution 5, to

---

[a] See Appendix, No. I. pp. 264 to 272.

[1] i.e. the jawbone of an ass: see Judges 15: 14–17.

be nominated by the said Most and Right Reverend President and Vice-Presidents.¹

Well but (says some surly Guinea-Subscriber)—*these men, in the choice of whom we had none of us any share—is it for these men to do what they please with the money we furnish? and are we ourselves to have nothing to do with the disposal of it?*

Oh no, to be sure—(answers some lawyer or lawyer-tutored priest)—*Oh no, to be sure*—for, by Resolution the 4th, the management (you *see)* is theirs *and not* yours: *it is theirs and theirs* only. *And why should you grudge it them?—For they—do not you see it?—they are* your own Committee. *You and they are* the Society, *and they are* your Committee. *Great men as they are,—and, out of the Royal family, where will you find greater, or so great?—Great men as they are!—Such is their condescension, they claim to be nothing more. Great men, and so condescending to boot!—is it for such as you to fly in their faces, and act as if you were their superiors?—You their superiors—and not they yours?*

In this fictitious election, thus it is, that with relation to these self-chosen *Elect*, the supposed *Electors* are superior and inferior at the same time: superior as touching the furnishing of the money, inferior as touching the disposal of it: superior to the purpose of shew and appearance; inferior, or rather nothing at all, to every real purpose:—to every real purpose, but above all to the purpose of keeping open the door of the instruction, to all persons, by whom,—for their own sake, and that of the whole people of which they form a part,—it is so much needed.

But why—when facts are before us—why tax imagination for suppositions?—He would have been dealt with—this impertinently intruding guinea-man at Sion-College²—he would have been dealt with—exactly as, at the intended courtly meeting at Maidstone, the truth-obtruding *journeyman-watchmaker* was dealt with by the Whig Member, between whom and the Tory Member the representation of the County of Kent³ is so commodiously divided.[a]

[a] Kentish Chronicle, 18th June, 1816, in Cobbett's Register, 29th June, 1816, p. 808.⁴ 'Here one of the populace had the *effrontery* to remark, that only two hands

---

¹ For the Resolutions see *First Annual Report of the National Society*, pp. 6–8, and pp. 164–5 n. above.
² The annual meetings of 1812 and 1813 were held at Sion College.
³ i.e. Sir William Geary (1756–1825), MP for Kent 1796–1806, 1812–18, and Sir Edward Knatchbull (1758–1819), MP for Kent 1790–1802, 1806–19, respectively.
⁴ The *Kentish Chronicle* of 18 June 1816 contained a report of a meeting held at Maidstone on 17 June 1816, at which it was proposed to send a message of congratulation to the Royal Family on the marriage on 2 May 1816 of Princess Charlotte Augusta of Wales (1796–1817) to Prince Leopold of Saxe-Coburg (1790–1865), but the meeting ended in confusion and the motion was

Of this fiction, as of all such lawyer-begotten frauds, confusion is among the inevitable, as well as relatively useful and desirable, and desired consequences. Instead of the proper appellation, viz. *Governing* or *Managing body*, the appellation *General Committee* being employed—employed in the first instance—and thereafter, dropping the word *General*, the word *Committee* alone,—one consequence is—that to what is really a Committee, the term *Sub-Committee* is thereafter attached. In those places in which this word *Sub-Committee* is employed, improper as the appellation is, no confusion however is produced by it. But, as often as for the designation of the governing body the word *Committee* is employed, on every such occasion,—on pain of misconceiving the matter, and taking the body so styled for the body there styled a Sub-Committee,—what you have to do is—to remember that this which is called *a Committee*, viz. *of the Governing body* is—not a *Committee* of the governing body, but the governing body *itself*.

But, without some special motive—and that a pretty strong one—a man does not choose to keep his attention and memory thus upon the rack for hours together. Nor would even all this pains suffice: for, to thicken the confusion, to this sort of body called a *Sub-Committee*, is also applied the appellation *Committee*:[a] and thus it is that, through-

---

were held up, except by the High-Sheriff and his friends. Sir William Geary then challenged this man as to his condition in life, when he turned out to be a journeyman watchmaker, who was only a lodger in the town.' The proposed addresses in question (it is insisted, p. 818.) 'purported to be the addresses of the Nobility, &c. . . . . and *Inhabitants:*' . . . . The watchmaker, 'it is added . . . . had lived at Maidstone not above two years, and was only a lodger.'

[a] Thus, in Report I. p. 23, the same body which is styled '*the Sub-Committee for Building*' is presently afterwards styled '*the Building Committee.*' So likewise in Report II. p. 5. we have '*the School-Committee,*' and *that* before any mention is made of *Sub-Committees:* and immediately after the word '*Sub-Committees,*' instead of the *Sub-Committee for Building* we have '*the Committee for Building.*' So again in the next page (p. 6.) we have '*their Committee*' (i.e. the Committee's Committee) '*of Correspondence:*' and moreover in the same page '*a finance Committee:*'—in p. 14. '*School Committee*' twice; in p. 16, twice; in p. 17, once: and in pages 15 and 16, a '*Committee of Ladies:*'—in all which instances, after due consideration, it will appear that what is meant by *Committee* is *Sub-Committee*. And thus it is, that throughout,—as far as depends upon the Reverend and most Reverend penmen,—the two ideas, for the distinguishing of which the terms *Committee* and *Sub-Committee* are in one place held up to view in form and ceremony, are, by what is done in so many other places, so effectually confounded.

---

lost. The article from which Bentham quotes, entitled 'To the men of Kent, On their late rejection of Addresses of Congratulation to the Royal Family, on the subject of the Marriage of the Princess Charlotte of Wales', reprints the report, and goes on to praise the actions of the inhabitants of Maidstone: see *Cobbett's Weekly Political Register*, vol. xxx, no. 26 (29 June 1816), cols. 801–32.

out the whole of this business, the personality of the real agents in it is kept involved in a perpetual cloud: which is the very thing that was to be done.

PART V.

BAPTISM AND SPONSORSHIP PROPER, WHEN INSTITUTED—BAPTISM USELESS, SPONSORSHIP IMPROPER, NOW.

OF this tract the main object is—to promote the passing a correct judgment on the nature and tendency of the formulary, which forms the subject of it. To this purpose it will not be necessary to enter into any part of the history of that same formulary, other than what is legible upon the face of it, together with a few such other particulars of Church history as are matter of universal and undisputed notoriety.

When, upon the accession of Elizabeth, and the re-substitution of the Protestant system to the Catholic, a set of formularies to be employed on religious occasions was framed,[1]—the interest of public peace concurred with this one particular interest, in recommending to the ruling few, the preserving, with as little change as might be, every institution which was not, on some particular account, in a particular way and high degree obnoxious: and the prepossession,— which, in the breasts of the uninformed and unscrutinizing multitude, *habit* had formed in favour of every thing, in which they had been accustomed to behold an object of respect,—was sufficient to present *change*, in so far as it went, in the character of a hazardous operation,—adherence to established usage as the course most favourable to general content and peace—in a word as the only safe one.

In the Romish ritual, mixt up with those notions, which, having been suggested by the temporal interests and interest-begotten prejudices of successive rulers, were of course subservient to those interests, others may be observed, which,—having been instituted in a state of things altogether different from that in which the religion of Jesus, and with it the authority of the successors of St. Peter, found itself seated on the throne,—had, though no longer suited to the times, been preserved from change, only because no special and urgent interest had been felt calling for a change.

Among these, the formulary here in question, viz. the *Catechism*,—

---

[1] The *Book of Common Prayer*, first authorized by the Act of Uniformity of 1552 (5 & 6 Ed. VI, c. 1), was re-authorized, with minor alterations, by the Act of Uniformity of 1559 (1 Eliz. I, c. 2).

together with the supposed more important formulary of *Baptism* by which it was preceded,—and the confessedly less important formulary of *Confirmation* by which it was followed,—formed so many links of a connected chain.

In the difference between the primæval and the subsequent states of Christian society, may be found the cause of those two leading features in the Catechism, of which the monstrosity will come to be displayed in the ensuing tract: viz. the unperformable obligation actually taken upon themselves by the *Sponsors*, and the obligation pretended to be imposed by them upon the child:[1]—of that monstrosity and palpable absurdity in the texture of the instrument, and of the ceremony in which it is employed, and of that immorality, which in the lips and breasts of those who bear a part in that ceremony, is the consequence of the continuance of the practices in question, in a state of things, which, in respect of the particulars in question, is so opposite to that, in which these obligations were at first instituted.[2]

At the time at which this *Sponsorship* had its rise, it had in utility and reason a foundation at least, and that altogether a natural and obvious one.

In those days, it was in the persons of adults rather than of infants—of infants no otherwise than in company with, and in the character of appendages to adults, that the religion of Jesus received its recruits.[3] To the condition of an adult, and to that alone, are any obligations such as those in question, adapted,—and with them the formulary in question, in so far as those obligations are contained in it. To this position, when once brought to view, who is it that can refuse his assent?

Be the society what it may into which a member is received, a precaution too obvious not to be in some degree attended to in it, is— the taking measures, such as the particular nature of the case points out, for avoiding to give admittance, in the character of a member, to any person other than such an one,—in whose instance a ground presents itself for expecting to see two conditions fulfilled:—the one a negative, the other a *positive* one: the *negative* one,—that of his not inflicting in any shape annoyance upon the Society, or any of its

---

[1] See pp. 204–11 below.

[2] In August 1816 Bentham declined to act as godfather at the baptism of Bentham Dumont Koe (1816–42), the son of his friend and amanuensis John Herbert Koe (1783–1860), stating that he 'could not endure to take a part in that abominable ceremony': see Bentham to John Herbert Koe, 7 August 1816, *The Correspondence of Jeremy Bentham*, vol. viii, ed. S. Conway, Oxford, 1988 (*CW*), p. 541.

[3] In early Christianity, the baptism of adults was performed to signify admission into the Christian community. Infant baptism was not practised until the third century.

members; the positive condition—that, in some way or other he will be contributory, to the purposes which in its formation the Society had in view.

In the early ages of the religion of Jesus, any society formed for the exercise of it was naturally and necessarily a select one: as a whole, it was surrounded with adversaries: at a very early period, it was split into parts called *sects;* and each sect beheld in some measure an adversary in every other. On the admission of a new member, the making such provision as the nature of the case admitted of for the fulfilment of the above conditions, was therefore an obvious and rational, not to say a necessary and unavoidable, exercise of prudence.

Thus useful and unexceptionable, at its commencement, and even for ages afterwards, was the institution of *Sponsors:* by this one institution it was, that provision was made for the fulfilment of both those conditions: for the *negative* one, by the very act performed by a man in offering himself as a *Sponsor;*—forasmuch as, even without any such positive and verbally expressed engagement, what no one could fail of perceiving is—that by the very act of proposing the individual in question for the purpose of his being received as a member, a degree of displeasure in the breast of the other members, towards any person by whose imprudence the Society had been loaded with the supposed burthen, would, in case of annoyance received either from his deportment or his character, be a natural result:—for the fulfilment of the *positive* condition, an undertaking to instruct him in the several principles and practices, essential or peculiar to the society, would be an expedient altogether obvious.

In the case thus brought to view, the candidate for admission being by the supposition, in an adult state,—no absurdity—no impropriety in any shape—was attached to an undertaking to any such effect: his consent to do whatever should on his part be necessary to the fulfilment of it, was necessarily implied in the act of his appearing in the character of a candidate: in the very act of solicitation, or even without solicitation, by a bare consent on his part to his being admitted. *Admit me into your Society,* says the Candidate.—*Yes, if you will do as we do,* say the Members. *So I will, as soon as I know how,* replies the Candidate. *I will shew him how,* says a Sponsor. In this short dialogue, the nature of the engagement,—and at the same time the plain and real use of the function of *Sponsor,*—stand expressed.

Widely different is the state of things, in which, under the Church of England,—not to speak of other Churches,—the formulary of baptism, with the institution of sponsorship included in it, is at this time of day employed.

For the practice of sponsorship, in the present state of the religion of Jesus—in a country in which it is established—supported, or even though it were but protected against injury, by government—there cannot be at any rate any general necessity,—nor even, as it should seem, any very considerable use.

By its father alone,—or some nominee of his, declared, or at any rate implied,—can a child be legally subjected to this ceremony. By the custom of the country and of the Church, it is almost immediately after birth—it is long before the dawn of reason—that it takes place. At this time of life, and for one-and-twenty years thereafter,—in the hands of that parent, or of his substitute as above, dwells the power,—and, unless by accident, the habit,—of giving direction to the conduct of the child.

On the part of the father, or any such substitute of his, any such sponsorship is neither necessary, nor so much as proper. The religion of Jesus, is it in his eyes a true religion? and that edition of it, which is in use in the Church of England, a proper mode? in the belief and practice of that religion, and in that mode, voluntarily, spontaneously, and without any such or any other engagement, will he bring up his child. In the eyes of this only proper judge, is that religion not a true one, or is this edition of it not a good edition? It is not right that by any external inducement, whether in the shape of reward, or in the shape of punishment,—by any such external inducement, howsoever disguised, he should be induced, or sought to be induced, to follow it.

Considered as undertaken by the father, or his substitute, whether upon the whole defensible or not, the propriety of this sort of sponsorship is at any rate not altogether destitute of plausibility. The object being desirable—in every point of view desirable—desirable in respect of temporal, desirable in respect of eternal welfare; the guardians of the whole community, shall they refuse to do what is in their power to promote it?

Thus stands the question, as applied to the father or his substitute. Be this as it may,—applied to any person or persons other than those two, it will be found replete with absurdity and immorality.

In number, the Sponsors are commonly three: two of the same sex with the child: the third of the opposite sex: to avoid confusion, it will be sufficient to speak of one. The course of conduct then, the maintenance of which for so long a course of years, is thus promised by him, what is it?—it is one which it never is either in his power or in his intention, so much as to commence. With the consent of his father or his substitute—yes, with that consent the power might be acquired by this person just as by any other: but, neither has he any

INTRODUCTION. PART V.

expectation that any such consent will be given to him, nor if given, has he any such intention as that of accepting it; nor, on the other hand, in the breast of the father or his substitute, has any such intention any place.

Among the three Sponsors, suppose three irreconcilable ways of thinking, on the subject of the religious instruction proposed to be given to the child—what in this case is the result? To this question there are two answers. One is in the spirit of the Church, viz. that no such *schism*—no such '*guilt,*' as his Lordship of London would call it[1]—is to be supposed: the other is in the spirit of sincerity and experience; viz. that as this office,—though without pay, and therefore reserved for the laity,—belongs to the catalogue of *sinecures*, there cannot be two modes of executing it.

Under these circumstances, not only does a man engage, as above, for a course of action to be persevered in by *himself*—a course upon which it is neither in his intention nor in his power so much as to enter—but moreover for the *child*'s entering upon, and to the last day of his life persevering in, *another* course of action—and that a different, though a correspondent one.

Over his own conduct he *has* power: over that other line of conduct, viz. that of the child, to which he thus engages to give direction, he has *not*, as he well knows, any power whatsoever. Under these circumstances, though what he could *not* do is—*actually* to exercise over the conduct of the child any influence, yet what he *could* do is—to *endeavour* to exercise the promised influence. But what he promises to do is—not simply to *endeavour* to exercise, but actually to *exercise* it.

Amongst other acts which he promises the child shall perform, is the act of *believing:* in the formulary,—in the lump, and no otherwise than by a loose and general description,—a set of propositions, (and, such propositions!) are brought to view; and all these the Sponsor promises the infant shall believe.

Of the compound of absurdity and wickedness mixt up in every such undertaking, nothing further will be said here: in the ensuing Commentary, something on this subject,—and what it is hoped will be sufficient,—will be found.[2]

In the tenor of the formulary, not only is the Sponsor made to take this rash vow, but the vow,—rash and absurd as it would be on the part of any person, on whom it could by possibility be obligatory,—is assumed to be obligatory on the infant, who took no part in it.

Of this supposed vicarious obligation, and the absurdity involved in it, something will be likewise found, as above.

[1] See p. 48 n. above.   [2] See pp. 204–11 below.

So much as to the Sponsorship referred to and necessitated by this Catechism: before coming to particulars, one word of general observation may suffice for the Catechism itself.

Considered as involving a declaration of persuasion in relation to a body of speculative religious doctrine—a declaration to be made, by a child but just emerged from infancy—by a being in whose mind the faculty of reason has but just begun to put itself forth—in the very nature of the species of composition called a *Catechism*, there is a peculiar, and that a flagrant, degree of inaptitude.

At this age, in relation to any such subject, a declaration of persuasion, what can it be but an *untruth?*—the habit of making such declarations, what is it but an habitual course of *lying?*—the obligation to which the child is thus subjected—the obligation of continuing in this course, what is it but an *obligation* to enter upon and continue in a *course of lying?*—If, by the helpless subjection and blameless ignorance attached to that age, the child itself stands exempted from all guilt,—can any such exemption be for a moment supposed to extend itself to any of those in whose situation no such excuse—no such cause of exemption—is to be found? To the open-eyed, and deliberate, and determined teachers and suborners of immorality in this shape?

Meantime an indication, which may already be given in this place is—that,—as of *this* formulary, so of every other formulary, and every other characteristic part of Church of England discipline and doctrine,—if not the *justificative*, the *final* and *efficient* cause, stands full in the face of every one who dares look at it: it may be seen in the situation of the rulers of the Church, and the sinister interest, that springs out of that source. Under every system of government, in proportion as it is corrupt, it is the interest of the ruling few that the intellectual, and thence the moral part of the public mind, should be in the most perfect and convenient state of depravation possible:—that, on the part of the *subject many*, in the words of his Lordship of London, the 'prostration of understanding and will'[1] should be as abject and as universal as possible: that, being themselves enured and habituated to the violation of all engagements and all other moral duties, the like violation, on the part of those their superiors, should on every occasion be in their eyes an object of indifference:—that—to take this one example out of a thousand—Church falsehoods and Church sinecures being regarded not merely as objects of indifference, but as sacred,—State falsehoods and state sinecures may at the least be regarded as objects of indifference. And, under a system of all pervading

[1] See p. 37 n. above.

INTRODUCTION. PART V.

corruption,—under which, while all *powers* are *real*, all *checks* are *nominal*,—these, though never reduced to writing, nor ever settled in *concert*—(for where *co-operation* without concert suffices, *concert*, having its dangers, is worse than useless)—these then are the terms—the too well established and by the ruling few too generally understood and fulfilled terms—of the so insolently trumpeted, and too really existing, *Alliance,—between Church and State*.

'I conclude,' (says Dr. *Bell*, Elements of Tuition, Part II. Edit. 1814, p. 377,)[1] 'I conclude with the conclusion of the *Instructions for the establishing and conducting Regimental Schools.*'[a]—Good: and to the present purpose a more apt conclusion could not be found. 'The attention,' (continues the doctor)—'the attention of every person, directing and superintending a school, is particulary called to watch over the moral and religious conduct of the children; and to implant in them, as well by daily practice, as by perfect instruction in the books recommended for that purpose, such habits as may best conduce to guard them against the vices to which their condition is peculiarly liable. In particular, the most rigid observance should be enforced of the grand virtue of *truth*, both for its own sake, and as supplying one of the readiest means of correcting vice of every kind. On this ground, a *lie* should never be excused; and a fault, aggravated by a lie, should always be punished with exemplary severity.'

Punished, say you?—Oh yes, good Doctor, punished they should be. Punished?—but who? the innocent or the guilty? the helpless infant, or the grey-headed suborners, and inexcusable authors of the unwitting and unwilling transgression of the thus gradually and insensibly corrupted innocents?

'Those portions of their religious books should be strongly rivetted in their minds,' continues the Reverend Doctor, 'which warn against lying,' .... then follows a list of other transgressions, of which lying, we see, stands at the head:—Oh yes, good Doctor, rivetted in their minds should those books be, by which this pander to all vices and all crimes, is warned against. But, out of those same tender and susceptible minds, with how much more anxious care should be

---

[a] Printed and sold *by Authority*, by W. Clowes, Northumberland Court, Strand, 1811. Price 6*d*.[2]

[1] Andrew Bell, *Elements of Tuition. Part II. The English School, or the history, analysis, and application of the Madras system of education to English Schools*, London, 1814, pp. 377–8.
[2] *Instructions for Establishing and Conducting Regimental Schools, upon The Rev. Dr. Bell's System, As Adopted at the Royal Military Asylum, Chelsea* was published at London in 1811 by the printer William Clowes.

kept the poison of that book, by which that vice of all vices is not only forced into practice, but inculcated as the first and most sacred of all duties?

THE
Church of England Catechism
EXAMINED.

Question 1.[1]

WHAT is your name?

Answer. (Pronouncing the child's name.)

Question 2. Who gave you that[2] name?

Answer. My Godfathers and my Godmothers in my baptism(1); wherein I was made a member of Christ, the child of God, and an inheritor of the kingdom of heaven(2).

OBSERVATIONS.

(1). {*Godfathers and Godmothers in my Baptism.*}—Thus far the answer appears not to stand exposed to any considerable objection: it being supposed, that to this examination no child is subjected, on whom the ceremony called *baptism* has not been performed. So far as this is true, the answer is nothing more than the statement of a matter of fact, of the existence of which, though, generally speaking, it is not possible the child should have any remembrance of it, it is but natural that he should feel himself assured by satisfactory and unsuspected evidence. But this blamelessness—it will soon be seen, whether it be of any long continuance.

(2). {*Wherein I was made,* &c.}—Already the contempt of truth, pregnant with those incongruities, of which that corrupt affection is so naturally productive, begins to manifest itself. In this formulary, styled *a Catechism*, will be found involved, though many of them tacitly, in a manner and without any sufficient warning, a system of assertions, prodigious in extent and variety, contained in another formulary, being the verbal part of a ceremony of prior date, called *baptism*. Of this anterior ceremony, the *examinee*, a child, commonly but just able to speak—a child, in which the faculty of reason[3] has as yet scarcely begun to develope itself—a child completely incompetent to the forming of any *judgment*, or so much as a *conception*, in relation to the matter contained in it, is made to take upon himself to pronounce the effect.

Here, then, the first lesson which he is made to learn, and *that* under the notion of forming his mind to the sentiment of *piety*, is a lesson, which, if it amount to any thing, and has any meaning, is a lesson of *insincerity:* and

---

[1] The questions and answers are taken from 'A Catechism that is to say an instruction to be learned of every person before he be brought to be confirmed by the bishop' in the *Book of Common Prayer.*

[2] Catechism 'this'.

[3] 1818 'name'. The text follows the 'Errata'.

which, in as far as it forms him to any thing, forms him to insincerity. For hereby what is the declaration which he is made to utter?—a declaration, asserting in the character of a true fact, the fact of his entertaining a persuasion which in truth he does not entertain, and which that he should entertain, is, in the nature of the case, not possible. When by Rousseau, on the occasion of the stories commonly put into the hands of children, under the name of *fables*, the practice, of thus drawing from the fountain of falsehood and misrepresentation the first aliment presented to the infant mind, was held up to view, and the absurdity and mischievous tendency of it displayed,[1] deep and extensive was the sensation produced by the remark, not less so the conviction and recognition of the justice of it. But if, in any such profane book of instruction, the admission of falsehood be incongruous, and the habit of regarding it not only with indifference but with approbation pernicious, how much more so in a book of religious instruction?—in a book professing to introduce men to the favour of the God of truth?[2]

Yes, if by misrepresentation—yes, if by falsehood, any real and *preponderant* good effect could be produced, such as could not be produced by any other means. But by this or any other of the falsehoods, so plentifully strewed all over this Catechism, and which will successively be held up to view, in what imaginable shape can any good be seen to flow?

Question 3.—What did your Godfathers and Godmothers then for you?

Answer.—They did promise and vow three things in my name(1): First, that I should renounce the devil and all his works(2), the pomps and vanity of this wicked world(3), and all the sinful lusts of the flesh(4): Secondly, that I should believe all the articles of the Christian faith(5): And, thirdly, that I should keep God's holy will and commandments, and walk in the same all the days of my life(6).

OBSERVATIONS.

I. *Things* is the name given to the *courses of conduct*, which are [t]he subjects of the vow here spoken of. But before we enter upon the consideration of these *things*, one *thing* presents itself as calling for consideration,—and that is the implied—the necessarily implied—assumption, that it is in the power of any person,—not only with the consent of the father or other guardian, but even without any such consent,—to fasten upon a child at its birth, and long before it is itself capable of giving consent to any thing, with the concurrence of two other persons, alike self-appointed, load it with a set of obligations—obligations of a most terrific and appalling character—obligations of the nature of *oaths*, of which just so

---

[1] Jean Jacques Rousseau (1712–78), Genevan writer and philosopher, had written in *Émile, ou de l'éducation*, 4 vols., Francfort, 1762, i. 135: 'Comment peut-on s'aveugler assez pour appeller les fables la morale des enfans? sans songer que l'apologue en les amusant les abuse, que séduits par le mensonge ils laissent échapper la vérité, & que ce qu'on fait pour leur rendre l'instruction agréable les empêche d'en profiter.'

[2] See, for instance, Deuteronomy 32: 4.

much and no more is rendered visible, as is sufficient to render them terrific,—obligations, to which neither in quantity, nor in quality, are any limits attempted to be, or capable of being assigned.

Every child, at its birth, is cast into bondage, under the power of three persons, who, for any provision that is made to the contrary, may have been self-chosen, and in practice frequently are. Even though these bonds were not more coercive than those of *temporal* slavery—of slavery in the *temporal* sense—this surely would be bad enough:—the notion of a power, derived from the Almighty, to cast men into such bondage, absurd and indefensible enough. But such bondage, what is it in comparison of the bondage actually supposed to be thus imposable and imposed? It is as the space covered by human life, to eternity: to that eternity over which the effects, here supposed to be produced by this bondage, are here supposed to extend.

Oh but, by our wisdom and our care (say the lawgivers, by whom this formulary was devised and imposed),—*by our wisdom and our care, against abuse of this power, provision—effectual provision—has, in and by this very instrument, been made.* . . .

Answer.—Yes: such provision as will be seen. But, in the mean time, and to authorize you to make this provision, what you have assumed,—and what for that purpose it was necessary for you to assume,—and *that* in the character of an universal proposition, is—that, by the Almighty, in consideration of that particular portion of wisdom, which, to *you in particular*, it has happened to be blest with—such power not only is *fit to be* given to *rulers in general*, but *has actually been* given to them:—and this, be they who they may, to *all* rulers: and sure enough, if, to the extent to which, to the purpose of the argument, it is necessary it should be assumed, this general proposition is granted, every proposition, necessary to the establishment of your own aptitude in particular, may be thrown into the bargain, as not being worth disputing about.

But, any such power—when, and on what occasion, was it ever given? where is any the least evidence, of any such gift, to be found?

A job for the casuists.—Here is an engagement taken—an engagement taken in the solemn and awful form of a vow—a vow made by the sponsors—that the child shall do so and so: a vow made by A, not that he himself, but that B, shall do so and so. B, in process of time, breaks the vow: for this transgression—for this breach of a *vow*—of a *promissory oath*—for this species of *perjury*, who is it that is to be punished? A or B? or some one else, and who else? If punished, in what *mode* and to what *amount*, punished? by everlasting flames in hell, or by any and what milder punishment?—Questions these, which, whenever this formulary is considered as any thing better than a parcel of words without meaning, will surely, now that, perhaps, for the first time the suggestion is made, be regarded as having some claim to answers. The persons thus dealing out eventual punishment at their own pleasure—viz. *the sponsors*—are they the persons, by whom, in case of a breach of the vow, the punishment is to be borne,—suppose the ordinary one of everlasting burning in hell fire?—if so, quere, of the whole number of persons who have been inveigled into the taking upon themselves this office, what is the number that will be saved?—What is the number?—*Answer.* None. For, whether its being kept inviolate is not as far from being possible as from being desirable, is what any rational eye will presently be in a condition to perceive. Upon the person, whom, in a state of helpless infancy, under the direction of the Church of England hierarchy, they have thus fastened upon and loaded with this burthen—is it upon this Jonas, that the lot of punishment will fall?[1]—What a case is his! and, in its effect, what sort of a boon is this, which is thus magnified!

II.—Thus much as to the *general principle* of the alleged engagement— now as to the subject matter of it.

Three, and but three, is the number here spoken of as the number of the things vowed and promised. But, of these *three* things, the first-mentioned is of itself a TRIPLE one, speaking of three things, or sets of things, as so many things which are to be renounced: as so many things, for the renunciation of which by the child (whatsoever be meant by *renunciation*), undertakers, under the name of *sponsors*, (or the child can not be a Christian), must be found, that will pledge themselves.

Mean time, without stopping as yet to take any clear view of the preceding *things*, no sooner is the last of them brought to view, than a question very naturally presents itself. Supposing this engagement fulfilled, can any thing else be wanting? 'God's holy will and commandments' kept, can any thing more be necessary? Is it in the nature of the case that even God himself should will or desire any thing more? The terms of the phrase, it must be confessed, are *general:* at the same time, for terms so comprehensive, few can be clearer or more easily intelligible.—'*A commandment*'—what sort of a thing *that* is, is among those things, which, by daily and hourly reference, are made known to every body. Sure enough, if every thing else had been equally clear, no such commentary as the present would ever have made its appearance.

Come we now to those other '*things*,' by which this last is so unnecessarily preceded.

In relation to these *first-mentioned* things, numbered first and second, the first observation that strikes the eye is—that, presented as they are in this manner to view, the child is bid to look upon them as so many distinct things:—upon each of them as something, which in its nature is distinct, and on this occasion specially contradistinguished, from the thing *last-mentioned*, viz. 'the keeping God's holy will and commandments.' If, all the days of his life, so it is that a man has been keeping this holy will, and these holy commandments,[2] what he has thus been doing, is he to understand then that it will be accepted as sufficient? Not he, indeed:—remain for him to do all these other things, whatsoever they may be.

These things, whatever they are, if so it be that it is in *pursuance*, as well as in consequence, of the engagement thus taken, that they are to be done by him, then so it is that to his doing them one thing more is necessary;

---

[1] See Jonah 1: 7.   [2] See Deuteronomy 17: 19–20.

which is, that he understand what they are: unfortunately, here, it will be seen, lies the difficulty,—and *that*, to an ordinary understanding, not to speak of extraordinary ones, it is much to be feared, an insuperable one.

Among the three things, or sets of things, that are to be renounced, first come '*the Devil and all his works.*'—The *Devil*, who or what is *he*, and how is it that he is *renounced?*—The *works* of the Devil, what are *they*—and how is it that they are renounced?—Applied to the Devil, who or whatever he is,— applied to the Devil's works, whatever they are,—what sort of an operation is *renouncement*, or *renunciation?*

To all these several words,—to one of them in particular, by which an idea, no less terrific than obscure and indeterminate, is wont to be excited,—what tolerably distinct ideas can rationally be expected to be attached, in the mind of infant simplicity and ignorance? When the holy person, whose name is next under the Sovereign's, seated on the pinnacle of theological science,—when the *Archbishop of Canterbury* himself is able to tell us who or what the Devil is, what are his *works*, and by what operation they are *renounced*,—they being all the while things distinct,—all of them,— as well from 'the sinful lusts of the flesh,' as from 'the pomps and vanity of this wicked world,'—then it is that it may be time enough to expect any tolerably clear, and practically useful idea, of all these mysteries, to stand attached to these words, in the infant mind, for the nourishment of which this composition, such as we see it, is the morsel first administered.

'*The Devil and all his works.*'—And in the first place, the Devil himself,—of whom so decided and familiar a mention, as of one whom every body knows, is made.—Where lives he? Who is he? What is he? The child itself, did it ever see him? by any one, to whom, for the purpose of the inquiry, the child has access, was he ever seen? The child, has it ever happened to it to have any sort of dealings with him? Is it in any such danger as that of having, at any time, to its[1] knowledge, any sort of dealings with him?—If not, then to what purpose is this *renouncement?* and, once more, what is it that is meant by it? Suppose him, however, to have actually renounced this Devil—that is, speaking of this Devil, to have said, *I renounce him*—in what condition is he, other than that which he would have been in, had no such renouncement been made?—The engagement, whatever it be, if any, which by this renunciation has been taken, by what *act* or acts is it that it would be *violated?*—This is surely among the things that would be worth knowing, were it only that a man might have it in his power to avoid the violating—the breaking—of this his engagement, without knowing, and for want of knowing, what it is.

'*The Devil and all his works!*'—Exists there any where any real being to which this name is applicable? If yes, exists there any sufficient reason for supposing that he ever made his appearance upon this earth?—ever made his presence sensible to, exhibited his person to the senses of, any human being that ever lived?

Not by unbelievers only, but by many a pious Christian, is the existence of

---

[1] 1818 'his'. The text follows the 'Errata'.

any such being not merely doubted of, but, for such reasons as to them have been satisfactory, utterly denied:—the sort of *being* mentioned under this name, being, in their notion of the matter, no other than an *allegorical* one; the passages, in which mention is made of him, so many purely *allegorical* or *figurative* expressions.

Figurative, and nothing more, was and is, according to them, the existence of this personage: figurative, and upon a line with that of *Jupiter* and *Juno*,[1] and the other inhabitants of the classical heaven, subjects or colleagues to those celestial potentates.

True, say certain fathers of the primitive Christian church. Yes; most exactly indeed upon a par were and are the Devils, great and small, with those *Gods* and *Goddesses*, great and small—with those *Dii majorum gentium*—with those *Dii minorum gentium*.[2] Strange, indeed, if they were not upon a par, when in truth they were and are the very same. Who?—yes—who were Jupiter and Juno, and the rest of them?—Who, but so many *Devils*, who, applying their influence to the inhabitants of this earth, caused themselves to be respectively worshipped under those classic names.

In these later times, to men of the deepest learning,—though among them it probably would not be easy to find many, if any, to join their suffrages on this question with those of the abovementioned fathers,—every thing relative to this personage, and in particular his existence, is matter of doubt and difficulty; and as between this and that one of them is matter of *dispute*. At the same time, even among babes and sucklings,[3] there is not one who is not qualified to decide upon it, and so well qualified as in this our Church to be forced to decide upon it, and to decide upon it accordingly.

To any such tender mind how indeed should it be matter of doubt or difficulty!—when, besides being assured of the existence of this personage by the earliest of all lessons, and highest of all authorities—(for that of *the Bible*,—a book of which the sense is to be taken upon the credit of this improved substitute, is but derivative)—not only his nature, but his very form is brought to view and made known by those *portraitures*, which are to be seen every where, and in particular in so many copies of the Book of Common Prayer, of which this Catechism forms a part.[4]

To the learned, as well as to the gay, among persons of riper years, such

---

[1] In Roman mythology, Jupiter was supreme ruler of the gods and mortals, and Juno, his consort, was chief of the goddesses.

[2] i.e. 'gods of the superior peoples' and 'gods of the inferior peoples'. The phrase *maiorum gentium di* is found in Cicero, *Tusculan Disputations*, I. xiii. 29, but is derived from the division of Roman senators into *patres maiorum et minorum gentium*.

[3] Psalm 8: 2; Matthew 21: 16.

[4] The devil commonly appeared in illustrations of Christ's temptation in the wilderness in Matthew 4: 1–11, the Gospel text for the First Sunday in Lent: see, for example, *The Book of Common Prayer, And Administration of the Sacraments, and other Rites and Ceremonies of the Church*, London, 1758, unpaginated; *The Book of Common Prayer, And Administration of the Sacraments, and other Rites and Ceremonies of the Church*, Cambridge, 1763, unpaginated; and *The Book of Common Prayer, and Administration of the Sacraments, and other Rites and Ceremonies of The Church*, Oxford, 1782, unpaginated.

portraitures, with the infinite variety of tales connected with them, are either subjects of merriment or objects of indifference. But, to the multitude of the young and uninformed, whose learning begins and ends with this so highly magnified summary, serious indeed is the idea attached to that tremendous sound. How many, from whose minds the horrific being,—of which, from the most unquestionable authority, the existence is thus certified,—is never absent! How many to whom this his ideal presence is sufficient to render *solitude*, at least when coupled with *darkness*, a situation of never-ceasing torment?[1]

(3). {*'The pomps and vanity of this wicked world.'*}—Pomps and vanity, *two* other sorts of things given here as *one* thing,—and that one, as well as the things preceding and succeeding, a thing to be *'renounced.'* Renounced?— By whom?—By every member of the Church of England without exception, and *that* with almost his earliest articulate breath.

As to the *vanity*, with or without the subjoined limitation, by which it is confined to *'this wicked world,'* being in itself the *vainest* of all *vain* words[2]— so completely *vain* as to be void of all meaning—it may, with that character attached to it, be dismissed.

But the word *pomp*—to this word is attached by usage—unvaried usage—a meaning somewhat more determinate and intelligible. Under the word *pomp* are comprised all those factitious appendages, by which factitious dignity,—when combined with the visible and tangible fruits and marks of opulence,—is, in the hands of the *ruling few*, employed to distinguish them from the *subject many*.

The *Monarch*, in the first place, is it not by *pomp* that he is intended and enabled to display and preserve his *dignity*, and therewith and thereby to maintain his *power?* The robes—the sceptre—the crown—the train of attendants, in so many forms and colours—armed and unarmed—if these be not the elements of *pomp*, what others are?

Not to speak of *Lords Temporal*, with their *titles*, their *coronets*, and their *armorial ensigns*, behold the Lords *Spiritual* with the *'fine linen'* on their shoulders, the *'purple'* on their *liveries*,[3] the *purple* and the *mitre* on their *equipages*. If not of *these* things, of *what* things is *'pomp'* made?

Of all these holy personages—these sitting and walking pageants—what one has there ever been, by whom all these *things* have not been thus solemnly *renounced?*—all these *things*, to which, disguised under the name of *decency*,[4] they now cling with such fond and undisguised affection:—these *things*, of which the very essence of their order is, according to them, composed, and by the taking away of which *the Church* would, according to them, be laid in ruins, and along with it *the State*.

That this so much magnified instrument of theatrical piety, is neither more nor less than a farce,—that nothing that is to be found in it need or ought to be considered as possessing any binding force,—that it is neither more nor less than so much sound without sense,—is not this the

---

[1] For Bentham's own 'torment' see Bowring, x. 21.
[2] See Ephesians 5: 6.
[3] See Luke 16: 19.
[4] See p. 86 & n. above.

CHURCH-OF-ENGLANDISM

comment, which, in that highest of all high places, the text receives from practice?

Such, then, being the judgment passed on it by the highest of all authorities, by what inferior authority—by what private individual—should any different judgment be passed upon it?

And this is the *'Instruction, which,'* (as it says itself in and by its title), is *'to be learned* of every person before he be brought to be confirmed by *the Bishop.'*[1]—By the Bishop? and by what Bishop?—by the self-same Bishop, who by the *'pomps,'* whatever they are, by which he is surrounded, manifests the contempt with which, by himself, this same *Instruction* is regarded: and who, at the very time, when the youthful votaries, whom he beholds at his feet, are passing examination under his eye,—and, under his authority, in and by the words thus forced into their mouths, made to declare the knowledge which they have of its contents, and the sentiments of veneration with which, by these same contents, they have been impregnated,—is all the while, in relation to these same contents, making manifest, if not his deliberate contempt of them, at least his ignorance or negligence.

(4). *'Sinful lusts of the flesh.'*—In this may be seen the *third* and last of the three *'things,'* or sets of things, which with its scarce articulate accents, the child, so lately in its cradle, is made to declare itself to have *'renounced.'*—Those *'lusts,'* which he has so decidedly *'renounced'*—those *'sinful lusts'*—what are they?—what, in his view of them, can they be?—Is it that the *'lusts of the flesh'* are, *all* of them, *'sinful,'* and as such to be comprised in the *renunciation?* or is it that, while there are *some* of them that *are* sinful, and as such are to be *'renounced,'* others there are, that are *not* sinful, and accordingly are *not* comprised in it?—These are among the secrets, which, howsoever here *mentioned*, are not here *made known*. But are they not *worth knowing?*—Are they not *necessary* to be known?—Are they not such as *must* have been known, ere the *'Instruction which is to be learned of* (meaning *by*) *every* person,' can, to *any one* person, be of any sort of use?

(5). *'Secondly, that I should believe all the articles of the Christian faith.*

Behold here another subject for a promise—for a promise in the shape of a *solemn vow*—in the shape of that sacred sort of instrument, which is neither more nor less than an *oath*, applied and adapted to this particular purpose. A promise?—to do what?—*to believe:*—a promise to believe an innumerable host of things,—and that without knowing what they are. For, be it observed, the thing to be believed is—not simply *the Articles*, but *all* the Articles. Follows, indeed, the *Creed*, called *the 'Apostles' Creed,'* the repetition of which is performed in answer to the presently following command—*'Rehearse the Articles of thy Belief.'*[2]—but in this Creed are they all contained? Not they indeed. For if they are, what is the *Nicene* Creed, and what the *Athanasian?*—both of them comprised in the *Liturgy*—that massy com-

---

[1] See p. 203 n. above
[2] See pp. 211–22 below.

pound, which the child is condemned to gulp down after he has swallowed this Catechism;—each of them as much a part of the Church of England Liturgy, and thereby of what passes among Church of Englandists for the repository of the Christian faith, as that, called the *Apostles' Creed*, is.[1]

Question 4.—Dost thou not think that thou art bound to believe, and to do as they have promised for thee?

Answer.—Yes, verily; and, by God's help, so I will. And I heartily thank our heavenly Father, that he hath called me to this state of salvation, through Jesus Christ our Saviour. And I pray unto God to give me his grace, that I may continue in the same to my life's end.

OBSERVATIONS.

Question. '*Dost thou not think*,' &c.—*Answer*. '*Yes, verily*,' &c.—Here then, not only do the authors of this formulary themselves advance this absurdity, but they compel the poor child,—as they have hitherto compelled so many millions—compelled, during so many successive generations, the far greater part of the population of the whole kingdom, and done what depended upon them towards compelling all future generations to the end of time,—compel him to[2] pronounce his assent to it, and his approbation of it.

Now then, once more, if so it be, that it is in the power of any three persons, under the name of *Sponsors*, to take possession of a child—a newborn child—and bind it, force it, to believe *this set* of Articles—how should it not be equally in their power to force it to believe any *other* set of Articles!—to believe, for example, the direct *reverse* of these same Articles!—If it be in their power, thus to force a child,—to force as many children as they please,—to believe a set of Articles which *they* call '*the Christian faith*,' how should it not be in their power to force it to believe a set of Articles, for example, of *the Mahometan* faith?

Here then is a notion, which strikes—(for does it not strike?)—at the root of all religion as well as all morality: and, forasmuch as, in giving utterance to this mass of absurdity, the child is forced to say that *he believes it*,—while, at his years, at any rate, to believe it is not possible,—thus it is that the duty and practice of *lying* forms part of every Church of England child's first lesson:—forms part?—Yes—forms a part, though but a part, of what he is *taught*,—but forms nearly the whole of what—let us hope at least—it is possible to him to *learn* from it.

Command, immediately following upon the fourth question—'*Rehearse the Articles of thy Belief*.'

Answer.—'I believe in God, the Father Almighty, Maker of heaven

---

[1] According to Art. 8 of the Thirty-nine Articles, the Nicene and Athanasian Creeds, as well as the Apostles' Creed, were 'thoroughly to be received and believed'. The Nicene Creed was recited during the Communion service, while the Apostles' Creed was recited in Evening and Morning Prayer, apart from thirteen feast days on which the Athanasian Creed was recited.

[2] 1818 'time,—to'. The text follows the 'Errata'.

CHURCH-OF-ENGLANDISM

and earth: And in Jesus Christ, his only Son our Lord, who was conceived by the Holy Ghost(1), born of the Virgin Mary(2), suffered under Pontius Pilate(3), was crucified, dead, and buried(4), He descended into hell(5); the third day he rose again from the dead, He ascended into heaven, and sitteth at the right hand of God the Father Almighty; From thence he shall come to judge the quick and the dead. I believe in the Holy Ghost(6); the holy Catholic Church(7); the communion of Saints(8); the forgiveness of sins(9); the resurrection of the body, and the life everlasting. Amen.'

OBSERVATIONS.[1]

The Apostles' Creed! This name, thus formally and universally applied—applied to a formulary, which, of those, by whom in that character it is forced into the mouths of children, there is not one, by whom any such notion is entertained, as that any one of those immediate disciples of Jesus had any, the smallest share in the formation of it!

Applied?—and by whom?—By the rulers of the English Church—of the Church of England, past and present,—by that Bench of Bishops, whose names stand at the head of an Association,[2] instituted for a set of purposes, of which the first in the order of time as well as of importance, is the causing the whole population to receive the formulary in that character.

An association, of which one main object is—to give currency to a *forgery!* to continue—and *that* for ever—to palm upon the rising generation as genuine an already exposed imposture. On the whole Bench sits there so much as a single individual, who will venture to declare, that he believes it *not* to have been a forgery? that he believes any one of those to have had a hand in it, in whose name it is thus put upon the whole people?

To all those who do not, with a critical eye, pointed to the questions of *verity* and *authenticity*, occupy themselves in the searching of the Scriptures, the immediate and sole looked-to evidence of that verity and authenticity, consists in the implied evidence, supposed to be bestowed upon it by those Right Reverend and well-paid witnesses. But here are these same witnesses, continually occupied in giving an attestation of authenticity, to a document, of the spuriousness of which they cannot but be, every one of them, fully conscious. If the religion of Jesus had no better ground to stand upon than this modern evidence, where would be the sort of regard due to it?

To give proofs, or so much as references to proofs, of its being a forgery—a generally exploded forgery—would be a mere waste of labour. *Pearson*—

---

[1] The following eight paragraphs appeared in 'Church of England Catechism Examined' at pp. 79–81, (i.e. immediately before the 'Recapitulation', p. 253 below), with the following note: 'NOTE.—*The Author being at a distance from the press, what follows on the subject of the Creed, was by accident omitted to be inserted in its more proper place, which was in p. 16, in which that part of the Catechism is spoken of.*' The passage has been restored to its proper place in the present edition.

[2] For Bentham's detailed criticism of the National Society for Promoting the Education of the Poor in the Principles of the Established Church see pp. 56–202 above.

CHURCH OF ENGLAND CATECHISM EXAMINED.

Bishop Pearson—whose comment on it is regularly included in the list of works, studied by all candidates for Church of England Ministry, into whose heads any such idea as that of rendering themselves, in an intellectual point of view, in any degree fit for their office, ever happens to find entrance,— *Pearson*—in styling it *the Creed*—knew it too well to venture, either in his title page, or any where else, to style it *the Apostles' Creed;* or so much as, in the way of insinuation, to give it to be understood, that the Apostles had, any of them, any thing to do with it.[1] '*The Creed* received in all ages of the Church,' (says he in his Epistle dedicatory): and thus far only did he venture to go beyond the truth, in speaking of it, except by this, viz. 'it is (says his Preface) generally taken to comprehend[2] all things necessary to be believed:'[3]—*the* Creed—as if he had never heard of more Creeds than this one: as if that Liturgy, of which it forms a part, did not, lest confusion should not be thick enough—force into men's mouths two other Creeds— the *Nicene* and the *Athanasian* (yes, the Athanasian!) by the side of it.[4]

For the first time—(pity the edition now on the table, though the *tenth*, does not enable any one to say exactly what that time was)—for the first time—observing what sort of a thing this tissue of dark allusions, taken in its own state, was,—he formed the generous resolution of rendering it intelligible: and in this endeavour, no fewer than four hundred closely printed folio pages, with more of microscopic notes than text, are employed: 'so that every one, when he pronounceth the Creed, may know, (says the good Bishop) what he ought to intend, and what he is understood to profess, when he so pronounceth it:'[5] so that now, to all those in whose instance to the labour of studying this *Exposition*, and the faculty of buying or borrowing it, has been added the felicity of understanding it, the text, in so far as the enterprize undertaken by the comment has been successful, has been rendered intelligible.

Creed and Exposition together, of those who but for it would have been damned, how many will have been saved by it? Of those who, if they had had it, would have been saved, how many will have been damned for want of it?—those included who will not have been rich enough either to buy or borrow it. When to each of these questions a satisfactory answer has been provided, then it is, that of its worth, a correct estimate, as well as conception, will have been formed.

This, together with both the other Creeds, and together with the spirit so[6] large a portion besides of the substance of her Liturgy, was by the Church of England received from her Holy Mother: among whose histories, that of the

---

[1] John Pearson (1613–86), Bishop of Chester from 1673, was author of *An Exposition of the Creed*, London, 1659. As he states below, Bentham refers to the tenth edition of the work published in 1715.

[2] Pearson, 10th edn. 'contain'.

[3] The quotations are taken from the dedication 'To the Right Worshipfull and Well-beloved The Parishioners of St Clements East-Cheape', and the preface addressed 'To the Reader', neither of which are paginated.

[4] See p. 211 n. above.

[5] See 'To the Reader', in *An Exposition of the Creed*.

[6] 1818 'spirit and so'. The text follows the 'Errata'.

CHURCH-OF-ENGLANDISM

pic-nic formation of this Creed by its putative fathers the Apostles, may be found in their proper places. The equally Established Church of *Scotland* is wiser and honester than to teach any of these Creeds.[1]

Of the three declarations of persuasion, which, under the name of *Creeds*, are all adopted into, and make part of the Church of England Liturgy, this,—which by universal confession falsely,[2] yet not the less universally, is called *the Apostles' Creed*,—is one.

In relation to this instrument, as here placed and employed, two questions naturally present themselves—

1. The set of opinions here stated as deduced from the text of holy writ, are they rightly deduced from holy writ? Do they in holy writ find a sufficient warrant?

2.[3] If yes, is it right and useful to take the whole of the instrument, as it stands,—and thus, at the tenderest age, force it into the mouths of children?

Of these questions, the first does not in any peculiar manner belong to this place: for the present at least it may therefore be dismissed.

In relation to the other question, a few observations may be not altogether without their use.

(1). {*Who was conceived by the Holy Ghost.*}—Not to dispute the matter of fact—the child—is it in the nature of the case that, of this *conception*, any conception at all should be entertained by the child, by whom the answer is lisped?

(2). {*Born of the Virgin Mary.*}—The like question to this clause.—Born of a Virgin?—Yes: viz. of a woman who was once a virgin: but, if *that* be what is here to be understood, so was every man that was ever born. Born without prejudice to her virginity?—she remaining after the birth as entirely a virgin as she was before? Is this a matter, the conception of which is, to a pupil, at such an age, in the number of things possible?—at such an age—not to speak of any less early age. Admitting the possibility, the attempt to convey an idea such as this, can it in any way be of use?

(3). {*Suffered under Pontius Pilate.*}[4]—To a child at such an age, the name of the Roman governor, under whose government the suffering took place—the remembrance of it, is it of any particular use?

(4). {*Was crucified, dead and buried.*}—*Crucifixion*—*burial*—in neither of these two facts is there any thing but what, at a very early age, a child may be capable of comprehending without much difficulty.—But death? the death of whom?—the death of a God?—What? a God? a God *of our own*

---

[1] The creeds were abandoned by the Westminster Assembly of Divines, and not included in the Church of Scotland Directory for the Public Worship of God or the Confession of Faith. The Apostles' Creed was, however, appended to the Shorter Catechism adopted by the Church of Scotland as 'a brief sum of the Christian faith, agreeable to the word of God, and anciently received in the churches of Christ'.

[2] 1818 adds '(1)' after 'falsely', but the enumeration appears to be redundant.

[3] 1818 omits '2.' The text follows the 'Errata'.

[4] Pontius Pilatus, Prefect of the Roman province of Judaea 26–36.

die?[1]—Much about this time, perhaps a little earlier, perhaps a little later, it may have happened to the child to hear of the Gods of the *heathens*—Gods in multitudes—not one of them subject to death. In such a case how inferior will this comparatively new God be apt to appear to him, in comparison of the least of these ancient ones? But if God the *Son* was thus mortal, what should preserve his Father from being mortal too? If it was the Son's turn to die at that time, may it not one of these days be the Father's turn? and then what is to become of the world, and all that live in it?

For the removal of this difficulty, what answer is left, but the doctrine of the *two natures?* Jesus (the child must be told) had two natures—the human and the divine: he was a man and a God, that is *the* God—for there is but one God—at the same time. It was the man only that was crucified, and, dying under the operation, was then buried. The God did not die: in the case of God, no such thing as death took place: it is not in the nature of God, that is to say, of the one God, to die. Well, then, while one of these persons, viz. the man, was dying, the other of them, the God, the one God, whereabouts was he?—Have a care, child, what you say. Two persons? no such thing. Man one, God one: these one and one, which you in your ignorance take for two, are not two persons: they are but one.—How but one person? One man, is not that one person? and one God, is not that another person? One and one, do they not make two?—In answer to any such questions, nothing remains but to chide the poor child for his ignorance—to insist upon his understanding in this case the difference between a nature and a person, and thereupon to plague him till he declares himself satisfied, that though Jesus had two *natures*, he had but one *person*, and that, in that instance at least, so far as *personality* was concerned, *a God*—no, not *a God*, but *God*—yes *God*, and man together, were one and the same.

Now, to any practical purpose, whether this or any part of it be true or no, is not, to child or man, worth inquiry. How should it be? For to human conduct, take it in any of these ways, what difference does it make? But, in regard to all this, or any part of this, to force a child to declare—to declare most solemnly and seriously, that he believes it: believes it just as he believes in the existence of the person, by whose words and gestures the words are forced into his mouth; and this in a case, in which any such belief is as plainly impossible! In this lies the mischief:—and, so long as in a habit of falsehood and insincerity, and that a universal one, there is any thing mischievous, this mischief will be as real, as the pretended belief is false.

(5). {*He descended into hell.*}—Of the matter of fact here asserted, the truth being admitted—(though for the admitting it no warrant was ever so much as attempted to be found in any part of Scripture, that bears any relation to Jesus, and though as well might it have been asserted, that, while a visit was then paid to *hell* by *Jesus*, a visit was at the same time paid to *heaven* by the *Devil*)—still, on this, as on so many preceding and so many succeeding occasions, comes the question—supposing the fact ever so well

---

[1] An allusion to Genesis 1: 26–7.

established, to what possible good use force a child, as soon as it can speak, to say that it believes this,—or so much as use any endeavours to cause it actually to believe any such thing?

When, against this proposition, the monstrous absurdity of it, coupled with its utter destituteness of all warrant from Scripture, is brought to view, the observation made by way of answer—and that probably enough a true one, is—that in this particular the *translation* is incorrect: for that in the original Greek the word, rendered in English by *hell*, did not, on this occasion, mean that which on every other occasion it is commonly understood to mean—viz. the abode, and place of torment, of the damned.[1]

But, besides that, of this observation, a necessary effect is to give birth to another question,—viz. if not *hell*, what other place then is, on this occasion, to be understood?—(a question, to which an answer would not, it is supposed, be very easy to be found),—another observation is, that, in the case of at least nine hundred and ninety-nine out of a thousand, of those, whose salvation is understood to be in so material a degree dependent—dependent, in some way or other—upon this Catechism,—no such mistranslation is known, or so much as suspected. In the conception of this vast majority,—the place of torment, appointed for the Devil and his angels,—*this* is the place, to which the visit of this Son of God—himself God—was, in his own divine person, paid.

Of this perplexity, added to so many other perplexities, what is the result? That,—in the minds of a very large proportion of the whole number,—a very large proportion, if not the whole, of this discourse, called *a Creed* and *the Creed*, produces the same effect as, and no more than, so much inarticulate sound. Not but that if, in the instance of the whole number, such were the case with *the whole* of this same creed, it would be all the better: always excepted the mischief of the lie which the child is taught and compelled to utter, in thus seriously and solemnly declaring that he believes it.

(6). {*I believe in the Holy Ghost.*}—Mere sounds without sense: mere words without meaning: not only void of all meaning, which to any *such young* person can be of any *use*—not only void of all meaning which to *any* person can be of any use,—but without any thing attached to them that can be called *meaning*.

What is the *Holy Ghost?—Answer.* The same as the *Holy Spirit.*

What then is the *Holy Spirit?—Answer.* The Spirit of God.

What then is this Spirit of God, that, when you believe [in] God, this should not be enough, but that you must believe in this Spirit of God besides? Believing in a man, what more do you do, by believing in his Spirit likewise?

'*The Lord be with you,*' says the Minister to the congregation in one part of our Liturgy. Not to be behind hand with him in piety or politeness, nor yet to give him back his compliment without variation, as if for want of words, 'And *with thy Spirit,*' returns the *Chorus*, under the command of the

---

[1] The Greek word $\alpha\delta\eta s$ (i.e. Hades), used in the New Testament, meant the underworld, the place of the dead, without any connotation of torment or punishment.

CHURCH OF ENGLAND CATECHISM EXAMINED.

Clerk.[1] In any such variation of the phrase, has imagination, in its extravagance, ever soared to such a height as to fancy itself to be possessing and employing a *re-agent*, having the effect of *decomposing* a human person, in such sort as to convert him, polypus like, into *two* persons, of which *himself* is one, and his *spirit* the other?

If believing in God be not enough, without believing in the Spirit of God besides, how came *this* to be enough? To believe in the Spirit of God, in addition to God himself, how can this be sufficient, when, besides the Spirit of God, according to the flowery texture of the same language and the same Scriptures, there are so many other things belonging to God, viz. the hand of God, the arm of God, the finger of God, the word of God, the power of God, the glory of God, and so forth:[2] each of them not less susceptible, than the Spirit of God, of a separate existence.—Oh, silly men—yes, if sincere, 'more silly than any sheep, which on the flowery plains shepherd did ever keep'[3]—ye string words upon words,—and then, for every word, believe, or pretend to believe, that a correspondent really existing object is brought into existence.

The Holy Ghost being, at the end of the account, something which is the same as God, and at the same time distinct from God,—and being something, in which, day by day, the child is obliged to say that he believes,—by the sense of this obligation, should it happen to him to be induced, to put himself upon the look-out for something determinate to believe in,—of such his inquiry, what, if any thing, will be the result?

In the same instructive prints, which present to his view the *Devil*, in the character of a black man, with horns to his head, and a tail to his rump,[4] he will behold a *pigeon*, hovering in a spot of light.[5] This *pigeon*, which, however, he will be taught to call not by this name, but by its other and more poetical name, a *dove*—this *pigeon* it is, that if any thing, will be the object of his belief.

One[6] God, whose picture *here* and *now* must not be drawn, but which when *here* it *was* drawn, *was*—and *there* where it is drawn, is—the picture of

---

[1] See, for example, 'The Order for Morning Prayer' and 'The Order for Evening Prayer', *Book of Common Prayer*.

[2] All these phrases except for 'arm of God' appear on numerous occasions in the Bible.

[3] See Ambrose Philips (bap. 1674, d. 1749), 'The Second Pastoral', first published in *Poetical Miscellanies: The Sixth Part. Containing a Collection of Original Poems, With Several New Translations*, London, 1709, p. 12:
    Ah silly I! more silly than my Sheep,
    Which on the flow'ry Banks I once did keep.

[4] See p. 208 & n. above.

[5] The dove, for example, appeared in illustrations for the baptism of Christ by John the Baptist as recounted in Mark 1: 9 and Matthew 3: 16 in *The Book of Common Prayer, And Administration of the Sacraments, and other Rites and Ceremonies of the Church*, London, 1758, and *The Book of Common Prayer, and Administration of the Sacraments, and other Rites and Ceremonies of The Church*, Oxford, 1782. The dove also appeared in illustrations for the coming of the Holy Ghost to the disciples in Acts 2: 3–4, from the Epistle text for Whitsunday; see, for example, *The Book of Common Prayer, And Administration of the Sacraments, and other Rites and Ceremonies of the Church*, Cambridge, 1763, unpaginated.

[6] 1818 'Our'. The text follows the 'Errata'.

an *old man*,[1]—*another God*, whose picture may be drawn, and is continually drawn, and when drawn is seen to be the picture of a *young man*—which God is likewise not only a God but also a man,—a *third* God, whose picture may be drawn, and being drawn, is seen to be the picture of the sort of *pigeon* called a *dove*,—these three Gods, who, man and *pigeon* included, make, after all, but one and the same object of belief, and that object *a God*,—these, when this system of instruction has been read, marked, learnt, and inwardly digested,[2]—comprise and constitute the *subject* of all this science—the *object* of the young child's belief—of that belief, of which he is forced to say that he entertains it.—That he entertains it?—why?—Even because, in an unthinking and half-hearing moment, three persons,—under the rod of the law,—to save him from the endless and inscrutable mass of temporal inconvenience, attached to the non-performance of the ceremony,[3]—undertook, by that which would be not only a *rash*, but a *flagitious*, were it any thing but a *senseless* vow, that, after having begun to entertain this belief, before he knew or cared what it was that he was thus entertaining, he would, to the end of his life, continue to entertain it.

(7). {*The Holy Catholic Church.*}—*The Holy Catholic Church.*—'*I believe in the Holy Catholic Church.*'—Not to speak of former times, what is it that *at present* a child can understand himself to have spoken of himself as doing, when he has declared that he believes in *the Holy Catholic Church?*—*I believe in God?*—Yes, this is what he *may* conceive himself to understand.—*I believe in God;* i.e. I believe in the *existence* of a God—and so in regard to *Jesus Christ*, and the *Holy Ghost*. But—*I believe in the existence of a Holy Catholic Church?*— For this same Church, of which, under the name of *the Holy Catholic Church*—*one* Holy Catholic Church, and no more than one—he is thus forced to speak, where is it that he is to look? If, by any such name as *the Catholic Church*, there be any thing that, on any other occasion, he has ever heard spoken of as being in existence, it will have been *the Roman Catholic Church:*—a Church, composed of *Roman Catholics*, who are the same men

---

[1] Before the Protestant Reformation, painted and sculpted religious images decorated English churches, including God portrayed as an old man, a pointing hand, or a ray of light. Protestant Reformers, however, condemned such images as a potential source of abuse and idolatry, and, taking the Second Commandment as their warrant, banned all images from churches: see, for example, Royal Injunction of 1559, §23, in *Tudor Royal Proclamations*, ed. P.L. Hughes and J.F. Larkin, 3 vols., New Haven and London, 1964–9, ii. 123; 1 Eliz. I, c. 2, §25 (1559); and the Thirty-nine Articles of the Church of England, Arts. 22 and 35. Puritans in the Long Parliament of 1640–60 later confirmed this stance: see 'An Ordinance for the utter demolishing, removing and taking away of all Monuments of Superstition or Idolatry', 26 August 1643, and 'An Ordinance for the further demolishing of Monuments of Idolatry and Superstition', 9 May 1644, *Lords Journals*, vi. 200–1, 546. Illustrations of religious subjects and histories were never banned in private places, such as homes and in books, and, by the time Bentham was writing, some religious images were permitted in English churches, though not images of God.

[2] See Collect from the Second Sunday in Advent, in 'The Collects Epistles and Gospels to be used throughout the year', *Book of Common Prayer*.

[3] The Corporation Act of 1661 (13 Car. II, Stat. II, c. 1) and the Test Act of 1673 (25 Car. II, c. 2) disbarred those who had not, within a specified time, received communion from holding offices in borough corporations and under the crown respectively. See also p. 289 n. below.

that are sometimes called *Papists*, and who, when they were in power, burnt as many of the good people called *Protestants*, of whom he himself is one, as for that purpose they could lay hold of. Now, as to the *Holy Ghost*, in whom the child has just been declaring himself to believe,—whatsoever is or is not meant by *holiness*,—that *Ghost*, without any difficulty, is *holy*. But this Church, composed as it is of the barbarous men called *Papists*, is this too *Holy?*—holy, even as the *Holy Ghost is Holy?*—On the part of the poor child, suppose any particle of thought to be bestowed upon the subject, how distressing must be the perplexity, into which he here finds himself plunged?—But no:—before it has arrived thus far, the plain truth of the case is—that, whether in the breast of a child, or in the breast of an adult, the faculty of thought, having found itself baffled and wearied out,—has, in despair, withdrawn itself from the whole subject,—leaving in the grasp of the conception and the memory, nothing but a string of sounds and characters, void of all sense.

(8). {*The Communion of Saints.*}—*The Communion of Saints?* One more puzzle: a riddle, which unhappily is not explicable, but which happily is not worth being explained.

The Communion of Saints—What is *a Communion?* What are *Saints?*—Saints, the poor child will soon have heard of.—There is St. Peter; there are the rest of the twelve Apostles, (Traitor *Judas* being excepted):[1] there are Jesus's four *Biographers*, decorated with the title of *Evangelists:* all or most of them more or less known to him by their portraits; all of them striking likenesses; and, though last not least, there is St. *Paul*, whose beginning had borne but too near a resemblance to the latter end of *Judas*.[2] In *the Communion,*—or, at any rate, in *a* communion,—the child may likewise, ere long, behold a thing which he has *heard of,* and moreover *heard*—a part of the Church service, called sometimes, for shortness, *the Communion* simply; at other times, without abbreviation, *the Communion Service.*—*Communion—Saints—belief*—putting together the ideas brought to view by these three words,—what, in relation to this matter, will be the little creature's belief?—something, perhaps, to this effect; viz. that, among the Apostles, and whatever other holy men used to be called *Saints*, it was a custom to join together in the performance of *the Communion Service;* of the Communion service,—worded, as he has seen it, or is about to see it worded, viz. in the *Church of England Liturgy.*

If this be an error, well would it be for the successive generations, by which the compound, here analyzed, is destined to be swallowed,—not to speak of those by whom it *has been* swallowed,—if, of all errors contained in it, this were the most pernicious one.

Saints, whose portraits he has there been used to see—that, like good Saints as they were, they used, all of them, to join in the performance of the Communion service—this may do for a time. But to believe in the

---

[1] For Judas's betrayal of Jesus see Matthew 26: 47–50; Mark 14: 43–6; Luke 22: 47–54; and John 18: 1–12.
[2] Before his conversion to Christianity, Saul (as he had then been known) had been notorious for his persecution of Christians: see Acts 7: 58; 8: 1–3; 9: 1–2.

CHURCH-OF-ENGLANDISM

Communion of Saints, is to believe in the Saints themselves:—and who are these Saints? To any[1] such question, should it ever happen to him to put to himself, what answer will he have to give?—Where shall he find it?—Where shall he look for it?—Sooner or later it may happen to him to look into the Calendar, that stands at the commencement of his Common Prayer Book, more especially as it is there that he will have to look for Holidays.[2] Looking into this treasury of consecrated idleness, he will find, that, to the original stock of Saints, he will have to add a list of modern ones; not to speak of Martyrs and Confessors, with whom this Catechism has happily abstained from burthening his memory and his conscience. Neither in this however will there be any great difficulty: and now, to his belief in the Devil will be added, his belief in *Saint Dunstan*, whose Church is established still in Fleet-street, and whose Saintship consisted in pulling the unclean spirit by the nose.[3] Here at any rate may be Saints enough to satisfy his believing appetite, so long as his studies are confined to the Common Prayer Book, of which this Catechism makes a part, and the Calendar, by which it is commenced, or preceded. But, by the Holy Scriptures—should they ever carry him so far—how will those ideas, which by the Common Prayer Book he had been led to form of Saints, be enlarged, and at the same time confused and troubled? On this head, are the Holy Scriptures—is the New Testament—are the Acts of the Apostles, to be believed? If so, then is every one a Saint, by whom the religion of Jesus is, or ever has been, or shall ever have been, professed. Read to this purpose the Acts of the Apostles: or, what is shorter—turn to any *Concordance*.[4]

If this be so, then in the number of these holy subjects or objects of his belief, he may have to place not only St. *Peter* and St. *Paul* with their contemporaries, as above, with such of their successors, as St. *Sutton* and St. *Vernon*, and St. *Howley*,[5] and St. *Burgess*,[6] and St. *Eldon*, and St. *Sidmouth*, and St. *Harrowby*,[7] and St. *Bailey*,[8] and St. *Stevens*,[9] and St.

[1] 1818 'Saints? Any'. The text follows the 'Errata'.
[2] For a list of the feasts and holy days to be celebrated in the church year see 'The Calendar with the Table of Lessons' which appears at the beginning of the *Book of Common Prayer*.
[3] According to his biographer Osbern, St Dunstan (d. 988), Benedictine monk and Archbishop of Canterbury from 960, when a young monk at work at a forge in Glastonbury, seized the devil (in the guise of a young woman) by the nose with his red-hot tongs. Depictions of Dunstan often included tongs as one of his attributes. The church of St Dunstan-in-the-West, Fleet Street, London dated from the eleventh century. St Dunstan's Day is 19 May.
[4] For the identification of Christians with saints see, for instance, Acts 9: 13, 32, 41; Romans 1: 7; I Corinthians 1: 2; and Philippians 1: 1.   [5] 1818 '*Howell*'. The text follows the 'Errata'.
[6] Charles Manners-Sutton, Archbishop of Canterbury; Edward Venables-Vernon, subsequently Harcourt (1757–1847), Archbishop of York from 1808; William Howley, Bishop of London; and Thomas Burgess, Bishop of St David's.
[7] Eldon, Lord Chancellor; Sidmouth, Home Secretary; and Harrowby, Lord President of the Council.
[8] Sir John Bayley (1763–1841), Justice of King's Bench 1808–30, Baron of the Exchequer 1830–4, and author of *The Book of Common Prayer, and Administration of the Sacraments and other Rites and Ceremonies of the Church . . . with Notes on the Epistles, Gospels, Psalms, and Lessons*, London, 1816.
[9] William Stevens (1732–1807), hosier, religious writer, and high churchman, Treasurer of Queen Anne's Bounty 1782–1807.

CHURCH OF ENGLAND CATECHISM EXAMINED.

Parke,[1] and St. *Wilberforce*,[2] and St. *Bernard*,[3] and St. *Milner*[4] the Protestant, and St. *Milner* the Catholic,[5] and St. *Hannah*[6] and St. *Joanna*,[7]—but St. *Napoleon* moreover, and St. *George*,[8] and St. *Ellenborough*,[9] and St. *Yarmouth* the *Orange-man*,[10] and St. *Headfort*,[11] and St. *Dudley Bate*,[12] and St. *Southey*,[13] and St. *Anti-Jacobin*,[14] and St. *Eclectic*,[15] and St. *Quarterly Review*.[16]

(9). {*The forgiveness of sins; the resurrection of the body; and the life everlasting.*}—On these several points, to the present purpose it seems scarcely necessary to bestow any very particular observations. Thus briefly and elliptically conceived, containing nothing but a mere indication of certain topics, as if touched upon in some other work, the phrases amount of themselves to nothing. The demand they present for explanation is obvious and undeniable; and in the whole body of that formulary, by not so much as a syllable in the way of explanation are they accompanied. Nothing of that sort is there in the *Creed* itself; as little in this *Catechism*, into which, for the instruction of young children, it is engrafted.

As such they add to the number of propositions or subject-matters, in relation to which, while it is impossible the child should entertain any belief concerning them, he is thus forced to stand up with all solemnity, and say, '*I believe.*'[17]

---

[1] Sir James Alan Park, Justice of Common Pleas.

[2] William Wilberforce (1759–1833), politician and philanthropist, MP for Kingston-upon-Hull 1780–4, Yorkshire 1784–1812, and Bramber 1812–25.

[3] Sir Thomas Bernard, philanthropist and co-founder of the Society for Bettering the Condition of the Poor.

[4] 1818 'St. *W. Milner*'. The text follows the 'Errata'.

[5] Isaac Milner (1750–1820), natural philosopher, evangelical, and Dean of Carlisle from 1791; and John Milner (1752–1826), Roman Catholic Bishop of Castabala and Vicar-Apostolic of the Midlands from 1803.

[6] Hannah More (1745–1833), religious writer, evangelist, and philanthropist.

[7] Joanna Baillie (1762–1851), playwright and poet, and since 1802, when the family were neighbours of Bentham's brother Sir Samuel Bentham (1757–1831) and his family in Hampstead, a friend of Bentham's.

[8] Napoleon Bonaparte (1769–1821), Emperor of the French 1804–14; and George III, King of Great Britain and Ireland from 1760.

[9] Ellenborough, Chief Justice of King's Bench.

[10] Francis Charles Seymour-Conway (1777–1842), styled Earl of Yarmouth 1794–1822, succeeded as third Marquis of Hertford in 1822, MP for Orford 1797–1802, Lisburn 1802–12, County Antrim 1812–18, and Camelford 1820–2.

[11] Thomas Taylour (1757–1829), styled Viscount Headfort (I) 1766–95, succeeded as 2nd Earl of Bective (I) in 1795, created Marquis of Headfort (I) in 1800, MP for Kells 1776–90, Longford 1790–4, and County Meath 1794–5, and Lord of the Bedchamber 1812–29.

[12] Sir Henry Bate Dudley (1745–1824), writer, journalist, and editor of the *Morning Post* 1775–80, founder and editor of the *Morning Herald* 1780–1804, in receipt of various Irish benefices from 1804 to 1812, Rector of Willingham, Cambridgeshire 1812–24, and Canon of Ely Cathedral 1817–24.

[13] Robert Southey (1774–1843), poet and reviewer.

[14] The *Anti-Jacobin Review*, founded in 1798, whose editor at this time was John Gifford (formerly John Richards Green) (1758–1818).

[15] The *Eclectic Review*, founded in 1805, whose editor and proprietor at this time was Josiah Conder (1789–1855).

[16] The *Quarterly Review*, founded in 1809, whose editor at this time was William Gifford (1756–1826).

[17] 1818 '*I do believe.*' The text follows the 'Errata'.

As to these three last-mentioned subjects, compleat the proposition—what in each instance you have, and all that you have, is composed of so many allusions—mere allusions. In the mind of him, whoever he was, by whom this formulary was penned, they had doubtless, every one of them, a *subject-matter* or *object*, more or less determinate—every one of them accordingly a *meaning*. But, in the mind of the so newly-born child,—in that mind, in which it is, generally speaking, impossible that the indeterminate portion of matter thus alluded to should have any place—what meaning can they, any of them, have? At bottom, what then is it that he is thus forced to declare? What but this, viz. that he believes in whatever is thus forced into his mouth, without knowing so much as *who* it is that put it where it is, much less *what* it is?

Question 5th.—What dost thou chiefly learn in these articles of thy belief?

Answer.—First, I learn to believe in God the Father, who hath made me and all the world(1).

Secondly, in God the Son, who hath redeemed me and all mankind(2).

Thirdly, in God the Holy Ghost, who sanctifieth me and all the elect people of God(3).

OBSERVATIONS.

To these three things may be added three others, which, with a degree of correctness, proportioned to the degree of the impregnation he has received from them, a child may make sure of learning;—and these are,—the art of *gratuitous assertion*—the art of speaking and writing without thinking—and the art of making *groundless inferences*.

(1). {*Belief in God the Father.*}—Yes: this is among the things which, supposing them *noticed*, are not incapable of being *learnt* from it.

(2). {*Belief in God the Son?*}—Yes, and this likewise. But—belief *in God the Son, who redeemed me and all the world?*—As to the fact of the *redemption;* had it been taken for the subject of an independent article of belief, no objection would, *here* at least, have been made to it. But the Creed called the *Apostles'* Creed?—this just repeated Creed?—from this discourse is the belief of any such thing as *redemption* to be learnt? Look at it, reader, once more: examine it from top to bottom. Of no such thing—any the slightest intimation will you find in it.

But *mankind, all* of whom the child is thus made to say he believes to have been redeemed—redeemed, along with himself, by Jesus—*they*, considering[1] the condition in which they will be seen to be placed, present some claim to notice.

Of this *redemption*, the *universality* any more than the *fact*, is not here

---

[1] 1818 '*they*, on considering'. The text follows the 'Errata'.

meant to be disputed. But, whosoever has been made to declare himself to be a believer in it, it might not have been amiss, it should seem, had some little provision been made, for preserving him from any such obligation, as that of declaring, on an eventually subsequent occasion, a directly opposite belief: viz. that of declaring, in solemn form, his belief of and in the entire contents of that other formulary, called the *Thirty-nine Articles*.—Of that test and treasury of Church of England orthodoxy, in *one* article, viz. the 18th, intituled, '*Of obtaining eternal salvation only by the name of Christ*,' 'Those (it is said) are to be held accursed, that presume to say, that every man shall be saved by the law or sect which he professed, so that he be diligent to frame his life according to that Law and the Light of Nature. For holy Scripture doth set out unto us (concludes the article) only the name of Jesus whereby men must be saved.'

Not to speak of any *former* portion of time,—of the whole number of human beings existing at *this* time upon this our earth, by far the greater number, it is manifest, can never have heard of any such person or name as *Jesus*. This great majority—are they capable of being saved, each of them '*diligently framing his life*,' in the terms of the article, 'according to the Law of Nature,' (i.e. it must be presumed, leading a virtuous life), or are they not?

Being, along with the rest of mankind, redeemed by Jesus, is a man *capable* of being '*saved*,' otherwise than 'by the name of Jesus?'—then is the article *false*.—Is he *incapable?*—then where is the use of such *redemption*, and what is a man the better for it?

Every man who takes what are called *Holy Orders*—every man whose name is entered in the books of either University—declares in writing his belief in *all* these *Articles*.[1] But, as hath been seen, no sooner does he thus declare, than, by such his declaration, he contradicts the belief thus expressed in and by this his *Catechism*.

By parental authority—by the compulsion, inseparable from the exercise, however directed, of that authority,—in a word, by *force*—by any thing but *argument* or *reason* applied to the understanding,—during a long and uninterrupted course of years, he is made continually to declare this to be his belief: thereupon, when the time for the purchase of a ticket in the Ecclesiastical Lottery, and with it the time for *Subscription* comes,—all on a sudden he turns short round, casts from him this his belief, and embraces the reverse of it.

All this with the most perfect, and the most exemplary *regularity:* and thus it is that *order, good order, regularity, decency*—sounds so sweet to the ears of *Orthodoxy, Despotism*, and their ever ready handmaid, *Mendacity*—are preserved.[2]

---

[1] A formal declaration of assent to the Thirty-nine Articles was legally required of all clergy taking office: see Canon 36 of the Canons of 1604, in *The Anglican Canons 1529–1947*, ed. G. Bray, Woodbridge, 1998 (*Church of England Record Society*, Vol. VI), pp. 318–21. Matriculants at the University of Oxford and graduands at the University of Cambridge were required to assent to the Thirty-nine Articles. For Bentham's comments on this practice see pp. 35–6 above.

[2] For Bentham's further discussion of this theme see *The Book of Fallacies*, pp. 232–5 (Bowring, ii. 441–2).

(3). {*Thirdly, in God the Holy Ghost, who sanctifieth me and all the elect people of God.*}—In explanation of the function called *sanctification*, thus allotted to God the *Holy Ghost*, what, in this instrument, is there to be found?—Just as much as in explanation of the function of *redemption*, just allotted, as above, to God the *Son*.

Whence then all this elaborate distinction of functions? all the work thus given to the carving knife? The Godhead being, as every body is supposed to know, or at least made to say, composed of three persons,—and, on the occasion in question, the plan being to give something to do for each,—thereupon, the less plainly incomprehensible functions of *creation* and *redemption* being already disposed of,—divided, as hath been seen, between the two other persons of this undivided Trinity, comes the question—what can we find for the Holy Ghost to do?—Answer. *Sanctification.*—Here, then, whatsoever be the meaning of it, here was a sort of *employment* found for him, every other being engaged.

Here, then, in this word we have the name of a sort of *process*, which the child is made to say is going on within him; going on within him at all times—going on within him at the very instant he is giving this account of it. This process, then, what is it? Of what feelings is it productive? By what marks and symptoms is he to know whether it really is or is not going on within him, as he is forced to say it is? How does he feel, now that the Holy Ghost is *sanctifying* him? How is it that he would feel, if no such operation were going on within him?

Too often does it happen to him, in some shape or other, to commit *sin;* or something which he is told and regarded to believe is *sin:* an event which cannot fail to be frequently, not to say continually, taking place, if that be true, which in the Liturgy we are all made so decidedly to confess and assert,—viz. that we are all—all of us without exception—so many '*miserable sinners?*'[1] In the *School room*, doing what by this Catechism he is forced to do, saying what he is forced to say, the child thus declares himself, notwithstanding, a *sanctified* person. From thence going to church, he confesses himself to be no better than '*a miserable sinner.*' If he is not always this miserable sinner, then why is he always forced to say he is? If he is always this same miserable sinner, then this sanctification, be it what it may, which the Holy Ghost was at the pains of bestowing upon him, what is he the better for it?

The child, into whose mouth these words are forced, does he not so much as suppose himself to feel going on within him any process, to which the word *sanctification* can be applied? If *not*, then what is it that this same *sanctification* means? and why is it that he is made to speak of the Holy Ghost, as performing or having performed it upon him, when he feels not any such thing, nor knows any thing about the matter?

Does he then feel or suppose any such particular operation going on with

---

[1] As part of the Litany to be said or sung after Morning Prayer on Sunday, Wednesday, and Friday, the phrase 'have mercy upon us miserable sinners' is repeated several times by both priest and worshippers: see 'The Litany', *Book of Common Prayer*.

CHURCH OF ENGLAND CATECHISM EXAMINED.

[in] him? If so, then must this sanctification be the receiving of that inward light, which certain of the people called *Methodists*, take upon them to speak of themselves as feeling within themselves.[1] By the rulers of the Church and their adherents, these Methodists are spoken of as *schismatics*, and a species of heretics.[2] Quere, such reprobation, how is it consistent with the declaration thus expressed and included in this Catechism?

To be *sanctified* is to be made *holy*. By the child, be he who he may, sooner or later, this point of information will have been received, if it has not been already. While giving this answer, *does* the child then feel itself *holy?*—If *not*, then why is it to be forced to say it does? If *yes*, then is it already a *Methodist* child: an arrant *Methodist*.

Question 6.—You said that your Godfathers and Godmothers did promise for you that you should keep God's commandments. Tell me how many there be.

Answer.—Ten.

Question 7.—Which be they?

Answer.—The same which God spake in the twentieth chapter of Exodus, saying, I am the Lord thy God, who brought thee out of the land of Egypt, out of the house of bondage.[3]

1.Thou shalt have none other Gods but me.

☛ Thereupon follow the other nine of these commandments.[4]

OBSERVATIONS.

Upon the face of this introduction, an appearance rather unfortunate presents itself. The child in question is not a Jew: neither he nor any of his forefathers were ever, in the manner thus alluded to, '*brought out of the land of Egypt.*' But it is to the Jews, and to that race alone,—to those, and the progeny of those, who were thus brought out of the land of Egypt,—that these Commandments are any where in the Bible represented as having been delivered.

How far, by a person professing the religion of Jesus they ought to be considered as binding upon him, is a subject of controversy, upon which it is not proposed to enter in this place.

One observation, however, there is, which, even in this place, claims admission,—and *that* by a title which it seems not easy to dispute. This is—that, in a discourse, which is intended for the instruction of *Christian* children, and which has for one of its objects the causing these Commandments to be regarded as binding upon Christians, it seems not altogether congruous to that design, to employ a form of words, upon the face of which it appears, that no person, not being of Jewish lineage, and at the same time of the Jewish persuasion in matters of religion, and therefore no child for

---

[1] It was more characteristically the Quakers, rather than the Methodists, who claimed to receive guidance from the 'inward light'.

[2] Bentham, no doubt, had in mind [Howley], *Charge delivered to the Clergy of the Diocese of London*: see p. 48 & n. above.

[3] See Exodus 20: 2.

[4] See Exodus 20: 3–17.

whose use this formulary was intended, is of the number of the persons to whom these Commandments were addressed.

In relation to this incongruity, what was the expectation, and consequent instruction, of the penners and establishers of this formulary?—that it *would* and *should*, or that it *would not* and *should not*, attract, in general, the notice, and engage the attention, of those who were destined to be impregnated with it?—impregnated with the *matter*, or, at any rate, with the *words* of it? *If yes*, then the expectation and intention was,—that, by those, by whom the words of this formulary were got by heart, no reliance should be placed in the *words*, of which it was composed; but that for the sense of it, they were to refer themselves to whatever construction the person, to whose guidance it was meant they should stand subjected, might at any time be pleased to put upon it:—*if no*, then the expectation and intention was,—that in this part at least—(and if in *this* part, how should it be otherwise in any *other?*) the place it occupied in men's minds would and should be that of an insignificant assemblage of words:—of mere words, not accompanied by correspondent ideas, and therefore not capable of exercising any influence on human practice;—on the conduct of those upon whose memories it was to be impressed.

But, in relation to this matter, let the *expectation* and *intention* have been what they may, what is likely to be the *effect?* The incongruity, *will it* be perceived? then in so far will the unfitness of this formulary for its purpose be perceived. The incongruity, will it *not* be perceived? it will then be, because,—in this particular part, as in the whole together,—it is not of a nature to take on the understanding any efficient hold, nor therefore to produce on life and conduct any beneficial effect.

Thou shalt not make to thyself any graven image, nor the likeness of any thing that is in heaven above, or in the earth beneath, or in the waters under the earth.[1]

OBSERVATIONS.

Upon the face of this commandment, two branches of art and science stand condemned and prohibited; viz. the *graphic art* in all its various modifications; the graphic art, and thereby, in great measure, the science of *natural history:* two branches of art and science; and thereby, among *men*, those by whom those branches of art and science are respectively practised and cultivated: on the one hand, *painters* and other such *artists*—on the other hand, *natural philosophers*.

True it is, that, immediately after the above, these are the words that follow:—'*Thou shalt not bow down to them, nor worship them.*'[2] Well then (it has been said) by this it appears, that in so far as concerns manual operation in any shape, in addition to the act of *bowing down to* and *worshipping them*, all that was meant to be included in the prohibition, was—not simply the act of *making* the sorts of things in question, but the act of making them for the *purpose* in question: viz. that of their being *bowed down to* and *worshipped.*

[1] Exodus 20: 4.   [2] Exodus 20: 5.

CHURCH OF ENGLAND CATECHISM EXAMINED.

Yes, verily: in this may be seen a signification, which must per force be put upon these words, in so far as a resolution has been previously taken, that whatsoever were the real meaning of the prohibitory clause, the act of *making*, as applied to the class of articles in question, shall not be *considered* as included in it.

But, upon the face of the words, as they here stand, is this the *true*, the *natural*, the *proper* sense of them? If so, then are the words designative of the sort of act first mentioned, viz. the act of *making*—then are the words—'*Thou shalt not make to thyself*'—to be considered as words void of meaning: then is the whole passage to be understood, as it would be if no such words were there.

But, for the taking of any such liberty with this passage where is the sufficient warrant? If with *this* passage that sort of liberty may be taken,—taken at pleasure, by any man who finds a convenience in so doing,—why not with any other, and every other?—This is the way that, now-a-days, so many religions are made. By omission, by insertion, by substitution—by *amendment* in every shape—a man makes a Bible of his own; and thereupon, with intimations given of divine vengeance in case of refractoriness, he calls upon mankind to bow down and worship it.

The writer, inspired or not inspired, by whom this passage was originally penned, was he so much less skilled in the import and management of his own language, as not to be able to give expression to a prohibition, which he *did* intend *should* take effect,—not to be able to give expression to this prohibition, without adding to it another and still more extensive,—and that a useless and pernicious one,—which he *did not intend* should take effect? Inspired or uninspired, had he not foresight enough to foresee (and surely no such gift as that of supernatural prophecy was necessary to enable a man to foresee) that such as is here contended for would be the signification put upon these words,—and in consequence to do what was so perfectly easy to do, for preventing any such sense from being put upon them, viz. to forbear inserting the words by which this supposed real intention was so plainly counteracted, and which could not be either necessary or conducive to any other purpose than that of counteracting it.

In truth, according to the plain and only natural import of the words, here are two sorts of acts, perfectly distinct from and unconnected with each other, that are successively taken for the objects of so many successive prohibitory clauses. *One* is—the act of *worshipping* the natural objects therein described, the *other* is—the act of *making* visible representations of these same objects.

True it is, that it is not in *this* order that the two prohibitions follow one another: it is in the reverse order: the prohibition of *making* any likenesses of the objects in question, this is the prohibition that happens here to have been first. And in this collocation it is—in the relative position thus given to these two prohibitive clauses, which in this their situation are, however, upon the face of them, no less completely independent of one another, than in the opposite situation they would have been—in this circumstance, insignificant as it is, may be seen the only shadow of pretence, that could be found, for a change so violent—for a misrepresentation so manifest.

All this while—as every body knows—in this country, in which the religion of Jesus is not only professed, but established, and even forced upon men by law,—under the same law the *making of graven images* is not only practised, and allowed, but by public authority encouraged; as well as in all other imaginable ways, 'the likenesses' of all sorts of things that are 'in heaven above, or in the earth beneath, or in the water (whatsoever there is of it that is) under the earth.' In this state of law and universal practice, while such as above is manifestly the import of this commandment,—a commandment, exhibiting not only in the character of a *divine* one, but of a divine one, binding not only upon the Jews, to whom it was delivered, but upon Christians, to whom it was not delivered,—is it not deplorable, that, in this country in particular, every Christian, belonging to the established religion, should thus be forced to declare his resolution to keep this commandment along with the rest;—this commandment, which no such Christian ever *does* keep, or entertain so much as a thought of keeping? or, except in and by this formulary, addressed to young children only, is ever called upon to keep?

To engage in any such task as that of writing a commentary on this Jewish code, forms not any part of the design of the present tract. That part of this Catechism, which is composed of the remaining eight of these commandments, has therefore been omitted.

Question 8.—What dost thou chiefly learn by these commandments?

Answer.—I learn two things: my duty towards God, and my duty towards my neighbour.

OBSERVATIONS.

Of a *commentary*, be the subject what it may, a proper,—and (it should seem) where, as here, censure is out of the question, the only proper,—use is—in so far as the text is, either with reference to all persons in general, or with reference to a particular description of persons, for whose use the commentary is intended, less perspicuous than might have been wished, to clear away the ambiguity or obscurity;—to wit, by bringing to view what, upon the consideration of the whole, presents itself as the true meaning— the meaning intended by the person of whose discourse the text is composed.

On a subject such as the present, if,—besides exhibiting the meaning which it was in the mind and intention of the author of the original work to convey,—the author of the accessory work in question takes upon himself to draw inferences of his own, in so far it is rather a *sermon* than a *commentary*. Be that as it may, in this case what he ought to do is—carefully to avoid confounding with the consecrated ground-work his own unconsecrated inference: and, in particular, in giving expression to his own inference, he ought to employ for that purpose other words of his own, chosen by himself for that same purpose; and not any such words of the original text, as will have the effect of causing this inference of his to be regarded not as his inference, but as so much matter already and actually included in the text; i.e. as constituting a part of that meaning, which, by means of that text, it had been the intention of the author to convey to his expected readers.[1]

Taken on the footing of an *independent* proposition, that in the main, at this time of day, it would be for the benefit of a professor of the religion of Jesus, to regard the above described duties as so many duties incumbent on himself, is not here less meant to be represented as a matter open to dispute. But that, in the character of *an inference*—an inference drawn from the tenor of the code here in question, any such proposition is correct, can not be admitted. The Jews—they and they alone—were the people to whom this code was addressed. In addressing himself, whether to his hearers or his readers, those, and those alone, were the people, which, on this occasion, could have been present to the mind of *Moses*, in such sort as to be considered as the people, with reference to whom the word *neighbour* was to be understood. But in those days, and on that occasion, who was *the neighbour of a Jew?* In general, every other Jew: but most assuredly no person other than a Jew. On that occasion, had the benefit of these commandments been meant to be extended to men in general, the word correspondent to the word *man*, and *not* the word correspondent to the word *neighbour*, would have been the word employed. If by *Moses*, of all men, men *in general*—all men without distinction—had been meant, what should have been *his* inducement to discard this most obvious of all words, and substitute to it a different word, the effect of which, in so far as any effect is given to it, is—to designate, to the exclusion of the whole remainder of the species, a comparatively minute portion of it.

Neighbour being a *relative* term—a word of *reference*,—no sooner is the *object* of reference changed, than, in this new case, it comes to be designative of a set of persons altogether different from those which in the first instance it was employed to designate. The sort of person, who, during the penning of the text, was in contemplation under the word *neighbour*, could be no other than a *Jew*. But, at this time of day, in so far as the word *neighbour* is used in its only proper sense, no Jew is the neighbour, much less the *only* sort of neighbour, of any child into whose mouth this formulary is forced. True it is that, when *Jesus* comes, he is represented as making *an amendment* to this code: declaring, on that occasion, that, by every one of *his* followers, not *Jews* alone, but every other man without exception, should, to the purpose of receiving the benefits proffered by him, be considered in the character of a *neighbour*.[2] With this explanation, true it is that, to the particular purpose in question, in the vocabulary of a follower of Jesus, the word *neighbour* becomes synonymous to the word *man:*—understand with this explanation, given

[1] The word 'neighbour' appears in the Ninth and Tenth Commandments: see Exodus 20: 16–17. The injunction to 'love thy neighbour as thyself' appears at Leviticus 19: 18.
[2] Bentham, no doubt, has in mind the parable of the Good Samaritan: see Luke 10: 29–37.

as it was by *Jesus*. But, to the explanation and extension, thus, at so vast a distance of time after the issuing of this code, given to it by Jesus, no reference is, in this formulary, to be found. In it the neighbour of the *Christian* is represented as being at all times the same sort of person as was the neighbour of the *Jew* in *Moses's* time; and the one as well as the other, as being the same sort of person as is designated by the word *man* at all times. Accordingly, presently after, viz. in the answer to the next question but one, the expression *all men* is slipt in,—and, without notice, is employed in the place of *neighbour:*[1] as if the two words had all along the same meaning: and thus, instead of the clear light, in which the whole matter might so easily have been placed, it is wrapt up in confusion and darkness.

Question 9.—What is thy duty towards God?
Answer.—My duty towards God is to believe in him, to fear him, and to love him with all my heart, with all my mind, with all my soul, and with all my strength; to worship him, to give him thanks, to put my whole trust in him, to call upon him, to honour his holy name and his word, and to serve him truly all the days of my life.

OBSERVATIONS.

On the subject of this answer, not a few are the questions that present themselves:—the questions,—pregnant, all of them, with doubts, if not with objections,—none[2] of them chargeable, as it should seem, with impertinence. But, as the suggestions conveyed by them have not for their result any imputation on the *morality* of the discourse;—as, supposing them well grounded, nothing beyond its character for wisdom is affected by them,—to frame the answers is a task that will be left altogether to the reader: nor, upon any of the subjects thus touched upon, will any more words be employed, than what have been found absolutely necessary for giving expression to the questions themselves.

1. Belief in God? what is it that is here meant by it? belief that God *exists*, or any thing, and what else?

2. Belief—an act of the understanding—ought it to be, or can it be made subject to the determination of the will?

3. If, in the mind in question, the existence of God is *already* the subject matter of *belief*, what need can there be to take it for a subject of *obligation?*—to rank it among *duties?*

4. If it be not, where can be the *effective ground*—the cause of fulfilment—in the case of the *obligation* thus supposed? Of what sort of matter can any such ground be composed?

5. In regard to *love*, on the supposition that, to the person in question, the object in question is not only an object of *fear*, but of a fear which is altogether boundless, in this case, of any such affection as is expressed by the word *love*, is the real existence, or any thing but the name and profession, compatible with such fear?

6. In particular, any such sentiment or affection as *love*, is it, in such a

---

[1] See p. 231 below.   [2] 1818 'some'. The text follows the 'Errata'.

place as the human breast, producible by, or so much as compatible with, all this *straining*.

7. Wherein, except in words, consists, on this occasion, the difference between *heart* and *mind*, and *soul* and *strength*?

8. By this accumulation of words, thus heaped one upon another, is any other idea conveyed, than that of the extreme difficulty of the task thus endeavoured to be imposed, viz. the task of *loving*?

9. Any such affection as that called love, where it really has place, does it ever happen to it to have for its accompaniment any such idea as that of *difficulty*?

10. Be the object what it may, he to whom the idea of *loving* it presents any such idea as that of difficulty, can he with truth be said to *love* it?

11. In the case of a young child—not to speak of maturer age—does it seem likely that, by all these words, any such *straining* should frequently be produced?

12. Supposing it produced, does it seem likely that any real good effects, with relation either to his own happiness, or to the happiness of those, whose lot may have placed them within the field of his influence, will result from it?

13. Be the person who he may, a determination on his part to put his *whole* trust in God, is it, if carried into effect, compatible with the practice of putting any *part* of his trust in the known and perpetually experienced and unquestionable operation and efficiency of *second* causes?

14. A *total*, or even considerable, though it were but *partial*, disregard to the operation of such *second causes*, would it be in any degree compatible with personal safety—with the preservation of health, of life, or of any thing that is worth preserving, whether to the individual himself, or to any other person or persons, whose lot it may be to stand in need of his assistance?

15. The exertions thus required, and perforce undertaken to be employed, in the endeavour to serve that *Being*, to whom all human service is '*unprofitable*,'[a] might they not with more profit be directed to the service of those weak creatures, whose need, of all the service that can be rendered to them, is at all times so urgent and so abundant?

Question 10.—What is thy duty towards thy neighbour?

Answer.—My duty towards my neighbour, is to love him as myself, and to do to all men as I would they should do unto me. To love, honour, and succour my father and mother. To honour and obey the king, and all that are put in authority under him. To submit myself to all my governors, teachers, spiritual pastors and masters. To order myself lowly and reverently to all my betters. To hurt nobody by word or[1] deed. To be true and just in all my dealings. To bear no malice nor

[a] Luke xvii. 10.—So likewise ye, when ye shall have done all those things which are commanded you, say, we are unprofitable servants; we have done that which was our duty to do.

---

[1] Catechism 'nor'.

hatred in my heart. To keep my hands from picking and stealing, and my tongue from evil speaking, lying, and slandering. To keep my body in temperance, soberness, and chastity. Not to covet nor desire other men's goods; but to learn and labour, truly to get mine own living, and to do my duty in that state of life, unto which it shall please God to call me.

OBSERVATIONS.

Of this long and wordy formulary, had the whole contents been of a piece with the answer thus given to this question, assuredly it would never have been taken for the subject of a commentary, wearing any such complexion as that of the present, or having any such conclusions for its result and practical inference.

Throwing out the greater part, or the whole of the rest, adding or not adding any thing in the place of the matter thus discarded,—were it proposed to retain the substance of this answer, some such little changes might perhaps be suggested, as need not despair of being received in the character of *amendments*. But, taken even as it stands, especially when consideration is had of the age in which it was penned, and above all, when comparison is made of it with the whole remainder of that of which it forms a part,—so beautiful does it appear, that the eye shrinks from any such task, as that of travelling over it in search of imperfections.

Question 11,[1] (put immediately after *the Lord's Prayer*),—What desirest thou of God in this Prayer?

Answer.—I desire my Lord God our heavenly Father, who is the giver of all goodness, to send his grace(1) unto me, and to all people.[2]

OBSERVATIONS.

(1) {*Grace.*}—Here is the Prayer; and in the whole tenor of it, from beginning to end, about any such thing or word as *grace*, not so much as a single syllable.

The misrepresentation thus made, is it an innocent one? On the mind of every man, by whom this formulary is regarded as unexceptionable, the effect of it—is it not—in conjunction with so many other causes which the same formulary sets to work,—to contribute towards the reconciling him to that convenient laxity of interpretation, which among religionists is so unhappily frequent,—and, with relation to all worldly interests, so convenient?

A subject-matter, of which every body sees that no mention is made in this

---

[1] 1818 '10'. The misnumbering of this and the following questions has been silently corrected.

[2] Catechism: 'people, that we may worship him, serve him, and obey him, as we ought to do. And I pray unto God, that he will send us all things that be needful both for our souls and bodies; and that he will be merciful unto us, and forgive us our sins; and that it will please him to save and defend us in all dangers ghostly and bodily; and that he will keep us from all sin and wickedness, and from our ghostly enemy, and from everlasting death. And this I trust he will do of his mercy and goodness, through our Lord Jesus Christ. And therefore I say, Amen, So be it.'

Prayer—this subject-matter, a child, who sees that it is *not* there, is made to declare—to declare in the face of a clergyman, or other person, under whom he is passing this examination,—and who, as well as he, sees that it is *not* there,—to declare, and to declare most solemnly, that it *is* there.

The lesson, thus forced into every Church-of-England mouth, suppose it to be productive of any fruits whatsoever,—is it possible that, under such instruction, a rooted and habitual depravation of the mental faculties, intellectual and moral, should not be of the number of those fruits? To repeat, as if it were true, that which, with his own eyes, he sees to be untrue, this is what from infancy a child is compelled to practise—this is what he is made to reckon among the number of his *duties*.

In addition to *grace*, another of the *things* which, they not being in this Prayer, the pupil is thus forced to declare himself to have found in it, is *death—everlasting death.*—Of *everlasting death*, what mention is there in this Prayer of Jesus?—Not any: nor yet so much as of what is commonly meant by *death*. Of *evil*, yes: and death (it may be said) everlasting death—is not this an evil?—Doubtless: at least if by *death* be meant—not the absence of all sufferance, but sufferance itself. But if this were a sufficient warrant for making the child say, that Jesus spoke of *death*, when no such word as *death* is to be found in what he said, so would it be for speaking of all other things, one after another, to which, with any propriety, the word *evil* could be applied, and thereupon saying of each, that Jesus had spoken of it.

As to *grace*, on this occasion, as on so many others—not to say *all* others—it is a mere *expletive;* adding nothing to the sense. Yet upon the ground of this expletive, systems have been built, controversies raised, swords drawn, and blood made to flow in torrents.

But, of this disastrous expletive, more will be seen presently; viz. when the modern inventions, called *Sacraments*, come to be laid upon the table.

Question 12.—How many Sacraments hath Christ ordained in his Church?

Answer.—Two only(1), as generally necessary to salvation: that is to say, *Baptism*(2), and the *Supper of the Lord*(3).

OBSERVATIONS.

(1). {*Two only.*}—Of the word *only*, the use—so all commentators are agreed—was to put an exclusion upon a parcel of other ceremonies, to which this revolted Church, the Church of England, had found the name of *sacrament* attached by the original Church from which she broke loose.[1]

But, as to *Christ*, the question being how many *sacraments* hath Christ ordained, the true answer would have been—none. For on what occasion, in the only language in which he spoke, is he represented as having employed

---

[1] According to the Roman Catholic Church, there were seven sacraments: baptism, confirmation, matrimony, holy orders, penance, eucharist, and extreme unction. Protestant reformers, who believed in the sufficiency of scripture for all matters of doctrine, recognized only two sacraments said to be ordained by Christ, baptism and the eucharist, a position adopted by the Church of England (see Thirty-nine Articles, Art. 25).

any word, to which the word *sacrament*, taken from the Latin *sacramentum*, corresponds in this our language?

Sacrament? what is it but a word of modern invention—a sort of metaphysical term, having certainly for its effect, probably for its object, the causing to be regarded as mysterious, two operations, in neither of which there was any mystery,—to be regarded as having a connexion with each other—and that connexion fraught with mystery—two objects, between which no such connexion, nor any connexion at all, had been established by Jesus.

(2). {1. *Baptism*}.—This operation was a *ceremony:* a ceremony, having for its object the serving to establish, and upon occasion bring to mind, the fact of a man's having been aggregated into the society formed by Jesus: the religious society, of which—God or man, or both in one,—he was the teacher and the head.

In an unlettered community, it was a sort of substitute for an entry in a *register* or *memorandum book*. By a too natural misconception, the mere *sign* or *evidence* of this aggregation was taken for the *efficient cause* of the benefits produced by it. Thereupon came questions, out of number, about the circumstances by which it should be accompanied:—1. whether the application of the water should be *total* or *partial?*—2. if partial, what fingers should be employed in it?—3. and what the *form* should be, that should be given to the wet mark made by it? &c. &c.[a] the principle of *nullity*—that inexhaustible source of uncertainty in all its excruciating shapes—that prime instrument of fraud and rapine—being borrowed from technical jurisprudence, and, in the character of a necessary *consequence*, attached to every deviation from the arbitrarily imagined and endlessly diversified standard of rectitude. In the same spirit, had the literary, and more durable expedient of a *Register-book* been employed, questions might have been started—whether, for the validity of the appointment, the *quill* should be a *goose*-quill or a *crow*-quill; the *paper, demy* or *foolscap*; the *binding, calf* or *sheep*.

[a] In the Russian Empire, by differences on this ground, persecutions and disastrous civil wars have been kindled.[1] By the sect, which, in the sixteenth century, under the name of *Anabaptists*, to the determination of performing the humectation in the *total* way, as it was performed by Jesus, added other particulars, some of which were not only absurd but deplorably mischievous—peculiarities not regarding ceremony but morals—prodigious were the miseries inflicted and suffered.[2]

[1] The liturgical reforms in the Russian Orthodox Church instituted by Nikon (1605–81), Patriarch of Moscow 1652–8, including the requirement that the sign of the cross be made with three fingers instead of two, caused divisions within the Church. The Old Believers, who refused to accept the reforms, were subjected to violent persecution.

[2] The sects of Anabaptists, which flourished in the sixteenth century, advocated the adult baptism of believers, and variously common ownership of property, polygamy, and non-participation in government. Anabaptists were denounced and violently persecuted by both Roman Catholics and Protestants, and it is estimated that, by the end of the sixteenth century, tens of thousands had been put to death.

CHURCH OF ENGLAND CATECHISM EXAMINED.

Christ *ordain* Baptism under the name and character of a *Sacrament?* If by *ordain* is meant the same as by *institute*—the same as *the having been the first to practise*, or *cause to be practised*,—he did not so much as *ordain* it in the character of a *ceremony*. Practise it indeed he did, and afterwards cause it to be practised. But, before he practised it, or caused it to be practised by or upon any one else, he submitted to have it practised upon himself, after it had been practised already upon multitudes. By John it had already been practised upon multitudes, before it was practised by him upon Jesus.[1]— Those who are forced to say this Catechism, why are they so much as suffered to read the New Testament? Can they read it without seeing this?

By whomsoever first invented and put in practice,—in its character of a succedaneum to an entry in a *Register-book*, it was an operation in every respect well imagined. In the country in which it was thus practised, heat was plenty, water scarce, writing and reading still scarcer, money not over plenty. Baptism,—whether by dipping, by sprinkling, or by both,—was then and there a pleasant operation. Wherever either a river ran, or a lake stood, it cost nothing. John took no surplice fees. Jesus took no surplice fees.[2] Whenever the existence of the Devil is fully proved, it will be proved that by that Ghost it was that these priests' fees were instituted, exactly at the same time with Judges' fees. Surplice fees are unknown in Scotland. By the Church of England only, not by the Church of Scotland, do the poor behold the gates of heaven shut against them.[3]

Question 13.—What meanest thou by the word sacrament?

Answer.—I mean an outward and visible sign of an inward and spiritual grace, given unto us, ordained by Christ himself, as a means whereby we receive the same, and a pledge to assure us thereof.

OBSERVATIONS.

Here, as already observed—here may be seen another example,—shewing how a semblance of something may be manufactured out of nothing. Two transactions—the performance of the ceremony of *Baptism*, and the utterance of a few words, stated as having been uttered by Jesus on the occasion of a supper at which he was present[4]—two transactions,—which, unless it be the identity of the person who bore the principal part in both, had nothing at all in common,—forced into conjunction; and a generic appellation—*the sacrament*—made, to serve as it were, for a box, for inclosing them, and keeping them together.—*Sacrament?* by whom was this word invented and made? By *Jesus?*—no more than it was by *Satan*. When thus made, what is the meaning given to this Rome-sprung vocable? In the English, and other dialects of the Teutonic, it is rendered by *holy:* it is

---

[1] For the career of John the Baptist up to and including his baptism of Jesus see Matthew 3: 1–17; Mark 1: 1–11; Luke 3: 1–22; and John 1: 19–34.

[2] The term surplice fee traditionally referred to the variable sum customarily paid to the officiating clergy for marriages and burials. Here Bentham also has in mind the fees which were customarily offered for baptism and the churching of women. See Burn, *Ecclesiastical Law*, 2nd edn., 4 vols., 1767, iii. 19–21.

[3] An echo of Matthew 23: 13.

[4] See pp. 244–6 below.

the holy thing. And *a holy thing*, what is it?—*Holiness?* the word *holiness*, what is meant by it? As a property belonging to the thing itself, be the thing what it may, just nothing. By a thing—by any thing whatsoever, of which, by the principle of association, the idea has happened to become connected with the idea of the Almighty Creator,—a connexion of which any one created thing is, and ever has been, just as capable as any other,—by any thing—by every thing to which any such accident has happened, is this mysterious property thus acquired.

Thus then—such has been the course taken by the manufacturing process—by the invention of this so much worse than useless generic term, a branch of false science—a portion of wayward school logic—has been manufactured. Being made to pass examination in this science, the unfledged parrot takes in the words that are forced into its mouth, and declares itself to *understand*, where there is nothing to be understood.

Under the name of '*a grace*,' a something—and that something 'good'—given unto us—given to every body—given alike to every man, whatsoever be his conduct—given as a thing of course,—by the mere ceremony: a pretended something, which, when examined by an unsophisticated eye, turns out to be in itself exactly nothing,—and even by the name thus given to it, is but *a sign*,—yet, by the description at this same time given of it, it is an *efficient cause!*

The Almighty laid hold of, and made to enter into a contract (under what penalty is not mentioned), pledging himself, binding himself, to give to this pretended *efficient cause* a pretendedly *real effect!* Thus it is that the sham science grows: thus it is that the wilderness is formed, in which the wits of those who are destined to travel in it, are destined to be lost.

Question 14.—How many parts are there in a sacrament?

Answer.—Two: the outward visible sign, and the inward spiritual grace.

OBSERVATIONS.

A compound made out of a *real* and *visible ceremony*, to which, by the force of imagination, is attached an *invisible* and *unintelligible* effect—such is the *whole:* and now comes the unfledged parrot, and with his tongue is required to split it into two parts.

Question 15.—What is the outward visible sign, or form in Baptism?

Answer.—Water(l); wherein the person is baptized(2) in the name of the Father, and of the Son, and of the Holy Ghost(3).

OBSERVATIONS.

(1).—Water the sign? No:—of itself water is not the sign of the thing in question—i.e. the transaction here in question—or of any thing else. Of the transaction in question, viz. aggregation to the society in question, the sign was a physical *operation:* not water itself, but the *application* of that liquid to the body of the person aggregated. For preserving the memory of the transaction in question,—instead of a transient operation, such as was the application of water to the body in question, suppose the object employed to have been an *entry* in a *Baptism book:*—of the transaction in question what would have been the sign?—not the *leaf* of the book in its *blank* state, but the *mark made*—*the words written*—on that leaf.

In itself nothing can be more trifling than such an inaccuracy: the real matter of regret is—that in this body of pretended instruction, composed by a man who understood not what he wrote, a child should be forced to declare himself to understand, that which, neither to himself nor any one else, is any thing better than unintelligible.

(2). 'Where*in* the person is baptized'—not where*with*, but where*in*—Alas! alas! what a scene of horror presents itself to view! The baptism then must be by immersion—by a thorough dipping—or it is no baptism.—The whole ceremony—all *null and void!* Of the myriads in a year, who, under the Church of England discipline, are *said* to be baptized, how many are the *really* baptized?—Not one!

All, all of us heathens! all a prey to Satan!—all children of wrath! (so we shall see the next answer saying)—all 'alive to sin!'—all 'dead to righteousness!'—the best works we ever do, or can do, no better than so many sins!!!

(3). {*In the name of the Father, and of the Son, and of the Holy Ghost.*}— Here we have a short string of sounds—sounds that are in use to perform the office of *names*—and, by the texture thus given to a mouthful of air, note well the effects produced! a human being rescued or not rescued from a state of endless torment! And, to such an operation, in the character of a *cause*,—by whom—by what—have such effects been attached?—By the deluded or deluding imaginations of a set of presumptuous and domineering men.—Under the name of *magic*, or some such name, state the same conceit as issuing from a heathen brain,—execration or derision, instead of awe and veneration, are the sentiments it calls forth.

Question 16.—What is the inward and spiritual grace?

Answer.—A death unto sin, and a new birth unto righteousness; for being by nature born in sin, and the children of wrath, we are hereby made the children of grace.

OBSERVATIONS.

Note well the sort of story that is here told.—The Almighty God,—maker of all things visible and 'invisible'—'of heaven and earth, and all that therein is'[1]—makes, amongst other things, a child; and no sooner has he made it, than he is '*wrath*' with it for being made.[2] He determines accordingly to consign it to a state of endless torture. Meantime comes somebody,—and, pronouncing certain words, applies the child to a quantity of water, or a

---

[1] See Colossians 1: 16 and Psalm 146: 6 respectively. The two passages are combined at the beginning of the Nicene Creed.
[2] For 'the children of wrath' see Ephesians 2: 3.

CHURCH-OF-ENGLANDISM

quantity of water to the child. Moved by these words, the all-wise Being changes his design; and, though he is not so far appeased as to give the child its pardon, vouchsafes to it *a chance*—no one can say *what* chance—of ultimate escape.—And this is what the child gets by being 'made'—and we see in what way made—'*a child of grace.*'

Thereupon comes the sort of *wit*, ghostly and ghastly, which, on such occasions, has been so plentifully played off: there we have *death*, and here we have *new birth:* death unto sin, new birth unto righteousness.[1] And in this wit we have a subject—not merely for *admiration*, but moreover for *belief:*— for belief, of the withholding of which, as if it were in the power of every man to believe or not believe what he pleased, the consequence is—what at every turn, and, upon every occasion, stares us in the face—a state of endless torture.

Question 17.—What is required of persons to be baptized?

Answer.—Repentance, whereby they forsake sin; and faith, whereby they stedfastly believe the promises of God made to them in that sacrament.

OBSERVATIONS.

Obvious indeed are the observations suggested by this answer. But forasmuch as by the next question these observations are themselves undertaken to be obviated, let this next question, with the answers which it is employed to call forth, be first heard.

Question 18.—Why then are infants baptized, when, by reason of their tender age, they cannot perform them?

Answer.—Because they promise them both by their sureties: which promise, when they come to age, themselves are bound to perform.

OBSERVATIONS.

{Perform *them?*}—Perform *what?*—Here may be seen a cloud of obscurity and ambiguity, derived from a sort of source—a purely grammatical one—such as in a composition so highly elaborated, and so abundantly examined, would not naturally have been looked for. Of such things as are in their nature capable of being '*performed*,' the *last* thing mentioned,—not to say the only thing,—is what is brought to view by the word *promises*. Yet, on a little reflection, these things, viz. *promises*, (it will be seen) can not be among the things here in view.—Why?—Answer—Because *God* is the person *by* whom these promises were stated as being made. But, not even in such a composition as *this*, can it have been supposed or pretended, that when God is the person by whom a promise is made, the person by whom that promise is to be performed is an infant.—An infant? Yea, *a just-born infant:*—the time allowed for performance being no longer than the interval between its birth and the age at which baptism is commonly administered: an interval commonly of between a week and a fortnight.

[1] An echo of Romans 5: 21, and, in essence, of Paul's theology.

CHURCH OF ENGLAND CATECHISM EXAMINED.

Look a little forwards however, and then a little backwards, and it will be sufficiently clear, that, though the *things* to be performed are indeed *promises*, yet the *person, by whom* they are to be performed, is—not the last[1] antecedent, viz. *God*, but the *infant:* the infant who is considered as the subject of the operation in question, viz. *baptism*. Why not *God* but the infant?—*Answer*, for this plain reason:—because the acts which are held up to view in the character of subjects of *promise* are '*Faith* and *Repentance;*' to wit, the Faith and Repentance above spoken of.

It is not, however, without some violence to *grammar*—some violation of the *rules* of grammar—that the language is here reconcileable to the rules of common sense. The *number* employed in the 17th question is the *singular* number.—'What *is* required:' the number employed in the 18th question, by which, with its answer, the answer to that 17th question is undertaken to be explained, is the *plural* number: '*Perform them,*' says the 18th question: promise *them*, says the answer to it. And this promise *them*, of what is it the representative? Why—as turns out immediately after—of two things. Here then, between question the 17th (i.e. the question, to which, it being, and with so much reason, considered, that explanation is wanting, explanation, such as we see, is accordingly given)—between this 17th question and question 18th (i.e. the question employed to explain it) a contradiction exhibits itself. Believe the *explained* question, there is but *one* thing required: believe the *explaining* question, there are two things—two very different things, both, required: viz. the *faith* and the *repentance*. These are the *them* which, viz. by *their sureties*, the children *promised:* these are the *them* which, viz. *by themselves*, they are to perform. For so it is, that according to this law and this divinity, they themselves are thus to be sureties for their own sureties.

From the grammatical, return we now to the religious ground: and thereon to what remains of the task which the poor child has to go through with.

Two things, as above, he is required to do: and *that* because once upon a time, without knowing any thing about the matter, he promised to do them: *he* promised, that is *other people* did, which comes to the same thing. These things are—to *repent* of *sin*, whether he has committed any or no: and to believe,—and that 'stedfastly,' whatever he may think of it,—what, for that purpose, is thereupon put into his hands. This is—that when, a few days after his birth, the Clergyman threw a little water on his face,—saying over him at the same time a few words without a meaning,—God was all the while making him *promises*, which promises might however as well have not been made, since nobody has so much as pretended to know what they were.

Another task, which his believing faculty is, at the same time, put to,—though without any express mention of it,—consists in the believing bad *principles* to be good *principles*, and bad *reasons* good *reasons*.

Example of bad *principles:*—that it is in the power of any *three* persons,

---

[1] 1818 'least'. The text follows the 'Errata'.

CHURCH-OF-ENGLANDISM

two of them being of the one sex and one of the other, by making, in the name of a new-born infant, a parcel of *promises,* to saddle it with a load of *obligations:* amongst others, that of believing,—how incredible soever, when the time comes, they may appear to him,—things upon things, which, had he not been thus saddled, he could *not* have believed.

Example of bad *reasons:*—that a man's having taken upon him to promise, that a child shall believe so and so, affords any reason for the child's believing as much, or so much as trying to believe it.

The point of *time,* at which these two exploits are to be performed—in this may be seen a point, in relation to which, if the babes and sucklings[1] should, any of them, succeed in forming to themselves any thing like a clear conception, they will have done more than seems to have been done by the sages, by whom this task has been thus put into their hands.

'*What is required of persons* AFTER *they have been baptized?*' Had the question stood thus, the meaning would have been clear enough. Thus however it, unfortunately, does not stand: instead of so doing, it stands thus:—'*What is required of persons* TO BE *baptized?*' In this way of putting it, the child's having done these things, that are thus 'required' of him, is what, in the language of lawyers, is called *a condition precedent* to his being baptized. These things, then, which he is to do before he is baptized—that is, before he is a *fortnight,* or perhaps before he is a *week* old—what are they?—The question has been already answered. He is to *repent*—to repent of the sins which, in nobody can say what numbers, in his way from the breast to the cradle and back again, he has already committed: and he is to believe—to believe with all his might, all the fine things which for that purpose have been provided. All this while, if so it be, that a child, almost as soon as born, may *promise* by proxy, why not *repent* and *believe* by proxy? The sponsors, when they have *promised* for him, why not as well *perform* for him? Having undertaken for the *performances,* as they are all along called,— viz. a quantity of *repentance,* and moreover, a quantity of *faith,*—who so proper as *they* to execute these several performances?

To a child of a week or a fortnight old, the finding sins of its own to repent of, may not be altogether so easy a task, as on this occasion seems to have been supposed:—to the good men and woman, or the good man and women, by whom all these promises are made for it, the matter may, every now and then at least, be a matter of much less difficulty.

The *order* in which these same two performances are required and expected to succeed one another;—in this may be seen another exemplification, of the muddiness of the fountain, from which all this instruction flowed. In the natural course of things, the *motive* comes before the *act.* If the course here prescribed were to be pursued, the *act* would take the lead: and then, with a manifestation of humility, of which any example would not easily be found elsewhere, up comes in the train of it the generating and directing *motive.* According to the scheme of Jesus, faith was of course every where the seed, repentance one of the fruits of it: it was because a man

---

[1] Psalm 8: 2; Matthew 21: 16.

believed—expected to experience the eventual fulfilment of the threats and promises held out to him—it was because a man believed that he was to repent,—not because he repented, that he was to believe. Into the conception of any man besides this *Catechism-maker*, did any such idea ever enter, as that of addressing threats and promises to a man, to no other purpose than that of making him do what he had done already? But, if the mind, in which both these fruits were to be produced by the genial virtue of this ceremony, was a new-born infant's, either of them would be as ready to come forth as the other: and thus the *Catechism-maker* is justified.

Question 19.—Why was the sacrament of the Lord's Supper ordained?

Answer.—For the continual remembrance of the sacrifice of the death of Christ, and of the benefits which we receive thereby.

OBSERVATIONS.

Of this answer,—keeping *in* that part for which a warrant is to be found in the text of the Gospel History,[1] and leaving *out* of it that part which, no such warrant being to be found for it, has been the work of imagination,—inserting at the same time such words of limitation as may be necessary to confine the proposition within the limits designated by the sacred text,—of this answer the purport might (it should seem) have stood thus expressed:—'For the continual remembrance . . . . of the death of Christ,' to be preserved in the minds of such of his disciples, as,—having been admitted by him into a state of peculiar intimacy, and, from time to time, sent out by him, from place to place, to preach his doctrine,—became distinguished by the appellation of his '*Apostles:*'—*Apostles*, in the Greek (the only language in which the Gospel history, or any part of it, has been handed down to us) meaning neither more nor less than *an Emissary*, or *Messenger*.[2]

As to '*the benefits which we receive thereby,*'—what, in this Catechism, they are said to be—what the child is forced to say he believes them to be—will be seen presently.

Moreover, in the act of *receiving*, as brought to view by the word '*received*,' is implied the act of *delivering:* as also, that he, by whom the act of delivering is to be performed, is a different person from him by whom the act of receiving is to be performed. A foundation being thus laid,—and that foundation having, in the words of the sacred history, a sufficient support,—and that not exposed to dispute,—now comes the superstructure, which is the seat of the deception, and which has no such support. This is—that to the act of *delivering*, one sort of person and one alone, is competent: viz. *a Priest:* a person, on whom a corporeal ceremony has been performed: a corporeal ceremony[3] from which a multitude of spiritual, supernatural,

---

[1] For the Last Supper see Matthew 26: 17–30 (esp. 26–9); Mark 14: 12–26 (esp. 22–5); and Luke 22: 7–39 (esp. 19–20).

[2] The Greek word αποστολος originally meant 'messenger' or 'ambassador'.

[3] 1818 'a ceremony'. The text follows the 'Errata'.

and mystical consequences are deduced:—the act of *receiving*—that alone is the *act*, whereunto, under the system, of which this Catechism makes a part, persons other than priests, are competent: nor even to this are the profane multitude competent, but subject to *exceptions*, drawn out of an inexhaustible mine of exceptions, which has been opened for that purpose:—a mine capable, in its origin at least, of being dug into to any depth, which the interest of those who opened it could require.

And thus it is, that, upon the ground of this *supper*, which, as the whole history declares, was neither more nor less than a mere social and farewel repast, taken with the utmost privacy;—a repast of which none were partakers, but the most confidential friends and disciples of the Master;—a repast, taken on the occasion of his foreseen and approaching fall;—upon this ground, and with so slender a stock of the most ordinary materials, has been erected a manufactory of *grace:*—of *grace*,—a commodity, which, being alike suited to every body's use, was to be sold to all who should be disposed to purchase it: a *manufactory*, carried on in different forms, under an imaginary perpetual patent, always for the benefit of the *patentees*.

Instead of domination for the purpose of degradation,—had useful instruction, and the melioration of moral disposition and conduct been the object,—and thereupon had some physical operation, performed by Jesus himself, and actually directed to that object, been looked out for, to be taken for a subject of imitation, and, for the above good purposes, converted into a ceremony,—in any such case, in the incident of the *feet-washing*, as related by Saint John, the founders of the Romish, and therein of the English Church, might have found what they wanted.

A little before the supper in question, there was another; if indeed it was another, and not the same. Be this as it may, at the supper spoken of by *John*, (by whom not the least intimation is given of the *bread-breaking,*) the same select disciples being present, Jesus sees reason to give them a lesson of humility. He therefore in his own person and deportment sets them an example of that virtue. He insists on washing their feet. Put to shame by a manifestation so striking of a disposition with which their own formed so disadvantageous a contrast, Peter resists: vain however is all resistance, and, upon the feet of all the twelve, the operation is performed.

To give to this ceremony a real importance—a practical object, no arbitrary inferences—no additions—would have been necessary: never was design more plainly, more impressively expressed.[a]

[a] St. John, Chap. XIII.

1. Now before the feast of the Passover, when Jesus knew that his hour was come that he should depart out of this world unto the father, having loved his own which were in the world, he loved them unto the end.

2. And supper being ended, the devil having now put into the heart of Judas Iscariot, Simon's son, to betray him;

3. Jesus knowing that the father had given all things into his hands, and that he was come from God and went to God;

4. He riseth from supper, and laid aside his garments; and took a towel, and girded himself.

While this comparatively insignificant one was sublimated into a *mystery*,—that really instructive ceremony, how comes it to have been passed over in such profound neglect?—How?—why for three perfectly intelligible reasons.—

1. Because it gave, to the self-created order of official persons, no privilege—no peculiar advantage.

2. Because the lesson, which it so plainly gives, is to them a lesson of condemnation.

3. Because, to the inventors of the *drinking ceremony*, drinking wine while others looked on, was an operation more pleasant than would have been the washing the feet of those same spectators.[1]

Here then are two contiguous suppers—two farewel suppers—or two incidents, related as having had place at the same supper. By the one, a lesson is given—a lesson pregnant with instruction, as plain as it is salutary,—and one, the applicability of which, and with it the utility, will endure as long as man endures. In the other, what is visible to every eye is—an incident, naturally interesting indeed in no mean degree to the individuals then present, but having neither interest nor meaning, as applied to any other individual; nor of itself calculated, or designed, to convey instruction in any shape whatsoever.—The universally important transaction is passed over in universal silence and neglect,—the other is converted into a mystery, with damnation—universal damnation, or thereabouts—at the bottom of it!

5. After that he poureth water into a bason, and began to wash the disciples' feet, and to wipe them with the towel wherewith he was girded.

6. Then cometh he to Simon Peter: and Peter said unto him, Lord, dost thou wash my feet?

7. Jesus answered and said unto him, what I do thou knowest not now; but thou shalt know hereafter.

8. Peter saith unto him, Thou shalt never wash my feet. Jesus answered him, if I wash thee not thou hast no part with me.

9. Simon Peter saith unto him, Lord, not my feet only, but also my hands, and my head.

10. Jesus saith unto him, he that is washed, needeth not, save to wash his feet, but is clean every whit; and ye are clean, but not all.

11. For he knew who should betray him; therefore said he, ye are not all clean.

12. So after he had washed their feet, and had taken his garments, and was set down again, he said unto them, Know ye what I have done to you?

13. Ye call me master and Lord; and ye say well, for so I am.

14. If I, then, your Lord and master have washed your feet; ye also ought to wash one another's feet.

15. For I have given you an example that ye should do as I have done to you.

16. Verily, verily, I say unto you, the servant is not greater than his Lord; neither he that is sent, greater than he that sent him.

17. If ye know these things, happy are ye if ye do them.

---

[1] The Roman Catholic doctrine of concomitance held that the body and blood of Christ was present in both the consecrated bread and wine, in consequence of which the wine was withheld from the laity. However, in the Church of England, communion in both kinds was administered (see Thirty-nine Articles, Art. 30).

Question 20.—What is the outward part or sign of the Lord's Supper?

Answer.—Bread and Wine, which the Lord hath commanded to be received.

OBSERVATIONS.

{*Hath commanded to be received?*}—Mark well the misrepresentation, of which this phrase is the chief instrument: seldom has a plan of misrepresentation been more subtilely contrived.

Had the passage stood in these words, *Which the Lord* . . . . *commanded to be received,*—stood in these words, without the word *hath,*—the answer would, as far as it went, have been unobjectionable: as far as it went, it would have been conformable to the sacred text. Mark well—without the word *hath:* for in this short word lurks the poison—the seed of the deceit.

It is by this word *hath* that the transaction is represented as meant to be applied to the *indefinite present:* i.e. to every *point of time*, at which it shall have happened to this account of it to find a reader, and to every individual *person*, by whom,—he being a believer in the religion of Jesus,—it shall have happened to be heard or read.

Such is the conception, which, by the authors of this Catechism, composed in the sixteenth century after the birth of Jesus, is endeavoured to be impressed: viz. that to the effect just described, a command delivered by Jesus, in the intention of its being considered as obligatory,—obligatory with a force equal at least to that of any of his moral precepts,—was addressed to *all* persons, by whom the religion taught by him should come to be professed:—to *all* of them, without distinction, to the end of time.

Such is the conception, which, by these men of yesterday, this part of the *history* of Jesus is represented as intended to convey. In *the history itself,* how is this same matter represented?

According to the history, who are the persons present?—a numerous assembly, as at the delivery of the sermon on the *Mount?*[1]—No:—but a chosen few, sitting with him in a private chamber: the twelve disciples, whose condition had been distinguished from that of the general body of his followers by marks of peculiar confidence, and whose life had been interwoven with his own by habits of peculiar intimacy.

'Ever and anon, when I am no longer with you,—and when after my departure, it happens to you—to you the chosen among my disciples—to meet together, on a convivial occasion as at present,—when the materials of the repast are before you, think of your departed master, think of this your last meeting (for such it will be) in my presence. Think of his now approaching death: think of the cause and fruit of it. When, for the purpose of the social repast, bread, such as that which I have thus broken, comes also to be broken, think of this body, which, for the part acted by me for your instruction, will, ere long, be broken and destroyed.

---

[1] For 'the multitudes' present at the Sermon on the Mount see Matthew 5: 1; 8: 1.

CHURCH OF ENGLAND CATECHISM EXAMINED.

'When the wine, whatever it be that stands before you, comes to be poured out, let it call to your remembrance his blood which will have been shed in that same cause'. . . .

With this evident sense before them, will nothing satisfy men but the grossest nonsense? Of the multitude of figurative expressions, to which scanty and unformed languages in general—to which the Jewish language in particular, with its dialects—were necessitated, or at least were continually wont, to have recourse,—is *this alone*, in spite of the plainest common sense, to be understood in the literal sense?

That, in his own hand Jesus held his own body, but in the first instance without the blood belonging to it; and having, by breaking it into eleven or twelve pieces, converted each of those *parts* into the *whole*, gave those his eleven or twelve bodies, one to each guest—he himself, with or without his body, looking on all the while to see them eat it,—and thereupon, immediately after gave to each of them the whole of his blood—viz. the wine which had just been poured out, and by him converted into blood,—the bodies, into which the bread had been converted, not having any blood in them,—that of all these self-contradictory extravagances the existence should be more probable than that, on an impassioned occasion, Jesus should have made use of a figurative expression—and that too in a language which scarce offered any other? In a barbarous age, and thence, under the influence of blind caprice, even in a more improved age,—under the Roman Catholic edition of the religion of Jesus . . . . Yes:[1] under such a system, in the admission given to any such style of interpretation, how little soever there may be of abstract reason, there is but too much of consistency.

But, under a government calling itself *Protestant*,—and oppressing *Catholics*, because they are Catholics, and, for these very extravagances, branding them with the name of *Idolaters!* . . . .[2]

Believe that Jesus, having held his own body in his own hand, gave to each of twelve men, the whole of that same body, and then saw them eat it, &c. &c.—Believe this, because Jesus is related to have said so?—Well then—(not to speak of *a way*[a]) believe that Jesus was *a door*—a door always

---

[a] John, xiv. 6. Jesus saith unto him, I am the *way*, the truth, and the life: no man cometh unto the father but through me.

---

[1] According to the Roman Catholic Church doctrine of transubstantiation, adopted by the Fourth Lateran Council in 1215, and reaffirmed by the Council of Trent in 1551 (Thirteenth Session, 11 October 1551, *Canons and Decrees of the Council of Trent*, p. 75), the bread and wine were transformed into the body and blood of Christ, although their physical character remained unchanged.

[2] Bentham probably had in mind the oath imposed by the Test Act of 1678 (30 Car. II, stat. 2, §3) which had to be sworn by commoners and peers to enable them to sit and vote in the Houses of Parliament: 'I *A.B.* do solemnly and sincerely, in the presence of God, profess, testify, and declare, That I do believe that in the Sacrament of the Lord's Supper there is not any Transubstantiation of the Elements of Bread and Wine into the Body and Blood of Christ at or after the Consecration thereof by any Person whatsoever: And that the Invocation or Adoration of the Virgin *Mary*, or any other Saint, and the Sacrifice of the Mass, as they are now used in the Church of *Rome*, are superstitious and idolatrous.'

CHURCH-OF-ENGLANDISM

open for as many men as pleased to '*go in and out*' *through it*:[a] for this too is among the things, which, in the same sacred books, it is related of him that he said. In the mouth of a Protestant, among Protestants, this argument, when addressed by them to Catholics, is relied on as conclusive. Conclusive? and against what? why, against this very cannibal story, of the truth of which every Church of England child is thus forced to declare itself persuaded.

Compared with this, the supposition about *the door* would be rational and probable. Consider *Bright* and *Lambert*:[1] the least of these great men had quantity of matter enough in his body, to admit of an aperture, through which, as through a door, a man of ordinary size might have passed without much difficulty. Believing and teaching the mystery of *Cannibalism*, will a man refuse to believe and teach this other mystery of the *door?* If so, what will his faith avail him?—When bread and wine, and body and blood, and every thing else is swallowed, still, unless he will swallow the *door* likewise,—still, if he is consistent, he is an *unbeliever;* he is still an *infidel*, and all that he has swallowed has been swallowed in waste.

Question 21.—What is the inward part, or thing signified?

Answer.—The body and blood of Christ, which are verily and indeed taken, and received by the faithful in the Lord's Supper.

OBSERVATIONS.

Body and Blood, *without* the Bread and Wine,—the Bread and Wine being metamorphosed into Body and Blood,—in the *pure* grimgribber of modern *technical* theology—in the theology of the *Roman* school—this is *transubstantiation*. Body and Blood, *with* the Bread and Wine—in the *adulterated* grimgribber—the produce of *Luther's* unmatured attempts to throw off the load of pernicious rubbish heaped up by the Romish school—this is *consubstantiation*.[2] In respect of absurdity, self-contradiction, and groundless inference,—between the *trans* and the [*con*],[3] is there so much as a shade of difference worth thinking of? On the *con* plan the mess has more matter in it than in the *trans:* and the more the worse.

'*Verily and indeed!*'—Danger is here foreseen,—and, it being foreseen, provision is thus made against it:—the danger, lest, here or there, the stomach of this or that intractable and refractory child, should, in the midst of all this instruction, be tempted to listen, in preference, to the testimony of his own senses: lest, accordingly, not finding in his palate the taste and consistence of *flesh*, any more than, under his eyes, the colour of *blood*, he should thereupon, notwithstanding all *assurances*, and the threatenings that

---

[a] John x. 9. I am the *door;* by me, if any man enter in, he shall be saved, and shall go in and out, and find pasture.

---

[1] Edward Bright (d. 1750) and Daniel Lambert (1770–1809) were both noted for their corpulence: at his death Bright weighed 42 stone, and Lambert nearly 53 stone.

[2] Martin Luther (1483–1546), German Protestant reformer, believed in the co-existence of the body and blood of Christ and the bread and wine.

[3] 1818 '*sub*'.

CHURCH OF ENGLAND CATECHISM EXAMINED.

may be seen glittering in the back-ground, be perverse enough to harbour doubts of his own *Cannibalism*. Of the reiterated intensity of these *asseverations*, the object is—to keep out, if possible, all such *doubts*.

Question 22.—What are the benefits whereof we are partakers thereby?

Answer.—The strengthening and refreshing of our souls by the body and blood of Christ, as our bodies are by the bread and wine.

OBSERVATIONS.

In itself, a puzzling one indeed is the question here. But—answers such as this—let *these* be received as answers, no question can be a puzzling one.— Souls refreshed by a body and a quantity of blood?—Oh yes: if the body were but a *metaphorical* body, the blood but *metaphorical* blood, and the refreshment but *metaphorical* refreshment, in that case there would be no difficulty. By that which is *metaphorical, any thing* may be done: Yes, *any thing;* for that which is *metaphorical* is—*any thing*. But the body—is it then a metaphorical body?—Not it indeed. It is the *real* body: the blood is the *real* blood;—or how could they be '*verily and indeed taken?*' the *refreshment,* which a true Church of England soul takes by the *eating* of this *body,* and the *drinking* of this blood, is either no refreshment at all, or it is the same refreshment, that the soul of a New Zealander takes when he has been fortunate in battle:[1] when,—as a clergyman of the New Zealand religion, whatever it be, would phrase it,—'the Lord has delivered the enemy into his hand.'[2]

Nay, but it is only by that part of the meal which is composed of the bread and the wine, that our bodies, (says somebody), *are here said to be 'refreshed.'*— True: but the *body* and the *blood* are not the less said to be *taken:* i.e. taken, if into any thing, into our bodies: '*verily,*' (lest any thing like doubt on the subject should be suffered to remain)—'*verily and indeed taken.*' When thus *taken,* true indeed it is, that it is to the refreshing of our *souls,* that *that* part of the *chyle,* which is extracted *from* it, is applied. But, as to the *verity,* with which it must have been *taken,* the particular application thus made of it, makes not any difference: whatever part of man's person it goes to the refreshment of,—to produce this refreshment, whatever it is, *taken* it must be:—*taken?* yes, and *digested* likewise:—or how can any thing like *refreshment* be afforded by it?

To make all points not only *plain and clear,* but moreover smooth and easy,—on *this,* as on so many other occasions, the word *spiritual* is at hand. In a *carnal, temporal,* sense, not exactly true, *conceditur:* but besides the *carnal, temporal* sense,[3] for this, as for all other words for which it is wanted, there is a *spiritual* sense: and, if in this *spiritual* sense the thing be, as it *is,* true,—then, in this same *spiritual* sense, it is not only *as well* as if it were true

---

[1] According to James Cook, *A Voyage towards the South Pole, and round the world. Performed in His Majesty's Ships the Resolution and Adventure, In the Years 1772, 1773, 1774, and 1775,* 2 vols., London, 1777, i. 245, New Zealanders ate their enemies slain in battle.
[2] See, for instance, Genesis 14: 20.
[3] 1818 'source'. The text follows the 'Errata'.

in the *carnal* sense, but much better: better, viz. by the amount of the *superiority*—the undeniable superiority—of *things spiritual* over *things temporal:*—not to speak of *persons.*

So convenient is the use—so admirable the virtue—of the word *spiritual.* By it whatsoever things are *false* may at pleasure be made *true:* false in a *carnal*—false in a *temporal* sense—yes, so let them be:—still, in a *spiritual* sense, they are not the less capable of being true: whereupon, in that purer and superior sense, if there be any *convenience* in their being true, true they are.

To perform this metamorphosis, you couple the word *spiritual,* as above, with the word *sense.* This done, take any proposition that you please, the more absurd the better:—a still more absurd one, than the above *cannibal* proposition, if—which it will hardly be found to do—the nature of things affords any where a more absurd one.—Proposed by itself, and without that support, which the adjunct in question has in store for every absurdity, the falsity of it is, in the mind of any man in his senses, too glaring to admit of its finding so much as a momentary acceptance. Thus it is with it in its *natural* sense. To the word *sense,* add the word *spiritual,* and now, instead of being absurd and *false*—false to a degree of palpable absurdity—it requires nothing but a simple assertion to render it true. Have you any such thing in hand as *a mind,* to subdue,—to soften,—to weaken?—a mind, which you want to convert into a species of wax, ready to be moulded at any time to your purpose, whatsoever that purpose be?—here then is your way to go to work upon it. Take in hand one of these absurd propositions—the more palpably absurd the better—try it upon the man in the first place, *without* subterfuge: try it upon him in its *natural* sense. If in that sense you find him swallowing it, so much the better:—but, if you find him giving it back to you immediately, unable or refusing to swallow it,—you then give it to him a second time, wrapped up in the words *spiritual* sense—a *spiritual* sense, (tell him) and no other, is the sense in which he is to understand it.

Alas!—the quantity of the good things of this wicked world, which, by men calling themselves *spiritual,* are every day consuming—would they but content themselves with the consuming of these same good things, in a *spiritual* sense,—leaving to the growers, and makers, and buyers, the consuming of them in a *carnal* sense,—how much less would there be to be seen of that *pauperism,* which, under the covering of prosperity, that glitters at and about the *head,* is, in the *heart* of the population, so plainly seen, as well as so severely felt!

Generally speaking, this *spiritual* sense—alias *nonsensical* sense—seems to be the opposite or negative of the *carnal* sense. Thus, for example, in this *cannibal* case;—viz. eating the body and blood of a man, or of a God, or of both together.—*Carnal* sense, *eating it: spiritual* sense, *not* eating it.

To this interpretation of the word *spiritual,* as applied to *sense,* give constancy and *consistency,* then, in so far as it is understood in this sense, there may be not much harm in it.—For, in that case, forasmuch as there is such a thing as *eating* the sort of food in question in a *spiritual* sense, so

CHURCH OF ENGLAND CATECHISM EXAMINED.

there will also be such a thing as *believing* in that same sense: and as, in a spiritual sense, *eating* is *not* eating,—so, in a spiritual sense, *believing* will be *not* believing.

On this plan, unspeakable will be the benefit both to *Faith* and to *Charity:* to *Faith*, because, on this plan, there is nothing whatsoever but may be believed—believed by all men and without difficulty:—to *Charity*, because, on this plan, throughout the whole field of divinity, the whole mass of any two men's opinions,—in a word, of all men's opinions,—may, on every imaginable point, be as opposite as possible, and brotherly love not in any the smallest degree lessened by it:—take any proposition whatsoever, A believes it in a carnal or temporal sense, B, and every body else that differs from A, believes it in a spiritual sense. Here then, if, by and with this mode of unity, *Faith* is satisfied, so still more easily and heartily is *Charity: Hope* need never quit them,[1] and thus every thing is as it should be.[2]

Question 23.—What is required of them who come to the Lord's Supper?

Answer.—To examine themselves, whether(1) they repent them truly of their former sins(2), stedfastly purposing to lead a new life(3), have a lively faith in God's mercy through Christ(4), with a thankful remembrance of his death(5), and be in charity with all men.

OBSERVATIONS.

Five distinguishable alleged *duties*, forming so many subjects of examination, are here observable: five *duties* or *obligations*, concerning which every child is forced to affirm and declare, that he is persuaded of their having been imposed by the Almighty—imposed upon the child himself, together with all his fellow Christians.

Concerning all these supposed duties, the first question that presents itself as proper to be made, is—in any one of the histories we have of *Jesus*, what ground is there for any such supposition, as that, in the character of duties to be performed on the occasion of any such ceremony, as that which, having been instituted by the Church of Rome, and retained by the Church of England, is here spoken of,—duties, to this effect, or to any other, were by Jesus meant to be imposed upon any person whatsoever; and in particular upon any person, into whose mouth the declaration, to the effect that has just been seen, has ever been, or is ever destined to be forced?—*Answer*.—Not any. The ceremony itself, a mere modern invention;—the duties, thus attached to it, a mere fiction;—a fiction, put forth in the teeth of those undisputed and undisputable texts of Scripture, in which nothing that bears the smallest resemblance to it is to be found. In these texts, the persons addressed, no other than the *twelve* chosen disciples, distinguished

---

[1] See I Corinthians 13: 13.
[2] An echo of Blackstone's phrase, 'Every thing is now as it should be', made in the context of a discussion of the offence of heresy at *Commentaries on the Laws of England*, iv. 49, but which Bentham took to be characteristic of Blackstone's attitude to the British political system as a whole.

CHURCH-OF-ENGLANDISM

by the name of *Apostles;*—no other disciples, or followers, being present,—or, so much as in the way of any the slightest and most general allusion, spoken of: even to these chosen few the act recommended, of such a nature,—a mere token and pledge of remembrance,—a social act of a purely convivial nature,—as scarcely to be capable of being taken for the subject of a duty. They *all* [ate],[1] they *all* drank:—thus say two of those three of his four biographers, by whom what passed at that supper is reported.[2] At that same time, he (Jesus himself) [ate][3] with them, if *Luke* is to be believed: consequently, according to the orthodox interpretation, [ate][4] and drank along with them his thirteenth part of his own body and his own blood: which doing, he said to them, on that same occasion, according to that same Luke; *'This do in remembrance of me.'*[a] A duty, if a duty it can be called, plainly and expressly confined to *twelve* persons, then living and then present: and, in their instance, no such *accessory* duties as are here set up—no nor any other accessory duties—added to it;—such being the exact state of the case,—with the acknowledged standard of belief and practice before their eyes, up start a set of men, sixteen centuries after,—and, without deigning to assert, do more than assert—for they pretend to take for granted,—that, upon all that ever professed, or ever shall profess, the religion of Jesus, a whole swarm of duties, viz. the swarm thus confidently delivered, were, on that same occasion, imposed by him.

If, without support from any history, true or false,—and, on the contrary, in the teeth of so many histories, which now are, and then were in every body's hands—all of them recognized, as constituting, in relation to this very subject, the sole standard of belief and practice,—if, under such disadvantages, such palpable misrepresentation has been made—such gross impositions, not only attempted, but, by the arm of coercive power carried into effect with success,—what limits can there be to the impostures, which, with the same support, may with like success have been attempted, on subjects, on which the power of imposture has found no such obstacle to check it?—*Tradition—Roman Catholic Tradition*—in this word—not to look any further—an indication is given of the sort of matter, in which an answer to this question may be found.

Under all these five heads of examination, and in particular under the first,—suppose however the answer were in the affirmative: on this supposition, various are the observations, which the answer would be apt to suggest, if considered in its several particular parts.

1. This supernatural recipe with what degree of frequency is it expected to be repeated? 2. Suppose it were *a week*—suppose it but once *a month*—

[a] Luke xxii. 15. 'And he said unto them, With desire *I have desired to eat this passover* with you before I suffer: 16. For I say unto you, I will not *any more* eat thereof until it be fulfilled in the kingdom of God.' Such being his declared desire, and the means being at hand, and no obstacle at hand, of course that desire was fulfilled.[5]

---

[1] 1818 'eat'. [2] See Matthew 26: 26–7; and Mark 14: 22–3.
[3] 1818 'eat'. [4] 1818 'eat'.
[5] Jesus' injunction 'this do in remembrance of me' is at Luke 22: 19.

suppose even the number of doses taken in a year still smaller.—Each time,—let the times follow one another ever so quickly,—here is '*a new life*' undertaken to be led:—such at least is to be, on each occasion, the 'stedfast purpose.' But, of any such new life—(whatsoever may be meant by a new life)—what on any occasion, according to the string of intimations thus given, will be the fruit or use?—Each time there is to be '*repentance*'—each time the repentance is to be '*true*'—yet, true as it is, each and every time it is to be of no effect: the penitent being, all along, in the same sad case, as if no repentance had taken place. Each time the *purpose*, how '*stedfast*' soever it be, is to be broken through, and the condition which the penitent is thereupon to be in, is to be exactly the same as if no such '*purpose*' had been resolved upon. For, if that purpose be to lead a life without sin, then, suppose the purpose adhered to, of what use would be the *new life?*—The *new* life—no:—the *old* life is on that supposition the only *good* one:—a *new* life?—whatsoever of *novelty* his life had in it, he would, on this supposition, be but so much the worse for it.

Mark well, that all the time this perpetual alternative of sinning and repentance is going on, 'lively' is to be the man's '*faith in God's mercy:*' lively, in other words, his assurance—that upon repentance, forgiveness will each and every time follow. Full of comfort, no doubt, for the time, will this assurance be. For time *present*, yes:—But on the *future*, on each such occasion, what, if any, will be, at all times, its *tendency*, and but too probably its effect? What but to give encouragement—and by encouragement birth—to sin?

In a word—to use a familiar, but not the less apposite, expression—at the end of each such supper, *a new score*, it appears, is to be considered as commenced; and, at the conclusion of each immediately succeeding one, such new score will, if the view thus given of the effect be a correct one, be considered as *rubbed off*. In an account of sins, any more than in an account of money, can there be any stronger, or indeed other encouragement to the running up of a fresh score, than the assurance of having it rubbed off *at pleasure:* rubbed off at any time, and at no other expense than that of a few words of course.

As to contrition, *grief, sorrow, penitence, repentance,*—whatever be the *words* employed,—for any such affection, what room does the nature of the case leave in the breast of a man, whose persuasion is—that he is dealing upon such terms? *Sin*, he may thus at all times have his bellyfull of: only one thing he must not forget, which is—that in some manner or other, between the time of his committing each such sin, and the time of the next supper of this sort that he partakes of, he must 'truly repent,' i.e. be sincerely sorry for it.—Take a mouthful of bread and a mouthful of wine—taking care that before they are swallowed, whatsoever sins it has happened to you to commit, since the *last* preceding mouthful of each was swallowed, are truly repented of,—vanished are all these sins: all these sinful acts are caused not to have happened, and every thing is as it should be.[1] Such is the virtue of this bread, and of this wine:—if not this, then what else is it?

[1] See p. 249 n. above.

CHURCH-OF-ENGLANDISM

Under or over the *Church of Rome*, certain Popes used for some time to be selling this sort of licence, (*indulgence* was in the language of technical theology, its appropriate name): and, in that Church, to a *Church-of-England* eye, it was of course every thing that was mischievous and abominable.[1] By these Popes it was granted indeed, but in retail only, at so much per sin, and at high prices: and, the higher the prices, the smaller the number of those, in whose instance it could be obtained, and thereby become productive of its mischievous effects. But, if even under the Church of Rome this licensing system was a mischievous one, under the Church of England, how much greater must not be the mischievousness of it? Under the Church of England, at so small a price as that of the Table offering, *if* any such there be, it is put into every hand that can afford to pay that small price:[2] and the whole mass of sins, which, between supper and supper, a man can see his convenience in committing—the whole mass, be they in spirit and number what they may, are thus included in one and the same *indulgence*.

Has it not *this* effect?—Well then, if it has *not*, *no* effect has it whatever:— and such, from beginning to end, is the perpetual alternative. *Justification*,— shadow of justification, the case affords not any: *apology, palliation*, this is all that can be made or done for it. That, when all is said and done, things may, by a dispensation of God's providence, produced by an act of God's mercy, turn out to be in that same state, in which they would have been, had nothing of this sort been either said or done,—such is the most favourable result, of which, under the guidance of the most prejudiced judgment, the most sanguine imagination can entertain a hope.

And, in that most favourable case, can it really be said to be thus destitute of effect?—Yes: but in no other sense than that, in which, after having, for a length of time, been employed, dose after dose, without success, in the hope of curing some disease, *opium* may be said to have been destitute of effect. The non-existence of *particular* effect—viz. of the particular *good* effect hoped for—is but too true. But, of a *general* effect—and *that* a most disastrous one—the *existence* is at the same time but too true—a prostration of strength—an universal debility—'that prostration of the understanding and will,'[3] by which the constitution is destroyed.[a]

[a] And the production of which is among the *declared* objects of the NATIONAL INSTITUTION, according to the form given to it by the BENCH OF BISHOPS; and in particular of the BISHOP OF LONDON'S labours in support of it. See the ensuing Appendix.[4]

---

[1] The sale of indulgences by the Roman Catholic Church for the remission of punishment, on earth or in purgatory, which had become a common practice from the twelfth century, was confirmed and reformed by the Council of Trent in 1563: see Twenty-Fifth Session, 4 December 1563, *Canons and Decrees of the Council of Trent*, pp. 253–4. The practice was condemned and prohibited by Protestant reformers.

[2] During the Offertory in the Communion Service, Deacons, Churchwardens, and other appointed persons collected alms from communicants for the poor, and other oblations, which were then placed on the altar or Holy Table.

[3] See [Howley], *Charge delivered to the Clergy of the Diocese of London*, p. 16, reproduced at p. 37 n. above.

[4] See Appendix I, pp. 257–311 below.

RECAPITULATION.[1]

On recurring to the Observations contained in the preceding pages, the following are the *vices* which will, it is believed, be found to have been proved upon this formulary, the peccant matter of which is, with a diligence unhappily so successful, injected, by the hand of power, into the breasts of the great majority of the population, at the very first dawn of the reasoning faculty—

I. BAD GRAMMAR. For a passage teaching bad grammar by example, see p. 238.

II. BAD LOGIC; viz.
  1. By inculcation of matter plainly useless. See p. 215 to 219.
  2. By inculcation of manifest surplusage. See p. 245. 246.
  3. By inculcation of matter plainly unintelligible. See p. 206 to 210. 214 to 222. 224. 225.
  4. By inculcation of propositions inconsistent with one another. See p. 209. 210.
  5. By inculcation of instruction, which is either erroneous, or at best useless. See p. 230. 231.
  6. By exemplification and consequent inculcation of the art and habit of gratuitous or unfounded assertion, and groundless inference. See p. 222. 223. 228. 229. 230.
  7. By inculcation of matter, repugnant to those thirty-nine Articles, to which the whole body of the Clergy—Bishops and Archbishops included—together with all other ruling and otherwise influential persons,—who become partakers of that course of education which is in highest repute, will, upon entrance into that course, after being thus impregnated with the repugnant matter of this formulary, be forced to declare their assent and approbation on record. See p. 222. 223.
  8. By inculcation of matter savouring of Popery. See p. 245 to 248.

III. Matter, the tendency of which is—to operate, in various *other* ways, to the depravation of the INTELLECTUAL part of man's frame, viz.
  1. Matter, by which the principle of *vicarious obligation* is inculcated: i.e. by which children are commanded to believe, that it is in the power of two or three self-appointed persons, by agreeing together, to oblige a young child, in conscience, to pursue to the end of his life, any course of conduct, which, at that time, it may please them to prescribe. See p. 205. 206.
  2. Matter, by which the young child is himself forced to utter *a rash*

---

[1] This Recapitulation is reproduced at 'Preface', pp. 40–2 above.

promise, binding him, during life, to pursue the course of conduct therein and thereby prescribed. See p. 210. 211.
3. Matter, by which the child is initiated in the art and habit of *lax interpretation:* i.e. of declaring, in relation to the discourse in question, whatever it may be, his persuasion, that such or such was the meaning, intended by the *author* to be conveyed by it: viz. whatever meaning it may at any time happen to suit the personal purpose of the *interpreter* so to convey, how wide soever of the import really so intended to be conveyed. See p. 232. 233 to 252.
4. Matter, by which the *intellectual* part of the child's frame is destined to be *debilitated* and *depraved* by groundless and useless *terrors*. See p. 207 to 209. 237.

IV. Matter, the tendency of which is to operate, in various other ways, to the DEPRAVATION of the MORAL part of man's frame: viz.
1. Matter, in the texture of which *Hypocrisy* is plainly discernible. See p. 209. 210.
2. Matter, by which *lying* is inculcated as a duty:—a duty, which the child is forced to declare himself bound to persevere in the performance of. See p. 203. 204. 211. 215. 224. 232. 233. 237.
3. Matter, by which *Imposture* may be seen to be promoted. See p. 233 to 252.
4. Matter, by which *Forgery* may be seen to be knowingly uttered. See p. 212. 213.
5. Matter, by which encouragement is given to sin and *wickedness in every shape*. See p. 250 to 252.

V. Matter, the tendency of which is to operate, in an immediate way, to the injury of the SENSITIVE part of man's frame.
Matter, by which groundless and useless terrors are infused, as above.

Such,—on the grounds all along referred to, and plainly brought to view,—is the character and tendency herein *imputed* to this Church of England formulary, with the matter of which every English breast is, by the government at large, under the guidance of the ruling part of the Clergy, designed and endeavoured to be impregnated: *imputed*, and with what *justice*, let any person in whose eyes either the morals or the understanding of the whole people of England are objects worthy of regard, and who at the same time has courage to look in the face truth, however unwelcome, and opposed by prejudices ever so inveterate lay his hand upon his heart and pronounce.

CHURCH OF ENGLAND CATECHISM EXAMINED.

Ill will towards men,[1]—towards all men, in whatsoever rank in life situated, with reference to him in whose breast the corrupt affection is evident—equal, superior or inferior,—this, taking the whole together, may now be added to the list of those fruits, the seeds of which are so thickly sown by this machine. Ill will and, from ill will, oppression and persecution:—oppression the *chronical* disease, persecution, the *acute:* oppression, universal, habitual, and sluggish; persecution particular and casual; according as opportunity happens to be favourable.

The genealogy is in this wise: From *imaginary* grace, imaginary *mystery*, imaginary *sacrament*, come imaginary *blasphemy*, imaginary *sin;* from imaginary sin, comes *real antipathy;* and from men, in ruling and otherwise influential situations, *real oppression* and *real persecution*, on that one part; *real suffering* on the other:—for, by the imaginary sin, is produced, in the ruling breast, along with the antipathy, a pretence for gratifying it.

GOOD MEN, GOOD SUBJECTS, and GOOD CHRISTIANS—such, and in these very words, are the *goods*, which,—in giving the explanation of his truly admirable, and beyond doubt *ultimately* and highly useful, system of intellectual machinery,—over and over again,—and always, by means of a set of instruments, of which this formulary is the earliest and beyond comparison the most extensively employed article,—over and over again:—and, as here, in *placard letters—Dr. Bell* undertakes for the manufacturing.[2]

Good men and *Good Christians!* and by means of a thorough impregnation with the matter of this formulary!—Yes: if, of *Good men* and *Good Christians*, the characteristic qualities are—*hypocrisy, lying, imposture, forgery, sin* and *vice* in every other shape.

Good subjects? Yes: if the *goodness* of the subjection be in proportion to the *abjectness* of it: for, of abjectness in the subjection of the *subject many* to the dominion of the *ruling few*, can any more conclusive exemplification be exhibited, than that which is afforded, by the practice thus persevered in, of the swallowing of matter, thus poisonous to the whole moral texture of man's frame?—*Good Subjects?*—Yes: if the *Good Subject* be a character purposely selected to form a contrast with that of the *Good Citizen:* a description, by which—though now so studiously marked out for infamy as descrip-

---

[1] An ironic echo of Luke 2: 14: 'Glory to God in the highest, and on earth peace, good will toward men.'

[2] See Andrew Bell, *Elements of Tuition. Part I. The Madras School*, London, 1813, pp. 49–50: 'But it is the grand aim of this seminary to instil into these children EVERY PRINCIPLE FITTING FOR GOOD SUBJECTS, GOOD MEN, GOOD CHRISTIANS; and that they are brought up in such habits as may render them most useful to their patrons and benefactors, to whom they owe such peculiar duty.'

tive of an enlisted partizan of *anarchy*—no Frenchman, in the most despotic æra of the monarchy, ever scrupled to designate himself.

GOOD MEN, GOOD SUBJECTS, and GOOD CHRISTIANS!—Yes: let us not only wish, but hope, and even believe—that in and from the mind-turning mill, invented and worked by *Dr. Bell*, all these good articles will in conclusion be manufactured and issued out for use. Manufactured?—but by what instrument?—By this formulary?—No: —but, if at all, *in spite* of it.

The greater the efficiency of this admirable instrument—the more capable in its own nature of being, in all its efficiency, applied to the best uses—the greater in the breast of a true lover of mankind will be the regret at seeing it, in the very first application made of it, employed in thus thickly sowing in the mind, at the earliest dawn of reason, the seeds of depravity in every shape.

For consolation one hope remains:—and this is—that, after having, with whatsoever success, been thus employed in the introduction of the disease, it may, in a maturer state of the faculties—such is the nature of the instrument—be, still more effectually as well as more worthily, rendered conducive to the extirpation of it.

APPENDIX. No. I.

REMARKS
ON THE OBJECT OF THE CHURCH OF ENGLAND RELIGION, AS AVOWED BY THE BISHOP OF LONDON.

A PROSTRATION of intellectual strength—a confirmed mental debility—in the review just given of the *Church of England Catechism*,—such, in conclusion, was the result brought to view, as being, how mischievous soever, the least mischievous effect, which, naturally speaking, it can reasonably be expected to have, when it has any, upon the generality of the minds of the children, into whose mouths it is forced.

While the pen was tracing some such words as the above, far enough was the penman from any such expectation, as *that* of seeing his conception expressed, in a manner so much more pointed and particular, and at the same time so completely apposite, in a Discourse which, after having passed through a pair of Episcopal lips, has, under the name of '*A Charge to the Clergy of London,*' (his diocese) been printed and[1] published under the Right Reverend author's official name.[2]

Expressed?—but in what character?—in the character of a disorder—an epidemic disease—of which the existence ought to be deplored, and, if possible, the continuance prevented?—No:—but in the character of a consummation devoutly to be wished,[3] and to the acceleration of which the utmost exertions of the official instructors of the people ought to be directed: directed by the instrumentality of this same Catechism, through the medium of the National Society Schools.

---

[1] 1818 'printed for and'. The text follows the 'Errata'.
[2] i.e. William, Lord Bishop of London: see the title page to Howley's *A Charge delivered to the Clergy of the Diocese of London.*
[3] *Hamlet*, III. i. 63–4.

Prostration of the understanding and the will—these are the words—the very words—therein employed, as expressive of the state of mind, regarded by the Right Reverend author, as being 'indispensable to proficiency in Christian instruction.' (p. 16.)

To present a picture of a set of men, *Unitarians* by name, of whom some are *Deists*, others *Atheists*, (p. 14), and the *rest* (including, as it should seem, all Christians, whose profession varies in any degree from that of the Church of England), as persons[1] 'on whom the charge of infidelity attaches in a certain degree,' (p. [16])[2]—has been the business of a few preceding pages. In the 17th he speaks of them as being 'generally' . . . . men of some education, whose thoughts 'have been little employed on the subject of religion; or who, *loving rather to question than learn*, have approached *the oracles of divine truth* without that *humble docility*, that *prostration of the understanding and will*, which are indispensable to proficiency in Christian instruction.'

Prostration of the understanding and will? Yes, says the reader perhaps—but *before* what? 'before those oracles of divine truth' just before-mentioned—viz. the Holy Scriptures. The limitation is a candid one—and but for what follows, might be not unreasonably taken for a just one: it is however by the *reader*, and not by the *writer*, that it is applied. It is that[3] sort of limitation, which, to save himself from the imputation of applying a Roman Catholic spirit to Protestant doctrines, it were to be wished he had made, rather than what he has actually made.

A mind, in which the *understanding* and the *will* are *prostrate*—no matter before *what*—is a mind in the lowest state of debility, which, without correspondent debility of body, can have place. Not more than the corporeal, can the mental part of man's frame be at once in a state of weakness, and in a state of strength. If to '*question*' any thing that is set before it is regarded as a *sin*, if to '*learn*,' without questioning, any thing that is set before it is regarded as a *duty*,—set before it, with the customary threats in the back ground, the *Catholic Catechism*, it is a *Catholic* mind;—set before it the *Koran*, it is a Mahometan mind.

Oh yes? Let God, in his own person, appear,—and, whether in speech or writing, deliver *his* oracles,—'*prostration*, of the understanding and will,' would then indeed be as reasonable as it would be universal.

But to no man, in these our times, does God make any such

---

[1] 1818 'England), persons'. The text follows the 'Errata'.
[2] 1818 '15'.
[3] 1818 'is rather that'. The text follows the 'Errata'

appearance; nor, if on this point either Jesus[a] or John[b] are to be believed, ever did he. If, therefore, on any occasion, to any thing, by the name of *'the oracles of divine truth'* any such prostration as a *prostration of the understanding and will* is performed, it is to man, and not to God, that it is performed.

Meantime the oracles, which, under the name of *the oracles of divine truth*, his Lordship has had in view,—and towards which, on pain of forfeiture of 'proficiency in Christian instruction,' he calls for 'that *humble docility*,' and that *'prostration of the understanding and will,'* which are indispensable to that same proficiency,—what are they?—The contents of the Bible, or of any part of it?—Not they indeed. They are what cometh out of the mouth of the Church of England Clergy:—viz. of that part of it, whose happy lot it is to be subject to his rule. (p. 23.) Ask his Lordship else.

After speaking of the National Society Schools, in all of which this Catechism is forced into all the scholars' mouths, and on this, as on so many other occasions, giving his flock to understand—that, all who do not profess what the Church of England professes, should by all those who do, be regarded as *enemies*, (p. 22)—he exhorts them to be persevering in giving direction to these Schools; (p. 23)[1]—and, in case of their being so, as it is his *trust* they will, looks forward with exultation to the blessed effects, which he is assured will follow. 'Your instructions and exhortations, received with *humble docility*—(humble docility once more, for nothing less will serve)—(humble docility for ever!)—received with humble docility, *as the oracles of God*, by congregations who revere in your persons the dispensers of divine truth, will no longer be wasted on a barren soil.'

Here then in this concluding passage, whatsoever veil either his Lordship's prudence, or the candour or partiality of some friendly

---

[a] John, vi. 46. Not that any man hath seen the Father, save he which is of God, he hath seen the Father.

[b] 1 John, iv. 12. No man hath seen God at any time.

---

[1] See [Howley], *Charge delivered to the Clergy of the Diocese of London*, pp. 22–3: 'In the mean while every populous village, unprovided with a national school, must be regarded as a strong hold abandoned to the occupation of the enemy.

'It would, however, be a fatal mistake to imagine that even complete success in the establishment of schools would supersede all farther necessity of vigilance and labour. The conduct of these institutions, so intimately connected with national welfare and the stability of our establishments, political, civil, and religious, requires the unremitted inspection of the wisdom which presided at their original formation. In abandoning the direction of a system, which, if neglected, will cease to be useful, if perverted, will be injurious to the community, but maintained in vigorous action on its true principles is pregnant with incalculable blessings, we should incur the just imputation of treachery to that sacred cause, which the Clergy, beyond any other description of men, by all the obligations of duty, by all the inducements of charity, are engaged to promote and cherish.'

hand, may, at an earlier period, have endeavoured, as above, to spread over his principles and his plans, over his wishes and his endeavours, is thrown aside, (thanks to the warmth produced by the inspiration of his own eloquence!); and here, in conclusion, may be seen, as the avowed object of his Lordship's endeavours, the establishment of a state of things, which, when described in plain English, is neither more nor less (for, what else is it?) than a system of slavery;—of intellectual, and thence, as a necessary consequence, of moral and corporeal slavery,—in which, his Lordship, and his Right Reverend Co-adjutors and Reverend Sub-adjutors, are to be tyrants and sub-tyrants,—all other, i.e. all profane Church of Englandists, in the character of subjects, and all non-Church of Englandists in the character of 'enemies,' slaves:—and, of this tyranny, the *National Society's* Schools—i.e. the *Bench of Bishops'* Schools—are to be the *instruments* in *one* sense,—and this *Catechism*, together with the rest of that body of formularies of which it makes a part—but *above*, because *before* all, this *Catechism*—is to be *an instrument*, in *another* sense. And whether, for such a design, it would be easy for the wit of man, to frame or devise a fitter or better-adapted instrument,—the reader has, for some time, been in a way to judge.

Not to speak of God himself,—who, as already above observed, is altogether out of the question,—let not any one imagine, that, if manifested towards the Holy Scriptures, or towards any object soever, other than the body of men in whose governance he acts so conspicuous a part,—the *prostration of understanding and will*, thus called for, would satisfy the holy zeal of this ruler of the Established Church,—that 'Established Church,' 'so justly considered (in p. 1) as *the* bulwark of pure religion, *the* pillar of divine truth.'

The 'Scripture'—is it the Scripture, that, in his Lordship's declared conception, is to be taken for the object of this 'prostration?' No: nor so much as for the standard of belief:—the standard of belief—the only practical and effectual standard of belief, and thence (p. 17) of conduct,[1] is the 'interpretation' put upon Scripture. This 'interpretation' is the interpretation put upon it (p. [15])[2] by certain *'laws:'* these laws are *'established laws.'* What established laws?—To this question,

---

[1] See ibid., p. 17: 'And never was there a period in our history, in which so strong a disposition prevailed to study the truths of Revelation, and to appreciate their value in the direction of human conduct.'

[2] 1818 '19'. See [Howley], *Charge delivered to the Clergy of the Diocese of London*, p. 15: 'The charge of infidelity indeed attaches in a certain degree to all who refuse their assent to any material doctrine deducible by the established laws of interpretation from Scripture; and great must be the force of that prejudice, which can overlook the inconsistency of arbitrarily imposing a meaning unwarranted by the usages of language, on a book to which all parties appeal as the standard and rule of faith.'

APPENDIX, NO. I.

in his Lordship's view, is it possible there can have been any other than one answer,—viz. the laws established by the Established Church:—'the Established Church,' the above declared *'bulwark of pure religion,'* the above declared *'pillar of divine truth:'*—that Established Church, whose *'doctrines'* alone are *'sound,'*[1] whose opinions and conduct alone are pure—pure (p. 1) from the *'guilt of schism.'*[2]

'Laws of interpretation' then there are, and these (according to his Lordship) 'established laws:' and, 'to all who refuse their assent to any material doctrine deducible from Scripture' . . . by these laws, 'the charge of infidelity' (according to his Lordship, p. 15) attaches in a certain degree; and 'great (continues he) must be the force of that prejudice, which can overlook the inconsistency of arbitrarily imposing a meaning, unwarranted by the usages of language, on a book to which all parties appeal as the standard and rule of faith.'—'Appealing to the Scripture as the standard and rule of faith'—is this then capable of exempting any party from the charge of infidelity?—Not it indeed, says his Lordship, as we now see.

On the other hand—those, whose *'instructions'* as well as 'exhortations' (on condition (p. 23) of their forcing into the mouths of children this Catechism with its accompaniments) ought to be 'received with humble docility as the oracles of God, by congregations who revere in their persons the dispensers of divine truth'[3]—against any such persons can any such 'charge' be made as[4] that of 'infidelity,' (p. 15), 'of prejudice,' of 'inconsistency,' of arbitrary imposition, 'of arbitrarily imposing a meaning unwarranted by the usages of language, on that book' (viz. the Scripture) 'to which all parties appeal as the standard and rule of faith?'—No, verily. After this, let any one say, whether it be to the *book*,—that book, by the appeal to which no other effect is produced than the keeping alive those contests of contending parties, to all of which, all but one, the charge of infidelity attaches,—let any one say, whether it be to any such dead letter, or to the instruction, of those holy and living persons, whose instructions ought to be

---

[1] See ibid., p. 1: 'The principal aim of all his [Randolph's] labours was the maintenance of sound doctrine and the security of the Established Church, which he justly considered as the bulwark of pure religion, the pillar of divine truth.'

[2] See p. 48 n. above.

[3] See [Howley], *Charge delivered to the Clergy of the Diocese of London*, pp. 23–4: 'Your instructions and exhortations received with humble docility, as the oracles of God, by congregations who revere in your persons the dispensers of divine truth, will no longer be wasted on a barren soil: and you will find unspeakable consolation, in contemplating the efficacy of your labours in the advancement and maintenance of those high interests, which have been confided by your Redeemer, as a precious deposit, to your especial protection and care.'

[4] 1818 'truth"—to any such person can any such "charge" as'. The text follows the 'Errata'.

'received as oracles of God,' that in his Lordship's view,—if they would save themselves from the charge of 'infidelity,' and from the predicament of being regarded and treated by this disciple of the meek Jesus as *'enemies,'* and by the reason as well as piety of the people, 'with contempt and horror,'[1]—men must, to all practical and effectual purposes, look for the standard and rule of faith, and of that *'conduct'* which is to be *'directed'* by that faith. (p. [17].)[2]

The Scriptures?—admitting them, for decorum sake, to have been, while page 16 was perusing, 'the oracles of divine truth,' these were at best but *dead* oracles. The oracles, *which*, or rather *who*, while page 23 was perusing, were viewed in spirit as 'the oracles of God,'—the oracles, in whose *'persons the dispensers of divine truth'* were to be *'revered,'*—these—(as, by those, upon whose substance they are fattened, is but too well felt)—are *living* Oracles.

From his Lordship's own declaration, as evidenced by his Lordship's own words, thus much is plain; viz. that, by him,—in addressing himself to the Clergy, of the diocese of which he is Bishop,—to the Clergy, his own subordinates,—their instructions being received with humble docility as the oracles of God is mentioned—not only as an event which would be the eventual result, of their taking, and persevering (as per p. 23)[3] in, the 'direction' of the schools in question,—the schools in which the first thing taught is this Catechism,—but as being a highly desirable event:—an event, desirable, not only to the world in general, but to them in particular, and that to such a degree as to serve them as a reward for the performance of the function thus recommended to their care.

In the character, in which he thus expresses his wishes, and uses his endeavours, to cause these instructions to be received,—did he—in the first place in the *composing*, in the second place in the *preaching*, in the third and last place in the *revising* for the press, this most deliberate, and perseveringly studied and considered, however inconsiderate, discourse—did he, or did he not, regard them as fit and entitled to be so considered—considered by all to whose ears or eyes it should ever happen to them to come? if no, then what is this but exhortation to, and conscious participation in, a system of imposture? If yes, then observe whether, according to his

---

[1] See [Howley], *Charge delivered to the Clergy of the Diocese of London*, pp. 14–15: 'the appellation of Deist became a term of reproach; and the licentious freethinker was identified in popular estimation with the professed atheist. The union of unbelievers, as a regular and ostensible party, was dissolved by this discomfiture; it was impossible to act with effect under a character which the reason and piety of the people regarded with contempt and horror: and, owing to this general disposition of the public mind, the direct attacks on religious and moral truth were for a long time few and feeble.'

[2] 1818 '67'.

[3] See p. 259 n. above.

APPENDIX, NO. I.

Lordship's views—those views in which, in and by this his published *Charge*, he is labouring, as far as may be in his power, to cause all men to be partakers—any regard which, at the suggestion of prudence, it may happen to him to have professed towards those dead 'oracles of divine truth,' be in effect any thing better than a mockery.

That the privilege of having their *'instructions . . . . received as the oracles of God,'* was meant by him to be considered as one that *ought to be,* any more than as one that actually *is,* confined to his own particular subordinates in the body of the Church of England Clergy, is an interpretation, which,—it may be averred without fear of contradiction,—no friend of his Lordship's would wish to see put upon these or any other words of his.—No:—in this same privilege, what he meant to give us to understand was, that the whole body of that Clergy should be sharers:—sharers?—yes: and, saving the regard due to their respective situations in the hierarchy, *equal* sharers.

But, according to that other position of his Lordship's, (p. 15), which has been already brought to view, there are certain 'established laws of interpretation from Scripture:' laws, not only established, but, in such sort, and so firmly established, that to disobedience to them—viz. to the act of 'all who refuse their assent to any material doctrine deducible . . . . from Scripture' by those same laws, 'the charge of infidelity'. . . . 'in a certain degree'. . . . 'attaches.' These 'laws of interpretation'. . . . 'established' then as they are, where else can it have been his meaning that we should look for them, than in those instructions, which, almost in the same breath, and no more than eight pages after, are thus spoken of by him as 'the oracles of God.'

But if the instructions—be they what they may—which, from time to time, are delivered, by a set of men, whose doctrines,—as often as, according to what *they* represent as being the established *laws of interpretation,* (meaning interpretation of Scripture) they take upon themselves to put an interpretation upon any passage of Scripture,— are, as it is declared by his Lordship they ought to be, received as the oracles of God,—where is the practical use or application—where the real influence—that any one can discover, and shew, to be left to Scripture?—To the eyes (suppose) of all others who look upon it, Scripture delivers this or[1] that 'material doctrine:' pursuing, as *they* declare, the 'established laws of interpretation'—the laws confirmed by themselves, and acted under, after having been established by their predecessors,—deducing from Scripture by those same laws all

[1] 1818 'as'. The text follows the 'Errata'.

their 'instructions,'—the doctrine they deliver is the direct opposite one. But 'to all who refuse their assent to any material doctrine so deducible, the charge of infidelity' (according to his Lordship, p. 15) attaches: by these same established laws of interpretation a material doctrine is thereupon actually deduced: and by the supposition, (no very improbable one), by all whose misfortune it is to be *dissenters* from the Church of England, assent to this same doctrine is refused. What, according to his Lordship, with his established laws of interpretation, is the consequence?—What, but that these unfortunate persons, little as they imagine it, are—all in the lump—*ipso facto infidels*. In such a state of things—under such an authority—what particle of effectual authority can any one shew to be still left to Scripture?—How can it, otherwise than subject to their good pleasure, serve on any occasion for the 'direction' either of belief or 'conduct?'[1] In this dead oracle may, perhaps, be seen *one* 'standard of truth'—*one* source of *direction:*—but in those living 'oracles of God'[2] is at all times to be seen *another*, from which—let the dead one say what it will—every man's belief and conduct is, on pain of *judgment of infidelity*, to take its direction, as often as they please.

In such a state of things, those same *dead* oracles of God, of what sort of deportment and affection are they—can they be—the object, other than outward grimace and secret mockery? while all the real authority—all the power—all the influence—is the property of these *living* ones!

Meantime these '*established laws of interpretation*,' what are they?—where are they to be found? Not to speak of the professors of Christianity at large—not to speak of the ruling members of established Churches in general—all of whom by these his Lordship's decrees stand already condemned and put aside as *infidels*—established by the Church of England itself or herself, are there any such laws?—If so it be, that his Lordship knows of any, which, established as he declares them to be—are universally, or though it were but generally, avowed, appealed to, and acted upon—the cause of Christianity, would it not have been somewhat better served by an enumeration given of them, or though it were but a reference made to them, than by a discourse, in which, on the occasion, and under the mask of an Episcopal Charge to the Clergy of one diocese, the whole body of the people—such of them as, while occupied in exercising upon the most important of all subjects that reasonable faculty which God has given to them, are not able to agree with one another, what to believe and what to disbelieve, are thus excited to regard one another with contempt and horror?

[1] See p. 260 n. above.   [2] See p. 261 n. above.

APPENDIX, NO. I.

Of any such established laws of interpretation,—laws established in the form of *written* or *statute* law,—the *text*, it is believed, would not be very easy to be found. But of the laws of interpretation,—established, in so far as, by practice, laws that have never been framed, may be said to be established,—laws established, in the form of *unwritten, alias* Common Law,—of laws of interpretation established in *this* way, and in particular by that Church, to which we are indebted for this Catechism,—a set, in which the whole body will be found comprized, may, though not in *tenor* (for of the laws of *Common Law* it is the characteristic property *not* to have any *tenor*) be *in purport* stated with sufficient accuracy.

One of them may be styled—the law of *virtual insertion:*—a law, in virtue of which, to the whole body of holy writ may be added—any body of doctrine, which, any number of centuries ago, in the most tyrannical times, happened to suit, or to be thought to suit, the present and temporal interests of the tyrants of these times: and moreover, any other body or bodies of doctrine, which may happen to suit the like interest, of his Lordship's above-mentioned living 'oracles of God,' in the[1] *present,* and in all *future* times.

Another is—the law of *omission,* or *virtual expunction:* in virtue of which,—by so simple an expedient as that of not[2] saying any thing about the matter—or in one word, *silence,*—any doctrine of Scripture, which is found to stand in the way of these same interests may be got rid of, and caused to be as if it never had been.

A third—*the* third—(for[3] beyond this the form of interpretation 'can no further go') is—the rule of *virtual substitution:* 'to make which third, they join the former two.'[4] Provided with these three rules as with so many thunderbolts, the living Oracles of God may now be seen to be pretty well equipped for laying *'prostrate,'* and casting down into the abyss of just *'contempt and horror,'* all such presumptuous men, who, *'loving rather to question than to learn,'*[5] might otherwise be found troublesome.

[1] 1818 'God," the'. The text follows the 'Errata'.
[2] 1818 'mere'. The text follows the 'Errata'.
[3] 1818 'third—is, (for'. The text follows the 'Errata'.
[4] See Richard Owen Cambridge, 'On meeting at Mr. Garrick's An Author very shabbily drest in an old velvet Waistcoat, on which he had sewed Embroidery of a later date', in *The Works of Richard Owen Cambridge, Esq. including several pieces never before published*, London, 1803, p. 350:
> Three waistcoats, in three distant ages born,
> The bard with faded lustre did adorn.
> The first in velvet's figured pride surpast;
> The next in 'broidery; in both the last.
> His purse and fancy could no further go,
> To make a third he join'd the former two.

[5] See p. 37 n. above.

CHURCH-OF-ENGLANDISM

[1.] As to *exemplifications*,—for exemplifications of the rule of *virtual insertion*, after the indications, which, in the review here made of the *Catechism*, have just been given, no person need, now at least, be at a loss, who either remembers, or is able to read that same Catechism. From beginning to end that formulary may be stated as being in some sort an exemplification of this commodious rule: but, should any more particularly limited exemplification be wanted, they may be found in the *Recapitulation*, under the head of *gratuitous insertion* and *groundless inference*.[1]

2. As to *virtual omission*,—for the exemplification of this one of the Church of England's laws of spiritual interpretation, as by the Holy Mother Church, so by the no less Holy Daughter,[2] all those texts are marked of course, the observance of which would, to the living Oracles of God, be in any shape matter of inconvenience.

In particular, all those precepts of Jesus, from which, (supposing any regard paid to them,) they being in a special manner addressed, to the persons chosen among his disciples, to serve in the character of *Apostles*,—any reduction in the articles of *opulence*, *power*, or *dignity*, would be apt to ensue, to these lineally descended spiritual children and successors of those same Apostles.[3]

In relation to this subject, in the history of Jesus, as delivered by his biographers the Evangelists, several very untoward passages (it must be acknowledged) are to be found: passages, by which, but for this expedient, no small degree of perplexity might have been produced.

One, for example—one very untoward passage, is,—and *that* most unfortunately, repeated by three out of these four inspired biographers,[a]—the passage, in which, to him who '*trusts in riches*,'

[a] Luke xviii. 18 to 30.	Matt. [ix.][4] 16 to 28.	Mark x. 17 to 31.
24. And when Jesus saw that he was very sorrowful, he said, How hardly shall they that have riches enter into the kingdom of God.	22. But when the young man heard that saying, he went away sorrowful; for he had great possessions.	22. And he was sad at that saying, and went away grieved: for he had great possessions.
25. For it is easier for a camel to go through a needle's eye, than for a rich man to enter into the kingdom of God.	23. Then said Jesus unto his disciples, verily I say unto you, that a rich man shall hardly enter into the kingdom of heaven.	23. And Jesus looked round about, and said unto his disciples, How hardly shall they that have riches enter into the kingdom of God.
26. And they that heard it	24. And again I say unto you, it is easier for a camel	24. And the disciples

---

[1] See p. 253 above.
[2] i.e. the Roman Catholic Church and the Church of England respectively.
[3] The Bishops of the Church of England were said to derive their authority in unbroken succession from the Apostles.   [4] 1818 'xxx.' is a slip.

APPENDIX, NO. I.

(not to go further—though the text does seem to go somewhat further) *salvation* is by Jesus himself declared to be—though not exactly, yet something very near to exactly—*'impossible.'* In all of them, 'it is easier (says he) for a camel to go through the eye of a needle than for a rich man to enter into the kingdom of God.' In one of them alone is to be found the explanation, in which all the *softening*, any where given to the severity of the sentence, is contained—'How hard is it for them that *trust in riches* to enter into the kingdom of God!' and, unfortunately, even in this account, the softening, instead of closing the discourse, is followed by the repetition of the sentence, clothed as above in all its rigour.—Well then—among them that *trust in riches*—among *them*, at any rate, no more will be seen entering into the kingdom of God, than there will have been seen *camels* going through the eye of a needle.

Call it *an hyperbole*—assume the utmost licence that distress of argument can gasp for—still, if by this be meant any thing, what is meant by it will be—that, to him who trusts in riches, admission into the kingdom of heaven will be more difficult, than if he did not trust in riches.

But, by *trusting in riches*, what is it that can have here been meant?—trusting in their procuring to the possessor the necessaries

said, Who then can be saved?

27. And he said, The things which are impossible with men are possible with God.

28. Then Peter said, Lo, we have left all and followed thee.

to go through the eye of a needle, than for a rich man to enter into the kingdom of God.

25. When his disciples heard it, they were exceedingly amazed, saying, who then can be saved?

26. But Jesus beheld them, and said unto them, With men this is impossible, but with God all things are possible.

27. Then answered Peter, and said unto him, Behold, we have forsaken all, and followed thee.

were astonished at his words. But Jesus answered again, and saith unto them, Children, how hard is it for them that trust in riches to enter into the kingdom of God.

25. It is easier for a camel to go through the eye of a needle, than for a rich man to enter into the kingdom of God.

26. And they were astonished out of measure, saying among themselves, who then can be saved?

27. And Jesus looking upon them, saith, With men it is impossible, but not with God: for with God all things are possible.

28. Then Peter began to say unto him, Lo, we have left all and have followed thee.

and conveniences of this life? trusting in *money,* for its procuring *money's worth?* money's worth in all its shapes?—*This* is a trust, which, to avoid putting in riches is not, to any man, who ever lived in a country in which money was in use, so much as possible. Not to believe that riches have *this* power, is to deny the truth of a multitude of facts, the truth of which is every day proved to him by the evidence of his senses. What then, if any, is the sense, that must be put upon this passage? What but this—viz. that, in the first place, it is not in the nature of *riches,* to render it more easy for the *possessor* himself to enter into the kingdom of heaven, than it would be if he did *not* possess them; in the next place, that as little is it in their nature to render it easier to him to persuade *others,* into that course of life, which will cause *them* to enter into that same kingdom, than it would be to him if *he* did *not* possess them. To speak more shortly—on the occasion here in question, by *trusting in riches* is meant, if any thing be meant, relying upon them in the character of *instruments of salvation,*—of salvation, either to the possessor himself, or to those on whom, to that end, his influence exerts itself.

But, the clergy of an *Established Church*—unless it be by their *riches,* in conjunction with their *powers* and their *dignities,* (of which presently) by what are they distinguished from the Clergy of a *Non-Established* Church? and, among Established Churches, unless by the *riches,* the powers, and the dignities possessed by some among them, by what are the Clergy of the *Church of England* distinguished from the Clergy of the *Church of Scotland?* As often as it happens to any of them to speak of the *security* of the Church, what else is it that they mean, but the preserving, without diminution, to those among them that are *rich* their *riches,*—to those among them who have power their *power,*—to those among them who have dignities their *dignities,*—to those among them, who have any of those good things in prospect, their *prospects?*—When it happens to any of them to speak of the *downfall*—the *destruction*—the *ruin*—the *subversion*—of the *Church,* or of the Ecclesiastical establishment,—of which the subversion of the religion of Jesus, if it be not the self-same event, is of course the immediate consequence,—what is it that they mean, unless it be the *divesting* of their *riches,* such of them as have riches,—of their *power,* such of them as have power,—of their *dignities,* such of them as have dignities,—of their *prospects,* such of them as have prospects. Now if *this* be not *trusting in riches,* in what *other* shape, by what *other* tokens, can *trust in riches* be made manifest?

Three times—not to say oftener—did the spirit of contentious ambition break out among the Apostles: as often was it repressed by

APPENDIX, NO. I.

Jesus, in almost the same words. *One* would be first or greatest—*another* would be first or greatest—and what to all of them was his answer? No one of you shall be greater than any other: let your contention be—not who shall possess most power, but who shall render most service.[a]

[a] FIRST TIME.

Mark ix. 33, 34, 35.	Luke ix. 46, 47.	Matt. xviii. 1, 2, 3, 4.
33. And he came to Capernaum: and being in the house, he asked them what was it that they disputed among themselves by the way? 34. But they held their peace: for by the way they had disputed among themselves who should be greatest. 35. And he sat down and called the twelve, and saith unto them, if any man shall desire to be first, the same shall be last of all, and servant of all.	46. Then there arose a reasoning amongst them which of them should be greatest. 47. And Jesus perceiving the thought of their heart, took a child and set him by him.	1. At the same time came the disciples unto Jesus, saying, who is the greatest in the kingdom of heaven? 2. And Jesus called a little child unto him, and set him in the midst of them. 3. And said, Verily I say unto you, unless you be converted and become as little children, ye shall not enter into the kingdom of heaven. 4. Whosoever therefore shall humble himself as this little child, the same is greatest in the kingdom of heaven.

SECOND TIME.

Matt. xx. 20 to 28.	Mark x. 35 to 45.
20. Then came to him the mother of Zebedee's children, with her sons, worshipping him, and desiring a certain thing of him. 21. And he said unto her, What wilt thou?—She saith unto him, Grant that these my two sons, may sit, the one on thy right hand, and the other on the left, in thy kingdom.... 24. And when the ten heard it, they were moved with indignation against the two brethren. 25. But Jesus called them unto him, and said, ye know that the princes of the Gentiles exercise dominion over them, and they that are great exercise *authority* upon them. 26. But it shall not be so among you: but whosoever will be great among you, let him be your minister. 27. And whosoever will be chief among you, let him be your servant.	35. And James and John, the sons of Zebedee, came unto him, saying, Master, we would that thou shouldest do for us whatsoever we shall desire. 36. And he said, What would ye that I should do for you? 37. They said unto him, Grant unto us that we may sit, one on thy right hand, and the other on thy left hand, in thy glory.... 41. And when the ten heard it, they began to be much displeased with James and John. 42. But Jesus called them to him, and saith unto them, ye know that they which are accounted to rule over the gentiles exercise lordship over them; and their great ones exercise authority upon them. 43. But so shall it not be among you; but whosoever will be great among you shall be your minister: 44. And whosoever of you will be the chiefest shall be servant of all.

On these texts, then,—meaning always in the virtual expunction of them—or rather in an interpretation put upon them by *the rule of contraries*—may be seen founded the whole *hierarchy*.—*Prebends, Canons, Deans*—these wallow in *riches*—contend which shall first be made a *Bishop*—and neither *render*, nor so much as *pretend* to render—so much as the least particle of service. *Bishops* and *Archbishops*—these wallow in a compost made of *riches, power*, and *factitious dignity*—assume the style of *royalty*—call their houses, *palaces*—call their arm-chairs, *thrones*—take *Dives*, as if in bravado, for their pattern—clothe themselves—yea and their very footmen also—'in purple and fine linen'[1]—strut about and look big—call aloud for *'humble docility'*—declare their *'contempt and horror'*[2] for every person who presumes to demur to the demand—talk of the service they are rendering—and this is the way in which they render it.

On this same occasion, to the *three* already mentioned established laws of interpretation, one *other* might perhaps have been added, viz. *the rule of contraries: Minister ye unto every one*, say the texts; *lord* it over no one. Let us *lord* it over every one, says the interpretation; let us *minister* to none.

[3.] Of *virtual substitution*, no further exemplification need be looked for, than the avowed, and pertinaciously defended practice of one of the *Bible-circulating* Societies: that association of the wise in their own generation,[3] by whom such care is taken, in as far as depends upon themselves, not to suffer the word of *God* to go abroad, without the word of *man* to speak for it.[4]

Along with the dead 'Oracles of divine truth,' (p. 16), lest a poison

28. Even as the son of man came not to be ministered unto, but to minister, and to give his life a ransom for many.

45. For even the son of man came not to be ministered unto, but to minister, and to give his life a ransom for many.

THIRD TIME.
Luke xxii. 24, 25, 26.

24. And there was also a strife among them which of them should be accounted the greatest.

25. And he said unto them, the kings of the Gentiles exercise lordship over them; and they that exercise authority upon them are called benefactors.

26. But ye shall not be so; but he that is greatest among you, let him be as the younger; and he that is chief, as he that doth serve.

---

[1] Luke 16: 19. [2] See pp. 37 n., 262 n. above.
[3] An echo of Luke 16: 8.
[4] Bentham probably has in mind the Society for Promoting Christian Knowledge, founded in 1698 to promote schools, the Bible, and Christian knowledge at home and abroad. Throughout the eighteenth century, the Society was the largest producer of Christian literature in England, publishing tracts and pamphlets on subjects such as baptism, confirmation, and private devotion, and distributing Bibles and the *Book of Common Prayer*.

APPENDIX, NO. I.

so dangerous should be without its antidote—care is, by these true sons of the Church, thus taken, to administer a corrective, made up about two centuries and a half ago; a corrective of which this Catechism composes either the most essential portion, or the whole.[1] Under the mask of an *accompaniment*, this corrective, it has been shewn already, is in effect and virtue—in every thing but the name, a *substitute*.

Into any company, *not* instructed in the deaf and dumb language—or even into any company that *has* been so instructed, send a deaf and dumb man that has *not* been so instructed, to what real use, but that of empty ceremony could be the presence of this unfortunate person? Were he a king?—Were he an emperor—where would be his power or influence?—To what purpose, then, can any such concomitancy be insisted upon, unless it be one or other of these two:—viz. that which the priests of Apollo at Delphi had, when those living *Oracles of* that *God* took upon themselves the trouble of declaring and expounding the will of the dead stone ones,[2]—or that which the rulers of Jerusalem had when they placarded Jesus, in the character of the king of the Jews?[3]

While as yet she remained in the womb of her holy mother, the prudence of the Church of England refused to suffer a poison so dangerous as that of the Scriptures to circulate in the body politic on any terms.[4] Now that, having eaten her way out of the body of that parent, of whose person she wants so little of being the express image, she turns upon her to bite, and even, if possible, to devour the womb in which she was conceived,—unable to annihilate the dreaded poison, she does that which answers her purpose less invidiously, and scarcely less effectually—she amalgamates with it her own antidotes.

Suppose now the Holy Mother (nor is this supposition at present altogether without foundation in fact)—suppose her, at any time, to circulate the pretended poison without any pretended antidote—which will then be the honestest—the Mother or the Daughter?

True it is, that all this about Churches is but allegory: equally true, that all profane allegory is but trumpery or imposture. But that

---

[1] The Catechism was included in the 'First Prayer Book of Edward VI', which, according to the first Act of Uniformity of 1548 (2 & 3 Ed. VI, c. 1), was to be used exclusively in the Church of England from the next Feast of Pentecost (9 June 1549).

[2] The role of the priests at Delphi was to interpret the often obscure oracles of Apollo, pronounced by the priestess, and made in response to requests for guidance.

[3] According to the accounts in Matthew 27: 34–44, Mark 15: 24–32, and Luke 23: 36–8, the purpose of the sign placed on the cross above Jesus was to mock him. The account in John 19: 19–22 is ambivalent.

[4] See p. 70 n. above.

CHURCH-OF-ENGLANDISM

Church, that self-styled 'excellent' Church[1]—in which every deficiency in merit is so amply made up by self-praise—what existence has *it* or *she*, but an allegorical one? and of an allegorical entity who can speak but in allegory?

If, stript of that power, which cannot be exercised but to be abused,—the well-fed children of this world, who, to save themselves from being seen to be what they are, take shelter—sometimes in the image of *an old building,* sometimes in the image of *a beautiful woman,* were bereft [of] the[2] mammon of unrighteousness[3]—all of them that now feed upon it—left in the plight in which they are,—take away the idol, what would there be to be *reviled,* to be *ruined,* to be *violated*—to be *overthrown,* to be *subverted,* to be *destroyed?*—But for allegory, where would be her *fathers,* her *sons,* her *children*—her *pillars,* her *buttresses,* her *ornaments?*—Where would be the most efficient as well as splendid portions, of the matter, of which all her defences are composed?

To return to his Lordship of London.—Speaking of the Bell Instruction Schools (p. 23), which, so far as established, are under the patronage of the National Society,—and in which, part,—and that the most efficiently administered part,—of the matter of instruction, is composed of the matter of this Catechism—'In[4] proportion to the success of your attention to this important point, the course of your ministry' (says he, p. 23, in that passage of which something has been said already)[5] 'will become *smooth and easy.* Your parishioners, from their infancy initiated in the principles, and inured to the practice, of pure Christianity, will crowd with pious affection to the altars of their Mother Church; and will have to regard the pretences and artifices of corrupt or illiterate instructors with indifference or disdain. *Your instructions* and exhortations' (continues he) '*received with humble docility as the oracles of God,* by congregations who revere in *your persons* the dispensers of divine truth, will *no longer be wasted* on a barren soil: and you will find unspeakable *consolation*' (concludes this Charge, p. 24) 'in contemplating the *efficacy* of your *labours* in the advancement and maintenance of those high interests, which have been confided *by your Redeemer,* as a *precious deposit,* to your *especial protection and care.*'

'*Smooth and easy?*' Yes, my good Lord of yesterday, worthy successor of the Lord of t'other day,[6]—in whose eyes, as well as

---

[1] See p. 29 n. above.
[2] 1818 'were, so far as concerns the'. The text follows the 'Errata'.
[3] Luke 16: 9.
[4] 1818 'Catechism.—"In'. The text follows the 'Errata'.   [5] See pp. 262–3 above.
[6] John Randolph, Howley's predecessor as Bishop of London. For Bentham's comparison of Randolph and Howley see pp. 154–8 above.

APPENDIX, NO. I.

your's, (p. 1), '*schism*' was '*guilt,*' in whose eyes 'the Established Church,' (more than half the opulence of which is obtained and received on false pretences—on the pretence of doing duty, accompanied with the determination to do none)—in whose eyes this nest and nursery of deliberate and lucrative falsehood was, as we stand assured by you, the storehouse 'of[1] divine truth,'—and 'whose endeavour' (p. 2) was to replace ecclesiastical discipline on its 'ancient footing'—smooth and easy, as your Lordship says, will be, if they perform the task you are thus recommending to them, this course of theirs—'the course of their ministry.'—Still more smooth and easy—no less smooth and easy than these[2] your Lordship's periods—will be the course of all those among them (that is to say, the great multitude) who will give themselves no such trouble.

Smooth and easy this course?—Strange indeed if it were not so. If not to *them*, to whom else should it be so? What other course is there that can be so? and how should it be otherwise?

The *Minister* receives his 20*l.* a year,[3] his 200*l.* a year, or his 2,000*l.* a year, for of this sort is the equality observed in the apportionment of their hire, among the labourers in this vineyard[4]—his 2,000*l.* a year for reading, or undertaking to read, with a determination not to read, *his* half of the Liturgy,—with or without a *Sermon*, which, if it be not an already printed one, but of his own composing, is so much the worse for being so.[5] The *Parish Clerk* receives his 5*l.* or his 10*l.* a year for reading *his* half of the same formulary.[6] The *members of the congregation*—such of them as can read and are so disposed—read the same string of words that the Clerk reads,—and these *Amateurs* perform gratis.

What the Minister reads, might just as well be read by the Clerk: what the Minister and the Clerk read, might just as well be read by any of the *National Society's* Scholars, as soon as their course of instruction in its schools is finished, or before: Doing this—i.e.

---

[1] 1818 '"the follower of'. The text follows the 'Errata'.

[2] 1818 'those'. The text follows the 'Errata'.

[3] The Act for the better maintenance of Curates of 1713 (12 Ann., Stat. 2, c. 12, § 1) stipulated that curates were to receive a salary of not less than £20 per annum. This sum was increased to £80 per annum by the Curates Act of 1813 (53 Geo. III, c. 149, § 7) introduced by Harrowby. For Bentham's examination of what he terms 'Harrowby's Bill' see Appendix V, §§ 2–3, pp. 499–525 below.

[4] For the parable of the labourers in the vineyard see Matthew 20: 1–16.

[5] For Bentham's discussion of the remuneration of the clergy see pp. 371–415, 499–525 below.

[6] The Parish Clerk assisted the priest during church services by leading the congregational responses and prayers, and reading the epistle. He could also assist in baptism, marriage, and burial, for which he received a fee. The remuneration of the Parish Clerk depended upon the custom of the parish in which he worked. See Joseph Shaw, *Parish Law: or, A Guide to Justices of the Peace, Ministers, Churchwardens, Overseers of the Poor, Constables, Surveyors of the Highways, Vestry-Clerks, and all others concerned in Parish Business*, London, 1733, pp. 42–4; and Burn, *Ecclesiastical Law*, 2nd edn., 1767, iii. 63–8.

CHURCH-OF-ENGLANDISM

reading this—(for what else is there that they are, any of them, under any obligation of doing?) Doing this, or doing neither this nor any thing else, 'the *Established Church* is'—i.e. the Ministers of the Established Church are, according to the system of poetico-architectural divinity, 'the pillars of divine truth. . . . But, the more pillars the edifice has, the more firmly it will be *established*.' Instead of troubling so many grown Gentlemen, whose time might in other ways be employed so much more agreeably to themselves,—instead of employing *them* to do this drudgery, why not turn it over at once to the scholars thus recommended to their care? So many scholars, who, having passed through one of these schools, would be thus employed, so many more *pillars* would the Church have for its supports. Of all the things, which the Reverend persons in question are, as such, under any obligation of performing—of all the things which they ever do perform, except it be here and there in the character of a work of *supererogation*, and receiving extraordinary laud for it,—is there a single one, which might not be done precisely as well—supposing their school-time well and successfully employed—by these '*babes and sucklings*.'[1] And, in this case, supposing the *manner of reading 'smooth and easy*,' is there any thing else that could fail to be so?

A zealous and diligent (every thing but a humble) servant of God—labouring, in season and out of season, to rescue souls from the jaws of Satan,—contending against a host of opposing adversaries, in the shape of 'corrupt or illiterate instructors,' full (p. 23) of 'pretences and artifices,'—struggling under loads of difficulties—difficulties raised (p. 18) by 'the joint machinations of infidels and sectaries, assisted by the indiscretion of short-sighted piety,'[2]—difficulties almost too great to be surmounted by human powers, but for such support as they are thus to make for themselves,—is not this the sort of image, which,—in the character of a faithful sketch of the situation of a Church of England Clergyman on the one hand—and, on the other hand, of the character of a parish, peopled by a Church of England laity,—it is his Lordship's object, in this part of his discourse, to set before men's eyes, and engage them to accept of?—To accept of such a picture as a true one!—as if that which is clear to every one else could be otherwise than clear to the author and publisher of this Charge, viz. that, except by the merest accident, in perhaps one parish out of

---

[1] Psalm 8: 2; Matthew 21: 16.
[2] See [Howley], *Charge delivered to the Clergy of the Diocese of London*, p. 18: 'if the joint machinations of infidels and sectaries, assisted by the indiscretion of short sighted piety, are calculated to excite alarm; the means of resisting a torrent enlarged by the union of waters, which, issuing in opposite directions from different sources, have at length fallen into the same channel, deserve our most serious consideration'.

APPENDIX, NO. I.

fifty or a hundred—every thing that savours of labour—of contention, of difficulty—every thing of this sort,—not only if regarded as existing in any considerable quantity, but if regarded as exemplified in any the minutest particle,—is purely imaginary and fictitious. In the recital either of the *periodical* or the *occasional* formularies—in the saying of his part in the Morning or Evening Common Prayer—with or without the additional twenty minutes labour of reading his sermon—in the performing of his part in the burying, christening, marrying, or married-woman-churching service,—what *opposition*—what difficulty in any shape—does or can any Church of England Minister ever experience?—In all this reading out of a book, what is there that, by any such ill-assorted cause as he brings to view, or by any other cause whatsoever, could, in any, the smallest degree, be rendered *smoother* or *easier* than it is? If every child without exception, that lives to the schooling age, were educated in these schools, could the performance of this reading task be by any possibility, in any degree, rendered smoother or easier to the Minister, or the Curate, by whom it is performed?

By any such consummation,—seriously as, on so many other accounts, it is to be wished for,[1]—how is it that, towards the removal of any of the *asperities* or *difficulties* thus alluded to—the only asperities or difficulties which (unless it be now and then the getting in of their tithes) the holy persons in question stand exposed to—any the smallest advance would be made? In all these formularies, where is the paragraph that would be *cancelled* by such a consummation? where is the paragraph that would be so much as *shortened* by it?

No:—so far is the thus assigned cause from being capable of contributing any thing towards the production of its assigned effect—viz. the diminution of the only sort of labour, which, unless by mere accident, and in the character of a work of *supererogation*, is ever performed, or so much as pretended to be performed,—the result of any such supposed increase in the piety and populousness of Church of England congregations, would be the exactly opposite effect:—increase, not diminution, of all labour really performed by a Church of England Ministry. The greater the number of those who, in the language of the *Howleys* and *Chateaubriants*[2] 'crowd with pious affection to the altar of their Mother Church'[3]—in plain English, after the sermon, repair to the Communion Table, to join in taking what is called *the sacrament*,—the

---

[1] An echo of *Hamlet*, III. i. 63–4, first quoted at p. 257 above.
[2] François-René, Vicomte de Chateaubriand (1768–1848), French Romantic writer, author of *Génie du Christianisme, ou Beautés de la religion Chrétienne*, 5 vols., Paris, 1802.
[3] See p. 272 above.

greater the number of the individuals, to each of whom his portion of the flesh-producing bread, and afterwards another of the blood-producing wine, would have to be distributed: yea, and moreover the greater the number of times, during which the appointed ghostly formulary, short as it happily is, would have to be repeated.[1] At the time of the millenium thus prophecied, suppose the number of communicants to be double what it is at present, would not this part of the duty—the part thus, as above, particularized—be doubled? Then, in the only quality of it, viz. *length*, which is susceptible of *care* and *difficulty*, instead of being made twice as '*smooth* and *easy*,' would it not be twice as *rough* and *difficult*?

In the article of *surplice fees*,[2] true it is, that, from the conversion of all dissenters into zealous and assiduous Church-of-Englandists, some advantage might accrue to some of the holy persons to whom this *Charge* was preached: viz. to such of them as, in the character of Curates, or in their bargains with their respective Curates, take to themselves the whole, or a part, of that mass of the mammon of unrighteousness,[3] from which the hand of a Clergyman of the *Church of Scotland* would recoil with disdain[4]—or, in his Lordship's language, with '*contempt and horror.*'[5] But, howsoever, by any such accession, the *course* which his Lordship speaks of—'*the course of the Ministry*' (p. 23) of his Reverend auditors—would be rendered *pleasant*, and in that sense '*smooth*,'—it would still,—in respect of the only sort of *labour*—and, in *that* sense, of *difficulty*—which is attached to it in the character of a *duty*,—be rendered—not the more '*easy*,' but the more *difficult*.

When,—stript of the veil of mystery and imposture in which, according to custom, they are bedizened,—they are presented in the garb of simple truth, such, it has been seen, is the substance of these episcopal effusions, with which the understandings of mankind, on the supposition of their having been reduced to a state sufficiently 'prostrate' viz. by the help of the old instrument of confusion—the Catechism, with its *et ceteras*,—and the Articles and their *et ceteras*,—though before the invention, and consequently

---

[1] i.e. the words spoken by the minister whilst administering the sacrament to the congregation. See 'The Order for the Administration of The Lord's Supper or Holy Communion', *Book of Common Prayer*: 'The Body of our Lord Jesus Christ, which was given for thee, preserve thy body and soul unto everlasting life: Take and eat this in remembrance that Christ died for thee, and feed on him in thy heart by faith with thanksgiving.

'The Blood of our Lord Jesus Christ, which was shed for thee, preserve thy body and soul unto everlasting life: Drink this in remembrance that Christ's Blood was shed for thee, and be thankful.'

[2] See p. 235 n. above.　　　　　　　　　　　　　　　　　　　　　　[3] Luke 16: 9.

[4] Surplice fees were not payable in the Church of Scotland.

[5] See p. 262 n. above.

APPENDIX, NO. I.

without the help of the new instrument of *instruction*,—are endeavoured to be impregnated.

In one way, then, and one way only,—viz. the way above hinted at,—could the universally wished for multiplication, of schools and well-reading scholars, be rendered in any degree conducive, to the causing the 'course of the ministry' in question to be smoother and easier than it is. This is—the placing the scholars in the *reading desks*, to read the Ministers' part in the *Liturgy*, and in the *pulpits* to read the *sermons;* or, instead of these modern effusions, which at best are liable to be tainted with the 'corruption' (p. 23) of the times, those venerable, and, by his said Lordship, in this very Charge, bepraised and lauded productions of good Queen Elizabeth's days—*the Homilies*,[a]—to which these modern effusions, (Oracles of God as they are, p. 23) are but inadequate, and not altogether undangerous, substitutes. This source of relief has been already proposed, and it will be seen to have the rarely exemplified merit of being a sure one.

What Church of England layman is there, whose ears have not been wounded with the groans of the Reverend Ministers of God's word, labouring under a load of *duty*, composed of services to be performed every seventh day, of the length of an hour, an hour and a half, or two hours each, once, twice, thrice, or—(for in one instance out of a hundred or two, such things have been known, incredible as it may seem) even as many as *four* times—nay, as *five* times, with *rides* or even *walks* between the *sittings* and the *standings*, and no more than six days out of the seven for repose![1] Call in but those *little*

---

[a] P. 21, in a Note. 'The several HOMILIES on Salvation, on Faith, and on Good Works,[2] are earnestly recommended to the repeated perusal and serious consideration of all Clergymen, as admirable specimens and models of this wise and salutary caution: viz. In touching on doctrines which are liable to perversion, ... to preclude' (says the text, p. 21) 'the possibility of misconception by clear and precise statements, and distinct explanations and cautions: and to frame your expressions with such scrupulous accuracy, that they may neither be wrested by the unstable, nor misunderstood by the ignorant and unwary.'

---

[1] In the story of the Creation in Genesis 1–2: 3, God laboured for six days and rested on the seventh.

[2] See 'An Homelie of the saluacion of mankynde, by onely Christe our sauior, from synne and death euerlastyng', 'A short declaracion of the true liuely, and Christian Faithe', and 'An Homelie, or sermon, of good workes annexed unto faithe', first published as Sermons 3, 4, and 5 respectively in *Certayne Sermons, or Homelies, appoynted by the Kynges Maiestie, to be declared and redde, by all persones, Vicares, or Curates, every Sondaye in their churches, where they have cure*, London, 1547, during the reign of Edward VI (1537–53), King of England and Ireland from 1547. A second volume of twenty-one sermons entitled *The second Tome of Homilees, of such matters as were promised, and intituled in the former part of Homilees*, London, 1571, was published during the reign of Elizabeth I. The two volumes were combined for later editions, appearing, for instance, as *Sermons or Homilies appointed to be read in Churches in the time of Queen Elizabeth of famous memory*, 4th edn., Oxford, 1816.

ones, to each of whom the *labour* might by *division* be reduced to any degree of minuteness,—do but this, and, for the relief of the at present so heavily-worked and heavily-groaning labourers in that spiritual vineyard, a seventh day of repose might be added to the six. Of the 'course of the ministry,' the smoothness and easiness would, by this relief, be raised to its *maximum*. The interest of *the Church*—that is, of the *paid part* of it—would thus in the highest degree be served: and the interest of *the Church*—that is, of the *paying part* of it, in what way would it be injured or disserved?—Let him who thinks he knows of any such way declare it.

The more seriously and thoroughly this proposal is considered, the more clearly it will be seen—that, except the novelty of it, the case affords no argument, capable of being set in opposition to it.

As to the above-acknowledged *works of supererogation*,—the performance of which in here and there an instance, is not meant to be denied—but which are not, nor in their nature, to any good purpose, ever can be, works of *perfect obligation*, and as such caused to be exacted to any thing like a sufficient extent,—they might and would, after the proposed arrangement, continue to be performed as at present; and the same *motives*, which, in the present state of things, suffice for the production of them, would, in the proposed state of things, exercise themselves with equal efficiency in the production of the same effect.

Such is the incontestable result and state of things, in so far as use is made of a once-for-all composed and for ever established formulary:—by any person who is able to read out in such manner as to be intelligible, every thing that, in the situation in question, any man can be made to do, is capable of being done: the art of reading—in that one art the one thing needful[1] is concentrated: every thing else, to which any such name as *art*, or *science*, or *knowledge*, is wont to be applied, is needless and superfluous: all money employed in the supposed or pretended purchase of the fruit of any such accomplishment, so much money bestowed in waste: in waste, even if any security were to be had for the possession of what is thus paid for:—a supposition, which, in the[2] present state of things, is notoriously an imaginary one.

Nay, but is there no difference between *good reading* and *bad reading?*—O yes—difference, much more than is to be wished. But when all *forms*—in both senses and pronunciations of the word[3]—all

---

[1] Luke 10: 42. [2] 1818 'this'. The text follows the 'Errata'.

[3] According to the entry for FORM in the unpaginated second volume of Samuel Johnson, *A Dictionary of the English Language*, ed. H.J. Todd, 4 vols., London, 1818, the word *form* in the sense of a class, or rank of students, was pronounced 'with *o* long, as if it were *foarm*'. Samuel Johnson (1709–84), author and lexicographer, first published *A Dictionary of the English Language* in 2 volumes at London in 1755.

APPENDIX, NO. I.

form and *forms* have been gone through, all *degrees* taken, all examinations passed, what reason is there for expecting, that, on the side of the ordained Minister, as compared with the *Bell-taught* and well-taught school-boy, any advantage will, in this particular, be found?—The *Holy Ghost*, who, at the word of command, so regularly passes from the hand of the Bishop into the head of the new Minister—with power to keep out of hell or let drop into it whom he pleases[a]—this Ghost, with all his holiness, is he *a Reading-master?*[b] If he be, it is more than ever he professed to be: and, from *Mr. Thelwall*, by whom the teaching of this art *is* professed,[1]— and whose professions in this way are performed, it is said, to the satisfaction of those who trust in them,—the art would be much more likely to be learnt. Among all the arts, and all the sciences, which, in the whole course of the career,—the literary, scientific, and spiritual career,—from the *petty form* at Eton or Westminster, up to the examining Chaplain's study,—the younger son, of a family that has a living in its gift, has been dragged through, and is supposed to be impregnated with,—is *the art of reading*—(meaning always the art of reading *with propriety*—the art which Mr. Thelwall teaches)—is any *such* art to be found?—Well then, in this art, the ordained and full-ripe Minister, with the Holy Ghost in his head, has never been instructed at all. The unfledged school-boy has been (suppose) instructed in it:—which of the two stands the best chance of being found *well* instructed in it?

[a] Extract from that part of the Church of England Liturgy, which is intituled, *The Form and Manner of ordaining of Priests.* 'The Bishop, with the Priests present, shall lay their hands severally upon the head of every one that receiveth the order of Priesthood; the Receivers humbly kneeling upon their knees, and the Bishop saying,
'Receive the Holy Ghost for the Office and Work of a Priest in the Church of God, now committed unto thee by the imposition of our hands.'—'Whose sins thou dost forgive, they are forgiven; and whose sins thou dost retain, they are retained.'

[b] A *Reading-master?* No:—a *Speaking-master?* Yes. So say the Methodist, the Quaker, yea, and the Minister of that Scottish Church, equally *established* with, and so much better established than, the English? A *Speaking-master*, all these men, how different soever in other things, do concur in beholding in their Holy Ghost. And by whom, and from whence shall this their pretension be contested with success? Not by the Church of Englandists, either from observation or from Scripture.[2]

---

[1] John Thelwall (1764–1834), political reformer, lecturer, and writer, had in 1809 established an Institute of Elocution in Lincoln's Inn Fields, London, where he taught elocution and speech therapy until 1818. His publications included *Mr Thelwall's Introductory Discourse On the Nature and Objects of Elocutionary Science; and the Studies and Accomplishments connected with the Cultivation of the Faculty of Oral Expression: with Outlines of a Course of Lectures on the Science and Practice of Elocution*, Pontefract, 1805, and *Selections and Original Articles, for Mr Thelwall's Lectures on the Science and Practice of Elocution*, Birmingham, 1806.

[2] According to St Paul, prophecy and speaking in tongues were both gifts of the Spirit: see I Corinthians 12: 10.

So much for the *smoothness and easiness*, thus professed to be looked for, in the character of a new and hitherto unexperienced blessing, from the new schools.

Meantime, is it not a lamentable spectacle—would it not be a lamented, if it were not so perpetual an one—to see the ruler of a Christian Church, in the face of a whole congregation, to every individual of which it is known that there is not a syllable of —— in what he is thus saying,—thus, with a continual appeal to the Almighty in his mouth,—holding up, in a solemn and deliberate discourse, an image,—of which, to his own perfect knowledge, as well as that of every body else, the very reverse is the ——? exhibiting it in audible signs, and thus, face to face, to his *Church*,—preaching thus to his Church, in one sense of the word *Church*, viz. to the *wolfish* part of the community in question; and then, in visible and permanent signs, to his *Church* in the other sense, viz. to the *sheepish* part?

But, such is the effect of that ——— to —— , which, through the medium of this Catechism, a Church-of-Englandist sucks in with his earliest breath: and which, by *Subscription* after *Subscription*, and *oath* after *oath*, at his entrance into the University, and thereafter at every gradation, is confirmed. A few pages back may be seen the Catechism, and here may be seen one of its fruits.—Sowing thistle-seed, can you expect figs, or any thing better than thistles?[1]

Over a Church thus constituted, no wonder if, in the view, and by the confession of those who are so well paid for propping it, there should be impending dangers.—'We are indeed exposed to dangers,' (says his Lordship, p. 13), 'and those of no ordinary magnitude.'—'*We*'—viz. his reverend subordinates, to whom this Charge was preached: for, *Church* being, according to the convenience of the person and the moment incessantly used, sometimes in one, sometimes in another of two opposite senses, viz. for the designation of one or other, sometimes even of both, of two opposite classes, viz. the rulers and the ruled—the plunderers and the plundered—hence it is, that, to every one who wishes to know what it is he means, interpretation is, on each occasion, necessary.

Exposed to dangers these rulers?—O yes:—so far as concerns the possession of their *rule*, strange it would be, if it were otherwise.—'Those dangers of no ordinary magnitude?'—not quite so clear, what the extraordinary magnitude may be which is thus hinted at.

The Church in danger?—O yes: if by *the Church* be meant either its system, in regard to doctrine, or its system, in regard to discipline, its

---

[1] An echo of Matthew 7: 16.

APPENDIX, NO. I.

system which gives a man from 20*l.* to 20,000*l.* a year[1] for professing to believe what he does not believe, and turns him out to starve for confessing himself to believe what he does believe.—Constituted as it is, without danger it never can be, until it is without existence.

The *cause*—the *cause* of the danger—about this alone, between one eye and another, if they be in any degree observant ones, can there be any difference?

'The opposite extremes of defect, or excess of religious belief and feeling,' (says his Lordship thereupon) 'prevail among us, in a variety of modifications and degrees, to an alarming extent. The partizans of these several errors,' (continues he), 'disjoined in all other respects, by discordancy of principle, sentiment, and ultimate views, are not the less disposed to unite in offensive alliance against the object of their common aversion, the Established Church.'[2]

Thus far his Lordship. Still the old story—always the same portion of truth—always the same portion of fiction—always the same inconsistency.

The Established Church the object of common aversion, to the partizans, of all the opinions, thus, as of course, lumped together by the name of *'errors?'*—O yes: true enough:—and how should it be otherwise? A nuisance of any kind, how should it be *otherwise* than an object of aversion to any one to whom it is a nuisance?

Those to whom this Church is an object of this common aversion, disposed to *unite* in offensive alliance against it?—In this may be seen the fiction, and *that* not only a stale, but even a self-refuted calumny.

Self-refuted? Yes, and in this same paragraph. Discordant one with another are all these different classes—discordant, as he himself observes, and as they necessarily are, or they would not be what they are, and are thus stated as being—'discordant in principle, sentiment, and ultimate views.'

Such being the discordance—and *that* a discordance which has had place from the beginning, from the time when they respectively began to be what they are,—and which, in the nature of the case, is destined to continue to the end, i.e. to the time when they shall respectively cease to be in existence,—where then is the *union*, or so much as the disposition to an *union?* where is the *alliance?*

In this fiction of an *union* and *alliance* may be seen the exemplification of one of those vulgar fallacies,—expressive tokens of a bad cause, and of the consciousness of its badness,—those fallacies, in

---

[1] i.e. from the minimum salary of a Curate to the income of the Archbishop of Canterbury: see p. 273 & n. above and p. 409 n. below respectively.
[2] [Howley], *Charge delivered to the Clergy of the Diocese of London*, p. 13.

the use of which these hirelings never tire: a fallacy, having for its object the kindling by a false imputation a flame of resentment,—and thus, besides affording a gratification to the dissocial appetite, creating a diversion, by which men's minds may be led astray from the original and proper object of consideration.

By *alliance* and *union*, the design is that the reader shall understand *concert*, and from this *concert* infer *sympathy:* and that thus these several persuasions,—amongst which the differences and disagreement is as wide as possible,—these several persuasions, and the men by whom they are respectively entertained, shall be confounded under one common and undiscriminating term of reproach and odium.

Atheists, Deists, Unitarian Christians, Independents, Baptists, Quakers, Presbyterians, Wesleyan Methodists, Whitfieldian Methodists,[1] Catholics, not to mention any others,—by all these several names, so many persuasions in respect of religious matters are expressed—all of them as decidedly distinct from one another, as is that of the regular members of the Established Church from any of them. Of all these, to the multitude of Church of Englandists, of whom the majority of the population are still composed, (not to speak of Jews, who, unbelievers as they are, are on these occasions out of the question,—and, as they write not much, either to attack the establishment or to defend themselves, are comparatively unobnoxious),[2] the *Atheists* are the most obnoxious, next to them the *Deists*, next to them the Unitarian Christians,—next to them, if not before them, the *Catholics*. Now, of this fallacy, and the misrepresentation couched in it, what is the object? To cause, as far as possible, all these different persuasions to be taken for one and the same, in the hope that, whatsoever *aversion* may, in any mind, happen to be entertained towards the *least* obnoxious, may, by the blessing of God, be thus refined and improved, into the *hatred* entertained towards the *most* obnoxious:—that the *Unitarian* Christian, for example, may be taken for a *Deist* in disguise, and as such hated;—that so the *Unitarian Christian* and *the Deist*, thus tied together, may be taken, both of them, for *Atheists* in disguise, and as such execrated.

'*Union? alliance?*' to what imaginable end should any such junction take place?—To give any increased effect to 'the common aversion towards the Established Church?'—to the production of any such effect, no such union or alliance is necessary: by no such union or alliance could any such effect be promoted.

---

[1] Followers respectively of John Wesley (1703–91) and George Whitefield (1714–70), evangelist.
[2] 1818 'inobnoxious'. The text follows the 'Errata'.

APPENDIX, NO. I.

In the whole system may be seen,—and if not seen already, shall, by every eye that has courage to endure the sight, be, ere long, seen,—one vast mass of corruption, of the existence of which, no small number of its own rulers have, of late days, shewn themselves in no inconsiderable degree sensible. From the whole together, there exists not that human being in the kingdom (to go no further) that is not, in a more or less direct way, a sufferer. Of those mischiefs, which, to his own observation and feelings, happen to be most obvious, this or that individual,—to which soever of those persuasions it may happen to him to belong,—gives, upon occasion, indication of this or that exemplification. But, to perform this useful office, what need has any such person, or any one person whatsoever, to join with any other? Assuredly with no one person of any one of all these persuasions, or any persuasion, has the matter of these pages been concerted.

So much for fictions:—now for realities.

Of these dangers,—the reality of which is not meant to be here contested, but on the contrary is meant to be subscribed to,—real sources, three in number, may without much difficulty be descried:—three sources, of no one of which any indication could indeed be reasonably expected from any such Right Reverend hand:—viz. the doctrine and discipline of the Church itself;—the view taken of it by the thinking part of those who have not yet separated from it;—and the mode of defence employed—and therein the sort of design manifested—the temper displayed, and the sort of language used—by its hired and worldlily-interested advocates.

[1.] Three distinguishable enough sources of danger; but the grand source of sources, the source from which all others flow—the source not only of danger but of destruction—sure and inevitable destruction—may be seen in itself—in its very essence: in its own original sin, for which no means of redemption were, or were meant to be, or are or ever can be, provided.[1]

1. In its *formularies*, of which this *Catechism*—the most extended in its application, and the most operative in its effect, is a specimen:—a specimen, to which all its other formularies are well matched.

2. In its 39 Articles, to which,—with an ever unpunishable, and even unprovable, mendacity,—all, who in that Church engage to apply and enforce the precepts and instructions of Jesus, are so needlessly and uselessly, without the shadow of a warrant from

---

[1] An allusion to the doctrine of Original Sin which holds that man has been in a state of sin since the Fall of Adam and Eve, recounted in Genesis 3.

Jesus, at once hired and forced, to profess an assent, recorded under their hands.[a]

3. In its setting up, in defiance of the most express commands of that Jesus whom it professes to serve[1]—in its setting up one class, of these pretended teachers of that religion, to exercise dominion over the rest, and at the same time to take, in the seat of temporal legislation that ruling part, for which their utter and universal incompetence is effectually manifested, by a prudential and almost universal silence: while the needlessness of any such anti-christian practice, is all along demonstrated by the example of that equally Established Church,[2] in which all useful regulations are as strictly

[a] Increasing to any required amount the quantity of real guilt, in the hope of doing away the appearance of it, with asseverations as vehement as were ever employed by Saint Peter to obtain credence for his denials of his Master,[3] they will protest and protest, that there is not, in the whole mass of that substitute to the Bible, one word they do not believe. Of the credence due to any such declaration, would you form a judgment? Carry your eye over the mass, if your patience will serve you so far—note with *Paley* the *multitude*—not forgetting the *extent*—of the propositions contained in it[4]—note the essential and utterly indispellable obscurity of the subjects themselves—note the obscurity of the manner in which they are handled—note the position and character of the age in which it was put together—learn and note the characters of the individuals under whom, and the individuals by whom, it was put together—note the vengeance, denounced and executed, upon all, by whom any such *love*, as that which, in his Lordship's eyes, (p. 16), is so *hateful*—the *'love rather to question than learn'*—was presumed to be manifested in relation to it—note the looseness, attached to the style of that generation, and even of so many less immature generations by which it has been succeeded—join with *Paley* in pronouncing unmendacious assent to be in such circumstances impossible; and then, instead of recommending the abolition of the obligation to declare assent, join, if you can, with that defender of fashionable Christianity, and preacher of loose morality and corrupt government, in recommending perseverance in the prescription and practice of the mendacity,—on condition of substituting in idea, to the declaration subscribed to, a totally different one, invented by himself, and cloathed in vague generalities for the purpose.[5]

---

[1] See pp. 268–70 above.   [2] i.e. the Church of Scotland.
[3] See p. 20 n. above.
[4] William Paley (1743–1805), theologian and philosopher, in *The Principles of Moral and Political Philosophy* (first published 1785), 12th edn., 2 vols., London, 1799, Bk. III, Pt. I, Ch. 22, i. 219, having stated that the Thirty-nine Articles were imposed by the legislature of 13 Eliz. I, c. 12, comments: 'They who contend, that nothing less can justify subscription to the thirty-nine articles, than the actual belief of each and every separate proposition contained in them, must suppose, that the legislature expected the consent of ten thousand men, and that in perpetual succession, not to one controverted proposition, but to many hundreds. It is difficult to conceive how this could be expected by any, who observed the incurable diversity of human opinion upon all subjects short of demonstration.'
[5] Paley goes on to state (ibid. 219–20) that the intention of the legislature of 13 Eliz. I, c. 12, was 'to exclude from offices in the church, 1. All abettors of popery. 2. Anabaptists, who were at that time a powerful party on the continent. 3. The Puritans, who were hostile to an episcopal constitution; and in general the members of such leading sects or foreign establishments as

APPENDIX, NO. I.

and universally obeyed and conformed to, as they are manifestly trampled upon by the *Rome-begotten* and *Rome-resembling* Church.

4. In the plain proof, which, to every eye that could endure to look at it, has all along been afforded—that, of the object looked to in the continuance given, along with as much as could, with worldly profit, be preserved of the Romish *doctrine*, to as much as could, with like profit, be preserved of the Romish discipline, neither the present nor the future well-being of *the subject many* ever formed a part: nor any thing, so much as the service, thereby rendered in appearance to the Monarchy, in reality to the private, personal, exclusive, and thereby sinister interest of the Monarch of that day,[1] in conjunction with his terror-struck and ever prostrate and prostitute instruments—the other members of the *unseen* and invisible, but not less severely felt, corporation of the *ruling few.*—Afforded? and by what?—By all the particulars, by which the discipline of the Church of England is distinguished from that which is common to all non-established Churches,—particulars, by which, even among established Churches, it is, with few exceptions, not less disadvantageously distinguished from the Church of Scotland:—afforded—1. by the monstrous *inequality* of the allotted salaries; (as if, upon being made an Archbishop, a man's stomach grew some hundred times as large as that of a Priest),—2. by the abundance of *sinecure salaries*, allotted where there exists not so much as the pretence of service,—3. by the multitude of *Pluralities*, for no one of which can so much as the shadow of a justification be pleaded, on any other supposition than that the same person is constantly existing and serving at the same moment in divers distant places,—4. by the establishment of so vast a mass of *remuneration*, in a state of utter *independency on service,*— undeniable as it is, that it is only in so far as it is dependent on service, that service can reasonably be looked for as the fruit of it:— abominations all of them unknown not only in all *Non-established Churches*, but in the equally *Established* Church on the other side of the Tweed.

5. In the proof afforded—that,—under a system of unvarying and everlasting formularies, the matter of which is, in respect of the task of utterance, divided between a functionary called a *Parish Minister* and a functionary called a *Parish Clerk,*—every penny in the way of *pay*, over and above that which suffices to engage the service of the lowest-paid Clerk, has from first to last been worse than simply

---

threatened to overthrow our own'. A person should not subscribe, continues Paley, if he 'finds himself comprehended within these descriptions', and unless he was 'convinced' that he was 'truly and substantially satisfying the intention of the legislator'.

[1] i.e. Henry VIII.

thrown away;—and that, by the *taxes*, imposed to supply the matter of this profusion, *that* oppression has been produced, the continuance of which is a scandal to the age, and that popular odium, which, in so far as it is pointed against the persons of *individuals*, who neither have it in their power to contribute to the remedying the abuse, nor take upon themselves to defend it, is misapplied and unjust,—but which, in so far as directed against *the system*, can never be sufficiently strenuous, so long as any particle of the mischief continues in existence.

6. In the mode, in which these pretended instructors are *fastened* upon the people who are supposed to be instructed by them, and *that* upon such terms as afford no relief in the case of the supposed instructor's becoming, or being from the first, what in half the parishes of the kingdom he always is, a nullity, or what in so many of them he is—a nuisance. The *money*, which, on pretence of the instruction, is exacted, the sole real object of regard; and that a *marketable* one:—human beings—the souls, in whose instance the difference between eternal felicity and eternal torment is supposed to depend upon the choice,—not having, so much as in appearance, any the least part in it, nor being so much as thought of, or even pretended to be thought of. The money, if not always the *sole*, always the *main* object: the *duty* or *service* (for by the courtesy of England[1] such it is called) for which it is given, at the utmost but an *accessory:*—an accessory,—and *that*, by all parties, regarded and spoken of, in the character of an incumbrance. Of the direct *ratio* of the quantity of *pay*, of the inverse *ratio* of the quantity of *service*, is composed the known and universally acknowledged measure of value in *a benefice:* meaning of that inferior sort, which is here in question:—a benefice, of which it is the hard lot to be incumbered— in name and appearance at least—with the care and charge of the troublesome and worthless articles, called *Souls*.[a]

---

[a] In the Scottish Church, for the most part, true it is that this one incongruity has place.[2] But—such, in that Church, is the organization of the judicial branch of the

---

[1] In law, the Courtesy or Curtesy of England was the custom of permitting a man whose wife had given birth to a live child to enjoy a widower's rights for his lifetime over any lands his wife brought to the marriage: see Blackstone, *Commentaries on the Laws of England*, ii. 126–8. Bentham, however, seems here to have a more generic meaning in mind.

[2] The traditional mode of appointing parish clergy in the Church of Scotland had been through patronage, frequently that of the local laird. This system had been abolished in 1649, restored in 1662, but abolished again in 1690 (*Acts of the Parliaments of Scotland*: Act 53, 19 July 1690, ix. 196–7). It was superseded by a system of nomination by parish elders and heritors (local property owners), with the final decision being made by the Presbytery within whose bounds the parish lay. This system was in turn abolished, and that of lay patronage restored, by the Church Patronage (Scotland) Act of 1712 (10 Ann., c. 12). The issue remained a contentious one throughout the rest of the eighteenth century, and for much of the nineteenth.

APPENDIX, NO. I.

*Seats sold like cattle at a fair—Seats—*or as, to strengthen the phrase, it is so frequently said—*constituents,* meaning their *suffrages*—formed, on a well-known occasion, to a quondam Westminster Scholar, at[1] that time a Representative of the University of Oxford, the subject of a declamation, in the character of *Speaker of the House of Commons:*[2] as if corruption were the more mischievous for being open and notorious. What, were such a *thesis* given to him, would this same orator find to say of *souls*—immortal souls—sold after the same similitude? For, souls—are they not as truly sold by Messrs. *Skinner and Dyke,*[3] as ever constituents were, or were meant

Ecclesiastical establishment,[4] as to render it plainly impracticable for any Minister who is unfit for the office to continue in it, and therefore as plainly not worth his while to enter into it: and, forasmuch as, where the faculty of choosing the instructor is shared amongst all who share in the benefit of the instruction, the possibility of unfitness on the one part is not excluded, and that of adverse dissention on the other part is let in, the mischief, whatever under that Church it may be, which stands attached to the case where the choice is in the hands of a single person, receives *some* compensation from the exclusion thereby put upon such dissention, and from those services (viz. superintendance of Schools, and of Poors' Funds)[5] which have no place in a Non-Established Church, a most ample one,—thence it is that, protected by custom and not heavily condemned by experience, the incongruity continues without any considerable complaint. But, under Church of Englandism, the mischief displays itself in all its force: it has neither compensation nor palliative.[6]

---

[1] 1818 'Scholar, then at'. The text follows the 'Errata'.

[2] See the remark made by Charles Abbot, a pupil at Westminster School 1763–75, MP for Oxford University 1806–17, and Speaker of the House of Commons 1802–17, during the debate on Curwen's Bill on 1 June 1809, reported in *Parliamentary Debates* (1809) xiv. 838: 'unless we now proceed to brand and stigmatize [the sale of seats] by a prohibitory Law, I am firmly persuaded that even before the short remnant of this Session is concluded, we shall see that Seats in this House are advertised for sale by Public Auction: And we shall have brought a greater scandal upon Parliament and the Nation, than this country has ever known since Parliament have had an existence.'

[3] Auctioneers at 87 Aldersgate Street, London.

[4] See p. 304 n. below.

[5] The Scottish poor law had evolved from the 1570s through a series of Acts of Parliament and Proclamations of the Privy Council, which were consolidated and confirmed in 1698: see *Acts of the Parliament of Scotland*: Act 40, 1 September 1698, vol. x, 177–8. In landward (rural) parishes, relief was administered by the kirk sessions. It was based on a combination of voluntary contributions (often called church-door offerings) and assessments levied on heritors, tenants, and inhabitants: however, as the heritors frequently agreed an informal assessment among themselves, obviating the need for a legal assessment, the system in practice tended to be voluntary. A network of parish schools, overseen by the kirk sessions and financed by assessments, had developed in the seventeenth century under the terms of an act of the Privy Council of 1616 and subsequent statutes: see ibid.: Act 5, 28 June 1633, vol. v, 21–2; Act 171, 2 February 1646, vol. vi, part i, 554; and Act 26, 9 October 1696, vol. x, 63–4. Many charity schools also existed, generally funded by voluntary subscriptions, church collections, and mortifications (bequests).

[6] In England the clergy had, as such, no direct statutory duties in relation to the administration of poor relief or the provision of education.

to be, by Lord *Clancarty* to *Lord Castlereagh?*[1] and this, under and by virtue of the constitution, of a Church, of which the Right Honourable and learned Gentleman, and another Right Honourable and learned Oxonian, his colleague,[2] are in every way such zealous supporters, as well as listed advocates.

Not that, under this part of the Constitution, there appears any clear reason for supposing that, upon the whole, in consequence of this sort of arrangement, souls are, in any the smallest degree, worse served, than they would be if no such thing were ever in existence. But why? only because where *descent* has such strong motives for choosing ill, and next to none for choosing well, *purchase* or chance will not choose worse. To form a true judgment of the mischief, ask of *a Methodist*, of *a Baptist*, of a *Unitarian*, of any other of the '*guilty*' sort of persons called '*Schismatics*,' (p. 1), what would be *his* feelings, were the *pulpit* of *his* Meeting to become an object of sale, as a Church-of-England pulpit is; and, if any person, weak enough to become a purchaser, could ever be found, how many of the seats beneath it would have occupants?

Upon the *Lay* part of the *Official Establishment* (*Parliament* included) corruption is continually charged, and too surely not without cause. But, were it as corrupt, as by those whose complaints against it are loudest, it is said to be, it would be purity itself, in comparison of the *Ecclesiastical*. Where would Buonaparte have been at this moment, if, like half the beneficed Clergy,—half the army, half the navy, half the officers of the revenue had been regularly paid for doing nothing?—It is only in the *religious* part of the Establishment, that neglect of duty—wilful, constant, predetermined neglect of duty—and with it obtainment of money on false pretences—is, by authority of the legislature, and of that Constitution, which, on these and so many other such accounts, can never be enough lauded,—sanctioned and established. That, for which, if done upon a small scale, and without a gown upon his back, a man would be condemned to hard labour on board the *Hulks*,—that same fraud, wearing on his back a gown, in which for that sole purpose he has clothed himself, he practises—not only without danger, but without shame.

---

[1] Richard Le Poer Trench (1767–1837), styled Viscount Dunlo (I) 1803–5, who succeeded as second Earl of Clancarty (I) in 1805, and was created Baron Trench in 1815 and Viscount Clancarty in 1823, when MP for Galway County 1798–1800 voted in 1799 against the proposed Union with Britain, but was then persuaded by Robert Stewart (1769–1822), second Marquess of Londonderry (I), styled Viscount Castlereagh 1796–1821, at that time Chief Secretary to the Lord Lieutenant of Ireland 1798–1801, later Foreign Secretary 1812–22, to support the Union. In return, Trench's father was created Viscount Dunlo (I) in 1801 and Earl of Clancarty (I) in 1803.

[2] Perhaps Nicholas Vansittart, who attended Christ Church College, Oxford, and graduated BA in 1787, MA in 1791, and received the degree of Doctor of Civil Law on 16 June 1814.

APPENDIX, NO. I.

Polluted by imaginary blood, swallowed at an imaginary altar, a layman,—ere he can be admitted to serve in the character of a public functionary, in this or that line of non-ecclesiastical duty,—is required by law to make, upon that same altar, a sacrifice of his sincerity to the Moloch of the Church of England.[1] But, besides that, in sacrificing his cock to *Æsculapius, Socrates*[2] did not declare his belief concerning the number of persons of which *Æsculapius* was composed,—the sacrifice which, under the dominion of former blindness, *law* was forced to require, a mixture of fear and shame keeps *government* from exacting: and thus, for a great part, the Non-Ecclesiastical part of the establishment remains uncontaminated by a pollution, from which the Ecclesiastical part cannot, without agony, behold it free.

To that part of the Laity,—to which, by the harvest it yields, *misrule* in all its shapes is, in some way or other, rendered a source of profit, and thence an object of proportionable affection—*reform*, in all its shapes, an object, though not of *'contempt,'* of *'horror,'* equal to the utmost which it has been or can be the endeavour of his Lordship to inspire,[3]—what is it that renders the Ecclesiastical branch of the establishment an object of so much inward affection and outward reverence?—What? but that in *that* part of the Establishment, they behold *sanctified*, and by sanctification protected, abuses so much beyond any, of the establishment of which, in their own branch, they durst suffer themselves to entertain so much as a ray of hope.—*Sinecures, Pluralities, Sale* or *Grant* of *Reversions*—Pay out of all proportion with service—pay without any service—pay without so much as pretence of service—factitious dignity, without merit and without use—shares in the sovereignty, without so much as the pretence of independence—all protected not only from reformation but reproach:—all these abominations not only *justified* but *sanctified*.

The Ecclesiastical Establishment—including the Bench of Bishops in the Upper House of Parliament—is necessary to the existence of the Constitution. In this proposition we behold a fundamental axiom or postulate. Obedience, passive and active, to

---

[1] The Corporation Act of 1661 (13 Car. II, Stat. II, c. 1) required all members of municipal corporations to affirm that they had received communion according to the rites of the Church of England within the year preceding their election. The Test Act of 1673 (25 Car. II, c. 2) required all holders of offices, civil or military, under the Crown, to receive communion according to the rites of the Church of England, and to deny the doctrine of transubstantiation. For Moloch see p. 93 n. above.

[2] After drinking the poison hemlock in 399 BC, Socrates asked his friend Crito to sacrifice a cock to Asclepius, the Greek god of healing: see Plato, *Phaedo*, 66.

[3] See p. 262 n. above.

the will of the Monarch, as signified or not signified by the Minister,—or, in default of signification, as guessed at by observations taken of his countenance or of the other signs of the times—obedience on the one part, without so much as trouble of command on the other—is the universal and incontestably constant habit of that holy Bench. Obsequiousness, thus constant and universal, is the fruit and conclusive evidence of equally constant corruption: obsequiousness to corruptive influence on the one part, exertion of it on the other. Therefore constant corruption is a vital and indispensable part of the Constitution of this country. In the series of these propositions behold the argument, so congenial to the understandings, and so dear to the hearts, of the parties to the *Grand Alliance:* the alliance discovered by Warburton between *Church and State.*[a]

In the confirmation given in England to the Romish system of Episcopacy, what was the end? the end, not only pursued, but declared to be in view? Was it the establishment of *Religion?*—of the religion of that Jesus, by whom all inequality among the teachers of his religion was so pointedly and repeatedly forbidden?[1]—No; but the establishing of *Monarchy:* of that form of government, to the establishment of which the sacrifice thus made of the religion of Jesus was, by the Royal adage, *No Bishop no King,*[2] declared to be found necessary.—Declared—and with what truth? In Scotland is George less effectually King than in England? Yet still has the cry of '*No Bishop no King'* been reckoned, deemed, and taken—and still will it continue to be deemed and taken—a sufficient warrant for this rebellion against the King of Heaven. Reckoned? and by whom?—by

[a] Some thirty years ago, or thereabouts, was published by *Dr. Watson*, then and still *Bishop of Llandaff,* a pamphlet, in the form of *a letter, to the Archbishop of Canterbury,* in which, in the character of a specific for this disease, abolition of *Translations* is recommended: meaning Translations from less opulent to more opulent *Bishopricks.*[3]—With about as fair a promise, might abolition of Translations from Homer and Virgil have been recommended. The remedy might have some effect, if no Bishop had either family or friend,—or any mode of being served or gratified, by Monarch or Minister, other than by a better Bishoprick.

[1] See pp. 268–70 above.

[2] The response given by James I to the demand made by the Puritans for reform of the episcopacy at the Hampton Court Conference held from 14 to 18 January 1604: see David Hume, *The History of England from the Invasion of Julius Caesar to The Revolution in 1688* (first published 1754–62), 6 vols., Indianapolis, 1983, v. 12.

[3] Richard Watson (1737–1816), Bishop of Llandaff from 1782, advocated the redistribution of income from richer to poorer sees on each occasion a richer one became vacant, thus removing the temptation for Bishops to seek translation to wealthier sees: see *A Letter to His Grace the Archbishop of Canterbury,* London, 1783. Bentham's copy of the work, the third edition of 1816, reprinted from the *Pamphleteer,* vol. viii, no. xvi (1816) 573–94, is at British Library shelf-mark C.T. 66 (1).

APPENDIX, NO. I.

the most holy among *the Saints:* and among them by *non-receivers* of the *Holy Ghost*, not less than by *receivers*.

'By their fruits ye shall know them.'[1] With a pencil, furnished by holy writ, are thus pourtrayed the characters of the two Churches.

Turn to those documents, by which the fruits of the two Ecclesiastical Establishments in Great Britain are displayed in so plain a shape, and in such lively colours. *Criminal offences* in a year—in *England*, so many; in *Scotland*, so many. Allowance made for difference of population. Under CHURCH OF ENGLANDISM more than *ten times as many* as under CHURCH OF SCOTLANDISM![a]

With all its vices, even CATHOLICISM yields to CHURCH OF ENGLANDISM, in its crime-producing virtue. Even in IRELAND,—where four-fifths of the population are under the CHURCH OF ROME,—the *Criminal Calendar* is not much more loaded, than it is in ENGLAND under the CHURCH OF ENGLAND.[2]

Translating, for his Lordship's accommodation, the simple truth into that language, in which his Lordship's eloquence is most at home,—the leprosy of the *Mother* has cleaved to the *Daughter*,[3] and in this latter generation, greater is the number of the *spots* in which it has displayed itself.

To complete the picture of the *Daughter*,—for the present at least, another picture may suffice.

Who is the *good shepherd?*—need it be answered?—need it be so much as asked?—He who can say—(John, x. 14.) 'I know my sheep, and am known of mine.'

---

[a] H. of Commons Returns of *Committals*, No. 45, 12 Feb. 1812: No. 84, 26 Feb. 1812: No. [246],[4] 22 May, 1812.[5]

---

[1] Matthew 7: 20.

[2] In fact, the proportion of the 15,865 persons committed to trial in Ireland from 1805 to 1810 to the total population of Ireland, estimated at this time to be 6,000,000, was, apparently, slightly smaller than that for England, where 28,608 persons had been committed to trial from 1805 to 1810 out of a population of 10,106,780, as given by the census of 1811.

The census taken in Ireland on 1 May 1813 produced inaccurate and unreliable results. According to calculations made in William Shaw Mason, *A Statistical Account, or Parochial Survey of Ireland, drawn up from the Communications of the Clergy*, 3 vols., Dublin, 1814–19, iii. pp. xxi, xlix, the population in 1813 was just under 6,000,000, and the ratio of Roman Catholic to Protestant was $2\frac{3}{4}$ to 1. William Shaw Mason (1774–1853), statistician and bibliographer, was Secretary to the Commissioners for Public Records in Ireland from 1810.

[3] An echo of II Kings 5: 27. [4] 1818 '240'.

[5] i.e. No. 45, 'Scotland. A Return of Persons, Male and Female, Committed, in the years 1805, 1806, 1807, 1808, 1809, & 1810, To the several Gaols in Scotland', 12 February 1812; No. 84, 'A return of the number of Persons, charged with Criminal Offences, Who were committed to the different Gaols in England and Wales, for trial . . . in the Years 1805,—1806,—1807,—1808,—1809,—1810,—& 1811', 26 February 1812; and No. 246, 'A statement of the number of Offenders committed to the several gaols in Ireland, for trial . . . in the years 1805, 1806, 1807, 1808, 1809, & 1810', 22 May 1812: see *Commons Sessional Papers* (1812) x. 217–32, 233–6, and v. 1005–6 respectively. At p. 93 above, Bentham calculates the ratio as more than eleven to one.

CHURCH-OF-ENGLANDISM

In the *Statistical View of Scotland*, published by *Sir John Sinclair*,—of every parish in that kingdom, in number near 900, a description is given by its Minister, and he a constantly *resident* one.[1] Of late, even of the parishes of *Ireland*, a like account has been begun to be published, and that an *official* or *demi-official* one.[2] In the case of England,—with that challenge, now for more than five-and-twenty years past staring every body in the face,—the utter impracticability of obtaining any such account,—notwithstanding the unavoidable disgrace and reproach, attendant on such impotence,—stands demonstrated. As to the *cause*, it may be fully seen in those House of Commons *Returns*,—on the subject of *Non-Residence*, and other subjects connected with it,—for which the public is indebted to the zeal and industry of *the Earl of Harrowby*.[3]—What a man knows nothing of, he cannot give an account of.

Such[4] as above is the *first* of the above-mentioned sources, of the *danger*,—which may be seen, and has been seen, hanging over the head of the *Church of England:* meaning the opulence, the power, the dignities, and the idleness—of the set of men who, under the notion of their inculcating the precepts of Jesus, are thus employed in trampling on them.

2. Of[5] these causes the *second* may be seen in the sentiments and affections, which, in the breasts of the members of the Established

---

[1] Sir John Sinclair (1754–1835), *The Statistical Account of Scotland Drawn up from the communications of the ministers of the different parishes*, 21 vols., Edinburgh, 1791–9, in fact contains 938 statistical accounts, which refer to 879 parishes (see xx. 555–79, and Appendix H, p. lxxxiii). Bentham took the figure of 'near 900' parishes from a table published in the *Edinburgh Almanack, and Imperial Register, for 1812*, Edinburgh, [1811], pp. 137–55, and abstracted at p. 481 n. below.

[2] While the work was not an official publication, Mason acknowledged the encouragement and patronage of Sir Robert Peel (1788–1850), statesman, Chief Secretary to the Lord Lieutenant of Ireland 1812–18, Home Secretary 1822–7, 1828–30, leader of the administration 1834–5, 1841–6: see William Shaw Mason, *A Statistical Account, or Parochial Survey of Ireland*, i. pp. v–vi.

[3] In *Substance of the Speech of the Earl of Harrowby*, pp. 41–4, Harrowby inserted the following four abstracts from the six that had been ordered by and presented to the House of Lords in May and July 1812 (see *Lords Journals*, xlviii. 844, 849, 1019, 1024–5): 1. 'Abstract of the Number of Resident and Licensed Curates, with the Amount of the Salaries of Curacies, according to the Diocesan Returns for the Year 1810'; 2. 'An Abstract of the Extract from the "Copies of Diocesan Returns for the Year ending 25th December 1810," ... distinguishing each Diocese, and stating the Number of Benefices under 150*l*. per Annum'; 3. 'Abstract of the Totals stated under each Head in the Returns made by the Archbishops and Bishops of every Parish, containing a Population of 1,000 and upwards'; 4. 'An Abstract of the "Copies of the Diocesan Returns for the year ending 25th December 1810," ... distinguishing the Number of Incumbents who are resident or doing their Duty, from the Number of those who are neither Resident nor doing their Duty'. Abstracts 1, 3, and 4 were subsequently printed in *Commons Sessional Papers* (1812), x. 151–4, 155–6, 157–8 respectively. For further discussion of these and other returns on non-residence see pp. 361–3 n., 389–90 n. below.

[4] 1818 '2. Such'. The enumeration is redundant.

[5] 1818 'Of'. The text follows the 'Errata'.

APPENDIX, NO. I.

Church itself,—meaning the *subject many*, who, in these their self-appointed, or worse than self-appointed instructors, are, instead of *servants*, in[1] direct contradiction to, and open contempt of, the ordinances of the God worshipped alike by all of them,[2] made to find *rulers*,—are entertained[3] in relation to those same rulers.

Whatsoever causes of aversion, actual or legitimate, attach upon the situation of *Non-Church of Englandists*, of all persuasions as above,—these, when compared with those causes of aversion, which attach upon such of the *subject many*, whose indigenous weakness, or adoptive weakness, or sinister interest, or interest-begotten prejudice, or indolence, or indifference, continue them upon[4] the list of members of that same holy Church, will be seen to be much more considerable. True it is, that to those strangers, as well as to these members, the same extortion, with the exception of such *surplice fees* as are avoidable,[5] is inevitably extended.[6] True it is, that from those strangers, as well as from Church of Englandists, is extracted their proportion of the annually extorted 100,000*l.*, added to Church benefices,[7]—without any the smallest security, exacted for the rendering of that service, on pretence of which, worthless as it is, the dole is given: and without any the smallest benefit in any shape, other than that which would accrue from the distribution of it among an equal number of helpless mendicants.—But, by those[8] strangers, from the Church-of-England Ministers, or their lordly rulers, no service, in any shape is looked for:—to those strangers, no service, in any shape, is ever by those same functionaries promised or professed to be rendered:—by those strangers, no *expectation* of good, in any shape, from that quarter, being entertained,—no *disappointment* is experienced: whereas, with here and there a

---

[1] 1818 '*servants*, made, in'. The text follows the 'Errata'.
[2] See, again, pp. 268–70 above.
[3] 1818 '*rulers*, entertained'. The text follows the 'Errata'.
[4] 1818 'continue upon'. The text follows the 'Errata'.
[5] i.e. fees paid to the officiating clergy for baptism, marriage, churching of women, and burial.
[6] Tithes, one tenth of agricultural and garden produce, were due, either in kind or as commuted money payments, from all those resident in a parish. Tithes were payable to the rector of the parish, or, in places where there was a vicarage, divided between rector (who might be a layman) and vicar.
[7] Queen Anne's Bounty, established in 1704 by 2 & 3 Ann., c. 11, ordered that the sum of money paid on taking possession of an ecclesiastical benefice, and the recurring annual charge, previously paid to the Crown under the First Fruits and Tenths Act of 1534 (26 Hen. VIII, c. 3), should thenceforth be paid to the Governors of Queen Anne's Bounty, who were to use the money to augment the maintenance of poor clergy. Additionally, commencing in 1809, Parliament made eleven annual grants of £100,000 to aid the work of the Governors. For further discussion of taxation and the Church see pp. 518–25 below.
[8] 1818 'these'. The text follows the 'Errata'.

casual exception, by the Lay Members of the Church, whatsoever expectation of good is expected, has disappointment for its consequence.

3. Remains, as and for the *third* cause or source of *danger* to this same holy Church, that which consists in the style and character of those its *defences*, of which this *Charge* may be set at the head.

To '*proficiency in Christian instruction*'—meaning always to the sort of proficiency of which the interpretation has already been given—viz. to that proficiency which (p. 23) consists in the belief that '*instructions and exhortations*,' delivered to the people by men standing in subjection to the author of this *Charge*, are the Oracles of God—true, indeed, it may well be, that '*humble docility*,'—that '*prostration of the understanding and the will*,'—(pp. 16 and 23)—yes, the humblest docility—yes, the most abject prostration—are '*indispensable*.'[1]

Sooner or later, however, what may peradventure happen, is—that, of a posture thus awkward, the understandings of men may, in a proportion more or less considerable, grow tired. If, by any cause whatsoever, a change so salutary should ever be accomplished,—then it is, that the spectacle thus exhibited—the open pulling off the mask—the unpalliated insult,—thus offered, to all whose docility may dispose them to meet it and prostrate themselves before it,—cannot surely be altogether without its influence.

By imputing any such *Romanism* to any Church of Englandist at present dead or living, what disservice could any *enemy* of this Church have done to it, comparable to that which this protector and *friend* is doing to it?—Imputed by an enemy, it would have been pronounced mere calumny, and vehemently disavowed. Here it is in black and white: and,—by one whose attachment to the system can no more be doubted of, than the power and opulence he draws from it,—avowed, and over and over again proclaimed.

To such *real* sources of *danger*, coupled with such a *professed defence*,—would it be of any use—would it afford any material addition in the way of instruction—to add the mention, of any of those other danger-increasing defences, with which, at present, by the inscrutable decrees of the Almighty, the Church is encompassed?—of a *Dr. Burgess, Bishop of St. David's*, who,—emulating the anatomist of antiquity, by whom the difficulty experienced, in finding living human bodies for dissection, was lamented as a proof of the *hardness of the times*,[2]—expresses a regret, the sincerity of which

---

[1] See pp. 37 n. and 261 n. above.
[2] Bentham's source may have been William Eden, *Principles of Penal Law*, London, 1771, pp. 71–2, where a passage entitled 'Of the Disposal of the dead Body of the Criminal'

APPENDIX, NO. I.

cannot be doubted of, at the thoughts of having it no longer in his power, to consign to *forfeiture of livelihood*, with *etceteras*,—followed, in case of constancy, by a three years' imprisonment,—those, whose optics fail them, in their endeavours to behold in the one God as many *God-persons* as he does.[a]

Would it be of use to add the mention?—Oh yes—to save labour, take the printed letter—of[1] a *Dr. Kipling, Dean of Peterborough*, who—to make a Priest of the Church of Rome[2] hold his pen and tongue, and thus promote (as it seems to him) the interest of the Church of England, assures him in black and white, that if he will not, by a certain day, prove what, according to this his statement, is unprovable, he will prosecute him, and have him punished, for saying of the *Church of England* that *it* or *she* is a new one: punished, for saying of the *daughter* that she is *younger* than the *mother* from whom she sprung, and whom, in the worst of her features, to the best of her power, she has ever strived to imitate.[b]

---

[a] See the Bishop's late miscellaneous pamphlet, (title not at this moment accessible) in which he performs one more '*Demonstration of the Trinity*,'—together with other achievements.[3]

[b] The following is a paragraph copied from the Monthly Magazine for July, 1815, p. 580.[4] In no subsequent number has any place been found, in which the document has been pronounced a forgery.

'The following letter was sent lately by Dr. Kipling, Dean of Peterborough, to the Rev. John Lingard, a Roman Catholic Priest:'—

Rev. Sir,

In your strictures on Professor Marsh's Comparative View,[5] occur these words

---

reproduces the following quotation: *Ubi, præ iniquitate temporum, vivos homines dissecare non licet*, i.e. 'When, because of the hardness of the times, it is not lawful to dissect living men'. Eden cites his source as Aulus Cornelius Celsus (*fl.* 14–37), in the proem to *De Medicina*. These precise words do not, however, appear there, and are probably a paraphrase. Celsus does refer to the practice of Herophilus of Chalcedon (*c.* 330–260 BC) and Erasistratus of Ceos (*c.* 315–*c.* 240 BC) of performing dissection on living criminals. See Celsus, *De Medicina*, Prooemium, 23: *Herophilum et Erasistratum, qui nocentes homines a regibus ex carcere acceptos vivos inciderint*, i.e. 'Herophilus and Erasistratus who laid open living criminals whom they received out of prison from kings'.

[1] 1818 'the composition—of'. The text follows the 'Errata'.
[2] For Kipling and Lingard see p. 49 n. above.
[3] See Thomas Burgess, *A Brief Memorial on the Repeal of So much of the Statute 9. and 10. William III. as relates to Persons denying the Doctrine of the Holy Trinity: addressed to all who believe the Christian Religion to be a True Religion, and who are desirous of maintaining the religious institutions of their ancestors. To which is prefixed, A Demonstration of the Three Great Truths of Christianity, together with Specimens of Unitarian Rejection of Scripture and of all Antiquity*, London, 1814, esp. pp. 19–23. The Doctrine of the Trinity Act of 1813 (53 Geo. III, c. 160) relieved Unitarians from the penalties which Bentham mentions and which were stipulated in the Blasphemy Act of 1698 (9 & 10 Wm. III, c. 32).
[4] *Monthly Magazine*, vol. xxxix, no. 270 (1 July 1815), 580.
[5] John Lingard, *Strictures on Dr. Marsh's Comparative View of the Churches of England and Rome*, London 1815, was a critique of Herbert Marsh, *A Comparative View of the Churches of*

'Conventional symbol of union, (p. 14). Union of unbelievers, as a regular and ostensible party, (p. 14). Faction again embodied, (p. 15). Infidelity in the garb of Christianity, (p. 16). Machinations of this enemy, (p. 16). Joint machinations of infidels and sectaries,' (p. 18).[1]—O horrible conspiracy! O miscreant enemies!—Among the *Howleys*, the *Burgesses*, the *Kiplings*, and their *etcœteras*—among all these unnatural enemies of their common Mother—the dear and 'kind Mother' which gave them birth—has there been any such concert?—Enquire—Yea, let *him* enquire, who has much time and little work, for it.—Without any the smallest need of conspiracy or concert,—by the same interest, afflicted by the same congenial blindness,—similar wounds may, with the same pious and kind intentions, be, at any time, and in any numbers inflicted.

But that,[2] among these two Right Reverend Defenders of the

once, 'new Church of England,'[3] and these oftener, 'the modern Church of England;'[4] that for both these expressions you are amenable to a court of justice, I infer from this extract, 'seditious words in derogation of the established Religion, are indictable as tending to a breach of the peace; as where a person said, *Your religion is a new religion; preaching is but prating, and prayer once a day is more edifying.*' Hawk. 7.[5] Besides, the Church by law established in this country is so inseparably interwoven with the British Constitution, that whatever is calumny upon the former must be calumny upon the latter. If however, you shall assure me, in the course of a few days, that within a reasonable time you will publish a vindication of this defamatory language, I will defer to prosecute you, not only until sufficient time has been granted you for that purpose, but also till an opportunity has been allowed the public to peruse my reply to it. By a vindication is here meant, complete proof of this position, that the structure of the Church of England, and the materials of which it is composed, are new and modern. Should it appear to be the general opinion, when the reasonings of us both shall have been maturely considered, that your vindication is complete, I will then make a recantation, and cease to be a member of the established Church. If by the generality of our readers it shall be thought defective, you will be summoned to answer for your offensive demeanour in Westminster Hall. It may justly be presumed, that before you ventured to issue forth your detractions, arguments to establish the position above mentioned, had been prepared with sedulity, and judiciously arranged. I therefore shall add, that by 'a reasonable time' you must understand a few months only.

T. KIPLING.

Peterborough, March 23, 1815.

England and Rome, Cambridge, 1814. Marsh (1757–1839), biblical scholar, was Bishop of Llandaff 1816–19 and Bishop of Peterborough from 1819.

[1] The quotations are taken from [Howley], *Charge delivered to the Clergy of the Diocese of London*.
[2] 1818 'inflicted. That'. The text follows the 'Errata', which inserts the paragraph break.
[3] See Lingard, *Strictures on Dr Marsh's Comparative View*, p. 56.
[4] See ibid., pp. 1, 34, 54.
[5] See William Hawkins, *A Treatise of the Pleas of the Crown*, Ch. 6, §6, i. 7.

APPENDIX, NO. I.

faith[1] and so forth, their Right Reverend Colleagues, and their Most Reverend Superiors,—in the arrangement, by means of which this same *Catechism* has already been to so great an extent, and is intended to be to the greatest possible extent, forced into the mouths, and if possible into the heads and hearts, of the rising generation,—not only co-operation but concert has had place, is proved by the so often published *Advertisement*,[2] garnished and sanctified by their respective signatures.

In this their advertisement, for money to buy and breed proselytes with,—*excellent* is the title conferred by these same Bishops, on their Church.—*Excellent?* in what *sense?* in what *eyes?*—

In certain senses—in certain eyes—the excellence of it will be found to be above dispute.

'*Our Church?*'—wherein shall we behold our Church?—1. In our *Archbishops* and *Bishops*, and their Spiritual Proxies the *Archdeacons?*—2. In our *Deans, Canons, Prebendaries*, and *Precentors?*—3. In the Parish *Ministers* and *Parish Clerks*—joint readers of the substance of this Catechism, with the tenor or substance of Creeds, Articles, and other Formularies, and all and singular other the established *substitutes* to God's word, thereunto appertaining,—the said Ministers, whether Rectors, Vicars, or Curates, being by the courtesy of England[3] styled Ministers of the said God's word?—4. In the '*humbly docile*' and '*prostrate*' laity, by whom all these living receptacles of the Holy Ghost are fed and pampered?—5. In the system of *Ordinances* and *powers*,—established for the extraction of the matter with which they are so pampered,—and for the securing that semblance of service which serves as the pretence for the extraction of that precious matter?—6. In the *edifices* in which this semblance of service is performed?

I. As to our *Archbishops* and our *Bishops*. That in their own and one another's *excellent eyes*, these holy persons neither do nor ever will cease to be sufficiently *excellent*,—never will the most 'malicious' of all those enemies, with whom his Lordship has been wrestling in spirit, have the 'malice' to dispute.

Correspondently excellent will the whole species be, in the eyes of those inferior dignitaries, and moreover of such other of the

---

[1] Defender of the Faith was a title conferred in 1521 on Henry VIII by Leo X, Pope from 1513 to 1521, in recognition of the treatise *Assertio Septem Sacramentorum adversus Martinum Lutherum*, in which Henry VIII defended the doctrine of the seven sacraments against the ideas of early Protestant reformers. The title was recognized by Parliament in 1544 (35 Hen. VIII, c. 3), since when it has been adopted by all English monarchs.

[2] For the 'Advertisement' see pp. 110–14 n. above.

[3] See p. 286 n. above.

Ministers of God's word, dumb and speaking, whose *hope* is to become partakers of that same excellence.

In like manner will the excellence of each individual *Dives*[1] be an object of *faith*, in the eyes of all those, to whom any of the crumbs expected to fall from his holy table are an object of *hope*.

Correspondently *excellent* will each individual of those Most and Right Reverend and holy persons be—in the eyes of the Monarch and the Minister, who from their *Hope*, christened by the name of *Gratitude*, receives, in the House of Lords, the fruits of that *'humble docility'* and *'prostration of understanding and will,'* which they would not have had to *preach*, if they had not learnt to *practise*.

II. *Deans, Canons, and Prebends!*—These receptacles of the matter of consecrated opulence,—and of that *dignity* which is the fruit of that holy opulence, and which, when hard pressed, takes refuge from reproach under the name of *decency*,[2]—how can *these*—to any eye avoid exhibiting in a variety of shapes, the image of *excellence?*—*they*, to each of whom belongs an *excellent stall*, in which he might any or every afternoon take an *excellent nap*,—and peradventure would, were it not that *excellent wine*, and the hope of *excellent good fortune*, in the *excellent cardroom* of some *excellent watering place*,—or some other similar occupation,—or the absence of all occupation,—is still more *excellent:* and, forasmuch as *smoothness* and *easiness*—the qualities, which by his Lordship, as hath been seen,[3] are held up to the view of amateurs, as constituting the *summum bonum* of a *Church-of-England Ministry*—are in this instance, in their persons, and for their benefit, smoothed up to the highest imaginable pitch of *excellence*.

III. *Parish Ministers*—be they *Rectors, Vicars*, or *Curates*—so they are but Church-of-England[4] *Priests*, in what eyes can they fail to display the lustre of *excellence*—they, the least of whom is *Reverend*—*they*, who at no time are more full of *wine*, than (witness their own testimony as above)[5] they are at all times of the *Holy Ghost*—*they*, who share with the Almighty in the prerogative of *pardon*[6]—that prerogative, to the assumption of which by *Jesus*, the *Pharisees* could not be reconciled by all his miracles[7]—that *prerogative*, in comparison of

---

[1] See p. 328 & n. below.   [2] See p. 86 & n. above.
[3] See p. 272 above.
[4] 1818 'but as Church-of-England'. The text follows the 'Errata'.
[5] See p. 279 & n. above.
[6] See the prayers for the 'Absolution or Remission of sins', pronounced by the priest at Morning Prayer, Evening Prayer, Holy Communion, and the Visitation of the Sick, in the *Book of Common Prayer*.
[7] For the conflict between Jesus and the Pharisees see, for instance, Matthew 12: 1–45, 15: 1–20; Mark 7: 1–13.

APPENDIX, NO. I.

which the correspondent prerogative of the earthly Monarch is but as one to infinity[1]—*they*, to whose forbearance *Satan* is indebted for whatsoever portion of the population of his kingdom is received by him from the Church of England—they, who sharing indeed with the profane laity the art and act of *eating* God, share only with one another and their Roman and Lutheran colleagues, the art and act of *making* him:—*they* who, while such of them as are not altogether equal to *Deans, Canons,* and *Prebends,* as touching their *repose,* are—all of them—equal to their respective *Parish Clerks* as touching their duties,—and who, while by God's *justice* they are, some of them, rendered inferior to those same Parish Clerks as touching their *benefices,* are—others of them—by God's *bounty,* rendered, as touching *their* benefices, superior to *Bishops;*—exhibiting in their glory, like the stars of heaven, such *excellent variety,* in what eyes can they, or any of them, fail or cease to display the lustre of *excellence?*

IV. *The Laity?*—who,—in the *eyes* of Archbishops, Bishops, and Archdeacons,—Deans, Canons, Prebends, and Precentors, possessors of benefices of all sorts and sizes,—and moreover in the eyes of the *patrons* of the same,—are so *excellently* well taught, as well as quite sufficiently well fed,—in what *eyes,* other than their own, can they ever fail or cease—all of them except the said *patrons*—to be *excellently* well fleeced and squeezed, and no less *excellently* gulled and duped.

V. *The Church?*—the system of *ordinances* and *powers* sanctified by that holy name—the purposes for which *these* were so plainly established are now in view:—was ever any system of ordinances and powers more excellently well adapted to its purposes?—Of the Church of Rome, by the excess of that zeal, with which it laboured to shine forth before men, a portion of the *excellence* has been sunk behind a cloud: of the Church of England the *excellence* shines as yet (but how much longer will it shine?) with undiminished lustre. The Church of England—so long however as she continues to be what she is, in what eyes can the attribute of *excellence* ever cease to be her due,—due to her *excellent* prudence,—or, at any rate, to her *excellent* good fortune?

VI. The *Edifices?*—in so far as she, now—it, is[2] composed of *edifices*—those edifices of stone, or brick and mortar—those compounds of stone or brick and mortar raised aloft—and containing,

---

[1] For the Royal prerogative of pardon see Blackstone, *Commentaries on the Laws of England,* iv. 391–5.
[2] 1818 'The *Edifices?*—It is, in so far as it is'. The text follows the 'Errata'.

CHURCH-OF-ENGLANDISM

each of them, *an altar*—each of them, not less truly than the temple of *Jupiter Ammon, a seat of sacrifice*[1]—all of them by *Episcopal consecration*, many of them by their *antiquity*, and some of them by their *vastness* and *magnificence*, fitted to be receptacles and sources of *sanctity*—by that mixture of *magnificence* and *antiquity*, of which, in the eye of the architect, *venerableness* is composed,—do they not serve *excellently* well, for the infusion of *that* element of sanctity into the breasts of those *holy* men, to whom they are respectively the *seats of empire*, and for bearing witness thereby to the authenticity of that *charter*, by which the keys of heaven and hell are vested in those *excellent* and holy hands?

Of the proof thus afforded, the probative force, is it not in the compound ratio of the *length*, the *breadth*, the *height*, the *splendor*, and the *antiquity* of the edifice? Always understood, that the style must be of that sort which is called *Gothic:* for, of true sanctity what proof can be afforded, by the Pagan gaiety of the architecture of Greece and Rome?

In the same ratio rises the degree of *excellence*, with which they serve in the character of *objects*, to travellers on the high roads, and to Country Gentlemen in the parks and gardens of this land: especially in the eyes of such of them as, in the character of patrons, are partakers of the sanctity thus composed.

In a correspondent ratio rises the degree of *excellence*, with which,—in virtue of their capacity of undergoing *ruin, destruction, downfall, desolation*, and *subversion*,—they serve, by those bonds of affection, which are to be found upon their altars, to bind the hearts of the laity to the *Church* in all its senses,—to call forth the ties of foreboding sympathy,—and to raise the flame of holy indignation, against all persons, by whom any such profanation is *compassed*, or, otherwise than for the prevention of it, *imagined.*[2]

Of the features of *excellence*, perceptible in the face and frame of this *excellent* Church, behold here the catalogue. His *Lordship of London*, by whom *understandings and wills are prostrated*[3]—his *Lordship of Lincoln*, by whom *Calvinism* is *annihilated*[4]—his *Lordship*

---

[1] The temple of Amun or Ammon, the chief Egyptian deity, identified with both the Greek Zeus and the Roman Jupiter, was located at Siwa in the Libyan desert.

[2] Under the Treason Act of 1351 (25 Ed. III, Stat. 5, c. 2), treason was defined as 'When a man doth compass or imagine the death of our Lord the King, or our Lady his Queen, or of their eldest son and heir.'   [3] See p. 37 n. above.

[4] George Pretyman Tomline (1750–1827), Bishop of Lincoln 1787–1820, was the author of *A Refutation of Calvinism; in which, the doctrines of original sin, grace, regeneration, justification, and universal redemption, are explained, and the peculiar tenets maintained by Calvin upon these points are proved to be contrary to scripture, to the writings of the antient fathers of the Christian Church, and to the public formularies of the Church of England*, London, 1811.

APPENDIX, NO. I.

of St. David's, by whom the *Trinity* is *demonstrated*[1]—the *Very Reverend the Dean*, in whose eyes the antiquity of a fictitious entity receives so satisfactory a proof from the threat of indictment in the King's Bench[2]—know they of any other *item* in the catalogue of the Church's *excellences?*—Know they of any other precise, distinct, intelligible feature or property in it, susceptible of the name of *excellence?*—if so, let them declare it.

Now—and now perhaps for the first time, it depends upon themselves, and each of them, to have a distinct view of the *danger* with which all this *excellence* is menaced:—this danger, let them avert it. Yea by all means in their power let them encounter it, saving always the *ultima ratio regum et sacerdotum*—the last and favourite *logic* of priests as well as kings[3]—the *logic*, by which all deficiencies in other logic are supplied—the *logic*, by which any one thing as well as any other is proved—the *logic*, with which opulence confutes poverty, foolishness wisdom, orthodoxy heterodoxy, and improbity virtue— the *logic*, with which *Daniel Isaac Eaton* was so recently and so effectually confuted, and reduced to silence[4]—the *logic*, which is so much better suited than that of *Aristotle*[5] to their understanding as well as their taste—to wit, *information* or *indictment*, as aforesaid.

Speaking of the American war[6]—'Disapproving this civil war,' (says the Edinburgh Review for June, 1815, p. 176),[7] 'Lord Barrington, for four years supported it by his vote, and by his official co-operation. And this example is now recommended to the imitation of the British youth by a venerable Prelate (his brother the Bishop of Durham)[8] with the weight that belongs to his station and his age. . . .

'In the very worst times of Roman slavery,' (continues the Reviewer), 'the great historian (Tacitus)[9] has imagined a speech

---

[1] See pp. 294–5 above.   [2] See p. 295 & n. above.
[3] Louis XIV (1638–1715), King of France from 1643, had the words *ultima ratio regum* engraved on his cannons, while the cannons of Frederick the Great (1712–86), King of Prussia from 1740, were engraved *ultima ratio regis*.
[4] Daniel Isaac Eaton (bap. 1753, d. 1814), radical writer and publisher, having published Thomas Paine, *The Age of Reason. Part the Third*, London, 1811, was charged with publishing a blasphemous and profane libel against the Christian religion. The trial took place before the Court of King's Bench on 6 March 1812, whereupon Eaton was sentenced on 15 May 1812 to eighteen months in Newgate prison, and to stand in the pillory once within a month of the sentence. See further p. 309 below.
[5] Aristotle (384–322 BC), Greek philosopher.
[6] i.e. the American War of Independence 1776–83.
[7] See *Edinburgh Review*, vol. xxv, no. xlix (June 1815), 172–8, at 176–8, reviewing *The Political Life of William Wildman Viscount Barrington, compiled from original papers by his brother, Shute, Bishop of Durham*, London, 1814. The passages in parenthesis and the italics are Bentham's. William Wildman Barrington (1717–93), second Viscount Barrington, was Secretary at War 1755–61, 1765–78, Chancellor of the Exchequer 1761-2, and Treasurer of the Navy 1762–5.
[8] i.e. Shute Barrington.   [9] Cornelius Tacitus (*c.* 56–*c.* 118), Roman historian.

for one of the sycophants and accomplices of Sejanus,[1] which many readers have considered as an exaggeration of the base principles of that gang of miscreants.—*Non est nostrûm æstimare quem suprà cæteros, et quibus de causis, extollas. Tibi summum rerum judicium Dii dedêre: nobis obsequii gloria relicta est.*'[2] "It belongs not to us to sit in judgment on persons preferred by you, or on the causes of that preference. To you the Gods have given supreme power: to us is left the glory of obedience."

'If such maxims were confined to grossly profligate persons, they would[3] excite no surprise, and they would produce comparatively little evil. But the mischief of the case is, that they are the natural growth of a deceived conscience, in men otherwise moral, who have lived in courts, and who have long been accustomed to exercise authority. A strong tendency towards such principles is the necessary result of their situation; and they find their way into the conviction of many, who have the discretion not to publish them to the world, and who have not perhaps the boldness to avow them distinctly to their own minds. In this respect the cause of the people is more unfortunate than that of authority. The extravagances of demagogues are necessarily public. They are instantly spread through every part of a country. They are quoted from generation to generation, by all those whose vocation it is to render liberty odious or contemptible. It is otherwise with the equally extravagant opinions of courtiers and statesmen. They conceal their obnoxious singularities; and *it is very seldom that we catch so clear a glimpse of the interior of their minds, as in this volume, which shews us a man who, if consistent with himself, must have been a partizan of despotism;* though, during his whole life, he must have employed the language of the British constitution, and often extolled its transcendent excellency. The favourers of absolute monarchy, indeed, must generally *dissemble their opinions*. Those of a more popular government must seek to publish and to disseminate them. The latter, therefore, can never be more numerous than they seem. The former always are: and[4] it is extremely probable that those who incline towards regal despotism, and whose measures would terminate in its establishment, are more numerous in England than the partizans of a mere democratical government; as it is quite certain, that in all ordinary times, they are far more dangerous from their rank, their wealth, their talents, and their influence.'

---

[1] Lucius Aelius Sejanus (d. 31), Roman statesman, was denounced as a traitor by Tiberius (42 BC–AD 37), Roman Emperor from 14 AD, and executed.

[2] See Tacitus, *Annals*, VI. 8. The following translation appears to have been supplied by Bentham himself.

[3] *Edinburgh Review* 'could'.

[4] *Edinburgh Review* 'are so; and'.

APPENDIX, NO. I.

Taking credit, and not altogether without cause, for the sagacity which has brought to light the unwarily betrayed secret of the *veteran* votary of despotism, the Reviewer could never at that time have laid his hands on this Ecclesiastical Manifesto, in which, drunk with new promotion as with new wine, the newly-enthroned brandisher of the crosier,[1] throwing off not only all 'veils,' and 'masks,' and 'disguises,'[2] but even those coverings which common decency would have joined with common prudence in keeping on, stalks forth,—with his mind at the end of his fingers, *in puris naturalibus*,—the avowed instrument, of the most rampant despotism that words can describe, or heart conceive,—and, together with his own secrets, betrays those of the *Associated Bench*, of whose association the real and ultimate objects cannot now be dubious.

It assuredly cannot be, without turning the ear of disbelief, to whatsoever testimony this modern Sacheverel[3] has been pleased to deliver, concerning his own principles—his own feelings—his own wishes—his own endeavours,—if any other man can succeed in persuading himself, that any thing,—short of that system of *passive obedience* and *non-resistance*, which, till the *Revolution*[4] came, and for so long afterwards, formed the part of the solemnly proclaimed creed of that University[5] of which his Lordship is so worthy a

---

[1] William Howley had been consecrated Bishop of London on 10 October 1813.

[2] [Howley], *Charge delivered to the Clergy of the Diocese of London*, pp. 14–15: '[infidelity] first burst on the astonished world, betraying its native deformity through a thin veil of metaphysical subtleties'; 'the advocates of deistical tenets were completely unmasked'; 'their disrespectful reflections on the person and actions of their Saviour, are distinguished from real Unitarians, and betray the true secret of the flimsy disguise which they have assumed as a cover from the odium of avowed infidelity'.

[3] Henry Sacheverell (bap. 1674, d. 1724) achieved fame as an apologist for the High Church and Tory party when impeached for sedition by the Whig-dominated House of Commons on account of a sermon preached at St Paul's on 5 November 1709, in which he defended the doctrine of non-resistance and argued that the Church was in danger from the Whig ministry. Following a celebrated trial, he was pronounced guilty by the House of Lords on 20 March 1710, but the sentence merely suspending him from preaching for three years was regarded as a triumph for him and the Tory cause.

[4] i.e. the Glorious Revolution of 1688–9.

[5] Following the discovery of the Rye House Plot to kill Charles II, the Convocation of the University of Oxford promulgated a Decree on 21 July 1683 (*Judicium Decretum Universitatis Oxoniensis Latum in Convocatione habita Jul. 21. an. 1683. Contra quosdam Perniciosos Libros Propositiones Impias*), condemning the tenets and writings of Whigs, dissenters, and papists, and asserted their loyalty to the King and adherence to the doctrines of passive obedience and non-resistance. Condemned books were burned, and copies of the Decree displayed in the Colleges. The Decree was read in full at Sacheverell's trial at the request of Constantine Phipps, one of Sacheverell's defence counsel: see *The Tryal of Dr. Henry Sacheverell, Before the House of Peers, for High Crimes and Misdemeanors; upon an Impeachment by the Knights, Citizens and Burgesses in Parliament Assembled, in the Name of themselves, and of all the Commons of Great Britain: Begun in Westminster-Hall the 27th Day of February 1709/10, and from thence continued by several Adjournments until the 23d Day of March following*, London, 1710, pp. 235–8, published by order of the House of Lords.

member,[1]—would be capable of satisfying the holy zeal which flames in his Lordship's breast.—It is to the *Puritans*, mostly if not exclusively, that, by the acknowledgment of *David Hume*,— much as the philosopher hated those religionists, and in great measure for this very reason,—we stand indebted, for whatsoever of those things called *liberties* are still, in practice, left to us,[2] and for the advantage of having gold for a covering to the rods by which we are ruled. Even to *David Hume*, those *enthusiasts*—those *sectaries*— those *schismatics*—those *men of guilt*,—(for, according to the *present* as well as the *late Lord of London* (p. 1), all *schism* is guilt)[3]—were known by the *liberties* which they gained for us, and left to us:—to his Lordship they are known only by '*the troubles they excited:*' for, to his Lordship, and those who think and act with him, every breast which presumes (p. 16) to '*question*' what it should '*learn*,' to harbour any such '*guilt*' as that of '*schism*,' or so much as (p. 2) any '*opinion . . . . which, even by remote consequences, might unsettle the faith of the inexperienced*,' is a fit object of '*exposure*,' and a declared source of '*trouble.*'

The Puritans, *exciters* of troubles!—*exciters* only! as if, so far as they have had power, they have not been *composers* of troubles likewise!— as if it were not by the composing of those troubles, which to that end they contributed to the excitement of, (for how else could any thing good have been done?) that *in Scotland* they succeeded at length in establishing that system of Church Government,[4] which,—if the *absence* of all Church management, daubed with the untempered mortar of *temporal power*, be not still better,—will, the more it is looked into, be the more universally and clearly seen to want little indeed of being a model of perfection:—which, to the most useful and important—and those *really performed* duties—unknown to the Church of England,—such as *inspection of Schools* and *management of Poors' funds*,—adds the merit of self-purification, and the blessing of purity, from all the abuses, such as *Creeds, Unchangeable Formularies, Reading without thinking, Sinecures, Non-Residence, Pluralities, Surplice fees, Palaces*,—sanctified seats of princely opulence,

---

[1] Howley matriculated at New College, Oxford in 1783, graduated BA in 1787 and MA in 1791, and was Canon of Christ Church, Oxford 1804–9 and Regius Professor of Divinity 1809–13.

[2] See Hume, *History of England*, iv. 145–6.

[3] See p. 48 n. above.

[4] i.e. the hierarchy of courts which constituted the presbyterian system of the government of the Church of Scotland: the Kirk Session, the lowest court, consisting of the minister and elders of the parish; the Presbytery consisting of the minister and an elder from each Kirk Session within its bounds; the Synod consisting of all members of the Presbyteries within its province; and the General Assembly, the supreme court, consisting of members appointed by every Presbytery.

APPENDIX, NO. I.

close by the side of the abodes of destitute penury:—penury so destitute, that not so much as the shadow of an excuse could be found for the continuance of it, if the uselessness of the service thus equipped and remunerated had not superseded the need of all excuse for the neglect of it:—the system (I say) of that Church (for now I am come back to Scotland) which now, for more than a century has scorned to endure, within its bosom, a set of puppets,[1] invested each of them with a portion of the sovereignty, to no other purpose than that of giving, to a notoriously dependent assembly, a mendacious colour of independence, covering interested servility with the cloak of gratitude.

Such were the *Puritans*—those '*schismatics*'—those *men of 'guilt'*—those *exciters of troubles;*—such, *in both kingdoms*, the *object*,—and such *in Scotland* the *result*—of the *troubles* they excited:—such in England *then*, and alas! *still*, the *demand* for troubles; for troubles having *the like object*, and, by like favour of Almighty beneficence, *the like result*.

Yes: could a similar consummation be here secured, might not a moderate portion of some of those things, reprobated by this prostrator of understandings and wills, under the name of *troubles*,—might not some of these *troubles*, suited to the improved character of the times—*troubles*, if composed of reasoning alone, and without slaughtering,—be well employed? Let any one, to whom either pure religion, pure morals, or pure government is an object of affection, think and judge.

A *mask* forsooth—a mask necessary (so his Lordship, p. 14, would persuade us) for the 'adversaries' of his Church?

The *Quaker*, the *Baptist*, the *Methodist*, the *Independent*, the *Presbyterian*, the *Unitarian Christian*, the *Deist*, the *Atheist*—as if any of all these had any the smallest need of, or use for, any such thing as a *mask*, for bringing to view the *corruptions*, as above, by which the Church of England remains assimilated to the Church of Rome,—distinguished *above* all other established Churches, and *from* all non-established ones?

Still the same endeavour to cause men to be condemned for opinions not their own! The *Christian Unitarian*—what support can he look to give to his Christian opinions by Anti-Christian arguments?—the Atheist—what support can he look to give to his Atheistical opinions by Theistical arguments?—by what can either of them defend his own opinions, but by arguments corresponding and adapted to these same opinions?—On the subject of religion, each of these—unless the Atheist be an exception—has some

---

[1] i.e. Bishops. Presbyterianism had finally been established in Scotland in 1690.

opinions in common with every other. Is it a fraud in him to bring to view the reasons by which these his opinions[1] have been recommended to him?—is this a *fraud* in him, merely because, in minds that entertain other opinions not entertained by himself, these reasons may happen to stand approved?

The *Quaker*, the *Baptist*, the *Methodist*, the *Independent*, the *Presbyterian*, the *Unitarian Christian*, the *Deist*, the *Atheist*, the *Church-of-England layman*—all these,—but, above all, this layman—find, in the shapes just mentioned, oppressors, and as such adversaries, in the Church-of-England *Clergy*, headed by the Church-of-England *Hierarchy:*—yes: all these; but, for the causes already brought to view, most of all the great body of Church-of-Englandists.—Without any endeavour at relief, am I to submit for ever to oppression, for no other reason, than that if I were to obtain relief, it might be shared with me by this or that other man, who, though he *feels*, happens not to *think*, as I do?

A *mask* indeed!—The Church-of-England receiver of the Holy Ghost—be he Church-ruler—Minister—or consecrated idler—to him, and to him alone, can any such implement be of use:—and, on his part, constant and incontestable is the demand for it.[2]

The poisons, which it is the sure effect of that formulary, so far as it has any, to infuse—poisons to the *intellectual*, poisons to the *moral*, poisons to the *sensitive* part of man's frame,—these poisons—not to speak of the remainder of that set of lengthened bead-rolls, of which it forms a part—have here in part been brought to view. To preserve his Lordship, for example, from the awkwardness of being *seen to see* these fruits of Church-of-England doctrine and discipline, or of being forced to shut his eyes against them, to save himself from seeing them—to such purposes *a mask* might perhaps be not altogether without its use.

The Creeds—all of them at war with reason, with Scripture, and with one another;—the everlasting and lengthened bead-rolls, heard or not heard, between sleeping and waking, while they are mumbled over without thinking;—the *Sinecures*, the *Pluralities*, the *Non-Residences*, the *outrageously-paid Benefices*, the *fornication-compelling*, and *birth* and *death-embittering Surplice-fees;*—the *gorgeous opulence* by the side of the *useless pittance*, indiscriminately attached in the shape of purchase money, to the same useless, if not unrendered, service;—the *intestine war*, so anxiously perpetuated in the hearts of the respective parishes, by the perpetuation of a mode of payment,

---

[1] 1818 'which his own opinions'. The text follows the 'Errata'.
[2] [Howley], *Charge to the Clergy of the Diocese of London*, 1812, p. 14: 'In the issue of the controversies which followed, the advocates of deistical tenets were completely unmasked.'

APPENDIX, NO. I.

established by the Church of Rome, when the *barbarism* combined with the *superstition* of the times, in giving to the most oppressive of taxes the character of an unavoidable one;[1]—Yes, for the countenance, which can look in the face abuses such as these, with a determination to deny either the existence or the mischievousness of them—for a countenance of such a complexion *a mask* may well be necessary!

Yes—necessary for any course of warfare in which abuses such as these are undertaken to be defended, will be not only a *mask*, or rather a *head-piece*,—but the whole armour of those *fallacies*, which Aristotle never dreamt of,[2] and which by the ingenuity of succeeding Sophists have been invented: fallacies, of which he who thinks it worth his while, may in the works of Court-and-Church-of-England polemics, and in particular in this *Charge*, find as many exemplifications as he need desire.

As for trade, so for religion,—different as they are in other respects, whatsoever may have been the case in the days of primæval barbarism,—the best thing that a government could *now* do, would be not to meddle with it, always excepted the purifying it from whatsoever portions of the *matter of wealth, power, or dignity*, in the shape of the *matter of corruption*, superstition has ever daubed it with. Revenue forces government to meddle with trade: but (witness America else), neither revenue nor any thing else forces government to meddle with religion.[3] The perfection of all Church management is the absence of all Church government. Witness all the sects: witness every sectary in the kingdom. In what sect, in the breast of what sectary, is religion a matter of indifference? In what sect does a man declare himself to believe any thing he does not believe? In what sect does a Minister extort money for doing nothing? In what sect is the service, taken by itself, spoken of as a hardship,—as matter of complaint,—and by the pay, and that alone, rendered just endurable? In what sect is a Minister paid for his service, the value of a penny more than by those to whom it is rendered it is thought worth? In what sect does the Minister insult the indigent, by the display of an opulence, wrung out of the bowels of indigence? Where is the sect that furnishes puppets, to act the part of free agents, for the benefit of the Monarch, in the farce of legislation? Where is the sect that furnishes inhabitants to the *Jails*, to the *Hulks*, or to the *Penal*

---

[1] i.e. tithes.
[2] For the fallacies which Aristotle did identify see *On Sophistical Refutations*, III–v, 165b–168a.
[3] The First Amendment to the Constitution of the United States (1791) provided that 'Congress shall make no law respecting an establishment of religion, or prohibiting the free exercise thereof'.

CHURCH-OF-ENGLANDISM

Colonies? Where would Penal Colonies, Hulks, or Jails, find inhabitants, but for the Church of England?

When to each of these several questions an answer has been given,—go then, ye hypocrites, take trumpet in hand, sound forth the guilt of schism, and command all men to fall prostrate before your Golden Image,[1] and its unrivalled *'excellence.'*

Before this paper is brought to a close, one thing yet remains to be presented to the consideration of those whom it may concern.

By this Bishop of London, the Clergy of his diocese are, in this his address to them, spoken of as so many persons whose 'instructions' ought with 'humble docility,' and 'prostration of the understanding and will,' to be received as the oracles of God:[2] and this without condition or limitation annext, such as that of their being conformable to the holy scriptures.

But this same Right Reverend person,—not only in this his address, exhibits himself as one having authority, in matters of doctrine and discipline, over these same spiritual persons and every [one] of them,—and prepared (p. 4) for 'asserting the rights of that authority against factious opposition or contumacious negligence,'—but, in point of law, as well as in fact, is actually so, beyond dispute or doubt, and knows himself so to be.

Hereupon comes a question or two, the title of which to consideration will not, it is believed, be found altogether easy to dispute.

1. Whether a Church-of-England Bishop,—who thus publicly and deliberately gives himself out as superior to those whose instructions are *the Oracles of God*, and to whom he thereby,—in the language noted by Jesus (John, x. 34) for its extravagance, when applied to men,—says, *'Ye are Gods,'* ought to be suffered, on any terms, or at any rate without public recantation, to retain either that purely ecclesiastical situation, the authority of which he has thus abused, or his temporal seat on the Bishop's Bench in the Upper House of the Legislature?

2. Whether, from such a quarter, such discourse be altogether consistent with mental sanity? whether the imputation of insanity be not the most lenient interpretation that can be put upon it? and, let sanity or insanity be the state of mind ascribed to him, whether by the text—*'his Bishoprick let another take'*[3]—a course proper to be pursued be not pointed out?

In what light—especially now that the matter has in this public manner been held up to notice—if those, to whom belongs the power

---

[1] For the setting up of the Golden Image see Daniel 3: 1–7.
[2] See p. 37 n. above.
[3] Acts 1: 20.

APPENDIX, NO. I.

of correcting such enormities, should leave them uncorrected,—and thus, by connivance, render themselves participators in those same enormities,—in what light will they merit to be regarded by the other members of the Church of England? and,—if by the whole body of the members of that Church such connivance should be left unremonstrated against and uncomplained of,—in what light will they merit, and in what light will they be likely, to be regarded, by all other Christian Churches—established and non-established?

Daniel Isaac Eaton was imprisoned and set in the pillory t'other day,—for no other offence, than the publication of a book, in which the title of Jesus to the character of God, and that of the Holy Scriptures to the title of true histories, was denied and argued against.[1] But, neither did *Daniel Isaac Eaton*, nor the writer whose work he was thus punished for publishing, ever give himself out as *superior to the Oracles of God:* nor was either of them furnished with a seat in the Upper House of the legislature, with a 10,000*l*. a year salary,[2] or any salary at all, in reward for, and in condition, and in consideration of his undertaking to do his utmost to cause the Holy Scriptures, and them alone, to be received as the Oracles of God. By *Daniel Isaac Eaton* no breach of trust was committed: his sin, whatever else it was, was the sin of ignorance.

The ribaldry of *Daniel Isaac Eaton* passed but for what it was worth: for, in his situation there was not any thing that could enable it, or tend to cause it, to pass for any thing more. *Daniel Isaac Eaton* was not of the number of those, who hold themselves as successors, and sole legitimate successors, to the distinguished few, of whom Jesus said, '*Ye are the salt of the earth.*'[3] *Daniel Isaac Eaton* was not, at that time, like them, '*set upon a hill,*'[4]—or at any time after, upon any typical hill, other than the hill of always intended disgrace, but not unfrequently eventual honour,—*the pillory*.

Meantime, were it only that the Court and its '*prostrate*' Ministry may be known for what *they are*, this their new-raised favourite cannot be too perfectly or extensively known for what *he is*.

It is no secret, in how high a degree, any impression produced by those arbitrarily designative characters of which spoken and written discourse is composed, is capable of being strengthened and deepened by those naturally imitative and representative ones, which it is the work of the pencil or the graver to delineate.

In a moderate compass, and without breach of unity, in one picture

---

[1] See p. 301 & n. above.
[2] According to the table reproduced at pp. 409–12 n. below, the income of the Bishop of London was £9,000 per annum.
[3] Matthew 5: 13. [4] Matthew 5: 14.

might be exhibited a view of the two *opposite religions*—the religion of *Jesus*, and the religion of the *Church of England*, as delineated by this its Bishop.

In the *back* ground, on one hand might stand *Jesus*, washing the feet of his disciples, as related in John, xiii. 1 to 17. In the fore ground, *on the right hand*, one group in *Charity-School Uniform*, in the prescribed attitude of *prostration*,—his Lordship, in his *palace*, seated on his *throne*, showering down, with dignified negligence, upon these little ones, his benedictions:—on the *left hand*, in costumes and postures indicative of various occupations,—but most of them with Bibles in their hands, or under their arms, and all of them with serious and reflecting countenances, another group,—his said Lordship spitting down upon them, through the magnificently Gothic palace window, labels inscribed with the words '*contempt and horror.*'

Thus much,—being,—with[1] the exception of the Scriptural, and surely not unappropriate, part of the subject,—nothing more than his Lordship's own discourse, expressed by the pencil instead of the pen,—it has[2] in it nothing more than what might be *painted* by the grave pencil of *Mr. West*:[3]—and, for the window of some Cathedral, eternized in glass by *Mr. Pearson*.[4]

An addition and exposition, to any such effect as the following,—*Hogarth* being, alas! no more[5]—could scarcely be added from any other than the *Holland* School:[6] and would require the *graver*, for giving expression to it.

At his Lordship's elbow, the Spirit,—who is so much better known to his Lordship than to the writer of these pages,—busy in supplying the Episcopal writing-table with '*laws of interpretation.*' On the remaining side of the back ground, *Dives*,—in that costume of his which has been taken for an *uniform* by the *Episcopal Bench*—viz. his *purple* and his fine *linen;*[7]—his eyes directed to his Lordship,—the

---

[1] 1818 'much,—it being,—with'. The text follows the 'Errata'.

[2] 1818 'pen,—has'. The text follows the 'Errata'.

[3] Benjamin West (1738–1820), American painter who settled in London in 1763, was noted for his large history paintings.

[4] James Pearson (*c.* 1740–1838), Irish glass painter, produced a range of religious and secular works on glass, some of which can still be seen in the windows of Brasenose College Chapel, Oxford, St Botolph, Aldersgate, London, and Salisbury Cathedral.

[5] William Hogarth (1697–1764), English painter and engraver, most noted for his satirical commentaries on contemporary life.

[6] The Dutch School of art, associated with the rise of the new Dutch republic in the seventeenth century, was characterized by portraits, landscapes, scenes of Dutch life, and still life. Amongst its most notable artists were Hendrick Avercamp (1585–1634), Pieter de Hooch (1629–84), Jacob van Ruisdael (*c.* 1628–82), Jan Steen (1626–79), and Johannes Vermeer (1632–75).

[7] See p. 270 above.

APPENDIX, NO. I.

finger of one hand pointing to his own parched tongue, on which the demand for water remains still unsatisfied,—his other hand pointing to a cushion of asbestos velvet, left vacant for the Right Reverend sitting-part, by his side.

APPENDIX, No. II.

LORD's SUPPER—NOT DESIGNED BY JESUS FOR GENERAL IMITATION—ITS UTTER UNFITNESS FOR THAT PURPOSE.

IN the body of this work, the ceremony commonly called *The Lord's Supper* came necessarily under review.[1] On that occasion its unfitness to be employed in that character was touched upon. Incidental and cursory was the consideration then given to it, and the mention accordingly then made of it. After a more thorough consideration—on the one hand, so convincing appeared the proof of its being completely destitute of all warrant from *Scripture*,—on the other hand, so deplorably *mischievous* in respect of the application made of it,—so great consequently the benefit, if at length the religion of Jesus could be cleared of so morbid an excrescence,—that in this volume a few more pages could not be refused—to the hope, however faint, of contributing something towards the rendering to the interests of religion, morality, and general happiness, so salutary a service.

On this occasion,—that nothing may be wanting, either to the solidity or to the clearness of the ground on which the opinion of the sincere reader is called for,—all that relates to that other scene, viz. the *feet-washing* scene, having for illustration been already brought under his eye (viz. in pages 242, 243),—what belongs to the *bread-eating* and *wine-drinking* scene will now be found in like manner brought to view.[a] And here, before he proceeds any further, he may

[a] Account of what passed at the Lord's Supper, as delivered by three of the four Evangelists:—John, silent.

Luke xxii.	Matt. xxvi.	Mark xiv.
7. Then came the day of unleavened bread, when the passover must be killed.	17. Now the first day of the feast of unleavened bread, the disciples came to Jesus, saying unto him, Where wilt thou that we prepare	12. And the first day of unleavened bread, when they killed the passover, his disciples said unto him, Where wilt thou that we go
8. And he sent Peter and John, saying, Go, and		

[1] See pp. 241–52 above.

APPENDIX, NO. II.

perhaps find a convenience in bestowing a second glance on what has been said on the two subjects in the place just mentioned: viz. in pages from 241 to 243 inclusive.

prepare us the passover that we may eat.

9. And they said unto him, Where wilt thou that we prepare?
10. And he said unto them, Behold, when ye are entered into the city, there shall a man meet you, bearing a pitcher of water; follow him into the house, where he entereth in.
11. And ye shall say unto the good man of the house, The master saith unto thee, Where is the guest chamber, where I shall eat the passover with my disciples?
12. And he shall shew you a large upper room furnished: there make ready.
13. And they went, and found as he had said unto them: and they made ready the passover.
14. And when the hour was come, he sat down, and the twelve Apostles with him.
15. And he said unto them, With desire, I have desired to eat this passover with you before I suffer:
16. For I say unto you, I will not any more eat thereof, until it be fulfilled in the kingdom of God.
17. And he took the cup, and gave thanks, and said, Take this, and divide it among yourselves:

for thee to eat the passover?

18. And he said, Go into the city to such a man, and say unto him; The Master saith, My time is at hand, I will keep the passover at thy house with my disciples.
19. And the disciples did as Jesus had appointed them, and they made ready the passover.
20. Now when the even was come, he sat down with the twelve.
26. And as they were eating, Jesus took bread and blessed it, and brake it, and gave it to the disciples, and said, Take, eat; this is my body.
27. And he took the cup, and gave thanks, and gave it to them, saying, Drink ye all of it;
28. For this is my blood of the New Testament, which is shed for many for the remission of sins.
29. But I say unto you, I will not drink henceforth of the fruit of the vine, until that day when I drink it new with you in my Father's kingdom.

and prepare, that thou mayest eat the passover?

13. And he sendeth forth two of his disciples, and saith unto them, Go ye into the city, and there shall meet you a man bearing a pitcher of water: follow him.
14. And wheresoever he shall go in, say ye to the good man of the house, The Master saith, Where is the guest chamber, where I shall eat the passover with my disciples?
15. And he will shew you a large upper room, furnished and prepared: there make ready for us.
16. And his disciples went forth and came into the city; and found as he had said unto them: and they made ready the passover.
17. And in the evening he cometh with the twelve.
22. And as they did eat, Jesus took bread and blessed and brake it, and gave to them, and said, Take, eat; this is my body.
23. And he took the cup, and when he had given thanks, he gave it unto them, and they all drank of it.
24. And he said unto them, This is my blood of the New Testament, which is shed for many.

First, then, as to the applicability of the bread-eating and wine-drinking scene to the condition of mankind at large.

The sort of commemoration, suggested by Jesus to the Apostles, was it intended—could it have been intended—to be practised by any persons other than those belonging to the company then and there present? *Answer.* Not it indeed: under the circumstances of the case it could not have been. In favour of the affirmative, in no one of the three historics is so much as a particle of evidence to be found. On the opposite side may be seen the most convincing evidence. From this last meeting—for such it was expected to be—all but the select twelve had by a necessary anxiety been excluded: from all but *them* it had been concealed: and even among them there was one too many.[1] The crisis was at hand. The fatal order had been issued, the endeavour was—on the one part to effect, on the other to avoid, the execution of it. Of this last endeavour the accomplishment had already become hopeless. The plan of the traitor had been settled.

In the mind of Jesus had any such design been entertained, as that of instituting a ceremony to be performed by his followers in all places and all times, would he in his address to these twelve have been so completely silent as to any such intention? Would he have abstained as he did from[2] giving any the slightest intimation of any such wish, as that by any one person in the company, communication of the matter should be made to any one person out of it?

When, by the same Jesus, those lessons of real and practical importance were delivered, the observance of which lies equally

18. For I say unto you, I will not drink of the fruit of the vine until the kingdom of God shall come. 19. And he took bread, and gave thanks, and brake it, and gave unto them, saying, This is my body, which is given for you: this do in remembrance of me. 20. Likewise also the cup after supper, saying, This cup is the New Testament in my blood, which is shed for you.	25. Verily I say unto you, I will drink no more of the fruit of the vine, until that day that I drink it new in the kingdom of God.

---

[1] i.e. Judas Iscariot, who would betray Jesus.
[2] 1818 'abstained from'. The text follows the 'Errata'.

within the competence of all mankind, did he on that occasion shut himself up with his confidential servants in a private chamber?—On the contrary, it was on an eminence that on that occasion he lifted up his voice: an eminence on which he was seen, and from which he was heard, by thousands.[1]

When it was really his intention, that those things, which in the first instance he had communicated to the select few, should by them be communicated to all, did he not say so?—did he not express himself in the most explicit terms? *'Go ye therefore and teach all nations:'* these, as reported in Matthew (xxviii. 19.)—*'Go ye into all the world, and preach the Gospel to every creature'* ... these, as reported by Mark (xvi. 15.) on that same occasion, were his words.

To *'all nations,'*—supposing it his intention (though he said no such thing) that it should be communicated to all nations,—would the exhibition of the Supper scene, any more than of the Church-of-England imitation of it, have been possible?—Not it indeed.

On that sad and deeply affecting occasion,—even to the select company then present, what is it then that was in reality commanded? *Remembrance*, and nothing more.—*Commanded*, shall we say? Say rather *solicited*. Sympathy—genuine sympathy—is it a subject for command? No. False expressions of it, yes: these *may* be extorted by fear: but the affection itself is not to be thus gained.

If on that occasion any thing was *commanded*, *what* is it then that was commanded? Is it a system of stated meetings, with a ceremony to be performed at each? No: not so much as any thing like so much as one single stated meeting. At *that* time, nothing more was called for to be done by them—nothing more, than the doing what they came fully prepared to do—taking with one accord that repast, for the taking of which they were come. For any *succeeding* point of time, what was at that same time called for? Remembrance, and nothing more. *'Do this'* ... were his words. Do what? Do what had just been done by all: viz. eating bread and drinking wine. But in this what was there that would not have been done by them of course, though no intimation to any such effect had been received by them? thus much they would have done of course for sustenance. *'Do this in remembrance of me:'*—i.e. *when*, for a *convivial* purpose, *at any future time, you meet any of you together, keep me in your remembrance—think and speak of me.* In a wish so natural—so simple—so completely devoid of mystery, behold the true and only meaning of this discourse, which by so sad a perversion of language—by so deplorable an exercise given to a disordered imagination—has been sublimated into a

---

[1] For the Sermon on the Mount, which Jesus preached to 'the multitudes', see Matthew 5–7.

mystery; and, in an endless train, inferences no less replete with mischief than with absurdity deduced from it!

The *bread*—was that intended and commanded by him thus to be eaten—eaten in ceremony *by all nations?*—was that intended by him to be eaten by 'every living creature?'[1] The *wine*—was it thus intended and commanded by him to be drunken?—drunken in ceremony by all nations?—drunken in ceremony by every creature?

There was indeed moreover the *'giving thanks;'* nor in this was there any thing but what might be done 'by all nations:'—by 'every living creature,' that on this occasion could have been in view. But neither in this is there any thing that could, on that occasion, have entered into the composition of the subject of the special command.

Among the people of that nation, *this* was an already established custom:[a] just as the *saying grace* before and after meat (in imitation probably of that same custom) has come to be among *us*. Accordingly, in no established form of the Christian Religion has this *giving of thanks* been regarded as either constituting the essence, or so much as entering into the composition of the essence, of what is called *the sacrament:* let any one so regard it,—and, in his view of the matter, the Sacrament of the Lord's Supper is eaten, as often as grace is said before or after a meal.

Breaking bread and eating it—putting wine into a cup and drinking it—to those to whom what is above was spoken,—oh, yes: both these performances were possible enough. But to all *nations?* How great the multitude—not to speak of *'creatures,'*—but of whole nations—to which neither of these performances has ever yet been possible.

Hunters and fishers—shepherds—husbandmen—by these names, taken in the three distinguishable degrees, which it has successively occupied in the scale of civilization, is the whole human race brought to view.[2] Hunters—fishers—shepherds:—to how many nations thus

---

[a] Mark, [viii.][3] 6, 14, 23.[4]—He (Jesus) took the seven loaves and gave thanks ... John, vi, 11.—When he (Jesus) had given thanks he distributed ... ib. 23.—They did eat bread after the Lord had given thanks ... Acts, xxvii. 35.—Paul took bread and gave thanks to God ... Romans, xiv. 6.—He that eateth, eateth to the Lord, for he giveth God thanks.

---

[1] Genesis 1: 21, 2: 19.

[2] For the division of mankind into three distinct stages of development—hunters, shepherds, and husbandmen—see, for example, Adam Smith, *An Inquiry into the Nature and Causes of the Wealth of Nations* (first published in 1776), ed. R.H. Campbell, A.S. Skinner, and W.B. Todd, 2 vols., Oxford, 1976, ii. 689–94.

[3] 1818 'vii.'

[4] The first quotation comes from Mark 8: 6. The second quotation given as '14, 23', refers to Mark 14: 23: 'And he took the cup, and when he had given thanks, he gave *it* to them: and they all drank of it.'

APPENDIX, NO. II.

denominated has not only the taste, but even the name, of both those fruits of husbandry been utterly unknown?

Even in the husbandman state, in how many nations, to the vast majority of the population, has not bread—this first of the two supposed necessary instruments of salvation—been at all times inaccessible? In the tropical countries—in five-and-forty graduated portions of the earth's surface—and those the best inhabited—out of the about a hundred and twenty habitable ones, either some unmanufactured grain, such as rice,—or some root, such as the yam or cassavi,—has all along occupied the place of this elaborated article of manufacture.

Still narrower are the limits of the climate which affords the fruit of which wine is made. Vain would be the observation, that, under the name of *wine*, any fermented liquor, affording an ardent spirit, may be comprized. The 'vine,' and that alone, is the plant, 'the fruit of'[1] which was on this occasion mentioned by Jesus, as the material of which the wine he was there speaking of—viz. wine of the sort of that which then and there stood before him—was made. The Apostles were not Chemists. Jesus himself was not a Chemist. Under the name of *wine*, no liquor, other than the fermented juice of grapes, was at that time and in that place known. Unless by a forced extension—and that of comparatively modern date—to no liquor, other than the fermented juice of grapes, is the name of *wine* applicable even now.

By hosts of missionaries—vying, yet harmonizing with each other—(delightful thought!) the religion of Jesus has, of late years, been carried to the remotest south and to the remotest east.[2] Heaven prosper their benevolent and pious labours! Heaven preserve them from the despotism that threatens to nip in the bud their precious fruits! This ceremony, what will they do with it? What indeed have they done with it? The new-created Lord Spiritual of Calcutta, who, armed with power, riches, and[3] factitious dignity, is sent out to condemn by his example the equality preached by Jesus—this newly commissioned Antichrist with his three Sub-Antichrists,[4] what will they do with it? Engrafting on the religion of Jesus the more acceptable religion of Bacchus, will they re-instate in his former

---

[1] Mark 14: 25.

[2] The Society for the Propagation of the Gospel in Foreign Parts, founded in 1701, sent missionaries to work in the American colonies and the West Indies, while the Church Missionary Society, founded in 1799, sent missionaries to work in Africa and Asia.

[3] 1818 'riches, opulence, and'. The text follows the 'Errata'.

[4] The East India Company Act of 1813 (53 Geo. III, c. 155, §§ 49–54) provided for the appointment of a Bishop of Calcutta and of the three Archdeacons of Calcutta, Madras, and Bombay respectively. Thomas Fanshaw Middleton (1769–1822) was consecrated as the first Bishop of Calcutta in 1814.

conquests this their favourite God?[1] The pay granted for these intruders, is it not burthen enough for those already over-loaded heathens? To furnish out the *working* subalterns of this company of *Sinecurists* with these exotic and costly implements of salvation, will not the pressure of that burthen receive yet further increase? Or will the discovery be made, that the religion of Jesus changes with the climate: and that the inebriating liquor, necessary as it is to salvation in England, may be dispensed with in Hindostan?

This ceremony—the performance of it, is it then really necessary to salvation? If yes, then,—knowing or not knowing (choose ye which) that to millions upon millions of human creatures the performance of it would not be possible,—Jesus prescribed it notwithstanding: foreseeing and intending, that, for want of their having performed this impossibility, they would and should continue, to all eternity, in a state of unutterable torment:—and this merely for want of their having performed this one impossibility, while of no other precept of his had the observance been thus placed out of their reach.

'*No:—not indeed absolutely* necessary, *but however highly* conducive . . . .' will this then be the answer? Slender indeed will be the support, which from any such answer the credit of the ceremony will receive. Instead of the absolute certainty of infinite torment, what we gain by the amendment is the substitution of a *chance*—a certain degree of *probability*. But here then the question still recoils upon us—what chance?—tell us what chance? and be the chance what it may, by the difference between that and certainty, if the certainty be unreasonable, and as such inadmissible, will the unreasonableness be varied any otherwise than in degree?

Yes to be sure—if such was really the pleasure of the potter, submission is all that is left to the 'clay.'[2] But that such was really his pleasure, on what ground is it that we are called upon to believe? Exactly on none at all: or rather—as an algebraist would say—less than none: for while there are no reasons for any such supposition, we have seen what reasons there are against it.

But, on all such occasions as the present, the resolve in the first place determined upon is, that the practice of man—of man in power—shall be justified: and, to give effect to this resolve, how great the dishonour thus cast upon God may be, they care not. *They*, they are the potters: God, the clay: to compass their end, Him they make what they please. And this end, what is it? Only that the

---

[1] It was said, for instance by Nonnus of Panopolis (*fl.* 450–70), *Dionysiaca*, XIII–XL, that Dionysus (whose Roman name was Bacchus), the god of wine and intoxication, had invaded India.

[2] An echo of Isaiah 64: 8 and Jeremiah 18: 6.

APPENDIX, NO. II.

'understandings and wills,' which they have laid 'prostrate,'[1] may in reality be as clay in these same impious hands.

Again.—If it were necessary to salvation, this same ceremony—to produce such its effect, with what degree of frequency—how many times, for example, in the compass of a twelvemonth—must it have been repeated?—What? is a man to be tormented to all eternity,—or though it were but for so much as a single moment,—only for having fallen short of the necessary number of times by no more than one? and this only because he knew not that which nobody ever told him of,—and which, without his being told of by somebody, it was impossible he should know?

Well then—if it be neither *necessary*, nor so much as conducive to salvation, why so determined, so persevering, and so vehement in your endeavours to force men to declare that they believe it is so, and if possible, actually to believe that it is so? On the one side stands the absurdity—on the other, the insincerity—on both sides the mischievousness—of this your practice:—take your choice.

Not only to these two out of the three great divisions of the human species,[2] have both these pretendedly necessary instruments of salvation been at all times inaccessible,—but even in the remaining division, one of those two elements, and *that* the one to which the greatest degree of importance has been attached,—has,—to a large part of the population, not to say the largest,—been in practice equally inaccessible. Throughout this region the liquid element,—such is the price to which by taxes it has been raised in every country, and, by the expense of carriage, in these in which it is an imported article,—it would, if permitted to be partaken of by as many as the solid element is partaken of, thus, by the extent of the demand, have been raised above the reach of the poorest, and thereby of the most numerous classes. In Catholic countries, this indeterminate cause of exclusion is indeed itself excluded. But how? even by a determinate and altogether invincible one: viz. by that, next to universal, exclusion,—by which the use of this more costly article is, on each occasion, confined to the officiating priest.[3] Moreover, by this way of settling the matter,—of the command thus ascribed to Jesus—and the application of it supposed, or pretended to be supposed, to have been designed by him to be extended to all mankind—one half is openly set at

---

[1] See [Howley], *Charge delivered to the Clergy of the Diocese of London*, p. 16, and p. 37 n. above.

[2] See p. 316 n. above.

[3] In accordance with the doctrine of concomitance, that the body and blood of Christ were present in both the consecrated bread and wine, the Roman Catholic Church withheld the wine from the laity.

nought. Whatsoever persons he commanded to become partakers of the *bread*, exactly the same persons did he command to become partakers of the *wine*. Yet such was the effrontery, or the blindness, of those, whoever they were, by whom the form given to the ceremony in those days of darkness was devised—their disobedience to one part of the supposed ordinance is as direct and palpable as disobedience can be, while their obedience to the other part is no less so in effect.

In Protestant countries indeed no such direct exclusion has place:[1] but here steps in the indirect exclusion, produced by the dearness of the article.

In England, true it is, that,—according to the code of ceremonial law, which, under the name of the *Rubrick*, is interwoven with the Liturgy,—wine for this purpose is to be provided at the expense of the *Parish*:[2] and by this arrangement, so completely of a piece with the whole system of pay for ecclesiastical service, those by whom the partaking of it would be regarded as a sin, as well as those by whom it is regarded as a means of committing sin with impunity,—high and low, rich and poor,—are forced to be contributors to the melancholy repast:—those who regard sin as annihilated by it, and those who regard sin as created by it.

By these oppressive means it is, that the costly and foreign liquor of inebriation and salvation is procured, and *in words* promised and held out to all: to the poorest (who are always the greater number) as well as to the richest: to *paupers*, as well as to the *rateable inhabitants* by whom they are supported.

But the poor—those whose poverty is certified by the state of their clothing and other tokens—are they really admitted to the altar—are *they* admitted to a sip of the precious liquor, thus metamorphosed into the still more precious blood?—Ah no: it cannot be: this would be incompatible with all notions of Church-of-England *decency*.[3] If they were, this repast—this *spiritual* repast—so much would it in that case have of carnal annoyance in it—would not be partaken of even by that comparatively small number of the rich, to whom it is not an object of complete and constant disregard. No: in the practice of that Church, among the distinguishing characters of which is the inexorable exclusion so copiously bestowed upon those, whose stock of the

---

[1] In the Church of England, for instance, the congregation received both the bread and wine: see Thirty-nine Articles, Art. 30. 'Of both kinds'.

[2] See the rubric inserted at the conclusion of 'The Order for the Administration of the Lord's Supper or Holy Communion' in the *Book of Common Prayer*: 'The Bread and Wine for the Communion shall be provided by the Curate and the Church-wardens at the charges of the Parish.'

[3] See p. 86 n. above.

APPENDIX, NO. II.

elements of Church-of-England decency does not enable them to pay for a seat in any one of its places of worship,[1]—well may any one be assured, that whatsoever encouragement, or even permission, is given for the drinking of rich wine at public expense, is, by some means or other, confined to those who can afford to pay for it.

In favour of the exclusion thus put upon the majority of Christians, an argument might even be urged, to which no[2] satisfactory answer might be very easy to be found. Of the quantity of real faith really lodged in the region of the heart, no very exact measure can be seen stamped on the countenance, or any where else. By the sensual love of the inebriating liquor, or by the love of profane laughter, a reprobate might at any time have been sent to the holy altar,—there to empty, at one draught, that cup, which had been prepared for as many sips as there had been guests expected at this ambiguous feast: and thus, to the words of the poetically inspired heathen,— *(pleno se proluit auro)*[3]—little as he ever dreamt of any such fulfilment—might be given—and with as much propriety as to so many other universally applicable passages—the character of a special prophecy.

All this while, against the assumed doctrine, by which the universal and habitual drinking of an inebriating liquor is numbered among the means of salvation, has the impossibility of any thing like universal performance ever presented itself to either Church—to Holy Mother, or to her still more Holy Daughter—in any such character as that of a conclusive argument? Never: no, never. Never in the thoughts of either Church has the condition of the poor—never in the thoughts of either of these self-styled *Christian Churches* has the condition of the great majority of those, who either are, or, if so it had pleased these holy phantoms, would have been Christians—had in reality the honour of a place: if it had, no such ceremony as this could possibly have been established. No:—for the great bulk of mankind, no more has *salvation* been ever intended by the Church-of-England Priest, than *justice*, or so much as the shew of it, by the English Lawyers. By the founders of Church-of-England Religion, had salvation been designed for any but the rich, *Bacchus* would never have thus been seated by the side of *Jesus*. By the founders of English law (not to speak of the upholders of it) had justice been designed for any but the

---

[1] The installation and upkeep of pews for the use of the whole congregation was charged to parishioners, but in practice the appropriation of pews by particular families for their exclusive use through payment of pew-rents, building costs, or long use, was widespread: see Burn, *Ecclesiastical Law*, 2nd edn., 1767, i. 328–35.

[2] 1818 'on'. The text follows the 'Errata'.

[3] Virgil, *Aeneid*, I. 738–9: *ille impiger hausit spumantem pateram, et pleno se proluit auro*, i.e. 'he valiantly drained the foaming cup, and drew a deep draught from the brimming gold'.

CHURCH-OF-ENGLANDISM

rich, no such abomination would have been known as either *Law-Taxes*[a] or *Law-Fees*.[b]

Is there after all no road to Heaven but through ceremonies?— Must we at any price have a ceremony? Well then, let *feet-washing*—let *mutual feet-washing*—be that ceremony. To save it from that contempt which is the too natural companion of familiarity, let us deal by it as the ceremony of Dipping—in Greek, *Baptism*—and for that same reason—has been dealt by. Instead of our own vulgar tongue, let the name of it be taken from a dead language, and—what may be still better—from that same consecrated language. Instead of *feet-washing*, let it be—as with the Latins—*Pediluvium*, or—as with the Greeks, *Podolusis*.[1] Thus then, for the commencement of the career of ceremony, we should have *Dipping*, alias *Baptism;* for the continuance of it, *Feet-washing*, alias *Podolusis*.

Compare, in this point of view, the *Pediluvium* with the *Sacramental Supper*,—and behold, on all points taken together, how greatly the aqueous ceremony has the advantage.

1. As to the *source*. The same in the one case as in the other is the *source* to which they are traceable.

2. From that same sacred source, for the bread-eating and wine-drinking ceremony, there is nothing stronger (it has been seen) than *solicitation* or *recommendation:* no expression of desire, to which with propriety can be given the appellation of *a command*. For the feet-washing—for the mutual feet-washing ceremony, there is not only a positive command,—but, of the operation prescribed, one exemplification, and that a most striking one,—exhibited, and the command accompanied with words by which it is anxiously enforced. 'If I then your Lord and master have washed your feet; ye also ought to wash one another's feet. For I have given you an example that ye should do as I have done to you.' (John, xiii. 14, 15.)

3. In the source from which the bread-eating and wine-drinking ceremony has been deduced, no morally useful lesson could (it has been seen) have been meant to be delivered. In the source from

[a] See Bentham's Defence of Usury, and Protest against Law-Taxes.[2]
[b] See Bentham's Scotch Reform.[3]

[1] The Latin word *pediluvium* means footbath, or the bathing of feet; Bentham seems to have coined the Greek word *podolusis* from the words πους (foot) and λουω (wash).
[2] *Defence of Usury; Shewing the Impolicy of the Present Legal Restraints on the Terms of Pecuniary Bargains*, London, 1787 (Bowring, iii. 1–29); 'A Protest against Law Taxes, shewing the peculiar mischievousness of all such impositions as add to the expence of an appeal to justice', London and Dublin, printed 1793, later published in 1795 (Bowring, ii. 573–83).
[3] *Scotch Reform; considered, with reference to the Plan, proposed in the late Parliament, for the Regulation of the Courts, and the Administration of Justice, in Scotland: with Illustrations from English Non-reform*, London, 1808 (Bowring, v. 1–53).

APPENDIX, NO. II.

which the feet-washing ceremony would be to be deduced, a moral lesson of the utmost practical importance—viz. *abstinence from ambitious contention*—or, in one word, *humility*—was meant to be—was most explicitly declared to be—delivered.

4. From the source from which the bread-eating and wine-drinking ceremony has been deduced, no special *morally useful* lesson has ever been so much as attempted to be deduced. *Immoral* lessons, yes: and those in abundance:—the efficacy of an inebriating liquor either in washing away sin,—or in causing it, after it has been committed, not to have been committed:—the encouragement thereby given to sin: the power assumed upon the strength of it, by the most egregious of sinners, in the character of a priest, to consign to heaven or hell whom he pleases; by means of that same power, the further power to *prostrate men's understandings and wills*[1] at his feet: to render them subjects to his will, and instruments to his lusts. From the source from which the mutual feet-washing ceremony would be to be deduced, which of all those immoral inferences could ever be deduced? What but the purest morality would ever be deducible?

5. From the source from which the bread-eating and wine-drinking ceremony has been deduced, were any morally useful lessons deducible, narrow at best in its application would be the virtue of that ceremony. The bread and wine, no lesson. Were the lesson ever so useful, to none but *wine-drinkers* would the benefit of it be extended or extendible. Excluded from it would be—not only the whole population of the whole torrid zone, but in the two temperate zones all that abject class of human beings, whose souls, in the eyes of the Holy Mother and Daughter Churches, have never been worth a thought,—and in whose instance,—in pursuance of a recent discovery, announced by the so deliberately declared judgment of a well-fed dignitary of the English Church,—as declared, in a confidential and efficacious address, to the congenial mind of a Bible-distributing Chancellor of the Exchequer,[2]—it has been found that neither *health* nor *life* have any greater claim to regard,—and who, that on all occasions they may be dealt with according to their deserts, have been marked out by him for constant and condign contempt under the name of *ale-drinkers*.[a]

---

[a] See, in 'Further Papers relating to Excise Prosecutions,' printed for the House of Commons, by Order, dated 28th March, 1816. No. 179, 2. in p. 5,—Letter 'From the very Reverend the Dean of Canterbury to S.R. Lushington, Esq. Secretary to the

---

[1] See p. 37 n. above.

[2] Vansittart was a member and supporter of many religious societies: he was, for instance, a Vice-President 1811–33, and President 1834–51 of the British and Foreign Bible Society, founded in 1804 to distribute vernacular bibles world-wide.

Treasury, dated Rectory House, Piccadilly, February 6, 1815;'[1] this very Reverend person, adding to that his rich sinecure, the rich and Court-embracing Rectory of St. James's. This letter has been communicated to the public at large in the Monthly Magazine for 1 July, 1816, together with one of several Representations from the Commissioners of Excise, (six in number,)[2] which this, followed by five other extra-judicial intercessions from that same number of individuals,[3] had the effect of setting at nought: in the judgment of these same Commissioners, this being *'an ex parte representation, totally false and groundless.'* For an offence committed by a Brewing Magistrate—a neighbour of this very Reverend person's—an offence whereby, in the judgment of these Commissioners, delivered on the ground of legal evidence, not merely the revenue is 'defrauded, but the health of his Majesty's subjects highly endangered . . . . an offence of which it is utterly impossible for a moment to believe he could be ignorant,'—the offender was under prosecution. In this letter, after a confession that the writer 'does not understand the nature of the business, the grounds of intercession are stated to be—that the offender has appeared to him to be a *useful* magistrate,—that the prosecution had (he fears) its source in malice,'—that '*the matter concerns only ale-drinkers:* and that to lessen the *influence* of a *useful* man unnecessarily is a great evil.'[4] *Influence—usefulness*—the import of these words in the vocabulary of the Treasury is no secret, and may be seen abundantly illustrated in the collection of cases of which this is one. Whom to apply to for impunity—through what channel—and on what grounds;—these are points on which, after perusal of these papers, a defrauder of the Revenue, whether he be or be not moreover a poisoner of his own customers, need not be much at a loss: at any rate, if, being a Magistrate to boot, he be, in the Treasury sense, a *'useful'* one. On the text *Render to Cæsar the things which are Cæsar's*,[5] may moreover be seen the interpretation put *at the Rectory of St. James's*.

So much for the Minister of religion: a word or two more as to the guardian of the Revenue.[6]—*House of Commons Papers*—'*Further Papers relative to Excise Prosecution*,' &c. Date of Order for printing, 28th March, 1816. Nos. 2 and 179. 1. *Treasury to Excise*, 23d November, 1814. '*Insanity and revengeful malice on the part of Mr. B.*' (the erroneously supposed prosecutor),[7] sole alleged cause, for directions 'to suspend all

---

[1] For the report of the case of John Abbott, a magistrate and brewer in Canterbury, accused of putting adulterating ingredients in his beer, and the letter from Andrewes, Dean of Canterbury, to Stephen Rumbold Lushington, Joint Secretary to the Treasury, in support of Abbott see 'Further Papers Relating to Excise Prosecutions; &c', *Commons Sessional Papers* (1816) xviii. 65–74, esp. 69. See also pp. 49–52 above and the Andrewes Appendix, pp. 537–75 below.

[2] The letter from Andrewes, and the letter from the Commissioners of Excise, dated 27 January 1815, signed by six officials, were reproduced in the *Monthly Magazine*, vol. xli, no. 285 (1 July 1816), 572–3. The letter from the Excise Office, from which Bentham takes the following two quotations, also appears at *Commons Sessional Papers* (1816) xviii. 68.

[3] i.e. the five letters, in addition to that of Andrewes, sent in support of Abbott: see *Commons Sessional Papers* (1816) xviii. 69–71.

[4] In his letter, Andrewes had written: 'I have just heard that my good neighbour, Mr. Abbott of Canterbury, is likely to get into some trouble respecting an information laid against him about his brewery, the nature of which however I do not understand. Ever since I have known him he has appeared to me so good a man, and so useful a magistrate that I should be very sorry to have that usefulness diminished by his being brought forward to the public in a matter which concerns only ale drinkers, and I fear has its source in malice.'

[5] Matthew 22: 21; Mark 12: 17.

[6] i.e. Vansittart, Chancellor of the Exchequer.

[7] It was believed by Abbott and his supporters that George Blake, a neighbour of Abbott, had made the accusation against him, but the Commissioners of Excise denied that Blake had

APPENDIX, NO. II.

Law Proceedings, until,' &c.—2. *Treasury Minute, 10th Feb.* 1815. Penalties incurred £3,252;[1] remitted, with the exception of £500 and the Crown's costs. Without specific evidence, and in the teeth of specific evidence, the delinquent's conduct pronounced, *'honourable to himself, and beneficial to the community.'*—'Extortionate demands and *malignant motives of the parties originally concerned in the prosecution,'* again recognized as the sole ground, and that a sufficient one, for the remission of the penalty in question, viz. £2,732, *minus* costs of suit.—3. Letter thereupon, viz. Treasury to Excise, 25th Feb. 1815, signed, *N. Vansittart, B. Paget, C. Grant, junior,*[2] 'requiring' the Excise Board to 'stay'—i.e. put an end to—'the prosecution,' upon payment as above.

So much for the individual proceeding in the individual case. Now as to the general grounds of it, in respect of reason, justice, policy, and probity:

Here[3] a portion of punishment is *remitted:* for *justification* of this remission, a circumstance brought forward as the *ground*—and that a sufficient one—is the alleged nature of the *motive,* by which the prosecutor was engaged to act in that capacity: the alleged motive being *enmity.* But a more completely and palpably irrelevant one, heart cannot conceive. On the supposition of guiltiness, the propriety of inflicting the punishment has been determined by the law: in case of not-guiltiness, the danger of conviction, and thence of undue punishment, can it in any the smallest degree be influenced by the *motives* by which the prosecutor was set to work?—Even in the situation of a *witness,* in no case has *enmity* been admitted as a ground of exclusion: Yet, so far as concerns matter of fact, on what has been said by the *witness* or witnesses depends altogether the fate of the defendant: but for that, let the *prosecutor* (i.e. his lawyer) have said what he will, it goes for nothing.

The motive or motives of the prosecutor being nothing to the purpose, an observation, which may seem[4] almost superfluous, is—that, were it not for this motive, or for another motive, which, when any objection at all applies, viz. in the case of a witness, is regarded by the law as an objection of a still stronger stamp,—viz. desire and eventual expectation of pecuniary gain,—no delinquent could ever be convicted—no penal law be productive of any effect. Yet this still more objectionable motive is the very motive which the law itself sets to work, to obtain prosecutors (not to speak of witnesses) and on which, on that occasion, it places its sole dependence.[5]

---

played a part in the prosecution. See the letter from the Commissioners of Excise to the Lords Commissioners of the Treasury, 27 January 1815, *Commons Sessional Papers* (1816) xviii. 68: 'We beg leave to acquaint Your Lordships, that George Blake, (whose papers are herewith returned,) is wholly unconcerned, either as Informer or Witness in the prosecution of the Memorialist, which is for one of the grossest and least pardonable offences, we conceive, that can be committed, videlicet, the using adulterating ingredients in his beer'.

[1] In his undated Memorial at *Commons Sessional Papers* (1816) xviii. 65–7, Abbott gives the total penalties with which he is charged as £2,420, not £3,252 as Bentham states here, and not £2,732 as he states below.

[2] Berkeley Paget, Commissioner of the Treasury 1810–26, and Charles Grant, Commissioner of the Treasury 1813–19.   [3] 1818 '1. Here'. The enumeration is redundant.

[4] 1818 'may alone seem'. The text follows the 'Errata'.

[5] Under many penal statutes, an informer was permitted to sue and receive whole or part of the penalty from a successful prosecution. Hence any penalty paid by Abbott, who may have been prosecuted for adulterating beer under 51 Geo. III, c. 87, §16, could, according to §35, be divided between the King and the person who informed. According to Common Law such informers were not, however, competent witnesses: see *R. v. Cobbold* in Lord Chief Baron Gilbert, *Cases in Law and Equity: Argued, Debated and Adjudged in the King's Bench and Chancery, in the Twelfth and Thirteenth Years of Queen Anne, During the Time of Lord Chief Justice Parker,* London, 1760, pp. 111–14. In turn, particular statutes ordered that evidence from

CHURCH-OF-ENGLANDISM

Oh, but (say perhaps the Right Honourable Guardian of the Revenue, and the Very Reverend Guardian of Religion and Morality[1]—for, even from benches has an absurdity, which thus lays an axe to the root of all government been heard)—punishment (say they) ought not to be inflicted upon a delinquent, if the prosecutor has been actuated by any[2] other than the purest motives: *pure philanthropy—public spirit, disinterested love of justice*—call them what you please: by that which it calls upon him to do in the capacity of a prosecutor, or any other,—whatsoever be the service which he renders to the public,—by these motives, and no others, ought he ever to be engaged to render it.—Well then, if so it be,—if in so disreputable, so irksome, and so expensive, a situation as that of *prosecutor* in a *penal action*, these heroic motives are not only extensively enough prevalent, but strong enough to procure a supply of public servants sufficient for public use,—how much more surely will they be so, for procuring it for the right honourable, and honoured situation of a *Chancellor of the Exchequer*,—or the reverend and revered situation of a *Rector of St. James*'s? But if so,—then, whatever pay is annext to either of these exalted situations, is it not so much thrown away?

As for enmity to the delinquent—if, for giving impunity to that same delinquent, the existence of an affection of that sort in the breast of the prosecutor be admitted as a sufficient ground, never for the exercise of so God-like a prerogative can a Chancellor of the Exchequer be at a loss. How should he?—for, if any thing can be, the very act of prosecuting, is it not of itself a sufficient proof of enmity?

Suppose then that, for the impunity given by this Guardian of the Revenue to those who defraud it, the sole ground thus alleged will be uniformly and impartially acted upon,—no such defrauder will be punished, the revenue will be extinct, and the government along with it. But, let all this talk be the genuine fruit of the Catechism,—let all this purity be hypocrisy,—let impunity be hopeless to all but the comparatively few, who have it in their power to make themselves, in the Treasury sense, useful,—the constitution is indeed poisoned, but the government remains.—Which was to be demonstrated.

Note that, having been begun by former Chancellors of the Exchequer, this scheme for selling impunity for electioneering interest was completed t'other day by the present one.—See the Debates of the Day on this subject, and the Acts of Parliament there spoken of.[3]

Note, lastly, that—so badly are Acts of Parliament penned—and will continue to be penned, till the style used in this country be changed for the style in use in every other—in revenue cases as in others, unless a power of remission be lodged somewhere, persons not guilty against the *spirit*, will but too frequently be punished

---

an interested witness should be admitted on the grounds that the law should not be rendered ineffectual by impossibility of proof: see Lord Chief Baron Gilbert, *The Law of Evidence* (first published 1754), 6th edn., 3 vols., London, 1801, i. 114–15.

[1] i.e. Vansittart and Andrewes.

[2] The 'Errata' gives 'by these any', but 1818 appears to make better sense.

[3] Power to remit penalties, fines, seizures, and forfeitures in customs and excise prosecutions had been vested in the Commissioners of Customs by 27 Geo. III, c. 32, §15 (1787), but this power had been transferred to the Lords Commissioners of the Treasury by 54 Geo. III, c. 171 (1814). In the House of Commons on 2 April 1816 Brougham had introduced a motion attacking the measure and had accused the Lords Commissioners of the unjustifiable exercise of their powers in remitting penalties in return for political support. In the course of his speech, Brougham cited the case of Abbott of Canterbury and the six letters submitted in his support, three of which were from Members of Parliament. Vansittart spoke against Brougham's motion, which was defeated. See *Parliamentary Debates* (1816) xxxiii. 854–82.

APPENDIX, NO. II.

From the source from which the feet-washing ceremony would be to be deduced, co-extensive with the whole human race is the moral lesson that would be deducible. Monstrosities and casualties excepted, every man has feet, every man has hands: water, or he will not live, must be within the reach of every man. Howsoever unworthy, no less number of feet—no nor yet of hands—has by the unsearchable decrees of Providence been given to the *paupers* than to the Dean—no, nor than to the Archbishop.

One circumstance, which has been proved to belong to the bread-eating and wine-drinking source, cannot but be admitted to belong to the feet-washing scene,—and that is its not being particularly intended to receive any application, beyond the select company in which it was exhibited.

Not that that human being has ever existed, in whose instance, on this or that occasion, the demand for a lesson of humility might not have had place. But, for the planting and propagating of this virtue, lessons addressed to the boundless multitude had already been given by Jesus. On the occasion on which this feet-washing scene was exhibited, all that was needed was accordingly all that was given:— viz. a lesson having for its object the keeping down that spirit of ambitious contention, from which on so many occasions, the peace, even of this select society in particular, had unhappily received disturbance.[1]

All the excellences above ascribed to the *feet-washing* ceremony being admitted to belong to it,—still it is only in the character of an indispensable institution, and on the supposition that—such being the hardness of men's hearts—the appetite for ceremonies is too keen to be left altogether ungratified,—it is only on this supposition, that at this time of day the establishment of any such ceremony can be seriously proposed. In a country such as this, for the institution of new ceremonies—especially religious ceremonies—the time is pretty well over. The ceremonies that are preserved and observed—it

under the *letter*, of the law. But, by leaving the power in the hands of the subordinate Boards, the object of corrupt influence could not have been accomplished. Of those Boards, on the one hand, the members are in a situation of independence: their seats are their's during good behaviour;—bating legal conviction of delinquency, for life:—on the other hand, they can and do hear evidence—special and appropriate evidence. The members of the superior board are such (need it be said?) so long as they do as they are bid, and no longer: as to evidence,—on any such subject, had they inclination, they have not so much as *time* enough to hear any:—unless proof of *usefulness* on the part of the offender be evidence; and of this evidence the whole is contained in the *names* of the intercessors. Being impossible to be put to, is it possible the power should have been designed for, any other than a bad use?

---
[1] See pp. 242–3 above.

CHURCH-OF-ENGLANDISM

is rather because they are old established, than for any other cause, that they are preserved. Proposed now for the first time, scarcely would the self-same ceremonies be endured. By the hand of power, scarcely with any better effect than deception—scarcely for any better purpose than the production of that effect—can a ceremony, in the character of a religious ceremony, have ever been instituted, or kept on foot.

Not that in any human society— not that in this country more especially—not that on the rulers of the Church-of-England most especially—a lesson of humility, supposing the effect in any degree correspondent to the design, could ever be altogether without its use. The misfortune is—that in this country,—in the instance of that class of men in whose[1] instance the use of it is most urgent,—the greater the demand for this virtue, the more hopeless would be the prospect of a supply:—oh yes! the more hopeless—howsoever impressive in its lesson, and whatsoever were the source from which it came!—Have they not the Sermon on the Mount?[2] Do they not feed with it their pauper children?—Have they not the parable of the *Camel* and the *Needle*?[3] Have they not always had before them the mutually feet-washing scene?[4] Have they not *Lazarus?* Have they not *Dives?*—Yes:—but with what fruit? Lazarus—Yes: to them it is Lazarus that is the object of scorn; Dives the object of imitation: universal, yea, and openly ostentatious imitation.[5]—Yea: though with the other Lazarus in his hand this Lazarus were to rise from the dead,[6] still would they cleave to their Mammon,[7] so long as any the least remnant of it remained to them.

Suppose, however, for argument sake, that the reverse of all this is true: suppose that the times admit of such a ceremony.—On a periodical appointed day, in public view—in the view of the largest multitude, to which a simultaneous view of the same object can be afforded—suppose the *Archbishop of Canterbury* repairing to one of the Hulks, and then and there, with his own super-consecrated hands, washing the feet of a dozen of the inhabitants. On a scene of this sort, could any want of proportion—could impropriety in any shape—be charged? Between the Archbishop and the vilest inhabitant of those receptacles, is the distance in point of worth so great as was that between Jesus—whether God or not God—and the best of

[1] 1818 'which'. The text follows the 'Errata'.
[2] Matthew 5–7.
[3] Matthew 19: 24; Mark 10: 25; Luke 18: 25.
[4] John 13: 1–17.
[5] For the parable of the rich man and Lazarus see Luke 16: 19–31.
[6] For the raising of Lazarus see John 11: 1–46.
[7] An echo of Matthew 6: 24; Luke 16: 13.

his Apostles?—Answer, ye Athanasians! Answer, ye Arians![1] Cease your groans! Cease your exclamations! Lay your hands upon your hearts, and answer if you can, with simplicity and truth!—By his own confession—his own most public confession, as often as he acts his part in the *Liturgy* portion of his Bead-roll—the Archbishop, is he not a '*miserable sinner?*'[2]—If (what will but too frequently be true) the *convict*, be he who he may—the man on whom a stone from the tower of *Siloam* fell[3]—is also a miserable sinner,—is it altogether so clear that he is a more efficiently, a more extensively mischievous sinner,—in how much greater degree soever a more miserable one,—than the *Archbishop?*—Unless it be the quantity of the mammon of unrighteousness[4]—of the matter of the renounced pomps and vanities,[5]—possessed by the Lord of the Palace, not possessed by the inmate of the Hulk,—exists there any scale of *sinnership*—exists there any scale of *miserableness*—by which the sinnership and the miserableness of the Archbishop can be measured, and shewn to be less—and by how much less—than that of the convict?

For four years last past and more, by means of the tissue of imposture which has here been brought to view, has not the Archbishop been engaged in the carrying on the scheme of antichristian exclusion which has here been also brought to view?[6] At any rate, in no such course of cool and persevering wickedness has the convict been engaged. Removed as he has been by his penal situation from so many of the temptations to sin,—perhaps penitent, and pure even in thought,—at any rate, pure in deed,[7]—perhaps neither in all this time has he been actively engaged in any fresh sin. In the *Archbishop* on the one hand, and in the *Convict* on the other, who shall say that the parable of the *Pharisee* and the *Publican* may not already have found its exemplification?[8]—Who shall say that in the same poor miserable sinner, that other parable, the parable of *Dives* and *Lazarus* will not find its exemplification, at another time

---

[1] Athanasius (*c.* 296–373) supported the doctrine of consubstantiality, promulgated at the Council of Nicaea in 325 and confirmed at the Council of Constantinople in 381, in opposition to the Arian doctrine of subordinationism that denied the full divinity of Christ.

[2] See p. 224 n. above.

[3] Luke 13: 4.

[4] Luke 16: 9.

[5] See pp. 50 n., 209–10 above.

[6] i.e. Charles Manners-Sutton, in his role as President of the National Society for Promoting the Education of the Poor: see pp. 160–8 above.

[7] An echo of the 'general Confession' from 'The Order for the Administration of the Lord's Supper or Holy Communion', *Book of Common Prayer*: 'We acknowledge and bewail our manifold sins and wickedness, Which we from time to time most grievously have committed, By thought, word, and deed'.

[8] Luke 18: 9–14.

CHURCH-OF-ENGLANDISM

and in another place? The *costume* of *Dives*, is it not the *costume* of the Archbishop, yea, even of his menial servants?[1]

Let all this be said,—let it even be admitted for true;—and let it moreover be admitted, that never in any case—supposing it accompanied with any promise of efficiency—a lesson of humility could be more needed,—still recurs the question—whether supposing it administered, to and in the person of any such exalted sinners, and in any such shape,—it really would afford any adequate promise of being productive of so desirable an effect. Unhappily to this question no answer presents itself in any other than a negative shape.

In some eyes, the effect would be—not so much humiliation as exaltation. So prodigious the distance between the point of extreme depression occupied for the moment, and the exalted position occupied the whole remainder of the year,—the humiliation of the extraordinary state would but serve as a foil to the splendor of the ordinary state. Condescension—is it not one of the forms, in which pride manifests itself and magnifies itself?

To give to the scene its full stage effect, the principal actor would of course be furnished out with all the several appropriate articles belonging to the property of the theatre to which he belongs:—the *lawn-sleeves*, the *crozier*, the *mitre*, and the *throne*:—in a word, (with the exception of the palace), the whole apparatus of the renounced 'pomps and vanities.' The other actors—or rather the *patients*—on whom the operation would be to be performed—would of course be the most comely individuals that could be selected out of the whole crew: and, for the occasion, that no infringement of the laws of Church-of-England decency[2] might be discernible, would be new clothed; and the feet,—by way of preparation for this sacramental and solemn purification by the holy and most Reverend hands,—made as clean as unhallowed hands could make them.

In other eyes—(and not improbably of this number would be the greater multitude)—the ceremony being a novel one, and the imposing gloom of antiquity being wanting to it,—the idea of ridicule would obtrude itself, and shut the door against those moral ideas, for the calling up of which the ceremony was instituted. The representative of Jesus—(and could there be a more dissimilar one?)—this false Christ—would be quizzed, in and by the surrounding and staring multitude: quizzed, and by none more rudely and jovially than by his counterfeit Apostles.

In a word, in an exhibition thus theatrical,—acted the virtue would

---

[1] The rich man was 'clothed in purple and fine linen': see Luke 16: 19.
[2] See p. 86 n. above.

APPENDIX, NO. II.

indeed be—but it would not be practised. What would be exhibited is—not the reality of it, only the appearance.

That the picture here brought to view is far from being altogether the work of imagination, is known to all who are in any way conversant with the ceremonies of the Holy Mother, whose good works in that kind, her revolted, though still on so many points obsequious, and sincerely sympathizing Daughter, has always been so well disposed to imitate. At Rome, on an appointed day, the Holy Father performs, in public view, and with no small solemnity, on the feet of his Cardinals (is it? or upon some less hallowed feet?) this emblematic ceremony.[1] Perhaps, in the account thus given, the quality—either of the passive feet or of the operating hands—is not exactly represented. Settle the point with greater exactness let those eyes, which have more strength and patience than those by which the present account has been guided. What is certain is—that, among the ceremonies of the Church of Rome, this proud lesson of humility possesses a not altogether unconspicuous place.

To this scene, which in the original had the purest morality for its undoubted object, how minute, however, is the importance now attached, in comparison of what is attached to that other scene, which even at the first had no moral lesson for its object, and which from first to last has had such and so much mischievous morality for its effect? But of this neglect is there any difficulty in discovering the cause? Oh no, it is visible enough. Of the lesson which in the original scene was intended to be given, suppose but the imitation to have had its proper and full effect—its proper and full effect upon every body—upon spectators as well as actors,—*equality* would long ago have been the result, and *hierarchy* no where visible but in history.

The real purpose—the purpose which, as thus acted, the scene was really designed to have—was therefore that of increasing, as above, not diminishing, the distance between the hierarchy on the one hand and the profane multitude on the other. As to ridicule, laughter would not *there* be unpunishable as *here*.[a]

[a] Since what is above was written, the following passage has been observed in the Evangelical Magazine for May, 1816, p. 189.[2]

FRENCH FANATICISM.—The ceremonies of the Last Supper being too painful for his Majesty,[3] who would have been obliged to remain long standing, it was Monsieur[4]

---

[1] The ceremony of washing the feet, known as the pedilavium, was performed on Maundy Thursday by the Pope, who washed the feet of twelve or thirteen poor priests, and by Bishops throughout the Roman Catholic Church.

[2] See *Evangelical Magazine, and Missionary Chronicle*, vol. xxiv (May 1816), 189, reprinting an article from *The Times*, 16 April 1816.   [3] Louis XVIII.

[4] Monsieur, a title traditionally given in France to the King's second son, in this case refers to the next younger brother of the King, namely Charles Philippe, Comte d'Artois (1757–1836), subsequently Charles X, King of France 1824–30.

CHURCH-OF-ENGLANDISM

Let us return to and conclude with the main subject—the bread-eating and wine-drinking scene.—Bible in hand, thus manifestly has the inapplicability of it to any *general* purpose—thus manifestly has the groundlessness and mischievousness of the Church of England ceremony deduced from it—as well as, in a greater or less degree, of any other ceremony deduced or deducible from it—been made apparent. Well, then—will condemnation—will so much as disuse of it be the consequence? Yes: if to established Churches—if even to any Churches, to whose tenets practice, howsoever blind and unreflecting, has given a certain degree of fixedness—the Bible were really the standard of opinion and practice. But to what established Church is the Bible the standard of opinion and practice? No: it is the very essential character of an *established Church,*—in so far as a written declaration of opinions is joined in by its members, and that declaration an unalterable one,—there exists in it a standard of opinion and practice, by which, as to every part to which that standard extends, the Bible has been turned into a dead letter, the modern composition in question being thus far established in the character of a *substitute* to it.

who filled the place of the King in this act of piety, practised by our Monarchs from time immemorial on Holy Thursday. Thirteen children of poor, but honest parents, were admitted to the honour of representing the Apostles. They were all in red tunics, and placed on benches sufficiently raised to enable the [Prince],[1] without stooping, to wash their feet, wipe them, and kiss them. Every child received from the hands of Monsieur a loaf, a small cruise of wine, thirteen plates, and thirteen five-franc pieces. The Dukes D'Angouleme and Berry[2] performed the functions of waiters, and brought the bread and wine and the meats. All these ceremonies were gone through with a piety and collectedness worthy the descendants of St. Louis.[3]

Times, April [16].[4]

---

[1] 1818 'Princes'. The text follows *The Times.*
[2] Louis Antoine, Duc d'Angoulême, and Charles Ferdinand, Duc de Berry (1778–1820), the sons of Charles Philippe, Comte d'Artois.
[3] Louis IX (1214–70), King of France from 1226, had been canonized in 1297.
[4] 1818 '17', following the incorrect date given in the *Evangelical Magazine.*

APPENDIX, No. III.

REMEDIES TO THE MISCHIEFS OF THE EXCLUSIONARY SYSTEM AS APPLIED TO INSTRUCTION.

A WHOLE volume of condemnation—and what (says somebody) is the practical inference?—What is it you would wish to see done?—By what you have been saying, if there be any truth in it, mischief, to an enormous amount, has been brought to view.—Have you then any thing, and what, to propose in the character of a remedy?

Yes, verily: or of all that has been written for the exposure of the supposed mischief, not a syllable would by this hand have ever been penned. Of whatever wounds it may have happened to it to inflict, not one has ever been inflicted to any other end, than that which in the wounds he makes the Surgeon has in view.

In the course of the above pages, in the character of *sources* of the mischiefs brought to view, two systems have been pointed out: 1. The *exclusionary system*, as applied to the business of *general instruction;* and 2. That system of *Church discipline*, which at present has place in the Established Church of England.

In the prosecution of this remedial design, the first mentioned, least extensive, and more easily remediable of the two masses of mischief, will come under consideration in the present paper: the other, in the next No. of this Appendix.[1]

As[2] to what concerns the exclusionary system:—according to the hands, by which if applied they will be applied, two very different remedies present themselves.

Supposition the first.—As far as can be done without passing condemnation on any part of the doctrine or discipline of the established Church, the present rulers of the Society, self-styled the *National Society*—or, (what would be incomparably better), *Parliament* itself—(for thus all-comprehensive is the prospect that has already begun to open upon the subject) are ready and willing to

---

[1] See pp. 343–493 below.   [2] 1818 '1. As'. The enumeration is redundant.

CHURCH-OF-ENGLANDISM

throw open the seats and sources of instruction, to all whose parents, &c. shall be willing to send them in.

Supposition the second.—Persevering in the support given to the exclusionary system, the powers in question refuse to give their hands to any measures, the effect of which may be to diminish in any degree the efficiency of it.

On the first supposition,—of the course to be taken, the steps are already in some measure marked out by the National Society itself.— Among its lesson books, some there are, to which, for any thing that appears, no person, professing any of the known modifications of the religion of Jesus, could consistently object. These are—those which, in the list printed in Report II. p. 193, and, without alteration, reprinted in Report III. p. 172,[1] are in the following order, respectively designated by the four appellations following; viz.

1. Sermon on the Mount.
2. Parables of our Blessed Saviour.
3. Miracles of Ditto.
4. Discourses of Ditto.

The Lesson-Books which, on this same plan of conciliation, would (it is supposed) be to be omitted, are those which, in those same places, are in the order in which they are here copied, designated by the four other appellations following: viz.

1. Broken Catechism.[2]
2. Ostervald's Abridgment.[3]
3. Chief Truths.[4]
4. Mrs. Trimmer's Teacher's Assistant.[5]

In addition to the above four last-mentioned, three other articles (being the only remaining ones) might perhaps—to judge of them by their titles in the above list—be found to require revision, for the purpose of expunging out of them all passages to which any denomination of Christians would by their known tenets stand engaged to object:—

1. National Society Central School-Book, No. 1.
2. National Society Central School-Book, No. 2.[6]
3. National Society Central School-Book, No. 3.

This done, every discourse, which is not either among the *Discourses* ascribed to Jesus by one or more of his four biographers, or among the accounts respectively delivered by them on the subject

---

[1] *Second Annual Report of the National Society*, p. 193, and *Third Annual Report of the National Society*, p. 172.
[2] *Church Catechism Broke into Short Questions.*
[3] Ostervald, *Abridgement of the History of the Bible.*
[4] *Catechetical Instruction: Being an Account of the Chief Truths of the Christian Religion.*
[5] Trimmer, *Teacher's Assistant.*
[6] See p. 64 n. above.

of his *Miracles*, would be discarded: and thus the exclusionary system would be done away in so far as regards the children of all parents, &c. professing the religion of Jesus: always understood, that to the lesson-books discarded, no such others as would stand exposed to the like objections, shall be substituted.

To give completeness to this remedy, what would further be requisite would be—the *abrogation* or *alteration* of the instrument which has for its objects the shutting the doors of all these seats of instruction against all persons who, not being Members of the Church of England, would be desirous of serving in them in the character of *Schoolmasters*. This is that which, in the Society's Report II., p. 197, is printed under the title of *Form of Certificate for Masters*, (No. IX.) and again, in Report III., p. 176., under that same title, (No. VII.)[1]

Abrogation or rather *alteration:*—for, for the purpose here in question, after the slight alteration necessary to the exclusion of the exclusion, what remains would not remain open to objection.[a]

The misfortune is—that, supposing the door of the system of instruction to have been opened thus wide, still there remains in this country a native class of religionists—nor *that* in number an inconsiderable one—for the admission of which the opening is not yet wide enough,—and this is—that of the *Jews*.

In regard to these, on this particular occasion, small is the number of words that will be necessary to bring to mind two observations which elsewhere have been enlarged upon, in speaking of the exclusionary system, considered in respect of all the applications that can be made of it. One is—that these are human creatures. The other is—that, by any mischief, which, having been committed by a Jew, had its origin in a deficiency of intellectual instruction on the part of such Jew, the suffering produced in the breast of a Christian, will not be less than it would have been had the transgressor been of Christian, or any other non-Jewish, race.[2]

---

[a] In Report III. p. [176.][3] Omit 1.—*'is a Member of the United Church of England and Ireland, as by law established.'*

2. *'and into the regularity of   attendance on the service of the Church.'*

To make the other requisite amendment in the description of the class of persons, whose attestation to the good character of the proposed Schoolmaster is required, to the words, *'Rector, Vicar,* or *Curate,'* add *or 'Minister of the Place of worship, at (here describe its local situation.) and by the society of Christians, calling themselves,* . . . . whereupon could follow the name of such Society: with an additional form of words, adapted to the purpose of giving admission to the people called *Quakers*, by whom, in their intercourse with the Holy Ghost, no official or professional person, under any such name as *Minister*, is employed.

---

[1] The 'Form of Certificate for Masters' is reproduced at p. 97 above.
[2] See pp. 61–2 above.
[3] 1818 '126' is a slip.

CHURCH-OF-ENGLANDISM

Thus far as to the *principle.*—As to the *mode*—that for the giving admission to this, or any other class of men,—the use of these records of the religion of Jesus, should, in a course of instruction, applied to those who otherwise would have *none*, under a government professing the religion of Jesus, be, in the framing of a set of lesson-books, omitted,—can scarcely be a proposable expedient. But—what, in case of a system of really national education established by the Legislature, may without scruple be proposed, is—a declaration, having for its object the affording to religionists of that profession a full assurance,—that, by sending their children to any one of these seats and sources of intellectual instruction, it will depend altogether upon themselves to continue or not continue them in the profession of the religion of their ancestors: for example, a clause inhibiting schoolmasters, and all other persons, from holding, in any such National School, any discourse tending to engage any scholar brought up in the Jewish persuasion, to relinquish the profession of the Jewish religion. Remain still the professors of other religions, and non-religionists at large. But, for the extending to their case the application of this security, a very few words—such as the words, *or any other persuasion on the subject of religion*—might assuredly be made to suffice.

In the security thus proposed to be afforded, a precaution to the following effect is, however, necessarily comprehended.—In the whole scheme of instruction, written as well as oral, whatsoever discourses in any way relative to the subject of religion are employed, matters must be so ordered, that by no scholar, in and by any of the words put into his mouth, shall any thing be said, as to what *he himself* believes, but only as to what,—under the name of *the Church* or *the Government*, or whatever other name may be regarded as more apposite,—those, by whose authority the instruction is administered to him, believe.

Not less necessary is this expedient to the exclusion of insincerity out of the mouths and bosoms of the children of Church-of-Englandists themselves, than to the avoiding to exclude from the benefit of the instruction the children of heretics and unbelievers.

Nor, by the care thus taken to avoid inculcating immorality, will religion be divested of any part of her salutary influence. Be the discourse in question what it may, if upon understanding that you yourselves believe it, the scholar believes it likewise, you have what you wish: but, if not, will you, by forcing him to say he believes it, cause him really to believe it? No:—of the words employed in that endeavour the only effect will be—the inculcating in him the habit of *lying,* and adding to the number of his duties the daily practice of that

APPENDIX, NO. III.

vice:—of that vice, which is the pander to all other vices and to all crimes.

In your classical schools you cause him to read what Cæsar has related of his victories over the Gauls.[1]—Nothing of all this do you ever force the child to say he believes: yet is it not, as of course,—and without any such certificate from Church or State in favour of it,—received by him as true?

Even where the narration has for its subject this or that act or discourse ascribed to Jesus himself, bad would still be the example, if—believing it or not believing it—(and to whom else could it be known that he did believe it?)—the child were forced to say he believed it. But, how much worse the example, where the act or discourse to which the declaration of belief is forced to be attached, is—not any discourse or act ascribed to Jesus, but this or that *inference* deduced from it—deduced from it by a set of presumptuous and tyrannical men,—while, by other men, in much greater numbers, inferences have been deduced to an effect directly opposite?

Cease to employ religion to eradicate morality—put but this bridle upon your passions—and all difficulties are at an end.

What is it that on this subject (naming it) *the Church of England teaches?*—Every thing that follows, being introduced by a question to some such effect as this,—thus while religion is planted, falsehood may, out of this part of the instruction at least, be eradicated.

What? shall we then suffer ourselves thus to be led by an enemy?—By no means: but thus led you could be—and blindly so, and by any enemy of yours at his pleasure, and that in every thing—in so far as any such determination were known to have been taken by you, as that of acting in contrariety to his declared wishes. Thus to lead you blindfold would cost him but a word: to the description of whatever course he would wish you to pursue, all he would have to do would be to attach a *negative*.

No:—for a warrant for turning away from the wickedness of the exclusionary system, of no such being as this apostate need ye know the existence. Look but to the *Bishop of Norwich*[2]—look but to *Sir Thomas Bernard*.[3] For a warrant for turning away from the wickedness of teaching children to tell lies, look into any one of your Bibles,[4]—if, while distributing them to others, you can bear to look into them yourselves.

---

[1] Gaius Julius Caesar (100–44 BC). Bentham had studied Caesar's *Commentarii de bello gallico* at Westminster School and at the University of Oxford: see *The Correspondence of Jeremy Bentham*, vol. i, ed. T.L.S. Sprigge, London, 1968 (*CW*), p. 17, and Bowring, x. 36 n. respectively.
[2] See p. 101 n. above.
[3] See pp. 99–101 above.
[4] Bentham may have had in mind such passages as Exodus 20: 16 and Revelation 21: 27.

That in situations so far superior to all effectual responsibility, salutary impression should be made,—on hearts so effectually preserved by their numbers from all sense of shame,—is almost beyond hope. By a clergyman of unblemished character—a Member of their own Church—*the Rev. Vicesimus Knox*—in seventeen successive editions—now for some forty years, or thereabouts[1]— the rulers of the University of Oxford have they not stood charged with keeping the whole body of their subjects—including all such Archbishops and Bishops as have passed through that school of corruption—constantly plunged—not in the *indictable crime* indeed, but not the less incontestably in the *sin*, of *perjury?* In all this time, any one of them, has he had the front to deny it? any one of them, has he ever manifested any desire of being cleansed from it? any one of them, for any thing that has ever appeared, has he ever had the heart to suffer any uneasiness at the thoughts of it? The sin is not an indictable one: and, with whatsoever justice stones from offended heaven might be showered down upon each guilty head, the hand by which upon earth the first stone will be cast[2] is never to be found.

When, under the conscious guilt of perjury, and subornation of perjury, symptoms of contrition shall appear,—then, if ever, may be the time, when, in the shape here pourtrayed, *Tyranny*, with *Hypocrisy* and *Imposture* for its supports, may be expected to relax its gripe.

Meantime one remedy there is—which, happily for the cause of religion and morality, is, and can never cease to be, in the hands of the very persons, who, though so far from being the only sufferers, are, in the most immediate and certain way, the sufferers, from this tyranny.

Hard indeed would be the condition of mankind, if, while Vice had all power at command, Virtue should be without resource. Hard indeed—if, by interested tyranny, instead of being a means of salvation, conscience were, at pleasure, and without power of resistance, convertible into an instrument of mischief. No. By any such means as that of a promise to perform it, can an act, which is in itself pernicious, be converted into a duty?—A promise extorted by force from an agent altogether incapable of resistance? If, with a pistol to my throat, I have promised to murder my father or my mother, does conscience require at my hands the performance of any such promise? No: if, in the vigour of full age, a promise to act wickedly is essentially void, how much more clearly so at an age, at which whatsoever words the ear has been filled with, are made to come out at the mouth without any power of resistance.

---

[1] i.e. Knox, *Liberal Education*: see p. 34 & n. above.
[2] See John 8: 7.

APPENDIX, NO. III.

Thus much as to *promises*. So in regard to *assertions*. By those fears of immediate and unendurable suffering, by which the child has been made to say, *I believe this* or *I believe that*—he at the same time not believing any such thing,—can it be made matter of *duty*—of moral or religious duty—to believe any such thing, or so much as to endeavour to believe it? If, by the fear of man, he has been made to persevere for years in the utterance of this untruth,—after his escape from this fear, would the fear of God be worthily employed, in continuing him in the utterance of this same untruth?

Thus much as to the *child* itself. Now as to its *parents*. A benefit of unspeakable value,—a benefit to which every member of the community has, for the sake of every other member, as well as his own sake, an equal claim,—is seized into the hands of interested tyranny, and participation of it is refused to all children, whose parents will not purchase it for them, at the price, which,—for the purpose of continuing all understandings and all wills in a state of prostration under this same tyranny,—is set upon it. This price consists in the utterance of a set of words expressive of the above-mentioned *void promises*, or of words expressive of the above-mentioned *untrue assertions*. By the utterance of no such void promises—by the utterance of no such untrue assertions do the mouths and the breasts from which they are thus forcibly and tyrannically extracted, contract—if when free they do but purge themselves of it, (for thus much has just been proved)—any such taint as that of sin or moral blame. By refusing to suffer it to give utterance to those empty sounds, shall the parent deprive his child—and by so doing deprive the whole community—of so unspeakable a benefit? By such refusal not only will he do this mischief, but by contributing to give effect to this same tyranny, he will have rendered himself an accomplice to it:—he will have been an instrument in its hands.

In the breast either of child or parent,—at that time, or at any succeeding point of time,—any such affection as *gratitude*, ought it to be excited by any such benefit, administered or proffered by such hands, and on such terms?

Indignation, on the contrary, should it not rather be the emotion of the moment? and this emotion, followed throughout life by the determination, by every practicable and moral means, to contribute to the rescue of the public mind from the gripe of this corruptive tyranny.

Happily the means are as simple and sure as they are obvious. Deny not to your children the proffered instruction: deny it not to them, even though these are the terms on which it is proffered. Poisonous, it is true, is the drug which has been purposely mixt up

CHURCH-OF-ENGLANDISM

with it: but, to extract the poison, and leave the instruction pure, depends upon yourselves.

Day by day, as the course of instruction proceeds, as the enemies of morality and religion proceed in administering the pestiferous compound, let a salutary counter-instruction be given to them:—an instruction how to separate from the poison the wholesome food, and 'feed on it in their hearts'—feed on it, 'with thanksgiving'[1] indeed,— but with a thanksgiving, of which a person very different from those their intended corrupters shall be the object.

From first to last, in speaking to your children concerning the instruction thus administered to them, let your discourse be to some such effect as this.—'The *arts* themselves which you are learning— (the arts of *reading* and *writing*), are in themselves pure, and they are useful beyond all price. Among the notions which they are employed to infuse into your minds,—and but for which they would never have been thus taught,—are many which (as you will see in proportion as you see any thing in them), teem with immorality added to absurdity, in a variety of shapes. As the stock of your knowledge, and the strength of your judgment receive their increase, judge—and let the judgment be your own—whether among the *assertions*, of which these men force you to declare your belief, there be not, in more or less abundance, such as are false—among the *opinions*, such as are absurd—among the *precepts*, such as, in proportion to the obedience paid to them, would be productive—not of good but mischief.'

'Whatever, then, under the name of *a Catechism* or any other they give you to *say, say it*—since so it must be: if, among the words thus forced into your mouths, the words *I believe* should meet your eyes or ears, say *I believe* accordingly. To the words with which they are accompanied, be they what they may, add (since there is no remedy) these inevitable words, as under the like pressure you would add them to a history of the Arabian Genii, or of the Grecian Gods. After this warning, it will not be matter of much difficulty to you to observe how different the sense of these much-abused words is, when thus applied, compared with what it is when employed in saying *I believe sugar is sweet, and vinegar sour—I believe my father and my mother love me, and that it is a pleasure to me to love them.* And above all— think not that,—because, under this compulsion, you are justified in saying *I believe*, where you do not believe,—you would be justified in the utterance of any such untruth where you are free.'

'As to your Master, by whose hand this compound of lies and

---

[1] See 'The Order for the Administration of the Lord's Supper or Holy Communion', *Book of Common Prayer*: 'Take and eat this in remembrance that Christ died for thee, and feed on him in thy heart by faith with thanksgiving.'

nonsense is thus forced into your mouth, be sorry for him as you are for yourself. He, like you, is under a force. To yourself, unless with the unwholesome mixture, the wholesome instruction would never have been administered: to him, unless on condition of offering it thus defiled, the faculty of administering the wholesome food would never have been imparted. In him behold, therefore, not only a friend, but a fellow sufferer. In those, by whom this force is put upon him—in those high-seated and irresistible enemies of virtue, happiness, and of whatsoever in religion there is that is true—in those men, be they who they may, behold his as well as your enemies—his as well as your oppressors.'

'Take then, in these arts, the arms, which,—in the hope of seeing you employ them, in conjunction with these your oppressors, against the cause of virtue, happiness, and true religion,—will be put into your hands. Take them, but with the determination of employing them—employing them on every favourable opportunity—and to the utmost of your power—not to any such wicked purpose as that for which they are given to you, but for the generous and virtuous purpose of the rescuing your fellow countrymen from the chains to which you were thus forced to submit your infant hands; to rescue *them* and yourselves from the shame and thraldom by which you and they are thus oppressed. Serve them—yes: since thus to serve them you will be compelled. Serve them? yes. But how?—even as *Baal*, as you have heard, or anon will hear,—was served by Jehu.'[1][a]

Prepared by timely, and sufficiently repeated warning, to some such effect as above,—the juvenile ear will receive with due distinction the wholesome part of the instruction,—and neither will the head be weakened, nor the heart corrupted, by any poison that shall have been mixt up with it.

[a] To some such effect as the above, by some Clergyman, or other leading Member of each non-established Church—in that particular form which in his eyes shall be best and fittest for the purpose, might not a short warning be drawn up, and delivered to every member of such Church, who, at any one of those Church-of-England Schools has already a child labouring under this yoke, as well as to every other such member, who has a child, by whom in future he might wish to see the benefit of the useful part of the instruction shared?

Let it not pass unobserved—that to the adoption and use of the remedy thus proposed in the present work, it is not necessary that, by him who adopts the remedy, any other part of this same work—no—not that so much as any one other opinion advanced in it—or any one word in it—should be approved. All that is necessary is—that, approving of *his own* opinions, he disapprove at the same time, in a sufficient degree, the opinions and practices, inculcated in and by any of the Church-of-England formularies.

[1] Having invited the priests and worshippers of Baal to an assembly, Jehu ordered his soldiers to massacre them and destroy the images of Baal: see II Kings 10: 18–28.

CHURCH-OF-ENGLANDISM

And thus too it is—that, at length, in the toils which they have spread for the innocent, the guilty, and none but the guilty, will be caught:—the mischief which they had imagined to do, will remain undone:—the good, which,—till the hope of converting it into an instrument of mischief opened to them, they beheld with no other eyes than those of contempt,—or, if not of contempt of *fear*,—the good which, but for that hope, they would have been the last to think of doing—*this* alone will continue to be done.

APPENDIX, No. IV.

REMEDY TO ALL RELIGIOUS AND MUCH POLITICAL MISCHIEF—EUTHANASIA OF THE CHURCH.

INTRODUCTION.—Under the religion of Mahomet, an auspicious prophecy has long been current—a prophecy by which its downfal is predicted, and can scarce fail to be accelerated.[1]

Under that other adversary, and too successful rival, of the religion of Jesus[a]—the religion of the Church of England—a similarly foreboding voice has for some time been heard.

In the *Quarterly Review* has now, for some years past, been seen an instrument of defence—not to speak of offence—set up and kept up by the votaries of corruption in all its forms, for the defence of the system, against whatsoever attacks shall peradventure be made on it: made on it from any quarter, but more especially from the sometimes prudently generous, but always calculating and balancing, policy of the *Edinburgh Review*.

In the Quarterly Review, for *March*, 1816, may be seen a portrait of the Church, in her present convulsed state:[2] the patient in almost her last agony: powder-of-post the best remedy, which the resources of the Doctor can supply him with.

---

[a] Supra. Introd. Part I. §9.[3]

---

[1] A prophecy predicting the downfall of Islam, to which Bentham refers, has not been traced. He may, however, have had in mind the coming of the false prophet, al-Masīh ad-Dajjāl, who will seek to lead people into disbelief, before the coming of Mahdī, who will bring justice and light to the world.

[2] The *Quarterly Review* was not published in March, but in January, April, July, and December. Bentham probably had in mind an article entitled 'Tracts on Baptismal Regeneration', which appeared in *Quarterly Review*, vol. xv, no. xxx (July 1816), 475–511, and examined the controversy between those who adopted the high church belief that the baptized infant was unconditionally regenerate, and those who adopted the evangelical belief that regeneration was conditional upon the baptized child's subsequent profession of salvation by faith. The controversy had been triggered by the Bampton Lectures at Oxford in 1812 given by the High Church clergyman Richard Mant (1776–1848), two of whose tracts on the subject were the main focus of the article.

[3] See pp. 82–7 above.

A picture of disease—of disease radical, mortal, and remediless—is a prophecy of death.

Well then, Messieurs Quarterly Reviewers,—uncrowned, but not unpaid 'Defenders of the faith, and so forth,'[1]—come and see,—and that a little more clearly than as yet you seem to have seen,—on what substantial ground this prophecy of yours is built.

Service—Pay—Discipline.—Under one or other of these heads may be condensed the most practical part of what presents itself in support of the demand for this *innovation:*—for this crowning *super-innovation*,—for which the system is quite sufficiently rotten, and for which the times will soon be ripe,—upon the innovation which, under the name of *the Reformation*, was, about 250 years ago, definitively made in the Church-of-England, by the Crown of England, upon the Church of Rome:—made—half *with*, half *against*, the good liking of whatever was good among the people of England: who, looking to see corruption extirpated in England, as it was extirpated or extirpating in Scotland, saw it only shifted in part from hand to hand, and shared between the Mitre, the Crown, and the two Houses.

§1.—*Plan of this Paper.*

Throughout the whole course of this Volume, and in particular in the body of it, viz. in pages from 277 to 307, there has been but too much occasion to bring and hold up to view, this or that particular exemplification of the worthlessness of the system of Church Government of which the formulary in question is one of the principal instruments and supports. In further proof of the utter rottenness of this same system—of its complete ripeness for dissolution—the following recapitulation,—with here and there, for the sake of regularity and roundness, a word or two of addition,—may perhaps, in the eyes of a sincere lover of his country and mankind, appear not altogether ill-bestowed.

The system may be considered either in an *absolute*, or in a *comparative* point of view: i.e. by itself, without referring to any object other than the *ends* to which it is supposed to be directed,—or in comparison with *other* systems, that may be seen professing to be directed to the same ends.

In an absolute point of view it may be considered, 1. in respect of the *ends* or *objects*, to the attainment of which it professes to be directed. 2. In respect of its actual *structure*, by means of which it professes to direct itself to the attainment of those same objects or

---

[1] See p. 297 n. above.

ends. 3. In respect of the *effects* actually produced by it, with reference to these same objects or ends.

The objects, to the attainment of which it may be seen, or, without injustice, presumed, to profess itself to be directed, may be comprehended under the following heads,—viz. 1. Advancement of *Piety*. 2. Advancement of Truth in *Doctrine*. 3. Melioration of the state of the *intellectual* part of the human frame. 4. Melioration of the moral part of the human frame, in the instance of the people taken at large. 5. Melioration, or at any rate preservation, of that same part in the particular instance of the Clergy. 6. Melioration of the state of *education* in all classes. 7. Increase or preservation of inward peace and comfort in the breasts on which it operates. 8. Preservation of the actual composition and disposition of the Government.

Service—Pay—Discipline.—Under these heads, for the purpose of the present brief review, will be comprised the arrangements, by means of which it professes to aim at the accomplishment of those[1] same objects.

As to the *effects actually* produced by the system, they will need no other nomenclature or arrangement than that which has already been given to the *objects* or *ends* above stated as professed to be aimed at. Of these *effects* a brief sketch has been drawn up, but, for the present, the limits prescribed by necessity to the present work forbid the insertion of it.[2]

As to those other systems which, in comparison with, and for the illustration of, the system principally in question, will all along be held up to view, they are—1. The equally *Established Church of Scotland*. 2. In one body (for, in relation to the three above-mentioned heads, viz. *service, pay*, and *discipline*,—they will be found to stand on all material points—all of them—on the same footing) in one body, accordingly, the several *Non-Established Churches:* understand of course *Protestant* Churches: for as to the original, and Universal Mother Church—the Church of Rome—no scrutiny into the particulars of her internal structure affords, to the present purpose, any promise of practical use.

For the mass of mischief here brought to view, nothing, in the character of a remedy, could present itself as affording any tolerable promise, but dissolution. *Cacothanasia*, bad death,—or *Euthanasia*, good death (to borrow a word from David Hume)[a]—under one or

[a] By Hume, in one of his Essays, the death of the existing constitution being considered as not far distant, absolute monarchy is stated as the form likely to be

---

[1] 1818 'these'. The text follows the 'Errata'.
[2] The text of the 'brief sketch' has not been identified, but for the corresponding marginal summary sheets see the Editorial Introduction, p. xiv above.

other of these names will the end of the system, whenever it takes place, be found characterizable.

The object here being of course to recommend that which presents itself as the *good* or *happy* death, in preference to the bad and afflictive one, the following section may serve to give an idea of the characteristic circumstance, by which the two modes of dissolution may be distinguished.

The mode and body of instruction and guidance, by means of the existing Liturgy, with the addition of Sermons,—is it by Church-of-Englandists generally approved of?—Assuming that it is so, it will be shewn—that, for the administering of this instruction and guidance, a distinct order of men, under the name of *Priests,*—according to the principles at present established in regard to *doctrine*, being completely useless,—and, for the keeping of this order of men to their duty, another distinct rank of men, under the name of *Bishops* and *Archbishops,*—of course equally useless,—thereupon, if both these classes of men were suffered to empty themselves by death without replenishment, the administering of instruction in this self-same *doctrine*, throughout the kingdom, without any variation, and with at least as much effect as at present, might be secured, so long as the government lasts;—secured, and *that* with a degree of plenitude and uniformity at present unknown,—and, so far as depends upon *Sermons*, with a degree of improvement altogether unquestionable, even by the most zealous Church-of-Englandists:—and that, thereupon, with increased security for the *identity*, and with increase, moreover, to the efficiency, of the body of instruction at present administered by the *Clerical* to the Lay portion of the Church, the whole of the Ecclesiastical income of England, with the exception of a portion altogether inconsiderable, might be applied in diminution of those intolerable burthens under which the nation sinks.

§2.—*Euthanasia—, in Contradistinction to Cacothanasia, what?*—Uti possidetis *Principle—Its Application to this case.*

Before any thing further is said, either of the demand for, or of the mode and means of, reformation,—sound policy joins with humanity

worn by it at its resurrection, and it is in contemplation of this result that the supposed approaching death is characterized by the name of a happy one.[1]

---

[1] See David Hume, 'Whether the British Government inclines more to Absolute Monarchy, or to a Republic' (first published 1741), in *Essays, Moral, Political, and Literary*, rev. edn., ed. E.F. Miller, Indianapolis, 1987, p. 53: 'Absolute monarchy . . . is the easiest death, the true *Euthanasia* of the British constitution.'

in paying homage to the saving grace of the *uti possidetis* principle.[a] In those *international* arrangements, by which war is terminated, *uti possidetis*—keep what each of you has got at present—forms but one out of a number of principles of pacification, among which the acting powers have to choose. In arrangements of internal national reform, in so far as concerns *money* and *factitious dignity*—in a word, as to every object of desire,—*power* excepted, which in this case can never be considered any otherwise than as held in *trust*,—the principle of *uti possidetis* admits of no other to stand in competition with it.

The case supposed to call for the application of this principle is this.—The Church of England system is ripe for dissolution. The *service* provided by it is of a bad sort: inefficient with respect to the ends or objects professed to be aimed at by it: efficient with relation to divers effects, which, being pernicious, are too flagrantly so to be professed to be aimed at. Taken in the aggregate, the *pay* allotted for that service is excessive: the distribution of it being *unequal* in the extreme, it is,—while in the higher parts of the scale *excessive* to a degree altogether monstrous,—in the lowest, though in no instance perhaps *deficient* with reference to what would be necessary for the purchase of such inefficient service, yet enormously so with reference to what would be necessary for the purchase of good and efficient service from the class of hands proposed and supposed to be engaged. The *discipline*,—having for its professed object the securing, in consideration of the *pay* given and received, the rendering of the service professed to be rendered,—is, with reference to that end, eminently, not to say utterly, inefficient; but with reference to divers bad effects—and that to a vast extent—eminently efficient:—such are the propositions,—proofs of which will here be brought to view: such are the grounds on which,—on the supposition that the *service* must be preserved, the dissolution of the whole remainder of the system is

---

[a] *Uti possidetis*—i.e. *as you possess:*[1]—understand as added, though not expressed—so, you shall continue—*after the peace in question, you shall continue to possess:—uti possidetis, possidebitis.*
See Bentham, par Dumont Legislat. civ. et penale ii. Ch. vii. p. 31. For the principle there laid down, the present appellative is here ventured to be proposed.[2]

---

[1] *Uti possidetis* is a technical term in Roman Law, but used here in a general sense.
[2] See *Traités de législation civile et pénale*, ed. Étienne Dumont, 3 vols., Paris, 1802, Pt. I, Ch. VII. De la Sûreté, ii. 29–32, esp. 31: 'Pour se faire une idée nette de toute l'étendue qu'il faut donner au principe de la sûreté, il faut considérer que l'homme n'est pas, comme les animaux, borné au présent, soit pour souffrir, soit pour jouir, mais qu'il est susceptible de peines et de plaisir par anticipation, et qu'il ne suffiroit pas de le mettre à l'abri d'une perte actuelle, mais qu'il faut lui garantir autant que possible ses possessions contre les pertes futures. Il faut prolonger l'idée de sa sûreté dans toute la perspective que son imagination est capable de mesurer.' Pierre Étienne Louis Dumont (1759–1829), Bentham's Genevan editor, produced five major recensions of his works: see p. 582 n. below.

called for,—including whatsoever regards the topics of *pay* or *discipline*.

On the supposition that,—taken in the aggregate, or at any rate, in a number of instances covering in the whole a great extent, it contains a portion of excess,—what, in respect of this excess, shall be the lot of the actual occupants?—Shall it be the same with that of the clerks, who, under the name of *Supernumeraries*, have, without compensation, been discharged from the service of the several *Boards?*[1]—or, without taking any thing from the individual comfort of any of the actual possessors, shall it be carried into effect, as far as possible, upon the *uti possidetis* principle: that is, at the charge of none but the unknown and unascertained individuals, who, but for the change, would have become their successors?—The answer here proposed is—upon the *uti possidetis* principle.

By the *uti possidetis* principle, as applied to the subject here in question, what is required is—that, on the occasion of the change in question, every individual interested be, as far as may be, saved from the sensation of loss. It is by the nature of the tenure in question, on which the possessions in question are held, viz. in respect of its *non-hereditariness*, that room is afforded for a reduction of pay—and *that* to a very ample amount—without any violation of this tutelary principle.

Immediately on resignation, amotion, or decease, of any and every possessor of a share of and in the mass of emolument in question, let that share fall in, into the hands of government: to be applied, in alleviation of the public burthens, or to any other more beneficial purpose, if any such purpose can be found. It will thus take the destination that ordinary property in immovables takes on failure of heirs: *escheat*, from the old French, *escheoir, to fall in*, is, in this latter case, the word.[a]

To patrons of benefices—of such benefices, the patronage of which is in private hands—compensation must, however, be made: made it must be, or the *uti possidetis* principle will in so far be violated. But in this there will be no difficulty. The income of a benefice given, the marketable value of it, as ascertained by sales, and even by auctions—is no less well known, than that of a head of 'cattle at a fair,'

---

[a] On the occasion of the pretended reform, by stat. 53 G. 3. ch. 149. §13. so far as concerns the interest of patrons, this dictate of justice was set at nought. See App. No. V.[2]

---

[1] According to *The Times*, 27 November 1815, the Lords of the Treasury had ordered the discharge of supernumerary clerks (appointed with the expectation of being placed on the establishment as vacancies arose) from government departments and public offices.

[2] See pp. 499–518 below.

and even rather more generally known than that of a seat in either House.[1]

On this plan, whatsoever unavoidable evil, in the shape of immediate suffering, is liable to result from *change*, is reduced to its *minimum*.

On this same plan, the provocation to resistance is, in like manner, *minimized:* and by this means, probability of success is so far *maximized*.

On the other hand, the good promised by the change is, it must be confessed, *not* maximized: it cannot come in otherwise than gradually, as possessors die off:—nor completely, till the longest continued possession has ceased.

But even taking into account the interests of *piety* and *morality*,—in respect of *certainty*—(viz. apparent certainty, with reference to human optics)—the *good* promised by the change, in all shapes taken together, cannot, it must be acknowledged, be with propriety placed, by any well-regulated imagination, on a level with the *evil*, which, in case of a violation of the *uti possidetis* principle, would be produced in all shapes taken together: the injury,—which, by the change would be done to the interests of piety and morality,—being, on this side also, taken into the account. This latter is not, like the pecuniary part of the benefit, capable of being expressed in figures: and sanguine indeed must be the estimate formed of the good expected, in this shape, if, under the convulsion that could not but be produced in that case by the enterprize, the gain to piety and morality would amount to an equivalent for the loss sustained in both those precious shapes.

At the Restoration, when, in conjunction with despotism, impiety and immorality were re-seated on the throne, true it is, that two thousand Church-of-England Parish Ministers of *that* day, were without compensation in any shape or degree, expelled—expelled at the instance and to the use of so many Priests, belonging to the Church which is *now* the Church of England.[2] But, unless it be that of the Church of Rome, where are any examples to be found so bad—so unfit to be taken for a pattern—as that of the Church of England?—

---

[1] An advowson, or right to present a clergyman to a parish or other ecclesiastical benefice by a lay patron, was a property right which could pass by gift, inheritance, sale, or auction. Such sales were advertised in newspapers, often with an indication of the annual income that could be expected from the benefice. See Blackstone, *Commentaries on the Laws of England*, ii. 21–4, and pp. 287–8 above.

[2] Around 2,000 clergy were ejected from their livings for refusing to comply with the provisions of the Act of Uniformity of 1662 (13 & 14 Car. II, c. 4), requiring all ministers to use the *Book of Common Prayer* of 1662, declare rebellion against the monarch illegal, and submit to episcopal ordination.

No: not a *pattern* was *that*, but a *beacon: not a pattern* to be pursued, but a *beacon* to be avoided.

Only to *value*, however, and not to *form*,—either according to reason or to custom,—can the *uti possidetis* principle be, in this case, understood to apply. When, for a public purpose of real or supposed utility, property belonging to individuals is deemed requisite to be employed, no scruple is ever entertained of causing it to change hands, so as what is regarded as being equal in *value* be given for it.

Accordingly, in what shape soever the income finds its way into the hands of the present possessor, whether, for example, in the shape of tithes or rent, no scruple need be made of selling it on public account, provided a government annuity to the full value be given for it. Income,—paid with a degree of regularity far short of that with which government annuities, granted for valuable consideration, are paid,— is regarded as a mode of remuneration sufficiently secure, in the case of the most necessary and incontestable service: sufficiently for those who risk life and limb, and health, for the purchase of it. To those to whose piety this security suffices not, give a draught upon *Melchisedec*.[1]

In the case of *tithes in kind*, the *form*, independently of the *value*, being an inexhaustible source of vexation and ill-will,—property in this form should never pass out of the hands of the present possessors, without being extinguished for the benefit of the productive hands, on which at present this burthen rests; and for enabling those, and all other persons interested, to purchase this relief, all such legal facilities as are either already in use,[2] or without injustice can be added to them, will of course be to be afforded.

On this occasion, the *uti possidetis* principle cannot, however, be fully carried into effect, unless due regard be paid to the *pretium affectionis*—the value of affection: that source of enjoyment and suffering, to the importance of which the Roman lawyers have been duly sensible,—the English as insensible as so many stocks or stones.[3] Say *pretium affectionis:* not because for English use Latin

---

[1] When Abram returned in triumph from defeating the raiders of Sodom and Gomorrah, Melchizedek, King of Salem and 'the priest of the most high God', brought out bread and wine and blessed Abram, who gave him a tithe of his victory spoils. See Genesis 14: 18–20. The priesthood of Jesus was later associated with that of Melchizedek: see Hebrews 5–7.

[2] A *modus decimandi* was a compensation, either pecuniary or in work or labour, made instead of payment of tithes in kind: see Blackstone, *Commentaries on the Laws of England*, ii. 29–31.

[3] Although the notion of *pretium affectionis* is firmly rejected in classical Roman Law (see, for instance, *Digest of Justinian*, xxxv. ii. 63), it was developed in the later Civil Law tradition (see, for instance, Samuel Pufendorf (1632–94), *De jure naturae et gentium* (first published 1672), Lib. 5, Cap. 1, §7, and [Henry Home, Lord Kames (1696–1782)], *Principles of Equity* (first published 1760), 2nd edn., Edinburgh, 1767, p. 80). The notion did enter discussion in the Court of

is better than English; but because an expression,—which, being borrowed from any foreign, is stuck into the vernacular language,—affords a better chance, than can be presented by any correspondent expression taken from the vernacular language itself, for laying hold of the attention and fixing itself on the memory. Of articles susceptible of the *pretium affectionis, instances* are—a *house*, that, for any considerable length of time, has continued in the occupation of the present possessors,—especially if money of his has been laid out upon it,—together with any *garden* or nearly adjacent field:—but, in addition to *these*, scarcely among *immovable* ones will any other articles be found.

Subject to the above restrictions, so far as public economy would not be disserved by the anticipation, no reason can be assigned why the sale of a source of ecclesiastical income,—sinecure or not sinecure,—need wait for a vacancy.

As to *tithes*, in so far as a *commutation* of property from *that* into this or that *other* shape is regarded simply as a measure of political economy,—having for its object the diminution of vexation and the increase of produce—what is manifest enough is—that to the benefit, of relief from pressure in that peculiarly inconvenient shape, consummation could not be given, without extending it to such tithes as are in *lay* hands. But, compared with that benefit, the benefit here in question stands on ground, though in some part coincident, yet, on the whole, much more ample:—for, to all the benefit which has place in that case, the measure here in question will be seen to add others, which in that instance have no place. Hence it is, that, between the one and the other measure, no sort of connexion in any degree *necessary* has place: without the other, either of them is capable of being carried into effect.

§3.—1. *Service.*

Taking in hand the Church-of-England system in the character of the alleged *cause*, let us now, under the above several heads, viz. *service, pay,* and *discipline*—observe what sort of tendencies it exhibits with respect to the production of what is desirable in relation to the also above-mentioned *ends:* what loss, if any, in relation to those ends respectively, would be produced by the abolition of the system,—and, to the making up of any such loss, what measures promise to be best adapted.

Chancery in the late-eighteenth and early-nineteenth centuries: see, for instance, *Campbell v. Walker* (1800) and *Coles v. Trecothick* (1804) in Francis Vesey Junior, *Reports of Cases Argued and Determined in the High Court of Chancery*, 20 vols., London, 1795–1822, v. 678–83, esp. 679, and ix. 234–53, esp. 246, respectively.

1. First as to *service*. By *service*, understand service in all shapes, in which, in relation to the above *ends*, or any of them, may be reasonably expected at the hands of a beneficed Clergyman, in return for the benefit which in the shape of the matter of wealth, or in any other shape, it may happen to the benefice to put into his hands.

Considered as that, of which, by the exercise of lawful power, the performance may in some degree or other, by some means or other, be rendered more or less probable,—*service* takes the name of *duty*.

Professional and *extra-professional*—to one or other of these heads may all services, expectable at the hands of a Clergyman, be referred. *Professional* duties, those for the performance of which, the character with which the clerical person has been invested, is supposed to have rendered him apt, to the exclusion of, or at the least in preference to, any person not invested with that character: *extra-professional*, those of which it is understood that they might with no less propriety be performed by any other person, taken at large.[a]

Services or duties of *perfect* obligation—services or duties of *imperfect* obligation—to one or other of these heads may be referred all *professional* duties. The distinction is already in use: it may be seen in Puffendorf and elsewhere.[1]

By duties of *perfect obligation*, understand all such duties, to the performance of which, by punishment or otherwise, a man may be compelled by the hands of law.

On request, or even on any adequate prospect of use, spontaneously contributing, in any shape, by advice and even by assistance, according as power suffices and occasion calls, to the welfare, everlasting and even temporal, of the several individuals committed to his charge—under some such words of general description may be comprehended the multifarious classes of duties, distinguished by the appellation of duties of *imperfect obligation*, considered by some

[a] Instances of *Extra-professional duties* are afforded by the reading of extracts from Acts of Parliament, Proclamations, or other discourses, the publication of which in this mode is prescribed by Government: also notices respecting marriages, briefs for collecting of alms, &c.[2]

[1] See Pufendorf, *De Jure Naturae et Gentium*, Lib. III, Cap. IV, §9. Obligatio perfecte aut imperfecte mutua, and also, for instance, Paley, *Principles of Moral and Political Philosophy*, 12th edn., Bk. II, Ch. X, i. 91–3; Bk. III, Pt. I, Ch. V, i. 132–3.

[2] Acts of Parliament, and announcements regarding matters such as repairs to highways, the poor rate, and land and property taxes, together with briefs, which authorized a collection for a designated charitable purpose by the churchwarden, were read after the Nicene Creed in the Communion Service. Marriage banns were read after the second lesson in the Morning or Evening Service. See Burn, *Ecclesiastical Law*, 2nd edn., 1767, i. 229, iii. 252, 257–8, and 'The Order for the Administration of the Lord's Supper or Holy Communion' and 'The Form of Solemnization of Matrimony', *Book of Common Prayer*.

APPENDIX, NO. IV. §III.

in England, and by all in Scotland, as being attached to the Clerical office.

Of *imperfect obligation* they are called—for such is the term in use—in so far as the performance of them, not being compellable by the hand of law, is no otherwise enforced, than by motives belonging to the religious or to the moral sanction.

Under the Church-of-England system, duties of perfect obligation are not to be found, other than those which are performed by the reading of certain discourses out of a book, unless it be the incidental performance of certain concomitant corporeal acts, in the way of *vesture, posture, gesture*, and *locomotion*.

Fixt or *variable*—to one or other of these two heads may be referred all the discourses thus to be read: *fixt*, the several portions of the *Liturgy: variable*, the discourses styled *Sermons*.

Thus, in the whole mass of the duties of an English Church-of-England Parish-Priest to the performance of all that part which is composed of duties of *perfect* obligation,—being the whole of what he can be compelled to perform—the whole of what any provision is made for his performing,—the whole of what there is any security for his performing—the whole which there is any reasonable ground for expecting to see him perform—and the whole of what, generally speaking, he does perform,—every human being that can *read* the discourses in question, is in some sort competent: competent in proportion to the degree of aptitude with which he is able and willing to perform *this act*.

Of the several portions of the above Liturgy, the reading is divided between the *Minister* and the *Clerk*:[1] of the *Congregation*, such members as are at once able and willing, join and read in unison with the Clerk.

As in the part read by the *Clerk*, there is not any thing which the *Minister* would not be equally able to read; so in the part read by the Minister, there is nothing which the Clerk would not be equally able to read:—in both instances the language is the same.

If that part which is now read by the Minister were by the Clerk read in addition to his own, the labour of his *lungs* would by the whole amount of it receive an increase: but to the quantity occupied of his *time* no addition would be made.

The whole quantity of time occupied by the whole of the service is not greater than that which, by Ministers of other Churches, established as well as non-established, is commonly employed in preaching and praying,—without intermission or relaxation, unless it

---

[1] For the duties of the Parish Clerk see p. 273 n. above.

CHURCH-OF-ENGLANDISM

be by psalm-singing performed by the congregation, with or without a Clerk to lead them.

In the shape of service of *perfect obligation*, whatsoever, therefore, under the Church-of-England system, is done by the *Parish Minister*, might—and that without any addition to the quantity of time expended—be done by the *Parish Clerk;* or,—if it be regarded as requisite that a sort of drama should be exhibited, with two different classes of persons for the performance of so many different parts,— to any *boy*, who has been made proficient in the reading of the Bible, the part of the *Minister* might be transferred: and *that* without disadvantage in any assignable shape.

No:—for, of the actual *Clerk* the mode of reading (says somebody) is but too apt to be improper and unexpressive: that of the *boy* might, with but too much reason, be expected to be still more so.

True: but so likewise—and *that* by the very nature of the case,—is that of the Minister. By the perpetual habit of reading the self-same portion of discourse, the attention is confined to the sound, and detached from the ideas: the mode of utterance is not, in this case, as in the case of *spoken* discourse, governed by the sense.

Comparing the Minister with the Clerk—the actual Minister with the actual Clerk, upon a candid consideration there would probably on the whole be found some pre-eminence on the side of the Minister. But this advantage, such as it is, can it be regarded as forming any thing like an adequate compensation for the difference between the average of the *pay* given to the Clerk and the *pay* given to the Minister? does it *vary* and keep pace with the variation in the quantum of the pay, allotted in different parishes for exactly the same quantum of service? Does it vary from the equivalent for 10*l*. to the equivalent for the 7,000*l*. a year, which, in a certain parish in the Isle of Ely, is said to be the amount of pay actually received by the Minister,[1] for which of course nothing is done, and by whom more is done than it might be altogether safe to state?[a]

True it is, that from instruction the art of apt and appropriate reading might, like other arts, be learnt: and if learnt, might, by an uncommonly strict and anxious attention, even though as here the

---

[a] Even by an anonymous writer,[2] this, though not as a fact, may, without impropriety, be mentioned as an object for inquiry.

[1] Algernon Peyton (1786–1868), Rector of Doddington 1811–68. The parish extended over sixty square miles and had become a prosperous agricultural area following the drainage of the Fens. Peyton was reputed to earn £7,000 annually, although William Wright, Letter V, 18 January 1814 (*Morning Chronicle*, 21 January 1814), claimed that the annual income was as much as £12,000 (see p. 471 below).

[2] i.e. Bentham, who had originally intended to publish this work anonymously.

APPENDIX, NO. IV. §III.

discourse read were everlastingly the same, be, for a length of time more or less considerable, retained.

True also it is, that for this last half century, or a little more, in all England there have generally been one or two intelligent men, who have made it a profession to be teachers of this art.[1]

But this is not among the arts so much as professed to be *taught*—much less among the arts actually *learnt*—at either of those highest seats of learning,[2] from which,—with very few exceptions, and those still less favourable to any chance of instruction in this art,—the Church-of-England pulpits and reading desks are supplied with occupants.

So much for the *Clerk*. But, transfer now the comparison to the actual and future probable Parish Minister on the one part, and the future probable *Bell-taught* and ulteriorly teachable Parish Schoolboy on the other part, the probability of pre-eminence will in every point of view be seen to be on the side of the Parish boy.

Into this boy, if it were worth while, the art of appropriate reading might, by instruction,—supported by premiums, suited in the moderation of their amount to the humility of his situation,—be infused: into the Parish Minister it cannot be infused. Unless it be by some accident too rare to be worth taking into account for any such purpose as the present,—in this shape no instruction has he ever received: if he has received any, soon, by the constantly operating attraction of gravity, as above, will it be pressed out of him: if he has not learnt it, never henceforward will he learn it: the days in which, if in any, any such labour would have been endurable, are long since past.

Thus much as to *power*. But *inducement*—possible cause of *inclination*—where is it? Unless it be in the minute number of those, to whom imagination may present this sort of proficiency as a possible cause of preferment—perhaps out of some score *one*—exactly no where. Nothing in this situation does a man suffer by the non-possession of this art: nothing would be his gain by the possessing it.

Among the duties of *perfect* obligation, remains the reading of the *variable* part of the mass of discourse, viz. the *Sermons*.

But to the reading of this *variable* part every person who is competent to the reading of the Bible, is no less competent [than][3] to the reading of the *first* part: the actual Parish Clerk, or the proposed Parish boy, no less than the Parish Minister.

---

[1] Thelwall, for instance: see p. 279 & n. above.
[2] i.e. the Universities of Oxford and Cambridge.
[3] 1818 'then'.

Of the proposed substitution, the result, it will be seen, would be at least as unexceptionable and beneficial in this case as in the other.

In regard to Sermons, two results are desirable: the one *positive*, the other *negative*. The *positive* is—that to every congregation, within any assumed space of time—say a year—shall be administered in this shape such a body of discourse as shall be, in the highest possible degree, *conducive* to the ends of religious instruction as above particularized.[a] The *negative* result is—that to that same assembly, within that same space of time, shall *not* be administered any portion of discourse that shall, in any respect or any degree be *adverse* to those same objects: or at any rate, that if, contrary to intention, any such pernicious instruction be administered, it shall in *quantity* as well as *quality* be as little pernicious as possible. Say, then, for memory's sake—*positive* end, useful instruction *maximized:* negative end, pernicious instruction *minimized*.

Under the existing system, for the accomplishment of the *positive* one of these two ends, no security at all is or can, in the nature of the case, be given: for the accomplishment of the *negative* end, a sort of apparent security, yes: viz. by means of the system of discipline. But of real efficiency, under the Church-of-England system, owing to the inaptness of the system of discipline, this security will be seen to have little more than the appearance. *See the section on Discipline.*[1]

Under the proposed system, to both those ends accomplishment might, and in this particular upon Church-of-England principles, be given with the utmost facility, and to a degree of perfection never before imagined, nor ever till now attainable.

At the time of the settlement of the Church under Elizabeth, the number of *Sermons* as yet published being very small, and moreover proportionably so, the number of such persons, as to the ability added the effectual inclination to compose such as should be at the same time useful to hearers in general, and acceptable to the ruling powers,—discourses, calculated for the conveyance of such instruction as was at that time thought expedient to be conveyed, were composed and printed by authority, under the name of *Homilies:*[2] and to each Parish Minister a general invitation was given, as often as should be agreeable to him, instead of a sermon of his own composition, to read one of these Homilies.[3]

[a] Supra, §2.[4]

---

[1] See §6, pp. 415–27 below.
[2] See p. 277 & n. above.
[3] Bentham perhaps had in mind Art. 35 of the Thirty-nine Articles, which asked ministers to read the Homilies 'diligently and distinctly, that they may be understood of the people'.
[4] See pp. 346–51 above.

APPENDIX, NO. IV. §III.

On three of these Homilies, viz. those 'on Salvation, on Faith, and on Good Works,' much laud and earnest 'recommendation' is bestowed by his present Lordship of London, viz. in p. 21 of his Charge so often mentioned.[1] And, considering that by the same authority, by which warrant was given for the substitution of these three to home-made sermons, warrant was given for the like use to be made of all the other Homilies in that same book, there seems little need of apprehension, that in a practice thus authorized any cause for condemnation should, even by so rigid a censor as this Right Reverend prostrater of understandings and wills,[2] be found.

Of these optionally employable discourses the number might receive any degree of extension, which in the eyes of government—whatsoever on this occasion be to be understood by the word *government*—might seem meet. If the portion of ground which, in the field of religion, was at that time covered by the aggregate mass of these *Homilies*, was sufficiently ample, much more would be the whole of the ground, covered by the aggregate mass of all the discourses which, under the name of *Sermons*, have been made public from that time to the present. Rich as is the stock of Church-of-England sermons extant, yet need not *Government*, whoever on this occasion he would be, confine himself within the bounds within which that stock, ample as it is, is confined. To the whole aggregate mass of all those discourses, which under that name, or of that nature, have at any time seen the light in any part of Christendom,—even the dominion of the Catholic Church not excluded,—this everlastingly orthodox, and everlastingly, as well as in every way '*Excellent,*'[3] though fictitious person, might, on this occasion, extend his researches: nor,—so well assured as he is of his own *excellence*, and, in every thing but the name, of his own *infallibility*,—skilled as he accordingly is in distinguishing, throughout the whole expanse of that field, whatsoever is poisonous from whatsoever is wholesome,—neither the name of *Catholic*, nor that of *Popish*, nay, nor even that of *Presbyterian*, need awaken his apprehension, or disturb his rest. Wide as would be the field which would thus be open to choice, neither within the bounds of this vast field need *choice*, it being *his own* choice, remain for ever, no nor at any time, confined. Sermons, rising still higher and higher in the scale of excellence, if possible, than the most excellent of the existing ones, might, from time to time, according to the arbitrage of the same ever excellent Judge, be added to the whole of the first

---

[1] See [Howley], *Charge delivered to the Clergy of the Diocese of London*, p. 21.
[2] See p. 37 n. above.
[3] See p. 29 n. above.

chosen stock, or in equal or greater quantity substituted to the least excellent portion of it.

But if, in quality of a succedaneum to home-made sermons, then present and then future,—a stock of fixt discourses, comparatively speaking, so scanty as is the *Book of Homilies*, (for in a moderate 8vo. they are all contained),[1] were at that time deemed—and consequently at that time were and still are—fit and sufficient to be employed,—with how much fuller and more incontestable assurance of sufficiency—yea, and of comparative perfection—might a substitute be formed, by a selection made at this[2] time of day, made by hands of acknowledged competency,—out of the entire stock of the discourses of this nature that have been published from the date of those same *Homilies* down to the present time?—To the collection thus proposed, give then the name of *The Collection or Book of Homily Sermons*.

By a single notice given, of *liberty* to employ at pleasure—and rather with praise on the score of canonical obedience, than dispraise on the score of indolence—in lieu of a home-made, or supposed home-made sermon, a sermon taken out of this collection, provision would in some sort be made for the accomplishment of the *positive* end above-mentioned. But, for the accomplishment of the *negative* end, an *injunction*, prescribing the *exclusive use* of this Collection of *Homily Sermons*, in lieu of all home-made Sermons, would be necessary: the prohibition of course not applying to the *printing* or *publishing* of any discourse of this *nature*, or in *that name*.

Nor yet, from the persons so deeply concerned in point of spiritual interest, need all exercise of private judgment, even upon the supposition of an exclusionary ordinance to the effect just mentioned, be taken away. For, in such a case, among jewels, all of them of the first water, the choice might surely, and without much danger, be left to any, even the least skilful hand. Let it be, for example, in the Churchwardens for the time being: each choosing a sermon by turns: in case of an odd one, supposing each to insist on the object of his choice, a precedent of unquestionable authority is at hand: let the one discourse in question be determined by the same arbitrage, by which—in the person of the posthumous Apostle *Matthias*—popularly elected successor to the traitor *Judas*,—a living fountain of eloquence, directed to the same ends—was set up.[a]

[a] Acts, i. [15][3] to 26.[4]

---

[1] *Sermons or Homilies appointed to be read in Churches in the time of Queen Elizabeth of famous memory*, 4th edn., Oxford, 1816, was octavo in size, and contained thirty-three sermons.
[2] 1818 'that'. The text follows the 'Errata'.
[3] 1818 '19'.
[4] Matthias was chosen by lot.

APPENDIX, NO. IV. §III.

To the taste of the rulers of *any* Established Church, an institution of this sort might naturally be not altogether uncongenial, the power of selection being of course, as it could not but be, lodged in their hands. From the pulpit, at any rate, the two great bugbears, *heresy* and *schism*, would thus be most effectually and for ever excluded. Nor yet against the proposed institution could any such imputation be cast, as that of shutting the door against improvement. For,—so long as the choice remained in the same official, and therein ever competent, and unerring, and (if such be their pleasure) infallible hands,—the door to improvement might,—and without any the smallest danger, would—remain as fully open as it ought to be: and whatsoever in this unquestionable wisdom shall, from time to time, come to be deemed *improvement*, and not *innovation*, (for at no time will innovation ever be endurable), will from time to time, and for ever, be accordingly made.[a]

In the days when the Church-of-England *Homilies* were first published, the time for tacking to the permission any such clause as the here proposed exclusive clause, including a prohibition put upon the reading of *home-made* sermons, was assuredly not come.

[a] Note that in this way, by means of this *one* institution,—in the judgment, and for the use, of the three equally Established and eternally conflicting Churches—the *English*, the *Roman Catholic*, and the *Scottish*,—might be constructed three systems of religious instruction—all different—each excellent, each pure to the utmost degree of purity—and, without danger of heresy or schism, each from the first to the last susceptible of ulterior excellence.

The time, at which the selection would, even in the first instance, come to be performed, being, at any rate on all subjects other than that of religious mystery, a time of comparative lucidity,—hence it is, that, even to a judgment by which all fixt forms without exception stood condemned, a Sermon taken out of a collection thus made, might be expected to present no inconsiderable probability, of being superior in value to an *average* sermon, delivered according to the existing practice, in the character of a *home-made* discourse. True it is, that, in the case of the *home-made* discourse, the time of delivery, and thence presumably the time of composition, would on each occasion be the then present time, i.e. on that same occasion the most lucid of all times. But in the judgments in question there seems little danger, that this advantage, such as it is, should be a match for the difference between individual and authoritative choice.

Under the Established Church of Scotland, neither the obligation, it being in this case altogether out of the question, nor so much as the unrestricted permission, to substitute a *Homily Sermon* to a home-made Sermon, could consistently be given: for of such a permission the effect would be that of an opiate, by which the life of piety, and with it of moral instruction, would be extinguished, and the whole Church reduced to that state of perpetual slumber in which it beholds its neighbour buried. But, for preserving the talent in unimpaired vigour, out of the whole number of sermons in the year, a number considerably short of the whole might suffice: and thus might provision be made for the incidental deficiencies which death, disease, and miscellaneous accidents conspire to render unavoidable.

But as surely, if it be not by this time come, always remembering the provision for continual addition proposed to be tacked to it, never at any time can it come.

In this as in so many other instances, thus it is that one and the same institution, which at one time would have been in a high degree mischievous, may, by change of circumstances, be rendered at another time clearly and highly beneficial. And yet there are those, who, thinking, or at least professing to have at heart the good of mankind, would, if they could, on the whole field of religion as well as government, shut an everlasting door against all change!

Come we now to the duties of *imperfect obligation*, as above defined.

Under the Church-of-England system, in here and there an instance,—one out of perhaps *a dozen* or *a score*,—a portion of time and labour, more or less considerable, may, in his own parish possibly, or even elsewhere, be seen employed in this [work][1] of beneficence by a Church-of-England Parish Priest. Instances of this sort are even known, and with heartfelt pleasure viewed, and with the most cordial respect and affection requited—by the author of these pages.

But when and where any such good habit obtains, it is only as it were *by accident:* and, though without the name, the footing on which it stands is exactly that of a *work of supererogation:*—a work of which, while the non-performance passes altogether without notice, the performance is considered as matter of extraordinary merit: merit so extraordinary, as to make atonement for the *eleven* or the *nineteen* instances, in which all those good things, which should have been done, are left undone.

Necessary to the performance of duty in this line is the possession of a correspondent stock of information in that line of appropriate science, which may be termed *Pastoral Statistics:* an acquaintance with the population of the parish, in respect of all those circumstances in which the faculty of exercising these beneficent and pious acts with advantage depends: and as a part of it, an acquaintance with all the several dwellings in the parish, together with the persons of their respective inhabitants. Inherent in the constitution of the Church of England, may be seen to be the branch of ignorance correspondent and opposite to this science: call it *anti-pastoral ignorance.*

In so far as it is the necessary consequence of *Non-Residence,* this ignorance, though in this case not the less vicious, may be referred to the known category of *invincible* ignorance.

[1] 1818 'walk'.

APPENDIX, NO. IV. §III.

Of the fulness of pastoral statistic knowledge, imagination cannot figure to itself a more complete, a more incontestable, a more honourable proof, than that which has so long been exhibited in and by the work edited by *Sir John Sinclair*. Parishes in Scotland, 895: of the state of every one of them an account more or less instructive: and of all these accounts not one but was furnished by the Minister either of the Parish itself,—or in case of accident,—for example, death or temporary infirmity,—by the Minister of some adjacent Parish.[1]

In and for England, whatsoever wishes may, under the influence of envy and shame, have been conceived towards the formation and delivery of any such account, have, by obvious impossibility, ever been rendered abortive.

Of this impossibility, as to a vast proportion of the whole number, the cause may be seen in the Returns made to the House of Commons on the subject of *Non-Residence*.[a]

[a] Among the papers, printed by order of the House of Commons, are to be seen Returns respecting Non-Residence for the three consecutive years, 1809, 1810, and 1811.[2] In those for 1809, 11,194 being given as and for the total number of *Incumbents*, and 3,836 as and for the total number of *Residents*,—this leaves, for the total number of *Non-Residents* in that year, though not summed up, 7,358. In the next year, 1810, the total number of *Incumbents* is sunk from 11,194 to 10,261: decrease 933. But while there is this decrease in the total number of *Incumbents*,— *Residents* and *Non-Residents* taken together,—the total number of *Residents* is increased from 3,836 to 4,421: increase 585: the total number of Non-Residents consequently diminished from 7,358 to 5,840: decrease 1,516. In 1811, the total number of Incumbents rises again: though short of the total number for the first year, 1809, by 393; it rises from 10,261—the number for the second year, 1810—to 10,801: increase 540: but, in this third year, 1811, while the total number of *Residents* increases no more than from 4,421 to 4,490—increase 69—the total number of *Non-Residents* increases from the 5,840 to 6,311: increase 471.

In each year, to some purposes, and, amongst the rest, the one here in question, allowance will require to be made for the case, which, in the Return for the year 1809, is, by the Bishop of Norwich, termed the case of *virtual residence*.[3] This is the case of those who, although the Parsonage House is not the place, or among the places, of their respective residences, are, in the Returns, stated as being persons who '*perform*

---

[1] For Sinclair, *Statistical Account of Scotland*, see p. 292 n. above, and for the figure of 895 parishes see p. 481 n. below.

[2] 'An Abstract of Returns respecting Residence and Non-Residence; For the Year ending the 25th March 1809', 'Abstract of the Number and Classes of Non-Resident Incumbents, And of the Number of Resident Incumbents, According to the Diocesan Returns for the Year 1810', and 'Abstract of the Number and Classes of Non-Resident Incumbents, And of the Number of Resident Incumbents, According to the Diocesan Returns for the Year 1811', in *Commons Sessional Papers* (1812) x. 159–62, 151–4, and (1812–13) xiii. 47–50, respectively.

[3] At the foot of the Abstract (see *Commons Sessional Papers* (1812) x. 161) is a copy of a note which had been annexed to the Diocesan Return of Norwich by Henry Bathurst, Bishop of Norwich: 'Besides the 353 Residents, there is a very large majority of the Non-Residents, who perform their own duty, and are therefore virtually Resident. This circumstance has not been accurately stated in the Return, but shall be rectified in future.'

CHURCH-OF-ENGLANDISM

Of *Non-Residence*, a necessary consequence is *Anti-pastoral Ignorance*. Unfortunately, not quite so necessary is the connexion between the two opposites:—between *Residence* and *Pastoral Know-*

the Duties of their Parishes.' Of these, for the year 1809, the number expressly stated as being in this case, is 565: to these add 105, that being the number whose case is stated to be that of '*Residence in a Mansion within the Parish*, belonging to Incumbent or Relative,'—in which case the performance of duty, though not expressly stated, may (it is supposed) be presumed,—(though in these cases, if it really had place, it seems odd enough that it should not have been so stated)—with this addition, the total number of these *Virtual Residents* for that year will be 670. For the year 1810, without the addition of the numbers contained in this uninclucled case, it appears to be—what in the Earl of Harrowby's Speech (pp. 3 and 19)[1] it is stated to be, 970; with the addition, (viz. 62)[2] 1032: for the year 1811, (which year, though the date of that Speech is 18th June, 1812, appears not to have come under his Lordship's cognizance)[3] it appears to have increased to 1433: with the like addition (added number 68) [1501].[4] The Earl of Harrowby not having numbered among the 'DOERS OF THEIR OWN DUTY,'—(to use his Lordship's words)[5]—those who though '*residing in a Mansion within the Parish*,' have taken out *Licences* for *Non-Residence*,—is it possible, that, after all, by none of the individuals belonging to this omitted class, though residing, all of them, within their Parishes, any part of the duty of it was done?—The question seems not altogether an unnatural one: for any answer to it, no other *data* are to be found. That, among the Incumbents returned as *non-resident*, a distinction should be made, in respect and in favour of those who, notwithstanding such their Non-Residence, '*perform*,' or '*do their own duties*,' is undeniable. Unfortunately, altogether vague, however, is the best information which it can afford. As to the duties of *perfect obligation*,—whether in the parish in question the Incumbent *resides* or *not*,—such duties, as by law he is obliged to do, it may be presumed he does: all these in both cases, but not any more in either case. If so, then are the duties of *imperfect obligation* the only ones, in regard to which *Residence* or *Non-Residence* can make any difference. In regard to these, so far as concerns the actual performance of them, very little difference probably has place; but, in regard to physical facility as to the performance of them, it is susceptible of variation upon a very large scale. Many are the cases in which two contiguous livings are held by the same person: in these instances it may happen, that the distance of the Parsonage *House* from the *Church*, which it does *not* belong to, is not so great as from the Church which it *does* belong to: thus stands the matter at one end of the scale: at the other end, stands the case in which the distance of the officiating Minister's place of residence from the Church of

---

[1] Harrowby introduced the debate to consider the report on amendments to the Stipendiary Curates Bill in the House of Lords on 18 June 1812: see *Parliamentary Debates* (1812) xxiii. 592–3. The Act for the further support and maintenance of Stipendiary Curates received the Royal Assent on 20 July 1813 as 53 Geo. III, c. 149. The speech was subsequently published as *Substance of the Speech of the Earl of Harrowby* (see p. 86 n. above), and it is from this that Bentham quotes. For Bentham's detailed notes on the speech see UC vi. 200–9 (16 April 1813).

[2] i.e. those said to be in 'Residence in a Mansion within the Parish, belonging to Incumbent or Relative'.

[3] The Abstract for 1811 was not ordered to be printed until 26 March 1813.

[4] 1818 '1801'.

[5] *Substance of the Speech of the Earl of Harrowby*, p. 19: 'there are also 970 Incumbents non-resident, but doing their own duty'.

ledge. The drawing-room, the dining-room, the cellar, the stable, the dog-kennel, of the Lord or Squire—with the state of all these agreeable receptacles, under the Church-of-England system, the most perfect acquaintance may, without any over-weening confidence, be expected at the hands of the Resident Minister, where there is any,—whether Rector, Vicar, or Curate: here is comfort *in præsenti;* here is hope of glory *in futuro*.[1] But the *poor* inhabitants and their wants,—not altogether unhonoured are they, if to the man of God as many of their names are known, as of those of his Lordship's hounds.

Compliments and observations on the place and the weather omitted, follows a dialogue between a zealous Church-of-England Bishop and the Oxford Graduate.[2]

Zealot.—What? Give a Parish boy the Holy Ghost? Give this urchin the power to remit or retain sins?

Graduate.—Why not? As to the Holy Ghost—whatever he or it is—either he or it is, or is not, at your disposal: if he or it is not, why pretend to dispose of him or it? If he or it is, what should hinder your giving him or it to the boy, as well as to them to whom you are in use to give him or it? As to the power of remitting or retaining sins,—produce this power of yours: shew any such restriction in it, as can prevent your giving it to the boy, or to any one else to whom you would please to give it? 'Whose soever sins ye remit, they are remitted to them; and whose soever sins ye retain, they are retained.' Thus said Jesus (John, xx. 23.) to his Apostles. If then ye are the same person, each of you, as one of those same Apostles, ye can, every one of you, remit sins—the sins of any sinning creature: if ye are the same person, each of you, as Jesus, ye can give to any rational creature this same power of remitting sins. In this case, ye can, with exactly as much ease, give this power to the Parish-Boy, as to the Parish-Minister.

Zealot.—Give it to the urchin?—Well:—suppose as much. But if he had it, would he not abuse it?

Graduate.—Not he indeed. If you yourself, for example, are Jesus, *that* will be your care; and not any the least danger is there of your

his Parish is so great, that, if not all his powers, all his reasonably expectable exertions, are exhausted by the riding to the Church once every Sunday to do the necessary duty there, and then back again. In any system in which the exigencies of the service constituted the standard of reference, two or three contiguous parishes would, in many instances, be united: and, in these instances, a proportionable number of cases of Non-Residence would thus disappear.

---

[1] *in præsenti*: at the present time; *in futuro*: in future.
[2] i.e. the author of *Church-of-Englandism*.

giving the power to any creature that will abuse it.—But neither will he, if, for argument sake, you are *not* Jesus. When, by a priest of your making the sins are forgiven, still it is always according to your *Rubrick*, and your formulary of *Absolution*. By the Rubrick effectual security is afforded, against all abuse in respect of the *occasion* on which the operation is performed, and by that means in respect of the *persons* on whom it is to be performed; and, by the formulary, against any abuse in the *mode* of performance. If he varies, this holy person, from the formulary, though it be but an iota, the operation is void, and the sins are not forgiven: ask Sir William Scott else, or Mr. Justice Bailey, or Mr. Justice Parke.[1]

Zealot.—Oh, but to give the boy these powers, would be to give him *Priest's Orders:* and he is not so much as in *Deacon's Orders.*[2]

Graduate.—*Priest's Orders! Deacon's Orders!* Where did you get these Orders? From *Jesus?* Alas! no. From whom then? Even from the *Whore of Babylon*, alias *Holy Mother Church*. Why did you ever quit her? Go back to her—get absolution from her and make your peace. From her you may have a whole heap more of *Orders*, one upon another: all of them under Deacon's, each of them conveying altogether as much inspiration as can be conveyed by Deacon's.[3] Turn to the *Acts of the Apostles*. What else was a *Deacon* but a manager of the common funds?[4] Whatsoever a *Deacon* was then, is not a *Churchwarden* now?—Well, if you cannot part with your *Deacon's* Orders, keep them then: it need make no difference. You *cumulate Divinity Degrees* (in your *Universities* I mean):—you *cumulate* the two *Divinity Degrees:*[5]—what should hinder your *cumulating* these two *Orders?*—True it is, that when, on his way to the priesthood, a man is as yet but a *Deacon*, he has no power of himself (you say) to forgive sins: all he can as yet do is to beg of God Almighty to forgive them,—

[1] At this time Scott was a Judge in the Consistory Court of London and Vicar-General of the Province of Canterbury, and Judge of the High Court of Admiralty, Bayley was a Justice of King's Bench, and Park a Justice of Common Pleas. All three were staunch supporters of the Church of England, and Scott and Park were members of the General Committee of the National Society for Promoting the Education of the Poor.

[2] In the Church of England, the diaconate was the lowest of the three major orders of ministry (the two others being the priesthood and the episcopate), and was regarded as a stage in preparation for priesthood. A deacon was permitted to read the gospel and to preach. See Burn, *Ecclesiastical Law*, 2nd edn., 1767, Ordination, §VI. Form and manner of ordaining deacons, iii. 37–8.

[3] The four minor orders in the Roman Catholic Church were acolytes, exorcists, lectors, and doorkeepers.

[4] The appointment by the Jerusalem Church of seven men to administer the widows' fund, recounted at Acts 6: 1–6, was traditionally understood to be the origin of the office of deacon.

[5] At the Universities of Oxford and Cambridge, students who had obtained their Bachelor of Arts and Master of Arts could proceed to the further degrees of Bachelor of Divinity and Doctor of Divinity. Since a degree in Arts was sufficient qualification for the priesthood, only a small number of those entering the Church qualified as Bachelor of Divinity or Doctor of Divinity.

who, therefore, on this particular occasion, is left to do as he pleases: accordingly, instead of the *Absolution*, what the *Deacon* reads is no more than a *Prayer:* it is only when, by having been made to receive the *Holy Ghost*, he the *Deacon* has been transformed into a *Priest*, that he receives this *power:* and then and thereafter it is, that, immediately upon his pronouncing the *Absolution*, the sins vanish off the score, whether God Almighty pleases or not:—or else where is the difference?—The implied confession thus put into the *Deacon*'s mouth—the confession of his own incapacity to pronounce the *Absolution*—of the incapacity he labours under, as to the forgiving the sins otherwise than with the help of the Almighty—is one of your contrivances—and a more ingenious one could not easily have been hit upon—for satisfying the people, that the *incapacity* will be changed into *power*, as soon as the *Deacon* is ripened into a Priest. The boy, be he ever so young,—if he says, or is supposed to have said his *Catechism*, you give him *Confirmation*. What then should hinder your giving him *Deacon*'s, and *Priest*'s, or any other *Orders*, at the same time?—It will be so much trouble saved: and, generally speaking, you are not overfond of trouble. After all, if it be more agreeable to you to take two ceremonies to do it in than one, so be it.

One word more. The power of forgiving or retaining sins, and thereby of sending any body to heaven or hell at pleasure being given, how came you—aye, and how do ye now continue to be—so barbarous, as to send men in such multitudes to hell—aye, or so much as a single one of them?—Why do you leave *any* man's sins unforgiven? Why do not you keep on forgiving sins as fast as they are committed, and thus send every body to heaven?

Zealot. Sir, we know better things. Sir, if I were to send to heaven a man who ought to go to hell,—*yourself*, Sir, for example,—this would be a sin, Sir,—and a most enormous sin,—and God would send *me* to hell for committing it.

Graduate. Not he, indeed: if you would but manage properly, as you might do without difficulty. Take to yourself, for example, one other man endowed with the same useful powers. At the same instant, each of you forgive, in one breath, all the sins of the whole world,—those of his partner included,—and in particular, for fear of mistakes, this last sin, which consists in the forgiving of all the other sins. This done, what sin is there left, for which God could send you to hell, or do any thing else to you that you would not like? Now then, if hell overflows, and heaven is almost a desert, with none but a few choice Church-of-Englandists to roam about in it, who is it that is to blame?—Who but you and yours?

Zealot. Alas! what is all this but *ridicule?*—And ridicule—can it, even in your own estimation, be considered as fair argument?—fit to be made use of as a *test of truth?*[1]

Graduate. That depends upon where it is fetched from—whether from without or from within. If from without, no: as if, for example,—in speaking of your notion about causing a man, by laying your hands upon his head, and speaking certain words to him, to receive the Holy Ghost,—I were to compare you to a juggler, who making as if he had put a ring into a box, gives it to a man to hold, who, upon opening it, finds there is no ring there. Here the way in which ridicule cast upon the serious and important subject is cast, is—by presenting to view along with it another subject, which is in itself a trifling one, and has not any connection with it, material to the purpose in hand.

But if it be by matter taken from the subject itself, and necessarily belonging to it, that the ridicule is reflected upon it, no argument can be fairer: nor can there be in this case a fairer *test of truth,*—i.e. a surer proof that what is given for true is not so,—than what is applied, when, by the matter thus drawn from the notion itself, the quality of *ridiculousness* is shewn to belong to it. Such is the case, in so far as any position, which is either a necessary *consequence* of the one in question, or necessary to be advanced to form a *ground* for it, is to a certain degree *absurd:* viz. to such a degree as to appear *ridiculous:*—the more palpably absurd it is, the more flagrantly ridiculous.

Thus as to this notion of yours—this notion of your having power to give power to other men to remit sins. What ground do you produce for it? What other than the above passage in *St. John's Gospel,*[2] in which he speaks of *Jesus* as conferring this power on his *Apostles.* Now then, (say I), there is only one supposition, on which, by his conferring it upon his *Apostles,* he has conferred it upon *you:* and that is—your being the same persons with those his Apostles. Necessary is an assumption to that effect to the proving of your having any such power: or—to take it the other way—assuming that, in consequence of what Jesus thus said to his Apostles, you have this power,—it follows that you are the same persons with those his Apostles. But—this notion of your being the same persons with those Apostles of Jesus—to such a degree, in my view of the matter, I must confess, is it an absurd one, that if it be not a ridiculous one, I know not where any such notion as a ridiculous one is to be found. To come then to the principal notion—viz. that of your having the power to remit sins, or to give to any body else that same power—the cause of the ridicule cast on it, is it any thing external and foreign to the notion

---

[1] Anthony Ashley Cooper (1671–1713), third Earl of Shaftesbury, had advocated the use of ridicule as a test of truth in *Sensus Communis: An Essay on the Freedom of Wit and Humour,* London, 1709. [2] John 20: 23.

itself? No: it is a quality, not only belonging to the notion itself, but inseparable from it: viz. its requiring this other undeniably absurd and ridiculous notion for a necessary support, or including it as a necessary consequence. Exhibit it with its necessary *supports* and *consequences*, no otherwise than by misrepresentation can *this*, or any other notion, which is thus in itself ridiculous, be made to appear *not* ridiculous.

Let but this be received as law, viz. that nothing that, in the exercise of their power, has on the subject of religion been advanced by men in power, is to be caused to appear ridiculous,—then may every thing which is not only most absurd, but most mischievous as well as absurd, be advanced by them without possibility of contradiction,—and, for want of refutation, assent by force of authority procured to the most pernicious notions, practice altogether governed by them,—and the public mind reduced to the state in which it is already in Spain, and, thanks to those who rule in England, will presently be in France.

Zealot.—Well, Sir, you seem to be talking all this while very much at your ease, but will you find it altogether so easy to exculpate this talk of yours from the charge of *blasphemy?*

Graduate.—This depends upon what you mean by *blasphemy*. If it be language intentionally expressive of, or proceeding from, disrespect towards the Almighty,—towards a being believed by myself to exist, and to be Almighty,—neither on this present occasion is any such blasphemy to be found in me, nor on any occasion in any man whatsoever has any such blasphemy been found, unless the man were absolutely and literally mad. Not being mad, no such sentiment towards the Almighty do I entertain,—of no such sentiment is this or any other language of mine intentionally expressive. In this sense then have I as easily as effectually exculpated this my talk from the charge of *blasphemy*. But, if this be not what you mean by *blasphemy*,—then, unless you mean by it something that, under that name, is punishable by law, or deserving of disapprobation at the hands of public opinion,—which is what I believe you would not find it very easy to prove,—call it by that name if it be any satisfaction to you, you have my free leave for it.[a]

---

[a] On every part of the field of religion—whether a man be in power or *not*—but more particularly if he *is*—this way of thinking, speaking, and acting, is unhappily but too generally prevalent. Whatsoever are the opinions which he entertains, or professes to entertain,—what he all along insists upon is—that they are God's, and as such ought by every man to be deemed and taken to be:—yes, and accordingly spoken of by every man who takes the liberty—a liberty on this hypothesis equally audacious and inconsistent—of contesting them: yes, and this at the very time, and

Zealot.—Oh, but the *decencies* . . . . ? Put this low-bred Parish-boy in the place of the University-bred and regularly ordained Priest, what will become of the *decencies?*

all the time, that he is contesting them: all this on pain of being subjected to the *punishment,* or at any rate to the *reproach,* of blasphemy.

Now then if so it be that the man in question—the self-constituted and untolerating censor—is the Almighty, then as above, true it is, that the language, by which any disrespect is cast upon any such opinion of his, *is* blasphemy: on this supposition, but not otherwise.

History speaks of a man, who, fancying, or pretending to fancy himself, to be *Jesus,* went about the country declaring himself so to be to every body who would hear him.[1] This man spoke out. For prostration of understanding and will, as towards himself, by this vagabond, supposing him impudent enough to call for obsequiousness in that shape, the ground was explicitly declared. Comes *his Lordship of London,* and,—addressing himself to the Clergy, his subordinates, and through them by means of the press to the public at large,—informs them of a case, in which obsequiousness in that same abject and unreserved form will be due to, and as such may be called for by, themselves.[2] To these men will it then really be due? Yes: if they be, each of them, Jesus,—but not otherwise. Thus then does he encourage and virtually command them, each of them, to give men to understand that he is Jesus.—Command them? How? in explicit terms as the vagabond did? No: only by necessary implication: nothing more: in that lies the only difference. To be himself the *one Jesus,* will even *that* satisfy him? Not it indeed: *Jesuses* must he have, and by hundreds, for his subordinates.

Dismissing the Bishop, take any controversialist at random, so he be a religious one, this assumption of his being *God*—every one who on the points in question agrees with him, a God—each of them the one only God—is but too apt to run through all his discourses, and to be among the postulates, which all his demonstrations take for their ground. Nor will even this satisfy him. For, when you have a dispute with him, you having the boldness to contest this or that one of his tenets,—what he virtually requires of you is—on your part a virtual admission that such is the case. Whatever assertions the tenet contains,—yes, and whatever assertions he comes out with, in defence of them,—they must be, all of them, deemed and taken to be so many assertions made by God, and on that supposition must the language employed by you in speaking of them be grounded. Supposing them then absurd,—and *that* to such a degree as to be ridiculous,—may you represent them exactly as they are? No. Will he endure that you should?—Not he indeed. For, as by the implied postulate he is God, his assertions are God's assertions, which being true, they cannot be, any of them, *ridiculous:* and to treat any of them as such is *blasphemy;* and you, so treating them, are a *blasphemer:* and blasphemers are such wretches, no treatment can be too bad for them. On every such occasion, all along, in giving expression to these opinions of his, he, on his part, takes care, of course, to employ

---

[1] James Nayler (1618–60), Quaker preacher and writer, was in 1656 charged with impersonating Christ and claiming divine status, and found guilty of 'horrid blasphemy'. There was no law by which he could be punished by death for this crime, so it was agreed that he would be whipped, exposed in the pillory, have his tongue bored through with a hot iron, and stigmatized on the forehead with the letter B for 'Blasphemy'. See *A Complete Collection of State-Trials, and Proceedings upon High-Treason, and other misdemeanours; from the Reign of King Richard II. to the End of the Reign of King George I*, ed. Sollom Emlyn, 6 vols., London, 2nd edn., 1730, ii. 265–72.

[2] See pp. 261–2 above.

APPENDIX, NO. IV. §III.

Graduate. Well then, as to the *decencies.* Unless by the *decencies* you mean the 10*l.* a year, or the 7,000*l.* a year,[1] or some intermediate sum given for doing something or nothing, on which subject some-such language as imports them to be so many just objects of the most prostrate veneration. In any defence he makes of them against any attacks, all along he thus keeps *taking for granted* that which is in dispute. In all this there is nothing but what, though not altogether logical, is, considering the nature of the subject, natural enough, and at least excusable. But neither will this satisfy him: for, on your part, the language used by you, in relation to these assertions of his, must be of such a sort as to convey an implied confirmation of the *grant.* In themselves they are so absurd as to be ridiculous. Representing them as venerable, what you would say of them would be a misrepresentation. Yet in this misrepresentation he insists that all along you shall join, or all your arguments are so much *blasphemy.*

The misfortune is—that if the notion a man has advanced is to a certain degree absurd and ridiculous, and it has fallen in your way to shew it so to be,—in so doing you have unavoidably been testifying towards the man himself a certain degree of *disrespect:* for in proportion as what, on any occasion, a man says, is seen to be ridiculous, in that same proportion does he become the object of the sort of sentiment called *disrespect.* Irritated by this disrespect—irritated, and, by the irritation, his judgment to such a degree disturbed, as to cause him, in the view he takes of the matter, to mistake one person for another—the disrespect thus shewn to him, and this notice of his, he fancies, or pretends to fancy, is disrespect shewn to the Almighty. To the Almighty?—Yes: if he and the Almighty are one and the same person—(a proposition which, by the bye, may as easily be true as that any three persons are but one):—Yes, if he and the Almighty are one and the same person, but not otherwise. But as for you, you for your part do *not* believe him to be the Almighty: therefore, whatsoever disrespect you may unavoidably have been testifying, it goes no further than your antagonist—it reaches not the Almighty.

That, to whatsoever object or objects applied, *three* and *one* are the same number, this, for example, (you say) is a notion so *absurd* as to be *ridiculous:* as such you accordingly, if you speak of it without misrepresentation, cannot avoid representing it.—Alas! (cries he) this is *blasphemy:* this is blaspheming the *Trinity:* this is blaspheming *God:* this is treating the Almighty with contempt.—Treat the Almighty with contempt?—not you indeed. With contempt enough indeed, what is but natural, and indeed scarce avoidable, is—that on this occasion something or other should be treated by you: for example, this notion of his—that in that instance, or any instance, applied to the same *object* (or *objects* shall we say?) *three* and *one* are the same number. After putting on this occasion *person* for *God,* as on other occasions he would put *person* for *a man,* to say that three *God-persons* are but one God, is exactly the same absurdity—exactly the same self-contradictory proposition—as to say of three *man-persons* (three brothers, for instance) that they are but one man: of a proposition thus self-contradictory,—by no evidence, that ever was contained in a book, or ever could be contained in a book,—can the truth be proved.—Away, away! cries he: what is all this but *blasphemy!*—And so the dispute ends, by his going to a lawyer for advice, whether he cannot give himself the satisfaction of seeing you punished,—and out of the Judge's tender mercy, forced to tell a barefaced lie under the name of *recantation,* to save yourself from further punishment.

This word *blasphemy,* in the meaning at present attached to it, for what sort of purpose is it employed? Only to serve as a cloak for some injury, which he, *by* whom

---

[1] i.e. the income of the Rectory of Doddington: see p. 354 & n. above.

thing will be said presently—the *decencies* have already been enumerated: the *vestments*, the *postures*, the *gestures*, and the *locomotions*.

As to the *vestments*, these you might give to the juvenile reader, if you thought it worth the while. Similar vestments—some of them at least—are actually worn at six or seven years old by boys in Cathedrals—in those magnificent,—and, except to the lust of the eye, so completely useless,—edifices, in which for six days out of the

the word is employed, labours thereby to do, *to* him to whose discourse it is applied: to render him an object—if not of legal punishment, at the least of public hatred, for expression given to this or that notion, opposite to those entertained, or professed to be entertained, by *him,* by whom the word is thus employed.

Considering the use which it has thus been put to, and the mischievous passions of which—and with but too much success—it is, almost as often as employed, endeavoured to be made the instrument,—great would be the service done to mankind, were it possible to extirpate it out of all language.

Next to the extirpation of it, is the laying the *root* bare. Like almost every other word that has been used with reference to *God* or *Gods*, it was of course first used with reference to *man*. Used with reference to man in the Greek (from which so large a part of the language of technical religion has been derived), compounded, as it were, of two words, one of which signifies *injury*, the other *reputation*, it meant neither more nor less than *injury to his reputation*. Blaspheming against man, was injury done to the reputation of the man. In this the only original sense of the word, blasphemy therefore against God was injury done to the reputation of God. Now then, as to *man*, by injury done to *his* reputation, man is indeed liable to be subjected to sufferance:—to sufferance in various shapes, varying in quantity upon a scale of almost indefinite length. But, by injury done to *God's* reputation, is *God* exposed to sufferance in those or any other shapes? No, says somebody: but, by notions which are unworthy of him, *injury* is in your phrase *done to his reputation:* or, in the more usual and proper phrase, *dishonour* is done to him, and *disrespect* shewn to him, and for that disrespect the offender ought to be punished. Such is the answer.—Here then, as above, look into this supposed *disrespect* towards *God*, what you will find in it is neither more nor less than disrespect towards some opinion entertained, or pretended to be entertained, *concerning God* by *man:* by man with *power* in his hands.

Take two men of irritable mould—set them a talking about God—and thence necessarily about his attributes,—the moment any difference of opinion has place between them—and that moment will never be far distant—each becomes, in the eyes of the other, *a blasphemer:*—to each it thereupon becomes clear, that the other ought to be punished: punished in the offending member: the only doubt being, whether, as has been sometimes done, it ought to be bored through with a red-hot iron,[1] or cut out. Inadequate, incorrect notions concerning God, are not they *unworthy* of him?—Yes. Did that man then ever exist, of whom, if he entertained any notions at all concerning God, it might not with truth be said, that he entertained *unworthy* notions of him? No: and yet, in the next breath, by the same man who thus says *no*, will punishment be called for to be inflicted on this or that other man, for the *unworthiness*, as above, of such his notions!

---

[1] See p. 368 n. above.

seven, the pleasantness of what is *sung* cannot so far atone for the insipidity of what is *said*, as to procure upon an average half a dozen voluntary yawners, in addition to the compulsory ones.

Remain the *postures*, the *gestures*, and the *loco-motions*—the marching and counter-marching—from *Reading-desk* to *Altar*—from *Altar* back to *Reading-desk*—from *Reading-desk* up to *Pulpit:* as if when reading his own stuff, or another man's stuff, on pretence of its being his own, it were necessary a man should exhibit himself as a higher man than when, under the name of a lesson—reading the word of God.

Well—keep them there—if you cannot part with them—the *postures*, the *gestures*, and the *loco-motions*. But, in all of them put together, what is there that a boy of fourteen would not serve for as well as a man of forty? Stupid indeed must the boy be, if after a couple of hours' drilling he be not as perfect in this part of the exercise as the man could be if he were fourscore.

Even in your Universities—where, along with perjury, ceremony is taught in such perfection,—immediately as he comes from school, is not a boy made what is called a *Bible Clerk?*[1] And this Bible Clerk, is it not his peculiar office in the Chapel every day, in the course of the service, to read, under the name of *first* or *second* lesson, a chapter or two out of the Bible? Being old enough and in every respect good enough to read the word of God, is he not old enough and in every respect good enough to read your Liturgy?—Whatsoever be *propriety* or *decency* in reading, is it of more importance that this Liturgy of your's, than that the word of God, should be read with propriety and decency?

The boy, *Chorister boy*, wears one sort of vestment: the boy, *Bible Clerk*, wears another sort of vestment. The *Chorister boy's* vestment is the exact miniature of your Priest's *Surplice*. This very gown worn by the boy Bible Clerk—this, or something scarce distinguishable from it, is used by many a Priest to read his sermon in. Thus you have *Precedent—Precedent* for every thing. *Reason*—it were in vain to shew her to you: but *Precedent*—her improved substitute, you and your brother the Lawyer have ever numbered among your Gods.

§4.—2. *Pay.*

In this case, as in others, the use, and only use of *pay* is the obtaining, in sufficient quantity, *service* of the requisite quality and degree of goodness.

---

[1] The Bible Clerk was a class of student in certain colleges at the Universities of Oxford and Cambridge, who read the lessons in chapel and said grace in the dining hall.

When, on such an occasion, and for such a purpose, mention is made of *pay*,—the fund, out of which it is considered as coming, must be understood to be a fund, composed of money extracted from such as,—but for the force of government applied in case of refusal,—would be unwilling contributors: in a word, levied by *taxation*. For, in so far as those, out of whose pocket it comes are willing, and for the obtaining of it no misrepresentation is employed, nor by the use thus made of it any injury done to any other person,—no reason can be assigned for wishing to see any limitation set to their expenditure, in this shape more than in any other.

But, for the purchase of service of the sort in question, viz. that which consists in the administering of instruction of the sort in question,—is it fit that, at the expense of the whole population—willing and unwilling taken together—is it fit that money should be taken? *Answer.*—If it be only in respect of its effects, in relation to his own welfare, that each man's conduct were considered, perhaps not.

But, to the mischief, which, by the misconduct of any one man, and so in the case of each man, may, for want of such instruction, be produced,—mischief operating in diminution of the happiness of others,[a]—scarcely can any limits be assigned.

Manifest it seems at any rate, that, if for instruction, in relation to this part of the field of thought and action, money ought not to be levied in the way of taxation, much less ought it for instruction, in relation to any other parts.

In so far as, among those who are in possession of receiving instruction of the sort in question, there are any who desire the continuance of it, this possession affords another reason—and *that*, it should seem, an irresistible one—for the continuance of it,—and thereby for the continuance of the *pay* necessary for the obtainment of it.

For the purpose of giving expression to the sort of relation, which ought to have place, between *service*,—supposed to be rendered, or required, by or on behalf of the public, on the one hand,—and *pay*, considered as employed, or employable, in the purchase of such service, on the other,—follow, in two corresponding pages, two corresponding sets of *maxims:* the one set expressive of those by which, in the view taken of the subject by the author of these pages,

---

[a] See Introd. Part II. § Mischiefs of Exclusion.[1]

[1] i.e. 'Introduction', Part II.—Exclusionary System of Instruction—its Establishment—its bad Tendencies, pp. 88–98 above.

practice ought to be governed;[a] the other, expressive of those by which it has been thought that, to an extent more or less considerable, practice has been and continues to be actually governed.

[a] The principles from whence these maxims have been deduced, are to be found, mostly, if not completely, as far as recollection serves, in Mr. Bentham's *Traité des Peines et des Recompenses*, as edited by Mr. Dumont, anno 1812, or thereabouts;[1] but, the work not being at hand, no particular reference can be made to it.

To a student in the art and science of legislation,—if among the thousand official legislators, or thereabouts, with their expectant successors and unofficial critics, any such person there be,—it might be a not altogether unuseful praxis, to take up the principles and maxims thus applied to Clerical, and make application of them to Lay, Offices.—As to the Edinburgh Reviewers, the principles laid down in the above book not being much more favourable to the interests of Placemen in expectancy than of Placemen in possession, they have, in their review of it, very prudently stopped at the subject of *punishment*, leaving that of *reward* untouched.[2]

[1] See *Théorie des peines et des récompenses*, ed. Étienne Dumont, 2 vols., London, 1811, Liv. II. Des Salaires, ii. 150–208.

[2] See the article, whose anonymous author was Henry Brougham, entitled 'Bentham's Theory of Punishments, by Dumont', in *Edinburgh Review*, vol. xxii, no. xliii (October 1813), 1–31.

OXFORD GRADUATE'S MAXIMS.

1. For the due rendering of *service* in respect of *office*, adequate *aptitude* and adequate *inclination*—*aptitude*, including *mental power*—are both necessary—neither suffices without the other.

2. For proof of the existence of adequate aptitude,—and in particular in the case of a functionary, who by his office is required to pray and preach in public,—*examination* performed in public is, generally speaking, the only adequate security.[a]

3. To the office, be it what it may, a quantity of *pay*, to any amount, may be attached, without adding either in *quantity* or in *quality*, to the value of the service, if any, which is rendered in respect of it.

4. Of the *pay* attached to office, the *magnitude* affords not of itself any security at all,—much less any adequate security,—for the rendering, in *any* quantity or of any quality, much less in *apt* quantity and quality, the *service*, for the rendering of which the office is professed to have been created and kept on foot.

5. Unless, in so far as adequate superiority, in respect of the *value* of the service performed, i.e. *quantity* and *quality* of it taken together, can be shewn to result from *superiority* of pay, the *less* the pay the better.

6. Unless, in so far as adequate superiority, in respect of *value*, i.e. quantity or quality of service performed, as above, can be shewn to result, from the employing of hands, paid at the public expense by money exacted from *unwilling* hands,—service ought rather to be received from *unpaid*,—if spontaneously offering,—or otherwise

---

[a] See Notes, p. 382.[1]

[1] In 1818 the note marker is placed at the end of Maxim 3, though it clearly belongs at the end of Maxim 2.

374

EXCELLENT CHURCH'S MAXIMS.

1. For the rendering of service in respect of an Ecclesiastical (or *Lay*) office, neither *aptitude* nor *inclination* are necessary. It suffices that the desire of the pay allotted for the purchase of the service is strong enough to cause a man to engage to render it: and this whether he does or does not intend to render it.[a]

2. For the possession of an Ecclesiastical (or *Lay*) office, neither aptitude nor inclination, with reference to the rendering of the service, for the purchase of which the office is professed to have been instituted and to be kept on foot, being necessary,—it is not necessary that, for the proof of the existence of adequate aptitude, any adequate *security* should be taken in any shape, nor therefore in the shape of *public examination*.[b]

3. The *greater* the quantity of *pay* attached to an Ecclesiastical (or *Lay*) office, be it what it may, the *greater* in *value*,—*quality* and *quantity* taken together into the account,—will be the *service* rendered by the possessor of it.[c]

4. The *magnitude* of the pay attached to an Ecclesiastical (or *Lay*) office, affords of itself an adequate security for the rendering, in adequate quality and quantity, the service, for the rendering of which the office is professed to have been created and kept on foot.[d]

5. The *greater* the quantity of *pay* is, which is attached to an Ecclesiastical (or *Lay*) office, the *better*. No quantity, how great soever, requires for the justification of it any determinate ground for the supposition, that extra-magnitude, in any degree, in the value of the *service* performed by the possessor of it, will be the result of any extra-magnitude in the quantity of the pay.[e]

6. So long as money, exacted by public authority from *unwilling hands*, can be found for the purchase of an engagement to render the service, it is not good that it be rendered either *gratuitously*, or for pay received altogether from *willing hands*.[f]

---

[a] See Notes, p. 387.

willing hands,—or from hands paid by contributions furnished by willing hands.[b]

7. Unless, in case of special and preponderant reason to the contrary, for the purpose of affording pay for the purchase of public service, contributions ought rather to be received from *willing*, than from *unwilling*, hands.

8. In no case, in virtue of any office, by the possessor of which as such, no laborious function is performed, nor any service rendered to the public, should money be received or paid at the expense of unwilling hands. In four words, *no service, no pay!* in two words, *no Sinecures.*[c] N.B. No public office having ever been created, but under the notion of service to be done in respect of it by the possessor,—every penny, received in virtue of an office, in which no labour regarded as serviceable to the public, is performed by the possessor, is so much received on *a false pretence.*

9. As the mass of pay, allotted to the office in question, for the purchase of the service attached to it, should not in the *whole* together be given and received, unless the whole of such service be rendered,—so neither should any *particle* of such mass of pay be given and received, unless a correspondent portion of service be rendered.

10. In respect of each portion of service required in virtue of any office, every *security* necessary to the causing it to be rendered should be taken.[d]

11. The classes, whose place in the scale of opulence is lowest, are those to whose exigencies in all shapes the service performed by a *Parish Priest*, as such, ought to be preferably adapted:—and this on a double account: viz. because it is in this instance that the need of such service,—and in particular of such service as is rendered by the performance of the duties of *imperfect obligation*,—is most pressing, and because it is of them that the greatest part of the population is composed.

12. In the situation of *Parish Priest*, the greater the quantity of the pay received by a man, the more powerfully is he drawn from, and set above, the habit of holding, and disposition to hold, intercourse with those persons, by whom, as above, in all respects, and in particular in respect of the duties of *imperfect obligation* his services are most needed.

7. For the furnishing of pay for the purchase of Ecclesiastical service, it is not good that contributions be received from none but *willing* hands: they ought to be exacted from *unwilling* ones.[g]

8. By the possessor of an Ecclesiastical (or *Lay*) office, in return for pay, be the amount of it ever so great, no service need in any shape be rendered. In three words, *Sinecures are necessary!* N.B. By the power, the opulence, the dignity, and the high connexion, of the person by whom the money is received, that mode of obtaining it, which on the part of a powerless, indigent, undignified and unconnected person would be justly punishable and accordingly punished, is rendered innoxious, justifiable, and beneficial to the state.[h]

9. By the possessor of an Ecclesiastical (or *Lay*) office, as, in return for the pay taken on the whole, be the amount of it ever so great, no service need in any shape be rendered, so neither in return for any *part* of it.[i]

10. If, in respect of any part of the service, so it has happened, that payment for it has been made and received by the *day*,—or, as in the case of services paid for by surplice-fees, by the *job*,—whereby the rendering of that part has been secured, while every other part has remained unperformed,—it is not necessary that the security thus found to be efficacious in these instances, or that any other efficacious security, should be extended to other instances.[j]

11. The classes, whose place in the scale of opulence is lowest, are those by whom it is either not at all necessary, or least necessary, that the service rendered by a Parish Priest, and in particular, that the service rendered by the performance of the duties of *imperfect obligation* should be rendered.[k]

12. In the situation of Parish Priest,—though, the greater the quantity of pay is which is received by a man, the more powerfully he is drawn off from, and set above, those classes of persons to whom the performance of his duties promises to be of the greatest use, and in particular in whose instance the need of that service, which is rendered by the performance of his duties of imperfect obligation, is at the highest pitch,—yet the quantity of pay cannot be too great:

13. To the Minister, who, on no occasion uses any *fixed form*, the talent of discoursing without book, and in a great degree without special premeditation, is necessary.

14. To the Minister, the whole of whose exigible duty may be performed by reading out of a book, no *talent* other than that which consists in *reading out of a book* is necessary.

15. For the purchase of that service, which consists of nothing more than the reading out of a book,—the least quantity of pay,—in return for which any person who is capable of reading, in an intelligible manner, such matters as, under the system of instruction in question, require to be read out of a book,—is sufficient.

16. Under the Church-of-England System,—for the performance of the duties of *imperfect obligation* no adequate security being given, or being capable of being given, nor any well-grounded expectation of their being generally and efficiently performed being capable of being afforded,—there remain only the duties of *perfect obligation;* and, these consisting in nothing but reading out of a book,—the quantum of pay necessary to, and proper to be employed in, the purchase of a stock of service, in each Parish, adequate to the securing the performance of all the clerical duties that can reasonably be expected to be performed in it, is no more than the least quantity sufficient to purchase the exercise of that sort and degree of talent, which is exercised by the reading, in an intelligible manner, out of a book.

because to whatever extent it may happen that no service shall in any shape have been received by them at his hands; yet *had* such service been rendered to them, the greater the quantity of pay received by him, the greater *would have been* the quantity of respect paid by them to *him*, and thence to the *religion* which he *professes* to teach.[1]

13. To the Ecclesiastical Minister, who, on no occasion, should use any *fixt form*,—the talent of discoursing without book, and in a great degree without special premeditation, would be altogether necessary. But, in the instance of a Church-of-England Ecclesiastical Minister, fixt forms having, by the providence[1] of the Church, been provided for every thing, no such talent is necessary.[m]

14. To the Ecclesiastical Minister, the whole of whose exigible duty may be performed by reading out of a book, no talent, other than that which consists in reading out of a book, is necessary: and, as at the hands of the sons or other near relations, though they be but the younger children, of noblemen and gentlemen of large fortune, whose chief or only pursuit is worldly and expensive pleasure, no such talent as that which consists in the discoursing without book, and in great measure without special premeditation, can reasonably be expected,—thence so it is that, for this reason of *modern* times, added to others which had place in former times, no service from any such functionary ought to be required other than such as is rendered by the reading out of a book.[n]

15. For the purchase of that Ecclesiastical service which consists of nothing more than the *reading out of a* book, the *greatest quantity of pay* that can be found actually employed in the purchase of an engagement to render it, be that engagement fulfilled or not, can never be too great.[o]

16. Although, under the Church-of-England system, for the purchase of a stock of service, by the rendering of which will be performed all that mass of duty, the performance of which is *exigible*, or, in return for any quantity of pay whatsoever, can reasonably be *expected*, so[2] it may be, that the quantity of *pay* really *necessary*, is no more than the *least quantity*, sufficient to purchase the exercise of that sort and degree of talent, which consists in the *reading out of a book*,—yet,—the chief if not the only object worth regarding, being to secure a more comfortable provision in this world for the higher and richer classes,—thence it is, that any *diminution* in the quantity of money at any time exacted from all classes, low and high together, to be employed as *pay* in the purchase of an engagement, fulfilled or not fulfilled, to render this sort of service, would, instead of a *benefit*, be

---

[1] 1818 'prudence'. The text follows the 'Errata'.
[2] 1818 '*expected;* so'. The text follows the 'Errata'.

17. For the purchase of instruction, to be administered, throughout the whole country to the poorer classes, for the benefit of the community at large,—whatever money is employed may,—if it be considerable enough to cause the obligation of contributing towards it to be felt as a burthen,—be, with less inconvenience, drawn from the *universal* than from a local *fund:* for, in this last case, the greater the amount, the greater the danger, lest in the breast of the forced contributors, the exaction should be considered as an injury, and the person by whom the amount of what is thus exacted is received, as the author of the injury: and, to the feelings,—of any person, in whose eyes the instruction thus administered is either useless, much more if pernicious, or the quantity of money exacted for the purchase of the instruction excessive,—the injury will be the greater, the more plainly useless, or the more highly pernicious the instruction is, and the more enormously excessive the quantity of pay exacted for the purchase of it.[e]

an intolerable *grievance:* and every *addition,* to the quantity of money so exacted and employed, is a public *benefit.*

17. How great soever, in a large proportion of the whole number of parishes, may be the quantity of money, exacted for the purchase of the service professed to be rendered by the performance of the duties professed to be performed,—and how great soever the number of the persons, in whose eyes either no service at all is rendered, or if any, none but what is useless, or even pernicious; and thence to their feelings in how great a degree soever injurious and afflictive,—yet, being at present taken in each parish out of a local fund, formed by contributions exacted from a certain class of the parishioners, it ought notwithstanding to be for ever drawn out of the local fund so constituted; because,—if *Reason,*—drawn from the *principle of utility,* i.e. from the consideration of the *feelings* of all persons concerned,—*Reason,* by which such commutation is prescribed—were to be taken for the standard of reference,—whatever is superfluous in the quantity of money exacted on this score, might come to be remitted, and the common interest of the *subject many* in that particular no longer sacrificed to the separate interest of the *ruling few,* who, in these masses of excessive pay, behold a source of opulence to themselves.[p][1]

---

[1] 1818 omits footnote marker.

NOTES TO THE GRADUATE'S MAXIMS.

[a] *To Maxim* 2.—Among Non-Ecclesiastical offices of all sorts, *Military* and *Non-Military* taken together, to some the security afforded by *public examination is* afforded already; to many more it *might be* applied with great advantage; to some it would *not* be applicable with preponderant, if any, advantage. But, to attempt any such thing as an arrangement of the whole system of offices under these three classes, belongs not to the present purpose.

[b] *To Maxim* 6.—The hands, at the expense of which payment is made, are not to be deemed *willing* ones, where service,—being, by order of government, appointed to be rendered, in the case in question, to an individual of the description in question,—would, in the event of his not paying what in the name of *a fee* is required of him, be refused to him.

So,—inasmuch as money paid on account of the public is raised by *taxes*, imposed on contributors, who, in an indeterminately large proportion, would not, to the amount required of them respectively, if to any amount, be contributors, if they could avoid it,—all money paid on account of the public is, to this purpose, to be considered as received from *unwilling* hands.

[c] *To Maxim* 8.—1. By every portion of pay thus bestowed a needless and useless burthen is laid upon the contributors.

2. Every portion of pay thus bestowed being so much *obtained on false pretences*, is obtained by that species of immorality, which,—in so far as it is practised by persons, who, in respect of the profit of it, are not in connexion with the members of the government,—is classed with crimes, and punished as such:—punished with *transportation*, or hard labour on board the *Hulks*. The crime called *Swindling* is a modification of it.

3. By the comparison and the contrast,—in the eyes of those persons by whom, in return for pay, the service is rendered—in all eyes, but more particularly in theirs,—the inequality renders their situation the less eligible. *More than I earn so hardly by my labour, that man receives for doing nothing* . . . What cause for discontent more natural or more just?

4. The persons, to whose profit the matter of reward is thus prostituted, become themselves, in so far as the true principles of government on this behalf are understood, the objects of odium, and *that* odium just. Being, to the amount of that profit, depredators, preying upon the substance of the people, they are regarded—and not without reason, as so many public enemies, to whose private interest the interest of the *subject many* is made a needless and useless sacrifice.

5. The persons, by authority from whom, as well as the persons by whom, and to whose use depredation is thus committed, being persons professing to act—to act on this same occasion in the character of trustees for the whole community—the sort of enormity thus committed by them is, on their part, a *breach of* such their *trust*. By the whole amount of the money which, after being levied, is thus wasted, and of the vexation produced in the levying it, the government by which it is levied and the waste committed, has the appearance of being—not to say *is*—a government of extortion, oppression, and tyranny.

NOTES TO THE GRADUATE'S MAXIMS.

6. By the establishment of the practice of *trust-breaking* in this case,—in the persons of a class of men, set apart for the purpose of affording instruction, and *example* in the way of *religion* and *morality*, to all other classes of the people,—more especially by the enormous *extent*, to which in this case it is carried,—not only a colour of justification, but a veil of *sanctity* is thrown over it: and encouragement and support is thus given to it, not only in *this* case, but in the case where the service, on pretence of which the pay received in virtue of office is of a *civil*, (meaning a *non-ecclesiastical*,) in contradistinction to an *ecclesiastical* nature;—in a word, to *all other* offices under government.

Ecclesiastical, or *non-ecclesiastical*, by what Church-of-Englandist can any censure be consistently passed on the practice of *Sinecurism?*

By what man, *Non-Churchman* or *Churchman*, can any censure be passed on *Sinecurism* without passing a proportionate censure on the *Excellent* Church?

Thus,—not merely by a participation, but by the receipt of an enormously superior sum, in the profit of guilt in this shape,—is the Excellent Church,—with all her sons, by whom any such affection is felt as that of *hope*—even thus is she *bribed*, and engaged by the bribery, in the defence of *fraud* and *depredation*.

7. In the case of this unpunishable, as in the case of punishable, depredation,—if, to the amount of so much as a single farthing, the levying and application of money to this purpose be to be *justified*, then, on equally good ground, may the levying and applying to the same purpose money to any amount whatever:—yes, to any amount, up to the last penny, that can by any means be exacted from a starving and sinking people.

8. Even in the *non-ecclesiastical* part of the field of government, the abundance of sinecure offices—undisguised and disguised together—with the enormity of the aggregate amount of the money thus exacted from the people under false pretences, is among the most prominent of the grievances, under which the people labour. But, if the ratio, of the aggregate of the pay allotted to these sham offices to the aggregate of the pay allotted to efficient offices, be made the object of regard,—in the *non-ecclesiastical* part of the field this ratio is as nothing, compared with what it is in the *ecclesiastical:* in the *sacred,* as it is called.

Where the service undertaken for is that of defending souls against the assaults of the devil, so it is that, in the instance of almost one half of the whole number of these members of the *'Church militant,'* in return for the pay received nothing whatever is done, or so much as endeavoured to be done:—at the post at which the service should be performed, the voluntarily inlisted soldier—the receiver of the pay—is never to be found. Here then, in this *sacred* army, almost one half of the soldiers are *deserters: deserters* receiving all the while pay as *effectives:* the *Bishops,* officers in this army—and the advisers of the Monarch, the Commander of it—conniving at the desertion, and concurring in exacting the pay, which, with full notice[1] of the desertion, they force the people to give to these notorious deserters: the *Bishops*—many if not most of them—and, with the connivance of the rest, and the concurrence of the advisers of the Crown—receiving, as will be seen, (see the section on *Discipline)*[2] in addition to the pay attached to their respective offices, other pay as *privates*, and in every instance in which they do receive it, acting the part of *deserters.*

Not to speak of those public servants, whose offices are included in the *civil* (meaning the *non-military* part) of the *civil,* (meaning,—for in this state is this part of the language,—the *non-ecclesiastical* part) of the field of government,—in what

---

[1] 1818 'notion'. The text follows the 'Errata'.
[2] See pp. 415–71 and especially pp. 453–7 n. below.

situation would the country have been, if, in the *Military* part, the enormity of the breach of trust committed by *sinecurism* had been equal to what it is in the *Ecclesiastical?* If, of the whole number of Officers and Privates, in the land and in the sea service taken together, whose engagement is to defend bodies and goods against the assaults of foreign enemies—enemies made of flesh and blood—almost half the number had been living constantly in a state of *desertion,* receiving their pay notwithstanding? Under the burthen of the whole of that vast establishment, of which this branch is of course by far the greatest and the most burthensome, the country is already sinking. But, on the supposition here in question, the amount of this part of the burthen would have been nearly double to what it is.

In the attribute *Excellent,*—thus in a public advertisement, bestowed by the Bench of Bishops upon the *Church,* of which *they* are at the head[1]—bestowed in as regular and solemn form as the corresponding abstract term *Excellency* is bestowed upon a certain rank of *Foreign Envoys,*—what less can be implied, but that, on the part of these *holy* persons—some *consecrated,* all in *Holy Orders*—morality, and *that* in a degree over and above any in which it is to be found in the same number of persons, belonging to the profane class,—is constantly to be found: these sacred persons—all in *palaces,* the *Archbishops* on *thrones,* as upon hills topped by mountains—being in profession set up to serve as examples—as so many burning and shining lights[2]—to all profane ones.

Such being the pretension, what is the real fact? Over and over again, in every page of this work it has been visible. Pre-eminence? yes: but in what scale?—In the scale of virtue? No. In what scale then?—Alas! if[3] *mendacity* and *insincerity,* as proved by *subscription*—[if][4] *breach of trust,* and *depredation,* as proved by *over-paid places*—[if][5] *obtainment on false pretences,* as proved by *Non-Residence, Pluralism,* and *Sinecurism*— be vicious,—in the scale of *vice:* the obtainment on false pretences the vice of the *greater* part; the mendacity and the insincerity the vice of the *whole* tribe. Of the two tribes of these domineering Churchmen, who all of them are, by their own confession, so many *'miserable sinners,'*[6] *that* by which the exclusive possession of the quality of *consecrated holiness* is arrogated to itself, the most pre-eminently and notoriously *miserable.*

Such is the Church—'that Established Church, which' (according to the Earl of Harrowby's Speech, p. 32) *'is the boast and the support of our country.'*[7] Such is the system, which, by the mouth and pen of this their spokesman, his fellow saints,—at so heavy an expense to the good people of England—and not only of England but of Scotland—yes, of Scotland, where the burthen is so completely without pretence,—have for so long a course of years been labouring in *their* way to support—to support, as will be seen,[8] by increase of mere unoperative existence, with increase of pay for the support of it, but without any the slightest endeavour to give increase to profitable service:—to service, profitable or unprofitable.

As to the persons to whose situations these maxims are applicable, they will be found to be as follows:

All[9] possessors of *Sinecures,* by whatsoever denomination distinguished: viz.

1. All *Deans, Canons, Prebendaries, Præcentors:*[10]
2. All possessors of Sinecure *Rectories, Vicarages,* or *Donative Curacies:*
3. All Rectors, all Vicars, all Curates of Donative Curacies, who, not having more

---

[1] See pp. 29 and 110 n. above.   [2] See John 5: 35.
[3] 1818 'of'. The text follows the 'Errata'.   [4] 1818 'of'.   [5] 1818 'of'.
[6] See p. 224 n. above.   [7] See p. 391 n. below.   [8] See pp. 518–25 below.
[9] 1818 '1. All'. The enumeration is redundant.
[10] 1818 '*Procetors*'. The text follows the 'Errata'.

NOTES TO THE GRADUATE'S MAXIMS.

service to perform than they are physically able to perform, *employ stipendiary Curates:*

4. All possessors of *overpaid* Rectories, Vicarages, and Donative Curacies, by the amount of the overplus:

5. All *Pluralists*, by the amount of the pay attached to the whole number of their benefices more than one:

6. All *Archbishops*, *Bishops*, and *Archdeacons*, unless and except in so far as service,—which, without them, would not be rendered with equal aptitude, quality and quantity taken together,—is rendered by them towards the maintenance of *discipline:* as to which see further under the head of *Discipline*.[1]

N.B. In the Church of Scotland, *Established* as it is, no instance of any of the above-mentioned abominations is to be found.

Of course, neither is there, nor can there be, in any *Non-Established* Protestant Church.

Behold what, on the subject of *Sinecures*,—at the very commencement of the half-emancipation from the yoke of Popery, of which they are a relick,—was the opinion—the pointedly declared opinion—of *Archbishop Cranmer*, Martyr and one of the chief heroes of the Established Church of England:[2]—declared in the very face of the bloody tyrant, under whose order a fresh batch of them had just been brought upon the carpet: it is taken from *Bishop Burnet*, who had the honesty to print it in his History of the Reformation.[3] If by *Cranmer*, instead of being thus pointedly condemned, the institution had been lauded, it would not have been more useful or justifiable than it is: the observations above called forth would not have been the less justly applicable to it. But many are the minds, by which,—while the most unanswerable reasons, drawn from the principle of general utility and the nature of the case, would be applied to them without effect,—the authority of an *Archbishop*, especially that Archbishop being a *Martyr*, and that Martyr *Cranmer*, may on such an occasion be found decisive.[a]

---

[a] From Burnet's History of the Reformation, vol. iii.

'A Letter of Thomas, Lord Archbishop of Canterbury, to Cromwell,[4] upon the new foundation of Canterbury.'[5]

AN ORIGINAL.

'My very singular good Lord,

'After my most hearty commendations, these shall be to advertise your Lordship, that I have received your letters, dated the 27th day of November, and therewith a bill concerning the Devise for the New Establishment, to be made in

---

[1] See pp. 415–71 below.

[2] Thomas Cranmer (1489–1556), Archbishop of Canterbury from 1533, had presided over the reformation of the English Church under Henry VIII and Edward VI. Following the accession of the Roman Catholic Mary I in 1553, Cranmer was imprisoned, found guilty of heresy, and burnt at the stake at Oxford in March 1556.

[3] See Gilbert Burnet, *The History of the Reformation of the Church of England*, 3 Pts., London, 1679–1715. In the following passage, from Pt. III, 'A Collection of Records, Letters, and Original Papers; with other Instruments Referr'd to in the former History', no. 65, pp. 157–9, Bentham has modernized the spelling, varied the punctuation and capitalization, and added italics. Gilbert Burnet (1643–1715), Scottish historian, clergyman, and Bishop of Salisbury from 1689.

[4] Thomas Cromwell (*c.* 1485–1540), created Baron Cromwell in 1536 and Earl of Essex in 1540, was Henry VIII's chief minister from 1532, but was convicted of treason and heresy by Bill of Attainder, and executed in July 1540.

[5] The letter is dated 29 November [1539]: see *History of the Reformation of the Church of England*, Pt. III, 'Collection of Records', no. 65, p. 159.

[d] *To Maxim* 10.—1. So far as concerns *quantity* of service, and in particular in so far as that quantity is measured by the quantity of *time* employed in the rendering of the service,—of the *securities* capable of being taken for the due rendering of service required in respect of office, the most simple,—and in proportion to the quantity of money at stake the most efficacious,—is that which is afforded, by taking the service in the least parcels or parts into which it stands naturally divided, and so, in the instance of each of those parcels or parts attaching to the act of rendering the service a proportionable parcel of pay.

2. This maxim is conformed to in so far as payment by the *day*, or by the *job* or piece, is the mode of payment employed. In so far as he is paid by the fees called *surplice fees*, a Parish Priest is paid by the *job*.[1] The indignity may afford a text for Saint *Howley*, Saint *Marsh*,[2] or Saint *Quarterly Review*. But the mode is not the less characteristically and appositely designated.

3. To the duties of *imperfect obligation* it is altogether inapplicable. For this reason it is not applicable either to the system of the Established Church of *Scotland*, or to the system of any *Non-Established* Church. But, neither is there in any one of these systems any *demand* for it. The object of it is accomplished by the system of *discipline*. See below the section on *Discipline*.[3]

---

the Metropolitan Church of Canterbury: By which your Lordship requireth my Advice thereupon by writing, for our mutual Consents. Surely, my Lord, as touching the Books drawn, and the Order of the same, I think it will be a very substantial and godly Foundation: Nevertheless in my opinion the PREBENDARIES, which will be allowed 40*l.* a-piece yearly, might be altered to a more expedient use. And this is my consideration; for having Experience both in times past, and also in our Days, how *the said Sect of Prebendaries have not only spent their time in much Idleness, and their Substance in superfluous Belly-cheer, I think it not to be a convenient State or Degree to be maintained and established, Considering first that commonly a Prebendary is neither a learner, nor a Teacher, but a good Viander*. Then by the same name they look to be chief, and to bear all the whole rule and Preheminence in the College where they be Resident: By means whereof *the younger*, of their own Nature given more to Pleasure, good Chear, and Pastime, than to Abstinence, Study, and Learning, *shall easily be brought from their Books to follow the Appetite and Example of the same Prebendaries, being their Heads and Rulers: And the State of the Prebendaries hath been so excessively abused, that when learned men have*[4] *been admitted into such Room, many times they have desisted*[5] *from their good and godly Studies, and all other virtuous exercise of preaching and teaching*. Wherefore, if it may so stand with the King's gracious Pleasure, *I would wish that not only the* NAME *of a* PREBENDARY *were exiled his Grace's Foundations, but also* THE SUPERFLUOUS CONDITIONS OF SUCH PERSONS. I cannot deny but that *the beginning of* PREBENDARIES *was no less proposed for the Maintenance of good learning and good Conversation of living, than* RELIGIOUS *men were: But forasmuch as both be gone from their first estate and order, and the one is found like offender with the other, it maketh no great matter if they perish both together: For to say the truth, it is an estate which* ST. PAUL, *reckoning up the degrees and estates allowed in his time, could not find in the Church of Christ.*'[6]

---

[1] See p. 235 n. above.

[2] i.e. William Howley, Bishop of London, and Herbert Marsh, Bishop of Llandaff. For Bentham's comments on the use of the title 'Saint' see pp. 219–21 above.

[3] See pp. 415–27 below.

[4] 1818 '*hath*'. The text follows the 'Errata'.

[5] 1818 '*dcsisted*'. The text follows the 'Errata'.

[6] St Paul refers to deacons and bishops: see Philippians 1: 1. There is no reference to prebendaries in the New Testament.

NOTES TO EXCELLENT CHURCH'S MAXIMS.

4. But, to the *Church of England* system,—supposing the duties of *perfect obligation* performed by the *juvenile reader* instead of the adult Minister,—it would be perfectly applicable, and the state of the case would require it. See also to this point the section on *Discipline*.

[e] *To Maxim* 17.—Note that,—until the abuse, consisting in the exaction of *excessive* pay instead of *least sufficient* pay, as above, shall have been removed,—the *locality* of the fund is in one respect an advantage: viz. by operating as a stimulus, towards engaging the forced contributors to employ their exertions for the removal of the abuse.

Strongly as in this way the sense of injury cannot but operate in *England*,—where the portion of the population, by which the injury is sustained, is not computed to form as yet more than about *one seventh* part of the whole,—how much more strongly must it not operate in *Ireland*, where the portion thus injured—Catholic and Protestant Dissenters together—are computed to form not less than *nine tenth* parts of the whole?

Lamentable indeed it is—that a religion,—so absurd and mischievous as is the *Catholic*, compared even with the least good, not to say the only bad, edition of the *Protestant* religion,—should in any country prevail to any such extent as that in which it prevails in *Ireland*. But, so long as the people, by whom it is professed, are continued in a state of oppression,—as they will be so long as in respect of any the smallest right whatsoever they are upon a footing inferior to that of any other sect,— so long, unless a system of irresistible compulsion be applied to them, will that pernicious sect continue, without any considerable, if any, diminution in its numbers. Suppose them, on the other hand, standing, as above, upon a footing of equality,— then would *Missionaries* from all the *active* sects of Protestants, pour in upon that neighbouring land, and make war upon the *Whore of Babylon*, as ardently as they do already upon *Mahomet* and *Bramah*, and with all the advantage, which comparative appropriate knowledge has over deplorably gross, and to a sad extent the very grossest, ignorance.

But, in that case, the inefficiency of Church-of-Englandism to every useful purpose would be still more glaringly manifest than at present: and the sluggard depredators, who fatten there upon the bread of idleness,[1] would be covered with still more conspicuously just reproach and shame.

Yes: it is *for* Church-of-Englandism, as well as *by* Church-of-Englandism, that Catholicism and Popery are kept on foot in *Ireland*.

NOTES TO EXCELLENT CHURCH'S MAXIMS.

[a] *To Maxim* 1.—Proofs of the adoption of this maxim in the Ecclesiastical department. 1. That to the rendering of service, so far as it is rendered by the mere possession of office, *inclination* to perform the duties of it is not regarded as necessary, is proved in and by as many cases as there are instances of *Non-Residence*.—See above, §3, p. 361.

2. That, to the rendering of this same service, appropriate and adequate *mental power* is not regarded as necessary, is proved by the following state of things. In both

---

[1] Proverbs 31: 27.

the English Universities,—viz. in Cambridge time out of mind, and in Oxford of late years,—for securing appropriate and sufficient aptitude with relation to that sort of service, which a man is understood to be rendering—rendering to himself, and eventually to the public—by the taking of an University degree, the act of undergoing *examination in public* has been deemed requisite, and accordingly has been and is exacted.[1] But, for any such purpose as that of securing aptitude, for the situation in which in the character of Minister of a Parish a man is understood to take upon himself the *cure of Souls*, no such security is exacted. Nor yet on the occasion of a man's receiving what are called *Holy Orders:* viz. a sort of *degree*, the taking of which has been rendered a necessary preparative to the capacity of undertaking any such *cure of souls*. For, this private degree is sufficiently taken, whenever, out of twenty-six Archbishops and Bishops, a man can find a single one, having out of a number of Chaplains *one* who, after conversing with him in secret, will, in the accustomed form, cause it to be understood, that in his opinion the candidate in question possesses, with relation to the state and condition of a Church-of-England Priest, a sufficient degree of aptitude.[2]

True it is—that, in many, and probably in most instances, either before or soon after the receiving of these *Holy Orders*, a man takes, or has taken, one or more of these *University degrees:* but equally true is it that to the receiving these *Orders* no such degree is necessary: and that in an unliquidated number of instances, these *Orders* are received by men by whom no such degree is ever taken.

True also it may be admitted to be, that,—for the rendering of any service, for the rendering of which any adequate security is afforded, or of the rendering of which any reasonable and sufficiently grounded expectation can be entertained,—the quality and quantity of mental power, of the existence of which adequate assurance may be obtained in the case of the *Bell-taught* school-boy as above, will, under the fixt forms of the Church-of-England, be sufficient: and that, consequently, any such additional mental power as is evidenced by the taking of any such degree, public or private, as aforesaid, is unnecessary and superfluous. But, on this head, such, as far as appears, has not as yet been the conception generally entertained, or at any rate generally avowed, any where in the Church-of-England: not the conception avowed, nor accordingly the conception acted upon, in the framing of the regulations, or in the establishing of the customs, by which that Excellent Church is governed.

So much as to *practice*. As to *theory*, on this as on every other part of the field of Church-of-England *discipline* (*service* and *pay* added or included), the public is fortunate enough to possess a generally received as well as authoritatively established body of doctrine, in the above quoted speech of the *Earl of Harrowby*, spoken in the House of Lords on the 18th of June, 1812, and afterwards published by his Lordship,[3] on the occasion and in support of one part of his grand system of reform, being the part which on that occasion passed into a law. Along with *legal* authority

---

[1] Examinations in the Universities of Oxford and Cambridge were traditionally oral and public. Since the sixteenth century the most able students at the University of Cambridge had been eligible for special mention in an order of precedence, and at the time Bentham was writing, there were three classes of honours for finalists. The Oxford examination statute of 1800 had introduced a provision for twelve men to be considered for honours, while subsequent amendments in 1807 allowed for all students worthy of honours to be ranked into two, and then in 1809 into three, classes.

[2] Before being presented to the Bishop for ordination, a candidate for the priesthood was examined in private by an Archdeacon: see 'The Form and Manner of Ordering of Priests', *Book of Common Prayer*.

[3] See p. 362 & n. above.

NOTES TO EXCELLENT CHURCH'S MAXIMS.

already effectually applied to this part, the whole system has for its support, in the shape of *intellectual* authority, besides that of his Lordship, that of the departed Saint, of pious and most zealous Church-of-England memory—*Saint Perceval:*[1] in the character of whose 'Executor' in this behalf, the noble Earl, on that occasion, acted, (Speech, pp. 1, 2),[2] and still continues to act. Of this abuse, if such it may be called, of this abuse, considered in a general point of view, or at any rate, of the continuance of it,—we have his Lordship's decidedly declared approbation. And here be it noted, once for all, that to abuse—to abuse in all its shapes—*silence*, from the mouth of a man, who, with Government at his back, comes out with a system of reform given as complete—*silence*, as surely as it ever gives *consent*—gives *confirmation*.

As to the particular supposed abuse here in question, after acknowledging with the most engagingly spontaneous candour, (p. [7]),[3] that 'Pluralities and Non-Residence,' (i.e. obtainment of money on false pretences), are certainly no necessary part of the establishment of a Christian Church; and that 'as far as he is aware, they are unknown to the laws of any Church but that of England;' in conclusion, however, his decided opinion is, (p. 21), that 'a strict injunction of universal residence would be neither practicable nor desirable.' Yet cases there are in which, speaking of Non-Residence, this practice (he says) is by no means 'creditable to the Church.' There are in number (out of the 4,339 cases of effective Non-Residence remaining after deduction of the 1,501 Virtual Residents as per p. 361) according to him 600, in which a Curate is employed, the living, (observes his Lordship), 'being *of small value.*' How any mischief, which is *not* produced by Non-Residence, where the living is of *great value*, should be produced by its being of *small value*, seems not very easy to discover. If the damnation of souls were an object worthy of regard, the residence of the Incumbent affording at the same time any chance of warding off so undesirable a result,—on any such supposition, forasmuch as the largest living will, generally speaking, contain the largest population, the cases where the living is large would, one should have thought, have rather been taken for the objects of his Lordship's censure. But on the day on which this speech was spoken, the attendance on the Bishops' Bench was (it may well be presumed) not a scanty one. In the Returns for the year 1810—being the year to which, as appears by the Tables printed at the end of it, this speech bears reference—*thirty-five* stands as the number of '*Livings held at this time by Bishops:*' considerably more than one a-piece for the four-and-twenty

---

[1] Spencer Perceval (1762–1812), Chancellor of the Exchequer 1807–9, and leader of the administration as First Lord of the Treasury from 1809 until his assassination on 11 May 1812. Perceval had, in 1805, 1806, and 1808, introduced Bills to impose residency on clergy and ensure adequate payment for curates, but the Bills had been defeated.

[2] See *Substance of the Speech of the Earl of Harrowby*, pp. 1–2: 'I am acting, in this instance, only as the executor of a much-lamented friend. It forms a part of that system of measures for strengthening the establishment of the Church of England, to which, amidst all the pressure of the complicated concerns of this country, he had most earnestly directed his attention. The other branches of this plan were not in sufficient forwardness to be submitted to Parliament; but this branch being distinct from the rest, and the Bill appearing to be in a state fit to be brought forward, it was his intention to produce it in another House during this present session. The execution of this purpose was not permitted to him. The same stroke which deprived the Crown of one of its most faithful servants, Parliament of one of its brightest ornaments, and private life of the most engaging pattern of every private virtue, at the same moment deprived the Church of its firmest and most enlightened friend. . . . Much as I regret that the administration of this part of his inheritance should not have fallen into better hands, I feel that upon every principle which united our opinions upon this important subject, it has unavoidably fallen into mine, and I am equally bound by duty and by feeling to spare no exertions in the discharge of a sacred trust.'

[3] 1818 '1' appears to be a slip.

Bishops.[1] Of these thirty-five livings, not many, it may well be imagined, could, in respect of their[2] smallness, afford matter for his Lordship's above-mentioned censure. A collection of the cases in which, according to the Latin proverb, *censure*—and not merely *moral* but *legal* censure—spares the *crows* and fastens exclusively on the *doves*,[3]—or, in more appropriate language, spares the *Diveses* and fastens exclusively on the *Lazaruses*,[4]—would assuredly not be a scanty one, and would form a not uninstructive illustration of the combined excellence of Church and State.

^b *To Maxim 2.*—See Note to Maxim 1.

^c *To Maxim 3.*—Proof, of the adoption of this maxim in the Ecclesiastical department, general practice and general understanding, as evidenced by the Act obtained and preparatory speech spoken in the House of Lords, and afterwards published by the *Earl of Harrowby*, as above, 18th June, 1812. In no part of his plan as exhibited in that speech, is any intimation given, that, in any instance, by *excess* of pay put into ecclesiastical hands,—how enormous soever the *pay*, and whether any *service* or none be rendered for it, and if any, how *minute* soever that service,— mischief in any shape is produced. Deficiency of pay—to the operation of that one cause—of that one and no other,—unless it be absence from the spot on which, if useful service in any shape were by the person in question rendered, it would be rendered,—is every imperfection ascribed, which, in his Lordship's view, presents any demand for remedy. In each of as many Parishes as possible, to cause a Parish Priest, viz. either Incumbent or Curate, to exist, and into the pocket of the Curate, at the expense of every *future Incumbent*,—and thence at the expense not only of every future, but eventually of the *present Patron*,—to put a sum of money, over and above that for which the Curate would have been ready and willing to undertake to perform the service—in the accomplishment of these two connected objects—the one of them partly by the means of the other—may be seen the whole texture of that plan of reform or improvement, by which, whatsoever was still wanting to the giving to the excellence of the Church-of-England system the finishing touches, was to be supplied. At the expense of *Patrons* and *Incumbents*, money to be put into the pockets of *Curates:* at the expense of the *public* at large, money to be put into the pockets of *Incumbents*, over and above that for which they would respectively have been willing to undertake to perform the service:—more money to be put into the pockets of *Architects*, to build fine buildings with, under the name of *Churches*:[5] upon the accomplishment of these two objects, together with another or two, consisting merely in the expenditure of money, without any security for the production of any good effect by means of it, will the whole force of the noble Earl's and his late Right Honourable friend's genius be found expended.

Money exacted from unwilling hands by force of law—money in such vast sums— and for what? For the advancement of piety and morality?—No: not so much as in profession in any part of this speech. For what then? For 'the preservation of the Church,' (p. 32): 'of that Established Church, which is *the boast and the support of our country*.' For the better accomplishment of this grand and primary if not sole object,

[1] See 'An Abstract of the "Copies of the Diocesan Returns for the Year ending 25th December 1810, presented to the House of Lords on the 20th May 1812;" distinguishing the Number of Incumbents who are Resident or doing their Duty, from the Number of those who are neither Resident nor doing their Duty', in *Substance of the Speech of the Earl of Harrowby*, p. 44.

[2] 1818 'its'. The text follows the 'Errata'.

[3] Juvenal, *Saturae*, I. II. 63: *dat veniam corvis, vexat censura columbas*.

[4] For the parable of the rich man and Lazarus see Luke 16: 19–31.

[5] For Harrowby's plans to build additional churches see pp. 396 & n. and 535–6 below.

NOTES TO EXCELLENT CHURCH'S MAXIMS.

the holy Proteus is on this occasion brought forward in its character of a *'Citadel.'* It has *'assailants from within and from without.'* It has *'outworks:'* it has a *'garrison:'* but it is in danger of being *'betrayed* by want of *discipline:'* and its *'garrison'* is in danger of being *'starved:'*[1]—*'a system of measures for strengthening the establishment of the Church of England,'*—such accordingly, at the very outset of the speech, (p. 1), is the system pursued: such its object—and even in profession its sole object—according to the account given of it by the noble author by whom it is introduced. This being the object—when, in relation to it, any such word as *service* is employed, of what sort can be the *service* meant? *Answer:* That sort of service which consists in contributing to the defence of this Citadel against those its assailants. That, in the expectation of the Noble Engineer, in whose eyes the demand for service in this shape was so urgent, the service thus desired would, in case of the adoption and execution of this his plan, be rendered, and being rendered, would be effectual, cannot be matter of doubt. But, for the causing this service to be rendered, what is the instrument to which he looks? *Answer:* Unless it be the sort of discipline, such as it is, which will be seen added for the prevention of *desertion,—money,* and nothing else: *money* to be put into the pockets of the *garrison:* money to be put into the pockets of Architects for the erection of more Citadels.

Such then being his plan, and such his own account of it, his maxim, the maxim on which he acts, may it not with truth, as above, be said to be this?—*The greater the quantity of pay attached to the office, be it what it may, the greater in value, quantity and quality taken together into the account, will be the service rendered by the possessor of it.* In *riches,* and without any such superfluous care as that about *performance of duty*—in *riches,* and with no other than the single exception above mentioned, is, on this occasion at least, the noble Christian's only trust: to *his* mind's eye, camels gallopping through the eyes[2] of needles[3] have doubtless been a familiar spectacle. On the part of the persons *militant,* of which this his garrison is composed, on what circumstances does this his trust repose itself? On any such qualification as 'respectability of character, exemplary discharge of duty, or a competent share of learning?' Not it, indeed. Of these, he expressly declares (p. 15), he is 'far from supposing that they are necessarily connected, or even connected at all, with the amount of the salary received.' On what then?—On the quantity of *respect* paid to the noble army of his Church militant: paid not only to officers but to privates. Respect?—Good. But *money*—the money by which every thing is to be done—is *that* respect? No. Put the question to a Sectary, the answer will be—that they are very different things. But in the Excellent Church, some how or other, it is for *money,* and nothing else, that respect, or any thing else that is good, is to be had. 'Men,' says his Lordship, (p. 16), 'are too apt to measure the respect they owe to persons, or to offices, by the respect which they see paid to them by the authorities to which they look up. What must they think,' continues he, (p. 16), 'of the value which is set by the Legislature upon the persons or the office of those to whose care the religion of the people is entrusted, when they see at how low a rate their services are estimated?'

What indeed is not said *directly* is—that when by a certain quantity of pay the

---

[1] See *Substance of the Speech of the Earl of Harrowby,* p. 32: 'My chief anxiety is, to draw to this subject the attention of your Lordships, to convince you that the call for that attention is the call of duty, as you regard the preservation of that Established Church which is the boast and the support of our country. It is assailed from within and from without. Some of its ancient outworks are, in the opinion of many of its warmest friends, no longer applicable to the circumstances of the times in which we live; but its citadel is strong; if repaired upon its own principles, it may resist every attack; let it not be betrayed by want of discipline, or by starving its garrison.'
[2] 1818 'eye'. The text follows the 'Errata'.
[3] Mark 10: 24–5.

CHURCH-OF-ENGLANDISM

functionaries belonging to this class are secured against *contempt*, the *respect* of the people will go on increasing, with every addition made to that quantity, whatever it may be: indirectly, however, it is not the less incontrovertibly insinuated. For, not only of the value set by the Legislature on the *persons* in question, but of the value set by the same supreme body on the *office* itself, the quantity of *pay* allotted to it is spoken of as the measure, and test, and conclusive evidence. But if so it be at any one part of the scale, how can it fail of being so at any other? That for this purpose any line ought to be or can be drawn at any point of this scale—of any such notion not any the slightest intimation is any where given. And to the 'value set by the Legislature, upon the office of those, to whose care,' (as his Lordship observes), 'the religion of the people is entrusted,' what bounds would he recommend to be set by any body? Boundless being the *value* of their office, boundless accordingly ought to be the *quantity* of their pay: *boundless*—though not in the absolute and abstract sense—yet thus far boundless, as to have no other limits than those which are set to it by the *ignorant impatience* of those out of whose pockets it must come.[1] Such is the logic of the Noble Advocate of Excellent Church: though disguised and guarded against every adverse grasp by so prudential an indeterminateness and slipperiness as has been furnished by his Lordship's skill in the arts of rhetoric. While to the eye of hostility or scrutiny it presents the semblance of a limited demand, it presents the substance of an unlimited one to all those '*understandings*' which the eloquence of his Lordship of London, seconded by the prospect of the good things of this wicked world, has laid '*prostrate*'[2] at the feet of Excellent Church.

Money then being, in his Lordship's eyes, as well as Excellent Church's, the one thing needful,[3]—in money her sole trust—the more she[4] has of it, the stronger her hold,—no wonder that, to the adding more and more to the bulk and strength of this holdfast, the force of his Lordship's ingenuity should be directed. Of the exclusive efficiency of this instrument, according to his Lordship's notion of it, can any further proof be wanting? Behold it then, in the very next paragraph, (p. 16). Of every species of *Sectaries* the rapid progress is recognized. To what cause is it ascribed? To the superiority of the service rendered—of the instruction administered—by these schismatics,[5] in comparison of that which is rendered by the Ministers of Excellent Church?—Of course to any thing rather than this. To what then?—to the superiority of the *pay* received by those schismatics, in comparison of that which is received by their Excellencies: 'How can we be surprised,' (says his Lordship), 'at the rapid progress of every species of sectaries (who are far from allowing the Ministers of their congregations to fall in point of income to a level with the Curates of the Established Church,) when so large a proportion of the Ministers of that Church are left in a state of abject poverty.'[6]—Superiority of pay? What? in any sectarian Church is there more factitious *dignity*, more *power*, and, above all, more *money* to be had—and that for *less work*, than in Excellent Church?—In his Lordship's view, (p. 16), the Church is a *lottery*.—What? in any sectarian Church are there any 25,000*l*. 14,000*l*. 10,000*l*., or so much as 1,000*l*. a year prizes? Strange then would it be, if, after so many testimonies, there could remain a doubt, that in the maxim, *the quantity of religion in the country will be as the quantity of the money put into the pockets of the Clergy and others for the support of it*, is contained the persuasion, which, with all his might, it has been, and continues to be, his Lordship's endeavour to impress into every mind that can be induced to receive it.

---

[1] See p. 493 n. below. [2] See p. 37 & n. above. [3] Luke 10: 42.
[4] 1818 'more money she'. The text follows the 'Errata'.
[5] See p. 48 n. above.
[6] *Substance of the Speech of the Earl of Harrowby*, pp. 16–17.

NOTES TO EXCELLENT CHURCH'S MAXIMS.

But, on this head, could any doubt be left by his *theory*, it may be seen effectually excluded by his *practice*.—It is in the case of *Curates* (it has been seen) that in this speech of his Lordship's this theory is advanced in the first instance: but, if once received as applicable to that case, then come two other and more profitable applications of it, first to the case of *Incumbents*, and then to the case of the money demanded for more *Churches*. As to the case of Curates, though *nominally* at the expense of *Incumbents*, it is really, (as hath been seen, and will be seen further), at the expense of *Patrons* alone, that the money for the *Curates* was to be and has been provided. But it is at the expense of the people at large—*Sectaries* included, who cannot so much as be expected to receive any part of the direct benefit from it,—that the money for the supposed underpaid *Incumbents* has been and continues to be provided; and, moreover, if the people will find patience, it is at their expense that the additional stock of *Churches* is about to be provided. The *Incumbents*—the only Incumbents—at whose expense the money is to be provided for *Curates*, will be the *future contingent* Incumbents: and by these the burthen will not be felt. But the *people*, on whom the burthen is, and will be thrown, are the *existing* people of the *existing* time, by whom it will be felt in all its pressure.

Another of the fallacies,—employed by his Lordship's rhetorick, in the endeavour to conciliate the affection of those on whom it depends, and to secure the patience of the people, under the system of unpunishable depredation to which he is devoting them,—may be seen in the just mentioned emblem of the *Lottery*, taken from *Adam Smith*. 'How can we expect, (says he, p. 16) considering the Church only as a profession, that men who have necessarily received a *liberal* education, and who ought to be men of *liberal* views, will continue to enter into a profession, in which the blanks bear so large a proportion to the prizes?'[1] And again (in p. 28), 'In this Lottery, they (the prizes) are indeed far less than the purchase money paid for the tickets:'— the Lottery accordingly is, in the words of Adam Smith, a *disadvantageous* one.[2] Of this emblem, what is the *moral?—Encrease* (such it is of course) *Encrease the aggregate value of the prizes*. Well, then, when this encrease is made, will you thereby have rendered your lottery a less disadvantageous one to the purchasers of tickets?—Most assuredly not: much more probably will you have rendered it a still more disadvantageous one.—Why? because the greater in number and value the aggregate amount of the prizes, the greater, and—such is the delusive quality of hope—in an indeterminately larger proportion than before, will be the number of the competitors—the number of the purchasers of the tickets. In this way, under the notion of making the lottery less and less disadvantageous, you may keep adding to the number and value of the prizes, till you have emptied the pockets of the people of their last shilling: and when this is done, it will still be more disadvantageous than ever. Such, where applied to professions, is the fallacy couched in this emblem of a *lottery*. In a *real* lottery, the *number* of the *tickets* is always *limited;* in which case, true it is, that if while the number of the tickets remains the same, you make any addition to the aggregate value of the prizes, then so it is, that by the whole amount of the addition, you render the lottery so much the less disadvantageous than it was before. But neither in the lottery of the Church, nor in any other of the pretended lotteries to

---

[1] The draws for the lottery were made from two rotary boxes (wheels of fortune), one containing all the lottery tickets sold, and the other an equal number of tickets of which some were prizes and some were blanks. One ticket was drawn simultaneously from each wheel.

[2] Smith, *Wealth of Nations*, ii. 562: 'It [the search after new silver and gold mines] is perhaps the most disadvantageous lottery in the world, or the one in which the gain of those who draw the prizes bears the least proportion to the loss of those who draw the blanks'.

CHURCH-OF-ENGLANDISM

which, for the like purpose, the emblem of a lottery has been applied, is there any limitation to the number of the tickets.*

d To Maxim 4.—Proof, among official men, general *understanding* and general *practice.*—See Note (*c*) to Maxim 3.

e To Maxim 5.—Proof, among official men, general *understanding* and *practice:* and see Doctrine of the Earl of Harrowby, as explained in Note (*c*) to Maxim 3.

f To Maxim 6.—See Note (*g*) to Maxim 7.

g To Maxim 7.—In the Non-Established Church, composed of the people called *Quakers,* the sort of service, which, in other Churches is rendered by hands specially appointed, and generally paid, is rendered by the unpaid hands of such of the Members of this Church as, from time to time, feel disposed to render it. But *Quakers* are *Sectaries:* and as according to the doctrine of the Bishop of London, all Sectaries are men of 'guilt,'[1] so according to the milder doctrine and language of the Earl of Harrowby—milder in form at least—it is not good that Church service should be rendered by, or received from Sectaries.[2]

---

a To all the several predatory professions, to which the ruling and influential few betake themselves, for the means of preying upon the subject-many—to the Politician's and the Lawyer's, as well as to the Established Churchman's—this emblem of Adam Smith has been a perfect treasure. Be the amount of the depredation ever so enormous, the whole class of depredators are converted, in the lump, from objects of just jealousy into objects of compassion and sympathy. No abuse, be it ever so excruciating, that it has not been employed, and with but too much success, to reconcile men to:—throughout the whole field of government, *sinecures, useless* places, *needless* places, and *overpaid* places:—in the department of judicature, the continually increasing aggravation of the miseries produced by the technical system of procedure;—*factitious delay, vexation,* and *expense,* manufactured by the hands of lawyers, for the sake of the profit made by them out of the expense. Under the shadow of this emblem, we have seen—yes, this very generation has seen—a *Chancellor* and a *Master of the Rolls,* 'combining and confederating,' to use their own jargon, to and with each other, to levy, and, under the name of fees, levying accordingly, without consent of Parliament, masses of money, more or less of which, through the channel of *patronage,* was to go into their own pockets.[3]—Levy money without consent of Parliament? On what ground? Because by the like hands, in the same manner, money has been levied once before.[4] Of the ground made in this case, what was the extent, in comparison of that which prevented not the condemnation of Ship-money, and the punishment of those Judges, by whom that imposition had been converted into an instrument of depredation. In the days of Charles the First, Ship-money found a *Hampden,*[5] but this is the reign

---

[1] See p. 48 n. above.   [2] See p. 392 n. above.

[3] An Order of the Court of Chancery issued on 26 February 1807 on the authority of Thomas Erskine (1750–1823), first Baron Erskine, Lord Chancellor 1806–7, and Sir William Grant (1752–1832), Master of the Rolls 1801–17, had sanctioned an increase of costs in the Court. See *Official Aptitude Maximized; Expense Minimized,* ed. P. Schofield, Oxford, 1993 (*CW*), pp. 61–2 n., 65 n., 212–21.

[4] The previous occasion had been an increase in fees in the Court of Chancery authorized in 1743 by Philip Yorke (1690–1764), first Baron and first Earl of Hardwicke, Lord Chancellor 1737–56, and William Fortescue (1687–1749), Master of the Rolls 1741–9: see ibid., p. 217 & n.

[5] In 1634 the ancient tax of ship money had been revived and extended by Charles I with a view to funding the Navy from the nation as a whole. In 1637–8 the legality of the tax was tested in a case involving John Hampden (1595–1643), with judges deciding narrowly in favour of the Crown. The tax became increasingly unpopular and was eventually declared illegal by the Ship Money Act of 1640 (16 Car. 1, c. 14).

NOTES TO EXCELLENT CHURCH'S MAXIMS.

Proof of the adoption given to this and the last preceding Maxim,—general *understanding* as expressed in the language of the *Earl of Harrowby*. It is among the *'dangers of our situation,'* that mention is made by him (p. 32)[1] of the increase in the number of dissenting places of worship, and the still greater increase in the number of dissenting Ministers.—'While the licences for the creation[2] of dissenting places of worship are increasing,' (says he), 'from the average of ninety per annum during the first fourteen years of the present reign, to an average of five hundred and eighteen, during the last fourteen years; and the licences for dissenting preachers in a still larger proportion; while there are 1,881 parishes, containing a population of nearly five millions of persons, in which the churches and chapels are 2,553, capable of containing only 1,856,000 persons, and the places of dissenting worship are 3,438; do not (continues he) let us shut our eyes to the dangers of our situation.' And in the next page, (p. 33), 'in the most populous parishes, places of worship, according to the Church of England, are notoriously deficient. The people have no option but the entire neglect of all divine worship, or the attendance upon a worship which makes them dissenters from the establishment.

'While the chapels of every sect, (continues his Lordship) are rising round them day by day, and inviting congregations by every species of accommodation, and by the repetition of their services at different hours, the parish church is open perhaps only once on the Sunday; is insufficient to accommodate the rich; and in too many places is almost shut against the poor.'[3] In any breast, in which either the religion of Jesus, or that morality which depends upon it, were a primary object of regard,—under the inability which the Church of England thus confessedly labours under, as to the affording to the people the benefits of divine worship according to the religion of Jesus,—the fact that there are *other* Churches by which the benefit of divine

---

of George the Third, and the race of *Hampden* is no more. In a British House of Commons, not a single voice to lift itself up against the levying of money without the consent of Parliament! Money levied without consent of Parliament, for private and personal use, levied by that tax, compared with which the worst of other taxes is a relief.[a] One of the confederates was once a *Soldier-Officer:* and there came out a pamphlet, proving that officer's pay was such as no gentleman could live upon.[4] Little could he then expect ever to find it in his power, in so smooth a manner, to reduce such theories to practice.

O rare emblem—emblem of a lottery!—a use for it this, which, with all their sagacity, the inventors of that ingenious instrument never could have imagined!

---

[a] See Bentham's Protest against Law Taxes.

---

[1] 1818 '(pp. 32–16)'. *Substance of the Speech of the Earl of Harrowby*, p. 32.
[2] Harrowby 'erection'.
[3] *Substance of the Speech of the Earl of Harrowby*, pp. 33–4.
[4] Erskine had purchased a commission in the 2nd Battalion of the Royal Regiment of Foot in 1768, and was appointed to the rank of Lieutenant in April 1773. He was the anonymous author of *Observations on the prevailing abuses in the British Army, arising from the corruption of civil government. With a proposal to the Officers towards obtaining an Addition to their Pay*, London, 1775, which exhorted officers to refuse to vote for any candidate at a Parliamentary election who would not support a petition of the Army to augment pay, and included petitions for signature and presentation to the House of Commons and the King. In September 1775 Erskine sold his commission in the Army, having in April 1775 been admitted to Lincoln's Inn and thereby commencing his legal career. For Bentham's contact with Erskine at this time see John Lord Campbell, *The Lives of the Lord Chancellors and Keepers of the Great Seal of England*, 8 vols., London, 1845–69, vi. 388.

worship, according to the religion of Jesus, is administered, should it not naturally, whatsoever preference were given to the Church-of-England form in comparison with these dissenters' forms, be, upon the whole, an object—not of regret, but of consolation?—But the religion of the Noble Earl is the religion of the Church-of-England: and the increased extent thus given to the benefit of divine worship, according to the religion of Jesus, is, to his Lordship, matter of pure regret, unassuaged, for any thing that appears, for any the least particle of consolation. All this is consistent: all this is National-Society principle. To hell let them all go, rather than seek otherwise than under our command the way to heaven.

Happily for the religion of Jesus, and that morality which depends upon it, and that happiness which depends upon this morality,—the good people of England, as his Lordship himself sees and shews, have given judgment against his Lordship of Harrowby, his Lordship of London, and these their schemes. If, among the different Protestant modes of the religion of Jesus, the mode of the Established Church of England were not, in respect of its tendency to promote the ends of religion, inferior in the eyes of the people at large to those other modes, additional places of worship in that mode, capable of holding more persons than those places of dissenting worship, would, in all this time, have been erected:—erected, and by the same honourable means; erected by voluntary contributions. In the period in question no doubt that by these same means, in number more or less considerable, places of Church-of-England worship have been erected. But, notwithstanding the prodigious difference in respect of pecuniary capacity and influence, so small is the number, shame has kept his Lordship and his coadjutors from holding it up to view.

Voluntarily they will not contribute any thing:—seeing this, his Lordship's plan—his Lordship's declared intention—is, if he can, to make them contribute by force.[a] But, along with all luke-warm Church-of-Englandists, included in that design is the intention of compelling all dissenters, thus to add to their already exacted contributions, towards the performance of a service, from which, if it were ever so good an one, they could not reap any direct benefit, and which, in their eyes, with what reason let it now be judged, is so far from being a good one.

[h] *To Maxim* 8.—General proof—universal understanding and universal practice.—Specific proof—opinion delivered in the Earl of Harrowby's Speech, as above.

Speaking of the Act of Henry the Eighth, by which *Non-Residence* was *disallowed* in some cases, but *allowed* in others,[1]—after saying (p. 20) that 'the extreme strictness and *universality*' of the disallowance 'had brought it into desuetude,' and without saying any thing in favour of an universal disallowance, in any case, or in any date of the Church, 'I am induced' (says he) 'by many considerations to think, that, in an

---

[a] *Extract from Morning Chronicle, June 27th,* 1816.

{House of Lords, June 26th.}

'Lord Harrowby moved for an Abstract of Returns respecting the Residence of the Clergy, and an Extract of Returns respecting the capacity of Churches and Chapels, as compared with the population of each parish, &c. His Lordship stated, that Parliament would be called upon next Session for some legislative measure, and for an act of munificence, with a view to the establishment, as far as possible, of a sufficient number of Churches and Chapels commensurate with the population.'[2]

---

[1] 21 Hen. VIII, c. 13 (1529).

[2] For Harrowby's request on 26 June 1816 for the abstracts see *Lords Journals* (1814–16) l. 789. The eventual result was the Church Building Act of 1818 (58 Geo. III, c. 45). For Bentham's further comments on this proposal see pp. 535–6 below.

NOTES TO EXCELLENT CHURCH'S MAXIMS.

establishment where the income of benefices bears[1] no proportion to the labour or importance of the cure, a strict injunction of universal residence could neither be practicable nor desirable.'

Speaking immediately after of *Pluralities*, 'I am equally averse' (continues he) 'to the abolition of pluralities;' (p. 21.) 'but the more I have considered the subject, the more firmly am I convinced that some *regulation*, by which the extent of pluralities and non-residence should either directly or indirectly be reduced, is essential to the existence of an Established Church in this kingdom.'—So far his Lordship: *Regulation?*—Yes:—for how trifling soever the regulation, whatsoever is *regulated* is thereby *confirmed*.

Regulate, and by regulation *confirm* the practice of *non-residence* and *pluralism?* Regulate then next, and by regulation confirm the practices of *shop-lifting* and *swindling*. So many instances of *Sinecurism*, so many instances of the safe-obtainment of money in large masses by false pretence. So many instances of *Non-Residence*, so many instances of *Sinecurism*.—So many instances of *Pluralism*, so many instances—of *Sinecurism*, of *Non-Residence*, total or partial,—and thereby of obtainment on false pretences. So many *benefices* possessed by one and the *same* Pluralist, so many instances, with or without the exception of *one*, of the obtainment of money, by this same person, on this same false pretence.

^j *To Maxim 9.*—See Note (^k) to Maxim 10.

^k *To Maxim 10.*—*Proof*, universally established practice—general understanding grounded on it, and the opinion of the Earl of Harrowby, as evidenced by the silence maintained in relation to this subject, as well in his plan of reform as in the Speech spoken by him on the introduction of it. Of 'surplice fees,' in p. 8, he makes explicit mention: but to no other purpose than the remarking, that 'it was impossible to comprehend them in one abstract.' And though it is by the officiating minister, that in every instance they are received,—by the Curate, as often as he is the officiating Minister,—by the Curate in whose hands it would have been in his Lordship's power to keep them in every instance, by a clause, prohibiting the Incumbent from ever taking them out of the hands of his Curate,—to Curates (p. 22) he gives enormous and constantly *disproportionate* sums, for an *'extent of labour'* in every other particular purely imaginary, (so it will soon be seen), suppressing all mention of these constantly *proportionate* remunerations.

^l *To Maxim 11.*—*Proof*, established *practice;* and, among Church-of-Englandists, an extensively, if not generally, prevalent *understanding*, of which that practice is effect and cause: moreover, recognition made of the existence of this practice by the Earl of Harrowby, where, as above, (Note (^g) in Maxim 7) he says, (Speech, p. 33) 'the parish church .... is insufficient to accommodate the rich, and, in too many places, is almost shut against the poor.'—According to a notion imputed to *Mahomet* and his followers, women have no souls:[2] according to an opinion thus proved, as above, upon Church-of-Englandists, the poor, 'in too many places,' either have no souls at all, or none that are worth saving from hell-fire. On this head see Note (^g) to Maxim 7. But the exclusion thus put upon the poor, whence comes it? Whence but from the fundamental principle, acted upon by the Church of England, at the period of what on that occasion is called the *Reformation?* viz. the sacrifice of the spiritual interest of poor and rich to the temporal interests of the rich.

---

[1] 1818 'bear'. The text follows the 'Errata'.

[2] It was widely, but erroneously, thought in Europe at this time that Muslims believed that women could not enter paradise: see, for instance, Charles de Secondat, Baron de Montesquieu, *Lettres Persanes*, 2 vols., Amsterdam, 1721, Letter XXII, i. 94.

^m *To Maxim* 13.—See Note (^c) to Maxim 3.
ⁿ *To Maxim* 14.—See Note (^c) to Maxim 3. *Proof,* established regulations; in particular, the Statute, called the *Act of Uniformity,* (13 and 14, c. 2. c. 4.)—practice established under and according to these regulations,[1]—and general understanding, in conformity to those regulations and that practice. See also Note (^a) to Maxim 1.
^o *To Maxim* 15.—See Note (^c) to Maxim 3.
^p *To Maxim* 16.—See Note (^c) to Maxim 3; and the scheme of the Noble Church Reformer on this subject, as noticed in Note (^c) to Maxim 3, and Note (^[lk])[2] to Maxim 10.
^q *To Maxim* 17.—See Maxim 14: and Note (^c) to Maxim 3.

---

[1] The Act of Uniformity of 1662 required all services of worship to be conducted according to the *Book of Common Prayer:* see p. 349 & n. above.
[2] 1818 'th' is a slip.

§5.—*Pay continued—Merit, whether produceable by Sinecures, &c.*

Zealot.—But *merit?*—What do you say to *merit?*—Surely has it all this while been altogether out of your thoughts! *Sinecures*—the great use of them—and is it not a sufficient use? is—to serve as *rewards for merit.* In this line of public service—(and can there be any other equally important one?) take away Sinecures, and other *liberally* paid offices, you leave merit without hope of reward; and, if thus you leave merit without hope of reward, is not this excluding it? In this line, or any other, do you know of any thing better than merit?—And can you have too much of it?—And, if you could, which you cannot, would you be *ungenerous* enough—*illiberal* enough—*unjust* enough—to have[1] it without paying for it?

Graduate.—Before all things it is necessary to have a meaning. When you talk of *merit*—of having Sinecures to give as *rewards for merit*—what I *do* understand is—that your wish is to have public money in this shape, to dispose of as may be most agreeable to you: what I do *not* understand is—on what *public ground*, for what public cause, you claim thus to have it at your disposal.

What, in my notion of the matter, is the only justifiable cause for the disposing of the matter of reward, in this or any other shape, is the *production of public service:* say—if in the sound of the word *merit* there be any thing particularly agreeable to you—say the *production of meritorious*, but be pleased to add, *beneficial, public service:* for *ordinary* service, *ordinary* reward; for *extra service*, *extra* reward: and, moreover, be pleased to remember, that in no shape, pecuniary or not pecuniary, can the matter of reward be bestowed by government, but that it is at the expense of the whole community that it is bestowed.

Production of public service—in this result then behold the only proper object, of reward bestowed on the sort of occasion here in question: bestowed by the trustees for the public;—bestowed at the expense of the public;—bestowed in an indefinitely large proportion, if not in the whole, at the expense of unwilling contributors.

A most pernicious,—and, at the same time, a most deplorably common, error,—is *that* by which the case of reward, administered as here at *public* expense, is confounded with the case, in which it is administered at *personal* expense: with the case, in which the party *by* whom it is administered is the party *at whose expense* it is administered. Administered at *personal* expense, *excess* is neither *probable* nor *mischievous:* be it ever so great, no person, other than the donor, can

---

[1] 1818 'leave'. The text follows the 'Errata'.

find in the magnitude of it any cause of complaint: and, by the supposition, no such cause does he find: administered at *public* expense, excess *is* constantly *mischievous*, and as constantly *probable*. *Liberality—generosity*—such are the attributes ascribed to the *gift*, and thence to the *giver*, in the case where, in respect of its magnitude, the disposition made of the good thing given in the way of reward, is an object of approbation to him by whom it is thus spoken of. Applied to reward, conferred at *personal* expense, these *eulogistic* appellatives are innoxious, and even beneficial: applied to reward, conferred at *public* expense, they are noxious; they are instruments of pernicious delusion; they are instruments in the hand of *misrule, peculation,* and *depredation. Liberality* at a man's *own* expense—*liberality* at *other* men's expense—what can be more opposite? In the *first* case, and in that alone, it is that *self-denial* can find place: in the *other* case, instead of *self-denial*, nothing is to be seen but *selfishness*. In the first case, the only tax imposed is the tax imposed by the giver upon his own *self-regarding* affection, imposed for the gratification of his own *sympathetic*—of his own *social* affections: so let him do, tax those his personal affections—as high as he pleases—you need not fear his *over-taxing* them: should he even do so, it is *his* concern alone—not any body else's.

These things considered, if it be at public expense, talk not of *rewarding merit*—talk not of *retribution*—talk not of *remuneration*—at any rate in the character of an *end* in view: of words of this complexion, by the indeterminateness of their import, the tendency is—to mislead men's minds, and to reconcile them to *misrule*, in the shapes of *waste, peculation,* and *depredation:* say always *production of public service,* or, if you please, *production of meritorious public service*. By either of these phrases, indication is given of the object, which, on the occasion in question, *is*, or *ought to be*, the sole and immediate end in view:—an object, which is at the same time a *test* of the propriety of the disposition made, and a *measure* of propriety for the quantity so disposed of.

By the word *merit*, what is the object really designated? Any *specific quality* in the subject? No: nothing but the *affection* with which, by him, by whom the word is employed, the subject is regarded,—unless it be the property which the subject manifests, in giving birth to the affection so excited and directed. A *libel* is any thing that a man does *not* like: *merit* is any thing he *does* like: *libel* is a word invented to enable men to waste *punishment* at pleasure: *merit* is a word invented to enable them to waste *reward* at pleasure.

For bestowing reward at public expense, on any occasion or in any shape, this then being the only proper object and immediate *end in view*—the only justifiable cause—viz. *production of public service,*—so it is that, with reference to the accomplishment of this object, rewards, in the shape now in question, viz. *Sinecures* and *Extra-paid* places, will be seen to be essentially improper: being not only *not conducive* to that end, but, with reference to the attainment of it, positively adverse and obstructive.

Uncertainty, unproportionality, abstractiveness or *seductiveness,* and *degradingness,*—in the combination of all these qualities, may the cause of the impropriety be seen in the case of *Sinecures;* in the combination of all of them but the last, in the case of *Extra-paid* places.

1. *Uncertainty:*—for it is by *existing,* not by *future contingent* bread, that man is kept alive. In the list of Sinecures, be it ever so long, and be the service ever so meritorious, so it may be, that no one article,—such as, for the *merit* and the *man* in question, can be spared,—shall have fallen in, till the man is dead, the service forgotten, or some other service performed by some other man, whose *service,* or whose *merit,* i.e. whose *person* is more acceptable.

2. *Unproportionality:*—for,—on the one hand, be the value of the *past* service to be rewarded, and on the other hand the value of the service producible by means of the reward, what it may,—so it is that, the value of the reward being *fixt,* and not capable of being adapted to the value of either of those services, the chances are indefinitely great, that in quantity it will be either *greater* or *less* than the proper one.[a]

3. *Abstractiveness* or *seductiveness: abstractiveness,* the property of drawing a man *out of* the meritorious course to which he should be attached; *seductiveness,* the property of drawing him *into* a course of dissipation: leading him into a life of idleness, or engaging him in the pursuit of what commonly goes by the name of *pleasure:* of pleasure in those shapes in which the sudden influx of the matter of wealth now for the first time enables him to purchase it. Of this effect the magnitude will indeed depend upon the relative magnitude of the lot of reward—the *Sinecure.* But, in the case in question, this magnitude is in many instances notoriously enormous.

4. *Degradingness:* of this quality, and its inherency in the very essence of a Sinecure, mention has been already made: the shape being such, that in this shape reward cannot be received by a man,

---

[a] By this circumstance, therefore, is a *Sinecure* distinguished from a *Pension.* A Pension is *not,* in its own nature, incapable of being adjusted—adjusted with any degree of nicety to the value of the service: a *Sinecure is.* No wonder: for it is not by any view of making application of them to any such purpose as that of a reward for real public service, that in any branch of the public service they have been produced.

without his aggregating himself to a class of men, in whose instance nothing but condign punishment is wanting to aggregate them to the class of notorious criminals.

In this quality of *degradingness* may be seen, as above, the only shade of difference, which, in this respect, has place between the case of a *Sinecure* and the case of an *overpaid* place, of the pay of which the *excess*, instead of being, for the benefit of the public, suppressed, is kept on foot, to be disposed of in the same manner that a *Sinecure*, so called, would be disposed of. Where the excess arises from the smallness of the quantity of *time* employed in the performance of the duties, the office is in fact, by the amount of the deficiency in the article of time employed in the performance of the duties of it, a *Sinecure*.

Thus much being thus proved, viz. that to the production of meritorious public service in *any* line, reward, in either of the shapes in question, more particularly in that of *Sinecure*, is essentially ill adapted, another proposition presents itself, the proof of which may be apt to appear a work of supererogation. This is—that in relation to the production of extra-meritorious public service in the line here in question, the tendency of purely *factitious* extra reward, not only in this shape, but in any shape, is *not conducive*, but *adverse* and *preventive*.

As to the *exigible* duties, it is only in and by *Sermons* that *extra-meritorious service* referable to this head can be rendered.

Matter and *delivery*—to one or other of these heads will be found referable, whatsoever *merit* is capable of having place in a discourse of any kind: whatsoever *service*, extra-meritorious or simply meritorious, is capable of being rendered by it. So far as it is by the reading of a fixt form, such as the Liturgy, that the duty is performed, so far under the head of *matter*, no place is left for merit on the part of any individual, present or future. So far as concerns *delivery*, whatever comes to be said in regard to the reading of a *Sermon*, will, without considerable variation, be applicable to the reading of the Liturgy.

I. As to *Sermons*, and the meritorious service which in respect of the *matter* of them is capable of being rendered, true it cannot but be admitted to be, that while *printing* was unknown or rare, factitious extra reward might by its application to extra-meritorious service in this shape have been not incapable of being employed with beneficial effect. But by that admirable art, so it is that, for merit in this, as well as so many other lines of public service, has been brought into existence a species of reward in the shape of *natural*, i.e. *naturally attached* reward, by which, in this country at any rate,—unless it be, in some such way as will be seen, in subordination to this *natural* reward,—whatever may have been or may be the case in other times or other places, the use of *factitious* reward has been done away.

By *natural* or *naturally attached* reward, understand any benefit which, without any thing done for the purpose, either by the hand of government, or by any other hand, finds its way into the hands of him by whom the service in question has been rendered.

On most parts of the field of literature, and on that in question in a greater degree than almost any other,—to a written discourse, by which extra-meritorious service is capable of being in any shape rendered to the public, is naturally attached a mass of reward in a *pecuniary* shape, dependent upon publication, and consisting in *author's profits*. A class of cases is not altogether wanting in which,—by reason that the benefit, howsoever real and important, does not in colours sufficiently strong present itself to the feelings of a sufficiently considerable part of the whole number of the persons benefited, or capable of being benefited,—this naturally attached reward fails of being adequate. But assuredly the case here in question belongs not to that class.

In most instances, and in particular in the present,—among the properties of this *natural* reward, *one* is—*that* of being more eminently exempt than any *factitious* reward can be from the danger of being *misapplied: another* is, that, in respect of *proportionality* with reference to the *value* of the service, it presents in general a fairer chance than is presented by any such *factitious* reward: a *third* is— that, in the very nature of the case, it comes all of it from *willing*, no part of it from *unwilling* hands: thence so it is, that no *suffering* is produced by it. Of these three desirable properties, the *last* cannot by any person be denied to belong to it. The two first *may* indeed:—but by whom?—By those to whom,—their own '*understandings* and *wills*,' together with the few others which are in league with them, being, in their eyes, the only '*understandings* and *wills*' worthy of being regarded otherwise than with contempt,—it is accordingly an object prudently concealed, or madly avowed, to keep in a state of '[*prostration*]'[1] those same faculties in all other men.

In the case of the proposed *Homily Sermons*, the conception has been seen to be[2]—that, without the benefit of any ulterior reward, natural or factitious, the utility of the service rendered to *Church-of-Englandists* in general by Church attendance, might, even in their own conceptions, be rendered in a very considerable degree greater than it is at present. Still, however, on this plan, service *in this same*

---

[1] 1818 '*protraction*' appears to be a slip. For Howley's phrase, 'prostration of the understanding and the will', see p. 37 n. above.

[2] See pp. 356–60 above.

shape, more and more useful, was not by any means out of view. Were the door of the proposed collection to remain inexorably shut against all future additions, the application of the existing stock of *natural* reward might, in a degree more or less considerable, be obstructed. But,—if, on this occasion, due attention being paid to the course naturally taken by the *natural* reward, the application of factitious reward be guided by it,—*factitious* reward might, in this particular way (it is supposed) be employed—not only without any ill effects, but even with positive good effect.[a]

[a] Five, it is believed, is the number of 8vo. volumes containing the Sermons published by the late *Dr. Blair*, of Edinburgh. Not till some time after the first, came successively the four others.[1] For each of the four he received, by agreement, from the firm of Millar and Cadell (since Cadell and Davies) 1,000*l*.: concerning the price paid for the *first*, nothing can *here* be said with certainty. After payment of these great prices, so vast was the profit made by the Booksellers, that, from an emotion of spontaneous generosity, they presented him with 1,000*l*. more.[2] The choice was given him of plate or money. He chose the money: it was paid him, to the knowledge of the writer of this article, by Sir William Forbes, banker, of Edinburgh.[3]

With the indications thus given, to serve as securities for substantial correctness,—the writer, though anonymous,[4] may venture to propose the anecdote as a subject for inquiry.

Instruction, in more shapes than one, may be derived from it.

1. To moderate desires, such as suit the subject and the profession, *natural* reward, in a quantity not incapable of operating with beneficial effect, is attached to meritorious service in this line and in this shape.

2. By *Church-of-Scotlandism*, with its 933 Parish Priests and no more,[5] service of greater value, in this line and in this shape, has been produced, than by *Church-of-Englandism*, with its 11,000 Parish Priests and more,[6] besides its hierarchy of Archbishops and Bishops, with *Sinecurists* dignified and undignified, possessors of extravagantly paid benefices,—all kept on foot under the notion of their being applied in remuneration and production of *extra-meritorious* service. By no Church-of-England Clergyman, Priest, Bishop, or Archbishop, even though Tillotson was one Archbishop,[7] has ever been produced a collection of Sermons, of which the number of purchasers, and thence necessarily of readers, has been near so great.

---

[1] Hugh Blair (1718–1800), Church of Scotland minister, author, and academic, published five volumes of sermons at London and Edinburgh in 1777, 1780, 1790, 1794, and 1801 respectively. The final volume was published posthumously, while the first volume had reached its twenty-second edition by the time of Blair's death.

[2] The work was published and sold by William Creech in Edinburgh, and William Strahan and Thomas Cadell in London. From the sale of copyrights, and cash gifts from the publishers, Blair reputedly earned over £2,000 from the four volumes published in his lifetime.

[3] Sir William Forbes (1739–1806), sixth Baron Forbes of Pitsligo, Scottish banker and benefactor.

[4] Bentham originally intended to publish the present work anonymously: see p. 7 & n. above.

[5] According to Bentham's own calculations, based on information published in the *Edinburgh Almanack, and Imperial Register, for 1812*, there were 944 parochial benefices in Scotland: see p. 481 n. below.   [6] See p. 361 n. above.

[7] John Tillotson (1630–94), Archbishop of Canterbury from 1691, published fifty-four sermons both separately and collectedly between 1671 and 1694. These sermons, together

APPENDIX NO. IV. §V.

Thus much as to *matter*. Remains *delivery*. Remains thereupon to be shewn, that, in regard to the production of *extra-meritorious* service in this shape, the tendency of factitious reward would be rather *preventive* than *promotive*.

So far as depends upon good *delivery*, nothing can be more assuredly attached to extra-meritorious service in the character of a preacher, nothing more certainly and exactly proportionate, than *natural* reward. The more impressive the delivery, the more auditors: the more auditors, not only the greater the quantity of reward reaped in the shapes of *admiration, respect*, and *reputation*, but, if the preacher chooses, the more money. Even under *Church-of-England-ism*, though not in *Parish Churches*, yet in *Chapels* built or hired on speculation, the truth of this, and even without prejudice to orthodoxy, has been experienced by many a Clergyman, much to his advantage.

In the established Church of *Scotland*, in the three first-mentioned acquisitions—viz. *admiration, respect,* and *reputation*, may indeed be seen all the rewards that a Clergyman can look for from this particular source. But in these shapes, refined as they are, is reward altogether without its value?—altogether destitute of operative and productive energy?

In the Non-Established Churches,—as, in the way of *natural* reward (*factitious* having in this case no existence), almost every thing depends upon *Prayers* and *Sermons*, *matter* and *delivery* together,—so accordingly in no small degree upon *delivery*.[a]

All this while,—though, under Church-of-Englandism, for *extra-meritorious service* in this shape—matter and delivery together—adequate natural reward, as above, is, to those to whom it appears worth their while to seek it, by no means unattainable,—yet, if the maximum of meritorious service in this shape were the object, the

---

3. Even in the conception of *Church-of-Englandists* themselves, instruction not unwholesome is not altogether incapable of being drawn, from a fountain, ecclesiastically speaking, *foreign* and *schismatical* as it is. For, unless in no small proportion to *Church-of-Englandists*, could any such vast number of copies have been sold? Assuredly in houses, zealously *Church-of-Englandist*, have they been found by the writer of these pages. Note that in the whole collection not so much as a single part (it is believed) can be found touched upon, that is in controversy between the two Churches.

[a] Of *delivery*, the component parts are *intonation* and *gesture*. As to *gesture*, from a man reading out of a book, scarcely would it any where be endurable. In England, scarcely, without much reserve, from a man preaching without book. Englishmen are not *Athenians*.

---

with a further 200 unpublished ones and other writings, were collected by Ralph Barker and published in fourteen volumes between 1695 and 1704.

Church to look to would, for the reasons already given, be—among Established Churches, not the *English,* but the *Scotch:* to which may be added, with little distinction, all the Non-Established Churches.

Yes: so far from producing it, the tendency of *Sinecures,*—of *factitious* reward, especially in any such large masses,—particularly in this line of service,—is—to *prevent* merit from coming into existence. To the natural reward as above described, in possession or in prospect, substitute now, or add a mass of *factitious* reward: a richer *living,* a fat *Deanery,* or a *Bishoprick:*—what will be the consequence?—The *factitious* reward—it will be at the hands of this or that high-seated[1] individual, in the character of Patron, that it will be looked for: instead of *being worshipped* by his congregation, the business of the Preacher will be to *worship* this giver of good gifts: to that object will all his attention and exertions be directed. This, while the reward is as yet but in *expectancy.* But, suppose it in *possession,* and no ulterior object of ambition in prospect, then not only in the line of *public service,* but in every other line, even in the line of *Patron-worship,* will exertions cease. The hope of the reward is what the exertions had for their cause: the *cause* ceasing, so does the *effect.*

Thus stands the matter so far as depends upon the performance of the duties of *perfect* obligation. Turn now to those of *imperfect* obligation—the *inexigible services* so often distinguished and explained. On condition of his residency then, and in proportion to the relative value which his charity, his zeal, and his intelligence, give to them,—*respect,* and, within a moderately extensive circle, *reputation,* will attach upon them, and constitute in the breast of the Parish Priest the *temporal* and human part of his reward. As[2] to *admiration*—of that sort which is the fruit of discourse, and in a more particular manner of oratory,—it belongs not to this part of his field of duty: but in lieu of it, he finds in *affection* a more appropriate, and to a pious taste a less suspected, and upon the whole a sweeter fruit.

Apply now the fatter *Living,* the fat *Deanery,* the fat *Bishoprick:* during expectancy, behold now the same *obstructive*[3] and *seductive* influence; *after possession,* the same *narcotic* and *sedative* influence.

What happens but seldom will yet happen now and then. Well then:—from admiration of the degree of perfection in which these *inexigible* services have been rendered by a *Parish Priest,* a Patron bestows upon him the adipose matter:—the rich living, the dignified

---

[1] 1818 'high-rated'. The text follows the 'Errata'.
[2] 1818 'reward; as'. The text follows the 'Errata'.
[3] 1818 '*destructive*'. The text follows the 'Errata'.

APPENDIX NO. IV. §V.

Sinecure, the Bishoprick. Suppose this for argument sake. Upon Parish Priests *in general* will the gift operate with any such general effect as that of producing increase of meritorious service in this same shape?—No: the most *commonly*, not the most *rarely* productive cause, is the cause to which by men at large, an effect is ascribed: the *gift* itself will be visible to all eyes; the *cause* of it to but a few: not *merit*, but what is called *interest*, will have the credit of it.

For rewarding *merit*—and perhaps, if pressed, for rewarding *meritorious public service*—this forsooth is the pretence on which ye ask for the disposal of these good gifts. Ah, hypocrites! is it for any such use that ye covet them? Unless it be to make the surer of *keeping* them for other uses, do ye ever put them to any such use?—Not ye indeed; ye know better things.[1]

Works of *supererogation* and *policy* excepted, as above, *interest* in some shape or other—by this familiar and comprehensive name may be expressed the efficient cause, to which in every instance the receipt of any such good gift may, without danger of error, be ascribed. By some modification or other of the art of *pleasing*, the clerical person has found favour in the Patron's sight: by good fortune or industry he has found the means of rendering himself in some way or other *useful* to him: *son, cousin, quondam preceptor, dependent*—to the Patron he bears some relation or other, which renders it either a matter of *profit*, or a point of *honour*, to make provision for him:—add the same cases, having place or relation to any near connexion or particular friend of the Patron. Lastly, but not[2] least appositely, in either House suppose *vote* and *speech*, or though it be but a *vote*, secured, during the life of the Parliament, to Monarch or Minister—secured in either case to *legitimacy*—by a dutiful and loyal use of so divine an attribute as that of beneficence.[3] Of all these causes,—to which more and more might be added,—is there any one that will not be recognized in the character of a more probable cause for the effect, than any such rare and magnanimous desire, as that of giving, in any line of office, sacred or profane, increase to meritorious public service?

Rich gifts in *this* shape are not well adapted to the production of extra-meritorious service in *any* line of office:—rich gifts in *any* shape are not promotive but preventive of extra-meritorious service in the line of *ecclesiastical* office. It is not for any such purpose that they were instituted: it is not for any such purpose that they are kept on foot. Of any one of these positions is the truth a secret?—No more

---

[1] Bentham is echoing Jesus's reproval of the scribes and Pharisees: see Matthew 23: 13–33.
[2] 1818 'Lastly, not'. The text follows the 'Errata'.
[3] See, for instance, Psalm 68: 19.

than the existence of *Saint Paul's Cathedral* within view from *St. James's Park*.[1]

Even by a man who in general piques himself upon conscientiousness or public spirit, will any scruple or mystery be made of their being obtained by him, or of him, by *interest?*—by *interest*, in some shape or other, as above particularized?

Meantime,—as the same activity, which is exerting itself principally in the more efficient art of *interest-making*, may, in the meantime, be exercising itself with more or less success in the less efficient art of preaching, each art lending encouragement to the other,—what, among such a multitude, might equally have been effected by a throw of the dice, may also be effected by the sort of state policy above spoken of: viz. in the multitude of cyphers setting down here and there a significant figure. While, by '*usefulness*' in the *Treasury* sense,[2] and by those other arts by which such eminences are most naturally gained, working himself up to *St. James's*,—even the recorded contemner of '*Ale-drinkers*,' and supporter of their '*poisoners*,'[3] was displaying, it is said, such pulpit talents, as reflected a certain degree of countenance on the countenance he was receiving.[4] And thus it is, that, as the hierarchy never has been, so never can it be in much danger of being altogether destitute of *merit:* of *merit*, to wit, of that quality and in that quantity, which will have enabled this or that Courtly writer, whose language is the language of harmonious exaggeration, to give a description of the *Bishops' Bench* in some such strain as may be found set by *Pope:*

> 'Ev'n in a Bishop I can spy Desert;
> 'Secker is *decent*, Rundel has a *Heart*,
> '*Manners* with *Candour* are to Benson giv'n,
> 'To Berkley, *every Virtue* under Heaven.'
> *Pope's Epilogue to the Satires*, Dial. ii.[5]

---

[1] i.e. the residence of Andrewes, as Rector of St James's, Piccadilly.

[2] See p. 324 n. above.

[3] For Andrewes' involvement in the case of Abbott the brewer see pp. 49–50, 323 & n. above, and pp. 539–46 below.

[4] For Andrewes' reputation as a preacher see, for instance, Revd George Pellew, *A Sermon preached in the Cathedral and Metropolitical Church of Christ's, Canterbury, on Sunday, June XII. M.DCCC.XXV. on the occasion of the Death of the Very Revd. Gerrard Andrewes, D.D. Late Dean of Canterbury, and Rector of St. James, Westminster*, London, 1825, pp. 12–15, esp. 12: 'As an eloquent and persuasive preacher of the Gospel, he was rarely, if ever, surpassed.'

[5] The lines originally appeared in Alexander Pope (1688–1744), *One Thousand Seven Hundred and Thirty Eight. Dialogue II*, London, 1738, p. 7, which later appeared under the title 'Epilogues to the Satires' in *The Works of Alexander Pope Esq.*, 9 vols., London, 1753 (see iv. 318–19). The clerics mentioned are Thomas Secker (1693–1768), Bishop of Bristol 1735–7, Bishop of Oxford 1737–58, Archbishop of Canterbury 1758–68; Thomas Rundle (1688–1743), Bishop of Derry 1735–43; Martin Benson (1689–1752), Bishop of Gloucester 1735–52; and George Berkeley (1685–1753), Bishop of Cloyne 1734–53.

APPENDIX NO. IV. §V.

In all this there may have been little or nothing that was not true. But supposing it all most correctly true, what would it prove in favour of the existence of Bishopricks? For being *decent*, having a *heart*, or having *manners* with *candour*, is there any necessity or use in giving a man from 1,000*l*. to 25,000*l*. a year? And suppose *Berkley* to have had *every virtue under heaven*, what,—out of the small circle in which he moved, and in which his virtue found his reward,—was the country the better for it? that part of it excepted which was embodied in his published works, and which also generated its own reward.[1][a]

[a] INCOMES of ENGLISH and IRISH BISHOPRICS, with intimations concerning the *interest*, by which they were most of them respectively obtained. From the Morning Chronicle for the [17th and 25th February, 1813].[2]

N.B. By the sums annexed are designated—not the whole Ecclesiastical incomes enjoyed by the respective Bishops, but the incomes belonging to the Bishopricks, exclusive of such *Sinecures*, and *Livings* converted by them and for their benefit into *Sinecures*, as are held with these same Bishopricks.

ENGLISH BISHOPRICKS: [17th February, 1813].[3]

Canterbury, *Duke of Rutland*'s cousin[4]	£ 20,000
York, *Lord Vernon*'s and *Harcourt*'s brother[5]	14,000
Durham, *Lord Barrington*'s uncle[6]	24,000
Winchester, late *Lord North*'s brother[7]	18,000
Ely, *Duke of Rutland*'s tutor[8]	12,000
London, Dr. Randolph[9]	9,000

[1] In addition to his works of philosophy, notably *A Treatise Concerning the Principles of Human Knowlege*, Pt. I, Dublin, 1710, Berkeley compiled *The Ladies Library*, 3 vols., London, 1714, which went through six editions in his lifetime, and *Siris: A Chain of Philosophical Reflexions and Inquiries Concerning the Virtues of Tar Water, and divers other subjects connected together and arising one from another*, Dublin, 1744, a reconciliation of metaphysics and medicine, which enjoyed very large sales as a home-medicine guide.
[2] 1818 '25th February, 1813, and 19th April, 1813' is incorrect.   [3] 1818 '19th April, 1813'.
[4] Manners-Sutton, Archbishop of Canterbury 1805–28, was the son of George Manners-Sutton (1723–83), whose brother John Manners (1721–70) was the father of Charles Manners (1754–87), fourth Duke of Rutland, and grandfather of John Henry Manners (1778–1857), fifth Duke of Rutland.
[5] Edward Venables-Vernon (subsequently Harcourt), Archbishop of York 1808–47, was the brother of George Venables-Vernon (1735–1813), second Baron Vernon, but the cousin of William Harcourt (1743–1830), third Earl Harcourt, who was the son of his mother's brother Simon Harcourt (1714–77), first Earl Harcourt. On the death of William Harcourt in 1830, Edward Venables-Vernon inherited Harcourt's estates and adopted his name.
[6] Shute Barrington, Bishop of Durham 1791–1826, was the uncle of Richard Barrington (1761–1814), fourth Viscount Barrington of Ardglass, who was the son of his brother John Barrington (bap. 1719, d. 1764).
[7] Brownlow North (1741–1820), Bishop of Winchester 1781–1820, was the half-brother of Frederick North (1732–92), second Earl of Guilford, styled Lord North 1752–90, leader of the administration as First Lord of the Treasury and Chancellor of the Exchequer 1770–82.
[8] Bowyer Edward Sparke (1759–1836), Bishop of Ely 1812–36, who was tutor to John Henry Manners, fifth Duke of Rutland, at Trinity College, Cambridge.
[9] John Randolph, Bishop of London 1809–13.

CHURCH-OF-ENGLANDISM

Bath and Wells, *Duke of Gloucester*'s tutor[1]	5,000
Chichester, *Duke of Richmond*'s tutor[2]	4,000
Litchfield, *Lord Cornwallis*'s uncle[3]	6,000
Worcester, Dr. Cornewall[4]	6,000
Hereford, *Duke of Beaufort*'s tutor[5]	4,000
Bangor, Son of *Queen*'s English master[6]	5,000
St. Asaph, *Lord Buckingham*'s tutor[7]	6,000
Oxford, Brother of Prince Regent's tutor[8]	3,000
Lincoln, *Mr. Pitt*'s secretary[9]	5,000
Salisbury, *Princess Charlotte*'s tutor[10]	6,000
Norwich, Dr. Bathurst[11]	4,000
Carlisle, *Duke of Portland*'s tutor[12]	3,500
St. David's, Dr. Burgess[13]	5,000
Rochester, *Duke of Portland*'s secretary[14]	1,500
Exeter, *Lord Chichester*'s brother[15]	3,000

[1] Richard Beadon (1737–1824), Bishop of Bath and Wells 1802–24, had charge of the education of William Frederick (1776–1834), styled Prince William of Gloucester until succeeding as second Duke of Gloucester and Edinburgh in 1805, at Trinity College, Cambridge.

[2] John Buckner (1734–1824), Bishop of Chichester 1798–1824, had been domestic Chaplain to Charles Lennox (1764–1819), fourth Duke of Richmond.

[3] James Cornwallis (1743–1824), Bishop of Coventry and Lichfield 1781–1824, fourth Earl Cornwallis from 1823, was the uncle of Charles Cornwallis (1774–1823), second Marquis Cornwallis, who was the son of his brother Charles Cornwallis (1738–1805), first Marquis Cornwallis.

[4] Folliot Herbert Walker Cornewall (bap. 1754, d. 1831), Bishop of Worcester 1808–31.

[5] John Luxmoore (1756–1830), Bishop of Hereford 1808–15, was tutor not to the Duke of Beaufort, but to Charles William Henry Montagu-Scott (1772–1819), fourth Duke of Buccleuch, at King's College, Cambridge.

[6] Henry William Majendie (1754–1830), Bishop of Bangor 1809–30, was a son of John James Majendie (1709–82), tutor to Queen Charlotte from 1761 to 1768.

[7] William Cleaver (1742–1815), Bishop of St Asaph 1806–15, was tutor to George Nugent-Temple-Grenville (1753–1813), third Earl Temple and first Marquis of Buckingham, at Christ Church College, Oxford.

[8] William Jackson (1751–1815), Bishop of Oxford 1812–15, was the brother of Cyril Jackson (1746–1819), tutor from 1771 to 1776 to George (1762–1830), Prince of Wales, Prince Regent 1811–20, and Frederick (1763–1827), Duke of York and Albany, the two eldest sons of George III.

[9] George Pretyman Tomline, Bishop of Lincoln 1787–1820, was private secretary from 1784 to 1787 to William Pitt the Younger (1759–1806), leader of the administration as First Lord of the Treasury and Chancellor of the Exchequer 1783–1801, 1804–6.

[10] John Fisher (1748–1825), Bishop of Salisbury 1807–25, was tutor from 1805 to 1817 to Princess Charlotte Augusta of Wales.

[11] Henry Bathurst, Bishop of Norwich 1805–37.

[12] Samuel Goodenough (1743–1827), Bishop of Carlisle 1808–27. William Henry Cavendish Cavendish-Scott-Bentinck (1768–1854), fourth Duke of Portland, attended Goodenough's school at Ealing from 1774 to 1783. [13] Thomas Burgess, Bishop of St David's 1803–25.

[14] Walker King (1755–1827), Bishop of Rochester 1809–27. In 1782 King had worked as a private secretary to Charles Watson-Wentworth (1730–82), second Marquis of Rockingham, leader of the administration as First Lord of the Treasury 1765–6, 1782. His brother John King (1759–1830), Permanent Under-Secretary of State at the Home Office 1791–1806, had, however, served under William Henry Cavendish-Bentinck (1738–1809), third Duke of Portland, Home Secretary 1794–1801.

[15] George Pelham (1766–1827), Bishop of Exeter 1807–20, was the brother of Thomas Pelham (1756–1826), second Earl of Chichester.

APPENDIX NO. IV. §V.

Peterborough, Dr. Madan[1]	1,000
Bristol, *Mr. Perceval*'s tutor[2]	1,000
Landaff, Dr. Watson[3]	900
Gloucester, Dr. Huntingford[4]	1,200
Chester, *Lord Ellenborough*'s brother[5]	1,000
Sodor and Man, Mr. George Murray, son of late *Bishop of St. David's, Duke of Athol*'s nephew in law, *Earl of Kinnoul*'s brother-in-law[6]	
	£169,100

IRISH BISHOPRICKS: 25th February, 1813.

Armagh, *Marquis of Bute*'s brother[7]	£14,000
Cashel, *Viscount Middleton*'s brother[8]	8,000
Tuam, *Marquis of Waterford*'s uncle[9]	9,000
Dublin, *Bishop of St. Asaph*'s brother[10]	12,000
Kildare, *Lord Balcarras*'s brother[11]	7,000
Meath, *Duke of Portland*'s private secretary[12]	6,000
Derry, *Lord Northland*'s brother[13]	13,000
Kilmore, *Marquis of Waterford*'s cousin,[14] about.	6,000
Elphin, *Lord Clancarty*'s brother[15]	10,000

---

[1] Spencer Madan (1729–1813), Bishop of Peterborough 1794–1813.
[2] William Lort Mansel (1753–1820), Bishop of Bristol 1808–20, was tutor to Spencer Perceval at Trinity College, Cambridge.
[3] Richard Watson, Bishop of Llandaff 1782–1816.
[4] George Isaac Huntingford (1748–1832), Bishop of Gloucester 1802–15.
[5] George Henry Law (1761–1845), Bishop of Chester 1812–24, was the brother of Baron Ellenborough, Chief Justice of King's Bench 1802–18.
[6] George Murray (1784–1860), Bishop of Sodor and Man 1814–27, second son of Lord George Murray (1761–1803), Bishop of St David's 1801–3, married Sarah Hay-Drummond (d. 1874), sister of Thomas Robert Hay-Drummond (1785–1866), eleventh Earl of Kinnoull. On 22 May 1813 Murray had been nominated Bishop of Sodor and Man by his father's eldest brother John Murray (1755–1830), fourth Duke of Atholl.
[7] William Stuart (1755–1822), Archbishop of Armagh 1800–22, was a brother of John Stuart (1744–1814), created Marquis of Bute (I) in 1796.
[8] Charles Brodrick (1761–1822), Archbishop of Cashel 1801–22, was a brother of George Brodrick (1754–1836), fourth Viscount Midleton (I).
[9] William Beresford (1743–1819), first Baron Decies, Archbishop of Tuam 1794–1819, was the uncle of Henry de la Poer Beresford (1772–1826), second Marquis of Waterford (I), who was the son of his brother George de la Poer Beresford (1735–1800), created first Marquis of Waterford (I) in 1789.
[10] Euseby Cleaver (1745–1819), Archbishop of Dublin 1809–19, was a brother of William Cleaver, Bishop of St Asaph.
[11] Charles Lindsay (1760–1846), Bishop of Kildare 1804–46, was a brother of Alexander Lindsay (1752–1825), sixth Earl of Balcarres.
[12] Thomas Lewis O'Beirne (1749–1823), Bishop of Meath 1798–1823, was chaplain and private secretary to the third Duke of Portland, initially in 1782 when Portland was Lord-Lieutenant of Ireland, and again in 1783 when Portland was First Lord of the Treasury.
[13] William Knox (1762–1831), Bishop of Derry 1803–31, was a brother of Thomas Knox (1754–1840), who succeeded his father Thomas Knox (1729–1818), first Viscount Northland (I), as second Viscount Northland (I) in 1818.
[14] George de la Poer Beresford (1765–1841), Bishop of Kilmore 1802–41, was a cousin of Henry de la Poer Beresford, second Marquis of Waterford (I), who was son of his father's brother George de la Poer Beresford, first Marquis of Waterford (I).
[15] Power Le Poer Trench (1770–1839), Bishop of Elphin 1810–19, was a brother of Richard Le Poer Trench, second Earl of Clancarty (I), first Baron Trench, and first Viscount Clancarty.

CHURCH-OF-ENGLANDISM

Killaloe, *Marquis of Ely*'s brother[1]	6,000
Raphoe, *Marquis of Waterford*'s brother, about[2]	9,000
Cork, *Lord Howth*'s brother[3]	5,000
Fernes, *Lord Roden*'s brother[4]	6,000
Down, *Lord Caledon*'s cousin[5]	6,000
Killala, Dr. Vershoegle[6]	3,500
Cloyne, Dr. Bennett[7]	5,000
Clogher, Dr. Porter[8]	7,000
Waterford, Dr. Stock[9]	6,000
Ossory, Dr. Kearney[10]	3,500
Dromore, Dr. Leslie[11]	5,000
Limerick, Dr. Warburton[12]	6,000
Clonfert, Dr. [Butson][13]	3,500
	£156,500

{From the Morning Chronicle, 25th Aug. 1813.}

'The vacancies filled up by *this* Administration (there is now one open)[14] on the Bench of *Bishops*, in *Ireland*, have been *seven;* of these, four were given to the *brothers* of the Marquis of Waterford, Earls Howth, Roden, and Kilkenny.[15] It will be observed, that the *Marquis of Waterford* has *three* mitres now in his family, the *Archbishoprick of Tuam*, and the *Bishopricks* of *Kilmore* and *Killaloe*.[16] How much "Virtue and Talent"[17] do these *Beresfords* possess. In the same way have the enormous Irish *livings* been disposed of.

---

[1] Robert Ponsonby Tottenham Loftus (1773–1850), Bishop of Killaloe 1804–20, was brother of John Loftus (1770–1845), second Marquis of Ely (I).

[2] John George de la Poer Beresford (1773–1862), Bishop of Raphoe 1807–19, was a brother of Henry de la Poer Beresford, second Marquis of Waterford (I).

[3] Thomas St Lawrence (1755–1831), Bishop of Cork 1807–31, was a brother of William St Lawrence (1752–1822), second Earl of Howth (I).

[4] Percy Jocelyn (1764–1843), Bishop of Ferns and Leighlin 1809–20, was a brother of Robert Jocelyn (1756–1820), second Earl of Roden (I).

[5] Nathaniel Alexander (1760–1840), Bishop of Down and Connor 1804–23, was a cousin of Du Pre Alexander (1777–1839), second Earl of Caledon (I), who was son of his father's brother James Alexander (1730–1802), created Earl of Caledon (I) in 1800.

[6] James Verschoyle (1750–1834), Bishop of Killala and Achonry 1810–34.

[7] William Bennet (c. 1746–1820), Bishop of Cloyne 1794–1820.

[8] John Porter (d. 1819), Bishop of Clogher 1797–1819.

[9] Joseph Stock (1740–1813), Bishop of Waterford and Lismore 1810–13.

[10] John Kearney (1744–1813), Bishop of Ossory 1806–13.

[11] John Leslie (1774–1854), Bishop of Dromore 1812–19.

[12] Charles Mongan Warburton (n.d.), Bishop of Limerick 1806–20.

[13] 1818 'Batson'. Christopher Butson (c. 1749–1836), Bishop of Clonfert 1804–36.

[14] Joseph Stock, Bishop of Waterford and Lismore, had died on 13 August 1813.

[15] i.e. the sees of Raphoe, Cork, Ferns, and Ossory respectively. Kearney, who died on 22 May 1813, was succeeded as Bishop of Ossory by Robert Fowler (c. 1767–1841), whose sister Mildred (d. 1830) had married Edmund Butler (1771–1846), created Earl of Kilkenny (I) in 1793.

[16] John George de La Poer Beresford was Bishop of Raphoe, and not Killaloe.

[17] Cf. George Rose, *Observations respecting the Public Expenditure, and the Influence of the Crown*, London, 1810, pp. 65–6: 'It has always been justly held in a free country, and particularly in this, to be one of its greatest privileges, that the chief aristocracy, as far as relates to the management of its public concerns, should be an aristocracy of talent and of virtue'.

APPENDIX NO. IV. §V.

'The vacancies (before the last)[1] that they have filled up on the *Bench*, in *England*, have been *eight;* the persons who have been selected have been the *Tutors* of the *Dukes* of *Buccleugh, Portland, Gloucester, Rutland*, the *brother* of the *Prince-Regent*'s *Tutor*, the *Secretary* of the *Duke of Portland*, and a *brother* of *Lord Ellenborough*.[2] The LAWS, in *England*, rival the BERESFORDS, in *Ireland;* for they have had *three* mitres. The present *Bishop of Chester's father* had the See of *Carlisle*, and his *brother*, the See of *Elphin*.[3]

'The *Deaneries, Prebends,* &c. have been chiefly got by the *Duke of Beaufort, Lords Harrowby, Brownlow*,[4] &c. for their *own connexions*. With the exception of the *Deanery of Canterbury*, bestowed upon a *popular preacher*,[5] we ask whether one of those good things has fallen upon a person recommended alone "by Virtue and Talent?"—N.B. Mask not yet dropped off.

'It is a moot point, whether the *Bishoprick of Waterford*, just vacant by the death of *Dr. Stock*, is in the *patronage* of the *Duke of Richmond* or *Lord Whitworth:* the latter, though sworn in Lord Lieutenant of Ireland before the English Council (it is contended) not being virtually invested with the Sovereign Authority of the Sister Kingdom, until he is also sworn into that high office before the Privy Council of Ireland also.[6] It is said, however, that the *brother* of the *Attorney-General* of *Ireland* is to be the new *Bishop* of *Waterford*.[7]

'The Bishopric of *Bristol* is about to receive a considerable addition to its episcopal revenue, through the means of the *Archbishop of Canterbury*, the valuable rectory of *Almondsford*, on the Severn, in the *patronage* of the Bishop of Bristol, having just become vacant, but the presentation to it devolving to his Grace, as an *option*, he has *liberally* wa[i]ved his right, on condition that it be annexed to the See in perpetuity, which will raise it from *six hundred* to *two thousand two hundred pounds* per annum.'

Engaging every successive *Bishop* of *Bristol* to obtain this same *Living*, on pretence of doing all the duty, with a fixed determination not to do any part of it—such is the *virtue*, which, under the name of *liberality*, is, by the candour of this Opposition writer, whoever he is, made matter of laud, for the benefit of his *Grace* of *Canterbury*. But, quære as to the matter of fact?—As to the obtainment of *Livings* by *Bishops*, see further under the head of *Discipline*.[8]

Morning Chronicle, 19*th Nov.* 1813.—'Ministers have rewarded their friend, Dr. Parsons, of Oxford, with the Bishoprick of Peterborough;—it is not forgotten with

---

[1] i.e. the vacancy occasioned by the death of Claudius Crigan (*c.* 1743–1813), Bishop of Sodor and Man from 1784, who had died on 5 April 1813. George Murray had been nominated to the see on 22 May 1813, and was consecrated on 6 March 1814 (see also p. 411 n. above).

[2] i.e. the sees of Hereford, Carlisle, Bath and Wells, Ely, Oxford, Rochester, and Chester respectively.

[3] George Henry Law, Bishop of Chester, was son of Edmund Law (1703–87), Bishop of Carlisle 1769–87, and brother of John Law (1745–1810), Bishop of Elphin 1795–1810.

[4] Henry Charles Somerset (1766–1835), sixth Duke of Beaufort; Dudley Ryder, Earl of Harrowby; and John Cust (1779–1853), second Baron Brownlow, later first Earl Brownlow.

[5] Gerrard Andrewes.

[6] Charles Lennox, fourth Duke of Richmond, Lord Lieutenant of Ireland 1807–13, and Charles Whitworth (1752–1825), first Earl Whitworth, Lord Lieutenant of Ireland 1813–17. Whitworth had been appointed Lord Lieutenant on 3 June 1813, and was installed in Dublin on 26 August 1813, the day after this article appeared.

[7] In the event, Richard Bourke (1767–1832) succeeded as Bishop of Waterford and Lismore in August 1813, while James Saurin (1759–1842), brother of William Saurin (1757–1839), Attorney General for Ireland 1807–22, later became Bishop of Dromore 1819–42.

[8] See pp. 453–7 n. below.

CHURCH-OF-ENGLANDISM

But—the few grains of wheat, which accident and policy concur in scattering in among the chaff,[1] do they do any thing like paying for the *manure?* In the Scottish Church, without this part of the expense, in the Non-Established Churches without any expense, you have all the wheat without any of the chaff. In the Scottish Church you have all *professional* services, *inexigible* as well as *exigible*, with most important *extra-professional* duties, all well performed:—not to speak of human learning. In the Non-Established Churches, though in *all* of them without the *extra-professional* services, and in perhaps the most populous of them without human learning, you have the *professional* services, *inexigible* as well as *exigible*, rendered; and under[2] circumstances of which a still more active zeal than in *any Established* Church, even than in that of *Scotland*, is a *natural*, not to say a *necessary* consequence.

Good my Lord, I have now, I hope, afforded your Lordship satisfaction as to the above six or seven points: viz. 1. That the probable production of public service, in some specific shape, and not *merit* at large, is the only proper *ground*, on which, at the expense of the public, the matter of *reward*, in any shape, can be bestowed:—2. That as in *every* line of public service, so more particularly in *this*, a *Sinecure* is, in every imaginable point of view, ill-suited to any such purpose as that of the production of meritorious public service:—3. That by none of the duties performed by a Clergyman of the Church of England can any such service be rendered, the production of which can reasonably be expected to be promoted by *factitious* extra reward in any shape, and particularly in the shape of *Sinecure* or *Extra-paid* office:—4. That,—for production of every the most valuable service, which in that situation and character can be rendered,—the reward which, by the very nature of the case, without any thing done by government, attaches upon the service, is *proper*, and, with or without a proposed slight exception, *sufficient:* 5. that of large masses of *factitious* reward,—whether in the shape of *Sinecure* or any other,—under Church-of-Englandism, the natural effect, so far from *causing* to come, is to *prevent* meritorious public service from

how much zeal he discharged the duties of the *Presiding Officer*, during *Lord Eldon*'s unsuccessful contest for the *Chancellorship* of the *University*.'[3]

---

[1] An echo of Matthew 3: 12; Luke 3: 17.
[2] 1818 'rendered under'. The text follows the 'Errata'.
[3] When Vice-Chancellor of the University of Oxford 1807–10, John Parsons (1761–1819) had proposed Eldon for the Chancellorship, but he had been defeated by William Wyndham Grenville (1759–1834), first Baron Grenville, Home Secretary 1789–91, Foreign Secretary 1791–1801, and leader of the administration as First Lord of the Treasury 1806–7. Parsons was consecrated as Bishop of Peterborough on 12 December 1813.

coming, into existence: 6. that (saving your Lordship's presence) instead of the giving existence to meritorious public service, the views of those by whom the continuance of Sinecures, and overpaid and useless and needless places is contended for, are of a nature altogether opposite: advancement of personal and private interest at the expense of public, the *end;* corruption, the *means:* that (to come to particulars) *Deaneries, Canonries, Prebends,* with their respective *et cæteras,* and moreover the *Incumbent's part* of the profit of Livings served by *Curates,* are plainly useless, and worse than useless:—that the difference between Curate's pay and the least pay for which any man or boy, that can read, would read what the Curate reads, is also useless; and that *Bishopricks* and *Archbishopricks,* unless any adequate use can be found for them under the head of *Discipline* (of which presently) are in a still worse case.

To your Lordship's universally acknowledged merit—to that demand for reward of the highest price, which is so illustriously visible in your Lordship's case—I bow with prostrate reverence:—but, on a case so *singular,* no true *general* proposition can be built.

§6.—III. *Discipline.*

Church discipline may be considered, in its exercise over the *Clergy,* or in its exercise over the people at large, i.e. over *Clergy* and *Laity* together; say for shortness, over the *Laity.*

In an Established Church, considered in its exercise over the *Clergy,* the proper use of it may be defined to be, so to order matters, that, in return for the *pay,* if any, *service* shall be rendered, such as shall in *quality* be conformable to the system established in regard to *doctrine,* and moreover *adequate* in respect of *quantity.*

1. First, as to the duties of *perfect obligation.—*

Under a *Liturgy, quality* being secured by the *fixt form,* if the *Parish-boy* be employed to read the *Minister's* part, nothing can be easier than to secure the performance of the service in due *quantity.* For the *stated* and *periodically recurring* parts pay him each time, as, for the *occasional* parts of the service, the Minister is paid at present; viz. by the fees called *surplice fees.* The paymasters may be the *Churchwardens.*

Under Church-of-Englandism, as to every part of the service but the *Sermons, doctrine* is secured by the *Liturgy.* By the here-proposed *authoritative Collection of Homily Sermons,*[1] it would be no less effectually secured in regard to *Sermons.*

In regard to both these parts of the service, for securing conform-

---

[1] See pp. 356–60 above.

ity on the part of the proposed *Parish-boy*, no great expense, either in money, attention, or talent, would be necessary.

In case of *involuntary* deviations, suspension, or in case of delinquency, repeated in such sort as to serve as conclusive evidence of inaptitude, *deprivation* might, by the governing body of the Parish, be inflicted without much difficulty. In case of *purposed* delinquency, through boyish malice, a proportionate application of the rod might be added. But, under the absence of all ordinary motives for purposed delinquency, naturally speaking, whatsoever is said about the rod, may remain a dead letter for any number of ages.

In a *Non-Established Church*, no apparatus is employed—no *official* establishment—no body of *coercive* laws—for the maintenance of discipline. With perfect *simplicity*, and with no less perfect *efficiency*, the discipline is exercised by the lay-members of the Church themselves; by the lay-members, in their character of voluntary contributors to the expense. If the service had ever failed to be performed, no member would have paid any thing: if for a time the service were to cease to be performed, for that same time at least, every member who thought fit so to do would cease to pay. But, this being the case, and universally seen to be the case, in no instance in any such Church does the service cease to be performed. Not for a year—not so much as for a day—is any such office a *Sinecure*. If, in respect of *quality*, it is, in the judgment of any such member, to a certain degree ill-performed, he stops his *attendance* and with it his *contribution*. This stoppage has, according to the amount of it, the effect of a legal penalty: but with this difference, viz. that by the endeavour, successful or unsuccessful, to cause a legal penalty to be levied, the burthen of litigation would to a certainty be laid upon the shoulders of both parties, while the success of the endeavour, be the offence ever so flagrant, would still be uncertain: whereas, in a Non-Established Church, no sooner, on the part of the Minister, does any thing, which, in the conception of a contributing member, is regarded as delinquency, manifest itself, than he withdraws his contribution, and, with the exception of the delay, vexation, and expense, attendant on litigation, this substraction has the effect of *a fine:* and of this fine, the *severity* is exactly as the *number* of the contributing members, by whom, in any such degree, as to call for punishment in this shape, what is done is regarded as constituting an *offence*.

Under the *established* Church of *Scotland*, a body of coercive laws, for the maintenance of discipline, has place: but, for the giving execution to those laws, no separate official establishment has place. With the assistance of a certain proportion of the *Laity*, the Clergy,—amongst whom inequality is no more established or suf-

APPENDIX NO. IV. §VI.

fered, than by *Jesus* it was among his *Apostles*,[1]—the Clergy, collected in *bodies*, exercise what little discipline needs to be exercised by them, over one another, considered as *individuals*.[2]

In this Church, discipline cannot, it is true, be in every instance exercised without litigation. But in this Church the form of procedure in these cases being,—not, as under the English Church, *technical*,—that is, teeming with *factitious delay, vexation*, and *expense*,—and established and kept up for the sake of the lawyer's profit upon the expense,—but *natural*,[a]—and thence pure of all those abominations,—the burthen of litigation is reduced to its *minimum*.

The use of judicial procedure,—or, in other words, of *litigation*,— bating the bad sense, which, by the blind feeling of the miseries produced by technical procedure, has been so indiscriminately attached to the word *litigation*—is to give effect to the *substantive* portion, or *main body*, of the law. If, of the ordinances contained in this *main body*, so it be that no *infringement* ever takes place, no demand can there ever be for *litigation:* suppose infringement, the demand will, in any given space of time, be as the number of the infringements. If,—while, in case of infringement, there are any persons, who at the same time possess and feel an interest in the execution of these ordinances, no instance occurs of any demand calling for their execution, such demand being capable of being made without any *delay*, vexation, or expense, to the demandant, other than that *minimum* which is inseparable from *natural* procedure,—it is a sign that no transgression ever takes place: and so, the less frequent the demand, the less frequent may the instances of transgression be justly concluded to be.

But, under the system of *technical* procedure transgression may be universal, and still no application for execution ever have place. And—not to speak of *State*—not very far from this is the situation of things under *Church* of England and its laws.

Moreover, in *this* may be seen the English of the *brutum fulmen*, ascribed, by the Earl of Harrowby, (p. 30) to *Ecclesiastical Censures*,[3]

---

[a] For the differences between *technical* and *natural* procedure, see Bentham's Scotch Reform, &c. throughout.

---

[1] See pp. 266–70 above.

[2] For Bentham's further comments on the hierarchy of courts in the Church of Scotland see pp. 304–5 above and pp. 481–2 n. below.

[3] See *Substance of the Speech of the Earl of Harrowby*, p. 30: 'It is evident, that until the laws of the Church, which prohibit Curates from officiating without licence, are generally enforced, all provisions for the increase of their salaries are nugatory. It is proposed, therefore, to substitute legislative enactments for the *brutum fulmen* [i.e. ineffective threat] of ecclesiastical censures; and to subject to the penalties for non-residence, every non-resident Incumbent who shall

CHURCH-OF-ENGLANDISM

i.e. to Church-of-England discipline. It is not that to the *thunderbolt*, when hurled, any thing is wanting to the rendering it as deadly as a thunderbolt need be. But the arm of the God is so formed as not to be put effectually in motion but by a certain mass of *fees:* and with no sufficient degree of frequency is the requisite mass to be found.

If, *without* a separate official establishment for the maintenance of discipline, discipline be maintained as well as, though it be no better than, *with* and under an establishment of this sort instituted and kept up for that purpose,—on this supposition any such establishment is at best but useless. But a proposition, the truth of which, to all who have any acquaintance with the two establishments, is perfectly notorious,—and into the truth of which no *Archbishop of Canterbury*, no *Bishop of London*, no *First Lord of the Treasury*, no *Chancellor of the Exchequer*, will venture to provoke, or so much as permit an inquiry,—is, that the degree, in which discipline is maintained in the two established Churches, is in the *Scottish* Church at the *top* of the scale of perfection, and, under the *English* Church, at the very *bottom of it*.

As to any demand that can have place for it—for the maintenance of discipline, the whole clerical part of the official establishment of England is therefore completely useless: and—to speak in particular—the several situations of *Archbishop, Bishop, Archdeacon*, and *Rural Dean*, have thus been proved to be completely useless.

Of the discipline exercised in the Church of England, the whole is *in name* exercised by *Bishops*. Of that which is thus *said* to be exercised by Bishops, part is really exercised by these same holy persons; part not by them, but by certain other persons, *inferior* but not *subordinate* to them, under the name of *Judges of the Bishops' Court*.[1]

The part which is exercised by these Judges is that part which, according to the distinction brought to view at the outset,[2] is exercised over the people at large, Clergy and Laity together.

Of the discipline *said* to be exercised by Bishops, happily for the *Laity*, over the *Clergy* alone is exercised now-a-days that part which is *really* exercised by Bishops.[3]

employ an unlicensed Curate, notwithstanding he may have a statutable exemption, or a licence for non-residence.'

[1] The Bishop's Court or Consistory Court was normally presided over by the diocesan Chancellor (combining the technically separate offices of Official Principal and Vicar-General), but it was always open to the Bishop to sit himself. No appeal lay to the Bishop from his Chancellor. [2] See p. 415 above.

[3] A sentence of deposition from a ministry, or deprivation of a living, could only be pronounced by a Bishop: see Burn, *Ecclesiastical Law*, 2nd edn., 1767, 'Degradation' and 'Deposition', ii. 122–4.

APPENDIX NO. IV. §VI.

Not efficient to any one good purpose, the discipline thus really exercised by Bishops is, on the whole of it, as far as it goes, efficient to the aggregate of all *bad* purposes. That aggregate is *despotism*.

Correlative to *despotism* is *slavery*. With *vice* in one form, the breast of the despot is filled by it: with vice in other forms, that of the slave. He who as towards one man acts the part of a despot, is but the more fitted for acting towards another man that of a slave. So many men as there are, one above another, standing in these relations one to another, so many links are there in the chain of slavery. To form a link, or any number of links, in such a chain, *'prostration of will,'* so long as it lasts, suffices. But, to render it perpetual, *'prostration of understanding'* is moreover necessary.—*Lord of London*, is it not?[1]

In whatsoever instance and to whatsoever extent, under or without the name of *judicature*, so it is that, in respect of happiness and unhappiness, the lot of one man is determined by another, if it be secretly, singly, and without appeal, this other is thereby constituted *a despot*. By publicity, so it be all-pervading, a check—and *that* in no inconsiderable a degree an effectual one—is applied to judicial power: more especially if the law, in the giving effect to which it is employed, be *really-existing*, i.e. *Statute* Law; in contradistinction to sham law, commonly called *Common Law*. Even in the darkness of secrecy, by *plurality* of Judges, a check is in some sort applied to despotism, since in proportion to the number, the secrecy is relaxed, and, in the event of improbity, each beholds in every other a *possible* accuser at least, in how small a degree so ever a *probable* one.

The Judge, by whom, *without*, or even though it be *with*, Statute Law—and that closely penned—for his guide, judicature is exercised, not only in secret and without appeal, but singly, is a despot complete. A Judge of this sort is every English Bishop. Of this despotism, the foundation having been laid of old, the edifice of late has been completed.—See Section 7.[2]

1. Examination, for *Orders* called *Holy*, i.e. for the liberty of scrambling for the loaves and fishes,[3]—on pretence of a man's having a God somewhere or other in the inside of him—say *Examination* for *Holy Orders*.[4] 2. *Licensing* for *Non-Residence*, i.e. for obtaining money on false pretences. 3. Keeping eyes shut or open at pleasure, to non-answer or false answer to questions, by a true answer to which a Non-Resident might expose himself to penalties.

---

[1] See p. 37 n. above.
[2] See pp. 428–59 below.
[3] An allusion to the story of the feeding of the five thousand: see Matthew 14: 15–21; Mark 6: 35–44; Luke 9: 10–17; and John 6: 5–14.
[4] See p. 388 n. above.

4. Apportioning of *Curates' Stipends:* i.e. power of taking money out of the pockets of Rectors and Vicars to put into the pockets of Curates. 5. Determining whether to the office of Parish Priest a man shall be allowed, or not allowed, to add the occupation of a Husbandman. All this judicature, behold it exercised by these Judges, acting not only in secret, but singly, and without appeal:—with an inconsiderable modification or two—too inconsiderable to be worth noticing in so general a view—exercised, the whole of it, in the way of despotism, if there be any such thing as despotism.

To weave, for the unrestrained despotism that is within, a cloak, composed of the appearance of self-restraint, is the work of hypocrisy and self-praise. The man takes his cue from, after having perhaps given his cue to, the Earl of Harrowby.[a] He turns up the whites of his eyes: he groans under the load: and, could his prayers be heard, this cup, as well as so many others, would be taken out of his hands:[1]— out of the hands that clench upon it.

Under a Bishop,—that is, as often as he pleases—and he always pleases;—under his *Chaplain,*—(for, whenever the exercise of a Bishop's power has any thing in it beyond amusement, it is turned down to underlings) be the candidate's inaptitude ever so complete, never can any thing, but the most consummate imprudence or mishap, debar him from the benefit of the desired visit from the Holy Ghost. *His* being the choice of the supposed examining *Bishop,* and thence of the really examining *Chaplain,*—thence it is, that, on the part of five-and-twenty out of the six-and-twenty Examining Chaplains,[2] or sets of Chaplains, the union of the most consummate skill and knowledge, with the most consummate probity, could not, to any such purpose as that of excluding inaptitude, be of any use, so long as there remained a twenty-sixth, at whose hands the requisite degree of indulgence might, by any means, be obtained. As in a *Catholic Confessor,* so in a Church-of-England Examining Chaplain, the reputation of facility,—that is, of the habitual violation of duty— the reputation, and thence the reality—is, in one shape or other, a source of profit. Before the Holy Ghost is received by him, fees most assuredly pass from hand to hand,[3]—fees to the amount of which

---

[a] Speech, p. 25.—'As the law stands at present there can be no part of the duty of a Bishop more *irksome* and invidious, than the general exercise of a discretion, unguided by the landmarks of law,' &c. O yes: so it is with human nature. Poor Emperors! poor Kings! poor Regents! how they all suffer!—which of them for a moment would be what he is, if his subjects did not force him to it?

[1] An echo of Matthew 26: 39; Mark 14: 36; and Luke 22: 42.
[2] i.e. Chaplains to the twenty-six Bishops.
[3] 1818 'pass from hand,'. The text follows the 'Errata'.

APPENDIX NO. IV. §VI.

there is not any limit—whatsoever be the pockets in which they ultimately find their rest.[1]

Under the Established Church of Scotland no license for the exercise of clerical functions is granted, but in consequence of a strict[2] and appropriate examination, performed in and by a *many-seated* judicatory, and *without fees*.[3] As to the *Holy Ghost*, he is not received by any body. Wherefore, according to Church of *England*, while in Church of *Rome*, every thing done with this or that exception, every thing done is valid; in Church of *Scotland* every thing done is void. In the whole Church of Scotland no such character as that of a *Priest* is to be found. By a man presuming to officiate in that character, every function that is performed is void. Be they ever so copiously sprinkled, all children, as well as all men and women, go to hell. Except in the profane way of digestion, no bread becomes flesh; no wine, blood. Fathers and mothers are all rogues and whores. All men and all women go to hell by a double title: firstly, as not being rightly *christened;* lastly, as not being rightly *buried*.

II. Remain, as and for the only clerical duties, to the performance of which the proposed juvenile reader would not be competent, the duties of *imperfect obligation*. But of these duties, neither do the Bishops enforce the performance, nor has it ever entered into their views to enforce it, nor have they it, nor can they have it, in their power to enforce it. In the nature of the case, by no sort of human power can it, with any tolerable degree of efficacy, be enforced, other than that by which it is enforced in the Established Church of Scotland, or that by which it is enforced in every Non-Established Church.

To a degree more or less efficient, without any factitious impulse from external force,—remains, in all places and at all times, in regard to these same duties, the *physical* power of performance.

Now then for a calculation: on the one side of the account, set down all those by whom, within a given space of time, the attribute of heroism will, in this Christian shape, have been exemplified: on the other side, those who, by the *looseness* of their lives, will have been rendered *scandalous*, and those who by *pride*, or *exaction*, or both together, will have been rendered odious:—on which of the two sides of the account will be found the largest numbers?—Note that, in so

---

[1] According to Canon Law, no Archbishop, Bishop, or Suffragan Bishop was entitled to receive either directly or indirectly a fee for ordaining priests. The only fees in association with ordination were payable to the Registrar of the Bishop for letters testimonial, and were to amount to a sum of not more than 10s. See Burn, *Ecclesiastical Law*, 2nd edn., 1767, iii. 39–41.

[2] 1818 'stout'. The text follows the 'Errata'.

[3] In the Church of Scotland, the Presbytery, consisting of ministers and elders from each parish in the area, supervised the training, probation, and licensing of ministers.

far as the aptitude of the whole system is the object of the inquiry, to the sinister side of the account will belong the number, of those in whose instance the odium has had no other cause than the exaction of that which, being legally due to them, would not but upon compulsion, have been paid to them: for here, though not the individuals, still it is the system that is in fault.

Note, that neither the dissoluteness, nor the pride, nor the exaction, *have* place in the Scottish Established, or *can have* place in any Non-Established, Church.

Thus rotten being the state of the discipline, bad as is the state of the service, which it pretends to support,—still worse would it be than it is, but for the aid it derives from *schism* and schismatics: from those men of *guilt*, whom the *prostrators of understandings and wills*— had they *their* will—would exterminate.[1]

Schism, it has been observed already, is conducive to *truth in doctrine*:[2] it is no less so to *goodness in discipline*. By the very nature of the case, a sort of *auction* is established. The article put up and bid for is *public favour*. The *bidders* are the several sects; led—such of them as have leaders—by their respective chosen instructors. The *auction* is a *perpetual* one: the *biddings* are in *good behaviour:* in whatsoever sort of good behaviour passes for the best; and which, if it be not in *every* point that which is most conducive to general happiness, differs not from it very widely, and, under the protection of *freedom*, will approach nearer and nearer to the mark continually, in proportion to the degree of freedom which has place. So many of these competitors, so many mutual *spies*—so many eventual *informers*—against that sect, in the conduct of which, if any such there be, mischief in any shape is to be found. *Spies—informers*—by these names are designated so many sorts of agents, to the function of which, necessary as they are in every government, the experience had of the ill use, which, in proportion as the government has been ill-constructed, has been made of them, has given an *ill name:* but, in the case here in question, there is no *ill* but in the *name*.

Of the service rendered in this shape by *schism*, due notice may be seen in *Adam Smith*.[3]

Such then is this branch of the Church Discipline. The subordinate Clergy are plagued by it: the people at large, Clergy and Laity together, are not served by it.

---

[1] See pp. 37 n. and 48 n. above.   [2] A reference, possibly, to p. 305 above.

[3] Smith argued in favour of the impartial treatment of all religions by the state, noting that where each man could choose his own religion, the teachers of religion would be obliged to exert themselves to maintain adherents, while their mutual competition would not only prevent any sect from becoming too large, but render each respectful of all others: see *Wealth of Nations*, ii. 792–3.

APPENDIX NO. IV. §VI.

With the discipline in no better a state than that of the English Church, suppose an English *Army*. The next moment, what would become of it?

In respect of discipline, between the three species of Churches, the case may be thus briefly, nor yet incorrectly, stated. In the English Established Church may be seen the *forms* of discipline without the substance: in the Scottish, *form and substance* both: in the *Non-Established* Churches no form, but nevertheless the *substance:* and this but the better, for being *without* the forms.

So much for Church discipline, considered as exercised over the Clergy; exercised for the purpose of securing the due performance of Church service. Now as to discipline called *Church Discipline*, considered as exercised over the people at large, Clergy and Laity together.

But, over the *Laity*, by Clerical hands, as such, to what good end should any discipline at all be exercised? Till a satisfactory answer to this question be found—and never will any such answer to it be found—so much as there is of this discipline exercised, or attempted or pretended to be exercised, so much is there of sheer abuse.

Take any of the acts, in the punishing of which this discipline is employed. For the punishment of it does any real demand exist? By whatsoever other judicatures other mischievous acts are punished, so may this be punished. Does no such demand exist? Then ought it not to be punished, by these, any more than by any other judicatures.

Turn to Blackstone, and you will find, that because, in the days of Popish darkness, for the punishment of certain offences, three sorts of judicatories were established, therefore for one and the same individual offence, there ought to be, as there are, three different sets of lawyers to prey upon both parties, offenders and injured parties together,—three separate lots of punishment, each sufficient of itself, each capable of being inflicted in addition to the two others.[1] For the same reason, if *thirty* different sets of lawyers were to be fattened, every supposed offender ought to be punished thirty times over, each time sufficiently for one and the same offence: all this to save the joint lottery of Church and Law from becoming a disadvantageous one.

If, in the customary style of vulgar nonsense, addressing himself to a notorious prostitute, a man bestows upon her the epithet *cursed*, calling her or not calling her *bitch*, taking him before a Justice of

---

[1] Bentham perhaps has in mind the right of appeal which lay from the Archdeacon's Court to the Consistory Court or Bishop's Court, and from there to the Court of Arches or Court of Appeal, held by the Archbishops of York and Canterbury: see Blackstone, *Commentaries on the Laws of England*, iii. 64–5.

CHURCH-OF-ENGLANDISM

Peace, she makes him pay,—for so says the law,—a shilling:[1] if, instead of *bitch*, he calls her *whore*, neither meaning any thing more, nor hurting her any more by the word *whore* than by the word *bitch*, she puts him into a court called *an Ecclesiastical Court*, and neither of them get out of it for less than some twenty, thirty, or forty pounds.[2]

The Ecclesiastical Court system is, as no one can deny, a remnant of that system of despotism called the *Roman*, alias the *Civil* law, topped by the law of Popery, called the *Canon* law: the whole of it as complete a nuisance as ever was established: the mode of proof employed under it as opposite as possible to whatever is acknowledged to be a proper one.[3] If it were ten times as bad as it is, men would not be wanting, who, if possible, would be ten times as hot and inexorable as they are in the defence of it.

After all, it is only by misrepresentation that these judicatories, bad as they are, are called *Ecclesiastical Courts*, the system of discipline which they exercise, *Ecclesiastical* or *Church discipline*, and that part of the system of law under which they exercise it, *Ecclesiastical law*. The men who in these Judicatures act as *Judges*, are not, unless by accident, and then in no other than *subordinate* situations, *Clergymen*.[4]

What then is it that makes this part of Church discipline so dear to Bishops, and to all others who look to become, or to make, Bishops? What is it that renders it so clear to them that without these judicatories no soul could be saved? Behold the cause. Though not themselves *Bishops*,—nor, unless as above in a few inconsiderable instances, so much as *Priests*,—the Judges of these Courts are appointed by Bishops; and, of that portion of the people's substance that can be squeezed out by the hands of those judicial Officers and their subordinates, a portion more or less considerable is employed in giving fatness to the *families* of Bishops.

Let the same Justice who levied a shilling for the word *cursed*, levy

---

[1] Accusations of slander were generally dealt with in Common Law courts, but if the slander involved spiritual matters such as disbelief or moral misbehaviour, including accusations of being a whore, the matter was dealt with in the ecclesiastical court. See Blackstone, *Commentaries on the Laws of England*, iii. 123–5; and Burn, *Ecclesiastical Law*, 2nd edn., 1767, 'Defamation', ii. 112–22.

[2] No penalty was paid upon a successful prosecution for slander in the ecclesiastical courts, but a penance for the sin was pronounced by the judge, and the guilty party would be required to pay costs. Fees were set for officials exercising ecclesiastical jurisdiction. See Burn, *Ecclesiastical Law*, 2nd edn., 1767, ii. 218–28, esp. 223–8.

[3] In the Ecclesiastical Courts evidence was collected in written form by a single judge in private: see Burn, *Ecclesiastical Law*, 2nd edn., 1767, ii. 46.

[4] To exercise jurisdiction in the ecclesiastical courts the candidate had to be 26 years of age, a Master of Arts or Bachelor at Law, learned in civil and ecclesiastical law, and subscribe to the oath of the King's supremacy and to the Thirty-nine Articles: see Burn, *Ecclesiastical Law*, 2nd edn., 1767, ii. 41–2.

APPENDIX NO. IV. §VI.

another or the same shilling for the word *whore*, you have at once a precedent, upon the model of which you may give exercise to what part soever there may be, if there be any, of the Church discipline exercised upon the people at large, that is fit to be exercised. So doing, you may transfigure all that portion of the hierarchy that belongs to it, into that state of beatitude which is called *Sinecure*. The misfortune is—that the *sine-cure* would in this case be also *sine pay:* and there would be the rub.[1] But,—be the case as it may in regard to this or that division of the *non-penal* part of the business,—for the profit made out of the *penal* part, compensation at the public expense, might be even more than adequate, and still not ill-bestowed.

On this part of the field, as in so many others, look, and behold imposture mounted upon imposture. Imposture, the notion—that, by money squeezed out by *clerical* hands, *souls* are mended more than if the hands were *non-clerical* ones: imposture, the pretence that the *hands* thus employed in the exaction of it *are* clerical ones. But, so long as the people will continue to lie with their heads in a bush, to be thus vexed and pillaged, where is the imposture, where even the violence, that will be grudged?

As in the profane judicatories, so in the sacred ones—as in all other Christian countries, so in England—*technical* procedure, cloaking itself in the name of *regular*, took for its main, if not for its sole object, maximization of delay, vexation, and expense: of expense, for the sake of the profit extractible out of the expense. Among such a cloud of other witnesses,[2] witness the Noble Lord, whose duty, if he did it, would be done by making entries in a book, and who in his share of this profit beholds, and clasps to his heart his *'freehold.'*[3] Witness again that Judge, who numbers among his duties, the duty of checking and punishing any exactions which may happen to be practised to his own use; to whom all those judicatories, by which natural justice is substituted to technical injustice, are as declaredly odious as 'hell is false;' and by whom, after his worthy predecessors, the requisite portion of law has been so modelled, as to transfer to the head[4] of the injured complainant, any punishment that may be due to the exacting and exaction-protecting Judge.

[1] An echo of *Hamlet*, III. i. 65. [2] Hebrews 12: 1.
[3] Charles George Perceval (1756–1840), second Baron Arden (I) from 1784, first Baron Arden from 1802, had in 1790 been appointed Registrar of the Court of Admiralty, an office to which he had held the reversion since 1764. Henry Martin (1763–1839), MP for Kinsale 1806–18, challenged Arden's tenure of the office in the House of Commons on 19 June 1812, alleging that Arden had made a profit of £30,000 per annum in fees, and £7,000 per annum in interest on securities (see *Parliamentary Debates* (1812) xxiii. 626–9). Subsequent legislation allowed Arden to retain the post until his death (53 Geo. III, c. 151, §13), whereupon the office was converted into a salaried post (3 & 4 Vict., c. 66).
[4] 1818 'hand'. The text follows the 'Errata'.

Would you be assured that profit thus extracted was at least a principal, if not the sole, object to the founders of English judicature, read *Adam Smith*, who unfortunately saw not, or at least has not discovered that he saw, any thing to object to it.[1] Would you behold in all its shapes the mischief of the system by which this profit is extracted, read *Bentham*, who, in his *Protest against Law Taxes*, has given a picture of them, and in his *Scotch Reform* has shewn by what *devices* the man of law contrived in this country to swell to so exalted a pitch the profit, and for the sake of it the mischief, producible from this source.[2]

Among the fruits of these devices, behold, as in matters between man and man, a denial of justice, so in respect of the enforcement of pastoral as well as so many other official duties, a palsy in the arm of justice,—and, in consequence of that palsy, among the Clergy a general neglect of duty, and towards those parts of the duty[3] which apply specially to their function, a generally prevalent and thoroughly confirmed habit of disobedience. In addition to reason operating upon experience, would you be assured of this by authority? call in once more the Earl of Harrowby. In the speech by which his Bill was introduced, 'ecclesiastical censures' pronounced (p. 30) as above, 'a *brutum fulmen:*'[4] in the preamble to his Bill (p. 36), the '*insufficiency*' of the laws declared: throughout the whole tenor of it, the power of enforcing observance being given exclusively to the Bishops, behold it concluding with a clause (p. 40), enacting, 'that Bishops shall exercise summarily, and without formal process or suit, the powers vested in them by this Act.'

Ecclesiastical censure an *inefficient thunder?* whence then came its inefficiency?—The laws in this behalf insufficient? whence came their insufficiency?—Is it that in the *substantive* part of the law there was any deficiency? No. Of penalties there was no want: of penalties, with reward upon the usual plan, to be sued for and upon conviction paid[5] to *Informers*.[6] But,—whatsoever would have been

---

[1] Having stated that in the days of Henry II (1133–89), King of England from 1154, 'the administration of justice, not only afforded a certain revenue to the sovereign, but to procure this revenue seems to have been one of the principal advantages which he proposed to obtain by the administration of justice', Smith did, in fact, go on to claim that the 'scheme of making the administration of justice subservient to the purposes of revenue, could scarce fail to be productive of several very gross abuses'. See *Wealth of Nations*, ii. 716.

[2] See *Scotch Reform*, pp. 11–30 (Bowring, v. 7–16).

[3] 1818 'body'. The text follows the 'Errata'.

[4] See pp. 417–18 above.

[5] 1818 'conviction be paid'. The text follows the 'Errata'.

[6] Under the Non-Resident Clergy Act of 1803 (43 Geo. III, c. 84, §12), penalties for non-residence could range from one-third to three-quarters of the value of the living, depending on the duration of non-residence. The whole of the penalty was to be paid to the person or persons who informed and sued for the sum.

APPENDIX NO. IV. §VI.

the weight of the penalties, supposing them inflicted, and out of them the Informers paid,—such was the expense and vexation attached to the purchase of an Informer's ticket in this part of the lottery of the law, that for generation after generation none of these tickets had found purchasers. At last an extraordinary concurrence of apparently favourable circumstances presented to one individual[a] a prospect of net profit in the event of his accepting the invitation held out by the law, and thus adding his labours to those of the Judge in the service of justice. He accepted it accordingly. He brought his actions. The consequence was—that, to give impunity to the delinquent, the power of Parliament being called in, was employed accordingly in breaking the faith of Parliament, and stopping the course of justice.

Nor, had compensation been given to the listed and then perfidiously discarded minister of justice, would it have been ill employed. Without desiring to see them enforced, the hypocrisy of a tyrannical Government had in the beginning imposed these duties. Each successive Government had, by its negligence, invited men to the violation of them. From first to last, so rotten has been the whole system, nothing but mischief could ever have been the result of whatever could have been done to patch it up.

At them once more, *Lord Folkestone!* humane, intrepid, generous Lord Folkestone![1] Piety, morality, whatever is good in government, call upon you with one voice. One more attack upon the *poison-tree.* Lay your axe now to the root:[2] think it not enough now to nibble at the branches. Open once more upon the listed advocates—the well-sworn and well-subscriptionatized advocates—of whatsoever is evil—adversaries of whatsoever is good. Opposite to you behold *Sir William.* Give him one other ague. Death to the *Church* in one of its many senses, that ague will be life to the *Church* in its only good sense: death to so many of the sins of the *ruling few,* it will be salvation to the welfare of the *subject multitude.*

---

[a] Mr. W. Wright, of whom further on.[3]

[1] In the House of Commons on 9 January 1812, William Pleydell-Bouverie (1779–1869), styled Viscount Folkestone 1779–1828, and afterwards third Earl of Radnor, MP for Downton 1801–2 and Salisbury 1802–28, drew attention to alleged abuses in the consistory courts. On 23 January 1812 Folkestone introduced a motion to appoint a committee to enquire into their reform, but withdrew it when Sir William Scott, a judge in the Consistory Court of London and Vicar-General of the Province of Canterbury, undertook to introduce a measure for the better regulation of the ecclesiastical courts, which was eventually enacted as 53 Geo. III, c. 127 (1813). See *Parliamentary Debates* (1812) xxi. 99–102, 295–319.
[2] Matthew 3: 10; Luke 3: 9.
[3] See pp. 428–71 below.

CHURCH-OF-ENGLANDISM

§7. *State of Discipline, as exhibited by authority, and elucidated by a Diocesan Secretary.*

Of the actual state of the Church, the picture exhibited in the under-mentioned *Tables*,[1] within these few years to and by Parliament, is too instructive to be suffered to pass altogether unnoticed even in so compressed a work as the present. Coupled with the arrangements made by Henry the Eighth at the commencement of that so imperfectly beneficial change, which for want of a better, is spoken of in England by the name of *the Reformation,* (of which presently), it proves (as will be seen) to demonstration, this fundamental truth, viz. that in the conduct of that change, on the part of the ruling powers, neither at the commencement, nor at any subsequent period, has the welfare, temporal and eternal,— say, for shortness, *the salvation of souls,* or, in one word, *salvation,*—been the *main* and *ruling* object, or end in view, of what has been done. To a sincere eye, that can endure to look the idea in the face, the only points, that will remain susceptible of a question, will be—whether in *any* degree, and if in any, in *what* degree, on this or that occasion, to the ruling powers of this or that time, this most sacred and most extensively public object was an object of regard.

The years for and during which the matters in question are exhibited in these Tables, are the three successive years, 1809, 1810, and 1811. 'An ABSTRACT of RETURNS *respecting* NON-RESIDENCE; *for the Year ending* 25*th March* 1809:'—such is the title of the earliest of these Tables: ABSTRACT *of the Number and Classes of* NON-RESIDENT INCUMBENTS, *and of the Number of* RESIDENT INCUMBENTS, *according to the Diocesan Returns for the Year* 1810: such is the title of the next succeeding one: and in the same form, with the exception of the name of the year, is that for 1811.[2]

It is in the copies printed by and for the House of Commons, that these Tables have been consulted:—date of the Order for that of 1811, 26th March, 1813.[3] Of no *later* date has any information on this subject been printed by the Order of the House of Commons. By the body of information thus collected, the object, by the contemplation of which the collection of it had been produced, had been accomplished: viz. the forming a ground for the *plan of reform,* or whatever else it is to be called, began by the late *Minister, Mr. Perceval,* and

[1] See pp. 440–1 below.
[2] For abstracts of diocesan returns dated 25 March 1809, 1810, and 1811 see *Commons Sessional Papers* (1812) x. 159–62, 151–4, and (1812–13) xiii. 47–50, respectively.
[3] See *Commons Journals* (1812–13) lxviii. 354, 946–7.

APPENDIX NO. IV. §VII.

supported, continued, and still continuing, by the *President of the Council*, the *Earl of Harrowby*.[1]

Of this valuable body of information—for such it will truly be seen to be—the immediate source and efficient cause may be seen in the Act of the year 1803: 43 G. III. c. 84. 7th July, 1803. For the various lights thus cast upon her whole fabric, Excellent Church appears to have been indebted to the confederacy of political saints, and, in an especial manner, to the pious policy and professional skill of *Sir William Scott*.[2] Among the schemes which for her confirmation appear to have been formed by this Holy Brotherhood, one was— the peopling with Curates a number, more or less considerable, of the *parsonages* deserted by *Sinecurist Incumbents*. For this and other purposes, an article of information, which, now for the *first* time, was deemed necessary to be possessed by any body, was—in each *diocese*, of the whole number of Incumbents, by whom, by reading over and over again a quantity of matter, out of a modern book, souls were to be saved, how many there were, whose bodies were occasionally to be seen, in the several places in which, if in this or any other shape *service* were rendered by them, it would be necessary they should be to render it,—and how many others, whose equally consecrated bodies, how replete soever with the Holy Ghost, were never at any time thus visible.

For this *service* it is that,—for the causing of it to be in every parish rendered, and rendered in a proper manner,—under the names of *Bishops* and *Archbishops*, a set of men, dressed out to this day in the popish habits of the fifteenth century, are kept in a Protestant House of Legislature,—where, every day, that there may be something for them to do, some one of them is seen mumbling over the same page or two, out of that same book, to unconscious ears.[3] For this service,—still more empty and unprofitable than the service for the enforcing of which it professes to be employed—for this service it is, that pay is received from about 1,000*l*.[4] to above 20,000*l*. a year,— with a more or less rich mass of patronage to each, for the enrichment of families and dependents,—and a seat for life in that Upper House of Legislation: besides additions to the pay of each to an indefinite amount,—in the shape of standing *Sinecures*, and *Cures*

---

[1] See p. 389 n. above.
[2] The Non-Resident Clergy Act of 1803, which had been introduced into the House of Commons on 6 April 1803 by Scott (see *Parliamentary History* (1801–3) xxxvi. 1514–15), required diocesan returns to be made, in the first instance for the year 1804 (see 43 Geo. III, c. 84, §25).
[3] Prayers were read at the start of each day's sitting by a senior Bishop in the House of Lords, and by the Speaker's Chaplain in the House of Commons.
[4] 1818 '10,000*l*.' The text follows the 'Errata'.

occasionally improved, as will be seen, for the purpose, into Sinecures.

To know whether a man, who in a particular place has service to perform, performs it rightly,—to know even so much as whether he so much as makes a show of performing it, two preliminary points of knowledge are necessary, viz. *who* the man is, and whether the place—the only place—in which such duty, if done, can be done, is at any time among the places in which his body is to be found. Under the system which the act found existing,—not, unless by accident, was so much as this preliminary stock of knowledge, slender and barren as it is, in the possession of any of these Right Reverend and Most Reverend *Figurantes* on the politico-religious theatre, whose sole essential duty, if they had any, would have been the causing of that other duty, such as it is, to be done.—Not any thing did they know about the matter: never had it been intended that they should: they found not in their hands any tolerably sufficient means for the obtainment of such knowledge. This ignorance, does it stand in need of proof? Behold it then in the Act: for, of the objects and functions of it, one part, and that a necessary one, is—not only the furnishing of that information by the Bishops to Parliament, but the antecedently necessary furnishing of this same information, by the Incumbents to these same Bishops.

The Act being thus necessarily brought to view—some sort of intimation, how brief soever, of the other matters, about which it occupied itself, may in this place be expected.—1. To give confirmation and extension to Non-Residence, with the complete and wilful neglect of duty therein included:—2. to authorize the conversion of *Cure* into *Sinecure*, for the purpose of putting, in addition to the regularly allotted revenues of their *Sees* and *Provinces*, more and more money, without stint, into the pockets of Archbishops as well as Bishops:—3. to establish by various means, in those holy hands, a pure despotism, placing under it the whole body of the *Non-Resident* Parochial Clergy and their Curates, together with an unlimited proportion of *Residents:*—4. to give to delinquency indemnity for the past, as well as security for the future,[1]—punishing at the same time with disappointment and loss such persons as, by invitation, had engaged in the service of the law, for the enforcing the execution of it upon delinquents;—these may be mentioned as the most material of the objects provided for in this Act, in addition to the giving

[1] An echo of the war aims enunciated by Pitt in the House of Commons on 25 April 1793, soon after the commencement of the French Revolutionary Wars: 'this country was justly entitled to proceed on the war against France, to repel her unjust attacks, and, if possible, to chastise and to punish her, and to obtain indemnification for the past, and security for the future'. See *Parliamentary History* (1792–4) xxx. 715.

APPENDIX NO. IV. §VII.

continuance to the already mentioned supply of *ecclesiastico-statistical* information, which will be seen exhibited in the ensuing Tables.[1]

July 7th, 1803, is the date given to this Act. March 25th, 1809, is the concluding day of the earliest year, for and in relation to which, any of the information which it undertook to bring to light, made its appearance: length of the interval between the issuing of the order and the time of the facts stated in the earliest document exhibited in consequence, near six years. April 18th, 1810, is the date of the *House of Commons' Address,* in compliance with which it was furnished by the *Council Board:* June 2d, 1810, is the date of the *Abstract* made of the above Returns by the Reverend Thomas Brooke Clarke,[2] by order of *that Board:* being the earliest of all the Abstracts, *three* in number, that have ever made their appearance, and the earliest of those same *three,* which will here be seen consolidated into *one.*[3] June 13th, 1812, and no earlier, is the date of the *House of Commons' Order,* from which, for the first time, it received the sort of half-publicity, which accompanies those unpurchaseable papers, the distribution of which is confined to the Members of that House.[4] Little less than *nine* years had thus elapsed, before any part of that information had transpired, the obtainment of which was one of the main objects of this Act:[5] and, when at last it did come forth, that it came forth teeming with gaps and misrepresentations—with both defects upon a prodigiously extensive scale—is what will be visible in an instant to any eye; visible by any the slightest glance at the difference between the numbers standing under the three different years, in cases where the real facts admitted not of any but a comparatively minute proportion of such difference. Even to this very day might the

---

[1] See pp. 440–1 below.

[2] Thomas Brooke Clarke was appointed Ecclesiastical Officer to the Privy Council, with the task of collecting and computing the diocesan returns requested by 43 Geo. III, c. 84, §25 (1803).

[3] See p. 463 n. below.

[4] Abstracts of the Diocesan Returns for 1807–8 and 1808–9 were ordered to be prepared by the House of Commons on 18 April 1810 (*Commons Journals* (1810) lxv. 306). Those for 1808–9 were presented to the House on 5 June 1810, when they were ordered to be inserted in the Appendix of the *Journal* (ibid. 452–3, 746). On 13 June 1812 these were again ordered to be inserted in the Appendix of the *Journal* and printed (*Commons Journals* (1812) lxvii. 425, 876–7; *Commons Sessional Papers* (1812) x. 159–62).

[5] Abstracts of the diocesan returns respecting non-residence for the years 1804–5, 1805–6, and 1806–7 had in fact been ordered to be prepared by the House of Commons on 13 April 1808 (*Commons Journals* (1808–9) lxiii. 266). They were laid before the House on 29 April 1808 (ibid. 279), and on 9 May 1808 ordered to be inserted in the Appendix of the *Journal* and printed (ibid. 303, 851–2; *Commons Sessional Papers* (1808) ix. 237–60). Abstracts of the diocesan returns respecting non-residence for the year 1807–8 were ordered to be prepared on 30 June 1808 (*Commons Journals* (1808–9) lxiii. 477), and with the returns from 1804 until 1807 were ordered on 25 May 1809 to be inserted in the Appendix of the *Journal* and printed (see *Commons Journals* (1809) lxiv. 343, 685–6; *Commons Sessional Papers* (1809) ix. 23–32).

nakedness of *Excellent Church* have remained concealed from all profane eyes, had not the zeal of some of her most devoted sons,—in an evil hour,—evil for Holy Mother, but proportionably auspicious for the public,—uncovered it, and commenced that display of it, which will here be seen, more or less extended.

In the exhibition thus made, why so many years omitted? Why? unless it be, that, in any anterior state, the nakedness would have been still more shocking to any observing eye.

From the *individual Returns*, made to such Orders as were in consequence sent from the several Bishops, were composed,—by the Reverend Divine, whose name is at the bottom of the Table for the year 1810,[1] or by some other person or persons,—these three *Abstracts*, the matters of which are respectively arranged under the general *heads* and *sub-heads*, that will be seen.

Whether, for any succeeding years, any views of the Church, on the same or any other plan, have been furnished to the *Privy Council*,—and, if so, from that Board to the *House of Lords*,— cannot here be stated. At any rate, no further information appears to have been called for by the House of Commons.[2]

In those Returns, the years in and for which the state of the Church, in the particulars in question, is exhibited, are those successive years 1809, 1810, 1811. By the side of each of the principal heads, which stand one under another in a vertical line, are given in a horizontal line, headed by the names of the several dioceses, figures expressive of the numbers of the persons, stated respectively from these same dioceses, as being in the predicament designated by these same principal heads. Occupying in each Table the largest[3] proportion of the whole space, and, not being needful for the present purpose, the contents of this subdivision are here omitted:—but, by means of this omission, room is left for the giving at one view, in so far as in those originals it is exhibited, the state of the Church for those same three successive years.

In these Returns, under the common name of *Incumbents*, the whole collective body of Rectors, Vicars, and Perpetual Curates, is cast, in the first instance, into two divisions, designated by two very instructive names, viz. *Residents* and *Non-Residents: Residents*, those by whom more or less, of that duty for which they receive their pay, is done or supposed to be done: *Non-Residents*, those by whom,—with

---

[1] i.e. Thomas Brooke Clarke.

[2] It was not until 1817 that further abstracts from the diocesan returns were ordered for 1812–13, 1813–14, and 1814–15, and subsequently ordered to be printed by the House of Commons: see *Commons Sessional Papers* (1817) xv. 142–9, 179–82.

[3] 1818 'large'. The text follows the 'Errata'.

the exception of a small proportion, distinguishable, though in these Tables not distinguished, by the appellation of *Virtual Residents*,—no part of that duty for which they receive pay is so much as *supposed* to be done: in other words, *Doers of duty* and *Non-Doers*. Such then, to use its own phrase, is the Army of *the Church Militant:* an army composed of *effectives* and *deserters:* the *effectives* receiving pay as such; the *deserters* also receiving pay as *effectives*, notwithstanding they are *deserters*.

How little allowance soever they can pretend to from the heavenly King whom they profess to serve, from his Vicegerent here on earth allowances to this effect have not only been received by them, but even granted to them without their asking.

Of this English manufactory of *sinecure* out of *cure* the center having long been erected by the *spiritual* Popes of Rome, founders of the primæval and Universal Church, the right wing (the center being at the same time condemned) was erected by the self-crowned *temporal* Pope, Henry the Eighth, *Defender of the Faith*, (i.e. of his own faith in all its successive forms)[1] founder of the new and local Church, self-styled *Excellent Church:*[2]—founder, viz. in and by the Act 21 H. VIII. c. 13.[3] Thus, for about 273 years, to the great convenience of those for whose accommodation it had been erected, had it enriched the scene,—when in the reign of the present Most religious King (for every King of England is, by the Act of Uniformity, and the Liturgy which forms a part of it, *Most religious)*[4]—it came to pass, that, for giving still further increase to that holy convenience, a *new wing* was added, viz. by the Act 43 G. III. c. 84. already mentioned. *Thirteen* or *fourteen* (for in this case numeration would not be found quite so easy as might naturally be supposed)—*thirteen* or *fourteen* is the number of *niches*, already under the name of *Exemptions*, provided in the *old* wing: about the same number, under the name of *Licenses*, in the *new* one: and,— so completely have the principles and taste of the *fundator incipiens* been imbibed and pursued by the *fundator perficiens*,[5]— that, until upon more particular examination the error was dis-

---

[1] See p. 297 n. above.
[2] For the phrase 'Excellent Church' see p. 29 n. above.
[3] The Clergy Act of 1529 (21 Hen. VIII, c. 13) regulated pluralism and non-residency.
[4] See 'A Prayer for the High Court of Parliament, to be read during their Session', *Book of Common Prayer*, which begins, 'Most gracious God, we humbly beseech thee, as for this Kingdom in general, so especially for the High Court of Parliament, under our most religious and gracious King at this time assembled. . . .'
[5] i.e. the 'instigating founder', namely Henry VIII, and the 'concluding founder', namely George III. For the legal distinction between *fundatio incipiens* and *fundatio perficiens* see Blackstone, *Commentaries on the Laws of England*, i. 468.

covered, the same date had actually been ascribed to both of them.[a]

By these preliminary remarks the eye of the general reader will, it is hoped, have been sufficiently prepared for the inspection of the ensuing Table. For the further elucidation of the subject, to some of the heads of information contained in it, *Notes* will be found subjoined.[1] Of these Notes, the matter will be found to be partly mere matter of observation, partly matter of information, resting on the authority of Mr. *W. Wright*, to whose successive Letters on the subject, as transcribed from the Morning Chronicle, of the years 1813 and 1814, reference is all along made: letters, seven or eight in number, the earliest bearing date Nov. 6th, 1813, and published in the Morning Chronicle of the 13th of that month, or thereabouts; the latest, 11th March, 1814.[2]

According to his own statement, he had then lately been *Secretary* to *four Bishops:* in the first instance to the late Dr. Randolph, then Bishop of London: afterwards, and it should seem, at the same time, to the then Bishops of *Ely* and *Norwich;* and one other—name and diocese not discernible.[3] By every one of these Prelates, except *Dr. Randolph*, he speaks of himself as having been neglected and ill-used.

On the strength of the information, obtained in the course of that holy service by this quondam Secretary, it is, that, in the year 1811, against a considerable number of Incumbents, those actions, which gave so much disturbance to the wisdom of Parliament, were brought,—for the recovery of penalties supposed to have been

[a] Of *Exemptions* likewise a folio page full is added. See No. V. of this.[4]

---

[1] See pp. 442–59 below.
[2] William Henry Wright (1753–1828), author and clergyman, incumbent of the parishes of North Stoke, Ipsden, and Newnham Murren, Oxfordshire 1800–28, wrote eight letters to the *Morning Chronicle* on the subject of clerical non-residence:
Letter I, dated 6 November 1813, published 13 November 1813.
Letter II, dated 17 November 1813, published 20 November 1813.
Letter III, dated 29 November 1813, published 17 December 1813.
Letter IV, dated 3 December 1813, published 20 December 1813.
Letter V, dated 18 January 1814, published 21 January 1814.
Letter VI, dated 26 January 1814, published 16 February 1814.
Letter VII, dated 6 February 1814, published 4 March 1814.
Letter VIII, dated 10 February 1814, published 11 March 1814.
[3] According to his own account, Wright was appointed Secretary to the Bishops of Ely, Oxford, Norwich, and St David's in 1805, mainly to cope with the demands of government for information on the residence of clergy. Although he ceased his employment for the Bishop of St David's sometime after 1809, Wright continued to work for the Bishops of Ely and Norwich, and for John Randolph, when he was Bishop of Oxford 1799–1807, Bishop of Bangor 1807–9, and finally Bishop of London from 1809. See 'Petition of Mr. Wright against the Clergy Residence Proceedings Bill', 20 November 1813, *Parliamentary Debates* (1813–14) xxvii. 168–72, and Wright's Letter I, 6 November 1813 (*Morning Chronicle*, 13 November 1813).
[4] See pp. 497–9 n. below.

APPENDIX NO. IV. §VII.

incurred by violation of those laws which had for their object, real or pretended, the preventing of the sort of *desertion* above spoken of.[1]

To repel the imputation of his having chosen for his victims delinquents who were such in *form* only, and not in *substance,* 'in any action,' (says he, Lett. 4th. 3d Dec. 1813) 'which I have caused to be commenced against persons holding two benefices, if they can prove that they resided constantly on one, and performed the proper duty, and had a resident and licensed curate on the other, whereon he also performed the duty according to law, I will (under the sanction of the court, by whose authority I am always guided) in such cases accept a nominal penalty.'

Of those actions, what was the consequence? Judgment? No: but denial of justice. In pursuance of a Bill, brought in by Mr. Bragge Bathurst, 17th Nov. 1813,[2] an Act of Parliament was passed, giving impunity to delinquents, violating the public faith pledged by Parliament to the individual, by whom the invitation given to engage in the service of religion and law had been accepted, leaving him, for any thing that appears, without compensation in any shape for the loss, the trouble, and the ill-will, he had drawn upon himself by the confidence so unhappily placed by him in the justice of Government.[3]

In the last, or last but one, of these letters, ulterior information is announced and threatened.[4] No such ulterior information, however, made its appearance. The letter-writer's circumstances, as described by himself, considered,—the probability seems to be, that the intimation was not given altogether in vain, and that, by holy policy in some shape or other, the pen of the too inquisitive and active Secretary was saved from the eventually intended trouble.[a]

[a] Of *Mr. Wright's* published letters, as above, the date of the last is 11th March, 1814. Relative to his part in the business, the latest printed document that has been found, is a Petition of his to the House of Commons, which in the Votes of the 21st April, 1814,[5] stands as follows:

---

[1] According to Wright's counsel, who had been called to the bar of the House of Lords on 26 November 1813, Wright had brought 200 prosecutions against clergy: see *Parliamentary Debates* (1813–14) xxvii. 199.

[2] Charles Bragge Bathurst (1754–1831), MP for Monmouth 1790–6, Bristol 1796–1812, Bodmin 1812–18, and Harwich 1818–23, introduced the Non-Resident Clergy Bill, intended to stay prosecutions against clergy under 43 Geo. III, c. 84, on 17 November 1813: see *Parliamentary Debates* (1813–14) xxvii. 128–31.

[3] In fact, three Acts were passed in response to actions against members of the clergy: 54 Geo. III, c. 6 (6 December 1813), which stayed the proceedings until 20 April 1814; 54 Geo. III, c. 44 (19 April 1814), which stayed the proceedings until 20 May 1814; and 54 Geo III, c. 54 (18 May 1814), which discontinued the actions.

[4] In the postscript to Wright's Letter VIII, 10 February 1814 (*Morning Chronicle*, 11 March 1814), he announced: 'In my next, I will point out the Laws and Constitutions of our Ancestors, to prevent dilapidations.'

[5] See *Votes of the House of Commons*, no. 54 (21 April 1814), pp. 396–7. The petition is

CHURCH-OF-ENGLANDISM

'Ordered, that the Report from the Committee of the whole House, on the Bill to discontinue proceedings in certain actions already commenced, and to prevent vexatious suits against Spiritual Persons under an Act passed in the 43d year of His present Majesty,[1] be taken into further consideration upon Monday next.

'A petition of *William Wright*, of Bridge-Court, Westminster, in the County of Middlesex, Gentleman, was presented and read; setting forth, that, under the sanction of an Act of Parliament, made and passed in the 43rd year of the reign of his present Majesty, intituled, "An act to amend the laws relating to spiritual persons holding of Farms, and for enforcing the Residence of spiritual persons on their Benefices, in England," the Petitioner commenced divers actions against Clergymen for the recovery of part of the penalties, to the payment of which they had by their own neglect become liable; and the Petitioner was induced to believe that himself, or any other person who might sue for the same, would find that encouragement and protection, to which, by the laws of this Country, he was led to believe himself entitled; and that the Petitioner never had any desire, or ever sought to imprison the persons of the Clergy, as hath been imputed to him, he being well aware that he was prohibited from so doing by the 17th section of the said Act, it being therein provided that no execution shall be levied against the body of any spiritual person for any penalty, if the same can be recovered within three years by sequestration of the benefice; and that the representations made by the Clergy derogatory to the character of the Petitioner as a Christian and a gentleman, of his having entrapped them, nourished or engendered their offences, or kept back their licences or notifications, he most solemnly declares are untrue; so far from which, the *Petitioner* did at great trouble *prepare a faithful abstract of all the Statutes in force respecting residence, and added thereto forms of notification, and Petitions for licences of non-residence*,[2] *which at his own personal expense, he caused to be printed and distributed gratis, not only to the Clergy of the dioceses wherein he acted as Secretary, but also to the Clergy of other dioceses; and that he did also at his own personal expense, from the month of April,* 1806, *to the month of April,* 1813, *cause advertisements to be inserted in the provincial newspapers, and circular letters to be written to the Clergy, for the purpose of acquainting them with the necessity there was for them to renew their licences, if the cause which created their existence still continued, and to request others of the Clergy to deliver the notifications required by the said Act;* and that so conscious is the Petitioner of the rectitude of his conduct, that *he invites the whole body of Clergy, against whom he has commenced actions, to adduce a single case in evidence at the Bar of the House, of his ever having entrapped any of them, nourished or engendered their offences, or kept back either their licences or notifications; and that the Petitioner has commenced actions for penalties against Clergymen in twenty different dioceses*, and therefore his researches are not confined to the four dioceses in which he had been employed as Secretary, but *his information has been derived, not only from an extract published by authority of the Right honourable the House of Lords*,[3] *which was introduced to his attention by a dignitary of the Church, who complained that such a publication should be permitted by Government, as it held up a large proportion of the Clergy to prosecution,*

---

reproduced in *Parliamentary Debates* (1813–14) xxvii. 462–5. Wright had previously presented two petitions to the House of Commons, on 20 November 1813 and 31 March 1814: see ibid. 168–72, 396–7, respectively.

[1] i.e. the measure which would be enacted as 54 Geo. III, c. 54.

[2] See 'On the Residence of the Clergy in England, and Holding of Farms. An Abstract of the 43d of George III Cap. 84 with Observations, Forms of Petitions for Licences and Notifications.' The Advertisement at the front of the work is signed by Wright and dated 24 March 1806.

[3] See p. 438 n. below.

APPENDIX NO. IV. §VII.

but also from many long, tedious, and expensive journeys, which the Petitioner has made, in order to elucidate the subject; and that, since the Petitioner has commenced actions for penalties under the before mentioned Act, not only clubs and associations of the Clergy have been publicly convened, for the purpose of defeating the Petitioner in his legal claims, which combination the Petitioner humbly submits is contrary to the known Law of the land, but also *several of the Clergy have caused friendly actions to be commenced against themselves, in order, if possible, to defeat the Petitioner's vested rights;*[1] and the Petitioner is informed that some of them have consulted Counsel whether they could not avoid the penalties to which they were liable, by a resignation of their benefices, and retaking them; and that the *Petitioner feels perfectly satisfied that the House will not lend its aid to deprive him of a right so sacred as that which is vested in him by a recent Act of the Legislature, framed by the united wisdom of both Houses of Parliament,* (poor Petitioner! little, if sincere, did he know Honourable Houses) and that no measures will be adopted by the House to abridge him of the penalties under the said Act, upon the *ex parte* reports which have been communicated to the House; and that the Petitioner has not only, by the means aforesaid, been put to a very considerable expense in putting the Clergy in possession of the Law of the Land on the subject, and in obtaining the necessary evidence and information in support of his said actions, but has by their neglect, in not renewing their licences, *sustained an annual loss of at least £300 during nine years in which he was Secretary to four Lord Bishops;*[2] *the Petitioner therefore places himself under the protection of the House, and prays* that the Bill to discontinue Proceedings in certain actions already commenced, and to prevent vexatious suits against spiritual persons, under an Act passed in the 43d year of His present Majesty, may not in its present shape pass into a Law, and that *he may be heard, by himself or Counsel, against the said Bill, and be allowed to produce such evidence as he may be advised,* or that the House will be pleased to grant him such relief as to them shall seem meet.

'Ordered, That the said Petition do lie upon the Table.'

Here, then, amongst so many other things, has been seen, on the one part, the offer—(Oh, impious offer!) to uncover—a corner at least—of the nakedness of Holy Mother Church: on the other part, in the depth of the silence with which the offer was received, the horror which such an impiety could not fail to produce.

From that time to the present, it appears not, from any document that has been found, that the public has heard any thing from Mr. Wright: by this silence, and that alone, the hope is produced—that in some unknown way and proportion, compensation may have been received by him for the course of expense and labour he had, as above, been led into, by so unfortunate a supposition as that the faith of Parliament was a safe object of reliance. By a careful search made into the documents of the *time* by a learned friend, the author is assured, that, antecedently to those actions brought by Mr. Wright, it was in certain prosecutions grounded in the original statute of Henry the Eighth, and commenced, probably by some other person, at some time anterior to the year 1801, that the whole system of *sham-reform,* that will be seen unfolded, took its rise: that accordingly the first Act that was passed in consequence was the Act 41 G. III. c. 102. which was a temporary Act, and for its object had no

---

[1] The practice of commencing a prosecution to prevent others from doing so was barred by 4 Hen. VII, c. 20, and the practice of commencing a prosecution with the object of settling the matter privately was barred by 18 Eliz. I, c. 5, §4. See Blackstone, *Commentaries on the Laws of England,* iii. 160, iv. 135–6.

[2] To obtain a licence for non-residence, clergy had to pay a fee of £10 to the Secretary of the Bishop: see 43 Geo. III, c. 84, §19.

other than the stopping of these same prosecutions.[1] By the 42 G. III. c. 86. brought in by Sir William Scott, it was continued, and again by the Act 43 G. III. c. 34. the Bill for which was brought in by the same Right Honourable son of Excellent Church;[2] whereupon came the Act of the same year, c. 84.[3] of the efficiency of which for giving security and increase to *Non-Residence*, under the notion of '*enforcing* Residence,' ample proof will here be seen.

Thirtieth of July, 1814, (54 G. III. c. 175.) is the date of the latest Act on the subject of Excellent Church that has been found. In this Act, the provision made in the former Act of the 43 G. III. c. 84. after all the pains taken, to hammer it into a '*brutum fulmen*' being still, by some nervous temperament or other, been found too formidable, was (by §10, 11) limited to a 20*l.* penalty[4] (a sum scarcely sufficient to cover with any assurance the difference between costs allowed on taxation and costs out of pocket): care being taken, by a cloak very ingeniously woven in the texture of the preceding section,[5] to enable a merciful Bishop to save from the gripe of the Informer any penitent sinner, whose 'prostration of understanding and will'[6] shall have been sufficiently profound. But,—if, instead of 20*l.*, the pay thus offered to an Informer were 200*l.*,—after what has passed, by what Informer will a ticket in this part of the lottery of the law ever be purchased? Surely by no one, whose attention common prudence has directed to the history of the part taken by Government in this business. Seeing that as often as a ticket of this sort has been purchased, all shame being cast aside, the whole power of Government has been employed in destroying the value of it, what he will see, if he has eyes, is—that, in any such case, to put trust in the Government of this Country, framed as it is at present, would be not only to lean on a broken reed,[7] but to kick against the pricks.[8]

As to the paper above spoken of by Mr. Wright, by the name of the *Extract published by authority of the House of Lords*,—against which paper the complaint had been made, that it held up a large proportion of the clergy to prosecution,—it seems to have been the same of which mention is made in the fourth of his above-mentioned Letters; date of the Letter, or of the Morning Chronicle in which it was published, 3d December, 1813: 'The extract of Diocesan Returns, ordered to be printed by the House of Lords, contained only 1742 Benefices, and of them, 383 Incumbents were stated as fit objects of prosecution; besides 430 demanding inquiry previous to an action being commenced.'[9]

---

[1] By 41 George III, c. 102 (1801), all proceedings against clergy were stayed until 25 March 1802.

[2] Introduced by Sir William Scott, the two Acts further extended the stay in proceedings until 8 April 1803 and 8 July 1803 respectively.

[3] i.e. 43 Geo. III, c. 84.

[4] By the Clergy Penalties Act (54 Geo. III, c. 175, §§ 10, 11), penalties for non-residence were set at £20, whereas by the Non-Resident Clergy Act (43 Geo. III, c. 84, §12), penalties for non-residence might rise from one-third to three-quarters of the value of the living, depending on the duration of non-residence, with the whole of the penalty payable to the person or persons who informed and sued for the sum.

[5] Bentham presumably has in mind 54 Geo. III, c. 175, §6, rather than §9, which permitted the respective Archbishop or Bishop to remit the whole or any part of the penalty.

[6] See p. 37 n. above.

[7] Isaiah 36: 6.

[8] Acts 9: 5; 26: 14.

[9] See Wright's Letter IV, 3 December 1813 (*Morning Chronicle*, 20 December 1813). The paper of the House of Lords has not been identified.

APPENDIX NO. IV. §VII.

In regard to these actions, if any person there be, in whose view of the matter it is evident, that no duty, which by these deserters from the service of their God, would have been performed, had they been at their posts, would have been of any real value,—that to their parishioners no less than to their God, they would have been unprofitable servants,[1]—and that, howsoever condemned by their invisible Commander-in-chief, such their desertion had, by a long continued course, partly of open allowance, partly of connivance, been authorized and encouraged by the only power, to which it is the custom of *Excellent Church* to have regard,—it will be in a correspondent degree evident, that if on this score any blame attaches upon Parliament, it can only have been in respect of the nonallowance of adequate compensation at the public expense: a neglect, in consequence of which the burthen threatened by law to transgressors was transferred from their shoulders to those of the too credulous individual, who, by invitation from Parliament, had been engaged in the service of justice.

The impunity thus given to transgressors,—while *punishment* in every thing but the name was inflicted on those who, at the call of Parliament, had loaded themselves with expense in the endeavour to bring them to punishment,—will at any rate be a lesson to those who otherwise might have been disposed to 'put their trust in princes,'[2] whose engagements have been thus openly and deliberately violated: and, in this state of things, it may be inquired, whether, from any penalties appointed in their laws, the professed reformers of Church discipline have themselves either expected or desired any real effect, other than that of giving the appearance of efficiency to a system of discipline, for which no real efficiency was designed.—Follows now the *Table*.[3]

---

[1] An echo of Matthew 25: 30.
[2] An echo of Psalm 146: 3.
[3] Bentham has compiled the following table from the sources listed at p. 361 n. above.

CHURCH-OF-ENGLANDISM

ABSTRACT of RETURNS respecting NON-RESIDENCE, for the under-mentioned Years, ending 25th March.

Form and Arrangement of Abstracts, by Order of Council.	1809.	1810.	1811.
I.—Exemptions.			
1. Residence on other Benefices([a])	1,240	[1,846][1]	2,059
2. Official Chaplaincies[a]	37	41	24
3. Chaplains to privileged Individuals([b])	32	21	41
4. Ecclesiastical, Collegiate, and Cathedral Offices[b]	281	251	250
5. Officers in the Royal Chapels of St. James's and Whitehall	—	—	—
6. Readers[c] in his Majesty's Private Chapel at Windsor	1	—	1
7. Preachers and Readers in the Inns of Court[d] or at the Rolls	11	8	8
8. Public Officers and Tutors in the Universities of Oxford and Cambridge	69	67	55
9. Resident Fellows in ditto[e]	47	38	34
10. Provost of Eton, Warden of Winchester, Fellows of both	13	30	24
11. Schoolmasters and Ushers of Eton, Westminster, Winchester, &c.	8	5	5
12. Students residing in Oxford or Cambridge, under 30[f]	7	—	12
13. Exemptions not notified([c])	817	363	155
14. Livings held by Bishops, 1809. See No. 30, iv.	26	—	—
II.—Licences.			
15. I. Infirmity of Incumbent or Family([d])	465	389	396
16. II. Want or unfitness of Parsonage Houses([e])	944	941	1,068
17. III. Residence in a Mansion within the Parish belonging to Incumbent or relative	105	62	68
18. IV. Incumbents possessing small Livings, licensed to Curacies	210	170	168
19. V. Schoolmasters or Ushers of Endowed Schools	159	122	133
20. VI. Masters or Preachers of Hospitals	19	4	5
21. VII. Endowed Preachers or Lecturers	30	24	19
22. VIII. Licensed Preachers in Proprietary Chapels	14	16	14
23. IX. Librarians of the British Museum, Sion College, and Trustees of Lord Crew's Charity	5	3	4
24. X. Incumbents residing in the neighbourhood, and doing duty[g] ([f])	565	348	301
25. XI. Unenumerated cases, confirmed by the Archbishop([g])	54	35	26
26. XII. Unenumerated cases within the Archbishops' Dioceses([h])	—	—	5

[a] In the Returns for 1810 and 1811, *Chaplains*.
[b] In 1810, 1811, *Officers*.
[c] In 1810, 1811, *Reader*.
[d] In 1810, 1811, *and*.
[e] In 1810, 1811, *Oxford and Cambridge*.
[f] In 1810, 1811, *thirty years of age*.
[g] In 1810, 1811, *Performing the Duties of their Parishes*.

[1] 1818 '1816'. The correct figure is given in the table at p. 463 n. below.

APPENDIX NO. IV. §VII.

Form and Arrangement of Abstracts, by Order of Council.	Non-Residents' Numbers, in Years		
	1809.	1810.	1811.
III.—Cases which could not be included among Licences or Exemptions.			
27. I. Absence without Licence or Exemption(i)	672	650	1,033
28. II. Dilapidated Churches(k)	[23][1]	34	56
29. III. Sinecures and Dignities not requiring Residence(l)	[233]	70	68
30. IV. Livings held by Bishops(m)	[26]	35	21
31. V. 4. Vacancies(n)	—	74	96
32. VI. 5. Recent Institutions(o)	[0]	54	33
33. VII. Held by Sequestration(p)	—	91	78
34. Miscellaneous Cases not included in the preceding Classes(q)	[1271]	38	51

TOTALS.

	1809.	1810.	1811.	1809.	1810.	1811.
Incumbents exempted by Statutes without Licence	2,589	2,671	2,668			
Whereof are stated as performing the Duties of their Parishes	—	—	—	—	244	173
Incumbents exempted, under Statute or otherwise, by Licence	2,826	2,114	2,207			
Whereof are stated as performing the Duties of their Parishes	—	—	—	565	747	685
Incumbents 'Absent' (i.e. Non-Resident) without Exemption or Licence	—	1,017	1,385			
Whereof are stated as performing the Duties of their Parishes	—	—	—	—	5	14
Incumbents whose cases are stated as 'miscellaneous,' and not included in the preceding Classes	—	38	51			
Whereof are stated as performing the duties of their Parishes	—	—	—	—	2	60
Totals of those stated as performing the duties of their Parishes	. .	. .	. .	565	998	932
Total of the above cases of Non-Residence	7,358	5,840	6,311			
And cases of alleged Residence	3,836	4,421	4,490			
Totals of Incumbents reported as Non-Resident or Resident	11,194	10,261	10,801[2]			

---

[1] Although omitted from 1818, this and the following four figures in the column are given in the table at p. 463 n. below.

[2] 1818 transposes the final three figures from the 1810 and 1811 columns. The text has been silently corrected. The figures appear correctly at p. 361 n. above and in the table at p. 463 n. below.

NOTES

TO THE ABOVE NON-RESIDENCE TABLE.

[a]1. {*Residence on other Benefices.*} Speaking (Lett. 1. 6th Nov. 1813)[1] of the persons against whom he had brought those actions of his, which were stopped by Parliament, 'they are also,' says Mr. Wright, 'against some who have been returned as resident, but who are not so, and many of those holding one, two, or three livings, from some of which they claim exemption, in consequence of residence on others, which' {residence} 'they do not perform.'[a]

[b] 3. {*Chaplains to privileged individuals.*} The *privilege* is—that of depriving a certain number of Parishes, increasing with the dignity and sanctity of the privileged person—depriving them of the service, which, but for this dignity and sanctity, would have been rendered to the souls of the inhabitants, by those who are, by authority of the church, ([21][2] H. VIII. c. 13. §13 to 21. §24.) deemed their most proper pastors; leaving the souls to take their chance in each instance, for having or not having more or less of the service of a make-shift substitute, hired at the lowest price for which any one is to be hired. Besides *Peers* and *Peeresses* with their *children*, and *official men* in abundance, *six* is the number of Parishes in which a man may give this advantage to the Devil if he is a *Bishop; eight*, when he is an *Archbishop*. Of the persons, to whom, under the name of his *Chaplains*, the privileged person is entitled to give the profit of this injury, the number is, according to his rank, from one to eight, as above. Increasing, it seems, in proportion, in the first place, to his *sanctity*, and, in the next place, to his *rank*, is the weight with which his soul gravitates on towards the pit of hell, increasing, consequently, in the same proportion the quantity of spiritual labour necessary to stop him in his descent. Such, it should seem, is the principle, and is it altogether an inapposite one?

[c] 13. {*Exemptions not notified*, 817, 363, 155.} In these instances no exemption being notified, how and whence comes the existence of any such thing to be known to the person by whom in this case the Return is made, and who, it is supposed, is the Bishop of the Diocese? To those who are in the secret must the question be addressed, by any person whose desire it is to know how this matter stands. To us who are *not* in the secret, the decreasing series, exhibited by the three years, viz. 817, 363, and 155, seems remarkable enough: it looks as if this or that *stimulus*, by which more and more of these defaulters had been awakened out of their lethargy, or frightened out of their contempt, had by degrees been found.

Confront this *decreasing* series with the preceding *increasing* series of the cases of *Residence on other benefices*, 1240, [1846, 2059],[3] and the succeeding *decreasing* then *increasing* series of cases of '*Absence without License or Exemption*,' 672, 650, 1033: not to speak of the *decreasing* series of the numbers of Incumbents residing in the neighbourhood and doing duty: viz. 565, 348, 301. Is it in the nature of the case that truth and veracity should in all these instances—or in any one of them—have accompanied the variation in these numbers?

---

[a] As to this matter, see further, under Note ([1]), to *Absence without License or Exemption*.[4]

---

[1] Wright's Letter I, 6 November 1813 (*Morning Chronicle*, 13 November 1813).
[2] 1818 '25'.   [3] 1818 '1816, 2057'.   [4] See pp. 448–51 n. below.

NOTES.

^d {15. I. *Infirmity of Incumbent, or Family:* 465, 389, 396.} Follows what, on this subject, we have from *Mr. Wright*, Lett. VI. January [26]th,[1] 1814:[2]

'Now ill-health of the Incumbent himself, or his wife or daughter, is a common pretext, when no other legal cause can be found of avoiding residence. Of *twenty-two* licenses granted in one diocese, for this reason, *three only* of the persons are in a state of health to warrant it, and the benefices from which they so absent themselves are very valuable. Whether the nineteen, whom I thus challenge as using false pretences, deserve the imputation, will best appear by the mode of life they adopt. Some live in town during the winter; and, although night-air certainly cannot benefit a valetudinarian, they may be constantly seen at card-parties, routs, or the theatre. In summer, enjoying the amusements of fashionable watering-places, whilst, too often, their Curate, by the parsimonious stipend they afford him, is, with a numerous family, in a state of the greatest poverty. Others have beneficial schools in the neighbourhood of London. Others are continually to be met with near their residence in more pleasant parts of the Country, enjoying the sports of the field, or vigilantly endeavouring to detect some poor countryman, who may have an unfortunate inclination to taste game! Others may be seen most days driving their own carriage! Some are in debt, and some are Curates near the Fens! and all, to observers, seem perfectly healthful; yet a certificate from a medical man is deposited with the Bishop that they are not so; probably it is six or eight years before, when there might have existed a degree of temporary ill health, but after the cause ceases, the same plea is continued, and a license once granted is renewed as a matter of course.'

^e {16. II. *Want or unfitness of Parsonage Houses*, 944, 941, 1,068.} Behold here a number, little less than one-tenth of the whole number of Parsonage Houses: a number considerably greater than the whole number of Parishes in Scotland, in no one of which is any such thing as a Parish without a Parsonage, or an uninhabited Parsonage, to be seen.

With reference to *Parsonage House*, after the word *want*, steals in the word *unfitness;* unfitness furnishing a cloak unbounded in extent for the exercise of Right Reverend despotism. To the Reverend friend of the Right Reverend arbiter, what Parsonage, that is not more agreeable to him than any other residence he could have, can be otherwise than unfit?—here, exercise is found for Right Reverend *beneficence*. For a man, who, by 'non-prostration of understanding and will,' is troublesome, what pig-stye, having the name of a Parsonage, can be otherwise than fit?—Here exercise is found for the severity of Right Reverend *justice*.

'In one diocese,' (says Mr. Wright, Lett. II. Morning Chronicle, 20th Nov. 1813)[3] '*one-third* of the Parsonage Houses were returned to be in bad repair.' Thus far Mr. Wright. This it should seem must, in each instance, have been for the purpose of serving as an excuse, true or false, for *Non-Residence*. On what other occasion could a statement to this effect have been called forth?

^f {24. X. *Incumbents residing in the Neighbourhood, and* (per Abstract of 1809) *doing duty:* (per Abstracts of 1810 and 1811) *performing the Duties of their respective Parishes,*—565, 348, 301.} Out of Section 19 of the above-mentioned Act of 43 G. III. c. 84. viz. the self-styled *Residence-enforcing* Act (for such in the title it professes to be) sprung the class of *Licenses* granted to the class of *Non-Residents* thus described. In so far as regards *Non-Residence*, this Act may be seen to have two objects; 1. To give increase to the population of *Sinecurist Incumbents*, and thereby to

---

[1] 1818 '6th'.
[2] Wright's Letter VI, 26 January 1814 (*Morning Chronicle*, 16 February 1814).
[3] Wright's Letter II, 17 November 1813 (*Morning Chronicle*, 20 November 1813).

give *in reality increased* extent to a state of things so agreeable and convenient to Excellent Church: 2. To establish, in the minds of those who are not in the secret, the *persuasion* that the wish and endeavour has been all along to *diminish* the extent to which Sinecurism, in that same convenient and agreeable state, had been carried.

For the accomplishment of the principal of these two general objects, two specific objects have, with indisputable success, been pursued: to the original colony of these Sinecurists, planted by the Act of Henry the Eighth,[1] viz. Sinecurists by *Exemption*, two others, it will be seen, have now, by or under this self-styled Residence-enforcing Act, been added, viz. *Non-Residents*, alias Sinecurists by *License*, and *Non-Residents*, alias Sinecurists by *connivance:* of which latter a little further on.

For the effectuation of the minor of these two general objects, viz. that of making a *cloak* for the principal one, besides the words in the title, viz. 'and for enforcing the Residence of Spiritual Persons on their Benefices,'[2] the following is the turn given (it will be seen with what ingenuity) to the language in the above-mentioned 19th Section. In the first place comes a description given of the *general* situation, common to all the persons to whom (but to them alone), in the cases thereupon particularly enumerated, it shall be lawful to grant licenses. This general situation is—what?—That of all Incumbents whatsoever, in what part soever, of the kingdom, or even of the globe, resident?—Oh no. What then? *Answer.* That sort of situation alone, which is not in any instance so remote from the Parish, from which the pay is received, but that, in some shape or other,—to the amount of some part or other, though not to the amount of the whole, of what is regularly due,—benefit might by the inhabitants be received from the pious labours of the Incumbent. For the producing a conception to this effect, it will be seen how dexterously the following words are contrived:—'It shall be lawful for any Bishop to grant Licenses to any Spiritual Persons' (describing them) 'to reside *out of the proper House of Residence, or out of the Parish*, and *within such distance therefrom* as the case may appear to such Bishop to require, if, *upon the consideration of all the circumstances* of any such case, such Bishop shall, *in his discretion*, think the same *fit* and *proper:*'[3] and thereupon immediately comes the description of the several *specific* cases, nine in number, in which, on the above *condition*, as above insinuated, and not otherwise, the indulgence in question may be allowed.

Now this condition, what is it?—what but that, notwithstanding the licenses, a man's actual residence shall still be, in relation to his Parish, within what may for shortness be termed *service-admitting* distance. Distance, viz. with reference to the place—the only place—in which, in consideration of the pay received, duty in any shape is by him by whom it is received to be performed—service in any shape to be rendered,—is a circumstance, which the Bishop is, by the express terms of the Act, required to take into *consideration*. But, to what purpose, take it at all into consideration, unless so it be, that in which ever of the nine cases in question the Incumbent be, his residence will still, under and notwithstanding any such License, be within service-admitting distance? For, let it but be understood, that by the Incumbent, when thus licensed '*to reside out of his proper House of Residence, or out of the Parish*,' he may, by his License, be put into such a situation, as not to have it so much as in his power to perform any sort of duty, legally exigible or legally inexigible, from which the Parish can be supposed to receive from him any sort of benefit,—let this be understood, as well might his residence be at the *antipodes* as at any lesser distance.

---

[1] i.e. 21 Hen. VIII, c.13.
[2] The full title of the Non-Resident Clergy Act (43 Geo. III, c. 84) was 'An Act to amend the Laws relating to Spiritual Persons holding of Farms; and for enforcing the Residence of Spiritual Persons on their Benefices in *England*.' [3] 43 Geo. III, c. 84, §19.

NOTES.

What then, in regard to the exercise to be given to this power, was the conception, which we who are not in the secret were to be led to entertain ourselves with?—what? but that, in no case whatever—not even in any one of the nine cases thereupon so particularly described—was an Incumbent to be licensed to reside either out of the proper place of residence, i.e. the *Parsonage*, or at any rate out of the *Parish*, unless the place, in which, in virtue of such License, he took up his residence, were in some sort within the above-explained *service-admitting* distance.

Such then was the expectation meant to be raised. Of any one of the distinguished and variously titled persons, by whose piety this clause was got up, can there have been so much as a single one, who ever meant it should be fulfilled? The answer may be found in the residences of about as many Incumbents as have received those Licenses.

Such then being the intention and the effect, observe now in what way the intention is fulfilled—the effect produced.—Of the preceding nine statutable grounds,—coupled with the immediately succeeding unstatutable and spurious one, which necessitated this explanation,—behold then the practical result.—If the Incumbent be in any one of those nine cases, his Spiritual Lordship, if such be his pleasure, and not otherwise, be the distance what it will, grants him a License *under* the Act: if not in any one of them, then, under the notion, true or false, of his being in this case, so does he out of his own head, and without any warrant from the Act.

Thus much as to the *Act* itself. Turn now to the *Abstracts*, and in them, under the head of *Licenses*, observe the *twelve* causes of License that have been deduced from it:[1] and in particular this *tenth* cause,[2] which will be seen to have been added by Episcopal effrontery to the insufficiently exercised authority of Parliament.

On the subject of discipline, Church and State together, this article may, when compared with the Act, be seen to present upon the face of it, a picture rather more extensive as well as instructive, than any which, when this body of information was called for, was probably intended to be very generally conveyed. Taking it for correct, here may be seen, and at one view, not only under what sort of discipline *Bishops* are, as in relation to *Parliament*, but moreover what sort of discipline *Parliament* itself is, as towards that *public*, in which that same Parliament, in one of its parts, professes itself in some sort to be dependent.

In the Act in question—being the law in which these licenses originated—the only law under which they have been, or can be legally granted—in Section 19—*nine* cases are, as above, described, in which, and in which alone, with the exception of two others, in the next section (Section 20.) distinguished, as above, by the name of '*Unenumerated Cases*,' the granting of these Licenses, after the regard paid as above to *distance*, is allowed.[3] These *nine* are the nine which, under the general head of *Licenses*, may be seen standing in the Table.[4] In the Abstracts of these several Years, after these *nine*, each of which, provided always that due regard be paid to the circumstance of distance, as above, and not otherwise, has its ground and warrant in the Act, comes this *tenth* case, thus simply and coolly inserted—this *tenth* case, for the warranting of which, not even in the most vague and unexplicit manner, is so much as a single syllable to be found in the Act.

Now then, what upon the face of these three successive Returns we see asserted, is this plain matter of fact, viz. that, on the grounds thus described, so it was, that, in every one of the instances, under the heads of the several Dioceses specified and particularized in figures,—viz. that in all the several instances above-mentioned,—by

[1] i.e. nos. 15–26 on the Table, p. 440 above.
[2] i.e. no. 24.   [3] i.e. nos. 25–6.   [4] i.e. nos. 15–23.

CHURCH-OF-ENGLANDISM

the Bishops of these several Dioceses, Licenses for Non-Residence were actually granted to those same numbers of Incumbents. Of any of these Right Reverend Prelates is this true? Well then, in every one of those Right Reverend Guardians of Ecclesiastical Discipline, and Members of the Upper House of Parliament, of which it is true, may be seen a self-constituted legislator, acting on his own single authority: setting thus his own power above the power of Parliament.

By the men of law, and other political saints, by whom a part was taken in the penmanship of this Act, was the above-described state of things which has been the result, foreseen and intended, and such their intentions mutually communicated? If so, in these same pious persons we have so many successful conspirators, conspiring for the establishment and maintenance of this corrupt system of pay without service, on pretence of souls-saving—conspiring, to permit, and cause to be committed, on the part of the order of Bishops, an usurpation of and upon the authority of Parliament. Was it that no such intention, or that no such communication did indeed take place?—then at any rate,—unless while year after year, so many accordant pictures of Excellent Church, viewed in this point of view, were successively hung up in the *Council Chamber* and in both Houses, these same pious persons were all the time fast asleep,—we have, with or without conspiracy, so many *connivers* at the clandestine transfer thus made of the authority of Parliament.

The Earl of Harrowby in particular—the indefatigable servant of Excellent Church,—in whose breast, in conjunction with that of the departed Saint,[1] this Act, and every thing else which, for the advancement of Church-of-England piety, has in this pious reign been done, or attempted in Parliament, took its rise,—the Earl of Harrowby, for the purpose of whose Act for the putting Incumbents' money into the pockets of Curates, this body of information was called for,—by whom it has been sifted to the bottom, been commented upon in his Speech, and in the pamphlet containing that same Speech re-methodized and re-edited,[2]—is it by mere accident, that his eyes have, for any thing that appears, been thus long shut against this contempt of Parliament—this usurpation—to which those pious labours have given birth and continuance?—If among those who have the power, there be any one who has the curiosity to learn how these matters stand,—let him address himself to these pious persons whom the Votes, or other public prints, present to view, as having taken a part in this pious business, and in particular, in the Upper House, to the *Earl of Harrowby;* and, in the Lower House, to *Sir William Scott.*

On the occasion of this exercise of legislative power, it may be matter of curiosity to observe the various parts taken, in the three successive years, by the several potentates:—

I. *Four,* and no more, abstained from it altogether. These (taken all along in alphabetical order) were, 1. Bath and Wells; 2. St. David's; 3. Gloucester; 4. Rochester.

II. *Eight,* having taken up the sceptre in the beginning, kept it in hand to the last. These were, 1. Bangor; 2. CANTERBURY; 3. Chester; 4. Durham; 5. Exeter; 6. Hereford; 7. Litchfield and Coventry; 8. Winchester.

N.B. In both these lines of conduct may be seen *consistency,* though operating in such *opposite* directions.

III. *Five,* having taken up the sceptre, and kept it in hand the two first years, let it drop the last. These were, 1. St. Asaph; 2. Carlisle; 3. Landaff; 4. Lincoln; 5. YORK.

IV. *Five,* having taken it up the first year, let it drop the second, and did not

---

[1] Perceval: see p. 389 & n. above.
[2] For Bentham's comments on Harrowby's role in the passing of the Curates Act of 1813 see pp. 388–9 n. above.

NOTES.

afterwards resume it. These were, 1. Ely; 2. *London!* 3. Norwich; 4. Peterborough; 5. Worcester.

V. *Three*, having taken it up the first year, dropt it the second, but took it up again the third. These were, 1. Bristol; 2. Chichester; 3. Salisbury.

VI. *One*, having shrunk from the enterprize the first year, plucked up courage enough the second, but lost it on the third. This one was *Oxford*.

Another curious state of things is—that which may be learnt from a confrontation made of this *article* (X) with the several *sub-articles*, if so they may be styled, in each of the *Abstracts* for 1810 and 1811, (in each of them the same *four*),[1] in each of which such multitudes are stated as *'performing the duties of their Parishes.'* Between these cases and the one principally here in question, wherein consists the difference?—In both,—in so far as the Returns are true, the Incumbents 'perform *the* duties,' i.e. *all* the duties: but the difference is—that, in the principal article, they are stated as *residing in the neighbourhood;*—whereas, in the *sub-articles*, no statement to that effect is contained. But, if this be true, viz. that in all these instances the 'duties' which they were bound to 'perform,' were all of them, by the several Incumbents, in their several Parishes, really 'performed,' what is there that should have deprived so many holy men of the benefit of a License any more than these others?—In the one case, exactly as good a warrant did the Act give as in the other: viz. none in either.—Clouds upon clouds! every thing is wrapt up in clouds. The solution, is it this? In the cases designated by the *principal article*, the Incumbent applied for a License, and thus obtained it: in those designated by the *sub-articles*, no application, consequently no License; but, to save reputation of Holy Church, Bishops spoke for so many Incumbents, who feared, or thought it not worth their while, to speak for themselves. As to this spontaneous mercy, see further Section 8, Note.[2]

[g] {25. XI. *Unenumerated Cases confirmed by the Archbishop:* 54, 35, 26.} In the Act of the 43d of the King (c. 84.), after all those which have been seen in the Table, manufactured, and set up under generic heads,—the pretence for leaving the souls to shift for themselves, while the money allowed for taking care of them is pocketed, not being found sufficiently numerous,—a sweeping clause (§ 20.) was provided, allowing every Bishop to manufacture other pretences in any number, on condition of getting his superior, the Archbishop, to join with him.

Had any thing better than the extension of ecclesiastical despotism been intended,—annexed to this relaxing clause would have been some provision for taking into consideration, from time to time, the *individual* cases as they arose, and out of them forming *general* ones, to add to the above list. But, by Excellent Church despotism, two capital purposes are at once served; viz. conversion of cure of souls into *sinecure*, for the accommodation of the *ruling few*, and the service due to the same separate and sinister interest, by the extension given to corrupt and corruptive influence.

Of the ulterior grounds for non-performance of duty, thus left to the indulgence and ingenuity of Bishops, checked by the severe sanctity of Archbishops, the following case, stated by *Mr. Wright* (Lett. IV. 3d Dec. 1813, in the *Morning Chronicle* of some days afterwards)[3] seems to have been given as a specimen:—'I have now

---

[1] The sub-category of non-resident incumbents who were said in the 'Abstracts' for 1810 and 1811 to 'perform the Duties of their Parishes' in fact appears on five occasions, once each under 'Exemptions', 'Licences', and 'Miscellaneous Cases', and twice under 'Cases which could not be included under Licences or Exemptions'. Bentham has consolidated the two latter in the Non-Residence Table, p. 441 above.

[2] See pp. 462–5 n. below.

[3] Wright's Letter IV, 3 December 1813 (*Morning Chronicle*, 20 December 1813).

before me' (says this quondam Episcopal Secretary) 'an authentic[1] document, which states, that a *license* was granted to a Clergyman for Non-Residence, and, on looking for the cause, it is returned "outlawed."'

[h] {26. XII. *Unenumerated Cases within the Archbishop's Diocese;* 0, 0, 5.} Every Bishop having for his Ecclesiastical Superior one of the two Archbishops,—where the allowance for setting up the additional pretence-manufactory was, in the first instance, given to a Bishop: and, for form sake, to keep up the idea of subordination, and give to holy idlers the appearance of something to do, there was an use in requiring the concurrence of this his Superior. But the Archbishop having no Ecclesiastical Superior, and yet having not only his *Province*, but, within that Province, a *Diocese* of his own, what was to be done in his case? The answer was obvious. High as it is, the sanctity of a Bishop not being as yet at the highest point, requires a *check:* in the still higher sanctity of the Archbishop a competent check is provided. But, in the Archbishop, sanctity is at the very highest point: no check therefore is necessary for it. While Dr. Manners Sutton was as yet but Bishop of Norwich,[2] holy as he was in life and conversation, (inquire at Norwich else) exemplary in the discharge of all episcopal duties, still, though never sinning, he was not yet unpeccable. But now he is Archbishop of Canterbury, and never had St. Thomas Becket[3] a more worthy successor. For the two first of the three years thus employed in the preparation of the new system for the reformation of discipline, the Canterbury and York pretence-manufactories, notwithstanding the advantage which a *single-seated* has over a *many-seated* discretion, seems by some cause or other—say by a somewhat over-delicate conscience—say by doubts borrowed from a neighbouring woolsack[4]—kept at a stand. But in the last of the three years it may be seen set to work.

[i] {27. I. *Absence* (i.e. Non-Residence) *without License or Exemption:* 672, 650, 1,033.} On the part of Incumbents, *False Return* and *Non-Return;* on the part of Bishops and Archbishops, *connivance;*—in these may be seen three different yet intimately connected forms of transgression, blessed fruits of the original sin in which Excellent Church was conceived, and of the sham discipline which sprung from it.

Of *False Return*, express indication will not be expected to be found upon the face of any of these authoritatively published documents: still less of *connivance* on the part of those holy persons. Cases of *Non-Return* are the cases, which in these Tables have for their denomination the words *'Absence,'* (i.e. Non-Residence) *'without License or Exemption.'*

In one or other of the several possible ways, an Incumbent (suppose) is, and determines to continue, a transgressor of the laws: of those holy laws, which he hears, and sees, and feels were never intended to find obedience. 1. To avoid paying to his Curate a forced price,[5] he forbears to take out the license which the law in its wisdom requires, to warrant an Incumbent in casting off upon another person the cure of the souls, for the taking charge of which he has, by his own acknowledgement thus expressed, been overpaid: 2. Holding *two* livings, and being entitled to a dispensation for holding them on condition of submitting to a certain degree of residence on one or both of them, and not meaning to submit to any degree of

---

[1] Letter IV 'authorized'.

[2] Manners-Sutton was Bishop of Norwich from 1792 to 1805, before his translation to Canterbury.

[3] Thomas Becket (1120–70), Archbishop of Canterbury from 1162.

[4] i.e. from Lord Chancellor Eldon.

[5] According to the Non-Resident Clergy Act of 1803 (43 Geo. III, c. 84, §20), if a licence was granted for the incumbent to live outside his parish, the Bishop was authorized to assign an appropriate salary to be paid to the Curate appointed to carry out the duties of the incumbent.

NOTES.

residence in either, he avoids—in the first place to take out any *dispensation*, and in the next place to make any *Returns* to the questions put to him. For if, a return being made, that return were *false*, by the falsehood he might be exposed—possibly to *punishment*, and at any rate to shame: if *true*, thereby to *penalties*.

3. If the number of livings be greater than *two*, in which case he may be termed an *Ultra-Pluralist*, or *Unjustifiable Pluralist*, as in the other case a *Simple Pluralist*, no dispensation being allowed, what he exposes himself to is (by 21 H. VIII. c. 13. §9, 10.) forfeiture of all livings but that which came into his possession last.[1]

Such are the dangers, to which, in these several cases, a man would expose himself, were he to pay canonical obedience to the orders—to make *answer* to the inquiries—so received from his Bishop.—To what then does he expose himself by *silence?*—To nothing: to nothing at any rate, unless it be his misfortune to stand, on some special account, in bad odour with the Right Reverend arbiter of his fate.

In the case of *Simple Pluralism*, justification may, viz. by dispensation, (with fees for the same),[2] be attained. But in the case of *Ultra-Pluralism*, neither by dispensation nor by any thing else, can, to any legal purpose, any such holy work be accomplished. By one and the same *Ultra-Pluralist*, the number held of benefices with cure of souls amounts, (for of this will be seen alleged instances), amounts (suppose) to *seven*. On this supposition, no return of more than *two* can he make to the mandate, whatever it is, with perfect safety: for, on a perusal of the whole collection of Returns, it might in this case be seen that, all *seven* being in *one* hand, all but the last are thereby, as above, forfeitable. This well-fed man of God, what course then will he take in consequence of the queries sent to him from his Bishop or his Bishops? Either he will let them lie all together unnoticed, or—making answer as to *two* out of the *seven*, he will leave in that same predicament the other *five*. In the first case, *seven*, in the other *five* will have been the number added by this one *Ultra-Pluralist* to the above totals of 672, 650, and 1,033.

Note here—in the last of the three years, the number swelling to more than half as much again as it was in either of the preceding ones. Whence so extraordinary a swell?—Whence?—unless it be that,—finding the contempt, thus put upon the orders of their superiors, thus for two successive years unpunished and unnoticed,—all such delinquents, whose cases were most desperate, and least susceptible of true declaration or probably successful misrepresentation, betook themselves to *silence:* to *silence*, as to an asylum, in which the best chance for impunity was to be found.

At the same time, for want of a sufficiently correct and commanding view of the situation in which he stands, fearful of what may be the consequence of an apparent *contempt* thus manifested by silence, many an one (it will be manifest) there has been, who, seeing that by *true returns* he would expose himself to punishment in one way, and by *non-return* in another, has had recourse to *falsehood*.

And here, in a more especial manner than in the case of Simple *Non-Return*, comes the demand for *connivance:—connivance*, (of which presently), on the part of Right Reverend and Most Reverend eyes.

As to this matter, the following exhibits an alleged case of Non-Return, as reported by Mr. Wright (Letter II. Morning Chronicle of 20th Nov. [1813]).[3] 'A Rector,

---

[1] The Clergy Act of 1529 provided that any person holding a benefice with cure of souls (beyound a certain value), and who took another living, had to vacate the first (§ 9), and that the patron had thereupon to present another cleric to the living (§ 10).

[2] According to the Non-Resident Clergy Act of 1803 (43 Geo. III, c. 84, § 19), a fee of no more than 10s. was payable to the Secretary or officer of the Bishop issuing the licence, together with any stamps required by law.

[3] 1818 '1816'. Wright's Letter II, 17 November 1813 (*Morning Chronicle*, 20 November 1813).

CHURCH-OF-ENGLANDISM

holding two livings by dispensation, one with 500*l*. the other 400*l*. per annum;—the Incumbent lives 200 miles off, and has no resident or licensed Curate; nor has he thought it worth his notice to state to the Bishop, why he is Non-Resident according to 43 G. III. c. 84. §25, 26.'

On the subject of *Pluralism* and *Ultra-Pluralism* taken together, 'In one diocese,' (says *Mr. Wright*, Letter V. January [18th],[1] 1814),[2] 'in one diocese, there are about 216 Clergy, who each hold *two* livings; 40, who hold *three* each; 13, who hold *four* each; 1, who holds *five;* and 1, who holds *six*, besides *Dignities* and *Offices:* and although many of these, thus accounted *single* benefices, are two, three, four, or five Parishes *consolidated*, yet great part of these Pluralists do not reside in any of their preferments.'

The same Ultra-Pluralists are (it should seem) the persons whom Mr. Wright has in view when he asks (Letter IV. 3d Dec. 1813, Morning Chronicle),[3] 'How are these Pluralists to be returned in March next to his Majesty in Council? are they to be called resident in each living? If so, the list of Residents will appear very respectable: but it is not a new mode of increasing their numbers: or are they to be returned as excepted from the operations of the laws?'

'I will prove,' (says he, Letter VII. March 4th, 1814, Morning Chronicle),[4] 'I will prove that there are Pluralists holding more than *seven* benefices and dignities.'

In these cases of *Ultra-Pluralism*, whereabouts are the eyes of the *Archbishop*, when he grants, if so it be that he does grant, to one and the same person as many *dispensations, minus* one, as he has livings; and those of the *Bishop*, when he grants, if so it be that he does grant, to this same extra-meritorious person, the same number, or any part of the same number of *licenses*, viz. licenses for *Non-Residence*, including licenses for the same number of *Curates?* Here we have in one station the sin of *Ultra-Pluralism* (a sin the guilt of which is as real, as that of *Simony* is imaginary), in two other stations, the sin,—converted by the sanctity of the station into the virtue,—of connivance.

Number of these self-confessed inexcusable deserters of duty, A° 1809, no greater than 672; A° 1810, no greater than 650; A° 1811, swelled all at once to 1,033. In the increase—the great and sudden increase—thus acquired by the goodly fellowship of pretenceless truants, may be read the revelation of divers mysteries, by which all attempt at interpretation might otherwise have been set at nought. 1. '*Incumbents residing in the neighbourhood and doing duty*,' numbers shrunk from 565 (A° 1809) to 348! (A° 1810); and from 348 (A° 1810) to 301, A° 1811:—silence, where the same purpose may equally be accomplished by both, being in some eyes, and in some cases, more eligible than either rank mendacity, or an excuse irrelevant or insufficient upon the face of it:—2. 'Unenumerated cases, confirmed by the Archbishop, shrunk from 54 to 35, and from 35 to 26:'—thus much, besides the several other instances of contraction in less striking proportion, which a glance at the Table will bring to view, in the cases by which this case is preceded. Add to these the following out of those that follow it: 3. '*Sinecures, and Dignities not requiring Residence*,' number shrunk from 233 to 70! and from 70 to 68:—4. '*Livings held by Bishops*,' after an increase in one year from 26 to 35, shrunk from 35 to 21:—5. '*Recent Institutions*,' number from 54 (A° 1810) shrunk to 33:—6. '*Held by Sequestration*'—(an article of unpleasant aspect) number from 91 (A° 1810) shrunk to 78.

As to the '*Unenumerated cases*,'—as the two last of the above string of twelve cases

---

[1] 1818 '10th'.
[2] Wright's Letter V, 18 January 1814 (*Morning Chronicle*, 21 January 1814).
[3] Wright's Letter IV, 3 December 1813 (*Morning Chronicle*, 20 December 1813).
[4] Wright's Letter VII, 6 February 1814 (*Morning Chronicle*, 4 March 1814).

NOTES.

of license are styled—(not that any of the *others* have any *numbers* prefixed to them either in the *Act*, or in any one of the *Abstracts*)—as to these two cases of arch-licentiousness without a mask,—who, that felt aright the ground he stood upon, would lay 'understanding and will prostrate'[1] before his Bishop—his high-seated, and, except by accident, unknown and unknowing Bishop—much less, in the first place, before this Bishop, and then, in the event of this first sceptre's being held out to him, the still more highly and tremendously exalted Archbishop,—when, without any part of this compound of peril and humiliation, the same impunity might so easily be secured—secured by sitting still and silent?

Thus when, for giving allowance and increase to *Non-Residence*, the whole stock of excuses had been exhausted, so small a part of which, in the eyes of any one to whom salvation of souls were an object would, one should have thought, have been worth a straw,—the whole budget of the excuses, which so well exercised an invention as that of the Right Honourable and learned draughtsmen, assisted by all the experience and ingenuity of the host of reverend and other pious persons interested, could frame—and when even this was deemed not sufficient, without a power given to each Bishop with the concurrence of his Archbishop, and to the Archbishop without the concurrence of any body, to give allowance to this dereliction of sacred duty, in any case at pleasure, in which, after all the exercise thus given to experienced and interested ingenuity, not so much as the shadow of a pretence for it could be found,—after all this, in *connivance* was universally viewed, it thus appears, the surest, and to all parties (those excepted whose souls are at stake) the most convenient ground, on which this system, for the eradication of what little discipline, or regard for duty, might here and there have otherwise maintained its footing, could be erected.

Such, in itself and in its consequences—its natural (and *can* it be said its unforeseen or unintended?) consequences—is the *Act*, to which the *Right Honourable Sir William Scott*, by whom the Bill for it was brought in, has not scrupled to prefix the title of, '*An Act to amend*, &c. . . . . *and for enforcing the Residence of Spiritual Persons on their Benefices in England:*'—of the Most Reverend Fathers in God, the Archbishops—of the Right Reverend Fathers in the same God, the Bishops—divers concurring in, no one objecting to, the bestowing upon it this *same* instructive and memorable title.

^k [28. II.][2] {*Dilapidated Churches*, 23, 34, 56.} [29. III.][3] {*Sinecures and Dignities not requiring Residence*, [233],[4] 70, 68.} In one respect, these two classes of the 'Cases of Non-Residence which could *not* be included among Licenses or Exemptions,' possess a joint claim to notice. Such, in the Return for 1810, being the second of the three years, is the character ascribed to both of them,—well then—this same character, is it the character that was ascribed to them in the first of these same three years? Oh no: in the accounts of that year they are both of them placed under the general head of *Licenses*.

Amidst this contrariety of statement, how then stands the fact?—Is it that, in this first year 1809, by the respective Bishops, Licenses were granted to so many Incumbents for the alleged cause, that the Churches belonging to their respective Parishes were in a state of dilapidation? and to so many others, because[5] the Sinecures or Dignities of which they were respectively possessed, (the same being, all of them, Parochial Benefices) did not require Residence? If so, bold indeed were the hands by which, for any such causes, Licenses were signed: for of

---

[1] See p. 37 n. above.
[2] 1818 '13. I.'   [3] 1818 '14. II.'   [4] 1818 '33'.
[5] 1818 'became'. The text follows the 'Errata'.

451

CHURCH-OF-ENGLANDISM

neither of them is any, so much as the most distant, hint to be found in the Act:—in the only Law by which, on condition of *License*, allowance is given to *Non-Residence*.

Thus then must have falsehood existed somewhere: the only question is, where. An Incumbent, to whom his Bishop had not for any such cause granted a License, did he state himself, and to the Bishop himself, as having on this ground received a License? or, the framer of this Abstract for 1809, knowing that no such Return had been made, did he, viz. to the number which thus stands annext to the case, state such Returns to have been made?—If so, was it of his own motion, or at the suggestion of any, and what other person or persons that, by that Reverend Person, the false statement was thus made?—And so in the next case, viz. the case of *'Sinecures and Dignities not requiring Residence.'*

A propos of *Dilapidated Churches*.—If, to every Parish, *Residence* of a person thus replete with the Holy Ghost be—of itself, and independently of all duty done—so great a blessing,—how is it that (not to speak of *License*—*that*, as above, being plainly destitute of all ground)—how is it that, by a sort of *moral* title, *Exemption* comes to be allowed on the mere ground of the non-existence, or non-repair of the *Church* alone, so long as the *Parsonage* is not incapable of affording a lodging to the Holy Ghost?—The Church—it is not in the Church that, with this inmate in his breast, the man of God has his daily habitation. Destitute of these benefits, for the administering of which no place, other than that consecrated edifice called *the Church* could have been an allowable situation—deprived accordingly of the benefit of *direct* instruction,—the need which the Parishioners have of instruction by *example*—in a word, of whatsoever other benefits may be found derivable from this sanctifying Residence, is it not so much the more urgent?

To this, should he feel disposed to give it, the *Earl of Harrowby* might find his answer. It is not, he might say, by Excellent Church at large, that any such anxiety for the diminution of Non-Residence has ever been testified: no: with me, and the departed man of God, whose mantle I have upon my shoulders[1]—it is with the chosen band that on this ground have been acting along with us—it is in our breasts that all this anxiety took its rise: the Act commonly called the *Curates' Act*[2]—the Act in which this pious affection sought and has obtained relief—the Act for a ground for which this information was obtained,—it is *our* Act.

Good, for the *Earl of Harrowby*. But *Excellent Church*, in what sort of a plight does this defence place her *Excellency?*

In what sort of plight does it place those highly exalted persons behind the curtain, under whose direction these *Abstracts* were framed? In their judgment this case formed a class apart—a case which did *not* come under the last preceding case, intituled *'Absence without License or Exemption.'* It stands at the head of a list of cases, all which were, upon the face of them, understood to present a colour of justification: of justification in a *moral*, though not in a *legal* point of view.

Now as to the *numbers*—the numbers exhibited under each of these heads, in the three respective years:—as to this part, note well the amount of the draught made upon our faith.—First, as to *Dilapidated Churches*.—Anno 1809, of the Churches which, from the first erection of these sacred edifices, have fallen into this deplorable state, the whole number found remaining in it at the close of this year, no more than 23:—at the end of one single year more, viz. 1810, that number swelled to 34, almost half as many again; increase 11: next year, viz. 1811, number 56, increase 22; number of the increase doubled:—from these data, calculate—any person, to whom a calculation of this sort would afford amusement—at what Anno Domini England would be left without so much as a single Church in it.

---

[1] i.e. Perceval.   [2] i.e. 53 Geo. III, c. 149.

NOTES.

Next as to *Sinecures and Dignities not requiring Residence*. Note here that,—notwithstanding the word *Sinecures*, and the word *Dignities* substituted in some of these cases to the word *Sinecures*,—what may be averred without much danger of error is—that all these benefices are so many *parochial* benefices: benefices, i.e. masses of profit extracted out of the pockets of so many sets of parishioners, encumbered with so many of these holy persons, so properly styled *Incumbents:* if not, no place could they have had in these Returns. The case then must be—that, with the constantly operating and all-embracing benefit of Episcopal discipline, by persevering neglect of pastoral duty, fostered by Episcopal connivance, so many *Cures* of souls must have been improved into *Sinecures:* in these, as in other Parishes, the inhabitants paying for having their souls saved, and in these, as in other Parishes, no service to any such purpose performed:—no service—no, nor so much as the pretence and form of service.

Being then so many *Parochial Benefices*, these *Dignities*, how has it happened to them *not* to require Residence? Is it that these cases are so many cases of *Exemption?* Not they indeed:—if they had been, then of course under this or that one of the thirteen cases so intituled, would they not, every one of them, have thus been entered; leaving no matter to be placed under any such head as this. Is it that they are so many cases in which Licenses have been granted? Yes, says the Return for 1809: no, says the Return for 1810, and, after it, that for 1811.—Search all *Scotland* over, not one will you find of these Sinecures: as little any one of these *Dignities*. Visionary and fanatical are the notions entertained of *Dignity* by these schismatics! With them it consists in fulfilment of duty: not in idleness pampered by depredation. And, imbued with the same wild notions, need scarce be said, are all the *Non-Established Churches*.

Now, as to the numbers in the different years. Anno 1809, first year of these Returns, no fewer than 233. Comes the next year, 1810,—vanished are all but 70: *third* and last year, two more gone: remain at this time no more than 68. By these Returns, if Truth kept company with them, no bad service might thus be done: the best thing that, as to this matter, could happen, would in that case be—that *all* Parochial benefices should be Sinecures.

'*Where is your pretence for putting these cases under the head of Licenses?*'—by some such question, put by somebody, after the Return for 1809 had been made up, and before the Return for 1810 had been finally settled—by some such troublesome question, it seems to have been, that the difference between the 233 and the 70 was made to vanish. Meantime the 163 Sinecurists and Dignitaries, thus unmasked and dislodged, what became of them? In what other of all these lurking holes of *evasion* or *falsehood* did they take refuge? or was it in the last desperate resource, *silence?*—helpless and perilous silence?

ᵐ 30. IV. {*Livings held by Bishops*, 26, 35, 21.} See No. [14].[1] By every man by whom the pay attached to a Parochial Benefice is received,—he neither performing, nor so much as intending to perform, the duty, in consideration of which it is allotted to him,—so much money (when shall the occasions for the repetition of this position cease?) so much money as has been received by him, has been *obtained on a false pretence*. If the power given to Bishops had really among its objects the *salvation of souls*, and thence the causing that *instruction* to be received by the people, for the administering of which the *pay* is appointed, among the first of these objects, in the order of necessity, would surely have been—the taking care, that,—while, for want of sufficient pay to an instructor, there were a fellowship of individuals, to whom that instruction could not be administered,—there should not be any person, on whom, in

---

[1] 1818 '13'. 1818 then adds '30. IV.', which seems redundant.

CHURCH-OF-ENGLANDISM

consequence of, and as it were in recompense for, the false pretence of rendering such instruction, any such money should be bestowed.

Not content with conniving at this mixture of rapacity and mendacity in others—not content with conniving at immorality in this double shape—here, out of the whole number of Bishops and Archbishops, viz. 26, here may be seen a large, probably the greater, proportion, practising it themselves for their own benefit.

Number of livings held by Bishops, as per Returns, Anno 1809, 26: Anno 1810, 35: Anno 1811, 21: all of them stated as cases of Non-Residence: and therefore cases in which no duty is performed, in return for whatever money is thus received. Here, in the first of these three years, the number of masses of pay received upon this false pretence, is exactly equal to the number of the Right Reverend Lords by whom in this way they are respectively received: here then, if so it were that they received, each of them, what, upon an equal division, would be his part in the plunder, here would be exactly as many 'miserable' and habitual 'sinners'[1] in this shape, as there are self-pretended receivers of the power of giving to others the power of forgiving sins. In many instances, indeed, so enormous are the masses of pay attached to these disguised half-sinecures, which would be so highly improved by being turned into undisguised and complete ones—that in these instances no such appendage is ever added. But, the total number of the masses thus obtained being given,—the less any one Bishop has, the more there is which remains for some other or others of these propagators, as well as receivers of the Holy Ghost.

Another curious enough circumstance is—that, while in the first of the three years the number of livings stated as thus held is but 26, and in the last of them but 21; in the second of them no less is it than 35. One thing is certain, viz. that in no instance would a living, *not* held by a Bishop, be stated as being held by any such Right Reverend and grasping hands: whereas, nothing is more easy than that in any numbers they should be *actually* so held, without being *returned* as being so held. If, to any such plain questions as these which have been seen, a Bishop cannot or will not obtain an answer, from an Incumbent who is nothing higher than a *subordinate*, much less will he, or can he from a *brother Bishop*. Among the holy persons,—by each of whom, of the money paid in a parish, for the salvation of the souls belonging to it, a good nine-tenths was pocketed, while the business is turned over to any underling that will undertake the job for the remaining tenth,—*Salvation of souls*, forsooth!—what a jest must it not have been in such a company? Ah! *quantum nobis profuit ista de Christo fabula!*[2]

One Bishop check misconduct in another Bishop! As well might you expect to see a Judge occupied in striking off the amount of a law expense, which would have gone into his own or a brother Judge's pocket.

Yes, *that* it does:—the principle, upon and by which this accommodation is provided and secured, presents an irresistible claim to notice. Under the allied Excellencies, scarcely will you find any where a high, and as the phrase is, responsible office, in which matters are not so arranged, that if a man misbehaves in it, and in particular if he commits waste or depredation in it, so it is that in the

---

[1] See p. 224 n. above.

[2] This remark is attributed to Pope Leo X by his secretary Cardinal Pietro Bembo (1470–1547), in John Bale, *Acta Romanorum Pontificum*, Basel, 1558, Liber VII, no. 163, p. 382, where it is given as *Quantum nobis ac nostro cœtui profuerit ea de Christo fabula, satis est seculis omnibus notum*, and in translation (by John Studley) in John Bale, *The Pageant of Popes, Contayninge the lyves of all the Bishops of Rome, from the beginninge of them to the yeare of Grace 1555*, London, 1574, Bk. VII, no. 163, p. 179^v, as 'All ages can testifie enough howe profitable that fable of Christe hath ben to us and our companie'.

NOTES.

tribunal, which has cognizance of his offence, one seat is secured to the delinquent, and the others are occupied by men, who being sharers with him in the same sinister interest and fellow-feeling, would, in case of punishment, or *restraint* imposed upon him, be in some way or other his fellow-sufferers. Is he a Lord of the Treasury? Is he a Lord of the Admiralty?—A seat he must have, either in the House of Lords, by which,—or in the House of Commons, at the instance of which,—if tried, he must be tried. Is he a Welsh Judge, a Master in Chancery, or a Master of the Rolls, the House of Commons is open to him. Is he head Judge of International Law?[1] is he head Judge of Ecclesiastical Law?[2] the same Honourable House is open to him, and never fails to receive him. Is he at the head of the Criminal Law?[3]—that to any amount, through other names, he may to his own use receive the plunder of the prisoner and the distressed—that to this and all other purposes the very idea of responsibility may be excluded, and despotism made perfect, he is regularly and constantly seated in the only tribunal in which he can be tried.[4] Is he Chancellor? that all remedy to the abuses, by which he and his confederates profit, may be hopeless, he not only *sits in* that same judicatory, but *governs* it.[5]

Judica teipsum[6] (in the story told by *Blackstone*, out of the *year Book*) said the Cardinals to the sinning Pope, who, in compliance with so polite an invitation, after judging himself, condemned himself to be burnt, and, being burnt accordingly, was burnt into a *saint*.[7] The *judica-teipsum principle*—be this then the name of that all-extensively and all-efficiently ruling principle, which, under the allied Excellencies, is so little spoken of, so universally and effectually acted upon,—and of which the convenience and the security it affords are so well felt and understood in confidential situations.

In the instance here in question, thanks to this same *judica-teipsum* principle, such is the state of the sort of tool called *Parliament*, that, in the last but one of the spiritually reforming Acts, passed in the reign of his present Most Excellent Majesty, (43 G. III. c. 84.) may be seen, in so many words, the clause or section following:—
'XLI. And to the intent *to avoid all doubts*, be it enacted, that no *Archbishop* or Bishop having, or who shall have any Dignity, Prebend, Benefice, Donative, or *perpetual Cure*, shall, by reason of *Non-Residence* upon the same, be subject or liable to any penalties or forfeitures.' Under the thus anxiously craved shelter of this clause, conceive now an Archbishop,—with his 20,000*l.* a year, or his 14,000*l.* a year, besides his patronage,[8]—fastening upon a Curacy, and pilfering it of a part of the pence belonging to it!—Yes: *impunity* they have got: but what have they got along with it? the word is present to every eye: it begins with the same letter, and need not be completed.

Now,—if the service, the performance of which the system of discipline pretends to secure, were of any use, or the discipline were in any other respects capable of operating with any effect,—let it be imagined on what ground, in case of delinquency in any shape, in the breast of an Incumbent with lawn sleeves to his gown, any such apprehension could be entertained, as that of experiencing either punishment or

---

[1] i.e. of the Court of Admiralty.
[2] i.e. Dean of the Arches (the judge of the Archbishop of Canterbury's Prerogative Court sitting in St Mary-le-Bow).
[3] i.e. Chief Justice of King's Bench. [4] i.e. the House of Lords.
[5] The Lord Chancellor was *ex officio* Speaker of the House of Lords.
[6] i.e. 'judge yourself'.
[7] See Blackstone, *Commentaries on the Laws of England*, iii. 301 n. The story of the Cardinals and the Pope was retold in an action of trespass brought by Thomas Chase, Chancellor of the University of Oxford, against himself in 1430.
[8] For the incomes of the Archishops of Canterbury and York see p. 409 n. above.

CHURCH-OF-ENGLANDISM

check, at the hands of a Right Reverend brother, sitting on the same bench and arrayed in the same robes?

With these sleeves on his arm,—and his 20,000*l*. a year, or his 14,000*l*. a year for keeping them washed,—conceive a man taking the pay of one of these Curacies, with the pretence of doing the whole duty of it on his lips, and in his heart the determination not to do any part of it; and thus pocketing the best part of the pence belonging to it. Conceive, at the same time, on pretence of taking in to wash these same symbols of purity, a woman, who had obtained a pair of them, selling them and going off with the money? Is there a *fifth clause* provided for her security? Would she be safe? Not she indeed: no license for swindling in that shape. No license for it in any shape to any of the swinish multitude.[1]—Shut up in one of the gaols would the swindling washer-woman be, or shipped off to one of the *Penal Colonies*.

Well now, after all the anxiety shewn, as above, and pains taken accordingly, in this Act of 1803, *to avoid 'all doubts,'* yet so it is, that, at the distance of above five years after the administering of this opiate, viz. in the year 1809, being the first year of these *Returns*, and thereafter in the years 1810 and 1811, *doubts*,—wheresoever bred, perhaps on that same sacred bench, perhaps on the neighbouring wool-sack,[2]—swarmed as much as ever. *Exemptions* is the head under which the case of *'Livings held by Bishops'* figures in the first of these three years: yet, some how or other, spite of this doubt-dispelling clause, when the Returns come to be given in for the next year 1810, this ground was regarded as being no longer tenable. Under what general head was it then ranked? Under that of 'CASES *which could not be included*' (thus peremptory is the language) *'among* LICENSES *or* EXEMPTIONS:' and, in the next of the three years comprised in these revelations, the same melancholy conviction still continued. By the 41st clause impunity was indeed given: but, some how or other, under the circumstances of the case,—this case of *Livings held by Bishops* being too scandalous to have found admission even into the original Act—the Act of Henry the Eighth,—simple impunity had come to be regarded as not quite sufficient for the purpose.

This vacillation in opinions, is it in this that we are to look for the already above-remarked variation in the numbers of the three successive years? Anno 1809, *twenty-six*, and no greater, the number of these who could muster up courage enough to declare, that their case is of the number of those which are to be seen on the list of Exemptions. In the next year 1810, a class of cases being established, under the acknowledged description of 'Cases which could *not* be included among Licenses or Exemptions,' all twenty-six now with one voice joined in the confession of their former sins, and to these six-and-twenty miserable sinners[3] were now added *nine* others, whom the shame, so well suited to their condition, had prevented from claiming an exemption, the title to which had been disallowed by conscience. Thus much as to the two first of these three years. Comes the last, and now,—out of the thirty-five, or whatever greater number was the real one,—twenty-one, and no more, abide by this self-condemning statement, all the rest seeking refuge along with the horde of delinquent Incumbents, in a declaredly penal and palpably unjustifiable silence.

Mark here another trait in the policy of the high Allies. For thus super-over-fattening these already overfattened idlers in reality, labourers only in appearance,—avowed Sinecures—benefices without Cure of Souls—could not be spared: these were wanted for other purposes. In each instance, that one *body* might be thus

---

[1] This phrase was used by Edmund Burke (1730–97) in *Reflections on the Revolution in France* (first published 1790) to describe the poor: see *The Writings and Speeches of Edmund Burke. Vol. VIII: The French Revolution 1790–1794*, ed. L.G. Mitchell and W.B. Todd, Oxford, 1989, p. 130.

[2] See p. 448 n. above.

[3] See p. 224 n. above.

NOTES.

pampered, *souls* by hundreds were thus accordingly to be put to spare diet, and (for such is all along the supposition built upon and acted upon) that diet of inferior quality;—of no better than the breath of *Curates:* and, out of those who, but for this usurpation, might at least,—and (if the parsonage happened to be elegant and pleasantly situated) would perhaps—have been Residents, the number of Non-Residents was thus augmented.

God, it is evident, was not thus served for nought.[1] A Deanery, for example, could not have come but out of the treasury of Court favour and Crown influence. But a fat Living, derived from some inferior and private source, might, peradventure, be already in the possession of the man of God, upon whose refusing shoulders the super-sacred lawn was predestinated to be forced: in this way, while pious *merit* was rewarded, the dictates of no less pious *economy* were at the same time observed: and, how high and sincere the regard was that was paid to that useful virtue, let any one judge, from the magnitude of the scandal to which, for the benefit of thus giving increase to it, their allied Excellencies scrupled not to expose themselves.

So true is it, that, under those High Allies, so far as concerns the predatory class of offences, not to speak of others, punishment is for that malefactor alone, whose offence is upon a small scale: impunity, security, and dignity, for him whose offence is upon the largest scale. And in the excellent feature thus common to both Excellencies may be seen what the attachment of so large a part of their admirers and supporters has for its *'fundamental feature.'*[2]

Under an absolute Monarchy there is but one licensed depredator; and, forasmuch as what in this way is taken *by* others is so much taken *from* him, it is his care,—in so far as to his political power he adds intellectual and active personal power adequate to the task,—to reduce to its minimum their respective shares. But, under this mixed monarchy, in the state to which it has been brought, to the quantity of the matter of *wealth* thus devoured by the arch-depredator must be, and is added a quantity of the same precious matter, to be employed in the shape of matter of *corruption*, to purchase, by the possession or the prospect of it, at the hands of the self-styled Trustees of the People, by whomsoever appointed,—and of individuals, governed by an interest separate from and adverse to that of the people,—the habitual breach of their acknowledged trust: and hence the notion, so studiously propagated, and, among those who behold their profit in it, so cordially embraced, that constant and almost universal corruption is of the essence of the constitution,—that, spite of the proof given by the *American United States* to the contrary, government cannot be carried on by any other than corrupted hands,—and that, to substitute uncorruption to corruption, would be to substitute anarchy to government.

ⁿ {31. V. *Vacancies;* 0, 74, 96.} On one account this head may be worth notice, viz. as being perhaps the only one of these thirty-three heads by which, in some just shape or other, reproach is not cast upon the system by which they are furnished. For the preceding year 1812, eleven is the number of vacancies, which the *Edinburgh Almanack* of the year 1813 exhibits in the 933 parochial benefices of the Scottish Church:[3] in this *one* particular is the proportion between the two Churches not marked by any difference, greater than that which in such a case might be expected to be made by the hand of chance.

---

[1] An echo of Genesis 29: 15.

[2] For Bentham's use of the phrases 'fundamental principle' and 'fundamental truth' see pp. 397 n., 428 above respectively.

[3] See the *Edinburgh Almanack, and Imperial Register, for 1813*, Edinburgh, [1812], pp. 143–61. Bentham refers to the *Edinburgh Almanack for 1812*, reckoning 944 benefices, at p. 481 n. below.

CHURCH-OF-ENGLANDISM

⁰ {32. VI. *Recent Institutions;* 0, 54, 33.} Of this locution the import may perhaps not be apparent to every eye at first glance. *Institution,* coupled with *Induction,* being the ecclesiastical term employed to designate the taking possession of the benefice: the intimation meant to be conveyed by these words appears to be—that, in each of these instances, the Incumbent having so recently come into possession, had not as yet had *time* sufficient to make the necessary preparations for his residence. But, supposing a man to have had no legal cause of allowance for Non-Residence,—no legal title to exempt him from the obligation of doing his duty,—and at the same time determined *not* to do it, rather than appear without excuse, what he would of course do is—to lay hold of this circumstance, and out of it make an excuse referable to this head. Under the above-mentioned head of *Infirmity of Incumbent* or Family, Mr. Wright has shewn how easily and frequently, under a friendly Bishop, a case of *infirmity* may, from an acute, be improved into a chronical case:[1] and to a case of *Recent Institution,* under the like auspices, the like convenient extension need not be despaired of.

ᵖ {33. VII. *Held by Sequestration:* 0, 91, 78.} Principally, if not exclusively, the individual cases included under this specific head will have been cases, in which the Incumbent being *insolvent,* possession, at the instance of some creditor or creditors, had been taken of the benefice, to raise money for the discharge of the debt. Only by Church-of-Englandism could such a class of cases have been furnished. Under the Church of Scotland no such remedy has place. Why? because, under that Established Church, no *demand* for it has ever been known to have place. On the part of a Church of Scotland Parish Priest, supposing insolvency even to have place, the object upon which the remedy would attach would be his *person;* and as to *property,* his *private* property, and not his *benefice.*

ᑐ {34. VIII. *Miscellaneous Cases not included in the preceding Classes:* 0, 38, 51.} In this may be seen another very convenient niche, well adapted to the purpose of serving as a lurking hole to an individual case that would not bear description.

Note, that of these eight cases, styled '*Cases which could not be included among Licenses or Exemptions,*' the two only ones which have place in the Return for the *first* year, viz. 1809, are that of '*Absence without License or Exemption,*' and that of '*Livings held by Bishops.*'[2] But, in the Return for 1809, we have a general head, denominated MISCELLANEOUS CASES, and the number subjoined to it as high as 1250.[3] Under this general head will of course have been included in that year the individual cases designated by the six particular heads added in the years 1810 and 1811.[4] In the Returns for the years 1810 and 1811, the numbers under these six particular cases are no more than, for the year 1810, 361; for the year 1811, [382];[5] corresponding to the number 1271 in the year 1809, will, in the year 1810, be 1011;[6] and, in the year 1811, 403.[7] Compare these numbers with the number for the year 1809, viz. 1271. Here we have another instance to add to the variations brought to view under Note (¹) p. 450.—

Thus,—wheresoever, for the accomplishment of the prime object of Excellent Church, viz. *pay without service,* there was any thing in the case that seemed to afford so much as the faintest shadow of a pretence,—the budget of pretences, vast and shameless as it was, not being yet large enough for a demand altogether insatiable,—which, having been established by the Act of *Henry the Eighth* has now been

---

[1] See p. 443 n. above.   [2] i.e. nos. 27 and 30 on the Table at p. 441 above.
[3] See *Commons Sessional Papers* (1812) x. 160–1, where the figure is given as 1271, as Bentham states below.
[4] i.e. nos. 28–9, 31–4.   [5] 1818 '401'.
[6] i.e. nos. 27–9, 31–4.   [7] i.e. nos. 28–34.

NOTES.

distinguished by the name of EXEMPTIONS; a place (we see) was found for it among the contents of the new budget now established under *George the Third*, for this same pious purpose, under the head of *Licenses*. Yet even this—we see how far it was from being sufficient:—for of the three successive years, the Returns give, as Cases of *Absence without License or Exemption*, for the year 1809, 672: for 1810, 650; for 1811, no fewer than 1,033. Such was the number of the instances, in which, upon the face of this statement, the inexecution of the laws, and, consequently, the inefficiency of the system of discipline employed for giving execution to them, stands demonstrated.

The last, of the three successive years respecting which these Returns had been exacted, was of course the year in which it might be expected, that, by the new and additional instrument of discipline, consisting in the call thus made for these notifications, its utmost effect would have been produced. Yet, in these last of the three years, the number of these *pretenceless* instances of dereliction of duty is more than half as great again as in either of the two preceding years: it amounts to more than *one-sixth* of the whole number of cases of absence.

In all these several particulars, had the Returns, furnished by these Bishops, exhibited marks of the most perfect accuracy, it would not have followed that to any useful purpose discipline was maintained by them; or that in that, or any other respect, this order of men was of any the smallest use. But,—forasmuch as to these shepherds of the professed shepherds of souls, their immediately subject flock, composed mostly of wolves in sheep's clothing, were, generally speaking, personally, as well as in every other particular, unknown,—thus it is that, generally speaking, no sort of care of them can they have been in use to take.

In these several documents, under whatever heads the matter of abuse may be found exhibited, thus much should all along be borne in mind, viz. that, in respect of *quantity*, the representation thus given cannot possibly have gone *beyond* the truth, but may, to an indefinite amount have fallen *short* of it.

§8. *Ulterior Information from Mr. Wright.*

Thus far the ground we have been treading upon is sure:—Acts of Parliament and official documents. For the ulterior lights which follow, we must, in the first instance, content ourselves with the authority of the above-mentioned *Mr. Wright*, whose opportunities of information have at any rate been unquestionable. If not themselves in any instance conclusive evidence, to any one who to the power adds the wish to bring to light any such completely satisfactory evidence, they may at any rate serve to furnish subjects for inquiry. In favour of their verity an universally applying and notorious article of *circumstantial* evidence applies: in the face of Excellent Church have they been standing now for about these three years, and not in all this time, in any instance, has denial been from any quarter opposed to them.

In the manufacture of Parochial Sinecurism has already been seen one of the capital objects of Church-of-England policy. Of the nature of Exemption and License, and the use made of those two chief instruments in the carrying on of that valuable branch of manufacture, a conception sufficiently correct and extensive for the purpose has already, it is hoped, been conveyed. Of the nature and virtue of *connivance*, a conception could not have been rendered quite so clear from the *Abstracts* alone, as it will, it is believed, be found to have been rendered by those same Abstracts, elucidated by the explanations, for which we are indebted to the quondam Diocesan Secretary.

Connivance supposes *delinquency:* in its import the word bears an implied reference to delinquency in some shape or other, towards which this sort of countenance is shewn: the person by whom it is shewn being a person, in whose hands, for the prevention of such delinquency, power has been placed,—instead of employing it to that end, he connives at the delinquency: while it is staring him in the face, he keeps his eyes shut, that he may have to say he has not seen it.

Diminishing Non-Residence being the *declared* object of the system of legislation and administration pursued, giving *increase* to it, as hath been seen, the *real* object,—the instrumental and subservient modes of delinquency, towards which the *conniving eyes* will be turned, will be those, the object and tendency of which is to give increase to it. In the present case, relation being had to certain inquiries, having for their object the exposure and proof of the *principal* delinquency, viz. *Non-Residence,*—the two *instrumental* and subservient modes of delinquency here in question are, as

APPENDIX, NO. IV. §VIII.

above observed, *False Responsion*, in the present case *False Notification;* and *Non-Responsion*, in this same case, *Non-Notification*. By *true Responsion*—by *true Notifications*—the principal delinquency would, in the cases in question, be confessed: therefore, by Notification in this shape, the forbidden purpose could not be effected. By *Non-Notification*, the party so transgressing would, in a direct way, expose himself to the penalties, such as they are, which have been provided: this, therefore, is not the *immediate*, but the *last* resource. The immediate and most promising resource is *False Notification*. For, by this expedient, unless and until the falsity shall have been discovered, the principal delinquency remains concealed from view. Now, if matters be so ordered, that, in each instance of delinquency, in no more than one hand can the necessary union, of *power* with *adequate inducement*, and thence with *inclination*, be found,—while, in the breast of the only person, whose *power* is adequate to the purpose, *adequate inducement* is generally *wanting*,—the consequence is—that, as often as it is so, *connivance* will be the state of the eyes, with which delinquency, in the desired shape in question, is regarded by him,—and the delinquency will as constantly be safe.

From the nature of the Episcopal situation it will be seen, that, in the state of things in question, towards delinquency in the shape in question, a general habit of connivance might naturally have been expected and depended upon: from the disclosure made by the *Abstracts* it will in a general way be seen, that, to a vast extent, such connivance cannot but have been manifested. In the statements made by *the Diocesan Secretary*, individual instances, and other evidences of such connivance, will be visible.

First, as to the general probability. In and by this pretendedly reforming Act, (43 G. III. c. 84.) followed up and supported by the other Act, of a ten years' later date, (53 G. III. c. 149.)[1] power being given to the *Bishops*, in their respective Dioceses, under the declared design of their enforcing the ordinances of the law,—despotism, and that without any exception worth regarding, in the purest and most perfect character,—is the shape in which, as already observed, that power has been conferred. In that part of the field of action which has been marked out by these two Acts, wheresoever delinquency has place, the Bishop is free to punish and repress it if he pleases:—he is equally free to leave it unpunished, and thus to authorize and encourage it, if he pleases. Wheresoever the latter is his pleasure, *connivance*, as hath been seen, is the name of the means, by which the desired effect is produced.

[1] i.e. the Non-Resident Clergy Act of 1803 and the Curates Act of 1813.

That, of the unbridled liberty, put into the hands of the mitred despot by this despotism, a general habit of connivance, towards delinquency in the shape in question, cannot but be the result,—will be sufficiently manifest to every eye, by which the state of *interests* in this part of the field of action is contemplated. That, throughout the whole of the Establishment, *pay* should be *maximized*,—on the other hand, *labour* and *inconvenience*, in every other shape, *minimized*,—is the particular interest common to every individual who has a place in it. Of the doing, otherwise than under the spur of the most cogent necessity, any thing by which either of these two so intimately connected objects may be counteracted,—the effect, on the part of a Bishop, or any other person, to whose office the duty of enforcing the laws is nominally attached,—will be, in the first place, to hurt that common particular and sinister interest in which he has so large a share; in the next place, to expose him to the ill-will of every individual, and of the connexions of every individual, whose individual interest is in a particular manner made to suffer by the act of coercive power so exercised.

Imagination cannot figure to itself a case, in which, unless by accident (of which presently) the indulgence given by such connivance, should not, on the part of every individual, in that so perniciously exalted and arbitrarily disposing situation, be of the two opposite lines of conduct the only one that can rationally be expected. True it is, that, at all times, among persons in such a number, situated in such a rank of life, some one or other small number may naturally be looked for, in whose breasts more or less of real regard for the professed ends of the establishment has place. But, even in these instances, no reasonable expectation of a conduct, different in this behalf from that of the majority, can reasonably be entertained. Strange, indeed—strange and not reasonably expectable in such a situation—must be any such blindness, as should prevent a man from seeing, that,—while, by the giving execution to the laws, individual *suffering*, in no small quantity, cannot but be produced,—it is not in the nature of the case that *real good* should in any shape be accomplished. Thus, even in the most generous as well as enlightened mind, sympathy—*social affection*—will be operating on the side of particular interest,—and connivance and indulgence, on the one part, impunity on the other, will be the general result.[a]

[a] To take any thing like an exact measure, of the whole of the field which may be seen to afford room for connivance—to make up any thing like a complete account of the classes of cases looking up to the Episcopal palace for conniving mercy—would be no easy task: under any of those general heads, to attempt to discover the individual instance in which so virtuous a vice had manifested itself, would be an

APPENDIX, NO. IV. §VIII.

altogether impracticable one. For a general conception, the following sketch may serve:[1]

	INDIVIDUAL CASES, in Years		
	1809.	1810.	1811.
1. Absence without License or Exemption	672	650	1,033
2. Residence on other Benefices	1,240	1,846	2,059
3. Exemptions not notified	817	363	155
4. Infirmity of Incumbent or Family	465	389	396
5. Want or Unfitness of Parsonage-House	944	[941][2]	1,068
6. Incumbents residing in the Neighbourhood, and doing Duty	565	348	301
7. Unenumerated cases, confirmed by the Archbishops	54	35	26
8. Dilapidated Churches	23	34	56
9. Sinecures and Dignities not requiring Residence	233	70	68
10. Livings held by Bishops	26	35	21
11. Recent Institutions	0	54	33
12. Miscellaneous Cases	1,271	38	51
Totals open to Connivance, viz. as towards *Non-Notification* and *False Notification*	6,310	4,903	5,268
Totals of Non-Residents	7,358	5,840	6,311
Totals of Residents	3,836	4,421	4,490
Totals of Residents and Non-Residents together	11,194	10,261	10,801

N.B. The three last totals are here given for the purpose of shewing the respective *proportions* between them and the first.

Of all these articles, the most curious one seems to be that which has for its title, *Exemptions not notified*. The grounds of indemnity so sure—the notification of it so simple and so easy, yet no notification made!—the Bishop,—at whose hands, if at any, and at whose hands alone, punishment, in case of the non-existence of any such exemption, could, if in any case, be seriously apprehended,—ready at all times to receive every such notification: yet, in the several years, by no one of all this prodigious number of thus wantonly tran[s]gressing men of God, any notification made. In so many hundreds of instances,—the party, whose safety is at stake upon the evidence, never troubles his head about the matter: the Judge—*he* it is who, at his own instance, is at the pains of collecting this exculpatory evidence: no man in this Utopia cares any thing for himself; the Judge—the Judge—and he alone it is, that cares for every body. All this while, whence is it that he can have come by his knowledge of the fact—this so unprecedently indulgent Judge? The exemption that has '*not*' been '*notified*'—(for such in all these instances is expressly declared to be the case)—how is it that he has come to the knowledge of it?—Ænigma upon ænigma! Mystery upon mystery!

The solution, is it, peradventure, this?—for no other can be found. Conscious of his not having in any shape any allowance for his Non-Residence—satisfied all the while that on no such account will harm in any shape happen to him—there sits the holy Sinecurist in perfect composure,—not making any notification, nor ever troubling his head about the matter. On the other hand, the *Bishop*, conceiving

---

[1] The following table presents a summary of the 'Abstract of Returns respecting Non-Residence' at pp. 440–1 above.   [2] 1818 '943'.

the reputation of Holy Church to be more or less concerned—the *Bishop* it is—who, in each instance, takes upon himself the pious task of supplying the deficiency, and,—from the circumstance of the non-production of any ground of exemption, inferring the existence of a proper one,—gives accordingly in this way his attestation of the fact.

Of the two modes of delinquency, viz. Non-Responsion and False Responsion, brought into action by the nature of the system,—for the sake of clearness it may perhaps be worth while, in the above list of cases, to endeavour to distinguish which it is that has place,—and thence, in case of *Episcopal connivance*, which it is that is the *object* of the connivance. Of these cases, two present themselves as being, upon the face of them, cases of *Non-Responsion*, viz. by *Non-Notification:* these are, *Absence without License or Exemption*, and *Exemptions not notified:* the rest as being,—in so far as delinquency in the principal shape, viz. unjustifiable Non-Residence, with or without Ultra-Pluralism, has place,—cases of *False Responsion*, viz. by *False Notification.*

In the case of *Exemptions not notified*,—if the only conceivable account of the matter be, as above, the true one,—then so it is, that in the instances, which, in the several years 1810 and 1811, gave rise to Non-Notification on the part of *Incumbents*,—not only *connivance*, viz. as towards transgression in this shape,—but *Falsehood*, committed by a *False* Return, knowingly made to the Head of the Church in Council,—was the fruit, on the part of *Bishops*.

If then, on the part of an English Bishop, reputation for veracity were worth maintaining, here would be an occasion for maintaining it: if, in that same holy quarter, exemption from the imputation of mendacity were worth securing, here would be an occasion for securing it. But, on the part of these consecrated persons, is any such reputation regarded as worth maintaining? Among so many manifestations, common to all, let the practice of the University of Oxford, in regard to the constantly and universally violated oaths, promising obedience to the Statutes—let the practice, of such of them as have been trained to holiness in that perjury hot-bed, speak:[1]—suppose them all, without exception, not merely *perjurers notorious*, but *perjurers convict*, who is it that would care? Would *Excellent Church* be the *less* Excellent? Not she indeed, but, contrariwise, the *more* Excellent. To out-vociferate the cry of *Corruption*,—the greater the demand for vociferation, the religious world would ring but the louder with the cry of *Excellence:* the more completely and more notoriously dry-rotten the whole fabric, the more money would be called for—called for by the united voices of the living Saints, and the ghosts of the departed ones—for the support of it.[2]

Behold now the comparison.—Under Church-of-Scotlandism, or in all Scotland, anno 1811, as in every year, total number of beneficed Clergymen, (of whom not one Non-Resident, not one Sinecurist, much less one delinquent Sinecurist) 944.[3] Under Church-of-Englandism, anno 1811, and thence by the latest divulged accounts,—self-confessing, openly transgressing, incorrigible, and authoritatively reported delinquents,—Non-Residents, Sinecurists, Pluralists, and Ultra-Pluralists together, in the shape of Incumbents,—absent, i.e. Non-Resident without License or Exemption, 1,033; besides to the number of 155 others, whose Exemptions,—most likely falsely pretended,—remained, whether truly or falsely supposed to exist, unnotified: the Act, by which such notification had for form sake been required,[4] being thus treated by them with the contempt so justly due to it:—the contempt which, from beginning

---

[1] See p. 34 & n. above.   [2] For the 'saints' see pp. 219–21 above.
[3] For Bentham's calculation of this figure see p. 481 n. below.
[4] i.e. the Non-Resident Clergy Act of 1803.

APPENDIX, NO. IV. §VIII.

That, of the general and regularly established system of connivance, an occasional and particular suspension, howsoever rare, is not altogether out of the nature of the case, has already been observed. Two *causes*, and two causes alone, present themselves as adequate to [t]he production of such an effect.

One is, on the part of the mitred despot, particular *ill-will* or *adverse interest*, as towards this or that particular delinquent. Of this first case, however, were instances ever so abundant, scarcely through any channel, on any occasion, or in any way, could any such be brought to light, much less in such a work as the present, in which no individual security for correctness can be afforded. But, by the very nature of the case, all possibility of proof—of completely conclusive proof at any rate—is precluded.—Let the conduct of the despot take which of the two opposite directions it will,—*Virtue*, in some shape or other, is always at hand to furnish it with an efficient cause. Is it connivance? the virtue is *Tender Mercy*:[1] is it restraint or punishment? the virtue is Love of Justice, or in one word, *Justice*. Sir Hudibras, such was his eloquence,

> 'could not ope
> 'His mouth, but out there flew a trope.'[2]

In Fairy Land, princesses are upon record, whose mouths could not open, but a still more substantially brilliant produce, composed of pearls, rubies, and diamonds, was the result. In the English hierarchy those exaggerations of fiction are every day left behind. A Church of England Bishop can neither shut his eyes nor open them, act or forbear to act, do something or do nothing, but out springs some virtue out of the consecrated bosom. When in the secret recesses of his palace, he is occupied in determining the lot of sinning Incumbents, *Mercy* (it has been seen) and *Justice*—are the virtues which court his choice. When in the House of Lords, seated on the sacred Bench, he lifts up his holy eyes to heaven,—he beholds on the right hand *Gratitude*, on the left hand *Patriotism*. But *Gratitude* having *Hope* for her support, it is only the leavings of this Patrician that are picked up now and then by the Plebeian Virtue. The object of *Gratitude* is embodied in the person of the earthly and living Monarch, Vice-gerent and express image of the

to end, it was not only formed, but intended to provoke. Add, to these authoritatively declared and authoritatively protected delinquents, the other, and probably greater part, composed of undeclared and undiscoverable, and still more carefully and effectually protected delinquents, as above.

---

[1] An echo of Luke 1: 78; James 5: 11.
[2] Samuel Butler, *Hudibras*, Pt. I, Canto 1, 81–2.

heavenly one: poor *Patriotism* has for her support no better an image than that of the many-headed monster, ycleped the *Swinish Multitude*.[1]

Of the other cause,—being that which operates, in the case, in which, for the interest of the whole system, and of all that fatten upon it, a sacrifice is understood to be necessitated,—one example presents itself to every eye.—In the Tragi-comedy of the *Curates' Act* has been seen, and will be seen again, the Noble Reformer, in the character of Arch-Sacrificator, sacrificing to Excellent Church a holocaust of Incumbents, to make a feast for Curates.

By this explanation we are prepared for the exemplifications which have been given of divers ulterior corruptions by the Diocesan Secretary:—corruptions in themselves more or less different, but all of them flowing from one common source.[a]

[a] On the subject of *connivance*, and thereupon of veracity and sincerity, the following home-questions, addressed to the Archbishops and Bishops, appeared in the Morning Chronicle of 27th Nov. 1813: no notice, in print, it is believed, was ever taken of them by any body:

'1. Will the Archbishops and Bishops, in general, or any of them, say, that they ever corresponded candidly with each other about any individual case, to ascertain whether they were imposed on or not?

'2. Will they severally say, that the whole of the persons returned by them as licensed, were at that time actually so?

'3. Will they, or any of them, say, that the whole of the persons returned as Resident, even resided within their respective parishes?

'4. Will any of them say, that the whole number, which each of them returned as exempt, made their Notifications?

'5. And were not all the Bishops desired by the Archbishops, under an Order of the Privy Council, to return those as not notified who had so neglected to send Notifications?'

'In the same diocese' (says Mr. Wright, Jan. 6th, 1814),[2] 'twenty-eight licenses have been granted, because "the house is unfit;" eighteen of these benefices had formerly fit houses; and, as the favourite motto of churchmen is, *Nullum tempus occurrit Ecclesiæ*,[3] they ought to be so now; and seven are unfit because they are let.... Two of the twelve had, by being consolidated, two parsonage-houses each. One Incumbent obtained a License by stating that he was Vicar of ———, and that he had no parsonage-house on his said Vicarage. He was correct, for he has none on his Vicarage, but it is on the Chapelry, which has been, time immemorial, annexed to it! He was instituted previous to the 43 G. III. and took the oath to reside, and had no License for the Residence till after that Act passed.

'The late Honourable Dr. Yorke, Bishop of Ely,'[4] (says the same Mr. Wright, March 11th, 1814)[5] 'on receiving False Returns from some of his Clergy on these

---

[1] See p. 456 n. above.
[2] Wright's Letter VI, 26 January 1814 (*Morning Chronicle*, 16 February 1814).
[3] i.e. 'time does not run against the Church'. Wright appears to be alluding ironically to the legal maxim *nullum tempus occurrit regi*, i.e. 'time does not run against the Crown'.
[4] James Yorke (1730–1808), Bishop of Ely 1781–1808.
[5] Wright's Letter VIII, 10 February 1814 (*Morning Chronicle*, 11 March 1814).

APPENDIX, NO. IV. §VIII.

I. *False Notification.*—As to falsehood in Notifications, 'It is not only against *Pluralists*,' (says *Mr. Wright*, Lett. I. 6th Nov. [1813],[1] Morning Chronicle, 13th Nov. or thereabouts,)[2] 'not only against *Pluralists*, who have neglected to get *Licenses* for Non-Residence, but against many who have neglected to make the proper *Notifications*, according to law,' (this is the case of *Non-Notification*,) 'of their exemption from Residence; which exemptions, even if notified, would be of a very *equivocal* nature: and others who have returned *false notifications.*' Such, he then goes on to say, are those against whom his actions were brought: 'as also others, who have been returned as *Resident*, but who are not so; and many of those holding one, two, or three livings, from some of which they claim exemption, in consequence of Residence on others, which' {Residence} 'they do not perform.'

For general presumptive proof of alleged falsehood in Notifications, see above, Section 7, Note (ᶜ), to 13. *Exemptions not notified:* for particular alleged instances of vice in this shape, see Note (ᵈ) to 15. I. *Infirmity, &c.* and Note (ⁱ) to 27. I. *Absence without License, &c.*[3]

II. *Falsehood in Statements made to Bishops for obtaining Licenses.*— 'A Vicar,' (says Mr. Wright, Lett. II. Morning Chronicle, 20th Nov. 1813)[4]—'A Vicar, who obtained a License from a Bishop for Non-Residence on one living, stating that he was going to live near another living in a different part of the kingdom. On inquiring for him at the place where he was supposed to[5] reside, he was gone to a more fashionable part of the country. His License has been expired two years, and his Curate neither licensed nor resident.'

III. *Perjury* and *Bond-breaking*, viz. by Non-Residence, or other non-performance of duty, the performance of which has thus been professed to be secured by a *promissory oath*, or a *bond*, or both.

matters, wrote under such Return, in the most decided language, the statement he had received from the Rural Deans, and sent it back to the Clergyman so attempting to impose upon him, and requested those officers to see that the reparations were completed. Indeed, in 1787, he publicly expressed his high sense of the assistance he had received at their hands, and the benefit their exertions were to the Diocese.'

'The system of evasion' (says he, Jan. 18th, 1814)[6] 'has risen to an alarming height, and even men who by their offices ought to be the foremost in repressing or exposing any deception attempted to be practised on the Diocesans, are themselves guilty of the most flagrant misrepresentations and contempt of the laws; while their Curates, and those of other opulent Incumbents and Pluralists, of three, four, five, six, and seven, benefices and dignities, have remained unlicensed.'

---

[1] 1818 '1815'.
[2] Wright's Letter I, 6 November 1813 (*Morning Chronicle*, 13 November 1813).
[3] See pp. 442 n., 443 n., 448–51 n. above, respectively.
[4] Wright's Letter II, 17 November 1813 (*Morning Chronicle*, 20 November 1813).
[5] 1818 'to to'. The text follows the 'Errata'.
[6] Wright's Letter V, 18 January 1814 (*Morning Chronicle*, 21 January 1814).

As to the *truth* of the matters of fact, in this as in all these other instances, it must rest upon the credit of *Mr. Wright*.

True or not, however, in these particular instances,—under Excellent Church, perjury will, on every safe and profitable occasion, be an incident but too truly probable. It is among the practices which, as hath been seen,[1] the Church of England clergy are trained up in and to in the preparatory situation. It is among her principles—it is what you will hear from every mouth—that things of this sort, (meaning *promissory oaths, subscriptions, test-ceremonies*, and so forth,) are all *matters of form:* and that, as such, they may without scruple be violated, as often as advantage or convenience in any shape is to be got by it. In any such predicament as that of having, for example, taken an oath on admission into the University of Oxford, promising constant observance of a set of regulations, many of which are, by every one who has ever taken the oath, continually infringed,—if conscience be too callous to need for its repose this or any other sedative, at any rate for putting aside the imputation of standing self-condemned, some short phrase or other, to serve as a plea, will always be necessary: and a more commodious one than this the nature of the case seems not to admit of. Among these same statutes, are some, the observance of which would be impossible: others, such that, by the observance of them, some mischief and no good would be produced: and thus a justification is found for violating others, of which, while the observance is both possible and beneficial, the non-observance is mischievous.

For cover-seeking falsehood, *Jesuitry* has long been proverbial: but, between Jesuitry and Church-of-Englandism, more especially in this Oxford edition of it, where has been the difference? The sin, over which these Romanists have never ceased to throw a cloak, these Church-of-Englandists commit openly, and at their ease. In the practice of *insincerity*, shame has never altogether quitted the school of *Loyola:*[2] it seems to have been reserved for Excellent Church, and more particularly for the University of Oxford, to regard that vice, in all its unpunishable forms, as a matter of indifference.

Follow now the facts from the pen of Mr. Wright, Lett. II. Morning Chronicle, 20th Nov. 1813:—

'The number of those who have neglected their duty, in contempt of the law, and *in direct violation of solemn oath and bonds*, are far more than can be contemplated without a considerable degree of alarm.'

---

[1] See p. 34 & n. above.
[2] St Ignatius Loyola (1491–1556), founder of the Society of Jesus.

APPENDIX, NO. IV. §VIII.

'A Vicar, on whom the great tythes of the benefice were settled many years ago, "in order to encourage him,"—they are now worth near 1,200*l*. per annum: when he was instituted, *he took an oath to reside*, which, although not administered since the Act of the 43d of his present Majesty, (being prohibited by section 37.) yet he having taken possession previous thereto, is not absolved from it, nor has he any legal cause of absence.'—What Mr. Wright means, of course, to give us to understand of this Vicar, is—that, notwithstanding this oath, he never did reside. Quære, by whom, and on what authority, was an oath to this effect administered?

'A Rector, holding *two* valuable Rectories, together about 1,200*l*. per annum, by dispensation, to obtain which he gave bond to the Archbishop, that he would constantly reside on one, and keep a Resident Curate on the other, himself preaching on the benefice where he did not reside thirteen sermons every year.' N.B. This is according to the form of a dispensation for Pluralism given in Burn's Ecclesiastical Law, title *Plurality*.[1] 'He obtained *Licenses* for a statutable cause *from both, kept a Curate on one*, who *served both* for 84*l*. but, his Licenses for Non-Residence being expired, and there being some doubt in the Bishop's mind, whether he had any regular Curate, the Licenses were not renewed: he of course became liable:' {viz. to an action: and against this alleged delinquent we are to conclude was one of Mr. Wright's actions brought.}

IV. *View of the Bishops' Bench, by this Secretary to four Bishops.*—'At a Committee of the Bishops,' (says Mr. Wright, Lett. I. Nov. 6th, 1813)[2] 'after a deliberation of nearly two years, it was decided that each Bishop should give his Secretary an annual sum of money. I have received it from not one of them, except my late lamented patron, the Bishop of London:' {Randolph.}

'Commiseration may have been given,' (says he, Lett. VII. March 4th, 1814,)[3] 'but it was all I ever received from any one, and that would have been unnecessary, if the sums had been paid which were acknowledged to be my due, for the extra-official business I transacted during nine years, for the dioceses I was employed in by order of Government. Although some part of it was for the advantage of the Clergy, the Bishops endeavoured to throw the whole expense upon Government; and Government (after allowing them printed franks, and, in several instances, papers to any extent from the King's Printing Office) considers that the Bishops ought to furnish the

---

[1] See 'Plurality', in Burn, *Ecclesiastical Law*, 2nd edn., 1767, iii. 87–103, esp. 101–2, where the form of the dispensation mentioned by Wright is given.
[2] Wright's Letter I, 6 November 1813 (*Morning Chronicle*, 13 November 1813).
[3] Wright's Letter VII, 6 February 1814 (*Morning Chronicle*, 4 March 1814).

required particulars at their own charge, and therefore, at present, I, and other Secretaries, remain unpaid.'

'Two Secretaries have, within the last ten years, fallen victims to the consequences of depression of mind arising from a want of sufficient income.'

V. *Quantity of actual Duty reduced by habitual Neglect;* viz. even of legally exigible Duty,—by subtraction of half, or of some yet larger proportion of the number of times at which, in the compass of the year, the *stated* parts of the Church-of-England service ought by law to be performed.

'In one diocese, *one-third* of the livings have had the duty within a few years reduced from *twice* each Sunday to *once*.'

'A Vicar who holds a consolidated living (and took the oath to reside) worth about 200*l.* per annum . . . had a license for non-residence, expired near two years: lives four miles off: holds also another vicarage, (*whereon he took the oath* to reside,) within these few years there was a house on this also: its value was about 150*l.* per annum: now there is said to be no house, and the duty on each is reduced from twice each Sunday to once.'[1]

VI. *Ely Diocese. State of its Discipline anno* 1813, *compared with the year* 1728. {From Mr. Wright's Letter V. Jan. 18th, 1814.}[2] 'The following statement of one small diocese, of which I have with infinite trouble, collected the particulars, for every parish except four, from *authentic* sources, will prove the necessity of some serious enquiry as to the performance of those sacred duties for which such large sums are paid out of the labours of the industrious.'

In 1728.	In 1813.
'On 140 livings 70 Resident Incumbents.	'On the same 140 livings, 45 Resident Incumbents.
'Thirty-five who resided near and performed the duty.	'Seventeen who reside near and perform the duty.
'Thirty-one curates who resided in the parish or near it.	'Thirty-five curates, some of whom reside seven, eight, ten, or twelve miles off.
'The population was 56,944 souls. The duty was performed 261 times every Sunday.	'The population is 82,176 souls. The service is performed about 185 times every Sunday.
'And their Income was 12,719*l.* per annum.'	'And their Income is now 61,474*l.* per annum.'

---

[1] This extract is taken from Wright's Letter II.
[2] Wright's Letter V, 18 January 1814 (*Morning Chronicle*, 21 January 1814).

APPENDIX, NO. IV. §IX.

Extract of a Letter, signed, *An Apologist:*—Morning Chronicle, 1st February, 1814:[1]—

After accusing Mr. Wright, in general terms, 'of fallacious and malignant conclusions'—'The Diocese,' (he says) 'if I am not mistaken, is *Ely*. In this Diocese,' (continues he) 'is the University of Cambridge, and the churches are more generally served, or the livings held, by Members of that University. These gentlemen are resident in their respective Colleges, and all the Statutes applied to Residence have recognized a just respect for literature, and have granted indulgences to men thus engaged in its pursuit.'—Is this genuine? or is it not Mr. Wright himself in disguise?

'I cannot,' (says he,) 'make out from what documents Mr. W. has acquired his statement of the relative amounts of the Ecclesiastical Revenues of this Diocese in the year 1728 and at the present time.... The increase of a Rectory, from 800*l*. to 12,000*l*. a year, arose,'.... 'from drainage of fens.'[2]

§9. *Vices of Excellent Church recapitulated.*

In the next section, that which presents itself as the best and easiest mode of effecting the change,—which, by the nature of the case, appears to be so imperatively demanded,—will, in its general features, be brought to view. Of the radical corruptions and other imperfections, of which the demand is composed, a conception not altogether uninstructive will, it is hoped, by this time have been conveyed. But,—the examination having insensibly drawn itself out to a length, so much beyond what at the outset was expected to be found necessary,—a summary recapitulation, in the form of a list of these same corruptions and imperfections—say in one word *vices*—of which the fabric of Excellent Church has been seen to be composed, may, it is hoped, for the purpose of a simultaneous view, be found not altogether without its uses.

I. VICES *having relation to* DOCTRINE.

I. 1. *Infallibility*, virtually and to every practical purpose, ascribed to a set of men, on no other ground than that of the temporal power possessed by them: men, in whose time the state of the human mind, in the scale of improvement, was to such a degree low, that scarcely on any other subject than this, confessedly the most obscure of any, is it at present an object of regard: all hope of correction being thus as effectually as possible taken away from whatsoever errors it may have happened to them to have fallen into. Say, for shortness,

---
[1] The letter is dated 27 January 1814.
[2] For the Rectory of Doddington in the Diocese of Ely see p. 354 n. above.

prostration of understanding and will, before the blindly assumed infallibility of a comparatively unenlightened age.[a]

II. 2. To an extent, proportioned to that on which these men of imputed infallibility may at present be deemed to have fallen into error,—the existing generation of professed instructors in matters of religion,—and the people at large, in quality of their pupils,—are, one and all,—by *Catechisms*,[b] *Creeds*, and *Subscriptions* to articles of faith, together with *fixed* forms of devotion, replete with practically useless tenets, on subjects, many of them, confessedly out of the reach of human comprehension,—forced into probable *error* and certain *insincerity*,—engaged to keep themselves debarred from the free exercise of their judgments,—and pledged to the delivering, as being in their eyes right and true, those tenets, to which it may, to any proportion, happen to be in those same eyes wrong and false; and to reject, as wrong and false, tenets which in those same eyes may come to be right and true.

Perpetuity endeavoured to be given to that mixture of error and insincerity,[c] *which was a necessary result of an assumption so unsuitable to human weakness.*

II. VICES *having relation to* SERVICE.

III. 1. *Spiritual* Instructors and guides in matters of religion, appointed,—not by those for the salvation of whose souls it thereby becomes their duty to labour,—but, each of them, generally speaking, by some one stranger, whose own appointment is at best the work of chance,—and whose interest it is, to the extent of whatever number of relatives he may have, for whom he stands inclined by worldly interest or affection to make provision, to provide for them in this way, notwithstanding any degree of unfitness by which it may happen to them to be characterized: this interest being the stronger, the more palpably they are unfit for every occupation to which the successful exercise of intelligence or active talent is necessary. *Instructors and guides in religion, appointed by persons more likely to appoint unfit than fit ones.*

IV. 2. *Fixed forms* established for every thing: and these exclusively allowed: ideas, if ever imbibed, soon evaporating,—remains a *caput*

[a] Chargeable (this vice, No. 1.) to the Scottish Established, but not to any of the Non-Established Churches.

[b] So far as concerns *Catechism* and *Subscription*, but with the exception of *Creeds*, this vice has been found chargeable on the Established Church of Scotland, though not to so great an extent as to that of England. See further on.[1]

[c] See Note [b], p. 472.

---

[1] See pp. 478–80 n. below.

APPENDIX, NO. IV. §IX.

mortuum composed of *signs. Thought excluded from instruction and worship by the exclusive establishment of fixed forms.*

V. 3. In large tracts of country, under the name of *Extra-parochial places*, the benefit of the instruction and worship, such as it is, never communicated to the inhabitants.*

To whole districts (viz. all extra-parochial ones) *the benefit, such as it is, denied.*

VI. 4. In many parishes, the whole population left without a Church to resort to,—though in these, as in other places, religious instruction and worship, otherwise than in a Church, continues to be treated as a crime.* *Parishes without Churches: worship out of a Church not the less a punishable crime.*

VII. 5. In a large proportion of the whole number of the parochial districts, the districts left without a dwelling-house for a Minister; while, in respect to exposure to punishment for Non-Residence, he has been left upon a footing of no less danger than if there were no such obstacle to his Residence.* *Parishes without Parsonages: yet Residence, if not in a Parsonage, as punishable as Non-Residence.*

VIII. 6. In a great multitude of instances,—the capacity of the house of worship, compared with the number of the parishioners, so [small],[1] that to a large, and even to by far the largest part of that number, participation in the benefit of religious instruction and worship has thus been suffered to become physically impossible.* *Parishioners excluded by want of Church-room.*

IX. 7. In many instances, the parochial district so large, or the situation of the place of worship so far from central, that, to a large proportion of the inhabitants, participation in religious instruction and worship has thus been rendered either impracticable, or to such a degree inconvenient, as, on that account, to be generally given up.* *Parishioners, excluded by remoteness of the Church.*

X. 8. In the edifices for religious instruction and worship, the disposition made of the space very generally such as, in a large proportion, to put an exclusion upon the *unopulent many*, by the over-accommodation afforded to the *opulent few*. *Poor, excluded by over-accommodation to the rich.*

XI. 9. For want of adequate motives for performance, such as would be, and elsewhere are, afforded by an apt system of discipline, duties of the inexigible class left generally unperformed. See *Discipline*.[2] *For want of motives, inexigible duties left generally unperformed.*

---

* See Note, p. 474.

[1] 1818 'large'.   [2] See pp. 421–2 above.

III. Vices *having relation to* Pay.

XII. 1. In a vast proportion of the whole number of parochial districts,—regard being had to the exigency of the service, particularly in the primæval age of almost universal ignorance,—the scantiness of the pay such, as to render the engagement of an adequately instructed and constantly resident Minister, altogether hopeless.

By scantiness of pay, engagement of an adequately qualified resident Minister rendered hopeless: or, Pay, too small for subsistence.*

XIII. 2. The pay,—while, as in the case of other taxes imposed for public purposes, exacted of necessity from unwilling hands,—yet not, as mostly in the case of taxes imposed for other public purposes, taken from an universal fund,—but so taken from a local fund, that, in the individual so paid at his expense, each neighbour beholds the sole author of the suffering produced on his part by the exaction; while, in many instances, by the person so paid for it, either service is not rendered, or, if rendered, is seen to be of little or no worth, compared with the price so paid for it,—and palpably excessive, when compared with the pay received for the like service in other parishes.*

By misassessment of the pay, the receiver rendered odious.

XIV. 3. From the nature of the subject-matter on which it is imposed, the mischief of the tax enhanced by unprofitable vexation,—and by the prohibition which, to an indefinite extent, it has the effect of putting, upon that application of labour which would have been the most profitable. *The tax by which the pay is levied, (viz. a tythe on produce) unprofitably vexatious, and frequently, in regard to the most profitable application of labour, prohibitive.*

XV. 4. In a great number of the districts, the pay, by so enormous an amount, viz. from twice to some score times—greater than in others, in which no reason can be assigned for regarding it as insufficient, (service not inferior either in quantity or in quality, being in those same districts performed for it,) that, in the eyes of the people from whom it is exacted, the difference constitutes a burthen imposed upon them without need or use: money exacted to no purpose but to be wasted. *Pay, by excess oppressive.*

---

* The vices, thus distinguished by an asterisk, are all of them such as would, in the nature of the case, be capable of being removed by money: and for the exaction of money for these purposes there cannot be, on the part of the supporters of Excellent Church, any want of readiness. But, by the correction of these unessential imperfections, supposing them corrected, the other vices, that belong to the essence of the system, would they be removed, or so much as diminished? Consider well the list, and you will find that, so far from being diminished, the mischievous efficacy of the whole system would be increased: to an enormous degree the pressure of the expense increased, and, in return for this increase of pressure, no good effect produced.

XVI. 5. In a great number of the districts, the pay to such a degree excessive,—as, by enabling a man, to invite him to expend the greater part of it in pleasures, or pursuits, not only foreign, but adverse to the service: no adequate motives, if any, being at the same time provided, for securing, on his part, the adequate performance of his duties. *Pay, by excess seductive.*

XVII. 6. For exigible services of the *occasional* class, pay, in the instance of each service, exacted in equal quantity from the richest and the poorest,—and thence, to the poor, oppressive. *Pay, by disproportionality excessive.*

XVIII. 7. By pay,—received without performing or intending to perform any part of the duty, on the pretence of performing which it is exacted,—the parochial offices in question, about half of them, more or less, say about 6,000, converted into Sinecures. *By bad discipline, Cures corrupted into Sinecures.*

XIX. 8. In masses of various sizes,—some of them as far as some dozen or even score of times as large as many an one, for which the entire duty of a benefice is performed,—lots of pay established, as if for spiritual service, but without any such service, either rendered or so much as prescribed. *Pay without service, in originally established Sinecures.*

IV. Vices *having relation to* Discipline.

XX. 1. By the name of *Bishops*,—with *Archbishops* over them, and *Archdeacons* under them, together with *Chancellors, Commissaries, Surrogates*, and other Judges appointed by them,—and, in the way of technical procedure, cognizance taken,—not only of matters bearing relation to religious *doctrine* and *service*, but of matters purely temporal, having no relation to either: (See above, Section 6.)[1] viz. the *Official principal* and *Dean of Arches*, appointed by the *Archbishop of Canterbury*,[2] the Chancellors appointed by the respective Bishops,[3] with *et cœteras* upon *et cœteras:* the whole constituting such a perfect mass of uncertainty and confusion as baffles all description:—so many orders of official persons, with masses of pay more or less enormous, preserved out of the trappings of Popery, under the pretence of their preserving *discipline,* viz. causing *service,* apt in quantity as well as quality, to be universally performed: though, all the time, it is by these very men, that the discipline has been brought

---

[1] See pp. 415–27 above.

[2] The united offices of the Archbishop's Official Principal and the Dean of the Arches were held by a judge appointed by the Archbishop to the Court of the Arches, which received and determined appeals from all inferior ecclesiastical courts.

[3] The Chancellor was the judge appointed by each Bishop to his Consistory Court.

CHURCH-OF-ENGLANDISM

into, and kept in, the ruinous state in which it has just been viewed.—*Discipline, destroyed by Bishops, &c.—paid at enormous rates, on the pretence of their preserving it.*

XXI. 2. To these Bishops and Archbishops, seats preserved in the Supreme Body of the temporal government: their situation by this means rendered such as,—while it would draw aside their attention from, if they bestowed any upon, their spiritual duties,—thereby, if the performance of them were of any use, depriving men's souls of the benefit of that use,—fills them with pride and ambition; and sets them to exercise temporal dominion over their fellow priests, and [over][1] their fellow Christians, in direct contempt of so peremptory and pointed a prohibition as that delivered by Jesus to those of his followers whose successors they pretend to be.[2]—*Bishops, &c. exercising temporal dominion in contempt of Jesus.*

XXII. 3. Bishops,—whose service, if any were rendered by them, would consist in the preventing their respective subordinates from receiving pay without performing the service for which it is appointed,—committing in the face of day, and for their own profit, the same sordid sin which they profess to prevent in others.—*Bishops, to their own use converting Cure of souls into Sinecure.*

XXIII. 4. In pursuance of a recently perfected system, the powers of these Prelates exercised in a manner completely despotic: viz. singly, secretly, without need of discussion before or by others,—without need of reason assigned by themselves,—in some cases without any appeal, in all without effectual appeal,—and on their part without personal responsibility in any shape.—*Bishops, exercising over their Parish Priests a recently established corrupt despotism.*

XXIV. 5. On principles purely Popish,—for no other purpose than, in open contempt of the plainest and most peremptory prohibitions of Jesus,[3] to give increase to the mass of emolument, temporal power, and factitious dignity, with which they are cloathed,—a separate and altogether useless body of *substantive law*,—with a correspondent system of *procedure* and *judicial establishment*—kept on foot, to no better purpose than that the patronage of the judicial establishment may be continued in the pre-eminently unfit hands of Bishops: complication, plainly useless, and palpably inexcusable,—and with it proportionable uncognoscibility,—thence to good purposes inefficiency, and to bad purposes efficiency,—being thus secured to the rule of action. *Law and judicature, complicated and corrupted, to swell by patronage of judicial offices the pomp of Bishops.*

---

[1] 1818 'other'.
[2] See pp. 268–70 above.
[3] See pp. 266–8 above.

APPENDIX, NO. IV. §IX.

XXV. 6. Fees exacted from individuals,—the very poorest not excepted, and in their instance capable of operating with prohibitory effect,—for each of the several occasional parts of the service, viz. Baptisms, Marriages, Churching of Women, and Burials: these being services, with the exception of the ceremony of Churching, taken for the subjects of the evidentiary documents on which family rights in general are made to depend: services, on the performance of which, according to intimations more or less determinately expressed, and more or less generally conveyed and received, the chance of salvation is moreover in some way or other dependent. *By fees exacted by Priests, the poor excluded in reality from temporal rights, and pretendedly from salvation.*

XXVI. 7. In whatever instances the mode of exercising the discipline is not, as above, despotic,—fees in like manner exacted: fees, i.e. money, exacted in the way of taxation, by the receivers for their own benefit; and having, as in the case of other taxes, the effect of a prohibition, excluding every one who is not able to pay them from all participation in the benefit, to the receipt of which they are attached.—*By fees, all but the rich excluded from justice.*

There stands Excellent Church. Behold her in *puris naturalibus*. These are among her *vices*. More, at any time, if wanted. Enquire, as above, of the Diocesan Secretary.[1] Who shall make up the *per contrà* side of her account? Who shall make out the list of her *Excellencies?*—Come forward, *Dean Kipling;*—Come forward, *Dean Andrews;*—Come forward, *Bishop Burgess;*—Come forward, *Bishop Marsh;*—Come forward, *Bishop Howley;*—Come forward, *Archbishop Sutton;*—'Defenders of the Faith and so forth.'[2]—Come forward, Legion,[3]—Saints of all sorts and sizes, buttoned up into unity in the waistcoat of *the Quarterly Review*. Shut up your common-place books;—blow aside your metaphors of all work, your bubble generalities;—speak plain for once, if you dare and can;—examine the uncorrupt side of your Diana,[4] if you can find it.—Take counsel together; give in with one accord the list of all her Excellencies:—or do they not already stand summed up in the one grand total—*Decency?*[5]

Think not out of the invisibility of your challenger[6] to make a plea for silence. The strength of his cause is not in *his* force but in *your* weakness. If in the title page his name and description stood at full length, by how much the shorter would be this list of *Vices?*

[1] William Wright.
[2] See p. 297 n. above.
[3] See Mark 5: 9; Luke 8: 30.
[4] i.e. source of profit: see Acts 19: 24–8.
[5] See p. 86 n. above.
[6] An allusion to Bentham's original intention to publish *Church-of-Englandism* anonymously.

Of the above vices, though of late years under Excellent Church herself, in the hands that have been mentioned, some of the most flagrant may be seen to have received increase,—yet when viewed in the lump, and without any distinction which in this place would be worth remark, they may be stated as constituting so many symptoms of the hereditary disease, brought by her into the world from the womb of her Holy Mother, once of Babylon, now of Rome.

Of these same vices, what is there that will be found chargeable upon any Protestant *Non-Established* Church?—not one.—From no small number of them, where it is on the footing of a *visitor* only, and not as *mistress* that she has place, even Holy Mother herself may be seen to be free. May she not, reader? Take in hand the Table,[1] and look over it in this view.

Of all these same diseases, two and no more in reality, one other in appearance, have been found not yet purged off, in the constitution of the Established Church of Scotland. The two real (it has been seen already)[2] are the two cardinal and intimately connected vices, which have been stated as having relation to doctrine, viz. 1. *Prostration of understanding and will* before the blindly assumed infallibility of a comparatively unenlightened age. 2. Perpetuity endeavoured to be given to that mixture of error and insincerity, which is the necessary result of an assumption so unsuitable to human weakness.[a]

[a] To the mischief, of an arrangement so palpably repugnant to common sense and sincerity—an arrangement which admits not of any thing like a justification, nor so much as an extenuation, other than the force of custom—of that power in which whatever is most flagitious has somewhere or other found its support—in a system in other respects so admirably conducive to the support of piety and morality,—it affords no small consolation to observe two most important defalcations: defalcations, by which taken together, the amount of it is reduced to a small matter, in comparison of that which has place under Excellent Church.

1. In the first place, of whatever there may be of *insincerity*, the practice is but the act of a moment; viz. the moment at which the signature, expressive of the assent, is attached: that moment over, room remains open at all times for the application of a proposition, which (it is hoped) will have been found sufficiently established in a former part of this work (viz. Preface, p. 38.), that, without breach of sincerity, a man may entertain, and without violation of any engagement, declare and maintain, opinions to any amount contrary to those, his assent to which had at any former point of time been declared and recorded. It is not—this bitter dose—it is not,—as in and by the fixt forms of Excellent Church,—in the shape of *Creeds*, of *Prayers*, and in so many other shapes, on every occasion of devotion, brought up again and reswallowed.

2. In the next place, to the Clergy—less than a thousand in number,—with no other addition than that of the Professors in the four Universities—all or most of them—is the obligation and practice of swallowing the poison, such as it is, confined:

---

[1] See pp. 440–1 above.   [2] See pp. 471–2 above.

APPENDIX, NO. IV. §IX.

neither to the *Laity* at large, nor so much as to the *Lay Students* in the *Universities*, does it extend itself.[1]

In the case of the first institutors of this practice, a sort of extenuation cannot but present itself: viz. that perhaps in no sect of Christians,—*Protestants* any more than *Catholics*, or members of the *Greek* Church,—was any instance in those days to be found, of a set of men exempt from the same mixture of blind diffidence and blind confidence. On the part of each man diffidence in the rectitude of his own opinion; confidence in the opinions entertained, or supposed to be entertained, by a set of men frequently unknown to him:—confidence in the rectitude of a man's own first thoughts; diffidence in the rectitude of the same man's more and more mature thoughts to the end of life. *Second thoughts are best*, says the familiar proverb, grounded on the experience of every thinking moment of every man's life. No;—say the establishers of these institutions: *first* thoughts alone are good for any thing: all subsequent thoughts put together are nothing worth.

In the situation of the first Reformers, and other founders of free Churches— without being acquainted with each other's opinions on the points of controversy, they could not in their perilous contest with the supporters of existing establishments, act in concert with each other, nor therefore with any tolerable prospect or chance of success: a *confession of faith*, or something equivalent, was therefore in their situation, generally speaking, necessary. In the composition of this bond of union, two errors are in the present instance visible. One is—instead of *minimizing* the number of points decided upon,—*maximizing* it, and thereby maximizing the field of probable disagreement: the other was—the omitting to give to the measure the declared character of a *temporary* one, subject to revision in happier times: in times calmed by security, and enlightened by a course of reflection and experience.

By the circumstance of the vastness of the body of doctrine,—coupled as it is with that of the immaturity of the age at which it was penned,—it seems not altogether easy to say whether the combined folly and immorality of the practice are increased or diminished. Supposing the mind to apply itself to the subject, they are surely increased: if in any respect they be diminished, it must be by the consideration of the palpable grossness and manifest impossibility of the belief thus professed to be entertained: the utter incredibility of any proposition, by which, in the universality expressed by it, the declaration should be seriously asserted to be sincere. It is on this ground, that, in the instance of the Church-of-England, the practice in question is vindicated, or rather apologized for, by *Paley*. 'No man alive ever could believe all this: therefore there is no harm in any man's solemnly and publicly declaring that he does believe it, every tittle of it:'—such is the argument.[2] But the apology, such as it is, what does it amount to?—what, but a declaration, that,—among these professors of piety and pure morality—of which if sincerity forms not a part, it seems difficult to say what other virtue does,—insincerity of the grossest kind is nothing less than universal: that, to the extent of this practice, the *profession of piety* has the *practice of immorality* for its universal accompaniment. And, from an imputation from which, otherwise than by the means above proposed, it is so impossible for them to free themselves, have they nothing to fear in the event of their continuing exposed to it?—What have they to fear from the casting it off? What have they *not* to fear from the continuing under the

---

[1] Persons seeking ordination in the Church of Scotland had to subscribe to the Confession of Faith (for which see pp. 57 n., 69–73 above), as did, in theory, Professors in the Universities of Aberdeen (strictly speaking King's College and Marischal College were independent institutions), Edinburgh, Glasgow, and St Andrews.

[2] For Paley's argument to this effect in relation to subscription to the Thirty-nine Articles see p. 284 & n. above.

reproach of it? Instead of *piety*, will it not be by *vice* that they will thus stand distinguished from the *Laity:* that Laity, whom it is their profession to guard from vice?

By this universality,—supposing it to have place,—true it is, that the *comparative* weakness and guilt, and thence the *scandal*, will be done away,—in the instance of this Church, as in the instance of all other Churches: but, by any such circumstances, or by any other, can such weakness and guilt, when *absolutely* considered, be truly said to be removed? And, to the founders of the institution—to them alone—not to any person by whom it is purposely kept up at present—does this extenuation, such as it is, apply itself.

To this sad disease of the intellectual as well as moral part of man's frame,—so simple and so gentle, yet so effectual, is the remedy which the nature of the case presents, that—considering that it applies not to the Established Church in question alone, but to every other Established Church—the mention of it must not, even in this place, be omitted. Preserving the self-same formulary,—viz. in the present instance, the *confession of faith*, containing the *two Catechisms*, the *long* and the *short* (so they are distinguished)—to the set of words expressive of belief, substitute a set of words expressive of a *promise* never to *teach* or to *utter*, in any place of public worship, any doctrine contrary to any thing therein contained. Not that, by an engagement to this effect taken in itself, any error, if any there be to be found in that vast body of abstruse doctrine, would thus be purged off. But,—for the correction of all such error, all other places—and in particular all *printers*' workshops—remaining open,—that, sooner or later, these weak parts, whatever they may be, would drop off by degrees,—is a prediction, the fulfilment of which seems as natural and probable as the hope of it is delightful. Thus,—by a cathartic, or rather an alterative, the mildness of which will surely not appear disputable,—the *immorality*, which is the only really foul spot in the case, would be carried off at once:—and whatever there may be of *error*, be made gradually and imperceptibly to evaporate.

By no acceptance given to an amendment to this effect, would any acknowledgement of insincerity be made, any self-condemnation be passed, any humiliation be incurred. From every man,—if any such man there be now living, by whom, to every proposition without exception contained in the book in question the firmest assent is given,—might even the proposal to this effect come, as completely free from all inconsistency, as from any one, if any such there were, by whom not so much as one single proposition in it were believed. 'These' (he might say) 'from the first were, and now to the last continue to be, *my own* opinions. Of all who dissent from any of them, the opinions are consequently, in proportion to the degree of their distance from these of mine, in my eyes erroneous. But, what I know but too well is—that among persons, possessing means of right judgment not inferior to my own, for every one that agrees, there are many more that disagree with me. Under these circumstances, is it in the nature of the case, that of every one of the whole number of these persons, by whom all this vast assemblage of opinions is professed to be entertained,—persons, by every one of whom a comfortable subsistence for life, which otherwise he could not have had, is obtained—the belief applies to it with the same universality as my own?—If not, then, of the continuance of the obligation in question the effect is—to give birth—and to what good end?—to a perpetual course of insincerity:—of insincerity, and where?—in the bosoms of a class of men, in whose instance not only the practice, but the bare suspicion of that vice is more pernicious than in the instance of any other.'

What?—among so many, and those surely not ill-paid, professors of piety and the purest morality, shall there be no one who will be preserved by shame, from the reproach of leaving altogether to a layman the praise of standing forth the only advocate of sincerity in a Christian Church?

3. The one which is such scarcely otherwise than in appearance, is the one designated by the words '*Instructors and guides in religion, appointed by persons more likely to appoint unfit than fit ones.*'—In this case, why only in appearance? *Answer.* Because that which is in appearance a complete appointment, is in reality nothing more than an *initiative*, controuled and capable of being defeated by a *negative* in other hands:—by an independent, apt, and efficient negative, actually controuled, and by all *candidates*, as well as by all Patrons, universally known to be so.[a]

[a] To the English reader, the following sketch of the state of the Patronage in the Established Church of Scotland may be matter of curiosity, if not of use. It has been made out from one of the lists annually published in the *Edinburgh Almanack*.[1] In it, the persons and classes of persons of different descriptions, in whose hands the patronage of the several parochial benefices appears to be vested, are as follows; the subjoined figures being expressive of the number of benefices possessed by them respectively; viz.

1. Individuals	590
2. The Crown	250
3. Individuals and the Crown alternately	30
4. The Town Councils of various Towns	41
5. The Parishioners at large	13
6. The University of St. Andrew's	7
7. The University of Glasgow	1
8. The University of St. Andrew's and an individual alternately	1
9. The University of St. Andrew's and the Crown alternately	1
10. The Town Council of Edinburgh (the Parishes being outlying)	3
11. The Town Council of Glasgow (the Parishes outlying)	1
12. The Directors (Quære, of what?)	2
13. The Heritors (Land-owners) of the respective Parishes	2
14. The Kirk Session (governing body, corresponding to the Vestry) of the Parish	1
15. In litigation	1
	944
Deduct Parishes	895
Add Churches styled Collegiate, each having two Ministers	49
Total number of Parochial Benefices as above	944

1. The great difference turns upon the difference between the description of the persons by whom the *examination* is performed, and thereby that test of aptitude applied, without which admission into the order of men in question cannot take place. Under Excellent Church there is but one person to examine, and of that sole Judge the candidate himself has the choice, and at this trial no other person is ever present. *See above*, §[6].[2] The test is therefore in this case but a sham. Under the Church of Scotland, the tribunal by which so important a species of judicature is

---

[1] Bentham extracted and catalogued the following material from 'Clergy of Scotland', *Edinburgh Almanack, and Imperial Register, for 1812*, pp. 137–55. This may have been the edition of the *Edinburgh Almanack* that was sent to Bentham at Ford Abbey: see Bentham to John Herbert Koe, 19 August 1816, *Correspondence (CW)*, viii. 551.

[2] 1818 '7'. See pp. 419–21 above.

In the above portraits,—drawn in miniature indeed, but from the life,—not to speak of Scotland, behold now on the one hand the picture of *Excellent Church*, on the other hand the picture of *Schism:*—the picture, in which are comprehended all those Churches, of which, in the declared opinion of the present Bishop of London, Dr. Howley, the members are, all of them, as such, in a state of constant '*guilt*.'[1] Such excellence and such guilt—which then is most eligible?

§10. *Facienda in the way of Reform.*

Of the vices by which the system of Excellent Church has been found distinguished, such as presented themselves, twenty-six[2] in number, as being on this occasion worth putting upon the list, have just been brought to view: by every one of these, so far from being subservient, it will have been seen to be rendered adverse to the joint interests of piety, morality, and economy: by every one of them, distinguished from the system common to all Protestant Non-Established Churches: by all of them but two, and those it is hoped exercised, is a *many-seated* one: the Presbytery of the *Presbytery bound* in which the benefice is situated:[3] a many-seated and open judicatory, which while in some measure it sets the lead to, is at the same time checked and controled by, the opinion of the people at large: the acts of this judicatory being moreover in this as in other cases subject to ulterior tribunals, one above another, viz. the Synod of the *Synodical bound*, and lastly, to the General Assembly: tribunals in every one of which a number of Laymen in considerable proportion have seats: and moreover,—in addition to the examination before the Presbytery,—service, consisting of a prayer and sermon, the sermon sometimes, the prayer constantly, pronounced either in the Parish Church before the congregation, or in the Presbytery room before the Presbytery, in an open audience. In this case then, that which in name and to a first appearance is an *absolute* choice,—is in effect, but an *initiative*, subjected to a negative: and *that* negative applied—not arbitrarily, but on a judicial inquiry, performed with the substance as well as the forms of judicature.

2. In one respect,—viz. that of security for intellectual aptitude, so far as depends upon *appropriate learning*,—this Established Church possesses, it is evident, an indisputable advantage over the generality even of Non-Established Churches. But if, generally speaking, in respect of this qualification,—which, after all, is but a collateral and not an effectual one,—the Clergy of the Scottish Established Church have the superiority over those of the English Non-Established Churches,—it is not in the nature of the case that, in the essential article of *appropriate zeal*, the superiority should not in general be on the other side. Of these the two qualifications, which is it that with reference to the great ends in view, is the most effectually conducive? A question this of no small importance in itself, but which, considering that under Excellent Church there is no tolerable security for either, belongs not to the present purpose.

---

[1] See p. 48 n. above.   [2] 1818 'twenty-five'. The text follows the 'Errata'.
[3] For the appointment of ministers in the Church of Scotland see p. 421 & n. above.

not very difficultly removable, from that of the Established Church of Scotland.

Of the plan, a brief sketch of which here follows, the design is to shew how this same system may be most effectually purged of all those vices:—how that which is at present corruption may put on incorruption.

On this occasion, with joint aim,—to *two* antagonizing yet not irreconcileable objects—both of them leading and all-comprehensive objects—has the endeavour been all along directed.

Main or *positive object.*—To place the business of religious instruction and worship in England upon a footing as beneficial to the joint interests of piety, morality, and economy, as the nature of the case admits of.

Secondary or *negative object.*—In so doing, to produce as little disturbance as possible to established habits, expectations, and prepossessions.

Both these objects being steadily and constantly kept in view,—for guiding the pen in the pursuit of them, the following rules have presented themselves in the character of *leading principles*.

I. In regard to *doctrine*.
    1. Respecting doctrine, let no change be attempted by the hand of government.

II. In regard to *service*.
    2. In so far as in *service doctrine* is involved, no change: let the established *fixt forms* of discourse be preserved inviolate.
    3. On the occasion of such change as the principle of preserving *doctrine* without change leaves liberty for making in regard to *service*,—let all established *habits* and *prepossessions* be conformed to, so far as is consistent with the essentials of the reforming change.

III. In regard to *pay*.
    4. Service, in perfect conformity to the now established doctrine being continued on its present footing, let all pay,—over and above what is necessary to the securing the performance of that service according to the fixt forms,—be defalcated, and applied to the real exigencies of the State.
    5. Let the change be so ordered, that all particular pecuniary interests existing at the time, whether in possession or fixt expectancy, shall rather be gainers than losers: and so in regard to *powers* and *dignities*.

IV. In regard to *discipline*.
    6. The existing system of discipline having been shewn to be

adverse rather than subservient to the three great interests in question, let it, as the existing functionaries drop off, drop off along with them:—and in the same gradual way let a system, characterized by the joint attributes of efficiency, simplicity, and frugality, take its place.

Leading Provisions of the proposed Reform.

I. *In regard to* Doctrine.

[I.] 1. Abolition of all recorded Declarations of belief concerning Doctrine.

II. *In regard to* Service and Pay.

II. 1. On death or removal of Incumbent, if there be no Curate, Parish Clerk to read, in addition to his own, the Minister's part of the Service; the proposed *Homily Sermons* included. (See § [3].)[1] For the additional labour, length of time employed not being increased, let half as much of his present pay be allotted, out of the Poor's Rates.[2]

III. 2. Power to Vestry to appoint for this form any other person as their choice, suppose a boy who has made himself perfect in reading in a parish school, but with no greater pay than that given to the Clerk.

IV. 3. The Clerk or other successor to the quondam Minister to be ordained or not ordained as to the constituted authorities shall seem meet. N.B. Already a sort of person called a *Clerk in orders* is not without example under the Church of England.[3]

V. 4. Of the *surplice fees*, these being paid mostly by the lower classes, let the part added in each instance to the Clerk's fee be less than as above:[4] instead of half as much, say one-fourth as much, or rather in lieu of both the Clerk's and Minister's fees, the smallest piece of coin being paid by the party or parties for making the entry in the Register, let the present amount of the Clerk's fee, with the above addition, be charged upon the Parish.

VI. 5. Instead of the Clerk, or substitute to the Clerk as above, Power to the Vestry to choose a Minister ordained upon the present footing. But, to the formation of his pay, none to contribute but those who choose to do so.—N.B. The Minister is at present (it is believed)

---

[1] 1818 '4'. See pp. 355–60 above.

[2] The poor rate was a tax on the occupiers of property raised by each parish to fund poor relief. Regulations regarding the poor rate were consolidated in 1597 (39 Eliz. I, c. 3), and re-enacted in 1601 (43 Eliz. I, c. 2). This method of funding poor relief was abandoned in 1834 (4 & 5 Will. IV, c. 76).

[3] A Rector or incumbent could appoint an ordained priest or deacon as Parish or Church Clerk, a practice later regularized by 7 & 8 Vic., c. 59, §2 (1844).

[4] i.e. less than the proportion allotted for reading.

chosen by the Vestry in some of the London Parishes: a Lecturer, i.e. an additional Preacher, certainly is.[1]

VII. 6. In each Parish, reserving to the present Church service the days and hours customarily employed therein, power to the Vestry to allow the use of the Church to any person or persons at pleasure for the purpose of divine worship, according to any form of the religion of Jesus.

VIII. 7. In the case of an Incumbent having a Curate, if it be in the situation of the Incumbent that a vacancy happens in the first instance, let the duty and pay of the Curate be continued to him so long as he continues Curate; the remainder of the pay of the Incumbent lapsing into the General *Church Reform Fund*, to be composed as hereinafter mentioned:[2]—if it be in the situation of the Curate that the vacancy happens, then let the duty be performed by the Clerk or other person as above; the Incumbent retaining his share of the pay, and the Curate's lapsing into the Church-Reform fund.

IV. *In regard to* DISCIPLINE.

VIII. 1. On death or removal of a Bishop, power to the Crown to nominate (suppose) an Archdeacon of that or any other Diocese,—to execute, without seat in the Lords, all other powers, with the title of *Vice-Bishop;* and out of the profits, from the[3] Church-Reform fund, a salary, commensurate to time and labour employed, without regard to dignity.

IX. 2. On a vacancy in the office of Vice-Bishop, power to the Crown to appoint a successor.

X. 3. On death or removal of an Archbishop, power to the Crown to nominate either a Bishop or an Archdeacon,—to exercise, without seat in the House of Lords, all other powers, with a salary, on the same principles as above.

XI. 4. As Incumbents and Curates die off, let Vice-Bishops' sees be consolidated.

V. *In regard to the* CHURCH-REFORM FUND, *and the masses of Pay of which it is to be composed.*

I. *Lands how to be disposed of.*

XII. 1. On the death or removal of an Archbishop or Bishop, let the lands and houses belonging to the Province or See be taken

---

[1] See Burn, *Ecclesiastical Law*, 2nd edn., 1767, 'Lecturer', ii. 347.
[2] See pp. 485–93 below.
[3] 1818 'profits out of the'. The text follows the 'Errata'.

possession of by the Escheator,[a] to be sold by auction: the produce to go to the Church-Reform fund. Till sale, profits to be paid into the existing *Augmentation Offices*.[1] No lot to be knocked down at a price below what will be sufficient at the time to purchase a government annuity equal to the then existing annual value.

XIII. 2. So, on death or removal of any Dean, Canon, Prebendary, Precentor, or any other such Sinecurist, holding in *severalty*.

XIV. 3. Power to any existing Archbishop, Bishop, or Sinecurist, to join in the sale of the immovable property, or any part of it, and in lieu of the present income, to accept for life the government annuity purchased with the produce of the sale. N.B. In this way very considerable additions to existing income would in many instances be to be made.

XV. 4. In a Chapter holding its possessions jointly,—on death or removal of any member, let his share be paid in as above to the *Augmentation Offices*.

XVI. 5. Power to majority of the Chapter to join in sale as above, and convert the whole property into government annuities as above.

XVII. 6. So in regard to Fellows, of University and other Colleges.

XVIII. 7. Adequate compensation to Scholars entitled to succeed to Fellowships; and to Scholars in endowed Schools entitled to succeed to Scholarships and Fellowships in Universities.

XIX. 8. On death or removal of Incumbent having no Curate, like provision in regard to Glebe belonging to Livings.

XX. 9. On death or removal of Incumbent having glebe and Curate, let the pay of the Curate be continued to him, till his death or removal, in the form of a government annuity, without expense; together with the Parsonage, if occupied or let by him.

---

[a] (Escheator.) For this purpose the office might need be revived.[2]

[1] The offices of the Governors of Queen Anne's Bounty had been based in Dean's Yard, Westminster since 1735. The Governors administered the payment of grants to augment the maintenance of poor clergy, traditionally collected from First Fruits and Tenths formerly paid to the Crown, supplemented at this time by an annual grant of £100,000 from Parliament. See p. 113 n. above and pp. 518–25 below.

[2] The Escheator, an office which dated from the 1230s, was a royal dignitary appointed annually by the Lord Treasurer for each county or pair of counties to protect the sovereign's rights and revenues, and to hold an inquisition to establish the sovereign's feudal dues following the death of one of his tenants. Escheators also supervised lands made vacant by the death of an Archbishop or Bishop, whereupon the Crown was entitled to any profits from the land until a new appointment was made. From 1541 the work of the Escheators was dealt with in the Court of Wards and Liveries, but the office fell into disuse when the Court was abolished by the Long Parliament in 1645 and the abolition confirmed in 1660 by 12 Car. II, c. 24.

APPENDIX, NO. IV. §X.

II. *Pecuniary dues, how to be disposed of.*

XXI. 10. On death or removal, as above, let Easter-Offerings cease.[1]

XXII. 11. Other pecuniary dues, not saleable,—or if saleable, till sale,—let them be paid into the Augmentation Office, as above.

III. *Tythes in Kind, how to be disposed of.*

XXIII. 12. On[2] death, or removal of Incumbent, let all *tythes in kind* cease. In lieu of them let an assessment be made, payable, by the occupant, in the manner of the Land-Tax. The assessment to be made as in the case of the present Assessed Taxes: in case of alleged excess, power to Occupant, Landlord, intermediate Lessee, or other person interested, to appeal to a Jury sitting at the Quarter Sessions. Against *overcharge*, viz. by alteration in the value of money, or value of the land in question and its produce,—provision by re-assessments periodical or occasional: but, in no case any *increase* to be given to this commutation-tax, on the score of any increase in the value of the produce.

XXIV. 13. Where the patronage is in the hands of an individual or individuals,—on sale of *glebe* or *pecuniary dues*, let a proportionable part of the purchase-money be given to the Patron, in compensation for the Advowson: so in the case of *tythes in kind*, a government annuity, equal in value to his share of the purchase-money, which the annual produce of the above-mentioned commutation-tax would fetch, if sold in the manner of the Land-Tax.

XXV. 14. Where the patronage is in the hands of the Crown, let no such allowance be made to the Patron. By this means that vast mass of the matter of wealth, operating in the hands of the Chancellor, in the shape of matter of corruption, would be sunk, and the Constitution relieved from the pressure of it.[3]

XXVI. 15. With a view to compensation on this score,—the several cases, in which the patronage is in the hands of corporate bodies of different descriptions,—to be considered; and, according to the nature of each body, compensation allowed or refused.

XXVII. 16. To a Patron,—having, at the passing of the Act, a son of not less than—say fourteen years of age, whom he was breeding up for the Church, for the purpose of his being presented to the benefice,—on oath made to this effect, on the sale of the several

---

[1] Offerings were due to the priest from each parishioner at Easter, Christmas, Whitsun, and on the feast of the dedication of the parish church. It was traditional at Easter for each communicant to pay the sum of 2d., and each household in London to pay 4d. See the rubric at the end of 'The Order for the Administration of the Lord's Supper or Holy Communion', *Book of Common Prayer*, and Burn, *Ecclesiastical Law*, 2nd edn., 1767, 'Offerings', iii. 19–21.

[2] 1818 '12.—1. On'. The figure '1' is redundant.

[3] The Lord Chancellor enjoyed the right of presentation to all the livings of the Crown under the value of £20 per annum: see Blackstone, *Commentaries on the Laws of England*, ii. 47.

elementary parts of the value of the living, as above, let extra compensation be made.

XXVIII. 17. After death or removal of an Incumbent,—let no tythes in kind, not at *that* time received or claimed, be at any time claimed on behalf of the *Church Reform* fund.

XXIX. 18. Where, instead of being in fee-simple, the whole in one hand,—the value of the Advowson is, in any way, by will, settlement, or otherwise divided amongst divers persons interested,—let division be made of the compensation money accordingly.

XXX. 19. To augment the reward for *real* service, and, at the same time, save University Colleges from dilapidation and University Towns from desolation,—in regard to a certain proportion of the Fellowships in each College, power to the Crown, on the death of a Fellow,—instead of causing his share to be received at the Augmentation Office,—to nominate to the vacant situation a wounded or superannuated officer in the sea or land service:—the officer giving up his half-pay and every other allowance.[a]

XXXI. 20. On the death or removal of any *Scholar* on the foundation, power to the College, and in their default, to the Crown, to allow to any such land or sea officer, without his giving up his half-pay or other allowance, the gratuitous use of the chamber so become vacant.[b]

[a] Within the memory of man, not only have Fellowships and Scholarships been added to existing University Colleges, but new University Colleges founded.[1] How blind the imitation! how deplorable the infatuation! as if Protestant monks were of any more use than Popish ones. *Learning*, indeed? Has learning been the object? For ages no *need* has there been of the supposed purchased learning: from first to last, never has there been any *security* for it.

[b] To *the Church*—in every honest sense of the word *Church*—not to speak of any such meritorious public servants as above—by giving to any *other* person whatever any one of the Church Sinecures, original or factitious (that would not be given in augmentation of insufficient pay to an officiating parish priest), would any injury or detriment be done?—To religious instruction the defender of the country has not contributed any thing:—true: but as little has the idler, so inappositely styled *reverend*.—By the defender of the country as such, *no* dishonour has been cast upon the clerical profession: upon *the Church*, in[2] that sense of the word *Church*. But by the Reverend Sinecurists, dishonour *has* been cast upon the Church:—if to any body of men it be a dishonour to have among them—and in the scale of opulence even at the head of them—a set of depredators, obtainers of money on false pretences. A Clergyman, who is never to officiate any where, he surely is the last man by whom any mass of pay so deserved should be obtainable. Where a Curate is kept, the pay of the benefice is divided between the Curate and the Incumbent:

---

[1] Worcester College, Oxford (formerly Gloucester Hall founded in 1560) was founded in 1714; Hertford College, Oxford (formerly Hart Hall founded in 1282) was founded in 1740; and Downing College, Cambridge was founded in 1800.

[2] 1818 'or'. The text follows the 'Errata'.

APPENDIX, NO. IV. §X.

For illustration of the applications proposed to be made of the above-mentioned *leading principles*, the above-mentioned proposed *leading provisions* will, it is hoped, be found to suffice.

Ireland! Ireland!—He that has the courage, let him apply all this to the case of Ireland.

Spoliation of the Church!—Plunder of the Church!—Subversion of the Church!—Destruction of the Church!—Oh horrible! . . . .

Spoliation, plunder, subversion, destruction, of a fictitious entity!— Well, all fictitious entities that ever were figured, suppose them despoiled, plundered, subverted, destroyed at one stroke: where would be the objection, so long as no *real entity* of the class of existing persons were found, that would be the worse. Of these individuals what one is there that would in any way be the worse for it? To persons in *possession*—to persons having right in *expectancy*— the option of either retaining simply what they have, or adding to it— such throughout, as to them, would be the effect of it.

On whom then does the loss by the spoliation fall? Upon those persons who, *but* for the change in question, *would*, to obtain this or that share of the money, have passed themselves off for receivers of the Holy Ghost. Deplore their fate?—deplore then along with it the fate of the hapless innocents, who, had a certain man intermarried with a certain woman, would have come into existence.

Remain as the only description of persons who would be real sufferers from the change,—those Clergymen, in whose bosoms, at the commencement of it, or at the time of the first authoritative proposal of it, any special hope of preferment, over and above what they were in possession or fixed expectation of, should have already taken root. Being indisputably real,—and this independently of the existence of merit in any shape in company with it,—to every feeling mind which contemplates it, the eventual mass of suffering thus circumstanced, cannot but be matter of well-grounded regret. By no such mind will this part of the subject be contemplated with any such apathy, as that which was manifested by Saint Perceval and his still living and flourishing Executor,[1] who,—to find money to put into the

between the Curate who does every thing, and the Incumbent who does nothing. In this case, according to the ceremonial of Excellent Church, it is necessary that, by every person who *officiates*, the ceremony called *taking Orders* shall be performed. Be it so: but the one who *never* does officiate, to what *use* should he take Orders: to what *effect* can he, but to disgrace them? As matters stand at present, where would be the mischief done to any body or any thing, if every Patron of a living were allowed to put into his own pocket the Incumbent's share, with power of appointing the Curate, so long as he conforms to the obligations imposed by law on a Reverend Incumbent, who, in this same way, turns over his duty to a Curate?

---
[1] i.e. Spencer Perceval and Harrowby.

pockets of unexpecting Curates, being bent upon stripping Incumbents, some of them of nearly half their income,[1]—went to work upon them, upon the true *Procrustes* plan,[2] plane in hand, as if they had been so many deal-boards.

But, how truly soever matter of *regret*,—compared with the evil put an end to and the positive good produced,—in whose eyes, unless it be those of the sufferers themselves and their immediate connexions,—by what, even the most feeling and scrupulous mind, can any mass of evil of this description be, with any propriety, regarded as constituting matter of *objection?*—By the signature of *peace*,—in an infinite variety of shapes, an incomparable greater body of expectation is always defeated, and suffering of the same kind created, than would be by the here-proposed change: yet, that, for the exclusion of this suffering, war ought to be carried on for everlasting—is surely more than ever expressed itself in the form of a serious proposition,—how numerous soever may have been the breasts by which the correspondent wish has been entertained.

Alas! it is not hope of future increase to present opulence, but even all tolerable assurance of present subsistence, that, by the late change, though it be from war to peace,[3]—the products of peace having been anticipated and consumed in unjust war,—has been torn out of human bosoms in such countless multitudes!

Yet true it is, that of this concluding plan, death of Excellent Church has from the very first been the acknowledged object. Death?—Yes: but of what part belonging to her? Her *Doctrine?*—No: *that* is left by it untouched: left to all those by whom it is approved:—left to them to make the most of it.—Her *Service?*—No: that is left to her not only untouched but better secured than ever: the performance of it secured with a degree of uniform regularity never hitherto exampled. Her *Doctrine?* Once more, no: that is embodied in her *Service:* and, her service remaining untouched, her doctrine—so much as is embodied in her service—is left untouched along with it. What is not embodied in the service is contained in her *Articles*.[4] These Articles then, if it be any satisfaction to her votaries, let them be added to the *Service*, and any number of times, in the year or the day, read as part of it: subscribed at those same times, or at any other times, by as many as please, though not by any who do not please: subscribed, but neither from hope of gain

---

[1] For Bentham's discussion of the scheme sponsored by Perceval and Harrowby to reduce the incomes of incumbents and thereby raise the pay of curates see pp. 499–518 below.

[2] Procrustes forced his victims to lie on a bed, and then either stretched their limbs or cut portions off in order to make them fit the bed: see Diodorus Siculus, *Library*, IV. lix. 5.

[3] An allusion to the ending of the Napoleonic Wars in 1815.

[4] i.e. the Thirty-nine Articles of the Church of England.

for doing so, nor from fear of loss or suffering for not doing so: subscribed,—and command by authority being obtained,—(and would it be refused?) made poetry by the Poet Laureat,[1] set to music by the reverend and fortunate performer on the violincello,[2] or any more accomplished and successful votary of St. Cecilia,[3] if any such be to be found: sublimed into poetry, sanctified by sacred music, and in this attire added to the royal psalms.

If neither over her *service*, nor over her doctrine, would the proposed death have dominion,[4] over what part then?—What part? What but that which, from first to last, has by all doctors been considered as her *vital* part, even that *part* in her which is of gold. Of gold, according to the most authentic accounts, was one of the thighs of the philosopher Pythagoras:[5] of the same precious matter is the heart of Excellent Church. In the Royal Navy,

'Hearts of oak are our ships, hearts of oak are our men;'[6]

according to one of the most popular of our Tyrtæus's:[7] not less incontestably of gold is the heart of Excellent Church. Worshipped as she is,—for what else is it that she is ever worshipped, by those whose 'understandings and wills lie prostrate'[8] at her feet?—Pass by a couple of men of the labouring class in conversation,—note the words for half a minute,—*beer* is sure to be one of them:—that which *beer* is to those real labourers in the vineyard of industry, *benefice* is to these pretended labourers in the vineyard of the Lord[9] on the seventh. Sit down in a company of Church-of-England Clergymen, or in any company where there are two such Clergymen: what are then and there the topics?—Belong they to religion?—to morality?—to literature?—No. *One* you may be assured of, and *that* the one which calls forth the most universal and lively interest:—that on which neither tongues nor ears can ever tire:—the value of this and that one of those good things which are called *livings*, and of those still better things which are *above* livings:—those good things for which the appearance of something is by somebody to be done, and

---

[1] The Poet Laureate was Robert Southey, who had been appointed in 1813.
[2] Not identified.   [3] St Cecilia is the patron saint of church music.
[4] An echo of Romans 6: 9.
[5] Pythagoras showed proof of his supernatural status by displaying his golden thigh: see, for example, Iamblichus, *On the Pythagorean Life*, xxviii. 135, 140.
[6] 'Heart of Oak', a song celebrating naval victories against the French in 1759, was written by David Garrick (1717–79), and set to music by William Boyce (bap. 1711, d. 1779) for the afterpiece *Harlequin's Invasion, or, A Christmas Gambol*, first presented at Drury Lane on 31 December 1759. The song was very popular with sailors, and subsequently became the unofficial anthem of the Royal Navy.
[7] Tyrtaeus, a Spartan poet of the seventh century BC, who composed martial songs for the Spartan army.
[8] See p. 37 n. above.   [9] See Matthew 20: 1.

those still better things for which not even *that* is by any body to be done.

The life then of this Excellent person being in her gold,—taking away her gold, you take away her life: her life you divest her of, and instead of it put on death: here then is *Thanasia*. But that death is a most easy one: an easier one was never imagined in Sybaris.[1] Here then is *Euthanasia*. No spasm: no convulsion: a death which no man will feel:—a death for which all men will be the better, and scarce a man the worse.

Yes:—this will indeed be,—if any one there ever was (in the gravest and most important sense), a death unto *sin:* yea, and at the same instant a new life unto righteousness.[2]

Of the money, which upon this plan would by degrees find its way into the proposed fund,—the quantity applicable to the exigencies of the public—the benefit which accordingly would thus be produced in the shape of economy—would not be inconsiderable.

But in this case even *that* benefit is but a secondary one. In regard to religious doctrine and instruction, no immediate or certain change, it is true, *would* (it has been seen) be—because, consistently with liberty and sincerity, no such change *could* be made by it. But the great mischief of which the system is the perennial source—the mischief done by it to morality and good government—would be cleared away: to morality, by the perpetual dominion which has been exercised by the above-mentioned confederacy of *vices:* to good government, by the support, which, through the medium of corrupt and corruptive influence, has been seen given to despotism.

Of the produce of the fund thus created, the most obvious application is the transfer of it to the *Sinking Fund*.[3] But to this it would be but as a drop to the ocean: and of no such addition can any expectation have ever been entertained by the public creditors.

For *public instruction* at large, other funds there are, and those amply sufficient,—if of the masses absorbed by the peculation of trustees, and of those misapplied by the ignorance of former ages, a proper application be now made to that use. To the Education-Committee of the House of Commons,[4] honest and intelligent men

---

[1] Sybaris, a Greek city in Southern Italy founded *c.* 720 BC, was noted for its wealth and luxury. The city was destroyed by the neighbouring colony of Croton in 510 BC.

[2] Bentham was, perhaps, recalling Paul's teaching in, for instance, Romans 6.

[3] The Sinking Fund, having been established by Robert Walpole (1676–1745), first Earl of Orford, in 1717 in order to reduce the National Debt, had been revived by William Pitt in 1786 (26 Geo. III, c. 31).

[4] The Committee appointed on 21 May 1816, at the request of Brougham, to inquire into the Education of the Lower Orders in the Metropolis (see *Parliamentary Debates* (1816) xxxiv. 633–6) included Samuel Romilly and Francis Burdett (1770–1844), radical MP for Westminster 1807–37, close friends of Bentham. It reported on 20 June 1816, and, amongst other measures,

look on this occasion with wistful, yet—considering on whom every thing ultimately depends—little expecting eyes.

Relief from taxes—this is the application which, in the state to which the country has been reduced, presents a claim superior to every other.

From taxes? Good. But from what taxes? From those of which, while the apparent mischief is greatest, the real mischief is least?— From a tax on intoxicating liquors, for example?—No: but from those taxes which are in the contrary case:—of which the prohibitory effect operates on those benefits, the value of which is at the same time greatest in reality, and, by contingency or remoteness, rendered least obvious, or least acutely sensible, to unscrutinizing eyes: taxes prohibitive of health, justice, communication: communication for supply of *commercial* wants—communication, for supply to the most crying of all wants—remedy against misrule.[1]

Under what tax will men be least *impatient?* this has been the question—this the only question—with the man of finance. Under what tax will men's *sufferings* be *least?*—under what greatest? This (says he to himself) is *their* concern, not mine. Thus it is that the activity of power has taken its direction from the undisguised object of its contempt—the impatience of ignorance. *'Ignorant impatience of taxation!'*[2] as if, supposing in their breasts the least spark of feeling for a nation's misery, the ignorance of those *by whom*, could ever have been exceeded by the ignorance of those *on* whom the taxes have been imposed!

By a supply such as that here in question—a supply which, how moderate soever it may prove, would come from a quarter to which official expectation can scarcely have ever directed itself—is presented one of those rare occasions, on which, on the field of taxation, it is possible for inveterate error to receive any considerable remedy. But on this, as on every other quarter of the field of political abuse, where?—where, alas! are the hands, to which remedy can be looked for with any ray of hope?

---

recommended the establishment of a commission to receive evidence on the management of educational foundations throughout the country (see ibid. 1230–5, and 'Report from Select Committee on the Education Of the Lower Orders in The Metropolis: with the minutes of evidence taken before the Committee', *Commons Sessional Papers* (1816) iv. 1–324), which led eventually to the formation of the Charity Commission which sat from 1818 to 1837.

[1] Bentham no doubt had in mind the stamp duties on newspapers, which had been increased in 1815 (55 Geo. III, c. 185).

[2] Bentham is alluding to a remark made by Castlereagh in the House of Commons on 13 February 1816 in a debate on the military estimates (*Parliamentary Debates* (1816) xxxii. 455): 'He felt assured that the people of England would not, from an ignorant impatience to be relieved from the pressure of taxation, put every thing to hazard, when every thing might be accomplished by continued constancy and firmness.'

APPENDIX, No. V.

RECENT MEASURES OF PRETENDED REFORM OR IMPROVEMENT—THEIR INUTILITY AND MISCHIEVOUSNESS.

INTRODUCTION.

IN the last section but one of the preceding number of this Appendix, has been presented to the consideration of the sincere Reader an exposure of the *Vices* under which the system of Excellent Church was regarded as labouring.[1]

In the last section, a compressed sketch of those arrangements, which have presented themselves in the character of *remedies*:[2] the most conducive to the great ends in view of any that could be found.

Meantime, by the hand of power, the existence of imperfection, in some shape and degree, having been recognized,—in the character of a system of remedies to such acknowledged imperfections, or, to speak authentically, 'a system of measures for strengthening the establishment of the Church of England:' (Speech of the Earl of Harrowby, p. 1.)[3] a set of arrangements of a widely different nature have been devised: arrangements, some of which have already been carried into effect; while others (as hath been seen, p. 396) have in general terms been announced as being still in preparation: a storm, which, having long been brewing, is, or at least has been, on the point of bursting upon our heads.

A standard of reference and comparison—a standard,—by reference to which may be ascertained, in the first place, what, in a system directed, or professed to be directed, to the proper ends, wears the character of *vice* or other *imperfection*,—in the next place, what arrangements promise to be best adapted to the removal of these imperfections,—having been, as above,—established,—thus it is that, supposing that standard to be what it aims at being, what

---

[1] See pp. 471–82 above.   [2] See pp. 482–93 above.   [3] See p. 389 n. above.

APPENDIX, NO. V. INTRODUCTION.

remains to be performed, of the task of applying to it the several authoritative arrangements in question, need not occupy much ulterior space.

Of the government plan, begun upon by the political Saints about twenty years ago, and still pursuing,—the leading measures, will, it is believed, be found all of them referable to one or more of the seven heads following, viz.

1. *Increasing*, on pretence of *diminishing*, the number of Non-Resident Incumbents.

2. *Increasing* the number of *Resident Curates*.

3. To that end, out of the pockets of *Incumbents* and Patrons, taking money, and forcing it into the pockets of *Curates*.

4. For increasing the value of English Livings, exacting from the population of the three kingdoms the annual sum of 100,000*l*.

5. Regulating the occupations of agriculture, in the case of a Parish or other Priest.

6. Over Incumbents and Curates lodging DESPOTIC *power* in the hands of *Bishops*.

7. Announced, and remaining to be executed. From Christians and others, of all persuasions, money to be exacted sufficient to render the number of Church-of-England Churches 'commensurate to the whole population.'[1]

The following are the statutes by which the above-mentioned objects have, with the exception of the one last-mentioned, been pursued:—

1. The Statute, 36 G. III. c. 83, 14th May, 1796, intituled 'An Act for the further support and maintenance of Curates within the Church of England; and for making certain Regulations respecting the appointment of such Curates, and the admission of persons to Cures augmented by Queen Anne's Bounty, with respect to the avoidance of other benefices.'—Call it for shortness *the Act of* 1796; or, *the first Curates' Act;* or, *Curate-pampering Act*.

2. The Statute, 43 G. III. c. 84, 7th July, 1803, intituled, *'An Act to amend the Laws relating to Spiritual Persons holding of Farms; and for enforcing the Residence of Spiritual Persons on their Benefices, in England.'*—Call it for shortness the Act of 1803; or, if its title to the appellative should be found to have been made good, *the first sham Residence enforcing Act;* or, *the first Non-Residence promoting Act*.

3. The Statute, 53 G. III. c. 149, 20th July, 1813, intituled, 'An Act for the farther support and maintenance of Stipendiary Curates.'—Call it for shortness *the Act of* 1813; or, *the second Curates' Act;* or, *Curate-pampering Act*.

---

[1] See p. 396 n. above.

4. The Statute, 54 G. III. c. 175, 30th July, 1814, intituled, 'An Act to explain and amend several Acts relating to Spiritual Persons holding of Farms; and for enforcing the Residence of such Persons on their benefices, in England, for one year, and from thence until six weeks after the meeting of the then next Session of Parliament.'—Call it for shortness *the Act of* 1814; or, with the proviso above-mentioned, *the second sham Residence enforcing Act;* or, *the second Non-Residence promoting Act.*

5. By Statute, 56 G. III. c. 6, 22d March, 1816, the last-mentioned Act is continued, without amendment, until the 5th July, 1816.

6. And, by Statute, 56 G. III. c. 123, 1st July, 1816, to 5th April, 1817.

Follows now, under the above heads, a small part of the multitude of observations which have been suggested by the provisions made in relation to them.

§1.—I. *Giving Increase to the Number of Non-Resident Incumbents.*

Of the additions which thus recently, under the head of *Licenses*, have, by the Act, 1803, 43 G. III. c. 84, being 'An Act to amend, &c. and for *enforcing* the Residence of Spiritual Persons on their benefices,' been in that shape openly made to the multitude of Non-Residents, and thereby of Sinecurists,—evidence stands already on the face of the official abstracts, as herein reprinted in Section 7 of No. IV. of this Appendix, p. 440. Of the additions which, to an unlimited amount (for the augmentation of Church-of-England decency),[1] have altogether, without warrant, been made to the same goodly fellowship of the eaters of the bread of idleness,[2]— viz. by the so studiously organized, so carefully nursed, and so religiously pursued system of Episcopal connivance,—some account may already have been seen in the 7th and 8th sections of that same number.[3] Nor yet is this the whole, or so much as the most prominent part, of that which, in this same Act, self-styled an *Act for enforcing Residence*, has been done for the increase and establishment of Non-Residence. In a still more straight, direct, and open manner, as well as in a, beyond comparison, more commodious *shape* than through the medium of a *License*,—(an indulgence refusable, and not to be granted but upon conditions),—has the same accommodation been afforded and extended, by additions made to the original stock of *Exemptions*, as established by Henry the Eighth.[4] That, after having done all this for the swelling of the account of Non-Residence, a set of

---

[1] See p. 86 n. above.   [2] Proverbs 31: 27.   [3] See pp. 428–71 above.
[4] i.e. 21 Hen. VIII, c. 13 (1529): see pp. 433–4 above.

APPENDIX, NO. V. §I.

men, or so much as a single man, should, in any situation, be found so intoxicated with uncontroled power, as to conclude with affixing to the Act by which it is done the title of an '*Act for enforcing Residence*,' presents itself as a matter of fact in its own nature so difficultly credible, that, for the satisfying the Reader that the case is *really* so, a simple reference presented itself as hardly sufficient. Lest misconception or misrepresentation should be suspected, the following Note gives a reprint of the section (43 G. III. c. 84. §15.), from which the copy, made by Henry of this part of the Popish system of indulgences, has, in these times of No-Popery! received its enlargement.[a]

[a] The numeral figures here inserted are not in the Act: they are inserted for distinction sake, and for relief to the Reader's eye in its travels through the labyrinth:—the break by which the first figure is preceded, makes the distinction between the old matter and the new.

'§. 15. And be it further enacted, That no spiritual person having, or holding any office, in such manner as the same under any of the provisions of the said first recited Act,[1] or of an Act, passed in the twenty-fifth year of the reign of King Henry the Eighth, intituled, An Act that every Judge of the High Courts may have one Chaplain beneficed with Cure;[2] or of another Act, passed in the twenty-eighth year of the reign of King Henry the Eighth, intituled, The Bill for Non-Residence of Spiritual Men and their Benefices;[3] or of another Act, passed in the thirty-third year of the reign of King Henry the Eighth, intituled, An Act for the Chancellor of the Duchy of Lancaster and others to have Chaplains;[4] would exempt such spiritual persons from Residence, or from the penalties and forfeitures in the said Acts contained for Non-Residence;—1. Or actually serving as a Chaplain of the House of Commons;—2. Or as Clerk of his Majesty's Closet;—3. Or as a Deputy Clerk thereof, during the time of their respective attendance;—4. Or as a Chaplain-General of his Majesty's Forces;—5. Or Brigade-Chaplain on foreign service;—6. Or Chaplain on Board any of his Majesty's Ships;—7. Or of his Majesty's Dock-Yards;—8. Or in any of his Majesty's Garrisons;—9. Or Chaplain of his Majesty's Corps of Artillery, during the times of attending the duties of such offices respectively;—10. Or as a Chaplain to any British Factory;—11. Or in the Household of any British Ambassador, or public Minister residing abroad, during the time of his actually residing in such Factory or Household, and performing there, at all due times and seasons, the duties of such his office;—12. Or as Chancellor, or Vicar-general, or, in his absence, the principal Surrogate or Official in any Ecclesiastical Court of any Diocese, whilst they are residing in the places where their respective offices are exercised;—13. Or as Minor Canon, or Vicar Choral, or Priest Vicar, or any such other public officer in any Cathedral or Collegiate Church, during the times for which they may be required by the Canons, or local Statutes thereof, to reside at such Cathedral or Collegiate Church, and actually reside and perform duty at the same;—14. Or as Deans, Sub-Deans, Priests, or Readers, in his Majesty's Royal Chapels, at St. James's and Whitehall;—15. Or as Reader in his Majesty's private Chapel, at Windsor or elsewhere;—16. Or as Chaplain at the Royal Military Asylum, at Chelsea, or Royal Military College, at High Wycombe, or Teacher at the Royal Military Academy, at

---

[1] 21 Hen. VIII, c. 13 (1529). [2] 25 Hen. VIII, c. 16 (1533).
[3] 28 Hen. VIII, c. 13 (1536). [4] 33 Hen. VIII, c. 28 (1541).

Woolwich;—17. Or Chaplains at the Royal Hospitals, at Greenwich and Chelsea;—18. Or as Chaplains to the Royal Hospitals for Seamen, at Haslar and Plymouth, whilst they shall respectively reside and perform the duties of their respective offices;—19. Or as a Preacher or Reader in any of the Inns of Court, or at the Rolls;—20. Or as Bursar, Dean, Vice-President, or public Tutor, or Chaplain, or other such public officer, in any College or Hall, in either of the Universities of Oxford or Cambridge, during the period for which he may respectively be required, by reason of any such office, to perform the duties of any such office, and actually shall perform the duties of the same;—21. Or as Public Librarian, or Public Registrar, or Proctor, or Public Orator, or other such public officer, in either of the said Universities during the period for which he may respectively be required, by reason thereof to perform the duties of any such office, and actually shall perform the duties of the same;—22. Or as Fellow of any College in either of the Universities, or of Eton or Winchester College, during the time for which he may be required to reside by any Charter or Statute, and actually resides therein;—23. Or as Warden or Provost of Eton or Winchester College, during the time for which they may be respectively required, to reside, or shall actually reside therein;—24. Or as Schoolmaster or Usher in the same, or as Schoolmaster or Usher of Westminster School;—shall be liable to any of the Pains, Penalties, or Forfeitures, in the said first recited Act, or this Act contained, for or on account of any Non-Residence on any Dignity, Prebend, Benefice, Donative, or Perpetual Curacy, any thing in the said Act, or this Act, contained to the contrary notwithstanding.'

Note well the estimation in which salvation of souls is held by the penners of this clause. With the exception of a small part—a part which, till of late, was, if not still is, as small as a man could be had to serve for—the pay allotted for the salvation of souls is stripped off from the labour, and given to every Incumbent who is fortunate enough to obtain any one article in the above-mentioned enormous list of preferments. This detachable mass of pay, is it needless to the purpose of salvation? Then why leave it attached?—Is it needful?—Then with what colour [of][1] decency, other than Church-of-England decency, presume to attach it?

Included, in no small proportion, in this list of preferments are a set of complete Sinecures. Here then, on no other ground—for no other merit—than the good fortune of his having, by the necessary breach of probity, obtained *one* Sinecure,—so it is, that, from an office of matchless importance and supposed laboriousness, a man is suffered to strip off the greater part of the pay, allotted to it under the notion at least of its being necessary: to strip off as great a part of its pay as possible,—and out of it, for his own benefit, to carve *another* Sinecure.

Take the converse of this case. Of the whole number of benefices with cure of souls, in the instance of the greater part, the quantity of pay attached to the office is declared to be insufficient. Well then, was ever any such proposition made, as that of taking any one of these useless offices, and, in a permanent way, attaching the whole, or any part of the pay of it, to any one of these supposed insufficiently paid soul-saving and laborious offices? Never, never—who is there that would have endured it? This would be robbing Excellent Church, stripping her of her jewels—stripping her of every thing to which she owes her Excellence?—Oh no: where addition to pay is to be made, it must be—not by substraction from Sinecures, but by addition to the taxes.

As to persons already in possession—under the thus existing system of almost universal delinquency, to have bestowed upon them the most perfect indemnity—to have continued to them by law a possession obtained by breach of law—yes: all this might and would have been well: in all this there would have been nothing but what

---

[1] 1818 'or'.

§2.—II. *Increasing the Number of Resident Curates.*

III. *To that end, out of the pockets of Incumbents and Patrons, taking money, and forcing it into the pockets of Curates.*[1]

For this part of the system, the person to whom Excellent Church is principally indebted is, as already observed, p. 388, the Earl of Harrowby. For the principal *provisions*, see in the *second Curates' Act*—the Act of 1813;[2]—for the *reasons* on which they were grounded, see his Lordship's Speech.[3]

On an occasion such as this, salvation of souls being, of course, in every body's mind—if not in truth, at any rate in profession, the *ultimate* end in view,—in the character of *intermediate* ends, two objects, in themselves altogether distinct, appear to have engaged, in close conjunction, more or less of his Lordship's attention: viz. 1. On the part of the class of official persons in question, viz. *Curates*, securing appropriate *official aptitude*. 2. In default of habitual *Residence* on the part of the *Incumbent*,—securing, in as many instances as may be, the performance of that article of ecclesiastical duty on the part of the *Curate*.

In regard to *official aptitude*, though in this as in other cases, it is not itself exactly the same thing as *money*,—yet, as hath been shewn already (App. No. IV. §4. *Pay)*,[4]—according to his Lordship's theory, expounded by this his Lordship's practice, the degree of this aptitude being exactly as the quantity of money,—thus it is that, by seeing what he has done for securing the money, we shall see what he has done, and the whole of what he has either done or endeavoured to do, for securing the aptitude.

3. First then, in regard to the money: and thereupon as to the fund might have been justified by the *uti possidetis principle* (See App. No. IV. §2, p. 346). But in an Act, calling itself *An Act for enforcing Residence*, thus wantonly to go to work, and heap together, in addition to the one originally and so unwarrantably established by Henry the Eighth,[5] a still more enormous mass of Non-Residence,— ... once more, what assurance! Not only are probity and sincerity thus violated, but consistency. If giving despotic power over the rest of the Clergy to Bishops be a right thing,—as in the case of the other batch of indulgences, established in the shape of *Licenses*, it is assumed to be,—why not in these cases likewise give to good discipline the same supposed security?—why not subject this tribe of Incumbents, as well as the other, to the same supposed salutary yoke?

---

[1] In 1818, this sentence appears in the body of the text, though it seems better placed as part of the section title.
[2] 53 Geo. III, c. 149 (1813).
[3] *Substance of the Speech of the Earl of Harrowby.*
[4] See pp. 371–98 above.
[5] 43 Geo. III, c. 84 and 21 Hen. VIII, c. 13 respectively.

out of which it is to come. The pockets, those *into* which it is to come, being the pockets of Curates, those *out* of which it is to come are the pockets of Incumbents:—that is to say, of the future race: (for, as to the existing stock, much against the bent of his Lordship's stoicism, by some of his own friends (p. 18)[1] they have been saved from his Lordship's gripe:) meantime, on the death or removal of each existing Incumbent, out of the pocket of the existing Patron, if then he be in existence:—for thereupon down falls the value of the Advowson, in a scale ending at 0, or somewhere thereabouts.

Without the aid of this, his Lordship's liberality,—money was all along finding its way, and would have continued to find its way, from the one pocket into the other: call this *the free amount:*—the money which his Lordship provides is therefore not the *whole* amount in each instance paid and received, but the *difference* between the *free* amount and the *whole* amount: call it the *forced addition.*

Next as to the *quantum* of the *whole* amount.[a] In the first place comes a lowest *minimum:* the least sum that, under the name of Curates' salary, is to be paid and received in any circumstances. This is 80*l.* a year: and, as in the instance of this lowest, so in the instance of each hereinafter mentioned minimum, the *whole profit* of the living, if it be less than the *minimum*, goes out of the pocket of the Incumbent into that of the Curate instead of it.[2]

Above this comes a series of *minimums,* rising one above another according to circumstances. If the number of the parishioners amount to three hundred, the addition to the lowest minimum is 20*l.*; total 100*l.* (Section 7): number five hundred, addition to minimum 40*l.*; total 120*l.*: number a thousand, addition to minimum 70*l.*; total 150*l.*

Ipso facto fixations and augmentations, the above: to these (Section

---

[a] In the account of this profit are surplice fees to be comprized? No answer in the Act.[3] Charming nest for doubts! Is it not, Lord Endless?[4]

---

[1] See *Substance of the Speech of the Earl of Harrowby,* pp. 18–19: 'It has . . . been our object to obviate, as far as we were able, in framing the provisions of the Bill now before your Lordships, those objections which had been most strongly pressed against the preceding Bills. Those objections were chiefly, the application of its provisions to Incumbents actually in possession, and the increase of the influence given to the Bishops over their Clergy. Limited as that Bill was to livings of above 400*l.* per annum, I did not feel the weight of the first of those objections; and even if its provisions had been more general, I should not have felt the latter: but they were both urged with great force by persons who would otherwise have been friendly to the object of the measure; and it was thought therefore highly desirable to remove them.'

[2] See 53 Geo. III, c.149, §7.

[3] For Harrowby's comment on the calculation of surplice fees see p. 397 n. above.

[4] Lord Endless was Bentham's nickname for Lord Chancellor Eldon who, as Bentham wrote, 'never settles any thing' and 'never ends any thing': see Bentham to John Frauncis Gwyn, 31 July 1818, *Correspondence* (*CW*), ix. 230, 231. For Eldon's 'doubts' see pp. 448 n., 456 n. above.

13) succeed two discretionary ones; seat of the discretion, the holy bosom of the Bishop.[1] Incumbent's profit, 'exceeding' 400*l*., even though *numbers* fall short of the three hundred, discretionary addition as high as 20*l*. (p. 10), total as high as 100: Incumbent's pay, as before, exceeding 400*l*. (p. 17); then, if numbers amount to five hundred, fixed addition, as above, 40*l*., total fixed salary 120*l*.; discretionary addition as far as 50*l*. more; total *maximum* 170*l*. Incumbent's profit, as before, 400*l*.; then, if numbers amount to one thousand, fixed addition, as above, 70*l*.; total fixed salary (p. 10) 150*l*.; discretionary addition as high (p. 17) as 50*l*. more: maximum 200*l*. All this over and above the use of the parsonage, of which presently.

So much for additions, fixed and discretionary. Then come[2] (Section 11, 12) certain discretionary *deductions*, for *taxes*, and *repairs;* seat of the discretion, Right Reverend bosom, as before.

At the same Right Reverend discretion (by Section 10) further deductions, where the Incumbent is 'Non-Resident, or incapable of performing the duties from age, sickness, or other unavoidable cause;'[3] in the License, statement of the *existence* of 'special reasons'—the reasons themselves consigned to a *secret Register:* a separate book not inspectable, but with leave of 'Bishop, Ordinary, or other proper authority.'

At the same Right Reverend discretion, where a Curate is allowed to serve two parishes, or three parishes (by Section 9) deduction as far as 30*l*. from each, but so that in no one the remaining salary shall be less than 50*l*. or the whole value of the benefice.[a]

---

[a] Suppose *three* livings, profit in each above 400*l*., population in each above a thousand: under this 9th section, coupled with sections 7 and 13, Curate may, if Bishop pleases, have out of each, 200*l*.; out of all together, 600*l*.: the Incumbent in each being left with 200*l*. and a fraction. In the scale of absurdity this is the highest point, and this too high to be probable:—but, below it might be found no small number of probable ones.

Profit of living, suppose 449*l*.: population more than 1000. Of Curate's salary, the minimum is 150*l*., Bishop may make it 200*l*.: by leaving in the pockets of the parishioners the odd 49*l*. and thus reducing Curate's maximum to 150*l*., Incumbent may save 1*l*.: regard for his own pecuniary interests, kindness towards his parishioners, desire of their esteem and good-will, dislike towards the deputy thus forced upon him, indignation at the oppression to which he is subjected by this law—which is there of the above causes that might not of itself suffice to produce the effect? So far as concerns the easement thus given to the parishioners, here—thanks to the husbandman's sleep—here we have wheat springing up among the tares sown by him.[4]

Endless would be the task of particularizing all the doubtful or indubitably incongruous cases, liable to spring out of the complicatedness of a mass of

---

[1] In the remainder of this paragraph Bentham paraphrases either §7 or §13 of 53 Geo. III, c. 149.
[2] 1818 'came'. The text follows the 'Errata'.
[3] 1818 'cause,'. The text follows the 'Errata'.
[4] See Matthew 13: 24–5.

To the above are added various provisions, adapted to particular cases,—forming a body of detail which, for any such purpose as the present, it seems needless to bring to view.

Anxious is the care taken to prevent the Curate from keeping out of his pocket any part of the salary which it is determined he shall have: agreement to any such effect (Section 15) declared void: to any part of the *forced addition*, not received by him, not only does the Curate himself remain, but moreover his personal 'representatives' remain, entitled, with treble costs: debt and costs to be put into the respective pockets, in a summary way, by the Bishop. Along with 'the gross value of the benefice,' Incumbent applying for License is, among other things (Section 18), to state, 'what salary he proposes to give to his Curate.' To Incumbent, no License for Non-Residence without such statement: to Curate (Section 19), no License to serve as Curate, till such statement has been given in by Incumbent.—For the concealment of these particulars, another *secret Register*.

To persons who, in virtue of *Exemptions*, stand *ipso facto* and without *License*, entitled to the indulgence of Non-Residence,—the above obligations are, in one way or other, extended. Howsoever entitled to this privilege, never *by law* has an Incumbent had it in his power to enjoy it without the existence of a Curate to do the duty:— No Curate, no Non-Residence. By the Act of 1796 (Section 6), power was given to the Bishop to deprive of his Curate any Incumbent, even though exempt by *ipso facto* exemption: first he was to force a License into the Curate's pocket: then, on his taking it out again (which he might do whenever he pleased) Incumbent, thus remaining without a Curate, remained without the benefit of the Exemption: bound thereupon either to give up the benefice, or to do the duty of it himself. Upon the back of this obligation,—the imposition of which was thus left dependent upon the discretion of the Bishop,—comes a clause in this Act of 1813 (Section 19), forcing, or seeming to force, the Bishop to impose it: 'it shall not be lawful' (says the Act) 'to the Bishop to grant the requisite License to the Curate, unless the Incumbent has given in to him the statement required.' And here we have a third *secret Register*.

So much for *securing official aptitude:* now as to the provision for *insuring Residence*. By the Act of 1796, power was given to the Bishop for allowing to the Curate the use of the Parsonage, *if* he chooses to have it:[1] to the same Right Reverend person, by this Act of 1813 arrangement, the uselessness and mischievousness of which will be seen as we advance.

---

[1] 36 Geo. III, c. 83, §1.

(Section 3), power is given to *make* the man occupy it, when he does *not* choose it.

On a short view of this mass of complication, of which such features only as seemed most prominent could here be offered to the Reader's eye, several subjects for observation have been presented:—1. The elements of *official aptitude* in this case, according to his Lordship's[1] view of them. 2. The principle of making *agreements* for other people. 3. The considerations on which the *gradations* in the amounts of forced salary have been grounded. 4. Under such a system as hath been seen in regard to *service*, the importance attached to *Residence*. 5. The confining of the *indulgence* to the *richer* benefices. 6. On the part of the whole system, the probability it presents of being *efficient* with reference to any of its professed purposes.

I. *Elements of official Aptitude in this Case—what the proper ones.*

The situation of a Curate being the official situation in question, what in that situation, in his Lordship's conception, are the elements of official aptitude?—Answer. *Liberality of education; liberality of views;* and *decency of appearance*. 'How can we expect,' (says he, p. 16, in a passage already above referred to,)[2] 'how can we expect, considering the Church only as a profession, that men, who *have necessarily received a liberal education*, and who *ought to be men of liberal views*, will continue to enter into a profession, in which the blanks bear so large a proportion to the prizes?[a] How can we expect that persons, whose incomes hardly afford the means of subsistence, will be able to keep up that *decent appearance* which is almost indispensably necessary to secure the respect of their parishioners?'—Not indeed in the way of *direct assertion* is it that these endowments are, with reference to the office in question, presented, we see, in the character of *elements of official aptitude*. But is it the less true, that in this character it is that they are presented?—No, indeed, for such they are *assumed* to be: and, whatsoever be the strength given to *direct assertion*, that with which *assumption* operates is still greater. How opposite to *liberality*, any state of things in which there is any deficiency in them!—in Excellent Church sense, which is the only endurable sense, how opposite even to *decency*—to common decency! And,—except that it increases with the money put into the reverend pocket,—let a man read this speech of his Lordship's ever

---

[a] If, for so many past hundreds of years, they have continued to enter into it, why not for any number of *future* ones?

[1] i.e. Harrowby. [2] See p. 393 n. above.

so often, no other indication will he find in it concerning the elements of *official aptitude*.

Different—he cannot but confess—far different—is the conception, which, with reference to this same office, it has been the lot of the Renegado Graduate[1] to have formed to himself, in regard to these same *elements of aptitude*.

Duties, as above,[2] are all of them either *exigible*, or *inexigible:* at every turn comes the *demand* for this analysis: at every turn came the analysis, and lays bare Excellent Church to the very bone. All character notoriously scandalous out of the question,—for all *exigible* duties, through the virtue of the *fixed forms*, any one man, so he can but read, is as good as any other—any one *boy* as good as either: the part that remains unemployed of the *Parish Clerk*, as good as either the whole boy or the whole man.

Not so as to the *inexigible* duties: with reference to which, a few words on the subject of official aptitude shall here be said:—the Reader being still besought to bear in mind, that the field of Church-of-England dominion is not a field, in which, under *any* system of arrangement, they can ever, on any tolerably substantial ground, be expected to be possessed and manifested: always excepted what has been already mentioned as the rare product either of accident or policy,—here and there a Christian hero amidst a swarm of idlers.

Appropriate *active talent*, appropriate *learning*, appropriate *zeal*, appropriate *humility*—these, in the breast of a Christian Priest,—be he Incumbent, be he Curate, be he Priest of a Church, in which the abomination of *Sinecurism*, and the visible sign of it—the name and office of *Curate*—is unknown,—these may be stated as the elements of official aptitude: appropriate *active talent*, praying and preaching without book,—in season and out of season,—from the head and heart, and not from the eye:—appropriate *learning*, viz. in that shape, in which that man, and he alone possesses it, who has the Bible at his fingers' ends:—appropriate *zeal*, that zeal which has for its object the salvation of souls, not the catching of the loaves and fishes:[3]—appropriate *humility*, viz. that which, so far from spurning them, seeks out with preference, the ignorant, the indigent, the ill-mannered, even the profligate, so long as the endeavour to give increase to their welfare in any shape, spiritual or temporal, affords a ray of hope; seeking out always the souls, whose need of the physician is greatest, in preference to those, whose demand, if any, for his assistance, is least imperative.

---

[1] i.e. Bentham himself.　　　　[2] See pp. 352–3 above.
[3] An allusion to the story of the feeding of the five thousand: see Matthew 14: 15–21; Mark 6: 35–44; Luke 9: 10–17; John 6: 5–14.

APPENDIX, NO. V. §II.

Sir (I hear his Lordship saying), *what is the sort of Curate you have been finding for me? Your man—he is no better than a Sectary, or a Methodist.* May be so, my good Lord: for, in truth, very different are the functions we have been thinking of: I, that of saving souls: your Lordship, that of occupying, with graceful decency, the place opposite to your Lordship's at your Lordship's table.

Possession of *profane* learning—is *that* what his Lordship meant by 'liberality of education?' Is that the endowment which it was his wish and endeavour to secure to his Curate? Surely it cannot be unknown to him by what means, somewhat more effectually than by the possession of so much money, it may be secured to a man: if not, it is high time he should learn it. The *examination,*—the *public* examination,[1]—by which, in the Universities, trial is made of a man's aptitude for a *degree*—let examinations such as these be employed as trials of a man's aptitude, in the respect in question, for a Curacy,—a trial of this sort would be a somewhat better security than is afforded by the word *liberality,* when employed by lips such as his Lordship's, in the designation of the sort of education which a functionary of that sort ought to have:—instead of confining it to the *road* which leads to a University degree, let him set up the *turnpike* either at the entrance into the road which leads to each particular parochial benefice, whether in the shape of an Incumbency or a Curacy,—or at that earliest stage, at which the road leads in common to *all* such parochial benefices at once: viz. exactly at the very point, at which, to a real and efficient barrier, the indulgence of the Bishop's Chaplain substitutes a phantasmagoric image. Without the examination, the *liberal education,*—that is, if it means any thing, the having, for a certain length of time, existed within the precincts of the University,—will not do any thing:—in a word, let him establish in England, and for the English Church, that trial and that test which is so notoriously and universally efficient and sufficient in the Scottish—establish the examinations, you may do any thing: and the *liberal* education, with the Universities in and by which it is administered, may, without much loss, be dispensed with.

II. Next as to the *forced agreements:*—

On an occasion such as this, to what possible good use can the force—the coercive force—of government be employed? In what possible way can it be thus employed without producing a net balance on the side of mischief? Suffer the parties to settle the matter between

---

[1] See p. 388 n. above.

themselves, both will have been contented, or no agreement will have been made. Enter Marplot with his regulation,—and now, in so far as it has any effect, out of every two parties one is, as with but too much cause he may be, discontented,—feeling the money forced out of his pocket, and thus in a double way a sufferer: first by the loss, and then[1] by the sense of the injury that caused it. Marplot, shall we say? or rather Machiavel in the disguise of Marplot?[2]

But what matters it who is contented, and who not? The great ends are accomplished: the Curates' *pay* increased, with it increases the security for his *official aptitude*, and with it the *probability*—(a sad word *that*—leave it to the mathematicians: no; instead of it, spite of self-contradiction, say the *certainty*)—of the salvation of souls.

III. *Thirdly, as to the Gradations in the amounts of Salary.*

One principle is—*the richness of the benefice:* and, if free agreement must stand excluded, and if there must moreover be increase, *this* principle, at any rate, seems an unobjectionable, as well as an obvious and simple one. The more money a man has,—*cæteris paribus*, the more he can afford to part with. How small soever, on the one part the benefit, on the other part the burthen is at any rate the less.

It was too simple and too rational to be abided by. Upon the back of this are mounted two other principles: and new complication is produced, and confusion thickened. In the first place (p. 22) comes '*extent of the labour;*' the advantage of 'making the remuneration bear some proportion to it:'—but, no sooner is it started, than it is discarded for another, which in his Lordship's view it '*may best be inferred from:*' and that is, 'number of the parishioners.'[3] At this time his Lordship (not to speak of the hearers and non-hearers, whose persuasion was led captive by his eloquence) his Lordship must surely have been nodding: for, in the real nature of the case, nothing will any one find by which any ground is afforded for this inference.

---

[1] 1818 'and himself then'. The text follows the 'Errata'.

[2] Bentham is alluding to two characters from English theatre whose names had particular associations. Marplot, a character in the play *The Busie Body: A Comedy*, by Susannah Centlivre (bap. 1669, d. 1723), first performed in 1709, was described in the Dramatis Personæ as someone who 'generally spoils all he undertakes, yet without Design'. Used by other playwrights, the name became synonymous with someone who accidentally spoils or hinders any undertaking. English Renaissance playwrights used the name Machiavel (after Niccolò Machiavelli (1469–1527), Florentine statesman, author of *The Prince* written in 1513) to personify an intriguer or schemer.

[3] *Substance of the Speech of the Earl of Harrowby*, pp. 22–3: 'In order to make the remuneration bear some proportion to the extent of the labour, which *prima facie* may best be inferred from the number of parishioners, it is proposed to raise the minimum to 100*l.* per annum, where the population exceeds 500 persons; and to 150*l.* per annum, where it exceeds 1000.'

Here then, for measuring out the quantity of the pay, are two quite different standards set up—set up close together—and to neither of them is any regard paid. All this while, in the practice of this same office, stood before the Noble Reformer's eyes an arrangement, which he had but to copy, and the two standards would, both of them, have been conformed to,—and, without labour, or so much as thought, the remuneration been carved out and adjusted to the two standards with almost mathematical nicety. Two species of service he might have seen, *stated* and *occasional:* the *stated*, the reading of the Minister's part in Morning and Evening Service, with or without a sermon: the *occasional*, the reading of the Minister's part in the several offices for Marriage, Churching of Women, Christening, and Burial. In the stated parts of the service, for the remuneration of which the forming a scale of gradations has imposed such a tax upon his Lordship's genius, the *extent of the labour* varies not an iota: not an iota either with any other circumstance, or with the '*number of the parishioners.*' in the *occasional* parts, it varies very exactly with the number of the parishioners. For the *stated* parts of the service, the pay allotted is in each Curacy a fixed quantity, viz. a fixed salary: for those occasional parts of the service, the quantity of pay varies with, and is in exact proportion to, the number of the occasions in which, as above, the service is performed: a fee, called a *surplice fee*, being paid on each. Allotting in every parish the same salary, to that part of the labour which, in every parish, is, or at least should be, the same,—had the proportioning of remuneration, in regard to those parts of the service of which the number performed in the year varies in different parishes, and *that* upon a wide extended scale, been the object really in view,—nothing would have been easier. The salary allotted for the unvarying part of the labour being the same in every parish,—in any given parish suppose the amount of these fees to be such as is deemed sufficient, the object is already accomplished: suppose it not deemed sufficient, all that would have been wanting would have been to count the fees of each sort as they stand on the Parish Register, and from the Parish Fund, to make to each such fee such addition as should be judged requisite.—Not that this plan of arrangement would be a good one: for, in comparison with that mode, which his Lordship found in universal use, and giving universal content,—and which, at his Lordship's instance, Parliament has been at such pains to prohibit,—it is obvious how bad an one it would be. Parishes might be found, in which the surplice fees do not yield so much as 2*l.* a year: others, in which they yield more than 200*l.* and, in those which do not yield the 2*l.*, a Curate it is intended shall live.—Not that the plan would be an endurable one: but what is the point, and the only point in question, it would be in exact conformity to these his Lordship's rules.

Did ever any such notion occur to his Lordship, as that of its being better for the souls that the Service—the *stated* parts of it—should be performed *eight* times a month,—viz. on each Sunday Morning and Evening Service both than only,—as in some parishes,—according to the Diocesan Secretary,—*once* a month?[1]—No, never:—at any rate in the character of a desirable arrangement: for, if it had,—with the same simplicity and certainty might it have been accomplished, in the case of the *stated* as in the case of the *occasional* Services;—and thus remuneration made to bear not merely '*some proportion*'—and we have seen how rough an one—to *imaginary* extent of labour, but a proportion—and that to any degree of nicety an exact one—to *real* extent of labour.

No: this would have been too simple:—no force put upon men's wills,—no violation of property,—no nullification of agreements,—little exercise for legislative power:—none for legislative wisdom:—above all, no subjecting of the greater part of the whole body of Parochial Clergy—officiating and not officiating together—to the arbitrary will of six-and-twenty important idlers, dressed up to look wise:—Residence,—*that* Residence which it is either found impossible to enforce, or determined not to enforce, *by* Bishops,—would be enforced, and with the utmost degree of certainty, and, with every desired degree of constancy, *without* Bishops.

'Extent of labour, *primâ facie*, best inferred from the numbers of the Parishioners!'—What reasoning!—yet upon the sole strength of it is, that from 80*l*., through four or five straggling gradations—wide-stretching gradations—has Parliament, at the instance of Lord Harrowby, raised, or made a shew of raising, the pay of this office to as high as 200*l*. Upon the strength of this same reasoning, Saint *Perceval* and *Sir William Scott*—such, if we may believe his Lordship (p. 23), was the force of it upon their minds—would have swelled the amount as high as to 250!²

On this occasion, presents itself to recollection an old book, which,—were it only to save appearances,—cannot be too seriously recommended to the perusal of the Noble Reformer, with whom appearance is every thing. This old book is called the *New Testament*:—if, in the library of Lord Harrowby, no copy of it happens to have place, his friend, Mr. Vansittart, who has copies plenty to

---

[1] See p. 469 above.
[2] See *Substance of the Speech of the Earl of Harrowby*, pp. 23–4: 'This will not, I trust be thought too high, when I remind your Lordships, that in the Bills brought in by Sir. W. Scott and Mr. Perceval, this maximum was in particular cases carried as high as 250*l*. per annum.'

APPENDIX, NO. V. §II.

dispose of cheap,[1] can help him to one. A story is there told by one *Jesus of Nazareth:* it is that of certain *labourers in a vineyard.*[2] At different hours of the same day, different gangs had come in, each gang making its agreement for the same price. The time for payment came,—as if they had been reading the speech of Lord Harrowby,—those who had come in earliest began to grumble:—why grumble (said the husbandman with whom they had made the agreement), you have all of you that which you agreed to take? no force upon any of you: why should you have any more?—True it is, that, for the same money, those who came in after you, have indeed laboured less: but what are you the worse for it? By excusing them from so much labour I did them a kindness indeed: but giving you, as I do, what you were content to take,—it being the whole of what I promised,—I did you no injury:—is it for your eyes to be evil, because I am good? In the declared judgment of Jesus this answer was a good one, and ought to be regarded as a satisfactory one. Not so, in the judgment of the Earl of Harrowby, Sir William Scott, and their fellows: they knew better things. And so did Excellent Church,—and so did all those of her sons,[a] whose concurrence was given to these clauses!

If, after all, this theory of Excellent Church's, thus adopted and applied to practice by the Noble Reformer, be a sound and true one,—viz. that, to souls of parishioners, chance of salvation is as the quantity of money, in the shape of official pay, put into the pocket of the Parish Priest,—(Incumbent or Curate makes not, it is presumed, much difference)—on this supposition, a plain course is marked out, for all those to take, who to a belief in this theory, add a due regard for their own souls. In the Isle and Diocese of Ely, indication has already been given of a Parish, in which the quantum of this soul-saving Mammon rises as high as 12,000*l.* a year.[3] To this most fortunate part of that fortunate island should these men then repair and take up their abode. Here would be a spot on which to plant the Bench of Bishops!—Here would be a spot on which, at any rate as often as religion were the order of the day, Parliaments should be held!—Here would be a spot for a new Cathedral, with its Dean and Chapter: the Dean some Bishop, who, in addition to his Bishopric, has not yet Sinecures enough:—the Chapter—of whom could it be better composed than of the penners of the Quarterly Review? more particularly such of them as have niches already in other Chapters.

[a] Supra, App. IV.[4]

[1] For Vansittart's association with the British and Foreign Bible Society see p. 323 n. above.
[2] Matthew 20: 1–16.
[3] For the income of the Rectory of Doddington in the Diocese of Ely see p. 354 n. above.
[4] See pp. 343–493 above.

For increase of sanctity, Church of England Saints flocking in from all quarters to this blessed spot, the whole surface would thus be covered with a great city,—a new Jerusalem:[1]—were it only by *Easter-offerings*,[2] the quantity of that holy matter, with which, in this holy office, official aptitude, and with it assurance of salvation to souls increases, would there receive a prodigious increase: the whole surface being covered by house by the side of house, each portion of it would be covered by story mounted upon story, until at length the force of gravity, without need of any such interposition as we read of in the parable,[3] should set limits to the increase.

IV. *As to the Benefit to be expected from such Residence.*

The means employed are (as will be seen) as they could not but be, of a compulsory nature. If, in any determinate and assignable shape, there were any security, or sufficient reason, for the expectation, that by, or in consequence of, a Church-of-England Minister's Residence in the Parish in which he serves as Curate, in contradistinction to any other spot of his own choice, any real service could be rendered to mankind,—here would be a good to set against the mischief from the compulsion, whatever it be. But, for any such expectation what sufficient or substantial reason can be found? Employ here the necessary and so often mentioned analysis. Of the duties incumbent on that office, all such as are of *perfect* obligation might, to a much greater extent, and to much greater certainty, be performed (it has been shewn) by the Parish Clerk alone, than at present they are by the Parish Clerk and a Minister together:[a] and, as for duties of *imperfect* obligation, the fulfilment of them, is it, in any degree worth regarding, probabilized by Residence? That there scarce exists a diocese, in which a number of instances of their being, in a more or less considerable degree, performed, would not be[4] to be found, seems altogether probable.[b] But, in whatever instance any degree of

---

[a] Supra, App. No. IV. §3. *Service:*—§ [10].[5] *Facienda.*[6]

[b] Under the system of corruption and misrule, partly from accident, partly from policy, thus it will be always happening, that, throughout the establishment, out of some large number, of those who are placed in official or other elevated situations, there shall be some one in whose instance a portion of merit, real or supposed, absolute or relative, is to be found. Thus, on the Bench of Bishops, out of the six-and-twenty, you have commonly one or two at a time, whose characters, whether by design or accident, keep up the reputation of the order from sinking outright.

---

[1] The 'new Jerusalem' is described in Revelation 21.   [2] See p. 487 n. above.
[3] Bentham perhaps had in mind the parable of the foolish man who built his house upon sand (see Matthew 7: 26–7), or possibly the building of the city and tower of Babel (see Genesis 11: 1–9).   [4] 1818 'would be'. The text follows the 'Errata'.
[5] 1818 '4.' is a slip.   [6] See pp. 351–71, 484–5 above.

performance is given to them, such performance is on the whole *a work of supererogation*. In respect of reputation, it is of course, by all parties interested, made the most of: speak of the general worthlessness of the system, these instances, rare as they are, are produced as proofs to the contrary:—and thus it is, that, by the support given to the totality, of a system essentially and radically bad, more general mischief, beyond all comparison, is done, than what is equal to the greatest good, which, in the small number of particular instances in question, is or can be done by the fulfilment of these duties. When a system is to a certain degree bad,—the worse it becomes, the better: the worse the more scandalous,—and the more scandalous, the nearer the abuse is to its remedy.

All this while, under Church-of-Englandism, is it really in the nature of the case, that, in the situation of Curate, not to speak of that of Incumbent, Residence in the Parish should, generally speaking, be productive of any clear benefit in any shape to the Parishioners?—In the Army—in the Army properly so called—hope of preferment is, no doubt, really necessary to the securing of appropriate service:—in the metaphorical Army of the *Church militant*,—in the 'Noble Army' of these supposed 'Martyrs' to their sacred duty,[1]—scarcely can any thing be more adverse than that hope, to the constancy and perfection of correspondently appropriate service. Incumbent or Curate, rich or poor,—pursuit of *pleasure*—of *pleasure* in the ordinary sense of the word—is the natural, the ordinary, the principal, business of the Church of England Parish Priest:—if rich, the pursuit of his own pleasure at his own expense:—if poor, the pursuit of the pleasures of every man, in whose patronage the eye of ambition can descry a ray of hope.

In the Scottish Established Church no such pursuit of pleasure will you see. Why?—because in that Priesthood there is no such opulence as enables the Priest to pursue it at *his own* expense:—and because in that Church there is no such thing as *preferment:*—no preferment for a man to pursue, *while* pursuing, and *by* pursuing pleasure, as above, at the expense of *others*.

In the Priesthood of any *Non-Established* Church still less can there be any such pursuit of pleasure. Why?—because while there is *not* any such opulence, there *is* at the same time hope of *preferment:* so opposite may, under different circumstances, be the effects produced by the same cause.—Of preferment?—yes: but whence?—from the favour of this or that individual in the character of Patron?—No: but

---

[1] The phrase 'the noble army of Martyrs' occurs in the hymn 'Te Deum Laudamus', part of 'The Order for Morning Prayer', *Book of Common Prayer*, and is thought to be an allusion to the 'great multitude' described in Revelation 7: 9–17.

from increase in the numbers of the congregation:—from the increase in *that* favour, of which appropriate good service is—if not absolutely the sole, at all times the most probable and promising, cause.

Against the number of these, whose character, by such works of supererogation as have just been mentioned, is rendered heroic, set down on the per contra side those whose character,—by dissipation, and incongruous behaviour in other shapes,—is rendered scandalous:—on which side is the balance most likely to be found?

V. *Confining to the richer Benefices the Indulgence of Non-Residence.*

Thus much as to what is professed and placed in front, viz. augmentation of Curates' pay,—augmentation of the number of Resident Curates. Another part of the plan there is, that comes in as it were by a side wind: being that which, in a wholesale way, disposes of the fate of a group of Incumbents, nor that a small one. These are they, in whose case, on the occasion of the conversion, which to their own profit they make of *Cure* into *Sinecure*, the quantity of money stripped off from the profit of a benefice is, according to the measure taken of it by the eye of opulence, comparatively small: upon an average, according to his Lordship (p. 22), not more than 54*l.* a year:[1]—in this case, '*the practice*' (he says, p. 21), 'is by no means creditable to the Church:' accordingly he puts an end to it:—*if the whole pay does not amount to what in my judgment is proper for you to allow to your Curate, no Sinecure must you carve out of it:—serve the benefice yourself, Sir, or give it up.* Upon any such petty scale (I think I hear his Lordship say) *depredation shall have no License from me. I will not suffer it. I have no sympathy for it. A paltry sum! What son, what brother of mine, would stoop so low as to pick it up?*—And now comes the demand for a *dictum*, in which the most engaging frankness is employed in smoothing away the austerity of rigid discipline:—'*Pluralities and Non-Residence,*' says he (p. 7), '*are certainly no necessary part of the Establishment of a Christian Church.*' Nobly said, my Lord; but suppose the amount two, three, ten times, a hundred times, as much—does the magnitude of the wrong convert it into right? *Oh yes* (says his Lordship); *to be sure it does, so as the sum is but large enough* (p. 21): the case is then reversed: the thing is become an object: it would suit a son or a brother of mine very well:—it may save my estate a

---

[1] According to *Substance of the Speech of the Earl of Harrowby*, p. 22, the average income of a benefice was £89, while the average income of a curate was £35. Bentham's figure of £54 for the average 'profit of a benefice' is the difference between the average income of a benefice and that of a curate.

rent-charge—the arrangement is a useful one:—a man of my rank may find his convenience in it:—I see nothing in it that is not *creditable*. Accordingly, no sooner is the plunderage swollen to this interesting pitch, than he and his associates hold out to it a protecting hand: they authorize and confirm it,—for so to do is the chief part of the business of this suite of statutes. Comes now the demand for those two aphorisms, by which this part of the account is settled. 'A strict injunction of universal Residence' (says he, p. 21) 'would neither be practicable nor desirable. I am equally averse to the abolition of *Pluralities.*'

Apply this reasoning to depredation, in any of those hazardous shapes, in which, Noble Lords and Honourable Gentlemen, having so many sure and safe means at command, have no need of practising it, and in which it has accordingly been all along punishable. If it exceed not—say the sum of 5*l.*—the plunder of a shop (suppose) is regarded by them as not worth stooping for. Here then comes the demand for the candid acknowledgement, and the maxim of rigid discipline. Plunder of a shop to so low an amount as 5*l.* is a practice that would be 'by no means creditable' to the House, or to any member of it. The practice of shoplifting, to any such petty amount, 'is certainly no necessary part' (p. 7), 'of the establishment of a Christian Church,' any more than of good order, legitimacy, prerogative, or privilege. But, at some point in the scale above this, it has risen to such an amount as to catch the eye, and produce a sense of *pruritus* in the hand. Now comes the time for the maxims of liberality and indulgence: practised in the manner in which shoplifting is practised by Noble Lords and Honourable Gentlemen,—'*a strict injunction of universal*' abstinence from it (p. 21) would neither be practicable nor desirable.

Behold here a line of distinction that runs all over the field of depredation:—it is a right thing or a wrong thing, according as the shape, in which it is practised, is or is not of the number of those shapes, in which a member of the corporation of the *ruling few has* or has *not* need and opportunity of having recourse to it. To convert to his own use the contents of a shop, no need has he of any such uncreditable and hazardous practice, as that of snatching them out through the shop window, and running off with them. He gives his orders for them openly and above board:—they roll into his house from all quarters:—he exhausts Bond-Street:[1]—he borrows money to the right and left:—he buys land:—he settles it on his family:—the land goes to his family:—the loss remains to his tradesmen and to his

---

[1] Bond Street, which ran from Piccadilly to Oxford Street in London, was noted for its expensive shops.

CHURCH-OF-ENGLANDISM

vendors:—a just punishment to each of them for judging of his probity from his situation and expenditure, and for not knowing to what extent he was in the same way cheating the others.

In the eyes of *Sir Samuel Romilly*, depredation in this shape is '*by no means creditable*' to Noble Lords or Honourable Gentlemen. Session after session he therefore tries to put an end to it. Taught by the superior authority of *the Master of the Rolls*, Noble Lords and Honourable Gentlemen pronounce as often—that, '*a strict injunction of universal*' abstinence from swindling in that shape '*would neither be practicable nor desirable.*'[1]

Follow the scent thus given you, honest Reader, if you have the courage,—hunt over the *Viner*[2] and *the Statute Book*,—soon will you find distinctions of this sort, in quantity sufficient to fill a volume. When you have done so, call then upon the Noble Lords and Honourable Gentlemen, beg of them to give up these things;— what you will then find will be—that, depredation, when committed in a *liberal* shape, is part of the privilege of Parliament: that as for you, you are a Jacobin and a Leveller, and that it is *anarchy*, and not *common honesty*, that you want to introduce.

VI. *Prospect of Efficiency with regard to the professed Purposes.*

A consideration, which in this view should never be out of mind, is—that of this, as of every other part of the *licensing* system, the efficiency depends altogether upon the conception, which it may happen, on the one part, to the Incumbent,—on the other part, to the Curate, to be entertaining,—concerning the need they respectively have of any such mutually troublesome yoke: and whether to any very considerable extent, and for any considerable degree of permanency,—under so well organized and well-established a system of connivance, as may have been seen,—any very strong conception of such need is likely to have place,—will be for any Reader to judge, whose patience has, in the last preceding Number of this Appendix, carried him through the 7th and 8th Sections.[3]

The date of this second Curates' Act, viz. the year 1813, being posterior to that of the latest of the three Returns, of which the

---

[1] Romilly introduced the Freehold Estates Bill into the House of Commons on 28 January 1807. The measure, which would have made freehold estates, upon the death of the possessor, liable for the payment of simple contract debts, was opposed by Sir William Grant, Master of the Rolls, on its Third Reading on 18 March 1807, whereupon it was defeated (see *Parliamentary Debates* (1806–7) viii. 561–3 and (1807) ix. 159–65). Romilly reintroduced the measure in 1814 and 1815; on both occasions it passed the Commons, but was lost in the Lords after meeting opposition from Eldon (see *Parliamentary Debates* (1814) xxviii. 748–50 and (1815) xxxi. 1036–9).

[2] Charles Viner, *General Abridgment of Law and Equity*, 23 vols., London, 1741–57.

[3] See pp. 428–71 above.

Abstracts have been seen, viz. 1811,[1]—this charge of connivance in one place and neglect of duty in another, has, it may be seen, for its ground,—when applied to any time subsequent to the date of this last Act,—not any particular matter of fact, nor in short, any thing stronger than mere presumption and inference. Well then, inquire of the Diocesan Secretary, and see what *he* says as to the matter of fact.

Twentieth of July, 1813, is the date of the Act: 6th of November following comes from Mr. Wright a letter,[2] of which so much as relates to this subject is in the words and figures following:—

'In spite of the Canon Law and injunction of Archbishops, out of 439 Curates, employed for Non-Resident Incumbents, only 100 {of them} are *licensed;* and of the 439, only 116 are *Resident,* either in the parish or Parsonage-House, a very small proportion of them in the latter.'

Six months after the passing of the Act had already elapsed;—all that time had it had for the production of its effect;—when the public received from this same Diocesan Secretary the following additional information:—

'Indeed' (says he, Letter V. 18th January, 1814),[3] 'such is the dislike of these persons to place their Curates in a more independent situation, that the Curates' Act, so laudably brought forward last session, remains in most dioceses unattended to, although the Bishops are now so stimulated by this beginning of what I intend to do, that they are sending circular Letters in all directions from their Secretaries and even Chaplains.'

All this was unquestionably true; for never has it been questioned. These were among the facts, of which, if untrue, the untruth would in course have been made manifest, had any acceptance been given to his offer of being examined, as embodied in his Petition of the 21st of April in that same year, herein above reprinted.[4]

Such, from this part of the plan, being the prospect of advantage,—neither can the *price* exacted for it, still less the price which, had it depended upon the Noble Reformer, would have been exacted for it,[a] be left wholly without notice.

[a] Speaking of objections made by persons in the main friendly to the measure, 'those objections' (says he, p. 18) 'were chiefly the application as to Incumbents actually in possession; and, &c. . . . limited as that Bill was to livings of above 400*l.* per annum, I did not feel the weight of this.'

---

[1] The Abstracts for 1811 (*Commons Sessional Papers* (1812–13) xiii. 47–50) were ordered to be printed on 26 March 1813. The Curates Bill was introduced by Harrowby on 5 June 1812, and received the Royal Assent on 20 July 1813.
[2] Wright's Letter I, 6 November 1813 (*Morning Chronicle,* 13 November 1813).
[3] Wright's Letter V, 18 January 1814 (*Morning Chronicle,* 21 January 1814).
[4] See pp. 435–7 n. above.

Flaming indeed on this occasion was his zeal for Excellent Church: icy his sympathy, if he had any, for the sufferings of individuals. An Incumbent, whose Curate had been in use to be content with 35*l.*,[a] would,—if his living produced him more—though it were but a farthing more—than 400*l.*, have, all of a sudden,—in lieu of the less than ten per cent. income-tax, which on this score he had been in use to pay, leaving him 365*l.* a year—(to which income his expectations of him and his family had been allowed to attach themselves from two to fifty years or more together), would have found this tax raised upon him to 50*l.* per cent.:—would, in a word, have found himself stripped of half his income.[1] By some persons of more feeling, or more consideration than zeal,—this part of the project was, it seems, defeated: of the imaginary benefit, the commencement was,—in the instance of each benefice,—postponed to the death or removal of the Incumbent: and thus, though the intended benefit to the reputation of Excellent Church was thus cut down, so much of the burthen as had been intended for the shoulders of Incumbents was taken off. Still, however, as above noticed, a Patron,—who, upon the death or removal of the existing Incumbent, had a son in readiness to receive the living, with a neat income of 365*l.*,—will upon that event have found it reduced, as above, to 200*l.* Insensible to the idea of the thunderstroke above-mentioned, no wonder the Noble Lord's sympathy should be in the same state, with regard to this loss, for which the Patron and his son may have had more or less time to prepare themselves.

But the Noble Reformer has found a theory for all this: and by this theory his breast has found a coat of mail provided for it. It lies (this theory) in the word *property*. 'But' (says he, p. 6) 'this, it is said, is a violent transfer of property. My answer' (continues he) 'is, that it is no violation or transfer of property at all; . . . our property in our freehold estates is absolute; that of the Church is conditional.' Thus far the Noble Reformer. *Violation of Property?*—Is that then the heart and substance of the objection?—Not it indeed. The objection is—that, without equivalent good in any shape, here is so much *human suffering produced*. In that, and that alone lies the evil; and if this be *not* an evil, does his Lordship know of any other that *is?*—This evil, is it removed, or so much as lessened, by the

---

[a] According to his own statement (p. 9), among those livings alone that are under 150*l.* a year, he found no fewer than 600 in which the salary was, upon an *average*, no more than 35*l.* a year: consequently, in about half the number of instances, more or less below that mark.

---

[1] See pp. 501–2 n. above.

employing of this word, or that other, in designating the operation by which it is produced?—All the property in the world, what is it worth, but for the sensible good produced by it, or the sensible evil produced by the want of it?

Now,—if, to take effect during the lives of the occupants, or even though it were not till after their respective deaths,—any man had (some Lord Stanhope, for example)[1] stood up with a proposal to abolish in the lump the great State Sinecures, or the great Church Sinecures,—what would the Noble Reformer have said to it?—would it have been any thing less than Jacobinism?—Yet, by an abolition of these nuisances, not to take place till after the death of the occupant,—not an atom of individual suffering—unless the cessation of indeterminate longing be to be placed to the account of suffering—would be produced.

But the treasury of corruptive influence—this, in the eyes of the ruling few—sacred and profane together—is the ark of the covenant:[2] this is not to be touched:—on this depends the constitution for its existence. Why?—because by the *one will* ought all other *wills* to be determined:—to *one interest* ought all other *interests* to be sacrificed:—before that one *will*, accompanied or not by *understanding*, ought all other *wills* and all *understandings* to be laid and to be kept 'prostrate.'[3]

So intimate is the connexion between *sinister interest* and *interest-begotten prejudice*—of the sincerity of the Noble Reformer there seems no particular ground for entertaining any doubt:—and the same may be said of the Right Honourable Reformer,[4] whose executor it is his boast to have been; as well as of an indeterminate proportion of those who in this, and other parts of the field of government, have been acting with them, and brought the affairs of the country to their present pass. Of their sincerity there seems little reason to doubt:—but on that account have they been the less mischievous, or are they—such of them as we are still burthened with—the less dangerous?—Alas! no: but by so much the more so. The more sincere, the more ardent and pertinacious. If (what seems not altogether improbable) it should seem to them that the salvation of their own souls depends upon their pursuing to the uttermost the principles thus acted upon as above, what are we—what are we, the

---

[1] Charles Stanhope (1753–1816), third Earl Stanhope, had been one of the most outspoken supporters of the French Revolution and advocate of Parliamentary reform and religious freedom.

[2] The Ark of the Covenant, the most sacred religious symbol of the Hebrews, was believed to represent the Presence of God: see Exodus 37: 1–5; Hebrews 9: 4.

[3] See p. 37 n. above.

[4] i.e. Spencer Perceval: see p. 389 n. above.

subject-many—the better for their religion and their sincerity?—Alas! we are all the worse for it.

§3.—IV. *For Increasing the Value of English Livings, exacting from the Population of the Three Kingdoms the Annual Sum of* 100,000*l.*

The history of the fund, to which this comes as an addition, presents some curious enough particulars.

Ever since the year 1703, being the third year of Queen Anne, that same original fund has been in existence.[1] It is composed of the produce of a part of the taxes[2] first imposed on ecclesiastical benefices in general:[3] imposed originally[4] by the *Popes;* and, by King Henry the Eighth and his Protestant successors, continued in quality of successors to these same Catholic rulers. The hold taken by the Popes had been unsteady and incomplete. Henry included within his grasp (26 H. VIII. c. 3.) all ecclesiastical benefices without distinction: *First Fruits* were the whole income of the first year; *tenths*, were a ten per cent. *income-tax* upon the income of each succeeding year. The amounts being of course, from the first, as low as individual self-defence on the spot, struggling against distant tyranny, could contrive to make them,—and for the decrease in the value of money no correspondent increase being ever made,—thus it is, that, upon an average of twelve years, ending with the year 1814, the sum total annually received from the whole number of benefices in England,—with the exception of those which, by the Act of Queen Anne,[5] were exempted, in consideration of their not yielding more than 50*l.* a year, money of that time,—amounted[6] to no more than about 14,000*l.*: (14,037*l.* 17*s.* 10$\frac{1}{4}$*d.*)[7]

Various topics of observation here suggest themselves:—1. Worthlessness of the original object;—2. Insufficiency of the means originally provided;—3. Amplitude of the means more properly applicable to the same object;—4. Wastefulness of the new addition, anno 1809.

---

[1] Queen Anne's Bounty, named after Anne (1665–1714), Queen of England, Scotland, and Ireland 1702–7, Queen of Great Britain and Ireland from 1707, was established in 1704 (2 & 3 Ann., c. 11), to augment the incomes of poor clergy.

[2] 1818 'of taxes'. The text follows the 'Errata'.

[3] As Bentham goes on to explain, the Bounty was funded from the First Fruits and Tenths previously paid to the Crown, but thenceforth paid to the Governors of the Bounty of Queen Anne, to assist in the maintenance of poor clergy. See also pp. 293 n., 486 n. above.

[4] 1818 'general, originally'. The text follows the 'Errata'.   [5] i.e. 5 Ann., c. 24 (1706).

[6] 1818 'year,—money of that time, amounted'. The text follows the 'Errata'.

[7] See 'Papers relating to Queen Anne's Bounty, and to Parliamentary Grants, for the Augmentation of the Maintenance of the Poor Clergy: 1703–1815', *Commons Sessional Papers* (1814–15) xii. 381–520, at 385, recording sums received at the Exchequer for First Fruits and Tenths for the years 1803 to 1814.

APPENDIX, NO. V. §III.

I. First, *as to the worthlessness of the original object.*

—What was that object?—salvation of souls?—increase in the value (quality and quantity taken together) of the official service?—No such thing: for, from that time down to the present,—now upwards of a century,—not of so much as a single step, taken towards the production of any such increase, are any traces to be found. 1. Appropriate *qualification*, on the part of the Incumbent. 2. Increase or security given to the number of *times* in the year on which *service* shall be performed. 3. *Residence* of a Minister within or near the Parish:—in relation to no one of these points, by authority of government, has any condition been ever established, or sought to be established.—Statutes at Large—Burn's Ecclesiastical Law—no trace of any such thing any where.

Among the papers printed by order and for the use of the House of Commons,—in and for six successive years, from 1810 to 1815 inclusive, may be seen papers, having each of them for its title, '*An Account of the Steps taken by the Governors of Queen Anne's Bounty, towards the sum of* 100,000*l. granted by Parliament for the Relief of the Poor Clergy.*'[1]—in no one of them is any such trace to be found.

Among these same House of Commons documents for the year 1815, may be seen a folio of 139 pages, with this title:—'*Papers relating to Queen Anne's Bounty, and to Parliamentary Grants for the Augmentation of the maintenance of the Poor Clergy.*' 1703–1815. Date of the order for printing, 27th February, 1815: No. 115.[2]—Throughout this whole volume, the same sacred silence. Of the host of saints, by which that Honourable House is sanctified,—not one, at whose instance, information in relation to the attention shewn to any one object except the money, was obtainable.

The number of souls saved will be as the aggregate amount of the money put into the pockets of the established Clergy:—such, once more, is the fundamental principle:—such has been the principle acted upon from the first—acted upon to the last—acted upon throughout the whole of the ecclesiastical department. To so many others that have been seen add this further proof, of the dominion exercised over practice by the *maxims* herein-above ascribed (App. No. IV. §4)[3] to Excellent Church.

Of any steps, in any one instance, taken by any person or persons,

---

[1] Parliament made eleven annual grants of £100,000, commencing on 5 September 1809, to aid the work of the Governors of Queen Anne's Bounty for the years 1809–16, 1818–20. For the first six papers see *Commons Sessional Papers* (1810) xiv. 99–102, (1810–11) x. 471–2, (1812) x. 163–6, (1812–13) xiii. 53–6, (1813–14) xii. 149–52, and (1814–15) xii. 521–4.

[2] i.e. *Commons Sessional Papers* (1814–15) xii. 381–520.

[3] See pp. 375–81 above.

towards the forwarding of any one of the above-mentioned essential objects,—the only trace that has been found shall here be mentioned:—it consists in the following passage in one of those letters of the Diocesan Secretary so often mentioned, viz. Letter II. Morning Chronicle, 20th Nov. 1813:[1]—

'On a recent proposal, by the Governors of the Bounties of Queen Anne, to augment some livings, *if the duty was increased*, one Incumbent proved satisfactorily, that, if he received the augmentation, and caused the duty to be performed once *every Sunday*, instead of *once a fortnight*, he should receive two pounds per annum less than he received without the augmentation;—another, where the duty is only *once a month*, not only declined the augmentation, with an *increase of duty to once a fortnight*, but stated, as other Churches were near, he thought it would be a good plan to *dilapidate* the Church entirely,—so that he wanted to get rid of the duty altogether,—but he did not say one word about giving up the living, although a small one.'

II. *Insufficiency of the means originally provided.*

III. *Amplitude of the means all along more properly applicable to the same object.*

From the days of Henry the Eighth, down to those of Queen Anne, not any the slightest symptoms of concern in relation to this matter: where, in the eyes of the retainers of the Monarch and *their* retainers, the pay, clogged as it was with the duty, was not worth their acceptance,—souls and their salvation were not worth a thought. The throne being filled by a weak woman, up steps Excellent Church, and seats itself by her side. The produce of the above-mentioned antique assessment is now, by the piety of the Queen, bestowed in augmentation of the small benefices. Pompous is the language in which the grant is announced and established. What does it amount to?—In round numbers, 14,000*l.* a year and no more.[2]

Not to speak of Bishoprics and Archbishoprics—among the twenty-six nests of acknowledged idlers, styled Chapters, headed by Deans,—more than one might be mentioned, each of which would, by its suppression, or at any rate with the addition of one other, have furnished towards this same object a larger contribution.

By the suppression of no one of these seats and sources of corruption, would any tax on the public have been imposed. By

[1] Wright's Letter II, 17 November 1813 (*Morning Chronicle*, 20 November 1813).
[2] See p. 518 & n. above.

that in question, as by every other manifestation of Royal *bounty*, a tax to the annual amount of it has been imposed: for, royal revenue being never sufficient for royal bounty, taxes are the means by which the everlasting deficiency is everlastingly supplied.

In regard to efficiency with reference to the ends in view,—whatever were these ends, the prospect afforded by such a contribution was altogether ludicrous. A calculation may be seen in Burn's Ecclesiastical Law, title, *First Fruits and Tenths*. At the time of making it—(the time not specified, nor is the omission any great loss)—226 was the number of years that would have elapsed, before the arrival of the day, on which,—on the supposition that livings, *under* the value of 50*l.* a year, money of the then present time, were the only ones to which the augmentation was to be applied,—they would—the whole number of them—have been raised *up to* that amount.[1]

Here then came a dilemma.—Salvation of souls being the professed object,—the money thus bestowed, under the notion of its operating in the character of a means towards that most important end, would it, with reference to that end, be in any degree efficient?—would it be altogether inefficient?—On neither supposition is any such remotely operative arrangement a defensible one. Is it in any degree efficient?—what is to become of souls before the instrument of salvation has been in readiness to operate?—why are these to be left unsaved, any more than those, if any, who will have to come after them?—Is it altogether inefficient?—The money thus bestowed is then, the whole of it, with reference to the ends in question, bestowed in waste. And, at the end of the 226 years, what, in point of pecuniary sufficiency, is produced? Of no one of the several Reverend principals in question, does the pay as yet amount, to one-fourth part of that which, at present, in the declared opinion of Parliament, the deputy of every such principal would have, if his quantum of pay were sufficient.[2]

IV. *Wastefulness of the recent Addition, Anno* 1809.

Paper money being plenty, political piety not less so, shame alone scarce,—May 20th, anno 1809, comes from the throne a message, calling upon Parliament, by one magnanimous effort, to fill up the gulph almost at once.[3] For a certain number of years, 100,000*l.* each

---

[1] Burn, *Ecclesiastical Law*, 2nd edn., 1767, 'First fruits and tenths', §IV. First fruits and tenths appropriated to the augmentation of small livings, ii. 248–9: '[C]omputing the clear amount of the bounty to make fifty five augmentations yearly, it will be 339 years from the year 1714 (which was the first year in which any augmentations were made) before all the said livings can exceed 50*l.* a year. And if it be computed, that half of such augmentations may be made in conjunction with other benefactors (which is improbable) it will require 226 years before all the livings already certified will exceed 50*l.* a year.'   [2] See pp. 500–1 above.

[3] The King's Message Respecting the Clergy, requesting that Parliament find a method to

year,—the thing is done.[1]—100,000*l.* a year?—what is 100,000*l.* a year?—compared with our expenditure on objects of infinitely inferior importance, a mere drop added to the ocean. Thus it is that, by every instance of past or present waste, argument is made, and that a conclusive one, for any future waste.[a]

On this head, to say any more in this place than has been said already—would be but repetition or anticipation.—100,000*l.* a year thus thrown out of the window! and what is the result?—Of the plan, such as it is, the completion is accelerated:—but the principle—the vicious principle—remains in all its absurdity,—and, with the acceleration given to the pretended benefit—to the[2] unfelt benefit—the too real and severely felt burthen is proportionably increased: the

---

[a] Well:—why, all of a sudden, at more than a hundred years distance, outbid, and to such a degree, the piety of the High-Church Queen?—The answer is ready. Oh (says the Earl of Liverpool), *(Cobbett's Debates*, xiv. 830–832)—this is for a 'class of men who, of all others, were *most* serviceable to the country!'[3]—Say you so, my Lord?—why then they are more serviceable—every man of them—than *Marquis Camden* with his 23,000*l.* a year;[4] or even *Lord Arden*, with his freehold 38,000*l.*:[5] something more than this 38,000*l.* is therefore the least part any of them should have.—Here may be seen a specimen of the reasoning, on the ground of which expenses are incurred and taxes imposed.—It shews how the money has gone, is going, and will continue to go—unless and until . . . . it is needless to add the rest.—Speech from his Lordship—Address accordingly, *nemine contradicente.*

But these, it may be, are but the Reporter's words.—Yes, so it may be. But, by these same Reporters, how much oftener are not speeches mended than marred?— Well then—compare the reasoning, as above, with the reasoning in the Earl of Harrowby's Speech—the produce of his own closet:—see whether in respect of closeness, between the imputed reasoning of the First Lord of the Treasury, and the undoubted reasoning of the Lord President of the Council,[6] there be much to choose.

---

accelerate the operation of Queen Anne's Bounty, was presented to the House of Commons on 26 May 1809 and to the House of Lords on 30 May 1809: see *Commons Journals* (1809) lxiv. 352, and *Lords Journals* (1809–10) xlvii. 319.

[1] See p. 519 n. above.

[2] 1818 'benefit—the'. The text follows the 'Errata'.

[3] The debate in the House of Lords of 1 June 1809 on the King's Message Respecting the Clergy is at *Parliamentary Debates* (1809) xiv. 830–2, and the comment by Robert Banks Jenkinson (1770–1828), second Earl of Liverpool, leader of the administration as First Lord of the Treasury 1812–27, is at col. 831.

[4] John Jeffreys Pratt (1759–1840), second Earl and first Marquis Camden, Lord Lieutenant of Ireland 1795–8, Secretary for War and Colonies 1804–5, Lord President of the Council 1805–6, 1807–12, had in 1780 been appointed one of the Tellers of the Exchequer, an office from which, by 1808, he received an annual income of over £23,000 (see 'Third Report from the Committee on Public Expenditure', *Commons Sessional Papers* (1808) iii. 427). At the beginning of 1817, Camden voluntarily relinquished the profits and emoluments arising from the Tellership, but retained a salary of £2,500 per annum.

[5] See p. 425 & n. above.

[6] i.e. Liverpool and Harrowby respectively.

APPENDIX, NO. V. §III.

burthen thus increased, and still the interest of the existing stock of souls sacrificed to that of their future contingent successors.[a]

[a] According[1] to the short account, given, in Cobbett's Debates, xiv. 830–832, of a speech of the *Earl of Harrowby*'s in the Lords, June 1, 1809,[2] on the occasion of the King's Message—1703 being the year in which the *First Fruits and Tenths* were allotted to this purpose, 203 years, reckoning from that year, was the length of time, that would have elapsed, ere all the livings then under 50*l.* would, out of that fund, be raised up to 50*l.*: 510 more, (together 723), ere all the livings then under 100*l.* would be raised up to 100*l.* But, with this 100,000*l.* in his hand, viz. with this sum once paid, or with the 100,000*l.* a year, (it does not exactly appear which) '*much gratified*' was the Noble Lord, by the thoughts that the original 203 years would be reduced to 39 or 40: at the end of which time no living would remain of less value than 50*l.* a year. Well, but this 50*l.* a year—a sum which, by 30*l.* a year, fails of being sufficient for the lowest paid Curacy—when this is gained, what is it that is gained?—and how stands the matter in regard to the time necessary to raise the 50*l.*, as above, to 100*l.* a year? '*Gratification*' being the object, the period would have been rather too distant, had the fixation of it been committed to calculation. It was, therefore, left to *imagination*:—a more pleasant accountant than *Cocker*.[3] By 50*l.* even then, will the provision be short of the sum, spoken of in the character of a *minimum*, in the Royal Message, by which the measure was introduced:—by 50*l.*? yea, and by 100*l.* a year, short of the sum, which, when the living is ever so little more than 400*l.*, *may*, out of it, be allowed to a Curate. See above, pp. 500, 501.

The grant was to be once for all: it was to be *annual* and *continual:* the one or the other, according as Honourable Gentlemen and Noble Lords should please.[4] Continuity, *i.e.* perpetuity, gave universal pleasure. True it is, that, in the Lords, symptoms of opposition had for the moment broke out. In argument accordingly (the determination being all the while otherwise) 100,000*l.* once paid was to be the whole: to that sum did the prudential arithmetic of the Earl of Harrowby *then* confine itself: the 39 or the 40 years accordingly was the time, during which '*the most serviceable men in the whole country*' would have to wait for this minute part of what was their due. Yet, six days after, 7th June, 1809, Annual Register for 1809, pp. 171, 172,—by the Chancellor of the Exchequer[5] no secret is made of its being destined for *perpetuity:* accordingly, the 39 or 40 years are now shrunk to 4 years. Resolution, unanimous. Chancellor of Exchequer's 'satisfaction, great.' '*Suggestions* for improvement, and the formation of a *system* (he said) would be considered afterwards.'[6] So far Mr. Chancellor of the Exchequer:—these *suggestions*, this *system*, and the proof that the men in question 'were of all others the most *serviceable to the country*' will all

---

[1] In 1818, the present note appeared at the conclusion of §3, prefaced by the remark: '**** Note, mislaid for the moment, intended to have been tacked to the end of the paragraph in p. 523, concluding with the words "contingent successors." Subject of it, the time, at which the benefit to the future contingent souls may be expected to receive its completion.'

[2] See *Parliamentary Debates* (1809) xiv. 832.

[3] Edward Cocker (1632–76), schoolteacher, and author of works on penmanship and arithmetic, including *Cockers Arithmetick, Being A plain and familiar Method suitable to the meanest capacity for the full understanding of that incomparable Art, as it is now taught by the ablest School-Masters in City and Countrey*, London, 1678.

[4] See *Parliamentary Debates* (1809) xiv. 831–2.

[5] i.e. Spencer Perceval.

[6] See *The Annual Register, or a View of the History, Politics, and Literature, For the Year 1809*, London, 1811, pp. 171–2, and *Parliamentary Debates* (1809) xiv. 920–2.

CHURCH-OF-ENGLANDISM

In the whole of this business taken together, one circumstance there is, capable of being regarded as a source of satisfaction,—and it is the only one.—This is—that, of the mass of money thus designed to be wasted, a proportion—and *that* by much the larger one—is yet capable of being saved. Of the 700,000*l*. thus furnished within these seven years, nothing (it appears) but the *interest* hath as yet been thus applied;—as to the principal, having been invested in Government Annuities, it remains untouched:—capable of being applied to better purposes. Old fund and new fund together,—there remains, at the disposal of the Governors, to the value of about 1,200,000 3 per cents. Particulars are not worth loading the page with:—the sources from whence this conclusion has been deduced, are the annual papers above spoken of, and the large mass of papers of Feb. 1815, p. 8.[1]

To this heavy and immediately imposed burthen,—imposed for future contingent, nor that any thing more than ideal benefit,—not a parallel, but a contrast, is afforded by the augmentation given the year after to the underpaid benefices of the Church of Scotland.[a]

Out of the 944 parochial benefices belonging to that Established Church,[2] the number of those of which the stipends remained below the annual sum of 150*l*., was 170:[3] to raise every one of them up to that mark, the sum required was 8,713*l*. 6*s*. 8*d*. By a Statute of the year [1810][4] (50 G. III. c. 84), 10,000*l*. was accordingly provided for that useful and altogether unexceptionable purpose.

Useful and unexceptionable?—how so?—if the annual 100,000*l*. granted for the English Clergy, was useless and indefensible?—Answer, in few words:—1. Under Excellent Church,—*Service*, over and over again proved unprofitable, or little better:—under Scottish

come out the same day. Whatsoever the men themselves may be, to the grand object from which every thing proceeds, and to which every thing tends—to the corruptive influence of the Crown, this job for the raising of their income will in no small degree be '*serviceable*.' In no small proportion are the livings thus enriched, in the gift of the *King*, that is, of the *Chancellor*. No *doubts* appear, on *this* occasion, to have issued from the official manufactory of *doubts*.[5]

[a] Taken from the House of Commons Paper, intitled Report of the number and value of the stipends of the Scotch Clergy under 150*l*. per annum: made out under the inspection of the Moderator of the General Assembly of the Church of Scotland.—Date of the order for printing, 23d March, 1810, No. 161.[6]

---

[1] See p. 519 & n. above.
[2] For Bentham's calculation of this figure see p. 481 n. above.
[3] In fact, the figure was 172: see *Commons Sessional Papers* (1810) xiv. 108.
[4] 1818 '1800'.
[5] For Lord Chancellor Eldon's patronage of ecclesiastical benefices see p. 487 n. above, and for his doubts see pp. 448 n., 456 n. above.
[6] See *Commons Sessional Papers* (1810) xiv. 103–10.

APPENDIX, NO. V. §IV.

Church, eminently and incontestably profitable: exigible duties well performed; inexigible performed, and universally performed. 2. Under Excellent Church, the *benefit* looked to from the augmentation, if not altogether ideal, at any rate future contingent as well as remote: under Scottish Church, immediate. 3. For Excellent Church, the amount of the *burthen* imposed on the United Kingdom, ten times as great as that imposed for the Scottish Church: while the population of England is not more than between five and six times that of Scotland.[1]

In regard to Scotland, one regret still remains: it is—that to the 8,700*l.*, 17,000*l.* more was not added. Though, in comparison with what it is in England the temptation is as nothing,—still, while the profit of some benefices being as high as 300*l.*, that of others has been no higher than 40*l.*,—hope of translation, and thence the pursuit called *preferment-hunting*, scarcely even in Scotland can have been altogether without example: scarcely even can it reasonably be expected to be completely so, where the difference is as great as it still remains, viz. the difference between 150*l.* a year (the present minimum) and the 300*l.* In the Scottish Church, give but money enough—and a very moderate sum will suffice—the appetite for translation may be every where and completely extinguished—not only actually extinguished, but manifestly seen to be so.

But, under Excellent Church, while Bishoprics and Archbishoprics remain, what is the number of hundreds of thousands—not to speak of millions—that would be necessary?—Calculate, any one, who has curiosity and leisure.

§4.—V. *Regulating the occupations of Agriculture, in the case of a Parish or other Priest.*

Note first the inconsistency as well as inutility of the apparent endeavour:—note afterwards the real and sinister object at the bottom of it.

Unless by license from a Bishop, a Clergyman not to act as a husbandman—nay nor so much as to take a few square yards to add to his garden, how scanty so ever may be the allotment attached to his parsonage![2]

A Parish Priest forbidden to act as a farmer? What inconsistency! what hypocrisy!—When was hypocrisy ever so blind? That which it not merely allows, but on pain of starvation forces him to do, it at the

---

[1] According to the census of 1811, the population of England and Wales (excluding those serving in the Army and Navy) was 10,106,780, and that of Scotland 1,804,864: see *Commons Sessional Papers* (1812) x. 171–4.
[2] See 43 Geo. III, c. 84, §§ 4–5.

same time forbids his doing, punishing him in case of his doing it: punishing him, unless it shall have happened to him to have obtained a license, the obtainment of which is at the same time made to depend—not on his own will, but on the free and unconjecturable will of another person, in whose breast personal interest may, in any imaginable shape, set up an inexorable bar to it.

To take the word *farmer*,—since upon this word, with its conjugates *to farm* and *farming*, every thing must turn. Of that which a farmer, as such, does, what is there that from first to last a Parish Priest is not by law, not only allowed, but on pain of perishing for want, compelled to do? A *farmer*, in one sense of the word, is, indeed, he who, by a species of contract, takes to *farm, i.e. to cultivate*, a quantity of land belonging to another person, paying him *rent* for it. In another sense, however, a man is said *to farm his own land:* and, so far as it is his own land alone that he farms, no such contract has place. But—the quantity and quality of the land occupied, and the manner in which it is occupied, being the same in both cases, what difference can it make to piety—what to official duty, whether a man does or does not pay rent for it?

In the *contract*, therefore, it can not be, that the objection lies, to the complex course of operation, whatever it be, for the designation of which the word *farming* is employed?—No: it is in the *occupation:* in the occupation in which, in consequence of such contract, the sort of man in question will be engaged.

And—that occupation—what is it?—what but the very occupation, which, from first to last, the sort of man has been forced to pursue— by the law itself forced to pursue—on pain of perishing?

Glebe and *tithes*—in one or other of these shapes was Parish Priests' pay originally received all over the kingdom. In one or other of these shapes, or in both together, received it was at the first in every *country* parish, without exception: and in the greater part of the whole number of parishes, in these same shapes, or in one of them, does it continue to be received or receivable, down to this day.

In so far as it is in the shape of *glebe* that the pay is received by him, the occupation of this functionary, unless he lets the land to farm to others, must be that of an agriculturist: in so far as it is in the shape of *tithes*, and, (as in most cases they are,) these tithes are the tenth part of the produce of *land*,—in this case likewise his occupation can not but be that of an agriculturist: the very occupation, for the exercise of which, land is taken to farm.

Increase of *piety*—increase of the quantity of *time* and *labour* proper to be employed in official *duty*—in these—one or other, or both of them—may all the pretences alledged, or rather insinuated—the pretences for the sort of restraint in question—be found.

Buying, producing, selling—to these three may the operations of the farmer—profane or sacred, impious or pious—be reduced.

1. As to *buying*—it is not in *buying* that the rub can lie:[1]—buying is an operation which the most Reverend person in existence, the Archbishop of Canterbury—which the 'most religious' person in existence, the King of England[2]—can not be exempted from the performance of.

2. As to *producing*,—unless he can find somebody to take the land of him to farm, (which is what he is never by law required to do, nor has ever in his single power to do,) from this glebe of his, in so far as it is out of *that* that the pay is to come,—by this glebe of his, unless it be by extracting *produce* from it, how is any thing that can serve for pay to him to be obtained?

3. Remains the operation of *selling*. But, the produce of his glebe, so far as he is paid in glebe,—and his tithes, when it is in kind that they are taken by him, unless it be from his *selling* of them,—how is it that, (with the exception of that part of each, which it is in his power with the help of his family to consume)—how is it that any thing that can serve for pay to him can be obtained by him? Neither by corn, nor by grass, could either his own or his wife's nakedness be covered,[3] with any tolerable degree of decency: the first horse or ass they met with in their way to Church would expose them to shame. By *fig-leaves*, yes;[4] but by no law—Ecclesiastical, Common, or Statute—is the husbandman any where compelled, as yet, to grow figs for fig-leaves.

With *piety*, therefore,—in the judgment at least, either of the founders or the upholders of the Parochial Priesthood,—no one of these three operations, of which the occupation of a husbandman is composed, can be inconsistent.

Supposing any one good thing aimed at,—remains as the only good thing that can have [been][5] aimed at by these restraints, increase of the quantity of time and labour employed in the performance of these same sacred and *official duties*. Of official *duties*, meaning always in the shape of *duties of imperfect obligation*, as above distinguished:[6] for, as to duties of *perfect* obligation, consisting in the reading of what is to be read,—for the performance of these,—in so far as it is intended they should be performed,—modes of coercion, rather more direct and efficient than any that can be

---

[1] An echo of *Hamlet*, III. i. 65.
[2] See p. 433 n. above.
[3] An echo of Leviticus 18: 1–18.
[4] See Genesis 3: 7.B.
[5] 1818 'heen'.
[6] See pp. 352–3 above.

CHURCH-OF-ENGLANDISM

applied by the mere interdiction of husbandry management, are actually in force. Now then, as to this point—what is the least additional quantity of land, the occupation of which would suffice, to produce the bad effect, of preventing the fulfilment of these obligations;—of preventing it in the instance of a Parish Priest, by whom, but for this cause of seductive avocation, these same obligations would be fulfilled?—Such is the problem, the solution of which has, by State piety, enlightened by State wisdom, been committed for solution, to the piety, enlightened by the wisdom, of each Bishop. This problem solved,—the quantity next below this noxious quantity at which the corruptive quality has its commencement, would be the quantity, the license for which could never experience a refusal, from that tender mercy,[1] which finds so sure an abode, in every such Right Reverend breast.

Another problem.—One Parish Priest (suppose) there is, who, in the produce of glebe, or in tithes, has 7,000*l*. (or 12,000*l*. a year, is it?)[2] to dispose of, for the purpose of converting it into pay for his own use: another, for the like holy purpose, has 10*l*. a year and no more. The Priest whose sacred means of maintenance amount to 10*l*. a year and no more—suppose him under the temptation of taking a farm of a hundred a year, in hopes of making a correspondent addition to it in that profane shape. By which of the two concerns would the greatest force of seductive avocation be applied? by the 110*l*. a year, or by the 12,000*l*. (or though it were but the 7,000*l*.) a year?

The Priest, who has the 7,000*l*. a year in produce to dispose of, disposes of it without need of applying for a license: the Priest who has but 110*l*. a year to dispose of for the same purpose, why is it that he has been forced to make application for a license?—to make application for it, and to depend upon the uncontrolled will of his Bishop for the receipt of it?[3]

Thus much as to the case of the Parish Priest. But neither is there any want of Priests, who are *not* Parish Priests; and who, for not being *that*, any more than any thing else that is of any use, are full as well paid, as if, in that shape or some other, they were of ever so much use. Holy as they are, those persons not being charged with duty in any shape, here there is an instance, in which avocation from duty, if

---

[1] See Luke 1: 78.

[2] An allusion to the income of the Rectory of Doddington in the Diocese of Ely: see p. 354 n. above.

[3] The Non-Resident Clergy Act of 1803 (43 Geo. III, c. 84, §§ 4, 5) permitted members of the clergy without any or without sufficient glebe lands to take farms, providing they obtained written consent from the Bishop.

APPENDIX, NO. V. §IV.

that be the evil to be prevented, has no place. Yet, in this instance, no less than in the other, for the prevention of the evil, be it what it may, is the same burthen of decision, imposed on the piety, enlightened by the wisdom, of the Bishop.

Well then—if so it be, that, by *selling*, with or without *producing*, the produce of land, the hands of a son of Excellent Church are really rendered unclean,—an effectual mode of preventing this uncleanness—a real remedy, such as it is, is, as it always has been, at the command of those same hands, by which that sham remedy was applied. Laying out of the case the case of *glebe*,—which in comparison is but as a mole-hill to a mountain,—this remedy—(need it be mentioned?) is *commutation of tithes*. By this means the *inconsistency* could at any rate be done away. If then, under the notion of securing either *piety* or *fulfilment of sacred duty*,—husbandry, in the case of a Priest, doing duty or not doing duty, were prohibited simply and absolutely,—nothing objectionable would remain but the *absurdity* and the *hypocrisy:* if, instead of being simple and absolute, the prohibition were rendered dissoluble by a *license*, nothing would remain but the *absurdity*, the *hypocrisy*, and the *despotism:* the barefaced erection of a system of despotism, *to*—not to say *for*—the corruption and demoralization of all parties concerned:—*subject many* as well as *ruling few*, in all their various shapes, included.

Now then for a few questions.—

The Clergy of the Established Church of *Scotland*—are they, any of them, engaged in farming? and if any, are any of them, in any and what degree or shape, the worse for it?

The Clergy of the *Non-Established* Churches—are they—any of them—engaged in farming? What temptation so ever there may be in it, do any of these men stand in need of penal laws, or Bishops, to keep them out of it?

Look at the plan above proposed in this work.[1] The *Parish Clerk*—or the *Bell-taught School-boy*—could *he* be a farmer? would there be any need of penal laws, for keeping *him* out of the business? together with Bishops, for keeping him *out* of it, or letting him *into* it?

From which of the two opposite courses has *piety*—has *sacred duty*—most to fear? from patriarchal, though it be profit-seeking industry? or from prodigality?—from carefulness in the shape of husbandry? or dissipation in the shape of fox-hunting, shooting, gaming, drinking, or amorous intrigue?—In which place has it most peril to encounter? in the market-house, or in my Lord's dining-room, with my Lady's drawing-room by the side of it?—

---

[1] See pp. 484–5 above.

Questions these as fit for the meridian of the British Forum,[1] as unfit for that of either House.

Of these inconsistencies, flagrant as they are, we shall not have far to look for the cause. For covering the cherished profligacy, a veil of sanctity was therefore requisite. For decency—Church-of-England *decency!*[2]—something in the shape of a veil was thought necessary: but, so the shape were in that sense *decent*, no matter how thin the texture.

A pretence was found in the already mentioned statute (21 H. 8. c. 13.). In this most curious effusion of transparent hypocrisy,—antecedently to those provisions by which, 'For the more quiet and virtuous increase and maintenance of divine service, the preaching and teaching the word of God, with godly-and-good-example-giving ... the increase of devotion and good opinion of the lay-fee toward the spiritual persons,' sinecurism was established,—eight sections full of details and words (§ 1 to 8.) are occupied in the labour of preserving from this profanation the sacred brotherhood. For giving effect to all this piety, the force of penalties was of course employed. When, by the malice of Informers, the peace of Excellent Church came, as above,[3] to be disturbed,—that part of the Act had, along with the rest, engaged the notice of those invited servants of the law. By the Act of 1803, for defeating their endeavours in that service, arrangements of a temporary nature were, in this as in the other cases, provided.[4] That done, common sense and common honesty called for a pure repeal. Policy,—beholding matter, capable of being employed with advantage in the composition of the yoke which was in preparation, took up this part of the Act with the rest, and in the manner that will be seen, converted it to that pious use.

§ 5.—VI. *Over Incumbents and Curates, lodging despotic power in the hands of Bishops.*

In Number IV. of this Appendix, § 6, p. 419, four occasions may be seen,[5] on which, the means that appear to have been employed for the attainment of this end, come into operation:—Examination for Holy Orders—Licensing for Non-Residence—Apportionment of

---

[1] A radical debating club founded in London in 1806 by John Gale Jones (1769–1838), which had closed in 1810 after Jones had been imprisoned for criminal libel, but which had reopened in 1815.

[2] See p. 86 n. above.   [3] See pp. 437–8 n. above.

[4] The Non-Resident Clergy Act (43 Geo. III, c. 84) provided that proceedings against non-resident clergy should be stayed (§§ 1–3), and that no penalty should be made for non-residence before 1 January 1804 (§ 42).

[5] Bentham in fact gives five such 'occasions' at pp. 419–20 above.

APPENDIX, NO. V. §V.

Curates' Stipends—Determining, in the instance of each Parish or other Priest, whether he may have, or shall not have, land in his occupation, and the produce of land under his management.

I. *As to Examination for Holy Orders:—power thereupon of granting or refusing admission.*

Confined as it is in its exercise to a single point of time,—in the character of an instrument of eventual vexation, this power can scarcely be in any considerable degree formidable:—the result being—(see p. 420) habitual and general laxity and inefficiency in the whole system of the discipline, not undue severity in the exercise of it.

II. and III. *As to Licensing for Non-Residence, and Apportionment of Curates' Stipends.*

It is by the joint operation of the powers exercised on these two occasions, that, among Incumbents who are Non-Residents, of all those, whose condition is that of an habitual and never repentant sinner, men's *wills* have so plainly been endeavoured to be kept, and doubtless in no inconsiderable proportion are kept, in a state of '*prostration*' at the feet of their respective Bishops.[1] Of these, the number indicated by the above discussion, seems to be—about one half of the whole number of existing *Incumbents.*—To these add, without any exception, the whole body of *stipendiary Curates*.

IV. *As to the determining, in the instance of each Parish or other Priest, whether he may, or shall not, have land in his occupation, or the produce of land under his management.*

Respecting the *origin* of this power, and the *principle* on which it has been *conferred*, see the last preceding section.[2]

In respect of its *extent*, and *incidental* consequences, this power has much more of efficiency in it, than to a first view may be obvious. In the class of *Incumbents*,—especially the more opulent,—are to be seen, in no small proportion, those who, to the sacred office of *Parish Priest*,—converted or not, as above, into a *sinecure*,—add the profane office of *a Justice of the Peace*. In the exercise of this profane office, such of their *wills* as, by the virtue of their sacred office had been laid *prostrate*, as above, at the feet of the Bishop, found their way of course, and without need of any special intimation, on every '*decent*'[3] and '*useful*'[4] occasion, from those holy feet to the feet of the Minister:

---

[1] See p. 37 n. above.
[2] See pp. 518–25 above.
[3] See p. 86 n. above.
[4] See pp. 50–1 n., 323–7 n. above.

viz. in the first place, these same holy *wills* themselves,—and, in the next place, along with them, in general, the wills of those, whose lot, in virtue of the powers attached to that Lay Office, is more or less at their disposal: and, in particular, the keepers of those houses of general resort, in which, in so large a proportion, along with the bodies, the minds of the people receive their food.—And here may be seen one of the knots of the family *alliance*, by which *Excellent Church*,—and her not much less Excellent Sister, *State*,—are knit together in such mutually delightful harmony.

Bent down together under the double yoke, all these amphibious functionaries, by an attraction altogether natural, aggregate themselves to the class of *'useful Magistrates:'*[1] Magistrates *useful*, in that official sense of the word, the explanation of which, may, in the *Plan* of this work, pp. 49 to 52, be found in the joint case of the worshipful poisoner, and the Very Reverend the declared scorner, of *ale-drinkers*.[2]

In this way it is, that—by the same sacred hands, by which, without prejudice to his Godhead, the body and blood of a God are put into the mouths of prostrate sinners,—indication may, on each proper occasion, be given—given to Victuallers and others—of the side on which it is proper to vote at Parliamentary and other Elections.

Judicature—and in so many instances to the value of a man's whole subsistence—judicature exercised by a Judge, acting singly, in secret, without need of discussion or examinable evidence,—and without appeal, unless it be to another such Judge, acting in the same unbridled manner—such is the sort of judicature committed to each Bishop.[3]—Now if this be *not despotism*, what else *is* despotism? If, acting in such a situation, a *Judge* be not a *despot*, who else is? If this be not *establishing* despotism, in what other way can despotism be established? If for its *object* the power thus conferred had not the establishment of this despotism, what other and better object had it? what other and better object could it have had?

Looking this objection, together with another, in the face—'seeing it *urged with great force*,' and even *by those who would otherwise have been 'friendly to the object of the measure*,'—'even if the *provision had been more general*, (says the Noble Reformer, p. 18)[4] *I should not have felt it*:' *'I should not have felt it*,' (says he) and this is all he deigns to say of it. In the *President of the Council,* behold here then a man, who

---

[1] See pp. 50–1 n. above.
[2] i.e. John Abbott, the Canterbury brewer and magistrate, and Gerrard Andrewes, Dean of Canterbury.
[3] See pp. 418–20 above.
[4] *Substance of the Speech of the Earl of Harrowby*, pp. 18–19.

APPENDIX, NO. V. §V.

brings in, and causes to be passed into an Act, what he calls (p. 1.) 'a system of measures for strengthening the establishment of the Church of England;'—and who, upon its being observed to him, that, by this system, the greater part, if not the whole of the Clergy of the Established Church are put in subjection, under the individual and arbitrary will of six and twenty men of their own order, laid prostrate by this and other means, under the separate, sinister, and corruptive influence of the Crown,—coolly observes, that 'even if these provisions had been more general, he should not have felt the objection!' Such are the *laws* by which—such the *men* by whom—we are governed!—Men whose uncontested object—men whose thus avowed object it is—to hold their fellow-subjects—to hold an entire class of their fellow-subjects in a state of the most abject servitude!—An entire class! and what class? even that class, on whose instructions it is moreover their avowed object to cause all the others to depend, for their eternal, and in the mean time for their temporal, welfare. Thus then have they been suffered to take into their power the whole stock of this '*salt of the earth*:'[1]—to take it into their power—and to what purpose, but to poison it?

Oh but, (says his Lordship) despotism *is indeed your word, but* 'influence'—*nothing more than* 'influence'—*is mine.*[2] *If then so indeed it be, that, by any opponents of mine in the House, establishment of* despotism *was objected to my system, no such account of it have you from me.—Influence—increase of the influence given to the Bishops over their Clergy—increase given to the influence of lawful and acknowledged superiors over their respective subordinates.—In the case in question, any more than in any other, what in all this is there that ought to be regarded as an objection?—an objection, and that too a peremptory one?*

O yes, my good Lord, *influence* is that, which this Act of yours has laboured to produce:—influence?—yea, and as your Lordship acknowledges, '*increase of influence.*' But, by being *influence*, is *despotism* the less *despotism?*—One species of *influence* indeed there is which is *not despotism:* for it is not *power:*—this is the influence of *understanding* on *understanding:*—it is the sort of influence, which, at this moment, this pen is employing its endeavours—its honest howsoever weak endeavours—to exercise. Moreover, other species of influence there are, which are *not despotism*, though they *do* come under the denomination of *power:* such is the influence exercised by a *Judge*, as such, when exercised under those

---

[1] Matthew 5: 13.
[2] See *Substance of the Speech of the Earl of Harrowby*, p. 18: 'Those objections [to previous Curates Bills] were chiefly, the application of its provisions to Incumbents actually in possession, and the increase of the influence given to the Bishops over their Clergy.'

CHURCH-OF-ENGLANDISM

checks, by which *judicature* is distinguished from *despotism:*—from the exercise of power altogether *arbitrary.*—The power, exercised under a body of laws, according to which, on payment of so much a head, if tried and convicted, (which he will never be,) a man is allowed, because he is white, to kill, because they are black, as many slaves, of his own or any body else's, as he pleases[1]—*this* too is *influence:*—but is it the less *despotism?* With or without his name to it, suppose a man addressing to your Lordship a letter, saying—*Before the Session is at an end, bring in a Bill, for blowing up Excellent Church, instead of patching it up and varnishing it, or I will deal with you as your departed friend was dealt with*[2]—by no such flagitious attempt to exercise *influence* over it, would your Lordship's steady and intrepid mind be wrought upon:—true: but that which by the supposition would be attempted to be exercised, would it with the less strict propriety be susceptible of being designated by the name of *influence?*

The instrument, by which the will of that Assembly,—the use of which, if it had any, would be the exercising a control over the servants of the Monarch,—is laid and kept constantly and *legitimately* prostrate at their feet,—is not *influence* the name by which it is called? called as universally as *arsenic* is called *arsenic?*—As easily as the name of *influence* has been given to parliamentary corruption, as easily might the name of *sugar* have been given to *arsenic;* as it has actually been to a poison extracted from *lead:*[3]—but the drug itself, would it be the less poisonous?

Call it *influence*—good, my Lord, and welcome: but, if its *mode of operating* be considered, continue as you began—speak out boldly and honestly—prefix to it the adjunct *despotic*—call it *despotic influence:*—if its *effects* on the character and conduct of both parties be considered, prefix to it the adjunct *corruptive*—call it *corruptive influence.* On these conditions—and is there any thing unreasonable in them? On these conditions—but not otherwise—not any the smallest objection on this occasion, will there be, to the use of the word *influence.* But, with this accompaniment—with an accompaniment thus explanatory—will your Lordship's avowed *insensibility* to the objection still remain?—remain not only unshaken but avowed?

---

[1] Bentham is most probably alluding to the laws of South Carolina. The Act for the Better Ordering of Negroes of 1740 provided that any person convicted of the wilful murder of a slave was to pay a fine of £700 and was forbidden to hold public office, and any person convicted of killing a slave in heat or passion, or by undue correction, was to pay a fine of £350: see *The Statutes at Large of South Carolina*, ed. T. Cooper and D.J. McCord, 10 vols., Columbia, 1836–41, vii. 410–11.

[2] An allusion to the assassination of Spencer Perceval on 11 May 1812.

[3] i.e. sugar of lead, a poisonous white crystalline compound used in dyeing.

APPENDIX, NO. V. §VI.

§6.—VII. *Announced, and remaining to be executed. From Christians and others of all persuasions, money to be exacted, sufficient to render the number of Church-of-England Churches 'commensurate to the whole population.'*

Of the announcement here in question, the evidence may be seen in No. IV. of this Appendix, p. 396.

Great, and every day increasing, is the number of churches, provided by the piety and liberality of so many congregations of the sincere and zealous followers of Jesus. But, the contributions of which the fund is composed, being purely and exclusively voluntary, one capital one among Excellent Church's maxims, viz. maxim the 7th, (p. 377) is violated. In the collection of the money, no *power* is exercised. Moreover, the congregation,—being mostly schismatics,—are, as such, men of '*guilt*;'[1] worshippers of God, and not of the English hierarchy. Hence the determination already announced—announced at this season of unprecedented distress[2]—the determination to exact more money, for the erection of more of these costly edifices.

But, to every new Church there must be an Incumbent at least, if not an Incumbent and a Curate. For every Incumbent there must be a Parsonage House, with Out-Houses, Garden, Field more or less ample, and other appurtenances: nor can the House be habitable without furniture.

For the number of the new Churches requisite, the *Population Tables* will of course be the standard of reference resorted to: for,—whatsoever *knowledge* there may be to the contrary,—the *presumption* will of course be—so many inhabitants of a certain age and upwards, so many members of the Established Church, all eager to crowd into the new Churches.

Before building and after building, the Churches and the Parsonages will form a foundation for more wholesome and coercive laws:—laws for forcing the unwilling to pay Ministers for serving in them;—laws for forcing the Ministers to give unnecessary pay to their Curates: laws for preventing Ministers, when they have received the pay, from going off with it to spend it elsewhere:—to spend it elsewhere without service,—without rendering that service, which, wherever rendered, is, if rendered, in the very nature of it so unprofitable.

A prophecy will here be hazarded. No such application will ever be

---

[1] See 48 n. above.
[2] Bentham was writing at a time of economic depression and high unemployment.

CHURCH-OF-ENGLANDISM

made.[1] How unable so ever to procure removal of established abuse, reason is sometimes sufficient for preventing, or at any rate for checking, increase.

Spontaneously on this subject the lips of the Noble Reformer will never open themselves: interrogated at any time, his answer will be—*this is not the time.*

Unhappily, from no inspired pen does this prophecy come. Should it be disfulfilled, then will be the time, for all men, in whose eyes waste is indefensible,—hypocrisy, fraud, and extortion, odious,—to come forward and remonstrate! Presbyterians, Independents, Quakers, Baptists, Unitarians, Catholics, Jews—all worshippers of God according to conscience—all these, but above all, all honest Church of Englandists—then will be the time for them to make themselves seen and heard.

Prepare for that day, Earl of Harrowby! Prepare for that day, Lord Viscount Sidmouth! Prepare for that day, Commander of the faithful, Duke of York!

FINIS.

---

[1] In fact, the Church Building Act of 1818 (58 Geo. III, c. 45) established the Commission for Building New Churches. In their 36th and final Report, dated 8 July 1856, the Commissioners announced that 615 churches had been built, and 21 more were in the course of erection (*Commons Sessional Papers* (1856) xviii. 65–78, at 65). The work of the Commissioners was transferred to the Ecclesiastical Commissioners for England on 1 January 1857 (19 & 20 Vic., c. 55).

EDITORIAL APPENDIX: THE ANDREWES APPENDIX

Appendix N° III.[1]
Dean Andrews and Mr Vansittart. Affections manifested by them towards the people—from the papers of the House of Commons.[a]

§1. *Only Ale-drinkers.*

Of the sort of disposition which it is the tendency of Church of Englandism in general, and its chief instrument the Catechism in particular, to produce in the minds of those who are impregnated with it, one feature, in the person of one rich Sinecurist, has already been brought to view: one feature, viz. in modern language, intolerance: in scripture language, hatred, malice and all uncharitableness.[2]

The other feature is more complicated.

In two different situations, the one a sacred, the other a profane one, may the effects of the cause in question be seen exemplified in the present instance.

To the Church it belongs to walk before: to the state to follow after. Next after the Blood Royal, next before the Lordship of the Lord High Chancellor, walks the Grace of the Archbishop of Canterbury. With the Church let us, therefore, commence.

The case is in this wise. Against John Abbot of the City of Canterbury Esqre, Brewer and Justice of the Peace for the County in which that City stands, at the instance of the Commissioners of Excise, a prosecution called an information was pending in the Court of Exchequer 'for the using (say these Commissioners) adulterating ingredients in his beer, whereby (continue they) not merely the revenue is defrauded, but the health of his Majesty's subjects highly endangered.'[3]

---

[a] Session 1816. N° of the paper 179. Date of the Order for Printing 28 March 1816. Title: Further Papers relating to Excise Prosecutions.[4]

---

[1] This is the full text of an Appendix which Bentham at one point intended to print as part of *Church-of-Englandism*. Thinking that its inclusion would make the text too lengthy, he decided to exclude it, but gave summaries at pp. 49–52 and 323–7 n. above. For further details see the Editorial Introduction, pp. xvii–xviii, xxv above.

[2] For Bentham's comments on Dean Kipling see p. 295 & n. above.

[3] See *Commons Sessional Papers* (1816) xviii. 68.

[4] See 'Further Papers Relating to Excise Prosecutions; &c.', *Commons Sessional Papers* (1816) xviii. 65–74. The papers in question, which, as Bentham states, were ordered to be printed by the House of Commons on 27 March 1816 (*Commons Journals* (1816) clxxiii. 248), concerned the case of John Abbott, a magistrate and brewer in Canterbury, accused of adulterating his beer. The case was cited in the House of Commons on 2 April 1816 by Brougham in the course of the debate on his motion on the remission of excise prosecutions (*Parliamentary Debates* (1816) xxxiii. 854–82, esp. 863–7, 874).

To the purpose of obtaining the stoppage of the course of justice in his favour, the Defendant Mr Abbot, applies by Memorial to the Lords of the Treasury,[1] backing his application with private and some of them very familiar letters in his favour to Mr Lushington, Secretary to the Treasury,[2] from six Gentlemen, four not Reverend, topped by two Reverend, in the list of whom the Very Reverend the Dean of Canterbury, who, moreover, is Rector of St James's, and as such dates his letter from the Rectory House in Piccadilly, stands at the head.[3] To these essential letters are added for form's sake two Affidavits, one from himself, the other from a servant of his, a Coachman.[4]

Of the guilt of the Defendant in whose behalf he applies to save him from trial in respect of the offence above described, this Very Reverend advocate does not speak of himself as entertaining so much as a doubt. Under these circumstances the most prudent course a man can take is to avoid, if possible, understanding any thing about the business in which he thus interferes, and to declare that in this endeavour he has succeeded. Such accordingly is the declaration made by this very Reverend Mediator and Advocate.[5]

Why, then, thus interfere? Answer—'To prevent evil.' For, says the very Reverend divine—so profound his wisdom—so delicate his

---

[1] See ibid., 65–7.

[2] Stephen Rumbold Lushington, Joint Secretary to the Treasury 1814–27.

[3] As well as from Andrewes, whose letter was printed first, other letters on Abbott's behalf were sent by John Baker (?1754–1831), MP for Canterbury 1796–7, 1802–18; John Bowes Bunce (c. 1775–1850), Vicar of St Dunston's, Canterbury 1801–50; Sir William Curtis (1752–1829), MP for the City of London 1790–1818; Sir Edward Knatchbull, MP for Kent 1790–1802, 1806–19; and Joseph Marryatt of Great George Street, London: see *Commons Sessional Papers* (1816) xviii. 69–71.

[4] For the affidavits from Abbott and his coachman John Croker, both dated 19 November 1814, see ibid. 67–8.

[5] In the text, Bentham has noted at this point, 'Here quote the Letter', indicating that it should be inserted in a note. Andrewes's letter appears at *Commons Sessional Papers* (1816) xviii. 69 as follows:

> 'From the very Reverend the Dean of Canterbury, to S.R. Lushington, Esq.
> Secretary to the Treasury.

Dear Sir,

I HAVE just heard that my good neighbour, Mr. Abbott of Canterbury, is likely to get into some trouble respecting an information laid against him about his brewery, the nature of which however I do not understand. Ever since I have known him he has appeared to me so good a man, and so useful a magistrate that I should be very sorry to have that usefulness diminished by his being brought forward to the public in a matter which concerns only ale drinkers, and I fear has its source in malice; for I will venture to say Mr. Abbott has not in reality been to blame. I have taken the liberty of mentioning this to you, because I think it my duty to prevent evil; and to lessen the influence of a useful man unnecessarily is a great evil; and if by producing this letter to those whom it may concern you can serve him and the public, I shall be much gratified. Have the goodness to excuse my giving you this trouble, and believe me, dear Sir, to be, with very great respect, your faithful, and obedient servant,
Rectory House, Piccadilly,
February 6, 1815

Gerrard Andrewes.'

conscience—'I think it my duty to prevent evil.' What evil? The evil of defrauding the Revenue? No: in his catalogue of evils, evil in this shape has no place: in his edition of the Bible, the text commanding the rendering unto Cæsar the things that are Cæsar's[1]—or at least in his remembrance—is not to be found. The evil of highly endangering the health of his Majesty's subjects? No: nor this neither, for in his eyes this, as we shall presently find him declaring, in little less than express terms, does not possess the character of an evil. What evil then? Answer.—That sort of evil which consists in the lessening of *'influence:'* for a maxim derivable from this same receptacle of piety and fountain of wisdom is that 'to lessen the influence of a useful man unnecessarily is a great evil,' and 'ever since I have known him (but without saying how long that is) he has appeared to me,' continues the Dean, 'so good a man, and so *useful* a Magistrate that I should be very sorry to have that usefulness diminished by'—and so forth.

Influence, to what particular purpose applied, useful—in what particular way useful? this is not said, nor is it necessary. To whom was this letter addressed? to the Secretary of the Treasury: and of what sort of Treasury will be seen presently. By whom was it addressed? By his acquaintance the Dean of Canterbury, and moreover the Rector of the Parish of which every thing that is Princely—every thing that is courtly—every thing that is official—is parishioner.[2] For so it is—and without any mystery—the possessor of the overpaid place and the sinecure—the place for which little is done and that little useless—and the place for which nothing at all is done, or so much as undertaken to be done—these two, are, as is the custom, *one.*

What, [as][3] above, the very Reverend intercessor does not venture to say is that his *protegé* has not been guilty of the offence with which he stood charged. But what he does venture to say [is] that, be that matter as it may, his said *protegé* 'has not in reality been to blame.' Guilty of defrauding the revenue and of endangering the health of his Majesty's subjects? Guilty of injuring the fair trader—of picking the pockets of his Majesty's subjects with one hand, and poisoning them with the other—and yet not to blame?

Of this purity from blame, two causes, though not in form and as such asserted, are not the less plainly intimated: one is that the persons whose health is injured are *'only ale-drinkers:'* the other is, that it was in *malice*—in malice in the heart of a somebody not

---

[1] Matthew 22: 21.
[2] Andrewes, as well as being Dean of Canterbury, was Rector of St James's, Piccadilly. For the proximity of the Rectory to St James's Palace see p. 50 n. above.
[3] MS 'has'.

mentioned—that the chance, such as it has proved to be, of the applying a check to the practice of defrauding the revenue and endangering the health of his Majesty's subjects took its rise. 'I should be very sorry to have that usefulness diminished by his being brought forward to the public in a matter which concerns only ale-drinkers, and I fear has its source in malice, for I will venture to say Mr Abbot has not in reality been to blame.'

Now, then, in the class of persons stiled *Ale-drinkers*, what is there—what can there be—that should render a matter which concerns none but them not worth attending to—an evil to which no persons but them are exposed to not worth preventing?

For an interpretation we must once more have recourse to the two correspondent situations—the situation of the person addressing and the situation of the persons addressed. In the drinking of ale—if it were ale in contradistinction to wine and ardent spirits (in a case of this sort water is unfortunately out of the question)—is there any harm? No, surely: for if there were, so good a man—and he a useful magistrate to boot—would never have been concerned in making it. No—need it be mentioned? the uninjuriousness of the practice consists in this—viz. that the persons injured by it are such as belong to no other class than that which, by the class to which the two parties to the correspondence belong, is denominated by such a variety of synonyms—such as the mob, the vulgar, low people, the people whom nobody knows, the swinish multitude,[1] the people who have no business with the laws but to obey them;[2] to obey them, viz. while those whose business it is to enforce them, violate them.[3]

One thing any body may here venture to say, which is down that very Reverend throat no such vulgar liquor as ale ever found its way; for in the opposite case, what concerns those throats down which it does find its way would not have been regarded as a matter of such entire indifference.

Some inference may, moreover, be drawn in relation to the Honourable and Right Honourable throats to whose sympathies and antipathies this same address was made. But except in so far as the very reverend throat be an exception, the distinction here in view was not improbably not between those who drink wine alone and those who drink ale alone, but between those who drink ale alone, not being able to afford any thing better, and those who,

---

[1] See p. 456 n. above.

[2] In the debate on the Treasonable Practices Bill in the House of Lords on 11 November 1795, Samuel Horsley, Bishop of Rochester, stated that, 'he did not know what the mass of the people in any country had to do with the laws but to obey them': see *Parliamentary History* (1795–6) xxxii. 258.

[3] Bentham has marked the following two paragraphs for possible deletion.

drinking ale or perhaps something smaller for the digestion and health's sake drunk during dinner, drink wine, smuggled or not smuggled, afterwards. Not that by their dinner-digesting beverage their Lordships would be better pleased to be poisoned than by their after-dinner solace. But that, howsoever it might happen to them to apply to Canterbury for brawn, they would never think of looking that way for ale.

As to the other consideration which has had its share in reconciling the very Reverend bosom to those supposed evils which have appeared so serious to less indulgent minds, viz. the fear that malice had had a share in the giving birth [to] detection, it is a consideration which, in the other class of bosoms above-mentioned, appears to have acted with equal weight. And this brings us to the Right Honourable and, though not Reverend, not the less pious Chancellor of the Exchequer.[1]

By[2] a Member of the religion of Jesus, by a dignatory of the Church, by the Rector of that parish which, on the list of the parishes of the Metropolis, stands first in dignity, to find sentiments such as these avowed—avowed in signs not susceptible of misconception or explanation—in signs which may endure as long as the use of the press endures and find their way to every spot to which the productions of that vehicle of unperishable information find their way—this is one of those facts in the viewing of which the eyes can scarce give credit to themselves.

As to the entertaining of the sort of affection in question, the difficulty is—among the ruling few, not to find those by whom they are entertained, but to find those by whom affections of any other sort are entertained. No: the difficulty—the only difficulty—there is, is, among so many by whom they are entertained, in finding so much as a single one by whom they are avowed. On the part of the person addressing, for the production of so extraordinary a phænomenon so irreconcileable with the most ordinary rules of prudence, two conditions must have concurred: the most thorough impregnation with the antisocial principles thus displayed; and a confidence clear of all doubt in the party to whom they are avowed.

---

[1] i.e. Nicholas Vansittart, Chancellor of the Exchequer 1812–23.
[2] In the text preceding this paragraph, Bentham has noted: 'Morn. Chron. 13 Apr. 1816. Poetical version of this letter by T.G.A. but instead of Abbot, the name is *Green*.' The poem, which appeared in the *Morning Chronicle* as Bentham describes, was headed 'Epistle from the Very Rev. the Dean, to the Right Hon. Charles Arbu–thn–t', and ended with the comment, 'A prose edition of this letter was read to the House of Commons by Mr. BROUGHAM, in the debate relating to certain relaxations of the *Excise Laws*.' Charles Arbuthnot (1767–1850), MP for East Looe 1795–6, Eye 1809–12, Orford 1812–18, St Germans 1818–27, St Ives 1828–30, and Ashburton 1830–1, was Joint Secretary to the Treasury 1809–23.

As to the affections themselves, by what account that can be given can justice be done to them? Affections of equal and undistinguishing benevolence and philanthropy are the affections in the inculcation of which the religion of Jesus owes confessedly its only title to favour in the eyes of any part of the population of a state—the governors or the governed. The affections avowed in this letter, of what sort are they? of a sort diametrically opposite to those affections by which that religion distinguishes itself from every other.

Follow this very Reverend and, it is said, eloquent parson to the theatre of his eloquence—listen to him while in the pulpit taking for his text the parable of Dives and Lazarus[1] or a portion of the Sermon on the Mount.[2] What unction! what devotion! what glowing periods! Follow him now to his study—stripping off his Christianity and charity with his gown and cassock, and writing a letter to a Minister begging impunity for a defrauder of the revenue and a wholesale poisoner of the people: impunity for the gain that is to be made by it— for one who keeps his Coach by the sale of liquid poison? Nay, but why not? says this man of God. But these people, the only people whose health can any way have been concerned in this case, what signifies what becomes of them? They are '*only ale-drinkers.*' If the rank of life they belonged to were the rank of wine-drinkers, it would be another thing. But who cares or need care any thing about them?

Only Ale-drinkers. The phrase is short: but never surely was phrase more expressive. When a man speaks at length and plainly, comment—paraphrase—may be unnecessary and at any rate stands exposed to the imputation of injustice. But when so much more meaning is conveyed than is expressed—when the essence of a page is condensed into two words, what is involved must be enveloped, comment must be made, or truth can not be brought to light, justice can not be done.

Only ale-drinkers. That, in the instance of a multitude of persons, to an indefinite amount, injury to health—injury of that sort which is the effect of a slow poison—[has been produced]—such is the position, of the truth of which a persuasion, so far from being denied, is implicitly asserted and avowed.

Only ale-drinkers. By the word only, if any where it ever means any thing, a distinction is here made, and in pursuance of it the population of the country divided into two opposite classes: the one composed of those who do not, the other of those who do, drink ale in a proportion so considerable as that, by such unwholesome drugs as the brewer may find his account in employing in the manufacturing of it, bodily health is in their instance liable to be injured by it. In a word, by a

[1] See Luke 16: 19–31.   [2] See Matthew 5–7.

mode of speech not the less familiar for being figurative, by non-ale-drinkers being understood people who are rich enough to have a claim to regard in the breasts of men in office, or, to speak in generals, the rich, by ale-drinkers are meant all such as are not rich enough to possess that advantage, or, in one word, the poor: or rather, for the anathema is more extensive, those who have not wealth enough to be numbered among the rich.

Now if, of all that has just been developed, there be any thing that is not implicitly but necessarily contained in these two words—of all this—if any thing less than all this is meant by them, what is it? what different interpretation can the ingenuity of man find to put upon them?

In vain would it be asked, why draw any severe inferences from a couple of unguarded words, employed in the course of confidential intercourse between friend and friend?—why seek thus to take any such cruel advantage of an unguarded word or two?—

No: true, by the imprudence it is that the disclosure is made: not so that the nature of them is in any the least degree changed. By many a man have such affections been entertained without their having ever been expressed: by no man can any such affections by whom they have not been entertained ever have been expressed. By many a man who did not believe in Jesus has been said, I do believe in Jesus: but by no man who at the time believed in Jesus has it been said, I do [not] believe in Jesus.[1]

What if, at the very moment of writing these two words, so it shall have been that the predicament in which the very Reverend the writer had placed himself was exactly the same as that for which St Paul reproves his disciples among the Corinthians?[2] What if the unguardedness should have had this for its cause? What if, after settling the matter after a Downing Street dinner with his Right Honourable friend,[3] the case was that this letter was penned at the writing table in the next room to which, for this purpose, he had made a momentary digression? The supposition is possible: nor, to judge from the mere circumstantial evidence afforded by the words themselves, and without any support from direct evidence, does the supposition present itself as containing any thing very improbable.

---

[1] The corresponding marginal summary paragraph clarifies the sense of the passage: 'Effect of such unguardedness—not utterance of sentiments not entertained: but over-confident thence imprudent disclosure of sentiments really entertained.

'No believer in Jesus says I believe not in Jesus.'

[2] In the corresponding marginal summary paragraph, Bentham is more explicit: 'Suppose him drunk as Paul's supper-drinking Corinthians.' For Paul's admonition of the Corinthians for drunkenness at the Lord's Supper see I Corinthians 11: 20–1.

[3] Vansittart had offices in Downing Street, Westminster.

But supposing it established: would the essentials of the case be found [to] receive any the smallest alteration? Would the inward and invisible cause by which this outward and visible sign was produced be done away?[1] No: not more so than if, instead of Burgundy and Champagne by bottles, nothing had been drank better than ale, and that in glasses. To the affections which in the fullness of the heart the mouth speaketh,[2] what is it, asks the Greek epigram, that is done by wine? does it generate them? No: it does but manifest them: if, being drunk, you are now for the first time seen to be wicked, it is not that this is the first time of your being wicked, but this is the first time that your wickedness has been discovered.[3]

Drunk or sober, good Mr Dean, the words are yours—the sentiments, but for which those words would never have slipt your pen, are no less so.

Now, then, of the *prostration of the understanding and will*,[4] in the production of which the Catechism is the instrument avowedly employed, what in the present instance—what as applied to the present purpose—is the use? Amongst others, it is this: that should it happen to the people, or any part of the people, to see a Minister's dependent's dependent poisoning them for the sake of the money that is to be got by doing so, and for the sake of maintaining himself in power, a Minister encouraging the poisoner to pursue his course, they may, in the dejection which results from their abasement, confess within themselves that it is what they were made for, and what, on pain of damnation, they are bound to submit to and acquiesce in.

§2. *Vansittart.*

That such were the sentiments of the very Reverend the Rector of St James['s] is altogether certain: that the like were the sentiments of the Right Honourable Gentleman for whose edification they were intended may be set down as little less so.

To the Treasury Chambers it was that this letter found its way on its dispatch from the St James's Rectory House in Piccadilly.[5]

In the breast of the Chancellor of the Exchequer, the letter of the very Reverend Sinecurist found what it reckoned upon, a receptacle full of sympathy. Yes—of sympathy. But for whom? the individuals

---

[1] An echo of the 'Catechism', *Book of Common Prayer*: 'What meanest thou by this word *Sacrament?* ... I mean an outward and visible sign of an inward and spiritual grace given unto us'.

[2] An echo of Matthew 12: 34; Luke 6: 45.

[3] *Anthologia Palatina*, XI. ccxxxii.　　　　　　　　　　　　　　　　　　[4] See p. 37 n. above.

[5] The letter was addressed to Lushington, Secretary to the Treasury.

for whom poison was preparing while the fraud was putting upon the revenue? Oh no: these were no better than ale-drinkers. The whole stock of that precious balm was engrossed by the good and 'useful' man in whose favour the Coach, which had so long been rolling on the profits of trade thus carried on, afforded sufficient evidence of his not belonging to any such vulgar herd.

In due form of office, and with that sort of philosophy with which all evidence of public distress is heard by him, Mr Vansittart sits by and either hears or dictates the minute in which the Commissioners of Excise are stated as representing the defendant to be 'under prosecution for putting unlawful and poisonous ingredients into the beer brewed by him, in which (says the Minute, viz. in that Report) the Commissioners state that the representations of the party are false and groundless, and that in their opinion he is not entitled to the least favourable regard.'[1] By Mr Vansittart, for the condition of the individuals in a number altogether indefinite who at the moment might be lying on the bed of sickness, while the good and useful author of it was rolling about in his Chariot, is so much as a single sign of thought vouchsafed?—No more than by the Emperor of Morocco. All his sympathies are engrossed by the 'person whose character and conduct (says the same Minute) are stated to have been so honourable to himself, and beneficial to the community:'[2] of all honourableness and beneficiality, be it observed, there is not a tittle of evidence [other][3] than the vague generalities got up for the purpose by the very Reverend Court Sinecurist and his Co-intercessors.

From that of an associate, says the proverb, may a man's disposition be known; much more from the language of an associate and his own together. True it is that, if, without further evidence, the terms of a letter were to be regarded [as] conclusive evidence against the person addressed, it would thus be put into the power of every man to ruin every other. Much in every case, and in some cases every thing, will depend upon the reception given to the letter by the person to whom it is addressed: upon any thing which is *said* or any thing which is done in pursuance of it.

Said, in pursuance of a letter so circumstanced—*said*, in any direct way in the sort of record called a Treasury Minute, nothing, without a violation of all forms, could have been. But in the Minute of which, on this occasion, the entry is brought to light, maxims—maxims of deep policy—are contained, and among those maxims not a tittle is to be found that does not stand as evidence—circumstantial indeed, for

[1] See Treasury Minute, 10 February 1815, *Commons Sessional Papers* (1816) xviii. 72.
[2] See ibid.
[3] MS 'or'.

direct could not have appeared—circumstantial but not the less conclusive evidence, of adoption given—no, not so much of adoption, as of already established agreement with the contempt so frankly avowed by the Court and Courtly Minister of the Gospel for the whole body of the poor, together with no inconsiderable portion of the middling classes, under the scornful name of ale-drinkers.

On the 23^d of November 1814 it is that, by command of the Lords, Mr Lushington, Secretary to the Treasury, addresses the Commissioners of Excise, inclosing a Memorial from the said Mr Abbot and 'the numerous documents which', says the letter, 'accompany the same,' [and] directs them to suspend all Law Proceedings in regard to a prosecution commenced against him at the suit of the revenue. Why suspend these law proceedings? The reason stands avowed. Somewhere or other, on the one hand, there exists a certain Mr Blake, on the other hand, there exist numerous documents (viz. the accompanying documents) 'strongly indicative of insanity and revengeful malice on the part of' this same Mr Blake.[1]

This Mr Blake, what relation bears him to the cause? that of a witness—an expected witness? even that would afford no reason for preventing trial: it would be a reason for coming to trial: for, then, all this insanity and malice might be produced and made to testify against him.

Is he so much as prosecutor or informer? no, nor this neither.[2] But the suspicion is that some evidence in it not capable of being objected to has been brought to light.

Now, then, as to motives in general, and malice in particular, considered as having place and operative in the situation of prosecutor, the Oxford Graduate[3] has found certain considerations which it is his wish to submitt to the consideration of two classes of persons, viz. Chancellors of the Exchequer, and Judges in general, and in particular to the twelve, and most particularly to the Chief Justice, of the King's Bench,[4] but moreover to Mr Justice Bailey, and Mr Justice Park,[5] in whom is all Church-of-England holiness.

1. One is that, in a case of alleged delinquency, the motives by which the prosecutor, the informer or the plaintiff, whatsoever be his

---

[1] See ibid., 65.
[2] See Excise Commissioners to the Lords Commissioners of the Treasury, 27 January 1815, ibid., 68: 'We beg leave to acquaint Your Lordships, that George Blake . . . is wholly unconcerned, either as Informer or Witness in the prosecution of the Memorialist.'
[3] i.e. the author of *Church-of-Englandism*: see p. 7 n. above.
[4] There were only four Justices, including the Chief Justice, of King's Bench. By the twelve judges or justices, Bentham had in mind the Justices who presided over the Courts of King's Bench, Common Pleas, and Exchequer.
[5] Bayley was Justice of King's Bench 1808–30, and Park Justice of Common Pleas 1816–38.

stile and title, have been actuated are not worth knowing, for that they are nothing to the purpose.

2. That they are not capable of being known: a consideration of which the importance, though if it stood alone it would be decisive, is altogether superseded and put out of Court by the preceding one.

3. That they are as plainly and constantly the resource of every Chancellor of the Exchequer whose wish it is, for the exercise and extension of favouritism or corrupt influence, to stop prosecution, and of every Chief Justice of the King's Bench whose wish it is to defeat justice.

4. That in the character of a ground for exemption, it is the sure and constant resource of every Defendant who is too plainly guilty to have any other.

1. In the first place, then, the quality of the motive is in this case nothing to the purpose. By the badness of a species of motive is meant, if it means any thing, its leading to mischievous results. But in this case, by the supposition, the act is good, or else justice is not good: for the result is furtherance of justice.

But, if he suborns witnesses . . . . . O yes: but this is no part of the case: subornation is not the name of a motive, but the name of an act. And in the present case, that in the way of subornation any thing was done or so much as attempted, is not so much as insinuated.

2. In the next place, the motive is a thing altogether incapable of being ascertained.

The motives by which the business of life is carried on—the motives on which the existence of the species depends—the motives on which the execution of *justice*, or what is called *justice*, depends— are all of them what, in the language of the Treasury and King's Bench, are termed bad motives: desire of money is what the execution of justice in matters called civil, and in matters called *penal* in so far as rewards are proffered, is dependent upon: ill-will, with or without supposed provocation, in which latter case it is called revenge, or, in the language of crafty malice, 'revengeful malice',[1] or by some other such opprobrious name of which the language of common-place rhetoric affords such multitudes, is what the execution of justice in matters called *penal* is dependent [upon]. Here we have the self-regarding and the dissocial affections: remain the social. Deducting family affection and personal friendship, affections exceeded in universality as well as extent by the self-regarding ones or the species would long ago have been extinct, remain social affections acting upon a large scale. But social affections acting upon a large scale and prevailing over dissocial or self-

[1] See p. 548 above.

regarding is heroic virtue: and to come to the present case, prosecuting for the mere benefit of the state—in the teeth of all the odium, the labour and expense attached to the situation of prosecutor, especially prosecutor for an offence by which no individual feels himself particularly injured—and not for the sake of reward in any shape, or gratification of ill-will from any cause, would be heroic virtue.

The Treasury, the King's Bench or the Attorney General, are they prepared to say the one that they will not institute, the other that they will not give effect to, any suit in which it shall appear that the prosecutor is exposed to the operation of any motive other than such as come under the operation of heroic virtue? The Treasury, who every Session come to Parliament and obtain Acts offering rewards—pecuniary rewards—for services to be rendered by men in the character of prosecutors,[1] are they prepared to say that they insist upon it as a condition *sine quâ non* that the inducements thus offered shall be offered without effect?

To affirm that heroic virtue as above explained has no existence any where would betray an ignorance of human nature not much less flagrant, than to say that it has existence every where. For a virtue which is not rare, heroic is no proper name.

At the expence of between £500 and £600, a man nicknamed the Monster, whose sport was to go about the streets wounding women, was some four-and-twenty years ago prosecuted to conviction by John Julius Angerstein now living.[2] But every man in general must be not only as benevolent, as public-spirited and desirous of well-deserved reputation, but as rich as this Angerstein—in short, he must be a sort of monster of the opposite description—ere a Treasury Secretary or an Attorney General can have any the slightest warrant for supposing that the business of justice can be carried on by prosecutions so produced.

3. This sort of irrelevancy is the natural resource of every Chancellor of the Exchequer whose wish it is, for the exercise and extension of favouritism or corrupt influence, to stop prosecution,

---

[1] Under many penal statutes, an informer was permitted to sue and receive the whole or a part of the penalty from a successful prosecution. Hence any penalty paid by Abbott, assuming that he was being prosecuted for adulterating beer under 51 Geo. III c. 87 (1811), §16, would, according to §35, have been divided between the King and the person who informed.

[2] John Julius Angerstein (*c.* 1732–1823), insurance broker and connoisseur of art, paid 5 gns. to the subscription set up at Lloyd's Coffee House in April 1790 to catch the man, nicknamed the Monster, who had been attacking women in London. It was variously reported that Angerstein had, moreover, offered in public bills and in the press sums of £20, £50, £100, and 135 gns., some of which were subsequently paid to witnesses. See, for instance, *The Times*, 17 and 22 April 1790, and *An Appeal to the Public, by Rhynwick Williams, containing Observations and Reflections on Facts, relative to his very extraordinary and melancholy case*, London, [1792], pp. v, ix, 33, written by Renwick Williams, who had been convicted of the offence.

and of every Chief Justice of the King's Bench whose wish it is to defeat justice.

If this plea be admitted as valid in itself, it is at all times in the power of every person in either of those situations, to the extent of the power attached to those same situations, to give effect to every such wish in every case.

Words tortured by lawyers are among the instruments, and among the most efficient of the instruments, employed by lawyers for torturing their betters.[a] In the slang vocabulary of Westminster Hall, prodigious is the number of the words applicable and applied to this most convenient purpose.

Among the most useful, if not absolutely the most useful, of all these tortured and torturing words is the word *malice*. Delightful word! with this sword in your mouth, for it has two edges, you destroy many an innocent, you save every criminal you please.

You impute malice to him, and for the malice thus imputed, you send him to be hanged.[1] In the situation of Juryman, or in any other situation, no man of common sense or honesty would imply it: those who, in your place before you, on pretence of declaring it, made that law which no man is suffered to know and every man is persecuted for not knowing,[2] look upon themselves accordingly to imply it.

In this way, with malice in your mouth, to say nothing of your heart, you put to death or otherwise destroy the innocent or venial offender whose ill-fate has rendered him the object of your malice.

Still more at your ease, you save the guilty object of your corrupt favour, punishing and mortifying at the same time, in the situation of prosecutor,[3] the object of your corrupt malice.[b]

---

[a] *Durum est torquere voces ad hoc ut torqueant homines.* Bacon *ab Augm. Scient.*[4]

[b] On an information, *the prosecutor must come with clean hands.*[5] This is another of your slang phrases. Whether the hands be clean in the figurative sense is not in the

---

[1] For the distinction between express and implied malice in relation to homicide see Blackstone, *Commentaries on the Laws of England*, iv. 198–201.

[2] Bentham's allusion is to the Common Law, and the doctrine that judges did not make law, but declared it: see, for instance, ibid., i. 68–73.

[3] For remedies against malicious prosecution see ibid., iii. 126–7.

[4] An adaptation of Francis Bacon, *De Augmentis Scientiarum* (first published 1623), Bk. VIII, Aphorism 13: *Durum est torquere leges, ad hoc ut torqueant homines*, i.e. 'It is a cruel thing to torture the laws, that they may torture men.' Bentham alters *leges* (laws) to *voces* (words). See *The Works of Francis Bacon*, ed. J. Spedding, R.L. Ellis, and D.D. Heath, 14 vols., London, 1857–74, i. 806.

[5] An allusion to the legal maxim that 'a man must come into a court of equity with clean hands', given its standard formulation by Sir James Eyre (bap. 1734, d. 1799), Baron of the Exchequer 1772–87, Chief Baron of the Exchequer 1787–93, Chief Justice of Common Pleas 1793–9, in *Dering v. Earl of Winchelsea* (1787), reported in Samuel Compton Cox, *Cases determined in the Courts of Equity, from 1783 to 1796 inclusive*, 2 vols., London, 1816, i. 318–23, at 319.

Oh, in the mouth of high-seated hypocrisy, what a useful word is the word *malice!* While every corrupt desire is gratified by it, the praise of purity—of exquisite moral sensibility—is reaped by it. No effect—howsoever desirable and necessary in itself—no effect will he be concerned in the production of but through the purest instruments. Not only his Law Officers, who let themselves out to hire to every man—to injured or injurer—are pure, not only his Chief Judges, who, before they were Judges, were Law Officers, are pure, but even his very prosecutors, or they shall be prosecutors without effect, shall be all pure. For the purchase of their services he offers them money, but such shall they all be, it shall not have any effect upon them. They shall be such men! He will put butter and honey into every man's mouth,[1] and it shall not melt there.—No: never shall evil be done by him, that good may come.[2]

4. In the fourth place, this plea is the constant resource of every Defendant whose guilt has deprived him of every other.

Yes, and how should it be otherwise? Except in cases which are not only seldom exemplified, but impossible to ascertain the existence of smallest degree more to the purpose than in the literal sense.—What? because, supposing the uncleanness real, one man has been guilty of an offence, is that a reason why another offence should go unpunished? Well then, when it suits you to protect guilt, how do you proceed? You turn to the prosecutor and look at his hands: if there be any the smallest and faintest spot on them, your pretence is found.

But it is a pretence that never can fail. For the ill-will, alias the malice, alias if you please the revengeful malice, always does exist: and in this case the implication which is so convenient to you can never fail to be true. True? how should it be otherwise? True it was—and let him prosecute these pages as libellous if he pleases—true it was in the case of the man by whom the Monster was brought to justice. Ill-will was among the affections excited in his breast by the spectacle of that barbarity: satisfaction at the thoughts of the retribution inflicted on the Monster was among the affections kindled by the success of this costly exertion of benevolence.

If, for giving exemption to a delinquent, malice in the breast of the prosecutor is a just ground, the Monster suffered unjustly. Produced by provocation, malice is bad enough: how much worse, how much more horrible, when utterly destitute of any such excuse! From the man whom he thus pursued to destruction, had Angerstein ever so much as fancied himself to have received any the slightest injury? Yet for the bringing this man to destruction, from five to six hundred pound did he keep on expending of his own money, such was the perseveringness, the implacableness, of his malice! The prosecutor's own Solicitor, had the question been put to him when the Defendant came up for sentence, could not have denied it.

Irritated at the spectacle of so much virtue, and the more convinced of its reality, the more sharply stimulated and anxiously determined to disprove its existence, what a field, supposing the matter of fact known or suspected, what a field to an | | for the exercise of his eloquence!

---

[1] An echo of Isaiah 7: 15.   [2] Romans 3: 8.

where they are exemplified, in point of fact the plea is true: ill-will, or as lawyers, where they mean any thing, where they know what they mean—which is not always the case—where they say malice, malice is the very efficient cause without which prosecution never could take place. Look at the criminal calendar—prosecutions and consequently prosecutors—every year by thousands. High and low—rich and poor—these men are they, every one of them, men of heroic virtue? [Oh][1] yes, the drinkers of wine: such of them alone excepted as are opposers of Administration, i.e. of the Government, i.e. of all government, i.e. Levellers, Jacobins and Atheists. Oh yes, those who are enabled by sinecures to drink wine and send acceptable intercessions. But those whose drink is no better than ale—are all these, men or women of heroic virtue? [Does] the having had his pocket picked, or his shop pilfered from, render a man, a man of heroic virtue?

How should it not be their refuge? The maxim that malice on the part of the prosecutor affords a sufficient ground for giving impunity to an offender is a maxim they find established: established in almost every mouth, and through sinister interest or interest-begotten prejudice in but too many breasts: established, we have seen, by whom, and how and for what cause.[a]

---

[a] Yard—Store-room—Closet—Vat—Barrel—box—whatsoever be the nature and name of the receptacle, let the contents of it be ever so amply fraught with mischief, nobody who has not access to it can afford any evidence or information of those contents. In manufactories in general, but more particularly in a manufactory in which any thing illegal is carried on, nobody has access but the persons who, whether under the general name of recruits or under some other more particular name, are employed in it. Whatsoever illegal practices are carried on in it, by no such servant, for any such purpose, or to any such effect, as that of bringing the offence and the offender to justice, can any such evidence or information be afforded without his subjecting himself to the imputation which, in current language—such is the imperfection of that instrument—may bear the name of treachery:—yes: and in vulgar and narrow minds be apt to subject him to the odium attached [to] that name.

To all this, the framers of the body of revenue laws—not to speak of other laws—have been more or less sensible: and strange indeed it would have been if, in any instance, they had not been so. Accordingly their object—their all-pervading object—has been to establish in every such track of delinquency a perpetual and manifest source of this species of treachery—to strew the spot all over with mantraps and spring guns. Such is the object and such, when not prevented by vulgar prejudice in low or corruption in high places, is the effect of the rewards offered for information to informers.

In thus taking the only chance for the accomplishing of a necessary purpose, what to [so] vast an extent has been done by the legislature, is it wrong or is it right? . . . Of treachery, the effects and tendency are different, and even opposite, according to the

---

[1] MS 'Of'.

Among the foremost of its objects, this tract has the shewing the influence which, as far as it prevails, the Church-of-England system in nature of the transaction and occasion on which it manifests itself. On the occasion of every transaction which is innoxious, treachery is improbity and vice: in every transaction which is preponderantly noxious, treachery, if not laudable, is at least not ill-laudable. Fidelity among persons engaged in innoxious transactions is one of the bonds by which that society is kept together. Among persons engaged in noxious transactions, not adherence to engagement, but violation of engagement—not *fidelity*, but *treachery*—for such must be the word untill language shall afford some other not thus unfitted for use—is another of the bonds by which the same object is secured.[a]

Yes: but where delinquency is not only criminal but noxious, fidelity to accomplices in it is not virtue, but persevering wickedness: treachery, if such must be the word for the sacrifice of accomplices, is not vice, but an atonement for wickedness.[b]

To return. Of the Church formulary, what is the main subject.—One of its main

---

[a] To such a degree may a government be corrupt that to subvert it or to endeavour to [subvert][1] it, howsoever highly punishable and thus criminal to subvert it or endeavour to subvert it, so far from being vice, may be heroic virtue. In some men's view of the matter, this may be the case with Mr Vansittart's government. But is it so in the view he takes of it?

[b] To that general sinister interest which they possess in common with the rest of the ruling and influential few, the man of law add[s] a more particular sinister interest of his own which in some of its operation is liable to afford more or less of obstruction to the more extensive sinister interest in which he is but a sharer. Legislators, by the laws of their own making—by the branch of law called the statute law—legislators, as above, offer rewards for evidence. By that more efficient and only immediately and surely efficient branch of law which, under the name of common law or unwritten law, is of their making, Judges annul and repeal in effect that law and declare that, if any such reward will be earned by it or is expected for it, the evidence shall not be heard.[2] For £50 a man will speak the truth: therefore he will perjure himself for the same money: such is their logic, no man by whom advantage in any pecuniary shape can be expected will ever speak truly: no man will by advantage in any other shape be induced to speak untruly: by no man in whose instance the profit obtainable by falshood is manifest will deception ever fail of being produced: by no man in whose instance the advantage obtainable by falshood is undiscovered and undiscoverable will deception ever be produced. Of this stamp, each provided with a cluster of groundless and inconsistent exceptions by which half its efficiency is eaten out, are composed their laws of evidence.

The contempt thus habitually put by the Judges upon the legislature, had it in this instance been productive of its full effect, the state would long ago have fallen to pieces. In a system of all-pervading corruption, in so far as any abuse receives its correction, it is not by any wholesome remedy, it is by an abuse operating in another direction: it is by a counter-abuse. More bad or less bad, fraud in some shape or other is the instrument by which every thing is done. Once upon a time, a bond was forged: don't involve yourself with the plague of prosecution, said a lawyer, forge a

---

[1] MS 'destroy'. Bentham presumably intended to amend 'destroy' to 'subvert', as he had earlier in the phrase.

[2] For the position of informers under statute and Common Law respectively see pp. 325–6 n. above.

general, and in particular this formulary,[1] which is the first stone of it, has on the moral character of those who have been bred under its influence. In a work of limited extent, the quantity of matter which uses is to habituate men to falshood in every shape in principle and in practice: if in the shape of perjury, so much the better: since he who boggles not at it in this shape will not, it may well be supposed, boggle at it in any other. By a set of twelve Jurymen, of whom from one to eleven are perjured as often as there is a difference of opinion, a smuggler is convicted on the testimony of a witness or two who, if, on being questioned as to what brought them there, they were not prepared to perjure themselves, would not be there. Within these four months the law and the Gospel of the English Catechism have received their compleat fulfilment. The system of Jury perjury—the system of judicial perjury produced by torture—has been established in Scotland.[2] The English lawyer has sung his inward *Nunc dimittis*, for now in the whole island is not a neck of land that may not be seen defiled by perjury.

---

release. Remedy being throughout unendurable, this is the principle on which, in every case, whatever palliative is applied is composed.

The contempt thus habitually put upon the legislature by Judges and as habitually submitted to by legislature, had it in this instance found no counter-abuse—had it in this instance been productive of its full effect, the springs of nourishment being thus dried up, the body politic would long ago have sunk in death. Counteracting, instead of obeying, the acts of their lawful superiors, they saw with conniving eyes the underlings of their own class counteracting theirs. The result—a division of labour was effected: the process of furnishing evidence was divided between two hands. The hunters set on by the legislature found it necessary to hunt in couples. Under the name of an informer, I., who knew nothing about the matter, gave the information and, in case of success, claimed and was supposed to pocket the reward. W., a man who knew every thing that was known about it, and whose appearance but for the reward would have been an effect without a cause, an act without a motive, received it without claiming it.

Out of this system of inconsistencies was made to flow that flood of troubled waters in which lawyers, for their game, love to fish. Of the many who offend, some are prosecuted: of those who are prosecuted, some are let off by corruptive influence for the benefit of the Chancellor of the Exchequer and his creatures, some are let off by quibbles for the benefit of the lawyers, as foxes are let off lest the breed should be lost, and Chancellor Rosslyn's prophecy is fulfilled: No cause is so desperate as to [be] indefensible.[3] The fair trader is thus starved: the consumer more and more heavily taxed; but still the system holds together, and so long as it does hold together, every thing is as it should be.[4]

---

[1] i.e. the Catechism.

[2] The Jury Trials (Scotland) Act of 1815 (55 Geo. III, c. 42) had extended trial by jury to civil cases in Scotland.

[3] Commonly attributed to Alexander Wedderburn (1733–1805), first Baron Loughborough and first Earl of Rosslyn, Solicitor General 1771-8, Lord Chancellor 1793–1801, the exact source of the quotation remains obscure. It may have arisen from a comment made by Wedderburn in the House of Commons on 3 December 1777 on the surrender of the British forces under John Burgoyne (1722–92) to the Americans at Saratoga in the previous October: 'The calamity, he could not deny, was great; but he could not infer from it that our condition was desperate'. See *Parliamentary Debates* (1777) vii. 102.

[4] An echo of Blackstone's phrase, 'Every thing is now as it should be', made in the context of a discussion of the offence of heresy at *Commentaries on the Laws of England*, iv. 49.

CHURCH-OF-ENGLANDISM

can be allotted to this purpose must be proportionably limited: and on such an occasion matters already public are the only matters which, especially by an anonymous writer, can with propriety be employed.

In the instance of the bulk of the community, evidence as conclusive as it is deplorable has been brought to view in and by the proportion of the number of prosecutions for criminal offences in England under the influence, if it has any, of the Episcopal Church of England compared with the number of prosecutions of the same description in the same time under the influence of the Presbyterian Church of Scotland.[1]

In the instance of the rulers of this Church, the like evidence has been furnished in the gross by a view of the manner in which the Society self-stiled the National Society—having for its Members all the Bishops—those who are not Bishops being in so small number that, with the assistance of any one layman whom they can depend upon, they have the whole power for ever in their hands[2]—having these for its operating hands, and for its avowed object the consigning immediately to what in their view of the matter is guilt, not to speak of its everlasting consequence perdition, all whose parents shall have declined to bend their necks under the corruptive yoke— is conducted: and in detail by a view of the characters respectively displayed in the writings of one leading Bishop and two distinguished Deans.[3]

What remains is to produce an example of the effect produced by the same system on the moral disposition of the same leading official person among the laity.

For this purpose, no other equally fair or more instructive sample could have been found than what will be seen afforded by the person on whom alone in effect depended the operations of that Board of Administration on which all the others are dependent.

This Board is the Treasury Board. This person is the Chancellor of the Exchequer: for as to the First Lord or Member of that Board,[4] when the two Offices which are most commonly held together happen to be in different hands, though on every occasion entitled to preside, and in this case to preside is to dictate, in the present instance he has not offered himself to view.

---

[1] See p. 93, 291 & n. above.

[2] For the membership of the National Society as set out in its constitution see p. 46 & n. above.

[3] The Bishop is Howley, Bishop of London, author of *Charge delivered to the Clergy of the Diocese of London* (see pp. 257–311 above), and the two Deans are Kipling, Dean of Peterborough, author of the letter to John Lingard reproduced in Appendix I, pp. 295–6 n. above, and Andrewes, author of the letter to Lushington on behalf of Abbott.

[4] i.e. Liverpool.

At the time in question, the Chancellor of the Exchequer was, and he still is, the Right Honourable Nicholas Vansittart. The Earl of Liverpool is a Nobleman of exemplary piety and warm affection for the Church of England. Mr Vansittart is a Gentleman of at least as warm and undoubted an affection for that same Church—and if possible of still more exemplary piety: for Mr Vansittart has presided and edified by his eloquence a Bible-distributing Society,[1] and no such Society has as yet been edified by the eloquence of the Earl of Liverpool.

Piety is in some breasts a cause of morality, in others a substitute to virtue, and an atonement made for the want of [it]. In the instance of an official person so situated, it is a question of no small interest to determine, as far as the evidence goes, in which of the two characters the affection operates with most effect.

What if it should appear that, while he was signing impunity, it was not in the nature of the human mind that in his there should have been the smallest doubt about guilt? that for granting the impunity thus granted, there was not so much as the shadow of a pretence? that on grounds equally good and pure, impunity, on all occasions, and at all times, may be granted to every public poisoner or every other revenue delinquent without exception, whose understanding and will are found to be, or can thus be made to be, prostrate at the feet of those at whose feet the understanding and will of this Chancellor of the Exchequer have, by the means known to his Lordship of London, been lain prostrate?[2] What if it should appear that, if in the present case corruption be not proved, corruption, though ever so real, can never be proved in any case in which money in the form of money can not be proved to have passed into the corrupted hand?

Question for the Casuists, or in default of Casuists, for the British Forum.[3] Supposing that in the situation of a Brewer, or in that of a Chancellor of the Exchequer, defrauding the revenue, or highly endangering the health of his Majesty's subjects, or stopping the course of justice, were sins—not that in any of the catalogue of sins given by St Paul,[4] any such sins, *totidem verbis* at least, are to be found—supposing, however, for debate or argument sake these were sins, to make a full atonement for those sins, in such sort, after their being committed, as to cause them never to have been committed, how many copies of the Bible, at what price each bought by other

---

[1] For Vansittart's connection with the British and Foreign Bible Society see p. 323 n. above.
[2] See p. 37 n. above.
[3] For the British Forum see p. 530 & n. above.
[4] See 1 Corinthians 6: 9–10; 1 Timothy 1: 9–10.

people's money, would require to be distributed? By a grain or two of bread added to a drop or two of wine—properly knelt to, and stiled, and prayed over, that these and any other sins in any number may, at any time after commission, be caused to have never been committed—all this is out of the question. But with all his piety, while the sacred Table is as far off as St James's Church is from Downing Street, a Chancellor of the Exchequer can not be so constant an attendant as he would wish to be: and in less time than what intervenes between the eating of the bloodless flesh and the drinking of the fleshless blood, orders might be signed for the distribution of a string of bibles that would reach from Downing Street to New South Wales.

On so useful and laudable a practice as the dissemination of the seeds of good learning and good morals, far be it from these pages to convey any sentiments other than those of approbation and applause. But while these good things which are done so easily are done, other good things should not be left undone, much less such bad things done.

Three names being, by the forms of that office, necessary to the legality and efficiency of every Act issued as the Act of that Board, three names are accordingly subjoined to the instrument by which the purpose in question was effected.[1] Of these, that of the Chancellor of the Exchequer, signed N. Vansittart, is the only one which shall here be brought to view. To encumber the page with the names of two living substitutes to as many mechanical automatons would not only encumber the page, but lead to false conclusion. Two puisnes attend in a sort of rotation: the hand of each applies itself to every thing that is done: of the mind of any one, any application made would in effect be useless, and in appearance an act of presumption and impertinence. The use of them is, at the Board to sign, in the House to speak, if, like Mr Vansittart, he has the gift of tongues,[2] and at any rate to vote. He who this day refuses either signature or vote is turned adrift the next tomorrow: what can be said, what need be said, more?

Boards of two very different sorts are afforded by the system of Administration: the uncorrupt and the corrupt: for, for shortness sake and saving due explanations, by these names they may be designated. The uncorrupt sort are filled by Members sitting during good behaviour; the corrupt by Members sitting during pleasure.

To the uncorrupt class belong the Boards of Excise and Customs:

---

[1] In addition to Vansittart, the Treasury Minute of 10 February 1815 was signed by Berkeley Paget, Commissioner of the Treasury 1810–26, and Charles Grant, Commissioner of the Treasury 1813–19: see *Commons Sessional Papers* (1816) xviii. 72.

[2] See I Corinthians 12: 10.

to the corrupt, the Treasury Board and the Admiralty Board. The Members of either the Excise Board or the Board of Customs, being, in so far as concerns their respective powers and salaries, independent, were they to have seats in the House of Commons they might, bating accidental causes of dependence, vote and even speak according to the dictates of their respective consciences. They are accordingly excluded from the House of Commons.[1]

The puisne Members of the Treasury Board and the Admiralty Board being in a state of the most perfect dependence, they are accordingly never any one of them without a seat in that same Honourable House.

Such is the perfection to which the 'prostration of understanding and will,' that ever blessed state which characterizes the Utopia of his Lordship of London, has been exalted in that seat of Government.

A matter which, though not quite so notorious as it ought to be, is what no man will be found hardy enough to set his hand to the denial of is—that a great part, not to say the greater part, of that business which is passed upon the nation as the free act of that House is the act of a majority which, but for a set of puppets, thus dressed up in men's cloaths, would not have existed: the few in whose instance any chance exists of their having wills of their own being either outnumbered or, by indolence or despair of use, excluded by men to whom the same number of the King's Life Guards would be a cheaper, an unimpostrous, an unhypocritical, an undeceptitious, and in every respect whatever a most advantageous and desirable substitute.

To represent the Boards above stiled uncorrupt Boards as absolutely uncorruptible would be a misrepresentation on every other supposition than that of the Members, or at least the majority of them acting on each occasion, as being utterly destitute of all relations, friends and dependents, or capacity of advancement for themselves: all that is meant, because all that ought to be meant, is that in this instance uncorruption is possible, whereas in the other instance it is not possible.

In addition to so many other instructive lights, this single case will have the effect of displaying the effects of what difference there is in the constitutions of the two sorts of Boards.

The uncorrupt Board, the Excise Board, will be seen remonstrating—in terms of honourable energy—remonstrating against so

---

[1] Since 1694 those farming, managing, or collecting duties or taxes (5 & 6 Will. & Mary, c. 7, §57), and since 1700 those appointed as commissioners of the excise and customs (11 & 12 Will. III, c. 2. §150 and 12 & 13 Will. III, c. 10, §89), had been debarred from standing as Members of Parliament: see Blackstone, *Commentaries on the Laws of England*, i. 169.

notorious a partiality—so pretenceless a stoppage of justice. Mr Vansittart, not to speak of the two puisnes buttoned into that one waistcoat—Mr Vansittart will be seen taking cognizance of that representation—and, without so much as the shadow of a pretence, stopping justice. And in this may be seen a pattern of that justice and of that purity which every one whom it may concern may on every occasion see reason to expect at those hands.

No—that there is not—not so much as the shadow of a pretence. That which for form sake is put forward to them to serve in the character of the required shadow is not by themselves believed to be true, and, if it were true, would be nothing to the purpose.

It is composed of two Affidavits. The one is from the Defendant himself: the other is from a servant of his, his Coachman.[1]

In his own affidavit, except that he never had known any thing at all of his own business,[2] what the Defendant says is a confession that a certain quantity of unlawful ingredients (3 lb) was, upon a search made by the Officers, really found upon his premises. Thus much he confesses.[3] But the quantity may have been ever so much greater for any thing he ventures to say to the contrary, and yet the smallness of the quantity, in addition to the fact of his never knowing any thing about his own business, and the supposed malignity of a person with whom the information is supposed to have originated, is the only ground made for the requested stoppage of the course of justice.

What is the fact? the 3 lb was 14 lb and the 14 lb is the remainder of a stock of 56 lb.[4]

What says the Coachman? That in the course of their search the Officers came to a place where he kept some Cow-powders: and from the circumstance of the Coachman's keeping Cow-powders in one place, the inference which he and his intercessors expect Mr Vansittart to draw is that nothing that is sworn by any number of

---

[1] For the two affidavits see p. 540 & n. above.

[2] In his affidavit, Abbott states that he 'had not been brought up to trade or business of any sort or kind whatsoever, and was at that time and still is entirely ignorant of the art and mystery of brewing': see *Commons Sessional Papers* (1816) xviii. 66.

[3] Abbott claimed that the officers of excise, when they searched his premises, found 1lb. of cow-powders and 3lb. of heading.

[4] See Excise Board to Lords Commissioners of the Treasury, 27 January 1814, *Commons Sessional Papers* (1816) xviii. 68: 'It appears to have been the constant practice at the Memorialist's Brewery to put drugs into the Brewing Copper, and the Officers upon searching the premises found two pounds, not one pound, as he states, of prepared powers; and instead of 3 lb. as represented 14 lb. of vitriol or copperas in two boxes, which if full would have contained 56 lb. These were found concealed behind some hurdles in a small paddock in the open air, where, from their dry and clean state, they could have been lodged only a very short period, and in all probability they had been removed during the time of the search.'

eye-witnesses of his keeping unlawful ingredients in any other place can be true.

Such was the opinion of Mr Vansittart: for in no other point of view has the affidavit any the slightest relation to the purpose. Whether in this opinion there was any thing erroneous, let his conduct state. For when called upon to produce his grounds for stopping the law, this is in the number of those grounds.

Here are two grounds—two principles—confessedly acted upon by Mr Vansittart: and he need but act up to his principles upon either of those grounds and the destruction of the revenue and the arrival of state bankruptcy follows as a necessary consequence.

1. The one is, as above, that the fact of the operativeness of the only motives by which (except in a case which scarce ever happens) the law can ever be carried into effect affords on every occasion a sufficient ground and reason for preventing the law from being carried into effect. Unless evidence be furnished, no effect can be given to the law: but where ruin to him against whom it operates will be the consequence, the very act of furnishing it is conclusive proof of malice.[1] The only persons by whom any thing that has place in the premise in question can ever be known—the only persons who have access to it—are the delinquent's servants. A servant instrumental to the ruin of his master? what can be more malicious?

Mr Vansittart's wish is to preserve the revenue. Mr Vansittart's wish is to see offences by which the revenue would be destroyed prevented. Mr Vansittart's wish is that such as are committed and detected shall be punished—but the means without which no such offence can ever be detected, Mr Vansittart will not suffer to be used.

To exculpate himself from the imputation of an intention to destroy the country by destroying the revenue, what will this sworn guardian of the revenue find to say? will it be this? Oh, but I do not mean to give impunity to every body—to all delinquents without distinction: only to such as are useful to me or mine: only to a few particular friends and their friends and their friends' friends.

2. The other is—that on condition of never knowing any thing of his own business, a man may defraud the revenue and injure the health of his fellow subjects in any way in which, and to any extent to which, he can make a profit by it. Of not knowing any thing about his own business, or rather of saying that he does not.[2]

Well, let them then be believed. For eight-and-twenty years he has

[1] The Treasury Minute of 10 February 1815 referred to 'the extortionate demands, and malignant motives of the parties originally concerned in the prosecution': see ibid. 72, and p. 563 n. below.

[2] For Abbott's self-confessed ignorance of the business see p. 560 n. above.

CHURCH-OF-ENGLANDISM

been carrying on his own business without knowing any thing of the matter.[1] By thus knowing nothing about the matter, he has risen from penury to the condition of one who keeps his equipage, is in the commission of the Peace, and keeps company with Court Sinecurists who despise Ale-drinkers. By thus knowing nothing about his own business, he is to have all the profit: but he is to have no part of the loss: for when the means by which he rose are at last brought to light, and, but for a stoppage of the law, loss would be the consequence, in steps a pious Chancellor of the Exchequer and, with the advice of the Court Confessor, stops it. A loss and what loss? a loss by which a small portion of the profit would be done away—a loss to be incurred by a forfeiture the total of which, if proved, could not amount to more than £2,620.[2] And what is that to a man who figures away in his equipage?

3. Another reason for giving impunity to the delinquent has been found by one of his six protectors, Sir Edward Knatchbull. He is sorry he has been found out. In the language of Sir Edward's rhetoric, 'it has certainly preyed upon Mr Abbot's mind, so much as to reduce him almost to death's door.'[3]

This ground has been adopted and embellished by Mr Vansittart. Adopting likewise the language of the St James's Casuist—weighing evil against benefit in the scales furnished to him by that Confessor[4]—he pronounces that 'more of public evil than benefit would result from the humiliation and extreme punishment of a person whose character and conduct are stated to have been so honourable to himself and beneficial to the community.'[5]

Extreme punishment! now what is this extreme punishment? transportation? pillory? would not any one be apt to suppose that it were at least the pillory? Whereas the truth is that, in its extremity, it amounts to no more than payment of the amount of the difference between the £500 which, together with 'the Crown's costs', he is to pay in the way of composition,[6] and the £2,620 which is the utmost that is charged, and which—such is the over-laxity of law accusation on the one hand, and such the over-strictness of the rules of evidence on the other—one may well be assured is manifestly a great deal more than would have been found capable of being proved.

Humiliation indeed?—No—this is among the dreams of M^r

---

[1] In his affidavit, Abbott states that he had bought his brewing business twenty-eight years previously: see *Commons Sessional Papers* (1816) xviii. 67.

[2] According to Abbott's Memorial, he was liable to forfeit the sum of £2,420 if found guilty of the charges against him: see ibid. 65–6. Bentham appears to have miscalculated.

[3] See ibid. 70.   [4] See p. 540 n. above.

[5] See the Treasury Minute, 10 February 1815, *Commons Sessional Papers* (1816) xviii. 72, and p. 547 above.

[6] The Treasury Minute, 10 February 1815, ordered that Abbott's prosecution 'be stayed upon the payment of the Crown's costs and a fine of 500*l*.': see ibid. 72.

Vansittart. After taking his chance for being convicted, had the lottery of the law been unfavourable to him, humiliation—except in so far as paying the difference between forfeited money and compensation money is humiliation—humiliation he would have paid none.

No: the humiliation [in] which, in his sentimentality and his sympathy, this Chancellor concurrs with the delinquent and his other friends, this and this alone is the humiliation suffered by him. The humiliation which is the result of convicted guilt—of secret guilt dragged into daylight—this is alike inflicted upon him in both cases. This is included in the very ground—in the avowed ground—of the act by which comparative impunity is granted to him.

No: the humiliation—the real humiliation—what this consists in is the having, to save a few hundred pounds, laid himself prostrate at the feet of a William Curtis—of a Gerrard Andrews—and, to compleat the climax, of a Nicholas Vansittart.

4. Another plea is that this offence was the first.[1] A man's not having been prosecuted for more offences than one, a reason for not punishing him for that one! When, under the maxims avowed and acted upon by Mr Vansittart, no smuggler or other offender whatever, though offending every day of his life, could ever suffer for so much as one offence without a miracle? Without a miracle, though offending every day of his life, no man can be convicted of so much as one offence, and here is Mr Vansittart who insists that, where he is disposed to give impunity, no man shall be punished for any one offence unless and untill he has been convicted of some number—and he does not say what number—more than one.

5. To compleat the humiliation, observe the good advice—the sermon—which it has now been the hard lot of the defendant to hear from the Treasury Chambers: read it in the Treasury Minute. Prudence requires a man to inspect his own concerns—every man ought to prevent the offences of his Managers[2]—branches of the still sublimer and more extensive maxim—every man ought to do what he ought to do—or, in the language of the 3^d form of Eaton and Westminster, *Omnes homines qui vivent in hoc orbe rotundo debent semper esse boni et nunquam esse mali.*[3] But in this particular branch

---

[1] See ibid.: 'My Lords are of opinion, that this the first instance of offence against the laws by his agent does not call for a rigorous infliction of legal penalties upon the master'.

[2] See ibid.: 'Notwithstanding the evidence submitted to their Lordships of the extortionate demands, and malignant motives of the parties originally concerned in the prosecution, My Lords cannot consent to absolve the Memorialist from all the consequences of his own misplaced confidence in his servants. A personal inspection of the concerns of his Brewery would have enabled the Petitioner to discover and prevent the offences of his managers, and to protect himself from the conspiring efforts of their resentment and treachery.'

[3] i.e. 'All men who live in this round world ought always to be good, and never to be bad.'

of it, St Paul, addressing himself in his Epistle to his disciples among the Thessalonians, had been before hand with the Chancellor of the Exchequer in this secret lamentation of one sinner over another. 'We beseech you, brethren . . .' says the Apostle of the Gentiles (I Thess. IV. 11) 'study to do your own business.' Why was not this given as a text to the Rector of St James's?

6. But, besides what has already been brought to view, 'evidence,' it seems, 'was submitted to their Lordships:' that is to Mr Vansittart. Perhaps so: though, if any, none but what, so perfectly ashamed of it are these Lordships, that they chose rather to disobey an order of the House of Commons than have it sent to the press. Evidence? but of what?—why, 'of the extortionate demands, and malignant motives, of the parties originally concerned in the prosecution.'[1] As well might they, in addition to the evidence afforded by the Coachman of the contents of his Cow-powders, have received evidence fixing the colour of the Coach in which, by a brewery thus conducted without his knowing any thing about the matter, he was enabled to pay his visits to his good neighbour the Dean of Canterbury. 'Extortionate demands—malignant motives—conspiracy—effects of resentment and treachery.' This in a Treasury Minute? Before this time was ever such rhetoric seen—after this time will ever such rhetoric be seen—in a Treasury Minute? In what place upon earth could all this indignant pathos have been penned? In what place, unless peradventure it were in the convivial chamber of the Treasury edifice at the end of the concluding bottle, amidst the mutual embrace and mingled tears of the sinner and the Bible-distributing forgiver of his sins.

A suppression of evidence has just been proved. But from any such quarter, by this or any other instance of suppression of evidence, where disclosure would be attended with inconvenience, let not any man be surprized. It has been proved at length that, upon the principles and in the practice of Church-of-Englandism, as often as the effect of evidence would be to bring to light malpractice on the part of its rulers, evidence ought to be suppressed. Throughout the whole of the Reports published of the proceeding of the National Society—of the Society under the government of the rulers of the Church—the day of the date stands suppressed.[2] In the practice of that Bishop-ruled Society of which he is so useful a Member,[3] Mr Vansittart seems to have learnt—though assuredly he [need][4] not have gone out of these his own Chambers to have learnt it—the

---

[1] See p. 563 n. above.   [2] See pp. 181–2 above.
[3] Vansittart was listed as a donor to the National Society for Promoting the Education of the Poor from 1811 to the time when Bentham was writing.
[4] MS 'had'.

propriety and honesty of suppressing babbling and inconvenient dates. Of the documents not suppressed in this paper of communications, all but two—no inconvenience having been apprehended from the disclosure—present the day of the date. These two are the two Memorials presented by the Defendant to the Treasury Board.[1] When presented, is it true that they had respectively no dates? Then, indeed, true it is that no dates in them have been suppressed. But the just inference is that they had dates, in which case their dates were suppressed. For if so it was that they had no dates, would not so extraordinary a deficiency have been noted? or rather, instead of being first connived at and then noted, would it not have been noted in the first instance, and been sent back to be supplied?

For what is a Memorial without a date? what, but an instrument in which, for the purpose of letting in any such falsification as the purpose may be found to require, a door for falsification has been left open.

At any rate, if, because it was not convenient to him to know, Mr Vansittart knew no more of the date of the day when his friends' several Memorials were presented to him than his friend knew of the business in which he made his fortune, still what Mr Vansittart—or somebody from whom he might have learnt whatever it was convenient to learn—could not avoid knowing was—on what days the same were respectively received.

A quantity of matter appearing in the character of evidence has just been mentioned as suppressed. But in so far, however, as irrelevance is a just ground for suppression, no charge of impropriety can attach upon it. Of the nature of the evidence thus suppressed, thus much, and no more than thus much, appears or suffices to demonstrate its irrelevance. It has for its declared object and sole declared object to prove that, in the words of the delinquent Memorialist, 'the informer's views in giving such information are for the sole purpose of extorting money from your Memorialist.'[2] In the margin of this paragraph of the House of Commons printed copy of the Memorial are the words, 'See Appendix.' In this may, moreover, be seen the only passage in which any reference is made to the Appendix. At the close of this paper, a man naturally looks for this Appendix. No such thing will he find. What he will find is, instead of it, these words '*˳* The Appendix is upon the Table of the House of Commons.'[3]

Now with all due submission to those whom it may concern—and

---

[1] For the two undated Memorials from Abbott see *Commons Sessional Papers* (1816) xviii. 65–7, 69.   [2] See Abbott's first undated Memorial at ibid. 67.
[3] Ibid. 73. Although ordered to be printed by the House of Commons on 29 March 1816 (*Commons Journals* (1816) lxxi. 254), the Appendix does not appear to have been so.

CHURCH-OF-ENGLANDISM

in particular the Right Honourable Charles Abbot, the Speaker of the Honourable House, upon whom the printing of documents printed in obedience to Orders of that Honourable House immediately depends—it follows not that because a document which a Board of Administration have taken for the ground of their proceedings is irrelevant and as such was incapable of entering into the composition of a proper ground—it follows not that because, to the purpose of affording an exculpation or extenuation for a defendant, the document was irrelevant, it was also irrelevant to the purpose of the enquiry whether, on the occasion of a grant of impunity given to such a Defendant by the Board of Administration, the conduct of such Board was justifiable. On the contrary, the more indubitably irrelevant was the document so acted upon, the more indubitably indefensible was the conduct of those who acted upon it.

Upon the face of this part of the business, what seems apparent, therefore, is—[1.] in the first place, that the irrelevancy of this Document, to which Mr Vansittart refers as forming one part of the ground of this proceeding, was so palpable that, in the opinion of his Right Honourable Colleague and Co-operator in the business of the National Society,[1] it was better that this document should remain concealed from all those who, in the language of the Rector of St James's, are no better than *Ale-drinkers*, and in the language of the Honourable House, whose Members have, by a fiction of the Honourable House, been chosen by them, no better than *strangers*.[2]

2. In the next place, agreeing with his said Right Honourable friend and Colleague in the maxim that more of public evil than benefit would result from the punishment of 'a person' (of any person) 'whose character and conduct have been stated' (by any competent person approved of as such by Mr Vansittart or any other Chancellor of the Exchequer, stated truly or falsely) 'to have been so honourable to himself and beneficial to the community,'[3] what appears is that, upon the principle, viz. another principle of the aforesaid St Paul, he that sows shall reap.[4] Be not deceived—it seemed to the Right Honourable Speaker to be but common and scriptural justice to the Right Honourable Chancellor, to give him the benefit of this his own work, and spare him, in so far as possible, the humiliation and extreme punishment of such an exposure—of an exposure by which he would have been exhibited as confederating and combining to and with a Defendant, to receive[?] from said Defendant, as and for

---

[1] i.e. Charles Abbot.

[2] 'Stranger' is a parliamentary term for any person who is not a member or official of the House of Commons.

[3] See p. 547 above.

[4] Galatians 6: 7.

a justification of a grant of impunity, a document which it was so impossible for any person really to have viewed in that light, that it was preferable at all hazard to suppress it.

No: there is no more evidence.—'The resentment and treachery,' 'the extortionate demands,' 'the malignant motives,'[1] of the sole and effective operation of which, though in its nature not capable of being known otherwise than by direct revelation from the searcher of all hearts to whom all hearts are known and from whom no events are hid,[2] Mr Vansittart is so sure of as if it had been revealed to him by an Apostle—on none of all these inscrutable matters, unless from a divine revelation or private whispers from this or that useful friend, could he have formed any conception at all otherwise than from these unavowable, and accordingly suppressed, documents: those documents of which he, and his Right Honourable friend for him, were so perfectly ashamed, and of the consequences of which, if disclosed, they were so justly apprehensive.

Now, instead of a Chancellor of the Exchequer who does these things in the way in which we see them doing by Mr Vansittart, suppose a Chancellor of the Exchequer doing them for bribes received in each instance in hard money by himself. The bribe-taking, would he be more noxious than the bible-giving, Chancellor? No: he would be much less noxious. Suppose all corruption-spreading Chancellors of the Exchequer of this bribe-taking sort, and no one of them of this bible-distributing sort:—the condition of the country, would it be worse in the supposed case than in the real case? No: it would be beyond all comparison less bad. The bribe-taking Chancellor, though by the supposition he has engaged in his bribe-taking, could not in the nature of the case long continue in it. Corruption, in the shape in which, to any efficient extent, it never can be committed, being by the sentimentality of the ruling few loaded with all the odium, while, in the only shape in which they can have any need of it, it receives their permitt—the bribe all this while not being susceptible of any such varnish as we see afforded by the generous indignation excited by 'the revengeful malice,' 'extortionate demands,' 'resentment and treachery' in this state of things, what could not be a secret to any body is—that if proved upon a Chancellor of the Exchequer, necessary prudence would prevent his friends and colleagues from stirring a finger in his support: he would be abandoned, as when stricken a deer is by the herd: he would be

---

[1] See p. 563 n. above.
[2] An echo of the Collect recited at the start of 'The Order for the Administration of the Lord's Supper or Holy Communion', *Book of Common Prayer*: 'Almighty God, unto whom all hearts be open, all desires known, and from whom no secrets are hid'.

abandoned, as the Saint Thornton, who went off with the public money which their piety had got for him, was abandoned by the other Saint Thorntons and the other Saints.[1] Understanding this—small indeed would be the number of bribes received into the bribe-taking Chancellor's store, before some delinquent, who, for a bribe of £100, after a course of undetected profit to the amount of £5,000, had upon detection been let off a forfeiture of £500, would come back to the bribe-taking Chancellor, and make reprisals. Full of 'extortionate demands,' made at the instigation of the most 'malignant motives,' he would come back and say to him with the most 'revengeful malice,' *Good Sir, give me back my £100, with £1,000 of your own to boot, or I will blow you.* The experiment succeeding—for how should it do otherwise?—repetition would be the word until the private Exchequer of the bribe-taking Chancellor would be left in a state of as perfect inanition as that public Exchequer of which the bible-distributing Chancellor has the care.

In this way it is that the bribe-taking Chancellor would be sure to be punished: the bible-distributing Chancellor, let him go on in the same way till all revenue is vanished, and all votes passed *nemine contradicente*, by what possibility can he ever be punished? for among those things which are most certain are some of those which, in the nature of things, never can be proved. Suppose it certain that, by the Rector of St James's, in the case of a Presbyterian or a man who had given a wrong vote in a Westminster Election—by Sir William Curtis, in the case of a man who had voted on the wrong side in a City of London Election—by Sir Edward Knatchbull, in the case of a man who had voted on the wrong side in an election for Kent or Canterbury—a man, by the malice of whose servant a quantity of unlawful ingredients had, for the first or only time, been dropped into a vat of ale—suppose such a man so circumstanced, being himself without reproach, had by all these worthies been left, with a wife and a dozen children, to stay in a jail till [. . .?]—for want of a word from any of them—or notwithstanding the most pressing instance from all of them—still more pressing than those which have here been seen, if possible—a Chancellor of the Exchequer would have left the law to

---

[1] The brothers Samuel Thornton (1754–1838), MP for Kingston-upon-Hull 1784–1806 and Surrey 1807–12, 1813–18, Robert Thornton (1759–1826), MP for Bridgwater 1785–90 and Colchester 1790–1817, and Henry Thornton (1760–1815), MP for Southwark 1782–1815, came from a wealthy mercantile family and maintained banking and mercantile interests, and, for a time all neighbours on Clapham Common, were members of the Clapham Sect involved in Wilberforce's campaign to end the slave trade. Robert Thornton, who was declared bankrupt in 1814, had fled to France under an assumed name, and then had gone to live in the United States of America: see *The Correspondence of George, Prince of Wales 1770–1812*, ed. A. Aspinall, 8 vols., London, 1963–71, vii. 280–1 n.

take its course, all these suppositions, all of them by the supposition certain[?] and verified—of any one of them, could so much as a single tittle be proved?—the question is self-answered.[1]

Five of these cases are to be found among the printed papers of the House:[2] in four of them, the independent Board is trodden under foot by M[r] Vansittart and his dependents on his dependent Board: in the fifth, which was the last, the stench of it was so foul that the nerves even of M[r] Vansittart could not stand it. Notwithstanding all these experiences, 'We are under no apprehension (say the Commissioners on this occasion) we are under no apprehension lest the present application of the revenue laws should be thought to require justification. It will be for your Lordships to determine whether you will interfere in a business judicially decided, and that in the manner proposed by the defendant himself; and will on *ex parte* and extra-judicial evidence stop a prosecution against persons repeatedly convicted of offences against the Statute for the protection of the Revenue. We shall think it our duty to proceed in due course of law, unless, as we trust will not be the case, we should receive Your Lordships' positive orders to forebear.'

Signed B. Sydenham, A. Phipps, G. Seymour (Lord George Seymour), W. Manley. Excise Office 28 Feb.[y] 1815.[3]

The case lingers till the 3 of Jan.[y] in the year 1816, on which day it concludes. Encouraged by the reception and compliance bestowed on former applications, the Defendants, Giles and John Davy, Brewers, at the borough of Lyme Regis in Devonshire, present a Memorial dated the 16th December 1815, which, in the Treasury Minute made thereupon, is entered as read on the 22[d] of that same month. On the 3[d] of the next month January goes to them a Treasury Letter informing them that this request can not be complied with.[4]

Not a page, one should think scarce a line, can ever issue from that Board without affording to him who has nerves to look into it information as instructive as it is disheartening.

Note the Treasury Minute as copied from their books, the Treasury Minute ordering a letter to be written; note the letter which goes in consequence. Their Lordships, M[r] Vansittart with his puisnes, prescribes the topics to be touched upon, M[r] Lushington, in his quality of Secretary, writes the letter and touches upon no

---

[1] In the text, Bentham has inserted the following heading above the next paragraph: 'Battle of the Boards.'

[2] For the case of John Gibbs of Emsworth, Hampshire, who contravened the salt laws, see *Commons Sessional Papers* (1816) xviii. 27–36, and for the cases of Solomon Leonard, brewer, of Bristol, Wolf Benjamin, soapmaker, of Leigh, Essex, and Giles and John Davie, brewers, of Lyme Regis, see ibid. 41–64. The case of Abbott is the fifth.

[3] See the case of Giles and John Davie, ibid. 61.

[4] See ibid. 61–2.

CHURCH-OF-ENGLANDISM

such topics. The House of Commons, while, with the exception of the too personally pressing Income Tax,[1] registering all his Edicts, can not entertain a more profound contempt for M[r] Vansittart than is manifested towards him by this his Secretary. Write to the parties, says M[r] Vansittart, acquainting them that my Lords see no grounds whatever for diminishing the penalties which they have (been?) 'adjudged to pay, or for extending to them (the parties) any further indulgence than they (their Lordships) have already granted.'[2]

Well, then, [of] the opinions thus expressed—expressed in the words *'no grounds whatever,' 'penalties adjudged'* and *'further indulgence'*—in the letter he writes to the parties, is any intimation to be found? None whatever. What their Lordships have ordered him to write, he will not write—what he does write is what they did not order him to write: 'they' (meaning their Lordships) can not comply with your request.

Disobedience such as this, one might have hoped, would have been sufficient. No: it is not sufficient: it must be seasoned with falshood and that a glaring one. M[r] Lushington, had he his Catechism open before him, could not have shewn himself more effectually impregnated with the spirit of it. I am commanded, says he, by my Lords to acquaint you—then follow the words that they can not comply with your request.

True it is that, if so it be that, over a bottle, a quorum of their Lordships, a number not less than three, said to him—Lushington— you must write so and so—never mind the minute, on this supposition, but on no other, on the part of said Lushington, there was no direct falshood: nothing worse than a fraud—a fraud consisting in the endeavour to cause those whom it concerned to believe that the letter thus written had for its warrant a Treasury Minute, he well knowing at the time that it had no such warrant.

But if so it be that Treasury Minutes are thus dealt with, the consequence must be that a book containing these Treasury Minutes has no better title to regard than a Report made in the name of the Bishops, the Chancellor, the speaker and others under the direction of the Archbishop of Canterbury.[3]

Note that, like every thing else which passes through the hands of a Ministry, all this, as well as if it had been ever so correct, passes

---

[1] Vansittart's proposal to continue the Property Tax Act of 1803 (43 Geo. III, c. 122), introduced to fund the war with Napoleonic France and amended in 1805 and 1806 (45 Geo. III, c. 15 and 46 Geo. III, c. 65), was defeated in the House of Commons on 18 March 1816 by 37 votes (*Parliamentary Debates* (1816) xxxiii. 451).
[2] See *Commons Sessional Papers* (1816), xviii. 62.
[3] An allusion to the *Annual Reports* of the National Society: see pp. 186–94 above.

upon the House of Commons.—But constituted as it is constituted, what is it that will not pass upon a House of Commons?

Note, moreover, that of the two conflicting Boards, the dependent and the independent one, an enquiry not altogether unworthy of notice is whether, in the nature of things, it be possible that if what is said by the one has any claim to regard, it be possible that any thing that is said or done by the other should have any such claim. Four times grounding themselves on regular evidence, the Excise Board, to whose competence the cause properly and originally belongs, declare the application—the application made for mitigation or exemption—altogether groundless. The dependent Board—which, for causes too palpably obvious to need mentioning, has made the two Houses give them as to this matter a jurisdiction concurrent with that of the Excise Board[1]—what tokens of regard does it pay to these regular and necessary representations from the independent Board? altogether as much as if the Hulks, and not an independent Board, had been the quarter from which they came. The Excise Board, is it then such a mass of corruption that no statement that ever comes [from][2] it has any the smallest claim to notice? Let any one say whether, on any supposition other than this, the conduct of the dependent Board can be justified or so much as palliated.

Of these two Boards, the dependent and the independent, either the one or the other must be a perfect nuisance.

Take notice that, of the evidence on which the independent Board all along acts, the shape may at any rate have been trustworthy: nor does any ground appear for supposing it to have been otherwise—whereas the evidence on which the dependent Board grounds the contempt it puts upon the independent Board is essentially untrustworthy, not received where any better is to be had by any one who does not mean to do wrong, extra-judicial and on one side only, and of this notice is on each occasion sounded in their ears.

On this occasion, one source of the deepest regret and the most acute compunction must not be dissembled. It is that by dragging the corruption into day light, information of its existence may be given to no one can say how many of those in whom the disposition to profit by it exists or may be thus created, but who by that ignorance of the real state of the Constitution, which is so general and so deplorable, might otherwise have been kept from profiting. In this point of view,

---

[1] In July 1814 jurisdiction in the matter of excise prosecutions to commence, continue, or stay proceedings, to restore goods seized, and to remit penalties forfeited before or after conviction, which had previously resided with the Commissioners of Excise and Customs, had been extended to the Lord Commissioners of the Treasury (see 54 Geo. III, c. 171).

[2] MS 'to' contradicts the evident sense of the passage.

the case is like that of an indictment preferred against a gaming-house or a house of ill-fame.

No, it is not without extreme grief and regret that this pen can bring itself to be contributory to the circulating, among those whose interest will prompt them to avail themselves of it, any such suspicion, and that a suspicion supported upon such grounds—as that, on condition of getting some two or three Members of Parliament or any other influential persons whose 'wills or understandings' be 'prostrate'[1] at the feet of such a person as Mr Vansittart or of any other person in his place, they may defraud the revenue to any extent they please: and this in the teeth of representations from those who alone have it in their power to obtain, in relation to a business of this sort, so much as a single tittle of trustworthy evidence—from the Members of one of the very few Boards among the Members of which any degree of independence, which is as much as to say any tolerably adequate degree of regard for truth and justice, can with any tolerably grounded assurance be looked for: of representations by which, being so justly characterized by the appellation of 'an ex parte representation,' the representations are 'declared to be totally false and groundless.'[2]

But such in this country, and under the constitution in the state in which it lingers, is the deplorable alternative. Publish the corruption, you encrease it: yet to conceal it would be still worse. Display the mischief, the chance of remedy is next to nothing. But until it is displayed, and fully displayed, all remedy is absolutely impossible.

Yes: ruin is ready to burst on every hand: every day the causes of it are operating with ever-accumulating force. Ireland has long been bankrupt: by no less a sum than | | a year, the whole revenue she affords has been insufficient for discharge of the interest of her debt.[a]

---

[a] The Minister sees this, acknowledges this, stops enquiry, yet pretends not so much as to have a remedy.[3]

[1] See p. 37 n. above.
[2] See Excise Board to the Treasury, 27 January 1815, *Commons Sessional Papers* (1816) xviii. 68: 'Under circumstances of so flagrant a nature we cannot think the Memorialist [i.e. John Abbott] entitled to the least favourable regard; but we shall consider it our indispensable duty to renew the proceedings against him, and bring the same to issue with all possible dispatch, unless we should have Your Lordships positive orders to the contrary; so perfectly satisfied are we of the validity of the evidence now in our hands for convicting the offender; and we regret that the case has been so far delayed from an ex parte representation totally false and groundless.'
[3] Bentham has indicated his intention to insert a reference at this point.
In the debate in the House of Lords on 2 April 1816 on a motion that a committee be appointed to take into consideration the state of Ireland, Liverpool, the leader of the administration, had rejected the appointment of both a Committee of the whole House and of a Select Committee. A financial statement, given by Buckingham, showed that since 1812 the

Hindostan, with her fifty millions of heavy taxed and vainly groaning subjects, has long been in the same state. Every incessantly deteriorating dependence the country has, and she is cursed with numberless ones, is, by the amount of the whole cost of the official establishment for government and defence—constant and occasional, in peace and in war—so much loss to the country. Ireland hanging upon her—Hindostan hanging upon her—every Colony which she is made to support, that the Liverpools and the Vansittarts may have the pleasure and the profit of sending their dependents to govern it, hanging upon her with continually encreasing pressure— the penal Colony pressing upon her with a weight of not less than £200,000 a year, for the Convict part of the population, which might have been maintained without expence,[1] were sent to the antipodes that they might be maintained at this expence—all these millstones hanging upon her neck, Britain may be expected every day to sink under the load. In the already manifested fate of Ireland and Hindostan may be seen the hourly impending fate of Britain. While the Liverpools and the Vansittarts of those days were settling the composition of the undivided and incomprehensible Being, the Roman Empire transplanted into Greece was crumbling into ruins. While, in consummation of their exertions, [the] British Empire is on the point of falling to pieces, the Liverpools and Vansittarts of the present day are paving the earth with Bibles.[2]

Throughout the whole field of government, the interest of the ruling and influential few is in a state of diametrical opposition to the interest of the subject many: and it is on the operation of this sinister interest that the lot of the country and every man in it is on every occasion determined. It is in the interest of the subject many that in no one instance either an overpaid place or a sinecure or a needless place should have existence. It is the interest of the ruling few, and of all those who look up to them for a share of the plunder, that needless places and overpaid places and sinecures should be as abundant, and each of them as profitably burthensome, and, with the exception of a few of the speaking ones, as unfitly filled, and the business of them done as badly, as possible. Out of Britain and Ireland, for the defence of Britain and Ireland, an army is altogether as needful on the Moon

---

annual charge of Ireland's National Debt had been greater than the net revenue paid into the Exchequer. See *Parliamentary Debates* (1816) xxxiii. 804–41. Reports of the debate appeared in *The Times* and *Morning Chronicle* of 3 April 1816.

[1] Bentham has in mind his own panopticon prison scheme.

[2] In the margin, the following incomplete fragment appears at this point: 'While with one and the same army the Castlereaghs are sowing the seeds of hourly expected wars, and crushing beyond hope of resurrection the constitution by the revival of which the only chance of salvation is presented'.

as in France or in Hindostan, or any other part of this our planet. The ruling few have an army: the subject many have none. As yet, with only now and then a violation of detail, the forms of the Constitution are observed. In London, as 18 centuries ago in Rome, they will continue to be observed, as long as by their apparent observance, the needful mischief can be done, with less trouble than by their open violation. In London, as at Rome, they will not be observed a moment longer. In what is doing in France, in what is done in Spain, in what is doing or will soon be doing and done every where else but in Republican America, read what is doing and will ere long be done in England.[1]

In France, the Deputies of the subject many are nominated by the Monarch openly: they are nominated by force. In Britain, thin and transparent as is the covering, they are nominated covertly, or if not nominated by him, bought by a mode of purchase which, because it is not bribery, is unpunishable. Oh what a blessing it would be if, instead of being nominated as here and now by fraud, the pretended deputies of the people—stiled representatives because known not to have been deputies—were, as in France, nominated by force. Oh what a blessing it would be if, of both Houses, no Members being bought by [unpunishable][2] influence, as many as by possibility could be were bought and sold by punishable bribery! Here would be impunity in name, punity in effect. What we have is punity in name, and in effect that impunity in which draining, vulgarly called fructifying, dependencies, groundless wars and endless waste, and the ruin which is impending, have their cause.

When remedy in every other shape is hopeless, the last remedy left to an oppressed subject many is in that form of petition by which alone they can be let into the knowledge of each other's minds. Of this last remedy, by a decision still more pretenceless, if possible, than that of the distributor of stamps and bibles, another Abbot, not the vendor of unwholesome and smuggled ale, but a disciple of the same School, has, during the sleep of the pretended watchdogs of the Constitution, had courage to rob an unconscious people.[3] Signatures,

---

[1] In the margin, Bentham has noted at this point: 'The few to whose optics it is discernible that government, as it has so long been carried on, is neither more nor less than a system of regulated plunderage—these few, whom to a view of the mischief could add any such intelligence and activity as should afford a hope of remedying it—these few, instead of bearing a hand to stop the plunderage, lie gaping for a share of it.'

[2] MS 'unpublishable'.

[3] Following the presentation by Francis Burdett on 3 March 1817 of over 500 petitions for Parliamentary reform, 468 of which were printed, Abbot, in his role as Speaker, on 12 March 1817 upheld the rule first made in 1656 and in accordance with similar decisions taken on 6 May 1793 and 30 June 1813, that petitions must not be printed before presentation to the House of Commons. See *Parliamentary History* (1792–4) xxx. 786; *Parliamentary Debates* (1813) xxvi.

though in the hand-writing of the several petitioners, are all void: why?—because, in the matter and prayer of the Petition, for saving the useless delay, vexation and expence of multiplied manuscript, that art which in no other cases finds so much as an Abbot to condemn it, was in this case, as in every other case it would have been, employed. On what ground either of reason or even of precedent—of that authority which, being the work of the conspiracy of the ruling few against the subject many, has been so frequently and so naturally in a state of opposition to reason—on what ground, either of reason or of precedent, did or can this last and most insidious and most malignant violation of the rights, even the acknowledged rights, of the people find so much as the shadow of a pretence? Absolutely in none. Two liberties, that of the press and that of petitioning, are thus crushed to pieces by this one stroke. Yet the Whigs, seeing in none of these petitions any petition for the transferring into their hands the power and practice of misrule, sit still and silent and connivent and demonstrate the share they possess in the conspiracy ever carried on against the subject many by the ruling few.

993–7; (1817) xxxv. 859–63, 998; and [John Hatsell], *Precedents of proceedings in the House of Commons; with observations* (first published 1781–6), 4 vols. London, 1818, ii. 189 n.

THE
BOOK OF CHURCH REFORM:
CONTAINING THE MOST ESSENTIAL PART
OF
Mr. BENTHAM'S
'CHURCH OF ENGLANDISM EXAMINED,' &c.

EDITED BY ONE OF HIS DISCIPLES.

TABLE OF CONTENTS.

§1. *Disorders (Political and Moral) of the Church.*
§2. *Remedies for the above-mentioned Disorders.*[1]

---

[1] For the text of these sections see 'Church-of-Englandism', Appendix IV, §§ 9–10, pp. 471–93 above, and Collation D, pp. 605–12 below.

PREFACE.

Reader.—The Book of Church Reform.—Whence comes this title?

Editor.—From that of Dr. Southey's work intituled *The Book of the Church*.[1]

Reader.—And why, for the extract you have thus made, take in this way a title from that Book?

Editor.—Because the title so worded is of use to our purpose, and that in more ways than one. It helps to draw attention to the plan of Church Reform we are re-editing; and, moreover, to satisfy people that it is a needful and unexceptionable one.

Reader.—To draw attention?—Yes: that I can conceive well enough; but as to satisfying people about what you mention, how is that to be? In that work of Mr. Bentham's, his object was, to overturn the Church, as the phrase is, and to leave the spot vacant. Dr. Southey's, in that work of *his*, to give support to that same venerable fabric, as another phrase has it. By whatsoever support may have so been given to that same fabric, how is it that aid has been given to the endeavours that have been made to overturn it? To a plain man this is not altogether obvious.

Editor.—Strange as at first glance this may seem to you, on a second view you will find it to be not the less true. In the following extract you will see Mr. Bentham doing two things; making proof of the evil effects produced by the English-Church-part of the Official Establishment of the country, without one single good effect; and to all these evils proposing in detail an effectual, and that the most appropriate, remedy. Doctor Southey's work had for its object the making people think that no change ought to be made in this same fabric, or whatever else it is to be called: this object it had, or none. Well, then; when he published this Book of his, there lay upon his table that same Book of Mr. Bentham's; upon that same table on which it had been lying for five or six years.[a] What then said he to it? What said he of it? Just nothing: No; nor from anything to be found in that same Book of Doctor Southey's would any body be led to know, or so much as imagine, that any such book as this of Mr. Bentham's ever had any existence. Of all the alleged evil effects of the establish-

---

[a] Date of publication of Church of Englandism—1818: date of the Book of the Church—1824.

[1] Robert Southey, *The Book of the Church*, 2 vols., London, 1824.

PREFACE

ment in question Mr. Bentham's book makes proof: of any one of them does Doctor Southey's book contain any disproof, or so much as an attempt at disproof? Disproof? No: nor so much as a *denial*. Mr. Bentham's book, in proposing the one indispensable remedy— namely, the pulling down the venerable fabric, and leaving the spot unoccupied,—shows in detail how the materials may be disposed of to the best advantage; and in what manner evil in any shape may be prevented from mixing itself with the remedy: in other words, how the proposed change may be effected, and not a particle of injury to property, or of human suffering in any shape, be produced by it. To all this what says Dr. Southey? Just nothing. How so? because he saw that of all that had been so advanced by Mr. Bentham, not any the smallest part was there that was not incontrovertible.

Reader.—To the discernment and tact of the learned Reviewer and Poet Laureate complimentary enough, it must be confessed, is this same surmise of yours: a tribute of admiration; and, as far as appears to me, no more than is justly due. But the compliment thus paid—is it not at the expense of his reputation for sincerity that it is thus paid?

Editor.—To be sure it is: how can it be otherwise? But what of that?

Reader.—Why, Sir, if that be the case, has he not then but too just ground to complain of you?

Editor.—Good Sir! none at all; not that, had he ever so much ground for such complaint, it ought to prevent us from rendering to the public the service we think we are thus rendering. But the case is, that on this score he has no ground at all for complaint against us: for, what cause can he or any man have for complaint against us, or any man, from the saying anything of him by which he will not be set so much as a peg lower in the estimation of the public, as at present constituted?

Every practising Barrister—is he not, as such, an open professor of insincerity? Is he not (as Junius says) 'an indiscriminate defender of *right* and *wrong*,'[1] and (as Bentham adds) 'by the indiscriminate utterance of *truth* and *falsehood*.'[2] Every one of the great Westminster-Hall Judges—the twelve, the fifteen, or the eighteen Judges,[3] take

[1] See *The Letters of Junius*, ed. J. Cannon, Oxford, 1978, p. 323, Letter LXVIII. To Lord Chief Justice Mansfield (21 January 1772): 'As a practical profession, the study of the law requires but a moderate portion of abilities. The learning of a pleader is usually upon a level with his integrity. The indiscriminate defence of right and wrong contracts the understanding, while it corrupts the heart.' The author was almost certainly Philip Francis (1740–1818), who, using the alias of Junius, wrote a series of over sixty letters in the *Public Advertiser* from 1768 to 1772.

[2] See *Rationale of Judicial Evidence, specially applied to English practice*, 5 vols., London, 1827, v. 108 (Bowring, vii. 415): 'The indiscriminate defence of right and wrong, by what is it kept up, but by the indiscriminate advancement of truth and falsehood?'

[3] The twelve were presumably the justices of the three Common Law courts, namely the Court of King's Bench, the Court of Common Pleas, and the Court of Exchequer; the fifteen

BOOK OF CHURCH REFORM

which number you will—has he not been a practising Barrister? and to the skill employed by him in that same *defence* and *utterance* is he not supposed and asserted—is he not generally even wished—to have been indebted, for his elevation to that same situation of opulence, dignity, uncontrolled and irresponsible power. Among all the qualifications regarded as desirable in the case of such a Judge, is there any other that is susceptible of determinate and incontrovertible proof?

Reader.—This Book of the political philosopher's (you take upon you to say) had been all that while lying upon the Poet Laureate's table. Good Sir! how do you know this?

Editor.—How can it have failed to be there? A work bearing for its title *Church of Englandism Examined, &c.* written by the author of the *Fragment on Government*,[1] the *Introduction to Morals and Legislation*,[2] the *Springs of Action Table*,[3] the *Defence of Usury*, '*Swear not at all*'— with so many *et cæteras* upon *et cæteras*, preceded or followed by those numerous works of his which, through the medium of the French language, had so long been spreading light all over the civilized world[4]—is it possible that for such a length of time it should have remained a subject of ignorance, or an object of indifference, to a Reviewer by profession?—to an eye so discursive and discerning as that of Doctor Southey? Ask the learned Doctor about this if you have really any doubt about it: ask him, and see what he will say to you.

Well, then—in this state of things what does this professed literary Champion of the Church? He does what, in the war of the sword, an able general, a Duke of Wellington[5] for example, would have done in

---

were the judges of the Court of Chancery in addition to these twelve; and the eighteen the three Justices added to the Common Law courts by the Act for the more effectual Administration of Justice of 1830 (11 Geo. IV & 1 Will. IV, c. 70) in addition to these fifteen.

[1] For *A Fragment on Government*, first published at London in 1776, see *A Comment on the Commentaries and A Fragment on Government*, ed. J.H. Burns and H.L.A. Hart, London, 1977 (*CW*), pp. 391–501.

[2] *An Introduction to the Principles of Morals and Legislation*, ed. J.H. Burns and H.L.A. Hart, London, 1970 (*CW*), was first published at London in 1789.

[3] For *A Table of the Springs of Action*, printed in 1815 and first published at London in 1817, see *Deontology together with A Table of the Springs of Action and Article on Utilitarianism*, ed. A. Goldworth, Oxford, 1983 (*CW*), pp. 79–115.

[4] Numerous editions of Bentham's works had been translated into French by 1831, most notably the five major recensions edited by Dumont: *Traités de législation civile et pénale*, 3 vols., Paris, 1802; *Théorie des peines et des récompenses*, 2 vols., London, 1811; *Tactique des assemblées législatives*, 2 vols., Geneva and Paris, 1816; *Traité des preuves judiciaires*, 2 vols., Paris, 1823; and *De l'organisation judiciaire, et de la codification*, Paris, 1828.

[5] Arthur Wellesley (1769–1852), first Viscount (1809), first Earl (1812), first Marquis (1812), and first Duke of Wellington (1814), in command of British, Portuguese, and Spanish forces, had achieved a series of victories over the French in the Peninsular War 1808–14, and had finally defeated Napoleon at Waterloo on 18 June 1815. He had more recently led the administration as First Lord of the Treasury 1828–30.

PREFACE

his place: he sets himself to *create*, or *make a diversion*, as the phrase is: to draw men's attention from the only object of intrinsic and real importance—namely, the state of the establishment in question at the present time, and the conduct and character of the members of it, by directing that same attention to the state of this same establishment in various former times, and the conduct and character of the members of it in those same former times.

Wherefore it is that, be the man who he may, his being or having been a Barrister in indiscriminate practice is, in the opinion of Mr. Bentham, a blot upon his scutcheon: and whatsoever claim he may have to the sort of indulgence shown to the woman taken in adultery,[1] still however this same man is beyond comparison less fit for a trust of any kind than the same man would have been if that same blot had not had place: and therefore so it is, that the Judges made upon his model will, as soon as the term of the first apprenticeship expires, have served their apprenticeship all of them on the Bench—none of them at the *Bar*.[2]

Then as to religion, and the religion of Jesus in particular, and more particularly the Church of England edition of it, and most of all the University of Cambridge, one of the two head schools of it—look at the University of Cambridge. Is there not a functionary—a paid functionary—put into and kept in an office by the style and title of the *Christian Advocate*?[3] And the Christian Advocate—can he advocate the religion of Jesus according to any edition of it other than that published by what, on this occasion, is called Church of Englandism?—that is to say, by the rulers of the Church of England? Well, then, in taking upon himself that same style and title of *Christian Advocate*, did he not—this sacred Advocate—profess the same indifference between *right* and *wrong*, and *truth* and *falsehood*, as is entertained and professed by all profane Advocates? And a late Christian Advocate, for example, in his defence of Church of Englandism against an attack made upon it by a work intituled *Not Paul but Jesus*, did he not give a signal and incontestible exemplification of that same indispensable and universally not merely tolerated, but positively belauded, indifference.[4]

---

[1] John 8: 1–11.

[2] For Bentham's proposals for the recruitment and appointment of judges see 'Constitutional Code', Ch. XII, §§ 28–9 (Bowring, ix. 525–32).

[3] The office of Christian Advocate, inaugurated in 1803, was funded by an endowment from the estate of John Hulse (1708–90), who left instructions directing that the position should be dedicated to the defence of Christianity.

[4] Thomas Smart Hughes (1786–1847) was author of *A Defence of the Apostle St. Paul against the Accusation of Gamaliel Smith, Esq. in a recent publication, entitled, 'Not Paul, But Jesus'*, Part I, Cambridge, 1823, and *On the Miracles of St. Paul. Being Part II. of a Defence of that Apostle against the Accusation of Gamaliel Smith, Esq. in a recent publication, entitled, 'Not Paul, But*

And therefore it is, that in so far as it is *established*, every thing that is called *religion* is, if sincerity be any part of morality, in irreconcileable enmity to morality: establishment of religion meaning, whatever else be meant by it, the employing, in a direct way or in an indirect way, reward and punishment, one or both, in inducing men to profess to entertain this or that opinion, how adverse to it soever may be the opinion entertained by them respectively in reality.

And therefore it is, that, when in any country the existing Temple of Imposture is pulled down, Mr. Bentham would not, if it depended upon him, have any other erected in the room of it; but, on the contrary, he would have the spot it was built on left vacant: left in the state it is in in the Anglo-American United States,[1] where, population for population, there is beyond comparison more regard for religion than in England—the chosen seat of insincerity, with its Church-building jobs *à la mode de Harrowby*.[a]

But before you have done with insincerity, good Sir, forget not to look at the Houses, or either of them—the Honorable and Right, or Most Honorable.—Look at the Debates, and, above all, look at the inexorable abhorrence with which secresy of suffrage, the capital instrument in the manufactory of sincerity, is clung to! and see whether it be possible for men to have more finished models of insincerity than are there to be found: and whether to say of this learned and skilful Defender of the Church of England faith and so forth, that he is a proficient in the art and practice of insincerity, is saying any thing worse of him than that he is a successful imitator of the practice of the most learned and illustrious practitioners, Noble and Honorable, that, in either of those excellent assemblies, are to be found. Thus stands the matter at present; but when Reform comes, the further it is carried the less will be the need, use, and demand, for insincerity on all sorts of subjects: and thus will improvement in the field of politics, and in that of morals, go on hand in hand.

As to discernment—so far as regards discernment, sincerity out of the question, not inconsiderable is the interest we have in the

---

[a] For a well-deserved exposure of these jobs to public indignation, see Mr. Bentham's Pamphlet hereinafter-mentioned.[2]

Jesus', Cambridge, 1824. According to *A Defence of the Apostle St. Paul*, pp. iii–iv, Hughes had been elected to the office of Christian Advocate in December 1822, and while preparing the first of his yearly publications in fulfilment of his duty to answer cavils and objections brought against natural or revealed religion, he had been handed *Not Paul, but Jesus*, with a view to his responding to it.

[1] The First Amendment to the Constitution of the United States, adopted in 1791, stipulated that Congress should pass no law respecting the establishment of religion.

[2] No pamphlet is in fact mentioned below, though for Bentham's comments on the building of new churches see 'Church-of-Englandism', Appendix V, §6, pp. 535–6 above.

PREFACE

reputation of the learned Doctor: for proportioned to the acuteness of that discernment is the probative force of the evidence given by him, as above, of the incontrovertibility of every thing that in the work in question had been advanced by Mr. Bentham.

And now, Sir, should opportunity present itself, ask Dr. Southey, or at any rate be pleased to ask yourself, whether in all this, any regard to the character and feelings of the learned Doctor has been wanting? And, in so far as we have thus dealt with him, no doubt do we make of our having the approbation of Mr. Bentham: for to this effect has, on all occasions, been the *language* of Mr. Bentham; whatsoever deviations from it may here and there have been made by this or that one of the disciples of his school; and as to Mr. Bentham (as is known to all men in proportion as he is known to them) to say that such is his *language*, is to say that such are his *opinions*.

So much as to Dr. Southey. Another gentleman who, though in a very different way, is rendering powerful assistance to our cause, is Mr. R. M. Beverley—a Gentleman of whose pamphlet, intituled a 'Letter to his Grace the Archbishop of York, on the corrupt state of the Church of England,'[1] the Morning Chronicle of June 11, 1831, speaks as having on that day arrived already at a *seventh Edition*.[2]

Of the attack made by him on the tottering fabric, justice calls peremptorily for the acknowledgment that it is conducted with spirit, wit, and eloquence. But by it the demand for the present reprint is not in any degree superseded. Striking and expressive as is this pamphlet of Mr. Beverley's, excursive and desultory will be seen to be his exposure of the corruption he has taken in hand. Methodicalness and all-comprehensiveness, not being aimed at by him, have of course not been attained. Then comes his plan of *reform*, which accordingly may be seen to be in a correspondent degree immethodical; and however justifiable, unjustified and incomplete.

Under these several heads, compare it now with the ensuing work of Mr. Bentham. This being all-comprehensive and correspondently methodical, whosoever may feel disposed to look at the one and the other of the two works at the same time, will do well to begin with reading the work of the experienced Jurist: and then, after taking note under each head of the several Disorders charged by him on the establishment, with the proof given of their existence respectively, to take in hand the pamphlet of Mr. Beverley, and, under that same head, note what is said by *him:* and so as to the *remedy*, as proposed and described under the head of each of its parts, by Mr. Bentham.

---

[1] R.M. Beverley, *A Letter to his Grace the Archbishop of York, on the Present Corrupt State of the Church of England*, Beverley, 1831.

[2] Beverley's pamphlet had reached its sixteenth edition by the end of 1831.

This task we had made some progress in performing for our readers; but, upon re-consideration, preferred the leaving the performance of it to themselves.[1]

In saying this of Mr. Beverley, that he has not done that which he has not professed to do, and which we are confident he did not so much as intend to do, we hope and trust we have not done to him any *injury*, or to that cause which belongs to him and us in common, any *disservice*. In and by what we are thus saying in relation to his work, we call to it most explicitly the attention of our readers: and to such as have not yet read it, we venture to promise much entertainment, and no inconsiderable quantity and variety of appropriate instruction from the perusal of it.[2]

---

[1] In his own copy of Beverley's work, at BL shelf-mark C.T. 66 (16), dated 14 June 1831, and inscribed 'Given this copy by Joseph Hume M.P. to J.B: this being one of 50 which the Author had sent to Hume to distribute', Bentham has inserted running heads: for example, 'Church of England a machine of Antichrist', p. 16; 'Solemnity and *Humbug* Twins', p. 17; '*Piety* everywhere more than among Bishops', p. 18; 'Christianity *"would it were part &c. of the* law of the land"', p. 21; and 'New Church building Jobs', pp. 22–3.

[2] For the continuation of the work see 'Church-of-Englandism', Appendix IV, §§ 9–10, pp. 471–93 above, and Collation D, pp. 605–12 below.

[CONCLUSION]

On this occasion, an opportunity presents itself of giving diffusion to a principle, which, whatsoever may have been its *'habitation'* in the *minds* of men, had never yet in the *language* had a *'name'* till it received one from the hand of Bentham. It is the *non-disappointment principle;*[1] to which, on some occasions, may require to be substituted a name springing from the same root—the *disappointment-minimizing principle.* Corresponding *rules*, which this principle is connected with and gives indication of, these—Rule 1. In the disposition which you (the Legislature) make of money, money's worth, or other objects of general desire, avoid as far as possible the production of any *disappointment* whatsoever. Rule 2. Where this *complete* exclusion of disappointment is not possible, so order matters that the quantity of disappointment you produce or suffer to remain (as the case may be) shall be as *small* as possible.

By this principle, so far as regards the possession of these same objects of desire, on the occasion of every disposition made of them by the hand of power, *right* and *wrong* are assumed to depend on the effect which the disposition in question has upon *human feelings:* upon the several pains and pleasures of which it is productive. Any thing which you call *your own*—the coat, for example, which you have on your back—why should you be maintained in the use and possession of it till you choose to part with it? Why should you be permitted to make use of it, all other men interdicted from making use of it, or disturbing you in the use of it? Why? *Answer.*—For this reason—as you, ever since you have had it, have been in expectation of continuing to make use of it, thence it is that, if by any man it were taken away from you without your consent, you would experience the sensation of *disappointment,* and that sensation a painful one, from the loss of it; whereas, in relation to this same garment, no such expectation having ever been entertained by any person other than yourself, no such pain has been produced in the mind of any other man by the consideration of his not having this same garment, nor will be produced by his continuing not to have it.

What is here said with relation to any man's coat, will, with equal truth and propriety, be considered as applicable to whatsoever other portion of money's worth a man has the possession or *fixt expectation*

---

[1] Bentham had discussed the 'disappointment-preventing principle' in his review of James Humphreys, *Observations on the actual State of the English Laws of Real Property, with the Outline of a Code,* London, 1826, which first appeared in the *Westminster Review,* vol. vi, no. xii (1826), 446–507, but was then published separately as *On Mr. Humphreys' Observations on the English Law of Real Property, with the Outline of a Code, &c.,* London, 1827 (Bowring, v. 387–416).

of, by means of any title whatsoever; and (to come to particulars) by means of any act by which he has been constituted a member of the Ecclesiastical Establishment: applicable to this, as also to whatsoever portion of property having, under the name of *tithes* for example, been in former days, as above,[1] in Ecclesiastical hands, has found its way into *lay hands* as they are called: meaning thereby all hands that are *not* Ecclesiastical hands.

As to the *coat*, such of our readers as have been readers of Dean Swift's History of the Three Brothers, Peter, Martin, and John; to each of whom their father, by his will, left a certain garment of this name,[2] will see that the present is not the first application that has been made of it to ecclesiastical purposes.

As to the name *non-disappointment* principle, or *disappointment-minimizing* principle—what other form of words was ever heard or seen so clear, so intelligible, so satisfactory, so *homecoming* to all men's businesses and bosoms? This offspring of his mind—the immediate descendant of the now all-pervading *Greatest Happiness Principle*, Bentham has long employed on all occasions: never did he disgrace his lips or his pen with the empty sounds, so abundantly and unhappily current in Houses, Honourable and Right Honourable. Sometimes contrary to *every* principle of justice—sometimes (with display of superior intellectual aptitude in the shapes of *knowledge* and *judgment*) contrary to the *first* principles of justice, says the current jargon, when the occasion is thought to have come for speaking in opposition to this or that arrangement or other measure. Contrary, indeed! and to what? to a list of articles, no one of which did any man ever see or hear, in existence or in description; no one of which, were a million offered for it, would he, or any man, be able to produce.

To other reformists, pretended or sincere—to all reformists, the sensibility of whose frame is of a temper opposite to his own—to them does Bentham leave it to operate upon human feelings, as if they were plates of iron or deal-boards: to them, who care not to the amount of how many thousands of men, women, and children they deprive of the comforts of life, or consign to a premature grave, when they have found this or that vague generality phrase, which, meaning

---

[1] See 'Church-of-Englandism', Appendix IV, §2, pp. 350–1 above.

[2] Jonathan Swift, satirist, and Dean of St. Patrick's Cathedral, Dublin from 1713, was the author of *A Tale of a Tub* (first published at London in 1704), a satire on the development of the Christian religion in Europe. The Father in his will leaves each of his three sons a coat (Christianity), with a warning that the coats are not to be altered. The three sons, (St) Peter, Martin (Luther), and Jack (John Calvin (1509–64), French Protestant reformer), representing respectively the Roman Catholic Church, the Church of England, and Protestant Dissenters, change the appearance of their coats, quarrel, and separate.

to each man that which it is most convenient to him it should mean, promises to furnish a cloak for his barbarity, and serve him in the character of a pretence.

How long, rather than borrow common-sense from Bentham, will this nonsense, so completely and repeatedly exposed by him, continue to be in use?

The case is, that these sounds can be got by heart, and, on occasion, come out with, by many a Pretty-Poll in Small-clothes,[1] into whose head common-sense, and sound reasoning, could never find admittance.

The proposed measure is contrary to the non-disappointment principle—this is an assertion which is susceptible of truth and falsehood: this is an assertion which, if agreeable to truth, constitutes one of the most incontrovertible and convincing of arguments. Taking, for example, Church property from any possessor of it, without giving to him that which to the feelings of a man so situated would be an equivalent, would produce in his mind a pain of disappointment—a pain which, so long as the property were left to remain in his hands, would not have place anywhere. And so in regard to property in any other shape or in any other hands.

Familiar to every parliamentary ear, thence to every newspaper-reading eye, is the phrase, *vested rights:* herein-above may be seen whatever *sense* is at the bottom of that *sound.*

Uti possidetis (in English *as you possess*) is a phrase which, on similar occasions, is in use to be employed on questions of international law, and on occasion of arrangements made for the disposal of portions of territory between one government and another. The name, *non-disappointment principle,* not having then been as yet invented, the phrase *uti possidetis* may be seen employed on an occasion of this sort in the original edition of '*Church of Englandism Examined.*'[2]

Just as these pages are sending to the press comes in a document, in and by which the baneful effects of the corruption, extortion, and oppression, produced by the so-called religious branch of the Official Establishment of England, are depicted in plain, but not the less striking colours. It bears for title 'UPPER CANADA. Copy of a Petition to the Imperial Parliament, respecting the Clergy reserved Lands and the King's College in that Province, agreed to at a Public Meeting at York (the capital) on the 10th of December, 1830; with documents

---

[1] The term 'Pretty Poll' referred both to a parrot and to an attractive child.
[2] See 'Church-of-Englandism', Appendix IV, §2, pp. 346–51 above.

relating thereto.' Place where printed not mentioned: year when printed, 1831.[1]

Of the prayer of this Petition the terms are as follows:—

'That the Ministers of all denominations of Christians may be left to be supported by the people among whom they labour: .... —that all political distinctions on account of religious faith be done away:—that all ministers of religion be removed from all places of political power in the Government:—that the Charter of King's College,' (the University of the country) 'be modified so as to exclude all sectarian tests and preferences; and that the proceeds of the sale of the lands heretofore set apart for the support of a political clergy, be appropriated to the purposes of general education and various internal improvements.'

In this same Petition, the only passage that presents itself as calling for amendment, is that which, after complaint made of the oppression and extortion exercised, by rendering the intervention of a priest necessary to the giving validity to the contract of marriage, proposes, by way of remedy, the letting in the priests of all other sects into a participation in the benefit derived from that same abuse. In a note to a passage in §2 of this work,[2] we have shown, that whatever cause the priests of the several sects may have for being well satisfied with this remedy, small indeed is the share possessed in that same satisfaction by their respective congregations. This passage is that, the omission of which is indicated by dots. . . . .

Selected by a glance, the rapidity of which has been matter of inexorable necessity, a few other particulars afforded by this interesting document must not be omitted.

For professing to believe in the thirty-nine Articles of Church of Englandism, given to the priest of that sect, real property to the amount of 3,760,000 [acres][3] being one-seventh part of the whole territory of the province; value 376,000*l.* a year, also 200,000*l.* and upwards over-paid, and 1,000*l.* a year for sixteen years![4] The flock of

---

[1] For a version of the pamphlet see *Upper Canada. Copy of a Petition to the Imperial Parliament, respecting the Clergy Reserved Lands, and the King's College, In that Province, agreed to at a Public Meeting at York, On the 10th of December, 1830; with Copies of other Documents relating thereto*, London, 1831. The version to which Bentham refers has not been identified.

The petition was presented to the House of Commons by Joseph Hume on 14 October 1831, when it was ordered to be printed: see *Parliamentary Debates* (1831) viii. 774–81. For a copy of the petition see *Commons Journals* (1830–1), lcccvi. Part II, 917–18.

[2] See Collation E, pp. 613–18 below. [3] 1831 '*l.*' is a slip.

[4] According to the petition, 'one seventh of the arable lands of the Province' had been estimated 'at 3,760,000 acres, and the annual revenue arising from said lands for a century to come at £.376,000', while an endowment of 225,944 acres made to King's College, York amounted to 'upwards of £.200,000', in addition to 'an annual appropriation of one thousand pounds for sixteen years' granted by the Imperial Parliament.

this so highly-remunerated believer not constituting more than a small part of the whole population of the province.[1] As to the Gods, which for all this are to be worshipped and glorified, in England as yet no more are there of them than three; in British India they have 33,000,000:[2] for less than that immense price—the Upper-Canadian price—so paid by Sir Robert,[3] the right honourable minister, had such been his pleasure, might have obtained worship for the same, or any other number of Devils into the bargain. To this union of Church of England piety and munificence, the Upper Canadians, such was their perversity—such their ignorant impatience of taxation[4]—raised objections. Of these objections, so long ago as May the 22nd, 1827, communication was made by 'Letter to the Under Secretary of State for the Colonies; for the information of Lord Goderich, then Secretary for the same' {p. 24}.[5] As to Sir Robert, to this application, down to the last moments of his political life, he remained inexorable.

Page 26, 27. Some time before the 22nd of March, 1828, was by Sir Robert and Lord Goderich intended to be erected, and stocked with functionaries, a *University* in manner following:—Chancellor, the Governor of the Province or his substitute; President, a Church of England Clergyman; that Church of England Clergyman the highest in authority in the whole province—that is to say, the *Archdeacon*; the regular Suffragan or Substitute to a Bishop, Upper Canada not being as yet deemed ripe for being *Bishop-ridden*. Professors, seven, and no more; every one of them a 'subscriber to the thirty-nine Articles'—

---

[1] According to the petition, the Select Committee of the House of Commons on the Civil Government in Canada appointed in 1828 had stated that the adherents of the Church of England constituted a small minority of the population (see *Commons Sessional Papers* (1828) vii. 375–733, at 385).

[2] i.e. the Holy Trinity of orthodox Christianity and Hindu deities respectively, though the number of the latter was often given as 330m., rather than the 33m. cited by Bentham.

[3] Sir Robert Peel.

[4] For Castlereagh's remark to this effect see p. 493 n. above. The remark gained notoriety when Thomas William Coke (1754–1842), later first Earl of Leicester of Holkham, Whig MP for Norfolk, chided Castlereagh with it in the House of Commons on 20 March 1816: see *Parliamentary Debates* (1816) xxxiii. 457–9; A.M.W. Stirling, *Coke of Norfolk and his Friends. The Life of Thomas William Coke, First Earl of Leicester of Holkham, containing an account of his ancestry, surroundings, public services & private friendships, & including many unpublished letters from noted men of his day, English and American*, new edn., London, 1912, p. 340.

[5] See 'A Letter addressed to R.J. Wilmot Horton, Esq. by the Rev. Dr. Strachan, Archdeacon of York, Upper Canada, dated 16th May 1827; respecting the State of the Church in that Province', *Commons Sessional Papers* (1826–7) xv. 515–20. Though addressed to Horton, the letter is 'for the information of Lord Goderich', namely Frederick John Robinson (1782–1859), first Viscount Goderich and first Earl of Ripon, Chancellor of the Exchequer 1823–7, Secretary for War and Colonies 1827, 1830–3, First Lord of the Treasury 1827–8, and Lord Privy Seal 1833–4.

The precise version of the text from which Bentham quotes has not been traced, though it is presumably the same source as that quoted above which contains the petition itself.

composed of these Professors and no other persons the *'College Council.'*

So far as it goes, all this is Sir Robert in perfection:—one arrangement alone was wanting to render the *Peelianism* complete—for each of the several Professors, a qualification of the manducatory, or say the *convivial* kind, rendered 'requisite and necessary, as well for the body as the soul:'[1] for this purpose some great hall to be appointed, such as that of one of the Inns of Court in London, in which in the course of three years every Candidate should have eaten *dinners* to the number of, and not less than, a hundred— and that that labour, when accomplished, being succeeded by repose, for and during not less than three years more; of these two branches, the *manducatory*, and the quiescent, the whole of the qualification being composed.

Reader.—Good Sir! what is this I hear? Are you not jesting with me? what is at the bottom of this jest? Excuse me, Sir! for I really do not understand what it is you would be at.

Editor.—Kind Sir! all this is no more than the exact truth. In and for the situation of Police Magistrate of the Metropolis, such, and no other, was the qualification which Sir Robert enacted and established, as necessary to secure [on] the part of those functionaries the requisite quality and quantity of appropriate aptitude;[2] a security, for the sake of which it was, that in his love of justice 'he thought it not robbery' to double the original quantum of the remuneration attached to that same office;[3] all which truths, with the addition of many more of the same complexion, stand demonstrated in Mr. Bentham's publication entitled *Official Aptitude Maximized, Expense Minimized*; and in particular in that part of it which bears

---

[1] See 'The Order for Morning Prayer' and 'The Order for Evening Prayer', *Book of Common Prayer*.

[2] In a speech delivered in the House of Commons on 21 March 1825, introducing 'A Bill to amend an Act for the more effectual Administration of the Office of Justice of the Peace in and near the Metropolis', Peel had stated, in relation to the qualifications necessary for appointment as a metropolitan police magistrate: 'The law had fixed no limitation with respect to the previous education of persons appointed to the office of magistrate; but he thought the committee would be pleased to hear, that a limitation on that point had been prescribed by the Secretary of State. Neither his noble predecessor in office (lord Sidmouth), nor himself, had ever appointed a person to fill the office of magistrate, who had not been a barrister of three years' standing.' See *Parliamentary Debates* (1825) xii. 1128–30. Sidmouth had been Home Secretary 1812–22.

[3] The Metropolitan Justices Act of 1792 (32 Geo. III, c. 53) had established the salaries of magistrates at £400 p.a. Their salaries had been raised to £500 p.a. by 42 Geo. III, c. 76 (1802), and to £600 p.a. by 54 Geo. III, c. 37 and c. 187 (1814). Peel's proposal was to raise their salaries to £800 p.a. and hence Bentham's reference to its doubling. Peel did not use the words 'not robbery', but stated that, 'a salary of 800*l.* a year was not more than a fair remuneration for the practice which a barrister must abandon, when he undertook the duties of a magistrate': see *Parliamentary Debates* (1825) xii. 1130.

for title 'Observations on Mr. Secretary Peel's Speech on the Police-Magistrates Salary-raising Bill.'[1] The arrangements in question being taken, and the correspondent Statute enacted,[2] by Sir Robert, in full despite of all that Mr. Bentham could do by those same *Observations* and remonstrances, all which, as may be seen in that pamphlet, was, before the passing of the Act, lying on Mr. Official's table. Of this improvement the success has been such as might and ought to have been expected, from the probity, the genius, and the discernment of the Right Honourable patron of the measure.

With the exception of this one feature, which is peculiar to Sir Robert, such, as has been seen, is the character of the Canadian Church of England Education system, to which Lord Goderich, by whom it had been approved in the old Cabinet, remains in the new Cabinet,[3] to give support, enlargement, and, if such be the pleasure of the Church of England Gods, perpetuity.

So much for the education of the male sex. For the female sex, what could a man find to match with it? What, but a High Boarding School, with Governesses, Sub-Governesses, and Teachers selected from the most distinguished houses of easy virtue that the Metropolis of the Mother Country affords.

THE END.

---

[1] See *Observations on Mr. Secretary Peel's House of Commons Speech, 21st March, 1825, Introducing his Police Magistrates' Salary Raising Bill*, London, 1825, and reproduced in *Official Aptitude Maximized; Expense Minimized: as Shewn in the Several Papers Comprised in this Volume*, London, 1830: see *Official Aptitude Maximized; Expense Minimized (CW)*, pp. 157–202.

[2] Justices of the Peace, Metropolis Act of 1825 (6 Geo. IV, c. 21).

[3] King's College, York had received its Charter on 15 March 1827 (see *Commons Sessional Papers* (1828) vii. 724–7), in the interministerium following the death of Liverpool on 17 February 1827 and before the appointment on 12 April 1827 of George Canning (1770–1827) as leader of the administration as First Lord of the Treasury and Chancellor of the Exchequer. Robinson (afterwards Viscount Goderich) had been Chancellor of the Exchequer 1823–7 in Liverpool's administration, had then been appointed Secretary for War and Colonies by Canning, and finally had been reappointed to the latter office in November 1830 by Charles Grey (1764–1845), second Earl Grey, leader of the administration as First Lord of the Treasury 1830–4.

COLLATIONS

The collations print all variants (including variations in punctuation, spelling, italics, and capitalization) between the 1818 edition of *Church-of-Englandism and its Catechism examined*, on which the present text is based, and the 1817 printed version and each of the published extracts of 1823, 1824, 1825, and 1831. The following point should, however, be noted. In the text, double inverted commas indicating quotations are replaced with single inverted commas, and single inverted commas usually indicating quotations within quotations are replaced with double inverted commas: the same convention has been adopted in the collations—consequently where a single quotation mark appears in this collation, the original employs double; and *vice versa*.

In the first column of the collations, the first figure refers to the page number(s) in the present edition, the second figure to the line number(s): hence 366, 15 refers to page 366, line 15.

A. CHURCH-OF-ENGLANDISM AND ITS CATECHISM EXAMINED (1817) COLLATION

Collation: Church-of-Englandism and its Catechism examined: preceded by strictures on the Exclusionary System, as pursued in the National Society's schools: interspersed with parallel views of the English and Scottish Established and Non-established Churches: and concluding with Remedies proposed for Abuses indicated: and an Examination of the Parliamentary System of Church Reform lately pursued, and still pursuing. By an Oxford Graduate, London: printed in the year 1817.

Note: The following printer's imprint appears on the recto of the title-page and at the end of the text following the 'Advertisement': 'J. M'Creery, Printer, Black-Horse-Court, London.' With the exception of the differences noted below, the remainder of the text is identical to the 1818 edition.

1, 19	PURSUING.
1, 20–1 *omits*	INCLUDING THE PROPOSED NEW CHURCHES.
1, 23–5 *replaces with*	JEREMY BENTHAM, . . . OXFORD, M.A. AN OXFORD GRADUATE
1, after 25 *adds*	PRINTED IN THE YEAR 1817
3, 8 *omits*	56
3, 14 *omits*	62
3, 15	I. A to
6, 1	Livings exacting
6, 4–11 *omits*	titles of Appendix V, §§ 4–6
6 *adds*	CORRIGENDA. Introduction, page 170, line 15, *for* Porteus *read* Randolph.[1]
7–27 *omits*	Preface on Publication
523–4 *omits*	note [a]
525, after 26 *adds*	ADVERTISEMENT.

WITH great concern the Printer finds it here necessary to state, that by some accident, with which he is not chargeable, the matter with which this work was to have been concluded has failed of coming to hand. At present, the source of information is at such a distance, that it is not possible for him to say at what time, or indeed if ever, the completion of it can be effected: thus much, however, he is enabled to say with certainty, that

---

[1] This correction is included in the 1818 Table of Errata: see the Editorial Introduction, p. xxviii above.

A. CHURCH-OF-ENGLANDISM

525–36 *omits* it consisted not of more than would have formed about half a sheet of this letter-press.
§§ 4–6[1]

---

[1] Strictly speaking, the reprinting of pp. 441–56 is a variant of the first issue of 1817, rather than an addition made to the published issue of 1818.

B. ON BLASPHEMY COLLATION

Collation: On Blasphemy. *The Examiner*, no. 525, 18 January 1818, pp. 34–5, and no. 526, 25 January 1818, p. 52.

Note: The text reproduces, in two parts, extracts from *Church-of-Englandism and its Catechism examined*, p. 367, lines 18–36; pp. 367–70 n.; p. 255, lines 10–15; and p. 365, line 43–p. 367, line 17 above.

367, before 18 *adds*	ON BLASPHEMY.
	Sir,—The topic of *Blasphemy*, considered as a subject for prosecution, having, in consequence of the late prosecutions, attracted that degree of attention which is so justly claimed by it, I take the liberty of sending to you for insertion, if you think proper, an extract relative to this subject, from a work, which comes from a pen not altogether unknown to you, and which, though it has for some time been in print, has never yet been published, but may at one time or other, perhaps, break through the shackles which hitherto have confined it.
367, 18	*Zealot*. Well,
367, 18	this time very
367, 20	blasphemy?
367, 21	*Graduate*. This
367, 21	blasphemy.
367, 23	Being
367, 25–6	occasion, in any manner whatsoever, has
367, 28	entertain, of
367, 29–30	sense, then, have
367, 31	blasphemy. But if
367, 31–2	blasphemy,—
367, 35	name: if
367, 36	it.
367, 37–370, 47	[Footnote appears as main text.]
367, 37	religion, whether
367, 37	*not*,—but
367, 38	*is*,—this
367, 40	is, that
367, 41	be; yes,
367, 42	liberty,—a
367, 43	inconsistent,—of
367, 43	them; yes,
367, 43–368, 4	very time that
368, 4	them; all
368, 5	rate, to
368, 5	*reproach* of

598

B. ON BLASPHEMY COLLATION

368, 5–6	[No paragraph break.]
368, 6	Now, then, if
368, 6	question,—the
368, 7	censor,—is
368, 7	language by
368, 8	blasphemy, on
368, 10	fancying or
368, 10	himself to
368, 10	Jesus,
368, 11	country, declaring
368, 15	them, by
368, 16	press, to
368, 19	Jesus, but
368, 21	Jesus. Command them? How?: In
368, 22	implication; nothing more; in
368, 23	that
368, 23	indeed; *Jesuses*
368, 26	God,—every
368, 27	God,—each
368, 27	God,—is
368, 29	him; for,
368, 30	him,—you
368, 31	is, on
368, 33	with in
368, 34	God; and
368, 35	you, in
368, 35	them, be
368, 36	*that* in such
368, 37	should? Not
368, 37	indeed; for,
368, 39	*ridiculous;* and
368, 39	blasphemy;
368, 40	blasphemer:
369, 8	him; for,
369, 11	ridiculous,—representing
369, 14	is, that
369, 15	be, in
369, 17	*disrespect;* for
369, 19	*disrespect*—irritated, and,
369, 20	him; in
369, 21	another, the
369, 22	him; and
369, 22	his he
369, 23	Almighty! Yes; if
369, 24	the by,
369, 25	one)—yes,
369, 25	are but one
369, 26	not
369, 28	antagonist; it
369, 29–30	number; this for example (you
369, 32	it. Alas!

599

B. ON BLASPHEMY COLLATION

369, 32	*blasphemy;*
369, 32	*Trinity;*
369, 33	*God;*
369, 33	contempt. Treat
369, 34	contempt! Not
369, 35	is that
369, 36	you; for example, that notion
369, 36	his,—that
369, 37	object, (or *objects*, shall
369, 37	say?)—three
369, 37	one
369, 39	a *man*,
369, 39	*God persons*
369, 40	absurdity,—exactly
369, 40	self contradictory proposition,—as
369, 41	*man persons*
369, 41	brothers for
369, 42	evidence that
369, 43	proved. Away,
369, 44	he; what
369, 44	*blasphemy!* And
369, 46	punished; and
369, 47	punishment!
369, after 47 *adds*	{*To be concluded in our next.*}
369, before 48 *adds*	ON BLASPHEMY
	{*Concluded from last week.*}
	TO THE EDITOR OF THE EXAMINER.
369, 48–9	what purpose
370, 9	do to
370, 9–10	applied; to
370, 10	object, if
370, 11	that action, opposite
370, 12	*him by*
370, 14	which, and
370, 14	success, it
370, 18	*God*, or
370, 20	derived) compounded,
370, 22	Blasphemy against man was
370, 24–5	Now, then,
370, 25	man,—by
370, 26	sufferance; to
370, 27	length;—but
370, 27	*God's*
370, 28	sufferance, in
370, 28	somebody; but
370, 29	is, in your phrase, *done*
370, 29	*reputation;* or,
370, 31	disrespect, the
370, 31–2	answer. Here, then,
370, 32	*God*. What
370, 34	*man;* by

600

B. ON BLASPHEMY COLLATION

370, 36	mould, set
370, 36	God, and
370, 37	attributes: the
370, 38	them,—and
370, 38	distant,—each
370, 39	a *blasphemer:* to
370, 39	clear that
370, 40	punished;—punished
370, 40	member;—the
370, 43	him? Yes.
370, 45	No; and
370, 47	above, if such
370, 47	notions.
370, 47 *adds*	* * * * * * * * * * * * * * *
255, 10	wise; from
255, 11	came
255, 11–12	*blasphemy;* imaginary *sin*, from
255, 12	sin comes
255, 14	other; for,
255, 16 *adds*	* * * * * * * * * * * * * * *
365, 43	*ridicule;* and ridicule, can
366, 1	argument, fit
366, 2	*test for truth?*
366, 3	from, whether
366, 4	no; as
366, 9	Here, the
366, 10	is, by
366, 14	it, then the
366, 15	fairer; nor
366, 15	be, in
366, 15	case, a
366, 15	*truth,* i.e.
366, 16	proof, that
366, 16	so, than
366, 21	*absurd,* viz.
366, 21–2	*ridiculous;* the
366, 23	yours,—this
366, 24	sins,—what
366, 27	Now, then,
366, 28	Apostles,
366, 28–9	you; and
366, 29	is, your
366, 31	or, to
366, 31	way, assuming
366, 33	power, it
366, 34	But this
366, 35	Jesus, to
366, 38	notion, viz.
366, 39	power, the

B. ON BLASPHEMY COLLATION

367, 1	No; it
367, 2	it, viz.
367, 10	ridiculous, then
367, 12–13	contradiction, and
367, 15	them, and

C. MOTHER CHURCH RELIEVED BY BLEEDING COLLATION

Collation: Mother Church Relieved by Bleeding; or, Vices and Remedies: extracted from Bentham's Church of Englandism, &c. examined: being matter applying to Existing Circumstances, and consisting of a Summary Recapitulation of the Vices, therein proved to have place in the existing system, and of the particulars of the remedial system therein proposed. London: printed and sold by Richard Carlile, 5, Water Lane, Fleet-Street, and 201, Strand. 1823. Price One Shilling.

Note: The text reproduces *Church-of-Englandism and its Catechism examined*, Appendix IV, §§9–10, pp. 471–93 above. The following printer's imprint appears at the end of the text: 'Printed by R. Carlile, Water-Lane, Fleet-Street.'

471, before 17, *adds*	MOTHER CHURCH RELIEVED BY BLEEDING*
471, 17	1. *Vices*
471, 18	I<small>N</small>
471 *adds note*	* The matter is here reprinted, without alteration, from the work at large: except that, to prevent confusion, the numbers expressive of the pages, and those expressive of the sections, are here omitted. The pages referred to in notes, are the pages in the Appendix to the work at large.
472, 23	but each
472, 34	thing;
472, 41	See Note, p. 7.
474, 36	and, for
474, 38	church,
477, 21	time if
477, 33	Excellencies;—or
478, 39	fixed forms
479, 22	upon, *maximizing*
479, 38	those professors
481, 6	controlled
481, 7	independant,
481, 8	controlled,
482, 9	II. *Facienda*
484, 8	declarations
485, 13	mentioned:—If
485, 22	profits out of Church-Reform
487, 3	saleable, or
487, 5	*kind*,
487, 14	but in

C. MOTHER CHURCH RELIEVED COLLATION

487, 23	fetch if
488, 37	Church;—if
488, 40	anywhere,
489, 2	above mentioned *leading*
491, 2	obtained—(and
491, 15	men.'
491, 24	Church of England
493, 24	whom, the

Collation: Mother Church Relieved by Bleeding; or, Vices and Remedies: extracted from Bentham's 'Church of Englandism.' &c. London: 1825. Printed for John and Henry L. Hunt, Tavistock Street, Covent Garden. Price One Shilling.

Note: The text reproduces *Church-of-Englandism and its Catechism examined*, Appendix IV, §§9–10, pp. 471–93 above. The following printer's imprint appears at the end of the text: 'Printed by C.H. Reynell, Broad Street, Golden Square.'

The text is exactly the same as the issue of 1823.

D. THE CHURCH OF ENGLAND CATECHISM EXAMINED COLLATION

Collation: The Church of England Catechism Examined. By Jeremy Bentham, Esq. A new Edition. London: 1824. Printed for John and Henry L. Hunt, Tavistock Street, Covent Garden. {*Price Half-a-Crown.*}

Note: The text reproduces *Church-of-Englandism and its Catechism examined*, 'The Church of England Catechism Examined', pp. 203–56 above. Nine pages of publisher's advertisements appear between the title-page and text. The following printer's imprint appears at the end of the text: 'London: Printed by C.H. Reynell, Broad-Street, Golden Square.'

203, 2	CHURCH OF ENGLAND CATECHISM
203, 4–5	1. WHAT
203, 12	*baptism.}—*
203, 13	objection; it
203, 14	supposed that
203, 14	subjected on
203, 20	seen whether
203, 21	(2.)
203, 22	incongruities of
203, 23	formulary styled
203, 29	develop
203, 35	thing and
204, 1	which, as far
204, 1	thing forms
204, 6	children under
204, 8	human mind,
204, 15	Truth?
204, 18	falsehoods so
204, 30	*conduct* which
204, 30–31	the subjects
204, 31	But,
204, 35	but without
204, 36	itself even capable
205, 2	terrific—obligations,
205, 2	quantity nor
205, 2	quality are
205, 3	be or
205, 8	power derived
205, 9	Almighty to
205, 12	life to
205, 12	eternity, over
205, 14	lawgivers by

D. CATECHISM EXAMINED COLLATION

205, 15	imposed)—*by*
205, 16	*has in*
205, 17	*instrument been*
205, 18	Yes; such
205, 22	wisdom which to
205, 22	*particular* it
205, 23	with, such
205, 24	them;—and
205, 27	proposition necessary
205, 28	particular may
205, 30	when and
205, 30	occasion was
205, 31	evidence of
205, 31	gift to
205, 38–9	*amount* punished?
206, 8	Jonas that
206, 9	this which
206, 15	renounced,—as
206, 16	which the
206, 16	*renunciation*) undertakers,
206, 17	*sponsors* (or
206, 17	Christian) must
206, 31	'*things*' by
206, 34	the the eye
206, 36	things—upon
206, 36	something which
206, 37	contradistinguished from
206, 38	If all
206, 39	life so
206, 39	will and
206, 43	*pursuance* as
206, 44	consequence of
207, 2	diffiulty,—
207, 6	*they*, and
207, 9	*renouncement* or
207, 11	idea no
207, 11	indeterminate is
207, 12	excited, what
207, 13	attached in
207, 18	'flesh' as
207, 20	clear and
207, 20	idea of
207, 20	mysteries to
207, 21	words in
207, 28	any dealings
207, 33	in had
207, 38	knowing and
207, 39	knowing what
208, 3	name being,
208, 8	*Juno* and
208, 15	Juno and

D. CATECHISM EXAMINED COLLATION

208, 22	difficulty, and
208, 29	lessons and
208, 31	nature but
209, 6	authority the
209, 7	many, to
209, 10	(3.)
209, 21	appendages by
209, 31	*Spiritual*, with
209, 35–6	not thus been solemnly
209, 37	affection;—these
210, 1	comment which,
210, 6	*which*' (as
210, 6	title) 'is *to*
210, 11	time when
210, 11	votaries whom
210, 12	feet are
210, 12	eye, under
210, 19	accents the
210, 23	are *all*
210, 23	them '*sinful*,'
210, 24–5	and such
210, 25	are that
210, 30	can to
210, 30	person be
210, 38	*Creed* called
210, 40	—But
210, 42–211, 1	compound which
211, 4	that called
211, 4	*Creed* is.
211, 5–6	believe and
211, 7	and by
211, 12	Answer.
211, 18	it and
211, 20	be that
211, 25	power thus
211, 34	lesson.—Forms
212, 12	those by
212, 13	one by
212, 15	any the
212, 17	present—by
212, 18	name stands
212, 19	importance is
212, 21	is, to
212, 24	declare that
212, 25	any of
212, 26	it in
212, 27	eye pointed
212, 30	authenticity consists
212, 30	evidence supposed
212, 32–3	authenticity to
212, 33	the seriousness of which

D. CATECHISM EXAMINED COLLATION

212, 38	labour.—Pearson—
213, 2	works studied
213, 5	*Pearson*, in
213, 5	*Creed*, knew
213, 6	page or
213, 7	understood that
213, 10	truth in
213, 14	enough, force
213, 23	intend and
213, 27	enterprise
213, 28	inelligible
213, 34	is that
213, 34	worth a
213, 34	estimate as
213, 35	conception will
213, 38	histories that
214, 1	Apostles may
214, 5	into and
214, 13	instrument as
214, 16	present, at least, it
214, 21	child by
214, 24	but if
214, 31	age the
214, 32	governor under
214, 37	What!
215, 3	case, how
215, 5	ones!
215, 8	world and
215, 11	God; that
215, 26	yes, *God*,
215, 32	it,—believes
215, 33	person by
215, 34	mouth, and
215, 34	case in
215, 35	impossible!—in
215, 37	real as
215, 41	Scripture that
215, 44	this as
215, 44–5	preceding and succeeding
216, 2	this, or
216, 7	incorrect; for
216, 8	word rendered
216, 8	not on
216, 9	occasion mean
216, 10	abode and
216, 10	torment of
216, 11	that of
216, 11	observation a
216, 12	is on
216, 12–13	occasion to
216, 14	found)—another

608

D. CATECHISM EXAMINED COLLATION

216, 14	that in
216, 15–16	thousand of those whose
216, 17	Catechism, no
216, 18	known or
216, 19	majority, the
216, 19	torment appointed
216, 20	place to
216, 22	ot her preplexities,
216, 23	That, in
216, 24	a *Creed*
216, 27	better; always
216, 37	believe this God,
216, 39	do by
216, 42	him either in
217, 1	clerk.
217, 1	imagination in
217, 2	extravagance ever
217, 5	one and
217, 7	God in
217, 15	word believe,
217, 19	as God and
217, 19–20	something in
217, 21	induced to
217, 24	prints which
217, 24	*Devil* in
217, 25	horns on his head and
217, 28	thing will
218, 1	*man;—another*
218, 3	*man;—a*
218, 8	digested, comprise
218, 16	would to
218, 17	life continue
218, 18	(7.)
218, 23	existence
218, 23–4	*Christ* and
218, 28	that on
218, 28	occasion he
218, 30	*Church*—a Church composed
219, 6	too, *Holy?*
219, 9	perplexity into
219, 11	child or
219, 12	out, has,
219, 13	subject, leaving
219, 13–14	memory nothing
219, 16	puzzle; a riddle which
219, 21	*Evangelists;* all
219, 25–6	likewise ere long behold
219, 27	sometimes for shortness *the*
219, 28	simply, at
219, 28	times without abbreviation *the*
219, 30	what in

D. CATECHISM EXAMINED COLLATION

219, 30	matter will
219, 32	Apostles and
219, 36	generations by
219, 37	compound here analyzed is
220, 5	Calendar that
220, 12	added his
220, 16	Calendar by
220, 17	commenced or
220, 17	But by
220, 22	Saint by
220, 23	Apostles; or,
220, 24	shorter, turn
220, 27–8	successors as St. *Sutton*, and
221, 3	*Napoleon*, moreover,
221, 4	*Orangeman*,
222, 6	But in
222, 8	place what
222, 19	in the
222, 22	others which,
222, 23	correctness proportioned
222, 29	likewise.—But belief
222, 31	*redemption*, had
222, 36	slighest
222, 41	*fact* is
223, 3	made for
223, 3	obligation as
223, 6	formulary called
223, 9	say that
223, 24	man, whose
224, 1	(3)
224, 16	word, we
224, 29	*School-room*,
224, 43–225, 1	within him
225, 2	*Methodists* take
225, 12	6th.—
225, 16	7th.—
225, 27	Egypt—that
225, 30	Jesus, they
225, 33	observation however there
225, 38	design to
225, 39	appears that
226, 7	or at
226, 34	*history;* two
226, 38	is that,
226, 42	prohibition was, not
226, 44	*viz.*
227, 8	*viz.*
227, 12	passage, where
227, 13	passage, that
227, 30	*viz.*
227, 42	question—this

D. CATECHISM EXAMINED COLLATION

228, 1	pretence that
228, 2	found for
228, 3	while, as
228, 3	knows in
228, 6	practised and
228, 14	Christian belonging
229, 29	*reference*—no
230, 5	*Moses'*
230, 7	*viz.*
230, 8	men
230, 10	light in
230, 20	questions, pregnant,
230, 22	But as
230, 27	employed than
231, 3	consists on
231, 3	occasion the
231, 6	conveyed than
231, 7	*viz.*
231, 17–18	those whose
231, 28	persons whose
231, 29	per force
232, 22	*Prayer*).—What
232, 23	prayer?
232, 31	man by
233, 5	lesson thus
233, 9	repeat as
233, 9	true that which with
233, 9	eyes he
233, 19	say that
233, 23	*grace* on
233, 27	But of
233, 27	*viz.*
233, 35	ceremonies to
233, 38	But as
234, 1	word to
234, 15	community it
234, 21	be that
234, 25	and in
235, 23	Sacrament?
235, 35	—made to serve, as
236, 35	14*th*.—
237, 13	baptism. The
237, 31	15*th*.—
238, 12	and upon
238, 14	16*th*.—
238, 23	17*th*.—
239, 2	clear that,
239, 33	is, *other*
240, 14	AFTER
240, 15–16	Thus, however, it unfortunately does
240, 34	To the

611

D. CATECHISM EXAMINED COLLATION

240, 38–9	exemplification of
240, 39	fountain from
241, 3 *inserts*	*paragraph break after* believe.
241, 10	18*th*.—
241, 22	disciples as,—
241, 26	History,
241, 27	*Emissary* or
242, 3	priests are
242, 8	is that upon
242, 26	question there
242, 28	*John* (by
242, 28	*bread-breaking*), the
243, 4	reasons:—
243, 6	privilege, no
243, 7	lesson which
243, 14	instruction as
243, 19	calculated or designed to
243, 23	poured
243, 35	therefore, said
243, 39	master, have
244, 6	misrepresentation of
244, 10	*received*, stood
244, 15	*i.e.*
244, 17	whom, he
244, 17	Jesus, it
244, 21	*viz.*
244, 27	conception which,
244, 36	you, and
244, 37	departure it
244, 37	you, to
244, 37–8	disciples, to meet together on
245, 8	wont to
245, 15	blood, *viz.*
245, 34	John xiv. 6.
246, 10	body to
246, 22	Wine, the
247, 21	when, as
247, 25	*bodies* (says
249, 32–3	other were
250, 28–9	impostures which,
250, 36	he answer
251, 25	opposite,
252, 2	licence (*indulgence*
252, 18	Justification,
252, 36–7 *omits*	See the ensuing Appendix.
253, 22	Thirty-nine
254, 35	endeavovred
254, 40	inveterate, lay
255, 3	superior, or

E. THE BOOK OF CHURCH REFORM COLLATION

Collation: The Book of Church Reform: Containing the Most Essential Part of Mr. Bentham's 'Church of Englandism Examined,' &c. Edited by one of his Disciples. 1831. London: 2, Wellington Street, Strand, Published at the Office of the Westminster Review, by Robert Heward; and sold by the Agents of the Westminster Review in all parts of the Kingdom.

Note: The text reproduces *Church-of-Englandism and its Catechism examined*, Appendix IV, §§9–10, pp. 471–93 above. The following printer's imprint appears on the verso of the title-page: 'T.C. Hansard, Printer, Paternoster-Row, London.' The following printer's imprint appears at the end of the text: 'T.C. Hansard, Printer, 32, Paternoster-Row, London.'

The work commences with the title page, 'Table of Contents', and 'Preface' reproduced at pp. 577–86 above.

471, 17 *omits*	§9. *Vices of Excellent Church recapitulated.*
471, 17 *adds*	BOOK OF CHURCH REFORM.
	§1. *Disorders, political and moral, of the Church.*
471, 18	In the following pages, that
471, 19	change in the constitution of the Church of England, which,
471, 20	demanded, will,
471, 21	corruption
471, 22	imperfections of
471, 22–7 *omits*	a conception not altogether uninstructive will, it is hoped, by this time have been conveyed. But,—the examination having insensibly drawn itself out to a length, so much beyond what at the outset was expected to be found necessary,—a summary recapitulation, in the form of a list of these same corruptions and imperfections—
471, 22–7 *adds*	for anything approaching to a complete conception the reader must unavoidably be referred to the work at large,* from which what follows is, the greatest part of it, extracted. Under the several heads of *Doctrine, Service, Pay* and *Discipline*, indication may here accordingly be seen made, of those several abuses, disorders, corruptions, imperfections—
471, 28	of the self-styled Excellent Church will be seen
471, 29	composed.
471, 29–30 *omits*	may, it is hoped, for the purpose of a simultaneous view, be found not altogether without its uses.

E. CHURCH REFORM COLLATION

471, 31 *omits*	I.
471 *adds note*	* Namely, 'Church of Englandism, and its Catechism examined,' &c. by Jeremy Bentham, &c. London, 1818.
472, 2	age.
472, 3 *omits*	II.
472, 7	Catechisms,
472, 16–17	true.—*Perpetuity*
472, 18	*insincerity*,
472, 21 *omits*	III.
472, 31–2	necessary.—*Instructors*
472, 34 *omits*	IV.
472, 36–7 *omits note*	
472, 38–40 *omits note*	
472, 41 *omits note*	
473, 1	signs.—*Thought*
473, 3 *omits*	V.
473, 5–6	inhabitants.—*To*
473, 8 *omits*	VI.
473, 11	crime.—*Parishes*
473, 13 *omits*	VII.
473, 15	non-residence,
473, 17	Residence.—*Parishes*
473, 18	*residence*,
473, 18	*non-residence*.
473, 19 *omits*	VIII.
473, 20–21	so small, that
473, 21	largest, part
473, 23–4	impossible.—*Parishioners*
473, 24	*Church room*.
473, 25 *omits*	IX.
473, 29–30	up.—*Parishioners excluded*
473, 31 *omits*	X.
473, 34	few.—*Poor excluded*
473, 36 *omits*	XI.
473, 38	Discipline.—For
473, 39	unperformed.*
473, 40 *omits note*	
473 *adds note*	* Of all abuses having relation to that set of operations which, under the Church of England system, goes by the name of *Service*, the most flagrant surely is that by which the presence of a Church of England priest, and his performance of a certain ceremony in which he bears the principal part, are rendered necessary to the validity of that species of contract on which the very existence of the human species depends. By this institution is created a power, for the creation of which not any the slightest ground in the precepts of Jesus, as recorded in the only history of them regarded as authentic—(namely that in the New Testament)—was ever so much as pretended to be found: accordingly, under the government of France, where that same

E. CHURCH REFORM COLLATION

religion is the religion of the community, no such power has place. For necessitating the intervention of a Priest of this or any other sect professing to teach and preach the religion of Jesus, no more reason has ever been, or ever can be found, than for necessitating the intervention of a teacher of the religion of Mahomet, or the religion of Brama.

474, 2 omits	XII.
474, 4	ignorance, the
474, 6–7	hopeless.—By
474, 8	or *Pay too*
474, 8	*subsistence*.
474, 9 omits	XIII.
474, 12	a universal
474, 18–19	parishes*.—By
474, 20 omits	XIV.
474, 24	profitable.—The
474, 27 omits	XV.
474, 33	use; money
474, 34	wasted.—Pay,
475, 1 omits	XVI.
475, 6	duties.—Pay,
475, 6	*excess, seductive*.
475, 7 omits	XVII.
475, 9	oppressive.—Pay,
475, 10	*disproportionality, excessive*.
475, 11 omits	XVIII.
475, 14	Sinecures.—By
475, 16 omits	XIX.
475, 19	service either
475, 20	prescribed.—Pay
475, 23 omits	XX.
475, 28 omits	(See above, Section 6.)
475, 30–31	Bishops with
475, 32	description: so
475, 37	time it
476, 4 omits	XXI.
476, 15 omits	XXII.
476, 21 omits	XXIII.
476, 28 omits	XXIV.
476, 35	bishops:
476, 39	action.—Law
477, 1 omits	XXV.
477, 10	dependent.—By
477, 11–12	and, pretendedly, from
477, 13 omits	XXVI.
477, 21–2	Enquire, for example, of
477, 27	*Sutton*;*—'Defenders
477, 38	title-page
477 adds note	* Most of these are gathered to their respective fathers.
478, 12	Reader?

615

E. CHURCH REFORM COLLATION

478, 12	Table and
478, 34–5	in 'Church of Englandism and its Catechism examined' (viz.
479, 44	it? What
480, 21	*printer's*
480, 37–8	persons possessing
480, 45	end—to
481, 6	controlled
481, 8	controlled,
481, 9	so.
481–2 *omits note*	
482, 2	now, on
482, 2	hand, the
482, 6	Howley,* the
482, 9 *omits*	§10. *Facienda in the way of Reform.*
482, 9 *adds*	§2. *Remedies for the above-mentioned Disorders.*
482 *adds note*	* Now Archbishop of Canterbury.
483, 10	*Positive*
483, 12	morality and
483, 14	*Negative*
483, 18	following suggestions have
483, 19	*leading rules.*
483, 24	service, doctrine
484, 11 *omits*	II.
484, 13 *omits*	(See §4.)
484, 16 *omits*	III.
484, 20 *omits*	IV.
484, 21	ordained, as
484, 24 *omits*	V.
484, 31 *omits*	VI.
485, 3 *omits*	VII.
485, 8 *omits*	VIII.
485, 16	Church Reform
485, 19 *omits*	VIII.
485, 22	profits of the Church Reform
485, 25 *omits*	IX.
485, 27 *omits*	X.
485, 31 *omits*	XI.
485, 31	Sees
485, 36 *omits*	XII.
486, 6 *omits*	XIII.
486, 8 *omits*	XIV.
486, 14 *omits*	XV.
486, 17 *omits*	XVI.
486, 20 *omits*	XVII.
486, 20	Fellows of
486, 21 *omits*	XVIII.
486, 22	Fellowships: and
486, 24 *omits*	XIX.
486, 26 *omits*	XX.
487, 2 *omits*	XXI.

616

E. CHURCH REFORM COLLATION

487, 3 *omits*	XXII.
487, 5	*Kind how*
487, 6 *omits*	XXIII.
487, 9	Taxes; in
487, 17 *omits*	XXIV.
487, 20	Advowson; so
487, 24 *omits*	XXV.
487, 29 *omits*	XXVI.
487, 33 *omits*	XXVII.
487, 34	age—whom
487, 36	oath* made
487 *adds note*	* At that time, when 'Church of Englandism,' &c. was published, Mr. Bentham had not as yet entered into the inquiry from which, amongst so many other interesting results, came this—namely, that of the ceremony styled *an oath* the effect is purely and in a prodigious degree mischievous. See *Petitions for Justice* and *Codification—*Device the 5th—Oaths for the establishment of the mendacity-necessitated; pages from 35 to 75: *Abridged Petitions*, pages from 18 to 29—Articles from 45 to 79.[1]
488, 3 *omits*	XXVIII.
488, 6 *omits*	XXIX.
488, 8	otherwise, divided
488, 10 *omits*	XXX.
488, 11	dilapidation, and
488, 18 *omits*	XXXI.
488, 26	indeed!
488, 37	Church;—if
489, 7	Oh, horrible! . . . .
489, 40	done, to
490, 11	incomparably
490, 34	Articles, then,
491, 8	*Service,*
491, 8	*doctrine,*
491, 15	men,'
491, 22–3	industry, during six days of the week, *benefice*
491, 26–7	religion? No:—to morality? No:—to literature?—
492, 5	*death:*
492, 6	*easy*
493, 14	communication for
493, 19	is, that
493, 24	whom, the
493, 33	hope?*
493 *adds note*	* Answer.—June 1831. To the Ministry of Earl Grey;[2] so long as it perseveres in the track upon which it has

[1] *Justice and Codification Petitions: being forms proposed for signature by all persons whose desire it is to see Justice no longer sold, delayed, or denied: and to obtain a possibility of that knowledge of the law, in proportion to the want of which they are subjected to unjust punishments, and deprived of the Benefit of their Rights*, London, 1829 (Bowring, v. 437–548, esp. 454–67, 513–16).
[2] Grey had become leader of the administration in November 1830.

E. CHURCH REFORM COLLATION

entered, and continues to promote the interest of the subject many, notwithstanding all opposition from any of the ruling few.

The work concludes with the text reproduced at pp. 587–93 above.

INDEX OF SUBJECTS

Note. The following is a unified index that refers to the texts of *Church-of-Englandism and its Catechism examined*, the Andrewes Appendix, and *Book of Church Reform*.

References to Bentham's notes are given by means of the page number(s) followed by the letter 'n.'

The symbol 'v.' is used to indicate 'as distinct from' or 'as opposed to'. Other abbreviations for frequently occurring words and phrases are as follows:

C.	Church
C. of E.	Church of England
C. of S.	Church of Scotland
govt.	government

ADVOWSON: money given to patron in compensation for, 487; where, divided, division of compensation money accordingly, 488; under Curates' Act, value of, falls, 500. *See* BENEFICE(S)

AFFECTION(S): middle classes held out as fit objects of antisocial, 50; test by which dissocial and social, may be distinguished, 54; avowed in Andrewes's letter diametrically opposite to those of religion of Jesus, 544; social, acting on large scale and prevailing over dissocial or self-regarding is heroic virtue, 549–50

AGRICULTURE: leading measures of govt. plan includes regulating occupations of, in case of priest, 495, 525–30

ALE-DRINKERS: health of, possesses not any title to regard, 51; human beings whose souls, health, or life have no claim to regard marked out by Andrewes for contempt under name of, 323 & n.; according to Andrewes, not worth attending to, 541–8; not regarded as men or women of heroic virtue, 553

ALLIANCE BETWEEN CHURCH AND STATE: Christianity employed in manufactory of corruption for cement to, 116 n.; terms of, 201; argument congenial to understandings and dear to hearts of parties to, discovered by Warburton, 290; in those who to office of priest add that of Justice of Peace may be seen one of knots of, 531–2

ANABAPTISTS: prodigious miseries suffered by, 234 n.

ANARCHY: good citizen marked out for infamy as partizan of, 255–6

ANNUITIES: property of C. of E. to be converted into, 485–6, 487; of money furnished to Governors of Queen Anne's Bounty, principal invested in, 524

ANTICHRIST: Lord Spiritual of Calcutta as newly commissioned, 317–18

APOSTLE(S): emissary or messenger meaning of, in Greek language, 241; persons addressed at Lord's Supper no other than, 249–50; spirit of contentious ambition among, repressed by Jesus, 268–9; not chemists, 317; if you are same person as one of, you can remit sins, 363; inequality not suffered by Jesus among, 416–17. *See* APOSTLES' CREED

APOSTLES' CREED: promise to believe, 210–11; not one by whom, forced into mouths of children notion entertained that Apostles had any share in formation of it, 212–14; usefulness of forcing, into mouths of children, 214–22. *See* CREEDS

APTITUDE: and inclination necessary v. not necessary for rendering of service, 374, 375, 387–90 n.; examination as test of, for clerical order in C. of E. v. C. of S., 481–

INDEX OF SUBJECTS

2 n.; according to Harrowby, degree of official, exactly as quantity of money, 499–502; elements of official, in situation of curate, 503–5; security for official, of curate increase with pay, 506; qualification enacted to secure, on part of police magistrate, 592–3

ARCHBISHOP(S): fraud in which, implicated, 190; wallow in compost of riches, power, and factitious dignity, 270; of Canterbury to wash feet of inhabitants of hulks, 328–30; set up to serve as examples, 384 n.; Archbishoprics worse than useless, 415, 418; for causing service to be rendered in every parish, kept in House of Lords, 429–30; may appoint eight Chaplains, 442 n.; connivance in non-residence, 447–51 n.; practising non-residence for own benefit, 454–7 n.; discipline destroyed by, 475–6; exercising temporal dominion in contempt of Jesus, 476; Bishop or Archdeacon to exercise powers of, on death or removal, 485

ARCHDEACON(S): discipline destroyed by, 475–6; to exercise powers of Archbishop on death or removal, 485

ARIANS: end put to oppression exercised upon, 49 n.

ARK OF THE COVENANT: treasury of corruptive influence in eyes of ruling few is, 517

ARMY: Erskine's pamphlet proving that officer's pay such as no gentleman could live upon, 395 n.; preferment necessary to securing of service, 511; out of Britain and Ireland not necessary for defence, 573–4

ATHANASIAN CREED: part of what passes among C. of Englandists for repository of Christian faith, 210–11; Liturgy forces, into men's mouths, 213. *See* CREEDS

ATHEIST(S): spirit of innovation of which atheism sure result, 122; most obnoxious to multitude of C. of Englandists, 282; can not defend opinions but by arguments corresponding to same opinions, 305–6; finds oppressors in C. of E. clergy, 306

ATHENIANS: in relation to gesture, Englishmen not, 405 n.

AUGMENTATION OFFICES: till sale of lands, profits to be paid into, 486; till sale, pecuniary dues to be paid into, 487

BAPTISM: proper when instituted but now needless, 45, 195–202; in ceremony of, child learns insincerity, 203–4; child loaded with obligations of most terrific character, 204–6; insuperable difficulty lies in child understanding things promised on his behalf, 206–11; object to establish fact of man's having been aggregated into society formed by Jesus, 234; in Russian Empire persecutions and civil wars kindled by differences on ground of, 234 n.; Christ did not ordain, in character of ceremony, 235; manufactured into sacrament, 235–6; in, water not sign of aggregation into society but physical operation, 236–7; must be by immersion, 237; effects produced by short string of sounds, 237; by, God vouchsafes child chance of escape from endless torture, 237–8; obscurity and ambiguity in promises to be performed by just-born infant, 238–41; by fees exacted for, poor excluded from temporal rights and salvation, 477. *See* CHRISTENING

BAPTIST(S): aversion entertained by C. of E. towards, 282; schismatics and men of guilt to C. of E., 288; finds oppressors in C. of E. clergy, 305–6; time for, to make themselves seen and heard, 536

BELL SYSTEM (OF EDUCATION): *see* NATIONAL SOCIETY

BENEFICE(S): as touching, some parish ministers rendered superior to Bishops, 299; mischievousness of outrageously paid, 306–7; compensation must be made to patrons of, or *uti possidetis* principle violated, 348–9; livings held by Bishops, 389–90 n., 453–7 n.; richer living during expectancy v. after possession, 406–7; in C. of E. v. C. of S., 457 n.; richness of, as principle for determining gradations in salary of curates, 506; govt. plan to confine indulgence of non-residence to richer, 512–14;

INDEX OF SUBJECTS

govt. plan for increasing value of English livings by exacting annual sum, 518–25. *See* NON-RESIDENCE; PLURALISM; PREFERMENT; SINECURE(S)

BIBLE: offence of Methodists in reading, 33–5; only fit lesson-book in Christian Free Schools, 58–62; Catechism made substitute to, 62–7, 208; policy to keep, out of sight, 70; in honour in England from 1648 to 1662, 72; should system of Lancaster spread, might prevail over Catechism, 90; by amendment man makes, of his own, 227; oracles of divine truth not contents of, according to Bishop of London, 259; standard of belief is interpretation put upon Scripture by Established Church, 260–72; C. of E. amalgamates poison of Scriptures with own antidotes, 271; Eaton denied title of true histories to Scriptures, 309; turned into dead letter in universities, 332; peculiar office of Bible Clerk to read, 371. *See* GOSPELS

BISHOP(S) in National Society, connivance of, in active misrepresentation, 52–3, 102–3, 153; education which forces children to say they believe what, paid for professing to believe, 159; fraud in which, seem implicated, 190; pomp of, 209–10 n.; system of slavery in which, are to be tyrants, 260; wallow in riches, power, and factitious dignity, 260; Bench of, in Upper House of Parliament necessary to Constitution, 289–91; title 'excellent' conferred by, on their C., 297–301, 384 n.; of Calcutta sent out to condemn by example equality preached by Jesus, 317–18; dialogue between zealous, and Oxford Graduate, 363–71; connive at desertion from army of C., 383–4 n.; livings held by, 389–90 n.; description of Bishops' Bench by Pope, 408–9; incomes of English and Irish Bishoprics, 409–14 n.; for maintenance of discipline situation of, proved useless, 418–21; for causing service to be rendered in every parish, kept in House of Lords, 429–30; furnishing information by, to Parliament on residents and non-residents, 430–1, 440–1, 442–59 n.; granting of licences for non-residence by, 444–7 n.; allowed to manufacture pretences for non-residence, 447–8 n.; connivance on part of, in false return and non-return on part of incumbent, 448–53 n., 461–2 & n.; practising non-residence for own benefit, 453–7 n.; suspension of general system of connivance due to ill-will on part of, towards delinquent, 465–6; Wright's view of Bench of, 469–70; discipline destroyed by, 475–6; exercising temporal dominion in contempt of Jesus, 476; to own use converting cure of souls into sinecure, 476; exercising over parish priests corrupt despotism, 476; law and judicature corrupted to swell pomp of, 476; on death of, power to Crown to nominate Vice-Bishop, 485; on death of, lands and houses belonging to see to be taken possession of by Escheator, 485–6; discretion of, to augment salary of curates, 500–1; residence would be enforced without, 508; spot on which to plant Bench of, 509; character of one or two, keeps up reputation of order, 510 n.; sum necessary to extinguish appetite for translation while Bishoprics remain, 525; unless by licence from, parish priest not to act as husbandman, 525–30; despotic power over incumbents and curates lodged in, 530–4. *See* ARCHBISHOP(S)

BLASPHEMY: and common law, 23–6; from imaginary grace, mystery, sacrament comes imaginary, 255; prosecution of Eaton for, 301, 309; if, be language intentionally expressive of disrespect towards Almighty, none found in Oxford Graduate, 367 & n.

BRAMAH: by course adopted by National Society support equally effectual might be given to religion of, 110–11 n.; Protestant missionaries make war upon, 387 n.

BRIBERY: bribe-taking Chancellor of Exchequer could not long continue, 567–9; blessing if members of Houses of Lords and Commons were bought and sold by punishable, 574

BRITAIN, GREAT: may be expected to sink, 573; army out of, not necessary for defence of, 573–4

INDEX OF SUBJECTS

BRITISH CONSTITUTION: temporal v. spiritual natures of, 8; inference that, will fall along with established C., 110 n.; neglect of duty sanctioned by, in religious part of establishment, 288; axiom that ecclesiastical establishment necessary to existence of, 289–90; depends on corruptive influence for existence, 517; general and deplorable state of, 571–2; forms of, will be observed so long as mischief can be done with less trouble than by violation, 574

BRITISH FORUM: questions for, 530, 557–8

BURIAL(S): no difficulty experienced by minister in performing burying service, 275; men and women go to hell by not being rightly buried, 421; by fees exacted for, poor excluded from temporal rights and salvation, 477; as occasional species of minister's service, 507

CAMBRIDGE, UNIVERSITY OF: Christian Advocate of, professes indifference between right and wrong, truth and falsehood, 583. *See* UNIVERSITY(IES)

CANADA, UPPER: baneful effects of corruption, extortion, and oppression produced by religious branch of establishment of England, 589–93

CANON LAW: ecclesiastical court system is remnant of Roman alias Civil Law, topped by, 424. *See* ECCLESIASTICAL LAW

CATECHISM (OF CHURCH OF ENGLAND): judgement pronounced on, far from favourable, 28; Bentham learned, 31–2; employed in National Society's Schools as instrument to produce docility and prostration, 36–7; vices proved upon, 40–2, 253–4; substituted to Bible in National Society's Schools, 43, 56–87, 91; virtues ascribed to baptism in, 45; contains matter tending to depravation of intellect, 47; nothing can contribute more to habit of insincerity than impregnation with matter of, 52; first censorial commentary applied to, 56–8; no tests of faithfulness of, to religion of Jesus, 67–73; badness of, in respect of matter, 74; badness of, in respect of form, 75–6, 146–53; framers conscious of badness of, in respect of matter, 77; imposers of, on schools conscious of badness of, 77–82; condemnation of system of exclusion in, 97–8; fictions of, cause of fondness with which it is hugged by priest and man of law, 191; and baptism, 195–200, 203–11; inaptitude of, considered as involving declaration of persuasion in relation to religious doctrine, 200–2; child compelled to pronounce assent and approbation, 211; and Apostles' Creed, 212–22; and belief in Father, Son, and Holy Ghost, 222–5; and God's commandments, 225–8; and duty towards God and neighbour, 228–32; and God's grace, 232–3; and sacraments of baptism and Lord's Supper, 233–52; ill will, oppression, and persecution as fruits of, 255–6; forced into scholars' mouths in National Society's Schools, 259, 261, 297, 340; exemplification of rule of virtual insertion, 266; composes essential corrective to Bible, 271; as source of danger and destruction to C. of E., 283; hypocrisy as fruit of, 326 n.; worthlessness of system of C. govt. of which, one of principal instruments, 344; tendency of, to produce hatred, 539; employed in production of prostration of understanding and will, 546; one of main uses of, to habituate men to falsehood, 554–5 n.

CATECHISM(S) (OF CHURCH OF SCOTLAND): C. of S. has longer and shorter, 57; contain quotations and references, 69–72, 78; Confession of Faith prepared by Westminster Assembly, 73–6 n.; C. of Scotlandists precluded from believing in religion of Jesus by, 85 n.; to words expressive of belief in, substitute words expressive of promise never to teach any doctrine contrary, 480 n.

CATHEDRAL(S): magnificent and completely useless edifices, 370–1; spot for new, in parish in diocese of Ely, 509–10

CATHOLIC CHURCH: *see* ROMAN CATHOLIC CHURCH

INDEX OF SUBJECTS

CHAPLAIN(S): Bishop's, and ordination of clergy, 420–1, 505; to privileged individuals exempt from residence, 442

CHRISTENING: no difficulty experienced by minister in performing, 275; men and women go to hell by not being rightly christened, 421; as occasional species of minister's service, 507. *See* BAPTISM

CHRISTIANITY: part and parcel of law of England, 25–6; C. of Scotlandists precluded from believing in, by Catechisms, 85 n.; regarded as state engine, 116 n.; infinite variety of opinions in, 117 n.; every one is saint by whom, professed, 220; cause of, would have been served by enumeration of laws of interpretation, 264; end of confirmation of episcopacy in England not establishment of, 290; view of, v. religion of C. of E., 309–11; carried to remotest south and east, 317–18; no sect of Christians exempt from mixture of diffidence and confidence, 479 n.

CHURCH BUILDINGS: C. as edifices in which service performed, 297, 299–300; money to be put into pockets of architects to build, 390–1 n.; at expense of people that additional stock of, to be provided, 393 n., 396 n.; Harrowby says, insufficient to accommodate rich and shut against poor, 397 n.; non-residence and dilapidated, 452 n.; in many parishes whole population left without, 473; parishioners excluded from benefit of religious instruction by want of room and by remoteness of, 473; money to be exacted to render, commensurate with population, 495, 535–6. *See* CATHEDRAL(S)

CHURCHING OF WOMEN: no difficulty experienced by minister in performing married-woman-churching service, 275; by fees exacted for, poor excluded from temporal rights and salvation, 477; as occasional species of minister's service, 507

CHURCH OF ENGLAND: *see* ENGLAND, CHURCH OF

CHURCH OF SCOTLAND: *see* SCOTLAND, CHURCH OF

CHURCH REFORM FUND: masses of pay of which, to be composed, 485–93

CIVILIZATION: degrees in scale of, by which human race brought to view, 316–17, 319

CIVIL LAW: *see* ROMAN LAW

CLERGY: two of Bentham's great-grandfathers were, 31; forced to declare assent to Thirty-nine Articles, 41, 223; taxation of, 91–2; morality of, compared to sectarian clergy, 117 n.; distinguished by riches, powers, and dignities, 268; ministry of, will be smooth and easy, according to Bishop of London, 272–80; advantage in reading on side of ordained minister v. school-boy, 278–9; and disappointment experienced by lay members, 293–4; display lustre of excellence, 298–9; oppressors of non-C. of Englandists and C. of E. laymen, 306; according to Bishop of London, instructions of, are oracles of God, 308; useless for administering instruction and guidance, 346; proper use of discipline exercised over, 415; duties of perfect v. imperfect obligation, 415–23; discipline exercised over, and laity together, 423–7; non-residence of, 428–71, 496–518; increasing value of livings of, 518–25; regulating occupations of agriculture of, 525–30; lodging despotic power in hands of Bishops over, 530–4. *See* ARCHBISHOP(S); ARCHDEACONS; BISHOP(S); CHAPLAIN(S); PREBENDARIES

COLONY(IES): population of penal, composed of human beings abandoned to ignorance, vice, and wretchedness, 93; C. of E. furnishes inhabitants to penal, 307–8; swindling washer-woman would be shipped off to penal, 456 n.; every, which country made to support hangs with increasing pressure, 573

COMMANDMENTS: *see* TEN COMMANDMENTS

COMMON LAW: and blasphemy, 11–12, 16, 23–6; lives and fortunes sacrificed to, 191; characteristic property of laws of, not to have any tenor, 265; sham law, 419; under, judges annul and repeal statute law, 554–5 n.

INDEX OF SUBJECTS

COMMON PRAYER, BOOK OF: calendar at commencement of, as treasury of consecrated idleness, 220

COMMONS, HOUSE OF: Reports in, penned by Chairman of Committee, 168–9; title and tokens of authenticity included in Reports of, 170; committee of whole, 187; returns on non-residence, 292; no further information on non-residence called for by, 432; honest and intelligent men look to Education Committee of, 492–3; members of Excise and Customs Boards excluded from, 559; members of Treasury and Admiralty Boards never without seat in, 559; blessing if members were bought and sold by punishable bribery, 574; abhorrence of secrecy of suffrage, 584; empty sounds current in, 588–9. *See* PARLIAMENT

COMMUNION: *see* LORD'S SUPPER

CONFESSION OF FAITH: *See* CATECHISM(S) (OF CHURCH OF SCOTLAND)

CONFIRMATION: with baptism and Catechism, formed links of connected chain, 196; if boy says Catechism, Bishop gives him, 365

CONSUBSTANTIATION: v. transubstantiation, 245–9

CORRUPTION: Catechism as instrument for corrupting intellectual and moral frame, 67–8; mass of, employing itself in fixing of adherents and purchase of converts, 113 n.; Christianity employed in manufactory of, 116 n.; exclusionary system characterized by intolerance and, 120; in proportion as govt. is corrupt, interest of ruling few that intellectual and moral part of public mind be in state of depravation, 200–1; not more mischievous for being open and notorious, 287; of lay v. ecclesiastical part of establishment, 288; vital and indispensable part of Constitution, 290; corruptions by which C. of E. remains assimilated to C. of Rome, 305; govt. to purify religion from, 307; University of Oxford a school of, 338; at Reformation, shared between Mitre, Crown, and two Houses of Parliament, 344; as means of advancement of personal at expense of public interest, 415; extension given to corrupt and corruptive influence, 447 n.; is of essence of Constitution, 457; exemplifications of corruptions given by Wright, 466; wealth operating in hands of Lord Chancellor in shape of, 487; support given to despotism through medium of corrupt and corruptive influence, 492; Constitution depends on corruptive influence for existence, 517; corruptive influence of Crown as grand object, 524 n.; name of influence given to parliamentary, 534; imputation of malice is resource of every Chancellor of Exchequer whose wish it is, for exercise of corrupt influence, to stop prosecution, 550–2; govt. may be to such a degree corrupt that to subvert it may be heroic virtue, 554 n.; in system of all-pervading, abuse receives correction by counter-abuse, 554–5 n.; system of administration affords uncorrupt v. corrupt boards, 558–60; by dragging, into day light, information given to those in whom disposition to profit by it exists, 571–2; baneful effects of, produced by C. of E. in Upper Canada, 589–93

CREEDS: at war with reason, Scripture, and one another, 306; instructors in religion and people at large forced into error and insincerity by, 472. *See* APOSTLES' CREED; ATHANASIAN CREED; NICENE CREED

CRIME: more than ten times as many criminal offences under C. of Englandism than under C. of Scotlandism, 93, 291 & n., 556

CURATES: *see* CLERGY

DEACONS: *see* CLERGY
DEANS: *see* CLERGY
DEATH: no mention of everlasting, in prayer of Jesus, 233
DEIST(S): Howley's picture of, 258; aversion entertained by C. of E. towards, 282; finds oppressors in C. of E. clergy, 305–6

INDEX OF SUBJECTS

DESPOTISM: slavery is correlative to, 419; purpose of Non-Resident Clergy Act to establish, 430; connivance towards delinquency result of liberty put into hands of mitred despot, 462; Bishops exercise corrupt, over parish priests, 476, 495, 499 n., 530–4

DEVIL: Jesus declared to be possessed by, 36; who or what is, and works, 207–9; visit paid to heaven by, 215; to child's belief in, will be added belief in St Dunstan, 220; proved that priests' fees instituted by, 235; all of us prey to Satan, 237; Satan indebted to forbearance of parish ministers, 298–9; in service of defending souls against assaults of, in instance of half of members of clergy nothing done, 383 n.; number of parishes in which Bishops and Archbishops may give advantage to, 442 n.

DISAPPOINTMENT-MINIMIZING PRINCIPLE: see NON-DISAPPOINTMENT PRINCIPLE; UTI POSSIDETIS PRINCIPLE

DISCIPLINE AND DOCTRINE: unfavourable opinions took rise in exercise given to, 32–9; contrast between C. of E. and C. of S. runs through whole field of discipline, 69; inaptitude of Catechism as declaration of persuasion in relation to doctrine, 200; system of C. of E. in regard to, in danger, 280–1, 283–92; poisons to intellectual, moral, and sensitive part of men's frame as fruits of, 306; advancement of truth in doctrine as professed object of C. govt., 345; discipline eminently efficient to divers bad effects, 347–8; authoritatively established body of doctrine on field of discipline, 388–9 n.; discipline considered in exercise over clergy v. over clergy and laity together, 415–27; state of discipline exhibited in diocesan returns of non-residence, 428–59; ulterior information on discipline from Wright, 460–71; vices of C. of E. having relation to doctrine, 471–2; vices of C. of E. having relation to discipline, 475–82; reform in regard to doctrine, 483, 484; reform in regard to discipline, 483–4, 485; laxity in system of discipline, 531

DISSECTION: difficulty in finding living human bodies for, lamented as proof of hardness of times, 294

DISSENTERS: whether right to enter Dissenting Meeting House, 31; conventicles protected by increasing multitude and intelligence of, 91; effect of compulsory proselytism of, 93–4; termed schismatics by Howley, 94; according to Howley, from C. of E. are infidels, 264; increase in surplice fees from conversion of, 276. See ANABAPTISTS; BAPTIST(S); DEIST(S); INDEPENDENT(S); METHODIST(S); NON-ESTABLISHED CHURCHES; PURITANS; QUAKER(S); UNITARIAN(S)

DOCTRINE: see DISCIPLINE AND DOCTRINE

DUTY(IES): towards God and neighbour, 228–32; alleged, which child forced to affirm imposed by Almighty, 249–52; clergy's neglect of, sanctioned in religious part of establishment, 288; of perfect v. imperfect obligation of clergy, 352–63, 510–11; performance of, of imperfect obligation by parish priest most pressing in instance of classes lowest in scale of opulence, 376, 377, 397 n.; no adequate security given for performance of, of imperfect obligation, 378, 379–80; payment by piece inapplicable to, of imperfect obligation of priest but applicable to, of perfect obligation performed by juvenile reader, 386–7 n.; inclination to perform, not regarded as necessary proved by non-residence, 387 n.; by amount of deficiency of time employed in, office is sinecure, 402; performance by clergy of exigible v. non-exigible, 402–15, 504; discipline exercised over clergy as to, of perfect v. imperfect obligation, 415–23; among clergy general neglect of, 426; clergy by whom, done v. not done, 432–3; perjury and bond-breaking by non-performance of, 467–9; quantity of, reduced by habitual neglect, 470; by pay received without performance of, half parochial offices converted into sinecures, 475; securing performance of, on part of curate as intermediate end of Curates'

625

INDEX OF SUBJECTS

Act, 503; under Scottish C. exigible, well-performed, and inexigible, performed, 524–5. *See* OBLIGATION; SERVICE

EASTER OFFERINGS: to cease on death or removal of incumbent, 487; quantity of, would receive prodigious increase, 510

ECCLESIASTICAL COURT(S): system is remnant of Roman alias Civil Law, topped by Canon Law, 424–5, 475–6; House of Commons open to head Judge of, 455

ECCLESIASTICAL LAW: kept on foot so that patronage of judicial establishment continued in hands of Bishops, 476; husbandman not compelled to grow figs for fig-leaves by, 527. *See* CANON LAW

EDUCATION: exclusion of one part of poor from benefits of, 88–98; grounds for hope that approbation of exclusionary system of, not general, 99–101; remedies to mischiefs of exclusionary system as applied to, 333–42; melioration of state of, as object of C. govt., 345; liberality of, as element of aptitude in situation of curate, 503; character of C. of E., system, 593; of male v. female sex, 593. *See* EXCLUSIONARY SYSTEM (OF EDUCATION); LANCASTERIAN SCHOOLS; NATIONAL SOCIETY

ENGLAND, CHURCH OF: Bentham enemy to, of which excellence declared, 29–30; Bentham's prepossessions in favour of, 30–1; Bentham's unfavourable opinions of discipline and doctrine of, took rise at University of Oxford, 32–9; to keep Bible out of sight is policy pursued by, 70; in danger, 90; Bible did not suit purposes of, 90–2; exclusion and proselytism pursued by, 92–6; benefit bestowed by Jesus' coming not intended by rulers of, for all mankind, 98; according to Bishop of London, all tenets different from those of, are schism, 111 n.; real worthlessness of, 113 n.; Christianity regarded as state engine employed in manufactory of corruption as cement to alliance of, and state, 116 n.; is but schism from original and venerable C., 117 n.; most deserving person under hierarchy of, 166; formulary of baptism employed under, 197–202; remarks on object of, religion as avowed by Bishop of London, 257–311; laws of interpretation established by, 264–70; real sources of danger to, 283–97; composition of, 297–300; catalogue of features of excellence of, 300–1; corruptions by which, remains assimilated to C. of Rome, 305; to admit poor to sip of wine incompatible with, decency, 320–1; euthanasia of, as remedy for religious and political mischief, 343–493; proof of utter rottenness of system of govt. of, 344–5; euthanasia of, recommended, 345–6; application of *uti possidetis* principle to case of, 346–51; loss produced in service, pay, and discipline by abolition of, and measures adapted to making up loss, 351–427; actual state of, exhibited in tables respecting non-residence, 427–59; ulterior information from Wright concerning non-residence, 460–71; vices of, recapitulated, 471–82; how, may be purged of vices, 482–93; leading measures of govt. plan for reform of, 494–6; giving increase to non-resident incumbents, 496–518; money exacted for increasing value of livings, 518–25; sinister object at bottom of endeavour to forbid priest to act as farmer, 525–30; despotic power lodged in hands of Bishops, 530–4; money to be exacted to render number of churches commensurate to population, 535–6; tendency of C. of Englandism to produce hatred, 539; as often as evidence would bring to light malpractice on part of rulers of, it ought to be suppressed, 564–5; object of Bentham to overturn, v. object of Southey to make people think no change ought to be made, 580–5; Beverley's plan for reform of, immethodical, 585–6; taking property of, from possessor without giving equivalent would produce pain of disappointment, 589; baneful effects of corruption, extortion, and oppression produced by, in Upper Canada, 589–93. *See* ALLIANCE BETWEEN CHURCH AND STATE; CATECHISM (OF CHURCH OF ENGLAND); CLERGY; DISCIPLINE AND DOCTRINE;

INDEX OF SUBJECTS

DUTY(IES); LITURGY; NON-RESIDENCE; PAY; PLURALISM; SERVICE; SINECURE(S); SURPLICE FEES; THIRTY-NINE ARTICLES

EQUALITY: inequality not established among clergy of C. of S., 416–17

ESCHEAT: as destination that property in immoveables takes on failure of heirs, 348; lands or houses belonging to province or see to be taken possession of by Escheator, 485–6

EUTHANASIA: of C. of E. as remedy to religious and political mischief, 55, 343–493; v. cacothanasia, 345–51; of C. of E. as death which no man will feel, 492

EVIDENCE: laws made by legislators offering rewards for, repealed by judges, 554–5 n.; act of furnishing, is conclusive proof of malice, 561; as often as, would bring to light malpractice on part of rulers, it ought to be suppressed, 564–5; trustworthy, acted upon by Excise v. untrustworthy, acted upon by Treasury, 571–2

EXAMINATION(S): for Holy Orders conducted in secret by Bishop, 419–20; in C. of S. no licence for clerical functions granted but in consequence of strict, 421; persons by whom, performed in C. of E. v. C. of S., 481–2 n.; public, to be employed as trials of aptitude for curacy, 505

EXCISE: as uncorrupt Board v. corrupt Treasury Board, 558–72

EXCLUSIONARY SYSTEM (OF EDUCATION): observation of, proximate cause of publication of *Church-of-Englandism*, 38; children of all who are not C. of Englandists stand excluded from instruction carried on in National Society Schools, 43, 88–98; grounds for hope that approbation of, not general, 44, 99–101; exclusionary acts work of Archbishop of Canterbury, 52, 102–3, 106–7, 160–8; remedies to, 54, 333–42; proofs of, 108, 109–22; essence of, included in word *proper*, 141–2; authors acting and consenting of, 153–68. *See* NATIONAL SOCIETY

EXPECTATION(S): negative object of reform: to produce as little disturbance as possible to established, 483; option of retaining what they have or adding to it would be effect of reform on persons having right in expectancy, 489. *See* NON-DISAPPOINTMENT PRINCIPLE; *UTI POSSIDETIS* PRINCIPLE

FARMING: *see* AGRICULTURE

FEES: no law, had justice been designed for any but rich, 321–2. *See* SURPLICE FEES

FEET-WASHING CEREMONY: advantages resulting from substitution of, to Lord's Supper, 53, 242–3, 310, 312–32

FICTITIOUS ENTITY(IES): C. of E. as, 301; no objection if all, destroyed, so long as no real entity the worse, 489

FIRST FRUITS AND TENTHS: Queen Anne's Bounty funded by, 518; calculations concerning, 521–3

GLEBE: power to convert, into govt. annuities, 486; on sale of, proportion given to patron in compensation for advowson, 487; priests' pay originally received in shape of tithes or, 526–8

GOD: every scribbler whose scribble put into Liturgy put upon level with, 25; profligate men make what they please of law of, 73; absurdity and presumption of putting men's word above word of, 84; falsehood in book professing to introduce men to favour of, of truth, 204; death of, 214–15; belief in, not enough without belief in spirit of, 216–18; questions pregnant with doubts on subject of answer to question what is duty towards, 230–1; holiness is property of thing of which idea connected with idea of Almighty Creator, 236; makes child and is wrath with it for being made, 237–8; person by whom promises stated as being made, 238–9; let, appear in own person, prostration would be as reasonable as it would universal, 258–9; C. of E. clergy as oracles of, 259–72, 294, 308; contempt of ordinances of,

INDEX OF SUBJECTS

293; parish ministers share in attributes of, 298–9; dishonour cast upon, 318; fear of, employed in utterance of untruth, 339; man insists that opinions he entertains are those of, 367–70 n.; arm of, put in motion by mass of fees, 418; without prejudice to Godhead, body and blood of, put into mouths of sinners, 532; time for worshippers of, according to conscience to make themselves heard, 536. *See* HOLY GHOST; TRINITY

GOSPELS: instruction, contain conducive or not to virtue, happiness, obedience, tranquillity, peace, salvation of souls, 98. *See* BIBLE

GOVERNMENT: partial application of maxims by which, rendered corrupt and despotic, 51; securing temporal well-being only proper ground for application of powers of, to religion, 94–5; nothing forces, to meddle with religion, 307; preservation of composition and disposition of, as object of C. govt., 345; by trust-breaking in case of clergy, encouragement given in case of all other offices under, 383 n.; abundance of sinecures in field of, is among most prominent grievances, 383 n.; to put trust in, would be to lean on broken reed, 438 n.; notion propagated that to substitute uncorruption to corruption would be to substitute anarchy to, 457 n.; leading measures of govt. plan for strengthening C. of E., 495; may be to such a degree corrupt that to subvert it may be heroic virtue, 554 n.; throughout field of, interest of ruling few in diametrical opposition to interest of subject many, 573–5; phrase *uti possidetis* employed in disposal of territory between one, and another, 589. *See* MONARCHY

GRACE: no mention made of, in Lord's Prayer, 232–3; turns out to be nothing, 236; what child gets by being made 'child of,' 237–8; upon ground of Lord's Supper has been erected manufactory of, 242; from imaginary mystery, sacrament, and, come imaginary blasphemy and sin, 255

GRAND LAMA: of today not truly one with, of other day than Bishop of London of same periods, 157–8

GREATEST HAPPINESS PRINCIPLE: non-disappointment principle is immediate descendant of, 588. *See* UTILITY

GREECE, GRECIAN, GREEK: words 'I believe' added to history of large part of Grecian Gods, 340; language of technical religion derived from, 370 n.; mixture of diffidence and confidence in members of C., 479

HEALTH: prosecution of Abbott for endangering, 539–48; atonement for sin of endangering, 557–8

HEAVEN: republicanism v. monarchy on subject on which difference between, and hell at stake, 73 n.; visit paid to, by Devil, 215; not in nature of riches to render it easy for possessor to enter into kingdom of, 266–8; keys of, and hell vested in excellent and holy hands, 300; no road to, but through ceremonies, 322; power of sending any body to, or hell at pleasure, 365; to hell let all go rather than seek otherwise than under command of C. of E. way to, 396 n.

HELL: republicanism v. monarchy on subject on which difference between heaven and, at stake, 73 n.; to what good use force child to say it believes Jesus descended into, 215–16; power of Holy Ghost to keep out of or drop into, whom he pleases, 279; keys of heaven and, vested in excellent and holy hands, 300; power of sending any body to heaven or, at pleasure, 365; to, let all go rather than seek otherwise than under command of C. of E. way to heaven, 396 n.; in C. of E. poor either have no souls or none worth saving from hell-fire, 397 n.; in C. of S. all men and women go to, 421; soul gravitates towards pit of, in proportion to sanctity and rank, 442 n.

HELOTS: deportment of, made to afford lesson of sobriety, 145

HERESY: offence of, charged upon Methodists at University of Oxford, 32–5; right of

628

INDEX OF SUBJECTS

burning heretics exercised by Henry VIII, Mary I, and James I, 155; effectually and for ever excluded from pulpit, 359 & n.

HINDUSTAN: has long been bankrupt, 573

HOLY GHOST: no conception of Jesus' conception by, entertained by child, 214; words 'I believe in,' void of meaning, 216–18, 219, 237; function called sanctification allotted to, 224–5; at word of command, passes from hand of Bishop into head of minister, 279; as reading v. speaking master, 279 & n.; in intercourse with, no minister employed by Quakers, 335 n.; whether, at disposal of Bishop, 363–7; never can any thing but imprudence or mishap bar candidate for ordination from visit of, 420–1. See GOD; TRINITY

HOLY SPIRIT: see HOLY GHOST

HOMILIES: see SERMONS

HULKS: population of, composed of human beings abandoned to ignorance, vice, and wretchedness, 93; C. of E. furnishes inhabitants to, 307–8; Archbishop of Canterbury to wash feet of inhabitants of, 328–30

HUMAN RACE: degrees in scale of civilization by which, brought to view, 316–17, 319

INCLINATION: and aptitude necessary v. not necessary for rendering of service, 374, 375, 387 n.

INDEPENDENT(S): aversion entertained by C. of E. towards, 282; finds oppressors in C. of E. clergy, 305–6; time for, to make themselves seen and heard, 536

INDULGENCE: selling of, mischievous to C.-of-E. eye, 252

INFLUENCE: preferment and seductive v. narcotic, 406; extension given to corrupt and corruptive, 447 n.; deanery could not come but out of court, 457 n.; support given to despotism through medium of corrupt and corruptive, 492; constitution depends on corruptive, for existence, 517; corruptive, of Crown as grand object, 524 n.; despotism not less despotism by being, 533–4; Andrewes interferes in Abbott's case in order to prevent evil which consists in lessening of, 541; imputation of malice is resource of every Chancellor of Exchequer whose wish it is, for exercise of corrupt, to stop prosecution, 550–2

INFORMER(S): motives by which, actuated are nothing to purpose, 548–9; treachery is effect of rewards offered to, 553–4 n.

INQUISITION: mode of inquiry employed at University of Oxford was mode employed under Catholic, 33–4; ancient footing of ecclesiastical discipline found in practice of Spanish, 155

INSTRUCTION: see EDUCATION; NATIONAL SOCIETY

INTEREST(S): love of money as branch of self-regarding, 21; Common Law is expression of will of men whose, in opposition to universal, 24; upon accession of Elizabeth, of public peace concurred with particular, 195; in proportion as govt. corrupt, of ruling few that intellectual and moral part of public mind be in state of depravation, 200–1; body of doctrine added to holy writ which happened to suit, of tyrants, 265; common, of subject many might come to be no longer sacrificed to, of ruling few, 381; needless sacrifice of, of subject many to private, 382 n.; is cause to which effect is ascribed by men at large, 407–8; corruption as means of advancement of personal at expense of public, 415; individuals governed by, adverse to that of people, 457 n.; particular, common to every individual who has place in establishment, 462; to one, ought all other, to be sacrificed, 517; of ruling few in diametrical opposition to, of subject many, 573–5. See SINISTER INTEREST

INTERNATIONAL LAW: House of Commons open to head judge of, 455 n.; phrase *uti possidetis* employed on questions of, 589

INDEX OF SUBJECTS

IRELAND: Criminal Calendar not much more loaded in, than England, 291; let leading principles of proposed reform be applied to, 489; has long been bankrupt, 572–3; army out of, not necessary for defence of, 573–4

JACOBINISM: spirit of innovation of which, sure result, 122; proposal to abolish sinecures would have been, 517

JAILS: see HULKS; PRISONS

JAPAN: Hollanders admitted as traders into Japanese Empire trampled on cross, 86–7; to Empire of, two Emperors, 118 n.

JESUITRY: falsehood of, v. C. of Englandism, 468

JESUS, RELIGION OF: see CHRISTIANITY

JEW(S): caution given by Jewish father on sending child to Christian Free School, 61–2; obscure allusion to Jewish Code in which contained Ten Commandments, 79; mockery of men by whom Jesus hailed 'King of Jews', 84, 271; Ten Commandments delivered to, alone, 225–30; figurative expressions to which Jewish language had recourse, 245; comparatively unobnoxious to C. of Englandists, 282; door of system of instruction to be opened to, 335–6; time for, to make themselves seen and heard, 536

JUDGES: under Common Law, annul and repeal statute law, 554–5 n.; indebted to skill employed in defence of right and wrong for elevation, 581–2; made upon Bentham's model will serve apprenticeship on Bench, 583. See JUSTICE OF THE PEACE; LORD CHANCELLOR; MASTER OF THE ROLLS

JUDICIAL PROCEDURE: use of, to give effect to substantive law, 417; main object of technical procedure: maximization of delay, vexation, and expense, 425–7

JUSTICE: motives on which execution of, depends are termed bad, 549–50; imputation of malice is resource of Chief Justice whose wish it is to defeat, 550–2; atonement for sin of stopping course of, 557–8; Vansittart stopping, without shadow of pretence, 560–1; contrary to first principles of, says current jargon, 588–9

JUSTICE OF THE PEACE: incumbents add office of, to office of parish priest, 531–2

KIRK: see CHURCH OF SCOTLAND

KORAN: catechism and articles attached to Bible v., 86; books useless if contents same with those of, worse than useless if different, 158–9; set, before mind in which understanding and will prostrate, it is Mahometan mind, 258

LANCASTERIAN SCHOOLS: monitorial system adopted and improved, 89; Bible put into action by, 90; put no exclusion on C. of Englandists, 112 n.

LAND TAX: see TAXATION

LAW: see CANON LAW; COMMON LAW; ECCLESIASTICAL LAW; INTERNATIONAL LAW; JUDICIAL PROCEDURE; LEGISLATION; PENAL LAW; ROMAN LAW; STATUTE LAW

LAWYERS: words employed by, for torturing, 551 & n.; sinister interest of man of law liable to afford obstruction to more extensive sinister interest, 554–5 n.; every practising barrister an open professor of insincerity, 581–2, 583

LEGISLATION: in farce of, C. of E. furnishes puppets to act part of free agents for benefit of monarch, 307; not unuseful praxis to student in, to take up principles applied to clerical and make application to lay offices, 373 n.

LIBERTY(IES): of press and petitioning crushed to pieces, 575

LITURGY: scribble put into book called, is put upon level with word of God, 25; pick out most absurd formulary from, 92; child condemned to gulp down, 210–11; forces Creeds into men's mouths, 213–14; in, all made to confess we are sinners,

INDEX OF SUBJECTS

224, 329; Bible Clerk good enough to read, 371; under, nothing easier than to secure performance of service, 415

LIVINGS: *see* BENEFICE(S); NON-RESIDENCE; PLURALISM; SINECURE(S)

LORD CHANCELLOR: and Master of Rolls levying money without consent of Parliament, 394–5 n.; sits in and governs House of Lords, 455 n.; matter of wealth operating in hands of, in shape of matter of corruption, 487

LORDS, HOUSE OF: Reports in, penned by Chairman of Committee, 168–9; titles and tokens of authenticity included in Reports of, 170; every day Bishop or Archbishop seen mumbling to unconscious ears, 429; Lord of Treasury or Admiralty must have seat in, or House of Commons, 455 n.; Archdeacon to execute powers of Bishop without seat in, 485; symptoms of opposition in, 523 n.; blessing if members were bought and sold by punishable bribery, 574; abhorrence of secrecy of suffrage, 584; empty sounds current in, 588–9. *See* PARLIAMENT

LORD'S PRAYER: with exception of, not a syllable of sacred text administered in Central Free School, 63, 66, 91; given as quotation by penners of Catechism, 69; no mention made of grace or everlasting death in, 232–3

LORD'S SUPPER: belief that custom of saints to join together in communion, 219–21; sacrament of, not ordained by Christ, 233–4; object of, was domination for purpose of degradation, 241–6; transubstantiation v. consubstantiation in, 246–7; spiritual v. carnal senses of meal composed of bread and wine, 247–9; ceremony of, is modern invention and duties attached a mere fiction, 249–52; communion and labour of clergy, 275–6; not designed by Jesus for imitation, 312–32

LOTTERY: when time comes for purchase of ticket in ecclesiastical, man casts from him belief expressed in Catechism, 223; in Harrowby's view, C. is, 392 n.; fallacy of emblem of, taken from Adam Smith, 393–4 n.; joint, of C. and Law, 423

LUTHERANS: share with C. of E. and Roman colleagues art and act of making God, 299

MAHOMET: by course adopted by National Society support equally effectual might be given to religion of, 110–11 n.; power of sponsors to force child to believe articles of Mahometan faith, 211; prostration of Mahometan mind, 258; under religion of, prophecy by which downfall predicted, 343; Protestant missionaries make war upon, 387; according to notion imputed to, women have no souls, 397 n.

MALICE: imputation of, in prosecution, 548–53, 561

MARRIAGE(S): no difficulty experienced by minister in performing marrying service, 275; by fees exacted for, poor excluded from temporal rights and salvation, 477; notices respecting, as instance of extra-professional duty, 352 n.; as occasional species of minister's service, 507; abuse of rendering intervention of priest necessary to giving validity to contract of, 590

MASTER OF THE ROLLS: and Lord Chancellor levying money without consent of Parliament, 394–5 n.; House of Commons open to, 455 n.

METHODIST(S): expelled from University of Oxford for heresy and frequentation of conventicles, 32–5, 38–9; spoken of as schismatics and heretics, 225; behold speaking-master in Holy Ghost, 279 n.; aversion entertained by C. of E. towards, 282; finds oppressors in C. of E. clergy, 305–6

MOHAMMED: *see* MAHOMET

MONARCH(S): by pomp that, preserves dignity and maintains power, 209; obedience to will of, is habit of Bishops, 289–90; prerogative of pardon of Priests v., 298–9; C. of E. furnishes puppets to act part of free agents for benefit of, in farce of legislation, 307; as Commander of 'C. militant,' 383 n.; allowances to desert duty

INDEX OF SUBJECTS

granted to incumbents from King, 433–4; object of gratitude embodied in, 465–6; taxes means by which deficiency in royal bounty supplied, 521; livings in gift of King enriched, 524 n.; deputies of people nominated by, openly in France and covertly in Britain, 574

MONARCHY: sincerity and carefulness of republicanism v. profligate and careless despotism of, 73 n.; end of confirmation to Romish system of episcopacy was establishing of, 290–1; according to Hume, absolute, form likely to be worn by Constitution at resurrection, 345–6 n.; depredation under absolute v. mixed, 457 n.

MOTIVE(S): no such thing as bad, 21–2; would in proposed state of things exercise themselves with equal efficiency, 278; punishment not to be inflicted if prosecutor actuated by any other than purest, 326 n.; performance of duties of imperfect obligation enforced by, belonging to religious or moral sanction, 353; in case of alleged delinquency, by which prosecutor actuated are nothing to purpose, 548–9; not capable of being known, 549–50

NATIONAL SOCIETY: Schools of, employed as instruments for production of humble docility and prostration of understanding and will, 36–7, 257–64, 272; from system of instruction carried on in Schools of, all who are not C. of Englandists excluded, 43, 88–98; grounds for regarding *Reports* of, as spurious and deceptive, 44–5, 52–3, 102–94; members of governing body of, 46; lists of books recommended by, 60 & n.; Catechism is substitute to Bible in Central Free School conducted in name of, 63–7; subscription to Thirty-nine Articles not yet put about necks of scholars of, 83; cause and ground of suspicion as to authenticity of *Reports*, 102–3; every thing material has been work of Archbishop of Canterbury or secretary acting under his orders, 106–9; proofs of system of exclusion, 109–22; non-existence of meetings of General Committee and Sub-Committees, 123–32; instruments represented as having received sanction of non-existent authorities not so sanctioned, 133–45; tokens of authenticity could not have been exhibited without glaring falsehood, 146–53; main actors in, 153–68; forms of disorder exemplified in *Reports*, 168–86; fraud involved in title of General Committee, 186–94; one main object of, to give currency to forgery, 212; prostration of understanding and will among declared objects of, 252 & n.; scholars of, might read what minister and clerk read, 273–8; remedies to mischiefs of exclusionary system, 333–42; principle of, to hell let them go than seek otherwise than under our command way to heaven, 396 n.; day of date suppressed in *Reports* of, 564. *See* EXCLUSIONARY SYSTEM (OF EDUCATION)

NICENE CREED: promise to believe, 210–11; Liturgy forces, into men's mouths, 213. *See* CREEDS

NON-DISAPPOINTMENT PRINCIPLE: corresponding rules connected with, 587; by, right and wrong assumed to depend on pains and pleasures of which disposition of objects of desire is productive, 587–8; immediate descendant of greatest happiness principle, 588. *See* UTI POSSIDETIS PRINCIPLE

NON-ESTABLISHED CHURCHES: held up to view in comparison with C. of E., 345, 385 n., 386 n., 478; natural reward in, depends upon prayers and sermons, 405–6; professional services rendered in, 414, 453 n.; hope of preferment in, from increase in numbers of congregation, 511–12; clergy of, not in need of penal laws to keep them out of farming, 529. *See* DISSENTERS

NON-RESIDENCE: in C. of E. v. C. of S., 292, 304–5, 306, 361; anti-pastoral ignorance consequence of, 360–3; inclination to perform duties not regarded as necessary proved by, 387 n.; in livings of great v. small value, 389–90 n.; practice of, regulated and confirmed, 396–7 n.; licence for, granted in secret by Bishop, 419–20, 530–1;

INDEX OF SUBJECTS

diocesan returns for, 428–59; ulterior information on, from Wright, 460–71; exposure of minister to punishment for, in parishes without parsonages, 473; govt. plan for increasing, on pretence of diminishing, number of non-resident incumbents and increasing number of resident curates, 495–518

OATH(S): power to load child with obligations of nature of, 204–6; promising obedience to Statutes of University of Oxford violated, 464 n.; non-performance of duty professed to be secured by promissory, 467–9

OBLIGATION: professional duties are perfect v. imperfect, 352; duties of perfect v. imperfect, attached to clerical office, 352–63, 378, 406; payment by piece not applicable to duties of imperfect, applicable to perfect, 386–7 n.; C. discipline exercised over clergy for securing performance of duties of perfect v. imperfect, 415–23. *See* DUTY(IES); SERVICE

OFFENCES: number of prosecutions for criminal, under C. of E. v. C. of S., 93, 291 & n., 556; three sorts of judicatories established for punishment of certain, 423

OXFORD, UNIVERSITY OF: Methodists expelled from, 32–5, 38–9, 91; Bentham's signing of Thirty-nine Articles at, 35–6, 38–9; passive obedience and non-resistance formed part of creed of, 303–4; rulers of, charged with keeping subjects plunged in sin of perjury, 338; practice of, in regard to oaths promising obedience to Statutes, 464 n., 468. *See* UNIVERSITY(IES)

PAINS AND PLEASURES: pursuit of pleasure is principal business of C. of E. priest, 511; right and wrong assumed to depend upon, of which disposition of objects of desire is productive, 587–9

PAPISTS: *see* ROMAN CATHOLIC CHURCH; POPE(S)

PARLIAMENT: right of governing in ecclesiastical matters without concurrence of, 155; locution 'Committee of whole House' found in practice of, 187; corruption continually charged upon, 288; Acts of, so badly penned that persons not guilty against spirit punished under letter of law, 326–7 n.; under Reformation, corruption shared between Mitre, Crown, and two Houses, 344; reading extracts from Acts of, as instance of extra-professional duty, 352 n.; Lord Chancellor and Master of Rolls levying money without consent of, 394–5 n.; furnishing information on non-residence by Bishops to, 430; unfortunate supposition that faith of, safe object of reliance, 437–8 n.; 439; discipline Bishops under in regard to, and, under as towards public, 445–7 n.; depredation part of privilege of, 514; as name influence given to parliamentary corruption, so might name sugar have been given to arsenic, 534. *See* COMMONS, HOUSE OF; LORDS, HOUSE OF

PATRONAGE: of judicial establishment continued in hands of Bishops, 476; sketch of, in C. of S., 481–2 n.; disposition of tithes where, in hands of individuals v. Crown v. corporate bodies, 487–8

PAY: interest of paid v. paying part of C. of E., 278; inequality of salaries, abundance of sinecure salaries, and establishment of remuneration in state of independency on service, 285; over that which suffices to engage clerk has been worse than thrown away, 285–6; measure of value of benefice composed of direct ratio of pay and inverse ratio of service, 286–9; intestine war perpetuated in parishes by mode of payment established by C. of Rome, 306–7; arrangement by which wine provided at expense of parish of piece with system of, for ecclesiastical service, 320; allotted for service excessive, distribution unequal, 347–8; pre-eminence in reading on side of minister as compensation for, given to clerk v. minister, 354; use of, is obtaining service of requisite quality and degree of goodness, 371–2, 399–415; maxims of Oxford Graduate v. Excellent C. on relation between service and,

633

INDEX OF SUBJECTS

372–81, 382–98 n.; for service rendered by Bishops and Archbishops, 429–30; corrupt system of, without service on pretence of soul-saving, 446 n.; to avoid paying curate forced price, incumbent forbears to take out licence, 448 n.; by every man by whom, attached to benefice received, money obtained on false pretence, 453–7 n.; vices having relation to, 474–5; Bishops profess to prevent subordinates receiving, without performing service, 476; leading principles of reform in regard to, 483; whether detachable mass of, needful or needless to purpose of salvation, 498 n.; govt. plan for augmentation of curates', 499–518; money taken out of pockets of incumbents forced into pockets of curates, 499–506, 516 & n.; under govt. plan, different standards set up for quantity of, of curates, 506–10; annual sum exacted from population for increasing value of livings, 518–25; parish priests', originally received in glebe and tithes, 526–9; despotic power lodged in hands of Bishops by appointment of curates' stipends, 530–1. *See* BENEFICE(S); SINECURE(S)

PENAL LAW: were it not for motives of enmity or pecuniary gain, no, could be productive of any effect, 325–7 n.

PETITIONING: as last remedy left to oppressed subject many, 574–5

PIETY: any thing that shall please, of bench to call Christianity will thereby be so, 25–6; advancement of, as object of C. of E., 345; interests of, served by *uti possidetis* principle, 349–50; system of C. of S. conducive to support of, 478 n.; by vices C. of E. rendered adverse to, 482–3; object to place religious instruction upon footing beneficial to, 483–4; in judgement of founders of priesthood, occupation of husbandman not inconsistent with, 527–9; increasing number of churches provided by, of sincere followers of Jesus, 535; as cause of morality v. substitute to virtue, 557

PLACEMEN: principles laid down not favourable to interests of, 373 n.

PLEASURES: *see* PAINS AND PLEASURES

PLURALISM: no justification for pluralities, 285; pluralities sanctified and protected in C. of E. establishment, 289, 306; C. of S. pure from abuse of pluralities, 304; Oxford Graduate's maxims applicable to pluralists, 385 n.; practice of, regulated and confirmed, 396–7 n.; dispensation in case of simple v. ultra, 449–50 n.; in C. of S. v. C. of E., 464 n.; Harrowby averse to abolition of pluralities, 512–13

POLICE MAGISTRATE: qualification enacted to secure aptitude on part of, 592–3

POOR: superintendence of poors' funds in C. of S., 287 n.; not admitted to sip of wine metamorphosed into blood, 320–1; fundamental principle of Reformation: sacrifice of spiritual interest of, and rich to temporal interests of rich, 397 n.; excluded from temporal rights and salvation, 477; under proposed reform, pay of Parish Clerk allotted out of Poor's Rates, 484; by ale-drinkers are meant, 545; contempt avowed by Andrewes for, 548

POPE(S): indulgence granted by certain, in retail, 252; manufactory of sinecure out of cure erected by, 433; taxes on benefices imposed originally by, 518

POPULATION: allowance made for difference of, criminal offences in England v. Scotland v. Ireland, 93, 291; burthen imposed by C. of E. v. C. of S. and, of England v. Scotland, 525; money to be exacted sufficient to render number of C. of E. churches commensurate to, 535–6

PREBENDARIES: set of idlers paid for doing nothing, 50

PREFERMENT: no, in C. of S., 511; in non–established C. from increase in congregation, 511–12; in Scotland preferment-hunting not altogether without example, 525. *See* BENEFICE(S)

PREJUDICE: that malice on part of prosecutor affords ground for impunity is maxim established through interest-begotten, 553

INDEX OF SUBJECTS

PRESBYTERIAN(S): difference between Presbyterianism and Episcopacy, 69; Scotchmen sent to convert Englishmen to Presbyterianism, 94–5; aversion entertained by C. of E. towards, 282; finds oppressors in C. of E. clergy, 305–6; time for, to make themselves seen and heard, 536. *See* SCOTLAND, CHURCH OF

PRESS: liberty of, crushed to pieces, 575

PRISONS: population of, composed of human beings abandoned to ignorance, vice, and wretchedness, 93; C. of E. furnishes inhabitants to jails, 307–8. *See* HULKS

PROPERTY: taking C., from possessor without giving equivalent would produce pain of disappointment, 589; for professing to believe in Thirty-nine Articles, real, in Upper Canada given to priest, 590–1

PROSECUTION(S): imputation of malice in, 548–53; number of, for criminal offences under C. of E. v. C. of S., 556

PROTESTANT(S): mode of religion of C. of E. inferior in eyes of people to other, modes, 396 n.; in, any more than Catholics or members of Greek Church, no set of men exempt from mixture of blind diffidence and confidence, 479 n.

PUBLICITY: check applied by, to judicial power, 419

PUNISHMENT: indemnity against, to all opinions respecting constitution of Godhead, 11; libel is word invented to enable men to waste, at pleasure; 400; three sorts of judicatories established for, of certain offences, 423; establishment of religion means, employed in inducing men to entertain opinion, 584

PURITANS: difference between Puritanism and impuritanism is that between management of equal many and domination of ruling few, 69, 71; as exciters of troubles, 71, 304–5; by acknowledgement of Hume, nation indebted to, for liberties, 304

QUAKER(S): behold speaking-master in Holy Ghost, 279 n., 335; aversion entertained by C. of E. towards, 282; finds oppressors in C. of E. clergy, 305–6; in intercourse with Holy Ghost no ministers employed by, 335 n.; in non-established C. composed of, service rendered by unpaid hands, 394 n.; time for, to make themselves seen and heard, 536

QUEEN ANNE'S BOUNTY: and parliamentary grants for augmentation of maintenance of poor clergy, 518–25

READING: of certain discourses duty under C. of E. system, 353–60

REAL ENTITY: no objection if all fictitious entities destroyed, so long as no, the worse, 489

REFORM: euthanasia as remedy to all religious and much political mischief, 54–5; facienda in way of, 482–93; inutility and mischievousness of measures of pretended, 494–536

REFORMATION: Protestant, made in C. of E. half with, half against, liking of people, 344; at, fundamental principle acted upon by C. of E.: sacrifice of spiritual interest of poor and rich to temporal interests of rich, 397 n.; for want of better name, change spoken of by name of, 428; confession of faith necessary for first Reformers, 479 n.

RELIGION: any system of, or no, might be forced into minds, 111 n.; in so far as established, is in enmity to morality, 584

REMEDY(IES): *see* REFORM

REMUNERATION: *see* PAY

REPUBLICANISM: conscientious sincerity of, forms striking contrast with despotism of monarchy, 73

RESTORATION: despotism, impiety, and immorality re-seated on throne, 349

INDEX OF SUBJECTS

REVENUE: prosecution of Abbott for defrauding, 539–42, 546–7; object of framers of, laws to establish treachery, 553–4 n.; atonement for sin of defrauding, 557–8; destruction of, necessary consequence of grounds acted upon by Vansittart, 561–2

REWARD(S): merit is word invented to enable men to waste, at pleasure, 400; in shape of sinecures and extra-paid places adverse to production of public service, 400–15; prosecuting not for sake of, would be heroic virtue, 550; treachery is effect of, offered to informers, 553–4 n.; laws made by legislators offering, for evidence repealed by judges, 554–5 n.; establishment of religion means, employed in inducing men to entertain opinion, 584. *See* PAY

RIDICULE: as test of truth, 365–7

RIGHT(S): of burning heretics exercised by Henry VIII, Mary I, and James I, 155; evidentiary documents on which family, made to depend, 477; option of retaining what they have or adding to it would be effect of reform on persons having, in expectancy, 489; sense at bottom of sound 'vested,' 589

ROMAN CATHOLIC CHURCH: Protestants stigmatized by dignitaries of C. of Rome, 50; Mrs Trimmer is to C. of E. what Blessed Virgin is to C. of Rome, 67; policy of, to keep Bible out of sight, 70; C. of Romanism in heart of Charles II, 72; Romanists rendered religion alarming to Japanese, 86–7; C. of E. in danger now as C. of Rome was three centuries ago, 90; by course adopted by National Society support equally effectual might be given to C. of Rome, 110–11 n.; perplexity into which child plunged by declaring belief in, 218–19; founders of Romish C. might have found useful instruction in feet-washing ceremony, 242; and the mystery of cannibalism, 245–7, 299; indication of imposture given in word Roman Catholic tradition, 250; prostration of Catholic mind, 258; inconvenient texts marked for omission by, 266; aversion entertained by C. of E. towards Catholics, 282; Catholicism yields to C. of Englandism in crime-producing virtue, 291; portion of excellence of C. of Rome sunk behind cloud, 299; feet-washing ceremony possesses place in C. of Rome, 331; Reformation of, 344; priest's and deacon's orders got from Holy Mother Church, 364; in Ireland, so long as people in state of oppression will Catholic religion continue without diminution in numbers, 387; hereditary disease brought by C. of E. from Holy Mother, 478; time for Catholics to make themselves seen and heard, 536

ROMAN LAW: Roman lawyers sensible to importance of *pretium affectionis*, 350; ecclesiastical court system is remnant of, topped by Canon Law, 424

RUSSIA: persecutions and civil wars kindled by differences on ground of baptism, 234 n.

SACRAMENT(S): none ordained by Christ, 233–4; generic appellation, made to serve for box for inclosing ceremony of baptism and few words uttered by Jesus, 235–6; as compound of real and visible ceremony to which is attached invisible and unintelligible effect, 236–8. *See* BAPTISM; BURIAL(S); CHRISTENING; CONFIRMATION; FEET-WASHING CEREMONY; LORD'S SUPPER

SAINTS: communion of, as riddle not explicable, 219–21

SALARY: *see* PAY

SALVATION: Christian beholds means of, in intellectual instruction, 88; whether instruction Gospel contains conducive to, 98; whether man capable of being 'saved' otherwise than 'by name of Jesus', 223; whether performance of ceremony of Lord's Supper necessary for, 318–22; not object of what has been done by ruling powers, 428; souls saved by incumbents reading out of modern book, 429; inhabitants paying for having souls saved and no service performed, 453 n.; power given to Bishops did not have, really among its objects, 453–4 n.; by fees

INDEX OF SUBJECTS

exacted by priest, poor pretendedly excluded from, 477; estimation in which, held, 498 n.; being ultimate end in view, intermediate ends of securing aptitude and performance of duty of curates engaged Harrowby's attention, 499; appropriate zeal of priest is zeal which has, for object, 504; chance of, is as quantity of money put into pocket of priest, 509, 519; where pay not worth acceptance in eyes of retainers of monarch, souls and, not worth thought, 520

SANCTION: performance of duties of imperfect obligation enforced by religious or moral, 353

SATAN: *see* DEVIL

SCHISM: according to Howley, all, is guilt, 48, 199, 272–3, 288, 304–5, 482; according to Howley, all tenets different from C. of E. are, 111 n., 115 n., 154; C. of E. but schism from original C., 117 n.; excluded from pulpit, 359 & n.; conducive to truth in doctrine and goodness in discipline, 422

SCHOOL(S): Bible only fit lesson book in Christian Free, 58–62; no substitute to Bible ought to be taught in Christian Free, 62–7; thorough impregnation with Catechism as condition of admittance to Free, 92. *See* EDUCATION; LANCASTERIAN SCHOOLS; NATIONAL SOCIETY

SCOTLAND, CHURCH OF: excellence of C. of E. compared with 48, 69; has longer and shorter Catechisms, 57; Catechisms as genuine abridgements of Bible, 70, 71–2, 73–6 n.; C. of Scotlandists believe in religion of Kirk and not religion of Jesus, 85 n.; wiser and honester than to teach Creeds, 214; clergy of C. of E. distinguished from clergy of, by riches, powers, and dignities, 268; needlessness of anti-Christian practice demonstrated by, 284–5; impracticable for unfit minister to continue, 286–7 n.; criminal offences under C. of E. v., 291, 556; description of every parish given by minister, 292, 361; govt. of, wants little of being model of perfection, 304–5; duties of imperfect obligation attached to clerical office, 352–3; institution of homily sermons under, 359 n.; abominations of C. of E. not found in, 385 n.; and production of sermons, 404 n.; admiration, respect, and reputation are rewards that clergyman can look for from extra-meritorious service as preacher, 405–6; professional services all well performed, 414; clergy collected in bodies exercise discipline over themselves as individuals, 416–17; no license for exercise of clerical functions granted but in consequence of strict examination, 421; duties of imperfect obligation enforced in, 421; neither dissoluteness nor pride have place in, 422; no parish without parsonage, 443 n.; vacancies in benefices of, 457 n.; sinecurism in C. of E. v., 453 n., 464 n.; vice having relation to doctrine chargeable on, 472 n., 478–82; efficient and sufficient test established in, for admission to benefice, 505; no such thing as preferment in, 511; augmentation given to underpaid benefices of, compared to C. of E., 524–5; question whether clergy of, engaged in farming, 529. *See* PRESBYTERIANISM

SERMONS: reading of, among duties of perfect obligation of parish minister, 355–60, 403–6, 484

SERVICE: establishment of mass of remuneration in state of utter independency on, 285; value of benefice composed of direct ratio of pay and inverse of, 286; expected from C. of E. ministers, 293–4; not provided by C. of E. is of bad sort, 347–8; tendencies exhibited by C. of E. with respect of production of desirable, 351–71; professional v. extra-professional, 352; of perfect v. imperfect, 352–63; parish-boy to undertake, 363–71; aptitude and inclination for rendering, 374, 375, 387–90 n.; rendered and quantity of pay, 374, 375, 390–4 n.; received from unpaid and willing hands, 374–6, 382 n.; for affording pay for public, contributions received from willing v. unwilling hands, 376, 377, 394–6 n.; in return for pay necessary v. unnecessary, 376, 377, 382–5 n., 396–7 n.; security to causing, to be rendered,

INDEX OF SUBJECTS

376, 377, 386–7 n., 397 n.; rendered by performance of duties of imperfect obligation to classes lowest in state of opulence, 376, 377, 397 n.; quantity of pay for, that consists in reading, 378, 379; sinecures to serve as rewards for meritorious, 399–415; considered in its exercise over clergy, proper use of discipline so to order matters that, rendered in return for pay, 415–23; knowledge whether man performs, rightly, 430; vices having relation to, 472–3; reform in regard to, 484–5; stated v. occasional, 507–9; unprofitable under C. of E. v. profitable under C. of S., 524–5. *See* DUTY(IES); OBLIGATION

SHIP MONEY: condemnation of, 394–5 n.

SIMONY: guilt of sin of, imaginary, 450 n.

SINCERITY: if, part of morality, established religion is in enmity to morality, 584

SINECURE(S): exclusionary system of education as indispensable instrument for preservation of, 112–13 n.; human learning annihilated to save, 159–60; C. of E. distinguished by number of sinecure salaries, 285; sanctified by ecclesiastical establishment, 289; in C. of E. v. C. of S., 304–5, 306, 464 n.; Oxford Graduate's maxim: no, 376, 382–5 n.; Excellent Church's maxim: are necessary, 377, 396–7 n.; as abuse that emblem of lottery employed with success to reconcile men to, 394 n.; whether merit producible by, 399–415; office of minister in non-established C. not, 416; judicial hierarchy of C. of E. may be transfigured into, 425; scheme for peopling with curates parsonages deserted by sinecurist incumbents, 429; additions to pay of Bishops in shape of, 429–30; objects of Residence-Enforcing Act: to increase sinecurist incumbents and to establish persuasion that endeavour has been to diminish sinecurism, 443–4 n., 496–8; conversion of cure of souls into, for accommodation of ruling few, 447 n.; and dignities not requiring residence, 451–3 n.; vices having regard to pay: cures converted into, and pay without service in originally established, 475; vice having regard to discipline: Bishops converting cure of souls into, 476; dishonour cast upon C. of E. by reverend sinecurists, 488–9 n.; elements of official aptitude in priest of C. in which sinecurism unknown, 504; by abolition of, after death of occupant, not an atom of suffering produced, 517; sinecurism established by statute, 530; interest of subject many v. ruling few on existence of, 573

SINISTER INTEREST: subject many whose, continues them upon list of members of C. of E., 293; intimate connection between, and interest-begotten prejudice, 517; that malice on part of prosecutor affords ground for impunity is maxim established through, 553; of man of law liable to afford obstruction to more extensive, 554–5 n.; on operation of, that lot of country determined, 573

SIN(S): phrase 'forgiveness of,' not accompanied by explanation in Catechism, 221–2; child confesses himself 'miserable sinner', 224; sinful acts caused not to have happened, 251–2; from imaginary, comes real antipathy, 255; of questioning any thing set before mind, 258; original, of C. of E., 283; Eaton's, was, of ignorance, 309; those by whom partaking of wine would be regarded as, forced to be contributors to Lord's Supper, 320; encouragement given to, by bread-eating and wine-drinking ceremony, 323; sinnership of Archbishop v. convict, 329–30; rulers of University of Oxford charged with keeping subjects plunged in, of perjury, 338; proposal to give parish boy power to remit or retain, 363–5; death to, of ruling few will be salvation to welfare of subject multitude, 427; guilt of, of ultra-pluralism as real as that of simony imaginary, 450; of insincerity in Jesuitry v. C. of Englandism, 468; atonement for, of defrauding revenue, endangering health, or stopping course of justice, 557–8

SLAVERY: avowed object of Howley's endeavours neither more nor less than system

638

INDEX OF SUBJECTS

of, 260; correlative to despotism is, 419; white man allowed to kill as many black slaves as he pleases, 534

SOULS: sold as constituents were by Clancarty to Castlereagh, 287–8; abject class of beings whose, never worth a thought in eyes of Holy Mother and Daughter Churches, 323; according to notion imputed to Mahomet, women have no, 397 n.; according to C. of Englandists, poor have no, or none worth saving, 397 n.; increasing in proportion to sanctity and rank is weight with which, gravitates to hell, 442. *See* SALVATION

SOVEREIGN: *see* MONARCH(S)

STATISTICS: inherent in C. of E., branch of ignorance correspondent and opposite to science of pastoral, 360–3

STATUTE LAW: indemnity to opinions respecting constitution of Godhead as against punishment under, v. Common Law, 11–12, 16–27; check applied by publicity to judicial power under, v. Common Law, 419; by, husbandman not compelled to grow figs for fig-leaves, 527; judges annul and repeal, 554–5

STIPEND: *see* PAY

SUBSCRIPTION (TO ARTICLES OF FAITH): fact asserted by, is that at moment of signature persuasion of person signing is that propositions true, 38–40 n., 54, 62; by, renouncement made of religion of Jesus, 87; mendacity and insincerity proved by, 384 n.; instructors in religion and people at large forced into error and insincerity by, 472. *See* OATH(S); THIRTY-NINE ARTICLES

SURPLICE FEES: unknown in Scotland, 235; advantage to some clergy in article of, from conversion of dissenters into C. of Englandists, 276; in C. of E. v. C. of S., 304–5, 306; in so far as paid by, priest is paid by job, 377, 386 n., 397 n.; parish boy employed to read minister's part of liturgy to be paid by, 415; by, poor excluded from temporal rights and salvation, 477; no answer in Curates' Act whether, comprized in account of salary, 500 n.; paid on each occasion service performed, 507

SYMPATHY: operating on side of particular interest results in connivance with non-residence on part of Bishop, 462

TAXATION: Bishops taxed themselves individually and taxed laymen along with them, 91–2; no law taxes had justice been designed for any but rich, 321–2; and purchase of service that consists in administering of religious instruction, 372; levying of money without consent of Parliament, 394–5 n.; by money exacted in way of, all but rich excluded from justice, 477; relief from taxes is application which presents claim superior to every other, 493; 'ignorant impatience of,' of Upper Canadians, 591. *See* QUEEN ANNE'S BOUNTY; TITHES

TEN COMMANDMENTS: as quotation in Catechism, 69, 79; incongruity of binding Christian children by employing, 225–6; upon face of, graphic art and natural history stand condemned, 226–8; inferences from, regarding duty towards God and neighbour, 228–32

THIRTY-NINE ARTICLES: heresy of Methodists consisted in different sense put on, than sense put on by interrogators, 33; time came for attaching Bentham's signature to, 35–6, 38–9; to subscribe to, is to utter enormously extensive lie, 62; no such security for orthodoxy as subscription to, yet put about necks of National Society's scholars, 83; by every subscriber to, religion of Jesus renounced, 85; belief expressed in, contradicts belief expressed in Catechism, 223; as source of danger to C. of E., 283–4; to be subscribed to by as many as please though not by any who do not, 490–1; for professing to believe in, real property in Upper Canada given to priest, 590–1. *See* OATH(S); SUBSCRIPTION (TO ARTICLES OF FAITH)

INDEX OF SUBJECTS

TITHES: intestine war perpetuated in parishes by, 306–7; property in form of, in kind should never pass out of hands of possessors without being extinguished, 350; commutation of, extended to such as are in lay hands, 351; on produce unprofitably vexatious, 474; how, in kind to be disposed of, 487–8; priests' pay originally received in glebe and, 526; and regulation of occupations of agriculture in case of priest, 526–9; application of non-disappointment principle to, 588. *See* PAY; QUEEN ANNE'S BOUNTY

TRANSUBSTANTIATION: v. consubstantiation, 245–9

TREACHERY: when vice v. virtue, 553–4 n.

TREASURY: Lord of, must have seat in House of Lords or Commons, 455 n.; Board of administration on which all others dependent, 556; as corrupt Board v. uncorrupt Boards of Excise and Customs, 558–72

TRINITY: identity of numbers three and one when applied to same object, 80; three Gods make one and same object of belief, 217–18; plan to give something to do for each of three persons of Godhead, 224; Father, Son, and Holy Ghost as short string of sounds by which human being rescued from endless torment, 237; Burgess expresses regret at having it no longer in his power to punish those who fail to behold in one God as many God-persons as he does, 294–5; absurdity to say that three God-persons are but one God, 369 n. *See* GOD; HOLY GHOST

UNDERSTANDING: prostration of, and will avowed object of endeavours of C. of E., 36–7, 47, 81, 112–13 n., 116 n., 153, 200, 252 & n., 258–60, 294, 298, 300, 308, 318–19, 323, 339, 357, 392 n., 403, 419, 422, 438 n., 451 n., 471–2, 478, 491, 517, 546, 557, 559, 572; argument which applies to, causes persuasion to be really entertained, 95

UNITARIAN(S): end put to oppression exercised upon, 49 n.; aversion entertained by C. of E. towards, 282; finds oppressors in C. of E. clergy, 305–6; time for, to make themselves seen and heard, 536

UNIVERSITY(IES): mendacity and insincerity sure effects of education at English, 36; every man whose name entered into books of, declares belief in Thirty-nine Articles, 223; art of reading not professed to be taught at, 355; divinity degrees cumulated at, 364; office of Bible Clerk in, 371; in, act of undergoing examination in public deemed requisite, 387–8 n., 505; in Scottish, subscription confined to Professors, 478–9 n.; and proposed reform of C. of E., 486, 488 & n.; intended to be erected in Upper Canada, 591–2. *See* CAMBRIDGE, UNIVERSITY OF; OXFORD, UNIVERSITY OF

UTILITY: if reason drawn from principle of, were taken for standard, interest of subject many no longer sacrificed to interest of ruling few, 381; reasons drawn from principle of, v. authority of Archbishop, 385 n. *See* GREATEST HAPPINESS PRINCIPLE

UTI POSSIDETIS PRINCIPLE: application of, to euthanasia of C. of E., 346–51; to have continued to persons in possession a possession obtained by breach of law would have been justified by, 498–9 n.; phrase *uti possidetis* employed on questions of international law, 589. *See* NON-DISAPPOINTMENT PRINCIPLE

VICES: proved upon Catechism recapitulated, 40–2, 253–4; of C. of E. having relation to doctrine, service, pay, and discipline, 471–82

WILL: prostration of understanding and, avowed object of endeavours of C. of E., 36–7, 47, 81, 112–13 n., 116 n., 153, 200, 252 & n., 258–60, 294, 298, 300, 308, 318–19, 323, 339, 357, 403, 419, 422, 438 n., 451 n., 471–2, 478, 491, 517, 546, 557, 559, 572

WOMEN: according to notion imputed to Mahomet, have no souls, 397 n.; education of male v. female sex, 593

INDEX OF NAMES

Note. The following is an index of names of persons and places appearing in the introduction, text, and notes; the last (whether Bentham's or the editors') are indicated by 'n.' Under Bentham's name, only references to his other works are indicated. For references to the Church of England, Church of Scotland, and other institutions, see the Index of Subjects.

Abbot, Charles, 1st Baron Colchester: 190 & n., 287 & n., 566–7, 574–5
Abbott, John: 50–1 n., 324–5 n., 326 n., 408 n., 532 & n., 539–44, 547, 548, 550 n., 556 n., 560–5, 569 n., 572 n.
Aberdeen, King's College: 478–9 n.
Aberdeen, Marischal College: 478–9 n.
Aberdeen, University of: 478–9 n.
Abraham: 61, 350 n.
Abram: *see* Abraham
Abû-l-Farağ: *see* Bar Hebræus
Adam: 283 n.
Adams, John Quincy: xix n.
Addington, Henry, 1st Viscount Sidmouth: 111 n., 220 & n., 536, 592 n.
Africa: 317 n.
Alexander, Du Pre, 2nd Earl of Caledon (I): 412 n.
Alexander, James, 1st Earl of Caledon (I): 412 n.
Alexander, Nathaniel, Bishop of Down and Connor: 412 n.
Alexandria, Library of: 158, 159 n.
Allen, William: 89 n.
al-Masīh ad-Dajjāl: 343 n.
America, American: *see* United States of America
Amun, Ammon: 300 & n.
Anabaptists: 234 n., 284 n.
Andrewes, Gerrard: xvii–xviii, xxv, 8 & n., 46, 48 n., 49–51, 323, 324–6 n., 408 & n., 413 n., 477, 532 & n., 539–48, 556 & n., 562, 563, 564, 566, 568
Angerstein, John Julius: 550 & n., 552 n.
Anne, Queen of Great Britain and Ireland: 518 & n., 520, 522 n.
Antarctic Circle: 19
Apollo: 271 & n.
Apostles, The: 213, 214, 219, 266 & n., 268–9, 313 n., 314, 317, 329, 332 n., 363, 366, 417
Arabia, Arabian: 340
Arbuthnot, Charles: 543 n.
Arctic Circle: 19
Arden: *see* Perceval
Arians: 49 n., 329 & n.
Aristotle: 301 & n., 307 & n.
Asclepius: 289 & n.
Ashley-Cooper, Cropley, 6th Earl of Shaftesbury: 127 & n., 129
Asia: 317 n.
Athanasians: 329
Athanasius: 329 n.
Atheist(s): 258, 282, 305–6, 553
Athens, Athenians: 23 n., 405 n.
Atholl: *see* Murray
Augustus Frederick, Duke of Sussex: 89 n.
Avercamp, Hendrick: 310 n.

Baal: 341 & n.
Babel, Tower of: 510 n.
Babylon: 478
Bacchus: 317–18, 321
Baillie, Joanna: 221 & n.
Baillie, Robert: 74–5 n.
Baker, John: 540 n.
Baker, Thomas: 159 & n.
Balcarres: *see* Lindsay
Baptist, Baptists: 282, 288, 305–6, 536
Barbary: 47
Bar Hebræus: 159 n.
Barker, Ralph: 405 n.
Barrington, John: 409 n.
Barrington, Richard, 4th Viscount Barrington: 409 n.
Barrington, Shute, Bishop of Llandaff,

INDEX OF NAMES

Salisbury, and Durham: 99 & n., 301 & n., 409 n.
Barrington, William Wildman, 2nd Viscount Barrington: 301 & n.
Bathurst, Charles Bragge: 435 & n.
Bathurst, Henry, Bishop of Norwich: 16 & n., 101 n., 337, 361 n., 410 n.
Bayley, Sir John: 220 & n., 364 & n., 548 & n.
Beadon, Richard, Bishop of Bath and Wells: 410 n., 413 n.
Beaufort: *see* Somerset
Becket, Thomas, Archbishop of Canterbury: 448 n.
Bective: *see* Taylour
Beelzebub: 36 n.
Bell, Andrew: 88 & n., 90, 112 n., 115 n., 122, 142 n., 201, 255–6, 272, 279, 355, 388 n., 529
Belsham, Thomas: 25 & n.
Bembo, Pietro: 454 n.
Benjamin, Wolf: 569 n.
Bennet, William, Bishop of Cloyne: 412 n.
Benson, Martin, Bishop of Gloucester: 408 & n.
Bentham, Alicia, née Grove, then Whitehorn: 31 & n.
Bentham, Jeremiah: 31 & n., 36
Bentham, Jeremiah (Senior): 31 & n.
Bentham, Jeremy:
 Analysis of the Influence of Natural Religion: xxiv n.
 The Book of Fallacies: 9 n., 223 n.
 Chrestomathia: xii
 'Church-of-Englandism examined': xiii–xiv
 A Comment on the Commentaries and A Fragment on Government: 582 & n.
 Defence of Usury: 322 n., 582
 De l'organisation judiciaire, et de la codification, 582 n.
 Deontology: 21 n., 582 n.
 A Fragment on Government, 582 n.
 An Introduction to the Principles of Morals and Legislation: 582 & n.
 'Jeremy Bentham to the Citizens of the United States': 26 & n.
 Justice and Codification Petitions: 617 & n.
 'Legislator of the World': 26 n.
 Not Paul, but Jesus: xxiv n., 583 & n.
 Observations on Peel's Speech: 593 & n.
 On Mr. Humphreys' Observations on the English Law of Real Property: 587 n.
 Official Aptitude Maximized; Expense Minimized: 394 n., 593 & n.
 Papers relative to Codification and Public Instruction: 26 & n.
 Plan of Parliamentary Reform: xi & n., 8 & n.
 'A Protest against Law Taxes': 322 n., 426
 Rationale of Judicial Evidence: 581 n.
 Scotch Reform: 322 n., 426 & n.
 'Swear not at all': xxii n., 35 n., 582
 A Table of the Springs of Action: 21 & n., 582 & n.
 Tactique des assemblées législatives, 582 n.
 Théorie des peines et des récompenses: 373 n., 582 n.
 Traité des preuves judiciaires, 582 n.
 Traités de législation civile et pénale: 347 n., 582 n.
Bentham, Sir Samuel: 221 n.
Beresford, George de la Poer, Bishop of Kilmore: 411 n., 412 n.
Beresford, George de la Poer, 1st Marquis of Waterford (I): 411 n.
Beresford, Henry de la Poer, 2nd Marquis of Waterford (I): 411 n., 412 n.
Beresford, John George de la Poer, Bishop of Raphoe: 412 n.
Beresford, William, 1st Baron Decies, Archbishop of Tuam: 411 n., 412 n.
Berkeley, George, Bishop of Cloyne: 408–9
Bernard, Sir Thomas: 99–100, 110 n., 221 & n., 337
Beverley, Robert Mackenzie: xxvi–xxvii, 585–6
Bexley: *see* Vansittart
Bishop Auckland: 99 n.
Blackstone, Sir William: 73 & n., 190, 249 n., 423, 455 n.
Blair, Hugh: 404 n.
Blake, George: 324–5 n., 548 & n.
Bonaparte, Napoleon, Emperor of the French: 221 & n., 288, 582 n.

INDEX OF NAMES

Bourke, Richard, Bishop of Waterford and Lismore: 413 n.
Bow Church: 149 n., 162
Bowring, Sir John: xxiv–xxv, 31 n.
Boyce, William: 491 n.
Bramah: 111 n., 387 n., 615
Bright, Edward: 246 & n.
Bristol: 19 n.
Britain, British: 69, 94, 97 n., 249 n., 288 n., 291, 296 n., 301, 302, 346 n., 573–4, 582 n.
Brodrick, Charles, Archbishop of Cashel: 411 n.
Brodrick, George, 4th Viscount Midleton (I): 411 n.
Brougham, Henry Peter, 1st Baron Brougham and Vaux: 89 n., 326 n., 492 n., 539 n., 543 n.
Brownlow: *see* Cust
Buccleuch: *see* Montagu-Scott
Buckingham: *see* Nugent-Temple-Grenville
Buckner, John, Bishop of Chichester: 410 n.
Bullock, William: 154 & n.
Bunce, John Bowes: 540 n.
Burdett, Sir Francis: xxiv, 492 n., 574 n.
Burges, Cornelius: 75 n., 76 n.
Burgess, Thomas, Bishop of St David's and Salisbury: 48–9 n., 154 & n., 220 & n., 294–5, 296, 300–1, 410 n., 477
Burgoyne, John: 555 n.
Burke, Edmund: 456 n.
Burn, Richard: 73 & n.
Burnet, Gilbert, Bishop of Salisbury: 385 n.
Burton, Francis: 130 n.
Bute: *see* Stuart
Butler, Edmund, 1st Earl of Kilkenny (I): 412 n.
Butler, Mildred, née Fowler: 412 n.
Butson, Christopher, Bishop of Clonfert: 412 n.
Byfield, Adoniram: 75 n., 76 n.

Cacus: 160 & n.
Cadell and Davies, Publishers: 404 n.
Cadell, Thomas: 404 n.
Caesar, Gaius Julius: 337 & n.
Caledon: *see* Alexander
Calvin, John: 588 n.

Cambridge, Downing College: 488 n.
Cambridge, George Owen: 130 n.
Cambridge, King's College: 410 n.
Cambridge, Trinity College: 409 n., 410 n., 411 n.
Cambridge, University of: 35, 223 & n., 355 & n., 364 & n., 371 & n., 388 n., 471, 498 n., 505, 583
Camden: *see* Pratt
Canada: *see* Upper Canada
Canning, George: 593 n.
Canterbury: 532 n., 543, 568
Canterbury, Convocation of: 91 n.
Capernaum: 269 n.
Carisbrooke Castle: 72 n.
Castlereagh: *see* Stewart
Catholic(s): *see* Roman Catholic(s)
Cavendish-Bentinck, William Henry Cavendish, 3rd Duke of Portland: 410 n., 411 n., 413 n.
Cavendish-Scott-Bentinck, William Henry Cavendish, 4th Duke of Portland: 410 n., 413 n.
Cecilia, St: 491 & n.
Celsus, Aulus Cornelius: 294–5
Centlivre, Susannah: 506 n.
Chard: 10
Charles I: King of England, Scotland, and Ireland: 33 n., 72 & n., 155 n., 394 n.
Charles II, King of England, Scotland, and Ireland: 72 & n., 303 n.
Charles X, King of France: 331–2 n.
Charles Ferdinand, Duc de Berry: 332 n.
Charles Philippe, Comte d'Artois: *see* Charles X, King of France
Charlotte, Queen of Great Britain and Ireland: 89 n., 410 n.
Charlotte Augusta of Wales, Princess: 192 n., 410 n.
Chase, Thomas: 455 n.
Chateaubriand, François-René, Vicomte de: 275 & n.
Chelsea, Royal Hospital: 498 n.
Chelsea, Royal Military Asylum: 497 n.
Chichester: *see* Pelham
China, Chinese: 87 n.
Christ: *see* Jesus Christ
Clancarty: *see* Trench
Clarke, Thomas Brooke: 431 & n., 432 & n.

643

INDEX OF NAMES

Cleaver, Euseby, Archbishop of Dublin: 411 n.
Cleaver, William, Bishop of St Asaph: 410 n., 411 n.
Cloots, Anacharsis: see du Val-de-Grâce
Cocker, Edward: 523 n.
Coke, Sir Edward: 73 & n.
Coke, Thomas William, 1st Earl of Leicester of Holkham: 591 n.
Colchester: see Abbot
Colchester: xvii n., 118–19 n.
Colls, John Flowerdew: xxvi & n.
Conder, Josiah: 221 n.
Constantinople, Council of: 329 n.
Cooper, Anthony Ashley, 3rd Earl of Shaftesbury: 366 n.
Corinthians: 545 & n.
Cornewalle, Folliot Herbert Walker, Bishop of Worcester: 410 n.
Cornwallis, Charles, 1st Marquis Cornwallis: 410 n.
Cornwallis, Charles, 2nd Marquis Cornwallis: 410 n.
Cornwallis, James, 4th Earl Cornwallis, Bishop of Coventry and Lichfield: 410 n.
Cranmer, Thomas, Archbishop of Canterbury: 385–6 n.
Creech, William: 404 n.
Crigan, Claudius, Bishop of Sodor and Man: 413 n.
Crito: 289 n.
Croker, John: 540 & n., 560, 564
Cromwell, Thomas, 1st Baron Cromwell, 1st Earl of Essex: 385–6 n.
Croton: 492 n.
Curtis, Sir William: 540 n., 563, 568
Cust, John, 2nd Baron and 1st Earl Brownlow: 413 n.

d'Angoulême: see de Bourbon
Davie, Giles: 569 n.
Davie, John: 569 n.
Davis, William: 130 n.
Dean, Forest of: 172 n.
de Berlaymont, Charles: 50 n.
de Bourbon, Louis Antoine, Duc d'Angoulême: 115 n., 332 n.
de Bourbon, Marie Thérèse Charlotte, Duchesse d'Angoulême: 115 n.
Decies: see Beresford

de Hooch, Pieter: 310 n.
Deist(s): 258, 262 n., 282, 305–6
Delphi: 271 & n.
Deshima: 86 n., 87 n.
Devil: xix, 204, 207–9, 215, 216, 217, 220 & n., 235, 237, 242 n., 274, 299
Devon: xviii
Dionysus: 318 n.
Dissenters: 91, 94, 264, 276, 303 n., 387 n.
Donatists: 71 n.
Draco: 23 & n.
Dublin: 100 n., 413 n.
Dudley, Sir Henry Bate: 221 & n.
Dumont, Pierre Étienne Louis: 373 n., 582 n.
Dunlo: see Trench
Dunstan, St: 220 & n.
Durell, David: 33 n.
Durham: 99
Dutch: see Netherlands
du Val-de-Grâce, Jean Baptiste, Baron von Cloots: 129 & n.

Ealing: 410 n.
Eaton, Daniel Isaac: 301 & n., 309
Eden, William: 294–5 n.
Edinburgh, University of: 478–9 n., 481 n.
Edward, Duke of Kent and Strathearn: 98 n., 101 n.
Edward VI, King of England and Ireland: 277 n., 385 n.
Egypt, Egyptian: 225, 300 n.
Eldon: see Scott
Elijah: 157
Eliot, Edward James: 99 n.
Elisha: 157
Elizabeth I, Queen of England and Ireland: 33 & n., 155 & n., 195, 277 & n., 356
Ellenborough: see Law
Ely: see Loftus
Ely, Isle of: 354
England, English: 25 n., 33, 36, 44, 69, 72, 74 n., 77, 90, 93 & n., 94–5, 102, 112 n., 117 n., 142, 151, 155, 167, 218 n., 254, 270, 286 & n., 287 n., 291 & n., 292, 297 & n., 302, 305, 318, 320, 321–2, 344, 346, 353, 355, 367, 384, 387 n., 396 n., 405 n., 409–11 n., 413 n., 418, 419, 423, 425, 426,

644

INDEX OF NAMES

428, 433, 465 n., 481 n., 483, 495, 518, 525, 535, 556, 574, 584, 591
Ensor, George: xx n.
Erasistratus of Ceos: 295 n.
Erskine, Thomas, 1st Baron Erskine: 394–5 n.
Essex: *see* Cromwell
Eton College: 279, 498 n., 563
Euclid: 26 & n.
Europe: 57 n., 397 n., 588 n.
Eve: 283 n.
Exeter: 152 n.
Eyre, Sir James: 551 n.

Fisher, John, Bishop of Salisbury: 410 n.
Folkestone: *see* Pleydell-Bouverie
Forbes, Sir William, 6th Baron Forbes of Pitsligo: 404 n.
Ford Abbey: xviii & n., xix & n., xxviii n., 10 & n., 94 n., 481 n.
Fortescue, William: 394 n.
Fowler, Robert, Bishop of Ossory: 412 n.
France, French: xvii n., 9 n., 115 n., 129 n., 256, 331 n., 367, 430 n., 491 n., 517 n., 568 n., 570 n., 574, 582 n., 614–15
Francis, Philip: 581 n.
Francis Xavier, St: 87 n.
Frederick, Duke of York and Albany: 410 n., 536
Frederick II (the Great), King of Prussia: 301 n.

Garrick, David: 491 n.
Gataker, Thomas: 74 n.
Gauls: 337
Geary, Sir William: 192 & n., 193 n.
Gentiles: 269–70 n.
George III, King of Great Britain and Ireland: 89 n., 221 & n., 290, 395 n., 433 & n., 459 n.
George IV, King of Great Britain and Ireland: 118 n., 161, 162, 410 n., 413 n.
George, Prince Regent: *see* George IV, King of Great Britain and Ireland
Gibbs, John: 569 n.
Gifford, John: 221 n.
Gifford, William: 221 n.
Gillespie, George: 75 n.
Glasgow, University of: 478–9 n., 481 n.

Glastonbury: 220 n.
Gloucester and Edinburgh: *see* William Frederick, 2nd Duke of Gloucester and Edinburgh
God: xxiii, 14 & n., 25, 36, 73, 80, 84, 89, 92, 97–8, 144, 166, 204, 205, 206, 211–12, 214–15, 216–18, 222, 224, 225, 228, 230–1, 232 & n., 234, 236, 237–9, 242 n., 245 n., 249, 250 n., 251, 252, 255 n., 258–67, 272, 274, 277 & n., 279 n., 280, 282, 293, 294–5, 297, 299, 305, 308, 309, 313–14 n., 316 n., 318, 339, 350 n., 363, 364–5, 367 & n., 371, 418, 439, 449 n., 451 n., 452 n., 457 n., 463 n., 517 n., 530, 532, 535, 536, 544, 567 n.
Goderich: *see* Robinson
Gomorrah: 350 n.
Goodenough, Samuel, Bishop of Carlisle: 410 n., 413 n.
Gouge, William: 74 n.
Gower, Stanley: 75 n.
Grant, Charles: 51 n., 325 n., 558 n.
Grant, Sir William: 394 n., 514 & n.
Great Britain: *see* Britain
Greece, Grecian, Greek: 49 n., 289 n., 300 & n., 322, 340, 479 n., 492 n., 573
Greenwich, Royal Hospital: 498 n.
Grenville, William Wyndham, 1st Baron Grenville: 414 n.
Grey, Charles, 2nd Earl Grey: 593 n., 617 & n.
Grindal, Edmund, Archbishop of Canterbury: 155 n.
Grote, George: xxiv n.
Grove, Alicia: *see* Bentham, Alicia
Grove, Thomas: 31
Guilford: *see* North

Hale, Sir Matthew: 25 n., 73 & n.
Halifax: 122
Hampden, John: 394–5 n.
Hampstead: 221 n.
Hampton Court Conference: 290 n.
Harcourt, Simon, 1st Earl Harcourt: 409 n.
Harcourt, William, 3rd Earl Harcourt: 409 n.
Hardwicke: *see* Yorke
Harrowby: *see* Ryder

INDEX OF NAMES

Haslar, Royal Hospital for Seamen: 498 n.
Hawkins, William: 73 & n.
Hay-Drummond, Sarah: 411 n.
Hay-Drummond, Thomas Robert, 11th Earl of Kinnoull: 411 n.
Hay, Thomas: 152 n.
Headfort: *see* Taylour
Hebrews: 517 n.
Helots: 145
Henderson, Alexander: 75 n.
Henry II, King of England: 426 n.
Henry VIII, King of England and Ireland: 155 & n., 285 & n., 297 n., 385 n., 428, 433 & n., 437 n., 458 n., 496, 497, 499 n., 518, 520
Heracles: 160 n.
Herle, Charles: 73 n., 74 n., 76 n.
Herophilus of Chalcedon: 295 n.
Hertford: *see* Seymour-Conway
High Wycombe, Royal Military College: 497 n.
Hindustan: 88, 318, 573–4
Hogarth, William: 310 & n.
Holland: *see* Netherlands
Home, Henry, Lord Kames: 350 n.
Homer: 290 n.
Hone, William: xxii & n., 24 & n., 25
Horsley, Samuel, Bishop of Rochester: 542 n.
Horton, R.J. Wilmot: 591 n.
Howard, John: 100 n.
Howley, William, Bishop of London: xii, xvi, 8 & n., 15, 36–7, 46, 47–8, 49 & n., 71, 81, 94 & n., 111 n., 115 n., 130 & n., 153–60, 168, 199, 200, 220 & n., 252 n., 257–65, 272–7, 280–1, 284 n., 291, 294, 296–8, 300–1, 303–11, 357, 368 n., 386 n., 392 n., 394 n., 396 n., 403 n., 419, 477, 482, 556 & n., 557, 559
Howth: *see* St Lawrence
Hoyle, Joshua: 74 n.
Hughes, Thomas Smart: 583 & n., 584
Hulse, John: 583 n.
Hume, David: 304, 345 & n.
Hume, Joseph: xxvi & n., xxvii n., 586 n., 590 n.
Huntingford, George Isaac, Bishop of Gloucester: 411 n.

Ignatius Loyola, St: 468 & n.
Independent(s): 282, 305–6, 536
India: 591
Ireland, Irish: xxvi, 15 & n., 20, 69, 94–5, 100 & n., 291 & n., 292, 387 n., 411–12 n., 413 n., 489, 572–4
Italy: 492 n.

Jackson, Cyril: 410 n., 413 n.
Jackson, William, Bishop of Oxford: 410 n., 413 n.
Jacobins: 553
James, St: 269 n.
James I, King of England, Scotland, and Ireland: 33 & n., 155 & n., 290 n.
James VI, King of Scotland: *see* James I, King of England, Scotland, and Ireland
Japan, Japanese: 86–7, 118 n.
Jeffreys, George, 1st Baron Jeffreys: 22 & n.
Jehu: 341 & n.
Jenkinson, Robert Banks, 2nd Earl of Liverpool: 522 n., 556–7, 572 n., 573, 593 n.
Jephthah: 39 n.
Jerusalem: 36 n., 271, 364 n.
Jesuits: 87 n.
Jesus Christ: xii, xvi, xix, 14 n., 34 & n., 36 & n., 38 n., 43, 49 & n., 53, 59, 60–1, 63, 64 n., 65–7, 72, 79, 82–3, 84, 85 n., 87, 91, 98, 109, 111 n., 137, 142, 143, 153, 189, 195, 196, 197, 198, 208 n., 211, 212, 215–16, 217 n., 218, 219 & n., 220, 222–3, 225, 228, 229–30, 232 n., 233–5, 240–5, 246–7, 249–50, 259, 262, 266–9, 271 & n., 272, 276 n., 283–4, 290, 292, 298 & n., 303 n., 308, 309, 310, 312–20, 321, 322, 327, 328–9, 330, 334–5, 336, 337, 340 n., 343, 350 n., 363–4, 366, 368 n., 386 n., 395–6 n., 407 n., 417, 454 n., 476, 485, 509, 535, 543, 544, 545, 583, 614–15
Jews, Jewish: xii, 49 n., 61–2, 79, 84, 225, 228, 229–30, 271, 282, 335–6, 536
Jocelyn, Percy, Bishop of Ferns and Leighlin: 412 n.
Jocelyn, Robert, 2nd Earl of Roden (I): 412 n.

INDEX OF NAMES

Johnson, Samuel: 278 n.
John, St: 144, 242, 259, 269 n., 312 n.
John the Baptist: 217 n., 235 & n.
Johnston, Sir Archibald, Lord Wariston: 75 n.
Jones, John Gale: 530 n.
Judas Iscariot: 219 & n., 242 n., 314 & n., 358
Junius: 581 & n.
Juno: 208 & n.
Jupiter: 208 & n., 300 & n.

Kames: *see* Home
Kearney, John, Bishop of Ossory: 412 n.
Kent: 192, 568
Kent and Strathearn: *see* Edward, Duke of Kent and Strathearn
Kilkenny: *see* Butler
King, John: 410 n.
King's College, York, Upper Canada: xxvii, 589–90, 593
King, Walker, Bishop of Rochester: 410 n., 413 n.
Kinnoull: *see* Hay-Drummond
Kipling, Thomas: xvii & n., 46 & n., 48 n., 49 & n., 50, 295 & n., 296, 301, 477, 539 & n., 556 & n.
Kirby, Sarah: *see* Trimmer, Sarah
Knatchbull, Sir Edward: 192 & n., 540 n., 562, 568
Knox, Thomas, 1st Viscount Northland (I): 411 n.
Knox, Thomas, 2nd Viscount Northland (I): 411 n.
Knox, Vicesimus: 34–5 n., 338
Knox, William, Bishop of Derry: 411 n.
Koe, Bentham Dumont: 196 n.
Koe, John Herbert: xi & n., xviii, xix, xx, xxi, xxii, xxiii, 196 n.

Lambert, Daniel: 246 & n.
Lambeth Palace: 164
Lancaster, Joseph: 89–90, 101 n., 112 n.
Latins: *see* Rome, Roman
Laud, William, Archbishop of Canterbury: xvii n., 155 & n.
Lauderdale: *see* Maitland
Law, Edward, 1st Baron Ellenborough: 11 n., 14–15, 17–24, 221 & n., 411 n., 413 n.
Law, Edmund, Bishop of Carlisle: 413 n.

Law, George Henry, Bishop of Chester: 411 n., 413 n.
Law, John, Bishop of Elphin: 413 n.
Lazarus: 328 & n.
Leicester: 122
Leicester of Holkham: *see* Coke
Lennox, Charles, 4th Duke of Richmond: 410 n., 413 n.
Leonard, Solomon: 569 n.
Leo X, Pope: 297 n., 454 n.
Leopold of Saxe-Coburg, Prince: 192 n.
Leslie, John, Bishop of Dromore: 412 n.
Levellers: 553
Libya, Libyan: 300 n.
Lincoln's Inn: 33 n.
Lindsay, Alexander, 6th Earl of Balcarres: 411 n.
Lindsay, Charles, Bishop of Kildare: 411 n.
Lingard, John: 49 & n., 295 & n., 556 n.
Liverpool: *see* Jenkinson
Liverpool: 25, 154 n.
Loftus, John, 2nd Marquis of Ely (I): 412 n.
Loftus, Robert Ponsonby Tottenham, Bishop of Killaloe: 412 n.
London: xviii, 13, 24 n., 31, 50 n., 63 n., 66 n., 88 n., 97 n., 101 n., 118 n., 120 n., 130 n., 132 n., 135 n., 154 & n., 164 n., 173 n., 174 n., 310 n., 443 n., 485, 487 n., 513 n., 540 n., 568, 574, 592
Londonderry: *see* Stewart
London House: 130 & n., 131, 164, 180 n.
Loughborough: *see* Wedderburn
Louis IX, King of France: 332 n.
Louis XIV, King of France: 301 n.
Louis XVIII, King of France: 115 n., 331–2 n.
Luke, St: 250
Lushington, Stephen Rumbold: 50 n., 323–4 n., 540 & n., 541, 546 n., 548, 556 n., 569–70
Luther, Martin: 246 & n., 588 n.
Luxmoore, John, Bishop of Hereford: 410 n., 413 n.

Machiavel: 506 & n.
Machiavelli, Niccolò: 506 n.
Madan, Spencer, Bishop of Peterborough: 411 n.

647

INDEX OF NAMES

Madras: 37 n., 88 n., 112 n., 119 n., 135 n., 137
Mahomet, Mahometan: 111 n., 158, 258, 343, 387 n., 397 n., 615 n.
Maidstone: 192 & n.
Maitland, John, 2nd Earl and 1st Duke of Lauderdale: 75 n.
Majendie, Henry William, Bishop of Bangor: 410 n.
Majendie, John James: 410 n.
Manley, William: 569
Manners, Charles, 4th Duke of Rutland: 409 n.
Manners, John: 409 n.
Manners, John Henry, 5th Duke of Rutland: 409 n., 413 n.
Manners-Sutton, Charles, Archbishop of Canterbury: xvi & n., xvii n., xxii & n., 8 & n., 10–16, 20, 24, 45, 46, 48 n., 52–3, 111 n., 113 n., 127, 128 n., 129, 134–6, 141, 142, 144, 145, 149 n., 153, 160–9, 180, 186, 188 & n., 220 & n., 328–30, 409 n., 413 n., 448 n., 477
Manners-Sutton, George: 409 n.
Mansel, William Lort, Bishop of Bristol: 411 n.
Mant, Richard: 343 n.
Marat, Jean Paul: 9 & n.
Margaret, Duchess of Parma: 50 n.
Marplot: 506 & n.
Marryatt, Joseph: 540 n.
Marsh, Herbert, Bishop of Llandaff: 295–6 n., 386 n., 477
Martin, Henry: 425 n.
Mary, Virgin: 67, 212, 214, 245 n.
Mary I, Queen of England and Ireland: 155 & n., 385 n.
Mason, William Shaw: 291 n., 292 n.
Matthias: 358 & n.
McCreery, John: xviii & n., xix, xxiii, 7 n.
Melchizedek: 350 & n.
Methodist(s): 32–5, 38, 91 n., 225 & n., 279 n., 282, 288, 305–6, 505
Mexico: 154 n.
Middleton, Thomas Fanshaw, Bishop of Calcutta: 317 & n.
Midleton: *see* Brodrick
Mill, James: 89 n.
Miller and Cadell, Publishers: 404 n.
Milner, Isaac: 221 & n.

Milner, John: 221 & n.
Mitford, John Freeman, 1st Baron Redesdale: 190 & n.
Moloch: 93 & n., 289 & n.
Montagu-Scott, Charles William Henry, 4th Duke of Buccleuch: 410 n., 413 n.
Moon: 573
More, Hannah: 221 & n.
Morocco: 547
Moses: 229, 230
Murray, George, Bishop of Sodor and Man: 411 n., 413 n.
Murray, John, 4th Duke of Atholl: 411 n.
Murray, Lord George, Bishop of St David's: 411 n.
Muslims: 397 n.

Nagasaki: 86 n.
Nayler, James: 368 n.
Neal, Daniel: 33 n., 71 & n.
Nelson, Horatio, 1st Viscount Nelson: 127 n.
Nelson, William, 1st Earl Nelson: 127 & n., 129
Netherlands, Dutch: 50 n., 86–7, 310 & n.
Newgate Prison: 301 n.
New Jerusalem: 510 & n.
Newport, Treaty of: 72 n.
New Zealand, New Zealander: 247 & n.
Nicaea, Council of: 329 n.
Nikon, Patriarch of Moscow: 234 n.
Nonnus of Panopolis: 318 n.
Norfolk: 152 n., 173 n., 174 n.
Norris, Henry Handley: 161 & n.
North, Brownlow, Bishop of Winchester: 409 n.
North, Frederick, Lord North, 2nd Earl of Guilford: 409 n.
Northland: *see* Knox
North Walsham: 152 n., 173 n.
Norwich: 152 n., 173 n., 174 n., 448 n.
Nugent-Temple-Grenville, George, 3rd Earl Temple and 1st Marquis of Buckingham: 410 n., 572 n.

O'Beirne, Thomas Lewis, Bishop of Meath: 411 n.
Omar, Caliph of Damascus: 159 n.
Orford: *see* Walpole
Ostervald, Jean Frédéric: 64 n., 67

INDEX OF NAMES

Oxford: 33 n., 385 n.
Oxford, Brasenose College Chapel: 310 n.
Oxford, Christ Church College: 288 n., 410 n.
Oxford, Gloucester Hall: *see* Oxford, Worcester College
Oxford, Hart Hall, Hertford College: 488 n.
Oxford, Queen's College: 28 n.
Oxford, St Edmund Hall: 33 n.
Oxford, University of: xii, 32–6, 91 & n., 223 & n., 287, 303 & n., 337 n., 338, 355 & n., 364 & n., 371 & n., 388 n., 414 n., 464 n., 468, 498 n., 505
Oxford, Worcester College: 488 n.

Paget, Berkeley: 51 n., 325 n., 558 n.
Paley, William: 284–5 n., 479 n.
Palmer, Herbert: 76 n.
Papists: *see* Roman Catholic(s)
Park, Sir James Alan: 165 n., 221 & n., 364 & n., 548 & n.
Parker, Matthew, Archbishop of Canterbury: 155 n.
Parma: *see* Margaret, Duchess of Parma
Parsons, John, Bishop of Peterborough: 413–14 n.
Paul III, Pope: 33 n.
Paul, St: 79, 219 & n., 220, 238 n., 279 n., 316 n., 386 n., 492 n., 545 & n., 557, 564, 566
Pearson, James: 310 & n.
Pearson, John, Bishop of Chester: 212–13
Peel, Sir Robert: 292 n., 591–3
Pelham, George, Bishop of Exeter: 410 n.
Pelham, Thomas, 2nd Earl of Chichester: 410 n.
Perceval, Charles George, 2nd Baron Arden (I) and 1st Baron Arden: 425 & n., 522 n.
Perceval, Spencer: 389 n., 390 n., 411 n., 428, 446 n., 452 n., 489–90, 508 & n., 517 & n., 523 n., 534 & n.
Peterborough: 296 n.
Peter, St: 20 & n., 38 & n., 79, 111 n., 195, 219, 220, 242, 243 n., 267 n., 284 n., 312 n., 588 n.
Peyton, Algernon: 354 & n.

Pharisees: 298 & n., 407 n.
Philip II, King of Spain: 50 n.
Philips, Ambrose: 217 n.
Philistines: 191
Phipps, Augustus: 569
Phipps, Constantine: 303 n.
Pitt, William (the Younger): 410 n., 430 n., 492 n.
Place, Francis: xix n., xx & n., xxi, xxiii, xxiv n., xxv–xxvi, 89 n.
Pleydell-Bouverie, William, Viscount Folkestone, 3rd Earl of Radnor: 427 & n.
Plumer, Sir Thomas: 165 n.
Plymouth, Royal Hospital for Seamen: 498 n.
Pontius Pilate: 212, 214 & n.
Pope, Alexander: 408 & n.
Porter, John, Bishop of Clogher: 412 n.
Porteus, Beilby, Bishop of London: 156 n.
Portland: *see* Cavendish-Bentinck; Cavendish-Scott-Bentinck
Portugal, Portuguese: 582 n.
Pratt, John Jeffreys, 2nd Earl and 1st Marquis Camden: 522 n.
Presbyterian(s): 282, 305–6, 536
Procrustes: 490 & n.
Protestant(s): 50, 98, 100 n., 219, 234 n., 245–6, 291 n., 297 n., 387 n., 479 n.
Pufendorf, Samuel: 350 n.
Puritans: 71 & n., 77, 155 n., 284–5 n., 290 n., 304–5
Pythagoras: 491 & n.

Quaker(s): 225 n., 279 n., 282, 305–6, 335 n., 394 n., 536

Radnor: *see* Pleydell-Bouverie
Radstock: *see* Waldegrave
Randolph, John, Bishop of London: 48 n., 94 & n., 114 & n., 115 n., 118 n., 130 & n., 154–60, 161, 162, 163, 164 & n., 168, 180, 188 & n., 261 n., 272–3, 303–4, 409 n., 434 & n., 469
Redesdale: *see* Mitford
Reynolds, Edward: 74 n.
Richmond: *see* Lennox
Ripon: *see* Robinson
Robespierre, Maximilien François Marie Isidore Joseph de: 9 & n.

649

INDEX OF NAMES

Robinson, Frederick John, 1st Viscount Goderich and 1st Earl of Ripon: 591 & n., 593 & n.
Roborough, Henry: 76 n.
Rockingham: *see* Watson-Wentworth
Roden: *see* Jocelyn
Rome, Roman: 208 n., 300 & n., 301–2, 318 n., 322, 331, 347 n., 350 & n., 573, 574
Roman Catholic(s): xii, 33, 53, 87, 100 & n., 115 n., 218–19, 234 n., 245–6, 258, 282, 291 n., 303 n., 387 n., 479 n., 536
Romilly, Lady Anne: xix n.
Romilly, Sir Samuel: xix–xxi, xxiv, 19 & n., 26, 492 n., 514 & n.
Rosslyn: *see* Wedderburn
Rousseau, Jean Jacques: 204 & n.
Rundle, Thomas, Bishop of Derry: 408 & n.
Russia, Russian: 234 n.
Rutherford, Samuel: 75 n.
Rutland: *see* Manners
Ryder, Dudley, 1st Earl of Harrowby: 8 & n., 86 n., 220 & n., 273 n., 292 & n., 362 n., 384 n., 388–98 n., 413 n., 417, 420, 426, 429, 446 n., 452 n., 489–90, 494, 499–500, 503–4, 505, 507–9, 512–13, 515–17, 522 n., 523 n., 532–4, 536, 584
Rye House Plot: 303 n.

Sacheverell, Henry: 303 & n.
St Andrews, University of: 478–9 n., 481 n.
St Botolph, Aldersgate: 310 n.
St Helena: 152 n.
St James's Park: 408
St Lawrence, Thomas, Bishop of Cork: 412 n.
St Lawrence, William, 2nd Earl of Howth (I): 412 n.
St Paul's Cathedral: 408
Salisbury Cathedral: 310 n.
Samson: 191
Sanzio, Raffaello: 94 n.
Saratoga, Battle of: 555 n.
Satan: *see* Devil
Saul: *see* Paul, St
Saurin, James, Bishop of Dromore: 413 n.

Saurin, William: 413 n.
Say, Jean Baptiste: xxiv & n.
Scotland, Scottish: 57 & n., 69, 70, 71, 72, 74 n., 77, 78, 85 n., 93 & n., 94–5, 214, 235, 268, 276 & n., 279 n., 284–5, 286–7 n., 290–2, 304–5, 344, 353, 359 n., 361, 384–5, 386 n., 404 n., 405–6, 414, 416, 418, 421–3, 443 n., 453 n., 457 n., 458 n., 464 n., 472 n., 478 & n., 481–2 n., 482, 483, 505, 511, 524–5, 529, 555 n., 556
Scott, John, 1st Baron and 1st Earl Eldon: 11 n., 14–15, 17–24, 190 & n., 220 n., 414 n., 448 n., 500 n., 514 n., 524 n.
Scott, Sir William, 1st Baron Stowell: 8 & n., 364 & n., 427 & n., 429 & n., 438 n., 446 n., 451 n., 508 & n., 509
Scroggs, Sir William: 22 & n.
Secker, Thomas, Archbishop of Canterbury: 408 & n.
Sejanus, Lucius Aelius: 302 & n.
Seymour-Conway, Francis Charles, Earl of Yarmouth, 3rd Marquis of Hertford: 221 & n.
Seymour, Lord George: 569
Shaftesbury: *see* Ashley-Cooper; Cooper
Sheffield: 122
Shepherd, Sir Samuel: 25 & n.
Sidmouth: *see* Addington
Siloam, Tower of: 329
Simon, father of Judas Iscariot: 242 n.
Simon Peter: *see* Peter, St
Sinclair, Sir John: 292 & n., 361
Sion: *see* Zion
Sion College: 120 n., 126 & n., 128, 129, 149 n., 192 & n.
Siwa: 300 n.
Skinner and Dyke, Auctioneers: 287 & n.
Smith, Adam: 393–4 n., 422 & n., 426 & n.
Smith, William: xv & n., xxii–xxiii, 10–27
Socrates: 289 & n.
Sodom: 350 n.
Somerset, Henry Charles, 6th Duke of Beaufort: 413 n.
South Carolina: 534 n.
Southey, Robert: xxvi & n., 221 & n., 491 n., 580–1, 582–3, 585
Spain, Spanish: 50 n., 117 n., 155, 367, 574, 582 n.

650

INDEX OF NAMES

Sparke, Bowyer Edward, Bishop of Ely: 409 n., 413 n.
Sparta, Spartan: 491 n.
Spencer, John, 1st Earl Spencer: 133 n.
Spencer, (Margaret) Georgiana, née Poyntz, Countess Spencer: 133 n.
Stanhope, Charles, 3rd Earl Stanhope: 517 & n.
Steen, Jan: 310 n.
Stevens, William: 220 & n.
Stewart, Robert, Viscount Castlereagh, 2nd Marquis of Londonderry (I): 288 & n., 493 n., 573 n., 591 n.
Stock, Joseph, Bishop of Waterford and Lismore: 412 n., 413 n.
Stowell: *see* Scott
Strahan, William: 404 n.
Stuart, John, Marquis of Bute (I): 411 n.
Stuart, William, Bishop of Armagh: 411 n.
Sussex: *see* Augustus Frederick, Duke of Sussex
Swift, Jonathan: 160 n., 588 & n.
Sybaris: 492 & n.
Sydenham, Benjamin: 569

Tabor, John: 31 & n.
Tabor, Rebecca: 31 & n.
Tacitus, Cornelius: 301 & n.
Taylor, Jeremy, Bishop of Down and Connor: 11 & n., 34
Taylour, Thomas, Viscount Headfort (I), 2nd Earl of Bective (I), and 1st Marquis of Headfort (I): 221 & n.
Temple: *see* Nugent-Temple-Grenville
Thelwall, John: 279 & n. 355 n.
Thessalonians: 564
Thornton, Henry: 568 & n.
Thornton, Robert: 568 & n..
Thornton, Samuel: 568 & n.
Thorpe, Essex: 118 n., 152 n.
Tiberius, Roman Emperor: 302 n.
Tibet: 158 n.
Tillotson, John, Archbishop of Canterbury: 404 n.
Tokugawa, Iemitsu, Shogun of Japan: 87 n.
Tomline, George Pretyman, Bishop of Lincoln: 300–1, 410 n.
Toronto: *see* York, Upper Canada
Tory: xi, 303 n.

Toyotomi, Hideyoshi: 87 n.
Trafalgar, Battle of: 127 n.
Trench, Power Le Poer, Bishop of Elphin: 411 n.
Trench, Richard Le Poer, Viscount Dunlo (I), 2nd Earl of Clancarty (I), 1st Baron Trench, and 1st Viscount Clancarty: 288 & n., 411 n.
Trimmer, Sarah, née Kirby: 64 n., 67
Tuckney, Anthony: 74 n.
Tweed, River: 285
Twisse, William: 74 n.
Tyrtaeus: 491 & n.

Unitarian(s): xxii, 10 n., 15 n., 37 n., 49 n., 258, 282, 288, 295 n., 303 n., 305–6, 536
United States of America: 26, 301 & n., 307 & n., 317 n., 457 n., 555 n., 568 n., 574, 584 & n.
Upper Canada: xxvii, 589–93
Utopia: 463 n., 559

van Ruisdael, Jacob: 310 n.
Vansittart, Nicholas, 1st Baron Bexley: xvii–xviii, 8 & n., 14 & n., 46, 48 n., 50, 51–2, 288 n., 323 & n., 324–6 n., 508–9, 539, 543 & n., 545 & n., 546–7, 554 n., 556–8, 560–70, 572–3
Venables-Vernon, subsequently Harcourt, Edward, Archbishop of York: 220 & n., 409 n.
Venables-Vernon, George, 2nd Baron Vernon: 409 n.
Vermeer, Johannes: 310 n.
Vernon: *see* Venables-Vernon
Verschoyle, James, Bishop of Killala and Achonry: 412 n.
Vines, Richard: 74 n.
Virgil: 290 n.
von Cloots: *see* du Val-de-Grâce

Wake, William, Archbishop of Canterbury: 58 n.
Waldegrave, William, 1st Baron Radstock (I): 130 n.
Wales: 93 n., 525 n.
Walmsley, Tindal Thompson: 45 & n., 97, 124, 129–30, 133–6, 138–45, 150, 151 n., 153, 161 n., 163, 166,

INDEX OF NAMES

168, 169 & n., 177 n., 179–80 n., 180, 183 n. 184 n., 186
Walpole, Robert, 1st Earl of Orford: 492 n.
Warburton, Charles Mongan, Bishop of Limerick: 412 n.
Warburton, William, Bishop of Gloucester: 116 n., 290
Wariston: *see* Johnston
Waterloo, Battle of: 582 n.
Waterford: *see* Beresford
Watson, Joshua: 124 & n.
Watson, Richard, Bishop of Llandaff: 290 n., 411 n.
Watson-Wentworth, Charles, 2nd Marquis of Rockingham: 410 n.
Wedderburn, Alexander, 1st Baron Loughborough and 1st Earl of Rosslyn: 555 n.
Wellesley, Arthur, 1st Viscount, 1st Earl, 1st Marquis, and 1st Duke of Wellington: 582–3
Wellington: *see* Wellesley
Wesley, John: 282 & n.
West, Benjamin: 310 & n.
West Indies: 47, 317 n.
Westminster: xviii, 12, 16, 31 n., 545 n.
Westminster Hall: 296 n.
Westminster School: 279, 287 & n., 337 n., 498 n., 563
Whig(s): xi, xx, 303 n., 575
White, Thomas: 120 n.
Whitefield, George: 282 & n.
Whitehorn, Alicia: *see* Bentham, Alicia
Whitgift, John, Archbishop of Canterbury: 155 & n.

Whitworth, Charles, 1st Earl Whitworth: 413 n.
Wight, Isle of: 72 & n.
Wilberforce, William: 221 & n., 568 n.
Wilks, John: 101 n.
Wilks, Mark: xxi & n., xxiii
William Frederick, 2nd Duke of Gloucester and Edinburgh: 410 n., 413 n.
Williams, Renwick: 550 n.
Wilson, Effingham: xxiii & n., 7 n.
Wilson, Thomas: 75 n.
Winchester: 152 n.
Winchester College: 498 n.
Wodehouse, John: 152 n.
Wood, Sir Matthew: 101 n.
Woodward, Alicia: 31 & n.
Woodward, William: 31 & n.
Woolwich, Royal Military Academy: 497–8 n.
Wright, John: 25 & n.
Wright, William Henry: 427 & n., 434–8, 442 n., 443 n., 447–8 n., 449–50 n., 458 n., 460–1, 466–71, 477 & n., 508, 515, 520

Yarmouth: *see* Seymour-Conway
York and Albany: *see* Frederick, Duke of York and Albany
York, Convocation of: 91 n.
Yorke, James, Bishop of Ely: 466–7 n.
Yorke, Philip, 1st Baron and 1st Earl of Hardwicke: 394 n.
York, Upper Canada: xxvii, 589

Zebedee: 269 n.
Zeus: 300 n.
Zion: 120 & n.